MEDICAL SELECTION OF LIFE RISKS

THIRD EDITION

MEDICAL SELECTION OF LIFE RISKS

THIRD EDITION

R. D. C. BRACKENRIDGE
W. JOHN ELDER

M
stockton
press

Published in the United States and Canada by
STOCKTON PRESS, 1992
257 Park Avenue South, New York, N.Y. 10010, USA

ISBN 1-56159-068-1

First published in the United Kingdom by
MACMILLAN PUBLISHERS LTD, 1992
Distributed by Globe Book Services Ltd
Brunel Road, Houndmills,
Basingstoke, Hants RG21 2XS, England

ISBN 0-333-53151-5

A catalogue record for this book
is available from The British Library.

Typeset and printed in Great Britain

Contents

Acknowledgements

First and foremost, we would like to thank the managements of Mercantile & General Reinsurance and Transamerica Occidental Life Insurance for the generous support afforded to us during the production of this third edition. As well as encouragement, we were given access to secretarial, copying and communications facilities without which our task as editors would have been much greater. We also wish to thank all the contributors who were invited to submit chapters for the new edition. They have given generously of their time and effort which we greatly appreciate and it has given us much pleasure to edit their work.

We would now like to thank a few persons individually for their help: Alex Duncan of the actuarial department of M & G London for producing two tables of UK life expectancy to be found in Part I; Paul Cooper and his team of underwriters in London and Cheltenham who assisted us in proofreading some of the later chapters; Sue Johnson and her colleagues for valuable secretarial assistance, despite their patience being sorely tried on a few occasions.

Finally, our thanks to our publishers for their helpful cooperation over the past two or three years of production. We particularly admire the way in which they have handled the difficult task of coordinating the work of two editors who are based thousands of miles apart.

R D C Brackenridge
W John Elder

The Contributors

Ian McLean Baird MD FRCP, Consultant Physician, Medical Spokesman, British Heart Foundation, London, UK

R D C Brackenridge MD FRCP(Glasg), Chief Medical Officer, Mercantile & General Reinsurance, London, UK

Maurice Brazeau MD FRCP(C), Associate Medical Director, Metropolitan Life Insurance Company, Ottowa, Ontario, Canada

Arthur E Brown MD, Formerly Vice President, Medical Selection and Issue, New England Mutual Life Insurance Company, Boston, Massachusetts, USA

Roger H Butz MD MPH, Vice President and Medical Director, SAFECO Life Insurance Company, Seattle, Washington, USA

Neil Cardoe FRCP, Chief Medical Adviser, Norwich Union Insurance Group, Norwich, UK

Leonardo Chait MD FACP FACC, Chief Cardiologist, The Pritikin Longevity Center, Santa Monica, California. Formerly Medical Director, Executive Life Insurance Company, Los Angeles, California, USA

Clifford Rose FRCP, Director, London Neurological Centre, Principal Medical Officer, Allied Dunbar Assurance, Swindon, UK

Richard S Croxson MB FRACP, Cardiologist, Chief Medical Officer, Mercantile & General Reinsurance, London, UK

Gordon R Cumming MD FRCP(C) FACC, Vice President and Medical Director, The Great West Life Assurance Company, Winnipeg, Manitoba, Canada

Arthur A DeTore MD, Vice President, Lincoln National Risk Management Inc, Fort Wayne, Indiana, USA

W John Elder MB BS MRCP DCH, Vice President and Medical Director, Transamerica Occidental Life Insurance Company, Los Angeles, California, USA

Polly Galbraith MD, Medical Director, Western Life Insurance Company, St Paul, Minnesota, USA

Robert K Gleeson MD FACP, Medical Director, Northwestern Mutual Life Insurance Company, Milwaukee, Wisconsin, USA

Robert L Goldstone MD, Vice President and Medical Director, Pacific Mutual Life Insurance Company, Newport Beach, California, USA

Roger F Harbin FSA, Vice President, SAFECO Life Insurance Company, Seattle, Washington, USA

Max L Hefti MD, Specialist Gastroenterologist. Former Chief Medical Officer, Swiss Reinsurance Company, Zurich, Switzerland

Brian R Kay MD, Department of Laboratory Medicine and Pathology, Mayo Clinic, Rochester, MN, USA

Michael W Kita MD, Vice President

and Medical Director, UNUM Life Insurance Company, Portland, Maine, USA

David Lawee CCFP FCFP, Director, Travel and Inoculation Services, Toronto Hospital, General Division, Toronto, Ontario, Canada

Maurice Lipsedge MD FRCP FRCP(Psych) DPM, Consultant Psychiatrist, Guy's Hospital, London, UK

Richard J Mackler MD FRCP(C), Associate Professor of Medicine, McGill University, Associate Medical Director, Mercantile & General Reinsurance, Montreal, Canada

Peter C Maynard ACII, Research Officer, Mercantile & General Reinsurance, Cheltenham, UK

R J Mills BSc PhD, Former Clinical Physiologist, Department of Respiratory Medicine, Royal Infirmary, Glasgow, UK

Howard L Minuk MD FRCP(C) ABIM, Chief Medical Officer, Mercantile & General Reinsurance. Medical Director, Prudential of America Life Insurance Company (Canada).

Eve Owen FCII, Underwriting Project Manager, Mercantile & General Reinsurance, London, UK

Robert D Rubens BSc MD FRCP, Professor of Clinical Oncology, Guy's Hospital, London. Chief Medical Officer, Mercantile & General Reinsurance, London, UK

James A Ryan, Jr MD FACP, Vice President and Chief Medical Director, Transamerica Occidental Life Insurance Company, Los Angeles, California, USA

Richard B Singer MD, Consultant to American Academy of Insurance Medicine. Formerly second Vice President and Director of Medical Research, New England Life Insurance Company, Boston, Massachusetts, USA

Harry A Woodman FSA FALU ChFC, Consultant Actuary, Formerly Vice President, New York Life Insurance Company, New York, USA

Introduction

Seven years have elapsed since the second edition of *Medical Selection of Life Risks* was published. During that time there have been several important developments in life and health insurance as well as in medicine. This third edition is therefore due, if not overdue.

Previous editions were written by a single author with expert advice from others when necessary. The field of insurance medicine has now become so vast that treatment of the subject within the covers of an international textbook is outside the scope of a single author. Accordingly, it was agreed with the publishers that the book should now be edited and individual authors, experienced in their particular sphere of insurance and medicine, should be invited to contribute chapters. In order to preserve a balance between North American and European practice the editorship has been shared between one based in London and the other based in Los Angeles. Each editor invited contributors from either side of the Atlantic in roughly equal numbers.

Past experience has been that readership of *Medical Selection of Life Risks* has been predominantly North American, a trend likely to continue. Consequently it was decided to conform to American spelling. Inevitably, a multi-contributor volume will contain differences in writing style but consistency has been maintained as far as possible. Both forms of biochemical measurement have been shown together in the tables and text but where only one type of unit is given the reader should refer to the table of conversion factors at the end of the book.

As before, the book is aimed at a variety of readers but primarily at doctors or physicians who wish to learn more about the intricacies of life insurance as it affects their day-to-day practice. Their interest will be stimulated in the selection of risks, both medical and otherwise, rating of substandard lives and, most importantly, the appreciation of long-term prognosis. Examining doctors will be helped to apply their clinical skills to the production of reports that are of maximum value to the life underwriter.

Although less pointedly, the book is also aimed at medical directors who will use it mainly as a reference or as a source of information on some obscure condition that does not appear in underwriting manuals. It will also serve as an invaluable guide to physicians who may be asked to deputize from time to time in the underwriting department. However, in our experience, the people who use the book the most — as a complement to the regular underwriting manual — are the lay underwriters, the backbone of the life insurance industry.

Outside the mainstream of the life insurance industry the book will be of use to brokers advising clients, solicitors and lawyers engaged in the business of

structured settlements, personnel managers of commercial companies and
actuaries of public authorities and businesses calculating disability pensions.

R D C Brackenridge
London

W John Elder
Los Angeles

September 1992

Preface

This third edition of *Medical Selection of Life Risks* has been enlarged by the addition of seven new chapters, three in Part I and four in Part II. These chapters have been neatly accommodated by slightly increasing the page size. However, the general format of the book remains the same as previous editions. Part I deals with the historical background and theoretical aspects of life insurance. Part II is devoted to the clinical and practical problems of selection and pricing of risks.

By absorbing the information in Part I, the uninitiated reader will learn a lot about the principles of risk selection and will be given a clear, step-by-step explanation of how substandard lives are classified and rated. A relatively new and growing facet of insurance, structured settlements, is explained by an expert on life table methodology, by an actuary and by a clinician dealing with the practical underwriting of these severely impaired lives. Finally, there is a chapter giving a glimpse into the future prospects of automated life underwriting of knowledge-based systems.

In addition to the updated chapters in Part II dealing with the system diseases, it has been necessary, in view of the importance of the subject, to include a separate chapter on the acquired immune deficiency syndrome (AIDS) and HIV positivity as it affects the life insurance industry generally and life underwriting in particular. The increasing importance of laboratory screening in risk selection has warranted another additional chapter on the subject. Two further chapters have been formed from expanded subject matter previously contained in the chapter on miscellaneous disorders, namely pregnancy and female genital disorders, and a review of drug abuse, alcohol and tobacco.

R D C Brackenridge
London

W John Elder
Los Angeles

PART I

CHAPTER 1

A HISTORICAL SURVEY OF THE DEVELOPMENT OF LIFE ASSURANCE

R D C BRACKENRIDGE
ARTHUR E BROWN

'Whenever there is a contingency, the cheapest way of providing against it is by uniting with others, so that each man may subject himself to a small deprivation, in order that no man may be subjected to a great loss. He, upon whom the contingency does not fall, does not get his money back again, nor does he get from it any visible or tangible benefit, but he obtains security against ruin and consequent peace of mind. He, upon whom the contingency does fall, gets all that those whom fortune has exempted from it have lost in hard money, and is thus enabled to sustain an event which would otherwise overwhelm him.'

Select Committee of the House of Commons, 1825

The earliest forms of insurance mainly concerned ships and their cargoes; the business was well established by the Middle Ages both in Great Britain and the continent of Europe. The first known life policy was issued in 1583 following strictly on the lines of a marine policy, but it was not until the late 17th century that efforts were made to meet the growing demand for life insurance.

Assurance was administered then by various societies under the tontine system, a tontine consisting of groups of people who banded together with the object of insuring their lives to make provision for their widows and children. Each member paid an entrance fee and an annual subscription which went towards the creation of a fund to meet death claims within the group, a proportion of the fund being set aside to cover the expense of running the scheme. Only the very young and very old were excluded from the tontines. Records show that this system was used by the Society for Widows and Orphans, and the Mercers' Company sponsored an insurance scheme run on similar lines to provide annuities for the widows of clergymen.

There were many abuses connected with life assurance as it was conducted in those days, one of the more serious being the practice of insuring a person's life without his knowledge. This allowed the more unscrupulous members of society to gamble on the lives of others which were at best none too sound, and many schemes failed financially for this reason.

It is clear that the failure of some of these earlier undertakings was due mainly to the lack of scientific selection of members. Thus the Traders Exchange House Office, founded in 1706 by Charles Povey, lasted only four years because most of the subscribers were bad lives and the dividend became so small that there were no inducements for new members to join or old ones to continue. Another company, also founded in 1706 but run on sounder lines, was the *Amicable Society for a Perpetual Assurance Office*, the first undertaking of its kind to be incorporated by Royal Charter. The number of subscribers was limited, and the rules regarding admission, premiums payable and amounts available for settling claims were strict. This society prospered until 1866 when it was absorbed into the *Norwich Union Life Insurance Society*.

The only other institutions empowered to transact life assurance at this time were the *Royal Exchange Assurance* and the *London Assurance*, both established in 1721, but selection of lives was still crude and was not founded on a scientific basis. The agents of the London Assurance were instructed in 1725 to interview the applicant in person and to have him prove his identity; the insurable interest was to be examined, and the applicant was to be asked whether he had had smallpox. The premium rates were determined accordingly but, even so, the business was still little more than a gamble.

The first serious attempt to establish population mortality rates was made by John Graunt, the son of a London draper, who in his spare time analyzed the records of the weekly christenings and burials in the City of London, the keeping of which had become an established custom since the plague of 1603. In 1662 Graunt published a book called *Natural and Political Observations made upon the Bills of Mortality*, and from this information he compiled a 'Table of Survivors' which was to be the forerunner of life tables. Graunt's efforts, although crude, were commendable for one who had received no special training.

Some years later Edmund Halley, the Astronomer Royal, made a study of the records of births and deaths which had been regularly kept in Breslau in Silesia since 1584, and in 1693 he published an essay called 'An Estimate of the Degrees of Mortality of Mankind drawn from Curious Tables of the Births and Funerals at the City of Breslaw'. The life table (*see* Table 1.1) that Halley prepared cannot be regarded as accurate, but it was the first work by a competent scientist using reasonably up-to-date statistics.

Table 1.1. Halley's life table.[a]

Age (years)	Expectation of life (years)	Age (years)	Expectation of Life (years)
0	33·50	45	19·22
5	41·55	50	16·81
10	39·99	55	14·51
15	36·86	60	12·09
20	33·61	65	9·73
25	30·38	70	7·53
30	27·35	75	5·99
35	24·51	80	5·74
40	21·78		

[a]Based on mortality experience in the city of Breslau during the years 1687–91.

Although Halley's work, along with that of Newton and De Moivre, his contemporary mathematicians, laid the foundations of actuarial science, it was not until the next generation that James Dodson, a pupil of De Moivre, showed that life assurance was practicable with premiums properly graduated according to age. Dodson was first and foremost a mathematician, and was elected a Fellow of the Royal Society in 1755 for his best known work *The Mathematical Repository*, but he soon turned his energies to the mathematics of life assurance.

In those days, the only forms of life assurance available were the year-to-year assurances granted by the charter corporations, and the small, variable death benefits provided by the 'Old Amicable'. Dodson, realizing that these arrangements were unsatisfactory and could be bettered, produced a treatise early in 1756 entitled *First Lecture on Insurances*, and in March of the same year he invited all those interested to meet him at the Queen's Head, Paternoster Row, in the City of London to explain to them the principles on which scientific life assurance could be run. There were several such meetings during which Dodson expounded his theories on how premiums should be calculated and how a life assurance fund would work out based on various assumptions. These principles, having been discussed by the group, were finally adopted, and the way was paved for the formation in 1762 of the *Society for Equitable Assurances on Lives and Survivorships*, which exists today as the *Equitable Life Assurance Society*. This was the very first life office to be run on true actuarial lines, and the original conception of mutual life assurance is still apparent today in the conduct of life business all over the world. Unfortunately Dodson died in 1757 and did not live to see the inauguration of the Society.

The original scale of premiums was based upon the bills of mortality for London in the years 1728–50 as calculated by Dodson. Later, in 1781, a modification of the Northampton Table, first published by Richard Price in 1771, was introduced for the Society's calculations. Richard Price was born in Bridgend, Glamorgan, in 1723, became a doctor of divinity and from 1758 lived at Newington Green, London, where he officiated as a minister of the English Presbyterian Church. He was elected a Fellow of the Royal Society in 1765 and was a friend of Joseph Priestley. Price's nephew, William Morgan, was appointed assistant actuary of the Equitable in 1774 and actuary in the following year.

While the first office of the Society for Equitable Assurances on Lives and Survivorships was being prepared in Nicholas Lane, six meetings of the directors took place at weekly intervals in the White Lion Tavern in Cornhill, where the first 27 proposals were accepted. It has been definitely established that the first office of the Society was the disused parsonage of St Nicholas Acons in Nicholas Lane, which stood immediately north of the graveyard. A plaque has now been placed there by the Corporation of the City of London to show that this was where life assurance started. The site is now occupied by the Lombard Street office of the National Westminster Bank.

Life assurance was then standing on the threshold of a new era in which mathematical reality had taken the place of chance. A further consolidation was the passing of the Life Assurance Act by Parliament in 1774. This did away with many of the old abuses such as speculation on the lives of others by persons who had no real interest in those lives.

The Northampton Table mentioned earlier is of special historic interest in the evolution of vital statistics. Various editions of this Table were published; the first, in 1771, was based on bills of mortality for the parish of All Saints over the period 1735–70. The fourth edition, generally referred to as The Northampton Table, which was published in 1783, was based on similar data over the period 1735–80. Both versions of the Table were used for the calculation of premium rates by the Equitable. By 1843 the Northampton Table had been largely abandoned for the calculation of premium rates.

Both versions of the Table were calculated essentially on the same basis. The basic data were the number of registered births and the number of deaths occurring during the period. The population was assumed to be stationary, and adjustments were made to allow for the effects of migration. Since many births were not registered the population was underestimated and, consequently, the resulting mortality rates were overstated.

Several years later, in 1837, the registration of births, marriages and deaths became compulsory in England, and the accumulated data enabled William Farr, the Compiler of Abstracts in the General Register Office, to develop a national system of vital statistics from which he published the first official English life tables in the Registrar General's Fifth Annual Report of 1843.

Life insurance in the USA had developed in a manner similar to that in England. Entry into fire and marine insurance stemmed from the American Revolution when Lloyds of London ceased to be available to US ships, thus the Insurance Company of North America, chartered in 1794 in the city of Philadelphia and the oldest stock insurance company in the USA, was formed to fill the gap. This was the first company to issue life policies in the USA when it wrote six temporary policies on the lives of ships' captains in charge of valuable cargoes on international sea routes. Even so, this type of business was strictly limited, being incidental to marine insurance.

It was not until 1809 in Philadelphia that the Pennsylvania Company for Insurance and Granting of Annuities started selling life insurance on a strictly commercial basis. This company is important historically because of the innovations which it introduced in its underwriting practice, some of which are still used today: notably the requirement of an application, or proposal, and a medical examination. Premiums charged were also based on the age of the applicant. Some time later, in 1823, the Massachusetts Hospital Life Insurance Company in Boston introduced a rate book.

Moorhead, in his book on the history of the actuarial profession in North America,[1] records that Elizur Wright, an actuary, invented the 'arithmeter' (a device to ease the work of calculation) and, as Commissioner of Insurance in the Commonwealth of Massachusetts, introduced 'fairness' in insurance with regulations such as those regarding withdrawal (surrender) values. Wright was also actuary of the Massachusetts Hospital Life Insurance Company and of the New England Mutual Life Insurance Company, and is known to have visited actuaries in England in 1844. In fact several exchange visits took place at about this time between actuaries from Great Britain and the USA; Charles Gill, a mathematician and actuary who had come over to the USA from England in 1831, returned to visit colleagues in England in 1851. Finally, in 1861, the American Experience Table was submitted. Elizur Wright died in 1885 after forty years of activity in life insurance as an actuary, state regulator and writer.

Nevertheless, life business at the beginning of the 19th century existed mainly to facilitate commerce by supplying finance on a credit basis, and therefore the needs of only a small, privileged section of the community were being met. It was not until the 1840s that the base of life insurance was eventually broadened, giving the industry an almost miraculous boost. Inspired by the concept of mutual insurance, which had been practised in England since 1762 by the Society for Equitable Assurances on Lives and Survivorships, two new life insurance companies – the Mutual Life Insurance Company of New York and the New England Mutual Life Insurance Company of Boston – began to transact business in 1843 on the mutual plan. In fact 1843 was a milestone in the history of life insurance in the USA, for it marked the beginning of a spectacular increase in the number of new companies formed and in the volume of new business transacted. After 1843 five more companies began to sell life insurance policies on a participating basis: the State Mutual Life Assurance Company of America in Worcester, Massachusetts in 1844, the New York Life Insurance Company and the Mutual Benefit Life Insurance Company of Newark in 1845, the Connecticut Mutual Life Insurance Company of Hartford, and the Penn Mutual Life Insurance Company of Philadelphia, both in 1847. All these seven companies grew in strength and have survived to the present day.[2]

The tremendous growth which occurred in the decades that followed coincided with a rapid increase in the population, which by now had become aware of the benefits of life insurance, and with an upsurge in the economic development of the country in relation to both agriculture and industry.

In Canada, the first company to start business was the Canada Life Assurance Company in 1847, later incorporated in 1849. In 1867, when Canada became the self-governing Dominion of Canada within the United Kingdom, Canada Life was still the only native Canadian company operating, although there were several branches of British and US companies all issuing life policies within the Dominion.

In Great Britain there was a steady growth in the number of life offices conducting business during the period 1800–70, but such was the uncontrolled nature of the growth that many offices had to close down, so that of the 192 companies operating in 1855 only 100 remained by 1870.

The first purely Scottish company to start life assurance was the Scottish Widows' Fund in 1815; there are records that an office transacting fire insurance opened a life department in about 1809, but this soon closed down due to lack of business. The Scottish Widows' Fund was followed by the Edinburgh Life Assurance Company in 1823, the Standard Life Assurance Company in 1825 and the Scottish Amicable Life Assurance Society in 1826.

Despite its obvious benefits to a community, life insurance in the mid-19th century was a luxury that could only be afforded by the relatively well-off, because of having to pay premiums annually, or even every three months, making insurance for the weekly paid worker virtually impossible. In 1854 a British parliamentary committee investigated the matter and recommended that insurance companies should make scientifically sound insurance available with premium payments adjusted to meet the needs of the working class. Thus 'industrial assurance' was born in 1854, when the Prudential Assurance Company in London inaugurated a scheme whereby life assurance cover was offered in return for a small weekly payment, the premiums being collected by an agent of the company who called at the home of the assured.

The utility of the scheme appealed to the working class, and industrial assurance grew to become a large and important branch of life business in Great Britain. It provided money to pay for burial expenses on the death of a member of the family, cash sums on maturity of an endowment policy and, for many industrial policyholders, it represented their only form of savings. Furthermore, it encouraged a spirit of thrift and sturdy independence in the working community, particularly in the north of England.

The success of industrial assurance in Great Britain was watched closely by insurance companies in the USA, at first with little enthusiasm. After prolonged arguments about the pros and cons of the matter, industrial insurance was eventually established in 1875 by the Prudential Friendly Society, later to become the Prudential Insurance Company of America. The initiative of the Prudential was soon to be followed by the Metropolitan Life Insurance Company of New York and the John Hancock Mutual Life Insurance Company of Boston, and thereafter the business snowballed.

Because of its inherent nature – a high occupational and class mortality coupled with high administrative costs relative to the small sums insured – industrial insurance is an expensive form of life cover. As a consequence early in the 20th century efforts were made to devise better methods of insuring the working population. These resulted in the introduction of a new and important form of life insurance, group life insurance, and the first plan was underwritten in 1911 by the Equitable Life Assurance Society of the United States. Group life insurance was the first major development in life insurance which was wholly a US innovation. Today, with certain modifications, it still holds an important place in the insurance of working populations throughout the world. The principle of group insurance is that life cover is granted to all employees of a firm or industrial organization without the need for evidence of health, other than that they be gainfully employed at the inception of the scheme. Administrative expenses are consequently much less than for individual industrial or ordinary life insurance, and the saving more than compensates for the slightly higher mortality cost experienced in group life schemes.

As life business expanded, the demand for experienced actuaries increased, and the Institute of Actuaries was founded in 1848 to foster the interests of the profession and to lay down standards. The status of the members was elevated when a Royal Charter was granted to the Institute in 1884. The sister body in Scotland, the Faculty of Actuaries, which was founded in 1856, was granted a Royal Charter in 1868. With the encouragement, it is said, of the many Fellows of the Institute and Faculty who had emigrated from Great Britain to the USA, the Actuarial Society of America was founded in 1889 to be followed some 20 years later by a similar body, the American Institute of Actuaries, in 1909. These two professional associations finally amalgamated in 1949 to become the Society of Actuaries.

In the earliest days of life assurance, it used to be sufficient for a candidate to appear before the board of directors who assessed his health by his appearance. Later a physician was sometimes invited to sit with and advise the directors, but as the volume of life business grew the state of health of applicants began to assume more importance in selection, and gradually a system of medical examination was evolved. The practice seems to have been started in 1809 by the Pennsylvania Company for the Insurance of Lives, but it was not established in Great Britain until some time before the middle of the century.

In view of the special techniques involved in medical selection, various professional associations and societies were eventually formed by physicians having a special interest in life insurance medicine in order that the medico-actuarial aspect of subjects bearing on their speciality could be discussed and experiences exchanged. Of these, the Association of Life Insurance Medical Directors of America (ALIMDA)*, founded 6 December 1889, is perhaps the most important and influential. The 34 medical directors representing 27 companies in 1889 grew to become 606 medical directors representing 363 companies and 46 branches in 1990, including physicians from Canada and other countries outside the USA. At its 100th annual meeting in October 1991 ALIMDA decided to change its name to the American Academy of Insurance Medicine (AAIM) to emphasize its educational mission and remove 'Life' from the title to reflect the wider interest of insurance medicine in recent decades. Besides an annual meeting at which scientific papers are read by speakers eminent both in the clinical and insurance fields, numerous committees and sub-committees of AAIM exist to deal with a wide variety of topics affecting the members, including professional and public relations, education, mortality and morbidity studies, and medical procedures relating to risk selection. The transactions of the annual meeting are published every year and distributed to the members. What started out as ALIMDA's 'Newsletter' in the 1960s has now developed into the much respected and informative *Journal of Insurance Medicine* under its recent editor, W. John Elder MD.

The American Life Convention, founded in 1906, was the oldest international association of life insurance companies in the USA and three provinces of Canada. In 1973 it merged with the Life Insurance Association of America to become the American Life Insurance Association, the aims and purposes of the two bodies having been identical for many years before. A further merger occurred in 1976 with the Institute of Life Insurance, the public relations arm of the industry, to form the American Council of Life Insurance (ACLI). The medical section holds annual meetings at various venues in North America at which papers having a bearing on life insurance medicine are read, and the proceedings are published annually. It also has committees; primarily these address matters of industry and regulatory concern to insurance medicine. Of particular note in the past decade has been their attention to the impact of AIDS and genetic testing on insurance.

In England the Assurance Medical Society, founded in 1893, holds evening meetings three times a year in London at which invited speakers read papers on subjects related to life and health insurance. Since 1985 biennial one-day medico-actuarial meetings have been held in London jointly with the Institute of Actuaries at which speakers from both professions are invited to address the fellows and members. In order to maintain a closer link with provincial members of the Society, one-day regional meetings are held annually at different venues of major insurance importance in the UK. These meetings are chaired by the president and are usually hosted by the local insurance company or companies. The speakers are normally drawn from among local physicians and chief medical officers. The proceedings of all those meetings are published annually in the transactions and distributed to members of the Society.

The first international congress for life assurance medicine (ICLAM) took place in Brussels in 1899. Subsequent congresses were held in Amsterdam, Paris and Berlin. The International Committee for Life Assurance Medicine was founded in Brussels in 1932. The aim of the organization is to promote international development and co-operation in insurance medicine. This is done in co-operation with the national insurance medical societies, mainly in the form of international congresses. The organization consists of an executive group, the Bureau with 8 members, and the Committee with representatives from 26 countries all over the world. During the congress in The Hague in 1989 it was decided to extend the Committee to cover disability and health insurance medicine. Three congresses have been held outside Europe: in Tel Aviv, Mexico City and, in 1986, Tokyo. In 1992 the congress was held for the third time in London, and in 1995 it is planned to take place in Washington DC.

COINTRA (Co-opération Internationale pour les Assurances des Risques Aggravés), founded in 1927, is an organization comprising several insurance and reinsurance companies from various European countries; it was set up to exchange ideas and information about the experience of substandard risks accepted for life and permanent health insurance. Conferences are held every three to five years at various venues in Europe at which papers of medico-actuarial interest are presented both by member companies and by invited speakers of repute in the insurance world. The transactions of these conferences are published and distributed to members.

MEDICO-ACTUARIAL INVESTIGATIONS

Since the establishment of these and other professional associations, a greater unanimity of opinion has grown regarding features important in the selection of life risks, and a system of tabulating clinical data from the medical examination of applicants has gradually evolved. What started out as 'judgmental underwriting' became 'scientific underwriting' based on sound actuarial figures. The first results were obtained from simple population studies and so-called 'collective investigations'; however, this rapidly progressed to large occupational and medical impairment studies. The first medical data gathered were those most easily obtained and related to urinalysis. Routine urine testing of life insurance applicants, which was introduced at the end of the 19th century, came to be regarded as so important that rapid advances were made in techniques for the detection of protein and sugar. In fact it was in this sphere that life insurance made a valuable contribution to clinical medicine at the time.

In those years it was the infectious diseases like tuberculosis, pneumonia, syphilis and the epidemics such as influenza and bubonic plague that were of primary concern. However, interest initially was focused on body build as a prognostic indicator, and work was completed on height and weight tables related to age and sex in 1897 and 1906; these were supplemented by tables published in the *Medico-Actuarial Mortality Investigation 1909–1912*.[3] Several further studies of build were carried out over the years culminating in the *Build Study 1979*.[4]

An equally important landmark was the introduction of sphygmomanometry early in the 20th century. The first instruments, which operated on the spring principle were rather unreliable, but from these a more accurate aneroid sphygmomanometer was developed by Dr O. H. Rogers, medical director of the New York Life Insurance Company, his model being the prototype of the Tycos instrument in use today.

When the custom of recording blood pressures had become established in life insurance practice some time after World War I, it became evident that the level of blood pressure bore a direct relationship to mortality; the higher the blood pressure in a group the higher the mortality. Several large-scale medico-actuarial studies conducted in North America between 1925 and 1979 have amply confirmed the impression.

These intercompany medico-actuarial investigations, beginning in 1909, were highly productive over the years and, besides build and blood pressure, covered many other major medical conditions as in the impairment studies of 1951 and 1983. In 1990 the second edition of *Medical Risks – Trends in Mortality by Age and Time Elapsed*[5] was published. This important work analysed follow-up studies gleaned from the insurance, epidemiological and clinical literature of the world and presented them in a form suitable to the needs of the life insurance industry.

Substandard insurance was slow to develop but was encouraged by the work of Oscar H Rogers and Arthur Hunter, medical director and actuary respectively of the New York Life Insurance Company, who devised a method of risk evaluation called the numerical rating system, which was described by them in a paper read to the Association of Life Insurance Medical Directors of America and the Actuarial Society of America in 1919. This method of measuring risk is now used universally, and its application can be seen in the medical chapters of this book. Rogers was also instrumental in developing the Medical Information Bureau (MIB), which he directed from 1902 to 1932. Most life insurance companies in North America subscribe to the MIB and feed factual information on substandard applicants into the system, which is kept highly confidential, and serves to protect member companies from fraud and the withholding of material information.

In the last quarter century, in addition to investigation and mortality studies, there has been much work on the marketing of new insurance products. Beginning in the 1950s the number of these products increased in a revolutionary fashion to include such things as group plans, sickness and accident policies, critical illness contracts (CIC) and long-term care (LTC) policies, split dollar plans, premium rates differing by sex and smoking habit, cost differential according to size of policy, structured settlements and others.

With the consolidating influence of national legislation from 1870 the business of life insurance has steadily grown, adapting itself to meet the current needs of the community, until today it is an important industry handling vast sums throughout the world. Life insurance is now a large source of personal savings in the western world, and a country's economy is assisted by the money that it provides to finance industrial expansion, new factories, government and municipal projects, and countless developments calling for fresh capital both at home and in the developing countries. From all of these a nation's standard of living benefits directly.

It is likely that the years ahead will be no less adventurous, particularly from the standpoint of health and longevity. In the USA, death rates from the major cardiovascular diseases have already declined dramatically in the past 25 years among persons of late middle age and older, and it is in this age group that exciting advances in the field of therapy might be expected to improve mortality in many other disease conditions, thus further extending expectation of life. Although the lifespan of man is still the same as it was in biblical times and is unlikely to alter, the number surviving to reach the biological limits of 80–90 years is bound to increase, bringing with it the social implications of age-related disablement and a reduction in quality of life. Associated with these efforts to increase longevity there will arise ethical and legislative matters that must be of concern to everyone; they too must be scrutinized closely, particularly in the areas of genetics and confidentiality.

LIFE INSURANCE IN SOME OTHER COUNTRIES

Scandinavia
Hans Dunér

Life insurance was first introduced in Denmark in 1842 with the establishment in Copenhagen of Statsanstalten For Livsforsikring. In Norway life insurance was introduced through Norske Liv which was founded in 1844, in Sweden through Skandia which was founded in 1855, and in Finland through Kaleva, founded in 1874.

In the beginning a medical examination of the applicant was not an essential requirement. The principle was that only obviously healthy and well situated people were approved. The applicant had to appear in person before the general manager of the company for a check up. However, gradually there was a need for a more professional evaluation of the medical risks and medical officers were involved. As the number of life insurance companies increased there was a greater need for liaison and co-operation between them. The first life insurance congress in Scandinavia took place in Stockholm in 1885, followed by a congress in Kristiania (now known as Oslo) in 1893, and in Copenhagen in 1904. The Swedish Association of Medical Officers of Life Insurance Medicine was founded in 1906. There has been a high degree of co-ordination of medical risk evaluation in the Scandinavian countries. In fact, in Sweden all life insurance companies used the same life underwriting manual until the middle of 1990. Competition in life business has also been restricted in Scandinavia in other respects, but changes are being implemented. For instance, the system of brokers is now quite common. Also, within the former strict limits for banking and insurance operations there is now a mutual shifting of traditional business focuses. Insurance products, such as unit-linked plans, which have already existed in other countries, were introduced in Sweden towards the end of 1990.

The Netherlands
H K de Raadt

The first insurance company to be established in the Netherlands was De Hollandsche Sociëteit van Levensverzekeringen in 1807. Initially this company only insured people of the upper strata of society. Consequently it resulted in a slow growth of approximately 4 percent on an annual basis. The total of amounts insured in 1810 amounted to approximately 1 million guilders, and in 1860 approximately 7 million guilders. In those days companies hardly paid attention to age and state of health. It was only in the second half of the 19th century that people got acquainted with actuarial techniques, which resulted in the introduction of so-called endowment and social insurances. A steady growth of the number of life insurance companies was visible. In 1890 there were already 70 life insurers with the total of capital sums insured amounting to 627 million guilders. The annual growth of 14 percent also attracted foreign companies; in 1900, already 51.

In the 20th century the large insurers increasingly applied themselves to the wealthy part of the population and left the social insurances to others. In an increasing degree, differentiation of premium took place, not only according to age and type of insurance, but also to state of health. Medical advisers were attracted, and became organized into an Association in 1910. They made it clear to the insurers that almost everybody was insurable, provided that they could obtain enough data to calculate the risk.

In 1923 the Association of Medical Advisers joined the Nederlandse Vereniging ter Bevordering van het Levensverzekeringswezen (Dutch Association for Promoting the Life Insurance System), which was also joined by the mathematicians in 1925. However, both associations quietly disappeared from this co-ordinating association in 1942, due to the fact that their opinion increasingly deviated from that of the insurers; calculating increased premiums on actuarial and medical grounds is incompatible with the way of thinking of a purely commercially operating company.

Meanwhile the medical advisers of non-life insurers organized themselves in 1971. Many advisers were members of both organizations, which resulted in a merger in 1980. The Association now has 155 members; they meet at least four times a year to discuss test cases. Every meeting is chaired by one of the insurance companies, the management of which gives a dinner party in the evening. The Association also organizes a continuing education course for more than one day and, in 1991 for the first time, a basic course of ten days. It is striving for a further specialization in order to gain an official recognition in the future.

Over the last few years the Association has increasingly stressed its distinctive features as a conversation partner for the government and insurers for the AIDS issue and genetic problems.

Belgium
P Lauwers

In Belgium the earliest records of some kind of life insurance go back as far as the 12th century. However, life insurance as it is known today started its development during the 19th century.

Group insurance began in about 1920, but its real boom began from about 1940–45 when its development was greatly encouraged by the introduction of tax advantages. A few years later, tax advantages were also applied to certain forms of individual life insurance, and since then the Belgian life insurance market has seen continuous development.

At present there are some 130 insurance companies, or groups of companies, in Belgium and approximately half of these are authorized to operate in the life branch. Composite insurers are permitted in Belgium.

Life insurance is basically a tariff market ensuring uniform rates, with only a very small number of companies applying lower premium rates, particularly in the group area. Several companies have started to market savings products which attempt to give the consumer a higher yield, and in some cases this is in co-operation with a bank.

For some time there has been a move to liberalize the Belgian life market. It is hoped that new regulations will take effect during 1991 which will free the premium tariff, allow development of flexible products such as Universal Whole Life, and authorize domestic companies to market unit-linked policies, known popularly as 'Branch 23'.

The market policy reserves amount to more than BEF 700 billion, which shows the important role played by life insurers in the country's economy. Roughly speaking, the assets representing those reserves are invested as follows: one third in government loans, one third in property and mortgage loans and one third in shares, bonds and so on.

Life premium income amounts to about 75 billion francs; that is approximately 30 percent of the overall premium income of the Belgian insurance market.

Since 1986 life insurance has seen an accelerated development mainly due to improved tax advantages. Almost 40 percent of premium income relates to group insurance, and some 60 percent to individual life insurance.

Germany
Othard Raestrup

The insurance industry in Germany is broken down into the public and the private sectors. Social insurance and private insurance have always been separate, but have also complemented one another. A meaningful co-existence has now developed between them: basic care is provided by compulsory annuity insurance, which is augmented by company pension schemes and individual additions in the form of private life insurance. Whilst membership in the classes of insurance required by law is mandatory, with its structure reflecting that of the general population, life insurance is voluntary, which might mean that disproportionately more ailing persons with a reduced life expectancy take out life insurance. This is the reason why the practice of classifying risks, which is the responsibility of company medical officers, was introduced in Germany at the end of the 19th century.

By 1903 a department of insurance medicine was established in the German Association for Insurance Studies. The successful and experienced chairman of the annual conference was Professor Florschütz, whose pioneering research laid the foundation for life insurance medicine in Germany. The numerical rating system was developed as a basis for risk assessment. During World War II all work came to a halt, and it was not possible to re-establish the department until 1950. The main area of research, to which Dr Kaewel devoted particular effort, was aimed at improving risk assessment on the basis of insurance medical analyses of diseases, disease groups and combinations, collected by the Central Statistical Office of the Association of Life Insurance Companies. With the assistance of German reinsurance companies, an individual method of assessment of exposed risks was developed which is still being constantly refined today through attention to all diagnostic, therapeutic, prognostic and epidemiological progress in medical science. Research is funded by the Association of Life Insurance Companies, and the journal 'Versicherungsmedizin', which provides up-to-date information for physicians, is also widely read outside the insurance industry.

Switzerland
Karl Werlen

Compared with other European countries the development of life insurance in Switzerland came relatively late. In the environment of a largely agricultural economy and patriarchal system of society, living in small towns and villages, the natural demands for security could be achieved with risks being absorbed by the 'community', following the principle of the extended family, artisan groups and guilds. It was those communities which first engendered organizations of a mutual or self-aid nature.

In the first half of the 19th century, with the onset of the industrial revolution in Switzerland, there was growing demand for individual provision. First attempts at setting up life offices failed and two companies were unsuccessful: the Allgemeine Schweizerische for dependants, widows and pensions, which was established in 1840, and the Schweizerische National-Vorsichtskasse for provident funds, established in 1841. Nevertheless, demand grew and was satisfied by some 20 German, English and French life offices.

The Swiss constitution of 1848 set the stage for a general boom in the economy. A relatively loose federation of individual states was superseded by a tightly knit confederation. A common currency, unification of measures, a central postal system, the abolition of customs duties between the individual states, and the development of a railway network created the necessary conditions for a positive development of the economy.

In 1857 the Schweizerische Lebensversicherungs-und Rentenanstalt (known today in English as the 'Swiss Life') was founded; it is still the largest Swiss life office. Then followed a spate of new life offices: La Suisse (1858), La Bâloise (1864), La Genevoise (1872), Pax (1876), and Patria (1881). In 1886 the first insurance supervisory act came into force, a law which was exemplary for other countries in continental Europe.

Following the collapse of the Swiss Life portfolios of some German insurers as a result of the German hyperinflation, some further local life companies were set up, for example VITA in 1922 and Winterthur Life in 1923, both subsidiaries of Accident & Liability Insurers.

Today, in 1991, 23 locally incorporated (of which a number are partly or wholly foreign owned) private life insurance companies actively write business; their premium income represents 57 percent of the total premium income of the private insurance industry in Switzerland.

Japan
Hiroshi Okamoto

The development of the life insurance industry in Japan has, of course, taken place within the context of larger historical trends. Japan's first life insurance company was established in 1881, just 14 years after Japan entered the completely new Meiji era. Efforts were made during this period to bring about the rapid modernization of Japan. It should be noted in particular that from the beginning company doctors were employed so that medical examinations could be done by qualified physicians. This played a major role in the advance of insurance medicine in Japan, and the first medical director, G. Indoh, laid the foundations for the development which followed. Nevertheless, this was a time when there was insufficient statistical data for mortality rates, and so the difficulties involved were enormous. In 1901 the Association of Life Insurance Medicine of Japan (ALIMJA) was established. Its first president was T Nakahama, who left a legacy of many great accomplishments. His diary is to be published very shortly to commemorate the 90th anniversary of the establishment of ALIMJA. Later, although Japan's insurance industry was significantly affected by the global economic turbulence of 1929, it continued its steady development. It seemed that both economically and culturally the country's foundation was firmly in place, but shortly afterwards Japan entered into a disastrous war.

After World War II Japan again entered a period of assimilation, but the wounds from the war were so great that until 1950 there were only ten lectures given at the Congress of Life Insurance Medicine of Japan. In 1950 the *Underwriting Manual* was published, a big step forward for numerical underwriting. During that same year the *Manual for Medical Examination* was published. In the postwar period, beginning in 1952, Japan has participated in the International Congress of Life Assurance Medicine (ICLAM).

From about 1955 the economy began to grow very quickly, and this also brought about rapid growth in the life insurance industry. Interaction with other scientific institutions also increased. From 1976 to 1979 joint research with the Japan National Railways (now known as JR) was undertaken into blood pressure. Since 1980 there has also been research with the Tokyo Women's Medical College into diabetes mellitus, as well as more recent research into ischemic heart disease. Over the last ten years research into prognosis of the human life span has advanced with lightning speed. In 1986 the ICLAM was held in Tokyo. There is, in fact, much interaction between Japan, the USA and Europe, as well as many other countries.

In 1991 ALIMJA celebrated its 90th anniversary, which also marked the introduction of the authorized diplomate system. This enables physicians to be accredited with a diploma in insurance medicine after 5 years of special study of the subject. A new textbook of insurance medicine in the Japanese language was also published at the same time. ALIMJA has been a member of the Japan Medical Congress since 1981, and with the introduction of the authorized diplomate system, the Association has now become an increasingly well regarded institution both in terms of its reputation and actual personnel. Membership exceeded 1,000 members in 1990 and the Journal of the Association of Life Insurance Medicine of Japan is published periodically. We are indeed fortunate to have grown along with the expanding economy on a scale never before experienced in Japan. However, it has been predicted that Japanese society will age increasingly rapidly, and therefore many challenges still lie ahead of us.

REFERENCES

1 Moorhead EJ. Our yesterdays: the history of the actuarial profession in North America, 1809–1979. Schaumburg, Illinois: Society of Actuaries, 1989.
2 Singer RB. Life insurance medicine: our heritage. *Trans Assoc Life Ins Med Dirs Am* 1989; 73: 214–18.
3 *Medico-actuarial Mortality Investigation 1909–1912*. New York: Actuarial Society of America/Association of Life Insurance Medical Directors of America, 1913.
4 *Build Study 1979*. New York: Society of Actuaries/Association of Life Insurance Medical Directors of America, 1980.
5 Lew EA, Gajewski J, editors. *Medical Risks – Trends in Mortality by Age and Time Elapsed*. Vols 1 and 2. New York, Westport, London, 1990.

*At the 100th Annual Meeting of ALIMDA at Marina del Rey in October 1991 it was decided to change the name of the Association to the American Academy of Insurance Medicine (AAIM) in order to emphasize its educational mission.

CHAPTER 2

FORMS OF LIFE AND HEALTH INSURANCE CONTRACTS

PETER C MAYNARD

BASIC TYPES OF LIFE POLICY

There are three different classifications of life insurance policies: term insurance, whole life and endowment.

The first, term insurance, consists of policies which are taken out as a means of insuring against the possibility of death within a specified period. The premiums payable are solely for the purpose of providing life cover as a form of protection.

Both whole life and endowment effectively make an investment that becomes payable at a future date, either on death or earlier. The premiums payable are for the purpose of providing a mix of life cover and investment and, as such, have cash or surrender values. In the case of whole life policies a payout will occur on the death of the life assured, whenever this occurs. On the other hand, an endowment policy will mature after a fixed period. Endowments thus pay on maturity or earlier death.

Term Insurance

The feature of term insurance is that for a relatively small premium a large amount can be assured. For term insurances up to about the age of 45, when mortality is low, premiums payable are very small; after middle life, when the mortality curve begins to rise, premiums are correspondingly higher. In the past most life offices would not offer this type of contract after the age of 65 in view of the much steeper rise in mortality experienced from this age, but today these older lives are considered acceptable.

By its very nature there is a certain amount of risk to the life company in term insurance. It has been established, particularly in North America, that there is a significantly higher mortality experience among people effecting term insurance contracts than among those holding endowment insurance. It seems likely that some degree of selection is exercised against the company in term insurance, and it is not altogether surprising that an applicant who has some reason to believe that his risk of dying is increased (for whatever reason) would wish to insure his life for as large a sum as possible at minimal cost. Thus the life company has to be particularly careful in the underwriting of term insurance proposals.

Term insurance is often issued for definite purposes (e.g. mortgage protection, school fees, death duty cover, credit insurance, etc). In such circumstances mortality experience is little different from that found in other forms of contract.

Term insurance is the most basic form of life insurance. There are a number of different types, and these are dealt with below.

Level Term Insurance

The simplest form is level term insurance. This contract provides that the life company will only pay the sum assured if the insured dies during the term of the policy. The sum assured does not vary during the policy term and once the policy has expired it has no value. This is one of the cheapest forms of life insurance, since the cover is only temporary and there is normally no surrender or cash value available on early termination.

Renewable Term Insurance

Some term insurances are 'renewable' in that on the expiry date there is an option to take out a further term insurance at standard rates without evidence of health, as long as the expiry date is not beyond, say, the age of 65. Each subsequent policy may have the same option. Whenever the policy comes up for renewal the premium will increase, since it is based on the then age of the life assured. Renewable policies are becoming more difficult to obtain due to the AIDS risk.

Convertible Term Insurance

This is term insurance with an option that enables the insured to convert it at any time during its existence to a whole life or endowment policy without further evidence of health. The premium for the new policy will be that normally applicable to a whole life or endowment policy for a person of the insured's age at the time of conversion. The premiums charged for convertible term insurance are slightly higher than for ordinary level term insurance to allow for the cost of the conversion option.

Decreasing Term Insurance

Term insurance of this type has a sum assured which reduces each year (or possibly each month) by a stated amount, decreasing to nil at the end of the term. It is normally used to cover a reducing debt, such as the capital outstanding on a house purchase mortgage, with the sum assured linked to the reduction in the capital outstanding under the loan. Although the cover decreases each year, the premium remains constant. Premiums for decreasing term insurance are generally slightly cheaper than for a level term insurance for the same initial sum assured and term.

Family Income Policies

Instead of having term insurance paying a lump sum on death, it is possible to have a policy which pays an income. This type of contract is known as a family income policy because it is intended to replace income that the insured would have produced for his family were he still alive. Family income benefit policies are relatively cheap because the cover, like that under decreasing term insurance, reduces over the term of the policy.

Whole Life Policies

A whole life policy pays a sum whenever the insured dies. It is a permanent policy, not limited to an expiry date as is a term insurance. A level premium is charged despite the fact that mortality is low before middle age and increases more rapidly afterwards. Theoretically, insurance for this rising mortality with age needs a small premium at younger ages and a larger premium in the later years. Such a variation in premiums would be rather inconvenient to apply, so the level premium, which was devised in the early days of life assurance in Britain, is charged throughout the term, enabling the life office to accumulate a reserve in the earlier years associated with low mortality in order to counteract the higher mortality in later life.

There are variations of the whole life contract in which premiums, instead of being charged throughout life, are paid only for a stated number of years, or cease at a stated age (e.g. at the age of 65 or 80), or as a lump sum payment at the beginning of the policy (the so-called 'single pay life'). The sum assured, however, remains payable only at death. In this type of policy, reserves are built up more quickly and, even after the payments cease, continue to increase by accruing interest.

Whole life policies can often be used as security for a loan, either from the insurance company or another lender.

Non-Profit Whole or Non-Participating Life Policies
A non-profit whole life policy has a level premium payable throughout life. It pays only a fixed sum assured, whenever death occurs. Nowadays very few non-profit whole life policies are purchased as they are perceived as poor value in comparison with with-profit policies.

With-Profit or Participating Whole Life Policies
These policies are almost the same as non-profit whole life insurance, the only difference being that the amount payable on death is the sum assured, plus whatever share of the life office's profits have been allocated up to the date of death.

Regular Premium Unit-Linked (UK) or Variable (USA) Whole Life Policies
These plans have become popular over the past ten years. Their main advantage is their flexibility, since they offer a variable mix between investment content and life cover.

There are many variations in the structure of investment fund linked policies. Major determinants are the tax laws and investment regulations of the countries in which the policies are sold. The essential feature is that part of the premium is paid into an investment fund and part is used to cover mortality and expense costs. The following describes the practice in the UK, but the principles underlying the structure of this unit-linked product are the same wherever insurance of this type is sold.

The policyholder pays regular premiums, which purchase units in one or more investment funds. Enough units are cancelled each month to purchase the guaranteed life cover. The initial level of life cover is set for the first ten years on the basis of an assumed growth rate in the fund to which the contract is linked. At the end of the ten years the policy is reviewed to see how the actual growth rate compares with the assumed growth rate. This determines whether the value of the units allocated at that time will be enough to maintain the sum assured. A few life companies undertake the first review at the end of five years rather than ten.

The action taken as a result of this review varies from company to company, but if the actual growth rate is higher than the assumed, the sum assured is usually increased. If it is lower, either the sum assured is reduced or the premium correspondingly increased. Further regular reviews are made, usually every five years, but possibly more frequently once the life assured reaches the age of 70 or 75.

If the policy is cashed in, the surrender value will be the bid value of the units allocated. If the total unit value overtakes the sum assured, then the higher amount will be payable on a death claim.

Endowment Policies

The third basic type of policy is the endowment assurance. Here, the sum assured is payable on a fixed date (the maturity date) or on the insured's earlier death. The standard non-profit endowment insurance provides a level guaranteed sum assured on death or maturity. Because there is certain to be a payout at some stage, endowment insurances have cash (surrender) values and can be used as security for loans, either from the life company itself or from other lenders, such as banks or building societies. Because of the rapid build up of cash value in most endowment policies very little endowment insurance is now sold in the USA, where it is considered as investment for tax purposes rather than as insurance.

The endowment policies described below are only really suitable investments if the investor does not want his money before the maturity date, and will not need to cash in the policy earlier. The best yield on an endowment policy is always obtained by waiting until the maturity date.

Non-Profit Endowments
This is the most basic form of endowment, with level premiums and a payout of a fixed guaranteed sum assured on maturity or earlier death. As in the case of whole life policies, relatively few non-profit policies are now sold.

With-Profit Endowments
Participation in the life company's profits can also apply to endowment insurance, where the amount payable on maturity or earlier death is the guaranteed sum assured, plus the bonuses. If the policy runs to maturity, bonuses will be higher than in the case of an earlier claim because they will have accumulated over a longer period.

Premiums are higher than for non-profit endowments, to reflect the greater benefits that are potentially payable. With-profit endowment contracts are the basic elements in many savings and house purchase arrangements.

Unit-Linked Endowments
Many regular premium unit-linked savings plans are written as long-term endowments or as ten-year endowments with an option to extend for further ten-year periods. These policies operate on the usual unit-linked principle, with premiums buying units in an investment fund, the performance of which determines the value of the policy on maturity or earlier surrender (although the latter event may incur some financial penalty). There is a minimum sum assured payable on death.

Unit-Linked Mortgage Plans

Many life companies now issue special unit-linked mortgage plans. These are similar to unit-linked endowment plans and provide a guaranteed sum assured on death, but not at maturity, where the sum assured payable is the bid value of the units. These plans incorporate review clauses so that the cost of the cover is measured periodically against the performance of the units.

A major drawback with unit-linked plans is that they may mature at a time when the value of the units is depressed. To reduce this risk many companies will recommend a switch into a safe investment, such as a cash or building society fund, five years before maturity. Most life companies will notify the life assured when the value of the units is equal to the guaranteed sum assured. This enables the loan to be repaid early from the proceeds of the policy if required.

Pure Endowments

A pure endowment is not truly a life policy, since it provides no life cover. The standard pure endowment is simply a contract that pays the maturity value if the life assured lives to the maturity date, but nothing if the life assured dies before that date. There is no life risk and thus no underwriting is needed. Some pure endowments have a surrender value, but many do not. Some offer a return of premiums on death before maturity.

Double Endowment Insurance

In this type of contract the survival benefit is twice the death benefit. Double endowment insurance is not as popular as it used to be, although some offices still offer it.

UNIVERSAL LIFE POLICIES

Universal life policies are a further development of regular premium investment-linked whole life policies. They are basically standard investment-linked whole life contracts but with a range of optional extras for total flexibility. The idea is that the policyholder pays what he likes, when he likes and chooses from the range of benefits. All premiums are paid into the selected fund(s) and each month the cost of whatever benefits currently apply is paid from the fund.

The range of benefits available usually includes the following:
1) Life cover.
2) An annual indexation option to adjust automatically the death benefit (and possibly other benefits) in line with the Retail Price Index.
3) The facility to increase further the sum assured at certain times (guaranteed insurability).
4) Waiving premiums during disability.
5) The option to take investment gain as income.
6) The facility to suspend premium payments (e.g. during unemployment).
7) Permanent health insurance cover.
8) Payment of the sum assured in advance in the event of total and permanent disability or diagnosis of a critical illness.

9) Payment of an income during hospitalization.

10) Doubling the sum assured in the event of death by accident (accidental death benefit).

11) The option to add a further life assured (e.g. on marriage). Benefits can often be added later as well as chosen at outset.

Most contracts provide for a regular premium, usually monthly, which can be increased or reduced as required, and also allow single premiums to be paid whenever desired. The new generation of investment-linked whole life and universal life policies are popular for family protection. Because they are very flexible they can be adapted to meet changing family circumstances.

In the USA variable universal life combines the investment features of variable whole life with universal life.

HEALTH INSURANCE

The aging population in the majority of developing countries around the world has led to increased pressure on state funding of health care. To combat this many governments have taken measures to encourage self-provision. The gradual change in emphasis from state to self-provision has led to growing interest in a variety of health products.

Critical Illness Cover

Critical illness cover is also known as, dread disease, recuperator life, revival life and living insurance.

This benefit was originally introduced by life offices in South Africa, and is now written in the UK and other markets. The sum assured is payable on the diagnosis of the first of a number of diseases that are specified in the policy, and is paid as an acceleration of all or part of the life sum assured; however, some companies now offer critical illness cover as a stand-alone policy. The object of the cover is to provide a cash sum, which the insured can use to mitigate the financial effects of coping with a serious illness and any resulting disability. Illnesses covered are typically myocardial infarction, coronary artery bypass surgery, stroke and cancer, although a number of companies have now extended the range to include impairments such as renal failure, major organ transplantation and paralysis.

Critical illness cover is often sold as an optional extra to universal life plans but a number of companies have made this, rather than the life cover, the key feature of their marketing. A few companies add critical illness riders to plans designed as protection for mortgage loans.

When considering an application various predisposing factors, as well as a history of any 'critical' illness, will be very important.

Permanent Health Insurance (PHI): Long-Term Disability Insurance (LTD)

Long-term disability due to sickness or accident may bring financial hardship to a person's family. Thus, many companies offer permanent health insurance (PHI) policies, called long-term disability (LTD) in the USA.

The object of the policy is to provide an income while the breadwinner is unable to work due to illness or injury. The first step is to decide what level of cover the family will need to continue living at the same standard. This may be affected by whatever benefits might be paid by an employer or under a pension scheme, which could possibly provide an acceptable level of income for some while. The benefits provided by the state must also be taken into account.

All PHI (or LTD) policies include a deferred or waiting period, which is the time between onset of disability and the commencement of income payments under the policy. The deferred period should be chosen to reflect the insured's circumstances; it is commonly three or six months, but can be as short as one month or as long as two years. The expiry date should be the insured's expected retirement date, since the policy is designed to cover his earned income and should thus continue for the whole of his working life.

Relatively common nowadays are unit-linked PHI policies, which operate in much the same way as many unit-linked life policies in that units are cancelled each month to purchase that month's cover. Regular reviews are undertaken to test whether unit growth has matched that made in the assumptions for the initial costing. When units have under-performed, an increase in premiums will be required to maintain the level of cover. When the units have performed better than the assumptions, a cash value will build up which may be surrendered or taken at the expiry of the plan.

PHI cover can be written as individual policies or as a group arrangement set up for a firm's employees. In the latter case the underwriting and administrative arrangements are often simplified by the operation of 'free cover' limits in the same way as a group life insurance scheme (*see* p. 000).

Private Medical Insurance

Private medical insurance provides cover for periods of illness when the policy-holder is receiving private medical treatment. Typically the following will be covered:
1) Hospital charges, including accommodation, nursing care, operating theatre fees, in-patient surgical dressings and drugs.
2) Specialists' fees for consultations and treatment, including fees for a surgeon, anesthetist or physician, diagnostic tests or physiotherapy.

Private medical insurance proposals may be underwritten in the traditional way, although it is usual to exclude conditions that directly or indirectly increase the risk to a significant degree. However, it is now common to dispense with full underwriting at outset and to rely on routine exclusion of pre-existing medical conditions.

The cover may take the form of individual policies or, for employees, a single group policy embracing a number of employees.

Long-Term Care

Long-term care insurance (LTCI) provides cover to meet the cost of personal and nursing care should it be required. As such costs can be substantial, this product also protects assets and safeguards inheritances for others. It is vital that the contract meets needs by providing realistic benefits, yet there have to be mechanisms to control frequency of claims and discourage fraudulent claims. There is a very good case for assessing eligibility for claim payment on the basis of degree of disability rather than service requirement; this can be achieved by assessing ability to perform various activities of daily living (ADL).

The length and content of an ADL list can be varied to suit different applications, but a workable list might read as follows:
1) Bathing.
2) Dressing.
3) Using the lavatory.
4) Continence.
5) Getting in and out of bed or a chair.
6) Feeding.

To fulfill the necessary criteria the insured must be unable to carry out a specified minimum number of these tasks. A further measure might be the requirement that assistance must be necessary to carry out the personal function, with the use of special equipment or appliances irrelevant.

It is usual to cover additionally the need for care or supervision arising through mental disorders, regardless of whether physical ADL criteria are fulfilled. However, cover may be restricted to organic brain syndromes such as Alzheimer's disease and other forms of dementia.

LTCI can be written as a stand-alone product or as a rider. Indeed LTCI is ideally suited as a rider to flexible whole life contracts. The payment of LTC benefits under such an arrangement represents advance payment of the sum assured. Compared with a stand-alone product the rider is inexpensive.

GROUP LIFE AND PENSION SCHEMES

The primary object of a group scheme is to secure a pension for employees at retirement age and life cover in the event of death before that time. The essential feature of a group life insurance scheme is that a number of employees are insured under a single contract arranged by the employer. Because the scheme is initiated by the employer the risk of selection against the insurance company is much less than in individual contracts; since the majority of employees will participate in the scheme, concession can usually be made by waiving evidence of health up to a maximum sum, such cover being termed 'free' cover. The amount of free cover granted depends on several factors, including the total number of employees participating, an even spread of the average sum assured over those participating and a minimum percentage of those eligible actually joining the scheme.

As the salaries of the various employees rise, so the amount of free cover may be exceeded; it is usual then for the insurance company to call for medical evidence of health from time to time. It may happen that one or two individuals are found to be uninsurable, but nevertheless they still remain insured under the terms of the free-cover limit at no increase in premiums. The only stipulation for free-cover is that the employee must be actively at work on the date of entry into the scheme. If he were absent because of ill health, free cover would not be granted until he had been actively at work again for a specified period or produced medical evidence showing full recovery from his illness.

A person not taking advantage of group life insurance when the scheme was initiated would be regarded with some suspicion if later he elected to enter. In the interim he may have developed some illness of a serious nature, or he may think he has developed one, and naturally wishes to obtain some life cover without medical evidence. In such circumstances the risk of antiselection is obvious, and medical evidence would usually be called for as a precautionary measure.

It is interesting that mortality experienced in group schemes is only slightly greater than in ordinary life insurance.

KEY-MAN AND OTHER BUSINESS PROTECTION POLICIES

Key-man insurance is cover effected by a business on the life of an employee who is vital to the continued profitability of the business. Examples of key men or women might be a sales executive generating valuable foreign contracts or, for a manufacturing company, a technical innovator responsible for a new product development. Often a key man is the person who has built up the business from scratch.

The loss of a key man through death or long illness could seriously affect a company's profitability in various ways, and key-man cover has evolved to provide some sort of financial recompense: the policy proceeds can be used to compensate for loss of profits, to finance the recruitment and training of a successor or, in the case of absence through illness, the employment of a locum. The sum insured and class of policy should be individually tailored to the needs of the company. The amounts involved are often substantial, and careful underwriting is necessary to ensure that there is insurable interest, that the level of cover is appropriate and that there is no moral hazard.

Key-man life policies are often term insurance of short duration, although longer duration policies (including certain whole life contracts) may be employed. The effects of prolonged illness causing absence from work can be dealt with in a number of ways. Key-man PHI is a very specialist form of health insurance cover, and typically runs for only a short period rather than to the retirement age of the life insured. An alternative solution is to use total and permanent disability benefit, which pays a lump sum in the event of the employee being unable to resume his job, the effects of which are potentially as serious as those arising from the employee's death. More recently critical illness policies have started to be applied to key-man situations, although there is some debate about how appropriate this form of cover is.

Other instances of life insurance used in business planning are partnership and directors' share protection arrangements. Life cover can enable a surviving partner or partners to purchase the share of a deceased partner from his estate, allowing them to keep full control of, and continue, the business. The exact details of partnership protection schemes vary, but the main requirement is a policy on the life of each partner under trust for the other partners; thus the survivors can readily exercise their right to buy out the deceased partner's share.

The death of a director-shareholder of a small private company can give rise to problems similar to those in a partnership. To prevent the shares passing to someone with no interest—or even unfriendly interests—in the company, a share protection scheme can be put in place, enabling purchase by the surviving directors. Once again, a policy on the life of each director held in trust for the others will provide the necessary funding.

INHERITANCE TAX PLANNING

Life insurance can be used to mitigate the often substantial liability for taxes levied on the estate of a deceased person or on the value of a gift made by a deceased person prior to death. The type of policy used depends on individual circumstances and, of course, legislation pertaining at the time.

One use of life insurance is to build up a tax-free fund outside the estate for beneficiaries after death. For example, an own-life policy effected by a parent under trust for children would mean that on death the policy proceeds would pass to the children free of tax. Alternatively a whole life policy (again under trust) can be a means of providing the beneficiaries of an estate with the funds to pay the necessary taxes, the sum assured being the approximate tax liability expected on death. If legislation provides that transfers between spouses are free of tax, then a liability may only arise on the death of the surviving spouse; the tax charge can be met by means of a joint whole life second-death policy effected by the husband and wife under trust for the estate beneficiaries.

Tax may be payable on gifts if the donor dies within a certain time after making the gift. The potential tax bill can be covered by a term insurance; the sum assured and duration should mirror the potential liability involved. The policy could be taken out by the donor under trust for the donee, or by the donee himself.

ANNUITIES

An annuity is a form of insurance contract in which, in return for a purchase price, the insurer agrees to pay a number of yearly or monthly installments. These payments usually commence immediately (immediate annuity) but they may begin after a specified period (deferred annuity). The annuity is normally paid throughout the lifetime of the annuitant, although instalments may cease after a specified period (or on the earlier death of the annuitant).

Payments under some annuities may be guaranteed for a number of years, regardless of the survival of the annuitant, but such a guarantee requires an increase in the basic purchase price.

The mortality experience of those who have purchased annuities voluntarily is lighter than under life insurance contracts because, generally, the former group have faith in their longevity and exercise a degree of selection against the life company. On the other hand, mortality under compulsory-purchase annuities, such as those in connection with pension arrangements, is higher because this group contains a significant proportion of impaired lives. It is not standard practice to underwrite annuity applications but insurance companies may specially assess and grant more favorable terms to under-average lives on request.

Although they have a variety of applications, annuities are most often employed in connection with retirement pension arrangements. They are also used by elderly people to convert cash reserves into extra income to supplement that from the state and other sources. Annuities can be used as a vehicle for funding nursing and other home care fees; logically this application should be refined by taking into account the health of the annuitant so that the purchase price accurately reflects the mortality risk.

Structured Settlements

Annuities have an important role to play in structured settlements. Common in the USA for some years and now being awarded with increasing frequency in the UK, structured settlements are financial arrangements used notably in connection with legal damage claims where the plaintiff has suffered injury resulting in significant disability. They are promoted as a more effective alternative to lump sum damage awards by providing lump sums together with an income throughout the lifetime of the plaintiff; the income payments can be arranged to increase as necessary to deal with the effects of inflation, and perhaps to deal with any future special needs associated with the victim's health. Structured settlements are a very specialized market because the medical histories involved are rarely seen in traditional life underwriting. Therefore each case requires careful and individual assessment to establish the annuity purchase price (*see* Chapters 4 and 6).

CHAPTER 3

PRINCIPLES OF RISK SELECTION AND CLASSIFICATION

HARRY A WOODMAN

This chapter is written from the US perspective; most of the principles and practices applicable in the USA also apply in Canada. Although there are differences in other countries, most practices are not so dissimilar that the reader cannot profit from the information in this chapter; general principles are likely to be the same.

One of the objects of underwriting should be to accept as large a proportion of cases as possible at standard premium rates, leaving only a small percentage of substandard lives to be rated according to the risk of the particular impairment present. Very few cases should be declined outright. The determination of individual risks acceptable to the company is called risk selection; the separation of groups of insurance risks into the categories of standard, and the degrees of substandard, is called risk classification. The company's underwriting policy-makers determine the risk classes and the underwriters assign each individual risk to the appropriate class.

The risk selection process starts with the agent, who has a responsibility, as well as a self-interest, to write applications only on people who need, and are likely to qualify for, insurance. The underwriter continues the selection process by obtaining information sufficient to determine whether or not the risk is acceptable.

RISK CLASSIFICATION PROCESS

After completing the selection process, the underwriter assigns the risk to one of the risk classes predetermined through the co-operative efforts of actuaries, medical directors and underwriters. The methodology used to determine risk classes based on mortality studies from various sources is described in Chapter 4. The risk classes include one or more standard classes (the standard class may be subdivided into preferred risks and the remainder), and several substandard classes (from three or four to as many as ten or twelve, depending on a company's marketing strategy). A premium is then determined for each class, and groups of risks expected to produce mortality at the level provided for by that premium are included in that class. The underwriter then determines the class to which each person should be assigned from the ratings developed for each impairment by the actuary-medical director-underwriter team.

There are certain risk characteristics that affect the level of mortality, and therefore the basic premium. For many years, the sole characteristic used to determine the basic premium for each insured was age. As age increases, the annual rate of mortality increases and the expectation of life (the average years of survival) decreases. In recent years sex and cigarette smoking habits have also been used to determine the basic premium for each insured. Females live longer than males, and nonsmokers live longer than smokers.

Table 3.1. Comparison of male and female expectations of life based on the 1975–80 ultimate (16th policy year and later) life insurance tables and the 1979–81 US life population tables, with expectations of life for male smokers and nonsmokers based on the 1980 CSO table (*see* pp. 44–6 and 'Note' *below*).

Age (years)	1975–80 ultimate		1979–81 population		1980 CSO (males)		
	Male	Female	Male	Female	Total	Smoker	Nonsmoker
5	–	–	66·29	70·53	–	–	–
15	60·57	65·92	56·52	60·72	56·93	53·47	58·83
25	51·25	56·21	47·37	54·16	47·84	44·51	49·68
35	41·80	46·50	38·20	41·71	38·61	35·38	40·35
45	32·39	37·03	29·22	32·76	29·62	26·57	31·15
55	23·58	28·03	21·08	24·65	21·29	18·68	22·44
65	15·83	19·72	14·21	17·60	14·04	12·13	14·70
75	9·66	12·31	8·90	11·67	8·31	7·26	8·58
85	5·35	6·73	5·13	7·18	4·46	4·16	4·51

Note The ultimate and US life population tables do not have subdivisions of data for smokers and nonsmokers. Therefore the 1980 CSO table is used to illustrate the expectations of life for male smokers and nonsmokers. The expectations of life in the 1980 CSO table are roughly the same as those in the 1979–81 life population tables. (The 1980 CSO table is a conservative life insurance table used for valuation purposes; it should not be considered as representative of aggregate life insurance experience.)

Expectation of life is a satisfactory way of measuring *average* periods of survival for *groups* of risks based on past experience. It is not a predictor of survival for an individual because of the many variables that can affect each person's lifetime.

The range of mortality for standard risks within each age-gender-smoking habits class is at least 85 percent to 125 percent of the average for that class. The better risks are those with excellent risk profile characteristics, particularly for coronary artery disease and accident. The poorer risks are those with poor risk profile characteristics, or with minor physical impairments or medical histories. If a company does not use gender and smoking habits in its classification of standard risks, the range of mortality would be from about 50 percent to 200 percent of the mortality rate for each age group; the lowest percentage would apply to female nonsmokers with excellent risk profiles, and the highest percentage would apply to male smokers with poor risk profiles.

Some companies divide the standard class by introducing a preferred risk classification instead of, or in addition to, the nonsmoker class. If preferred risk is used instead of nonsmoker, then nonsmoking is one of several criteria for preferred risk. If preferred risk is used in addition to nonsmoker, then nonsmokers with above average risk profiles are selected for preferred. The preferred risk classification may apply only to amounts above a certain minimum basis because only these large amounts have sufficient underwriting information to determine accurate classification of above average risks.

After classification by age, sex and smoking habits, the next step in risk classification is to provide for the extra mortality from those risks that have expected mortality beyond the limits of standard. In taking this step, it must be kept in mind that although certain risks have higher than average mortality, this excess mortality is not high enough to classify them as substandard. Moderate departures from average weight and blood pressure are accepted standard, as are medical impairments or histories of a relatively minor nature. This classification decision is governed by the previously mentioned objective of classifying the large majority as standard and declining very few. Approximately 90 percent of all applicants are classified as standard, about 6–7 percent substandard, and 3–4 percent declined. However, the percentages of standard, substandard and declined vary by issue age: from about 98 percent standard, 1 percent substandard and 1 percent declined at ages under 30, to about 60 percent standard, 20 percent substandard and 20 percent declined at the oldest issue ages. There is also a variation in these percentages by sex and smoking habits.

Medical Factors Affecting Risk Classification

The primary factor in classifying risks that are not standard is state of health. Medical impairments account for the substantial majority of substandard and declined risks, particularly at the older ages. It is the task of the underwriter to assess the degree of extra mortality that might be expected, and to make certain that the risk is placed in the same class as others having the same expected mortality. The appropriate ratings for impairments may be developed from the results of previous intercompany mortality studies, from studies of a company's own experience, from studies published in medical literature, and from current clinical opinion on prognosis in the light of developments in medical treatment and surgical procedures.

In addition to obtaining information about medical history and present health, companies utilize physical measurements (height-weight, blood pressure, pulse) and medical tests to determine whether there may be potential problems in apparently asymptomatic individuals, problems which may affect their life expectancy. These tests include laboratory examination of blood and urine, electrocardiograms and chest X-rays. Greatly expanded use of laboratory testing has been triggered by the concern about AIDS. The increased use of blood and urine test results has been helpful in refining medical selection.

Another factor associated with the overall medical evaluation of risks is family history, particularly of degenerative heart disease. Although few companies classify an individual as substandard solely on the basis of family history, it is often a factor in association with medical history, present health or medical tests.

The primary purpose of this book is to discuss the medical impairments that are important in risk selection. Part II is devoted to this purpose. However, there are a number of other factors taken into account in risk classification.

Other Factors Affecting Risk Classification

The same principle used in medical risk classification applies to other factors: minor increases in mortality risk are absorbed in the standard class and do not result in a substandard classification unless the risk is associated with a specific medical history. For example, aviation activity as a private pilot may not be ratable, but in combination with a history of heart disease or epilepsy it could result in a declination or the use of an aviation exclusion clause.

Occupation

Occupation was a major factor in underwriting before World War II. Since that time, technological advances in safety and improvements in working conditions have made most occupations insurable at standard rates.

Occupations that are considered hazardous, and that would be rated, are those involved in Pacific Coast lumbering, deep-sea fishing and diving, or in off-shore drilling; steeplejacks, crane operators, demolition workers, asbestos-processing workers, and workers in industries where there is a significant radiation hazard. Persons in occupations presenting a health or life hazard require special medical underwriting requirements to ensure that the effect of the hazard has not presented itself. There are also some occupations that present a life style hazard, such as bartenders and other employees of establishments where serving liquor is the primary source of income. Certain professional athletes and entertainers also present life style hazards; discretion is necessary when selecting these risks.

Certain occupations (such as the clergy and certain other professional and business occupations) have a better than average expectation of life. Some companies give credit for these occupations in their determination of preferred risk.

Hazardous Sports

An extra premium is usually required from those who participate in the most hazardous sports as either amateurs or professionals. Such sports include formula motor racing, motorcycle racing, skydiving, hang-gliding, scuba diving at depths over 50 feet, and mountaineering.

Aviation

Pilots and crew members of scheduled airlines are generally considered to be standard risks, along with private pilots who fly for pleasure. Other professional civilian pilots, and military pilots and crew members, are generally charged extra premiums. An aviation exclusion clause is used primarily for people in military training who may become military pilots.

Residence

People residing in, or travelling extensively to, underdeveloped countries may be subject to an extra premium because of poor sanitary conditions, prevalence of certain diseases, and insufficient access to medical care. Persons planning to travel to, or reside in, countries where there is political unrest may be declined.

Mortality differences between geographical areas within the same country are not recognized by premium differences. However, in the USA there are lower limits for laboratory testing in certain states because of the greater prevalence of HIV infection.

Cigarette Smoking

As previously mentioned (*see* pp. 31–3) cigarette smoking has become one of the major factors used in the classification of standard risks. Cigarette smoking is the cause of, or contributing factor to, many impairments, especially coronary artery disease, lung cancer, chronic obstructive pulmonary disease (COPD) and peripheral vascular disease. Careful consideration must be given to the classification of impaired risks who continue to smoke because the nonsmoker–smoker differential in the standard premium may not be sufficient to cover the additional mortality.

Life style

Excessive use of alcohol and drug dependence are other life style factors that are generally considered as part of the medical risk evaluation. Poorer alcohol risks and current drug users are usually declined.

Motor vehicle use can be a major risk hazard; persons with more than one or two recent violations are generally rated or declined, depending on the nature of the violation. The number of recorded violations usually represents only a small fraction of the number of the violations undetected. Persons with a poor motor vehicle record and a drink problem are certainly declined.

Combination of Hazards

This chapter suggests that medical selection of risks cannot be done without consideration of the entire risk. For some impairments the mortality from hazards other than medical may be unrelated to the mortality from the medical impairment. However, in many cases the combination makes the person uninsurable or at least suggests a rating greater than the sum of the parts.

INSURABLE INTEREST

To ensure that a life insurance contract is sound, the person who stands to benefit from the proceeds must have a *real* interest in the continued survival of the insured. The stronger this interest, the better the mortality experience is likely to be. Moreover, the sum payable under the insurance contract should not exceed the *real* financial interest. The evaluation of insurable interest is generally not the responsibility of the medical director. However, the medical director should be aware of any questionable insurable interest situation in order to help the underwriter make an overall evaluation.

Life insurance is normally bought for specific purposes: to provide continuation of income for dependents; to cover a home mortgage or other indebtedness; to lessen the impact of heavy estate taxes; to protect a business against the loss of a key person; to enable a business partner to buy out a deceased partner's share. When the reason for the insurance is not clear, the underwriter must be on guard, particularly if the amount applied for is large, and seek full details before proceeding. There are legal prohibitions against issuing a policy without insurable interest but these apply only when a person is purchasing insurance on another person's life. The key issue is not whether the transaction is legal, but whether it makes sense.

Even when the basic premise makes sense, the amount insured must also bear a reasonable relationship to the financial status of the proposed insured. If the insurance is likely to make the proposed insured worth more dead than alive at anytime during the duration of the contract, speculation must be suspected.

OBJECT OF RISK CLASSIFICATION

The object of risk classification is to protect the insurance company and control mortality experience by declining the severest risks (i.e. those with expected mortality requiring a premium that would encourage antiselection as it would be too high to be acceptable to most persons) and charging an extra premium commensurate with the expected extra mortality for insurable but substandard risks. Each person must pay a premium in proportion to the risk in order to maintain equity among all policy owners.

In the risk classification process, the classes of risk to be declined, to be issued insurance with a specified extra premium or to be issued standard insurance are determined by each company. These risk classes differ among companies according to their own experience and objectives. For example, one company may take a broad view of issuing insurance at standard rates to as many persons as possible, whereas another may be more selective in order to obtain a lower mortality experience and be able to be more competitive in its pricing. In general, a company cannot be overselective without discouraging the efforts of its agents, who are anxious to offer a reasonable premium to most of their customers.

Although risk classification is a very important and necessary function, it is not by any means the sole determinant of a company's mortality experience. Selection of risks helps to control antiselection, but it does not control the socioeconomic and life style characteristics of people in the markets in which a company operates. Nor does risk classification control the extent to which agents and brokers protect a company by doing a creditable job, both in field selection and in the presentation of clear, complete and accurate information (in the application itself and in the supplementary information attached to the application).

Therefore a company must provide products that are suitable for the markets in which its agents and brokers operate, and must train these field personnel well and encourage their allegiance. Company budgeting policy must provide sufficient funds to obtain adequate underwriting information and sufficient staff for underwriters to have enough time to evaluate the information properly. If an adequate underwriting appraisal is not completed, underwriting control will diminish, antiselection will be encouraged and a heavy excess mortality price will be paid.

EFFECT OF SELECTION

Because of the effect of selection, risks that are determined to be standard have a much lower mortality than the average for those in the population of the same age. This process identifies people with a moderate degree of extra mortality as substandard risks, and eliminates those with a high degree of extra mortality. The effect of selection is most apparent during the early policy years, but gradually wears off as insureds who originally met the conditions for standard insurance become substandard or uninsurable. Because of the initial selection process, however, the mortality of insured risks never reaches the level of population mortality.

The insurance company factors the lower mortality during the select period into its pricing, and the insured is therefore charged a much lower premium than if there were no selection process. At younger ages, relatively few people are excluded from the standard group and the effect of selection largely disappears after about ten years. At older ages, the effect of selection virtually never wears off.

For practical purposes, companies assume a select period of 15 or 20 years. During the select period, mortality experience is measured by issue age and duration. For example, insureds with current (i.e. attained) age of 45 who were issued policies 10 years ago (at the age of 35) have higher mortality at the attained age than insureds of the same attained age who were issued policies five years ago (at the age of 40). Due to the longer period from issue (the time of selection), a larger proportion of the issue-age-35 group has deteriorated and become substand-ard or uninsurable than those in the issue-age-40 group.

After the 15- or 20-year select period, all insureds are grouped by attained age; the mortality experience of this group is referred to as ultimate mortality. This means that in the previous example, when the insureds at the issue age of 35 and those at the issue age of 40 are at the attained age of 60, they are grouped together in determining ultimate mortality experience for that attained age, based on the assumption that the effect of selection has largely worn off.

Table 3.2 (*see below*), excerpted from the more complete Table 4.9 in Chapter 4, illustrates the tremendous effect of selection. Even the ultimate experience, which shows mortality after the major effects of selection have worn off, is substantially lower than population mortality.

Table 3.2. Comparison of deaths per 1,000 in the 1975–80 male Basic Tables select (1st, 6th and 11th policy years), ultimate (16th policy year upwards) and 1979–81 US white male population (*see* p. 60).

Age (years)	1975–80 select, policy year:			1975–80 ultimate (16th year upwards)	1979–81 US white population
	1st	6th	11th		
22	0·73	1·14	1·32	1·41	1·9
32	0·63	0·80	0·90	1·12	1·7
42	0·97	1·86	1·94	1·97	3·2
52	1·99	4·3	4·8	5·7	8·5
62	3·7	8·9	12·2	15·3	21·2
72	9·4	22·8	24·7	39·8	49·0

In addition to the issue age of the insured, the length of the selection period depends on the extent of selection. If the selection standards are minimal, as they are at younger ages (particularly for smaller amounts), the period of time before the select and ultimate approximately merge can be very short. Therefore, in measuring mortality where selection is minimal, a company may use a very short select period or none at all.

Antiselection

The term antiselection describes the factors that thwart a company's efforts to select risks in the way described in the previous pages. In the absence of selection, mortality experience would greatly exceed the level of population mortality, because a disproportionate number of poorer risks would choose to apply.

If a company has risk classes that are too broad or underwriting requirements that are too liberal, those risks who feel they can obtain a bargain will tend to take advantage of that company. For example, a person who is slightly substandard because of elevated blood pressure may look for a company that has broad standard limits, or that does not require a medical examination. On the other hand, risk classes that are too narrow will turn many risks away from that company and limit the volume of business written.

Another prevalent form of antiselection is non-disclosure, or misleading disclosure, of medical history. This may be deliberate, or can be done subconsciously, particularly if the agent or examiner asking the application questions is not thorough. Even when a medical examination is required, the nature of the impairment may be such that it is not detectable on examination. The company has some protection against 'material misrepresentation': the incontestability clause. However, this clause limits an action to the first two years following policy issue. (There is no limit to the contestable period in the UK.)

The incentive for antiselection is greatest for large amounts of insurance and for term insurance where the chance of gain is greatest in proportion to the premium invested. An individual can also select against several companies by applying for amounts in each that are within non-medical limits or within limits for some other requirement that may detect the antiselection.

DISABILITY WAIVER OF PREMIUM (WP) AND ACCIDENTAL DEATH BENEFIT (ADB)

In many cases the classification for life insurance determines the classification for WP and ADB. Generally persons with impairments in the lower substandard classes are charged an additional half or full multiple of the WP. Most of this extra charge is associated with the additional risk presented by the impairment, but part is needed to waive the higher total premium. For impairments in the higher substandard classes, WP is declined. For certain impairments with a high disability risk a higher charge is required, or WP may be declined for even the lowest life insurance rating. The underwriting concern is only about lengthy disability because the typical WP benefit provides for payments only after 6 months of total disability.

For most impairments in the lower substandard classes, the additional accidental death hazard is small and no extra charge is required. For most impairments in the moderate substandard classes an extra multiple is charged; for those in the highest classes, the ADB is declined. Some impairments present a greater risk of accidental death, either because a sudden episode may cause an accident or because the weakened condition of the individual may result in death from an accident that would have been survived by a healthier individual.

The WP and ADB classification process is similar for non-medical factors. However, the higher probability of disability and accidental death are likely to be of greater concern. Therefore, the need to charge an extra multiple for, or to decline, these benefits occurs more frequently than with medical impairments.

UNDERWRITING REQUIREMENTS

The extent of information routinely obtained based on age and amount is based on cost/benefit studies. These studies compare the cost of obtaining and processing the requirement with the present value of the mortality savings that would result from using the requirement. Therefore the extent of information may vary from a few questions about medical history on an application at a young age for a small amount, to very extensive information – including a full medical examination (in some cases two examinations), blood and urine tests, ECG and chest x-ray – on policies of large amounts, particularly at older ages. In many cases a statement from the proposed insured's physician is also routinely required.

The practice of accepting insurance without a medical examination (i.e. non-medical) became established in the UK in the 1920s and eventually spread to North America. For many years non-medical (medical history questions are asked by the agent rather than a doctor) was limited to smaller amounts at ages of 40 and under, but due to favorable experience was extended to quite large amounts in the early 1980s. Small amounts are currently issued over the age of 40, but the mortality experience has not been nearly as favorable as at younger ages. In the early 1970s many companies began substituting examinations by a trained technician (i.e. paramedical) for examinations by a physician. The technician obtaining the medical history and physical measurements (height and weight, blood pressure and pulse rate) is also able to collect blood and urine samples and use portable ECG equipment where required. Paramedical mortality experience has been favorable at ages up to 60 for non smokers and up to 45 for smokers but not at older ages, where a physician's examination is needed to detect abnormalities of heart and pulse rhythm and other signs of impairment that would only be apparent to a physician.

In addition to the routine requirements based on age and amount, underwriting requirements are suggested by the medical history or the physical findings on examination. The judgment of the medical director often determines to what extent further information is needed. This judgment is factored into the underwriter's decision as to whether the cost of the additional requirement and the delay involved are justified by the possibility of reaching a more favorable decision and increasing the chance of policy placement. This is often a difficult decision, particularly for a policy of moderate amount where the cost may often outweigh the benefit of the additional requirement; for larger amounts, the decision to obtain further information, provided there has been no substantial delay, is almost always justified. The decision whether or not to obtain an additional requirement will also be affected by the extent to which it may change the final underwriting action. If there is more than a slight chance that additional information may result in a declination, the requirement is usually obtained for protective reasons.

Attending Physician's Statement (APS)

The APS is the most useful single document in the underwriting assessment. However, there is often considerable delay in obtaining information because many attending physicians do not give insurance company requests high priority. Most companies try to be selective, keeping requests for APSs to those that will be the most useful. Therefore final underwriting actions are sometimes taken using medical histories without information from the attending physician, provided the amount is not large and the history is reasonably well-presented. In other cases the underwriting action may be based entirely on information given by the attending physician. In these cases the source of the information is protected by not disclosing the specific reason for rating, but by offering to provide this information to a physician named by the proposed insured.

The applicant's authorization for an APS is incorporated in the application form; the application is not processed without this authorization.

Medical Attendant's Report (MAR)

The MAR is the UK equivalent of the APS. It is particularly valuable in the UK because of the National Health Service's unique system of patients' medical records: a person's medical file, including specialist and other reports, is automatically transferred from one doctor to another whenever the person moves to a different part of the country and re-registers with a new doctor. Since continuity of medical records is preserved it is obvious that the MAR is a very valuable source of underwriting information, and it is used extensively by UK life insurance companies.

Medical Information Bureau (MIB)

The MIB has served insurance companies in the USA and Canada since the turn of the century. Its purpose is to prevent fraud and the concealment of important underwriting information.

Most companies are members and all member companies must report pertinent underwriting information to MIB. This includes the existence of a significant medical impairment or history and both favorable and unfavorable test results, but does not include the underwriting action taken by the company. Members interrogate the MIB as part of the underwriting process to determine if there is any record. This information may be used to assist the underwriting investigation; it may not be used as a basis for adverse underwriting action.

The form signed by the proposed insured as part of the application process authorizes the insurance company, among other things, to utilize MIB. The form also describes how the proposed insured can gain access to personal information on him in MIB files.

Other Sources of Information

Information is also obtained from non-medical sources. The primary source of such information in the USA is the investigative consumer report (inspection report). The insurance company engages a service to interview the applicant (as well as friends, neighbors, business associates and financial references) and to check court and motor vehicle records. The purpose is to gather information to assist in the medical, life style and financial evaluation of the proposed insured. The procedures for obtaining the information and protecting its confidentiality are contained in the US federal Fair Credit Reporting Act (FCRA).

Inspection reports are routinely obtained only for larger amounts. They are particularly helpful for evaluating financial need for insurance. They are also useful for developing information about medical history or obtaining the previously undisclosed name of an attending physician. Underwriters may also request inspection reports for smaller amounts in order to amplify information that has been developed during the underwriting process.

In some cases information is obtained solely by telephone interview with the applicant. The telephone interviewers may be employed by the insurance company or an independent service. Although the medical questions may be repetitive, this often jogs memory or conscience and produces information omitted from the application.

CAUSE OF DEATH

Cause of death is of interest to medical directors only as an indicator of the relative frequency of occurrence and mortality significance of impairments presented in the underwriting process. The use of cause of death can be misleading because the underlying cause, which is of primary significance to the underwriter, may not have been recorded on the death certificate. The death certificate, after the two-year contestable period, is the only routinely obtained source of cause-of-death information. (There is no limit to the contestable period in the UK.)

This is of particular concern in identifying AIDS as a cause of death. In many cases AIDS is not identified on the death certificate because of concern about possible stigma or because AIDS was ignored or overlooked as the underlying cause.

Table 3.3. Relative frequency of causes of death,[a] US standard life insurance experience (23 leading companies) in policy years 16 and upwards, 1978–83.

Age (years)	Cancer Male (%)	Cancer Female (%)	Cerebro-vascular Male (%)	Cerebro-vascular Female (%)	Heart and circulation Male (%)	Heart and circulation Female (%)	Accident and homicide Male (%)	Accident and homicide Female (%)	Suicide Male (%)	Suicide Female (%)	All other Male (%)	All other Female (%)
15–24	5·8	10·8	1·3	0·4	3·7	5·0	56·6	49·3	12·9	7·7	19·7	26·3
25–39	12·2	30·6	1·3	3·2	16·0	9·0	29·3	18·6	11·0	2·5	30·2	31·1
40–49	21·6	40·2	2·5	3·8	34·0	13·6	11·5	5·8	4·8	4·3	25·6	36·3
50–59	26·7	40·7	2·5	3·4	40·1	16·5	4·8	3·7	2·3	1·8	23·6	33·9
60–69	27·4	36·7	3·5	4·6	41·6	25·6	2·4	2·6	1·0	0·7	24·1	29·8
70–79	22·0	22·0	5·6	7·0	42·1	39·0	1·4	1·2	0·8	0·1	29·1	30·7
80+	14·3	10·6	4·3	11·9	45·0	46·2	1·6	1·1	0·3	0·1	29·5	29·1
Total	22·6	25·8	5·1	7·0	41·5	32·9	3·1	2·6	1·3	0·8	26·4	30·9

[a]The percentages for the six causes of death shown add horizontally to 100 percent for each sex.

Accidents, particularly motor vehicle, are the major cause of death at the younger adult ages. Applying risk selection to limit accidental deaths is virtually impossible, except for the most obvious situations involving hazardous avocations and occupations, poor driving records and abuse of alcohol and other controlled substances. As a result, the vast majority (about 98%) of young adult applicants are issued standard insurance. This percentage has been slightly reduced in recent years because of testing that has disclosed HIV infection.

At older ages cardiovascular disease and cancer predominate as the causes of death. Cardiovascular disease is decreasing in relative frequency and cancer is increasing but cardiovascular disease remains the primary cause of death among older insurance applicants. Moreover, there are many more signs and symptoms of cardiovascular disease than of cancer that can enable the medical director to reduce exposure to deaths from this cause.

REGULATORY AND LEGAL CONSTRAINTS

Until the 1970s underwriters were largely able to operate without governmental interference. Although most companies did not abuse this privilege, public concern developed about how companies used the information gathered in the underwriting process and the confidentiality with which it was maintained.

Model Privacy Act

The US Model Privacy Act was written in the early 1980s and has been adopted in about one quarter of the states, though most insurers comply with the Act's requirements in all states. The Act requires insurance companies to advise proposed insureds (or their physician if the information is confidential) of the reasons for any adverse underwriting action affecting them and, if requested, to provide them with the information that the decision was based on. It further stipulates that no insurance company may make an adverse underwriting decision on the mere fact of a previous adverse underwriting decision.

Insurance companies must also be prepared to respond to complaints made to state insurance departments, as well as to lawsuits brought by insureds and claimants. For these reasons it is very important that a complete and accurate file be kept showing the chronology of the underwriting process and the reasons for the underwriting actions taken. Documentation of this nature is much better than unsubstantiated explanations and rationalizations. Documentation at the time of underwriting action also forces the underwriter to provide a specific reason for his own action and thereby avoid action that does not have a logical and justifiable explanation.

Access to Medical Reports Act (AMRA)

This important piece of legislation came into force in the UK (except Northern Ireland) in January 1989. It establishes the individual's right of access to reports relating to himself that are made by medical practitioners for employment or insurance purposes. Within the meaning of the Act, a medical practitioner is one who is or has been responsible for the clinical care of the individual; therefore the act refers only to MARs and not to medical examination reports prepared by an independent doctor, or to paramedical examination reports.

Briefly, if an applicant wishes to exercise his rights under the Act, the medical attendant must be notified. A period of 21 days is then allowed for the applicant to contact the doctor in order to examine the report and, if necessary, request amendments to any part of the report that the applicant considers to be wrong or misleading. The doctor can either agree to such a request or refuse; if he refuses, the individual is then entitled to put his own views on the disputed entries in writing and have them attached to the report. If an applicant notifies that he does not wish to see the doctor's report, it can be despatched to the insurance company forthwith.

The delay inherent in the Act is a decided disadvantage to some applicants wishing to complete their business quickly, and it has been found that only about one to two percent of applicants exercise their right of access to the MAR.

DISCRIMINATION

Risk classification is a discriminatory process in which individuals are included in different risk classes according to the mortality expected. The persons in each class are expected to experience similar mortality; the expected mortality for each class is different. In this way each person pays his fair share and equity is achieved.

It is important that risk classification is based on *real* differences in mortality experience. That is, that unfair discrimination due to classification based on impressions that cannot be substantiated does not occur. There are laws in most states that prohibit discrimination based on sex, marital status, race, religion and national origin. Many states also prohibit discrimination based on sexual preference, which prevents companies using surrogates for sexual preference such as beneficiary or zip code as a basis for requiring HIV testing. Many states also prohibit (1) refusal, (2) limitation of coverage or (3) rate differentials based solely on physical or mental impairment unless such action is based on sound actuarial principles or actual or reasonably anticipated experience. Even when not required by law, it makes sound business sense to apply only fair discrimination practice in risk classification. Failure to exercise fairness and equity will cause the public, agents and underwriters to lose respect for the risk classification process in particular, and for the institution of life insurance in general.

Appendix

Table 3.4. Expectation of life (years) according to the 1975–80 Ultimate and the US Life 1979–81 Tables.

Age	1975–80 Ultimate Male	1975–80 Ultimate Female	US Life 79–81 Male Nonwhite	US Life 79–81 Male White	Age
0			65·64	70·82	0
1			66·01	70·70	1
2			65·10	69·76	2
3			64·16	68·81	3
4			63·22	67·84	4
5			62·26	66·87	5
6			61·29	65·90	6
7			60·32	64·92	7
8			59·35	63·94	8
9			58·37	62·96	9
10			57·39	61·98	10
11			56·41	60·99	11
12			55·43	60·00	12
13			54·45	59·02	13
14			53·48	58·05	14
15	60·57	65·92	52·52	57·09	15
16	59·61	64·94	51·57	56·14	16
17	58·67	63·97	50·63	55·21	17
18	57·73	63·00	49·70	54·28	18
19	56·80	62·03	48·78	53·36	19
20	55·88	61·06	47·87	52·45	20
21	54·95	60·09	46·97	51·54	21
22	54·03	59·12	46·08	50·64	22
23	53·10	58·15	45·20	49·73	23
24	52·18	57·18	44·33	48·83	24
25	51·25	56·21	43·46	47·92	25
26	50·32	55·24	42·59	47·01	26
27	49·38	54·27	41·72	46·09	27
28	48·44	53·30	40·85	45·17	28
29	47·50	52·33	39·99	44·24	29
30	46·56	51·35	39·13	43·32	30
31	45·61	50·38	38·26	42·39	31
32	44·66	49·41	37·40	41·46	32
33	43·71	48·44	36·54	40·52	33
34	42·76	47·47	35·69	39·59	34
35	41·80	46·50	34·83	38·66	35
36	40·85	45·54	33·98	37·73	36
37	39·90	44·58	33·14	36·80	37

Age	1975–80 Ultimate Male	1975–80 Ultimate Female	US Life 79–81 Male Nonwhite	US Life 79–81 Male White	Age
38	38·95	43·62	32·30	35·88	38
39	38·00	42·66	31·47	34·96	39
40	37·06	41·71	30·64	34·04	40
41	36·12	40·76	29·82	33·13	41
42	35·18	39·82	29·01	32·22	42
43	34·24	38·89	28·21	31·32	43
44	33·31	37·96	27·41	30·43	44
45	32·39	37·03	26·63	29·55	45
46	31·47	36·11	25·86	28·67	46
47	30·56	35·19	25·11	27·80	47
48	29·66	34·28	24·36	26·94	48
49	28·76	33·37	23·64	26·09	49
50	27·88	32·47	22·92	25·26	50
51	27·00	31·57	22·22	24·43	51
52	26·13	30·68	21·54	23·62	52
53	25·27	29·79	20·87	22·82	53
54	24·42	28·91	20·21	22·03	54
55	23·58	28·03	19·56	21·25	55
56	22·75	27·17	18·93	20·49	56
57	21·93	26·31	18·32	19·74	57
58	21·12	25·45	17·71	19·00	58
59	20·32	24·61	17·12	18·27	59
60	19·54	23·77	16·54	17·56	60
61	18·77	22·95	15·97	16·87	61
62	18·01	22·13	15·42	16·19	62
63	17·27	21·32	14·87	15·53	63
64	16·54	20·51	14·34	14·89	64
65	15·83	19·72	13·83	14·26	65
66	15·14	18·93	13·32	13·65	66
67	14·46	18·16	12·81	13·05	67
68	13·80	17·39	12·32	12·47	68
69	13·15	16·63	11·83	11·90	69
70	12·53	15·88	11·36	11·35	70
71	11·92	15·14	10·90	10·82	71
72	11·33	14·41	10·46	10·31	72
73	10·76	13·69	10·03	9·81	73
74	10·20	12·99	9·61	9·34	74
75	9·66	12·31	9·19	8·87	75
76	9·15	11·64	8·78	8·42	76
77	8·65	11·00	8·38	7·98	77
78	8·17	10·37	7·98	7·56	78

Age	1975–80 Ultimate Male	1975–80 Ultimate Female	US Life 79–81 Male Nonwhite	US Life 79–81 Male White	Age
79	7·71	9·77	7·59	7·15	79
80	7·27	9·20	7·21	6·76	80
81	6·85	8·65	6·86	6·39	81
82	6·45	8·13	6·53	6·04	82
83	6·07	7·64	6·24	5·70	83
84	5·70	7·17	5·96	5·39	84
85	5·35	6·73	5·69	5·09	85
86	5·02	6·31	5·42	4·80	86
87	4·71	5·91	5·17	4·54	87
88	4·42	5·53	4·92	4·29	88
89	4·14	5·17	4·69	4·05	89
90	3·88	4·83	4·48	3·83	90
91	3·64	4·50	4·27	3·61	91
92	3·40	4·19	4·07	3·41	92
93	3·18	3·88	3·88	3·22	93
94	2·96	3·58	3·72	3·05	94
95	2·74	3·27	3·59	2·91	95
96	2·51	2·95	3·49	2·78	96
97	2·26	2·61	3·40	2·67	97
98	1·97	2·23	3·31	2·57	98
99	1·62	1·78	3·23	2·48	99
100	1·16	1·23	3·15	2·39	100
101			3·06	2·31	101
102			2·97	2·24	102
103			2·86	2·17	103
104			2·73	2·09	104
105			2·57	2·00	105
106			2·37	1·88	106
107			2·09	1·72	107
108			1·72	1·48	108
109			1·21	1·11	109

Table 3.5. Yearly death rates per 1,000 according to the 1975–80 Ultimate and the US Life 1979–81 Tables.

Age	1975–80 Ultimate Male	1975–80 Ultimate Female	US Life 79–81 Male Nonwhite	US Life 79–81 Male White	Age
0			20·61	12·31	0
1			1·39	0·92	1
2			1·01	0·66	2
3			0·82	0·53	3
4			0·66	0·43	4
5			0·58	0·39	5
6			0·51	0·37	6
7			0·45	0·34	7
8			0·39	0·30	8
9			0·34	0·24	9
10			0·30	0·19	10
11			0·31	0·19	11
12			0·39	0·28	12
13			0·55	0·46	13
14			0·76	0·71	14
15	0·68	0·36	0·98	0·96	15
16	1·01	0·40	1·19	1·18	16
17	1·14	0·44	1·40	1·37	17
18	1·22	0·47	1·62	1·51	18
19	1·31	0·49	1·86	1·63	19
20	1·37	0·51	2·12	1·75	20
21	1·40	0·52	2·39	1·86	21
22	1·41	0·53	2·62	1·93	22
23	1·40	0·53	2·79	1·93	23
24	1·38	0·53	2·91	1·89	24
25	1·34	0·53	3·02	1·83	25
26	1·29	0·53	3·14	1·77	26
27	1·24	0·53	3·25	1·72	27
28	1·20	0·53	3·35	1·68	28
29	1·17	0·54	3·46	1·67	29
30	1·14	0·55	3·56	1·66	30
31	1·12	0·58	3·67	1·65	31
32	1·11	0·61	3·79	1·66	32
33	1·12	0·65	3·95	1·69	33
34	1·14	0·70	4·13	1·75	34
35	1·17	0·77	4·36	1·84	35
36	1·22	0·84	4·61	1·96	36
37	1·28	0·93	4·91	2·09	37
38	1·36	1·03	5·23	2·24	38

Age	1975–80 Ultimate Male	1975–80 Ultimate Female	US Life 79–81 Male Nonwhite	US Life 79–81 Male White	Age
39	1·45	1·15	5·57	2·40	39
40	1·56	1·29	5·95	2·61	40
41	1·70	1·45	6·38	2·87	41
42	1·87	1·62	6·87	3·16	42
43	2·07	1·79	7·43	3·48	43
44	2·31	1·96	8·07	3·82	44
45	2·58	2·14	8·77	4·20	45
46	2·89	2·33	9·52	4·63	46
47	3·24	2·52	10·36	5·14	47
48	3·61	2·72	11·28	5·73	48
49	4·02	2·93	12·25	6·39	49
50	4·45	3·17	13·23	7·06	50
51	4·92	3·43	14·24	7·75	51
52	5·44	3·71	15·31	8·50	52
53	6·00	4·04	16·48	9·34	53
54	6·61	4·40	17·74	10·27	54
55	7·27	4·80	19·05	11·25	55
56	8·01	5·23	20·39	12·27	56
57	8·82	5·70	21·74	13·38	57
58	9·73	6·22	23·12	14·64	58
59	10·75	6·78	24·59	16·05	59
60	11·89	7·37	26·19	17·62	60
61	13·17	8·00	27·94	19·33	61
62	14·57	8·67	29·81	21·19	62
63	16·07	9·38	31·72	23·16	63
64	17·71	10·15	33·61	25·23	64
65	19·50	10·99	35·45	27·38	65
66	21·47	11·91	37·33	29·68	66
67	23·65	12·92	39·36	32·18	67
68	26·05	14·03	41·71	34·95	68
69	28·69	15·25	44·45	38·05	69
70	31·57	16·63	47·54	41·48	70
71	34·68	18·21	50·84	45·16	71
72	38·00	20·04	54·21	49·01	72
73	41·60	22·17	57·42	52·95	73
74	45·54	24·65	60·46	57·03	74
75	49·90	27·53	63·56	61·46	75
76	54·71	30·86	66·99	66·42	76
77	60·03	34·69	70·83	71·80	77
78	66·85	39·07	75·38	77·62	78
79	72·18	44·00	80·88	83·94	79

Age	1975–80 Ultimate Male	1975–80 Ultimate Female	US life 79–81 Male Nonwhite	US Life 79–81 Male White	Age
80	79·02	49·48	87·72	90·99	80
81	86·36	55·51	95·78	98·86	81
82	94·12	62·09	104·33	107·33	82
83	102·35	69·22	111·90	116·13	83
84	111·41	76·90	117·81	125·23	84
85	121·31	85·13	124·06	135·07	85
86	132·05	93·91	131·54	145·92	86
87	143·63	103·24	139·45	156·91	87
88	156·05	113·12	148·05	167·74	88
89	169·12	123·55	157·29	178·75	89
90	182·61	134·53	166·21	190·58	90
91	196·52	146·06	175·27	203·89	91
92	210·85	158·14	185·99	218·64	92
93	225·60	170·77	198·66	234·53	93
94	240·77	183·95	212·29	250·61	94
95	256·36	197·68	225·54	266·17	95
96	272·37	211·96	232·74	280·01	96
97	288·80	226·79	239·44	293·11	97
98	305·65	242·17	245·63	305·45	98
99	322·92	258·10	251·35	317·03	99
100	340·61	274·58	256·62	327·84	100
101			261·46	337·91	101
102			265·90	347·24	102
103			269·96	355·88	103
104			273·67	363·84	104
105			277·06	371·17	105
106			280·14	377·90	106
107			282·95	384·07	107
108			285·50	389·71	108
109			287·82	394·86	109

CHAPTER 4

THE APPLICATION OF LIFE TABLE METHODOLOGY TO RISK APPRAISAL

RICHARD B SINGER

The purpose of this chapter is to present highly condensed descriptions of (1) life table methodology as used in follow-up (FU) studies, (2) the principal types of life table used as a standard or yardstick for comparative mortality, (3) an example of an FU study from which the indices of comparative mortality and survival may be derived by time elapsed, (4) an example of an FU study from which annual mortality rates may be averaged over multiple years elapsed, (5) mean age and estimate of mean expected mortality rate in cohorts with a wide range of age, (6) conversion of mortality ratios to a numerical rating, and relation of the excess death rate (EDR) to flat extra premiums, (7) life expectancy in medicolegal work and structured settlements, and (8) estimating statistical significance. It is important for the risk selection expert (whether a medical director (MD), lay underwriter, actuary or other specialist) to be able to examine, analyze and manipulate life table data with facility. This chapter attempts to provide the basic knowledge required, but facility will come only if the reader makes use of this knowledge in reading the other chapters of this book, and in applying the results of all types of mortality studies to his daily work. Additional description of the fundamentals of life table methodology may be found in the 1976 *Medical Risks* volume,[1] textbooks,[2] articles[3] and in course material of the Board of Insurance Medicine.[4]

LIFE TABLE METHODOLOGY

The life table is a device for displaying in a logical order the numbers of subjects counted alive at the beginning and end of consecutive time intervals following the common entry to FU, events (such as death) that occur during each FU interval, and rates of mortality and survival derived for each interval. Accurate counting is an essential ingredient of all FU studies. Excluding life expectancy data, there are 30 variables that might be considered in complete tables of comparative mortality and survival. Each variable must have a distinctive symbol. Although the symbols and number of variables may appear complex to the uninitiated, the variables have simple and orderly mathematical relations which can be readily learned. Furthermore, strenuous efforts have been made in the development of the format used in tables of comparative mortality to make the symbols easy to use and remember. Readers fearful of their lack of mathematical aptitude, take heart: you *can* master life table methodology and use it in your risk selection work.

Basic concepts in life table methodology may be summarized as follows. During any year of FU observation, the ith year, if all those living at the start (l_i) are followed to the end of the year, the status of the group at the end of the year is determinate in either of two ways: as deaths during the year (d_i) or as survivors living to the end of the year, $l_{i+1}=l_i-d_i$. The end of the ith year is the same as the start of the next consecutive, or $(i+1)$th year. If the duration from start of FU is designated by the symbol t (for time elapsed), the start of the ith year is at duration or time t_i, and the start of the $(i+1)$th year is at duration t_{i+1}, and t=0 at the starting point for all FU observation. Shorter or longer intervals are sometimes used, but the year is the most common unit of time for long-term FU studies. The FU interval may be designated by a set of consecutive numbers, i, but this number should be clearly distinguished from duration of time, t, because each interval has a starting and ending time, times which differ by the length of the interval, Δt. The interval is the basic unit of FU observation, from which the mortality rate is calculated as $q=d/l$ (if there were no subjects lost to or withdrawn from FU observation during the interval). Finally, q is a decimal that cannot exceed 1 (100 percent); it may have a minimum value of 0 if there were no deaths during the interval. Death and survival are complementary states, $q+p=1$. So, if the mortality rate, q, is known for any interval, the corresponding survival rate is known because of the relation $p=1-q$, and vice versa, $q=1-p$, if p is known. Cumulative survival is derived as the continued product of consecutive interval survival rates: $P=(p_1)(p_2)(p_3)$ . . .; cumulative mortality rate is derived as $Q=1-P$. It is necessary to derive Q as the complement of P because there is no mathematical relation that permits its derivation directly from the annual or interval rate, q. These are the fundamental relations for observed data in the life table, short of calculation of life expectancy.

In order to develop the fundamentals of life table methodology the extended table has been split into four shorter ones, each covering one aspect of the calculations involving the 30 variables mentioned above. The data have been taken from Abstract 312 of the 1976 *Medical Risks* volume,[1] which looks at male duPont employees aged 25–44 followed after acute myocardial infarction (MI). Early deaths have been included in these tables. In conditions with very high early mortality it is customary to exclude early deaths, and commence long-term FU at the end of the 'early' interval (often 30 days for acute MI patients), but in this example a constant duration (one year) has been maintained for all FU intervals, including the first. Notes on the derivation of the variable in each column are given in a key below the tables, and columns are numbered consecutively throughout the four tables. The reader is encouraged to prepare blank tables with the proper column headings and work through the calculations.

SEQUENTIAL LIFE TABLE CALCULATIONS

duPont Male Employees Aged 25–44 with Acute MI During 1956–61

The observed data in Table 4.1 are in columns 1–5; the exposure, E, is derived. In this chapter, and in mortality abstracts using this methodology, E must be given in units of person-years, so that they are additive over more than one interval. If shorter or unequal intervals are employed, allowance must be made to convert the interval number exposed to risk (NER) to exposure in person-years: if, for example, person-months are counted, NER must be divided by 12 (the months

Table 4.1. Observed data and calculation of exposure.

Interval number	Interval start–end	Number alive at start	Withdrawn alive	Number of deaths in interval	Exposure (patient-years)	Number alive at end
i	t to $t+\Delta t$	l	w	d	$E=l-0{\cdot}5w$	$l-(w+d)$
1	2	3a	4	5	6	3b
1	0–1 yr	252	39	70	232·5	143
2	1–2 yr	143	32	4	127·0	107
3	2–3 yr	107	31	6	91·5	70

Key to columns
1 Interval consecutive number.
2 Starting and ending times (t) of interval.
3a Number of patients (subjects), l, counted alive at start of interval.
4 Number, w, counted as withdrawn alive during the interval (because of end of FU or becoming lost to FU).
5 Number, d, of deaths counted during the interval.
6 Exposure, in patient-years (person-years), derived to give the average number exposed to risk during the interval. One-half of w is subtracted from l. Actuarial mathematics require that all deaths be given a full interval of exposure to risk ($0{\cdot}5d$ is not subtracted from l).
3b Number alive (surviving) to be counted at the end of the interval. This column is omitted from life tables because it is equal to the number alive at the start of the next interval (compare columns 3a and 3b).

in one year) in order to derive E as person-years. The value of E will be somewhat reduced if the interval duration used is shorter than one year. Shorter intervals are desirable to characterize a rapidly changing mortality or survival pattern, such as occurs in acute MI or stroke. However, for most chronic diseases the year is a suitable duration for FU observations. As we will see later, it may be expedient to combine several years into a longer interval, such as five years, in order to average results when the numbers of deaths per year are small (e.g. five or fewer per year). Most FU studies resemble this example in that subjects are entered over nearly all of the observation period — a full five years in this duPont study. To bring all subjects to a common entry point, $t=0$ at the time of the MI attack, will have the effect of producing a wide range of durations of FU, from less than one year to a maximum of five years. Thus, even if no subjects are lost to FU, w will be a considerable fraction of the number of entrants during each year of FU, and E will be smaller than l in each year. This produces what is called a double-decrement life table. It is important to distinguish such studies from a much smaller group of FU studies in which all subjects are followed to death or to a common minimum survival interval, such as five or ten years. In these studies $w=0$ in each interval, the life table is called a single-decrement table, and calculations of cumulative mortality and survival are simplified.

Note that all interval rates are annual rates in Table 4.2. If early deaths, within the first month, had been excluded, the starting point for long-term FU would have been one month (after the MI) and the duration of the first interval would have been 11 months or 0·917 years, instead of one full year. If the l and w appropriate to this interval had been used to derive the NER, this would have been for the 11-month interval. The symbol E in the column heading should be used only if the units are

Table 4.2. Calculation of observed mortality and survival rates.

Interval Number i	Interval Start–end t to $t+\triangle t$	Data columns 5 & 6 from Table 4.1 d/E	Interval rates Mortality $\delta=d/E$	Survival $p=1-q$	Cumulative rates Survival $P=(p_1)(p_2)..$	Mortality $Q=1-P$
1	2	7	8	9	10	11
1	0–1 yr	70/232·5	0·301	0·699	0·699	0·301
2	1–2 yr	4/127·0	0·031	0·969	0·677	0·323
3	2–3 yr	6/91·5	0·066	0·934	0·633	0·367

Key to columns
1, 2 As in Table 4.1.
7   Data for d from column 5 and E from column 6 of Table 4.1.
8   Annual (or interval) mortality rate $q=d/E$, as a decimal, 0 to (but not greater than) 1.
9   Annual (or interval) survival rate $p=1-q$, as a decimal, 0 to (but not greater than) 1.
10   Cumulative survival rate $P=(p_1)(p_2)(p_3)$ . . ., also a decimal not greater than 1.
11   Cumulative mortality rate $Q=1-P$, also a decimal, 0 to (but not greater than) 1. Note that cumulative rates are capitalized, but the same letters as q and p.

person-years. In this case with an interval duration of 11 months, this can be calculated as $E=(0·917)$NER. Then annual $q=d/E$, but interval $q_i=d/($NER$)$. The interval rate is the proper one to use to calculate cumulative survival from duration $t=$one month, the starting-point for a long-term FU excluding the experience of the first month. However, the annual mortality rate is the one needed to derive one index of comparative mortality, the excess death rate (EDR), as we will see shortly. Great care must be used to label column headings precisely and enter the proper values, E or NER, and the rates derived from them.

It is very important to select the table of expected rates that appears to be most appropriate to the group under observation, and this will be discussed below. The derivation of values of d' to match d in any observed subgroup specified by age, sex and interval of FU is a time-honored device of insurance mortality studies by impairment, as elegantly formulated by Rogers and Hunter at about the time of World War I.[5]

Column 3b is redundant, as previously noted. Other redundant columns in Tables 4.2 and 4.4 are those numbered 7, 17 and 20, which have been inserted in this sequence of tables for demonstration purposes. The various tabular formats used must be adapted to the data available in the published article and the organization of the results. The life table variables may be listed as follows:

Observed data: i, t, t, l, w, d, and their derived E and NER (seven variables).
Observed mortality rates: q (annual), q_i (interval), q (aggregate mean annual), q (geometric mean annual, $1-p$), Q (cumulative) (five variables).
Observed survival rates: p (annual), p_i (interval), $p=(p_i)^{1/.t}$ (geometric mean annual), $p=1-q$ (aggregate mean annual), P (cumulative) (five variables).
Expected rates: q', q'_i, q', q', Q', p', p'_i, p', p' and P' (ten variables).
Comparative indices: mortality ratio (MR), excess death rate (EDR) and survival ratio (SR) (three variables, not counting different methods of derivation).

Table 4.3. Expected mortality and survival rates and expected deaths (d′).

Interval Number i 1	Interval Start–end t to $t+\Delta t$ 2	Interval rates		Cumulative rates		Expected deaths $d'=(q')(E)$ 16
		Mortality q' 12	Survival $p'=1-q'$ 13	Survival $P'=(p'_1)(p'_2)..$ 14	Mortality $Q'=1-P'$ 15	
1	0–1 yr	0·0033	0·9967	0·9967	0·0033	0·77
2	1–2 yr	0·0036	0·9964	0·9931	0·0069	0·46
3	2–3 yr	0·0040	0·9960	0·9891	0·0109	0·37

Key to columns
1, 2 As in Table 4.1. Primes are used to distinguish expected rates and d'.
12   Expected annual mortality rates from 1959–61 US Life Tables, white male.
13   Expected annual survival rate, complement of q'.
14   Cumulative expected survival rate, continued product of successive p' values.
15   Cumulative expected mortality rate, complement of P'.
16   Expected deaths derived as product of E (column 6, Table 4.1) and q'. This gives the age/sex-matched d' corresponding to the observed interval d. Note that E, d and d' are additive for two or more intervals of FU data.

Table 4.4. Calculation of comparative mortality and survival.

Interval Number i 1	Interval Start–end t to $t+\Delta t$ 2	Observed/expected deaths d/d' 17	Mortality ratio $100d/d'$ 18	Excess death rate $1000(d/d')/E$ 19	Observed/expected cumulative survival P/P' 20	Survival ratio $100P/P'$ 21
1	0–1 yr	70/0·77	9100%	298	0·699/0·9967	70·1%
2	1–2 yr	4/0·46	870	28	0·677/0·9931	68·2
3	2–3 yr	6/0·37	1620	62	0·633/0·9891	64·0
1–3	0–3 yr	80/1·60	5000	174	0·633/0·9891	64·0

Key to columns
1, 2 As in Table 4.1.
17   Data for d from column 5, Table 4.1; data for d' from column 16, Table 4.3.
18   Interval mortality ratio, $MR=100d/d'$. For all three years combined, the aggregate mean mortality ratio, $MR=100\Sigma d/\Sigma d'=5000\%$, as shown on the bottom line. Mortality ratios are rounded off.[1]
19   Interval excess death rate, $EDR=1000(d-d')/E$, in extra deaths per thousand per year. Aggregate mean for 3 years, $EDR=1000(\Sigma d-\Sigma d')/E$, as shown on the bottom line.
20   Observed cumulative survival rate from column 10, Table 4.2, and expected cumulative survival rate from column 14, Table 4.3.
21   Cumulative survival ratio, $SR=100P/P'$. Note that cumulative mortality ratios as $100Q/Q'$ and interval survival ratios ($100p/p'$) are not shown in Table 4.4. Cumulative survival rates and ratios are the same for interval 3 as they are for intervals 1–3.

PRINCIPAL POPULATION AND INSURANCE LIFE TABLES

Both the US and English life tables are published in detailed form on a decennial basis. William Farr, a physician with a phenomenal aptitude for vital statistics, is due the credit for establishing the first reliable national life tables through his work at the General Register Office, starting in 1839 soon after the Office was established by act of Parliament (*see* Chapter 1). English Life Table Number 14 contains data for 1970–72. In the USA a national census has been taken decennially since 1790, but life tables for the USA have been published only since 1900, and were based on incomplete mortality data until 1936 because all of the 48 continental states were not included in the death registration area until that year (death registration has always been a state and not a federal function).

In a majority of published FU articles (exclusive of randomized clinical trials) observed mortality and survival results are presented without reference to any standard mortality. If the group observed can be reasonably considered to be a sample of the general population, then national or regional life tables should be chosen to derive race-, age- and sex-matched expected mortality and survival. However, if any degree of selection has been used to form the group under study, it is more accurate to utilize life tables with mortality lower than in the general population (*see* pp. 44–9). Table 4.7 contains extracts from the 1979–81 US Life Tables.

The decennial tables differ in two major respects from the tables published in the large annual volumes, *Vital Statistics of the United States*: the annual tables are based on deaths in a single year and, except for the census years, on post-censal population estimates. As the title indicates, the decennial tables utilize death counts over a three-year period centered on the census year. Each set of tables gives data for the total group population, and for males and females separately; there are four sets of tables by race: white, non-white, black and total population. Age, x, and the variables in the next three columns of Table 4.7 are familiar to the reader of the previous section. $_tL_x$ is an average of the number alive during each age interval, while T_x is the total of this average for the current age and all subsequent years of life for the cohort. The expectation of life, $\mathring{e}_x$, is calculated by dividing the total by l_x. It is evident that the derivation of life expectancy is a tedious process, involving the carrying of the life table calculations to an age (109–110), beyond the highest age shown in the tables, for which there were seven white male survivors, with an e_x of 1·97 years. Nevertheless life expectancy (or average duration of life) is characterized in the introductory text as the customary measure of longevity. Another measure sometimes used is the number of years to the duration at which the cumulative survival is 0·5 (derived from the l_x column), the 'probable lifetime', or median length of life.

The mortality rate for the first year of life (0·01231) is about 500-fold higher than the rate at age nine to ten years (0·00024); and on a short-term basis the neonatal rate is extremely high in the first day and decreases rapidly in the next few days and weeks, as shown at the top of Table 4.7. Note that the interval q values are for intervals of unequal length, ranging from one to 337 days (just over 48 weeks), but all of the life table calculations can still be carried out with consistency. If the mortality rate for the first day of life were sustained for the entire 365 days, the mortality rate for the first year would be 0·201 (instead of 0·01231), an annual rate that is not reached in white males until almost the age of 91. The minimum rate is seen in the pre-teen years; the rate rises rather rapidly in the teens, especially at ages 16–18 (the age at which most states begin to issue driver's licenses), to a level of 0·00193 at age 23, then decreases slightly to 0·00165 at age 31, after which the increase with advancing age is continuous. This 'hump' in the mortality curve in young adults is due to the high rate of death from car accidents and is much less prominent in young female than male drivers. In the approximate age range 40–85 years the annual increase in q is about 10 percent in both men and women. The rate then increases at a considerably slower pace than 10 percent per year, reaches a level of 0·305 at the age of 92 and is still under 0·400 at the age of 109. A similar pattern of q variation with advancing age is seen in other types of tables, such as insurance select and ultimate tables.

The wide variations in the mortality rate by race and sex are shown in Table 4.5, using age 50 as an example, from the 1979–81 US Life Tables. Sex differences persist at all ages, but at older ages racial differences are much smaller than at the age of 50.

Table 4.5. Comparison of mortality rate and life expectancy at age 50–51, by race and sex, 1979–81 US Life Tables.

Race and sex	Mortality rate, q	Life expectancy, e° (years)
White male	0·00706	25·26
White female	0·00376	30·96
Non-white male	0·01323	22·92
Non-white female	0·00688	28·59
Black male	0·01488	22·03
Black female	0·00765	27·84
Total male	0·00775	25·00
Total female	0·00416	30·69
Total population	0·00589	27·94

Differences between mortality rates in the life tables of industrialized nations tend to be much smaller than sex differences (*see* Table 4.6). However, mortality in less developed countries may be considerably higher than the rates in Table 00. With a steady and remarkable improvement since the end of World War II, mortality rates in Japan are now among the lowest in the world.

Table 4.6. National mortality rates per thousand, selected ages, by sex.

Nation/years	Male age					Female age				
	0	10	30	50	70	0	10	30	50	70
USA 1969–71	20·1	0·3	1·7	8·9	49·2	17·5	0·3	1·0	5·2	26·3
England (Number 13) 1970–72	19·8	0·3	1·0	7·4	55·5	13·2	0·2	0·6	4·5	27·8
France 1973–77	15·3	0·4	1·6	8·8	45·4	11·7	0·2	0·7	3·8	21·3
Switzerland 1968–73	16·9	0·3	1·2	6·2	45·0	13·0	0·3	0·6	3·5	24·8
Norway 1964	18·4	0·4	1·3	5·7	38·1	14·9	0·2	0·6	3·0	29·3
USSR[a] 1967–68	NA	0·8	3·6	10·2	46	NA	0·5	1·3	4·4	26
Australia[a] 1977	14·1	0·4	1·4	7·0	46	12·9	0·2	0·7	3·9	22
New Zealand[a] 1978	16·0	0·4	1·4	6·9	46	11·1	0·2	0·7	4·5	24
Japan 1980	8·3	0·2	0·9	4·6	35·0	6·6	0·1	0·6	2·5	19·3

NA = not available.
[a]Rates estimated from quinquennial averages, except at age 0–1.

Table 4.7. Extract from Table 5 of 1979–81 US Life Tables, White Males.[a]

Age interval	Proportion dying	Of 100,000 born alive		Stationary population		Average remaining lifetime
Period of life between two ages	Proportion of persons alive at beginning of age interval dying during interval	Number living at beginning of age interval	Number dying during age interval	In the age interval	In this and all subsequent age intervals	Average number of years of life remaining at beginning of age interval
1	2	3	4	5	6	7
x to $x+t$	$_tq_x$	l_x	$_td_x$	$_tL_x$	T_x	$\mathring{e}_x$
Days						
0–1	0·00438	100,000	438	273	7,081,671	70·82
1–7	0·00256	99,562	255	1,635	7,081,398	71·13
7–28	0·00139	99,307	138	5,709	7,079,763	71·29
28–365	0·00403	99,169	400	91,378	7,074,054	71·33
Years						
0–1	0·01231	100,000	1,231	98,995	7,081,671	70·82
1–2	0·00092	98,769	90	98,724	6,982,676	70·70
2–3	0·00066	98,679	65	98,646	6,883,952	67·76
3–4	0·00053	98,614	52	98,588	6,785,306	67·81
4–5	0·00043	98,,562	43	98,540	6,686,718	67.81
5–6	0·00039	98,519	39	98,499	6,588,178	66·87
6–7	0·00037	98,480	36	98,462	6,489,679	65·90
7–8	0·00034	98,444	34	98,428	6,391,217	64·92
8–9	0·00030	98,410	29	98,395	6,292,789	63·94
9–10	0·00024	98,381	24	98,369	6,194,394	62·96
.						
.						
.						
.						
.						
.						
50–51	0·00706	90,105	636	89,787	2,275,898	25·26
51–52	0·00775	89,469	693	89,122	2,186,111	24·43
52–53	0·00850	88,776	755	88,398	2,096,989	23·62
53–54	0·00934	88,021	823	87,610	2,008,591	22·82
54–55	0·01027	87,198	895	86,750	1,920,981	22·03
55–56	0·01125	86,303	971	85,818	1,834,231	21·25
56–57	0·01227	85,332	1,047	84,808	1,748,413	20·49
57–58	0·01338	84,285	1,128	83,722	1,663,605	19·74
58–59	0·01464	83,157	1,217	82,548	1,579,883	19·00
59–60	0·01605	81,940	1,315	81,283	1,497,335	18·27

[a]Source: *US Decennial Life Tables for 1979–81*, Vol 1, No 1, DHHS Publication No (PHS) 85–1150–1.

Secular changes in mortality are shown in Table 4.8 for selected ages in US white males in the period 1940–80. Rates of total mortality may not fully reflect the remarkable decrease in cardiovascular deaths over the age of 40. This important trend is discussed in Chapter 15. The decline, observed particularly in the USA and Australia, has not been seen to nearly the same extent in Great Britain and many European countries. A large decrease in deaths due to infectious diseases, including lobar pneumonia, tuberculosis and syphilis, occurred after the development and use of antibiotics at about the time of World War II. This effect was seen at all ages but was particularly prominent in young adults.

Table 4.8. Secular changes in mortality rates per thousand, US white males at selected ages, 1940–80.

Year	Age					
	0	10	30	50	70	90
1940	48·1	1·0	2·8	11·6	54·5	249
1950	30·7	0·6	1·8	10·1	50·3	229
1960	25·9	0·4	1·6	9·6	48·7	236
1970	20·1	0·3	1·7	8·9	49·2	213
1980	12·3	0·2	1·7	7·1	41·5	191

As an introduction to the concept of select mortality we can visualize mortality in any random sample of the general population as an aggregate rate, a weighted mean of a series of groups, a large fraction of persons in good health, and smaller fractions definable by progressively increasing excess mortality risks: many chronic, such as hypertension, some acute, such as a heart attack. The deaths in any year (or day of the year) therefore include both unexpected and, to some extent, deaths expected because of a chronic or acute risk factor. In the underwriting process for life insurance many of these risk factors are readily detectable, and applicants with the most severe risks can be declined for insurance. Even though the declinable group is a very small fraction of the pool of applicants or of the general population, this selection process can markedly reduce the age- and sex-specific mortality for a number of years. The reduction is at a maximum in the first year after selection and policy issue; the difference between the select rate and the ultimate rate at constant attained age diminishes progressively with interval from selection (policy duration). It is the practice of US and Canadian life insurance companies to utilize select mortality tables with separate rates for each of the first 15 years of policy duration. Experience for all policies with a duration greater than 15 years is then reported by attained age in a table of ultimate rates. In Table 4.9 rates are displayed from the 1975–80 Select and Ultimate Intercompany Tables (USA and Canada)[7] by attained age group, and compared with US white population rates.

The published select tables use entry age, but in Table 4.9 attained age has been used, so that rates on each horizontal row might be compared directly as rates for the same attained age. Thus the rate of 1·99 per thousand for men age 52

Table 4.9. Insurance Select and Ultimate mortality rates per thousand, 1975–80. Intercompany (USA and Canada), compared with 1979–81 US rates (white population), male and female.

Year of policy duration Attained age		Select rates			Ultimate	US white population
		1st	6th	11th	16th up	
			(entry age related to attained age)			
Group	x	x	$x-5$	$x-10$	$x-15$ up	x
			Males			
20–24	22	0·73	1·14	1·32	1·41	1·9
25–29	27	0·68	0·77	1·03	1·22	1·7
30–34	32	0·63	0·80	0·90	1·12	1·7
35–39	37	0·70	1·15	1·15	1·32	2·1
40–44	42	0·97	1·86	1·94	1·97	3·2
45–49	47	1·44	2·8	3·2	3·4	5·1
50–54	52	1·99	4·3	4·8	5·7	8·5
55–59	57	2·9	5·7	7·3	9·3	13·4
60–64	62	3·7	8·9	12·2	15·3	21·2
65–69	67	6·2	12·9	18·7	24·8	32·2
70 up	72	9·4	22·8	24·7	39·8	49·0
—	77	—	26·8	39·8	62·9	71·8
—	82	—	—	54·1	98·2	107
—	87	—	—	—	150	157
—	92	—	—	—	218	219
—	97	—	—	—	297	293
			Females			
20–24	22	0·32	0·42	0·53	0·53	0·6
25–29	27	0·31	0·42	0·54	0·53	0·6
30–34	32	0·39	0·58	0·64	0·63	0·7
35–39	37	0·50	0·91	1·00	0·98	1·1
40–44	42	0·73	1·43	1·70	1·71	1·7
45–49	47	0·98	2·2	2·5	2·6	2·8
50–54	52	1·23	2·8	3·5	3·9	4·5
55–59	57	1·57	3·8	5·1	6·0	6·8
60–64	62	2·2	5·2	6·9	9·0	10·7
65–69	67	3·0	7·1	9·5	13·5	16·0
70 up	72	5·1	9·5	14·6	21·1	25·2
—	77	—	15·8	22·6	33·9	40·2
—	82	—	—	34·4	65·7	69·5
—	87	—	—	—	108	115
—	92	—	—	—	164	177
—	97	—	—	—	234	252

(age 50–54 at entry) is only 46 percent of the 6th year rate (age 45–49 at entry), 41 percent of the 11th year rate (men age 40–44 at entry) and 35 percent of the ultimate rate (men age 35–39 or younger at entry). The ultimate male rate of 5·7 per thousand, in turn, is only 67 percent of the population rate for white males over a slightly later period of observation. These comparisons are illustrative of the impact of selection in reducing mortality, especially in the first few years after the selection is completed. The tables demonstrate that the effect persists beyond the arbitrary 15-year duration period chosen by the Society of Actuaries: there is a disproportionate increase from the 15th year select rate to the ultimate rate at the same attained age. This is attributable to the fact that the ultimate rate is based on mortality of policyholders with all policy durations from 16 years and up. Nevertheless outside North America actuarial practice in the use of standard issue mortality for comparison with mortality in impaired risks does not provide select tables with such a long select period. The English Institute of Actuaries does supervise preparation of intercompany select tables with a five-year select period. Insurance companies on the continent of Europe appear to use aggregate company mortality experience (rates based on all policyholders of the same attained age, regardless of policy divation), or even population mortality rates. One can presume that, when this is the practice, the actuary, medical director and underwriter somehow make allowance for the effects of selection in producing a lower mortality rate than the standard ostensibly used. Group life insurance mortality rates are also lower than population rates because the ability to hold gainful employment (with group life insurance benefits) is, in itself, a kind of selection, even though there is no effort to screen in the manner used for individual insurance.

'Antiselection' occurs whenever there is an opportunity for people with a poor risk to profit at the expense of better risks. This can result in inclusion (instead of exclusion) of very high risk cases in certain situations: for example, in the contractual conversion of group to individual insurance. This is shown in Tables 4.10 and 4.11, taken from an interesting article on selection.[8]

The explanation for the high mortality in the group conversion policies lies in the fact that few employees who are in good health take advantage of the opportunity to convert their group life insurance within the time limit, when their employment is terminated. Some do not feel a need to continue their insurance; others choose to submit evidence of insurability in lieu of conversion in order to obtain additional amounts or types of coverage not available in a group conversion, or simply out of loyalty to their agent, who would not have received a commission on the conversion policy. On the other hand, there is a powerful incentive for terminating employees with a high mortality risk to make this conversion, because they know it would be difficult and costly, if not impossible, to obtain life insurance by individual application. The group conversion policy may represent almost 100 percent policies with an increased risk, often a very high risk, such as advanced cancer or congestive heart failure. On this basis it is easy to understand the high mortality rates and ratios in the two right-hand columns of Tables 4.10 and 4.11.

TABLES OF COMPARATIVE MORTALITY BY TIME ELAPSED

Table 4.12 and some further tables used as examples are also taken from the experience of the duPont male employees with first MI (Abstract 312 in the 1976 *Medical Risks* volume[1]). However, other age and severity groups will be used, and the early deaths will be excluded, giving long-term mortality that extends from 30 days to five years after the MI. The format is more condensed than shown in some

Table 4.10. Effects of selection on mortality, male insured lives 1955–60.[8],[a]

Age group	US white male population 1959–61 (rate per thousand[b])	1st policy year		16th policy year upwards		Group insurance predominantly male 1960		Group conversion males 1959–67	
		Rate per thousand[b]	Ratio to US population	Rate per thousand[b]	Ratio to US population	Rate per thousand[b]	Ratio to US population	Rate per thousand[b]	Ratio to US population
30–34	1·7	0·6	32%	1·3	76%	1·3	76%	12·7	747%
35–39	2·5	0·9	35	1·6	64	1·8	72	15·1	604
40–44	4·1	1·5	37	2·7	66	3·1	76	19·9	485
45–49	6·9	2·2	32	5·1	74	5·3	77	28·5	413
50–54	11·6	3·2	28	8·3	72	8·6	74	43·4	374
55–59	17·3	4·3	25	13·3	77	13·9	80	67·8	392
60–64	26·9	6·7	25	21·6	80	21·3	79	93·1	346
65–69	39·3	10·2	26	33·0	84	32·8	83	119·9	305
70–74	56·2	14·8	26	50·0	89	50·5	90		
75–79	82·7			75·1	91	74·2	90		

[a]Source of basic data: publications of National Center for Health Statistics and Transactions of Society of Actuaries.
[b]Rates per thousand are probabilities of dying within a year.

Table 4.11. Effects of selection on mortality, female insured lives 1955–60.[8,a]

Age group	US white female population 1959–61 (rate per thousand[b])	1st policy year		16th policy year onwards		Group conversion females 1959–67	
		Rate per thousand[b]	Ratio to US population	Rate per thousand[b]	Ratio to US population	Rate per thousand[b]	Ratio to US population
30–34	1·0	0·5	50%	0·9	90%	17·1	1710%
35–39	1·5	0·5	33	1·3	87	20·4	1360
40–44	2·3	0·7	30	1·7	74	24·8	1078
45–49	3·6	1·2	33	2·9	81	31·1	864
50–54	5·6	1·4	25	4·5	80	41·3	738
55–59	8·1	2·2	27	6·7	83	57·2	706
60–64	13·3	3·2	24	10·0	75	70·8	532
65–69	21·0	5·1	24	16·8	80	81·0	386
70–74	34·6	7·4	21	33·4	97		
75–79	58·3			49·4	85		

aSource of basic data: publications of National Center for Health Statistics and Transactions of Society of Actuaries.
bRates per thousand are probabilities of dying within a year.

of the published tables, in keeping with current practice to reduce the volume of data presented in the tables. Withdrawals are not shown but have been used to derive E and NER. The high early mortality is shown by the observations that 61 of 252 men aged 25–44 died in the first 30 days after MI, 178 of 616 men aged 45–54 and 160 of 463 men aged 55–64 (30-day mortality rates of 24·2 percent, 28·9 percent and 34·6 percent respectively). As a consequence, mortality rates from 30 days to one year are considerably lower than the first-year rate shown in the Tables 4.12–4.14.

Mortality is still higher in the first year than in subsequent years, despite exclusion of the early deaths. In the first interval, NER$=434-0·5(83)=392·5$ (withdrawals not shown in Table 4.12). However, this is for an interval from 30 days to 365 days, or 0·917 year, so NER must be multiplied by 0·917 to obtain the exposure, E, 359·8 patient-years, as given in Table 4.12. Data for the withdrawals, w, are given in the abstract tables, but have been omitted from Table 4.12 to conserve space. Two aggregate means have been shown: one for duration 1–5 years and one for the total duration. Data for E, d and d' are added from the appropriate intervals to obtain the respective sums, from which the aggregate mean mortality rates are derived. Because of the disparity of the first year, the mean for intervals 2 to 5 (duration 2–5 years) is more representative of that period than is the overall mean: EDR is 37 per thousand per year and MR 420 percent in the former, but the overall EDR is 62 and overall MR 685 percent, as these means are heavily weighted by the high mortality in the first year.

TABLES OF COMPARATIVE MORTALITY BY AGE OR SEVERITY

Such tables are for all durations combined, or for combined intervals. The method preferred for these rates is an aggregate mean, but often it may be necessary to derive results from cumulative survival rates, P and P', or interval rates for more than one year, and then to obtain geometric mean values of p and q. Examples based on aggregate means for the age groups in the duPont experience are given in Table 4.13, separately for the first interval (30 days to 1 year), and then for duration 1–5 years. The data for men aged 45–54 are the same as those in Table 4.12. Comparative survival has been omitted from Table 4.13, to make room for the aggregate mean annual rates, $\bar{q}$ and $\bar{q}'$ (derived as $\Sigma d/\Sigma E$ and $\Sigma d'/\Sigma E$ respectively).

The experience of the duPont male employees has also been used to illustrate the use of cumulative survival rates to derive geometric mean annual rates, first for survival, then its complement, an annual mortality rate. Results are shown in Table 4.14 for two severity categories and the total cohort.

Survival rates, cumulative for the survivors at 30 days after the MI, have been derived from annual data by the life table method. If the FU period had consisted of five full years, the geometric annual mean of the survival rate at five years, P_5, would be $\sqrt[5]{P_5}\,P_5 = (P_5)^{1/5} = (P_5)^{0·2}$. The geometric mean for all cases would have been $(0·736)^{0·2}$ or 0·941. The complement of $\check{p}$ gives the annualized mean mortality rate $\hat{q}=1-0·941=0·059$, or 59 deaths per thousand per year. (This calculation is easily accomplished with a pocket calculator that has a function key to raise a number to any power; a decimal power less than 1 serves

Table 4.12. Comparative mortality and survival by time elapsed, duPont male employees aged 45–54, after first MI, 1956–61, deaths within 30 days excluded.

Number i	Interval Start–end t to $t + \triangle.t$	Number alive at start l	Exposure (patient-years) E	Numbers of deaths Observed d	Numbers of deaths Expected[a] d'	Mortality ratio $100d/d'$	Excess death rate[b] EDR	Cumulative survival Rate P	Cumulative survival Ratio $100P/P'$
1	30 d to 1 yr	434	359·8	43	3·34	1290%	110	0·890	89·8%
2	1–2 yr	308	274·0	12	2·84	430	34	0·851	86·7
3	2–3 yr	224	196·5	9	2·24	400	34	0·812	83·7
4	3–4 yr	160	129·5	7	1·61	435	42	0·768	80·2
5	4–5 yr	92	69·5	4	0·93	430	44	0·723	76·5
2–5	1–5 yr	308	667·5	32	7·58	420	37	0·723	76·5
1–5	30 d to 5 yr	434	1027·3	75	10·92	685	62	0·723	76·5

[a]Basis of expected deaths: 1959–61 US Life Tables, white male.
[b]EDR=1000 $(d-d')/E$, extra deaths per thousand per year.

Table 4.13. Comparative mortality by age, duPont male employees after MI, 1956–61, for two intervals: 30 days to 1 year, and 1–5 years.

Age at entry x	Alive at start l	Exposure (patient-years) E	Number of deaths Observed d	Number of deaths Expected[a] d'	Mortality ratio $100d/d'$	Mean annual mortality rate per thousand Observed $\bar{q}$	Mean annual mortality rate per thousand Expected $\bar{q}'$	Mean annual mortality rate per thousand Excess $(\bar{q}-\bar{q}')$
			30 days to 1 year					
25–44	190	156·7	9	0·51	1760%	57	3·3	54%
45–54	434	359·8	43	3·34	1290	120	9·3	111
55–64	305	249·3	28	5·11	550	112	20	92
All	929	765·8	80	8·96	895	104	11.7	92
			1–5 years					
25–44	143	317·5	13	1·29	1010%	41	4·1	37%
45–54	308	667·5	32	7·58	420	48	11·4	37
55–64	211	470·5	26	11·60	225	55	25	30
All	662	1455·5	71	20·47	345	49	14·1	35

[a]Basis of expected deaths: 1959–61 US Life Tables, white male.

Table 4.14. Comparative mortality and survival, duPont male employees after MI, all ages, average 30 days to 5 years, by hypertension and overweight.

Severity category[a]	Number alive at 30 days l	Cumulative survival rate		Survival ratio $100P/P'$	Mean annual mortality rate per thousand			Mortality ratio	
		Observed P	Expected[b] P'		Observed $\hat{q}$	Expected $\hat{q}'$	Excess $(\hat{q}-\hat{q}')$	Annual $100\hat{q}/\hat{q}'$	Cumulative $100Q/Q'$
All cases	932	0·736	0·932	78·9%	60	14	46	430%	390%
BP<150/94	666	0·780	0·933	83·6	49	14	35	350	330
BP>150/94	265	0·631	0·928	68·0	89	15	74	595	510
Normal weight	633	0·752	0·930	80·9	56	15	41	375	355
Overweight	298	0·705	0·933	75·6	69	14	55	495	440

[a]Hypertension is defined as two or more successive annual readings less than 150/94. Overweight is defined as more than 20 percent over ideal weight at last annual examination.
[b]Basis of expected survival: 1959–61 US Life Tables, white male.

as the exponent to extract a root.) However, the FU period is actually one month short of five years, or a total of 4·92 years. Hence the true exponent for the geometric mean is 1/4·92, or the decimal 0·203, and the rate is derived as $(0·736)^{0·203}=0·940$. The geometric mean annual mortality rate is 60 per thousand per year, as shown in Table 4.14. Two sets of mortality ratios are shown: one set derived from the annualized mortality rates, the other derived from the cumulative mortality rates. The latter, not given in Table 4.14, may be easily derived as $Q=1-P$ and $Q'=1-P'$. Note that Q/Q' ratios are always lower than mortality ratios based on mean annual q values, whether geometric or aggregate means. This is due to overestimate of expected annual exposure and deaths when there is excess observed mortality and the expected cohort is treated independently from the observed cohort. For this reason, when average mortality rates are derived, mortality ratios are based on these and not on cumulative rates. The final column in Table 4.14 is one that I would now ordinarily omit from any table in which the results are derived from cumulative rates. It should also be noted that aggregate and geometric mean annual mortality rates usually differ, because the weighting process (of annual values) is different in each method. This is discussed in the 1976 *Medical Risks* volume.[1]

OVERALL MEAN AGE AND ESTIMATING MEAN EXPECTED MORTALITY RATE

Clinical patient groups in FU studies are frequently reported with results for all ages combined, because the size of the cohort does not justify an age break-down. If only the mean age and range of age are given, without any age distribution, this creates two problems in the calculation of age- and sex-matched expected mortality: (1) the estimate of a mean q' for the entry year of FU, and (2) the progression of q' by time elapsed. The reason for this lies in the wide age range encountered in most such studies (e.g. a mean entry age of 55, with a range from 35 to 75). Mortality rates for children over the age of one and for young adults are very small, as we have seen, and they contribute relatively little to the mean q' of a group that includes many older adults. Because of the 9–11 percent annual increase in q' from about age 35 to 85, rates above the mean age contribute more to the mean q' than do the rates corresponding to ages below the mean age. The result is that the mean q' is invariably skewed to a value higher than the tabular q' corresponding to the mean age. The magnitude of the skewing depends on the age distribution, both the mean and the range of age for the group. With a range of ±20 years above and below a mean age of 55, the mean q' may be approximated by entering the life table at age 58, three years above the actual mean age. However, if the age range is narrow, as in decennial age groups, the central or mean age may be used to enter the life table to extract a q' very close to the mean derived from use of the annual ages and their weighted q' values. The wide age range is critical.

The problem of progression of q' with duration of follow-up is created by the changing age distribution of the survivors. As the survivors enter the start of each FU year, all are indeed one year older than they were in the previous year. However, mortality is higher at the older ages in the observed cohort, so that there are relatively fewer survivors at the older ages. As a consequence, the mean age of the survivors does not increase a full year with each year of follow-up, but at some lesser amount determined by the age pattern of mortality in the observed cohort. In six series of patients following coronary bypass surgery the annual increase in q' varied from 5 percent to as much as the increase of 11 percent per year in the expected mortality table. In post-MI patients the annual increase in q' was smaller, from about 3·5 percent to 7·5 percent per year. These results were derived from analysis of series of patients with coronary heart disease in Abstract 642 and other abstracts in 1990 edition of *Medical Risks*.[9] Unpublished similar analyses of data on patients with cancer of the colon, supplied by the National Cancer Institute from End Results Study Number 4, disclosed that both mean age and mean q' actually decreased in the second FU year, regardless of staging of the cancer, and subsequent increase was relatively slow. Thus in regional cancer in males the mean age was 66·1 years at entry, 65·2 years at the end of the first year (start of the second year) and still only 68·2 years at the end of the fifth year of observation (instead of 66·1+5·0, or 71·1 years of attained age, if all of the men surviving at duration five years had been 66·1 years at entry). The corresponding values for the mean q' were 0·0501 at entry, 0·0480 in the second year and 0·0565 in the year following five full years of observation. In cancer, therefore, the mortality pattern of mean q' with duration is quite different from the pattern in coronary heart disease. Empirical relations of this kind are not yet extensive enough to devise a general method of approximation of the change of q' with duration.

CONVERSION OF MORTALITY RATIO TO A NUMERICAL RATING

Most of the mortality abstracts derived from clinical FU studies give comparative mortality with an 'expected' yardstick based on mortality in the general population or some table other than the select tables used in insurance studies made by US and Canadian companies. If the mortality experience of a given company is equivalent to that shown in the intercompany select tables (*see* Table 4.9), then a mortality ratio based on the appropriate select rate does have a numerical correspondence with the substandard rating classification expressed as a percentage (standard equal to 100 percent). This is not true, however, for the studies in which population or other tables with higher expected mortality rates have been used to calculate q', d' and the corresponding mortality ratios. A detailed description of a method to convert such ratios to mortality ratios based on select rates has been reported.[10] The basic idea is to assume that the observed EDR is virtually constant regardless of the expected rates used. When both rates are expressed in the same units (decimal or deaths per thousand per year) an 'adjusted observed' rate, q_s, can easily be derived: $q_s = EDR + q_s'$. With q_s thus at hand, the mortality ratio (MR_s) based on select rates is $100 q_s / q_s'$. Table 4.15 illustrates the method and results for duPont men aged 45–54 (comparative mortality and survival results, with US population rates, are shown in Table 4.14). The upper part of the table contains the original data, with q' and d' derived from the 1959–61 US Life Tables. The lower part retains the EDR of the upper part, but substitutes the select q_s' for q', shows

Table 4.15. Derivation of mortality ratios based on select rates from original data, duPont Post-MI male employees aged 45–54 (*see* Table 4.12).

Interval Number i	Start–end t to $t+\triangle t$	Exposure (patient-years) E	Number of deaths Observed d	Expected d'	Mean annual mortality rate per thousand Observed $q=1000d/E$	Expected q'	Excess EDR$=q-q'$	Mortality ratio[a] $100q/q'$
				Comparative mortality from US Life Table rates[b]				
1	30 d to 1 yr	359·8	43	3·34	119	9	110	1220%
2	1–2 yr	272·0	12	2·80	44	10	34	440
3	2–3 yr	196·5	9	2·24	46	12	34	385
				Comparative mortality from insurance select rates[c]				
					$q_s=$EDR$+q_s'$	q_s'	same EDR	$100q_s/q_s'$
1	30 d to 1 yr	—	—	—	113	2·5	110	4500
2	1–2 yr	—	—	—	38	3·7	34	1020
3	2–3 yr	—	—	—	39	4·8	34	810

[a] Any differences from data in Table 4.12 are attributable to rounding off.
[b] 1959–1961 US Life Tables for the white male population.
[c] 1965–70 Basic Select Tables for males.

Table 4.16. Life expectancy approximation for a cohort with extremely high constant mortality rate of 0·3 per year, ages 10 to 30.[13]

Age	Number alive at start	Number of deaths each year	Average years lived, age x	Cumulative years lived to, P=0	Expectation of life (years)	Cumulative survival (end of year)
x	l_x	d_x	$L_x{}^a$	$T_x{}^b$	$\mathring{e}_x{}^c$	P_x
10–11	1000	300	850	2831	2·8	0·700
11–12	700	210	595	1981	2·8	0·490
12–13	490	147	416	1386	2·8	0·343
13–14	343	103	292	970	2·8	0·240
14–15	240	72	204	678	2·8	0·168
15–16	168	50	143	474	2·8	0·118
16–17	118	36	100	331	2·8	0·082
17–18	82	25	70	231	2·8	0·057
18–19	57	17	48	161	2·8	0·040
19–20	40	12	34	113	2·8	0·028
20–21	28	8	24	79	2·8	0·020
21–22	20	6	17	55	2·8	0·014
22–23	14	4	12	38	2·7	0·010
23–24	10	3	8	26	2·6	0·007
24–25	7	2	6	18	2·6	0·005
25–26	5·0	1·5	4·2	(12·0)	(2·4)	0·0035
26–27	3·5	1·0	3·0	(7·8)	(2·2)	0·0025
27–28	2·5	0·8	2·1	(4·8)	(1·9)	0·0017
28–29	1·7	0·5	1·4	(2·7)	(1·6)	0·0012
29–30	1·2	0·4	1·0	(1·3)	(1·1)	0·0008
30 up	(0·8)	(0·8)	(—)	(—)	(—)	0·0000
			Total L=2831			

$^a L_x = 0\cdot5\,(l_x + l_{x+1})$.
$^b T_x = L_x + $ Sum (all subsequent L_x values).
$^c \mathring{e}_x = T_x/l_x$ (values of T_x and e_x over the age of 24 are unrealiable in this table).

an adjusted 'observed' q_s as the sum of EDR and q_s', and the select MR_s as $100q_s/q_s'$. Note the effect of using a much smaller mortality rate: the mortality ratios become correspondingly larger. Use of the population expected rates would lead to a serious underestimate of the appropriate rating for the degree of excess mortality implicit in the EDR. Especially at ages under 50, the mortality ratio is much more sensitive to differences in expected q' than the EDR.

Just as a select mortality ratio may be considered equivalent to a table rating, so an EDR may be considered equivalent to a flat extra premium in dollars per $1,000 of insurance per year. It is also easy to develop a combination of flat extra and table rating, often used in ratings for applicants with a history of coronary heart disease. However, adjustment should be made if extra premiums are based on company mortality experience, and if the company mortality experience differs materially from the mortality rates in the intercompany basic select tables. Furthermore, this simplistic picture is only an approximation: in setting an appropriate rating the actuary must take into consideration (in addition to the excess mortality) other factors, such as expense, lapse rates, discount and interest rates, and anticipated future mortality. Such refinements are outside the scope of this chapter.

LIFE EXPECTANCY AND STRUCTURED SETTLEMENTS

Over the past decade the life insurance industry in North America has witnessed a remarkable growing demand for single premium annuities to provide for individual applicants with excess mortality risk ranging from extremely high levels (e.g. severely disabled patients, such as those in a persistent vegetative state of coma due to irreversible brain damage) to those with no extra risk at all (e.g. the healthy family of a person whose death was caused by negligence). Generally the premium is paid as the result of a lump sum settlement in a tort case. Specialist brokers make multiple applications to many of the more than 100 companies estimated in 1989 to be accepting this type of business; competition is therefore intense, and issue rates are very low. The term structured settlement (*see* Chapter 6) is appropriate for these litigation cases because there is often provision for an annual increase in annuity benefit payments to allow for inflation in the costs of medical and personal care above current levels.

Little has been written about the many complex problems involved in the estimate of the appropriate single premium for these annuities, but Dr Roger Butz arranged for an elective workshop on structured settlements after the end of the 1989 meeting of the Association of Life Insurance Medical Directors of America.[11] There were five presentations by Dr Butz and his fellow panelists, and the three that have been published will give the reader a good idea of the many interesting but difficult facets of this operation in an insurance company providing structured settlement annuities. The actuarial problems for premium setting are many: forecasting interest rates, the effect of economic inflation, mortality and expenses (including commissions and future income taxes). The medical underwriter is concerned only with the excess mortality. Although this may be in the realm of excess risk considered in issuing extra-premium life insurance, often an MD involved in this type of underwriting is confronted with high levels of excess risk that are entirely beyond the insurable limit. This is a totally new 'universe of discourse' in medical underwriting. Cases with spinal cord injury and severe brain damage appear to constitute more than half of the applications. Many of these entail EDRs of 100 or more extra deaths per thousand per year, and this level may be sustained for ten years or longer. Such mortality rates are associated with mortality ratios that are truly astronomical in magnitude — as much as 10,000 percent for children and young adults. In this sphere of very high mortality the time-honored medicolegal use of expectation of life, e_x, has been adopted as a measure of excess mortality that can be converted into an equivalent constant mortality ratio or an advancing of the actual age, either of which permit actuarial calculation of the discounted mortality portion of the premium cost. The actuary must choose whether to use an annuitant, insurance select or ultimate, or population table for expected deaths; once this choice is made, actuarial tables permit conversion from life expectancy to the equivalent mortality ratio or advance in actual age. The constant mortality ratio must be qualified, because at some age a high mortality ratio will produce a rate that exceeds 1·000, an impossible result. For example, a mortality ratio of 1,000 percent will produce a rate exceeding 1·000 in white males above the age of 81, at which age the tabular rate is 0·0989 (1979–81 US Life Tables). The pattern of mortality ratio of a high-risk cohort is invariably one of decrease with advancing age,[12] and the assumption of a long-term constant mortality ratio is much less realistic than assumption of a long-term constant EDR. At some older age it becomes necessary to graduate a high mortality ratio down to 100 percent of the tabular rate, regardless of which expected table is used. It is not appropriate in the space available in this chapter to describe the actuarial or underwriting methodology. However, in a single illustrative table the calculation of $\mathring{e}_x$ at an assumed very high constant mortality rate of 0·3 per year can be shown. This is of the order of the rates observed in severely handicapped patients with mental retardation (bedridden and requiring tube feeding) described in a recent report based on a state registry of patients with mental retardation.[13] The life expectancy table is shown on page 70 (Table 4.16).

Note that the total L_x in Table 4.16 slightly underestimates T_x because the calculations should be continued much further than the age of 30. However, the approximation error is small except for its effect on $\mathring{e}_x$ over the age of 25. The lower the EDR or mortality rate, the higher the age to which the life table calculations must be carried. Nevertheless the most accurate method of estimating $\mathring{e}_x$ in a high-risk case is to add values of EDR, from available follow-up studies starting at the patient's current age, to the appropriate values of expected q', year by year, to obtain an annual value of q, and from this to derive the complete life table (see Table 4.16). In addition, annual mortality ratios may be derived as $100q/q'$. This may be practical while the case is still in litigation, but not for the medical underwriter, because of the pressure for a speedy rating action.

An interesting property of $\mathring{e}_x$ in this type of high-mortality case its its relative independence of advancing age, as shown in the study of handicapped patients[13] already mentioned (Table 4.17 summarizes some of the results). The life expectancy does not decrease (until there are very few survivors) as the cohort advances in age because the very high mortality rate assumed remains constant.

Note the relative constancy of both the mortality rate and life expectancy over an age span of 29 years; both variables were virtually independent of age within this range. Group 1 consisted of 1,500 patients, group 2 of 4,513 patients and

Table 4.17. Life expectancy ages 1–30 in three severity grades of mentally retarded disabled patients.[13]

Group[a]	Annual Mortality Rate		Life Expectancy (years)		Cumulative Survival to Age 30
	Mean q	Range[a] Min–Max	Mean $\overset{\circ}{e}_x$	Range[a] Min–Max	P
1 Most severe	0·228	0·20–0·27	4·7	4·1– 5·4	0·0007
2 Intermediate	0·127	0·11–0·14	8·8	8·1–10·8	0·027
3 Least severe	0·037	0·02–0·06	21·3	18·8–23·4	0·323

[a]All patients were unable to walk. Group 1: immobile, required tube feeding. Group 2: immobile but could be fed by mouth. Group 3: some voluntary motion and able to take food from others.

group 3 of 997 patients (all ages, each group). The total number of deaths in group 3 was under 40. All of these patients were so disabled as to be totally dependent on others for personal care, yet there was a wide range in mortality and life expectancy over the three severity grades. For comparison, the mortality rate averaged 0·67 per year in the first two years after diagnosis of metastatic cancer of the colon (from the End Results Study Report Number 4, as given in Table 157d of *Medical Risks*.[1] This rate was for male and female patients, all ages combined. At duration 2–5 years the rate averaged 0·28 per year; at 5–10 years it averaged 0·11 per year. The average annual rate decreased steadily over the first five or six years, then tended to stabilize at a level similar to that reported in the group 2 patients in Table 4.17.

After this chapter was written a more detailed article on this subject has been published.

POISSON TEST

The time-honored statistical significance test used in insurance medical studies is the Poisson distribution applied to the number of observed deaths. Table 4.18 gives upper and lower confidence limits (CL) at the 95 percent and 90 percent levels for numbers of deaths from three to 100. Confidence limits or the confidence interval define a numerical range about the observed number of deaths: if the expected deaths, d', lie outside this interval, the difference from d is regarded as significant at the specified level; but if d' is within the interval, the difference is regarded as 'not significant'. For example, given 10 observed and 5·0 expected deaths, with an MR of 200 percent, the 95 percent CL for 10 observed deaths would be 4·8 to 18·4 (observed deaths). The corresponding 95 percent limits for the MR would be from 96 percent ($100 \times 4·8/5·0$) to 368 percent ($100 \times 18·4/5·0$). Since the 5·0 expected deaths exceed the lower limit of 4·8, and the MR of 96 percent is less than 100 percent, the excess mortality is not significant at the 95 percent confidence level. However, the observed MR is significant by the narrower 90 percent CL

Table 4.18. Confidence limits based on number of observed deaths, Poisson Distribution.[a,b]

Number of deaths observed d	Limits with respect to d				Limits as a ratio of d			
	95% limits		90% limits		95% limits		90% limits	
	Lower LL	Upper UL	Lower LL	Upper UL	Lower LL	Upper UL	Lower LL	Upper UL
3	0·6	8·8	0·8	7·8	0·21	2·93	0·27	2·60
4	1·1	10·2	1·4	9·2	0·27	2·56	0·34	2·29
5	1·6	11·7	2·0	10·5	0·32	2·33	0·39	2·10
6	2·2	13·1	2·6	11·8	0·37	2·18	0·44	1·97
7	2·8	14·4	3·3	13·1	0·40	2·06	0·47	1·88
8	3·5	15·8	4·0	14·4	0·43	1·97	0·50	1·80
9	4·1	17·1	4·7	15·7	0·46	1·90	0·52	1·74
10	4·8	18·4	5·4	17·0	0·48	1·84	0·54	1·70
11	5·5	19·7	6·2	18·2	0·50	1·79	0·56	1·66
12	6·2	21·0	6·9	19·4	0·52	1·75	0·58	1·62
13	6·9	22·2	7·7	20·7	0·53	1·71	0·59	1·59
14	7·7	23·5	8·5	21·9	0·55	1·68	0·61	1·56
15	8·4	24·7	9·2	23·1	0·56	1·65	0·62	1·54
16	9·1	26·0	10·0	24·3	0·57	1·62	0·63	1·52
17	9·9	27·2	10·8	25·5	0·58	1·60	0·64	1·50
18	10·7	28·4	11·6	26·7	0·59	1·58	0·64	1·48
19	11·4	29·7	12·4	27·9	0·60	1·56	0·65	1·47
20	12·2	30·9	13·3	29·1	0·61	1·54	0·66	1·46
22	13·8	33·3	14·9	31·4	0·63	1·51	0·68	1·43
24	15·4	35·7	16·5	33·8	0·64	1·49	0·69	1·41
26	17·0	38·1	18·2	36·1	0·65	1·47	0·70	1·39
28	18·6	40·5	19·9	38·4	0·66	1·45	0·71	1·37
30	20·2	42·8	21·6	40·7	0·67	1·43	0·72	1·36

32	21·9	45·2	23·3	43·0	0·68	1·41	0·73	1·34
34	23·5	47·5	25·0	45·3	0·69	1·40	0·74	1·33
36	25·2	49·8	26·7	47·5	0·70	1·38	0·74	1·32
38	26·9	52·2	28·5	49·8	0·71	1·37	0·75	1·31
40	28·6	54·5	30·2	52·1	0·72	1·36	0·76	1·30
45	32·8	60·2	34·6	57·7	0·73	1·34	0·77	1·28
50	37·1	65·9	39·0	63·3	0·74	1·32	0·78	1·27
55	41·4	71·6	43·4	68·9	0·75	1·30	0·79	1·25
60	45·8	77·2	47·9	74·4	0·76	1·29	0·80	1·24
65	50·2	82·8	52·3	79·9	0·77	1·27	0·80	1·23
70	54·6	88·4	56·8	85·4	0·78	1·26	0·81	1·22
75	59·0	94·0	61·3	90·9	0·79	1·25	0·82	1·21
80	63·4	99·6	65·9	96·4	0·79	1·24	0·82	1·20
85	67·9	105·1	70·4	101·8	0·80	1·24	0·83	1·20
90	72·4	110·6	75·0	107·2	0·80	1·23	0·83	1·19
95	76·9	116·1	79·6	112·7	0·81	1·22	0·84	1·19
100	81·4	121·6	84·1	118·1	0·81	1·22	0·84	1·18

aThe CL have been calculated in accordance with the traditional formula and definition of confidence interval for the Poisson distribution, as described in *Distributions in Statistics: discrete distributions*. (Dr Robert A Lew is thanked for his assistance in the preparation of this table.) When d exceeds 100, an approximation of the CL that is satisfactory for most purposes can be obtained by assuming a normal distribution. The formula is: 95 percent limits$=d\pm1\cdot96\sqrt{d}$, 90 percent limits$=d\pm1\cdot65\sqrt{d}$.

bTo obtain the lower CL, LL for a mortality ratio, MR, or a mortality rate q, multiply MR or q by the appropriate LL factor in the right-hand portion of the table. The upper CL, UL, for MR or q may similarly be computed by multiplying MR or q by the appropriate UL factor from the right-hand part of the table.

values shown in Table 4.18: from 5·4 to 17·0 deaths, with corresponding MRs of
108 percent to 340 percent. To achieve statistical significance for a given d, the
expected d' must be less than the lower CL as given in the table, and the mortality
ratio must exceed 100 percent.

Another way of assessing significance is to use a value of p to express the
probability that the difference is a random one. For a 95 percent CL value $p=0·05$,
and for a 90 percent CL value $p=0·10$. The footnotes to Table 00 indicate how the
two sets of CL values may be related to mortality rates and ratios. The selection of
$p=0·05$ as the level of significance to be used as a critical boundary between a
random difference and a significant difference in mortality (or of any other kind)
has been dictated by custom. Feinstein has discussed this problem in depth.[15] For a
description of the multitudinous significance tests in current use, the reader should
consult standard texts on the subject. The Poisson test will suffice in most mortality
studies in which a direct comparison can be made of an observed d with an expected
d'.

CONCLUSION

If this chapter has in some measure succeeded in explaining how life table
methodology may be applied by the medical underwriter to aid his task of mortality
risk classification, it should be understood that the subject matter is as extensive as
this presentation has been limited in scope. Many, many topics have been omitted
or described inadequately. In other chapters of this book the reader will find
myriad examples of results of FU studies being used to provide a rational basis for
underwriting selection and risk classification. Also, 1990 has seen the publication of
a new mortality reference monograph,[9] successor to the original *Medical Risks*
volume.[1] The new book was jointly sponsored by the Association of Life Insurance
Medical Directors of America and the Society of Actuaries, with technical and
other support from the Center of Medico-actuarial Statistics of the MIB, Inc.
Published in two volumes, it is twice as large, with nearly 400 abstracts. For
extensive further discussion of the techniques used in the design, conduct and
analysis of FU studies the reader should consult the published proceedings of a
1983 workshop sponsored by the American Cancer Society.[16] This contains
abundant material on topics and terms omitted from this chapter, such as
generation studies, case control studies, clinical trials, bias, regression analysis,
multivariate analysis, actuarial development of the life table and other topics.
Survival models and many statistical terms have been omitted from this chapter; a
good source for such subject matter is a text used for the fellowship examinations of
the Society of Actuaries.[17]

Life table methodology may be used for outcomes other than death. Any morbid
event that can be clearly defined may be substituted for death. The rates then
become an incidence or morbid event rate, and survival signifies 'free of a new
morbid event'. Mortality ratio becomes morbidity ratio, and EDR becomes an
excess event rate, when the development is on a comparative basis.[18,19]

REFERENCES

1 Singer RB, Levinson L (editors). *Medical Risks: Patterns of Mortality and Survival.* Lexington, Mass: Lexington Books, 1976; chapters 2 and 3.

2 Benjamin B, Haycocks HW. *The Analysis of Mortality and Other Actuarial Statistics.* Cambridge, England: University Press, 1970.

3 Cutler SJ, Ederer F. Maximum utilization of the life table method in analyzing survival curves. *J Chron Dis* 1958; 8: 699.

4 Pokorski RJ. Mortality methodology and analysis seminar — text. *J Insur Med* 1988; 20(4): 20.

5 Rogers OH, Hunter A. The numerical method of determining the value of risks for life insurance. *Proc Assoc Life Insur Med Dir Am* 1919; 7: 99.

6 Shryock HS, Siegel JS et al. *The Methods and Materials of Demography.* New York: Academic Press, 1976.

7 Society of Actuaries. 1975–80 Basic Tables. *1982 Reports of Mortality and Morbidity.* Chicago: Society of Actuaries, 1985; 55.

8 Metropolitan Life Insurance Co. Effects of selection on mortality. *Stat Bull* June 1971; 51:9.

9 Lew EA, Gajewski J (editors). *Medical Risks: Patterns of Mortality by Age and Time Elapsed.* New York: Praeger, 1990.

10 Singer RB. The conversion of mortality ratios to a numerical rating classification for life insurance underwriting. *J Insur Med* 1988; 20(2): 54.

11 Butz R et al. Structured settlement workshop. *J Insur Med* 1990; 22: 133.

12 Singer RB. Mortality follow-up studies and risk selection — retrospect and prospect. *Trans Assoc Life Insur Med Dir Am* 1978; 62: 215.

13 Eyman RK, Grossman RK et al. The life expectancy of profoundly handicapped people with mental retardation. *N Engl J Med* 1990; 323: 584.

14 Singer RB. A method of relating life expectancy in the US population life table to excess mortality. *J Insur Med* 1992; 24(1):32–41.

15 Feinstein AR. *Clinical Epidemiology.* Philadelphia: W B Saunders Co, 1985.

16 National Cancer Institute Monograph 67. *Selection, Follow-up and Analysis in Prospective Studies.* Bethesda, Md: NIH Publication No 85–2713, 1985.

17 London D. *Survival Models and their Estimation*, 2nd ed. Winsted and New Britain, Conn: ACTEX Publications, 1988.

18 Singer RB. Comparative morbidity — what are the prospects? *J Insur Med* 1988; 20(3): 47.

19 Singer RB. Morbidity abstract — recurrent MI in post-MI patients: the Framingham experience. *J Insur Med* 1988; 20(3): 54.

CHAPTER 5

THE RATING OF SUBSTANDARD LIVES

MICHAEL W KITA

'When you cannot measure [what you are describing], when you cannot express it in numbers, your knowledge is of a meager and unsatisfactory kind.'[1]

Lord Kelvin

Oscar Rogers and Arthur Hunter surely subscribed to the above belief of their scientific contemporary Lord Kelvin when they published in 1919 their 'Numerical Method of Determining the Value of Risks for Insurance'. Regarding the need for actual mortality data, they went so far as to say, 'if a person who is called upon to give an expert judgment of the value of a risk does not have data upon which to base a rating for the special hazard involved, he is equally unable to express an expert judgment anyhow.'[2] A bold statement perhaps, but Rogers and Hunter were zealous promoters of the general application of quantitative risk assessment to life insurance.

RISK CLASSIFICATION

Prior to the development of the numerical rating system, life insurance was almost exclusively concerned with accepting applicants who qualified as 'standard' risks and rejecting other risks. But with the advent of large-scale medical impairment studies at the turn of the century, the stage was set for measuring the excess mortality experienced by impaired (substandard) lives and relating it mathematically both to actuarial experience with, and medical expectations for, mortality and life expectancy. It was becoming clear that many substandard lives could be accepted for insurance as long as the rates they paid reflected the amount of extra mortality risk assumed by the insurer. Thus 'ratings' (extra premium proportionate to the amount of excess mortality risk involved) formed the basis for an approach to underwriting, whereby the insurer could not only qualify a risk (acceptable/ unacceptable) but quantify it (degrees of substandard). In so doing, insurers moved from the simplest form of risk classification (take/no take) to a more sophisticated form (substandard classes). If antiselection were avoided, and risks appropriately classified, the insurer could write profitable business in a broader insurance market, and the benefits of coverage could be extended to many more people than would otherwise have been eligible.

Numerical Rating System

What Rogers and Hunter did was to begin formalizing the risk-assessment thought process in a more quantitative way. They recognized that underwriting decisions, though not always (or easily) reducible to numbers, were also neither magical nor the result of some unique and inscrutable wisdom. Rather, such decisions represented the systematic weighing of certain favorable and unfavorable risk variables which, tempered by experience and judgment, resulted in a summary assessment of the risk. These factors and their weights could be assigned numerical values, and then combined according to certain rules. Their use promised greater consistency and speed of decision making in cases where the key risk variables could be specified and where mortality risk could be measured or estimated.

In simple terms, the standard risk is assigned a value of 100 percent (i.e. one unit of risk). Unfavorable risk factors, conditions, or impairments expected to produce excess mortality risk are added to that baseline risk. For example, if a person has two independent impairments, A and B, each with a known 50 percent increased risk of death compared with standard lives, a rating of +100 percent would be added to the basic (standard) risk of 100 percent to recognize the total mortality risk expected (i.e. twice the standard risk, or 200 percent). In other words:

Basic (standard) risk	100%	
Extra mortality risk associated with impairment A	+50%	
Independent extra mortality risk associated with impairment B	+50%	ratings
Overall (final) mortality risk	200%	

Note that each impairment rating is +50 (read as 'plus fifty') and equates to an amount of extra premium required to cover the expected excess-mortality cost. Each rating is preceded by a plus sign to show that the increase is one of excess

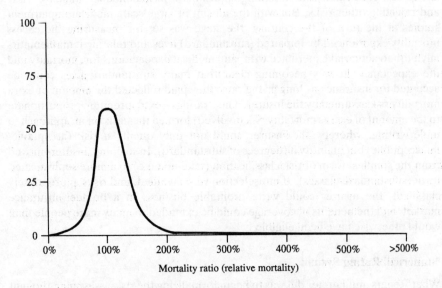

Fig. 5.1. Distribution of mortality risk among life insurance applicants

mortality, but the +50 actually constitutes a debit to the applicant since it will result in extra premium being charged. By the same token, if this applicant had some characteristic associated with unusual longevity, then a credit might be considered (e.g. −25 or 'minus twenty-five'), and factored into the assessment arithmetically. Subsequent chapters of this book describe how specific medical conditions are quantified to yield appropriate ratings.

If the impairments, A & B, were not independent, the ratings would be combined in some other fashion than by simple addition. For instance, if the impairments interacted over time in some co-morbid or synergistic fashion, their effect would need to be scaled higher than the simple sum of the two ratings. On the other hand, if the impairments were somehow mutually associated (interdependent), the net rating would need to be reduced to something less than the sum of the two. Actuarial experience and clinical judgment dictate most combinatorial solutions, but summation at least permits the calculation of a suitable rating for initial underwriting consideration.

Rating by Table
In Example 1 the final rating was 200 percent, but mortality risk is a continuum (*see* Fig. 5.1) and ratings could take on any value. In theory, final ratings of 201 percent and 199 percent could also exist. In practice, however, ratings cannot be refined to this degree and have evolved grouped into classes or 'tables'. A common scheme is to organize risk classes in increments of +25 percent, as, for example:

$$\text{Table A} = +\ \ 25\% \ (125\%)$$
$$\text{Table B} = +\ \ 50\% \ (150\%)$$
$$\text{Table C} = +\ \ 75\% \ (175\%)$$
$$\text{Table D} = +100\% \ (200\%)$$
$$\vdots$$
$$\vdots$$
$$\text{Table P} = +400\% \ (500\%)$$

According to such an arrangement, the hypothetical applicant in Example 1 would correspond to Table D (and be rated +100 or 'four tables'). Different companies choose differently which substandard risk classes they will use, some having all 16 tables (e.g. A to P) and others only a handful of them (e.g. +50, +100, +150, +200, +300, +400). Still others use groupings that are not based on multiples of +25 at all. A further discussion of alternative approaches can be found in the 'Table Ratings' section (*see* pp. 89–92).

Many risks at the upper end of the spectrum (e.g. more than +400) are considered speculative risks. Depending on an individual company's risk tolerance, such applicants may be declined coverage, or they may be referred to special risk carriers, offered coverage only on a limited or experimental basis, or offered coverage with a reinsurer's participation in the risk.

The vast majority (93–94 percent) of applications for life insurance in the USA are accepted as standard risks.[3] Most applicants are determined to be standard without any need for complicated calculation of debits and credits. The major underwriting effort focuses on the 6–7 percent of applications that are not approved standard: the 2–3 percent that are considered for offers but ultimately declined, and the 4–5 percent that are made substandard offers. Figure 5.2 shows how the risk continuum of Figure 5.1 sorts into risk classes. Of substandard issues in the USA, 82 percent are extra-rated for medical reasons (36 percent cardiovascular-renal, 14 percent weight related, 32 percent other medical reasons) and most of the remaining 18 percent for other-than-medical reasons.[3] The medical selection of life risks remains a crucial ingredient of the overall risk selection process, and the primary focus of substandard underwriting is the medically substandard risk.

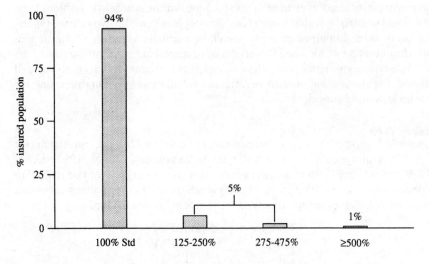

Fig. 5.2. Distribution of ratings among life insurance applicants

Dimensions of Standard

Since substandard risk is both defined and quantified in relation to standard risk, it is helpful to have clearly in mind some of the nuances of 'standard'. Whilst standard risk is the basic unit risk, or 100 percent, it should be understood that this is the implicit central risk for the standard class — a class that is a mixture of some risks whose mortality is less than 100 percent (80 percent or 90 percent of standard) and some whose mortality is more than 100 percent (e.g. 110 percent or 120 percent of standard) (*see* Fig. 5.3). Just how broad the standard class can be and still meet standard actuarial pricing assumptions is a matter each company decides (*see* Table 5.4, for hypothetical examples). Since mortality patterns for females differ widely from those of males, and non-smokers from smokers, a company may take its broad standard class and differentiate it into more than one standard grouping. The dashed and dotted lines in Figure 5.3 show how a composite curve for a single 'standard' population centered on 100 percent could, in fact, consist of two overlapping populations, differing slightly in risk according to a particular factor: female vs. male, or non-smoker vs. smoker. Each of these separate populations (e.g. standard male, standard female) would have its own particular base rate to which any additional substandard ratings would apply. Carried one step further, a company could have four standard populations: male smokers, male non-smokers, female smokers and female non-smokers.

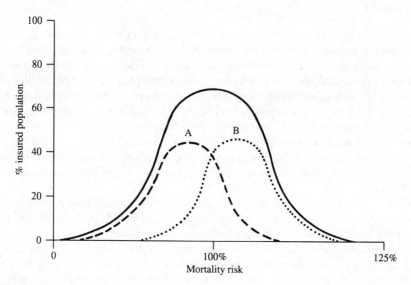

Fig. 5.3. The standard group.

Another approach to risks in the region near standard is to consider those with appreciably better-than-standard mortality expectations to be 'preferred' risks. Such risks might include female non-smokers or people who possess only mortality 'credits' against the base rate of 100 percent. Some companies will offer such individuals 'preferred' (superstandard) rates of premium. Note, however, that if such lives are carved out of the class of standard lives, then the distribution of remaining lives in the class will have its new average weighted a little more toward substandard than before, and pricing assumptions would need to recognize this.

In insurance parlance, 'standard' connotes an applicant with an acceptably normal or average profile of mortality risks: health history, risk factors, family history, avocations and the like. The criteria for deciding what is standard will be different for industrial life vs. ordinary life insurance, and for individual (whole) life vs. group (term) life insurance: the products and their intended markets differ, so the rates necessarily differ along with their concept of standard.

Standard, then, can have several meanings (just as 'normal' can have several different meanings[4]): (1) acceptable at standard rates of premium for the insurance product in question; (2) satisfying the eligibility standards of the underwriting department; (3) possessing similar mortality risk to that of other members of the standard class, experienced or expected; (4) acceptable unconditionally (as applied for). The standard rate of premium payable at each age and for different types of policies is calculated from the basic tables of mortality in use at the time. A policy may sometimes be called standard when it receives standard rates of premium, but when, in fact, it has been issued for a reduced benefit amount or subjected to some additional policy constraints that would not encumber a typical standard policy. Conversely, a policy may be treated as standard for purposes of dividends and non-forfeiture values and yet be substandard in price (e.g. carry a temporary 'flat extra' rating).

Substandard

Substandard lives are sometimes referred to as impaired lives, although the impairment in question may not be a condition that is currently impacting health or reducing functional capacity. Some impairments (high cholesterol, family history, high blood pressure) operate as risk factors, predisposing to premature mortality in some people, though not predicting eventual risk in everyone. Such factors, if present at the time of underwriting, represent specifiable and measurable risk concerns, but ones with a relative probability of future impairment, as opposed to imminent or inevitable consequence. A risk can be medically substandard for a variety of reasons. Preventing antiselection, and matching the right amount and terms of extra premium to the degree of substandardness, is why risks are identified and classified.

At a particular point in time and with regard to a particular insurance product, a risk decision is made based upon the disclosed state of health of the applicant in light of the existing state of medical knowledge about future (mortality) risk. For individual-life insurance the risk decision is a final, one-time decision (barring such things as lapse reinstatement or contestability). For group-life insurance it is a decision whose terms can be revisited at each renewal. But the key variable affecting each life insurance decision is mortality risk, and the extra ratings applied to substandard business chiefly reflect the mortality costs associated with specific impairments. Quantifying excess mortality and the factors governing it, and anticipating the pattern of mortality over time (loss distribution), are what the rating of substandard lives addresses.

Comparative Mortality

The underwriting of substandard lives uses comparative mortality to judge substandard risk. Simply put, in order for a condition to be viewed as substandard, mortality observed among those people having the condition must be greater than the mortality otherwise expected. And in order to know what mortality to expect, a reference mortality experience must be available.

Information about expected mortality exists in both graphical and tabular form in many clinical and insurance studies. Graphical data can generally be converted to life table form. Although life tables are all conceptually similar, not all life tables are the same. Some tables are for a particular year; others may cover a five- or ten-year time period. Some tables use a direct (fixed interval) or actuarial method; others use a Kaplan-Meier (variable interval) approach. Some are complete (single decrement) tables, and others account for censored lives (lapsed or withdrawn) in double decrement fashion. Some tables are raw or basic experience; others are smoothed or graduated and may even contain margins or loads (like an actuary's valuation table). Tables may be extremely comprehensive or they may be abridged in various ways.

Although Table 5.1 is far from exhaustive, it hints at the variety of life table data available for comparative mortality purposes. Chapter 4 discusses many of the finer points of how mortality comparisons can be made, and a quick glance through *Medical Risks*[5,6] can rapidly acquaint the interested reader with the multitude of sources that can be used for comparative mortality purposes.

Table 5.1. Terms used to describe features of life table data available for comparative mortality purposes.

Commonly used mortality rates	Reference populations for expected mortality	Some types of tables
age-specific	US population	Annual
age-sex-specific	Cohort	Interval
		(e.g. decennial)
impairment-specific	Individually insured	Select
untreated	lives	Ultimate
treated	Standard	Aggregate
	Substandard	Abridged
	Group lives	Valuation

Ultimately, the mortality comparison of interest to insurers is a comparison of excess mortality with insured lives. Insured lives have been through a selection process that screens or selects for favorable mortality risk. Even group life shows a 'selection effect', since being actively at work at the time of underwriting is an important health status screen. The selection process for individual life insurance is even more thorough, and results in select-lives standard mortality experience that is far lower than general population or even group mortality.

The mortality rates shown in Table 5.2, adapted from Singer[7] and Woodman (*see* Chapter 3), are those expected for males aged 42. They are the annual mortality rates (per thousand) according to four different but roughly contemporaneous life tables (*c* 1980). Entry age differs from the attained age (42) in those instances where a life insurance policy has been in force (policy duration). It equals attained age in those instances where there is no policy (e.g. US male population) or where it has just been issued (policy duration equals zero). 'Select' and 'Ultimate' refer to select-period and ultimate-period mortality experienced by persons selected as standard risks for individual life insurance. 'Group Life' refers to mortality experience among people selected as standard risks for group-life insurance. 'US Population' refers to mortality experience among persons from an unselected population.

Table 5.2. What mortality rate is expected for a 42-year-old male? (showing the effect of selection).

	Individual Life				Group Life[c]	US Population[d]
	Select[a]			Ultimate[b]		
Entry age	42	40	37	27	42	42
Policy duration	0	+2	+5	+15	0	–
Attained age	42	42	42	42	42	42
Mortality rate[e]	1·0	1·6	1·9	2.0	2.2	3.6

[a]1975–80 Basic Select Individual Life.
[b]1975–80 Basic Ultimate Individual Life.
[c]1975–79 Group Life.
[d]1979–81 US Population.
[e]Per thousand per year.

Table 5.2 illustrates the following points: (1) any of these mortality rates could be cited as an 'expected' rate, but the rates are clearly not identical, and care must be taken, when describing excess mortality, to make sure it is being compared to the relevant 'expected' mortality; (2) insured lives (whether individual or group) have lower mortality rates than the general population, owing to the effect of selection; (3) the effect of selection gradually diminishes with time (see select rates at higher policy durations), but even ultimate rates show some residual effect.

Isolating Impairment-Specific Mortality

To gauge the magnitude of substandard mortality risk, the impairment-specific mortality associated with the condition must somehow be isolated or separated from the baseline mortality that would otherwise be expected. Simplistically, there are two ways in which this can be done.

One way is by direct comparison. In a population consisting of insured lives, one can measure the mortality effect of the impairment in question, and compare it directly with the mortality experienced by a similar group that lacks the impairment. Ideally the groups would be alike in all respects but the impairment in question. An example of this approach would be an industry study (e.g. intercompany study) of insured lives.

Another way to measure the effect is indirectly. The mortality effect might have been observed in a general population as, for example, in a clinical study. After adjustment for the expected mortality for such a general population (mortality in the absence of said impairment), the impairment-specific mortality that has been isolated can then be related to an insured-lives population.

Either way, the mortality effect that is isolated becomes a measure of incremental risk.

Incremental Risk

Incremental risk can be expressed in two basic ways: as an incremental difference, or as a proportionate change.[8] In insurance parlance, these are called excess death rate (EDR) and mortality ratio (MR) respectively.

Suppose q and q' represent observed and expected mortality rates respectively — observed *with* an impairment (I) and expected *without* the impairment. Suppose further that the groups giving rise to q and q' are similar insured lives populations, alike in all important respects except the presence or absence of the impairment. Then the difference ($q-q'$) will be equivalent to the impairment-specific excess death rate (call it q_I) and would be arrived at by the direct comparison method described above.

Now suppose another pair of mortality rates, q_{US} and q'_{US}, represent the mortality observed in the US population with the same impairment (I) as above, and the mortality expected in the US population without the impairment. The difference ($q_{US}-q'_{US}$) will be the same q_I as before, only this time it will have been derived 'indirectly', that is, on a population other than insured lives. If added to the insured lives q', however, it will generate a mortality rate, q, equivalent to what would be observed if the impairment was studied in a select group of insureds.

So, regardless of how it is derived, an impairment-specific mortality rate becomes the basis for assessing the substandard risk (the incremental risk of death) as expressed in a MR or EDR. Mathematically, these measures of incremental risk may be expressed as follows:

$$EDR = [q-q']1000 = [(q'+q_I)-q']1000$$
$$= q_I(1000)$$
$$= \text{impairment-specific extra death rate}$$

$$MR = [q/q']100 = [(q'+q_I)/q']100\%$$
$$= 100\% \quad + (q_I/q')100\%$$
$$= \text{standard} + \text{impairment rating}$$

Since death rates are commonly reported per thousand, EDRs are calculated by taking the difference in rates and multiplying by a thousand to get whole numbers. Similarly, since a ratio usually yields a decimal expression, MRs are usually calculated by taking the ratio of two mortality rates and multiplying by a hundred to get a whole number (expressed as a percentage).

If a person applying for insurance has several impairments, he will have more than one q_I, and his degree of final substandardness will reflect the total excess mortality risk, combined arithmetically or otherwise, according to the independence of the various risks involved.

Other questions that may need to be addressed include:
1) Over what duration or span of time (five years, ten years or longer) are the estimates of q, q' and q_I accurate or meaningful?
2) when can annual rates be used, and when are aggregate or geometric annual mean rates necessary or desirable?

The interested reader is referred to other sources for consideration of the methodologic issues.[9]

RISKS

Risk has been used in previous paragraphs as if the term were self-explanatory, but some discussion would be helpful. When insurers engage in risk classification and risk selection,[10-12] they are primarily attempting to differentiate standard mortality risks from excess risks, and stratify the insurability of the latter. In this broad sense, risk equates to liability or exposure: if a policy pays a death benefit of $1,000,000 then ultimately this amount is what is at risk when the final underwriting decision has been made. Risk classification creates risk classes of comparable mortality (i.e. all risks that are assessed at +100, whether their type of impairment is cardiac, neurologic or some sum of debits, are expected to have twice standard mortality risk). If a standard risk has particular likelihoods or probabilities of death in the next n years, then a +100 risk has twice those probabilities. Risk selection (i.e. underwriting) then involves looking at a proposed risk (an applicant at risk of dying and the death benefit at stake), sizing up the nature and severity of the mortality risk involved, and assessing the proper risk class and premium.

Rates and Probabilities

Sometimes 'risk' is used in a way that seems interchangeable with a mortality rate or probability of dying, but this can cause some confusion. Some rates do express probability. An annual rate of mortality, q, is a true rate, being deaths per year, but it is also, mathematically speaking, a probability estimate representing the likelihood of an event (death) occurring over a specified duration (one year), and taking on values over the bounded range from 0 to 1. However, since not all rates are probabilities, and since some rates may take on any value from zero to infinity, it is important to distinguish between a rate and a probability. Strictly speaking, a rate is the measured occurrence of an event per unit of time, and a probability is the likelihood of occurrence within or over a specified length of time. An annual mortality rate determined from experience is the basis of predicting expected annual mortality probability of a comparable cohort.

Of particular interest in matters of mortality is the instantaneous mortality rate, μ_x, also called the force of mortality. By differential calculus it is the first derivative or limiting value of the survival curve evaluated at a point in time. Whereas q_x looks at the risk of dying over the next annual interval (x to $x+1$), μ_x looks at the instantaneous mortality rate operative at age x. μ_x is not a probability, but as an instantaneous rate it may take on values greater than 1. Inasmuch as it is independent of an arbitrary age interval, μ_x is considered a more fundamental measure of mortality than q_x. It is a key variable in traditional survival curves like the Gompertz equation and Makeham's law. These theoretical curves are used for fitting raw data into a mortality pattern. Useful ways of estimating μ_x from q_x exist and are well covered in actuarial sources.[13,14]

Forces of Mortality

Ultimately it is the pattern of mortality, the distribution of deaths over time (how many occurring early or prematurely, and how many occurring late) which life insurance tries to model and for which it tries properly to price its policies, standard and rated. It has long been recognized that death is primarily a function of age, with greater chance of dying, year to year, at higher ages than younger, after the initial high period of infant mortality is passed. If one plots percent survival (y-axis) against years since birth (x-axis) for any large population, the general shape of the resulting survival curve is as shown in Figure 5.4. Percent survival takes values from 100 percent to 0 percent, and so is mathematically equivalent to a probability; years since birth is the independent variable, age (x-axis).

This classic shape follows Gompertz's law,[15] named for the mathematician, Benjamin Gompertz, who devised a formula in 1825 that was a close approximation to a population survival function. He considered μ_x a measurement of man's susceptibility to death and proposed that it increased by geometric progression with age. In 1860 William Makeham made a refinement to Gompertz's work yielding a yet closer fit of the theoretical model to observed population survival curves. This function, called Makeham's Law, is a complex formula in which μ_x is part of an exponent of e (standard actuarial texts discuss this in detail), and has the form $\mu_x = A + Bc^x$. Although μ_x is called the force of mortality, Makeham shows μ_x to be itself composed of component forces. Very crudely speaking, the 'A, B, Cs' of mortality are the weights given to Accident, Behavioral hazards (environmental and public health factors, such as smoking, acquired diseases, and controllable or correctable risk factors) and Cellular aging operating at any age x. The rating of substandard lives is mostly to do with the quantification of mortality risk associated

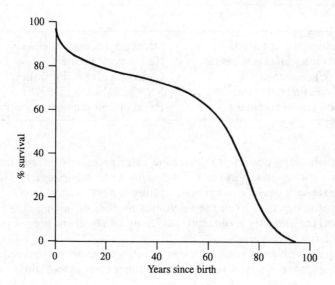

Fig. 5.4. Typical Gompertz-type survival curve.

with the 'B' factors. These 'B' factors (hazard exposures, medical impairments and any important co-morbidities) might be thought of as hastening the aging process or hastening premature death.

The important thing to note is that there are families of survival curves — curves for general populations, curves for insured lives and curves for impairment subsets of different kinds — that can be constructed. Cumulative survival curves, which are used by clinicians, are the complement of cumulative mortality curves, as used by actuaries. The survival functions, which relate life to death, allow one to infer both the expected mortality to be incurred (mortality rates) and the expected years of life remaining (life expectancy). Any two survival curves, or relevant portions of them, can be compared; alternatively their life tables (the tabular versions of the curves) can be compared. No surprise, then, that the customary approaches to debiting excess (premature) mortality — rating by means of table ratings, flat extras and debt/lien (using comparative mortality), or the adjustment of age (using comparative life expectancy) — make explicit use of these facts and relationships.

Patterns of Mortality

What general patterns of mortality — mortality different from expected insured-lives standard mortality — are there? Some typical patterns of level and incidence of excess mortality are shown in Table 5.3. Woodman kindly contributed the table and many of the ideas in this section.[16]

Table 5.3. Patterns of excess mortality.

Pattern	Example
Level number of extra deaths	Occupational/avocational accident
Level percentage of excess deaths	Respiratory disease
Decreasing percentage	Cancer; recent major surgery
Slowly decreasing percentage	Myocardial infarction
Slowly increasing percentage	Heart murmur; diabetes; overweight

It is theoretically possible to determine extra premiums for any impairment, based on a rating (mortality) table applicable to that impairment. Such tables could, if extensive enough, individualize ratings across all ages. However, such an approach is impractical given the enormous number of pricing classes it would require and the difficulty in obtaining sufficient data to define precise patterns for every impairment at every age.

To keep the number of pricing classes and rating tables within reason, companies generally use two primary systems to cover a range of extra mortality:

1) A system with multiple table classes (e.g. Tables A–P, as discussed earlier) that reflect a level or slowly increasing percentage of standard mortality. Most medical impairments, and other rating factors for which extra mortality is a relatively constant percentage of standard mortality at most ages, lend themselves to these multiple table extras.

2) A system with several levels of flat extra premiums — for example, 2·5–20 per mil (1,000) of face coverage (i.e. units of currency per 1,000 units insured) — that reflect situations where there is either a constant number of extra deaths per thousand or a decreasing percentage of standard mortality. Sometimes flat extras arc applied to medical impairments with high short-term initial mortality following a recovery, and would accordingly be temporary (e.g. five to ten years). Alternatively, a flat extra could be used to cover hazardous activities involved in certain occupations or avocations, in which case they may be permanent, or applicable at least until the termination of the hazard.

Although the use of one system or the other, by itself and without further embellishment, may be sufficient to address many risks, there are several refinements that sometimes merit consideration. The first is a sliding scale approach whereby flat extras or table ratings, initially high, are progressively reduced with advancing age or policy duration, often eventually to standard. For instance, the flat extra, instead of being a fixed amount (e.g. 5/mil) for a fixed term (e.g. five years), may be graduated (e.g. 5/mil for two years, then 3/mil for two years, and standard thereafter). Likewise, table ratings may be higher at younger ages or soon after recovery or last attack, and scaled down in subsequent time periods. A temporal sliding scale (ratings that attenuate with the passage of time) can obviate the need for periodic reconsiderations of the applied rating.

Another refinement would be to issue flat extras in combination with multiple table ratings. For instance, certain cardiac impairments can have substantial acute mortality and less severe long-term mortality, and the mixture of risk can be suitably addressed with either temporary or diminishing flat extras added to a fixed or reducing table rating.

Flat extras and table ratings are themselves based on related yardsticks of comparative mortality, the EDR and MR respectively. Alone or together, flat extras (temporary or permanent) and table ratings (fixed or variable) encompass most risks, and do so quite directly. They offer fairness to the applicant, tailoring the rating as individually as the mortality data for the risk class or group permit, and flexibility for the underwriter, avoiding an unmanageable number of tables or decision trees to have to sort through.

Two other risk management options exist for the life underwriter — adjustment of age, and imposition of debt or lien — which are rational approaches for unusual client needs or business situations, but which address the mortality risk indirectly. These will be discussed further in later paragraphs.

Table Ratings

As discussed earlier in this chapter, table ratings are based in theory on mortality ratios $[MR = 100\,(q/q')]$ where observed mortality for the impairment in question is related to expected mortality 'impairment free'. Table ratings are most useful for impairments with a level or slowly increasing percentage of standard mortality (*see* Table 5.5). Table ratings are also used in conjunction with temporary flat extras for some impairments with slowly decreasing percentage.

Different companies construct their table ratings differently, depending on their products, markets, experience and their risk tolerances. Table 5.4 shows three hypothetical companies with different schemes for their substandard classes. Company A has ten substandard classes beyond standard. It takes as standard anything from -15 to $+20$ (85 percent to 120 percent) and has ranges of ratings that are centered on the table rating for the class. Company A takes risks up to 550 percent.

Company B considers as standard anything from -20 to $+25$ (80 percent to 125 percent) and takes cases up to 1,000 percent. It uses 750 percent as its highest rating

Table 5.4. **Rating classes for three hypothetical companies (giving the range acceptable to that class).**

Company A	Company B	Company C			
		Under 30	30–39	40–49	50+
100%(85–120)	100% (80–125)	100% (to 140)	(to 135)	(to 130)	(to 125)
125% (125–145)	140% (130–150)	150% (to 185)	(to 175)	(to 170)	(to 165)
150% (145–160)	170% (155–185)	200%	(up to 250)		
175% (165–185)	210% (190–235)	300%	(up to 350)		
200% (190–210)	270% (240–300)	450%	(up to 500)		
225% (215–235)	350% (305–400)	600%	(up to 750)		
250% (240–275)	450% (405–500)				
300% (280–325)	750% (505–1000)				
350% (330–375)					
400% (380–450)					
500% (455–550)					

table and rating classes are not multiples of 25 percent. Company C has five substandard classes. It takes as standard some risks up to 140 percent, but only if under the age of 30. It has different definitions of its upper limit of standard, according to the age range of the applicant. Likewise, its first substandard class, 150 percent (+50), has different upper limits for the class, depending on the applicant's age. But its remaining substandard classes have the same ranges. The highest risk it will insure is up to a table rating of 600 percent.

Most of the table ratings in subsequent chapters are in multiples of 25 percent, for this is a common convention. Occasionally an impairment rating will be given as a range (+50 percent to +100 percent), and generally the higher rating is applied if the proposed insured is younger (e.g. below 35), has total debits and a degree of severity on the high end of the range for the risk in question, or if the time since occurrence, treatment, or recovery is chronologically closer to the next higher rating category.

Although a table rating of 200 percent may be twice the standard rating of 100 percent, the final premium charged does not equate to twice the standard gross premium.[12] This is because the mortality cost is not the only component of the premium charged. A rating of 200 percent does imply a mortality risk twice that expected of the standard group; and it does imply a mortality cost twice the net mortality cost of the standard group. However, the final amount of gross substandard premium charged will typically reflect whatever different or incremental costs are involved in substandard acquisition, maintenance, reconsideration, lapse and reinsurance arrangements. For term insurance the relationship of substandard to standard premium will be much closer to the percentage rating because there is no need to hold a large reserve against distant future claims.

Flat Extras

The other primary way of addressing substandard risks is by means of flat extras. As mentioned previously, flat extras are based, in theory, on excess death rates [EDR $= (q-q')1000$]. This type of approach is most useful for impairments with a level number of extra deaths (e.g. constant EDR) or rapidly decreasing percentage extra mortality. Flat extras are also used in conjunction with multiple table ratings in some impairments with slowly increasing percentage (see Table 5.5).

Flat extras may be temporary, as in the case of initially high risk decreasing with time (such as treated cancer, myocardial infarction, attempted suicide and surgically treated peptic ulcer disease). If the impairment has very steep initial mortality (e.g. most cancers), insurance is postponed for one or more years and then offered with flat extras. The extras are applied for several years until mortality has levelled off and roughly approximates expected survival for standard insureds.

Flat extras may be permanent if the risk is constant or ongoing, as in the case of accidents related to a chosen occupation or avocation. However, if and when the risk exposure ends, the flat extra can also be terminated, unless, as with some toxin exposures, there is a residual risk to cover.

The EDR, upon which flat extras are based, is less sensitive to variations in age than the MR. The effect of age on MR and EDR is well shown by Singer[7] (see Fig. 5.5). Since mortality rates naturally increase with age, the denominator of

Table 5.5. Rating methods theoretically consistent with particular patterns of excess mortality.

Mortality pattern/risk situation	Rating method
Level number of extra deaths	Permanent flat extras
Level percentage	Multiple table ratings
Decreasing percentage	Temporary flat extras
Slowly decreasing percentage	Multiple table plus temporary flat extras
Slowly increasing percentage	Table ratings, addition of years to age, or graduated death benefit
Heavy early risk, or as alternative to a decline	Rating by debt or lien

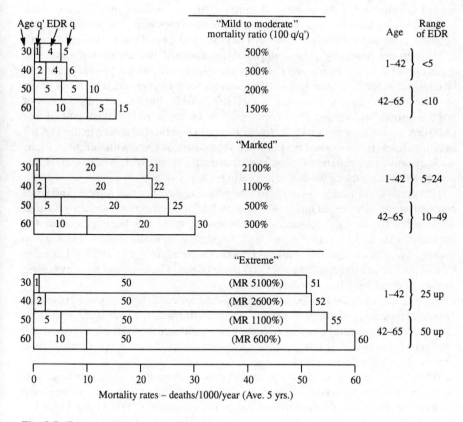

Fig. 5.5. Degrees of excess mortality.
Reproduced with kind permission of the author and the *Journal of Insurance Medicine*.

the MR and the subtrahend of the EDR are constantly increasing, but the effect on the MR (because it is a ratio) is more pronounced. A handy rule of thumb for expected annual mortality rates (q') for insured lives during the initial five-year select period is 1, 2, 5 and 10 per thousand (per year) corresponding to insured males of entry ages 30, 40, 50 and 60 respectively. As can be seen, an EDR of 4 at age 30 corresponds to a mortality ratio of 500 percent [(4+1)/1] but that same EDR at age 50 corresponds to a mortality ratio of 180 percent [(4+5)/5]. Accordingly, flat extras are often the rating method of choice for impaired elderly lives (over the age of 65).

Although practices vary from company to company, a commonly used approximation is to consider each increment of 1 (per thousand) in EDR roughly equivalent to an extra 1 per thousand (in face coverage) as flat extra premium. In some texts this is called a flat extra of 1/mil (mil being the abbreviation for thousand in Latin). For example, an EDR of 5 might be reflected in a flat extra rating of 5/mil, if the pattern of mortality associated with the EDR made such a flat extra (permanent or temporary) preferable to a table rating.

Adjustment of Age

Because of the inverse relationship between mortality rates and life expectancy by way of the survival curve or survival function, there is some general equivalence between saying someone of age x has a certain excess mortality, and saying that that person has the same life expectancy as a person aged $x+n$. Thus a 40-year-old with a 250 percent mortality ratio compared to standard has about the same life expectancy (29 years) as a healthy (standard) 49-year-old. Such a 40-year-old might be considered for insurance at the standard rates for a 49-year-old. This is not to say that the life span of any individual is itself predictable, but only that by the law of large numbers an average life expectancy can be projected. Adjustment of age (addition of years to age) was historically the rating method of choice in the UK for impaired lives. It has worked best for risks that slowly increase with duration, or, as an alternative to flat extras for insuring impaired elderly lives, where experience data may be inadequate for numerical rating.

This method continues to see some limited use today. For this reason, and since estimation of life expectancy is performed in connection with structured settlements by disability insurers and others, a table has been placed in the appendix (Table 5.6) relating age and degree of substandardness (MR%) to average life expectancy. These are updated Institute of Actuaries 1967/70 Ultimate tables, and they closely match 1980 CSO Basic tables. These are not annuity tables, but are derived from basic mortality tables.

Adjustment of age is also occasionally utilized for crediting non-smokers and/or females, especially if there is no base-rate distinction (i.e. separate standards classes for these differentiators). In these cases subtraction of age is performed and the 'superstandard' or preferred risks are treated as if they were younger than chronological age ('age setback').

Whilst tabular derivation of life expectancy is computationally exacting, it is worth mentioning in passing that a rough estimate to life expectancy can be based on a declining exponential approximation to life expectancy (DEALE). DEALE lends itself to quick curbside calculation suitable for some underwriting purposes. Although it makes certain approximations (including its use of μ_x interchangeably with q_x), it does give results, even at young ages, within 12 percent of results yielded by conventional Gompertz curves.[17,18] Its chief value may be as a means of quickly combining mortality rates from several independent medical conditions, or when utilizing q_x data from populations whose survival curves already have shapes approximating declining exponential curves (e.g. cancer survival).

Debt or Lien

The final method of making substandard offers is by imposing a debt or lien. This amounts to a return to the company of part of the death benefit; if viewed in this way, it could be said to run contrary to the primary purpose of life insurance. On the other hand, in those cases where the applicant is otherwise a declinable risk, life insurance on such terms may be preferable to no insurance at all. Such applicants may be willing to share in the risk with what amounts to an early-years deductible from the face benefit.

In the USA the debt or lien method is seldom used or permitted, although some individual pension-trust plans have employed this method. In the UK some endowment assurance laws are written using this approach. The debt or lien is generally a constant proportion of the face value of the policy, diminishing the payable benefit by the amount of the debt. The debt typically reduces evenly over the term of the contract, creating a kind of graduated benefit. A common formula for calculating the debt is $100K/100+K$, where K = the table rating that might have applied. For example, a rating of +50 would yield a debt of (100) $(50)/(100+50)$ = $5000/150 = 33$ percent. Therefore in the first year only 67 percent of the face cover would be payable. If this were a ten-year endowment contract, the debt might decrease at 3·3 percent per year, with the full benefit payable at the end.

A variation of sorts on this theme is frequently used in life insurance written by mail without underwriting. The parties agree that liability for the first few years of the contract is limited to refund of premiums, and thereafter to the face value of the benefit.

Comparison of Methods

How do the four methods compare? A hypothetical 40-year-old who is +150 (250 percent) would be rated six tables (150 percent), using mortality ratios (table ratings) as the basis for assessing extra premiums. Assuming the relevant mortality rates yielding 250 percent were 5 and 2 per thousand (q and q') respectively, the EDR would be 3 and the flat extra charged might be 3/mil for a period of time. Using Table 5.7 in the appendix, a 250 percent 40-year-old has a comparable life expectancy (29 years) to a 100 percent (standard) 49-year-old, and the approach might be to offer him a 49-year-old's standard rates. The advancement of age would be nine years. A debt or lien, meanwhile, might be assessed at (100) $(150)/(100 + 150) = 60$ percent, diminishing evenly to zero over the life of the contract.

Disability

Although the subject of this chapter is life insurance, a word must also be said about disability, since waiver of premium for disability, and even occasionally the payment of some disability benefits, can feature in life policies. The way an impairment is assessed for mortality differs in some respects from how disability (morbidity) risk is evaluated. Most conditions of consequence to life and longevity also have disability implications. But some conditions of little or no life insurance consequence, like spinal disk disease and anxiety disorders, can still be of appreciable disability significance. Also, whereas death is a permanent event, disability can involve recovery and even recurrence, and therefore provides more chance for antiselection. Furthermore the definition of total disability may vary from one company to another. Finally, whereas mortality data are fairly abundant, morbidity data are more scant, and because disability is often occupationally contexted a morbid event may be disabling for some occupations but not others.

Suffice it to say that the underwriting of the disability elements in life policies has important differences from the underwriting of mortality risk, although there are many analogies in the data collection and analytical process. A company may offer waiver of premium (WP) riders only on standard business, but theoretically one could offer rated (substandard) WP riders on applications where the base policy (life) carries an acceptably small table rating or flat extra, or where the WP rider can be subjected to its own disability underwriting.

Insurance Medicine and Clinical Medicine

Insurance medicine is an evolving discipline based largely on the interpretation of medical data as it pertains to prospective medico-actuarial risk. The medical director (MD) or underwriter's perspective may occasionally differ from that of the practising clinician. For example, clinicians talk of survival rates or percentage survival when reporting the long-term results of medical or surgical studies. In insurance medicine, mortality rates and mortality ratios are used as the basis for costing life insurance. The difference in perspective can be shown in the following example. If a clinical study shows a 95 percent five-year survival rate for a condition, the clinician will perceive this as indicative of low-risk and highly favorable prognosis. A 95 percent five-year survival translates to five percent, 5-year mortality, or 50 deaths per thousand people exposed to risk. A mortality rate of 50/1000 over five years is (crudely) about 10/1000 per year. If the group studied was one composed of 40-year-old males, the mortality rate expected for standard select insurance risks would be only 2/1000 per year (approximately). Thus the mortality ratio for the condition (10/2 = 500%) is highly substandard, even though the statistic '95 percent five-year survival' seems such a favorable statement about the condition in question.

An annual mortality rate of 2/1000 per year would result in ten deaths over five years. The cumulative mortality would then be 1 percent, and the five- year survival rate in this group would be 99 percent. The difference between 95 percent and 99 percent seems small (only a 4 percent difference) but the mortality ratio is substantial (500 percent). It is important when judging prospective risk to relate statistical information to the particular facts and context which apply, and to communicate the risk analysis as clearly as possible to clinicians and others whose initial frame of reference may not be identical.

Dynamic Concept of Substandard

Woodman has keenly articulated[19] the business implications of the evolution over time of changes in underwriting philosophy about what constitutes a substandard case. The advent of blood, urine and ECG testing has progressively redefined and repartitioned the standard, substandard and decline proportions of new business at a time when the secular trend toward overall mortality improvement has generally continued. The impact of HIV-positivity on mortality risk has had significant implications for insurers, and the epidemic continues to unfold. Yet despite uncertainties and change, evolving approaches to substandard underwriting have historically been quite successful, as reports like those of McCracken & Davis,[20] and the results of the *Medical Impairment Study 1983*,[21] have suggested.

SUMMARY

In summarizing this chapter it is hard to improve on the words of RDC Brackenridge from his second edition of this book:

'Persons in the substandard group have some impairment, usually medical, either in their past history, family history or present health which is likely to shorten life, and it is the task of the underwriter to assess the degree of extra mortality which might be expected, and to make certain that the risks are placed in groups comparable with others having the same expected mortality. The appropriate ratings for various impairments may be estimated either from the results of previous mortality studies of those impairments, from the experience of the individual life office concerned or from the trend of current clinical opinion regarding the progress of the impairments in question in the light of developments in therapeutic techniques.'[22]

Substandard underwriting uses life table methodology and survival analysis to derive mortality rates and quantify excess mortality. These are used as the basis of table ratings, flat extras, adjustment of age, and imposition of debt or lien, the four basic ways that substandard offers are crafted. Scientific and systematic application of these principles permits underwriters to reach explainable, marketable decisions that can be viable to their companies and valuable to their clients.

Two tables of expectations of life appear on pp. 101–3: Table 5.8 is from the UK, Table 5.9 from Japan.

APPENDIX

Life expectancy bears no simple relationship to MR or EDR, and for this reason tables for life expectancy that relate age to increasing degrees of substandardness are useful to the MD. Table 12 in the second edition of *Medical Selection of Life Risks* had this value for estimating life expectancy for structured settlement purposes and second-survivor life.[22]

In this appendix two tables are offered. Table 5.6 is an expanded and updated version of the second edition's Table 12. Table 5.7 is a similar table, giving life expectancy at quinquennial ages for progressively higher EDRs. Reasons for sometimes preferring a tabulation by EDR to that by MR are given in two recent articles.[23,24]

In both Table 5.6 and Table 5.7 life expectancy has been rounded to the nearest whole number. Institute of Actuaries Ultimate is a five-year ultimate table. Neither Table 5.6 nor Table 5.7 is an annuity table, and both are based on male mortality assumptions. Upward or downward adjustment of life expectancy for other assumptions (e.g. female sex, smoker etc) would need to be made by the user of the table. Appreciation is expressed to Alex Duncan of M & G London for the initial work on Table 5.6; appreciation is also expressed to Michael Cowell, FSA, for help in extending Table 5.6 to age 100 and in preparing Table 5.7.

Table 5.6. Life expectancy by incremental MR. Average expectation of life in years at quinquennial ages from 20 to 100 for different constant MRs (mortality ratio expressed as a percentage). Standard is 100 percent.[a]

Age	100%	150%	200%	250%	300%	400%	500%	1000%
20	56	52	49	47	45	43	41	34
25	52	48	45	43	41	38	36	30
30	47	43	40	38	36	34	32	26
35	42	38	35	33	32	29	27	22
40	37	33	30	29	27	25	23	17
45	32	28	26	24	22	20	18	14
50	28	24	22	20	18	16	15	10
55	23	20	17	16	15	13	11	7
60	19	16	14	12	11	9	8	5
65	15	12	11	9	8	7	6	3
70	12	9	8	7	6	5	4	2
75	9	7	6	5	4	3	3	1
80	7	5	4	3	3	2	2	1
85	5	4	3	2	2	1	1	<1
90	4	2	2	1	1	1	1	<1
95	3	2	1	1	1	<1	<1	<1
100	2	1	1	1	<1	<1	<1	<1

[a]Basis of standard mortality is Institute of Actuaries 1980 Assured Male (five-year) Ultimate table [IoA AM80(5)], which closely approximates 1980 CSO Male Non-smoker Basic table (80 CSO MNS).

Table 5.7. Life expectancy by incremental EDR. Average expectation of life at quinquennial ages from 20 to 100 for different constant EDRs (excess death rates expressed as deaths per 1,000). Standard is EDR = 0.[a]

Age	EDR=0	1	2	5	10	20	50
20	56	55	53	49	42	33	18
25	52	50	49	45	40	31	18
30	47	46	44	41	37	30	17
35	42	41	40	37	34	28	17
40	37	36	35	33	30	25	16
45	32	32	31	29	27	23	15
50	28	27	27	25	24	20	14
55	23	23	23	22	20	18	13
60	19	19	19	18	17	15	11
65	15	15	15	15	14	13	10
70	12	12	12	12	11	10	8
75	9	9	9	9	9	8	7
80	7	7	7	7	6	6	5
85	5	5	5	5	5	5	4
90	4	4	4	4	3	3	3
95	3	3	3	3	3	2	2
100	2	2	2	2	2	2	2

[a]Basis of standard mortality is Institute of Actuaries 1980 Assured Male (five-year) Ultimate table [IoA AM80(5)], which corresponds closely to 1980 CSO Male Non-smoker Basic table (80 CSO MNS).

REFERENCES

1 Thomson W (Lord Kelvin). In: Bartlett's *Familiar Quotations*. Boston: Little Brown, 1980; 594.
2 Rogers OH, Hunter A. Trans Soc Actuaries 1991; 20, part 2: 277.
3 Life Insurance Fact Book: American Council of Life Insurance 1990. Washington DC; 113–14.
4 Murphy EA. *The Logic of Medicine*. Baltimore: Johns Hopkins Press, 1976.
5 Lew EA, Gajewski J (eds). *Medical Risks: trends in mortality by age and time elapsed*. New York: Praeger, 1990.
6 Singer RB, Levinson L, (eds). *Medical Risks: patterns of mortality and survival*. Lexington, MA: Heath, 1976.
7 Singer RB. The conversion of mortality ratios to a numerical rating classification for life insurance underwriting. *J Insur Med* 1988; 20 (2): 54–61.
8 Feinstein A. *Clinical Epidemiology: the architecture of clinical research*. Philadelphia: Saunders, 1985; 126.
9 Singer RB, Kita MW. Guidelines for the evaluation of follow-up articles and preparation of mortality abstracts. *J Insur Med* 1991; 23 (1): 21–9.
10 Shepherd P, Webster AC. Selection of Risks. Chicago: Society of Actuaries, 1957.
11 Black K, Skipper H. *Life Insurance*. Englewood Cliffs, NJ: Prentice Hall, 1987.

12 Cummins JD et al. *Risk Classification in Life Insurance*. Boston: Kluwer-Nijhoff Publ., 1983.
13 Marx A. A life insurer's interpretation of survival rates. *Annals of Life Insurance Medicine* 1967; 3: 4.
14 Bowers NL et al. *Actuarial Mathematics*. Chicago: Society of Actuaries, 1986.
15 Jordan CW. *Life Contingencies*. Chicago: Society of Actuaries 1982; 1–2.
16 Woodman HA. Life insurance extra premiums for substandard risks. Study notes for the Society of Actuaries, 1988.
17 Beck JR et al. A convenient approximation of life expectancy (The 'DEALE'). *Am J Med* 1982; 73: 883–8.
18 Pauker SG, Kassirer JP. Decision analysis. *N Engl J Med* 1987; 316: 255.
19 Woodman HA. Are all substandard risks still substandard? *On the Risk* 1988; 5 (1): 23–4.
20 McCracken BH, Davis EE. Mortality in substandard life insurance. *J Insur Med* 1991; 23 (1): 8–11.
21 *Medical Impairment Study 1983*. Vol 1. Boston: Society of Actuaries and Association of Life Insurance Medical Directors of America, 1986.
22 Brackenridge RDC. *Medical Selection of Life Risks: a comprehensive guide to life expectancy for underwriters and clinicians*, 2nd ed. New York: Nature Press, 1985; 18.
23 Singer RB. A method of relating life expectancy in the US population life tables to excess mortality. *J Insur Med* 1992; 24 (1): 32–41.
24 Kita MW. Life expectancy. *J Insur Med* 1992; 24 (1): 47–9.

Table 5.8. Curtate expectation of life (e$_x$) according to the AM80 and AF80 (male and female permanent assurances 1980) ultimate tables. [a]

Age (years)	Male e$_x$ (years)	Female e$_x$ (years)	Age (years)	Male e$_x$ (years)	Female e$_x$ (years)	Age (years)	Male e$_x$ (years)	Female e$_x$ (years)	Age (years)	Male e$_x$ (years)	Female e$_x$ (years)
20	55.8	61.4	35	41.3	46.7	50	27.1	32.4	65	14.9	19.3
21	54.9	60.4	36	40.3	45.7	51	26.2	31.4	66	14.2	18.5
22	53.9	59.5	37	39.3	44.8	52	25.3	30.5	67	13.5	17.7
23	52.9	58.5	38	38.4	43.8	53	24.4	29.6	68	12.8	17.0
24	52.0	57.5	39	37.4	42.8	54	23.6	28.7	69	12.2	16.2
25	51.0	56.5	40	36.4	41.8	55	22.7	27.8	70	11.6	15.5
26	50.0	55.5	41	35.5	40.9	56	21.9	26.9	71	10.9	14.8
27	49.1	54.5	42	34.5	39.9	57	21.0	26.0	72	10.4	14.1
28	48.1	53.6	43	33.6	39.0	58	20.2	25.2	73	9.8	13.4
29	47.1	52.6	44	32.6	38.0	59	19.4	24.3	74	9.2	12.7
30	46.2	51.6	45	31.7	37.1	60	18.6	23.4	75	8.7	12.0
31	45.2	50.6	46	30.8	36.1	61	17.8	22.6	76	8.2	11.4
32	44.2	49.6	47	29.8	35.2	62	17.1	21.7	77	7.7	10.8
33	43.2	48.7	48	28.9	34.2	63	16.3	20.9	78	7.2	10.2
34	42.3	47.7	49	28.0	33.3	64	15.6	20.1	79	6.8	9.6
									80	6.4	9.0

[a]Based on data from the Continuous Mortality Investigation Reports no. 10, published by the Institute of Actuaries and the Faculty of Actuaries.

Table 5.9. Mortality of policies on standard lives, based on Japanese Experience Table 1979–80.[a]

Age (years)	Japanese Experience Table 1979–80 Male		Female		Age (years)	Japanese Experience Table 1979–80 Male		Female	
	Deaths per 1,000	Expectation of life (years)	Deaths per 1,000	Expectation of life (years)		Deaths per 1,000	Expectation of life (years)	Deaths per 1,000	Expectation of life (years)
0	1·28	75·01	1·27	81·17	45	2·88	32·17	1·64	37·68
1	1·06	74·10	1·01	80·27	46	3·23	31·26	1·78	36·74
2	0·85	73·18	0·75	79·35	47	3·58	30·36	1·93	35·81
3	0·67	72·24	0·53	78·41	48	3·92	29·46	2·11	34·88
4	0·54	71·29	0·37	77·45	49	4·25	28·58	2·28	33·95
5	0·46	70·33	0·26	76·48	50	4·59	27·70	2·46	33·03
6	0·41	69·36	0·21	75·50	51	4·96	26·82	2·64	32·11
7	0·38	68·39	0·20	74·51	52	5·38	25·95	2·82	31·19
8	0·35	67·42	0·19	73·53	53	5·87	25·09	3·01	30·28
9	0·29	66·44	0·17	72·54	54	6·43	24·24	3·23	29·37
10	0·25	65·46	0·15	71·56	55	7·05	23·39	3·47	28·46
11	0·24	64·48	0·14	70·57	56	7·70	22·55	3·74	27·56
12	0·26	63·49	0·13	69·58	57	8·40	21·73	4·07	26·66
13	0·31	62·51	0·15	68·58	58	9·17	20·91	4·44	25·77
14	0·42	61·53	0·19	67·60	59	10·06	20·09	4·86	24·88
15	0·58	60·55	0·25	66·61	60	11·06	19·29	5·34	24·00
16	0·76	59·59	0·31	65·62	61	12·19	18·50	5·88	23·12
17	0·95	58·63	0·37	64·65	62	13·42	17·73	6·49	22·26
18	1·09	57·69	0·41	63·67	63	14·77	16·96	7·17	21·40
19	1·17	56·75	0·43	62·70	64	16·32	16·21	7·95	20·55
20	1·19	55·82	0·44	61·72	65	18·04	15·47	8·83	19·71
21	1·15	54·88	0·44	60·75	66	19·96	14·74	9·82	18·88

Age				
22	1·09	53·95	0·45	59·78
23	1·03	53·00	0·46	58·80
24	0·98	52·06	0·49	57·83
25	0·95	51·11	0·51	56·86
26	0·92	50·16	0·53	55·89
27	0·90	49·20	0·54	54·92
28	0·88	48·25	0·55	53·95
29	0·87	47·29	0·56	52·97
30	0·87	46·33	0·60	52·00
31	0·89	45·37	0·65	51·03
32	0·94	44·41	0·71	50·07
33	1·00	43·45	0·77	49·10
34	1·08	42·49	0·83	48·14
35	1·16	41·54	0·90	47·18
36	1·26	40·59	0·96	46·22
37	1·36	39·64	1·02	45·27
38	1·47	38·69	1·09	44·31
39	1·60	37·75	1·16	43·36
40	1·73	36·81	1·23	42·41
41	1·88	35·87	1·30	41·46
42	2·07	34·93	1·37	40·51
43	2·29	34·01	1·44	39·57
44	2·57	33·08	1·53	38·63

Age				
67	22·10	14·03	10·94	18·07
68	24·49	13·34	12·21	17·26
69	27·15	12·66	13·64	16·47
70	30·12	12·00	15·26	15·69
71	33·42	11·36	17·08	14·92
72	37·10	10·73	19·14	14·17
73	41·19	10·13	21·46	13·44
74	45·74	9·54	24·08	12·73
75	50·80	8·97	27·03	12·03
76	56·43	8·43	30·36	11·35
77	62·67	7·90	34·12	10·69
78	69·60	7·39	38·34	10·05
79	77·27	6·91	43·10	9·43
80	85·78	6·45	48·45	8·83
85	143·64	4·45	86·82	6·18
90	235·79	2·95	153·76	4·11
95	373·23	1·90	264·91	2·62
100	556·23	1·21	433·46	1·61
105	1000·00	0·50	650·04	0·99
108			780·83	0·72
109			1000·00	0·50

aSource: Mortality Investigation Committee of the Life Insurance Association of Japan.

CHAPTER 6

STRUCTURED SETTLEMENTS

JAMES A RYAN, JR.
ROGER F HARBIN

BACKGROUND AND OVERVIEW

A structured settlement is an arrangement by which payments that constitute damages on account of personal injury are made over a period of time, possibly for the lifetime of the injured party, rather than as a single lump sum. Wrongful death is included in the meaning of personal injury, in which case compensation is paid to one or more survivors.

These arrangements may be voluntary, in the case of pre-trial settlements; they may be made in lieu of appeal after an award is rendered; or they may be imposed upon the parties by statute or by judicial authority, which most commonly occurs in the case of settlements involving minors. The arrangements may be unfunded, in which case the defendant agrees to make a future set of payments out of its then available funds, or it may be funded by means of the purchase of an annuity contract or other suitable assets. Annuity contracts have become the favored funding instruments because life insurance companies price them aggressively and make available a broad range of options, allowing for flexibility of settlement design.

History and Early Use

The earliest use of structured settlements probably occurred when an injured plaintiff was told that the defendant had no money to pay the claim, and the plaintiff was offered payment in instalments as an alternative to filing claim in bankruptcy court. The earliest recorded use occurred during the 1960s. At that time the drug thalidomide was associated with birth defects among Canadian children. The drug company involved quickly exhausted its insurance coverage, and began to settle cases through agreements to compensate the victims over their lifetimes rather than through one-time cash settlements.

In the USA the first settlements occurred in the early 1970s but remained fairly rare because of uncertainty over the tax treatment of the payments. When a plaintiff receives a lump sum in settlement of damages for personal injuries, the lump sum is free from federal income tax, but any future investment income earned on that lump sum is taxable income. The Internal Revenue Service issued a revenue ruling in 1979 concerning structured settlement arrangements. This ruling established that if the claimant has no right to the discounted present value of the award and has no right to rearrange the established schedule of payments, all income will be received tax free. In addition, to qualify for tax-free status the claimant is precluded from any right of ownership in the funding annuity. This clarification, along with a sudden and unprecedented rate of growth in the frequency and size of injury awards throughout the country, sparked a period of rapid expansion in the use and public recognition of structured settlements.[1]

Expanding Use

Although complete statistics are not available, it has been estimated that in 1979 about $150 million of annuity premium was received by life insurers from third party sources for funding periodic payment obligations. By 1991 this amount was approaching $3 billion. Structured settlements are now a normal business practice for most casualty insurance companies and many self-insured corporations. These comments are based on the North American experience. We realize there will be increasing international interest in this field, which will affect business practices of the insurance community in other parts of the world.

This rapid growth can be attributed to the fact that a properly devised structured settlement can have advantages for all parties involved.[2] In particular, society benefits from an arrangement by which a plaintiff can be restored, at least monetarily, to the condition which existed before the injury or loss occurred. The use of lump sums for this purpose has proven to be inadequate, in that it is not always possible to invest and manage money over the period in which it is needed. Thus there is a growing recognition among the public, courts and legislators that periodic payment settlements constitute good social policy.

Advantages for the Plaintiff

A basic advantage of periodic payments for plaintiffs is the ability to match the income to be received with the loss incurred. This includes future medical expenses and loss of income. A second advantage involves the management of funds. This is attractive to plaintiffs who lack financial expertise, particularly the ability to budget their spending. It is argued that the average lump sum settlement is spent by the plaintiff in a period of five years. Periodic payments also afford the plaintiff federal income tax savings that do not exist with a lump-sum award. In the USA periodic payments are entirely free of income tax, so taxation of what would otherwise be investment income is avoided.

Structured settlements are often the result of a pre-trial settlement. When the defendant arranges and the plaintiff accepts a settlement that recognizes federal income tax savings, and when compromise can be reached at an early date, the plaintiff benefits from not being required to incur the time, expense, emotional trauma and risk of a trial.

There are also disadvantages to the plaintiff. One of these involves the fixed nature of future payments. Should inflation increase to high levels, the periodic payment schedule, which does not adjust, may fail to provide an adequate income. This can be partially offset by payment schedules designed to increase or be augmented by future lump sums. Another risk to the plaintiff involves the ability of the obligor, who is either the original defendant or its assignee, to continue to make the required payments. Should that entity fail, the plaintiff must stand in line with the other creditors for payments, possibly at a reduced level.

Advantages for the Defendant

The major inducement for defendants and their casualty insurers to use periodic payments is cost savings. To the extent that paying by means of a structured settlement results in a higher after-tax income to the plaintiff, this creates a divisible benefit.

When this benefit is shared between the defendant and plaintiff, the defendant is able to settle a case at a lower net cost, and the plaintiff is able to receive a higher after-tax income. In addition, because of other advantages available to the plaintiff (primarily protection of the funds against early dissipation) an astute defendant will be able to negotiate cost savings for providing these advantages.

There are also disadvantages for defendants. Rather than paying a lump sum and closing its books on a claim immediately, a periodic payment obligor must set up administrative procedures to pay claimants over long periods of time. This requirement can be lessened by the purchase of a funding instrument, such as an annuity contract, and by directing the life insurance company issuing the contract to make the payment to the injured party.

It is also possible that as terms of periodic payment settlements become publicly known the sum of future payments to be made will become the amount discussed. This could lead to an inflated perspective of the value of periodic payment settlements and result in higher future damage verdicts. For example, in a recent case in Canada an annuity was purchased for $250,000. It provided for $100,000 per year, increasing at 3 percent compounded annually, beginning on the 18th birthday of an infant plaintiff. If the plaintiff lived to the age of 82, a total of $19.5 million would be paid. The press reported that a settlement for $19.5 million had been reached.

The Structured Settlement Agent or Broker

A sizable industry has grown up around the negotiation and settlement of damage awards and the marketing of annuity contracts as funding instruments. The industry is dominated by a few specialist firms performing this service as a full-time occupation. Consultants for these firms normally contact defendant organizations and offer to provide their services in the negotiation of settlements and arranging for funding annuity contracts.

These structured settlement specialists are compensated only by the commission earned on the sale of annuity contracts. The agent or broker markets his services by indicating that if success in negotiating a settlement is not achieved then no commission or expense payments will be due. In this sense it is similar to a contingent fee arrangement. In exchange for the prospect of earning a commission on the sale of an annuity the specialist contributes much of the expense and effort of conducting negotiations between the parties, while maintaining a semblance of neutrality.

The Life Insurance Company Issuing the Funding Annuity

Life insurance companies issue the annuities to fund structured settlements because casualty companies are generally not permitted to do so under state or provincial regulations.

For the life insurance company there is potential for writing a profitable line of business involving fixed liabilities. This permits the development of a portfolio of assets which can be matched to the liabilities without the risk of disintermediation of funds during periods of high interest rates. The duration of assets involved in backing a structured settlement annuity portfolio tends to be extremely long, which can balance shorter duration investments purchased for other products.

On the negative side, to the extent that statutory reserves exceed net premiums, the company's surplus is depleted by writing single premium annuities. The marketplace is also an extremely competitive one, in that the agent or broker represents several companies and shops each case for the lowest available price. The company is also exposed to significant reinvestment risk: the duration of liabilities may extend to fifty years or more, requiring reinvestment of excess cash flows in earlier years. Also, the company faces exposure to litigation arising out of improper acts by its agents, or failure to pay contract benefits in a timely fashion. To assure proper benefit payments the company will be required to spend significant sums on sophisticated administrative and benefit payment systems.

Immediate Annuities

Single premium immediate annuity contracts issued by life insurance companies have become the instrument of choice for funding structured settlements. These contracts allow a great deal of flexibility, and the life companies have developed efficient administrative systems for making future payments.

Design Alternatives
There are various designs of structured settlements, the number limited only by the ingenuity of the negotiator settling the case. A typical design might include a life annuity benefit stream, possibly with a certain period, to replace lost income. If dependents were relying on the injured party for support, then a certain period guarantees that those dependents would continue to receive money for the stipulated period even after the death of the injured party.

Another life income could be provided to meet future expected medical costs. This frequently does *not* include a certain period, so that the benefit payments are maximized. In the event of the death of the insured party, future medical expenses will no longer be incurred. In addition to the above streams of benefits, payments may provide for education of children, retirement income or any unforeseen future expenses.

Selection of a Life Company
An important concern on the part of all parties is the selection of the life insurance company. The market for structured settlements is extremely price competitive, and a small differential in assumed pricing interest rates makes a substantial difference in ultimate price. Therefore, companies that are willing to accept a riskier investment portfolio can find themselves at a price advantage. It is important that all parties recognize that there is a degree of risk involved in achieving the lowest possible price for the annuity contract.

In addition to price, there are concerns about quality of service. The first payment will be very carefully observed by the plaintiff to ensure that the life carrier can be relied on to meet its obligation of making payments on time. If one or more payments are late, complaints will be promptly levied against the life insurance company, the defendant, and the agent or broker.

Annuity Contract Pricing Considerations

Interest

To determine the interest rate that a company can use to price its annuity contracts, it is necessary to determine what portfolio of assets could be constructed that will have the desired characteristics. These include generating a cash flow that meets the expected liabilities as closely as possible under all future interest scenarios. The duration of assets needs to be as long as possible because liabilities often extend as long as 50 years or more; this is much longer than other insurance products, even immediate annuities sold as retirement income supplements. Because an asset portfolio can seldom be constructed with a duration beyond 30 years it is necessary to make an assumption about the interest rate at which excess cash flows, in the early years of the portfolio, can be reinvested. Since this is unknown some conservatism is appropriate.

In addition to duration, quality of assets is important. Some companies may choose to include high-yield bonds in their investment portfolios. Although this can result in more competitive prices if the added yield is fully reflected in pricing, the company should exercise great care to retain some portion of the extra yield to compensate itself for incurring added investment risk.

Mortality

For those future benefits involving a life contingency it is necessary to determine an appropriate mortality assumption. Retirement annuities, which involve significant self-selection, are normally priced using annuitant mortality. Most companies that offer settlement annuities believe that a significantly reduced element of self-selection is present. Therefore, a mortality assumption more like population mortality is frequently used.

Expenses

Having determined the net premium, it is necessary to increase it to provide for costs associated with issuing the contract and paying commissions. If the total cost of acquisition were 6 percent, for example, the net premium would be divided by 0·94 to determine the gross premium. In addition, if the contract is sold in a state which levies a premium tax on immediate annuities, then the net premium needs to be increased by an amount sufficient to pay the premium tax.

Miscellaneous

Other pricing considerations include changing interest rates, federal income taxes and competition.

Substandard Underwriting

The use of substandard annuities for structured settlements is a relatively recent development. It is important to recognize that the underwriting of substandard annuities is not simply an extension of the decades of experience and techniques which the life insurance industry has developed. Fundamental differences exist.

Mix of Impairments

The mix of impairments seen in applications for substandard annuities is entirely different from that experienced with life insurance applicants. Brain and spinal cord injuries make up the majority of the annuity applicants, and the more traditional problems of obesity, elevated blood pressure, diabetes, heart disease and so on make up a very small portion. This results in several key issues:

1) The life insurance industry has no experience of mortality for individuals with severe brain, spinal cord or similar impairments.

2) The clinical literature about mortality for these impairments is poor or scanty. In some cases the literature about certain impairments was derived from cases accumulated many years ago and fails to account for changes. Cases currently being underwritten may use mortality data and assumptions going back 50 to 75 years.

3) Significant 'shopping' occurs. In many cases applications are submitted to 10 or 15 different companies. The chances of actually placing a case on a competitive underwriting basis are so slim that it is possible that some placed cases represent the occasional errors in the underwriting process. This uncertainty calls for careful periodic review of underwriting posture.

4) Future medical advances are likely to reduce mortality below current levels, as new treatments, or even cures, are found.

Information Submitted to the Company

The materials provided for underwriting these annuities are of variable quality and volume. In general the information submitted by the broker is based on whatever medical information has been accumulated in the course of preparing the case for trial. This information may be obsolete or limited, or it may be so diluted that only limited information can be gleaned by leafing through pages of depositions, including legal arguments, that are of no interest to the underwriter.

Underwriting Techniques

In underwriting annuities the age used to determine the purchase price is adjusted to reflect the biological or physiological age of the individual, not the chronological age. The pricing is then done by entering the appropriate annuity rate table at the new assigned age. Although this method may lack precision, it is administratively simple and usually gives acceptable results.

A significant challenge is posed by the delay experienced before a realistic assessment of mortality outcomes can be achieved. Many of the conditions do not result in an immediate elevation of mortality, so assessment of the accuracy of underwriting is delayed considerably. In life insurance underwriting, the goal is to avoid antiselection at early durations, with much of the underwriting effect 'wearing off' within five years and nearly all the effect wearing off by the end of 10 or 15 years. Therefore, it is possible to determine mortality experience on any underwritten block of life business within a relatively short period.

In addition, the benefit payable may progressively increase with time due to the inclusion of an inflation factor in the benefit schedule. Thus, errors in underwriting become magnified over time.

Additional Concerns

At the time a case is underwritten, the medical director (MD) usually does not know whether there will be a life contingency involved, if a particular case will be placed or how large it is likely to be. With life underwriting, the requirements necessary for reaching a decision can be altered, based on the significance of the case in terms of eventual risk; but with a substandard annuity it is possible to have no idea at the time of underwriting if the case is $25,000 or $2·5 million.

Successful companies spend the time and apply the expertise needed to develop rational underwriting standards; they document these in a manual to ensure consistent handling, and make adjustments as more information becomes available. It is necessary to develop a good impairment coding system and a tracking system for regular assessment of mortality experience by impairment as time passes. The Society of Actuaries has produced a system of impairment coding for use in intercompany studies of this line of business (*see* p. 116).

MEDICAL UNDERWRITING ASPECTS

As already mentioned, the distribution of impairments seen is very different from that encountered in life insurance underwriting.[3,4] About 40 percent of the cases underwritten involve cerebral insults, 25 percent are spinal cord injuries, 15 percent are due to other trauma, and only 15–20 percent result from other medical problems. The summaries that follow describe the issues encountered in the first two categories.

Cerebral Impairments

The following is a summary of the structured settlements experience of one major US life insurance company over the past several years, with emphasis on one of the principal types of medical conditions encountered, cerebral impairments. This category constitutes 40–50 percent of the substandard cases referred to us and illustrates the difficulties and limitations faced in arriving at a reasonable estimate of life expectancy.

Transamerica Occidental Life has been in the structured settlements business for approximately seven years, and currently receives between 500 and 600 cases per month for consideration of substandard offers. These cases are reviewed by one of our experienced life underwriters, who has been assigned to this area since its inception and who has been working full-time on this activity for several years. About 10 percent of the cases he reviews are referred to the medical department to ensure it agrees with the offer. Other companies may rely on their MD to review the majority of these cases because of the difficulty in obtaining and training life underwriters for this line of business. Even experienced underwriters find this is a very different application of their knowledge and aptitude.

We use 1980 population mortality/life expectancy tables to arrive at a rated age. The tables show life expectancy for ages one to 100, male and female, for mortality ratios from 100 to 2,500 percent. The estimated life expectancy is translated into a rated age. We generally estimate a mortality ratio in milder impairments, life expectancy in more severe impairments (above 500 percent mortality), and both approaches in many cases to see if our decision makes sense. We rely on insurance and clinical judgment since there are so few helpful statistical studies in this arena. We seek to be consistent and conservative and limit our offer to a six-month period. We do not consider the interest assumptions or type of annuity plan in reaching the medical decision, although we do realize that these are major items affecting the final offer.

Underwriting Cerebral Impairments
In general, etiology is a minor factor, degree of damage being the major consideration in assessing risk.

Causes of cerebral impairment can be listed as follows:

1) Traumatic head injury (the majority): motor vehicle accidents, falls, gunshot wounds.
2) Anoxic encephalopathy
   a) Prenatal, perinatal, neonatal.
   b) Cardiorespiratory arrest: surgery, anesthesia, non-head trauma.
   c) Drowning or near-drowning.
3) Infections: meningitis, encephalitis.
4) Vascular insults: strokes, aneurysms.
5) Metabolic disorders, drug intoxications, tumors.

Factors in determining degree of impairment are as follows:

1) Motor impairment
   a) None.
   b) Fine co-ordination problems.
   c) Hemiparesis, hemiplegia.
   d) Quadriparesis, quadriplegia (wheel chair confinement, bedridden).
2) Cognitive function impairment
   a) Mild: poor memory, judgment etc.
   b) Moderate but functional in sheltered environment.
   c) Organic brain syndrome.
   d) Personality disorder, psychosis.
   e) Persistent vegetative state (PVS).
   f) Comatose (less common than PVS).
3) Seizure disorder: severity, control.
4) Presence of a shunt: effect, revisions, infections.
5) Level or quality of care.
6) Infections: urinary, respiratory, skin.
7) Presence of gastrostomy and/or tracheostomy.

Underwriting Requirements
It is essential to have medical information. We do not accept summaries or depositions from legal sources. Bias must be considered in reports solicited by either side in the controversy. Unedited depositions from a treating or examining

physician may be useful. We do not quote if the damaging event is very recent or if the medical data are not reasonably current.

Ratings

There is a wide spectrum of ratings, depending on the factors listed above. Cases with mild residuals may be standard; moderate impairments fall in the 200 to 400 percent mortality range; severe residuals such as PVS may call for a 15- to 20-year life expectancy estimate.

There are some special problems in risk assessment which should be mentioned.
1) Very young ages: it is difficult to evaluate the degree of impairment and retardation, and the prospects for improvement; future advances in medical care should also be considered.
2) Stability of status and time span since insult.
3) Effects of underlying diseases, especially in the older age groups.
4) Advanced age: this is a problem because we generally hesitate to estimate a life expectancy of less than 10 years, which limits the increased mortality ratio we can comfortably use.
The effect of age on a severe impairment such as PVS can be illustrated as follows:
1) A 65-year-old man has a normal life expectancy of 14 years. A 500 percent mortality assessment translates to 4·6 years of life expectancy, which is probably too short. A 300 percent mortality estimate (seven year expectancy) is more realistic.
2) A 25-year-old man in PVS may have a 20-year life expectancy (compared with the normal 47 years), which equates to 1,250 percent mortality.
3) A 10-year-old child with a similar degree of cerebral damage may have a 15- to 20-year expectancy, which translates to a mortality ratio of 2,500 percent or more.

Spinal Cord Injuries

Chait and Wilmot discussed this subject in a paper published in the Journal of Insurance Medicine in 1990.[5] They emphasized the importance of the anatomical level of the spinal injury, and its degree of completeness after a recovery plateau, in estimating life expectancy and/or mortality ratio. Available clinical studies often do not make these distinctions, and the longer term studies do not fully include the beneficial effects of recent improvements in medical care.[6,7]

A Canadian study, which included input from Manufacturers Life, appears to be the most useful for our purposes.[8] The 1983 paper included a fourth follow-up of a large group observed since 1945. The relative mortality rate was estimated at 186 percent for incomplete paraplegics, 209 percent for incomplete quadriplegics, 318 percent for complete paraplegics and 767 percent for complete quadriplegics. In the last group there is obviously a wide variation in mortality rate/life expectancy, depending on the exact level of injury and the presence or absence of respirator dependency. If the level is C-3 or above, the mortality ratios are well over 1,000 percent.

Causes of death are respiratory, cardiovascular, renal, suicide, cancer, liver disease and alcohol abuse. Deaths from renal disease are decreasing, but those from suicide and substance abuse are increasing.

Other factors in estimating life expectancy are the quality and level of care, emotional adjustment, living arrangements, degree of rehabilitation, work status, and history or presence of complications.

SUMMARY AND TRENDS

Development of the Business

From the early beginnings less than 20 years ago, structured settlement annuities have grown to a line of business actively solicited by about 100 insurers in North America. In recent years more than 10,000 cases annually have been settled in this way. The average single premium is nearly $200,000. Analysts expect the market to almost double in the next five years, largely due to increasing awards arising from malpractice and product liability litigation.

Changing Markets

Currently the markets for structured settlements are primarily related to personal injury lawsuits, medical liability cases (against physicians, hospitals and pharmaceutical manufacturers) and workers' compensation awards. The number and size of these settlements continue to increase. In addition, we see expanding markets developing in areas such as non-pharmaceutical product liability (foods, additives, cosmetics etc), environmental hazards, toxic clean-up judgments and multimillion dollar lottery winnings.

Medical Advances

On the one hand, new medical conditions are being recognized that may have tort implications, such as the eosinophilia-myalgia syndrome related to use of L-tryptophan. On the other hand, there are advances in diagnosis and treatment that are likely to have significant effects on the life expectancy of impaired individuals. A short list could include organ transplantation, gene substitution, more sophisticated vascular surgery, and improved anti-cancer agents. These and other medical developments need to be kept in mind when estimating life expectancy, especially in relatively young individuals.

REFERENCES

1 Harbin RF. Structured settlements, course I-441U study notes, *Society of Actuaries*, 1991.
2 Moylan RJ, Meredith RA, Holmes JS. The 'structured' settlement. *Trans Assoc Life Insur Med Dir Am* 1984; 68: 81–5.
3 Chait LO, Teitelbaum N. The medical underwriting of substandard life annuities. *J Ins Med* 1983; 14(3): 27–9.
4 Butz RH. The epidemiology of severe injuries in structured settlement applicants. *J Ins Med* 1986; 18(3): 2–16.
5 Chait LO, Wilmot C. Long term life expectancy in spinal cord injury. *J Ins Med* 1990; 22: 136–9.

6 DeVivo MJ, Fine PR, Stover SL. The prevalence of SCI: a re-estimation based on life tables. *SCI Digest* Winter 1980; 3–11.
7 De Vivo MJ et al. Seven-year survival following spinal cord injury. *Arch Neurol* 1987; 44: 872–5.
8 Geisler WO, Jousse AT, Wynne-Jones M, Breithaupt D. Survival in traumatic spinal cord injury. *Paraplegia* 1983; 21: 364–73.

IMPAIRMENT CODING

ANNUITANT INFORMATION

AGE _____

SEX _____

CONTRACT NUMBER _____

REVIEWING PHYSICIAN _____

DATE REVIEWED _____

DIRECTIONS: CHOOSE A MAXIMUM OF 3 IMPAIRMENTS WHICH APPLY TO THIS ANNUITANT. PLACE A NUMBER NEXT TO EACH IMPAIRMENT CHOSEN RANKING YOUR CHOICES IN ORDER OF SIGNIFICANCE FROM 1 TO 3 (A RANKING OF 1 HAVING THE MOST SIGNIFICANCE).

1. NEUROLOGIC (0100)

Spinal Cord Injury

	Quadraplegia Complete	Quadraplegia Incomplete	Paraplegia Complete	Paraplegia Incomplete
C 1-3	0101	0102		
C 4-8	0103	0104		
T 1-12			0105	0106
L 1-5			0107	0108

_____ 0109 Brown – Sequard

Encephalopathy

MILD: ambulatory, near-normal I.Q., continent, swallows

MODERATE: not mild or severe

SEVERE: vegetative, immobile, profound mental retardation, incontinent, tube-fed

BIRTH/CEREBRAL PALSY

	TRAUMATIC	HYPOXIC	OTHER
Mild	0110	0112	0113
Moderate	0114	0116	0117
Severe	0118	0120	0121

_____ 0125 CVA/Stroke
_____ 0126 Seizure
_____ 0127 Alzheimer/Dementia
_____ 0128 Multiple Sclerosis
_____ 0129 Neuromuscular Diseases
_____ 0130 Other Neurologic

2. CANCER (0200)

	Localized or Non-Metastatic	Metastatic
Neurologic	0201	0216
Breast	0202	0217
Lung	0203	0218
Skin	0204	0219
Urologic	0205	0220
Gastrointestinal	0206	0221
Hematologic	0207	0222
Female Genital	0208	0223
Male Genital	0209	0224
Endocrine	0210	0225
Bone	0211	0226
Soft Tissue	0212	0227
Head & Neck	0213	0228
Lymphoma	0214	0229
Other Cancer:	0215	0230

3. RHEUMATOLOGIC / ORTHOPEDIC (0300)

_____ 0301 Collagen–Vascular Disease
_____ 0302 Rheumatoid Arthritis
_____ 0303 Intervertebral Disc Disease

Amputation

	Upper	Lower
Unilat.	0304	0305
Bilat.	0306	0307

_____ 0308 Other Rheuma/Ortho

4. RESPIRATORY (0400)

_____ 0401 Chronic Obstructive Pulmonary Disease
_____ 0402 Pneumoconiosis
_____ 0403 Other

5. PSYCHIATRIC (0500)

_____ 0501 Depression
_____ 0502 Manic/Depressive
_____ 0503 Schizophrenia
_____ 0504 Organic Pain Syndrome
_____ 0505 Chronic Pain Syndrome
_____ 0506 Suicide Attempt
_____ 0507 Post Traumatic Stress Disorder
_____ 0508 Other

6. ENDOCRINE / METABOLIC (0600)

_____ 0601 Diabetes Mellitus
_____ 0602 Obesity
_____ 0603 Other

7. GENITO-URINARY (0700)

_____ 0701 Chronic Renal Failure
_____ 0702 Dialysis
_____ 0703 Other

8. INFECTIOUS DISEASE (0800)

_____ 0801 HIV Infection/Asymptomatic
_____ 0802 HIV Infection/ARC
_____ 0803 HIV Infection/AIDS
_____ 0804 Other I.D.

9. DRUGS (0900)

_____ 0901 Tobacco
_____ 0902 Alcoholism
_____ 0903 Cocaine / Derivatives
_____ 0904 Heroin / Derivatives
_____ 0905 Other

10. GASTROINTESTINAL (1000)

_____ 1001 Liver/Cirrhosis
_____ 1002 Pancreas
_____ 1003 Crohns
_____ 1004 Ulcerative Colitis
_____ 1005 Other

11. CARDIOVASCULAR (1100)

_____ 1101 Congenital

Coronary Artery Disease / Ischemic Heart Disease

New York Heart Classification

_____ 1102 Class I
_____ 1103 Class II
_____ 1104 Class III
_____ 1105 Class IV
_____ 1106 Unknown

_____ 1107 Valvular disease
_____ 1108 Cardiomyopathy
_____ 1109 Hypertension
_____ 1110 Peripheral Vascular Disease
_____ 1111 Cor pulmonale
_____ 1112 Other CV

12. HEMATOLOGIC (1200)

_____ 1201 Polycythemia
_____ 1202 Hemophilia
_____ 1203 Other

13. ENVIRONMENTAL (1300)

_____ 1301 Burns, Mild (0% – 49%)
_____ 1302 Burns, Moderate (50% – 79%)
_____ 1303 Burns, Severe (80% +)
_____ 1304 Toxins / Poisons
_____ 1305 Other

14. GENETIC (1400)

_____ 1401 Down's
_____ 1402 Other

15. TRANSPLANTS (1500)

_____ 1501 Heart
_____ 1502 Heart/Lung
_____ 1503 Liver
_____ 1504 Kidney
_____ 1505 Pancreas
_____ 1506 Bone Marrow
_____ 1507 Other

16. MISCELLANEOUS (1600)

_____ 1601

ADDITIONAL NOTES ON ANNUITANT

CHAPTER 7

LIFE UNDERWRITING WITH KNOWLEDGE-BASED SYSTEMS

ARTHUR A DETORE

A crucial skill for success in insurance risk management is underwriting. It is a very complex decision making process involving the manipulation of many types of information on multiple levels. The actuarial design of the product, abnormalities which increase the likelihood of loss and the quality of the available data must be weighted and used to resolve underwriting problems. This must be done in the context of a competitive market environment while balancing the expected loss with the expected investment income from the use of the pooled funds. Often, the underwriting decision is based upon incomplete and uncertain information. Nevertheless, the quality and consistency of underwriting has a direct, long-term impact on the insurer's bottom line, because the proportion of income paid for claims is greater than that paid to cover administrative expenses.

The medical director (MD) has always been an integral part of this decision making. In most insurance companies today underwriting is a manual process. Even though insurance products are designed with multiple considerations, many companies have not realized how the data involved in the decision-making process of underwriting is related to the pricing and other aspects of the product. In the past, companies could define products with simple actuarial designs and minimal underwriting and do very well. This is not possible in today's competitive, investment-oriented marketplace. Ways to enhance the underwriting process have evolved with the use of new technologies, especially information technology. The tools of information technology will play a much more important role in insurance and risk assessment as the amount and complexity of available information increases. Knowledge-based systems and artificial intelligence (AI) are two such tools.

ARTIFICIAL INTELLIGENCE (AI)

Knowledge-based systems are the product of research in AI. The term artificial intelligence was coined by Dr John McCarthy of Stanford University's School of Engineering in 1955 at a workshop of computer scientists at Dartmouth University. AI is now considered to be the branch of computer science whose goal is to program computers to perform tasks that, if done by a person, would require intelligence or the ability to adjust thinking to a new situation.[1] As an academic science, AI has several branches, including natural language processing, computer vision, automatic programming (machine learning), robotics and knowledge-based systems. Each corresponds to what could be called an 'intelligent' activity.

Natural language processing is the ability of computers to understand idiomatic spoken and written language. This allows people to talk to computers in the same way that they talk to other people. Computer vision is the capacity of a computer to process an image or picture and return a description of it. Automatic programming or machine learning is the ability of computers to program and reprogram themselves. Although currently there are programs which can induce new information from information fed into them, the goal of automatic programming is to have the computer itself determine what data it should review and what conclusions it should reach. Robotics is the ability of computers to sense, measure, create and respond to changes in the environment to perform physical tasks that were traditionally performed by people. This is one of the most advanced areas of AI and one which has been very successful commercially, especially in manufacturing.

KNOWLEDGE-BASED SYSTEMS

Knowledge-based systems are computer programs that solve problems in a non-procedural or opportunistic manner using knowledge from human experts to simulate human reasoning. They are also called expert systems or inference-based programs. The intelligent activity they emulate is problem solving and knowledge rather than just information used for their processing. What is the basis for this distinction? Information exists by itself, without a context; knowledge has the added dimension of being put into perspective or utilized in a skill or task. For example, a list of blood pressures would be information; reading a list of blood pressures, determining that they were elevated and making the connection that the elevated blood pressures require treatment is utilizing knowledge about blood pressure.

In knowledge-based systems, the knowledge is derived from human experts and the program simulates human thought processes, not by going in a step-by-step or procedural manner but by varying the decision making on the uniqueness of the information in a non-procedural manner. This is done by programming the heuristics or rules of thumb that experts use to search through large amounts of information. The approach is different from the algorithmic, detailed process of conventional programs and allows for complex decision making to be programmed in a way not possible before.

Medical knowledge-based systems have been written to interpret pulmonary function tests,[2] review clinical pathological conferences in internal medicine,[3] determine appropriate chemotherapy for certain cancers,[4] diagnose rheumatological disease,[5] and evaluate patients with suspected transient ischemic attacks.[6] A recent prospective study showed that the diagnostic accuracy of one program was better than that of the ward team and equivalent to that of consultant physicians for inpatient diagnostic challenges.[7]

Development of Knowledge-based Systems

Most often, knowledge-based systems are created by using programs called 'shells', which are software packages designed to develop knowledge-based systems in many areas of knowledge or domains.[8] They contain the generic components of a knowledge-based system, and the programmer must put in the specific knowledge about the problem as well as the general guideline for how to solve it.

Conceptually there are two ways this can be done: inductively or deductively. Inductive knowledge-based system shells create knowledge-based systems from processing example cases. If a knowledge-based system for interpreting electro-cardiograms were being developed with an inductive shell, then examples of the electrocardiograms with the interpretations would be presented to the program along with the parameters to examine. The program would infer the relationship among the parameters to determine the final interpretation.

The advantage of inductive shells is that they are very easy to use. The disadvantage is that once problems become very complex and the relationships among the parameters are not in a one-to-one correspondence these systems are not able to handle the complexity. This is especially true in pathophysiological or model-based reasoning, such as the diagnosis of congestive heart failure, in which the heart is viewed as a pump.[9]

Deductive knowledge-based system shells allow knowledge to be directly programmed, usually using 'if . . . then' rules or related sets of data called objects. If a deductive knowledge-based system were being written to interpret electro-cardiograms, then the explicit principles of interpretation, such as measuring the PR interval and correlating the P waves with the QRS complex, would be directly programmed into the system along with the underlying pathophysiological concepts. Because of the ability to program directly very complex relationships and reasoning, deductive knowledge-based systems enable the creation of systems that can deal with highly complicated problems.

A recent review of the diagnostic reasoning of physicians discussed the processes used in different situations. It described three main strategies: probabilistic reasoning, causal reasoning and deterministic reasoning.[10] Only the deductive approach to knowledge-based system development allows for the programming of all three of these. The disadvantage is that more expertise is required to program these types of systems and most experts are unable to develop these systems without assistance.

Neural Networks

An AI technology also used for automated decision making is neural networks. These are computing systems made up of a number of simple, highly connected hardware elements that process information by changing the intensity of the interactions among the components. Their design was fashioned after neurophysiological studies of animal brain tissue, in which brains were shown to be composed of neurons highly interconnected with multiple other cells in a network; hence the name.

Neural networks are not only structured differently from knowledge-based systems, they also work differently. They process information in parallel rather than sequentially. That is, when information enters, many elements process it at the same time. A network starts with a certain electrical equilibrium among the component elements. As the electronic information arrives, it changes the intensity of the connections so that the electrical current runs differently and the electrical output changes. The information is stored in the nature of the connections rather than in any one area.

Currently, unlike biological neural networks, artificial neural networks must be set up with the proper connections and 'trained' before they can be used. This involves giving many examples to the system so that it can readjust its connections to function in the desired way. In this way they are superficially similar to inductive knowledge-based systems; structurally they are quite different.

Neural networks are not yet in widespread commercial use. They do, however, have much potential. They could allow systems to 'learn' by updating their performance in processing new examples. Paul Harmon, an AI consultant, and others have suggested that neural networks will not replace knowledge-based systems but that the two will be complementary. Neural networks are very good at pattern recognition (similar to what the right side of the brain does in recognizing faces); knowledge-based systems are better for analytical processing (similar to what the left brain does).[8]

Knowledge Engineering

The purpose of knowledge engineering is to ensure the knowledge-based system solves problems as an expert does. It is the component of knowledge-based system development focused on the cognitive process of the human expert versus the technical aspects of the system. For inductive knowledge-based systems and neural networks the system itself defines the knowledge from the example cases. For deductive knowledge-based systems a knowledge engineering process must be completed. This can be viewed as having three distinct stages. The first, knowledge acquisition, defines the expert's knowledge, both the background knowledge and the heuristics the expert uses in practical application of the knowledge. This is usually done by interviewing the expert. In the development of an underwriting knowledge-based system, experienced underwriters and MDs are interviewed by a knowledge engineer, and asked to explain their reasoning as they review cases. The second stage, knowledge modeling, involves structuring the knowledge in programmable form. This requires the knowledge to be expressed in concise statements that can be entered into the knowledge-based system shell. The final stage, knowledge encoding, is the actual programming.[8]

These steps emphasize that knowledge engineering is not primarily concerned with the process of computer systems but with the cognitive processes of expert decision makers. Sometimes the expert is able to go through this process himself, but most often another person more skilled in interviewing and organizing knowledge, a knowledge engineer, will need to do this. In very complex domains, such as underwriting, the best knowledge engineers are underwriters or MDs who are already familiar with underwriting knowledge and have been trained in the process of knowledge-based system development.

Insurance Work Station Processing

As discussed, insurance is an information-intensive industry that requires a great deal of knowledge and problem solving to manage risk appropriately. Therefore, knowledge-based systems are well suited to the industry.

Information technology will have an expanding role in insurance as data becomes more appreciated as a corporate asset. However, to leverage it, users must be electronically linked. The raw data must be transformed into information and knowledge. In this way, technology creates competitive advantage.

Although isolated areas for advanced technology can be identified, a comprehensive view is necessary. To manage risk profitably, information must flow through an insurance company in the same way that raw materials flow through production plants. This can be accomplished by incorporating knowledge-based systems into work stations (i.e. computers set up with the software needed by professionals to collect and process their specialized information). How can this be done? Collection of information begins with the agent or broker. A preliminary processing system in the producer's work station starts the electronic flow of information. Data is collected from the proposed insured using a sales knowledge-based system that performs a needs analysis and correlates this information with the types of products available to achieve the best match. Other components of the work station develop the proposal and the application, and identify requirements. All of this information can be transmitted to the home office within seconds for continued processing.

Without additional input, the underwriting work station automatically correlates other sources of information, such as the company's alpha index and Medical Information Bureau (MIB) codes. Underwriting and issue will often be completed at this work station solely by the knowledge-based system. Cases needing review by an underwriter or MD can be distributed electronically along with images of additional documents, such as the attending physician's statements. This work station contains the decision-assistance knowledge-based systems for the medical, financial, and non-medical aspects of the case. It also monitors the status of each case and co-ordinates pricing and underwriting for a given product.

Once an underwriting decision has been reached, the information flows to an administrative work station where the policy data is maintained. From here policy changes can be made and claims paid. All underwriting, administrative and claims data is in turn forwarded to a comparative analysis work station. This station contains statistical modeling tools and has access to external databases for monitoring and studying results that update the underwriting system. This information then flows to actuarial work stations with knowledge-based systems for pricing, product design, reinsurance and product performance monitoring. Demographic and trend information could also be shared with marketing knowledge-based systems to study the competitive environment. Finally, the economic aspects of these decisions are collected by a financial work station that monitors financial results and a company's investment portfolio to accurately match assets and liabilities.

This entire flow can be visualized as a large mainframe computer with tremendous memory storage serving as a reservoir of information linked by data to the work stations. Each professional only views the subset of data needed to perform his task. Conceptually this is centralized data management with decentralized knowledge processing.

Historical Perspective

The use of information technology and specifically knowledge-based systems in underwriting has developed through generations of systems, which have progressively increased in complexity.

First Generation: Screening Systems

These were developed by larger companies in the 1970s to decrease general expenses. They allowed for the entry of information from the application, and screened out or accepted clean non-medical cases which were previously handled by manual jet screening units. The remainder of the cases were referred to underwriters.

Second Generation: Information Display Systems

These appeared in the mid 1980s. They were designed to save underwriters' time and thereby improve productivity. Information display systems allow the underwriter automated access to various sources of information, such as underwriting manuals, medical terminology, lists of medications and other underwriting guidelines. These systems replace the need for multiple volumes of handbooks. They allow rapid access to the information that an underwriter needs.

Third Generation: Initial Underwriting Systems

These systems were developed to improve service to the field by approving some cases automatically and eliminating cases not needing review by an underwriter. Because they require complex knowledge-based systems for their processing they have only been available for the past few years. Initial underwriting systems extend the capability of the first generation systems and go beyond screening to identify underwriting problems, automatically underwrite some cases, and pre-process other cases for underwriters by ordering information 'for cause', such as attending physician statements (APSs). The advanced third generation systems can also do initial underwriting with requirements such as medical examinations, inspection reports and laboratory test results. Some can even do discrepancy processing (i.e. comparison of the decisions based on the information on the application and information from other sources, noting and dealing with discrepancies, such as unadmitted histories).

Fourth Generation: Knowledge-based Decision Assistance Tools

These relatively new systems provide underwriters with knowledge-based systems to underwrite complex impairments and help them manage their administrative workload. They have been designed to enhance the risk selection process. Their use by underwriters can help manage mortality expenses by applying consistency to the underwriting process.

Fifth Generation: Total Underwriting Systems

The fifth generation of underwriting systems encompass and surpass the previous systems. They integrate all the components discussed above into a single system; they also include a management information system for the entire process. This is the essence of the underwriter work station, which, as discussed above, would be integrated into the entire administrative flow for its greatest impact.

Components of a Total Underwriting System

A total underwriting system needs to address the entire decision making process of underwriting, which starts at the time an application is completed and does not end until a policy is issued. The system needs multiple components for each of the essential functions.

Initial Data Entry

This is where information from the application is entered into the system. Depending upon the specifics of the company and its field force, data may be entered from an agent's laptop computer, at a regional marketing office or at the home office. Information from the agent's report, requirements ordered in the field and MIB information could also be entered for processing.

Screening

The second component is screening. This involves taking applications and sorting them into two groups: clean ones and those in need of further processing. This is fairly simple processing. Screening checks that applications need no further requirements, have all medical and non-medical questions answered properly, are within certain age and amount limits, and have acceptable finances and an appropriate beneficiary. Approved cases are sent directly to the administration system.

Initial Underwriting

Applications that are not approved by screening flow into the next component, initial underwriting. This series of knowledge-based systems defines underwriting problems and determines why the case required further processing. It checks for age and amount requirements and examines the financial, non-medical and medical aspects of the case, as well as the interactions among them. It decides if there is sufficient information to deal with the problems it has defined. For instance, if a proposed insured admits to a minor illness two years ago, the system will allow the case to pass through for most ages and amounts, unless the provider of the service was unusual. However, if there is a history of angina, the system will not try to approve the case but will refer it to an underwriter. Prior to its referral, the system determines requirements, such as an APS or ECG, and identifies the appropriate underwriting guidelines. In this way the initial underwriting deals with cases not needing an underwriter's attention and preprocesses those it cannot approve.

Requirement Processing

Since underwriting is an iterative process with information from many sources being reviewed at different times, a total underwriting system permits information (from requirements such as the medical examination, blood work, etc) to be entered into the system directly from the provider or by home office personnel. Processing requirements is similar to initial underwriting, except that discrepancy processing is done by comparing the details of the information from the application with those received later. In this way data from different sources is compared to uncover new problems. If there is a significant history or physical finding on the examination that was not admitted on the application, it is noted and the appropriate work-up is ordered. If no problems are discovered, cases can be automatically approved without consulting an underwriter.

Workflow Tools

Underwriters need certain tools to process their cases administratively. A total underwriting system provides these. They include front-end tools, back-end tools and status functions.

The front-end workflow tools keep track of cases, their requirements and underwriting problems. The in-tray function accesses cases electronically assigned to the underwriter. Rather than getting a stack of files, the underwriter now deals with an electronic stack of cases. For each case there is a detailed underwriting status with identifying data, as well as underwriting problems and their actions. Other tools allow the underwriter to manipulate, track and change the underwriting problems and requirements of a case. There is also an electronic notepad for the underwriter; this can be integrated with an electronic mail system for field communication.

The back-end workflow tools assist in the final administrative details of a case: forms to be signed, post-issue requirement preparation, reporting of MIB codes and the process of requesting reinsurance.

The status function lets non-underwriters review selected case information. An agent's status reveals the data from the application, as well as the requirements and whether they have been received.

Information Display

The information display component gives on-line access to underwriting guidelines with several types of automated searches to improve the access of information. It also makes available other underwriting references, such as medical dictionaries and drug references.

Impairment Knowledge-based Systems

The next component is the impairment underwriting knowledge-based systems. These programs deal with impairments such as high blood pressure, diabetes, cancer, respiratory disorders, aviation, ECG abnormalities and coronary heart disease. Their logic is patterned after the knowledge and thought processes of expert MDs and underwriters. Information is requested from the record and a rating is suggested. If underwriters choose, these will guide them through the detailed decisions needed to underwrite impaired cases.

Management Reporting

This component generates administrative and other reports on the decisions made within the system. Reports can be created by management from the database of information.

Benefits

Underwriting systems have many benefits. For underwriters they limit the number of cases that need to be reviewed, because the system is able to process them without intervention. In this way the technology improves the work of underwriting by eliminating unnecessary routine cases. Several companies have developed knowledge-based systems for this purpose and have been very pleased with the results. As one underwriting officer stated, 'This gives the underwriters time to deal with more complex and time-consuming cases . . . which was one of the reasons for installing the system.'[11] Furthermore initial underwriting knowledge-based systems decrease the number of times a case needs to be reviewed by an underwriter, because requirements are ordered and processed by the system prior to the underwriter seeing the case.

For the producer, service is greatly improved. This is possible because some applications can be approved by the system almost immediately, without having to be seen by an underwriter. One company that has integrated this type of system with its field offices is able electronically to approve applications in less than 15 minutes.[12] Also, the sales process can be helped by determining all requirements (both those required for 'age and amount' and those necessary for a specific cause) immediately so that producers do not have to contact an applicant a second or third time for additional information.

Knowledge-based systems can improve underwriter productivity in other ways with workflow management tools. Although these systems do not do any underwriting themselves, they do manage the paperwork in the ordering and keeping track of requirements. Such tools decrease the clerical work of underwriters and improve the workflow in underwriting departments by eliminating unnecessary paper flow.

As well as saving underwriters unnecessary work, knowledge-based systems can provide decision-assistance tools in the risk classification process. Impairment underwriting knowledge-based systems are sophisticated decision-support tools. They assist in the determination of ratings by prompting the user for information and correlating that information with underwriting guidelines and the programmed thought processes of expert underwriters. They serve as an excellent training tool for the junior underwriter and assist experienced underwriters in very complex cases.

In addition to helping in the actual underwriting decision making, knowledge-based systems can assist the underwriting manager with the overall underwriting process. Once information has been entered into an knowledge-based system, it becomes available for management reporting and decision making. This allows underwriting managers to follow the screening of cases by the knowledge-based system, as well as the ordering of requirements and the rating of impairments. These decisions can be tracked according to agent, agency or underwriter so that underwriters can interact better with the producers with whom they work; underwriting managers can also more effectively manage the underwriters who report to them. Previously unavailable management information tools are made readily available, as is information on specific underwriting decision making.

Impact on the Medical Directors (MD)

An underwriting knowledge-based system integrated within the new business department helps to maximize the impact of the medical department's support of the underwriting process. This can be done by the creation of an MD's work station that has access to the underwriting system, tools for searching the medical literature and other computerized data bases, and other medical decision-support programs.

As consultants with work stations within an integrated network, MDs can interpret ECGs, TVCs, laboratory results and other diagnostic information; they can access case material to assist in interpretations and then recommend ratings or further work-up while delivering specific messages to the underwriter. They can also review APSs with questions and deliver messages on the conclusions and the ratings.

Any cases that are diagnostic, or rating dilemmas that fall outside the underwriting guidelines or the system's logic, can be electronically referred to the MD who can access the medical literature and other data bases to form a better opinion. Case material forwarded to the MD for review can be referred back to the underwriter with references and messages and be kept as part of the record after the decision is made. All this can be done remotely or face to face, depending on how the workflow is designed.

This process enhances the educational role of the medical department. MDs can forward to underwriters articles and other references about their cases to individualize underwriters' education. This can be further enhanced by tracking the types of cases that are referred to the medical department, to direct underwriting education specifically to the topics of importance. Also, the strengths and weaknesses of specific underwriters could be determined by reviews of referrals and individualized tutorials could be developed.

Most importantly, MDs will play a vital role in the development and maintenance of the knowledge within underwriting systems. As the system generates underwriting data in the form of ratings and requirements, studies can be carried out by the medical department to assist in the modification of the system and to ensure that the system reflects appropriate medical judgement.

Non-technical Considerations

This chapter has focused on the technical aspects and benefits of knowledge-based systems for underwriting. However, any new technology has non-technical considerations as well. These include the inappropriate use of technology, cost effectiveness and the social aspects of the use of technology.

To be useful, a technology must provide the solution to a business problem. It is inappropriate for MDs and managers to ask the question 'Where can I use knowledge-based systems or other new technologies?' This type of thinking emphasizes the technology and not the solution. A better set of questions to ask when looking at the underwriting and new business area is 'What are the problems: expenses, service, inefficient workflow, training, mortality?' and 'Can knowledge-based systems help solve them?' A knowledge-based system that is not focused on the business issues will not add value to an underwriting department.

The next consideration is cost. A key management question should be 'If this system will address underwriting problems, is the solution cost effective?' The cost of implementing and using a new technology should be balanced by the benefits; otherwise there is no advantage of its use. For underwriting knowledge-based systems the cost of developing and maintaining the knowledge must be weighed against the value of the benefits. Companies must also consider their underwriting and data processing resources in the decision about the cost effectiveness of building or purchasing such systems.

The last consideration is the social and organization impact. Technology always affects people. Within an organization the introduction of new technology brings about changes. This creates a new set of management issues, especially if the rate of change of the organization is faster than the ability of the employees to become familiar with the technology.[13] New technologies can greatly impact the marketing and legal environment of companies. The implementation of new technologies must be managed appropriately to avoid difficulties.

Role of the Medical Director (MD)

Because MDs are a vital part of the underwriting process they must take a strong role within their companies in the evaluation and implementation of knowledge-based systems and other new technologies that affect the medical aspects of the new business and risk classification process. This can only be done if MDs are aware of the technologies, knowledgeable in their application, and involved in their implementation and use.

REFERENCES

1 Arnold WR, Bowie JS: Artificial intelligence: a personal, commonsense journey. Englewood Cliffs, N.J. Prentice-Hall Inc 1986.
2 Aikins JS, Kunz JC, Shortliffe EH, Fallat RJ. PUFF: an expert system for interpretation of pulmonary function data. Comput Biomed Res 1983; 16: 199–208.
3 Miller RA, Pople HE Jr, Meyers JD. INTERNIST–I, an experimental computer-based diagnostic consultant for general internal medicine. N Eng J Med 1982; 307: 468–76.
4 Hickman DH, Shortliffe EH, Bischoff MS, Scott AC, Jacobs CD. The treatment advice of a cancer chemotherapy protocol advisor. Ann Intern Med 1985; 103: 928–36.
5 Kingsland LC III, Lindberg DAB, Sharp GC. Anatomy of a knowledge-based consultant system: AI/RHEUM. MD Comp 1986; 3: 18–26.
6 Reggia JA, Tabb DR, Price TR, Banko M, Hebel R. Computer-aided assessment of transient ischemic attacks. Arch Neurol 1984; 41: 1248–54.
7 Bankowitz RA, NcNeil MA, Challinor SM, Parker RC, Kapoor WN, Miller RA. A computer-assisted medical diagnostic consultation service: implementation and prospective evaluation of a prototype. Ann Intern Med 1989; 110: 824–32.
8 Harmon P, Maus R, Morrissey W. Expert systems: tools and applications. New York: John Wiley & Sons Inc 1988.
9 Szolovits P, Patil RS, Schwartz WB. Artificial intelligence in medical diagnosis. Ann Intern Med 1989; 108: 80–87.
10 Kassirer JP. Diagnostic reasoning. Ann Intern Med 1989; 110: 893–900.
11 Jones DC. Insurer's underwriting staff gets 'expert' help. National Underwriter, October 5, 1987: 3.
12 Conversano J. Expert system lightens underwriters' work load. Resource May/June 1988: 6–8.
13 Baker JH. Information technologies: strategic opportunities for the life insurance industry. Trend Analysis Program. American Council of Life Insurance. October 1988.

CHAPTER 8

APPLICATION PROCESSING

EVE OWEN

Each insurance office has its own culture, which is reflected in the way it administers the business it receives. The following remarks are therefore of a general nature and illustrate the main features of processing applications for life insurance, from the initial proposal to the policy issue. First it is necessary to consider the standard forms used in assessing any application for life insurance, and then look at the various stages of the procedure.

APPLICATION FOR LIFE INSURANCE

Once agreement has been reached on the purchase of life insurance, the applicant must complete a questionnaire known as a proposal or application form; this will form the basis of the contract of insurance with the insurance company. The questions on the proposal are designed to give the insurance office sufficient information to set up its records and begin the assessment of the risk from an underwriting point of view. The questions include name, address, date of birth, occupation, and details of past and present health. The applicant will also be asked to give details of any previous life insurance applications, and details of family history and life style (i.e. smoking habits, alcohol consumption, foreign residence and hazardous avocational pursuits).

In the case of applications for larger than average sums insured, currently at around £250,000 or $500,000, the applicant will be asked to provide information about his financial status, and closer examination of the insurable interest under the policy will be required; for very large amounts independent confirmation of this information will be needed. In North America inspection reports, sometimes called investigative consumer reports, are used for larger sums insured. They are prepared by consumer reporting agencies and contain information about the applicant's occupation, personal habits, avocations and finances. To prepare an inspection report the investigating agency contacts and interviews the applicant, his friends, neighbours and business associates.

Because of the growing costs and time delays, inspection reports prepared by professional agencies are used less often; many insurance offices now use their own home office personnel, or even the underwriters themselves, to gather information by talking directly to the applicant over the telephone.

MEDICAL EXAMINATION

The applicant has a duty by law to disclose any information which may be considered relevant in the assessment of his application for life insurance.

However, human nature being what it is, there is often a significant amount of non-disclosure of important facts. This, together with the possibility that the applicant is genuinely unaware of any serious medical problem, is the reason why most insurers operate age and sum-insured limits, over which they automatically request an independent medical examination. Most offices also have a lower limit at which they automatically request a medical history report from the applicant's own doctor. In the UK this report is known as a medical attendant's report (MAR), and in North America and the continent of Europe as an attending physician's statement (APS).

Larger sums insured and older applicants may indicate the need for additional routine investigations, such as electrocardiograms (ECGs) (resting and/or exercise), chest X-rays (CXRs), blood profiles and urine analysis. There is also a routine requirement for HIV antibody tests at around the level that most companies routinely obtain medical examinations. If any of these routine requirements reveal adverse features, additional medical reports may be called for.

Choice of Examiner

Since the information obtained from medical examination is one of the important links in the chain of evidence on which underwriting is based, taking a careful history and accurately documenting the physical examination are essential. It is a fact that companies with a panel of hand-picked doctors throughout the country show a better mortality experience in their standard risk portfolios than companies employing doctors on a casual basis, some of whom may have little experience of what is required.

In North America it has been found that the most suitable medical examiners are younger physicians who have received a thorough postgraduate training for several years, and who, in addition to hospital appointments, have established themselves in private practice with their own offices and equipment. They are generally keener and show a greater interest in the work. Before a doctor's name is sent to the home office for inclusion on the panel for a particular area, the branch manager must be satisfied that the doctor has the necessary qualities and qualifications, as well as sufficient time to see the company's clients. After a period of probation, the physician may then be accepted as an approved examiner. This is the ideal situation, but in recent years there has been great difficulty in having applicants medically examined, due to the combination of a shortage of medical manpower and an increasing volume of life business. To overcome this difficulty some life insurance companies have been using paramedical organizations to obtain basic underwriting information on certain classes of applicants. Paramedical examinations are discussed in more detail later (see Chapter 10).

In the UK, where the pattern of medical practice differs somewhat from that in North America, life offices depend largely on general practitioners to carry out medical examinations, particularly in smaller towns and rural areas; throughout the country there are excellent, well qualified general practitioners who are sufficiently interested in life assurance work to learn the special techniques required to produce a first-class report. Such examiners are a boon to underwriting departments: a great deal of time and money could be saved if all offices maintained panels of approved examiners; offices could also issue booklets containing helpful guidance on some of the more important pieces of information to be gathered during examination.

As in North America, spiralling cost of medical evidence has forced offices to look at alternative approaches, and examinations by paramedics look set to take off in the UK in 1992 or 1993.

Medical Attendant's Report (MAR): Attending Physician's Statement (APS)

A report from the applicant's private physician or medical attendant may be obtained when certain information, disclosed in the medical examination requires confirmation or amplification. The medical attendant is asked to give a brief summary of the illnesses that he has attended the applicant for, and any relevant information from his records. This, together with the results of any investigations (radiological, cardiographic or biochemical) performed, is enormously helpful for reaching an equitable underwriting decision. However, obtaining written reports from attending physicians is time consuming and sometimes an irritation for the doctor. This has resulted in widespread use of copying services, with complete copies being made of the doctor's, a clinic's or hospital's file relating to the applicant.

In countries with a comprehensive medical service provided by the state, a MAR or APS is particularly valuable, because each member of the population is registered with a single doctor for general care, and medical records have continuity throughout that person's lifetime; the file follows automatically whenever he moves and registers with another doctor. In the USA continuity of medical records is sometimes less satisfactory: people often consult different physicians in their locality for different complaints, and if a person moves house his medical file does not necessarily follow.

To compensate for the sometimes inevitable deficiencies in information from attending physicians, life insurance companies in the USA have developed underwriting techniques based on current information from the medical examination together with any necessary ancillary tests. Also, most companies subscribe to the Medical Information Bureau (MIB), which maintains a record of applicants' medical impairments reported by other companies in the past.

Access to Medical Reports Act 1988 (AMRA)

Under this Act, in the UK a person applying for life insurance has to give his consent to the insurance company before it can write for a MAR. He also has the right to see the report before it has been sent to the insurance office or at any time within the following six months. The applicant may refuse to give consent to his doctor to pass on certain details from records, and in some circumstances it may be necessary for the insurance company to decline the application for insurance if consent is not forthcoming. Complying with the Act presents insurance companies with a considerable administrative burden (*see* Chapter 3, p. 42).

MARKETING AND SELLING INSURANCE

Insurance companies employ a range of different methods of marketing and selling their products. As life insurance usually has to be actively sold rather than simply being bought by the client, life insurance salesmen have to work hard to find potential customers and convince them that they need to purchase life cover.

Independent Financial Advisers

These are professional insurance salesmen who have specialist knowledge and who are able, because they are independent, to recommend the products best suited to their clients' needs from a range of companies they do business with. They are regulated by a strict code of conduct. In the USA the term 'financial adviser' is increasingly used, but 'broker' is still used to describe an independent salesman, specializing in insurance requiring attention to particular aspects (large amounts, medical impairments, legal settlements etc).

Direct Sales Forces

It is now becoming usual for insurance companies to have their own direct sales force. This is made up of employees who sell only the products of the company they represent. They are very often recruited from outside the life insurance industry for their proven selling ability, and are trained by the company in the basics of life insurance and the products of the office they represent. They are usually commission based, and are sometimes provided with a 'financing arrangement' until their commission earnings become a living wage.

Tied Agents

The third large distribution channel is the tied agent. This is usually a bank or building society which finds customers through the normal course of business and recommends one particular life insurance company. This is a very important source of business in the UK, with most large building societies now tied to a particular insurance company.

Branch Office

To improve the service provided to clients and gain maximum presence throughout the countries where a company operates, branch offices and regional offices are strategically sited in the main centres of population. Branch offices are predominantly sales offices and are used by the salesmen as a base to obtain appointments and complete their administration. The development of computer technology has meant that many branch or regional offices are now linked by networks to the main computer at head or home office, allowing many routine functions to be decentralized.

The branch office is the collecting point for new insurance applications. The branch administration staff check that details are complete and note whether any automatic medical requirements are indicated; they then apply for any necessary MAR or APS. The salesman is advised if the applicant needs a routine medical examination and any additional tests. Having completed the routine checking and requested any automatic medical requirements, branch staff forward the applications to head or home office.

Head Office: Home Office

When the application papers are received at head or home office, the application details are input into the computer to set up the policy records, and the medical documents relating to the application are checked by underwriting clerks who mark off any abnormal or unusual features. It is then the task of the lay underwriter to attach the numerical ratings applicable to each impairment. If the medical evidence seems straightforward, a proposal may be accepted as standard, or rated substandard, without reference to the chief medical officer (CMO) or medical director (MD).

Many large insurance companies now employ electronic data processing (EDP) to screen their applications and medical evidence. So-called 'clean' cases are passed through the computer, and appropriate policies processed and issued automatically without further human intervention. Cases rejected by the computer are sorted out into their various categories; those with medical impairments are then assessed individually by the life underwriters. The more complicated medical problems, and applications for insurance involving large sums of money, are usually considered by the lay underwriter in consultation with the CMO or MD of the company. If no further medical evidence is considered necessary, the favourable and unfavourable features are weighed and the rating, if any, decided.

In some cases further ancillary investigations may need to be carried out to clarify the clinical picture; for example, a blood glucose test might be required if unexplained glycosuria is reported on examination, an ECG if there is a history of chest pain suggestive of myocardial ischemia, or further estimations of blood pressure if the original readings are high or borderline.

Chief Medical Officer (CMO): Medical Director (MD)

In the UK it is customary for the CMO of a company to be retained on a part-time basis; the larger life offices may employ several part-time medical officers. The CMO is usually a consultant physician who is familiar with the particular problems applicable to life assurance, and this, along with a wide experience of general medicine, makes him very valuable to the office. A few CMOs devote most of their time to life insurance medicine as a speciality and rather less to purely clinical work, their services being retained by several offices. In addition to advising on underwriting, the CMO may carry out medical examinations when a difficult or unusual problem has to be settled, or when very large sums of money are to be assured. Such examinations may be carried out either at head office or his own rooms.

In North America, where life insurance companies are generally larger than in other countries, the MD is usually full-time. He and his assistant medical directors tend to be much more involved in the underwriting policy of the company, and have more time for statistical research and the investigation of mortality among the policyholders.

All the medical matters connected with life assurance are strictly confidential, the results of the examination being the property of the life office. The applicant must be given no indication by the examiner of the likely outcome, favourable or otherwise. Indeed, the medical examiner is not really in a position to express an opinion, since other medical evidence that he is unaware of might be made available to head or home office from a different source, altering the clinical picture entirely. If, however, some serious fault requiring medical attention is discovered during the course of the life assurance examination, most companies will notify the applicant's own doctor, so that he can take appropriate action in the interests of his patient.

The introduction of HIV antibody testing in life underwriting has highlighted the need for the CMO or MD to be prepared to talk with the applicant's doctor.

It is customary for companies to deal sympathetically with a family doctor's request for information to help him advise or treat his patient, especially if the applicant was declined, or accepted as substandard. The company is, of course, under no obligation to give reasons why a patient was declined or the premiums loaded, but can confine any information to points of fact. In the USA the customer's right to know why an adverse action has been taken is becoming increasingly pervasive. This means that the MD must explain to the attending physician, and sometimes even to the applicant, why the insurance decision was made.

Senior Underwriter
Although, in theory, the final authority to issue a policy rests with the board of directors or president of a company, this responsibility is invariably delegated to the senior underwriter, except possibly in cases of exceptional interest or those involving very large sums of money. The CMO or MD will make recommendations, which the underwriter can accept, vary or reject. The final decision rests with the senior underwriter.

PART II

CHAPTER 9

THE CONCEPT OF HEALTH AND DISEASE

R D C BRACKENRIDGE

LONGEVITY

Longevity and the factors involved in it are very relevant to the business of life assurance. Heredity and environment are the major factors, although the relative importance of each has been disputed.

It has been said in the past, and the argument is still heard, that there is no reason, given ideal conditions, why man should not live well past 100 years. Several biological analogies have been quoted in support of this contention; Fisher[1] mentions two relevant experiments. The first was one in which no natural death was found in a culture of paramecium in 8,500 generations, equal to one quarter of a million years of human life, the culture thriving as well at the end as at the beginning of the experiment. The second was performed in the 19th century by Alexis Carrel, a French biologist, who claimed that fibroblasts taken from the heart of a chick embryo could be kept alive indefinitely by washing out the poisons generated by the life process and by protecting them against infection and food deficiency. This claim was later refuted by Hayflick, working at Stanford, University, California, who repeated the experiment and discovered that Carrel's cells divided immortally because every so often he was adding fresh fibroblasts to the culture. The fact is that chick or even human fibroblasts do not keep growing immortally but age and die after about 50 or 60 doublings, which is a few more than they would have to perform during the life of the animal they came from.

Aging and Senescence

Aging is a time-related process and an intrinsic property of all species; it starts at birth and progresses throughout life. Provided that all noxious or feral environmental influences could be avoided and all diseases eliminated, death ideally would then take place at the upper limit of the life span of any particular species. In the human, this ideal is unlikely to be achieved, although survival has gradually increased through the ages due to continuing improvements in hygiene, education and medical advances (*see* Fig. 9.1).

Pure aging, however, is complicated by the phenomenon known as senescence, which, in iteroparous species like man, becomes apparent in the post-reproductive period and advances gradually as age increases, predisposing to death from accidents and disease.[2] The immune mechanisms of the body become compromised due to the effects of involution of the thymus; some cell types lose their capability of replication; presbyopia occurs as the lens of the eye loses its elasticity; and brain-mediated changes in endocrine function bring about, among other things, the menopause in women and similar, though less obvious, changes in men.

Environmental influences are also of great importance in determining the span of life, particularly when they are of an adverse nature and act on people showing more marked senescent changes. These influences may be chronic, as in long-standing cigarette smoking or alcohol abuse, or short-acting, as in severe psychic trauma. Thus, since senescence is a universal and intrinsic feature of the human species, the obvious way of reducing excess mortality would be to concentrate on correcting harmful influences in the environment.

Olshansky et al[3] attempted to estimate the amount of mortality reduction that would be required to achieve extreme longevity (80–120 years) and concluded that if hypothetical cures for the major degenerative diseases (cardiovascular and cancer) became available, overall mortality could be reduced by 75 percent; even so the authors considered it highly unlikely that life expectancy at birth would ever exceed the age of 85.

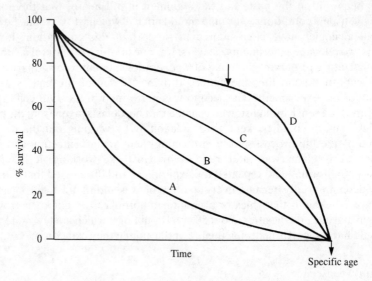

Fig. 9.1. The effect of improvements in hygiene on survival in humans and other iteroparous animals. People or animals living under feral conditions die at a constant rate from diseases and accidents (A). As conditions improve and death from diseases and accidents decreases, survival curves become more rectangular (B–D). Senescence can be defined as that part of the life span after the shoulder of the survival curve of individuals living under close to ideal conditions (arrow on curve D). Note that all survival curves cross the time axis at the same point (specific age), which is the theoretical upper limit of the species' life span. In the case of humans, this is between 115 and 120 years.
With kind permission of Dr J L Kirkland.

Much of our modern knowledge of the process of aging comes from research into molecular biology. The aging body loses some of its functions, particularly of self-adjustment and self-repair, which it had when young. This is due to loss of information in the cells themselves. Basic information is contained in deoxyribonucleic acid (DNA) which is responsible for storing the genetic code. Genes are made of DNA, the function of genes being to specify the sequence of amino acids that make up a protein. The protein may be an enzyme or part of a cellular structure such as connective tissue, skin or blood cells. Messenger ribonucleic acid (mRNA) conveys the blueprint of the genetic code from the nucleus to the site of protein synthesis on the ribosomes in the cytoplasm, where the amino acid sequence is manufactured.

During their lifetime cells may suffer damage to their DNA due to chemicals, ionizing radiation or viruses; mRNA will carry the damaged information, and consequently it will be translated into proteins or a new generation of cells which will in turn be abnormal. These errors in copying are repetitive and can escalate to such an extent that the cells may be treated as foreign by the body and attacked in much the same way as incompatible grafts.

In healthy youth, the body has a mechanism that can detect and rectify cell damage, which may only involve one isolated group of cells. With senescence, however, the quality-control mechanism appears to deteriorate, and the catastrophic escalation of abnormal cells emanating from the faulty RNA blueprint can result in serious organic disease, such as fibrinoid necrosis of the arterioles, inflammation of connective tissues or neoplasia itself. It is known that mortality due to cancer and blood vessel disease begins to increase from about the age of 45, long before true old age. If premature aging and chronic disease have to be regarded partly as the result of somatic mutation, it is equally necessary to emphasize the converse of this hypothesis: there must be some highly efficient mechanism by which the germ cells do *not* age prematurely. Thus it can be assumed that in people of sound constitution there is some efficient in-built mechanism for scrutinizing chromosomal damage of any sort that can either be corrected or immediately localized. This mechanism naturally becomes weaker as the natural span of human life approaches its limit, but why it should fail at relatively young age is the subject of the most intensive research.

All the evidence points to the importance of longevity in the parents as being a factor in the longevity of the offspring. Alexander Graham Bell found that the average age at death of those whose parents had both reached 80 was 52·7 years, whilst the average age at death of those whose parents had died below 60 was 32·8 years. Dublin et al[4] found in life insurance studies that the lowest mortality ratios were recorded for those whose parents were both living when insurance was issued, and the highest ratios occurred among those with both parents dead.

Although there is this close relationship between longevity of parents and offspring, it would be of great interest to know exactly what share is due to inherited biological soundness of stock and what share should be credited to environmental advantages enjoyed by offspring of the more long lived. The survival of parents to old age in most cases means a more protected and more favorable life for the children. Conversely, premature death of a parent or parents, even from accident, may mean the breaking up of the home, poor care for the children and even poverty. Any attempt to weight each factor separately is almost impossible because the influence of heredity and of environment are so closely interwoven.

It seems possible, however, that in the case of an early death of one or both parents, environment may be the more important factor in determining the potential length of life of the offspring. Man's increasing control over his environment, particularly regarding public health (e.g. improvements in nutrition and housing, and in the control of infection) has tended to mask the effects of heredity, especially in the younger age groups, where even those with a poor genetic composition can now be kept alive. Improvement in longevity of the general population in recent years is disproportionate to the negligible changes that have occurred in biological stock over a relatively short period, and must be ascribed to improvements in environmental conditions.

Around the middle of the 20th century the state of personal hygiene tended to be static and even retrograde; in the postwar period populations in the West were beginning to enjoy better living standards, but with them came the hazards of over-complex living and working conditions in urban communities together with various over-indulgencies (diet, smoking, alcohol and lack of exercise). At this time premature mortality from coronary artery disease, stroke, and cancer of the lung and bronchus reached alarming proportions. Realizing the seriousness of the situation, health authorities in the USA mounted vigorous campaigns to educate the public in the benefits of healthy living, especially about limitation of the amount of saturated fat and cholesterol in the diet, quitting smoking and taking regular physical exercise. Propaganda about the hazards of high blood pressure and the necessity for its control was continually fed to the population and, with the emerging availability of efficient antihypertensive drugs, mortality from stroke and hypertensive disease gradually fell until it is now at a very low level. Likewise, age-adjusted death rates from the major cardiovascular diseases has declined in the USA by more than 34 percent since about 1965.[3] It would appear, therefore, for the time being at least, that improvements in mortality at ages of 50 and over will be due almost entirely to two environmental factors: public health and advances in medical science.

MORBIDITY

The factors influencing morbidity are closely related to those influencing length of life; thus the pattern of disease occurring in a group of people is a very good guide to the probable life expectation of that group and may also be a useful prognostic index for individual cases. It is important, therefore, in life assurance work to be aware of the importance of different types of illness and to understand why they arise and the significance of their appearance in any particular applicant.

Illness or disease is not a state that occurs wholly by chance or bad luck. Those who have been endowed with a good biological constitution have the ability to resist disease much better than those who have not. In an epidemic of some virulent infection, such as poliomyelitis, the whole population, though at risk, is never completely overcome. Similarly, every top executive does not develop coronary thrombosis, hypertension or a duodenal ulcer. Also, the majority of those who develop influenza are well again within a few days whereas others may be incapacitated for several weeks, despite the fact that the infecting micro-organism and its virulence are the same.

What, therefore, is the basis of the biological constitution that enables the majority to escape infection in an epidemic, or to avoid the development of coronary thrombosis or duodenal ulcer despite the stresses of their occupation? What are the factors that predispose others to succumb? The answers to these questions could lead to a better understanding of the pattern of morbidity in man, and might also be helpful in estimating survivorship for life assurance purposes.

The manifold factors that decide the larger issues of health and disease in ourselves, our homes, our community and our nation are too complex as yet for comparable analysis, but the problem may be simplified for the purpose of illustration and still be of practical value to the clinician and to the underwriter dealing with selection for life assurance.

Constitution

The term 'constitution' or 'biological constitution' will be used frequently in this text, and some clear definition must be made at the outset. Constitution (or phenotype) may be defined as the totality of the physical and mental qualities and functions resulting from the interplay between heredity (genotype) and environment, which determine the general bodily health, the reaction to adverse circumstances, the resistance to disease and the personality of the individual.

Inheritance is determined by the genotype or pattern of genes at the moment of conception, and this may itself contain a varied number of mainly favourable or unfavourable characteristics. The environment may also be mainly favourable or unfavourable. Nurture is the provision or availability of all those factors in the environment – physical, psychoemotional or intellectual – that are predominantly favourable in their influence on the development of constitution, whereas lack of some or all of those nurturing factors would have an opposing and adverse effect on development.

Although environmental influences can affect constitution to some extent throughout life, the major moulding for good or bad takes place in the early formative years of infancy, childhood and adolescence; only minor changes can take place in the basic pattern after that. This is the constitution with which the individual has to sustain himself throughout the rest of his adult life, and its quality determines how he will react to his future environment.

The forces of environmental stress are always potentially damaging, and stimulate a physiological defence mechanism (i.e. the adaptation reaction). If the constitution is sound, the mechanism is successful in eliminating or minimizing any damage; if the constitution is unsound, the mechanism is overwhelmed, leading to the development of pathological lesions, presumably by a mechanism causing mutation of DNA in the cells of a target organ or tissue, and uncensored replication of abnormal proteins.

So, according to the genotype and the number of favourable and unfavourable environmental influences acting throughout life, the constitution may develop a pattern by which, over shorter or longer periods, health or disease may be experienced.

It has been shown (see p. 139) that one of the damaging influences in the maturing years is the death of one or both parents, due principally to environmental effects, but the actual cause of death itself is still very significant in that it may imply the existence of a bad genetic quality likely to be passed on to the offspring, and which along with any modifying factors in early environment would play its part in the formation of the biological constitution. An early parental death, even when the offspring is adolescent and well past the impressionable period of childhood, still has a bad genetic implication, particularly in deaths from certain causes. Causes that seem to be particularly conducive to unfavourable morbid traits in offspring are those involving the central nervous system, such as brain tumor, multiple sclerosis, Parkinsonism and presenile dementia. Other causes of death that are almost as unfavourable are carcinoma of stomach in either parent, or carcinoma of other organs in the mother alone.

There is also no doubt that the attainment of a sound constitution depends on a stable family unit consisting of both parents of good stock, sisters and, in the case of a male, at least one brother all enjoying robust health. On the other hand, there are several unfavourable factors in the early environment that have been found from experience to predispose to the development of an unsound constitution. One of the more important is neurosis in one or other parent, which inevitably results in domestic unhappiness and insecurity for the child. It is also very common to find that an only child, or the only boy among sisters, lacks a sound constitution unless his hereditary stock is extremely good and if it is not, the combination of poor genotype and the almost inevitably adverse environmental influences pertaining to the family situation can be very damaging indeed to the individual.

In the examination of young applicants, family history may be uninformative because insufficient information is known to the candidate; his parents usually would be relatively young and may not have developed any pathological condition sufficiently significant in the eyes of a young applicant. Also, if a parent has died when the applicant was an infant, the precise cause of death is very often unknown. In such circumstances the full value of family history is often lost.

Action and Reaction

The action of the forces of environment and the reaction of the bodily defence mechanisms may aptly be illustrated by a simple analogy from civil engineering.

A bridge built to sound structural design, employing the best of materials and workmanship, would outlast its guaranteed life, sustaining all sorts of stresses within or even above the specified limits. If we compare a bridge with the human organism, then the materials and design would represent hereditary characteristics, and the workmanship the early environmental moulding of these characteristics. The finished structure would then have a quality that could be compared with human biological constitution. In the case of a sound bridge, no amount of stress – represented by the volume of traffic passing over it – could cause damage, and the only possible chance of a crack appearing in the structure would be by applying a force far in excess of that which the bridge was guaranteed to withstand. So in a person of sound constitution, it would require some really excessive environmental insult to produce signs or symptoms of disease.

If, however, the bridge has been built to a faulty design, the materials used in its construction are not up to standard and the workmanship is not of the best, then trouble can be expected sooner or later. This bridge might be capable of withstanding the strain of ordinary traffic conditions but would be liable to develop cracks if the load should become heavier, despite the fact that it was still within the limits guaranteed by the engineer. Again applying the analogy to man, the faulty materials and design would in this case represent bad genetic traits, and the faulty workmanship an unfavourable early environment. The cracks in the structure would represent symptoms or signs of disease, which may appear as the result of only moderate environmental stress.

In both the bridge and the human organism, stress cracks tend to appear at the point of maximum weakness, which is usually genetically determined (i.e. target systems); thus disease of the respiratory tract in offspring is common when there is a history of, say, chronic bronchitis or emphysema in either parent. Similarly, Type II diabetes in forebears predisposes to the development of diabetes in offspring. Other appropriate examples come easily to mind.

A bridge that has to be continually repaired after use by even the lightest traffic would be a poor bridge indeed; sometimes the same state of affairs exists in man. A history of recurrent sickness over a long period would usually imply a rather poor biological constitution, especially if the precipitating factors were very ordinary and of a degree that would as a rule cause little or no impact on an average healthy individual. In such cases, a glance at the family history and a brief inquiry into the circumstances of early childhood would probably reveal sufficient reason for the recurrent lapses in health.

In order to make the contrast perfectly clear, the ideal bridge or better-than-average life has been compared with the faulty bridge or substandard or bad life. In underwriting, however, one is dealing mostly with average lives, which make up about 80 percent of the total (the remainder being accounted for by better-than-average, substandard and declined lives), so that if the analogy is to be applied correctly it is necessary to think in terms of an average bridge. Just as an average structure would require maintenance and repair of small or moderate defects due to occasional extraordinary stresses, so would the average healthy life suffer from occasional sickness not usually of a serious or life-endangering nature, and still be good enough to be classified as a standard risk.

Stress Diseases

A stress disease or disorder has been defined as one that has arisen because of failure to adapt successfully to a situation, or inability, often for subconscious reasons, to solve a frustrating problem. The term is still applied to only a few of the more obvious and easily understood conditions (e.g. anxiety reactions, dyspepsia and tension headache) but several of the more complex disorders have also been recognized as being stress-induced (e.g. rheumatoid arthritis and the collagen group of diseases). In fact, most disease, whether functional or organic, mental or physical, can probably be traced to faulty adaptation, the mechanism of which is in continuous activity in response to environment.

The extent of failure of adaptation depends, as has been pointed out on previous pages, on the severity of environmental stress on the one hand, which is always translated into psychical stress by the receptor areas of the brain, and the quality of personal biological constitution on the other; the type of illness resulting can range from the most insignificant and temporary to the most severe and fatal. The mechanism whereby a breakdown in adaptation is transformed into recognizable symptoms or actual tissue pathology is one of the most fascinating problems in modern medicine; at the moment it is the subject of intensive research by immunologists and molecular biologists.

Neuronal transmission by way of the vegetative nervous system is probably the simplest pathway by which the psyche affects the soma in response to faulty adaptation. As far back as 1935, Zondek[5] drew attention to the effect of emotional disturbance on certain bodily functions, such as metabolism, circulation, menstruation and appetite, and showed that changes in function were under the control of the vegetative nervous system with its nuclei in the hypothalamus. Faulty adaptation can, therefore, alter the rhythm of the functions under its control (e.g. sleep, respiration or pulse rate).

A hormonal mechanism linking environment with somatic disease was established when Selye, in 1941, demonstrated how depletion of certain steroid hormones in the adrenal cortex following a breakdown in adaptation could lead to non-specific inflammatory changes in certain tissues. Later, Hench and his co-workers,[6] applying Selye's theory, were able to reverse the inflammatory changes of rheumatoid arthritis by the administration of cortisone or its stimulating hormone corticotropin (ACTH). Other corticosteroid fractions have since been isolated and are in common use today as immunosuppressive agents.

As mentioned earlier, intensive research is currently being focused on the relationship between somatic mutation and chronic disease. Severe environmental stress – infective (particularly viral), traumatic (ionizing radiation, chemical poisons, drugs) or possibly psychological – can cause damage to the genetic molecule. Experimentally, viral DNA can be linked with host DNA in certain strains of mice to alter the genetic code and produce leukemia, and Burkitt's lymphoma in humans is almost invariably associated with the Epstein–Barr virus, although it is not yet definitely proven to be the cause. Somatic mutation can give rise to 'forbidden' clones of cells which, if not suppressed, can multiply catastrophically and produce antibodies against certain of the host's tissues causing widespread cell damage. Many diseases are now known to be due to this autoimmune reaction, such as Hashimoto's thyroiditis, acquired hemolytic anemia, Addison's disease, disturbances of lipid metabolism, atheroma, intravascular thrombosis, ulceration of the alimentary tract and probably cancer. Even the phenomenon of immunity and susceptibility to bacterial or viral invasion – a problem as yet unsolved – is dependent on good or faulty adaptation, whatever the final mechanism may turn out to be.

Despite the universal prevalance of the unsound biological constitution, medical science is becoming increasingly skillful at repairing the stress cracks in the human bridge. Advances in public health, together with social measures by enlightened governments all over the world, are tending to ease at least part of the load of environmental traffic, with the consequent improvement in general mortality. If, in addition, it were possible to alter for the better genes carrying unfavorable characteristics (genetic engineering), premature deaths in late middle life and early old age might be largely eliminated, thus extending length of life for the great majority to the biological limit for the human species (*see* p. 138).

THE CHANGING PATTERN OF MORTALITY

Comparison of the life tables of 50 years ago and now reveals the striking improvement in mortality that has occurred particularly in younger age groups over a relatively short period; an improvement due almost entirely to elimination of infectious diseases as a significant cause of death. Improvement in the age group 45–65, although much less, is also due not only to fewer deaths from infection but also to other advances, such as better medical, surgical and diagnostic techniques, and changes in personal hygiene.

Elimination of infectious illness as a major cause of mortality has had the effect of increasing the longevity of many young individuals possessing an inferior constitution, some of whom would otherwise have succumbed had it not been for the availability of chemotherapeutic drugs and antibiotics. As these people grow older they eventually enter the dangerous age group (from the age of 45 onwards) when the degenerative and neoplastic diseases begin to take their toll, and for which no outstanding therapeutic countermeasures have yet been found. It is not surprising, therefore, that many of those constitutionally susceptible persons will be caught prematurely in the finer meshes of the net comprising those more mortal diseases. In other words, the basically unfit now live on, only to be challenged later by a stiffer examination.

The pattern of diseases affecting man may be depicted by a spectrum (*see* Fig. 9.2). The simplest forms of disease – the protozoal and bacterial infections – occupy the extreme left-hand end, followed successively by diseases that become increasingly complex in etiology and pathology the further to the right in the spectrum they appear. The extreme right-hand end of the spectrum is occupied by the degenerative tissue disorders. As medical science advances, improvement in mortality will be seen to spring from the successful control, first of the simplest diseases at the extreme left of the spectrum, followed successively by those immediately adjacent in a left to right direction.

The bacterial diseases have been progressively conquered by sulphonamides, penicillin and the broad-spectrum antibiotics, the first to succumb being the gram-positive bacteria, followed by the gram-negative, and later by others of higher

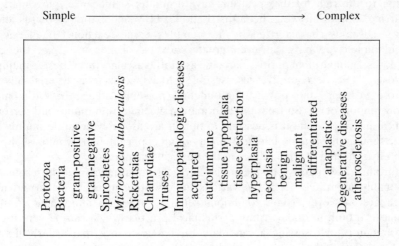

Fig. 9.2. Spectrum showing the transition of disease types from the most simple to the most complex.

order. Spirochetal diseases have also been controlled to a large extent, and in the past 30 years tuberculosis has been tamed by chemotherapy.

The first recognition of a compound with potent antiviral activity came in 1957 with the discovery of interferons. Since then various synthetic anti-virals against specific viruses have been developed, notably acyclovir, which is active against herpes simplex virus 1 and 2 and varicella zoster. With the recognition of the retrovirus human immunodeficiency virus (HIV) 1 and 2 as a cause of AIDS, much research has gone into the production of a suitable antiviral agent. Partial success has been achieved by the drugs zidovudin and foscarnet, which can prevent HIV replicating, but they do not eliminate the infection itself (*see* Chapter 28).

In recent years outstanding advances have been made in the chemotherapy of germ cell malignancies of the testis, teratoma and choriocarcinoma, trophoblastic disease in the female and Wilm's tumor in infancy, but beyond this there have been no significant advances in the treatment of other cancerous tumors. Limited success has been achieved in the prevention of atherosclerotic disease of the heart by public and personal health measures, but the back of the problem has yet to be broken.

SIGNIFICANCE OF DISEASE TYPES

The severity of an illness, as well as the type of illness suffered, is a good indication of an individual's personal quality of resistance. The more complex the pathological process, in other words the further to the right of the spectrum (*see* Fig. 9.2) it appears, the more significant becomes its importance for future morbidity and long-term mortality. Thus the simple bacterial infections at the extreme left of the spectrum have little importance in relation to immediate or long-term mortality, whereas diseases caused by the higher order of viruses further to the right of the spectrum have a greater significance, particularly if occurring sporadically (e.g. hepatitis B and C, HIV and cytomegalovirus infections). Diseases characterized by the complex tissue reactions of allergic or autoimmune type have an even greater adverse significance (e.g. the collagenoses, glomerulonephritis, sarcoidosis, intravascular thrombosis, multiple sclerosis). The degenerative diseases of cell aging, such as arterial atherosclerosis, cancer, and physical and mental presenile states, have the most serious import of all. So from the information gleaned from family and personal medical histories alone it is possible to obtain a reasonably accurate impression of the temperament and biological quality of an applicant. This would usually be faithfully reflected by the findings of the physical examination.

Mortality associated with the major medical impairments can be estimated reasonably accurately from the various underwriting manuals in current use. There are, however, some conditions often regarded as minor and of little significance both in underwriting and clinical practice which can be very useful discriminators in assessing a candidate for life assurance, particularly if they have occurred within a short period of application. Therefore, more attention might be paid to some of those subtleties that otherwise would go unnoticed unless specially looked for. By drawing attention to these conditions, there is no intention of implying that an individual would be a substandard life if he has a history of one, or even two or three of them. Their significance must be viewed in the context of the whole clinical picture, which, if borderline, would enable a better appraisal of the risk to be made both for permanent health and life contracts.

Perennial Rhinitis, Hay Fever

Rhinitis, whether of the perennial or pollen type, is usually regarded as more of a nuisance than anything more profound. However, people with such a history usually suffer infections badly, as was shown by Bendowski,[7] who made a personal study of the reactions of a large group of allergic patients in general practice during an epidemic of Asian strain influenza, comparing them with a similar group of non-allergic subjects. It was found that the allergic patients were more severely affected by the infection and developed bronchitis, asthma and pneumonia much more readily; the incidence of after effects was also much higher. The rhinitis sufferer reacts similarly to other infectious and non-infectious diseases and is generally more prone to excessive morbidity, and possibly slightly increased mortality.

Dermatoses

As a broad group, dermatoses or eczematides are almost always the external manifestation of a faulty adaptation to stress. All are localized to the skin and are of no danger to life in themselves; some may be markers of systemic disease in target organs that have become involved as the result of maladaptation to the same stress factor that produced the skin lesion.

Piles, Proctalgia, Pruritus Ani

Anal symptomatology is apt to embrace a rather heterogeneous group of conditions, ranging from the most serious to the most benign. Excluding neoplasia, these conditions are usually considered to be of little importance in themselves as regards danger to life, but when the symptoms they produce are demanding they should be viewed with some reserve, for they seem to be associated with some underlying emotional disturbance with a frequency that is more than coincidental. So if the history is recent, the medical examiner should be alerted to the possibility of incipient pathological processes developing elsewhere in response to the same stress force, particularly in people of known brittle constitution.

Thrombophlebitis, Phlebitis

In the *1951 Impairment Study*[8] a mortality ratio of 140 percent was found in the group of insured lives with a history of phlebitis, not just of recent onset but at any time prior to application. This was an unexpected finding, but it underlines the fact that such a history should not be too readily dismissed when assessing the long-term prognosis of applicants for life insurance.

In addition to the better known factors predisposing to thrombophlebitis, a personal or constitutional susceptibility also seems to be necessary for the full development of this potentially dangerous lesion. To those clinicians who enquire carefully into the environmental circumstances immediately preceding the onset of intravascular thrombosis, a history of psychic trauma of some form or another is almost always obtainable. It may be that there is a failure of adaptation in susceptible persons, which sets in motion some mechanism not yet wholly understood, resulting in abnormal coagulability of the blood. Harper[9] has made some observations on the biopathology of the condition. It has been shown in the rabbit that there is an increased coagulability of the blood when it is frightened, being a reflex defence mechanism enabling the animal to preserve its blood volume by efficient coagulation if wounded; the same evolutionary mechanism is perpetuated in man and can be brought into play under adverse conditions of environment. Careful observations over many years convinced Harper that, in certain cases, fear or lack of confidence by a sensitive patient plays a significant part in the onset of phlebothrombosis. These individuals have a temperament that disposes them to worry and to feel abnormal fear and anxiety, and one is reminded of the great increase in thrombophlebitis of the leg veins in those who used air-raid shelters in London during World War II. They sat for long periods on rather uncomfortable benches, the occurrence of thrombosis being attributed to prolonged immobilization in an uncomfortable position, but the influence of fear in those of susceptible constitution was never examined.

Many nervous patients react unfavorably to the often unconcealed events of a general ward and the fear of an impending operation; it is patients of such temperament who are especially vulnerable to phlebothrombosis when immobilized. Although thrombosis may sometimes occur spontaneously in an apparently healthy vessel, it is more common for it to occur on surfaces where the vascular endothelium has been damaged by phlebitis or trauma.

It would be true to say that once a person has shown himself susceptible to intravascular thrombosis, further episodes are more likely to occur, possibly in a position that could threaten life. It follows, therefore, that a history of phlebothrombosis in an applicant for life assurance must be viewed rather critically in the light of the findings of the *1951 Impairment Study*[8] and also in relation to the circumstances of its occurrence, and the type of person in whom it occurs.

Intervertebral Disc Syndrome

Ever since Mixter and Barr[10] demonstrated the role played by the prolapsed nucleus pulposus in the production of sciatic and other root pain, the materialistic view that the condition is a purely mechanical one has held sway, and observations of the older school of physicians indicating a close association between sciatica and emotional conflicts were forgotten. In recent years, however, the pendulum has begun to swing back, albeit rather slowly and grudgingly. Of all the joints in the body the spine is probably the best protected, particularly in the lumbar region (by powerful muscle groups). Moreover, healthy discs do not prolapse. So is there some prior pathologic process at work that affects the intervertebral unit causing the annulus to rupture in response to some, often minor, stress applied to the spine in an unguarded moment? Depression is a not infrequent accompaniment to disc lesions, and this is usually ascribed to prolonged, painful symptoms following the prolapse. This is undoubtedly true in some instances, but it is more likely that the depression is reactive to the psychic trauma that initiated the pathologic process in the intervertebral disc and annulus in the first place. Close enquiry will often reveal a history of some unsettling life event prior to the onset of symptoms of a prolapsed disc: for example, a death in the immediate family, a financial crisis, or sometimes lesser personal problems.

Hanraets[11] who has had a vast experience of the subject, takes the view that intervertebral disc lesions are not the strictly localized conditions previously thought, but are usually manifestations of a widespread degenerative process affecting not only the spine, but often the whole patient, including his psychological reactions. He found that the determining factors were mainly congenital anomalies, injury and an inherited diathesis. Although a history of prolapsed disc as such is of little interest to the life underwriter, it is of great importance to the underwriter dealing with permanent health insurance, since 'bad backs' feature prominently in the list of claims for disability.

Squint

Squint is a disorder that tends to originate in early childhood, being due to functional inco-ordination of the extraocular muscles traceable to abnormal tensions arising from a faulty family environment. The late effect of neglected squint is often an amblyopic or partially amblyopic eye. When a medical history is otherwise negative, the finding of squint or amblyopia is sometimes a useful guide to the biological constitution of an applicant.

Congenital Malformations

The presence of congenital malformations, even the most trivial, appears to be associated with an unusually high incidence of psychosomatic and related illnesses that have a manifest relationship to environmental stress. Why this should be so is not clear, but there is evidently some link with bad hereditary characteristics. Recent work by geneticists has shown that in conditions such as Marfan's syndrome there is a close genetic linkage of superficially trivial anatomic characters with grave hereditary pathologies. Even variations in relative length of the toes or the presence of supernumerary nipples have a significance. Harper,[9] who has made careful personal observations of patients with supernumerary nipples over many years, is convinced that those with well-marked skin vestiges are especially liable to illness manifestly precipitated by stressful situations. But, as is often the case, it is difficult to say how much the pattern of these illnesses is genetically determined and how much is due to environmental influences. Out of 191 personally observed cases of diabetes, Harper[9] found supernumerary nipples present as follows: perfect, 9; significant, 48; doubtful, 12. Disregarding the doubtful examples, the incidence of this congenital abnormality in the series is over 30 percent, compared with a generally accepted incidence of about 1 percent in the general population. This is significant beyond any doubt, and such lesions, however trivial they may appear to be, should be recorded; they should lead to a close search for other impairments, congenital or otherwise. It is useful to remember that it is usually the first-born male who bears the brunt of congenital defects.

An hereditary characteristic that is easy to examine and code is the color of the iris. An interesting observation has been made by Sutton,[12] who tested the pain reaction of 403 consecutive subjects to a reasonably constant stimulus – the dentist's drill – and compared it with iris color. He found that the more blue the eyes the less the reaction and as the color changed through blue-grey, green, hazel, light brown and dark brown so the reaction to pain increased. On retesting the findings were consistent. Despite Sutton's findings, it is likely that environmental influences early in life play an equally important role in determining a person's threshold to pain. Nevertheless, it might be informative to study the frequency and duration of morbidity in relation to iris color in those disorders where pain is the presenting symptom, particularly the indeterminate type of pain often labeled fibrositis, backache or soft tissue rheumatism.

Arcus Senilis: Corneal Arcus

In a way, the term arcus senilis is a misnomer: although the marginal ring of grey, fatty material that is deposited in the substance of the cornea is certainly seen more often in old age, the early stages also occur not infrequently in the young. On the other hand, the incidence of arcus senilis increases with age, and over the age of 60 it is a very common finding. Arcus senilis may be said, therefore, to be a sign of aging and, when it occurs in the young, a sign of premature aging, albeit only at the cellular or enzymatic level concerned with lipid transport, and then possibly only episodic in relation to isolated but recurring stressful situations.

In most young people seen by the author, some only in the third decade, there was a consistent association between the presence of a corneal arcus and chronic tension states, often manifesting as physical disorders. An apt analogy may be drawn from forestry. If the cross-section of a felled tree is examined, the rings formed annually during growth can be seen. By inspecting these for a malformed ring, the expert can identify a year in which the tree was under climatic stress.

Friedman and Rosenman[13] found that arcus senilis occurred frequently in those showing a behavior pattern characterized by an intense, sustained drive to achieve self-selected (but usually poorly defined) goals, profound inclination and eagerness to compete, persistent desire for recognition and advancement, continual involvement in multiple and diverse functions constantly subject to time restrictions, habitual propensity to accelerate the rate of execution of many physical and mental functions, and extraordinary mental and physical alertness. On the other hand, no close association was found between arcus senilis and those having a diametrically opposed behavior pattern.

A feature even more striking than the difference in incidence of arcus senilis was the fivefold increase in incidence of coronary artery disease in those of the former behavior pattern group compared with the latter. Despite the fact that a corneal arcus is one of the manifestations of Types II and III hyper-lipoproteinemia, it is unusual to find a consistently raised serum cholesterol level in individuals discovered by chance to have a corneal arcus, presumably because the stressful event that caused a temporary elevation of circulating lipids and deposition in the corneae at the time has now passed. Nevertheless, it is always worthwhile checking the lipoprotein profile when an arcus is found at an earlier age than expected.

HEALTH SCREENING

The examples presented above are only a few among many of the impairments which, although minor in themselves, are often warning signs of an underlying disorder of the whole organism and which, to the discerning, signify possible excess morbidity and mortality. Their appearance is probably of more interest to physicians engaged in preventive medicine and in the selection of applicants for life and health insurance than to clinicians whose primary concern is with patients who are already ill. Nevertheless, prognostic signs that have a bearing on future health and that are found in individuals who are apparently well (or even in patients undergoing investigation of symptoms) should be heeded; correction of possible underlying defects by, for example, changes in life style or other interventions could benefit many who might otherwise fall victim to later disease.

It was against this background of preventive medicine that regular medical checks gained popularity, first with large companies and corporations wishing to minimize sickness and premature deaths among key executives. Later a similar service was extended to other employees. Today, health screening has become established as an important feature of the current medical scene with services being provided by specialized units utilizing a vast array of investigational procedures. General practitioners, too, whose armamentarium is less imposing, provide just as valuable a service.

Health screening has been criticized by some as an unnecessary luxury which is barely cost-effective when applied to a well population. This might be so if examinations are carried out too frequently on people whose initial screening has been shown to be unexceptionable. On the other hand, if these examinations are sensibly spaced considering age and findings on initial screening, they can be valuable for checking risk factors and the progress of other medical conditions found previously, thus leading to prompt correction when necessary. In these circumstances the health and efficiency of the individual can be greatly enhanced.

JOB SCREENING

Where certain occupations demand people of high caliber, it should be possible to make an initial screening of candidates with information obtained from a full medical examination similar to that for life insurance supplemented by past medical records from the attending physician. The resulting data should be sufficient to identify individuals having the necessary physical and psychological properties required for the job. A final selection could then be made using specialized screening tests appropriate to the particular occupation. Some of the highly responsible jobs for which aspirants need the most careful selection are captains or pilots of civil and military aircraft, commanders of nuclear submarines and astronauts.

CONCLUSION

Although the purpose of this chapter has been to show how the good and bad points of biological constitution can be picked out and analysed, the good being extolled to the detriment of the bad, it must be remembered that the aim has been to identify the potentially long-lived from the short-lived, to separate the better-than-average from the average, and the average from the substandard. It cannot be denied, however, that there frequently exist some excellent qualities, even genius, in those of poor biological stock. Through the ages, valuable contributions have been made to literature, poetry, the theatre, science and medicine by people who because of constitutional inferiority have died young. On the other hand, the ideal individual from the point of view of longevity is often a very dull person, and life would probably be terribly uninteresting if everyone were cast in the same perfect biological mould; an assured span of 100 years might be no recompense for the loss of the infinite variety in all walks of life which characterizes the world as we know it today. Eugenics may after all have some disadvantages.

REFERENCES

1 Fisher I. Am J Pub Health 1927.
2 Kirkland JL. Insurance and the elderly: biological and clinical considerations in risk estimation. On the Risk 1990; 7 nl: 29–31.
3 Olshansky SJ, Carnes BA, Cassel C. In search of Methuselah: estimating the upper limits to human longevity. Science 1990; 250: 634–640.
4 Dublin LI, Lotka AJ, Spiegelman M. Length of Life, revd. edn. New York: The Ronald Press, 1949.
5 Zondek H. The Disease of the Endocrine Glands. London: Edward Arnold, 1935.
6 Hench PS, Kendall EC, Slocumb CH, Polly HF. Mayo Clin Proc 1949; 24: 181.
7 Bendowski B. Asian influenza (1957) in allergic patients. Br Med J 1958; 2: 1314.
8 1951 Impairment Study. New York: Society of Actuaries, 1954.
9 Harper RMD. Evolution and illness. Lancet 1958; 2: 92.
10 Mixter WJ, Barr JS. Rupture of the intervertebral disc with involvement of the spinal canal. N Engl J Med 1934; 211: 210.
11 Hanraets PMRJ. The degenerative back and its differential diagnosis. Amsterdam: Elsevier, 1959.
12 Sutton PRN. Association between colour of the iris of the eye and reaction to dental pain. Nature 1959; 184: 122.
13 Friedman M, Rosenman H. Association of specific overt behavior pattern with blood and cardiovascular findings. Blood cholesterol level, blood clotting time, incidence of arcus senilis, and clinical coronary artery disease. JAMA 1959; 169: 1286.

CHAPTER 10

THE MEDICAL EXAMINATION

R D C BRACKENRIDGE
RICHARD S CROXSON

Although it is not the intention of this chapter to teach clinical methods, several of the more important points in the history taking and physical examination that are especially important from the life insurance point of view are dealt with in some detail.

The chapter concentrates on data derived from medically examined business, which in the UK is still the favored method of gathering underwriting information. In North America paramedical examinations now outnumber medically examined business, and these are discussed later in the chapter. Non-medical business —medical data derived from the application alone, or in conjunction with a medical attendant's report (MAR) or an attending physician's statement (APS)—will not be discussed here.

It is not commonly realized that the medical and other confidential reports pertaining to a proposal for life assurance provide a unique and comprehensive socioclinical record of an individual that is not normally obtainable in any other field of medicine. The records include details of personal sickness from early life, including any special examinations or investigations carried out, a fully documented family history, a thorough clinical examination covering all systems, and independent observations on personal habits, business morals, financial status and domestic circumstances. When properly conducted, the medical examination itself probably allows for a more complete appraisal of an individual than many examinations carried out in ordinary clinical practice, since the latter tend to be concerned more with the presenting illness to the exclusion very often of other conditions not of immediate importance. The value of an accurate detailed history and observation of physical signs cannot be over-emphasized; it is the physician's 'secret weapon' in practice. Nothing he does pays greater dividends in relation to the time spent (or costs less) than a meticulous clinical examination, and this is even more true today, when there is a tendency to devalue accurate clinical information in favor of high technology investigations.

The examination for life assurance does in fact provide a very satisfying clinical exercise, the equivalent of which can rarely be achieved in the ordinary day-to-day routine of general practice, mainly because of pressure of work and lack of time. It is not often that a completely documented personal history, family history and physical examination can be carried out on a patient outside the unhurried atmosphere of consulting practice. However, it provides a valuable opportunity for those general practitioners interested in life insurance medicine to develop a technique of examination that is perfectly adaptable to ordinary clinical practice and that, being comprehensive, is much appreciated by patients.

The whole examination should take no more than half an hour on average, possibly 40 minutes for difficult cases and a little less for straightforward ones. It is advisable to work to a set plan both for history taking and physical examination, so that each system is considered in turn, keeping to the same routine for each patient. By so doing, very few important details should escape detection.

If additional investigations are requested by home office, either because of the sum insured or to elucidate a prior abnormality in the applicant's history, it is convenient and cost effective to try and obtain such information at the time of examination, which may mean the inclusion of, for example, urinary screens, blood tests, electrocardiograms and lung function tests. It is also an ideal time to obtain a sample of blood, saliva or urine for HIV antibody testing if requested by the company, and to carry out pre-test counseling. HIV antibody testing is now accepted as standard practice for sums insured above a certain limit; current North American and UK practice is discussed at length in Chapter 28.

Having completed his report the examiner should, by studying the number of deviations from ideal that have occurred, be able to assess fairly accurately the type of person he has examined, his mental status, his general adaptability, whether or not he tends to react abnormally to stress (either by functional or organic illness), and what his outlook might be. In compiling his report, the examining doctor should also ask himself if what he has written will be understood by other physicians. Have important points in the history been amplified? Have the reasons for any specialized investigations performed in the past been made clear? Has comment been made on deviations from normal in the physical examination?

Each life office has its own medical report form which has been evolved over the years, and which very often reflects the individuality of the office and the particular likes and dislikes of the chief medical officer (CMO). Ideally report forms should be designed to elicit the maximum amount of relevant information from personal history in as few well chosen questions as possible. Many forms do succeed in this aim, but there are a few that are so ill-planned as to be tiresome and needlessly time consuming.

PERSONAL HISTORY

After entering details of name, age and marital status, the occupation of the applicant should be noted as precisely as possible. Some occupations that may in fact be hazardous are often disguised in general terms such as company director, manager or foreman; such non-descriptive designations should always be qualified by the type of work the applicant is engaged in.

In eliciting medical history it is best to avoid a general enquiry about past events: unlike a private patient seeking advice, an applicant for life insurance is only going to disclose his medical history in response to specific questions. A common reply to too general an inquiry is 'minor illnesses only', but what may seem minor to the examinee may turn out to be significant when viewed in the context of the examination findings as a whole. Further information about so-called minor illnesses should always be sought so that their significance, or otherwise, can be appraised by the examining physician himself.

The following plan of questioning has been found useful by the author for immediately and quickly eliciting the major features in medical history, thus providing a framework on which the finer details of historical events can then be hung. Enquiry should be made regarding:

1) All surgical operations that may have been carried out.
2) Any serious accidents or injuries.
3) Hospitalization or institutional care for any other reason.
4) When the applicant last consulted his own or any other doctor, and for what reason (an important piece of evidence).
5) Consultations with, or investigations by, any other doctor or specialist on an out-patient basis, or routine health screening examinations.
6) What treatment, if any, is being prescribed or taken currently.
7) How much time has been lost from work in the past three years and the reason for this.

This plan would usually enable an examiner to elicit nine-tenths of significant history, and further enquiry regarding the systems not already touched upon should make it reasonably complete.

When documenting an event in medical history the date or year of its occurrence should always be stated and also the duration of symptoms or incapacity. In reports received by head office one sometimes sees answers such as 'indigestion' unqualified by dates or further amplification, and as such would be of little or no value to an underwriter. The history should be qualified by a brief description of what the applicant means by indigestion, the relieving and aggravating factors, how long it lasted, what investigations were carried out and with what results.

Similar remarks apply to the very commonly reported symptom 'pain in the chest', which could mean anything from insignificant musculoskeletal twinges to the pain of ischemic heart disease. A few pointed questions about the site of pain, its severity, character, radiation and relationship to effort, respiration, posture and food should enable the examining physician to form some opinion of its significance, whether obviously atypical, possibly suggestive of a cardiac origin or almost certainly ischemic heart disease (e.g. typical effort angina). Such information would enable the CMO to decide whether to disregard the symptom altogether or to seek further information from the applicant's attending physician, or to arrange further tests, such as an exercise ECG. Under the heading X-rays or other specialized investigations, one should always state the reason why an investigation was carried out, if this has not already been indicated in the history: for example, a chest X-ray may have been taken either as a purely routine procedure, such as mass miniature radiography, or because of some morbid symptom, such as hemoptysis. The date and result of the most recent chest X-ray examination should be recorded since knowledge of even a negative report would convey useful information to the underwriter, indicating that no serious pathology existed in the lungs at the time and that the heart size and contours were also normal.

Finally, a note should be made of the applicant's tobacco and alcohol usage, the latter qualified by the number and type of drinks consumed per day or week (*see* Chapter 30), the amount of exercise taken and participation in any unusual leisure activities.

FAMILY HISTORY

It is important to obtain as accurate a family history as possible since the information is of definite value to the underwriter: very often a decision to accept a borderline life as standard or substandard may ultimately depend on the family history. Although an applicant may state that his parents are alive and well, it is good practice to enquire if they have ever suffered any important illness in the past, such as a stroke, myocardial infarction or depression. Too often one sees the terms 'not known' or 'natural' entered under cause of death. In such circumstances, particularly if the parents died prematurely, the underwriter would have no option but to put the worst interpretation on the cause of death, causing an injustice to be done through no fault of the applicant. He should be encouraged to recall even the approximate details of a death in the family, such as the nature of the terminal illness, the organ or organs involved, and whether death was sudden and unexpected. The examiner may then be able to make some interpretation of the cause of death that would be useful to the underwriter.

Applicants are sometimes reticent about disclosing a suicide in the family and try to disguise the fact by using the term 'accident'. When a death is reported as accidental it is always best to qualify it by cause (e.g. road or rail accident, scald or burn, electrocution, drowned while bathing, etc). If suspicion still remains that a fatal accident may have been self-inflicted, one should ask what was the coroner's verdict.

If the applicant is married it is sometimes helpful to know the age and health of the spouse, and the ages and health of any children.

The significance attached to the various causes of death and ages at death as it affects selection is discussed under the appropriate impairments in later chapters.

PHYSICAL EXAMINATION

The first part of the examination report deals with a general description of the applicant, his height, weight, and measurements round the chest and abdomen. From these details the life underwriter can obtain at a glance a good mental image of the examinee.

Height and Weight

Ideally the most accurate record of build would be obtained by measuring barefoot height and naked weight, but to do so would be needlessly time consuming and inconvenient. In practice it has been found that to weigh in normal indoor clothes and shoes, and measure height in shoes with ordinary heels is a perfectly satisfactory method of documenting build. This allows reasonable consistency between examiner and examiner, company and company, and between companies in different countries. All mortality statistics of insured lives relating to build have been calculated on height and weight measured as stated, and rating tables, which are largely based on these statistics, use similar criteria of measurement. Moreover, the method has the advantage of convenience both for applicant and examiner. The weight of a man's indoor clothes and shoes is remarkably constant, about 6 to 9 lb (2·7 to 4 kg) depending on build, and the heels of ordinary shoes measure ¾ to 1 in (2·0 to 2·5 cm). If by the dictates of fashion the heels of some men's shoes are found to be extraordinarily high (or in the case of women), one has no option but to measure height without shoes; this fact should be stated in the report so that the underwriter can adjust the measurement before entering the build rating tables.

Well designed report forms always ask whether height has been measured with or without shoes, and request that weight be measured in ordinary indoor clothes with shoes.

General Description

For the physical examination the applicant should be stripped to the waist with trousers or skirt loosened or removed. Any lesser exposure is bad practice, for sooner or later some important physical sign in the region of the neck or lower abdomen will be missed. Moreover, the applicant will obtain a rather poor impression of the thoroughness of the examination.

An adequate description of the applicant in as few words as possible is quite an art, and one which has to be cultivated. The main points to record are as follows: (1) the type of build, whether light, medium or heavy, and whether the bony mass is big or small; (2) the amount and distribution of any excess weight, and whether this is composed mainly of fat or muscle or both; (3) whether active and athletic looking or flabby; (4) whether the complexion is fresh and healthy or sallow and pasty. Any suggestion of plethora of the face or conjunctivae should be recorded.

By classifying body build according to morphological type, a mental picture of an individual can be conveyed with the use of only one or two descriptive terms; Sheldon's classification[1] of body physique is probably the most widely known and succinct of these. He divides morphological characteristics into three main components: endomorphy, mesomorphy and ectomorphy (i.e. fatness, muscularity and linearity) (see Fig. 10.1). A person may exhibit the extreme characteristics of one type to the exclusion of the others, or there may be a combination of two types in varying proportions (see also pp. 198–200). The main characteristics of each of the three main components are listed below.

Endomorphy

There is general roundness and softness of the body with central concentration of mass, the abdominal and thoracic volumes predominating over the extremities, and the abdomen predominating over the thorax. The limbs are short and tapering and the extremities weak, the hands and feet being comparatively small. The thighs and upper arms are rounded and 'hammed', and muscle relief is absent. The head is large and almost spherical in extreme cases, and the face wide. Bony projections are not seen, and there is loss of dimpling at the lateral aspect of the buttocks. The endomorph has pubic hair of feminine distribution; there is often hair at the breasts and over the scapulae, and sometimes over the deltoids. The external genitals are typically hypotrophic.

Ectomorphy

This is characterized by linearity and decentralization of structure. The trunk is relatively short and the limbs relatively long. The abdomen is flat and shallow, whereas the thorax is long relative to the abdomen. Drooping of the shoulders is a constant feature, and they are narrow and lack muscular relief. The limbs are long, especially in relation to the distal segments, giving the appearance of weak thighs and upper arms. The muscles are slight and thready, with no tendency to bunching. In the head the most constant finding is a relatively small facial mass as compared with the cranial, and the features of the face are uniformally small, sharp and fragile. It presents a triangular appearance, the apex being at the chin. The lips are delicate and thin. The pubic hair may vary greatly and may be of either masculine or feminine distribution. The external genitals have typical linear hypertrophy.

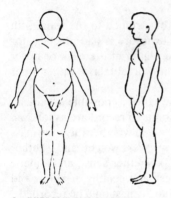

1. EXTREME ENDOMORPHY

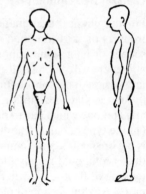

3. EXTREME ECTOMORPHY

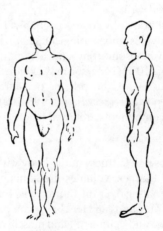

2. EXTREME MESOMORPHY

Fig. 10.1. Build types. (1) Extreme endomorphy, (2) extreme mesomorphy, (3) extreme ectomorphy.

Mesomorphy

The typical characteristic of mesomorphy is the squareness and hardness of the body. It is rugged, massive and muscular, the bones being large and prominent, with the muscles thrown into relief. There is no central concentration of mass as in the endomorph, and the limbs are strong, being as bulky in the distal segments as in the proximal. Thoracic volume predominates over abdominal, and the waist is relatively slender. The head varies in size but is generally of the cubical type, the bones being heavy and prominent. The facial mass is comparatively great compared with the cephalic. The skin is thick and coarse, and the pubic hair has the masculine distribution. The external genitals are compact and of average development.

In order to classify any particular individual, Sheldon[1] used a seven-point scale for each component of the build, each component being designated by three digits, the first representing endomorphy, the second mesomorphy and the third ectomorphy. The numeral 7 indicates the greatest number of characteristics and 1 the least (e.g. 171 indicates extreme mesomorphy, 225 strong ectomorphy and 515 ectomorph–endomorphy); but for the purpose of describing build in the medical examination report for life assurance, it would be unnecessary and indeed impossible to be so precise, since the seven-point scale can only be determined by certain measurements from specially positioned photographs. All that is necessary to provide a good general picture of the build is a word or phrase qualifying the main component or components present: for example, extreme endomorph, moderate endomorph, mesomorph–endomorph (i.e. a person showing the same number of features of both mesomorphy and endomorphy, with little or no ectomorphy) or ectomorph–endomorph (i.e. the same number of features of both ectomorphy and endomorphy, with little or no mesomorphy). It is desirable that this terminology should come into general use to describe the build of an applicant; it has the advantage of terseness, is unambiguous and is understood throughout the world.

Some relationship exists between somatotype and a susceptibility to certain diseases, but so far this has not been sufficiently well defined to influence materially the selection of lives for assurance.

Under general description, any outstanding features should also be noted, such as exophthalmos, thyroid enlargement, dyspnea or cyanosis, frequent cough, or the presence of an arcus senilis (particularly in people under the age of 60). It is important to notice whether the applicant is composed or nervous.

Chest Expansion and Girth Measurement

Measurement of the chest and abdomen completes the general physical picture. The chest expansion is an important piece of evidence, and as much care should be taken with its measurement as with blood pressure. In many of the reports one sees this is unfortunately not the case, and, being so, very little weight can be placed on it unless the examiner is known to be reliable or has made special comment when there has been undue deviation from average. In many cases the examinee is not instructed properly in the execution of the maneuver, with the result that ridiculously low readings are often recorded. In males an average reading is 2¾–3¼ in (7·0–8·3 cm). If anything lower is found a second attempt should be made, making certain that the lungs are completely exhaled and that inspiration is maximum. The abdominal measurement should be taken at the level of the umbilicus with the applicant relaxed and breathing naturally. A list of average chest expansions for different heights and ages is shown in Table 10.1.

Table 10.1. Average chest expansion of assured lives of different ages.

Height[a]	Chest expansion[b]					
	16	20–24	25–29	30–39	40–49	50 and over
5ft 0in (1·52)	2·8 (7·1)	2·8 (7·1)	2·8 (7·1)	2·7 (6·9)	2·7 (6·9)	2·3 (5·8)
5ft 4 in (1·63)	2·9 (7·4)	2·9 (7·4)	2·9 (7·4)	2·8 (7·1)	2·8 (7·1)	2·4 (6·1)
5ft 8in (1·73)	3·1 (7·9)	3·1 (7·9)	3·0 (7·6)	2·9 (7·4)	2·9 (7·4)	2·7 (6·9)
6ft 0in (1·83)	3·2 (8·1)	3·3 (8·4)	3·1 (7·9)	3·0 (7·6)	3·1 (7·9)	2·9 (7·4)

[a]Height in normal shoes in feet and inches (in metres).
[b]In inches (in centimetres).

Apart from obvious causes of poor chest expansion, such as ankylosing spondylitis, severe pulmonary emphysema or deformities of the chest (either congenital or surgically determined), there are other causes that are not always obvious, the commonest being a general state of emotional tension, leading in turn to increased tone of skeletal muscles that cannot easily be relaxed. Impaired chest expansion due to this cause is often accompanied by a higher than average blood pressure. Chest expansion in females should be measured at the upper level of the breasts.

Cardiovascular System

Accurate reporting of the clinical signs in the cardiovascular system is one of the most important tasks in the whole physical examination, and the ultimate disposal of an application for life assurance often depends on the nature of the data reported by the medical examiner. From the life underwriting point of view, the basic information required for assessment of a risk should include the following: the pulse rate and its regularity; the state of the peripheral arteries; the blood pressure; the location, by measurement, of the apex beat or left border of the heart; the heart sounds; and a full description of any cardiac murmurs. The reason for stressing the importance of these basic data is that nearly all of them have been the subject of mortality studies in the past. Therefore even if the medical examiner is unable to offer an interpretation of abnormal physical signs, and if a cardiologist's opinion is not available, the underwriter would still be able to classify an applicant in a broad mortality group by referring to the appropriate sections of a rating manual.

Additional information, especially when there is arterial hypertension, proteinuria or glycosuria, should include a description of the optic fundi and the state of the pulses in the lower limbs (by palpation), and auscultation for bruits over the femoral and carotid vessels.

Tachycardia

It should be remembered that a medical examination is often quite an event in a person's life, particularly if it is carried out by someone he does not know. There is therefore probably some degree of apprehension associated with a medical examination for life insurance, though this is not always detectable clinically by any abnormal physical signs. Some people, however, owing to their particular constitutional make-up, may react with an initial elevation of the pulse rate which, in many cases, falls to within acceptable limits after a short rest. The pulse rate should be recorded accurately with a watch, and it is quite sufficient to count the rate over 10 seconds, expressing the result as beats per minute. In this way any alteration in the rate over 30–40 seconds can be detected, and the degree of lability and recovery of the pulse rate estimated. The upper limit of the strictly ideal pulse rate lies no higher than about 72 beats per minute; in the absence of other obvious causes a rate higher than this usually reflects a state of emotional lability of a greater or lesser degree. In the fast pulse classifications of both the 1951 and 1983 impairment studies[2,3] mortality ratios were shown to increase as pulse rates increased over 90 per minute, and deaths by cause, which were more than the average expected, were equally divided between cardiovascular diseases, suicide and cancer. For the purpose of risk selection, debits usually start when the average pulse rate reaches 96 per minute, the higher the rate above this level the greater the debit. It is important, therefore, to re-count the pulse at least once, preferably at the end of the examination, if the initial rate is 96 per minute or higher.

It is often reported that a particular applicant is always nervous when examined by a doctor, and this is put forward as an excuse for a persistently fast pulse rate, sometimes in the region of 120–132 per minute; this is not a valid argument for disregarding an abnormal tachycardia, for such a state of affairs indicates a faulty reaction to stress which may occur in response not only to a medical examination, but to any difficult situation in life. In general, such people are substandard risks.

Bradycardia
A slow pulse does not have the same extra mortality significance as does a fast pulse. As a group, those subject to dyspepsia, peptic ulceration or other conditions dependent on excessive parasympathetic tone generally have slower than average pulse rates, varying from 54 to 66 per minute. A very slow pulse is characteristic of the young athletic adult in full training, particularly where the sport entails prolonged physical endurance, such as long-distance running. Pulse rates of 36–48 per minute in these people are by no means uncommon, and, are perfectly acceptable in the circumstances.

Still, a very slow pulse rate (in the region of 40 per minute) should always alert the examiner to the possibility of heart block or sinoatrial disease, especially in older, or younger unathletic, applicants, or to rate-slowing drugs such as betablockers. It would be helpful to the underwriter if the medical examiner were to test the reaction of the heart rate and rhythm to brisk exercise, since physiological sinus bradycardia can sometimes be differentiated clinically from a dysrhythmia by this means. If doubt still remained, an ECG would be necessary to be quite certain about the type of rhythm present.

Irregularity of the Pulse
Sinus arrhythmia is a normal phenomenon and can be disregarded; but when it is marked and clinically difficult to differentiate from ectopic beats or atrial fibrillation, response to simple exercise, such as straight leg raising, will usually clarify the situation.

The commonest cause of a pulse irregularity is ectopic beats; the clinical teaching that infrequent ectopic beats occurring in ambulant subjects with no history or signs of heart disease have no serious prognostic significance is also reflected in underwriting practice. The benign nature of ectopic beats occurring at rest in an otherwise healthy individual would be even more definitely established if they disappeared when the heart rate is increased by exercise.

On the other hand, experience gained by coronary care units in recent years indicates that frequent ventricular ectopic beats that occur after a myocardial infarction often precede the onset of ventricular fibrillation, especially when they are of the R-on-T variety and occur in salvos of two or three beats at a time. In life underwriting it is usual to take a less favourable view of frequent and persistant ectopic beats, particularly if they do not become less frequent following exercise. In such circumstances, if an ECG is not available to define the type of ectopics present and the state of the myocardium, a rating would be justified.

When ectopic beats are present, the medical examiner should report their frequency at rest as so many per minute or as one in so many normal beats, and at the end of the examination he should exercise the applicant and report whether the ectopics disappear, become less frequent, remain unaltered or increase in frequency.

The completely erratic rhythm of atrial fibrillation is usually fairly easily recognized, but at times it may be confused with frequently occurring ectopic beats in a basically sinus rhythm. When there is doubt it is sometimes possible to distinguish one from the other by observing the effect of exercise on the heart rhythm. If the irregularity at rest is due only to ectopic beats the basic rhythm after exercise will usually become recognizably regular, whereas if due to atrial fibrillation it will remain completely irregular.

Blood Pressure

As stated earlier, the higher the blood pressure level in observed groups the higher mortality becomes, so it is hardly surprising that the level of blood pressure has become a very important parameter in risk evaluation. To determine the correct level of blood pressure for underwriting purposes for any one individual is far from easy: unlike height, weight and girth, which are relatively static measurements at any given time, blood pressure can vary, sometimes widely, during the course of a few hours or even minutes, depending on the personality of the individual being examined and on his reaction to his environment. Also important in determining the final blood pressure to be used by the underwriter is the actual technique of its measurement, and the method of approach by the medical examiner to the whole problem of elevated blood pressure.

The mercury gravity sphygmomanometer is the most reliable recorder available for the clinical measurement of blood pressure. Once it is calibrated, recalibration is unnecessary unless some mercury is spilled accidentally from the reservoir. It is essential to check from time to time that the meniscus of the mercury is exactly at zero when the manometer is perpendicular.

When measuring blood pressure the position of the subject, whether recumbent on a couch or sitting upright in a chair, is probably immaterial. What is of prime importance is the position of the antecubital fossa in relation to the level of the heart. Mitchell et al[4] demonstrated the error that can occur in the blood pressure measured by the indirect method when the level of the antecubital fossa is higher or lower than the level of the heart or 'phlebostatic axis' (defined as the junction between the lateral border of the sternum and the fourth intercostal space). The error can be considerable, leading to spurious and misleading data when used for evaluating blood pressure risks.

The effect of arm level is largely explained by hydrostatic pressure, and when the antecubital fossa is at a level higher or lower than heart level the error in the observed blood pressure can be predicted from the standard formula for calculating hydrostatic pressure in a column of blood:

$$\text{hydrostatic pressure} = \frac{\text{distance in mm}}{13 \cdot 6} \times 1 \cdot 05 \, \text{mm Hg}$$

where 'distance' is the measurement between the auscultatory point in the antecubital fossa and the fourth intercostal space at the sternal border. If, for example, the blood pressure is measured with the forearm 15 cm below the heart level, which is not outside the bounds of possibility, it can be calculated from the above formula that the observed blood pressure, as read on the manometer scale, will be approximately 11 mm Hg too high. An error of this dimension is serious enough at the best of times, but would be even more so in an applicant whose true blood pressure is already raised or borderline, and would almost certainly lead to an unjust rating.

Physicians undertaking medical examinations for life insurance are strongly recommended when taking blood pressures to position the forearm so that the antecubital fossa is at the level of the fourth intercostal space at the sternum when the applicant is sitting, or at the midthoracic level when supine.

Needless to say, accurate reading of the mercury level as it falls in the manometer is important. In clinical work there is a tendency for physicians to report blood pressures with a digital preference of 5 mm Hg, but this should be avoided in life insurance reporting as it lacks precision. Instead it is preferable to measure blood pressure to the nearest 2 mm Hg, and this is perfectly feasible if due care is taken.

It is important too that there should be uniformity in the method of reporting blood pressure, particularly the diastolic phase, so that there is consistency in underwriting risks within a company, and, even more important, that there is consistency between company and company when data are to be pooled for statistical analysis.

Many years ago North American life insurance companies decided to use exclusively the fifth phase of the Korotkoff auscultatory sounds (i.e. the point when all sounds cease) to denote the diastolic blood pressure, as the fourth phase (i.e. the point of change from loud to soft muffled sounds) is frequently difficult to define with accuracy, and indeed is often absent, coinciding with the fifth phase. Now the practice of using the fifth phase diastolic for underwriting purposes is almost universal. This, of course, does not imply that the fifth phase diastolic pressure is nearer to the true diastolic pressure, as measured directly by intra-arterial cannula, than the fourth phase, for it is not. Holland and Humerfelt[5] confirmed that the differences between direct and indirect methods of blood pressure estimation are less for the diastolic fourth phase than for diastolic fifth phase. They also found that the differences between intra-arterial and cuff diastolic fifth phase were more closely correlated than for fourth phase. In other words, the point of cessation of sounds was rather easier to define than the change of sounds.

For statistical purposes it is immaterial that the fifth phase diastolic is further from the true diastolic than the fourth phase, so long as the fifth phase readings are consistently used. All the large-scale blood pressure studies of insured lives that have been carried out have been calculated on the basis of fifth phase diastolic pressure; blood pressure rating tables, being largely derived from these studies, also use the fifth phase.

The life underwriter is frequently presented with additional blood pressures from the attending physician, or from a specialist or clinic, which will be used together with blood pressure data from his company's own medical report in calculating the final blood pressure for rating purposes. Since it is usual in clinical practice to report diastolic blood pressure at the fourth phase, these additional readings have to be adjusted to fifth phase diastolic before averaging: this is done by subtracting 5 mm Hg from the fourth phase readings, which is the average difference between fourth and fifth phases at different levels of blood pressure.

Arterial blood pressure should always be recorded in the medical report form as systolic, diastolic fourth phase and diastolic fifth phase: 160/100-96. If there is no recognizable change of sound, or if the fourth and fifth phases coincide, it should be recorded as 165/98-98. By doing so the medical director (MD) reading the report at head office is left in no possible doubt about the meaning of the figures, and confusion is thereby avoided.

Except for blood pressure readings taken during the course of an illness or during the investigation of some suspected disease, those recorded during the life assurance examination will probably be the highest of the normal range for any particular person. This is mainly due to the fact that the medical examiner is often a stranger to the applicant, leading inevitably to some degree of apprehension, however slight. It is a good plan to leave the actual recording of blood pressure to as late in the examination as possible, so that the applicant has time to adjust himself to the strange conditions and become better acquainted with the examiner. Blood pressure readings so obtained are known as casual readings, and it is the casual blood pressure which is always used for life underwriting.

There are certain misleading practices in the reporting of blood pressure which are seen from time to time in the course of underwriting and which should be avoided. These are listed below.

1) A solitary elevated blood pressure reading should never be reported without repeating the estimation, preferably after the examination has been completed and the applicant has rested quietly for a few minutes. If no further measurements are made and reported, it can result in considerable inconvenience both to the applicant and the life office, for inevitably a further series of blood pressure readings will have to be arranged with an independent examiner so that a more accurate assessment of the applicant's blood pressure status can be made.

2) It is very misleading to the underwriter if only the lowest blood pressure of a series is reported; quite erroneous conclusions may be drawn which could result in the applicant being placed in a more favorable rating category than he should, to the detriment of other policyholders. It is important that the degree of lability of a blood pressure should be known, and the decision as to the appropriate blood pressure level of a series to be chosen must be left to the MD, who may have on file

evidence of blood pressure readings recorded by other medical examiners or even by the medical attendant.

3) Perhaps less serious is the practice of recording only the average of a series of blood pressures, but again, the underwriter would wish to know the degree of lability of the blood pressure, and this can only be judged when all the readings are recorded.

4) When further blood pressure readings have to be taken because the initial one was high, it is helpful to the underwriter if the medical examiner notes the pulse rate opposite each blood pressure recorded, as any change in the pattern of the systolic and diastolic blood pressure can often be explained by an increase or decrease in the heart rate.

Low blood pressure, when the systolic is 100 mm Hg or below, is not associated with any extra mortality if the subject is otherwise healthy. Pathological conditions that cause hypotension are unlikely to be encountered in applicants examined for life insurance, except possibly Addison's disease, but this would be readily recognized once the examining physician's suspicions were aroused. However, it is always worth repeating the blood pressure recording if the initial systolic pressure is below 100 mm Hg, if only to verify that the technique of the original estimation was not at fault. There is increasing evidence that systolic blood pressures below 100 mm Hg are associated with increased morbidity,[6] and hypotension is a much-treated continental European syndrome; as such it could be a marker for caution in disability insurance.

When an applicant is under treatment for hypertension with antihypertensive drugs, the usual routine of recording blood pressure should be followed, but in addition it would be informative to take a separate reading with the applicant standing, so that the postural effect of the drugs on the blood pressure can be assessed.

When the circumference of the upper arm is much greater than average due to obesity or muscular development, the blood pressure recorded by the indirect method is likely to be several millimetres higher than the true level, owing to technical reasons which will be discussed later. In such circumstances the medical examiner should report the fact that the circumference of the upper arm is unusually great so that the MD can make whatever adjustments to the blood pressure he thinks necessary. If a large cuff is available it is helpful to make extra recordings with this, as such pressures will be more accurate.

Examination of the Heart

Size

It is important to make as accurate an estimation as possible of the size of the heart, since significant cardiac enlargement can seriously worsen the prognosis of coexisting hypertension, valvar defects or ischemic heart disease. Clinical estimation of heart size is best made by using the apex beat as a guide, having first determined that the mediastinum is central by the usual clinical methods. The point of maximum thrust of the apex beat should be recorded as so many inches (or centimetres) from the midline in the appropriate interspace. It should be emphasized that it is quite impossible to judge the distance accurately enough with the eye, and a tape or other measure should always be used. A simple and convenient measuring scale can be made by marking off the stethoscope tubing at 3, 3½ and 4 in, or corresponding centimetres, from the chest-piece end. The advantage is that the scale is immediately available, thus allowing the measurement of the apex position to be made quickly without the inconvenience of having to leave the couch side to search for a tape measure.

The apex beat is sometimes difficult to find in certain individuals, and it may be necessary to palpate both in full inspiration and expiration. If still elusive, the left border of the heart should be determined by percussion, and the measurement taken from there. Occasionally even this maneuver is impossible, due either to the presence of pulmonary emphysema or gas in the fundus of the stomach; as a last resort, particularly in cases where it is essential that some idea of the size of the heart be known, palpation of the apex should be attempted with the applicant lying in the left lateral position. If located by this method, it should be remembered that there will be a shift of the heart of from ¾ to 1½ in (1·9 to 3·8 cm) to the left depending on age, and this should be allowed for in estimating the apex position in recumbency. Particular care is necessary in estimating heart size in elderly applicants due to thoracic skeletal changes.

The advantage of measuring the apex beat from the midline is that an absolute figure is obtained which, when related to body build, can be used to determine whether or not there is cardiac enlargement and, if enlarged, the degree (*see* Table 10.2).

It is common clinical practice to estimate the size of the heart by relating the apex beat to the left midclavicular line, the normal position being medial to it. If the midclavicular line is drawn accurately, it is a reliable guide to heart size. In practice this is never done, so the position of an apex beat or left cardiac border reported in this manner generally lacks precision, and its use is not advised in the medical examination for life assurance.

Normally the distance of the apex beat from the midline varies from 2¾ in (7·0 cm) in very lightly built adolescents to 4½ in (11·4 cm), or a little more, in heavily built males. When there seems to be some disparity between the position of the apex and the weight of the applicant its relation to the nipple line in males should be stated. An apex 4½ in (11·4 cm), or a little more, from the midline may not necessarily signify enlargement so long as it is in or medial to the left nipple line, but if lateral to it, enlargement would be certain, and even more so if the maximum

Table 10.2. Distances of cardiac apex from midline representing the upper limits of normal heart size at different weights.[a,b]

Weight	≤126 lb (57·0 kg)	≤150 lb (68·0 kg)	≤175 lb (79·5 kg)	≤200 lb (90·5 kg)	≤225 lb (102·0 kg)
Apex beat from midline	≤3½ in (8·9 cm)	≤4 in (10·2 cm)	≤4¼ in (10·8 cm)	≤4½ in (11·4 cm)	≤4¾ in (12·1 cm)

[a]When chest expanded exceeds 40 in (102 cm) increase the limit by 10 percent; when chest expanded less than 32 in (81 cm) decrease the limit by 10 percent.
[b]Slight heart enlargement: up to ½ in (1·3 cm) above upper limit of normal. Moderate heart enlargement: up to 1 in (2·5 cm) above upper limit of normal. Marked heart enlargement: over 1 in (2·5 cm) above upper limit of normal.

impulse were in the sixth interspace. In the hyperdynamic heart a forceful apex beat may sometimes appear to be about ½ in (1·3 cm) further to the left than it really is, giving the impression of cardiac enlargement when, in fact, there is none.

Character

The forceful, thrusting apical impulse of left ventricular hypertrophy (usually secondary to systemic hypertension, aortic stenosis or hypertrophic cardiomyopathy) may also be accompanied by a palpable fourth heart sound.

A more accurate method of determining the size of the heart is by teleoradiogram or a posteroanterior radiograph of the chest with the X-ray tube positioned 6 ft 6 in (2 m) distant from the subject. This is often requested by head or home office if a particular cardiovascular problem has to be evaluated, or as a purely routine part of the medical evidence when the sum assured is substantial. Methods of calculating various degrees of cardiac enlargement from a chest radiograph are described in Chapter 15.

Auscultation

The examining physician need not be an expert cardiologist to produce a comprehensible account of what he hearts on listening to the heart; although he may not always be able to interpret the signs he has elicited, this would not necessarily detract from the value of his report, provided he has documented his findings faithfully.

Certainly no difficulty should arise in interpreting the sounds of a healthy heart or even the well recognized murmurs of some of the more gross valve defects, such as the presystolic murmur and mid-diastolic rumble of mitral stenosis, the rough basal midsystolic murmur and thrill of aortic stenosis, or the early diastolic murmur of aortic incompetence. On the other hand, some murmurs are notoriously difficult to interpret, in particular the systolic murmur, which has been a diagnostic mare's nest ever since auscultation of the heart was first practised. It is this murmur that causes most difficulty in underwriting (and clinical practice), usually because too little information is given about it by the medical examiner. What can an MD advise his underwriter to do when a heart murmur is described as an 'apical systolic murmur' and nothing else? Most systolic murmurs are not in fact due to organic heart disease but are functional, although not always benign when viewed from the standpoint of long-term mortality; this would depend on the nature of the functional disorder causing the murmur. On the other hand, some systolic murmurs having an organic basis have little hemodynamic significance as far as the heart itself is concerned (for example, the midsystolic ejection murmur due to an atheromatous and dilated ascending aorta beyond a normal valve).

Some of the better designed medical report forms have a 'heart questionnaire' in which the important features of a murmur can be ticked off quickly in the appropriate boxes; this, together with a diagram of the anterior chest on which the apex position and the location and transmission of a murmur can be drawn, is of great value in assisting the CMO to assess the significance or otherwise of a murmur. The more important characteristics of a systolic murmur to be reported are listed below.

1) The area over which the murmur is heard and the point of maximum intensity.

2) The degree of intensity or loudness of the murmur.

3) The timing of the murmur, whether of short duration in early, late or midsystole, or long and pansystolic starting immediately after the first sound and continuing right into the second sound.

4) Conduction of the murmur, whether to the left axilla or above the right clavicle, or elsewhere.

5) The quality of the murmur, whether soft, blowing or rough, and whether low, medium or high-pitched.

It is important to try to estimate the loudness or intensity of a systolic murmur because it has been established by impairment studies that the louder the murmur the higher the mortality. A system of grading systolic murmurs according to intensity as proposed by Levine[7] in 1933 is very helpful for underwriting and is easy to use (*see* Table 10.3). The intensity of a murmur should be recorded thus: grade 1 (of six) or grade 3 (of six) or, alternatively, grade 1/6 or grade 3/6.

Table 10.3. Classification of systolic murmurs by intensity (after Levine).[7]

Grade	Intensity	Significance
1	Just audible	Almost always insignificant
2	Soft: easily heard	Very likely insignificant
3	Soft to moderately loud	Depends on other data
4	Loud	
5	Very loud	Denote cardiovascular disease of
6	Heard by unaided ear	greater or lesser severity

Another system of grading the intensity of murmurs using a four-point scale is popular among clinicians; when used in the life insurance report the grades should always be qualified by the scale (e.g. grade 2 (of four) or grade 2/4) to differentiate it from Levine's system.

The timing of a systolic murmur provides a valuable diagnostic clue to the nature of the causative lesion, and all systolic murmurs may be divided into three main types:

1) Midsystolic ejection murmurs caused by the forward flow of blood through the aortic or pulmonic valves and ventricular outflow tracts.

2) Pansystolic murmurs due to regurgitant back flow from ventricles to atria through incompetent valves, or to left-to-right shunts through a ventricular septal defect or patent ductus arteriosus.

3) Late systolic murmurs due to mitral or tricuspid regurgitation, often the hallmark of mitral valve prolapse when it follows a midsystolic click.

Ejection murmurs swell up to a crescendo about midsystole and invariably end before the second sound. These murmurs are caused by the turbulent flow of blood under the following conditions:

(1) stenosis of valve or outflow tract, (2) increased rate of ejection through the valve, (3) valvular damage without stenosis, (4) dilatation of the vessel beyond the valve, or (5) combinations of these factors.

Regurgitant systolic murmurs are usually pansystolic on auscultation and are caused by the flow of blood from a chamber or vessel that is at a higher pressure throughout systole than the receiving vessel or chamber. Except for functional tricuspid incompetence, which occurs in any case only in obviously diseased hearts, pansystolic murmurs are due to organic or structural heart disease. Functional systolic murmurs are virtually always flow murmurs arising in the left or right ventricular outflow tracts, and are thus ejection in type. The physical principles governing the production of cardiac murmurs are fully described by Leatham[8,9] and amplified in relation to Doppler echocardiographic findings by Popp.[10]

When there is a history of rheumatic fever and the heart sounds at rest appear to be normal without the presence of an audible murmur, the applicant should always be exercised and re-examined as he lies in the left lateral position. An unsuspected slight mitral stenosis is sometimes brought to light by this simple maneuver. This technique may also help to clarify murmurs and added heart sounds that are otherwise difficult to evaluate at rest, when the increased intensity allows more accurate positioning within the cardiac cycle.

The interpretation of a cardiac murmur, whether it be functional or organic, is a matter for the experience of the medical examiner. Even when he is in doubt the CMO or MD may still be able to make an interpretation if the clinical signs have been fully described as suggested, for he will often have the advantage of additional information to guide him, such as previous clinical reports, an ECG, radiograph of the chest and an echocardiogram. A normal echocardiographic study will confirm that a clinically doubtful murmur is functional and can be disregarded.

Examination of the Peripheral Vessels

If the clinical history is featureless and the examination appears to be straightforward, no minute investigation of the peripheral arterial system is required; it is usually sufficient to check one or two main points. Examination of the pulse at the radial and brachial arteries and assessment of the state of the vessel walls have already been mentioned, and femoral artery pulsation should always be sought during routine examination of the abdomen. Absent or greatly diminished and delayed pulsation on both sides in a young person who has an elevated blood pressure may be due to coarctation of the aorta, and occasionally a previously undiagnosed case has been discovered because this simple clinical sign was elicited. The often difficult and time consuming examination of the pulses at the ankles need not be carried out as a routine in the examination for life assurance unless there is a history suggestive of intermittent claudication, or if there is disparity in the amplitude of the femoral pulses or one leg is found to be obviously colder than the other when the limbs are routinely examined.

Although it is not always specifically requested, it is good practice to examine the optic fundi in all cases. This provides valuable information on the state of the vascular system, especially when there is hypertension or when glucose or protein is found in the urine. It would also be an essential part of the examination when there is a suspected neurological abnormality.

In describing cases of arteriosclerosis, the grading of the fundal appearances recommended by Keith et al[11] may be used (*see* Table 10.4). Alternatively a simple description of the state of the vessels may be made, noting the presence or absence of hemorrhages, exudates or papilledema.

Table 10.4. Classification of retinal appearances in hypertension.

Grade	Features
I	General narrowing of the arterioles with varying caliber and increased reflex
II	Further reduction in arteriolar caliber and constriction of the veins where crossed by the arterioles
III	Addition of exudates and/or hemorrhages
IV	Papilledema

When varicose veins are present, the main points to note are the distribution (whether in the thighs or below the knees, or both), whether they are slight, moderate or severe, and whether there is evidence of old or recent thrombophlebitis, varicose ulceration or eczema, or edema. The presence of edema should elicit a statement from the examiner concerning signs of congestive heart failure (e.g. increased JVP, hepatomegaly and rales); a definite observation as to their absence is helpful. It would be unusual, however, for insurance applicants to present in congestive cardiac failure.

Respiratory System

Before proceeding to the examination of the chest, the structures in the neck should be examined, noting any enlargement of lymph nodes or the thyroid gland, and defining the course of the trachea in the suprasternal notch. The importance of accurate measurement of the maximum expansion of the chest has already been stressed (*see* p. 159).

After inspection the hands should be run lightly over the chest wall seeking any abnormal lumps, paying particular attention to the axillae. Deformities of the thorax should be noted; these are commonly due to congenital malformation, such as the funnel deformity of sternal depression, pigeon deformity (either unilateral or bilateral), or kyphoscoliosis. When any of these deformities are present, their degree (whether mild, moderate or severe) should be stated and, in particular, whether any displacement of the heart and mediastinum exists resulting from sternal depression. The physical signs in the lungs and pleura should be reported in the usual manner, and any departure from normal noted.

Alimentary System

Examination of the abdomen should follow the usual routine of clinical practice, but particular attention should be paid to the state of the liver and spleen, since most diseases causing enlargement of these organs have a very significant effect on long-term mortality.

Liver

It is probably true to say that a normal liver can never be palpated during ordinary quiet respiration and, according to most authorities, it can be palpated only rarely even at the height of a deep inspiration. Bearn and Pilkington[12] examined the abdomens of 200 healthy young adults (100 males and 100 females) between the ages of 18 and 24 in order to find out which structures could be felt and how often. At the height of inspiration, one or both observers could feel the liver in only two males and eleven females, and in all of those the edge was soft and ill defined. These findings are, of course, not necessarily applicable to older age groups.

When a liver is palpable, it is essential that the medical examiner should report whether it is so on (1) quiet respiration or (2) at the height of deep inspiration. The consistency of the liver should also be stated (whether soft, firm or hard) and whether the edge is ill-defined or sharp; most importantly, the distance that the lower edge of the liver descends below the right costal margin in the nipple line should be measured and recorded in the report.

Sometimes a simple diagram showing the relationship of an enlarged liver to the subcostal angle and the umbilicus is very helpful for visualizing the verbal report.

Spleen

A normal spleen is, of course, never palpable even on deep inspiration, and if it can be felt the same procedure of reporting as for the liver should be employed (e.g. 'the tip of the spleen just palpable on deep inspiration', 'palpable' 3 cm below the left costal margin on deep inspiration' or '8 cm below the left costal margin on quiet respiration'). The consistency of the spleen should also be stated. By reporting in this way, precise information about the size and condition of the spleen is conveyed to the MD.

When there is a history of dyspepsia, an attempt should be made to elicit tenderness by deep palpation over the stomach, pyloric region, duodenum or gall bladder. The point where tenderness is most frequently found is slightly to the right and below the umbilicus, the surface landmark of the first part of the duodenum. If unequivocal, with a definite history of indigestion, an active ulcer, or at least duodenal congestion and irritability, may be inferred.

Hernia

If a hernia is discovered on examination, the main points to note are how long it has been present, the size and extent of the protrusion, and whether it is easily reducible. It is only when a hernia is irreducible or when immediate surgical correction is contemplated that the underwriter should be concerned.

Rectum

A rectal examination is not requested routinely in the life examination report, but when there have been recent, unexplained symptoms of signs suggestive of rectal pathology, urinary obstruction or tumor, it should be done as a matter of course. Since life insurance is now considered more frequently for older people, it may become sensible to carry out a rectal examination on those over the age of 60.

Urogenital System

A few features in the urogenital system require special attention. Digital examination of the prostate in suspicious circumstances has already been mentioned, and examination of the contents of the scrotum should always be carried out as a routine. If a hydrocele is found, a note should be made of how long it has been present because, if of recent onset in a young male, it may be the first sign of an underlying testicular tumor. On the other hand, a hydrocele that has been present for several years is likely to be benign.

An undescended testicle, being a precancerous condition, should always be noted in the report.

An enlarged, thickened or calcified epididymis may be the only clinical evidence of past tuberculous infection, and it may be a valuable piece of evidence when the clinical picture is viewed as a whole. If, for example, constant proteinuria has also been demonstrated, the likelihood that it is arising in a kidney previously damaged by tuberculosis is great.

In the case of female applicants the breasts should be examined where there is a history of previous pathology, and the nature of any lumps or surgical scars described. Pelvic examination, on the other hand, should never be carried out during the routine medical examination for life insurance. Significant menstrual disorders, such as amenorrhea, should be documented, together with the outcome of any recent smear tests. Information should be sought about the number of previous pregnancies or miscarriages, including the date of the last, and whether or not there were any complications, such as toxemia of pregnancy or conditions requiring cesarean section. If the applicant is pregnant at the time of examination an estimation of the duration of pregnancy should be made.

Urinalysis

A urine specimen must always be tested; if the applicant is male it should be passed in the presence of the examiner. If, in the case of nervous subjects, the specimen has to be passed in an adjoining room or toilet, the examiner must be satisfied that the urine is that of the applicant. A specimen of urine brought to the examination in a bottle must never be accepted unless it has been specially requested, as in the case of an early-rising specimen.

The important abnormal constituents to be sought are protein, glucose and blood, the tests for which are described elsewhere (see pp. 517–25), but any other unusual features of the urine should be recorded. A hazy urine that does not clear on the addition of a little acetic acid or gentle warming is an abnormal finding in males and may indicate the presence of pus or bacilli. However, this is a common finding in a non-catheter specimen from a female, and may usually be disregarded so long as it is slight and there is no protein present. Urine of unusual colour, or even fluorescent, may be due to drugs or various dyes used in the manufacture of sweets and candies.

If abnormal constituents are found in the urine on ordinary 'side-room' testing, further tests, including microscopic examination by a clinical pathologist, may be required to help clarify the significance of the original finding. In North America it is customary for insurance companies to have the examining physician forward a sample of urine to home office for full analysis if abnormal constituents have been found, if there is a blood pressure problem, or if the sum insured exceeds a certain amount. The testing of urine by specialized laboratories for the detection of nicotine and illicit drugs is useful and may be requested by home office when the circumstances demand it, but the usefulness of screening the urine for the presence of medicines such as oral antidiabetic drugs, diuretics and betablockers is questionable.[13] When proteinuria has been found in an ambulant specimen and the applicant is under the age of 30, it is important that one of the specimens retested should be passed immediately after rising from bed in the morning, so that the relatively benign condition of orthostatic proteinuria is not overlooked.

Central Nervous System

A routine examination of the pupils and their reactions, along with the deep reflexes at the knees and ankles, is all that is usually requested in most examination reports for life assurance, but if any other abnormal physical signs are apparent, or there is a history of neurological disease, the report should be amplified. If, for example, there is a previous history of retrobulbar neuritis, diplopia or other symptoms suggestive of multiple sclerosis, the report should include a comment on the presence or absence of any of the classical signs of the disease (e.g. slurring of speech, nystagmus, intention tremor, inco-ordination and abnormality of the abdominal reflexes, plantar responses and optic discs). Likewise, when an applicant has had poliomyelitis, traumatic paraplegia or a peripheral nerve lesion, any residual neuromuscular or sensory deficit should be described fully, and the degree of functional disability of locomotion or bladder control noted.

Constitution

Probably the most important observation of all, and one which is not usually specifically requested in most report forms, is an evaluation of personality, temperament and constitution. These have an undoubted influence on future health and longevity, and are probably just as important to record as many of the physical signs that have been discussed. The behaviour pattern will almost always be found consistent with the findings on examination, personal medical history, family history and environmental background generally.

Summary

When the examination has been completed, the findings must always be summarized, and it is a good plan to make a mental note of all the features that deviate not only from average but from ideal (for example, a borderline blood pressure, a chest expansion less than it should be or the presence of any congenital anomalies). By using the ideal life as a guideline for comparison, no significant abnormalities are likely to be overlooked and any weak links in the constitutional chain will thus be thrown into bolder relief. Many minor impairments may not be particularly meaningful judged individually, but considered in aggregate they may amount to an appreciable score in terms of extra mortality.

It is a mistake to omit comment on a medical examination that appears to be completely featureless; attention should be drawn to the good points as well as the bad, for a completely blank report may arouse suspicion in the underwriter's mind that the examination has been hastily and superficially carried out without due appreciation of the issues involved. Intelligent comment on the examination findings, even of average or better than average lives, indicates that the medical referee is fully conversant with the principles of medical selection.

With such a large proportion of life business now being conducted on a non-medical basis, most applicants who are sent for medical examination have some impairment or suspected impairment that will require careful assessment; therefore the medical examination cannot be regarded as a purely routine task. To some physicians accustomed to dealing with grosser pathological problems, many of the so-called impairments elicited during the course of an examination for life insurance may seem trivial; nevertheless they may have a distinct significance for length of life.

Prognosis is an art that is acquired not only from long experience, but also from attention to bodies of data, often thought by some to be insignificant, gleaned from a patient's complete clinical dossier. The form of the medical examination used in the selection of lives is ideally suited to the detection of these minor deviations from average and may be particularly helpful in difficult clinical problems. These advantages are, of course, not always apparent to the clinician who tends to view a patient and his disease at much closer range, making it more likely that he will miss valuable clues that lie outside the immediate field of investigation; these are clues that can often help to establish the consistency, or otherwise, of a diagnosis and allow a more rational prognosis.

PARAMEDICAL EXAMINATIONS

W John Elder

In North America during the 1960s medical examinations for insurance by physicians were becoming increasingly costly and there were annoying delays in getting them done. In 1967 Dr Charles Pope introduced the concept of replacing examinations by physicians with examinations done by nurses or medical technicians, hence the term paramedical examination.[14,15] Obviously these examinations were less expensive, and they were done at centers established for the purpose in metropolitan areas to make scheduling of appointments easier for agents and applicants.

The original idea was for the paramedical personnel conducting the examination to take the medical history, record height, weight, pulse and blood pressure, do a phonocardiogram and a pulmonary function test, and obtain blood and urine specimens. The thinking was that phonocardiography and pulmonary tests would replace heart and lung evaluation by a doctor, and a panel of blood tests would compensate for the medical pieces missing from the paramedical examination. In addition, if age or amount required it, a resting ECG could be done. Throughout the first decade this new paramedical examination became accepted by life insurance companies, although some modifications occurred. The phonocardiogram was dropped early, largely for technical reasons; and the pulmonary function test was used infrequently, partly because of technical inconsistencies but more significantly because medical underwriters did not appreciate the value of the test. Blood testing was not often requested in these early years, probably because underwriters were not sure how to apply the results to risk classification. Another change from the original concept was to swing away from fixed centers and develop a mobile capability, so that the service became available for applicants at their homes or offices, and for those who lived in less densely populated areas.

By the early 1980s paramedical examinations were widely used; there were a few big companies providing the service nationally or regionally, and a multitude of small operations. The major problems were poor quality controls and great variability in examiner ability. This became particularly important when the impact of AIDS on insurance was appreciated and a huge demand for phlebotomists occurred to obtain the necessary blood specimens. After much activity by insurance medical and underwriting organizations, insurance companies and the larger paramedical companies, quality control and much-needed attention to selection and training of paramedical staff were brought about. Most of the small operations were absorbed by the large companies or went out of business. Now most insurance companies operating nationally use only up to half a dozen paramedical companies for all their paramedical examinations, and are satisfied that this provides a good, manageable and cost effective service.

Approximately 80 to 90 per cent of insurance physical examinations are done by paramedicals in North America today, but physicians continue to examine for large-amount applications and for special circumstances (e.g. when there is a history of a medical impairment). Early doubts concerning accuracy of information provided by paramedicals have largely disappeared. In fact, almost the opposite has happened: paramedicals seem to have a lower tendency than physicians to edit a medical history because they think it is not relevant for insurance, or to round down a blood pressure.

Intercompany and intracompany studies have shown that mortality and claim experience with paramedical examinations was noticeably worse than that with physician examinations until the early 1980s, but in recent years differences have been slight. The Society of Actuaries has published studies which include comparison of experience with medical and paramedical business up to 1986.[16] The paramedical experience continued to be significantly poorer in the age group 0–9 years, and mildly worse over the age of 40, demonstrating the value of medical examinations in age groups where a paramedical is less likely to spot an abnormality. Insurance company MDs exerted considerable influence on the industry to help achieve these beneficial changes.[17]

REFERENCES

1 Sheldon WH. Varieties of human physique. New York: Harper, 1940.
2 1951 Impairment Study. New York: Society of Actuaries, 1954.
3 Medical Impairment Study 1983. Boston: Society of Actuaries and Association of Life Insurance Medical Directors of America, 1986.
4 Mitchell PL, Parlin RW, Blackburn H. Effect of vertical displacement of the arm on indirect blood pressure measurement. N Eng J Med 1964; 271: 72.
5 Holland WW, Humerfelt S. Measurement of blood pressure; comparison of intra-arterial and cuff values. Br Med J 1964; 2: 1241.

6 Wessely S, Nickson J, Cox B. Symptoms of low blood pressure: a population study. *Br Med J* 1990; 301: 362–5.
7 Levine SA. The systolic murmur. Its clinical significance. *JAMA* 1933; 101: 436.
8 Leatham A. Auscultation of the heart. *Lancet* 1958; 2: 703–8.
9 Leatham A. Auscultation of the heart. *Lancet* 1958; 2: 757–65.
10 Popp R. Echocardiography review. *New Eng J Med* 1990; 323 (2) 101; 323 (3) 165.
11 Keith NM, Wagener HP, Barker NW. Different types of essential hypertension: their course and prognosis. *Am J Med Sci* 1939; 197: 332.
12 Bearn JG, Pilkington TRE. Organs palpable in the normal adult abdomen. *Lancet* 1959; 2: 212.
13 Chait LO. Is urine testing worthwhile for insurance purposes? *J Ins Med* 1988; 20, No 2: 38–9.
14 Bullock DE. Paramedicals — past, present, future. *J Ins Med* 1988; 20, No 4: 62–4.
15 Reeder CL. The evolving insurance paramedical business. *J Ins Med* 1988; 20, No 4: 65–7.
16 Committee on individual life insurance. 1. Mortality under standard ordinary insurance issues between 1985 and 1986. *Soc of Act Reports*; 1990: 9–14.
17 Vale B. Paramedical examinations. *Trans Assoc Life Insur Med Dir Am* 1972; 56: 278–82.

CHAPTER 11

THE USE AND INTERPRETATION OF LABORATORY-DERIVED DATA

BRIAN R KAY
MICHAEL W KITA

Every day we rely on numbers to guide our judgment: values from laboratory tests, intervals on ECGs, percentages of coronary artery stenosis on catheterization reports and so on. However, there are dangers lurking behind blind reliance on numbers.

Multiphasic screening as a laboratory tool has grown enormously in the past few decades due to technical advances, entrepreneurial enthusiasm, and the need to screen for HIV disease.[1] This growth in the number of laboratory tests used for screening purposes has meant that people involved with risk selection have had to be aware of the definition of a 'normal' value, sensitivity, specificity and predictive value. The first part of this chapter is designed to outline basic principles underlying the rational use of laboratory-derived data and is drawn heavily from a Journal of Insurance Medicine article by Michael W Kita.[2]

PROBABILITY

Probability is the likelihood of something happening, expressed on a scale of 0 to 1 (0–100 percent). Probability is simply a means of quantitatively expressing uncertainty or risk.

Conditional probability is the likelihood of something being the case given that something else is already the case. Conditional probability statements would include the following: (a) the likelihood of having a positive test result, given the presence of a disease, and (b) the likelihood of having a disease, given a positive test result. Note that 'a' and 'b' are not the same thing: 'a' describes the sensitivity of a test, and 'b' the predictive value of a positive test result. These concepts will be explained and developed further.

As Figure 11.1 shows, the process of deciding the significance of a test result is a process of revising probabilities. In the absence of other information, you begin with the general population prevalence for a disease or condition, assuming that the person could reasonably belong to that population. Then, in the light of the relevant history and physical examination, the initial 'population prevalence' is modified to come up with an 'effective prevalence' based on the totality of information at hand. This effective prevalence becomes the 'prior probability' of disease (i.e. the probability of disease prior to conducting the next diagnostic test).

After the test is done, its result is factored into an estimation of disease likelihood and a 'post-test probability' of disease is calculated.

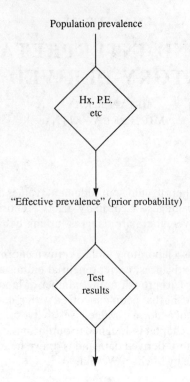

Fig. 11.1. Evaluation process.

EXPECTED VARIATION

To understand test results it is important to be aware of the several sources of expected variation, including biologic variation, sample variation and analytic variation.

Biologic variation refers to variability of test results due to age, sex, diurnal variation, pregnancy, fasting state and other such biologic factors. Sample variation refers to the variability caused by specimen handling (spun or unspun, time in the tube, exposure to heat or cold, etc.) and processing. Analytic variation refers to variability due to test methodology (e.g. type of assay) and the inherent accuracy and precision of the technique. Accuracy refers to the degree to which the lab result is identical to the actual or absolute value (e.g. when compared to a known 'standard'); precision refers to the reproducibility of a test result on repetitive runs.

For a given test the person attempting to interpret the test result needs to factor in all such sources of variation in order to interpret a test result as abnormal and to judge whether the abnormality is of clinical or underwriting significance.

REFERENCE RANGES

Reference ranges are constructed from groups of presumably healthy people but may include individuals with diseases that are subclinical or presymptomatic.

Optimally the reference range should represent only healthy people. But any reference range has some unhealthy people in it, which is one reason why graphs of the test results of healthy and diseased populations commonly overlap instead of cleanly separating. Another reason for overlap is that the diseased population includes a spectrum of disease, with mild and early cases often toward the low end and more severe cases at the upper end.

Even though the reference group is the presumably healthy group, not all of its members are considered 'normal'. Rather, the 'normal' part of the reference range is defined as the central 95 percent of the reference population. This gives rise to another phenomenon of testing: the possibility that someone who is healthy may have an abnormal test result due to chance alone and not to any significant condition. In other words, if a single routine (not for a medical indication) laboratory test is performed on an individual, and 'normal' is defined as the middle 95 percent of usual test results, there is a 95 percent probability of the result being normal and a 5 percent probability of it being abnormal, due to just chance alone. What happens in a battery of tests? Assuming the battery of tests is a chemistry profile (e.g. a Chem-15) and that each of these tests is mutually independent then the chance of being normal on all 15 is only 0·95 to the 15th power ($0·95^{15}$) or only 46 percent. Thus the chance of being abnormal on at least one test is 54 percent.

Abnormal results due to chance effects of multiple simultaneous testing tend to be borderline abnormalities that hover near the margins of the 'normal' range. Such results tend to normalize (regress toward the mean) on repeat testing, but at first glance they can cause considerable confusion for medical directors (MDs) or underwriters.

VALIDITY

A valid test is one which is appropriate for the intended purpose. Gamma- glutamyl transpeptidase (GGTP) as a test for diabetes performs poorly; this is because it is not valid for that purpose. Glucose measurements as tests for diabetes, however, have validity for that purpose.

Few tests are unique discriminators of one condition. Although GGTP is most often used for assessing liver function, it is present in other tissues and can occasionally be elevated due to renal disease, for instance. If the GGTP were elevated due to renal disease, it would then be a false positive test for liver disease. This is not because there is anything false about the GGTP having been elevated, but rather because it is giving false and misleading information about the condition under consideration, namely liver abnormality. To take a slightly different example, although an elevated GGTP level commonly arouses suspicion for alcohol-related impairment, taken alone it is not unique to, or even highly predictive of, alcohol-related disease because elevations can and do occur for other reasons. This does not make it a bad test for underwriting purposes because most of the other causes of significant elevations of GGTP also have important morbidity or mortality concerns to the underwriter; but for establishing alcoholism alone, the GGTP by itself is of limited value.

SENSITIVITY AND SPECIFICITY

Sensitivity means 'positive in disease': the test is positive when the disease is present. A highly sensitive test is one which gives a positive result when the disease is known to be present.

Specificity means 'negative in health': the test is negative when the disease is absent. A highly specific test is one which gives a negative result when the disease is known to be absent.

Most people think that when a test is specific for a particular disease, it is diagnostic of the disease being present. Actually sensitivity is the word best used to describe a test being strongly associated with the presence of disease.

DISTRIBUTION OF RESULTS

If we were to graph the test results of a group of disease-free people against the range of values they could have for that test, we would get a curved distribution of results. This would be the reference population (the population that is presumed not to have the disease in question).

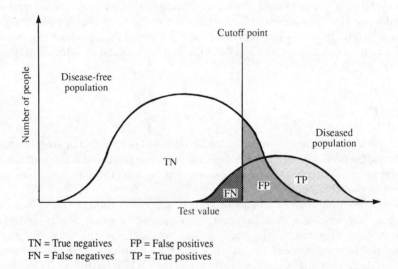

TN = True negatives   FP = False positives
FN = False negatives   TP = True positives

Fig. 11.2. Distribution of results for diseased and disease-free populations.

A second group of people, the diseased population, will also have a certain distribution, and the two curves will typically overlap (*see* Fig. 11.2). If we now define a particular value of the laboratory test as the cut-off line above which we will classify the result as abnormal, there are four groups of people. The cut-off line divides the non-diseased population into two parts: those below the cut-off who are the true negatives (TN = the lab result is negative, and the people are truly non-diseased), and false positives (FP = those non-diseased people who would falsely

a) No overlap = 2 populations (clean seperation)

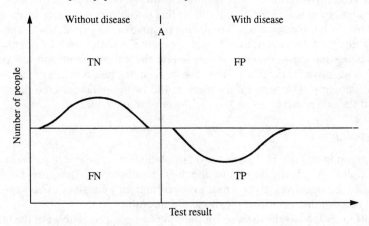

b) Partial overlap = 4 subgroups

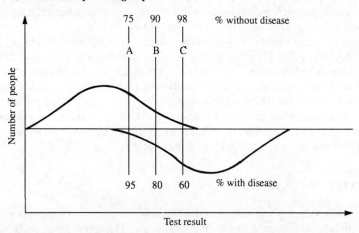

c) Full overlap = "one" population (nested)

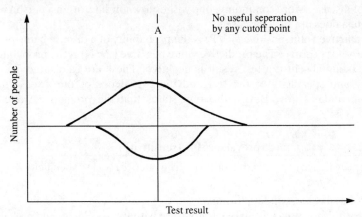

Fig. 11.3. Decision points.

be called abnormal because their results are above the cut-off). Likewise the diseased population is divided by the cut-off line into two parts: the true positives (TP = those with the disease who are testing positive or abnormal, above the cut-off point), and the false negatives (FN = those members of the diseased population who are being missed because they fall below the cut-off point and are being classified as negative for the disease). As can be seen, the relative sizes of these four groups of people will depend on the sizes of the two populations, the degree of overlap of the two populations and where the cut-off line is placed.

Decision Points

The top graph in Figure 11.3 shows two populations with no overlap. Therefore decision point 'A' clearly separates the two populations. There are no false positives or false negatives. Everyone is properly and truly classified. This would be a 'perfect test' for distinguishing the disease in question.

The bottom graph has the diseased population as a complete subset of the larger non-diseased population. No value of the test — not 'A', not anywhere — helpfully separates the groups. It would have no value for distinguishing between these two populations and would not be valid for that purpose.

In the middle graph there is significant overlap, and decision points could be placed at 'A', 'B' or 'C'. This is a 'typical test'. Decision point 'C' would result in high specificity (a high number of true negatives) but low sensitivity (a high number of false negatives). Decision point 'A' would have high sensitivity (a high number of true positives) but low specificity (a high number of false positives). This is the inevitable trade-off when dealing with tests used to discriminate conditions in populations that have overlap. It is hard to get both high specificity and high sensitivity out of a given cut-off level for a particular test.

PREDICTIVE VALUE

Sensitivity and specificity are indices of the diagnostic aspects of a test: how well the test performs in the presence or absence of disease. However, these indices only deal with the situation in which there is already knowledge of the presence or absence of disease. More commonly, one wishes to know how often a person with a negative test does not have disease.

The predictive value positive (PVP) is the probability of a disease being present if a test result is positive. The predictive value negative (PVN) is the probability of a disease being absent if a test result is negative. These are calculated from the sensitivity and specificity of the test and the prevalence of the disease in the population under study. Bayes' theorem states that the predictive value of a positive test is:

$$\frac{(\text{prevalence}) \times (\text{sensitivity})}{(\text{prevalence}) \times (\text{sensitivity}) \times (1 - \text{prevalence}) \times (1 - \text{specificity})}$$

The PVN has a corresponding formula.

Note that this formula has three variables: sensitivity, specificity and prevalence of disease in the population. The most often overlooked variable is prevalence. As illustrated by Kita,[2] following a treadmill positive for 1 mm ST depression in a 50-year-old male American, the post-test likelihood of disease ranges from 19 percent to 96 percent. In this example the wide range is due solely to varying the assumed disease prevalence (i.e. the pre-test likelihood of disease). Therefore one must know not only a great deal about the qualities of the test result but also be able to understand the test result in the appropriate context.

DISEASE PRESENCE; DISEASE PROPENSITY

Most clinical tests are used to determine a patient's probability of presence of disease. For example, the role of treadmill testing is to determine the likelihood of the patient having coronary disease, not the likelihood of the patient developing coronary disease.

In contrast, some tests may be used to predict the likelihood of future occurrence of disease. The degree of patient risk for the disease can be discrete or continuous. A test that presents a discrete risk gives a 'yes' or 'no' answer; the patient does or does not have the predisposition. An example of a discrete risk for future presence of disease is the genetic test for Huntington's disease (assuming the genetic test for Huntington's disease reaches a point where the test is perfect). This test segments a heterogeneous population of family members at high risk for developing Huntington's disease into two homogeneous categories: those who will develop the disease and those who will not.

A test for continuous risk gives a result that may fall anywhere along the line and that does not separate the population into groups of those who are at risk and those who are not. Serum cholesterol is an example of continuous risk. As cholesterol level increases, so does the risk of coronary disease. Predisposition tests for discrete risks are more accurate than those for continuous risks. For example, many people see the test for Huntington's disease as a way of detecting a 'ticking time bomb'. For this particular disease the metaphor probably fits. However, it may not fit for other diseases or other tests. Most predisposition tests are of a continuous nature. Most diseases have many and varied causes. Diseases like atherosclerosis and cancer are multifactorial. Their development is the result of many influences, each influence acting in a complex way. The trend toward using laboratory tests to determine the propensity of disease may have its zenith in the future with genetic tests.

GENETIC TESTS

Tests that identify genes are known as genetic tests. At present these are available for only a small number of genetic disorders. However, technology is rapidly being developed that may soon permit the identification of many of the genes responsible for illness. Genetic testing may become standard practice within the medical community by the year 2000.

Genetic tests may be of great benefit to society. But, as pointed out by Pokorski,[3] any use of genetic tests by insurers would present complex ethical, medical and social issues which insurers would have to take into account. As attending physicians commonly perform more and more genetic tests, insurers may need to obtain those test results to prevent antiselection.

If, at some future time, insurers decide that they must order genetic tests of their own, it is hoped that MDs and underwriters will ask specific questions which have been formulated to evaluate these genetic tests in the risk selection process. In addition to sensitivity, specificity and predictive value, these are:

1) Is the test cost effective, safe and convenient for screening large numbers of insurance applicants?

2) Is the test understood and accepted by the medical community?

3) Can the test readily be done by the reference laboratories used by insurance companies?

4) Does the test deal with an impairment that has significant morbidity and/or mortality implications?

5) Does the impairment occur frequently enough within the insurance buying populace to justify broad screening?

6) Does the test improve the equity of the underwriting process by more accurately assigning individuals to appropriate risk classes?

7) Does the test enhance value to the consumer by keeping insurance costs low and product availability high for the great majority of insurance applicants?

TUMOR MARKERS

It is likely that tumor marker screening tests will soon be available for use by the insurance industry. There are both distinctive advantages and disadvantages of such tests.[4] The development of tumor marker tests was covered at the 1991 ALIMDA meeting,[5,6] together with a brief account of one company's early experience with tumor marker screening.[7] The present use of tumor markers in clinical medicine was reviewed and the possible implications for insurance discussed at an insurance Tumor Marker Forum in 1992.[8] This is an overview of the potential and the pitfalls.

Tumor markers are laboratory tests that indicate a significant likelihood that a malignancy is present. In clinical use some tumor markers have had stunning success. Human chorionic gonadotropin (HCG) is a superb marker to follow hydatidiform mole and choriocarcinoma. Likewise alphafetoprotein has revolutionized the prognosis of malignant germ cell tumors of the testis following orchidectomy. Carcinoembryonic antigen (CEA) was one of the earliest tumor markers and has been useful in monitoring patients with colonic and rectal cancer. Prostatic-specific antigen (PSA) is an excellent test for monitoring the effectiveness of therapy for prostatic cancer and for determining the clinical stage of disease. For underwriting purposes, tumor markers that have been ordered by a clinician have been used to evaluate whether there is evidence of residual or recurrent malignant disease.

However, there is a difference between using a laboratory test for clinical purposes and for screening purposes. Quantitatively, the main difference is that of the usefulness of the test. As already mentioned, the disease prevalence plays an important role in determining the likelihood of someone having a disease, given a positive test result (predictive value of a positive test). That is, given the low prevalence of malignancy in the general population, a tumor marker test would have to have a very high specificity to be of use. In addition, elevation of a tumor marker is a continuous risk of malignant disease. Many results may be modestly elevated. Drawing a cut-off level where test results are above the normal range and yet not so high as to be diagnostic for cancer may be difficult. Furthermore it may be that it is the responsibility of the insurance company to notify the applicants, even if the test result is only minimally abnormal, to allow them to seek medical attention while their malignancy may be in an early, potentially curable stage. This would almost certainly mean many needless expensive and uncomfortable diagnostic procedures being performed. In addition, the meaning of an elevated tumor marker level in the presence of a negative evaluation would be problematic. From a societal point of view, widespread screening for malignancy may result in more people being denied insurance or having insurance postponed. If this reaches a high level, the popular perception of the insurance industry as offering a useful utility that is good for most of society may be in jeopardy, causing lawmakers to rethink their attitude about the insurance industry.

At the same time, it should be mentioned that as cardiovascular deaths decrease there has been an increase in cancer mortality; the insurance industry is seeing an older population with a higher incidence of malignant disease. Furthermore, in the underwriting process we have relatively good screening tests for cardiovascular diseases and some other impairments but very few underwriting tools to evaluate the cancer risk. Development of diagnostic tools to detect malignant disease would have a potential to decrease mortality. If the reduction of mortality were greater than the cost of the test, there would be a great financial incentive to perform such tests. In addition, the potential for early detection, when malignancies are possibly curable, could result in a more favorable perception of the insurance industry by the public.

The future use of tumor markers in screening is unclear. Their predictive abilities and costs will vary considerably. The potential benefit to insurers and applicants may be great. At the same time, characteristics of the tests and the implications for society must be kept in mind.

CHAIN OF CUSTODY

Chain of custody is the term given to a series of steps that are taken to prevent tampering with the specimen from the time that it is collected until the test result is reported by the laboratory. This first gained importance in testing for substance abuse, because of the potential for legal action. Chain of custody procedure documents the location and handling of the specimen from collection to disposal. This procedure aims to ensure that there is no tampering with the specimen, that there is documentation of each and every individual who handled the specimen, that unauthorized access to the specimen was not possible and that the specimen belonged to the individual identified on the label. When testing for substances of abuse for insurance purposes, most paramedical firms and laboratories require chain of custody procedures. In addition, many laboratories check for adulteration of urine specimens.

LIVER ENZYME (FUNCTION) TESTS

Specific laboratory tests and their attendant ratings are discussed in the sections of this book under specific organ systems. Liver function tests have been discussed with regard to clinical meaning in the appropriate chapter. However, this chapter looks at the interpretation of liver function tests used for screening purposes.

The liver enzymes most commonly encountered are: (1) serum glutamic oxaloacetic transaminase (SGOT), also known as aspartate aminotransferase (AST); (2) serum glutamic pyruvic transaminase (SGPT), also known as alanine aminotransferase (ALT); (3) gamma-glutamyl transpeptidase (GGTP); and (4) alkaline phosphatase.

Concurrent elevations of AST and ALT are usually caused by liver cell damage which allows the enzyme to leak out. The degree of elevation generally parallels the extent of liver cell damage.

GGTP is an inducible enzyme. The level of the enzyme reflects exposure to substances such as alcohol or medications. It is very sensitive for the early detection of liver disease. However, GGTP is not pathognomonic for any single disease. Elevations of GGTP may reflect many different liver impairments (including hepatitis, fatty liver, carcinoma, cirrhosis and a variety of infiltrative diseases) and several medications. GGTP is often associated with alcohol abuse. Repetitive and/or excessive alcohol use induces the liver cells to make GGTP. However, three drinks per day or less may not affect the test. In addition, isolated episodes of binge drinking do not normally have an effect on the GGTP. Even if alcohol consumption is discontinued, the GGTP remains elevated for several weeks.

There is a continuing search for screening tests with better sensitivity and specificity for alcohol abuse. The recently introduced desialylated transferrin (DST) may be the most useful of those currently available. Transferrin, used for the transport of iron, is synthesized primarily in the liver, and it is thought that alcohol interferes with the normal attachment of sialic acid to the transferrin molecule, thus creating DST. A few drinks taken daily for a month may cause a raised DST, which may remain detectable for 15 to 30 days after intake has ceased, clearing more quickly in younger people. Primary biliary cirrhosis and organic solvents can cause a raised DST.

Alkaline phosphatase is elevated in conditions that obstruct the bile ducts. Elevations are usually associated with serious disease.

It should be kept in mind that most mortality studies are based on a specific underlying impairment. Therefore the greatest accuracy in underwriting results from determining the impairment causing the abnormality. Obesity, hypertriglyceridemia and diabetes are frequently associated with elevated liver enzymes. Many medications are also associated with elevations.

After attempting to determine the impairment or condition causing the elevation, one should look for factors and characteristics suggestive of alcohol abuse. These would include suspicious behaviors (e.g. driving while intoxicated etc.) or medical reasons (e.g. recurrent gastritis, history of drug abuse, pancreatitis etc.)

Rating

Alcohol Abuse Not Suspected

| | AST or ALT[a,b] | | |
	Normal or unknown	≤1·5 times normal level	1·6–2·5 times normal level	≥2·6 times normal level
GGTP				
Normal or unknown	0	0 to +50	+100 to +200	Postpone
≤1·5 times normal level	0 to +50	+50	Refer to MD	Postpone
1·6–2·5 times normal level	+50 to +150	+100 to +200	Postpone	Postpone
2·6 times normal level	Postpone	Postpone	Postpone	Postpone

[a]If both ALT and AST are elevated, refer to MD.
[b]Higher ratings apply at higher levels.

Alkaline phosphatase elevated:
To 1·5 times normal level:
No other liver enzyme elevated — usually standard.
One other elevated — rate as for GGTP/AST/ALT elevations (*see* above).
Two or more elevated — usually postpone.
Other — usually postpone.

Serum bilirubin elevated:
No elevated liver enzyme(s) — rating for familial hyperbilirubinemia applies (*see* pp. 569–70).
Other — usually postpone.

Alcohol Abuse Suspected
Follow alcohol abuse underwriting guidelines (*see* Chapter 30).

SUMMARY

Knowledge of the use and interpretation of laboratory data is critical to underwriting. Although laboratory data are of great value, they are subject to limitations. MDs and underwriters must know the limits of reliability and usefulness of a test result for a particular proposed insured. The future of diagnostic technologies offers intriguing challenges to the risk selection process. Only by careful, thoughtful and knowledgeable processes shall we be able to meet those challenges.

REFERENCES

1 Butz R. Life Insurance and the laboratory: introduction. *J Insur Med* 1988; 20(2): 3–4.
2 Kita MW. Drawing conclusions from test results. *J Insur Med* 1990; 22(4): 270–8. (Also correction in *J Insur Med* 1991; 23(1): 33.)

3 Pokorski RJ. The genetic testing debate. *J Insur Med* 1988; 20(3): 42–4.
4 Chambers D. Tumor marker screening tests pose dilemma for insurance industry. *Medical Resource* 1990; 2: 1–3.
5 Taylor CR. Clinical use of tumor markers. *Trans Assoc Life Ins Med Dirs Am* 1991; 75: 65–8.
6 Morton DL., Gupta RK. Potential for tumor markers as screening tools for early cancer diagnosis. *Trans Assoc Life Ins Med Dirs Am* 1991; 75: 69–80.
7 Ryan JA. Preliminary experience with tumor markers. *Trans Assoc Life Ins Med Dirs Am* 1991; 75: 81–2.
8 Tumor Marker Forum. Sponsored by American Academy of Insurance Medicine. *J Ins Med*, Supplement 1992.

CHAPTER 12

BUILD

R D C BRACKENRIDGE
I MCLEAN BAIRD

In the earlier days of medicine, physicians became adept at diagnosis after recognizing that different characteristics of build tended to be associated with certain diseases: the thin and cadaverous with phthisis; the plethoric with apoplexy; and the bulky and pallid with dropsy. The tendency for the same build and the same diseases to run in families was also recognized. It is not surprising, therefore, that in these early days insurance companies attached considerable importance to the appearance and build of an applicant, but with advances in medical science it became unnecessary to rely on physical appearance alone for the estimation of the risk involved. Nevertheless, the information conveyed by build is still important today; excessive body weight is often the sole physical manifestation of a faulty constitution which otherwise may only be suspected, either because of an unfavourable family history or the pattern of previous sickness.

Before mortality statistics relating to build were first published in the USA in 1903,[1] underweights were considered to be much poorer insurance risks than overweights, mainly due to the high death rate from tuberculosis. At that time the influence of substantial overweight on mortality was not fully realized, and the fat individual with a rubicund complexion was considered to be a well-nourished and healthy fellow; but publication of mortality statistics regarding body weight changed these ideas, and soon the overweight applicant was obliged to pay for his disability with an extra premium.

In about the middle of this century, the emphasis began to shift mainly because of the elimination of tuberculosis as a significant factor in mortality, and underweight, far from being an adverse feature, gradually gave rise to a more favourable mortality experience in most age groups than average weight itself. This was clearly demonstrated in the *Build and Blood Pressure Study 1959*,[2] where the lowest mortality ratios were consistently associated with underweight, very often to appreciable degree.

Surprisingly this trend was reversed in the *Build Study 1979*[3] with mortality tending to show a rise in those who were 20 percent or more underweight. The reason for this is not altogether clear but may have been due to a change in the sampling of individuals studied between the 1959 and 1979 studies. Also there was a higher incidence of early mortality in the underweights of the 1979 study.

Table 12.1. Average weights (in pounds) of men of varying ages (15–69).[a]

Height[c]	Weight[b] (lb)							
	15–16	17–19	20–24	25–29	30–39	40–49	50–59	60–69
4ft 10in	93	106	112	116	120	121	122	121
4ft 11in	98	110	117	121	124	126	127	126
5 ft 0in	102	115	121	125	129	131	132	130

Height[c]	Weight[b] (lb)							
	15–16	17–19	20–24	25–29	30–39	40–49	50–59	60–69
5ft 1in	107	119	126	130	133	135	136	135
5ft 2in	112	124	130	134	138	140	141	140
5ft 3in	116	129	136	140	143	144	145	144
5ft 4in	121	132	139	143	147	149	150	149
5ft 5in	127	137	143	147	151	154	155	153
5ft 6in	133	141	148	152	156	158	159	158
5ft 7in	137	145	153	156	160	163	164	163
5ft 8in	143	150	157	161	165	167	168	167
5ft 9in	148	155	163	166	170	172	173	172
5ft 10in	153	159	167	171	174	176	177	176
5ft 11in	159	164	171	175	179	181	182	181
6ft 0in	162	168	176	181	184	186	187	186
6ft 1in	168	174	182	186	190	192	193	191
6ft 2in	173	179	187	191	195	197	198	196
6ft 3in	178	185	193	197	201	203	204	200
6ft 4in	184	190	198	202	206	208	209	207
6ft 5in	189	195	203	207	211	213	214	212
6ft 6in	195	201	209	213	217	219	220	218
6ft 7in	201	207	215	219	223	225	226	224

[a]Data from *Build Study 1979*.[3]
[b]Graduated weights in indoor clothing.
[c]In normal shoes.

Table 12.2. Average weights (in kilograms) of men of varying ages (15–69).[a]

Height[c] (m)	Weight[b] (kg)							
	15–16	17–19	20–24	25–29	30–39	40–49	50–59	60–69
1·47	42·0	48·0	51·0	52·5	54·5	55·0	55·5	55·0
1·50	44·5	50·0	53·0	55·0	56·0	57·0	57·5	57·0
1·52	46·5	52·0	55·0	56·5	58·5	59·5	60·0	59·0
1·55	48·5	54·0	57·0	59·0	60·5	61·0	61·5	61·0
1·57	51·0	56·0	59·0	61·0	62·5	63·5	64·0	63·5
1·60	52·5	58·0	61·0	63·5	65·0	65·5	66·0	65·5
1·63	55·0	60·0	63·0	65·0	66·5	67·5	68·0	67·5
1·65	57·5	62·0	65·0	66·5	68·5	70·0	70·5	69·5
1·68	60·5	64·0	67·0	69·0	71·0	71·5	72·0	71·0
1·70	62·0	66·0	69·5	71·0	72·5	74·0	74·5	74·0
1·73	65·0	68·0	71·0	73·0	75·0	75·5	76·0	75·5
1·75	67·0	70·5	73·5	75·5	77·0	78·0	78·5	78·0
1·78	69·5	72·0	75·5	77·5	79·0	80·0	80·5	80·0
1·80	72·0	74·5	77·5	79·5	81·0	82·0	82·5	82·0

Height^c (m)	Weight^b(kg)							
	15–16	17–19	20–24	25–29	30–39	40–49	50–59	60–69
1·83	73·5	76·0	80·0	82·0	83·5	84·5	85·0	84·5
1·85	76·0	79·0	82·5	84·5	86·0	87·0	87·5	86·5
1·88	78·5	81·0	85·0	86·5	88·5	89·5	90·0	89·0
1·91	80·5	84·0	87·5	89·5	91·0	92·0	92·5	90·5
1·93	83·5	86·0	90·0	91·5	93·5	94·5	95·0	94·0
1·96	85·5	88·5	92·0	94·0	95·0	96·5	97·0	96·0
1·98	88·5	91·0	95·0	96·5	98·5	99·5	100·0	99·0
2·01	92·0	94·0	97·5	99·5	101·0	102·0	102·5	101·5

^{a}Data from *Build Study 1979*.[3]
^{b}Graduated weights in indoor clothing.
^{c}In normal shoes.

Table 12.3. Average weights (in pounds) of women of varying ages (15–69).[a]

Height^c	Weight^b (lb)							
	15–16	17–19	20–24	25–29	30–39	40–49	50–59	60–69
4ft 6in	85	87	89	95	101	105	109	111
4ft 7in	89	91	93	98	104	108	112	114
4ft 8in	93	95	99	103	107	111	115	117
4ft 9in	97	99	101	106	110	114	118	120
4ft 10in	101	103	105	110	113	118	121	123
4ft 11in	105	108	110	112	115	121	125	127
5ft 0in	109	111	112	114	118	123	127	130
5ft 1in	112	115	116	119	121	127	131	133
5ft 2in	117	119	120	121	124	129	133	136
5ft 3in	121	123	124	125	128	133	137	140
5ft 4in	123	126	127	128	131	136	141	143
5ft 5in	128	129	130	132	134	139	144	147
5ft 6in	131	132	133	134	137	143	147	150
5ft 7in	135	136	137	138	141	147	152	155
5ft 8in	138	140	141	142	145	150	156	158
5ft 9in	142	145	146	148	150	155	159	161
5ft 10in	146	148	149	150	153	158	162	163
5ft 11in	149	150	155	156	159	162	166	167
6ft 0in	152	154	157	159	164	168	171	172
6ft 1in	155	157	159	163	168	172	175	176
6ft 2in	158	160	162	166	172	176	179	180
6ft 3in	161	163	165	170	176	180	183	184

^{a}Data from *Build Study 1979*.[3]
^{b}Graduated weights in indoor clothing.
^{c}In normal shoes.

Table 12.4. Average weights (in kilograms) of women of varying ages (15–69).[a]

Height[c] (m)	Weight[b] (kg)							
	15–16	17–19	20–24	25–29	30–39	40–49	50–59	60–69
1·37	38·5	39·5	40·5	43·0	46·0	47·5	49·5	50·5
1·40	40·5	41·5	42·0	44·5	47·0	49·0	51·0	51·0
1·42	42·0	43·0	45·0	46·5	48·5	50·5	52·0	53·0
1·45	44·0	45·0	46·0	48·0	50·0	51·5	53·5	54·5
1·47	46·0	46·5	47·5	50·0	51·5	53·5	55·0	56·0
1·50	47·5	49·0	50·0	51·0	52·0	55·0	56·0	57·5
1·52	49·5	50·5	51·0	51·5	53·5	56·0	57·5	59·0
1·55	51·0	52·0	52·5	54·0	55·0	57·5	59·5	60·5
1·57	53·0	54·0	54·5	55·0	56·0	58·5	60·5	61·5
1·60	55·0	56·0	56·0	56·5	58·0	60·5	62·0	63·5
1·63	56·0	57·0	57·5	58·0	59·5	61·5	64·0	65·0
1·65	58·0	58·5	59·0	60·0	61·0	63·0	65·5	66·5
1·68	59·5	60·0	60·5	60·5	62·0	65·0	66·5	68·0
1·70	61·0	61·5	62·0	62·5	64·0	66·5	69·0	70·5
1·73	62·5	63·5	64·0	64·5	66·0	68·0	71·0	71·5
1·75	64·5	66·0	66·0	67·0	68·0	70·5	72·0	73·0
1·79	66·0	67·0	67·5	68·0	69·5	71·5	73·5	74·0
1·80	67·5	68·0	70·5	71·0	72·0	73·5	75·5	75·5
1·83	69·0	70·0	71·0	72·0	74·5	76·0	77·5	78·0
1·85	70·5	71·0	72·0	74·0	76·5	78·0	79·5	80·0
1·88	71·5	72·5	73·5	75·5	78·0	80·0	81·0	81·5
1·91	73·0	74·0	75·0	77·0	80·0	81·5	83·0	83·5

[a]Data from *Build Study 1979*.[3]
[b]Graduated weights in indoor clothing.
[c]In normal shoes.

BUILD STUDIES

Studies of mortality among insured lives according to variations in weight date back to *The Specialized Mortality Investigation*[1] of 1903, which was followed by the *Medico-Actuarial Mortality Investigation 1909–12*[4] published in 1913, the *Supplement to the Medical Impairment Study 1929*,[5] the *Build and Blood Pressure Study 1959*,[2] and the *Build Study 1979*.[3] The *Build and Blood Pressure Study 1959* covered almost 4½ million lives traced for nearly 20 years. However, it included only a few statistics on extreme overweights and those with very high blood pressures. The *Build Study 1979* likewise covered approximately 4½ million lives traced for 22 years. It, too, included only scanty data on extreme overweights (*see* Tables 12.1–12.4).

It has been possible for the first time to compare the experience among insured lives according to build with the corresponding figures for a large sample of the general population of the USA. This latter experience derives from the American

Cancer Society's Cancer Prevention Study. Begun in 1959 it traced for some 12 years about 750,000 men and women, initially free of heart disease, related impairments, cancer and marked loss of weight. The results of this study according to variations in weight closely match the findings for overweight men in the *Build and Blood Pressure Study 1959*,[2] and for underweight men the findings in the *Build Study 1979*[3] (*see* Table 12.5). The similarity of findings for insured men and women

Table 12.5. Comparison of average weights in various studies.[a]

| Age | Height[b] | Weight[c] | | |
		Build Study 1979 (1950–71)	Build and Blood Pressure Study 1959 (1935–53)	American Cancer Society Study[d] (1959)
Men				
25	5ft 4in (1·63)	141 (64·0)	139 (63·0)	–
	5ft 8in (1·73)	159 (72·0)	153 (69·5)	–
	6ft 0in (1·83)	178 (80·5)	169 (76·5)	–
35	5ft 4in (1·63)	147 (66·5)	146 (66·0)	147 (66·0)
	5ft 8in (1·73)	165 (75·0)	161 (73·0)	162 (73·5)
	6ft 0in (1·83)	184 (83·5)	179 (81·0)	179 (81·0)
45	5ft 4in (1·63)	149 (67·5)	148 (67·5)	149 (67·5)
	5ft 8in (1·73)	167 (75·5)	165 (75·0)	164 (74·5)
	6ft 0in (1·83)	186 (84·5)	183 (83·0)	182 (82·5)
55	5ft 4in (1·63)	150 (68·0)	149 (67·5)	149 (67·5)
	5ft 8in (1·73)	168 (76·0)	166 (75·5)	164 (74·5)
	6ft 0in (1·83)	187 (85·0)	185 (84·0)	182 (82·5)
Women				
25	5ft 0in (1·52)	113 (51·5)	111 (50·5)	–
	5ft 4in (1·63)	128 (58·5)	123 (56·0)	–
	5ft 8in (1·73)	142 (64·5)	138 (62·5)	–
35	5ft 0in (1·52)	118 (53·5)	121 (55·0)	117 (53·0)
	5ft 4in (1·63)	128 (59·5)	132 (60·0)	131 (59·5)
	5ft 8in (1·73)	142 (66·0)	146 (66·5)	145 (66·0)
45	5ft 0in (1·52)	123 (56·0)	127 (57·5)	121 (55·0)
	5ft 4in (1·63)	136 (61·5)	140 (63·5)	136 (61·5)
	5ft 8in (1·73)	150 (68·0)	155 (70·5)	150 (68·0)
55	5ft 0in (1·52)	127 (57·5)	130 (59·0)	125 (56·5)
	5ft 4in (1·63)	141 (64·0)	144 (65·5)	141 (64·0)
	5ft 8in (1·73)	156 (71·0)	160 (72·5)	156 (71·0)

[a]Data from *Build Study, 1979.*[3]
[b]Height in normal shoes in feet and inches (in metres).
[c]Weight in indoor clothing in pounds (in kilograms).
[d]Adjusted from height in bare feet to approximate height in shoes.

drawn from the general population suggests that the mortality observed among insured men can be used as a guide for men in the general population for a variety of impairments.

The *Build and Blood Pressure Study 1959*[2] and the *Build Study 1979*[3] together comprise unique information regarding the mortality of insured lives according to variations in weight. Such information does not extend much beyond weights in excess of 60 percent above average nor to blood pressures in excess of 175/105 mm Hg. It is invaluable, however, for life insurance companies in their underwriting and calculation of premium rates for substandard risks.

A mortality study of overweights insured by the Cologne Reinsurance Company was reported in 1969.[6] The study, which covered the years 1948–66, showed that mortality associated with overweight as the sole impairment remained relatively low for eight years and only then started to show a modest rise. However, an extension of the above study covering the years 1948–74 was reported to COINTRA in 1977.[7] This rather surprisingly showed only very slight increments in mortality with increasing duration among insured subjects with uncomplicated overweight. On the other hand, the mortality observed in the overweight group with hypertension was considerably higher (about 50 percent) than that in the overweight group without hypertension.

Analysis of the Build Study 1979

The average weights of men in the *Build Study 1979*[3] exceed the corresponding weights in the *Build and Blood Pressure Study 1959* by 2–8 lb (0·5–4 kg) in their 30s, and by up to 5 lb (2·5 kg) in their 50s, the smallest differences being for short men and the largest for tall men. Men in their early 20s recorded average weights in the 1979 study that are from 4 to 15 lb (2 to 7 kg) greater than the corresponding weights in the earlier study. The average weights of women in the 1979 study have decreased by about a kilogram in their 30s and by 2–7 lb (1–3 kg) in their 50s as compared with the earlier study, but the average weights of women in their early 20s have increased by 3–5 lb (1·5–2·5 kg).

The mortality ratios of overweight men classified by ranges of absolute weight are not significantly different in the 1979 study from those in the earlier study (*see* Table 12.6), but men who are markedly overweight (i.e. those 30–60 percent above average weight) experience lower mortality in the *Build Study 1979* than in the *Build and Blood Pressure Study 1959*; their mortality ratios in the 1979 study are from 10–30 percentage points lower, the differentials increasing with mounting overweight (*see* Table 12.7). Consequently a new schedule of ratings has been prepared to take into account the changes in mortality exhibited in the *Build Study 1979* (*see* pp. 210–11).

The mortality ratios of overweight women classified by percentage departure from average weight exhibit somewhat smaller decreases from the earlier study.

By contrast, men weighing 20 percent below average recorded 10–15 percent higher mortality in the *Build Study 1979* than in the *Build and Blood Pressure Study 1959* (*see* Table 12.7). The optimum weights for men in the 1979 study appear to be about 10 percent below average weight. Women weighing

20 percent below average registered about 10 percent higher mortality; their optimum weights also seem to lie about 10 percent below average weight.

Mortality ratios of overweight women are relatively lower than those of

Table 12.6. Comparison of mortality ratios in relation to standard experience by absolute weight in Build Study 1979 (BS) and Build and Blood Pressure Study 1959 (BBPS).

Weight ranges[a]	Mortality ratios (%)					
	Short men[b]		Medium men[c]		Tall men[d]	
	BS	BBPS	BS	BBPS	BS	BBPS
105–114 (47·6–51·7)	120	110	115	113		
125–134 (56·7–60·8)	105	96	110[e]	89	107	94
145–154 (65·8–69·9)	102	95	99	90	99	82
165–174 (74·8–78·9)	108	113	96	100	91	90
185–194 (83·9–88·0)	120[e]	125	109	113	100	94
205–214 (93·0–97·1)	145	139[e]	125	125	110	114
225–234 (102·1–106·1)			139[e]	144[e]	135[e]	130[e]
245–254 (111·1–115·2)					155	

[a]Weight ranges in pounds (in kilograms).
[b]Average weight 150 lb (68 kg).
[c]Average weight 170 lb (77·1 kg).
[d]Average weight 190 lb (86·2 kg).
[e]Graduated mortality ratio.

Table 12.7. Mortality ratios in relation to standard experience by departure from average. Comparison of Build Study 1979 (BS), Build and Blood Pressure Study 1959 (BBPS) and American Cancer Society Study (ACS).

Departure from average weight (%)	Mortality ratios (%)					
	Men			Women		
	BS	BBPS	ACS	BS	BBPS	ACS
Below						
20	105	90	110	110	99	100
10	94	95	100	97	95	95
Above						
10	111	113	107	106	109	108
20	120	125	121	110	121	123
30	133	142	137	125	130	138
40	150	167	162	136		162
50	171	200	210	150[a]		200
60	195[a]	260				

[a]Graduated mortality ratio.

overweight men, the differentials ranging from 10 percentage points for weights 20 percent above the average to about 20 percentage points for weights 50 percent above average (*see* Table 12.7).

Mortality by Cause

Men weighting 20 percent above average experienced mortality from all causes in the 1979 study that was 20 percent above the standard 100 percent. Their death rates from coronary disease were about 15 percent higher, from diabetes about 150 percent higher and from digestive diseases about 20 percent higher. Men weighing 40 percent above average recorded mortality from all causes approximately 50 percent greater than standard (equal to 100 percent). Their death rates from coronary disease and from cerebrovascular accidents were about 60 percent higher, from diabetes more than 400 percent higher, and from digestive diseases about 120 percent higher.

Incidence of Mortality

The incidence of mortality associated with overweight tends to be late. The *Build and Blood Pressure Study 1959*[2] showed that among moderately overweight males the percentage extra mortality remained relatively low, about 20 percent in the first five years after issue of insurance, rising slightly in the next five years and continuing upwards over a period of another ten years to about 35 percent. Among markedly overweight males, percentage extra mortality followed a similar pattern but was more pronounced, rising to nearly 85 percent after 15 years had elapsed (*see* Fig. 12.1).

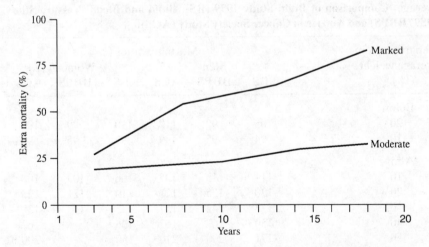

Fig. 12.1. The incidence of mortality among males who were moderately overweight and markedly overweight. [Source: *Build and Blood Pressure Study 1959*.[2] Graph adapted from *Statistical Bulletin*. New York: Metropolitan Life Insurance Company, November 1968].

This late incidence of mortality permits a certain amount of leniency in the underwriting of overweight lives whose policies will mature at a relatively early age, say 60 and under, and when the plan is of the endowment type standard rates may even be granted to applicants who are as much as 30–35 percent overweight.

Increasing Average Weights per various Heights for Men

A study of men insured by the Metropolitan Life Insurance Company[8] shows how average weights for men have increased over a quarter of a century, from 1941 to 1967, especially for men of above average height. Among short men there was little significant change in weight between 1941 and 1967. The average weights of men 5 ft 6 in to 5 ft 8 in (1·68 to 1·73 m) increased by about 4 lb (2 kg) between this period. The average weights of the men 5 ft 9 in to 5 ft 11 in (1·75 to 1·80 m) rose by 7 lb (3 kg) and those for the men 6 ft 0 in to 6 ft 2 in (1·83 to 1·88 m) by 8 lb (3·5 kg). It was among the younger men (ages 18–34) that the larger increases in weight were recorded.

Men usually reach their full heights by their mid-20s and after age 40 decrease by about 0·4 in (1 cm) in each decade thereafter.

Overweight in Combination with Other Impairments

When rateable overweight occurs together with other impairments, such as arterial hypertension, heart and circulatory disorders, diabetes, proteinuria or a family history of cardiovascular-renal disease, the extra mortality associated with overweight plus the other impairment is always somewhat greater than would be expected by summing the extra mortality for each. Depending on the degree of overweight, usually when greater than 20 percent, the sum of the rating for each impairment has to be increased by a factor of up to one quarter. The combination factors appropriate to each impairment will be discussed in the relevant chapters.

Fluctuation in Weight

Body weight is amazingly well regulated in the normal adult. With a daily variation of about 2 lb (1 kg) it remains constant for weeks, months or years in spite of changes in diet, climate and activity, and constancy of weight over a period of years is usually a good indicator of continuing normal health. Deviation, and particularly recent substantial deviation, from an individual's norm may signal serious disease, and this is true of gain in weight as well as loss.

In one who is substantially overweight a very large amount of weight can be lost quite quickly by strict dieting. In the person of average or below average weight a substantial loss, however, should arouse suspicion of serious underlying disease, and unless an adequate explanation for the loss were forthcoming it would be justifiable for an underwriter to postpone acceptance for life assurance for a period in order to protect the company against an early claim.

Rapid increase in weight would be an equally adverse situation which should alert the suspicion of the underwriter until it is adequately explained. Certain changes in life style can influence weight. Taking to drinking or giving up smoking may both lead to obesity. In certain types of person psychological trauma may lead to a rapid gain in weight; this, in part, may be due to the kind of drug being used in treating the depressive illness which results. Chlorpromazine, lithium carbonate and amitriptyline have all been implicated in causing weight gain in subjects being treated for depression, possibly because they produce a craving for carbohydrate-rich foods. Rarely a rapid gain in weight may be due to an endocrine tumour.

So the message to the life underwriter is clear: if the circumstances associated with a rapid increase or decrease in weight are not satisfactorily explained, an application for life insurance should be postponed for a short period to allow time for further investigations to be made, or simply to observe developments.

Mortality and Weight Reduction

The problem of how to deal with applicants who have reduced their weight by dieting sometimes arises, and doubts are often felt as to the validity of disregarding previous weight and rating in the weight group to which they now belong. Nevertheless, this would seem to be the correct procedure. An investigation by Dublin and Marks[9] showed that among insured lives that were rateably overweight, mortality did in fact become less when weight was reduced adequately by design. A similar investigation in the *Build and Blood Pressure Study 1959*[2] confirmed these earlier findings, for with a few exceptions, mortality among men who reduced their weight was appreciably less than that which would have been expected in their original weight groups. In most classifications by age and duration, the overweights who reduced showed mortality ratios which did not exceed 100 percent. However, in a few instances, notably for short men weighing 195–214 lb (88·5–97 kg) at issue and for tall men weighing 215–234 lb (97·5–106 kg), mortality ratios were of the order of 125 percent, which would probably be nearer 130 percent when computed from the time they become eligible for standard insurance.

It seems, therefore, that most overweights who have reduced to within average limits can be insured at standard rates, although in practice one would be happier if it were known that weight had been maintained at the reduced level for a reasonable period, say six months to a year, before doing so.

SOMATOTYPES AND MORTALITY

Owing to the absence of necessary data, large-scale mortality studies of insured lives have been unable to take into account the different builds or somatotypes, or in other words the relative proportions of fat, muscle and bone making up excess weight. However, some allowance is usually made in underwriting for the crude weight distribution deduced from the measurements round the chest and abdomen (*see* Table 12.8). This is done on the assumption that obesity is usually reflected by a large abdominal girth relative to the mean chest girth, and that the non-obese or less obese overweight has a small abdominal girth relative to the mean chest girth.

Table 12.8.   Credits and debits for abdominal girth in relation to expanded chest for various degrees of overweight. All ages up to 60. (*See* **Build ratings pp. 210–11.**)

Degree of overweight (%)	Less than expanded chest by 3 in (7·6 cm) and more	Equal to or up to 2¾ in (7·0 cm) more than expanded chest	Exceeds expanded chest by 3 in (7·6 cm) or more
Under 20	− 5	+ 5	+10
21–35	−10	+10	+15
36–50	−15	+15	+20
51 and over	−20	+20	+25

Those whose excess weight consists mainly of muscle and bone with little or no fat, and whose weight distribution is good, are generally considered to be better risks than those of the same height and weight who are obese. This means in effect that the overweight mesomorph is a better risk than the endomorph of corresponding weight. This impression has not been proved statistically, and may in fact be a fallacy, since it is well known that the mesomorph, possibly because of his temperament and behaviour pattern, is particularly prone to cardiovascular disease. Garn et al,[10] compared a group of young persons who had suffered a myocardial infarction with a similar group of healthy controls, and came to the conclusion that it was the endomorphic mesomorph (i.e. the dominantly muscular person with a good deal of fat) who was most prone to coronary artery disease. The same workers also showed that in groups of mesomorphs and endomorphs who had suffered coronary incidents both had higher than average levels of serum cholesterol and uric acid, but that it was the mesomorphs who had the greater excess of cholesterol, while the endomorphs had the greater excess of uric acid. Sanders,[11] in a well controlled experiment, attempted to show that the significant factor in coronary disease is excess fat rather than excess weight. He investigated a group of 48 white hospital patients with recent onset of ischemic heart disease, who were all free from complications and in whom the diagnosis had been confirmed by ECG. These he matched with a group of 52 healthy males selected at random from the files of a National Health Service practice. Body fat was measured by skinfold thickness at various sites using skinfold calipers. The result of the study showed that although there was no significant difference in weight between the group of patients with uncomplicated coronary artery disease and the group of healthy controls, the 'coronary' patients were found to have a significantly increased mass of body fat.

Parnell,[12] using Sheldon's FML (fat, muscularity and linearity) scale to denote somatotype (*see* p. 157), discussed the question of relative proportions of fat and muscle in overweights in relation to longevity. Those whose weights are much above average come from two main groups: the mesomorph-endomorphs (e.g. 532) who are predominantly fat; and endomorph-mesomorphs (e.g. 352) who are predominantly muscular with excess supporting fat. Parnell considered that there is a difference in mortality between these two types of build. Whereas somatotype 117, the pure ectomorph, gains little or nothing in weight throughout life, a common mid-range somatotype (e.g. 343) may be expected to gain some 16 percent by the age of 48; the heaviest gainer of all, somatotype 741, can add 56 percent to his weight at age 18 by the time he is 38, and may only survive longer if he actually reduces weight.

The mid-range somatotypes (443, 343, 353 and 344) comprise 22 percent of the white male population and represent man as he would like to be portrayed, the ideal figure. Their weight gain curves show no sign of falling off before their 70s, and this may indicate that their biological lifespan is longer than three-score years and ten, probably nearer 80 years, and for type 344 even that could be a conservative estimate.

In contrast to the mid-range types with a rating of 4 or 5 for mesomorphy, types 424, 425 and 524 (i.e. endomorph-ectomorphs), even when they are average weight for height, all show a downturn in their weight gain curves starting at about age 53, some earlier, thus indicating a curtailed longevity.

Parnell suggested that life insurance companies could obtain more meaningful mortality statistics regarding build by adding a third parameter, namely body fat as measured by skinfold thickness, to the conventional height and weight. Not all overweights are obese; some moderate overweights are predominantly muscular. On the other hand, many who are of average weight are technically obese, and there is evidence that mortality varies with the type of body build. Height and weight may be used to provide an index of linearity or ectomorphy, but it is clear that by themselves they afford no means of distinguishing weight in the form of fat from weight in the form of muscle.

Parnell's suggestion seems a reasonable one, but the drawback is that few medical referees possess the necessary calipers for measuring skinfold thickness and, until they do and until a uniform technique of measurement is adopted throughout the life insurance industry, it has little chance of being added to the medical examination as a standard procedure. There is no reason, however, why skinfold thickness should not be included as an obligatory measurement in paramedical examinations since most paramedical units are already equipped with the necessary calipers. Thereby at least some insurance statistics could be accumulated which in time could prove or disprove the value of this additional datum in the assessment of mortality associated with build.

1983 Metropolitan Height and Weight Tables[13]

The Metropolitan Life Insurance Company has been producing height and weight tables for many years. The first tables based on the lowest mortality for women and men were published in 1942 and 1943 respectively, to be followed some 16 years later by the 1959 Metropolitan Desirable Weight Table which was compiled from data derived from the *Build and Blood Pressure Study 1959*.[2] The most recent tables, the 1983 Metropolitan Height and Weight Tables, were based on the findings of the *Build Study 1979*[3] and take into account the narrowed gap between average weights and weights based on lowest mortality that had occurred since 1959. Although increased, the 1983 weights still fall below average weights indicating that it is wiser to weigh less than the average rather than more. The weights published in earlier Metropolitan tables used to be called 'ideal' or 'desirable', but because of various misinterpretations of their meaning these terms have now been dropped and replaced with 'weights at which people should have the greatest longevity – or least mortality'. It is important to realize that these weights are not used for underwriting purposes or in the computation of premiums.

The 1983 Metropolitan Height and Weight Tables (*see* Tables 12.9 and 12.10) are

Table 12.9. 1983 Metropolitan Height and Weight Tables for men and women according to frame, ages 25–59 (feet and inches, pounds).[a]

Height[b]	Small frame	Weight[c] (lb) Medium frame	Large frame
		Men	
5ft 2in	128–134	131–141	138–150
5ft 3in	130–136	133–143	140–153
5ft 4in	132–138	135–145	142–156
5ft 5in	134–140	137–148	144–160
5ft 6in	136–142	139–151	146–164
5ft 7in	138–145	142–154	149–168
5ft 8in	140–148	145–157	152–172
5ft 9in	142–151	148–160	155–176
5ft 10in	144–154	151–163	158–180
5ft 11in	146–157	154–166	161–184
6ft 0in	149–160	157–170	164–188
6ft 1in	152–164	160–174	168–192
6ft 2in	155–168	164–178	172–197
6ft 3in	158–172	167–182	176–202
6ft 4in	162–176	171–187	181–207
		Women	
4ft 10in	102–111	109–121	118–131
4ft 11in	103–113	111–123	120–134
5ft 0in	104–115	113–126	122–137
5ft 1in	106–118	115–129	125–140
5ft 2in	108–121	118–132	128–143
5ft 3in	111–124	121–135	131–147
5ft 4in	114–127	124–138	134–151
5ft 5in	117–130	127–141	137–155
5ft 6in	120–133	130–144	140–159
5ft 7in	123–136	133–147	143–163
5ft 8in	126–139	136–150	146–167
5ft 9in	129–142	139–153	149–170
5ft 10in	132–145	142–156	152–173
5ft 11in	135–148	145–159	155–176
6ft 0in	138–151	148–162	158–179

[a]Basic data from *Build Study 1979*.[3]
[b]In shoes with 1 inch heels.
[c]In indoor clothing weighing 5 lb for men and 3 lb for women.
With permission of the Metropolitan Life Insurance Company.

shown according to body frame: small, medium or large. A simple approximation of frame size can be made by measuring the distance between the medial and lateral epicondyles of the humerus with the forearm supinated and raised to an angle of 90° with the humerus. This is best done with a caliper, although a thumb to fingertip measurement is probably near enough for the purpose. Table 12.11 shows the range of elbow breadth measurements for men and women of medium frame at various heights. Measurements lower than those listed indicate a small frame while higher measurements indicate a large frame.

Table 12.10. 1983 Metropolitan Height and Weight Tables for men and women according to frame, ages 25–29 (metres and kilograms).[a]

| Height[b] (m) | Weight[c] (kg) | | |
	Small frame	Medium frame	Large frame
		Men	
1·58	58·3–61·0	59·6–64·2	62·8–68·3
1·59	58·6–61·3	59·9–64·5	63·1–68·8
1·60	59·0–61·7	60·3–64·9	63·5–69.4
1·61	59·3–62·0	60·6–65·2	63·8–69·9
1·62	59·7–62·4	61·0–65·6	64·2–70·5
1·63	60·0–62·7	61·3–66·0	64·5–71·1
1·64	60·4–63·1	61·7–66·5	64·9–71·8
1·65	60·8–63·5	62·1–67·0	65·3–72·5
1·66	61·1–63·8	62·4–67·6	65·6–73·2
1·67	61·5–64·2	62·8–68·2	66·0–74·0
1·68	61·8–64·6	63·2–68.7	66·4–74·7
1·69	62·2–65·2	63·8–69·3	67.0–75.4
1·70	62·5–65·7	64·3–69·8	67·5–76·1
1·71	62·9–66·2	64·8–70·3	68·0–76·8
1·72	63·2–66·7	65·4–70·8	68·5–77·5
1·73	63·6–67·3	65·9–71·4	69·1–78·2
1.74	63·9–67·8	66·4–71·9	69·6–78·9
1·75	64·3–68·3	66·9–72·4	70·1–79·6
1·76	64·7–68·9	67·5–73·0	70·7–80·3
1·77	65·0–69·5	68·1–73·5	71·3–81·0
1.78	65·4–70·0	68·6–74·0	71·8–81·8
1·79	65·7–70·5	69·2–74·6	72·3–82·5
1·80	66·1–71·0	69·7–75·1	72·8–83·3
1·81	66·6–71·6	70·2–75·8	73·4–84·0
1·82	67·1–72·1	70·7–76·5	73·9–84·7
1·83	67·7–72·7	71·3–77·2	74·5–85·4
1·84	68·2–73·4	71·8–77·9	75·2–86·1
1·85	68·7–74·1	72·4–78·6	75·9–86·8
1·86	69·2–74·8	73·0–79·3	76·6–87·6
1·87	69·8–75·5	73·7–80·0	77·3–88·5
1·88	70·3–76·2	74·4–80·7	78·0–89·4
1·89	70·9–76·9	74·9–81·5	78·7–90·3
1·90	71·4–77·6	75·4–82·2	79·4–91·2

Height[b] (m)	Weight[c] (kg)		
	Small frame	Medium frame	Large frame
		Men	
1·91	72·1–78·4	76·1–83·0	80·3–92·1
1·92	72·8–79·1	76·8–83·9	81·2–93·0
1·93	73·5–79·8	77·6–84·8	82·1–93·9
		Women	
1·48	46·4–50·6	49·6–55·1	53·7–59·8
1·49	46·6–51·0	50·0–55·5	54·1–60·3
1·50	46·7–51·3	50·3–55·9	54·4–60·9
1·51	46·9–51·7	50·7–56·4	54·8–61·4
1·52	47·1–52·1	51·1–57·0	55·2–61·9
1·53	47·4–52·5	51·5–57·5	55·6–62·4
1·54	47·8–53·0	51·9–58·0	56·2–63·0
1·55	48·1–53·6	52·2–58·6	56·8–63·6
1·56	48·5–54·1	52·7–59·1	57·3–64·1
1·57	48·8–54·6	53·2–59·6	57·8–64·6
1·58	49·3–55·2	53·8–60·2	58·4–65·3
1·59	49·8–55·7	54·3–60·7	58·9–66·0
1·60	50·3–56·2	54·9–61·2	59·4–66·7
1·61	50·8–56·7	55·4–61·7	59·9–67·4
1·62	51·4–57·3	55·9–62·3	60·5–68·1
1·63	51·9–57·8	56·4–62·8	61·0–68·8
1·64	52·5–58·4	57·0–63·4	61·5–69·5
1·65	53·0–58·9	57·5–63·9	62·0–70·2
1·66	53·6–59·5	58·1–64·5	62·6–70·9
1·67	54·1–60·0	58·7–65·0	63·2–71·7
1·68	54·6–60·5	59·2–65·5	63·7–72·4
1·69	55·2–61·1	59·7–66·1	64·3–73·1
1·70	55·7–61·6	60·2–66·6	64·8–73·8
1·71	56·2–62·1	60·7–67·1	65·3–74·5
1·72	56·8–62·6	61·3–67·6	65·8–75·2
1·73	57·3–63·2	61·8–68·2	66·4–75·9
1·74	57·8–63·7	62·3–68·7	66·9–76·4
1·75	58·3–64·2	62·8–69·2	67·4–76·9
1·76	58·9–64·8	63·4–69·8	68·0–77.5
1·77	59·5–65·4	64·0–70·4	68·5–78·1
1·78	60·0–65·9	64·5–70·9	69·0–78·6
1·79	60·5–66·4	65·1–71·4	69·6–79·1
1·80	61·0–66.9	65·6–71·9	70·1–79·6
1·81	61·6–67·5	66·1–72·5	70·7–80·2
1·82	62·1–68·0	66·6–73·0	71·2–80·7
1·83	62·6–68·5	67·1–73·5	71·7–81·2

[a]Basic data from *Build Study 1979*.[3]
[b]In shoes with 2·5 cm heels.
[c]In indoor clothing weighing 2·3 kg for men and 1·4 kg for women.
With permission of the Metropolitan Life Insurance Company.

Table 12.11. Elbow breadth measurements for men and women of medium frame at various heights.[a]

Height[b]	Elbow breadth
Men	
5ft 2in–5ft 3in (158–161 cm)	2½–2⅞ in (6·4–7·2 cm)
5ft 4in–5ft 7in (162–171 cm)	2⅝–2⅞ in (6·7–7·4 cm)
5ft 8in–5ft 11in (172–181 cm)	2¾–3 in (6·9–7·6 cm)
6ft 0in–6ft 3in (182–191 cm)	2¾–3⅛ in (7·1–7·8 cm)
6ft 4in (192–193 cm)	2⅞–3¼ in (7·4–8·1 cm.)
Women	
4ft 10in–4ft 11in (148–151 cm)	2¼–2½ in (5·6–6·4 cm)
5ft 0in–5ft 3in (152·161 cm)	2¼–2½ in (5·8–6·5 cm)
5ft 4in–5ft 7in (162–171 cm)	2⅜–2⅝ in (5·9–6·6 cm)
5ft 8in–5ft 11in (172–181 cm)	2⅜–2⅝ in (6·1–6·8 cm)
6ft 0in (182–183 cm)	2½–2¾ in (6·2–6·9 cm)

[a]Source of basic data: Data tape, Hanes I – Anthropometry, goniometry, skeletal age, bone density, and cortical thickness, ages 1–74. National Health and Nutritional Examination Survey, 1971–5, National Center for Health Statistics.
[b]In 1 inch (2·5 cm) heels.
With permission of the Metropolitan Life Insurance Company.

RELATIONSHIPS OF WEIGHT TO HEIGHT AND GIRTH

It is sometimes necessary for a life underwriter to reconcile height, weight and girth measurements recorded in the medical examination report. With a knowledge of two of the three variables the third can be calculated from tables compiled by the Society of Actuaries from a sample of over 65,000 men who were included in the *Build and Blood Pressure Study 1959*[2] (*see* Tables 12.12 and 12.13). Of all males, 90 percent may be expected to fall within the ranges of weights shown, and these tables are especially useful in checking reported weights when they appear to be otherwise inconsistent.

SURGICAL TREATMENT OF OBESITY

The medical treatment of massive obesity is generally unsatisfactory and this has led to the introduction of various surgical techniques in an attempt to improve the permanence of weight loss. The following is a brief account of the surgical procedures in common use, their effectiveness, complications and long-term mortality.

Jaw Wiring

This procedure allows only the ingestion of liquid forms of food, and if the wires are left in place for as long as six months weight loss of 50 lb (22·5 kg), or more, is possible. However, many follow-up studies have shown that when the wires are removed most of these individuals return to their original weight. Jaw wiring is useful nevertheless in preparing grossly obese individuals for one of the other surgical procedures and so reducing an operative mortality which might otherwise be considerable. There are no important complications of jaw wiring alone.

Intestinal Bypass Operations

These account for the greatest number of surgical procedures being carried out for weight reduction. The two currently used are end-to-side and end-to-end jejunoileostomy leaving about 40 cm of jejunum and 10 cm of ileum for functional absorption. There are several other modifications. Weight loss stabilizes in two to three years and averages 30 percent of initial weight. In those who survive the early postoperative period the long-term success rate is generally excellent and, according to Bray,[14] 90 percent of those patients were satisfied with the results obtained despite side effects. From the pooled figures of several clinics mortality in the first month after operation is 2–3 percent, although it can reach 14 percent in units performing only a few operations per year.

Table 12.12. Ranges of weights (in pounds) associated with height (in feet and inches) and girth for males, 1935–53.[a,b]

Sum of girth measurements[c]	Weight[d]					
	Ages under 40			Ages 40 and over		
	Lower limit	Expected weight	Upper limit	Lower limit	Expected weight	Upper limit
Height[e] = 5ft 3in						
80	81	97	112	82	98	114
90	102	117	132	101	117	133
100	122	137	152	120	136	151
110	142	157	172	139	155	170
120	162	177	193	158	173	189
130	182	197	213	177	192	208
140	202	218	233	195	211	227
150	222	238	253	214	230	246
160	243	258	273	233	249	265
170	263	278	293	252	268	284
Height[e] = 5ft 9in						
80	89	106	123	90	107	125
90	111	128	145	111	128	145
100	133	150	167	131	149	166
110	155	172	189	152	169	186
120	177	194	211	173	190	207
130	200	216	233	193	211	228
140	222	238	255	214	231	248
150	244	260	277	235	252	269
160	266	282	299	255	273	290
170	288	305	321	276	293	311

Sum of girth measurements[c]	Weight[d]					
	Ages under 40			Ages 40 and over		
	Lower limit	Expected weight	Upper limit	Lower limit	Expected weight	Upper limit
Height[e] = 6ft 3in						
80	97	115	133	98	117	135
90	121	139	157	120	139	158
100	145	163	181	143	162	180
110	169	187	205	165	184	203
120	193	211	229	188	206	225
130	217	235	253	210	229	248
140	241	259	277	233	251	270
150	265	283	301	255	274	293
160	289	307	325	278	296	315
170	313	331	349	300	319	338

[a]Data apply to measurements in the nude.
[b]Source: Committee on Mortality under Ordinary Insurance and Annuities (1966), Society of Actuaries.
[c]Chest at inspiration, plus chest at expiration, plus abdomen (in inches).
[d]When subjects have been weighed in ordinary outdoor clothing the following deductions should be made to obtain naked weight: at height 5 ft 4 in, 7 lb; at height 5 ft 5 in to 5 ft 9 in, 8 lb; at height 5 ft 10 in or more, 9 lb.
[e]Before entering the table, 1 in should be deducted from the height of men wearing normal shoes.

Table 12.13. Ranges of weights (in kilograms) associated with height (in centimetres) and girth for males, 1935–53.[a,b]

Sum of girth measurements[c]	Weight[d]					
	Ages under 40			Ages 40 and over		
	Lower limit	Expected weight	Upper limit	Lower limit	Expected weight	Upper limit
Height[e] = 1·6 m						
203	36·5	44·0	51·0	37·0	44·5	51·5
229	46·5	53·0	60·0	46·0	53.0	60·5
254	55·5	62·0	69·0	54·5	61·5	68·5
279	64·5	71·0	78·0	63·0	70·5	77·1
305	73·5	80·5	87·5	71·0	78·5	85·5
330	82·5	89·5	96·5	80·5	87·0	94·5
356	91·5	99·0	105·5	88·5	95·5	103·0
381	100·0	108·0	115·0	97·0	104·5	111·5
406	110·0	117·0	124·0	105·0	113·0	120·0
432	119·5	126·0	133·0	114·5	121·5	128·0

| Sum of girth measurements[c] | Weight[d] | | | | | |
| | Ages under 40 | | | Ages 40 and over | | |
	Lower limit	Expected weight	Upper limit	Lower limit	Expected weight	Upper limit
Height[e] = 1·75 m						
203	40·5	48·0	56·0	41·0	48·5	56·0
229	50·5	58·0	66·0	50·5	58·0	66·0
254	60·5	68.0	75·5	59·5	67·5	75·5
279	70·5	78·0	85·5	69·0	76·0	84·5
305	80·5	88·0	95·5	78·5	86·0	94·0
330	90·5	98·0	105·5	87·5	95·0	103·5
356	100·5	108·0	115·5	97·0	105·0	112·5
381	110·5	118·0	125·5	106·5	114·5	122·0
406	120·5	128·0	135·5	115·0	124·0	131·5
432	130·5	138·5	145·5	125·0	133·0	141·0
Height[e] = 1·91 cm						
203	44·0	52·0	60·5	44·5	53·0	61·0
229	55·0	63·0	71·0	54·0	63·0	71·5
254	66·0	74·0	82·0	65·0	73·5	81·5
279	76·5	85·0	93·0	75·0	83·5	92·0
305	85·5	95·5	104·0	85·5	93·5	102·0
330	98·5	106·5	115·0	95·5	104·0	112·5
356	109·5	117·5	125·5	105·5	114·0	122·5
381	120·0	128·5	136·5	115·5	124·5	133·0
406	131·0	139·5	147·5	126·0	134·5	143·0
432	142·0	150·0	158·5	136·0	144·5	153·5

[a]Data apply to measurements in the nude.
[b]Source: Committee on Mortality under Ordinary Insurance and Annuities (1966), Society of Actuaries.
[c]Chest at inspiration, plus chest at expiration, plus abdomen (in cm).
[d]When subjects have been weighed in ordinary outdoor clothing the following deductions should be made to obtain naked weight: at height 1·63 m, 3·2 kg; at height 1·65–1·75 m, 3·6 kg; at height 1·78 m and more, 4·1 kg.
[e]Before entering the table, 2·5 cm should be deducted from the height of men wearing normal shoes.

There is a high rate of metabolic disorders following jejunoileal bypass, including liver disease, oxalate renal stones, osteomalacia, immune complex vasculitis and abdominal distension, the most serious of these being liver disease. Initially there is always a rise in the enzymes aspartate aminotransferase (AST) and alanine aminotransferase (ALT), also known as serum glutamic oxaloacetic transaminase (SGOT) and serum glutamic pyruvic transaminase (SGPT) respectively, but usually these settle to normal or near normal levels. This rise is due to fatty infiltration (steatosis) of the liver cells. However, a progressive rise in the transaminases and serum bilirubin is a danger signal. One percent of subjects ultimately develop irreversible liver failure and die; death can occur at any time, sometimes many years after the operation. Bray[13] considers that the only certain way of detecting progressive liver damage is to perform serial liver biopsies. If necessary, the bypass can be reversed. Oxalate renal stones occur in 20–30 percent of patients sometimes necessitating surgery, but most of the other complications can be corrected medically once they are recognized.

A study of intestinal bypass surgery for morbid obesity by DeWind and Payne[15] was analyzed in *Medical Risks*.[16] The subjects studied were 230 obese patients (59 men and 171 women) aged 16 to 55 who had jejunoileal bypass performed between 1963 and 1975. Those considered to be poor operative risks, unstable emotionally or socially, and those who were unable to agree to a reasonable period of follow-up and treatment were eliminated from the study.

Most patients remained under observation for more than 2 years with an average follow-up of about 5½ years; the longest follow-up extended to almost 14 years.

Mortality results

Twenty-three patients died at varying intervals postoperatively, most of whom were considered to have conditions related to or caused by the operation. Weight loss was variable but maintained a steady trend for two years, after which a moderate gain was observed. Maximum weight reduction was accomplished during the one-to two-year period.

The overall relative mortality among the 230 subjects under study was about 600 percent of the expected on the basis of US 1969–71 Life Tables. The mortality among males was higher than among females (*see* Table 12.14).

Table 12.14. Intestinal bypass surgery, analysis of mortality by sex.

	Number of patients *l*	Average length of follow-up (years)	Deaths		Mortality ratio[a] 100% (*d*/*d'*)
			Observed *d*	Expected[a] *d'*	
Men	59	5.7	10	1·43	700
Women	171	5.8	13	2·56	500
Total	230		23	3·99	575

[a]Expected deaths calculated on US 1969–71 Life Tables.

Gastric Partition and Bypass

Various techniques are used, but provided the proximal pouch holds no more than 50 ml and the outlet stoma is not more than 12 mm in diameter, weight loss of 44–110 lb (20–50 kg) can be expected in the first six months, with an average final weight loss of 30 percent of initial weight. Operative mortality is 2–3 percent. Stomal complications and vomiting are the predominant side effects, but there are virtually no long-term metabolic complications.

Truncal Vagotomy

This is a relatively simple operation leading to slow emptying of the stomach and retention of food. The effect is to cause early satiety with consequent weight loss, although to a lesser extent than with intestinal and gastric bypass procedures. The main complication is putrefaction of food if gastric stasis is excessive; this may necessitate a drainage procedure, such as pyloroplasty, for relief of symptoms. If so, weight is inevitably regained.

Rating

Any existing complications of obesity should be taken into account (e.g. diabetes mellitus, hypertension, left ventricular hypertrophy and gallstones). There should be an adequate period of postponement before acceptance to eliminate early postoperative deaths and to allow steatosis of the liver to stabilize. In jejunoileal bypass operations, rating should allow for the known late mortality from liver failure and the risks of renal stone disease.

1) Jejunoileal bypass; no complications.

Postoperative period	Rating
Under 1 yr	Postpone
Thereafter	+100[a]

[a]Add rating for current weight.

2) Jejunoileal bypass; increasingly abnormal liver biopsies/increasing transaminases and bilirubin – decline.
3) Gastric partition and bypass.

Postoperative period	Rating
Under 6 mth	Postpone
6 mth–3 yr	+75[a]
Thereafter	+50[a]

[a]Add rating for current weight.

4) Truncal vagotomy; with or without complications.

Postoperative period	Rating
Under 6 mth	Postpone
Thereafter	Rate for current weight

Appendix: Build rating tables

Height (m)	Weight (kg)										
1·43	<43	43–65	66–74	75–79	80–85	86–90	91–94	95–99	100–104	105–110	111–117
1·45	<44	44–67	68–75	76–81	82–87	88–92	93–97	98–101	102–106	107–113	114–119
1·48	<45	45–69	70–77	78–83	84–89	90–95	96–99	100–104	105–108	109–115	116–121
1·50	<46	46–70	71–79	80–85	86–91	92–97	98–101	102–106	107–112	113–118	117–124
1·53	<47	47–72	73–81	82–87	88–94	95–99	100–104	105–108	109–114	115–121	122–127
1·55	<48	48–73	74–83	84–89	90–95	96–101	102–105	106–110	111–116	117–123	124–130
1·58	<49	49–74	75–84	85–91	92–98	99–103	104–108	109–112	113–118	119–124	125–132
1·60	<50	50–77	78–87	88–94	95–100	101–105	106–110	111–114	115–120	121–128	129–135
1·63	<51	51–79	80–89	90–96	97–103	104–108	109–112	113–117	118–123	124–130	131–138
1·65	<52	52–81	82–91	92–99	100–106	107–111	112–115	116–120	121–125	126–133	134–140
1·68	<54	54–84	85–94	95–102	103–109	110–114	115–119	120–123	124–128	129–136	137–144
1·70	<56	56–86	87–97	98–104	105–112	113–117	118–121	122–125	126–131	132–139	140–148
1·73	<57	57–88	89–99	100–107	108–114	115–120	121–124	125–128	129–134	135–142	143–150
1·75	<59	59–90	91–101	102–109	110–117	118–123	124–127	128–131	132–137	138–145	146–153
1·78	<60	60–92	93–104	105–112	113–120	121–126	127–130	131–134	135–140	141–148	149–155
1·80	<62	62–95	96–108	109–116	117–124	125–130	131–134	135–138	139–144	145–152	153–159
1·83	<64	64–98	99–110	111–119	120–128	129–134	135–138	139–143	144–148	149–156	157–164
1·85	<65	65–100	101–113	114–121	122–130	131–137	138–141	142–146	147–152	153–159	160–168
1·88	<67	67–102	103–116	117–124	125–134	135–140	141–145	146–149	150–155	156–163	164–170
1·90	<69	69–105	106–119	120–128	129–137	138–144	145–149	150–153	154–159	160–167	168–175
1·93	<70	70–108	109–122	123–132	133–141	142–148	149–153	154–156	157–163	164–171	172–180
1·95	<72	72–111	112–126	127–135	136–145	146–151	152–156	157–160	161–166	167–175	176–184
1·98	<74	74–114	115–129	130–139	140–149	150–155	156–159	160–164	165–170	171–180	181–189
Rating[a]											
Under age 55	+25	Standard	+15	+25	+50	+75	+100	+125	+150	+200	+250
Age 55 and over	+25	Standard	+10	+15	+35	+50	+75	+100	+125	+150	+200

[a]Ratings of +25 upwards should be imposed for lives whose weight is less than the minimum levels quoted above. With severely underweight lives care must be taken to ensure that any serious underlying cause is excluded before acceptance.
Source: Mercantile and General Reinsurance Company.

Height	Weight (lb)									
4ft 8in	<94	94–144	145–163	164–175	176–188	189–199	200–208	209–218	219–229	230–242	243–257
4ft 9in	<96	96–147	148–166	166–179	180–192	193–203	204–213	214–223	224–234	235–248	249–263
4ft 10in	<98	98–151	152–170	171–183	184–197	198–209	210–218	219–228	229–239	240–254	255–268
4ft 11in	<100	100–154	155–174	175–188	189–201	202–213	214–223	224–233	234–245	246–260	261–274
5ft 0in	<103	103–158	159–172	173–192	193–206	207–217	218–228	229–238	239–251	252–266	267–280
5ft 1in	<105	105–161	162–182	183–196	197–210	211–222	223–232	233–242	243–255	256–270	271–286
5ft 2in	<107	107–164	165–186	187–200	201–215	216–227	228–237	238–247	248–259	260–274	275–290
5ft 3in	<110	110–169	170–191	192–206	207–221	222–232	233–242	243–252	253–264	265–281	282–297
5ft 4in	<113	113–174	175–196	197–211	212–227	228–238	239–247	248–257	258–270	271–287	288–303
5ft 5in	<116	116–178	179–201	202–217	218–233	234–244	245–253	254–264	265–276	277–293	294–309
5ft 6in	<120	120–184	185–208	209–224	225–240	241–252	253–261	262–270	271–282	283–299	300–316
5ft 7in	<123	123–189	190–213	214–230	231–246	247–258	259–267	268–276	277–288	289–307	308–325
5ft 8in	<126	126–193	194–218	219–235	236–252	253–264	265–274	275–282	283–295	296–312	313–330
5ft 9in	<129	129–198	199–223	224–241	242–258	259–270	271–280	281–289	290–301	302–319	320–336
5ft 10in	<132	132–202	203–230	231–246	247–264	265–277	278–287	288–295	296–308	309–325	326–342
5ft 11in	<137	137–209	210–237	238–255	256–273	274–286	287–296	297–304	305–316	317–334	335–350
6ft 0in	<140	140–215	216–243	244–262	263–281	282–294	295–304	305–312	313–326	327–345	346–362
6ft 1in	<143	143–220	221–248	249–267	268–287	288–301	302–311	312–321	322–334	335–351	352–369
6ft 2in	<147	147–225	226–255	256–274	275–294	295–309	310–319	320–328	329–341	342–359	360–375
6ft 3in	<151	151–231	232–261	262–281	282–302	303–317	318–328	329–337	338–349	350–368	369–386
6ft 4in	<155	155–238	239–269	270–290	291–311	312–326	327–336	337–344	345–358	359–377	378–396
6ft 5in	<160	160–245	246–277	278–298	299–320	321–333	334–343	344–352	353–366	367–386	387–405
6ft 6in	<164	164–252	253–285	286–307	308–329	330–342	343–351	352–361	362–374	375–396	397–416
Rating[a]										
Under age 55	+25	Standard	+15	+25	+50	+75	+100	+125	+150	+200	+250
Age 55 and over	+25	Standard	+10	+15	+35	+50	+75	+100	+125	+150	+200

[a]Ratings of +25 upwards should be imposed for lives whose weight is less than the minimum levels quoted above. With severely underweight lives care must be taken to ensure that any serious underlying cause is excluded before acceptance.
Source: Mercantile and General Reinsurance Company.

BODY MASS INDEX, WEIGHT DISTRIBUTION AND HEALTH RISKS
I McLEAN BAIRD

Definition

Overweight has always been difficult to define, and average weights evolved from the *Build and Blood Pressure Study 1959*[2] and *Build Study 1979*[3] were limited by restrictions: persons who were markedly overweight or underweight were often rejected by insurance companies, and the confounding effect of smoking on mortality was not taken into account when estimating the most desirable weight from the viewpoint of survival. Life insurance studies record weight in normal indoor clothes and height in shoes with ordinary heels, whereas most epidemiological surveys record weight and height in normal clothes without jacket or shoes.

The Body Mass Index (BMI), sometimes referred to as the Quetelet Index, has now become a widely used measure of degree of obesity; fully described in 1950[17] by Kemsley, the BMI is independent of height. It is calculated by dividing the weight in kilograms by the height in metres squared (kg/m^2), and a nomogram is available for rapid calculation (*see* Fig. 12.2). There is general agreement that a BMI over 30 is associated with increased mortality in both males and females; mortality rises steeply as the BMI approaches 40 (*see* Fig. 12.3).[18] Acceptable BMI ranges have been further subdivided according to age, a BMI of 19–25 for individuals of 19–34 years, and 21–27 for individuals over 35 years of age. The elderly (65–85 years of age) appear to be exempt from association of BMI and increased mortality, possibly because they are the survivors of a group of obese individuals, some of whom may have died from obesity-related illnesses.[19]

Prevalance of Obesity

In 1989 UK surveys by the Office of Population Censuses and Surveys showed that 8 percent of males and 12 percent of females had a BMI over 30[20] compared with 6 percent of males and 8 percent of females in 1980,[21] so the numbers of individuals who could be termed severely obese are increasing in the UK. In the USA Van Italie and Lew estimate that 12·4 million people are severely overweight as defined by a BMI of 31 for men and 32 for women.[22]

Coronary Heart Disease, Diabetes, Hypertension, Hyperlipidemia and Obesity

The Nurses Health Study of 115,886 nurses showed a strong positive relationship between obesity and the risk of fatal and non-fatal myocardial infarction, even when the relative risks are adjusted for smoking.[23] A BMI of greater than 29 was associated with a two to threefold risk of myocardial infarction, and this relative risk rose to twelvefold if the obese individual was a current smoker. Similar cumulative risks occurred in individuals who were obese and hypertensive (ninefold), diabetic (twelvefold) or hypercholesterolemic (eightfold). The Framingham study over 24 years found a twofold incidence of major coronary heart disease in men and women if the individual was obese.[24]

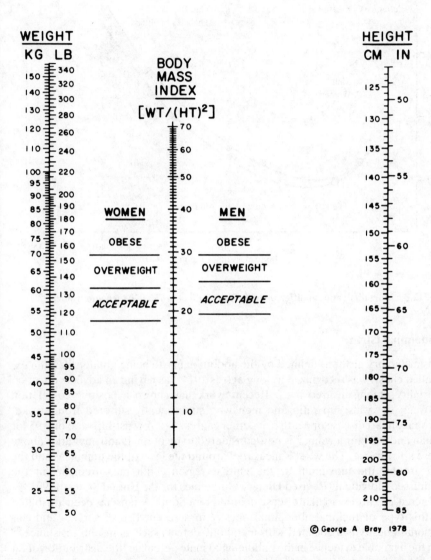

Fig. 12.2. Nomogram to determine body mass index. Place a ruler or straight edge between the body weight in kilograms or pounds on the left hand line, and the height in centimetres or inches on the right hand line. Body mass index is read from the middle line and is expressed as kg/m².
By kind permission of Professor George A Bray.

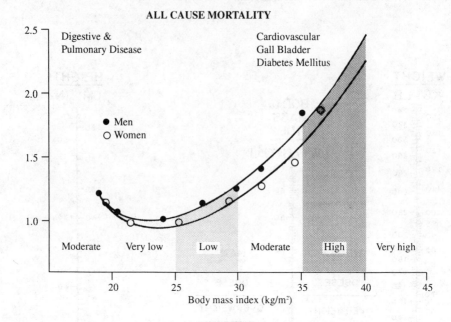

ALL CAUSE MORTALITY

Fig. 12.3. **Mortality ratios at differing body mass indices in 750,000 men and women.**[18]

Abdominal Girth

Unsatisfactory girth, as defined by the abdominal girth being greater than the expanded chest, was recognized as long ago as 1914[25] as having an adverse effect on mortality among insured lives. Recent work has shown a positive correlation between the waist-hip ratio and men who subsequently suffered from stroke, coronary heart disease or death from other causes.[26, 27] A waist-hip ratio of 0·95 for a man and 0·80 for a woman is now considered to be normal, and any ratios above these are adverse. The waist is measured around the level of the umbilicus and the hip around the maximum at the gluteal region, both measurements in the undressed individual (Revised Dietary Guidelines for the United States, 1990).

Increased cardiovascular disease in immigrant South Asians has been attributed to this type of regional abdominal obesity in a recent British survey, and this regional obesity is associated with metabolic defects such as insulin resistance.[28] On the available evidence in the middle-aged male or female, the distribution of fat could be a better predictor of cardiovascular disease than the degree of adiposity.

Mortality and Weight Loss

Very little data is available on severely obese subjects who have dieted and lost weight to within the normal range, but data from the *Build Study 1979*[3] indicates a reduction in mortality in obese men who have deliberately lost weight. Even a reduction of 22 lb (10 kg) will give immediate benefit in increasing exercise capacity and reducing blood pressure to normal levels.[29] Recent loss of weight without dieting is more likely to be due to disease; both men and women aged 60–69 years who had lost 10 lb (4.5 kg) or more within the 12 months preceding an application for life insurance experienced a mortality ratio of 186 percent.[30]

Disability Pensions and Obesity

A relatively minor degree of obesity with little impact on mortality has been shown to have a major effect on retirement from work and receipt of disability pensions due to cardiovascular disease or arthritis. Obese persons are up to four times more likely to have disability from arthritis of the knee or hip.[31]

Underweight

In the large Whitehall Study of 18,393 male civil servants, those who were underweight (a BMI less than 22) had an increased mortality, particularly in the 55–64 age group.[32] This may have been due to pre-existing disease unrecognized at the start of the survey.

Summary

1) Obesity as defined by a BMI over 30 is accompanied by increased mortality.
2) Increased abdominal girth is also a predictor of increased cardiovascular risk, and may be more important than actual body weight, particularly in men.
3) Other risk factors coinciding with obesity cause additive risks, cigarette smoking having the most pronounced effect.

REFERENCES

1 *The Specialized Mortality Investigation*. New York: Actuarial Society of America, 1903.
2 *Build and Blood Pressure Study 1959*. Chicago: Society of Actuaries, 1959.
3 *Build Study 1979*. New York: Society of Actuaries/Assoc of Life Insur Med Dirs of America, 1980.
4 *Medico-Actuarial Mortality Investigation 1909–12*. New York: Actuarial Society of America/Assoc of Life Insur Med Dirs of America, 1913.
5 *Supplement to the Medical Impairment Study 1929*. New York: Actuarial Society of America/Assoc of Life Insur Med Dirs of America, 1929.
6 Berger G, Garbsch K. *Proc 11th Internat Conf COINTRA* 1969; 2: 391.
7 Berger G, Garbsch K, Dehr R. *Proc 13th Internat Conf COINTRA* 1977: 221.
8 *Statistical Bulletin*. New York: Metropolitan Life Insurance Company. December 1970: 6.
9 Dublin LI, Marks HH. Mortality among insured overweights in recent years. *Trans Assoc Life Insur Med Dirs Am* 1951; 35: 235.
10 Garn SM, Gertler MM, Levine SA, White PD. Body weight versus weight standards in coronary artery disease and a healthy group. *Ann Int Med* 1951; 34: 1416.
11 Sanders K. Coronary artery disease and obesity. *Lancet* 1959; ii: 432.
12 Parnell RW. Somatometry and life assurance. *Trans Ass Med Socy* 1968: 141.

13 *Statistical Bulletin*. New York: Metropolitan Life Insurance Company. 1983 Metropolitan height and weight tables for men and women; Jan–Jun 1983: 2–9.

14 Bray GA. Surgical treatment of morbid obesity. *Trans Assoc Life Insur Med Dirs Am* 1978; 62: 106.

15 DeWind LT, Payne JH. Intestinal surgery for morbid obesity. *JAMA* 1976; 236: 2298–301.

16 Lew EA, Gajewski J. Eds. *Medical Risks: Trends in Mortality by Age and Time Elapsed*. New York, Westport CT, London: Praeger, 1990; 2: 13–61.

17 Kemsley WFF, Billewicz WZ, Thomson AM. A new weight-for-height standard based on British anthropometric data. *Br J Prev Soc Med* 1962; 16: 189–95.

18 Lew EA. Garfinkel L. Variations in mortality by weight among 750,000 men and women. *J Chronic Dis* 1987; 32: 563–76.

19 Rajala SA, Kanto AJ, Haavisto MV et al. Body weight and the three year prognosis in very old people. *Int J Obesity* 1990; 14: 997–1003.

20 The Dietary and Nutritional Survey of British Adults by the OPCS 1990. *HMSO*: 229–50.

21 On the State of the Public Health for the year 1980. *HMSO*: 78–9.

22 Van Italie TB, Lew EA. Overweight and underweight, in *Medical Risks: Trends in Mortality by Age and Time Elapsed*. Eds. Lew EA, Gajewski J. New York, Westport CT, London: Praeger, 1990.

23 Manson JAE, Colditz GA, Stampfer MJ et al. A prospective study of obesity and risk of coronary heart disease in women. *N Eng J Med* 1990; 322: 882–9.

24 Dawber TR. The Framingham Study. The epidemiology of atherosclerotic disease. Cambridge MA: Harvard University Press, 1980.

25 Mortality among insured lives showing medical impairments – defects in physical condition, in personal history or in family history. Part 1. *Medico-Actuarial Mortality Investigation vol IV*. (New York: The Association of Life Insurance Medical Directors of America and the Actuarial Society of America, 1914), 19–23.

26 Larsson B, Svardsudd L, Welin L et al. Abdominal adipose tissue distribution, obesity, and risk of cardiovascular disease and death. *Br Med J* 1984; 288: 1401–4.

27 Lapidus L, Bengtsson C, Larsson B et al. Distribution of adipose tissue and risk of cardiovascular disease and death. *Br Med J* 1984; 289: 1257–61.

28 McKeigue PM, Shah B, Marmot MG. Relation of central obesity and insulin resistance with high diabetes prevalence and cardiovascular risk in South Asians. *Lancet* 1991; 337: 382–86.

29 Ramhamadany PM, Dasgupta P, Brigden GS et al. Circadian variation of blood pressure in obese subjects on very low calorie diets. *Int J Obesity* 1990: 14: 43.

30 *1983 Medical Impairment Study*. Vol 1, Boston: Society of Actuaries and Association of Life Insurance Medical Directors of America, 1986.

31 Rissanen A, Heliovaara M, Knekt P et al. Risk of disability and mortality due to overweight in a Finnish population. *Br Med J* 1990; 301: 835–37.

32 Jarrett RJ, Shipley MJ, Rose G. Weight and mortality in the Whitehall study. *Br Med J* 1982; 285: 535–37.

CHAPTER 13

DIABETES MELLITUS

ROBERT L GOLDSTONE

Diabetes mellitus is a disorder of carbohydrate metabolism which results in hyperglycemia. There are multiple etiologic factors, generally involving a combination of a deficiency of insulin needed to bring glucose into cells and insulin resistance at the cellular level.

There is no one constant finding in diabetes mellitus except hyperglycemia, the hallmark of the disease. The disease has multiple metabolic abnormalities depending on its severity, and long-term complications involving eyes, blood vessels, kidneys and the nervous system may result. Uniformly and rapidly fatal until the discovery of insulin in 1921, it is now an insurable disease, with many markers (both laboratory and clinical) to aid the assessment of individual prognosis. Nonetheless, its behavior in different people may be quite random.

ETIOLOGY AND CLASSIFICATION

The National Diabetes Data Group classifies diabetes mellitus as either primary or secondary.[1] Primary diabetes includes those entities that do not have another associated disease as their cause. Primary diabetes is usually broken up into insulin-dependent diabetes (IDDM or Type I) and non-insulin-dependent diabetes (NIDDM or Type II). Both types appear to have a distinct genetic predisposition. In Type I, genetic susceptibility is brought out by an environmental agent. This is thought to activate an autoimmune pathway and destroy functioning insulin-producing beta cells. Overt hyperglycemia appears when a majority of these cells (approximately 85–90 percent) are destroyed.[2] Almost all Type I diabetics manifest their disease before the age of 30, although some older onset cases may behave like Type I onset. Type II usually involves a relative insulin deficiency combined with receptor resistance to circulating insulin. Classifications of diabetes follow:[3]

1) Type I or insulin dependent diabetes (IDDM); formerly called juvenile-onset or ketosis-prone diabetes.
2) Type II or non-insulin-dependent diabetes (NIDDM); formerly called adult-onset, maturity-onset or non-ketotic diabetes:
   a) Obese (~80%)
   b) Non-obese (~20%).
3) Secondary diabetes:
   a) Pancreatic disease (e.g. pancreatectomy, pancreatic insufficiency, hemochromatosis)
   b) Hormonal (excess counterinsulin hormones, e.g. Cushing's syndrome, acromegaly, pheochromocytoma)

  c) Drug-induced (e.g.thiazide diuretics, steroids, phenytoin)
  d) Associated with specific genetic syndromes (e.g. lipodystrophy, myotonic dystrophy, ataxia telangiectasia).
4) Impaired glucose tolerance (IGT); formerly called chemical, latent, borderline or subclinical diabetes.
5) Gestational diabetes: glucose intolerance with onset during pregnancy.

GENERAL CONSIDERATIONS

Type I usually begins by the age of 30. In the USA, data seems to point to a peak incidence between 13 and 15 years of age. When acute insulin-dependent diabetes occurs at later stages in life (e.g. after the age of 40) it may occasionally be classified as Type I because it shares certain characteristics with the younger age cases.

   When diagnosed, Type I diabetes tends to be rather rapid in onset (over a period of days), as opposed to Type II, which has symptoms slowly progressive often over a period of weeks. Excessive thirst and urination, dehydration and otherwise unexplained rapid weight loss are common. Use of exogenous insulin and rehydration is necessary to reverse this. Virtually all Type I diabetics must use insulin daily as a life-sustaining measure.

   There is significant extra mortality associated with IDDM. Individuals with IDDM have a mortality rate of approximately 3 per 1,000 under the age of 25, and 20 per 1,000 per year after the age of 25. Some 12 percent of juvenile IDDM patients die within 20 years of their diagnosis.[4] The death rate from renal and coronary disease, comprising almost one half of deaths, rises significantly after the age of 35, regardless of the duration of disease.[5]

   NIDDM also carries a substantial extra mortality. Many times this has to do with the normal diseases associated with aging rather than having acute metabolic compromise. Cardiovascular disease is a major cause of death in NIDDM as it often pre-exists the diabetes and, compared with normal controls,[5] appears to have a shortened survival curve after diagnosis.

DIAGNOSIS

When symptomatic, diabetes is an easy disease to diagnose. With the signs and symptoms of the disease and hyperglycemia over a given norm, the diagnosis is established with certainty. However, the diagnosis is not uniformly agreed on in the asymptomatic individual, who may have a normal fasting glucose but in whom abnormal glucose concentrations are found after stress or after a meal.

   The standard diagnostic tool for diagnosis of latent or chemical diabetes in the past was the oral glucose tolerance test (OGTT). A standard glucose load was ingested (usually 75 g, although studies have been done with anything between 50 g and 100 g) and blood samples were obtained at hourly intervals for four hours. A normal glucose tolerance is considered presumptive evidence against a diagnosis of diabetes. However, the predictive value of a positive test is uncertain: evidence suggests that the OGTT may overdiagnose diabetes, because a variety of stresses may produce an abnormal response. The discharge of ephinephrine is key to this, as it impairs insulin action and may account for a higher glucose concentration. Anxiety, inadequate diet or pre-test fasting techniques, lack of physical exercise and coexisting illness may all contribute to this.

In 1979 the National Diabetes Data Group of the National Institute of Health issued the following criteria for the diagnosis of using an OGTT with a 75 g glucose load:

a) Fasting (overnight): venous plasma glucose concentration > 7·8 mmol/l (140 mg/dl) on at least two separate occasions
b) Venous plasma glucose concentration > 11·1 mmol/l (200 mg/dl) at two hours postprandial and on at least one other occasion during the two-hour test.[6]

If the two-hour postprandial value is 140–200 mg/dl and one other value during the test (regardless of time) is obtained, a diagnosis of impaired glucose tolerance (IGT) is suggested. This has indicated to clinicians that people in this category are at increased risk of developing symptomatic diabetes (or occult hyperglycemia) sometime during their lifetime. However, most trials, though with limited experience over years, suggest that many individuals diagnosed with IGT (over two-thirds) never actually go on to develop frank diabetes. If the individual's life span were long enough and not shortened by various coexisting pathology or conditions, it is still possible that frank diabetes would occur over time. Consequently the OGTT usually raises more questions than it answers, and is more helpful when negative than when it is positive.

It is worthwhile to mention that venous whole blood concentrations are about 15 percent lower than plasma values. Tables 13.1–13.4 may be used as guides.

Table 13.1. Fasting blood glucose concentrations considered diagnostic of diabetes mellitus in non-pregnant adults.

Sample	Glucose value (mg/dl)	(mmol/l)
Venous plasma	≥140	≥7·8
Venous whole blood	≥120	≥6·7
Capillary whole blood	≥120	≥6·7

Table 13.2. Sustained blood glucose concentrations considered diagnostic of diabetes mellitus during OGTT.

Sample	Glucose value (mg/dl)	(mmol/l)
Venous plasma	≥200	≥11·12
Venous whole blood	≥180	≥10·00
Capillary whole blood	≥200	≥11·12

Table 13.3. Criteria diagnostic of IGT in non-pregnant adults.

Sample	Glucose value (mg/dl)	(mmol/l)
Fasting		
Venous plasma	<140	<7·8
Venous whole blood	<120	<6·7
Capillary whole blood	<120	<6·7
½-, 1- or 1½-hr OGTT		
Venous plasma	≥200	≥11·1
Venous whole blood	≥180	≥10·0
Capillary whole blood	≥200	≥11·1
2-hr OGTT		
Venous plasma	140–200	7·8–11·1
Venous whole blood	120–180	6·7–10·0
Capillary whole blood	140–200	7·8–11·1

Table 13.4. Normal glucose values in adults.

Sample	Glucose value (mg/dl)	(mmol/l)
Fasting		
Venous plasma	<115	<6·4
Venous whole blood	<100	<5·6
Capillary whole blood	<100	<5·6
½-, 1- or 1½-hr OGTT		
Venous plasma	<200	<11·1
Venous whole blood	<180	<10·0
Capillary whole blood	<200	<11·1
2-hr OGTT		
Venous plasma	140	7·8
Venous whole blood	120	6·7
Capillary whole blood	140	7·8

Laboratory Markers

We are now much better able to measure the degree of glycemic control than in the past, when random blood sugar and urine samples were the mainstay in assessment. Such samples are so circumstance-dependent and often atypical of long-term metabolic and glycemic status that they have relatively limited uses.

As already mentioned, random and fasting blood glucose values are often obtained for insurance purposes. When grossly abnormal they raise a high index of suspicion for potential problems. In establishing the diagnosis of diabetes they are quite helpful. However, cases being underwritten are often known diabetics and the assessment of metabolic control is the key.

Uncontrolled diabetes leads to a series of metabolic catastrophes, which may be fatal (*see* p. 223). Chronic poor control of diabetes gives rise to many chronic complications and conditions that also adversely affect mortality. Whilst there is still debate on how closely diabetics must have blood glucose values mirroring those of non-diabetics to avoid complications and poor outcome, it is universally agreed that poor control results in a marked decrease in longevity.

Diabetics by definition have physiologic abnormalities that result in significant differences from non-diabetics in their states of hyperglycemia and euglycemia, even given the same set of conditions. A random blood sugar estimation may give a distorted picture of long-term diabetic control given the circumstances preceding it: a good value does not infer that control is usually satisfactory and a poor one gives no assurances that control is always less than optimal. Even fasting blood sugar estimations are so affected by the circumstances (how long the fast was, whether diabetes was controlled or uncontrolled for that day or the preceding day alone, what type of diet was followed over the preceding days, etc) that they are of no value as a long-term predictor of metabolic consequences.

Glycosuria likewise has very limited usefulness in assessment of metabolic control. First and foremost, many conditions that have nothing to do with diabetes may cause the finding of glucose in the urine. Other sugars (e.g. lactose) must also be properly differentiated in the testing. The following conditions may cause glycosuria:

1) Diabetes mellitus.
2) Renal glycosuria.
3) Conditions causing rapid emptying of the stomach and rapid absorption of food (e.g. duodenal ulcer, vagotonia and hypertonic stomach, gastrectomy).
4) Hyperthyroidism.
5) Pheochromocytoma.
6) Cushing's syndrome, hyperadrenalism, administration of the corticosteroid group of drugs.
7) Increased secretion of diabetogenic hormone of the anterior pituitary, acromegaly.
8) Increased intracranial pressure, cerebral tumor, head injuries, early stages of subarachnoid hemorrhage.
9) Hemochromatosis.
10) Fanconi syndrome, or variants of it.

This illustrates that the finding of glucose in the urine does not necessarily make the diagnosis of diabetes. However, in an established diabetic can the amount of glucose found reliably predict the degree of control? Unfortunately, so many factors, even when diabetes is the only illness provocative for glycosuria, cause the value obtained to be unreliable. First, the glucose concentration in urine is always an average of what the kidney has spilled over from the last time the individual has urinated to the present sample obtained. As no one can reliably empty his bladder and then almost immediately produce another sample, the test is always a short-term average (perhaps a mixture of values) at different times. In addition, diabetes (and other related conditions) can alter the renal threshold for glucose, meaning that there is no one constant blood glucose value above which a kidney will consistently spill sugar into urine, and there may be glycosuria even in the face of normal blood glucose values. As can be seen, testing for glycosuria has very limited value.

Using fructosamine is a newer method for determining glycated serum proteins and is now included on most standard insurance laboratory determinations.[7] Fructosamine is a ketoamine, a derivative of the non-enzymatic reaction product of a sugar (usually glucose) to a protein (usually albumin). As the serum proteins measured have a half-life of between 7 and 22 days, it allows a more broad-based measure of glycemic control of 2–2½ weeks prior to the sample being drawn. Fructosamine has the advantage of being accurate despite hemolysis, lipemia or other problems with handling of the samples.[8] Its use gives a broader window through which to assess glucose control.[9]

Hemoglobin A_{1c} (HbA_{1c}) is still the standard marker for assessment of glycemic control. It first came into use as a marker in diabetic patients in 1971, when it was reported that a minor fraction of hemoglobin A was found to be significantly elevated in diabetic patients.[10] HbA_{1c} comprises 5–7 percent of the hemoglobin in the blood of non-diabetics. As the life of the red blood cell is the major determinant in this measurement, HbA_{1c} has the advantage of assessing control for six to eight weeks prior to the drawing of the sample. This makes it much less dependent on individual changes in diet, insulin or short-term control and allows a better long-term picture of control.

Fructosamine and HbA_{1c} correlate well in most cases with degree of diabetic control. Tables 13.5 and 13.6 give ranges of normal as well as correlative information.

Table 13.5. HORL glycemic control ranges, based on percentile ranges for less than 5,000 specimens.

Glycemic control	HbA_{1c} (%)	Fructosamine (mmol/l)
Excellent	<6·0	1·2–2·1
Good	6·1–8·0	2·2–2·5
Fair	8·1–10·0	2·6–3·0
Poor	>10	≥3·1

Table 13.6. HbA$_{1c}$ versus fructosamine and the clinical appreciation of diabetes control.[11]

Diabetes control	n	Fasting blood glucose (mg/d)	HbA$_{1c}$ (%)	Fructosamine (mmol/l)
Very good	11	109 ± 10	6·8 ± 0.2	2·20 ± 0·09
Good	34	167 ± 8	8·8 ± 0·2^c	2·67 ± 0·09^a
Poor	31	198 ± 15^b	9·5 ± 0·3^c	2·96 ± 0·12^b
Bad	37	274 ± 19^c	10·4 ± 0·2^c	3·46 ± 0·10^c

^{a}p < 0·05
^{b}p < 0·01
^{c}p < 0·0001

MORTALITY AND COMPLICATIONS

The diagnosis of diabetes carries with it an increased mortality, both from acute and chronic effects of hyperglycemia on the metabolic functions of the body and from complications caused by this on body organs. Before addressing complications, which have significant impact on longevity, studies have shown certain general factors that influence the selection of diabetic lives.

Mortality has been shown to be significantly greater in those who have expressed the disease earlier in life. Long-term Joslin clinic studies,[5] as well as insurance studies, have shown that mortality rates are significantly higher in those under the age of 30 at the time of diagnosis.[12] Males appear to have higher adverse outcomes at younger ages, but females appear to do less well with advancing age.

The findings showing that in older onset diabetics female outcomes lag behind those for males is interesting. Studies showed either an equal incidence in mortality ratios among men and women over the age of 50, or a higher ratio for women.[13,14] No specific hypothesis has been advanced for these findings.

The age of onset of complications for diabetes is probably the most significant factor in mortality; there is an extremely high rate of onset of complications at ages 13–15. As so many different adolescent developmental factors affect an acute onset of diabetes, this population cannot safely be offered insurance.

Albuminuria is an extremely unfavorable prognostic sign:[15] a study from the Equitable Life Assurance Society of the United States produced a mortality rate of over 1,000 percent in a group of followed declined diabetics with greater than 20 mg/dl of albuminuria.[16] A Lincoln National study produced similar findings: in diabetics who had only small to moderate amounts of albuminuria, the mortality ratio for issue age group 40–64 was almost 650 percent of standard, and for issue age group 10–39 almost 2,000 percent of standard.[17]

Diabetics treated with dietary controls alone or diet restriction plus oral medication show lower mortality ratios than insulin-dependent diabetics.[13,18] However, more recent clinical trials suggest that adult onset diabetics on insulin but under good control have mortality outcomes quite close to those treated with diet and oral hypoglycemics.

Table 13.7. Diabetic Mortality Study 1951–70.[a]

Age at application (years)	Entrants	Actual deaths	Expected deaths	Mortality ratio (%)
		Insured		
1–19	58		0·47	
20–29	414	17	3·75	453
30–39	776	41	16·63	247
40–49	940	58	40·79	142
50–59	616	64	43·71	146
60 and over	96	11	9·21	119
		Declined		
1–19	307	12	2·32	539
20–29	1308	153	11.59	1320
30–39	1514	210	29·70	707
40–49	2001	335	79·79	420
50–59	1773	386	126·88	304
60 and over	735	191	75·80	252

[a]Expected deaths based on Equitable's Select and Ultimate Mortality Tables 1958–63. Observed through 1971 anniversary of application.

Table 13.8. Diabetic Mortality Study 1951–70, issued and declined applications.[a]

Duration of diabetes at time of application (years)	Entrants	Actual deaths	Expected deaths	Mortality ratio (%)
Ages 1–19				
0–5	200	7	1·49	470
6–10	101	1	0·69	144
11–14	48	4	0·42	968
15–19	11	0	0·08	
20 and over	0			
All	360	12	2·68	448
Ages 20–29				
0–5	657	35	5·86	598
6–10	451	39	3·95	988
11–14	280	46	2·60	1766
15–19	208	28	1·76	1585
20 and over	110	18	1·10	1636
All	1706	166	15·27	1087

Duration of diabetes at time of application (years)	Entrants	Actual deaths	Expected deaths	Mortality ratio (%)
Ages 30–39				
0–5	1078	65	20·79	313
6–10	425	35	9·41	372
11–14	235	44	5·38	818
15–19	251	46	5·08	905
20 and over	268	61	5·38	1134
All	2257	251	46·04	542
Ages 40–49				
0–5	1695	193	65·90	293
6–10	559	85	25·17	337
11–14	212	34	10·08	337
15–19	182	36	9·04	398
20 and over	233	39	9·38	434
All	2881	387	119.57	324
Ages 50–59				
0–5	1477	225	106·84	211
6–10	445	106	33·16	320
11–14	164	46	11·36	405
15–19	119	40	9·44	424
20 and over	110	28	6·70	337
All	2315	445	167·50	266
Ages 60 and over				
0–5	478	103	48·67	212
6–10	165	46	19·78	233
11–14	52	16	4·86	329
15–19	52	24	6·08	395
20 and over	52	10	3·87	226
All	799	199	83·26	239

[a]Expected deaths based on Equitable's Select and Ultimate Mortality Tables 1958–63. Observed through 1971 anniversary of application.

DIABETES AND OTHER IMPAIRMENTS

Diabetes and Ischemic Heart Disease

There is a substantially higher death rate among diabetics with coronary artery disease than among controls with ischemic heart disease alone. The Framingham

Study has found that diabetes causes a twofold to threefold increase in the incidence of atherosclerotic disease.[19] The cause of the accelerated atherosclerosis is uncertain, although altered HDL:LDL levels, increased platelet adhesiveness and decreased prostacyclin synthesis are under investigation. Peripheral vascular disease, cardiomyopathy and stroke are also statistically higher in diabetics than controls.

Albuminuria: Proteinuria

In contrast with other impairments, the ten-year death rate of diabetics with albuminuria is almost four times that of matched controls. It appears that proteinuria, even at subclinical amounts, is a fair indicator of which diabetics will go on to develop renal impairment.[20]

Retinopathy

Retinopathy is a significant clinical prognostic sign. Early and advanced development of retinopathy appears to herald more widespread vascular changes, regardless of assessment of degree of control.[21]

Hypertension and Overweight

There is a direct correlation between blood pressure and mortality, as there also is between overweight and mortality. Their effects may be additive when both states are compromised in the presence of diabetes. Evidence at this point, however, fails to indicate that the mortality associated with either of these conditions is influenced by the presence of controlled diabetes.

Pregnancy

Pregnancy may cause alterations in blood glucose homeostasis due to the increase of circulating diabetogenic hormones (e.g. cortisol and epinephrine). Many pregnant women with abnormal glucose readings are managed by diet alone; some need insulin as the age of the fetus increases. In most cases pregnancy-induced diabetes does not require continued insulin after delivery and poses no underwriting concern, although there is debate whether or not the eventual incidence of diabetes mellitus is higher in the lifetime of these affected females.

RATING OF DIABETIC RISKS

Underwriting Requirements

In order to assess a case accurately, evaluation of the diabetic risk requires as much recent information, laboratory work and physician follow-up as possible. Besides a medical examination, and recent blood work with long-term parameters of glucose control if possible, the following information should be sought:

1) Date of onset of diabetes.
2) All medicine and insulin used and how often they are taken.

3) Assessment of control by laboratory markers and attending physician.
4) Frequency of diabetic coma or hypoglycemic reactions.
5) Degree and adequacy of physician follow-up.
6) Laboratory, ECG and other related studies if available (e.g. treadmill).
7) Nature and degree of any associated diabetic complications.

A diabetic questionnaire completed by the applicant should also be obtained.

Basic Ratings

Age of onset is a very important reflector of diabetic outcome in mortality studies. Basic debits for IDDM and NIDDM may be applied as follows:

IDDM or Type I:

Age at application	Basic rating
Under 15	Postpone
16–30	+250
31–50	+100 to +150
51 and over	Standard to +50

NIDDM or Type II:

Age at application	Basic rating
Under 30	Rate as IDDM
31–40	+100
41 and over	Standard to +50

Compliance and control are of key importance in applying these debits. Additional debits for poorer control may be applied as follows:

$HbA_{1c} < 7.5\%$
Fructosamine < 2.5 mmol/l $\Big\}$ no additional debits.

HbA_{1c} 7.6–8.5%
Fructosamine 2.5–2.9 mmol/l $\Big\}$ +50 to 75.

HbA_{1c} 8.6–9.9%
Fructosamine 3.0–3.3 mmol/l $\Big\}$ +100.

$HbA_{1c} > 10.0\%$
Fructosamine > 3.4 mmol/l $\Big\}$ decline.

The normal values for HbA_{1c} by chromatographic method are 3.0–6.0 percent; the normal values for fructosamine are 1.5–2.1 mmol/l.

In cases where the applicant's diabetic control is inadequate and no physician follow-up is obtained, declination is wise.

Impaired Glucose Tolerance (IGT)

IGT, gestational diabetes mellitus, medication- or situation-induced hyper-glycemia and previously abnormal glucose tolerance are all gray areas. Most individuals can be given standard insurance unless the potential for worsening of these states (or continual re-enactment of them) or the presence of worsening coexisting disease exists. Usually rating for the primary cause of the above situations will take this into account.

Additional Debits

When combined with diabetes, many diseases or states have a more adverse outcome than if mortality from the individual impairments were added separately.

Build and Blood Pressure

Slight abnormalities in blood sugar often occur because build is abnormal; normalizing build would actually bring blood glucose levels back to normal. Unless very significant, no added debits need apply. Applicants with markedly elevated blood pressure should probably be postponed in the presence of significantly abnormal blood sugars.

Physician Assessment of Control

Treating physicians' opinions on the control of diabetes often vary, depending on their skill and experience. The underwriter should be alerted to potential problems with compliance on the part of the applicant. Assessment of laboratory markers and complications should be combined with the physician's assessment.

Diabetic Ketoacidosis

If this has been present in the last three years (except at the time of onset of the disease), +50 to +100 should be added. Usually decline if there have been more than two episodes over this period.

Hypoglycemic Reactions

Frequent hypoglycemic reactions should carry an additional debit of +50. If the reactions are very frequent and severe, decline.

Albuminuria: Proteinuria

This finding increases mortality quite adversely.

mg/dl	Rating
To 20	+0
21–30	+50
31–50	+100
Greater than 50	Decline

Retinopathy
Mild (microaneurysms, background) – +0.
Moderate (exudative) – +50.
Severe (proliferative) – +100.

Coronary Heart Disease
When coronary heart disease and diabetes coexist, the coronary section of an underwriting manual should take precedence, with additional debits for diabetes being imposed secondary to the nature and severity of the disease in question. When coronary heart disease is regarded as a late complication of diabetes, always decline.

Alcohol Use
Excessive use of alcohol should be evaluated very carefully in the presence of diabetes. When alcohol criticism results in a +100 debit, it may be additive with the diabetes. If greater than +100, decline. Compliance with the diabetic regimen should be double-checked.

Cigarette Smoking
Smoking and diabetes combine to increase the tendency to develop vascular disease; an additional debit, usually +50, should be added where urinary nicotine levels are significant.

Glycosuria
Glycosuria as an isolated finding is quite unreliable in predicting severity of disease. When diabetes is already established as a cause, rate for diabetes. When glycosuria is a new and an only finding, levels of 0·2 g/100 ml call for a blood specimen or investigation of cause.

Other Underwriting Considerations

Certain complications, such as diabetic neuropathy and myopathy, may coincide with the disease. These complications usually, but not always, indicate suboptimal control of diabetes. As they are at times disability-provoking, they should be closely evaluated. If neuropathy is quite compromising, it may lead to significant peripheral vascular disease and loss of a limb.

Family history is often taken into account, especially when one or both parents or a sibling has died of diabetes-related complications. This is not necessarily ratable in itself if the individual is normoglycemic, though some companies will preclude the issue of a policy at preferred rates.

Mild diabetes is occasionally discovered on examination and during screening blood work as part of the insurance underwriting process. With adult-onset diabetes of minimal underwriting significance, the individual may be offered terms immediately, on the understanding that medical advice will be sought and appropriate treatment instituted. However, when diabetes is marked, even if of a more favorable type and prognosis, insurance coverage should probably be delayed until proper control and therapy are instituted.

REFERENCES

1 National Diabetes Data Group. Classification and diagnosis of diabetes mellitus and other categories of glucose intolerance. Diabetes 1977; 63: 843.

2 Under RH, Foster DW. Diabetes mellitus. In: Wilson JD, Foster DW, editors. Williams textbook of endocrinology, 8th ed. Philadelphia: Saunders, 1990 (in press).

3 Olefski JM. Diabetes mellitus. In: Wyngaarden JB, Smith LH, editors. Cecil textbook of medicine. Philadelphia: Saunders, 1985: 1320–41.

4 Harris MI. Classification and diagnostic criteria for diabetes and other categories of glucose intolerance. In: NIH publication No. 85. Diabetes in America: National Institute of Arthritis, Diabetes, and Digestive and Kidney Diseases. Washington DC: GPO, 1985, 1468.

5 Kroslewski AS, Warran JH Jr, Christleig AR. Onset, course, complications and prognosis of diabetes mellitus. In: Marble A et al, editors. Joslin's diabetes mellitus. Philadelphia: Lea and Fehriger, 1985.

6 National Diabetes Data Group. Classification and diagnosis of diabetes mellitus and other categories of glucose intolerance. Diabetes 1979; 28: 1039–57.

7 Johnson RN, Metcalf PA, Baker JR. Fructosamine: a new approach to the estimation of serum glycosylprotein. An index of diabetic control. Clin Chem Acta 1982; 127: 87–95.

8 Ludvigsen CW, Sprague G, Smith KM. Fructosamine: clinical usefulness and determination of reference ranges. J Insur Med 1989; 21(3): 203–9.

9 Baker JR, O'Connell JP, Metcalf PA, Lawson MR et al. Clinical usefulness of estimations of serum fructosamine concentrations as a screening test for diabetes mellitus. Br Med J 1983; 287: 863–7.

10 Trivelli LA, Ranney HM, Lai H. Hemoglobin components in patients with diabetes mellitus. New Engl J Med 1971; 284: 353–7.

11 Daubresse JC et al. Diabetes & metabolisme 1987; 13: 217–21.

12 1983 Medical Impairment Study. Vol. 1. Boston: Society of Actuaries and Association of Life Insurance Medical Directors of America, 1986.

13 Shenfield GM, Elton RA, Bhalla IP, Duncan LJ. Diabetic normality in Edinburgh. Diabete Metab (Paris) 1979; 5: 149–58.

14 O'Sullivan JB, Mahan CM. Mortality related to diabetes and blood glucose levels in a community study. Am J Epidem 1982; 116: 678–84.

15 Viberti GC, Jarrett RJ, Mahmed U, Hill RT et al. Microalbuminuria as a predictor of clinical nephropathy in insulin dependent diabetes. Lancet 1982; 1: 1430–32.

16 Klimt CR, Meinert CL, Miller M, Knowles HC Jr. University group diabetes program. Excerpta Med Int Congr 1967; Series No. 149: 261.

17 Cochran HA. Discussion. Insured diabetics. Trans Assoc Life Insur Med Dir Am 1968; 52: 238.

18 Krolewski AS, Czyzyk A, Kopczynski J. Mortality from cardiovascular diseases among diabetics. Diabetologia 1977; 13: 345–50.

19 Kannel WB, McGee DL. Diabetes and cardiovascular disease. The Framingham Study. JAMA 1979; 241: 2035–8.

20 Mogenson CE, Christensen CK. Predicting diabetic nephropathy in insulin dependent diabetic patients. New Engl J Med 1984; 311: 89.

21 L'Esperance FA Jr, James SA Jr. The eye and diabetes mellitus. In: Ellenberg M, Rifkin H, editors. Diabetes mellitus: theory and practice. 3rd ed. New Hyde Park NY: Medical Examination Publishing Company, 1983; 727–57.

CHAPTER 14

BLOOD PRESSURE

W JOHN ELDER

The association of raised blood pressure with extra mortality has been known for many years. It is one of the areas where study of insured populations by insurance company doctors has helped clinical medicine appreciate the significance of an abnormal finding in apparently healthy people.

In the early years of this century physicians were aware that a very high blood pressure presaged catastrophic events, such as stroke or renal failure, but the relationship between a moderately raised blood pressure and a shortened life expectancy was not appreciated until later. The statistical association of adverse mortality with averages of elevated blood pressures obtained from large numbers of people could not be applied to predict the future health of symptom-free individuals. The poor understanding of statistical significance among many clinicians in those days accounted for the frequent failure of doctors to comprehend why insurance companies charged their apparently fit patients with a mildly or moderately elevated blood pressure an increased premium for life insurance.

Although more detailed evidence of the relationship between blood pressure and mortality accumulated as the decades progressed, there was little that clinicians could do for their patients until effective therapies to reduce a raised blood pressure became available in the 1950s. As the range of medications broadened and the incidence of untoward side effects was reduced, it became acceptable to reduce the blood pressure in symptom-free individuals. It was then demonstrated that mortality improved to normal or near normal for people whose previously raised blood pressure was lowered to normal values. During this time the association between raised blood pressure and the incidence of cardiovascular and renal disease became increasingly evident, and the need developed to reduce a raised blood pressure to improve morbidity as well as mortality. Thus, elevated blood pressure became one of the early entities in the general concept of risk factors. This has led to a much greater appreciation of statistics by physicians in clinical practice and a better understanding of the reason why insurance companies rate mildly and moderately raised blood pressure.

PREVALENCE OF RAISED BLOOD PRESSURE

Raised blood pressure is present in many people throughout the world. In the US there are approximately 60 million people with hypertension. Efforts to improve detection, follow-up and education are achieving better control; by the mid-1980s about half were properly diagnosed and a third were receiving some form of hypertensive therapy. Diastolic hypertension is roughly twice as common in 50-year-olds as in 30-year-olds, and systolic hypertension increases greatly in prevalence after the age of 45, afflicting approximately 65 percent of the 65- to 74-

year-old age group. The prevalence of hypertension is higher among blacks (38 percent) than among whites (29 percent); the explanations given for this include heredity, higher salt intake and greater environmental stress. Hypertension is found more frequently in men (33 percent) than women (27 percent).

Today the prevalence of hypertension and elevated blood pressure are not necessarily the same. The wide use of therapies to reduce blood pressure has lowered its prevalence with respect to some definitions of hypertension; for example, the National Center for Health Statistics uses the term hypertension to include those with a raised blood pressure on examination and those without a raised blood pressure on examination but who reported on medical history that they are currently taking antihypertensive medication.

HYPERTENSION

Hypertension is divided into two categories: (1) primary, or essential, hypertension, and (2) secondary hypertension. About 95 percent have primary hypertension, which has no identifiable cause. The remaining small percentage have secondary hypertension for which, by definition, a cause is known. The causes of hypertension are as follows:
1) Coarctation of aorta.
2) Cushing's syndrome.
3) Drugs and hormones: amphetamines, oral contraceptives, estrogens, steroid or thyroid hormone excess.
4) Increased intracranial pressure.
5) Pheochromocytoma.
6) Primary aldosteronism: Conn's syndrome, idiopathic hyperaldosteronism.
7) Renal parenchymal disease: chronic pyelonephritis, congenital renal disease, diabetic nephropathy, glomerulonephritis, interstitial nephropathy, obstructive uropathy, polycystic disease, renin-secreting tumors, vasculitis.
8) Renal vascular disease.

Although the etiology of primary hypertension remains unknown, much has been discovered about the regulation of blood pressure. Normal blood pressure results from a balance of the resistance and capacitance of the blood vessels, cardiac output and blood volume. Balance is maintained through a series of feedback loops reacting to baroreceptors located throughout the circulation. The major mechanisms affecting control react to changes, causing the central nervous system to respond via the autonomic system or the adrenal medulla, and causing the kidney, which is particularly sensitive to alterations of volume, to respond via the renin-angiotensin-aldosterone system in association with the adrenal cortex or the renal kallikrein-kinin system. Abnormalities of each of these control mechanisms has been found in certain hypertensive conditions.

DEFINITIONS

There is no satisfactory definition of normal blood pressure; this is because morbidity and mortality increase linearly with increasing levels of either systolic or diastolic blood pressure. In 1960 Pickering[1] emphasized that hypertension is a quantitative not a qualitative disease, meaning that elevations in blood pressure represent quantitative changes in health on a continuous range. Any attempt to define normal blood pressure is made more difficult by the variations that occur within individuals with age, state of mind and physical condition. There is general agreement with the World Health Organization proposal that a systolic blood pressure below 140 mm Hg or a diastolic blood pressure below 90 mm Hg be called 'normal' for classification purposes. The Joint National Committee on Detection, Evaluation and Treatment of High Blood Pressure has a classification of blood pressure for adults over the age of 18 (*see* Table 14.1), which is particularly useful for consistency of evaluation and therapeutic guidance.

Table 14.1. Blood pressure classifications.[a]

Classification	Blood pressure (mm Hg)
	Diastolic
Normal blood pressure	<85
High normal blood pressure	85–89
Mild hypertension	90–104
Moderate hypertension	105–114
Severe hypertension	≥115
	Systolic (when diastolic BP <90)
Normal blood pressure	<140
Borderline isolated systolic hypertension	140–159
Isolated systolic hypertension	≥160

[a]Classification used by the Joint National Committee on Detection, Evaluation and Treatment of High Blood Pressure for adults aged 18 years or older.[2]

In childhood, blood pressure increases with age, reaching adult levels at about 18 years. The National Heart, Lung and Blood Institute has published criteria for children and adolescents.[3] Levels at or above which there is significant risk are: 116/76 mm Hg (three to five years of age), 122/78 mm Hg (six to nine years of age), 125/82 mm Hg (ten to 12 years of age), 136/86 mm Hg (13 to 15 years of age) and 142/92 mm Hg (16 to 18 years of age).

Blood pressure rises in most people as they become older. This is thought to be consequential to diminishing compliance of the arterial system as elasticity of the vessels decreases with normal aging. Levels of 160 mm Hg systolic and 100 mm Hg diastolic in people over the age of 60 are compatible with normal mortality rates of the general and insured populations. Nevertheless, mortality has been shown to be directly related to the height of the blood pressure in adults irrespective of age; therefore older people with lower blood pressures are likely to live longer.

TAKING AND RECORDING BLOOD PRESSURE

It is important for the blood pressure to be recorded accurately at the insurance physical examination. Unfortunately it is not always carried out with the care and attention it deserves, particularly by the casual or inexperienced examiner. The technical aspects of blood pressure measurement have been fully discussed in Chapter 10, so here it is necessary only to comment that clinicians have a tendency to round off levels to the nearest 5, or even 10, mm Hg. This practice may be less common now than it used to be because the statistical significance of a mildly or moderately raised blood pressure is more widely appreciated as a risk factor for cardiovascular disease. In the USA there is evidence that paramedical examiners record the blood pressure more accurately than physicians, as they do not have the clinical experience that may tempt a doctor to modify the readings. It is quite clear from many statistical and actuarial studies of mortality experience that significant differences are associated with only 2 mm Hg separations between reported levels of blood pressure. With diligence it is possible to achieve this degree of accuracy.

It is now almost universal insurance practice to use the systolic and diastolic fifth phase (cessation of sound) in the construction of blood pressure rating tables. Therefore it is important to make sure that the fifth phase is the diastolic pressure recorded at the examination. Some companies request the fourth (change of sound) and fifth phases to be recorded (e.g. 136/86–78), as this provides the medical director with additional information and prevents confusion; however, this would be unusual practice in North America.

The girth of the arm may modify the true systolic and diastolic readings, both being slightly higher the greater the circumference of the arm above average. Fletcher[4] found that when a group of overweight patients was dieted, an average fall of 15·5 kg (34 lb) produced an average diminution of arm circumference of 3·6 cm (1½ in), approximately 0·1 cm per kg. Hamilton et al[5] found that for every 1 cm of arm girth reduction a correction of −1·17 mm Hg for systolic and −1·14 mm Hg for diastolic should be applied when the indirect method of recording blood pressure is used. Therefore the error introduced by variations in arm circumference is slight and, for all practical purposes, may be disregarded unless arm girth is grossly abnormal.

SIGNIFICANCE OF RAISED BLOOD PRESSURE LEVELS

There is evidence from the Framingham study of a general population that a random isolated blood pressure reading is a good indicator of morbidity and mortality.[6] The simplistic explanation may be that this is blood pressure at which people live and is therefore an appropriate predictor of experience. However, most studies try to obtain an average of two or more readings, separated by a short period of rest if the initial level is raised. The Joint National Committee on Detection, Evaluation and Treatment of High Blood Pressure requires two readings to be taken on two separate occasions.[2] It is routine insurance practice to request a second or third reading after rest if the first reading is raised.

There has been much discussion over the years about the variability of blood pressure response of individuals to different physical and psychological stimuli. People whose systolic and diastolic pressures vary by less than 10 mm Hg to various stimuli can be called hyporeactors; if the variation is 10–20 mm Hg they are normoreactors; when it is more than 20 mm Hg they are hyperreactors. The highest of any particular individual's range of casual blood pressure is probably that first recorded during examination for life insurance, although it may not be abnormal. Here the person is subjected to a certain degree of stress in meeting an unfamiliar examiner, often in unfamiliar surroundings, and there is always some apprehension, even if only slight, about the outcome of the examination. This is an example of the so-called 'white coat syndrome'.[7] The person's feelings of stress are inevitable but far from unfortunate, since the casual blood pressure reading is of great value in assessing the reaction to environment, as long as the medical examination has been conducted pleasantly and calmly. It is reasonable to assume that the stress occasioned by a medical examination is not much more than might be expected in everyday life in business or domestic affairs.

BLOOD PRESSURE AND MORTALITY

For many years the life insurance approach to raised blood pressure differed from that of the clinician. Medical underwriters paid attention to relatively small increases in mortality, whereas physicians were involved with treating symptoms. Recently the actuarial concern for the adverse effects on mortality of small rises in blood pressure has merged with the medical attempt to preserve health and increase longevity. This progress is reflected in the history of studies of blood pressure in large groups of people; initially insured populations were studied, then both clinical and insurance investigations continued side by side, now there are many large population studies with an emphasis on the effects of treating raised blood pressure. Throughout all these studies medical science and the insurance industry have benefited greatly from each other's work.

In 1925 the Society of Actuaries and the Association of Life Insurance Medical Directors of America jointly published the first mortality study according to variations in blood pressure among insured lives.[8] This was followed by the *Blood Pressure Study 1939*,[9] the *Build and Blood Pressure Study 1959*[10] and the *Blood Pressure Study 1979*.[11] All the studies showed that mortality gradually increased above 125 percent for the insured population as blood pressure rose above 140/90 mm Hg, except for those over the age of 50, where slightly higher levels were associated with mortality within the standard range. The *Build and Blood Pressure Study 1959* was particularly important because it removed all doubt among clinicians and underwriters that insurance companies might have been too strict in their interpretation of blood pressure, especially at the borderline end of the scale.

The most recent study, the *Blood Pressure Study 1979*, involved about 4,350,000 policies issued to men and women during 1950–71. These were traced to policy anniversaries in 1972 (i.e. for periods of up to 22 years). Only about 420,000 of the policies involved blood pressures in the borderline range and only about 110,000 were in the definite high range, but the experience in these two ranges emphasized the need for treatment.

The salient finding of the *Blood Pressure Study 1979*, which was similar to that in earlier studies, was that even slight elevations of blood pressure were associated with significantly higher mortality than that among normotensive healthy people (*see* Table 14.2).

Table 14.2. Relative mortality of insured lives 1954–72, all ages combined, at various levels of systolic and diastolic pressure, compared with the mortality of standard life insurance risks taken as 100 percent.[a]

Systolic pressure (mm Hg)	Mortality ratio (%)		Diastolic pressure (mm Hg)	Mortality ratio (%)	
	Men	Women		Men	Women
Under 108	71	83	Under 73	85	87
108–117	77	90	73–77	92	96
118–127	89	93	78–82	99	103
128–137	111	107	83–87	118	114
138–147	135	121	88–92	136	132
148–157	166	135	93–97	169	167
158–167	206	169	98–102	200	181
168–177	218	178	103–107	258	208
178–187	232	278	108–112	244	195

[a]Source: Lew EA. *Trans Assoc Life Insur Med Dir Am* 1980; 64: 123.

The *Blood Pressure Study 1979* contained a most interesting section dealing with the effects of antihypertensive treatment. This was one of the earliest studies to report the beneficial effects of treatment on a large general population, and it had far reaching implications for underwriting treated hypertension. The number of policies was much lower than in the main study. It included 28,700 policies issued to men and women during 1950–71 (followed to 1972) where the codes indicated treatment for high blood pressure at the time of application for life insurance; the blood pressures coded were those at the time of application. To augment the number of cases with treated hypertension, a supplementary study was made of 4,200 additional policies issued to men and women during 1970–75 (followed to the end of 1976) where treatment was admitted on application. This latter experience provided an indication of the greater effectiveness of the more recently developed antihypertensive agents. Table 14.3 compares the mortality ratios of those being treated for hypertension with the mortality ratios of those not being treated in this way who had similar systolic and diastolic blood pressures at the time of application. Those being treated for hypertension, irrespective of their pretreatment blood pressure levels, had ratios equivalent or near to those with normal or untreated blood pressures.

Unfortunately the *Blood Pressure Study 1979* was not able to address hypertension present in combination with other impairments or to evaluate raised blood pressure in combination with smoking.

Table 14.3. Comparative mortality of treated blood pressures.[a]

Systolic pressure (mm Hg)	Treated cases (%)	All cases (%)	Diastolic pressure (mm Hg)	Treated cases (%)	All cases (%)
108–117	98	77	68–72	92	85
118–127	109	89	73–77	110	92
128–137	109	111	78–82	108	99
138–147	110	135	83–87	123	118
148–157	163	166	88–92	122	136
158–167	231	206	93–97	165	169
168–177	184	218	98–102	205	200
			103–107	228	258

[a]Source: Lew EA. *Trans Assoc Life Insur Med Dirs Am* 1980; 64: 123.

Another major contribution to the study of hypertension by the combined efforts of the Association of Life Insurance Medical Directors of America and the Society of Actuaries was medical and actuarial analysis of clinical, epidemiological and insurance studies, primarily published articles, containing survival data on medical impairments. This has resulted in the publication of two books: *Medical Risks: patterns of mortality and survival*,[12] published in 1976, and *Medical Risks: trends in mortality by age and time elapsed*,[13] published in 1989 and addressing the literature from 1976 to 1986. Both contained important sections on hypertension. In addition to the specific diseases addressed, these two books included information about actuarial medical methodology, which has broadened the understanding of the subject and has stimulated ongoing publication of studies in the *Journal of Insurance Medicine*, including work addressing hypertension.

The surveys in the USA by the National Center for Health Statistics since 1960 show little change in the prevalence of hypertension but a steady fall in the prevalence of elevated blood pressure, especially in those over the age of 50. These surveys also show an increase in those on antihypertensive medication, together with an increase in the smaller percentage whose hypertension is controlled on medication. These and other regional or more limited studies rarely report above 50 percent obtaining effective blood pressure control among those receiving antihypertensive medication. The progressively wider range of antihypertensive medications available probably explains the increasing proportion of those controlled. There are no studies of insured populations addressing prevalence or treatment, but it is probable that a higher percentage of insureds are taking hypertensive medication and that control is better than in the general population.

There has been a decline in cardiovascular mortality in the USA since 1950, particularly from stroke and, more recently, from ischemic heart disease. Although speculation continues about the reasons for this decline, there is agreement that control of elevated blood pressure with antihypertensive drugs has been a major factor. Many controlled clinical trials have demonstrated reduction in mortality from stroke, congestive heart failure and renal failure; the evidence for lower mortality from ischemic heart disease has been less definite, even conflicting.[14-20] The inconsistent findings on mortality from ischemic heart disease may be because of differences in the populations studied, varying severities of hypertension and complications, and differing approaches to therapy.

In 1979 echocardiography was added to the biennial examinations in the Framingham study and was found to detect left ventricular hypertrophy (LVH) in 16 percent of men and 19 percent of women in the entire population sample, fivefold to sixfold more frequently than with the electrocardiogram.[21,22] This finding reflects the high incidence of LVH with hypertension; more than 50 percent of elderly patients with essential hypertension were found to have LVH in one series.[23,24] LVH is known to be associated with ventricular arrhythmias and sudden death.[25] The long-term trials designed to evaluate treatment of hypertension have employed diuretics, vasodilators, reserpine and beta blockers, singly or in combination; these can cause undesirable effects on lipid levels or electrolyte balance predisposing to ischemic heart disease or arrhythmias. Increasing use of the newer angiotensin-converting enzyme (ACE) inhibitors and calcium channel blockers may lead to improvement in mortality associated with hypertensive therapy.[26]

INTERPRETATION OF BLOOD PRESSURE READINGS

The question arises as to which is the correct blood pressure reading of several to select for the purposes of underwriting. In the majority of cases there is no problem, as when the initial blood pressure on examination and any others from independent sources are strictly below 140/90 mm Hg; such levels would be associated with no extra mortality. On the other hand, the initial blood pressure reading may be higher than 140/90, and a further reading or readings taken after resting may show a fall, sometimes to within normal limits. In the same subject similar variations may be obtained when the blood pressure is rechecked by an independent examiner, or it may differ entirely. In such circumstances, which are not uncommon, the blood pressure level that will reflect the risk most faithfully will be the average of all the current readings available.

The validity of the method of averaging blood pressures in evaluating risks was tested by Pollack[27] and his colleagues of the Mutual Life Insurance Company of New York who made an investigation on policyholders who were substandard risks solely because of elevated blood pressure. The object was to find out whether lability of blood pressure was a significant factor in mortality and whether the company's method of averaging blood pressures (i.e. using a prior high reading and current examination readings) was a correct underwriting procedure. In this series of cases the highest and lowest systolic and the highest and lowest diastolic readings recorded within a period of six months were accepted as the range of blood pressure for that person, and for the purposes of rating, a strict average of both systolic and diastolic pressures was made. Mortality rates of those with labile blood pressure and those with non-labile blood pressure were compared after the observation period. From the results it was quite obvious that the mortality experienced in each group did not differ at all, the conclusion being that the method of averaging blood pressures was a correct means of arriving at an underwriting appraisal of the risk. It would, therefore, be manifestly wrong to accept as standard an applicant whose final resting blood pressure was 140/90 mm Hg but whose initial blood pressure was 160/100 mm Hg, unless a subsequent series of lower readings was such that the average of all came close to 140/90 mm Hg.

Hyperreactors

Two distinct patterns or combinations of systolic and diastolic blood pressures can be identified, each having a different significance for long-term mortality. The first is typified by a systolic blood pressure greater than 140 mm Hg and a diastolic blood pressure of less than, and commonly much less than, 90 mm Hg. The second is typified by a systolic blood pressure of about 140 mm Hg (or a little higher) and a diastolic blood pressure greater than 90 mm Hg. The first example illustrates hyperreaction of systolic blood pressure, which is usually accompanied by an increase in pulse rate and by an increase in the stroke volume output of the heart but by no elevation of diastolic blood pressure (cardiac hyperreaction). The second pattern is an example of the vascular type of hyperreaction in which there is increased peripheral vasoconstriction or resistance and little or no increase in cardiac output; this accounts for the predominant elevation of diastolic blood pressure and no, or only slight, elevation of systolic blood pressure.

Some evidence exists suggesting that the cardiac type of hyperreaction is not in itself indicative of subsequent development of diastolic hypertension or hypertensive disease, whereas the vascular type of hyperreaction is. Hines[28] quotes follow-up studies made on a group of patients at the Mayo Clinic who were subjected to a psychic pressor test (i.e. they were attending for the first time, and so were in unfamiliar surroundings, and their initial blood pressures were taken by a strange doctor). Among this group were 148 patients who had systolic blood pressure greater than 140 mm Hg but diastolic blood pressure less than 80 mm Hg. None of the 148 patients 20 years later had diastolic hypertension, hypertensive changes in their ocular fundi or any other evidence of hypertensive vascular disease.

Also, an entire group of patients attending the Mayo Clinic in whom the first reading of the blood pressure was used as a measure of response to a psychic pressor test was followed for ten to 20 years. The patients were classified as hyporeactors, normoreactors and hyperreactors according to their maximum diastolic pressure, and the initial reading was correlated with the subsequent development of hypertension. It was found that ten to 20 years later none of the hyporeactors had diastolic hypertension, a small number of normoreactors had diastolic hypertension and 57 percent of hyperreactors had significant diastolic hypertension (see Table 14.4).

Cardiac hyperreaction, which is basically a functional characteristic, must be distinguished from raised cardiac output due to systemic disease, and also from the raised systolic and relatively low diastolic blood pressure often found in old age when it is due to atheroma and loss of elasticity of the aorta and great vessels.

Despite the fact that these studies tend to confirm the widely held opinion that cardiac hyperreactors do not often develop diastolic hypertension and consequently must live longer than vascular hyperreactors, their mortality from all causes would still be somewhat higher than average. The method of calculating expected mortality from rating tables does, in fact, take into account both the

Table 14.4. Incidence of subsequent hypertension according to original diastolic blood pressure.

Classification[a]	Cases	Hypertension 10–20 yr later	
		Number	%
Hyporeactors	198	0	0
Normoreactors	878	31	4
Hyperreactors	446	254	57

[a]Diastolic blood pressure always less than 100 mm Hg. Hyporeactor, maximum diastolic pressure less than 70 mm Hg; normoreactor, maximum diastolic pressure 70–84 mm Hg; hyperreactor, maximum diastolic pressure 85–99 mm Hg.

systolic and diastolic blood pressure levels, although some adjustment may be necessary in individual cases.

EVALUATION OF BLOOD PRESSURE FOR RATING

When the blood pressure readings obtained on medical examination appear to be ratable in terms of the rating tables (a specimen of which is reproduced as Table 14.5), consideration should be given to obtaining a further series of readings, carried out possibly by an independent observer on another day. A series of three readings recorded over a period of about ten minutes as the applicant rests quietly allows a reasonably fair representation of the casual blood pressure. In this way a truer assessment of the overall blood pressure status can be made; whether or not the repeat readings are lower, higher or the same as those recorded originally, it is fairer both to the applicant and the insurance company.

In addition to blood pressure readings obtained at the original medical examination and any repeat examination, other readings may be available to the underwriter from different sources, such as the applicant's medical attendant, hospital or clinic reports, or from previous medical examinations by the same or other companies. Therefore when more than one blood pressure reading is available it is suggested that the procedure outlined below is followed in order to determine the appropriate level of blood pressure for rating purposes.

1) Disregard all blood pressure readings taken more than three years previously.
2) Calculate the average of the blood pressures taken on any one day within the previous three months and call these the daily averages.
3) Calculate the average of the daily averages for the previous three months and call this the current average.
4) Calculate the past average by forming the average of all blood pressure readings that are higher than the current average taken within the previous three years, excluding the past three months.
5) Due allowance can be made for past average blood pressures that are higher than the current average by weighting the past average one-third and the current

average two-thirds and adding the resulting figures together to form the rating average blood pressure. This can be done quickly using the following formula:

rating average $= B + \frac{1}{3}(A - B)$

where B is current average blood pressure and A is past average blood pressure.

Example:

past average blood pressure (A) = 190/112

current average blood pressure (B) = 160/100

therefore

rating average blood pressure $= 160/100 + \frac{1}{3}(30/12)$

$= 160/100 + 10/4 = 170/104$

There would, of course, be exceptions to the rule of averaging blood pressures if any readings are considered to be unreliable, either because of their source or because of the conditions under which they were taken (e.g. when a single high reading known to have been recorded under conditions of unusual stress appears among a series of consistently lower readings taken elsewhere, possibly by more than one examiner). Since the exceptional reading in this case is unlikely to have been a true casual reading, it would be excluded from the calculation of the average blood pressure.

Credits

There is no doubt that electrocardiography, echocardiography and radioscopy of the heart are extremely effective screening procedures in the selection of hypertensive risks, and when they are strictly normal substantial credits can be made against the rating for blood pressure, as indicated below.

Screening procedure	Credit		
	Up to +100[a]	+101 to +250[a]	Over +250[a]
Satisfactory ECG within 3 mth	−25	−50	−75
Satisfactory echocardiogram within 6 mth	−25	−50	−75
Satisfactory chest X-ray within 3 mth	−10	−15	−25

[a]Blood pressure rating.

Family History

Environmental factors apart, the chances of a person developing hypertension are increased twofold if both his parents are hypertensive; if he already has an elevated blood pressure, particularly of the diastolic phase, the likelihood of his developing

Table 14.5. Blood pressure ratings for male lives.[a,b]

Diastolic (5th phase) pressure (mm Hg)	Age	Systolic pressure (mm Hg)													
		136—140	141—145	146—150	151—155	156—160	161—165	166—170	171—175	176—180	181—185	186—190	191—195	196—200	201—210
85	Under 40	0	0	0	10	25	45	60	85	110	136	165	196	255	335
	40–49	0	0	0	0	0	20	40	60	80	100	125	160	215	300
	50–59	0	0	0	0	0	0	20	40	60	80	100	130	190	270
	60–64	0	0	0	0	0	0	0	15	30	50	70	100	160	255
	65–69	0	0	0	0	0	0	0	0	15	25	40	60	95	140
90	Under 40	0	10	20	30	45	65	85	105	130	160	190	225	275	340
	40–49	0	0	0	10	20	35	50	70	90	110	135	175	230	305
	50–59	0	0	0	0	0	15	30	50	70	90	110	145	195	275
	60–64	0	0	0	0	0	0	15	30	50	70	95	120	170	235
	65–69	0	0	0	0	0	0	0	15	25	40	55	75	100	140
95	Under 40	25	30	40	50	60	80	100	120	140	170	200	240	285	345
	40–49	0	10	15	25	35	45	60	80	100	120	150	190	240	310
	50–59	0	0	0	0	15	25	40	60	80	100	125	155	205	280
	60–64	0	0	0	0	0	15	25	40	60	80	105	135	180	235
	65–69	0	0	0	0	0	0	15	20	35	45	65	80	105	140
100	Under 40	55	60	65	75	85	100	115	135	160	190	220	260	300	350
	40–49	40	40	45	50	60	70	85	105	125	145	170	200	255	315
	50–59	20	25	30	35	40	50	60	75	90	115	145	180	220	285
	60–64	10	15	20	25	30	35	40	50	70	90	115	150	190	240
	65–69	0	0	10	15	15	20	25	30	40	50	70	90	110	145

105	Under 40	355	310	275	240	210	185	165	145	130	120	110	105
	40–49	325	270	220	185	160	140	125	115	105	100	95	90
	50–59	290	240	195	165	135	115	105	100	95	90	85	80
	60–64	245	195	160	125	100	80	70	60	60	60	60	60
	65–69	145	115	95	75	60	50	40	35	35	35	35	35
110	Under 40	365	330	300	280	260	235	215	195	180	175	170	
	40–49	330	290	260	230	210	190	175	160	150	145	145	
	50–59	305	260	220	195	175	160	145	135	135	135	135	
	60–64	250	210	180	160	145	130	120	110	100	100	100	
	65–69	150	125	105	95	85	75	70	65	60	55	55	
115	Under 40	370	345	325	310	295	285	275	265	260	260		
	40–49	335	315	300	285	270	255	240	225	225	225		
	50–59	315	290	275	260	245	230	215	200	195	195		
	60–64	260	240	220	205	190	180	170	160	150	150		
	65–69	160	145	130	120	110	105	100	95	90	90		
120	Under 40	380	365	350	335	320	305	295	285	285			
	40–49	350	325	310	300	290	280	270	265	260			
	50–59	330	315	300	290	280	270	260	250	245			
	60–64	270	260	250	240	230	225	220	215	215			
	65–69	160	155	150	145	140	135	130	130	130			

[a] For female lives use three-quarters of these ratings.
[b] Source: The Mercantile and General Reinsurance Company.

severe essential hypertension in the future is almost certain. From the point of view of practical underwriting, an applicant who is ratable on account of blood pressure is a rather worse risk if there is a family history of two or more deaths in parents or siblings under the age of 60 from cardiovascular-renal causes, whether these were associated with hypertension or not; an addition of +25 to +50 should be made to the blood pressure rating depending on age. Conversely if the family history is excellent, there being no evidence of cardiovascular-renal disease or hypertension, both parents being alive plus siblings including at least one brother, a credit of 25 can be allowed.

The Influence of Sex

Women with hypertension seem to fare so much better than men as regards mortality that considerably more latitude can be exercised in underwriting female lives with elevated blood pressure. From the results of comparative studies of death rates in men and women suffering from hypertension, it would be reasonable to assume that expected mortality in women with hypertension lies between 65 and 70 percent of that for men with equivalent levels of blood pressure.

Substantial Elevation of Blood Pressure

Up to now, the discussion has dealt mainly with uncomplicated, borderline and moderately raised blood pressure for which adequate mortality statistics are available, but the risk associated with substantially raised blood pressure (e.g. diastolic levels higher than 120 mm Hg) is not so certainly known. There are two reasons for this: first, there are relatively few people with such blood pressure levels; secondly, most of those who have would usually be declined for life insurance, thus being lost to statistical analysis. The statistics that do exist are usually reported by reinsurance companies that specialize in underwriting severely substandard lives; one such — The Mercantile and General Reinsurance Company in the UK — has from time to time been able to examine the mortality experience of its Blood Pressure Pool, which includes two groups of blood pressure that could be described as substantial.

The Blood Pressure Pool was formed in 1953 to insure lives with arterial hypertension who had no evidence of hypertensive complications, were not receiving antihypertensive drugs and had no other ratable impairment. No ceiling is placed on the level of blood pressure that is acceptable, but the higher this rises above 200/118 mm Hg the fewer are the applicants who can fulfill the criteria for inclusion in the Blood Pressure Pool because of the presence of hypertensive disease.

As the direct writing companies became more sophisticated in their handling of hypertension so the number of new entrants referred to the Blood Pressure Pool began to decrease steadily from the mid-1950s, and therefore the Pool was closed for new business as from 1 January 1981. Nevertheless the in-force portfolio has continued to be monitored at intervals, and the most recent experience covering the years 1961–1986 was reported to the 16th International Conference of COINTRA in 1989.[29] Table 14.6 shows the results for groups IV and V, which contain the highest levels of blood pressure. The expected pattern of mortality

Table 14.6. Experience of blood pressure groups IV and V, 1961–1986, of The Mercantile and General Reinsurance Company Blood Pressure Pool.

Group	Blood pressure (mm Hg)	Age at entry								
		Up to 50			50–59			60 and over		
		Actual deaths	Expected deaths[a]	Mortality ratio (%)	Actual deaths	Expected deaths[a]	Mortality ratio (%)	Actual deaths	Expected deaths[a]	Mortality ratio (%)
IV	185/113 to 199/117	13	2·8	464	31	18·5	168	40	39·4	102
V	200/118 and over	25	3·2	781	81	20·7	391	80	55·1	145

[a]Expected deaths per A 1967/70 Select.

ratios reducing with age and increasing with rising blood pressure levels at entry is again evident. The low mortality ratios at entry ages 60 and over is difficult to explain but may have been contributed to by the numbers of very elderly lives included in the study. Of some practical significance is the fact that the great majority of those found to have substantially elevated blood pressure on examination that had previously been unsuspected will almost certainly come under the surveillance of their attending physicians and be started on treatment, thus distorting the mortality statistics for substantial hypertension not under treatment at the time of application.

Complicated Hypertension

The ultimate effect of persistent and substantial hypertension is on the left ventricle of the heart, the kidneys and the peripheral vascular system; when complications have appeared the underwriting risk becomes considerably greater than that associated with similar levels of blood pressure with no complications. The stage of hypertensive disease may be recognized clinically by the appearance of LVH, proteinuria or exudative retinopathy. When the changes are early and equivocal, selection of risks can be greatly enhanced by electrocardiography, echocardiogram and radioscopy of the heart and, when necessary, by a test of renal function.

As a group, hypertensives with normal ECGs have a much more favorable mortality experience than hypertensives with abnormal ECGs. The effect of various degrees of cardiographic abnormality on mortality has been determined by Ungerleider[30] who studied insured lives of similar build, age and other characteristics, all with a blood pressure of about 160/110 mm Hg, the only variable being the ECG. Although this study reports on cases seen between 1929 and 1941, the results remain appropriate for insurance practice today. The findings of the study are shown in Table 14.7. Briefly, mortality was found to be 186 percent of average when the ECG was normal; with a questionable ECG (i.e. one that was not quite normal) mortality increased to 269 percent of average, and with an ECG pattern of left ventricular strain or hypertrophy mortality was 344 percent. Other abnormalities, including bundle branch blocks, produced even higher mortality ratios.

Table 14.7. The effect of cardiographic changes on the mortality of hypertensives.[a]

Group[b]	Average blood pressure (mm Hg)	Number studied	Actual deaths	Mortality ratio (%)
1	156/97	185	23	186
2	159/97	97	19	269
3	159/98	101	50	344
4	163/100	41	15	375

[a]Source: Ungerleider,[30] experience of Equitable Life Assurance Society between 1929 and 1941.
[b]Group 1, normal ECG; group 2, borderline ECG; group 3, ECG pattern of LVH; group 4, ECG evidence of myocardial disease with or without LVH.

Such is the value of electrocardiography in hypertension that a rating for blood pressure may sometimes be offset by substantial credits if the current tracing is strictly normal (*see* p. 241).

Blood Pressure and the Elderly Applicant

'Elevations of systolic blood pressure and diastolic blood pressure increase the relative risk of cardiovascular morbidity and mortality at least as much for elderly patients as young ones.' This statement was made in the 1988 Report of the Joint National Committee on Detection, Evaluation, and Treatment of High Blood Pressure.[31] Insurance impairment studies have shown that mortality associated with hypertension declines as age advances beyond 50 years, but life insurance statistics covering a large number of elderly people are lacking. As the blood pressure rating tables are based on insurance experience it is reasonable to continue to use them for life insurance underwriting, but further study may lead to some modification during the next decade.

ANTIHYPERTENSIVE TREATMENT

Symptomless Hypertension

Numerous studies have demonstrated that mortality associated with elevated blood pressure is related to the blood pressure level irrespective of treatment. The consensus of opinion now is that the most important criterion of risk is the blood pressure level at time of application. Certainly in the case of symptomless mild or moderate hypertension without evidence of hypertensive complications, most companies would rate on the current blood pressure (i.e. an average of all blood pressures recorded in the previous three months) and would be confident that this faithfully reflects the risk. Even when the pretreatment blood pressure is substantially elevated this rule should still apply, as long as there is no evidence of hypertensive disease at the time of medical examination. There are, however, one or two reservations to be made when underwriting substantial hypertension now under treatment:

1) Treatment should have been established for longer than three months. For periods of less than three months the pretreatment blood pressure level should be included in the averaging of the current blood pressure for rating.
2) The longer that definite hypertension has existed before treatment the more likely it is that hypertensive complications, such as atheroma of the coronary arteries, varying degrees of LVH and albuminuria, will have developed. If any of these complications have been reported by the attending physician prior to commencement of antihypertensive treatment, it would be advisable for the underwriter to determine the state of the cardiovascular system at time of application irrespective of the current blood pressure level. The best screening tests for this purpose, depending on the degree of previous hypertensive damage reported, would be a resting and submaximal effort ECG, radioscopy of the heart

and microurinalysis. Any rating for residual complications should be added to the rating (if any) for the current blood pressure.

3) Where antihypertensive treatment has been maintained satisfactorily for several years and clinical examination at application is normal, a history of substantial pretreatment hypertension with minor complications can generally be disregarded and the risk evaluated on the current blood pressure level alone.

Accelerated Hypertension; Secondary Hypertension

When the reason for instituting antihypertensive treatment was accelerated or malignant hypertension particular care should be exercised in selection. Secondary causes of hypertension, such as chronic pyelonephritis, should be rigidly excluded, and confirmatory tests showing normal renal function should be obligatory at the time of examination. Otherwise the criteria of insurability would be the same as for hypertensive disease of lesser severity.

The prognosis of several diseases exhibiting arterial hypertension as part of their syndrome, notably the chronic glomerular diseases, polyarteritis nodosa, chronic pyelonephritis and renal transplantation, has been markedly improved with the advent of efficient antihypertensive drugs. As in the case of symptomless hypertension, it is the level of treated blood pressure at the time of application that is the most important one in determining whether any additional rating to the primary impairment is necessary.

Similar remarks apply to hypertension associated with a history of cerebrovascular accidents, myocardial infarction and peripheral vascular disease. Before efficient antihypertensive drugs were available, the prognosis of these disorders made them virtually uninsurable. Now, with hypertension adequately controlled most would fall within the acceptable range of substandard risks.

SUMMARY

With the introduction of efficient antihypertensive agents and better understanding of their application, blood pressure has become a much less useful parameter of risk than it used to be. In the 1960s hypertension of more than slight degree would have been rated substandard as a matter of course, but today the same levels of uncomplicated hypertension can be treated and brought under control in most cases, transforming a substandard into a standard risk in a matter of weeks or months. Even when hypertensive disease is present, such as LVH and/or nephropathy, close control of the blood pressure over a longer period can reverse the pathologic changes, bringing the condition into a standard or near-standard category. Despite the efficacy of modern therapeutics, uncontrolled or poorly controlled hypertension still exists and remains an important risk factor for the development of cardiac, renal and cerebrovascular disease. Due weight should therefore be given to the rating of hypertension in these circumstances.

Although blood pressure may have been relegated to a lesser level of importance for risk selection it is still the duty of examining physicians or paramedics to make accurate recordings of the blood pressure at the time of examination without bias and without any attempt to interpret them. As in the past, high readings should be repeated after a short interval and all should be reported. Any further action should be left to the life underwriter.

REFERENCES

1 Pickering GW. *High Blood Pressure*. New York: Grune & Stratton, 1968.
2 Hypertension prevalence and the status of awareness treatment and control in the United States; final report of the Subcommittee on Definition and Prevalence of the Joint National Committee on Detection, Evaluation and Treatment of High Blood Pressure (1984). *Arch Intern Med* 1984; 1045.
3 Task force on blood pressure control in children: report of the second task force on blood pressure control in children. *Pediatrics* 1987; 79: 1.
4 Fletcher AP. The effects of weight reduction upon the blood-pressure of obese hypertensive women. *QJ Med* 1954; 23: 331.
5 Hamilton M, Pickering GW, Roberts JAF, Sowry CSG. The aetiology of essential hypertension. *Clin Sci* 1954; 13: 271.
6 Kannel WB. Some lessons in cardiovascular epidemiology from Framingham. *Am J Cardiol* 1976; 37: 269.
7 Pickering TG, James GD, Boddie C, Harshfield GA, Blank S, Laragh JH. How common is white coat hypertension? *JAMA* 1988; 259: 225–8.
8 *Blood Pressure Study 1925*. New York: Actuarial Society of America/Association of Life Insurance Medical Directors of America, 1925.
9 *Blood Pressure Study 1939*. New York: Actuarial Society of America/Association of Life Insurance Medical Directors of America, 1940.
10 *Build and Blood Pressure Study 1959*. Chicago: Society of Actuaries, 1959.
11 *Blood Pressure Study 1979*. New York: Society of Actuaries/Association of Life Insurance Medical Directors of America, 1980.
12 Singer RB, Levinson L (editors). *Medical Risks: patterns of mortality and survival*. Association of Life Insurance Medical Directors of America/Society of Actuaries, 1986.
13 Lew EA, Gajewski J (editors). *Medical Risks: trends in mortality by age and time elapsed*. Association of Life Insurance Medical Directors of America, 1990.
14 Smith WMcF. *Treatment of mild hypertension: results of a ten year intervention trial*. US Public Health Service Hospitals Cooperative Study, Group Circ Res 40 (Suppl 1) 1977; 98–105.
15 Helgeland MD. Treatment of mild hypertension: a 5 year controlled drug trial. The Oslo Study. *Am J Med* 1980; 69: 725–32.
16 Hypertension Detection and Follow-up Program Co-operative Group. The effect of treatment on mortality in mild hypertension. *N Engl J Med* 1983; 307: 976–80.
17 Report by the management committee: the Australian therapeutic trial in mild hypertension. *Lancet* 1980; 1: 1261–7.
18 Multiple Risk Factor Intervention Trial Research Group. Multiple risk factor intervention trial: risk factor changes and mortality results. *JAMA* 1982; 248: 1465–77.
19 Medical Research Council Working Party. MRC trial of treatment of mild hypertension: principal results. *Br Med J* 1985; 291: 97–103.
20 Amery A et al. Mortality and morbidity results from the European Working Party on High Blood Pressure in the Elderly Trial. *Lancet* 1985; 1: 1349–54.
21 Savage DD et al. The spectrum of left ventricular hypertrophy in a general population sample: the Framingham Study. *Circulation* 1987; 75 (part II): 1.
22 Levy D et al. Echocardiographically detected left ventricular hypertrophy: prevalence and risk factors. *Ann Int Med* 1988; 108: 7.
23 Messerli FH. Pathophysiology of essential hypertension and the role of combined alpha and beta blockade therapy. *Dateline: Hypertension* 1985; 3: 2.
24 Messerli FH. Essential hypertension in the elderly. *Lancet* 1983; 2: 983.
25 Savage D. Left ventricular hypertrophy as risk factor in sudden death (presented at 3rd Annual Meeting Am Soc of Hypertension). *Medical Tribune* 29 Sept 1988.

26 Gubner RS. Major new developments affecting treatment and prognosis in hypertension. *Trans Assoc Life Insur Med Dir Am* 1989; 73: 97–114.
27 Pollack AA, McGurl TJ, Plucinski TE. Hypertension in substandard insurance. *Trans Assoc Life Insur Med Dir Am* 1957; 41: 51.
28 Hines EA. Some aspects of the development and treatment of hypertensive diseases. *Trans Assoc Life Insur Med Dir Am* 1955; 39: 25.
29 *16th International Conference of COINTRA* 1989; 1: 33–43.
30 Ungerleider HE. The prognostic implications of the electrocardiogram. *Am J Cardiol* 1960; July: 35.
31 The 1988 Report of the Joint National Committee on Detection, Evaluation and Treatment of High Blood Pressure. *Arch Intern Med* 1988; 148: 1023–38.

CHAPTER 15

CARDIOVASCULAR DISORDERS

G R CUMMING AND RICHARD CROXSON

PART I: CORONARY HEART DISEASE

G R CUMMING

The purpose of Part I of this chapter is to expose the natural history of CHD, to identify risk factors for CHD and how they may impact on mortality, to outline methods of assessing the extent and severity of CHD and to estimate prognosis relative to a normal population. This is not an underwriting manual to use as an underwriting guide in day-to-day business, nor is the approach to underwriting necessarily conventional. Another purpose of Part I is to dispel the following myths concerning CHD.

1) If angina has been present 10–15 years the CHD is likely to be quite mild.
2) Angina is not nearly as serious a condition as a myocardial infarction.
3) After CABG, patients with three vessel disease do much worse than patients with two vessel disease.
4) Patients discharged from ICU as having non-cardiac chest pain are a standard risk.
5) In an exercise test 2·0 mm ST depression always indicates a worse prognosis than 1·2 mm ST depression.
6) A negative myocardial perfusion scan completely excludes the possibility of CHD when a GXT has been positive.
7) Horizontal ST depression is the only important parameter to monitor on a GXT.
8) Risk factors cease to be important after CHD has developed.
9) It is impossible to predict CHD prognosis accurately without an angiogram.
10) The best gage of myocardial ischemia is the angiographic appearance of the arteries.
11) Except for single vessel disease, CABG is always better than no CABG.
12) CHD is slowly progressive and unlikely to change in six months.
13) Atypical chest pains are not important.
14) Angiographic lesions that compromise the coronary lumen by less than 30 percent are not important.
15) Survival after PTCA is better than after bypass.
16) Coronary artery narrowing is irreversible.
17) Patients with impaired LV function do not do well after bypass.

INTRODUCTION

Coronary heart disease (CHD) is treacherous, as death or severe disability can occur suddenly in those with mild disease, and in those who are completely unaware that they have any disease. An early atherosclerotic plaque, compromising the coronary artery lumen only slightly, can be the site of an acute thrombosis, resulting in sudden death from arrhythmia, or a massive infarction leading to pump failure or severe residual impairment of ventricular function. A patient with a well healed myocardial infarction (MI) may develop ventricular ectopic activity that progresses to ventricular tachycardia and fibrillation, death occurring when cardiac damage is not severe, and perhaps with only one coronary artery being significantly narrowed.

Life underwriting of applicants with CHD needs to take those events that are unpredictable in the individual patient but predictable in a population of similar patients into consideration. There is a definite correlation between disease severity and long-term prognosis in patients with CHD. Most early deaths occur in patients with extensive disease in two or three of the major coronary arteries and in patients with severely impaired left ventricular function. There have been numerous survival studies with and without major interventions in patients with CHD, providing statistical evidence on which to base underwriting. Prognostication in CHD can be based on the extent and severity of the coronary artery narrowings, the degree of damage that has already occurred in the heart muscle, the presence or absence of electrical instability, the degree of ischemia brought on by stress, and the likely rate of progression of the atherosclerotic process.

The probability that a group of individuals currently without known disease will develop CHD in the future can also be predicted with a reasonable degree of precision from various risk factor studies.

Asymptomatic Applicants

Some applicants have extensive CAD, the prognosis is poor, but they will remain unrecognized unless a screening test is carried out. Some of these subjects are asymptomatic because they are inactive. A history of regular vigorous physical activity in an applicant is of definite value. The main screening test used at present is the exercise ECG.

A Glimpse into the Future

A most encouraging recent finding is that regression of atherosclerotic narrowings can occur in serial angiograms. Intensive dietary therapy can achieve this, but most patients will not follow the extreme dietary measures required. More recently Brown el al studied with repeat angiography three groups of patients with coronary artery disease (CAD) after an interval of 2·5 years. Those given conventional therapy (diet and colestipol) lowered low-density lipoprotein (LDL) cholesterol by only 7 percent, 46 percent showed lesion progression and only 11 percent showed lesion regression. Those given lovastatin and colestipol (or niacin and colestipol) had reductions in LDL cholesterol of 32–46 percent and increases in high-density lipoprotein (HDL) cholesterol of 15–43 percent. Progression of an atherosclerotic lesion occurred in only 21 percent, and regression in 32–39 percent. If treatment could begin earlier in all cases of CAD, it is possible that regression of the disease could be achieved in the majority.

The preservation of the myocardium has been the major goal of various treatment measures for all cases of MI in the past 20 years. Prevention of extension of the infarct can be obtained to some degree with measures that reduce clotting, such as heparin, warfarin, aspirin and dipyridamole. Reduction of myocardial oxygen demand is achieved with beta blockade. Reduction of superimposed coronary spasm is achieved with calcium channel blockade. Reduction of left ventricular work with angiotensin-converting enzyme (ACE) inhibitors has been shown to protect the left ventricle (LV).

In the past ten years there has been a flurry of activity in thrombolysis, which can result in aborting the infarction process completely if commenced early enough. Increased use of thrombolysis, extension to peripheral and rural hospitals and public education about the need for prompt treatment will increase in the coming years, and more effective thrombolytic agents will become available. This will decrease the extent of myocardial damage.

After thrombolysis the urgent application of angioplasty or bypass in appropriate cases may prevent subsequent problems for years to come. This causes considerable strain on angiography and bypass teams but the problems are likely to be solved.

Improved pharmacologic measures to reduce coronary spasm, protect the myocardium and stabilize arrhythmias will undoubtedly continue to be developed. Meaningful advances are needed particularly in the field of arrhythmia control and the prevention of sudden death. It may be that this problem will continue in its current unsatisfactory state. The only way to prevent sudden death in many patients may require prevention of extensive myocardial damage.

Balloon angioplasty of coronary narrowings was just the beginning of catheter intervention techniques, and advances will continue to be made in the use of stents, laser, ultrasound and other physical means of re-establishing a wide coronary artery lumen.

Continued refinement of bypass surgery techniques will result in improved survival rates, a reduction in the frequency of bypass occlusions and improved longevity.

Insurers can take some comfort in the fact there will be less CAD in the Western world in the coming years. In those who develop clinical manifestations of the disease, progress of disease will be halted or regression of arterial narrowings produced, and, failing that, methods of dealing with most of these narrowings will evolve.

Those underwriting the risk of death in patients with risk factors or with known CHD must rely on mortality studies carried out in the past, assuming that only a mild or modest improvement is likely to occur in the next 10–20 years. We cannot assume that reducing current risk factors will eliminate or even reduce mortality from CHD in years to come. In some Western societies mortality from CHD has already been reduced by 40–50 percent by a combination of decreased disease frequency and severity and better management; further gains cannot be assumed, and will depend on innovative research.

RISK FACTORS FOR CHD

Despite sophisticated measurements of blood lipids, emphasis on the dangers of smoking and elevated blood pressure, the risks of lack of physical activity and glucose intolerance, the main risk factors for CHD in Western civilization are age and male sex, factors we cannot modify, but factors that are built in to all mortality tables. For example, CHD was present in the Framingham population aged 35–44 in 4·1 per 1,000 males and 0·6 per 1,000 females, and by age group 75–84 the rates were 25·2 and 23·4 respectively.

Many risk factor studies compare the relative risk of coronary events between the bottom quintile for a given risk and the other four quintiles, dealing with risk factors singly or in various combinations. It is usually possible to show that for a single risk factor morbidity is up to three times higher in the top quintile, compared to the bottom quintile, for cholesterol or blood pressure. These high morbidity ratios are rather overwhelming, and on first approaching the risk factor studies such as the Framingham study there is a tendency for underwriters to give up in despair wondering, 'How can I rate an elevated cholesterol at 6·8 mmol/l (260 mg/dl) at 300 percent mortality?' Insurers do not divide their standard pool into quintiles.

The goal of most insurers is to market life insurance financial services to about 90 percent of the population at as low a price as possible and not to have a complex system with several levels of premium for this large standard pool. Some insurers, to gain market advantage, offer a special segment of the population an extra low premium for subjects at very low risk for all coronary risk factors, career risk, life style risks and other considerations. These companies must accept a higher mortality in their standard group because the overall mortality is not kept down by including some of these super-select applicants.

If we wish to devise a rating system using risk factors for coronary disease we must first establish company policy concerning what percent of the asymptomatic population we wish to offer standard rates. A fine tuning of the standard rates into several strata would likely cause public concern over the availability of inexpensive insurance.

Mortality debits can be assigned to the top quintile (or decile) values for factors such as cholesterol, HDL cholesterol and blood pressure. This discussion on risk factors will be simplified by addressing total mortality only, the main concern of life insurers. The majority of those who develop coronary disease manage to survive for many additional years, and excess mortality in subjects with risk factors is not as striking as excess morbidity. Table 15.1 summarizes pooled data from various studies. Mortality ratios comparing mortality of subjects with blood pressure and cholesterol in the fourth and fifth quintiles to mortality for the population as a whole are given.

The follow-up was about ten years, the studies took place in the 1960s (so they are not recent), the methodology was not standardized, only males were included in most of the studies, and subjects with diabetes, peripheral vascular disease, stroke and other illnesses (except for angina or infarction) were not excluded. The drawbacks are numerous. Several points deserve emphasis:

1) Age had a negligible effect on mortality ratios in this pooled data. Contrast this to patients post-CABG (coronary artery bypass graft).
2) ECG changes were of far greater importance than hypertension, high cholesterol or smoking.
3) Cholesterol over 7 mmol/l (268 mg/dl) increased mortality by less than 60 percent.

Table 15.1. Risk factors and total mortality pooling project, 8,503 men.[a]

Age	Mortality ratios (%)									
	Systolic BP		Diastolic BP		Cholesterol		Smoking (packs per day)			ECG	
	138–150	>150	88–94	>94	6·2–7 mmol/l (240–268 mg/dl)	>7 mmol/l (>268 mg/dl)	~$\frac{1}{2}$	~1	>1	Minor	Major
30–39	–	150	–	175	–	146	105	82	207	97	361
40–49	117	207	126	182	129	157	120	143	225	229	339
50–59	139	194	140	181	140	152	110	208	218	195	412

[a]Source: data from three work site studies (The Chicago Gas and Electric Companies and New York employees) and two population-based studies (Framingham and Tecumseh), utilizing data from Tables 601 A–F in *Medical Risks*.

4) Blood pressures from 138/88 to 150/95 increased mortality by less than 40 percent.
5) Smoking about one-half pack per day or less had little effect on total mortality. Heavy smokers had mortality ratios just over twice normal.

The ECG in this report was used to assess baseline mortality. The entire population with no ECG changes was considered to have standard mortality. Major ECG changes included right bundle branch block (RBBB), T-wave inversion, ST depression 0·5–0·9 mm, partial A–V block and frequent ectopic beats, changes that many medical advisors would consider being associated with only a slight extra risk. Mortality ratios for subjects with these changes were over 300 percent! Minor ECG changes included ST depression of less than 0·5 mm, flat or diphasic T-waves, PR longer than 0·21 mm, QRS voltage changes of left ventricular hypertrophy (LVH) without ST changes, and left axis deviation greater than −29°, changes which many medical underwriters currently ignore. These changes were associated with a mortality ratio of 200 percent after the age of 40.

ECG evidence of LVH occurs in hypertension, but the severity is not necessarily correlated with blood pressure levels, and some patients with minimal hypertension or normal pressures on treatment have LVH. Echocardiographic-calculated LV mass is predictive of mortality and cardiovascular events, and this technique identifies at least three times the number of subjects with LVH compared with the ECG. There is no uniform approach to using echocardiographic evidence of LVH in the underwriting process other than possibly to waive mortality debits for hypertension if the echo is normal. Regression of LVH occurs with ACE inhibitors or alpha-adrenergic blockers, such as prazosin, but not necessarily with beta-adrenergic blockers or calcium channel antagonists. The impact of regression of LVH on mortality is uncertain. Further information on total mortality and smoking in these populations is shown in Table 15.2.

Table 15.2. Pooling project, mortality ratios and smoking status at entry.[a]

Smoking status	Mortality ratio (%)
Never	68
Stopped for >1 yr	63
Cigar or pipe	79
½ pack per day or less	114
Approx 1 pack per day	169
>1 pack per day	218

[a]Source: data from three work site studies (The Chicago Gas and Electric Companies and New York employees) and two population-based studies (Framingham and Tecumseh), utilizing data from Tables 601 A–F in *Medical Risks*.

Smokers of more than one pack per day had a mortality ratio of over 330 percent compared with those who had never smoked but only 218 percent compared with the entire population.

Most insurers in North America have chosen to divide their individual life insurance applicants into smokers (those who admit to having had one or more cigarettes in the last year) and non-smokers (those who have not). Smokers' rates are currently 40–100 percent above a company's non-smoker rates. This system unduly penalizes the very light smoker and underpenalizes the heavy smoker, but administratively this division is the easiest to monitor.

Data covering mortality on smoking and cholesterol combined from the Framingham Study are summarized in Table 15.3.

Table 15.3. Smoking status, cholesterol and mortality, Framingham Study, 26-year follow-up.[a]

Cholesterol mmol/l (mg/dl)	Mortality ratio (%)					
	Males Cigarettes			Females Cigarettes		
	0[b]	2–19[b]	≥20[b]	0[b]	2–19[b]	≥20[b]
≤ 5·9 (225)	84	102	117	97	110	162
5·9–7 (226–269)	76	118	134	80	124	135
7–7·8 (270–299)	98	188	210	92	143	118
≥7·8 (300)	113	119	154	99	177	144
All	88	117	135	94	120	152

[a]Source: *Medical Risks*, tables 604 A–C.
[b]Cigarettes smoked per day.

Standard mortality was from a standard life insurance population. It is seen that a cholesterol value of 7 mmol/l (270 mg/dl) or more was associated with very little extra mortality in this population in the non-smokers. There is some unevenness in the data due to small numbers, which is why the authors of these studies were more comfortable discussing coronary events than total deaths.

Low HDL Cholesterol

This is considered an additional risk factor for CHD. HDL cholesterol (HDLC) accounts for 20–30 percent of total plasma cholesterol. Normal values should be at least 0·9 mmol/l (35 mg/dl). About 10 percent of North American males have values below 0·85 mmol/l (33 mg/dl), and 25 percent below 1·06 mmol/l (40·8 mg/dl). Only 7 percent of females are below this value.

Even subjects with total cholesterol under 5·2 mmol/l (200 mg/dl) have increased risk of CAD if their HDLC is low. HDLC is increased by high volume exercise participation, alcohol intake, cimetidine and estrogens, and is decreased by a febrile illness, obesity, high fat intake, beta blockers, retinoids and thiazides.

In the general population about 50 percent of the variability in HDLC is genetic, 50 percent environmental. There are a few rare diseases with low HDLC, such as Tangier disease, fish eye disease and familial HPAL.

Gemfibrazol and nicotinic acid may raise HDLC by 25 percent in subjects with values below 0·9 mmol/l (35 mg/dl). Bile acid sequestrates and HMG COA reductase inhibitors increase HDLC by 10 percent.

The laboratory measurement of HDLC is sometimes difficult, and reproducibility is not always good. In underwriting, an HDLC value consistently below 0·8 mmol/l (31 mg/dl) is just as serious as a total cholesterol above 8·5 mmol/l (327 mg/dl).

Cholesterol, Blood Pressure and Smoking in the MRFIT Study

The six-year mortality data from the more than 360 thousand men screened for the MRFIT Study provided a huge population in which to relate mortality to blood pressure, serum cholesterol and smoking status. In Table 15.4 the data from this study has been recalculated to be in line with insurance practices. Mortality rates are provided for the top quintile for serum cholesterol and the other 80 percent of the population.

Table 15.4. MRFIT Study: Comparison of CHD death rate in the top quintile to the lower four quintiles for major risk factors; deaths per 1,000 in six years, 356,222 men aged 35–37 years free of history of MI.

	Deaths per 1,000			
	Diastolic pressure <90		Diastolic pressure ≥90	
	Non-smoker	Smoker	Non-smoker	Smoker
Cholesterol quintiles 1–4	2·6	6·3	5·4	12·8
Cholesterol top quintile[a]	6·4	13·3	10·7	21·4

[a]Values of 6·4 mmol/l (245 mg/dl) or more.

Death rates from CHD ranged from 2·6 per 1,000 in six years for non-smoking men with diastolic blood pressure under 90 and cholesterol under 6·4 mmol/l (245 mg/dl), to 21·4 per 1,000 for smokers with diastolic blood pressure over 90 and cholesterol over 6·4 mmol/l (245 mg/dl). The risk ratio for three adverse risk factors versus zero risk factors was 8·2:1; for those with two adverse factors versus zero 4·1:1, and for cholesterol elevation only versus zero factors 2·5:1. These mortality ratios of 250–820 percent are higher than those found in the Framingham and pooling populations. This study is more recent than the others. The values emphasize that when more than one risk factor is present the risk is greater than the sum of the individual risks.

This general risk factor analysis does not include familial homozygous hypercholesterolemia or other uncommon lipid disorders. The newer lipid measurements, such as apolipoprotein or lipoprotein A, have not been considered. High triglycerides may be of some risk but have had an in-and-out history as being significant and will not be included.

Diabetes

The nine-year follow-up studies of the Chicago Heart Association Detection Project in Industry showed a high CHD death rate for people with diabetes at entry compared to those without (*see* Table 15.5).

Table 15.5. Nine-year CHD death rate for subjects with diabetes mellitus at entry age 35–64 years.

	Age-adjusted death rate per 1,000	
	Men	Women
No diabetes	23·7	3·6
Diabetes	111·5	30·8

In men diabetes increased the death rate from CHD by a factor of 4·7, in women by a factor of 8·5. However, death rate from CHD in diabetic men was 3·6 times the CHD death rate in diabetic women. Vascular complications are the major cause of death in diabetics and deaths from CHD are taken into account in Chapter 13. Many mild diabetics who might incur limited or no mortality debits for their diabetes have associated risk factors of hypertension, low HDLC and obesity.

Patients with hyperinsulinemia, insulin resistance, hypertension, hypertriglyceridemia and low HDLC have been grouped into a syndrome (syndrome X or Reaven syndrome); patients with these factors are at very high risk of CHD.

Some of these patients may have a close to normal glucose tolerance so that their insulin resistance is not apparent; at present the measurement of insulin resistance is not readily available.

Other Risk Factors

Other risk factors, such as vital capacity, resting heart rate (HR) over 100, abdominal fat distribution with abdominal girth greater than chest girth, and hostile type A personality, all have their proponents, but for various reasons have already been taken into consideration by most insurers.

The risk factor chart presented in this section (*see* Table 15.7) provides for a debit of 25 for impaired glucose tolerance, defined as fasting blood glucose of 6·1–7·8 mmol/l (110–140 mg/dl). Microalbuminuria is emerging as a significant indicator of future risk for vascular disease.

Risk Factors in Relation to the Decline in CHD Mortality

Whether the dramatic decline in total cardiovascular and coronary heart disease mortality between 1960 and 1970 was due to improved patient care or reduction in risk factors cannot be clarified. Risk factors may not have changed as much as is commonly believed, as shown in Framingham Study data on men aged 50–59 who died of causes other than CHD (*see* Table 15.6); there were negligible changes in cholesterol and blood pressure, and the number of smokers had increased.

Table 15.6. Risk factors, 1950–1970, for men aged 50–59 who died of causes other than cardiovascular disease, Framingham Study.

	1950	1960	1970	Change 1960–70 (%)
Cholesterol mmol/l (mg/dl)	5·6 (215)	6·1 (233)	5·7 (219)	−6
Systolic BP mm Hg	137	139	137	−1
Diastolic BP mm Hg	83	87	83	−4
% Hypertensive[a]	25	31	18	−13
% Smokers	67	54	68	+14
Cigarettes per day	17	16	18	+12

[a]Hypertensive = BP >160 systolic or 90 diastolic, or receiving antihypertensive medication.

At the same time, MI mortality for the first two years decreased by 50 percent, suggesting that improved medical care was responsible for a good portion of the decrease in CAD death rate.

It is possible to synthesize the above risk factor information into a rating system, and one such proposal is outlined in Table 15.7.

Table 15.7. Coronary risk factor underwriting schedule.

Risk Factor	Rating
Blood pressure[a]	
Under 120/80 — both	−15
Systolic pressure 140–150, diastolic pressure 88–95	+25
Under 140/88	Ignore
Cholesterol mmol/l (mg/dl)	
<4·7 (180)	−25
4·7–5·2 (180–200)	−15
5·2–6·5 (200–250)	0
6·5–7·2 (250–275)	+15
7·2–7·8 (276–300)	+30
7·8–8·5 (301–325)	+50
>8·5 (325)	See MD
HDL cholesterol	
Male Female	
>55 >65	−50
>46–55 >51–65	−25
36–45 41–50	0
30–35 35–40	+15
25–30 30–35	+25
<25 <30	+50

Risk Factor		Rating
Smoking[b]		
For companies with blended smoker/non-smoker rates		
$\leqslant$10		0
11–20		+25
>20		+75
For companies with separate smoker/non-smoker rates		
$\leqslant$20		0
>20		+35
Family history		
Both parents >70	No events	−25
1 parent coronary event	Under 60 male	+15
	female	0
2 parents coronary event	Under 60 male	+25
	female	0
Parent and 1 sibling coronary event	Under 60 male	+35
	female	+15
Parent and/or 2 siblings coronary event	Under 60 male	+50
	female	+25
ECG change		
T-wave flattening		+15
T-wave inversion, ST depression		+50
LVH voltage only		+15
LVH voltage and ST change		+75
Impaired glucose tolerance FBS 6·1–7·8 mmol/l (110–140 mg/dl)		+25
Normal treadmill with fitness in top 10%		−25

[a]For higher pressures use company blood pressure tables.
[b]Figures are cigarettes smoked per day.

Risk factors are totaled arithmetically if there are two adverse factors out of the four (smoking, high cholesterol, hypertension, family history). If there are three or four adverse factors, the total is multiplied by 1·33. For example, a male with BP 145/95, cholesterol 8·1 mmol/l (310 mg/dl), smoking 20 cigarettes per day with a negative family history would have debits of 25+50+0 or +75; adding 33 percent for three risk factors gives a total of +100, if the company had separate smoker/non-smoker rates. If the company had blended smoker/non-smoker rates, +25 is added for smoking, giving a total of +125; increasing this by 33 percent gives a total of +166.

Age and Risk Factors

Subjects age 60 or above with proven CHD have mortality ratios close to normal. There is a logistical problem in applying mortality debits for applicants who have risk factors only and no clinical evidence of CHD. Whilst age did not alter mortality ratio in some risk factor studies, and some studies in post-MI patients have emphasized the risk of continued smoking or elevated cholesterol regardless of age, it seems reasonable that debits for risk factors should decrease with age. The risk scores of Table 15.7 might be reduced by 25 percent for subjects over the age of 65. This is not to deny that risk factors are still important in the elderly, particularly in combination, and especially ECG changes of LVH.

In effect, everyone obtains a credit of 50 because few competitive primary insurers issue policies with debits of +50 or less.

Blood pressure higher than 150/95, with or without LVH by ECG or cardiac ultrasound, is discussed elsewhere (*see* Chapter 14).

Insurers have an obligation to their clients and to the public to promote preventative health measures. The industry's introduction of non-smoker life insurance rates helped to emphasize the dangers of cigarette smoking, and penalties for other risks may help drive home the importance of trying to correct those risk factors that can be altered. A patient complaining of a rating may make an attending physician pay attention to elevations in cholesterol and blood pressure that were previously written off as unimportant.

Body build is discussed in detail elsewhere (*see* Chapter 12). The pooling project found that weight in excess of 129 percent of desirable caused only a 20 percent increase in mortality and was less important than underweight. For that reason weight has not been included in risk factor analysis and is dealt with separately in most underwriting systems.

Family History

A detailed discussion of the familial aspects of CHD is not possible. It would appear that the familial incidence of CHD cannot be explained entirely on the basis of standard levels of known risk factors and that extra mortality is justified. When one knows that a Finnish study showed that if a male had an infarct before the age of 46 his normal brother had a 55 percent chance of developing CHD by the age of 55, it is obvious that an extra premium is fully justified for applicants with severely adverse family histories of CHD.

The *1951 Impairment Study* reported a mortality ratio of 141 percent for insureds who had reported two or more deaths in the immediate family caused by cardiovascular or renal disorders.

Risk factor modification may not reduce CHD mortality as much as is commonly taught. Using a computer model Tsevat et al predicted that the population increase in life expectancy in 35-year-old US men would be 1·1 years for blood pressure control, 0·8 years for smoking cessation and 0·7 years for reduction of cholesterol to below 5·2 mmol/l (200 mg/dl). For individual males the gains were predicted to be 2·3 years for smoking cessation, 1·1–5·3 years for blood pressure control and 0·5–4·2 years for lowering cholesterol to below 5·2 mmol/l (200 mg/dl). Eliminating CHD entirely would extend the average life expectancy of a 35-year-old male by only 3·1 years and a 35-year-old woman by 3·5 years, compared to the elimination of cancer extending expectancy by 2·5 years.

The Helsinki primary prevention trial has provided some alarming and disappointing results. During the second five years of follow-up the risk for death was 46 percent higher in the intervention group; for cardiac deaths it was 142 percent higher in the intervention group. The excess mortality in the intervention group could not be explained.

TYPICAL ANGINA PECTORIS (STABLE ANGINA)

Typical angina is a central chest discomfort, coming on with exertion and lasting only about five minutes after the exertion ceases. Angina comes on slowly, builds up for a minute or so, then gradually eases off. The pain varies considerably, with the following adjectives being applied: constricting, heaviness, tightness, squeezing, crushing, vice-like. Angina will occasionally last for up to 30 minutes.

Pain that is sharp or stabbing or that is a continuous ache is usually not due to myocardial ischemia. Some patients have little or no pain and have shortness of breath, or even just belching or emesis as their symptom of myocardial ischemia. The pain of angina typically radiates to the neck and jaw, the left shoulder or down the inner aspect of the left arm. The pain is characteristically relieved by nitroglycerine within six minutes. Over 90 percent of patients with typical chest discomforts coming on with exertion and requiring the patient to slow down or stop activity will have at least a 70 percent narrowing of one or more coronary arteries at arteriography. History is therefore important.

In the general population of asymptomatic adults over the age of 45 in North America about 4 percent have a significant coronary narrowing. In patients with non-anginal (atypical) types of chest pain about 15 percent have a coronary narrowing, so the patient with recurrent pain that seemingly is not angina cannot be totally dismissed.

The severity of typical angina is classified according to the degree of physical activity required to bring on chest discomfort. The Canadian Cardiovascular Society (CCS) adapted the system shown in Table 15.8. Insurers would not usually consider patients whose angina remains at Class 3, and never consider Class 4 patients.

Table 15.8. Canadian classification for angina.

Class	Description
1	No angina with ordinary physical activity such as walking or stair climbing.
2	Angina with walking more than two blocks or climbing over one flight of stairs at normal pace. Angina walking uphill, in the wind or cold, under emotional stress or after meals.
3	Angina with walking one to two blocks on the level at normal pace.
4	Inability to perform any physical activity without angina.

In some patients the chest pain, though not typical of angina, does have some of its features; for these features the term atypical angina is used. Examples are chest pain that is stabbing but that occurs with exercise and subsides with rest, or a squeezing pain that occurs at rest but not on exercise. About 50 percent of these patients have a significant coronary narrowing at arteriography.

The severity of the angina correlates poorly with coronary anatomy: some patients with mild symptoms have severe three vessel disease, others with only a 60 percent narrowing of one artery may complain of a disabling degree of severe chest pain on minimal exertion.

Of patients with severe coronary narrowings 20 percent have no chest pain. Silent MI is more common in diabetic subjects, perhaps because of damage to the autonomic nerves.

In the Framingham Study the annual mortality of subjects who had developed angina was about 4 percent, compared to 5 percent in patients who had had a non-fatal MI. Angina is minimally less serious than MI and our underwriting needs to reflect this. Many underwriting manuals give considerably smaller mortality debits for angina than for past infarction, regarding angina as much less serious than coronary disease. In part this may be because the diagnosis of angina included patients who had non-cardiac chest pain, chest pain with normal coronary arteries or angina only with extreme exertion, situations where prognosis is much better than it is for the majority of patients with typical angina.

Factors Affecting Mortality

Overall about 4 percent per year of patients with stable angina die, but if blood pressure and rest ECG are normal only 2 percent per year die. If hypertension is present and the ECG is abnormal 8 percent per year die. The extent of the CAD by angiography, LV function, presence or absence of rest ECG changes, the peak workload on an exercise test, current or past hypertension and the presence or absence of arrhythmia are of major prognostic importance. Mortality of those with ST and/or T-wave changes in the rest ECG is four times those without. Mortality of those with ST depression at a light exercise load is up to ten times higher than mortality in those without ST change at a more strenuous exercise workload. It is controversial whether those with over 2 mm ST depression fare worse than those with only 1–2 mm ST change. The amount of ST change is dependent on the protocol followed in the exercise laboratory; many laboratories terminate the test when there is 2·0 mm ST depression, whereas some directors encourage the subjects to continue as long as there are no other abnormal signs or symptoms. Patients with angina and no ST change on exercise may still have extensive CAD and early death. Patients who can do over 10 METs exercise have a low mortality of 1 percent per year; those who cannot do 5 METs work have a mortality exceeding 10 percent per year regardless of ST change.

Some patients with angina have no CAD at angiography. Their prognosis is close to normal. Subjects with 30–50 percent narrowings have about double the annual mortality of the general population; whilst these lesions are considered not hemodynamically important at the time, they are likely to progress and cause problems. Patients with narrowings of 70 percent or more have annual mortality rates that vary according to the number of arteries involved: 1–2 percent for one, 6 percent for two and 10 percent for three vessels or left main disease in the early studies. Greater degrees of LV dysfunction are associated with a worsening prognosis, and patients with congestive heart failure have a 16 percent annual mortality.

UNSTABLE ANGINA

Anginal chest pain that lasts longer than 15 minutes and that occurs at rest or with very little activity is called unstable angina. Previous terms used included preinfarction angina, intermediate coronary syndrome and coronary insufficiency. Also included in this syndrome is previously stable angina precipitated only with moderate exertion that now occurs with minimal activity, is more resistant to relief from nitroglycerine, with more intense symptoms and more radiation of the pain.

Angina that has been present less than one month is also included in this syndrome in some reports as it is not known whether or not this will become stable. If this new onset angina only occurs with 7 METs or more activity, it really does not belong in this category.

An ECG recorded during the episode of chest pain often shows ST depressions (sometimes elevation) that improve when the discomfort eases. If the ST changes persist for more than six hours it is likely that a subendocardial infarction has occurred. Some patients with unstable angina will have persisting T-wave inversions, but there should be no new Q-waves in the ECG, and serum enzymes should be normal.

Mild elevations in serum enzymes may indicate microinfarctions, or severe ischemic injury.

Treadmill testing is generally unwise in these patients with unstable angina outside a hospital setting, and coronary arteriography is usually carried out as soon as the diagnosis is entertained if it has not been done in the recent past and if the patient is a suitable candidate for interventional treatment with percutaneous transluminal coronary angioplasty (PTCA) or coronary artery bypass graft (CABG).

In some patients with severe coronary narrowings the unstable angina is due to small increases in demand for oxygen as with meals, emotion, transient blood pressure increases and transient catecholamine release. In other cases unstable angina is due to coronary artery spasm superimposed on coronary atherosclerotic lesions. At angiography the left anterior descending coronary artery (LAD) is most commonly narrowed, but in 10 percent of patients coronary angiography is negative. In many of these cases coronary spasm is responsible for the symptoms. If ST elevation occurs during the anginal pain and the angina occurs only at rest, the term Prinzmetal angina is used.

Patients with unstable angina are at high risk for serious complications. In-hospital mortality is 1–2 percent, and in the next year about 20 percent will have infarcted and 7 percent will have died. Some of these patients can be successfully managed medically; many are selected for bypass or PTCA. Insurance underwriting should be postponed for at least one year.

In patients with newly developed angina or worsening of previously stable angina not severe enough to be hospitalized, mortality is as high as 4 percent in the next six months. Underwriting should be postponed for six months in newly developed angina, and declined when there is worsening, until the situation is stable again and full investigation, including angiography, is available.

VARIANT ANGINA (PRINZMETAL ANGINA)

Prinzmetal angina is due to coronary artery spasm, either in arteries that are normal or near normal or at the site of an atherosclerotic plaque. The course is not always benign, the spasm can be prolonged enough to cause MI, and severe arrhythmias can occur during the spasm, including ventricular fibrillation. One-year mortality is about 15 percent; in these patients death is often sudden. With the discovery of calcium channel blocking agents, coronary spasm is usually preventable, and hospital admissions and investigations of this phenomenon have decreased considerably in the past ten years.

Many patients with Prinzmetal angina are women, and up to a third have normal coronary arteries. However, it cannot be assumed that coronary anatomy is normal without arteriography. In patients with and without atherosclerotic narrowings there is a tendency for coronary spasm to improve over time, and these patients may eventually become free of angina and no longer dependent on calcium channel blocking agents.

In proven cases of coronary spasm with normal coronary angiograms the chest pain is usually like angina in its site, quality and radiation, but frequently occurs at rest, often at night. The pain lasts longer than exercise-induced angina, but usually not longer than 15–20 minutes. The pain responds to nitroglycerine. Serious arrhythmia, often leading to syncope, occurs in up to 25 percent of patients. Exertional chest pain occurs in 25 percent. ECG monitoring during an attack of pain shows ST elevation in 90 percent of cases, ST depression in the remainder.

In patients having coronary angiography, spontaneous spasm is rare, about 0·2 percent. Catheter-induced spasm is to some extent related to technique, and occurs in up to 5 percent of all normal angiograms but in 38 percent of patients with a history typical for spasm. There is no consensus among angiographers as to what constitutes significant spasm. The strict criteria require a 70 percent narrowing of a previously clear artery with restoration to a normal lumen after nitroglycerine.

With ambulatory monitoring, painless ST elevation occurs in over 60 percent of cases. In patients with spasm and normal coronary arteries 60 percent of patients show spontaneous resolution with disappearance of all symptoms in three to four years.

Prognosis

Patients with episodes of marked pain not relieved early with nitroglycerine, accompanied by ventricular tachycardia A–V block, and syncope may develop MI and/or ventricular fibrillation and death.

Patients with major attacks would be declined as suitable risks until the disease became much less severe with a few mild episodes only.

Prognosis appears to be excellent in those with normal or only mildly diseased arteries, as long as serious arrhythmias do not occur during the attack. In a Cleveland Clinic series no cardiac deaths were recorded on follow-up. Waters et al reported on features associated with sudden death in variant angina, the most important being documented ventricular arrhythmias (VAs) during the spasm.

In patients with normal coronary arteries who have complete control of their symptoms for a period of one to two years on calcium antagonists a rating of +100 would seem reasonable.

In patients with spasm superimposed on coronary atherosclerosis the evaluation of risk is dependent on the extent of the atherosclerosis, with an extra debit of +75 being added for the spasm, until the symptoms have been completely under control for at least two to three years.

Severi et al followed 138 patients with variant angina, only nine without atherosclerotic narrowings. Seven patients died in follow-up, but by the end of the fourth year over half the patients were asymptomatic. Death was related to the severity of the underlying CHD.

Acute Chest Pain with Hospital Admission

Patients with chest pain deemed severe enough for report to a hospital emergency are often held overnight or for a few days, if only for medico-legal reasons. The standard investigation is ECG monitoring, and CPK and CPK MB measurements. If CPK is normal and the ECG is normal, the patient is discharged. The diagnosis they are given is at the discretion of the attending physician, and it may be non-cardiac chest pain, questionable coronary insufficiency, questionable coronary spasm or chest pain undiagnosed. In follow-up, from 1–6 percent of these subjects will infarct and 4 percent will return with proven coronary insufficiency. Underwriting these cases is a problem. Look for risk factors, obtain a treadmill test in select cases and postpone others for up to a year. They should not be totally dismissed as having normal hearts.

CPK MB band enzyme levels are considered sensitive and specific for myocardial necrosis. In patients who subsequently infarct, the initial CPK is often normal; serial values are required, this being the reason for admission. In about 20 percent of cases of chest pain that do not progress to infarction CPK is mildly elevated. It is uncertain if this reflects myocardial injury. If CPK elevations did occur it would be prudent underwriting to insist that at least a treadmill with thallium scintigraphy be obtained, possibly supplemented with a nuclear angiogram. An underwriting decision is often necessary without coronary angiogram results, and a protective extra premium may be necessary to cover the extra mortality present in a population of similar applicants.

MYOCARDIAL INFARCTION

Ignoring rare causes, all infarctions can be assumed to be associated with coronary atherosclerosis. In countries with a high incidence of CHD a man had a 20 percent chance of having a heart attack (infarction) by the age of 65. Out-of-hospital mortality is 20 percent, in-hospital 15 percent, and in the subsequent year 10 percent. Insurers usually enter the picture after this high early toll.

Infarction most commonly occurs in hearts with more than one narrow artery, but large infarcts can occur with single vessel occlusions in the absence of any disease in the other arteries.

Obstruction of the LAD leads to infarction of the anterior and apical parts of the LV wall and portions of the septum. Left circumflex (LCx) coronary artery occlusion causes infarction of the lateral and/or inferoposterior walls of the LV, and right coronary artery (RCA) occlusion is followed by inferoposterior infarction.

Thrombus formation at the site of an atherosclerotic plaque is the commonest cause of infarction. The plaque may have produced severe narrowing prior to the thrombus, but thrombi can occur on plaques causing only 25 percent loss of luminal diameter. After clot dissolution in patients with acute MI, coronary angiography reveals that in half of the cases the culprit lesion caused less than 60 percent stenosis.

Isolated right ventricular infarction is rare, but up to 20 percent of RCA occlusions are associated with right ventricular infarction as well as inferoposterior infarction of the LV.

Rupture of the heart at the site of infarction occurs most commonly three to five days after infarction and is not a problem faced by insurers, although occasionally the rupture seals over, a false aneurysm is formed and rupture may occur months or years later. Patients with true aneurysms over 2 cm in diameter are usually considered uninsurable.

A true aneurysm is a circumscribed out-pouching of the LV wall, present in 10 percent of survivors of infarction. Aneurysms are 1·0–8·0 cm in diameter; late rupture is very rare. Small aneurysms are not of great importance, but aneurysms greater than 3·0 cm expand during systole and steal some of the LV stroke volume, further reducing an already impaired ejection fraction. Clots form in aneurysms and also on the LV wall over the area of infarction, giving rise to systemic embolization.

LV function, measured by ejection fraction, declines after infarction in relation to how much myocardium was destroyed and whether or not there is an aneurysm. Wall motion studies using nuclear angiography, ultrasound or contrast angiography assesses the size of infarcts by the size of the non-contractile area on the LV wall. Long-standing severe coronary atherosclerosis may lead to impaired function from diffuse myocardial fibrosis. Patients with two or more separate infarctions have two or more areas of impaired LV function, often involving 40 percent or more of the left ventricular mass.

Of patients under the age of 35 who have MI, 15 percent have no obstructive coronary lesion at angiography. It is thought that infarction in these patients is due to thrombosis with spontaneous clot dissolution, due to spasm, or due to myocardial vulnerability, or combinations of these. Most of these patients have an excellent prognosis. Most insurers are skeptical about assuming risk in most patients under the age of 40 with prior infarction, but if such patients have had complete studies showing normal arteries, and careful follow-up shows no recurrence, limited residual damage and absence of risk factors over a three- to five-year period, an aggressive underwriting position is justified.

Prognostic Factors

Twenty-five percent of patients die within minutes to six hours of their heart attack. Those dying early do not have myocardial necrosis (i.e. infarction). Death is due to ventricular fibrillation in 90 percent of these patients. Some of these patients may have had a primary rhythm problem, not a coronary occlusion with developing infarction. About 75 percent of patients who have successful out-of-hospital resuscitation from ventricular fibrillation do not have evidence of infarction. After MI, up to 20 percent of subjects die within one to two hours, 17 percent in the next one to two days, and 8 percent in the next three weeks. There are numerous reports detailing the risk stratification of infarction victims who reach a coronary care unit, information that is of limited value to insurers. The two main prognostic factors are the extent of myocardial damage and the presence or absence of significant arrhythmia.

After leaving hospital (in seven to 30 days), the person recovering from infarction faces a 10 percent overall first-year mortality and a 5 percent annual mortality after that. Few patients with persisting heart failure survive five years. Most of those who die in the first year have either very poor LV function or severe three vessel disease. Whilst death is often sudden and due to ventricular fibrillation, the importance of ventricular ectopic activity (VEA) alone is uncertain because the majority of patients with significant dysrhythmia also have poor LV function. Two-year mortality is as low as 1 percent in subjects with near-normal LV function and normal heart rhythm. A low-level exercise test before hospital discharge can be helpful in predicting outcome. In one study those who completed the test and had no ST depression had a 2 percent one-year mortality, compared to a 27 percent one-year mortality in those with ST depression.

Various interventions available today have probably halved the mortality rates given above. Medical measures shown to improve survival in clinical trials include beta blockers, aspirin, calcium channel blockers, serum lipid reduction, smoking cessation and exercise rehabilitation. Bypass surgery is felt to improve survival in patients with left main disease, three vessel disease, three vessel disease with impaired LV function and probably in patients with severe two vessel disease.

The task of the underwriter is simplified if the patient with an uncomplicated acute MI has had an angiogram. When angiography is carried out routinely after acute MI, about 30 percent of subjects have one vessel disease, 30 percent two vessel disease, 30 percent three vessel disease, 10 percent left main disease and two-thirds have viable myocardium at risk. In some centers it is therefore routine to recommend angiography after any MI; other centers maintain that angiography is not necessary unless exercise testing with ECG, supplemented with perfusion scintigraphy and Holter monitoring, can show that the patients are at high risk.

Non-Q-Wave Infarction

This is defined as an acute infarction, confirmed by serum enzyme analysis, and evolving ST and T-wave changes in the ECG, but without pathologic Q-waves. Compared to patients with Q-wave infarctions, there is less myocardial necrosis, serum enzymes are not as high, there is a greater likelihood of a patent artery into the location and there is more residual provocative ischemia.

With thrombolysis therapy, more infarcts that would have become Q-wave infarctions remain non-Q-wave. Patients with non-Q-wave infarction are more prone to post-infarct angina and a higher incidence of repeat infarction.

The extent of coronary disease is about the same in Q- and non-Q-wave infarction, and the long-term mortality is about the same. One should not be misled into believing that prognosis is better in non-Q-wave cases; it may actually be worse in the first year after hospital discharge. Mortality in non-Q-wave infarction is improved with antithrombotic agents, calcium channel blocking agents and with interventions such as angioplasty or bypass.

Silent MI

This diagnosis is made when a resting ECG is found to show Q-wave changes consistent with a previous infarction in the absence of any admitted past acute event. The infarction may be truly silent, with absolutely no previous chest symptoms, or the subject may have had some chest pains that were not recognized as a cardiac problem. The ECG recognition of silent infarction is dependent on the predictive accuracy of the ECG in asymptomatic patients of the following patterns: Q-waves in leads 3 and AVF; Q-waves in leads 2, 3 AVF; QS-waves in leads V1–V3; QS in leads V1 and V2, small r in V4; QS in leads V1, small r in V2–V4; and QS in V1, small q in V2; Q-waves in leads 1 and AVL. T-wave changes alone may well be indicators of myocardial ischemia but are not usually considered in the diagnosis of CHD.

If there is an earlier ECG available for comparison, the interpretation of borderline changes is simplified. Although the ECG should ideally be a precise diagnostic tool, we often need to consider the clinical setting of age, sex and risk factors to help us decide whether or not a borderline pattern is probably due to past infarction. The diagnosis of a previous infarction can be supported by evidence such as perfusion scans, nuclear angiography or ultrasound, but such studies have frequently not been done and are not readily available to insurers.

Secondary Preventive Therapy

Pooled data from studies using beta blockers post-MI show that annual mortality is reduced by 25 percent for the first three years. After Q-wave infarction calcium channel antagonists do not lower mortality; in non-Q-wave infarcts they do. Aspirin may reduce vascular death by 23 percent. ACE inhibitors may prevent cardiac dilatation, preserve myocardial function and reduce mortality. It is difficult to consider medical management strategies in the evaluation of mortality.

SUDDEN CARDIAC DEATH

In approximately 20 percent of first coronary attacks the subject dies out of hospital, death being the first, last and only clinical manifestation of CAD. Sudden coronary death is due to a fresh thrombosis on an atherosclerotic plaque in 73 percent of cases, and due to arrhythmias in subjects with high-grade coronary stenosis in the remainder.

In the Framingham Study 40 percent of sudden cardiac deaths occurred in patients with known coronary disease. The death was sudden and unexpected at the time, but the patient was known to be at risk. By inference, the other 60 percent of sudden deaths must have occurred in subjects not known to have coronary disease.

Patients with 'hemodynamically unimportant' coronary narrowings are also at risk for sudden death. A 30–50 percent coronary lesion is associated with a ten times increase in the risk of sudden death compared to the general population. There is no completely satisfactory screening tool to identify asymptomatic subjects at high risk for sudden death.

Risk factor screening is a starting point. Some authors have recommended various fluoroscopy methods to identify coronary artery calcification, but this potentially useful tool is not currently in widespread use, and it would be awkward for insurers to introduce it. Near-maximal exercise testing will identify a group of subjects with a four- to sevenfold increase in coronary mortality over the next five years, but many cases of mild coronary disease have normal exercise ECGs.

The current gold standard for recognizing coronary atherosclerosis is the angiogram, but this diagnostic tool is not used in asymptomatic subjects. It is possible that new imaging methods, such as magnetic resonance, may soon become clinically applicable and allow non-invasive identification of arterial plaques. A real problem in CAD is that some of those who have their first infarction have a fresh thrombus developing on a plaque that is compromising the arterial lumen by less than 30 percent. These patients have limited collateral development, and an occlusion of a proximal LAD can have disastrous consequences, with either sudden death or extensive myocardial destruction. In the future it is possible that metabolically active plaques will be identified using various biological markers and new imaging tools, such as PET. Until this is possible, all insurers can do is pay attention to known risk factors. The reason for life insurance is to cover the unexpected, and included in this are sudden coronary deaths; the frequency of this in a given population is predictable. The incidence of coronary events, and death from coronary events, is on the decline in the USA, Canada and other areas, partly due to improvement in risk factors. It may be possible in the future to protect arteries further with agents such as calcium entry blockers to alter calcium dependent factors in the genesis of the atherosclerotic plaque.

Of patients who eventually die of CHD 50 percent die suddenly, usually as a result of ventricular fibrillation. The contribution of VEA as a risk factor for sudden death has been studied for years. Many patients with high-grade VEA have poor LV function, and poor LV function appears to be a more important predictor of eventual sudden death than VEA alone. It has yet to be shown that pharmacologic suppression of VEA can improve long-term survival, and some antiarrhythmia therapies may even lead to increased mortality.

Holter Monitor Studies and Sudden Death

Retrospective analyses of patients on Holter monitors show that ventricular tachycardia leading to ventricular fibrillation is responsible for most of the cases of sudden death, and bradyarrhythmias, usually due to sinus depression, are responsible for about 15 percent of sudden deaths. Holter monitors are usually performed on sick patients or patients with known or suspect rhythm problems, so this information does not tell us about mechanism of sudden death in asymptomatic subjects in the general population. Some cases of sudden death are due to *torsades de pointes* in patients on antiarrhythmic drugs. The proarrhythmic effect of some of these agents should make insurers extra cautious about accepting applicants requiring antiarrhythmic agents.

CHEST PAIN

Chest pain is a common reason for patients to see their doctors. In Framingham 16 percent of subjects reported atypical chest pain. Many other people have chest pain and never consult their doctors. Some of these patients have angina, but by far the majority probably have non-cardiac chest pain arising from the chest wall or esophagus. Some subjects are worriers, or their spouses are the worriers, and insist on a physician visit for any symptom that might mean cancer, stroke or heart trouble. Whether the attending physician reassures the patient on just a history or obtains an ECG, exercise test or other tests, or refers the patient to a cardiologist, depends on many factors which differ from doctor to doctor, and in the same physician, depending on the doctor-patient interaction. What is done often has little bearing on the objective assessment of the nature of the pain. Whether the consulting cardiologist obtains a coronary angiogram also depends on the doctor-patient interaction, and perhaps on the experience of the doctor in the last two months or on how full his slate is with patients having serious problems with their coronary circulation. The diagnosis of chest pain with normal coronary arteries can only be made if an angiogram is obtained. If the patient has absolutely regular coronary arteries with normal-sized lumen they are placed in the category of chest pain with normal coronary arteries — NCA. If they have a 30–50 percent narrowing of a coronary artery it is possible that this lesion is causing the symptoms, that the angiogram is deceptive and the true narrowing is 60–70 percent. A narrowing under 30 percent is not likely to cause symptoms, but such lesions can progress so that the situation is not perfectly benign.

If coronary angiograms are carried out in the patient with chest pain and are reported as normal, insurers can generally stop being concerned. The incidence of MI on follow-up is under 1·0 percent, and with ten years of follow-up cardiac death occurs in only about 0·6 percent. When the investigation is incomplete the insurer is faced with a guessing game. What is the risk of blindly accepting the physician's opinion that a chest pain is chest wall in origin, or esophageal, or psychogenic and due to stress? The insurer can pose a few simple questions to the applicant with a telephone interview, order a treadmill or obtain a full cardiac workup at the discretion of a consultant cardiologist. The attending physician often seems to have obtained a rest ECG and used this as a tool to reassure the patient, even though this test does not justify any reassurance.

Anxiety, depression or other psychiatric problems may be the reason why patients see their doctors with complaints of minor chest pains. Sorting out the cause of chest pain is complex and many patients have two or more kinds of chest pain, some due to myocardial ischemia and others seemingly non-cardiac. The physician who shows undue concern, obtains several tests and prescribes unnecessary nitroglycerine or other antianginal agents may enhance any illness behavior tendencies in the patient. In some patients the chest pain seriously interferes with their lives, and a coronary angiogram is done as a last resort just to show them it is not a heart problem. A normal study sometimes fails to alter these patients' illness behavior. A repeat coronary angiogram three to ten years afterwards is sometimes required to reinforce the reassurance.

Some insurers may wish to put a rating of +50 on the applicant who reports chest pain, to cover uncertainties about the diagnosis and prognosis. In some applicants we often wonder why a physician did not order any tests to rule out coronary disease when the patient consulted them for chest pain, particularly if there were two or more risk factors. It is unrewarding to second-guess the attending physician. If the history of chest pain is worrisome the insurer should not order a rest ECG but should take that extra step and obtain a treadmill ECG.

If coronary angiograms were obtained and are normal, patients with chest pain and normal coronary arteries can be placed in one of five groups:

1) Atypical chest pain: absence of exercise ECG change. Mortality in this group should be normal.
2) Atypical chest pain with ST depression on exercise ECG. The exercise changes are likely to be false positive and prognosis is normal.
3) Typical angina: absence of exercise ECG change. The cause of the symptoms is controversial, but the prognosis seems to be normal.
4) Typical angina with ST depression on exercise ECG. The diagnosis of syndrome X applies to this group. There may be subtle changes in myocardial perfusion, with abnormal perfusion studies, abnormal coronary flow reserve and microvascular changes. The existence and nature of Syndrome X is controversial. Prognosis is good but the occasional infarction and death have occurred. A rating of +100 would be prudent.
5) Rest chest pain with ST elevation: Prinzmetal angina. This type has been addressed (*see* pp. 266–7).

Atypical chest pain differs from typical angina in one or more ways, as follows: not uniformly precipitated by exercise; left-sided, not central; persisting longer than 15 minutes; may be relieved by nitroglycerine but not for five to ten minutes; sharp, lasting only a second; and associated with hyperventilation.

SILENT MYOCARDIAL ISCHEMIA

Silent ischemia refers to ST segment shifts in an ECG consistent with ischemia, and is divided into three types:

Type 1: Patients who have never had symptoms. Detection is usually by means of an exercise ECG. Prevalence is 2·5–10 percent of men aged 35–60.

Type 2: Patients who are asymptomatic after a proven MI. Prevalence of silent ischemia is about 20 percent. Detection involves low-level exercise testing or ambulatory ECG or both.

Type 3: Patients with both angina and silent ischemia. The prevalence of silent ischemia is about 40 percent in this group. The angina may be stable or unstable.

In Type 1 silent ischemia the risk ratio, comparing those with and without exercise ECG changes, for developing a coronary event is between 4:1 and 14:1 in various studies.

Type 2 patients with silent ischemia have an annual mortality of up to 6 percent. Mortality is the same in those with silent ischemia as it is in those with angina. Particularly ominous is a combination of low exercise tolerance, severe ST depression and three vessel disease.

Type 3 silent ischemia is also known as ambulatory silent ischemia. Before the 1970s silent ischemia referred to ST depression found on treadmill testing of asymptomatic subjects. When high quality ambulatory ECGs became available it was discovered that many patients with known CAD had episodes of ST depression during daily activities that were not associated with anginal pain. These episodes of ST depression occurred at lower HRs than required to initiate ST changes on treadmill testing. Eventually it was shown that these ST depressions were associated with altered ventricular function using radionuclide angiograms, and were therefore markers for ischemia. On the ambulatory ECG (Holter monitor) silent ischemia occurs most commonly after waking in the morning, peaks at noon, is at a low level in the afternoon, and lowest in the evening and night hours paralleling coronary deaths and infarction. These ST depressions are decreased by both beta blocker therapy and calcium channel blockers.

In patients with unstable angina on therapy, the occurrence of silent ischemia without recurrence of angina has been associated with a mortality four to nine times that of patients not having recurrent ST depressions after institution of therapy; and the risk of non-fatal infarction increased as much as 20 times, though patients with recent unstable angina are not acceptable risks for insurance. Once stable on treatment for some time, they may have a reasonable exercise capacity with treadmill testing and be free of anginal pain; but, unless the presence of their previous silent ischemia was recognized and reported to an insurer, a potentially poor prognosis may not be appreciated. It would appear that an ambulatory ECG in these patients with prior unstable angina separates out a group of patients who continue to have high mortality rates.

Patients with clinically stable angina, including cases that seem to be well controlled with few anginal episodes and an exercise capacity of 8 METs or more, also have episodes of silent ischemia. These episodes can occur up to 40 times daily; in patients who have these episodes silent ischemia is usually considerably more frequent than are episodes of ischemia with anginal pain.

The mortality in these patients with silent ischemia and stable angina is two to four times that of patients with similar degrees of angina and other parameters of their CAD. In some studies using multifactorial analysis silent ischemia has been a better independent predictor of outcome than was angiographic anatomy or treadmill test results.

Unfortunately clinical control of chest pain does not rule out the possibility of silent ischemia. Mulcahy et al found that one-third of their anginal patients on treatment adequate to eliminate their angina had silent ischemia, and this included those patients who had CCS Class 1 and 2 angina as well as those with Class 3 and 4 angina (see p. 265).

Silent ischemia is present in only about 10 percent of angina patients without treadmill evidence for ST depression. It is most common in patients who have ST depression at 6 METs exercise or less. A recent treadmill test is therefore helpful in identifying applicants who are most likely to have silent ischemia.

CORONARY ANGIOGRAPHY, CORONARY ARTERIOGRAPHY

The first selective coronary arteriograms were performed by F M Sones at the Cleveland Clinic in 1958. Prior to that, coronary arteries had been visualized by aortic root injections. Many major hospitals perform over one hundred coronary angiograms weekly, with indications that vary from minor chest pains of uncertain origin to incapacitating angina. Visualization of the coronary arteries is obtained in at least two separate planes, and often after nitroglycerine to exclude spasm. Interobserver differences in interpretation of angiograms are not uncommon and angiograms tend to underestimate disease severity, so even this diagnostic test has its imperfections. Some angiographic reports include a diagram with the site and degree of the atherosclerotic narrowings indicated; other reports provide narrative descriptions; and short reports just indicate the percent narrowing of the significant lesions in the three major arteries or their major branches.

Systems to score the overall ischemic impact of single and multiple coronary narrowings have been proposed. Relative scores were established to take into account the amount of myocardium that might be destroyed if the artery in question was occluded.

The earlier scoring systems had some deficiencies. A major lesion in a dominant coronary artery is more important than a similar lesion in a heart in which that artery is not perfusing a large area. The Gensini system provided similar ratings for the LAD and LCx, although a LAD occlusion may lead to considerably more ischemic damage than a LCx occlusion.

A major deficiency of coronary angiography and the scoring systems is that often only segmental lesions are scored and diffuse narrowing is sometimes difficult to recognize and not easily scored as there is no normal lumen against which to compare the observed arterial lumen.

A coronary artery that should have a uniform diameter of 2·5 mm has a stenotic area measuring only 0·5 mm. This is a stenosis of 2/2·5 or 80 percent. The cross-sectional area of the vessel before the stenosis is 4·9 mm^2, and at the stenosis 0.2 mm^2; the reduction area is 96 percent. The resistance to blood flow is proportional to the area, but the angiographer generally reports change in lumen diameter.

The Gensini system also gave modifying factors for the degree of obstruction. These factors were derived by estimating the decrease in blood flow that would result in a given decrease in a cross-sectional area of the artery.

Using a Cox model the Duke group have proposed a CHD severity index (*see* Table 15.9) based on the survival of medically treated patients. This index considers the number of diseased arteries, considering only those with stenosis equal to or exceeding 75 percent, the presence of severe stenosis (over 95 percent) and the presence or absence of severe proximal LAD narrowing. Because this index has been related to survival it is a useful starting point for assessing the comparative risk in medically treated patients.

Table 15.9. Duke index for CHD severity.

Extent of CHD	Index
Any stenosis <50%	0
1VD 50–74%	19
1VD 75–94%	23
1VD ≥ 95% not prox LAD	32
1VD prox LAD ≥ 95%	48
2VD 50–94%	37
2VD both ≥ 95% not prox LAD	42
2VD LAD ≥95%	48
2VD prox LAD ≥95%	56
3VD 50–94%	56
3VD one ≥95%	63
3VD prox LAD 75–94%	67
3VD prox LAD ≥95%	74
LMCA 50–94%	82
LMCA ≥95%	100

prox = proximal

Left ventriculography is carried out at the time of selective coronary angiography to assess global and segmental myocardial function and other anatomic details. It is preferably performed before the coronary artery injections because of the depressant effect of contrast materials on ventricular function. There is considerable interobserver variability in assessing segmental wall abnormalities and in eyeball estimates of overall contractility. Ventricular function can be normal despite severe three vessel disease. Hypokinesis is a segment with reduced inward motion during systole; akinesis is an area of no motion; dyskinesis is paradoxical outpouching during systole, usually associated with aneurysm. Serious complications of MI, such as rupture of the ventricular septum, a papillary muscle or large aneurysms, are revealed by ventriculography.

The various segments of the LV wall are labeled anterobasal, anterolateral, apical, diaphragmatic, posterobasal, septal, posterolateral and superolateral. Abnormalities of LV function can be classified as follows: normal, mild impairment (EF 50–60 percent), moderate impairment (EF 40–50 percent), one segmental area impaired, and severe impairment (EF under 40 percent and/or two or more segmental impairments).

Another indicator of LV function is the end diastolic pressure (LVEDP). This is normally 12 mm Hg or less. Values over 20 mm should be of concern, but if LV ejection fraction (EF) is normal and there are no akinetic segments, minor elevations of LVEDP are often disregarded.

Coronary angiography has proven to be an accurate indicator of prognosis. When the coronary arteries are normal at angiography, even in patients with symptoms or signs that led to the study, survival is the same as in a normal population. In patients with mild lesions not considered hemodynamically important (less than 50 percent), mortality ratio is as high as 266 percent, despite the zero rating given to this type of lesion in the Duke scale.

To improve the accuracy and consistency in the reporting of coronary angiographic results some laboratories measure stenosis with calipers rather than eyeball, and computerized methods are available that may eventually eliminate the up to 40 percent interobserver variations. These refinements will still underestimate the severity of atherosclerosis because it is a diffuse disease and not strictly segmental.

Despite its limitations, coronary angiography is the gold standard by which we estimate disease severity and, hence, prognosis, and also the diagnostic accuracy of the various non-invasive tools.

SCREENING OF ASYMPTOMATIC INSURANCE APPLICANTS FOR CHD

Screening with suitable tests would be useful in applicants with more than one risk factor, and in large amount cases because of the importance of CHD as a cause of premature death.

Our screening tools are crude, and include the rest ECG, a graded exercise test (GXT) and fluoroscopy for coronary calcification. The latter, which holds promise as a screening device, is seldom used.

Resting ECG

Abnormalities in the rest ECG are non-specific, but in the coronary age-group, arrhythmia, Q-waves, ST- and T-wave changes, abnormal axes, bundle branch blocks and other changes may be associated with CHD. In asymptomatic populations rest ECG changes are relatively weak predictors of increased mortality, as shown below in the examination of two studies.

The data in Table 15.10 are from a study of 18,403 male civil servants in Great Britain. ST depression, major and intermediate T-wave inversion and HR under 100 were not important prognostically in asymptomatic subjects. Left axis deviation, minor T-wave inversion, atrial fibrillation and left bundle branch block (LBBB) had limited but significant prognostic value in asymptomatic subjects.

Table 15.10. Prevalence and mortality of rest ECG changes, 18,403 male civil servants, Great Britain.

ECG finding	Prevalence per 1,000		Five-year coronary death rate per 1,000	
	A	S	A	S
Left axis deviation	28·9	44·1	20[a]	80[a]
ST depression:				
Major	0·9	5·8	0	390[a]
Intermed	3·7	26·3	20	110[a]
Minor	3·6	18·1	30	110[a]

ECG finding	Prevalence per 1,000		Five-year coronary death rate per 1,000	
	A	S	A	S
T-wave inversion:				
Major	0·1	0·8	0	0
Intermed	5·1	42·4	30	210[a]
Minor	27·9	60·1	30[a]	80[a]
Atrial fibrillation	2·1	15·2	70[a]	30
HR >100	24·3	20·2	10	120[a]
LBBB	13·7	27·6	30[a]	80

[a]Rate higher than in people without this ECG change p<0·05.
A = asymptomatic.
S = symptomatic on questionnaire.

Sox et al reviewed the world literature from the period 1970–1988 to assess the value of the rest ECG as a screening device (*see* Table 15.11). Any major ECG change was present in about 5 percent of the population, and mortality ratios varied from 200 percent to 300 percent.

Table 15.11. Relative risk of various ECG changes in general populations.[a]

	Prevalence	Relative risk of death	
		Mean	95% limits
Ventricular premature beats ≥ 10% of QRS	0·016	3·6	2·3–5·6
Left axis deviation >−30°	0·027	2·0	1·2–3·5
T-wave inversion	0·043	2·6	2·0–3·3
ST depression	0·014	3·4	1·6–6·9
Any major ECG change	0·049	3·6	2·6–4·8
Q-waves (Minnesota code 1·1–1·3)	0·014	4·6	2·8–7·6

[a]Based on the data collected from the literature by Sox et al.

T-Wave and ST Segment Abnormalities
Abnormal T inversions and ST changes occur in the absence of CHD and are of limited diagnostic value in isolation. Follow-up studies comparing men with T-wave inversion to those without have shown mortality ratios of 1·3:1 to 4·0:1. Some life underwriters may add +50 debits for such changes and remove these debits if a treadmill test is found to be normal. These changes are most worrisome in men aged 40–65 who have cardiovascular risk factors. They can largely be ignored in

men under the age of 40 and in women under the age of 50 in the absence of other indicators of cardiovascular risk.

ST depressions (Minnesota code 4:1–4) in men aged 35–64 are associated with risk ratios of 2–4:1 to 4·4:1 and can be assessed as T inversions. They are not diagnostic for CHD, but in general they indicate a slightly worse prognosis than T changes only.

Serial ECGs

A change in the electrocardiogram from one examination to another is occasionally of value to insurers. For ST and T changes, variations from one record to another are seldom helpful, but if changes are present in a current record not present previously, a treadmill test should probably be obtained.

Borderline Q-waves inferiorly, and QS or small r patterns anteroseptally, that represent changes from a previously perfectly normal ECG assume greater importance and usually signify that silent infarction has occurred.

Abnormal Q-Waves in the Absence of Clinical History (Presumed Silent Infarction)

In the Framingham Study silent Q-wave infarction patterns occurred in 0·8 per 1,000 men aged 45–54 and in 7·1 per 1,000 men aged 65–74. In various studies with four- to eight-year follow-up the mortality ratios, comparing men with Q-waves to men without Q-waves, ranged from 4·2:1 to 5·3:1, the mean being 4·6:1. One-fifth of infarctions in the Framingham Study were silent.

Obviously before considering insurance coverage for people with suspect silent infarction a full cardiac workup is required, the minimal assessment probably being a physical examination for signs of cardiovascular disease, an assessment of risk factors and a treadmill to assess functional capacity, signs of additional myocardium at risk and arrhythmia. When a prior ECG is not available for comparison, perfusion scans or tests for wall motion abnormalities may be required to determine if infarction has occurred. It is sometimes best to order a repeat rest ECG. QS complexes in leads V1–V4 can be produced by erroneous electrode positioning.

GXT

The symptom-limited maximal exercise test (GXT) has been discredited in underwriting circles as unsuitable as a screening tool in asymptomatic insurance applicants. The GXT in a general population of males aged 40–65 will be positive in up to 10 percent of subjects, equivocal in others, and of those with positive tests fewer than a third will manifest clinical CHD or death in the next ten years. In ten years two-thirds of those destined to develop CHD will come from those who had negative GXTs. The problem with specificity and sensitivity of the GXT in a population with a low prevalence of CHD, along with logistic problems, has led many companies to abandon routine use of the GXT or to restrict its use to applicants in excess of $2 million or $5 million. Logistic problems are encountered with delays for arranging a test that neither the applicant nor the agent want, along with the possibility of losing the case to a competitor that does not require a GXT. The test has been used much less since 1980 for these reasons, even though positive tests identify a population with a three to ten times higher chance of developing

CHD in the next five years compared to the population with a negative GXT. For some reason, everyone is relieved when the test is normal, even though two-thirds of those destined to develop clinical CHD in the next ten years will escape detection!

ST segment Changes

When the ST segment is normal at rest, a 1·0 mm ST depression that is horizontal or down-sloping of 0·08 seconds or longer is regarded as positive. Greater significance can be given to segments that are 2–4 mm depressed, but this is not as reliable a guide to severity of coronary stenosis as it is made out to be.

When the ST segment is up-sloping, the change may still signify ischemia. To distinguish the abnormal from the normal J-point depression with a rapidly up-sloping ST segment, which is clearly normal, various criteria have been used. The most frequently used are (1) an ST slope less than 1·0 mm/s coupled with 2·0 mm J-point depression or greater, and (2) ST segment still 1·0 mm below isoelectric level 0·08 seconds after the J-point.

ST segment changes are more frequently associated with ischemia if (1) they occur in leads V4–V6 rather than just leads 3, AVF, (2) they persist for longer than 60 seconds into recovery, (3) they occur in several as opposed to single leads, (4) the subject is over 40 and male. ST changes that occur at low exercise loads or at low HRs are more likely to be related to coronary stenosis.

Some computer exercise ECG programs calculate the ST depression per beats/ min increase in HR, and if this exceeds 0·015 mm multivessel CHD is suspected. (For example, if resting HR is 86 and 2·8 mm ST depression is observed at an exercise HR of 156, the ST depression is 0·04 mm/beats/min increase in HR.) Various other computer manipulations of the ST segment deviations are available.

If the ST segment during exercise is normal but ST segment depression develops during recovery, the change may be a postural effect or due to autonomic neurogenic factors, but it may be an indication of ischemia. It is helpful if the laboratory recorded an ECG prior to exercises in the standing position, to detect postural change, and after hyperventilation. If these maneuvers produced ST changes similar to exercise, the exercise changes are often discounted.

Other causes of ST depression in the absence of major CAD are digoxin, ventricular hypertrophy from any cause, hypertension, valvular disease, electrolyte changes, myocardial disease, mitral valve prolapse and previous pericarditis.

Is ST depression on exercise that is not due to coronary stenosis a marker for other problems that may be associated with increased mortality, such as myocardial disease, small vessel CHD and others? It is reassuring to note that in the CASS registry over 4,000 subjects had normal or near-normal angiograms, 125 had a positive GXT, 60 had a markedly positive GXT and survival in these 185 subjects was normal and identical to the other subjects with normal angiograms.

In LBBB the exercise test has some usefulness, providing information on fitness, maximal HR, presence or absence of angina and blood pressure response, but the ECG cannot be used to exclude ischemic change. The same is true in patients having WPW pattern in their resting ECG, unless this pattern disappears during exercise. The value of the exercise ECG in RBBB is debatable, but generally the ST segment remains stable in the limb leads and leads V5–V6 in the absence of coronary stenosis.

Most North American laboratories have settled on the routine 12-lead ECG for rest, exercise and recovery ECGs. The occasional laboratory still uses a single precordial lead, such as CM5; others record three leads during exercise and 12 leads at rest and in recovery. There are many computerized ECG outputs providing HRs and measurements of ST segment depression and slope of the ST segment from signal averaged ECG patterns. Lead CM5 was reported by Chaitman et al to identify 85 percent of the patients showing ischemic ST changes using a 13-lead system, so even the single lead exercise ECG does have considerable value.

To avoid motion artifacts the standard 12-lead system is modified with the right and left arm leads placed on the shoulders. If these leads are moved a little more medially the frontal axis shifts to the right by 25°, Q-waves in leads AVF may be lost and Q-waves may appear in AVL.

Type of Exercise
Some laboratories use a bicycle ergometer. There is no problem with this except that calculation of workload in METs is cumbersome and many subjects aged 50 and over cannot, or will not, approach their maximal HR, giving in to leg fatigue. The treadmill is the preferred mode of exercise in most North American exercise facilities.

What to Look for in Reading a GXT
1) Exercise modality (treadmill or bicycle).
2) Workload completed on the ergometer: kpm per minute or watts, the subject's weight on the treadmill, time completed and name attached to work protocol (i.e. Naughton, Bruce, Balke etc), treadmill speed and grade, estimated METs.
3) Maximal HR achieved.
4) Reason for termination: target heart rate, angina, fatigue, dyspnea, arrhythmia, claudication, orthopedic reasons, other.
5) Maximal ST depression in mm or mv. Slope of depression ST segment: (1) horizontal or down-sloping, (2) slowly up-sloping (less than 1·0 mm/s), (3) rapidly up-sloping (greater than 1·0 mm/s).
6) Workload at time ST segment first became 1·0 mm horizontally depressed.
7) Time of persistence of ST change into recovery.
8) Record of arrhythmias.
9) Resting blood pressure (often higher than that recorded by physician or paramedical examiner and an indication of stress-related pressure change).
10) Peak exercise blood pressure: normal at about 170/80 on treadmill, 200/90 on ergometer.
11) If ST change occurred during exercise, was a test for postural change or hyperventilation carried out?
12) Exaggerated atrial repolarization waves may be the cause of a false positive ST segment depression, and this can often be recognized.

Some reports conclude that the test was electrically positive (probably meaning horizontal ST segment depression 1·0 mm or greater) and clinically negative, meaning absence of anginal symptoms or angina equivalent.

A test recorded as equivocal usually means that J-point depression of approximately 2 mm was present, but ST segment was not perfectly horizontal and was not a clearly normal rapidly ascending segment.

In asymptomatic subjects a GXT may be ordered in the following situations:
1) CHD risk factors present.
2) Rest ST or T changes present, or borderline Q-waves.
3) Age and amount: age over 40 and applications for over $5 million.
4) Applicants with diabetes and/or vascular disease in limb or cranial arteries.

Safety of the GXT

The laboratory performing the exercise test, its medical director (MD) and its physicians should be fully accountable for quality control and patient safety. Clinical exercise facilities dealing mainly with patients who have CHD, often fairly severe, report one death and five non-fatal complications per 10 thousand tests. When an exercise test is requested, insurance applicants should be advised by their agents to report to the laboratory at the arranged time with running shoes, shorts or other loose exercise clothing, and to abstain from smoking and/or eating for three or more hours.

The degree of ST depression is of some importance, but has serious limitations because to a large degree it is governed by the effort the exercising subject is motivated to make and the procedure followed by the person controlling the test. Some middle-aged normal people unaccustomed to maximal exercise (perhaps never experiencing this since highschool, if then) seem determined to reach the end of an exercise stage (often stage 4 Bruce). ST segment response may be normal up to the last few minutes of the test, when the exercise becomes an obvious strain. In many of these tests the ST segment becomes normal within 30 seconds of stopping exercise. In such cases the ST depression may be duly recorded as 2·5 mm, and without knowing the circumstances this will be regarded as a strongly positive ST depression with a strong likelihood of serious CHD. If the test on the same person was carried out in a different laboratory where the same encouragement to go to exhaustion is not provided, the exercise would end two minutes earlier when fatigue became significant. ST depression at this stage could be under 1.0 mm.

The sensitivity and specificity values for the GXT and thallium scans has not been determined for populations with a 5 percent prevalence of CHD, and it is very likely that these values are so low that the positive predictive value of ST depression in an asymptomatic population, when the subjects exercise to near-maximal levels, is even lower than that suggested by some of the detailed tables and graphs calculated using Bayesian theory.

In many of the reported studies the sensitivity and specificity of the GXT in healthy populations has been calculated on the basis of coronary events, including the soft event, angina. When someone knows they have a potential ECG abnormality that may indicate CHD they are understandably on the alert for any chest discomfort. The higher frequency of chest pain developing in this population compared to the population with a normal GXT may not accurately reflect differences in the prevalence of CHD.

There are some clues that indicate ST depression may be a false positive: ST changes on exercise occur more frequently when there is 0·5 ST change at rest, or just a little scalloping of the ST segment; ST changes on exercise of questionable significance if there are ST changes before exercise on standing or after a minute of hyperventilation; ST changes that occur only in the last few minutes of exercise and revert to normal within 30 seconds of stopping exercise are more likely to be false positive. It is my observation that ST changes in populations of asymptomatic females occur with such frequency that the test is of dubious value other than for providing information on fitness. In females with a history of chest pain and with CHD risk factors ST changes are of greater importance; some studies in populations with a high prevalence of CHD have found very reasonable specificity and sensitivity values in females, but this is not the result in a population of asymptomatic low-risk females.

Instead of paying too much attention to the degree of ST depression, underwriters would be wise to look at the workload done. For example, McNeer et al reported that if exercise duration was 12 minutes or longer (over 13 METs), or HR exceeded 160 beats/min, less than 5 percent of subjects had two or three vessel disease, regardless of the magnitude of the ST change.

In clinical practice major ST change may lead to eventual coronary angiography and the diagnostic dilemma is solved, but in the asymptomatic subject the next step is often a myocardial perfusion scan or a nuclear angiogram or postexercise ultrasound study.

Diamond and Forrester calculated the likelihood of ST changes in mm being indicative of CHD based on the prevalence of CHD in autopsy studies, and the sensitivity and specificity of exercise ST change. At best, these calculations are based on several assumptions.

Table 15.12 from their data indicates that 1·0 mm ST depression in an asymptomatic female aged 47 has only a 2 percent chance of indicating CHD, making the underwriting decision simple. The asymptomatic male applicant for $5 million, aged 52, with 2·0 mm ST change has a 31 percent chance of having CHD. Some companies have a debit chart which might call for +100 mortality debits for this situation. Many applicants will not accept this without shopping around, and some companies would accept this risk standard without further testing. If we knew more details, such as workload and HR, duration of ST change into recovery and other risk factors, it might be clear that a standard offer is reasonable. If there were adverse factors, such as poor family history, hyperlipidemia and heavy smoking, +100 might seem too low. If a thallium scan was obtained and shown to be normal, a Bayesian chart could be used to show that the likelihood of CHD is below 5 percent. But if the workload, HR and other factors listed above were favorable, the requirement for a thallium could be waived. It is difficult to work all of these factors into an underwriting chart on GXT and ST depression; there is room for judgment.

Gould came to the conclusion that thallium stress testing had a sensitivity and specificity of only 65 percent, and suggested that previous values were too high related to sample bias and conservative interpretation.

In a population with a prevalence of CHD of 15 percent the requirement that both a GXT ECG and thallium scan be positive would mean that almost half of the patients with angiographically significant CHD would not be catheterized.

Analyses based on the sensitivity and specificity of perfusion scans of 85–90 percent may not be valid and a negative thallium scan does not rule out CHD.

Table 15.12. Post-test likelihood of CHD after GXT in asymptomatic patients.[a]

| Age | ST depression (mm) | | | | | | | |
| (years) | Normal | | 1·0–1·5 | | 1·5–2·0 | | >2·5 | |
	M	F	M	F	M	F	M	F
	No symptoms							
40–49	1	0	11	2	20	4	69	28
50–59	2	1	19	7	31	12	81	56
60–69	3	2	23	15	37	25	85	76
	Atypical angina							
40–49	16	3	64	25	78	39	97	88
50–59	25	10	75	50	86	67	98	95
60–69	32	21	81	72	90	83	99	98

[a]Source: Diamond and Forrester.

In an asymptomatic population without risk factors McNeer el al suggests that a positive test probably indicates CHD only 10–20 percent of the time, 80–90 percent of tests being false positive. A negative test is likely to mean that there is a 99·8 percent chance that the applicant does not have CHD.

In the MRFIT and Seattle Heart Watch studies only 5 percent of subjects with a positive GXT followed for six to seven years died or suffered MI.

The Lipid Research Clinics Mortality Follow-up Study performed submaximal GXTs in over 3,600 white males. After eight years mortality was 11·9 percent (22/185) in men with a positive test, 1·2 percent (36/2,993) in men with a negative test. In this population there were 58 deaths and the GXT identified 38 percent of those at risk. A strongly positive test (over 2 mm ST depression, during the first six minutes of exercise, at HR under 163 less 0·66 of age) identified a group with a cardiovascular mortality risk ratio of 15·6:1 before and 5·1:1 after age adjustment. The risk ratio for all-cause mortality was less, 7·2:1 before and 3·4:1 after age adjustment. A positive test in this population was a stronger risk factor for cardiovascular mortality than lipid measurements, smoking or hypertension, and was the equivalent of a 17·4 year markup in age! Therefore, despite drawbacks, there are obvious arguments that the GXT is valuable for insurance underwriting in asymptomatic patients.

Yosuf performed a meta-analysis of over 26 thousand exercise tests performed on asymptomatic subjects and concluded that a positive exercise ECG had a sensitivity of 37 percent, a specificity of 69 percent, but a predictive value of only 7 percent. People with a positive test have a fourfold greater risk of a coronary event, but two of every three events in a population occur in subjects with a normal test.

In the Baltimore aging study the 407 subjects with a positive GXT ECG also had thallium scans. Silent ischemia occurred in 2 percent of subjects aged 50–59 and in 15 percent of subjects over the age of 80. After five years cardiac events occurred in only 7 percent of subjects with positive tests. Of the cardiac events in the entire population 58 percent occurred in subjects with both tests normal. Therefore adding the thallium scans to the screening procedure did not increase the sensitivity of the screening procedure to an important degree.

There is a trend for the reports in the literature to become hooked on Bayesian analysis to assess the importance of a positive GXT, but when faced with an asymptomatic insurance applicant in a competitive situation probability analysis is only part of the answer.

The Duke group developed a nomogram based on GXT time, level of ST depression and occurrence of angina during the GXT to estimate mortality in four years' follow-up. This nomogram was developed following an outpatient population of patients referred because of suspect CHD. Underwood suggested that this nomogram could be used to estimate mortality ratios for insurance applicants, but he pointed out that most insurance applicants belonged to a different population than the outpatients referred to the Duke Cardiac Center.

Table 15.13 was calculated using the Duke nomogram in subjects of three ages, for GXT ST depressions of 1·0–2·5 mm and for three different exercise capacities. The subjects were assumed not to have had chest pain during the test. The mortality ratios calculated from this nomogram are very high for ages 45 and 55, even higher than ratios that might be used in patients with angiographic proof of severe CHD. It is obvious that this nomogram is of no value for estimating prognosis in the asymptomatic insurance applicant with a positive GXT.

The Duke GXT scoring system used the standard Bruce protocol with ST segment depression recorded 0·06 seconds after the J-point. Angina was scored zero if none during the GXT, 1·0 if angina occurred but did not shorten the GXT time, and 2 if angina caused the subject to stop exercising.

GXT score = exercise time −5 (maximal ST depression) −4 (angina index)

The four-year mortality was as follows: score $\geq$+5, 1.0 percent; score −10 to +4, 7 percent; and score <−10, 25 percent.

Table 15.13. Mortality ratios based on Duke nomogram from GXT positive exercise test, no angina.

| | Mortality ratio (%) | | | | | | | | |
| | Age 45 | | | Age 55 | | | Age 65 | | |
METs	7	10	12	7	10	12	7	10	12
ST 1·0	300	250	200	150	125	100	100	100	100
ST 1·5	500	300	250	250	150	125	100	100	100
ST 2·0	600	400	300	275	200	150	125	100	100
ST 2·5	750	500	350	375	250	175	150	100	100

NON-INVASIVE ASSESSMENT OF DISEASE SEVERITY AND PROGNOSIS IN APPLICANTS WITH KNOWN CHD

A fairly precise estimate of disease severity can be made without resorting to invasive testing (coronary angiography). The tools include clinical examination of

286 MEDICAL SELECTION OF LIFE RISKS

the heart and the vascular system, the resting ECG, a GXT with an ECG or with myocardial perfusion imaging or ultrasound, and nuclear angiography.

Rest ECG

Angina Pectoris

In patients with angina prognosis is worse in those with an abnormal resting ECG; even minor T changes double or triple the risk of infarction or death.

MI

Some resting ECG patterns are obvious indicators that severe myocardial destruction has occurred. Persisting ST elevation suggests aneurysm formation. Persistent wide Q-waves indicate more extensive damage than borderline Q-waves. Loss of R-waves extending from lead V1 to lead V6 with Q-waves indicates extensive anterior infarction with a poor prognosis. Inferior infarction carries a better prognosis than anterior infarction.

The Framingham Study provides not only risk factors information; because an entire population is available without referral bias, useful clinical information on disease outcome is also available. A rest ECG is often the only information available to insurers, and the pattern of this does have predictive information on survival after MI.

Table 15.14. Framingham Study: late resting ECG and mortality after infarction.

ECG pattern	Risk ratio for coronary death
Normalized ECG after infarct	1·0
Persistent Q-waves without other changes	1·8 NS
Persistent Q-waves with other changes	2·7[a]
Non-specific ST changes	3·5[b]
Non-specific T changes	3·3[b]
LVH voltage plus and ST change	7·7[b]
Bundle branch block	1·8 NS
Preinfarction ST changes	4·7
Preinfarction T changes	2·8
Preinfarction LVH	4·2

[a] $p < 0.05$.
[b] $p < 0.01$.
NS = not significant.

The risk ratios presented in Table 15.14 were adjusted for age and sex, and similar ratios pertained when systolic blood pressure, cholesterol and relative weight were included in a multivariate analysis. Those who normalized their ECG after infarction were given a mortality of 1·0, and the mortality ratios for those with residual changes show significant increases in mortality.

Smoking status was not considered, because of its failure to be of prognostic value post-MI in the Framingham population. In other post-infarction studies those who continued smoking had mortality rates two to three times those who did not smoke.

Only a minority of patients completely normalized their ECG after Q-wave infarction, 17 percent for inferior MI, 8 percent for anterior MI. Q-waves persisted in 70 percent after inferior MI and in 78 percent after anterior MI. Other abnormalities persisted in the remainder. The presence of LVH by both voltage and ST change carried the worst prognosis.

Of those having MI 25 percent had prior ECG changes. These were of considerable prognostic import, even to the degree of eliminating the post-MI pattern as a significant predictor of outcome. Prognosis was worse in those who had a previously abnormal ECG and then had ECG changes of infarction.

It is clear from this and other studies that normalization of the ECG after infarction is a favorable sign and is a factor that could be considered in underwriting.

There are systems for scoring the extent of MI or infarctions based on QRS analysis that are beyond the scope of this chapter.

GXT

Traditionally the mm of ST depression is usually mentioned as a marker of disease severity. This is not necessarily true. The degree of ST depression is very dependent on when an exercise test is terminated, and this depends on the exercise test supervisor, the attitude of the patient and whether antianginal drugs are being taken.

Some laboratories err on the side of safety: once the patient reports central chest pain the exercise test is terminated. ST segment depression at the time may be 1·0 mm, 2·0 mm or greater. Some laboratories automatically terminate the test when there is ST segment depression of more than 1·0 mm and the subject reports central chest discomfort; nothing further is required for a 95 percent or more certainty that CHD is present. Other laboratories ask the subject to continue exercising until their chest pain reaches the intensity that would lead them to stop exercise activities at home. This of course varies considerably from patient to patient: some continue with 5 mm ST depression, others stop with 1·0 mm. I regard the degree of exercise ST depression as a rather poor indicator of disease severity for these reasons, but this is not a popular opinion.

One of the best indicators of disease severity is the workload the patient can complete before having to stop, or the HR at the time of stopping because of angina. Table 15.15, from the report by McNeer et al, compares percent mortality in those who exceeded 12 METs exercise (10 percent) with those who completed less than 5 METs work (42 percent).

Prognostic Value

Table 15.15. Prognosis according to exercise test results.[a]

	Patients tested because of chest pain (% mortality)		CAD found on angiography (% mortality)	
	12 mth	48 mth	12 mth	48 mth
Exercise ECG				
Normal	1	6	8	10
Abnormal	8	20	8	23
Equivocal	4	12	9	26
Exercise duration and HR				
Stage 4 plus and HR >160	1	5	1	10
Stage 1 only and/or HR <120	15	22	16	42

[a]Source: McNeer et al.

In the coronary artery surgery study (CASS) a low exercise capacity was an independent predictor of increased mortality. This study also showed that patients with exercise ST changes had a worse prognosis than those without ST change, even with both groups having equivalent angiographic lesions. On the other hand, exercise-induced VEA was not associated with increased five-year mortality in the CASS study.

The treadmill can be used by the underwriter as a prognostic tool of considerable power, not just as a diagnostic aid to assess whether or not CHD is likely to be present. It would appear to be imprudent to offer life insurance coverage to any subject who, with a reasonable effort, could not do 5 METs work or increase their HR above 120 beats/min.

In underwriting applicants with known CHD it is important to recognize those who have severe two or three vessel or left main disease. Some of the GXT warning signs suggesting severe CHD are given below:

1) Horizontal or down-sloping ST depression of over 2·5 mm.
2) VEAs at HRs less than 130 when no arrthymia present at rest, accompanied by ST depression.
3) Ischemic ST changes of 1·0 mm or greater with exercise loads of only 3–5 METs. ST depression of greater than 0·015 mm per beats/min increase in HR.
4) Low maximal HR less than 120 not due to beta blockade or poor effort.
5) Systolic BP falling below the pre-exercise value by more than 10 mm Hg.
6) Very low exercise tolerance of less than 3 minutes, less than 6 METs even in the absence of ST change.

7) Ischemic ST changes persisting past six minute recovery.

8) Angina persisting for over five minutes after ceasing exercise, despite nitroglycerine.

For many years the purpose of an exercise test was to aid the diagnosis of CHD (i.e. to answer the question, 'Is CHD present or not present?'). This section looks at the use of GXT for assessing prognosis in applicants with known CHD. This is similar to the role played by the GXT in clinical medicine to assess disease severity, aid clinic decision making, direct therapy and gage the effectiveness of therapy.

Angiograms provide anatomic information of the coronary arteries, but how anatomic change influences cardiac function is not revealed by the angiogram. Perfusion scans assess the distribution of coronary blood flow, the exercise ECG monitors the electrical activity of the heart. Unfortunately the GXT exercise capacity is not a good measure of LV function. Some patients with EFs of 25 percent can last nine minutes on a treadmill test, others with EFs of 60 percent stop after three minutes. There are many explanations for this, including the observation that some patients can accommodate to a low cardiac output by greater extraction of oxygen and more efficient energy use.

At this time a well conducted GXT is the best measure of prognosis available to the life underwriter, and the important information is not the mm ST change but the working capacity in METs, and the work done or HR produced before ST signs of ischemia occur.

Nuclear Myocardial Perfusion Imaging

Exercise Thallium-201 Scintigraphy (Thallium Scans)
Thallium scintigraphy is performed as an adjunct to the conventional exercise ECG for specific indications, including the following:

1) When there are abnormal rest ECG patterns that would interfere with exercise ECG interpretation, such as LBBB, WPW pattern, rest ST and T changes.

2) When the exercise ECG does not agree with the clinical findings, suspected false negative and false positive exercise ECG tests.

3) When the exercise ECG is equivocal.

4) When it is uncertain that a previous infarction has occurred.

5) When greater accuracy (sensitivity and specificity) than an exercise ECG alone provides is required for patient management, as after PTCA.

Conduction of the Test
Near the end-point of a conventional exercise test the subject is given 2·0–3·5 mCi thallium-201 intravenously (the equivalent of 30 chest roentgenograms). Exercise is continued for another 30–60 seconds to ensure maximal myocardial hyperemia. The patient lies under a gamma counter and myocardial imaging begins five to ten minutes after the cessation of exercise. Images are obtained in anterior, left anterior oblique and extreme left anterior oblique projections. Recent modifications provide rotational cameras and computer reconstruction of tomographic

images — single photon emission computed tomography (SPECT). Normally the thallium is evenly distributed throughout the myocardium. In the early imaging, a zone of reduced thallium uptake indicates either an area of non-viable myocardium (infarction) or an area of under-perfusion (due to coronary artery obstruction). The images are repeated two to four hours later. Reversal of an early defect indicates that there is viable myocardium (not infarcted) and it is inferred that the exercise induced an area of under-perfusion or ischemia.

Diagnostic Accuracy

Compared to angiographic diagnosis of CHD, thallium scintigraphy has a sensitivity of 68–96 percent (average 84 percent), compared to 60–70 percent for the exercise ECG in the same patients. Specificity for thallium scintigraphy has been 65–87 percent, a modest improvement over the ECG. The sensitivity and specificity of both tests improves with increased frequency and increased severity of disease in the test population.

Results of the thallium test can also be equivocal. In cases that are not clearly normal or abnormal there is a continuum of 'possible under perfusion' to 'likely a small perfusion defect' to 'definite perfusion defect'. There are some problem areas of myocardium (inferoposterior wall and septum) that are more difficult to visualize because of attenuation of the gamma radiation by bone, large breasts or diaphragm. There is a move to substitute technetium for thallium in the hope of improving the images.

Prognostic Implications

Prognosis is worse if there are more than two areas of under-perfusion, as opposed to only single areas of under-perfusion.

Thallium scintigraphy can be used when a false positive exercise ECG is suspected. In 191 asymptomatic US aircrew with abnormal exercise ECGs, thallium testing showed 95 percent sensitivity and 91 percent specificity. In 92 asymptomatic females with positive exercise ECGs, thallium testing showed 75 percent sensitivity and 85 percent specificity when compared to coronary arteriography.

Notwithstanding the above reports, the predictive accuracy of a combination of the exercise ECG and thallium scintigraphy is dependent on the prevalence of the disease in the population being tested. The tests are most helpful in patients with an intermediate probability of disease. The detailed review of thallium scintigraphy by Kotler and Diamond suggests that physicians generally have more faith in the accuracy of this test and in the additional information it provides than can be supported by objective studies, especially in a population with low prevalence of disease. It may be that with the improved technology of the 1990s reliance on the accuracy of perfusion imaging is fully justified.

Thallium scintigraphy theoretically might surpass the exercise ECG in being able to identify patients with three vessel disease, showing more areas of ischemia. Performance of the test has sometimes been disappointing because (1) exercise may be limited by ischemic pain induced in the myocardial area served by the most diseased artery before the other areas become ischemic and (2) collateral flow may maintain perfusion; thallium tests show relative (not absolute) flow, so in the presence of global ischemia a thallium scan may appear normal.

After MI, patients with heart failure, poor LV EF, worrisome arrhythmias or continuing chest pain are easily recognized as being at high risk for death or other major events. Risk stratification is desired for the asymptomatic survivors of infarction. Those who are likely to do poorly should have coronary angiography followed, where advisable, with CABG or PTCA. On average, thallium testing has improved the sensitivity by 8 percent and specificity by 15 percent over exercise electrocardiography alone in various studies in terms of recognizing subjects with three vessel disease and areas of myocardium in jeopardy. Even with thallium testing, diagnostic accuracy leaves much to be desired, therefore the direction in many centers is to advise coronary arteriography after all cases of infarction.

Myocardial perfusion scans may soon be improved by using different agents; agents under current consideration utilize technetium-99 compounds. Gated SPECT images may soon provide measures of LV volume, contractility and segmental wall motion with the myocardial perfusion scans, eliminating the need for the additional procedure of nuclear angiography.

Myocardial Perfusion Imaging (MPI)

Dipyridamole Thallium Test

Some subjects are unable or unwilling to exercise at a sufficient workload to obtain a satisfactory treadmill or ergometer test. Arthritis or orthopedic problems, low fitness or lung disease, neuromuscular disorders, amputation, peripheral vascular disease, psychologic problems and central nervous system disease may all prevent or limit treadmill performance so that little exercise stress is produced. It is possible to substitute arm exercise for leg exercise but few laboratories are actually prepared to do this.

Dipyridamole dilates the coronary arteries and increases coronary blood flow in normals to three times control, greater than with exercise and more sustained. The subepicardial vessels are selectively dilated and 'steal' flow from the subendocardial layers. The limitations to thallium imaging are the same as for exercise: obesity, breast artifact and diaphragmatic uptake. Dipyridamole should not be given if there is known allergy; nor should it be given to patients on aminophylline, because this interferes with the action of dipyridamole. Test sensitivity and specificity in the diagnosis of CAD is claimed to be as high as 85–90 percent but this is highly dependent on the prevalence of disease in the population under study. Information on fitness, how the subject responds to the natural stress of exercise and knowledge about possible exercise-induced arrhythmia are lost. During the dipyridamole test chest pain occurs in a third of patients with ischemia, ST depression in 25 percent (less than that found with treadmill testing), but the thallium perfusion changes occur with increased frequency compared to exercise.

This test can also be used in patients with LBBB, WPW syndrome, LVH, patients on digoxin, where a false positive treadmill ECG may occur, and in patients on beta blocker who may not elevate their exercise HR sufficiently for a diagnostic treadmill test.

MPI after dipyridamole is used when a false positive or false negative treadmill

ECG is suspected in patients with multivessel CHD to decide which lesions are most hemodynamically significant; this helps plan angioplasty and clarifies risk stratification after acute infarction. MPI is useful in patients with claudication before surgery, patients with a high incidence of CHD who may be unable to exercise enough to fully stress the heart. MPI after dipyridamole will show ischemia in patients on full dose of beta blockers, calcium channel blockers and long-acting nitrates, whereas these medications may cause a treadmill ECG to be normal.

Radionuclide Assessment of Cardiac Function

Radionuclide Angiography

Radionuclide angiography is used to measure RV and LV EF, end diastolic volumes, cardiac output transit time and other functions. Computer construction of composite images from two to four cardiac cycles allows comparison of systolic and diastolic outlines to detect wall motion abnormalities. To increase resolution of the radionuclide, angiocardiogram counts can be obtained after there is equilibration of the radioactive material in the vascular system. Views are obtained in multiple projections to deal with overlapping heart chambers, and computer-generated views of left ventricular wall motion are made available to assess wall motion abnormalities.

Computer manipulations provide a means for detailed assessment of systolic and diastolic function that are not of practical insurance value at this time. Radionuclide angiography can be performed during and after exercise, performed on an ergometer in the supine position, to reveal exercise-induced wall motion abnormalities. The patient needs to maintain a difficult level of exercise for at least two minutes to collect an adequate number of counts; also, the patient must avoid motion of the chest, other than breathing.

Exercise Echocardiography

Nuclear studies are more costly and less readily available than cardiac ultrasound, and a large number of exercise studies are now carried out assessing immediate postexercise wall motion changes with 2-D ultrasound. Adequate images are possible in 70 percent of cases, but the technique is somewhat difficult to master and the chance of interobserver error greater than for nuclear angiography.

Wall motion abnormalities due to ischemia caused by exercise persist for a few minutes after exercise, so echocardiography can be obtained after exercise. Recent technical advances provide digital acquisition, elimination of respiratory artifact and the placing of pre- and postexercise images on the same screen for comparison. In experienced laboratories the sensitivity and specificity of the stress echocardiogram may equal that of SPECT thallium scans, but the quality of the examinations varies considerably; this is a problem that insurers cannot control, other than relying on studies carried out in well equipped centers.

CHD AFTER CABG

Bypass surgery patients are well suited for underwriting because full preoperative studies are available and regular follow-up can establish the success or failure of the procedure. For the 25-year longevity of this procedure those involved in the care of these patients have been trying to prove that they were accomplishing more than just relieving chest pain. As a result, numerous survival studies have been published.

The CABG operation involves placing a conduit from the aorta to one or more of the three major arteries, or their main branches, beyond an obstructing lesion to increase the blood flow into the heart muscle supplied by the narrowed arteries. The early operations used reversed saphenous veins from the legs, but in the last 20 years there has been increasing use of the left internal mammary artery (LIMA). The LIMA graft patency rate is 90–95 percent after ten years, compared to 70 percent for a saphenous vein; failure to use a LIMA graft is associated with increased mortality in the first ten years. The LIMA should ideally be used routinely for revascularization of the LAD. The patency advantage of using the LIMA (or the right internal mammary artery or arteries from below the diaphragm) to vessels other than the LAD has not been proven. Since the mid-1970s it has been appreciated that incomplete revascularization is associated with increased mortality; surgeons attempt to bypass the narrowings in all major arteries and their main branches that are 1·0 mm in diameter or larger. Sequential grafts may be made (one aortic connection with the vein going to two or three distal arteries) but this practice has possibly been associated with increased incidence of graft failure. An important consideration in CABG surgery is preservation of myocardial function; this has improved in the past 15 years.

An excellent review of late mortality postbypass in *Medical Risks* provides statistical information pertinent to underwriting. The CASS enrolled 19,907 cases between 1975 and 1978 from 15 centers in the USA and Canada; separate reports from each center were analyzed. Insurance underwriting is usually postponed for six to 12 months postoperative until the subject has returned to work or regular activities, and operative and early postoperative mortality will not be discussed. Current operative techniques have reduced perioperative mortality to 1–2 percent and have undoubtedly improved long-term survival beyond that shown by the current statistics, which are based on patients operated on before 1980. There is also increased effort being made to address the risk factors related to progression of disease.

After CABG surgery 90 percent of patients have clinical improvement with total absence or significant reduction of angina. Of subjects with prior ECG changes on exercise 50 percent no longer have exercise-induced ST depression; others are able to do more work on an exercise test before ST changes occur. Exercise tolerance is improved, but the impression of clinical improvement often exceeds that demonstrated by objective testing. The best evidence for reperfusion is obtained with thallium studies. Nowadays few patients have postoperative angiography unless they are having continuing or recurrent symptoms.

One of the objectives of CABG is to prevent future infarction. Unfortunately infarction was produced in the perioperative period in 5–15 percent of cases in early series, but the rate has been reduced to 2–5 percent in recent series. If the infarct is large, LV function may be worse than before surgery. Diagnosis of perioperative infarction is made by the appearance of new ECG changes (especially Q-waves), elevation of CPK MB band, pyrophosphate scan and new segmental loss of wall motion by echo or nuclear angiography.

Graft patency is an important consideration and is dependent on host factors, surgical skill, size and health of the coronary artery at the graft site and runoff. Patency rate six to 12 months after surgery is 70–90 percent. Graft occlusions in the first year are usually due to thrombus; later, a fibrous proliferation and atherosclerosis in the graft wall occur. Late graft occlusion occurs at a rate of 2 percent per year. Grafts with a low flow at the time of surgery are more likely to close. Progression of atherosclerosis in native coronary arteries distal to the graft will reduce flow rate and accelerate graft occlusion.

Failure Rate of CABG

Fitzgibbon et al performed serial angiograms, regardless of clinical progress, on 222 patients followed a mean of 9·6 years after CABG using vein grafts. Graft occlusion rates were 8 percent at one month, 13 percent at one year, 20 percent at five years, 41 percent at ten years and 45 percent at 11·5 years. In addition to the occlusions, at ten years 75 percent of the patent grafts had angiographic evidence of atherosclerosis and 26 percent had a greater than 50 percent reduction in graft lumen. Campeau reported 19 percent graft occlusion at five to seven years, 37 percent at 10–12 years, with 32 percent of patent grafts having greater than 50 percent reduction in lumen. In the Cleveland Clinic study, after 7·3 years 36 percent of grafts were occluded and 9 percent had narrowings of over 50 percent. Within ten years it can be expected that 65 percent of grafts will be either occluded or have developed significant narrowing. The greatest deterioration in graft function may occur between five and 7·5 years. In contrast to vein grafts, internal mammary artery grafts show ten-year patency rates of 90 percent. Improved surgical technique, use of antiplatelet agents and aggressive treatment of hyperlipidemia may reduce the problems with vein grafts. For various technical reasons vein grafts are still considered necessary for 80 percent of patients having CABG for multivessel CHD. In view of the above, does it make medical sense to apply a high insurance rating for the first ten years after a bypass and a lower rating after ten years?

Death after CABG is due to cardiac cause in 55 percent and to neurologic cause related to vascular disease in another 10 percent. Of the cardiac deaths 26 percent are sudden; the remainder are related to heart failure, acute in 49 percent, subacute 12 percent and chronic 12 percent. Subtle neurologic change may be present in 20 percent of patients three months after CABG but patients are not usually handicapped. Gross neurologic defects occur in 0·5 percent of patients under the age of 60 and in 5 percent of those over 70.

Mortality After Bypass

Table 15.16 summarizes five- and ten-year mortality ratios by age using data from five centers, as analyzed in *Medical Risks*. Comparative normal mortality was from group insurance data. Key points for underwriting are as follows:

1) Mortality ratios are prohibitive under the age of 40, and even with best case scenarios underwriting would be speculative. Many of these patients have diabetes or major degrees of hyperlipidemia. These patients seem to have an accelerated form of atherosclerosis. Only the exceptional patient with single vessel disease should be considered insurable.
2) Female relative mortality was much greater than male; underwriting before the age of 50 would be speculative.
3) The mortality ratios decline with increasing age. By the age of 70 or over, mortality for one month to five years and for five to ten years was better than the reference insurance population!
4) Mortality ratios are worse for the second five years compared to the first five years. Although it may make business sense to get a high premium income at the start, it does not make any medical sense to charge more premium income for the first five years after bypass, as is done in many rating manuals. When a subject applies for insurance seven years after bypass and escapes the early temporary extra of $5–15 per thousand, the subsequent fixed premium in this type of rating system may be inadequate to meet the risk. Whether the mortality rate from 11–20 years will continue to increase is uncertain, but it seems inescapable that it will, unless progression of atherosclerosis is halted and occlusions of both native and graft vessels can be prevented.
5) In males the mortality ratios from the age of 50 onwards are very favorable, even when there is no weeding out of the higher risks. When reviewing these mortality ratios it should be noted that all cases (including smokers and those with diabetes, high cholesterol, past and continuing hypertension, bad family histories, poor left ventricles and diffuse arterial disease) are all included.
6) Mortality ratios after 15–25 years are not available; how long this favorable mortality will persist is unknown.
7) A large series from the Texas Heart Institute confirms the higher mortality in females and a mortality below the reference population in males over 70 (*see* Table 15.17). Further studies of this problem show that body size and small arteries are the cause of the higher mortality in females, not gender.
8) An early series (1971–1973) from the Cleveland Clinic (*see* Table 15.18) shows the importance of LV function in overall survival. Five- to ten-year mortality ratios only are given. Mortality with severe LV impairment is prohibitive and most carriers deny coverage.
9) Mortality is often normal or better than reference population after CABG for single vessel CAD, as it was in the study shown in Table 15.19 from St Luke's Hospital, Kansas. In many series if there is no difference in ventricular function and revascularization is reasonably complete, there is little difference between two and three vessel disease groups for late mortality, as was the case in this Kansas study. Many underwriting manuals rate three vessel disease higher than two vessel disease, on the logical assumption that higher mortality is to be expected if the atherosclerotic process is more extensive. This does not necessarily follow. If the atherosclerosis is diffuse with poor runoff in the LAD and circumflex, but the RCA is normal, the patient will fare worse than the patient with segmental three vessel disease with good runoff and successful bypass. Note the low mortality ratios in general in this series.
10) Data from the Seattle Heart Watch (*see* Table 15.20) confirmed a mortality

below a reference population for patients having CABG for single vessel CAD, and a mortality that was the same for those with two and three vessel CAD. LV function represented as percent EF was of obvious importance, but in this series even the group with EFs less than 0·31 had only a 220 percent mortality ratio.

Table 15.16. Late mortality ratios after CABG, pooled series.[a]

Age at surgery (years)	Mortality ratios (%)			
	1 mth–5 yr			5–10 yr
	Males	Females	Combined	Sexes combined
<40	785	–	1130	1840
40–49	310	935	310	425
50–59	159	350	156	275
60–69	118	285	104	123
≥70	56	88	61	89

[a]Source: *Medical Risks*.

Table 15.17. Texas Heart Institute CABG surgery 1970–1981 (N = 22,284).[a]

Mortality ratios %			
Under age 70		70 and over	
Male	Female	Male	Female
223	330	87	235

[a]Source: *Medical Risks*.

Table 15.18. Cleveland Clinic CABG surgery 1971–1973, mortality ratios five to ten years postbypass (N = 2,703).[a]

LV function	Mortality ratios (%)
Normal	166
Mild abnormality	285
Moderate abnormality	415
Severe abnormality	670

[a]Source: *Medical Risks*.

Table 15.19. CABG St Luke's Hospital, Kansas, 1971–1976, four- to eight-year follow-up (N = 2,058).[a]

Number of vessels	Mortality ratios (%)
1	84
2	225
3	205

[a]Source: *Medical Risks*.

Table 15.20. Seattle Heart Watch one- to six-year follow-up of CABG, 1968–1974 (N = 1,880).[a]

Number of vessels	Mortality ratio (%)
1	64
2	144
3	164

Ejection fraction	Mortality ratio (%)
>0·5	107
0·31–0·5	168
<0·31	220

[a]Source: *Medical Risks*.

Table 15.21. Mortality ratios for Cleveland Clinic CABG, 1963–1965 (N = 598).[a]

	Mortality ratio (%)		
	0–5 yr	5–10 yr	11–15 yr
1 vessel	335	395	205
2 vessel	700	340	410
3 vessel	930	750	188
Left main	980	625	620
LV normal	455	355	210
Local abnormality	615	390	395
Aneurysm	1100	915	530
Diffuse	1730	865	300

[a]Source: *Medical Risks*.

Comparison of CABG and Medical Treatment Mortality

The 1991 publication of the American College of Cardiology/American Heart Association task force report on the guidelines and indications for coronary artery bypass surgery is an excellent source of current information on CABG and the comparison of mortality in medical and surgical treatment. An unsolved problem is that in the medical group 40 percent of subjects eventually had CABG or PTCA, but these were included in the medical groups.

Severity of angina before CABG does not influence subsequent mortality, but medically treated patients with severe angina have a higher mortality.

Objective evidence of ischemia with exercise ECG or myocardial perfusion studies does not alter late surgical mortality, but those with more severe ischemia do less well on medical treatment.

Unstable angina patients have greater survival with CABG than with medical treatment, even with the crossover that occurs.

Patients with three vessel disease have improved survival with CABG. Mortality

Table 15.22. Comparative mortality of CABG and medical treatment, from task force report.

	Mortality, 1–5 yr (%)	
	Medical	Surgical
GXT positive	11	4
GXT markedly positive	15	4
Unstable angina, 3 vessel	17	6
Left main, CASS 1989	31	10
3 vessel, no proximal, CASS 1989	23	17
3 vessel, 3 proximal, CASS 1989	27	10
Proximal LAD normal, European 1988	7	4
Proximal LAD stenosis, European 1988	10	4
3 vessel mild LV impairment	22	5
3 vessel severe LV impairment	30	17
Impaired LV function		
None	2·5	2·0
Moderate	7·3	4·0
Severe	17·8	7·0
Number of vessels		
1	2·0	1·8
2	4·0	2·0
3	8·0	3·0
LMCA	9·3	3·8
3 vessel disease		
Class I,II angina	21	6
Class III, IV angina	26	7

at five years in patients with Class I to II angina is 10 percent after CABG and 28 percent with medical treatment. Mortality at five years in patients with three vessel disease and Class III or IV angina is 13 percent after CABG and 41 percent with medical treatment.

Patients with left main disease under 90 percent do just as well after surgery as patients with three vessel disease; prognosis is so much better after CABG that no patient with LMCA disease today is advised to forego surgery.

The benefit of surgery is greater in patients with two or three vessel disease when the stenoses are proximal. Patients with proximal LAD stenosis before the first major branching do better with CABG than medical treatment. The more severe the LV dysfunction the greater the comparative benefit of surgery. The probability of survival after CABG and medical treatment is similar after 10–15 years. In the VA randomized trial of 1984 the comparative benefit of surgery over medical treatment, in terms of percent retention of potential lifetime, became zero after 16·1 years. The advantage of CABG over medical treatment was not altered by the age at surgery from ages 40 to 70.

In deciding on CABG or medical treatment in the clinical context, surgical and first-year mortality need to be considered. Insurers usually wait for one year after CABG before underwriting, to eliminate the early mortality from consideration. In Table 15.22 the first-year mortality has been eliminated, from both the medical and surgical values, as some of the medical cases would have had the same underwriting delay built in (i.e. past infarction, unstable angina, angina coming under medical control).

Table 15.23. CABG, European randomized trial, 1988; ten-year mortality comparison of CABG and medical treatment.

	Mortality (%)					
	1–5 yr		1–10 yr		5–10 yr	
	Med	Surg	Med	Surg	Med	Surg
Proximal LAD normal	9	8	17	20	8	12
Proximal LAD stenosis	18	7	36	25	29	17
GXT positive	11	4	23	16	12	12
GXT markedly positive	15	4	30	22	15	18

Limited data for ten-year follow-up was available to the task force, and the best available data was from the European randomized trial, 1988 (*see* Table 15.23).

If the proximal LAD was normal, there was no advantage of CABG in this trial, but LIMA grafts were not in general use. When proximal LAD stenosis was present, there was a large advantage of CABG from one to five years, and a smaller advantage from five to ten years.

The European study also compared the outcome based on the GXT results: positive or strongly positive. There was an advantage of CABG in the first five years but not in the next five years.

The results of the task force report and the ten-year follow-up of the randomized CASS study can be summarized, making three separate classes of patients:

Class 1: Definite advantage of CABG over medical treatment, with fewer deaths and no overlap at the 90 percent level of confidence.
All cases of LMCA stenosis over 50 percent even if asymptomatic.
All cases of three vessel disease and moderate or severe LV impairment, even if asymptomatic.
All cases of three vessel disease and Class 3 or 4 angina.
All cases of two vessel disease and proximal stenosis of a large LAD.
All cases of one vessel disease and proximal stenosis of a large LAD and mild or moderate LV impairment.

Class 2: Probable advantage of CABG over medical treatment, with fewer deaths and CHD events. The slight overlap at the 70 percent level of confidence would be likely to disappear with the enlargement of the statistical sample.
One vessel and two vessel disease, no symptoms with normal or mild LV impairment and stenosis of proximal LAD.
Two vessel disease without stenosis proximal LAD, with angina, with or without exercise ischemia, regardless of angina class.
One vessel disease without stenosis proximal LAD, with moderate or severe LV impairment.

Class 3: No proven advantage of CABG over medical treatment; all cases of one vessel disease and no stenosis of proximal LAD with normal or mild LV impairment, unless Class III angina present. In fact, with the ten-year randomized CASS study patients with a normal EF and mild stable angina, had a greater event free survival with medical therapy compared to CABG (76 percent as opposed to 66 percent).

The ten-year follow-up of the randomized CASS study showed no significant difference in ten-year survival (79 percent medical, 82 percent surgical in the overall group), but clearly those with severe disease and impaired LV function fared better after surgery. The crossover effect was significant: 6 percent of the medical group had surgery in the first six months, and by the end of the ten years 40 percent had had surgery!

In the task force report survival after CABG at one, five, ten and 15 years was 97 percent, 92 percent, 81 percent and 57 percent. At 15 years there was no difference in survival between medical and surgical patients. If we eliminate the early

Table 15.24. Mortality ratios calculated from pooled survival values from CABG trials for five-year intervals.

1st 5 yr		2nd 5 yr		3rd 5 yr	
Age	Ratio (%)	Age	Ratio (%)	Age	Ratio (%)
45	275	50	350	55	625
55	125	60	150	65	250
65	100	70	100	75	100

mortality, mortality for the first five years is 6 percent, for the next five years 11 percent, and for the next five years 24 percent. If we assume that mortality was due to CHD severity and not dependent on age, the mortality ratios for three ages are shown in Table 15.24.

Table 15.24 shows that the risk of CHD, especially after CABG, can easily be insured and that the mortality of older patients with CHD does not greatly exceed standard mortality. By eliminating the high-risk patients with extensive three vessel disease and severe LV impairment, insurers should feel confident about taking on applicants with known CHD.

There has been gradual evolution of information concerning the advantage of CABG over medical treatment, starting with no advantage in longevity over medical treatment, to advantage for LMCA stenosis only, to advantage in three vessel disease with impaired LV function. Now added to the above are any proximal LAD lesion, three vessel disease with impaired LV function, severe ischemia on exercise ECG and Class 3 or 4 symptoms. These advantages in mortality need to be considered in underwriting. It is not possible to assess patients with angina or previous infarction without coronary arteriography, although three vessel critical disease and LMCA stenosis can be ruled out with 90 percent certainty with a high workload GXT showing no or minimal ST change and/or a negative thallium scan.

Now that PTCA is in widespread use the picture is less clear. PTCA, as currently practised, is clearly not as successful in alleviating ischemia as CABG, nor in making the patient angina free, nor in reducing mortality in three vessel disease. In single vessel disease not involving proximal LAD or LMCA with normal LV function, there is probably little difference in survival between medical, CABG and PTCA treatments.

It follows that some patients with CHD are probably not suitable candidates for underwriting unless bypass is carried out: three vessel disease with mild impairment of LV function; two vessel disease with exercise-induced ischemia at 7 METs or less exercise; LAD disease with 90 percent narrowing, no infarction and ischemia at 7 METs or less exercise; and any applicant with EF less than 50 percent.

There is also concern for patients with single vessel proximal LAD stenosis who have not had surgery. In some applicants with CHD it does not make much difference whether or not they have had bypass when there is single vessel disease with 50–85 percent narrowing with no inducible ischemia at 8 METs exercise; nor if there is double vessel disease with no inducible ischemia at 8 METs exercise and normal LV function.

For applicants with severe CHD it makes sense to issue insurance if bypass has not been performed, but to allow for an improved mortality of about 25 percent for vein bypasses and about 50 percent for LIMA grafts. In this category would be triple vessel disease, 90 percent LAD narrowing with no ischemia at 8 METs exercise, and 70–90 percent two vessel narrowing with no ischemia at 8 METs exercise on medical treatment.

It goes without saying that applicants with LMCA cannot be considered prior to successful CABG; even then, they can only be considered if all other factors are favorable.

PERCUTANEOUS TRANSLUMINAL CORONARY ANGIOPLASTY (PTCA)

We are now faced with applicants who have had a variety of invasive procedures on their arteries, from simple ballooning to scrapers, cutters, rotating atherectomy devices, lasers and other devices, and the insertion of various stents. New methods have expanded the population of patients who can be considered for a therapeutic catheter procedure rather than bypass surgery, including those with long stenotic segments or complete occlusions. Currently, simple angioplasty is suitable for about 90 percent of patients selected for PTCA procedures. Some stents have been associated with a high rate of early occlusion. Patients who have had procedures other than simple PTCA with a balloon catheter are probably not suitable for underwriting given our current limited knowledge and follow-up.

Initially patients referred for PTCA had single vessel disease in proximal segments of the RCA, LAD or LCx. Prognosis in this group is excellent, regardless of the treatment. PTCA is currently also an option for patients with two and three vessel disease. Whether the procedure is as good as, or better than, CABG will be clarified on completion of ongoing comparative studies.

The ideal lesion for PTCA is less than 1·0 cm in length, concentric, accessible because it is proximal, not ostial, not angulated more than 45°, has little or no calcification, does not involve a bifurcation, has no thrombus and is not completely occluded. The balloon does not necessarily flatten the plaque; it certainly does not make it disappear, but the lumen is increased by fracturing the plaque and creating small dissections. On angiography it may appear that a near-normal channel has been produced, but in reality the contrast media is filling around and through fractures in the plaques, making it appear that there is little or no residual plaque. The initial success rate in the ideal lesion is close to 90 percent; there is a 1 percent incidence of infarction, a 1 percent need for CABG, and mortality is under 0·5 percent in experienced hands. Success is defined variously, one definition being that the luminal narrowing after the procedure is less than 50 percent, another that there has been a 50 percent reduction or greater in the degree of narrowing (i.e. from 80 percent to 40 percent). It is to be emphasized that the lumen is often not restored as much as might appear on the angiogram. Symptoms are immediately improved or they disappear and the patient can return to work in a week or sooner, but recurrence of significant stenosis starts immediately with some platelet aggregation and inflammatory cells, followed by aggressive smooth muscle proliferation. If restenosis is defined simply as a narrowing increasing by angiography to over 50 percent of vessel diameter, the rate of restenosis is at least 35 percent by six months, with a peak frequency at two to four months. After six months restenosis is less common, perhaps 2 percent per year.

For the patient with single vessel disease, long-term mortality is unlikely to be significantly changed by PTCA, unless there is a significant mortality from subsequent procedures. The risks are partly related to the anatomy of the lesion but also to the skill and experience of the operator.

When the lesions are about 2 cm in length, occur near a bifurcation where there is some thrombus formation, moderate calcification and vessel tortuosity, the success rate drops to 70 percent, the complication rate increases to 6 percent and the restenosis rate is still about 35 percent. When there is complete occlusion of the vessel of less than three months' duration, success rate is about 70 percent but the restenosis rate as high as 60 percent. However, if there is single vessel disease it can still be argued that these are important considerations for morbidity, but probably not long-term mortality.

PTCA is also performed in unfavorable cases, either because the patient wishes to avoid bypass, or the case is declined for CABG for various reasons, and symptoms justify a last-resort intervention. These cases have long lesions with diffuse atherosclerosis, tortuosity and calcification; a bifurcation may be involved and vessel angulation of 90 percent may be present. Success rate is less than 60 percent, complication rate 15 percent.

There has been considerable investigation into the identification of restenosis by non-invasive methods of treadmill ECG, such as treadmill with thallium or dipyridamole thallium scans, but the overall sensitivity is less than 80 percent and the treadmill ECG alone is unsatisfactory. The patient knows he has restenosis because angina recurs in half of those with restenosis by angiography.

If the patient is asymptomatic one year after PTCA and the treadmill with thallium is normal, it can be assumed that revascularization has been maintained. In the next seven years 3 percent per year will undergo repeat PTCA and 3 percent per year will undergo CABG.

The main drawback for insurance underwriting after PTCA is the 25–35 percent incidence of restenosis in the dilated vessel. In underwriting the CHD applicant who has had PTCA, the following are required:

1) Initial coronary angiogram report detailing coronary pathology and other details, as for post-CABG underwriting.
2) Report of the ballooning procedure: any occlusions, any infarction, any major dissection, need for emergency surgery, other complications if any.
3) Balloon result with immediate angiography:
a) What was the percent narrowing of diameter before angioplasty?
b) What was the percent narrowing of diameter after angioplasty?
c) Was a 50 percent or greater reduction in the degree of narrowing obtained (e.g. narrowing 80 percent before and 20 percent after, making a reduction of 60/80 or 75 percent)?
d) Was a pressure gradient measured across the vessel and did this change?
e) Was ballooning carried out on all narrowings? List the narrowings that were not treated.
4) Evidence for improvement, or lack of, in the first few months, such as symptomatic relief with disappearance of angina and improved treadmill performance with improved exercise ECG and myocardial perfusion scan.
5) Sustained improvement past six months with no recurrence of symptoms, a negative exercise ECG at high workload and a normal perfusion scan. A normal exercise ECG is, by itself, not sufficient to rule out a recurrent narrowing.
6) Although ideally it would be helpful to have follow-up angiographic results, this test is now reserved for those who have residual symptoms or perfusion defects on thallium testing.

Most companies prefer to postpone underwriting until at least a year has gone by.

Comparison of PTCA and CABG

The task force report reviewed preliminary evidence comparing CABG to PTCA in heterogenous groups of patients. After five years mortality was 3 percent for PTCA and 9 percent for CABG, but the PTCA group had 60 percent single vessel disease versus 4 percent in the CABG group. Multiple regression studies showed that any differences were not significant.

In patients over the age of 70 with three vessel disease, mortality after five years was 13 percent after CABG and 48 percent after PTCA. There was no contest over freedom from angina after five years: 72 percent for CABG and only 43 percent for PTCA.

In the task force report predictions were made for individual hypothetical situations, one example being a 65-year-old man with three vessel disease who was predicted to have a five-year mortality of 9 percent after CABG with a LIMA, 35 percent after medical treatment and 50 percent after PTCA.

Over the next few years hundreds of thousands of patients with CHD will have PTCA, and hopefully the place of PTCA as a treatment option will have support based on statistical data. Until then comparisons are suggested in Table 15.25.

Table 15.25. Comparison of CABG and PTCA for various conditions.

Condition	Comparison of CABG and PTCA
Single vessel disease, not LMCA	CABG with LIMA and PTCA with good result at 1 yr likely to be equal.
Two vessel disease	1 yr after, good result and complete revascularization proven by GXT and thallium scan: PTCA and CABG likely to be close to equal.
Three vessel disease	CABG superior to PTCA.
Recurrence of angina after single vessel PTCA	Assume stenosis just as bad as before the dilatation. Try to obtain comparative GXT endurance times.
Recurrence of angina after double vessel PTCA	Assume both areas of stenosis have returned to pre-PTCA status.
Normal GXT with thallium 1yr after PTCA	Assume that diameter of the stenotic segment is about the same as it was at the time of the immediate post-PTCA angiogram.

APPROACH TO UNDERWRITING

The 1985 edition of *Medical Selection of Life Risks* provides an excellent summary of insurers' early mortality experiences with underwriting CHD. In 1965 the industry changed from the level premium increase because mortality ratios and excess death rates varied considerably with age, although it could be argued that a more equitable assessment of actual risk is to have different mortality debits for each age group.

At first, insurers relied on clinical information only provided by history, sometimes supplemented by a resting ECG. Pooled information collected by Mercantile and General found mortality ratios in applicants with various degrees of CHD of 1000 percent under the age of 50, 400 percent for ages 50–59 and 125 percent for ages 60 and over, but other insurers reported ratios considerably lower. For applicants with angina insured by Lincoln National, mortality ratios were 344 percent for one to two years, declining to 200 percent by 11 years, and this was the era without CABG, routine exercise tests, beta blockers or even aspirin for CHD. Although credit can be given for astute underwriting, to have mortality rates this low the series must have contained a number of applicants who had non-coronary chest pain.

Rates suggested by Brackenridge as fairly common in the industry in 1985 for CHD were as follows:

Class	Rating
I	+75 and 7·5 per mil for 5 yr
II	+125 and 15 per mil for 5 yr
III	+200 and 25 per mil for 8 yr

The permanent mortality debit was to be increased by two-thirds for ages under 40, by one-third for ages 40–49 and decreased by one-third for ages over 60. Perhaps we are no closer to an ideal system today, despite considerably better information about our applicants and an improved understanding of CHD.

Many manuals and most insurers have separate underwriting categories for CHD, (such as angina, postinfarction, CHD with angiogram, CHD without angiogram, postbypass etc). The disease process is the same in all cases. Some patients with mild disease have had angiograms, many with severe disease have not. Silent ischemia is just as serious as ischemia with chest pain. The occasional patient with stenosis localized to the diagonal branch of the LAD coronary artery may have incapacitating angina. The fact that bypass or PTCA has been carried out cannot be used as an index for disease severity or prognosis. The risk of dying from CHD is a continuum, there are no stages or categories and many deaths are unpredictable. The underwriter must determine risk (1) based on what information is available from history, clinical examination and tests already obtained, and (2) by selectively ordering a few supplementary tests that are needed for risk determination (such as a GXT, but not including arteriography). If recent angiograms are not available, the severity of atherosclerosis must be predicted from indirect information, such as a current GXT or thallium scintigraphy. For underwriting purposes CHD risk can be categorized as very mild, mild, moderate, severe and very severe. The first category will have a mortality close to standard; patients in the last category have mortality rates in excess of 500 percent and are uninsurable.

It follows from the above that only one underwriting table is necessary for all CHD, whether or not an angiogram has been obtained, whether or not infarction has occurred, whether or not CABG has been carried out. Applicants can be placed in the various categories using the objective data available. The system needs to be flexible because marketing insurance is competitive and there is no right answer until the applicant is dead.

Determinants of Mortality Ratios

The prognosis in CHD depends on the following: extent and severity of arterial narrowing, the degree of LV impairment, the degree of inducible ischemia, the presence of electrical instability, and age and sex. These factors are related to some degree, but in many patients they are not closely connected. Examples would be:

1) Extensive LV impairment following a single LAD occlusion.
2) Exercise limited to 4 METs with 90 percent narrowing of LAD and no other lesion.
3) 4 mm ST depression with single vessel CHD.
4) No ST depression on exercise with extreme three vessel CHD.
5) 10 METs exercise capacity with severe three vessel CHD.
6) 10 METs exercise capacity with EF of 24 percent.

When using mortality ratios, age and smoking status are dominant factors that cannot be ignored. A 40-year-old non-smoker developing severe CHD and surviving 20 years to the age of 60 has a mortality ratio of over 700 percent; a 60-year-old smoker developing severe CHD and surviving 15 years to the age of 75 has a mortality ratio of only 150 percent; a 60-year-old male non-smoker following the same course has a mortality ratio of 250 percent.

Females develop CHD about ten years later than males but they do less well after bypass or angioplasty, possibly because of smaller arteries. An extra 100 mortality debit is required for females requiring these interventions. When using mortality ratios the greater longevity of females provides another hurdle for the medical underwriter. A female non-smoker aged 55 who is predicted to survive to the age of 75 has a mortality ratio of 350 percent, but if she is a smoker the ratio will be 275 percent. For a male smoker aged 55 predicted to reach the age of 75 the mortality ratio is normal, 100 percent.

Because of the complex interplay between age, sex and smoking status, it is useful for the MD, who estimates prognosis and then assigns a mortality rating, to have some idea of what this means in terms of survival. Table 15.26 is presented as a guideline, necessary when underwriting, using a mixture of statistics from medical reports and clinic judgment, and using a system dependent on mortality ratios. The dominant effect of age on mortality ratios cannot be overemphasized. Ten percent five-year mortality gives a mortality ratio of 1000 percent at age 35 and 100 percent at age 65. The approximate age the applicant must reach for each level of mortality for current insurance life tables is a useful guide for the MD with clinical experience. The 45-year-old with a 5 percent five-year mortality, assuming this risk to continue at the same 125 percent ratio, is predicted to reach the age of 78. The 55-year-old with a 15 percent five-year mortality, mortality ratio 375 percent, is predicted to reach the age of 70. More detailed tables of a similar nature can be provided by the actuaries for each age and sex and for smoking status.

These guidelines allow translating medical percent survival figures into approximate mortality classes.

The excess mortality due to CHD is presumed to be related to disease severity at the time of assessment and rate of disease progression, and is independent to some extent of age at assessment. This seems to be the case with CABG patients and perhaps most clinical categories. If the percent mortality from CHD is constant, the mortality ratio is markedly changed by age because of the increase in overall mortality from 2 per 1,000 at the age of 40 to 30 per 1,000 per year at the age of 70. Risks that seem unacceptable at the age of 45 become not unreasonable at the age of 55, and by the age of 65 the extra risks are relatively small.

Table 15.26. Mortality ratio guidelines for five levels of mortality in relation to age.

| Class number | 1 | 2 | 3 | 4 | 5 |
Description	Very mild	Mild	Moderate	Severe	Very severe
5-year mortality (%)	5	7	10	15	≥20
5-year survival (%)	95	93	90	85	≤80
Mortality ratio (%)					
Age: 35	500	700	1000	1500	≥2000
45	250	350	500	750	≥1000
55	125	175	250	375	≥500
65	100	100	100	150	≥200
Anticipated longevity					
Age: 35	64	55	53	49	≤44
45	71	68	65	58	≤55
55	78	76	74	70	≤69
65	83	83	83	81	≤79

For underwriting, the severity of CHD can be separated into five levels, from very mild to very severe, as in Table 15.27. Many applicants, particularly those with milder disease, will not have had invasive studies, and may not have had any recent investigation if they are relatively symptom free and satisfied with their current life style and functional capacity. It is recommended that all these subjects have at least a current GXT, otherwise it is not possible to assess risk. In some cases of older applicants for small policies risk can be assessed at what seems a fairly high mortality prediction with the offer to improve the rating should satisfactory objective information be provided by the applicant.

Not all factors will be present in the same risk category. An applicant whose physician states he is a Class 2 angina patient automatically becomes Class 4 severity if he has 3·0 mm ST depression on his ECG or a fitness level of −30 percent. An applicant having an apparent well-healed moderate-size infarction by ECG and who has an EF of 0·35 on echocardiogram is automatically in the very severe category. An applicant with mild angina (Class 2 CCS) is automatically in Class 5 if his coronary angiogram score, using the Duke system, is over 64. In applicants with angiogram results the highest severity class should be used. A

Table 15.27. Placing CHD applicants into five levels of risk.

Class number	1	2	3	4	5
Description	Very mild	Mild	Moderate	Severe	Very severe
Angina					
CCS Class	1	1	2	2–3	≥3
Rest ECG	Normal	Mild T, RBBB IAH	Moderate T, ST	ST depression	
GXT ST depression	1·0	1·0	0·1–0·5, 1·0–2·0	≥0·6, ≥3·0	≥2·0
GXT HR% maximum	≥90	≥90	≥80	≥70	≥70
GXT fitness	+10%	Normal	−20%	−30%	≥−30%
GXT angina	0	0	Some	Terminated	Terminated
Medication	0	Nitro	Various	Various	Various
Single infarction; no angina[a]					
CHF acute stage	0	0	0	0,+	0,+
Atrial fibrillation	0	0	0	0,+	
Rest ECG	Normal	Q, 2, 3, F, QV1–V2, T normal	Q, 2, 3, F, QV1–V3, small r V4, T changes	Same + ST changes	Both inferior and anterior changes, LVH with ST changes, ST elevation V1–V4

	Trivial defect	Small defect	Sizable defect		Several defects
Perfusion imaging					
Fixed defects, thallium scan	1 small	1 moderate	Sizable	2 or 3	≥3
Echo or RNA wall motion segments	55	50-54	45-49	40-44	<40
EF	0	10-25	26-45	45-63	64-100
Invasive studies available: coronary angiogram, Duke score					
LV angiogram					
EF	55+	50-54	45-49	40-44	<40
Wall motion segments	0	1	1-2	2-3	≥3

[a] If angina after single infarction, move up one or more classes depending on severity and GXT results.

class 3 Duke score but a Class 4 LV function score places the applicant in Class 4; a Class 3 Duke score but a Class 1 LV function score places the subject in Class 3.

The underwriting system proposed does not follow current industry standards. When a disease is chronic, usually with a downhill course, either gradually or in steps that are often catastrophic, it makes no medical sense to have a very high initial premium and then a low premium, so the practice of applying a flat temporary extra has not been followed. It seems particularly inappropriate to apply a flat extra for the first five or ten years after CABG and then a level premium at a lower level just when the various bypasses are likely to become clogged.

Some insurers follow the practice of using a temporary extra for the first five years after the last angina attack. Even if the client and the attending physician accurately recorded the last anginal attack this makes no medical sense in terms of measuring disease severity. The applicant may have been recently subjected to unusual physical exertion, such as rushing for an appointment or using stairs after an elevator shutdown. A second applicant with worse disease may have religiously avoided all activities likely to provoke chest discomfort.

Use of General Classification System

The use of this general classification system requires some judgment and flexibility because of the many variables. The reliability of the information needs to be taken into account. A person with three vessel CHD and all narrowings at least 75 percent has severe disease regardless of whether or not there has been infarction or angina. A person with an EF of 30 percent has severe disease whether his treadmill time was 4 or 12 minutes. A person with a 70 percent narrowing of the LAD with normal LV function has mild disease or at worst moderate, even though he may have angina with 4 mm ST depression at 6 METs work. The overriding data are the results of the coronary angiography. If a coronary angiogram has not been carried out, the applicant with angina and ST change at Stage I on the treadmill has severe disease until proven otherwise with an angiogram. The person with a major infarction with shock and CHF during the acute episode has severe disease, unless proven otherwise with at least nuclear angiogram at rest and exercise and, preferably, angiography. Any information showing an EF of under 40 percent places the applicant in the very severe disease category whether that information is from angiography, echo, nuclear angiography or implied from other studies, even a plain chest roentgenogram showing marked enlargement. This is regardless of the number of vessels narrowed or treadmill performance.

Flat Extras

For those who like the old system of flat extras, it is useful to see what this means in terms of mortality ratio, as that is our current method of expressing extra risk. The flat extra premium represents a considerably higher extra mortality debit for the younger applicant and the penalty for the non-smoker is double that for the smoker, which does not make much medical sense.

Table 15.28 shows that a $20 per mil temporary extra on a 65-year-old smoker is the equivalent of adding only about +65 to a mortality ratio. A 15 per mil temporary extra for a 55-year-old non-smoker is the equivalent of adding about

Table 15.28. Mortality ratio equivalent of flat extras: comparison of three ages, smoker versus non-smoker, males.

| Age | Cost $ per $1,000^a | | Approximate mortality ratio (%) equivalent to flat extra | | | | | |
| | | | 10 per mil | | 15 per mil | | 20 per mil | |
	Smoker	Non-smoker	Smoker	Non-smoker	Smoker	Non-smoker	Smoker	Non-smoker
45	5·40	2·70	185	370	275	550	370	740
55	11·40	6·60	100	175	150	225	190	300
65	30·80	15·80	30	60	50	100	65	125

[a] Approximate ten-year renewable term rates.

+225 to a mortality ratio. In the system this mortality debit is only applied for one to five years. Many insurers use this type of rating system and the reader is referred to their underwriting manuals. The information above is to show what this means in terms of mortality ratios.

GXT as the Main Factor in Underwriting

The key to underwriting applicants with known or suspect CHD is the GXT. It is not always possible to order nuclear imaging; it is awkward to arrange ultrasound tests (and quality is an unknown factor); it is not reasonable to expect angiography to be carried out for insurance purposes. The only measure insurers have apart from what has been obtained from the applicant's carers is the result of a current well conducted GXT.

1) Applicants with angiography in the past two years: objective information is available on coronary anatomy and LV function. A current GXT provides information on myocardium at risk and identifies those with rapid disease progression.

2) Applicants post-CABG: objective information is available on coronary anatomy and LV function before surgery. A current GXT assesses the completeness of revascularization, the likelihood that the grafts have remained patent.

3) Applicants post-MI, no angiogram: some measures of LV function may be available from hospital records at the time of discharge. The resting ECG will identify some applicants with severe damage where an automatic decline would be prudent. A current GXT provides invaluable prognostic information.

4) Applicants with angina, no angiogram: a current GXT is the most available tool to judge the severity of underlying CHD and provide prognostic information.

5) Applicants with risk factors: although the GXT lacks diagnostic accuracy, it will identify at least 40 percent of those at high risk of future coronary events; applicants with strongly positive tests are easily convinced to see their own physicians to finalize the diagnosis with nuclear scans or angiography.

Taking Medical Treatment Into Consideration

When a patient with fixed coronary stenotic lesions takes nitroglycerine his endurance time on the treadmill before angina is experienced, is increased before ST depression occurs, and the peak workload is also increased. The same is true after treatment with beta blocking drugs and calcium channel blocking agents. The degree of stenosis in the coronary arteries is not improved unless spasm was present. The work output of the heart is roughly proportional to HR multiplied by systolic blood pressure, and this product is often the same for the patient with coronary stenosis before and after medical treatment. With treatment, many patients with coronary stenosis no longer have angina and have no ST depression on their exercise ECG; they stop exercise because of fatigue or dyspnea.

A person who had angina interfering with daily activities (Class 3) five years ago, and who on treatment has only occasional angina (Class 1), is likely to have more severe arterial stenosis in his coronary arteries now than five years previously. It is difficult to know whether medical treatment alters prognosis a great deal. We know that patients with silent ischemia have a worse prognosis than those without. We don't know if, by eliminating the silent ischemia, we alter prognosis. We know that patients with Class 3 angina do worse than patients with Class 1 or 2 angina; we are uncertain that medical treatment to lessen the angina and convert this symptom to a Class 2 level does much to improve prognosis. CABG surgery has been the subject of clinical trials concerning prognosis; drug therapy has often not been subjected to the same prognostic trials. The end-point on drug programs is often the degree of improvement in symptomatology. Medical treatment, by reducing ischemia, does improve heart function. Contractility improves and exercise-induced wall motion changes revert to normal. Evidence is available that the failure of medical treatment to alleviate painless wall motion abnormalities induced by exercise identified a group of patients with adverse morbidity and mortality.

When the purpose of a GXT is to assist in diagnosis (CHD present or absent) the test should be performed after the patient has been off all medication for a few days, though patients stopping medication should be under close medical supervision. When the purpose of the GXT is to assess the efficacy of medical management and the freedom from ischemia the test should be performed while the patient is on his regular drug regimens. When the purpose of the GXT is to assess disease severity and prognosis a better idea of the disease severity can be obtained when the patient is off medications. Insurers cannot instruct applicants going for GXTs to change anything without the applicant's doctor's approval and supervision, and most often a GXT for assessment of severity and prognosis is performed with the patient continuing his regular medical regimen. Nitroglycerine is ideally not taken for a few hours before the test.

Signs of Progression of CHD

This subject is of sufficient importance to warrant discussion in this chapter.

CHD is often relentlessly progressive, even in patients who follow all the rules of diet, cholesterol and blood pressure control, smoking cessation and regular physical activity. The rate of progression is unpredictable. In underwriting applicants with known CHD it is important to look for indications of disease progression, some obvious and objective, others more subtle. If disease progression has occurred in applicants under the age of 60, high mortality is anticipated. Slow progression after the age of 60 may not increase mortality by more than 50 to 100 percent.

In one study of 168 patients who had three angiographic studies, 32 subjects showed progression in both intervals; in only nine subjects did progression occur in the same lesion (Bruschke et al, 1981). Disease progression should be suspected or confirmed in the following situations:

1) Angina with activities not previously causing angina. Angina where none had been present before.
2) Dyspnea with activities not previously causing dyspnea.
3) Appearance of any episodes of rest pain, especially with hospitalization and assessment at emergency center.
4) Infarction, whether from clinical information or ECG evidence.

5) Indirect evidence that may indicate decreasing cardiac function: retirement; change to a less demanding job (e.g. physical to office work); giving up of some activities (e.g. tennis, golf) or other decrease in fitness-related activities.

6) Need for antianginal medications. Need for alteration of dosage of cardiac medications or the addition of new medications.

7) Appearance of dysrhythmias not present before, or recent need to treat arrhythmia.

8) Objective evidence of ischemia occurring with less exercise. Decrease in treadmill work time more than expected from aging alone or a reduced fitness activity. Earlier appearance of ischemic ST changes in the treadmill protocol. Reduction in maximal HR by more than 10 beats/min.

9) Appearance of symptoms related to vascular disease elsewhere: claudication, cerebrovascular disease manifested by stroke, TIA, change in cognitive function, parkinsonism.

10) Deteriorating LV function from the results of comparable tests, such as repeat ultrasound studies or repeat nuclear angiograms.

11) Angiographic evidence of progression, including occlusion of a bypass vessel, new narrowings or progression of previous lesions in native coronary vessels. Even the need for angiography suggests that new and worrisome symptoms have occurred.

12) Results of thallium testing. Reappearance of reversible perfusion deficits or the appearance of new fixed or reversible perfusion defects.

13) The need for repeat bypass speaks for itself, as does the need for angioplasty at a different site and the need for angioplasty in a patient who had previous bypass.

Progression is often related to continuing risk factors, smoking, hypertension or lipid abnormalities.

Risk Factors in Patients with Known CHD

The rate of progression of CHD in the native coronary arteries and the rate of occlusion in the bypass vessels are partly related to the continuance of known risk factors. Some underwriting manuals reason that risk factor debits are not appropriate once clinical CHD has developed. This makes no medical sense at all. For example, in the Framingham study among subjects with prior MI those with a cholesterol above 7·1 mmol/l (275 mg/dl) had a risk ratio for death 2·6 times that for those with a cholesterol below this value. Several studies have shown that continued smoking increases the risk of death after MI and reduces survival after CABG.

I do not like insuring a patient who has a serious life-threatening disease who will not take a few simple steps to improve his chances of living and remaining functional. Many of our patients get the message after their first trip to the coronary care unit or their first session with their bypass surgeon, but others do not. The latter patient clearly requires additional debits for continuing risk factors. I advise our underwriters to automatically decline all applicants with significant CHD who continue to smoke 20 or more cigarettes daily. A cholesterol level remaining over 7·8 mmol/l (300 mg/dl) in a patient with two vessel CHD and prior CABG places the patient in a high-risk category regardless of the CABG result. The mortality debits for lesser degrees of continuing risk are covered in the risk factor section (*see* pp. 260–1), and these debits should be added to any CHD debits or built in to any mortality system.

Getting by with Limited Information

It is not prudent to order expensive medical tests for underwriting a $25 thousand insurance policy with an annual premium of $75. It is reasonable to make a high substandard offer to the applicant on the information available, and at the same time to indicate that it may be possible to reduce the rating should the applicant obtain favorable results in tests such as a treadmill, thallium, ultrasound or coronary arteriography.

For large amount insurance applications, in the $1–50 million range, the underwriter should obtain whatever information seems necessary for accurate risk stratification, short of coronary angiography. Some of these applicants may not wish to have additional tests, and competing companies may elect to get by without obtaining any additional tests for underwriting. This should be regarded as a business decision and not as sound medical underwriting.

Acute MI

Insurers usually postpone insuring the applicant with an acute MI for one year. Patients recovering from acute MI are discharged from hospital in seven to ten days, and it is common practice to perform a low-level (up to 7 METs) exercise test prior to discharge. A positive GXT is claimed to identify subjects with a high first-year mortality and/or reinfarction rate. Those with a positive GXT may be selected for early angiography. A quarter of patients at high risk can be identified in the first few days after admission to the coronary care unit. Predischarge EF fraction can be measured with ultrasound or nuclear angiography; if EF is less than 40 percent, angiography is recommended. Residual ischemia and ventricular function are the most important predictors of survival; that the risk of arrhythmias adds to the risk of death is uncertain. As yet, there has been no proven reduction in mortality using antiarrhythmic drugs, although the current amiodarone trial may show benefit. A newer assessment technique is the use of the signal-averaged ECG, and late potentials have been shown to correlate with the occurrence of ventricular tachycardia. Information from the intensive care unit (ICU) and on discharge of the post-MI patient is useful for underwriting, but a repeat assessment, including a GXT, should be obtained at the time of underwriting. The point is that there are often considerable medical details concerning the patient that are available for the asking from hospital records. The underwriter should not try to underwrite from the attending physician's statement (e.g. 'acute MI three years ago, no symptoms or problems since, recent ECG attached'). Risk stratification requires detailed information.

CHOLESTEROL

Historical Background

During the 1940s and early 1950s interest was focused on a possible relationship between blood cholesterol and the development of ischemic heart disease. In order to test the hypothesis several epidemiological studies were mounted, notably the Cooperative Study of the American Heart Association, reported in 1956, the Framingham Study of the US Public Health Service and Ancel Key's long-term study of Minnesota business and professional men at the Laboratory of Physiological Hygiene.

The follow-up results of these studies left no doubt about the link between total serum cholesterol and CAD, indicating that the higher the cholesterol level the higher the subsequent attack rate of clinical ischemic heart disease. Since the measurement of serum cholesterol is highly reproducible, it seemed to be ideally suited as a quantitative predictor of excess mortality in the selection of risks for life insurance, and by utilizing the follow-up results of the several epidemiological studies as a basis, experimental rating schedules were constructed by Gubner and Ungerleider and by Blackburn. Modifications of these were later adopted by most life companies for underwriting hypercholesterolemia when it was presented as part of the medical evidence.

Meanwhile the possibility of using other blood lipids as predictors of CAD was being investigated. Some observers reported that serum triglyceride also had a correlation with the development of arterial atheroma, whereas others found it to be unreliable when used as the sole predictive characteristic. The measurement of serum triglyceride has the disadvantage of being less reproducible than that of serum cholesterol, since it must always be carried out in the fasting state. Moreover hypertriglyceridemia due to chylomicronemia has no correlation with the development of vascular disease. It was not until 1967, when Fredrickson and his coworkers announced a new classification of the hyperlipoproteinemias, that the true association between serum cholesterol and triglyceride concentrations and ischemic heart disease became properly understood.

Fredrickson classified the primary hyperlipoproteinemias into five types, later increased to six by the addition of a subgroup. This proved, at the time, to be a valuable basis for the study of mortality and morbidity associated with the various types of lipid abnormality, and also for their rational treatment. However, neither Fredrickson's nor the WHO's classification of the hyperlipoproteinemias included the HDL hypothesis promulgated in 1975 by Miller and Miller linking atherogenesis to the metabolism of plasma HDL. Arising from this development, the measurement of HDL cholesterol is becoming increasingly popular, not only to avoid unnecessarily treating patients whose hypercholesterolemia is due to a high level of HDL, but also to help identify individuals with low levels who have a high risk of CHD. Table 15.29 shows the chief characteristics of the lipoprotein types.

The current recommendations for the detection, evaluation and treatment of high blood cholesterol in adults is contained in the National Cholesterol Education Programme Expert Panel Report co-ordinated by the National Heart, Lung and Blood Institute and builds on the work of the 1984 Consensus Development Conference on Lowering Blood Cholesterol to Prevent Heart Disease. This report provides practitioners with detailed recommendations and algorithms to assist with the development of therapy for individual patients both with diet alone and with drugs. It also indicates classifications based on total and low-density lipoprotein cholesterol, addressing counseling issues and the management of special patient and population groups.

Table 15.29. Characteristics of hyperlipoproteinemias.

Lipoprotein	Major lipid	Effect of increased levels	Type	Cardiovascular risk when levels increased	Xanthomas	Frequency
Low-density lipoprotein (LDL)	Cholesterol	Hypercholesterolemia	IIa	++	Tendon	Common
Very low-density lipoprotein (VLDL)	Triglyceride	Hypertriglyceridemia with low HDL	IV	+	Skin	Common
Low density lipoprotein + very low-density lipoprotein (LDL and VLDL)	—	Combined hyperlipidemia	IIb	++	Tendon	Common
Intermediate-density lipoprotein (IDL)	Cholesterol and triglyceride	Combined hyperlipidemia	III	++	Skin	Rare
Chylomicrons (CM)	Triglyceride	Hypertriglyceridemia	I, V	Not increased	Skin	Very rare
High-density lipoproteins (HDL)	Cholesterol	Normal plasma lipids or mild hyper-cholesterolemia		Low		Rare

Suggested ratings of hyperlipoproteinemias follow. They should be used in conjunction with Table 15.30 (*see* pp. 260–1), the coronary risk factor underwriting schedule.

Rating of Hyperlipoproteinemias

1) Triglyceride levels should be disregarded unless they exceed 20 mmol/l (1775 mg/dl), when a rating of +50 should be imposed.
2) Non-fasting triglyceride levels are an unsound basis for rating; all levels not confirmed as fasting should be viewed with caution.

Types I and V
Ratings should generally be for the underlying cause rather than the level of cholesterol or triglyceride, unless the latter exceeds the limit as detailed in (1) above. If full investigations have revealed an apparent cause and there are no associated impairments, no further rating is necessary.

Types IIa, IIb, III and IV
Ratings should be based on the average of all available cholesterol levels whether treated or not, with appropriate adjustments for HDL cholesterol when known.

Where HDL cholesterol is known divide the total cholesterol by the HDL cholesterol level:

$$\frac{\text{Total cholesterol}}{\text{HDL cholesterol}}$$

Result	Action	
≤6	Disregard elevated serum cholesterol	
>6 but ≤8	Rate in column A	
>8 but ≤11	Rate in column B	(*see* page 319)
>11 but ≤14	Rate in column C	
>14	Rate in column D	

Serum cholesterol						
mmol/l	Up to 6·25	6·26–7·0	7·01–7·8	7·81–9·75	9·76–11·7	11·71 up[a]
mg/dl	Up to 240	241–270	271–300	301–375	376–450	451 up[a]
			A	B	C	D
Age at entry						
Under 30	Standard	+25	+50	+75	+100	+150 up
30–49	Standard	Standard	+25	+50	+75	+100 up
50–59	Standard	Standard	Standard	+25	+50	+75 up
60 and over	Standard	Standard	Standard	Standard	+25	+50 up

[a]Levels higher than 14·3 mmol/l (550 mg/dl) should be regarded as highly suspicious of the familial homozygous form of hyperbetalipoproteinemia; refer to chief medical officer.

SUGGESTED REFERENCES

Alderman EL, Bourassa MG, Cohen LS et al. Ten year follow up of survival and myocardial infarction in the randomized Coronary Artery Surgery Study. *Circulation* 1990; 82: 1629–46.

Blackburn H. Proceedings of 47th Annual Meeting, Medical Life Section, American Life Convention 1959.

Brackenridge RDC. *Medical Selection of Life Risks*, 2nd ed. London: MacMillan, 1985.

Bruschke AVG et al. The anatomic evolution of coronary artery disease demonstrated by coronary arteriography in 256 non operated patients. *Circulation* 1981, 63: 527–36.

Burgess J H. Regression of coronary disease as a result of intensive lipid-lowering therapy and men with high level of apolipoprotein B. *N Engl J Med* 1990; 323: 1289–98.

Campeau L, Enjalbert M, Lessperance J et al. Atherosclerosis and late closure of aortocoronary saphenous vein grafts: sequential angiographic studies at 2 weeks, 1 year, 5–7 years and 10–12 years after surgery. *Circulation* 1983; 68 (Suppl II): 1–7.

Chaitman BR, Ryan TJ, Kronmal RA et al. Coronary Artery Surgery Study (CASS): comparability of 10 years survival in randomized and randomizable patients. *J Am Coll Cardiol* 1990; 16: 1071–8.

Chambers J, Bass C. Chest pain with normal coronary anatomy: a review of natural history and possible etiologic factors. *Progress in Cardiovascular Diseases* 1990; 33, No 3: 161–84.

Cohn PF. Prognosis for patients with different types of silent coronary artery disease. *Circulation* 1987; 75 (Suppl II): 3.

Cohn PF. Silent myocardial ischaemia. *Ann Int Med* 1988: 109; 312–17.

Deanfield JE, Shea MJ, Selwyn AP. Clinical evaluation of transient myocardial ischaemia during daily life. *Am J Med* 1985; 79 (Suppl 3A): 18–24.

DeBusk RF. Specialised testing after recent acute myocardial infarction. *Ann Int Med* 1989; 110: 470–81.

Detrano R, Froelicher VF. Exercise testing: uses and limitations considering recent studies. *Progress in Cardiovascular Diseases* 1988; 31, No 3: 173–204.

Detrano R, Gianrossi R, Mulvihill D, Lehmann K, Dubach P, Colombo A, Froelicher V. Exercise-induced ST segment depression in the diagnosis of multivessel coronary disease: a meta analysis. *J Am Coll Cardiol* 1989; 14, No 6: 1501–8.

Diamond GA, Forrester JS. Analysis of probability as an aid in the clinical diagnosis of coronary-artery disease. *New Engl J Med* 1979; 300: 1350–8.

Doyle JT. Epidemiologic aspects of the asymptomatic positive exercise test. *Circulation* 1987; 75 (Suppl II): 12–13.

Ellis SG, Fisher L, Dushman-Ellis S, Pettinger M, King SB, Roubin GS, Alderman E. Comparison of coronary angioplasty with medical treatment for single and double-vessel coronary disease with left anterior descending coronary involvement: long-term outcome based on an Emory-CASS registry study. *Am Heart J* 1989; 118: 208.

Fanelli C, Aronoff R. Restenosis following coronary angioplasty. *Am Heart J* 1990; 119: 357–68.

Fitzgibbon GM, Leach AJ, Kafka HP, Keon WJ. Coronary bypass graft fate: long-term angiographic study. *J Am Coll Cardiol* 1991; 17, No 5: 1075–80.

Fredrickson DS, Levy RI, Lees RS. Fat transport in lipoproteins: an integrated approach to mechanisms and disorders. *N Engl J Med* 1967; 276: 34, 94, 148, 215, 273.

Gaspoz J, Lee TH, Cook F, Weisberg MC, Goldman L. Outcome of patients who were admitted to a new short-stay unit to 'rule-out' myocardial infarction. *Am J Cardiol* 1991; 68: 145–9.

Gill JB, Ruddy TD, Newell JB, Finkelstein DM, Strauss HW, Boucher CA. Prognostic importance of thallium uptake by the lungs during exercise in coronary artery disease. *New Engl J Med* 1987; 317: 1485–9.

Goldschlager N, Sox HC. The diagnostic and prognostic value of the treadmill exercise test in the evaluation of chest pain, in patients with recent myocardial infarction, and in asymptomatic individuals. *Am Heart J* 1988; 116: 523–35.

Gordon DJ, Ekelund L, Karon JM, Probstfield JL, Rubenstein C, Sheffield T, Weissfield L. Predictive value of the exercise tolerance test for mortality in North American men: the Lipid Research Clinics Mortality Follow-Up Study. *Circulation* 1986; 74, No 2: 252–61.

Gould KL. How accurate is thallium exercise testing for the diagnosis of coronary artery disease? *J Am Coll Cardiol* 1989; 14, No 6: 1487–90.

Gubner RS, Ungerleider HE. Long-term prognosis and insurability in coronary heart disease. *Am Heart J* 1959; 58: 436.

Guiteras P, Chaitman BR, Waters DD, Bourassa MG, Scholl J, Ferguson RJ, Wagniart P. Diagnostic accuracy of exercise ECG lead systems in clinical subsets of women. *Circulation* 1982; 65: 1465–74.

Heimsimer JA, DeWitt CM. Exercise testing in women. *J Am Coll Cardiol* 1989; 1, No 6: 1448–9.

Henry PD. Calcium channel blockers and progression of coronary artery disease. *Circulation* 1990; 82: 2251–3.

Hollbenberg M, Zoltick JM, Go M, Yaney SF, Daniels W, Davis RC, Bedynek JL. Comparison of a quantitative treadmill exercise score with standard electrocardiographic criteria in screening asymptomatic young men for coronary artery disease. *New Engl J Med* 1985; 313: 600–6.

Hopkirk JAC, Uhl GS, Hickman JR, Fischer J, Medina A. Discrimination value of clinical and exercise variables in detecting significant coronary artery disease in asymptomatic men. *J Am Coll Cardiol* 1984; 3, No 4: 887–94.

Iskandrian AS, Hakki AH, Goel IP, Mundth ED, Kane-Marsch AK, Schenk CL. The use of rest and exercise radionuclide ventriculography in risk stratification in patients with suspected coronary artery disease. *Am Heart J* 1985; 110: 564–72.

Iskandrian AS, Hakki AH, Kane-Marsch S. Prognostic implications of exercise thallium-201 scintigraphy in patients with suspected or known coronary artery disease. *Am Heart J* 1985; 110: 135–43.

Isles CG, Hole DJ, Hawthorne VM, Lever AF. Relation between coronary risk and coronary mortality in women of the Renfrew and Paisley survey: comparison with men. *Lancet* 1992; 339: 702–6.

Jones A, Davies DH, Dove JR, Collinson MA, Brown PMR. Identification and treatment of risk factors for coronary heart disease in general practice: a possible screening model. *Br Med J* 1988; 296: 1711–14.

Kannel WB. Cholesterol and risk of coronary heart disease and mortality in men. *Clin Chem* 1988; 34: B53–9.

Kannel WB. Common electrocardiographic markers for subsequent clinical coronary events. *Circulation* 1987; 75 (Suppl II): 25–57.

Kannel WB. Prevalence and clinical aspects of unrecognized myocardial infarction and sudden unexpected death. *Circulation* 1987; 75 (Suppl II): 4–5.

Kansal S, Roitman D, Bradley EL, Sheffield LT. Enhanced evaluation of treadmill tests by means of scoring based on multivariate analysis and its clinical application: a study of 609 patients. *Am J Cardiol* 1983; 52: 1155–60.

Kemp HG, Kronmal RA, Vlietstra RE, Frye RL. Seven year survival of patients with normal or near normal coronary arteriograms: a CASS registry study. *J Am Coll Cardiol* 1986; 7: 479–83.

Keys A, Taylor HL, Blackburn H, Brzeck J, Anderson JT, Simonson E. Coronary heart disease among Minnesota business and professional men followed 15 years. *Circulation* 1963; 28: 381.

Kirklin JW et al. Summary of a consensus concerning death and ischaemic events after coronary artery bypass grafting. *Circulation* 1989; 79 (Suppl I): 81–9.

Kirklin JW, Akins CW, Blackstone EH, Booth BC, Califf FRM, Cohen LS et al. ACC/ AHA Task Force Report. Guidelines and indications for coronary artery bypass graft surgery. A report of the American College of Cardiology/American Heart Association Task Force on Assessment of Diagnostic and Therapeutic Cardiovascular Procedures (Sub-Committee on Coronary Artery Bypass Graft Surgery). *J Am Coll Cardiol* 1991; 17, No 5: 543–89.

Kotler TS, Diamond GA. Exercise thallium-201 scintigraphy in the diagnosis and prognosis of coronary artery disease. *Ann Int Med* 1990; 113: 684–702.

Kulick DK, Rahimtoola SH. Risk stratification in survivors of acute myocardial infarction: routine cardiac catheterization and angiography is a reasonable approach in most patients. *Am Heart J* 1991; 121: 641–56.

Lachterman B, Lehmann KG, Abrahamson D, Froelicher VF. 'Recovery only' ST-segment depression and the predictive accuracy of the exercise test. *Ann Int Med* 1990; 112: 11–16.

Lee TH, Juarez G, Cook EF, Weisberg MC, Rouan GW, Brand DA, Goldman L. Ruling out acute myocardial infarction. *New Engl J Med* 1991; 324: 1239–46.

Levy D, Garrison RJ, Savage D, Kannel WB, Castelli WP. Prognostic implications of echocardiographically determined left ventricular mass in the Framingham Heart Study. *New Engl J Med* 1990; 322: 1561–6.

Lew EA, Gajewski J (editors). *Medical Risks: trends in mortality by age and time elapsed.* Volume 1 and 2. New York: Praeger, 1990.

Lim R, Dyke L. Dymond DS. Effect on prognosis of abolition of exercise-induced painless myocardial ischaemia by medical therapy. *Am J Cardiol* 1992; 69: 733–5.

Lytle BW, Long FD, Cosgrove DM et al. Long-term (5–12 years) serial studies of internal mammary artery and saphenous vein coronary artery bypass grafts. *J Thorac Cardiovasc Surg* 1985; 89: 248–58.

Mackenzie BR. Positive exercise ECG and negative thallium — a standard risk? *J Insur Med* 1990; 22: 257–61.

Magarian GJ, Hickam DH. Non-cardiac causes of angina-like chest pain. *Progress in Cardiovascular Diseases* 1986; 29: 65–80.

Mark DB, Hlatky MA, Harrell FE, Lee KL, Califf RM, Pryor DB. Exercise treadmill score for predicting prognosis in coronary artery disease. *Ann Int Med* 1987; 106: 793–800.

Mark DB, Shaw L, Harrell FE, Hlatky MA, Lee KL, Bengton JR, McCants CB, Califf RM, Pryor DB. Prognostic value of a treadmill exercise score in out-patients with suspected coronary artery disease. *New Engl J Med* 1991; 325: 849–53.

Martin MJ, Hulley SB, Browner WS, Kuller LH, Wentworth D. Serum cholesterol, blood pressure and mortality: implications from a cohort of 361,622 men. *Lancet* 1986; 933–6.

McCormick J, Skrabanek P. Coronary heart disease is not preventable by population interventions. *Lancet* 1988; 839–41.

McHenry PL, O'Donnell J, Morris SN, Jordan JL. The abnormal exercise electrocardiogram in apparently healthy men: a predictor of angina pectoris as an initial coronary event during long-term follow-up. *Circulation* 1984; 70: 547–51.

Metcalfe MJ, Rawles JM, Shirreffs C, Jennings K. Six years follow up of a consecutive series of patients presenting to the coronary care unit with acute chest pain: prognostic importance of the electrocardiogram. *Br Heart J* 1990; 63: 267–72.

Miller GJ, Miller NE. Plasma high density lipoprotein concentration and development of ischaemic heart disease. *Lancet* 1975; I: 16.

Mock MB et al. Survival of medically treated patients in the Coronary Artery Surgery CASS registry. *Circulation* 1982; 66: 562.

Myers W et al. Surgical survival in the Coronary Artery Surgery CASS registry. *Ann Thorac Surg* 1985; 40: 246.

Non-Q-wave myocardial infarction (editorial). *Lancet* 1989; 899–900.

Okin PM, Bergman G, Kligfield P. Heart rate adjustment of the time-voltage ST segment integral: identification of coronary disease and relation to standard and heart rate-adjusted ST segment depression criteria. *J Am Coll Cardiol* 1991; 18: 1487–92.

Ornish D, Brown SE, Scherwitz LW et al. Can life-style changes reverse coronary heart disease. The Life-style Heart Trial. *Lancet* 1990; 336: 129.

Pepine CJ. Ambulant myocardial ischaemia and its prognostic implications. *Circulation* 1990; 81: 1136–8.

Phillips AN, Shaper AG, Pocock SJ, Walker M, MacFarlane PW. The role of risk factors in heart attacks occurring in men with pre-existing ischaemic heart disease. *Br Heart J* 1988; 60: 404–10.

Prognostic applications of exercise testing (editorial). *New Engl J Med* 1991; 325: 887–8.

Ryan TJ. A 10 year follow-up of single vessel angioplasty: some important lessons and lingering questions. *J Am Coll Cardiol* 1990; 16: 66.

Sapin PM, Koch G, Blauwet MB, McCarthy JJ, Hinds SW, Gettes LS. Identification of false positive exercise tests with use of electrocardiographic criteria: a possible role of atrial repolarization waves. *J Am Coll Cardiol* 1991; 18: 127–35.

Sargent P. Lesaffre E, Flameng W et al. Internal mammary artery: methods of use and their effect on survival. *Eur J Cardiothorac Surg* 1990; 4: 72–8.

Smith LR, Harrell FE, Rankin JS, Califf RM, Pryor DB, Muhlbaier LH et al. Determinants of early versus late cardiac death in patients undergoing coronary artery bypass graft surgery. *Circulation* 1991; 84 (Suppl III): 245–53.

Sox HC, Garber AM, Littenberg B. The resting electrocardiogram as a screening test. *Ann Int Med* 1989; 111: 489–502.

Sox HC, Littenberg B, Garber AM. The role of exercise testing in screening for coronary artery disease. *Ann Int Med* 1989; 110: 456–69.

Strandbery TE, Salomaa VV, Naukkarinen VA, Vanhanen HT, Sarna SJ, Miettinen TA. Long-term mortality after 5-year multifactorial primary prevention of cardiovascular diseases in middle-aged men. *JAMA* 1991; 266: 1225–9.

Technical Group of the Committee on Lipoproteins and Atherosclerosis. Evaluation of serum lipoprotein and cholesterol measurements as predictors of clinical complications of atherosclerosis. Report of a Cooperative Study of Lipoproteins of Atherosclerosis. *Circulation* 1956; 14: 691.

Tsevat J, Weinstein MC, Williams LW, Tosteson ANA, Goldman L. Expected gains in life expectancy from various coronary heart disease risk factor modifications. *Circulation* 1991; 83: 1194–1201.

Uhl GS, Froelicher V. Screening for asymptomatic coronary artery disease. *J Am Coll Cardiol* 1983; 13: 946–55.

Underwood II D. Quantifying estimated survival from exercise stress ECG. *J Insur Med* 1992; 24, No 1: 23–7.

Weiner DA. The diagnostic and prognostic significance of an asymptomatic positive exercise test. *Circulation* 1987; 75 (Suppl II): 20–1.

Wilson PWF, Cupples LA, Kannel WB. Is hyperglycemia associated with cardiovascular disease? The Framingham Study. *Am Heart J* 1991; 121: 586–90.

Wolfe CL. Silent myocardial ischemia: its impact on prognosis. *J Am Coll Cardiol* 1990; 15: 1004–6.

Wong ND, Levy D, Kannel WB. Prognostic significance of the electrocardiogram after Q wave myocardial infarction. The Framingham Study. *Circulation* 1990; 81: 780–9.

Yeung AC, Barry J, Orav J, Bonassin E, Raby KE, Selwyn AP. Effects of asymptomatic ischaemia on long-term prognosis in chronic stable coronary disease. *Circulation* 1991; 83: 1598–1604.

Zack PM, Chaitman BR, Davis KB, Kaiser GC, Wiens RD, Ng Grace. Survival patterns in clinical and angiographic subsets of medically treated patients with combined proximal left anterior descending and proximal left circumflex coronary artery disease (CASS). *Am Heart J* 1989; 118: 220.

PART II: OTHER CARDIOVASCULAR DISORDERS

RICHARD S CROXSON

ADVANCES IN CARDIOLOGY

The past three decades have seen spectacular advances in the diagnosis and treatment, both medical and surgical, of many heart and arterial disorders, with consequent improvement in the prognosis of individual impairments, many of which had been previously considered beyond the scope of life insurance. During this relatively short period we have seen the successful establishment of open heart surgery for the correction of congenital and acquired lesions, heart valve replacement, coronary angiography and coronary artery bypass surgery, cardiac pacemakers, endarterectomy for large vessel stenoses, and the medical management of cardiovascular disorders with betablocking drugs, calcium antagonists, ACE inhibitors, potent cholesterol-reducing agents and thrombolytic drugs.

Perhaps the most dramatic change since the last edition of *Medical Selection of Life Risks* was published in 1985 has been the rise of interventional cardiology (continuing, however, the need for team-work approach between the physician, radiologist and surgeon): coronary stenoses and occlusions may be treated by PTCA, laser techniques, atherectomy and the insertion of intravascular stents; and valvular stenosis may be relieved by balloon valvuloplasty, particularly in the field of pediatric cardiology, including umbrella closure of patent ductus arteriosus and defects in the atrial or ventricular septum, together with atrial septostomy and coil closure of undesired collateral vessels, even extending to intrauterine fetal intracardiac manipulations.

EVALUATION OF CARDIOVASCULAR RISK

When a cardiovascular abnormality exists and the diagnosis has been established beyond doubt, expected mortality in a group having that particular impairment can be assessed with reasonable accuracy. When, however, a cardiovascular abnormality is presumed to exist because of the reported presence of various abnormal signs and symptoms, but a precise diagnosis cannot be made on clinical grounds alone, it may still be possible to estimate the risk in any given individual by classifying him as belonging to one of several broad mortality groups according to the history and physical signs elicited on examination. This can be done because the principal impairments affecting the cardiovascular system, such as heart murmurs, history of rheumatic fever, heart enlargement, irregularities of rhythm and elevated blood pressure, have all been the subject of several mortality studies, and the significance of each in terms of extra deaths is known. The insurance statistics in the *Medical Impairment Study 1983*,[1] extended by the publication of *Medical Risks*[2] and supplemented by trends from clinical medicine with meta-analysis of clinical trials, now allow more confident prognostication, even in serious disorders.

PULSE RATE

Tachycardia (Sinus)

The importance of the pulse rate in life underwriting has already been mentioned in Chapter 10, but it can be restated that tachycardia not just due to obvious systemic disease may become a ratable impairment when the pulse rate on examination is consistently above 95 per minute, the risk becoming greater with increases in pulse rate above this level. Higher rates would require confirmation by electrocardiography of a sinus mechanism. The *Medical Impairment Study 1983*[1] showed that relative mortality was lower at ages under 50 in both sexes, whereas the Framingham Study allowed separation of the risk in relation to smoking status: the mortality of all male non-smokers with pulse rates over 87 per minute was 125 percent (119 percent for women); in light smokers the figures were 146 percent for men and 167 percent for women; figures for heavy smokers were 192 percent for men and 157 percent for women.

Numerical ratings applicable to various average pulse rates are shown below.

Pulse rate (beats/min)	Rating
96–100	Standard
101–110	+25
111–120	+50
Over 120	+75

BRADYCARDIA (SINUS)

No significance need be attached to slow pulse rates when there is no suspicion of cardiovascular disease (or if the individual is on betablocking drugs) and rates even below 40 per minute may be recorded in highly trained athletes. Care should be taken not to overlook second and third degree heart block when the pulse is very slow (below 40 per minute) and responds atypically to exercise. If in doubt a resting electrocardiogram, including a long rhythm strip, should be obtained.

CARDIAC ARRHYTHMIAS

Ectopic Beats: Extrasystoles: Premature Contractions

Ectopic beats give rise to the commonest form of pulse irregularity. They are present in 1 percent of standard electrocardiograms, and on 24-hour ECG monitoring they become more prevalent and complex with advancing age. Their frequent occurrence in hearts that cannot be shown by any other criteria to be diseased generally influences clinicians to attach little significance to ectopic beats of any sort in ambulant patients. Previous mortality studies on insured lives having ectopic beats at the time of acceptance have also indicated the generally favorable long-term prognosis for this type of arrhythmia, mortality ratios being within, or only slightly above, standard insurance limits. Despite these findings, most rating manuals still take a less than optimistic view of ectopic beats, judging them to be an extra risk; the more frequent the ectopics the higher the mortality, and the higher the mortality still if they should increase after exercise.

The hard line taken by insurance companies on ectopic beats has often been disputed, but doubts about their benign nature have been revived following a number of studies involving people with frequent ventricular ectopic beats (VEBs) in which an increased incidence of sudden death have been reported (e.g. the Tecumseh Community Study). These doubts have been reinforced by the knowledge that frequent ventricular ectopics in monitored patients with acute MI often appeared to herald the onset of ventricular tachycardia (VT) or fibrillation (the concept of so-called warning arrhythmias).

Much depends on the underlying state of the myocardium; if the heart is damaged ventricular extrasystoles (VEs) herald a poor prognosis. This is true for postinfarct patients, aortic stenosis, cardiac failure, mitral leaflet prolapse, the long QT syndromes and dilated and hypertrophic cardiomyopathies. VEs that appear during exercise are associated with an increased mortality rate in patients recovering from a heart attack, although their importance in patients with chronic coronary disease is less clear. It now seems likely that the adverse prognosis confirmed by extrasystoles in earlier community studies may be due to a subset of patients with pre-existing cardiac disease who weight the outcome of such surveys towards increased mortality.

Table 15.30. Mortality summary for different types of extrasystole.[a]

Type of extrasystole	Entrants	Actual deaths	Expected deaths	Mortality ratio (%)
Supraventricular				
Simple	83	15	12·69	118
Complex	39	6	6·22	96
Ventricular				
Simple	359	56	59·79	94
Complex	123	21	17·34	121

[a]Experience of Equitable Life Assurance Company, 1970. Source: Rodstein et al.[3]

Nevertheless, with the exception of postinfarction situations, it is on the whole unusual to obtain a history or find manifest signs of heart disease in people subject to ectopic beats. A mortality investigation reported in 1970 by Rodstein et al[3] confirms the favorable results of earlier studies and will be examined in more detail below. The study comprised 712 individuals insured by the Equitable Life Assurance Society between 1930 and 1956, and observed to 1968 or the year of termination of the policy by death. All were medically examined and all had ECGs showing one or more ectopic beats. The majority (604) would have been considered standard risks for insurance if the ectopics had been absent, and 108 cases would have been considered with a numerical rating of up to 95 percent extra mortality (because of other impairments) if the ectopics had been absent.

The main findings of the study may be summarized as follows: the overall observed mortality ratios in the group that would have been classed as standard risk except for the presence of ectopic beats showed no appreciable increase and fell within standard insurance premium classification. Similar normal mortality ratios were observed in subgroups with simple and complex supraventricular and ventricular ectopic beats. Complex ectopics were defined as having the following characteristics: aberrant conduction (supraventricular only), paired, multifocal, with postectopic T-wave inversion, on or close to the preceding T-wave (i.e. within 40 msec of the preceding T-wave), bigeminy or trigeminy; unifocal ectopics without any of those characteristics were classified as simple. There was no significant difference in mortality with age, nor between those who responded to exercise with an increase in the number of ectopics and those who had no change or a decrease in the number of ectopics immediately after exercise. There was a low incidence of sudden death among those with supraventricular ectopics. VEBs in the presence of other cardiac abnormalities and/or elevated blood pressure were associated with an increase in mortality in excess of the sum of the mortality of the separate impairments (*see* Table 15.31).

Table 15.31. Mortality of individuals with ventricular extrasystoles and other abnormality.[a,b]

Type of other abnormality	Entrants	Actual deaths	Expected deaths	Mortality ratio (%)
Blood pressure and/ or cardiac condition[b]	42	15	6·70	223
Abnormalities other than cardiac or blood pressure[b]	44	8	6·10	131

[a]Experience of Equitable Life Assurance Company, 1970. Source: Rodstein et al.[3]
[b]Rated up to 95 percent extra mortality.

A further study by Kennedy[4] in 1985 identified a group of patients who had VEs that were frequent (greater than 60 extrasystoles per hour) and complex (multiforms, couplets, VT or R-on-T beats) on 24-hour ECG monitoring. Over a follow-up period of about seven years the mortality rate was less than the standardized mortality rate of the equivalent US population and ran parallel to that of patients shown to have no or very slight lesions on coronary angiography.

Studies of US aircrew suggested that exercise induced extrasystoles in otherwise healthy men were benign; this was confirmed in the Baltimore Longitudinal Study in which volunteers underwent biennial assessment, including maximum treadmill stress testing for those with no clinical or ECG evidence of heart disease. A subset of this healthy group had frequent (10 percent or more of the beats in any one minute) or repetitive (salvos of three or more beats) VEs during exercise but an otherwise normal exercise test. Over a six-year follow-up period the mortality of subjects with exercise-induced extrasystoles was no different from that of an age- and sex-matched group of controls.

The *Medical Impairment Study 1983*[1] analyzed cardiac arrhythmias in 24,387 policies with 86 percent issued at standard and 14 percent at substandard premium rates; the majority of the arrhythmias were premature heart contractions. The overall experience was favorable, with mortality 105 percent of the expected based on 917 deaths among men and 107 percent of the expected based on 79 deaths among women. This indicated that in ostensibly healthy people premature contractions found on random examination carry little risk of extra mortality in the absence of other impairments. The general conclusion is that chronic ventricular arrhythmias occurring in the absence of otherwise manifest organic heart disease carry a benign long-term prognosis, although the outlook in newly occurring ventricular arrhythmias is less certain, as they may be early markers of organic heart disease.

Antiarrhythmic drug therapy may be effective in patients with symptomatic paroxysmal tachycardias or frequent ventricular premature beats, although suppression is rarely complete; in those patients with organic disease, intervention studies with specific antiarrhythmic drugs have yet to show that treatment of ventricular premature contractions can substantially reduce the risk of sudden death.

A further question arises relating to the value of treatment of asymptomatic ventricular premature beats in higher risk patients (post-myocardial infarction) with drugs, other than betablockers, that have been shown to have proven benefit. The Cardiac Arrythmia Suppression Trial (CAST) looked at three agents (encainide, flecainide and moricizine compared with placebo), all of which showed a significant ventricular premature contraction suppression rate. However, part of the trial was terminated early when it was shown that two of the three intervention arms with encainide and flecainide (class 1(c) agents) were associated with a higher risk of death and ventricular fibrillation.

Rating

Cardiographic evidence is undoubtedly valuable to the underwriter for confirming that an irregularity, particularly a complex one, is in fact due to ectopic beats and not to some other dysrhythmia of a more serious nature; it may also detect myocardial disease that is otherwise unsuspected. This being so, it should be remembered that one of the criteria necessary for inclusion in the Equitable's mortality study (*see* pp. 326–7) was an ECG, so the subjects studied were to some extent selected. Therefore the mortality ratios shown in Tables 15.30 and 15.31 are unlikely to be fully applicable to people in whom the diagnosis of ectopics has been made on clinical grounds alone. For this reason, it is appropriate to retain for use a schedule of ratings based on the frequency of irregular beats and their response to exercise when these are reported on medical examination alone. However, when clinical evidence is supported by an otherwise normal ECG substantial credits may be allowed as indicated below.

Rating for ectopic beats, extrasystoles or intermittent pulse; no ECG available:

Conditions	Irregular beats per minute		
	Occasional (i.e. 1–6)	Frequent (i.e. 7–20)	Very frequent (i.e. ≥21)[a]
Reducing or unaltered with exercise	0	+25	+75
Increasing with exercise	+25	+50	+125

[a]Including bigeminy and trigeminy.

ECG showing a normal tracing other than ectopics, whether complex or not — credit above ratings 50 points or sufficient to reduce to zero where applicable.

Ratable blood pressure or other ratable cardiac impairment — add appropriate rating directly to rating for ectopics.

ECG available and otherwise normal — credit to impairment allowing maximum points.

Paroxysmal Tachycardia

Paroxysmal tachycardia is a disorder of rhythm closely related to ectopic beats and may be defined as three or more consecutive beats at a rate greater than 100 per minute. It can be a difficult impairment to underwrite properly because one usually has to rely on the applicant's personal description of his attacks, their duration and frequency, age at onset and symptomatology in order to arrive at a reasonable evaluation of the risk. It is only by chance that the paroxysm is recorded on an electrocardiogram by the attending physician or during the medical examination for life insurance. More frequent or sustained paroxysms and those associated with important symptomatology are now likely to be studied at centers with specialist electrophysiologic techniques that may allow accurate diagnosis and treatment.

Paroxysmal Supraventricular Tachycardia (PSVT)

This is the most common cause of paroxysmal tachycardia in children and young adults. In most cases functional differences in conduction and refractoriness in the A–V node or the presence of an AV bypass tract provide the background for the development of PSVT, in which there is a continuous movement of an electrical wavefront through such a pathway (re-entry) involving the atrioventricular node or accessory atrioventricular connections. If either pathway is modified (by drugs, surgery or catheter ablation) and rendered incapable of sustaining conduction, re-entry is abolished. In some patients with accessory pathways that conduct in an anterograde direction pre-excitation of the ventricles occurs with short PR intervals and delta waves seen in the Wolff-Parkinson-White (WPW) syndrome. In certain of these patients rapid ventricular responses may develop during atrial fibrillation, occasionally of a life-threatening nature.

The usual history in PSVT is one of long duration with first paroxysms often dating back to adolescence. If attacks are short, infrequent and occur in an otherwise healthy individual with no known heart disease, the risk to life would be minimal; such an applicant would generally be accepted as standard. Prolonged or symptomatic attacks may require drug treatment or, if refractory, consideration of antiarrhythmic surgery or catheter ablation techniques. The recent use of catheter ablation with radiofrequency current has been associated with an extremely low rate of early complications; in one series of 164 patients there was a 99 percent success rate with those 9 percent in whom arrhythmia recurred within eight months, all of whom underwent a successful second ablation procedure. The *Medical Impairment Study 1983*[1] analyzed 8,361 policies, predominantly in people with mild infrequent attacks, and demonstrated a very favorable mortality, only 78 percent in those issued as standard risks; even those who had been insured at substandard premium rates recorded mortality rates close to those among standard insured lives.

Paroxysmal Ventricular Tachycardia

This occurs much less frequently and is far more serious than PSVT. It is one of the dangerous complications of acute MI, often degenerating to ventricular fibrillation, and in its paroxysmal form is generally associated with pre-existing heart disease, usually ischaemic. Only rarely does VT appear spontaneously in healthy people without evidence of heart disease, and in such cases it may pursue a benign course. Prevention of recurrent attacks of VT includes the use of drugs and antitachycardia pacing — including the use of a new device, the automatic implantable cardioverter defibrillator (AICD), which affords a back-up means of terminating unstable arrhythmias. Where activation electrophysiological mapping studies permit localization of the site of origin of the arrhythmia, surgical techniques can remove or isolate the abnormal focus identified at mapping.

Rating

Attacks of PSVT that are prolonged for several hours or even days, or in which the HR is excessively fast, can cause considerable distress due to congestive failure, and the risk associated with a history of attacks of such severity is significantly increased. Rating should be based on the frequency of prolonged attacks, severity of the resulting symptoms and the effectiveness, or otherwise, of prophylactic treatment, if used. The insurance risk is greatest when attacks are recent and continuing but diminishes with duration since the last severe or prolonged attack. Since the medical attendant is often closely involved with the emergency treatment of prolonged paroxysmal tachycardia, he will usually be able to supply valuable information to the underwriter about the attacks. The rating schedule presented below is appropriate for attacks lasting one day or longer, or for more than four major attacks yearly.

Time since last attack	Age at application		
	Under 46	46–59	60 and over
Within 1 yr	+150	+100	+50
2nd yr	+100	+50	+25
3rd–5th yr	+50	+25	0
Thereafter	0	0	0

Current ECG that is otherwise normal — credit.
Successful catheter ablation after one year — standard rates.
Cases of paroxysmal ventricular tachycardia of recent onset should be declined or postponed if last episode was within two years.

Atrial Fibrillation: Atrial Flutter

Atrial fibrillation is a common disorder of heart rhythm occurring in paroxysmal and persistent forms. It can be seen in normal subjects, particularly during emotional stress and following surgery, exercise or acute alcoholic intoxication. It occurs temporarily in patients with heart or lung disease who develop acute hypoxia or metabolic or hemodynamic derangements. Persistent atrial fibrillation usually occurs in patients with cardiovascular disease, most commonly rheumatic mitral valve disease, usually late in hypertensive cardiovascular disease, chronic lung disease, atrial septal defect and a variety of cardiac abnormalities including cardiomyopathies. It may be the presenting finding in thyrotoxicosis. When present without underlying heart disease it is usually called 'lone' atrial fibrillation and may represent the tachycardia phase of the tachycardia-bradycardia syndrome. It is rare in the young but reaches 3–5 percent frequency after the age of 60. The Framingham Study indicated that it resulted in a doubling of all-cause mortality and that there was an annual/incidence of 4–5 percent. In the normal heart the rapid ventricular rate in atrial fibrillation is the major cause of disability; in patients with compromised left ventricles loss of atrial contraction may contribute to low cardiac output and fatigue, and systemic embolization is increasingly recognized even in the absence of mitral valve disease. In recent onset atrial fibrillation, removal of the precipitating factor may restore sinus rhythm, otherwise cardioversion to sinus rhythm with intravenous verapamil, betablockers or amiodorone may be attempted before electrical cardioversion. In established atrial fibrillation, which is usually associated with increased atrial size, ventricular rate control with drugs (such as betablockers, digitalis or calcium antagonists) is required, and anticoagulation with warfarin or possibly aspirin considered.

1979 Atrial Fibrillation Mortality Study

A pilot mortality study of a single impairment, atrial fibrillation, was undertaken by the Association of Life Insurance Medical Directors of America and the Society of Actuaries in 1979,[5] utilizing MIB coded data covering the period November 1968 to June 1976. Completed questionnaires were received from 395 companies or regional offices, and 3,099 lives with 71 deaths were finally analyzed. From the results shown in Table 15.32, at least two very definite conclusions can be drawn.

Insurance applicants who have had paroxysmal or intermittent atrial fibrillation with no other definable impairments show no appreciable extra mortality.

Individuals with a history or findings of persisting atrial fibrillation show markedly increased mortality which is particularly striking in cases with coexisting mitral stenosis.

Requirements

When atrial fibrillation is discovered on examination or there is a history of paroxysmal attacks, full ancillary examinations with chest X-ray and ECG are advisable, unless information from the medical attendant makes this unnecessary (this will usually include a recent echocardiogram) or unless clinical examination itself reveals obvious causes for rejection, such as mitral stenosis. At later ages atrial fibrillation may be the only manifestation of thyrotoxicosis, and therefore a reliable test of thyroid function should always be included in the diagnostic screening.

Table 15.32. *1979 Atrial Fibrillation Mortality Study.*[5] **Expected deaths based on 1965–70 Select Basic Tables for males and females separately.**

Impairments	Number of lives[a]	Exposure (months)	Deaths Actual	Deaths Expected	Mortality ratio (%)	Extra deaths per 1000
Atrial fibrillation, constant, no other impairment	126	4609	11	1·418	776	25
Atrial fibrillation, constant, with:						
Mitral stenosis	23	981	7	0·043	1737	81
Coronary artery disease[b]	36	1375	4	0·571	701	30
Hypertension[b]	50	1886	7	0·971	721	38
Other impairments[b]	72	2914	4	1·056	379	12
Atrial fibrillation, paroxysmal or intermittent, no other impairments	1645	66728	13	14·509	90	−0·3
Atrial fibrillation, paroxysmal or intermittent, with:						
Mitral stenosis	27	947	3	0·232	1292	35
Coronary artery disease[b]	139	5261	7	2·184	320	11
Hypertension[b]	340	13665	5	4·100	122	0·8
Other impairments[b]	641	24884	10	6·067	165	2

[a]Male and female combined.
[b]Not included in previous categories.

Rating
Basic ratings for atrial fibrillation when there is no known primary heart disease or
thyrotoxicosis present are given below.
1) Established atrial fibrillation or flutter.

Age	Rating
Under 45	+150
46–59	+100 to +75
60–64	+50
65 and over	+25 to 0

Current ECG that is otherwise normal — credit.
2) Paroxysmal atrial fibrillation or flutter:
With no other impairment — standard.
With cardiovascular or other impairment — rate as established atrial fibrillation
(*see above*).

CARDIAC ENLARGEMENT

It is rare for cardiac enlargement to exist as an isolated abnormality; it is almost
always secondary to organic disease such as valve defects, congenital abnormalities, systemic or pulmonary hypertension, CHD or cardiomyopathy. Occasionally
enlargement may occur as a 'normal' finding in an endurance athlete, or
temporarily under conditions of severe stress (e.g. anemia, hypoxia or prolonged
paroxysmal tachycardia). The chamber or chambers enlarged will depend on the
particular lesion or disease present. Chamber dilatation is responsible for most of
the changes in size and contour, whereas myocardial hypertrophy results in wall
thickening with reduction of cavity size producing variations in cardiac contour.
Frequently hypertrophy and dilatation coexist.

For the purpose of underwriting, it is convenient to classify cardiac enlargement
as slight, moderate or marked. Even when the heart is slightly enlarged, mortality
is significantly higher than that associated with the causative lesion without cardiac
enlargement. Clinical estimation of cardiac enlargement is at best only approximate, but often it is the only guide available to the underwriter. If the position of
the cardiac apex or left cardiac border has been reported accurately as a measured
distance from the midline, the data in Table 15.33 may be used to determine
whether or not a heart is enlarged and, if so, by how much. An apex-to-midline
measurement 10 percent more than the upper limit of normal would indicate slight
cardiac enlargement; up to 20 percent more would indicate moderate cardiac
enlargement; a measurement above that would indicate marked cardiac enlargement.

Measurement of heart size can be made much more accurately from a
posteroanterior (PA) chest radiograph taken at a distance of 2 m, with the added
advantage that selective chamber enlargement may be inferred, alterations in the

Table 15.33. Distances of cardiac apex from midline representing the upper limits of normal heart size at different weights.[a,b]

Weight	57·0 kg (≤125 lb)	68·0 kg (≤150 lb)	79·5 kg (≤175 lb)	90·5 kg (≤200 lb)	102·0 kg (≤225 lb)
Apex beat from midline	8·9 cm (≤3½ in)	10·2 cm (≤4 in)	10·8 cm (≤4¼ in)	11·4 cm (≤4½ in)	12·1 cm (≤4¾ in)

[a]When chest expanded exceeds 40 in (102 cm) increase the limit by 10 percent; when chest expanded less than 32 in (81 cm) decrease the limit by 10 percent.
[b]Slight heart enlargement: up to ½ in (1·3 cm) above upper limit of normal; moderate heart enlargement: up to 1 in (2·5 cm) above upper limit of normal; marked heart enlargement: over 1 in (2·5 cm) above upper limit of normal.

aorta noted and the state of the pulmonary vasculature visualized. Apparent cardiac enlargement may be caused by pericardial effusions, epicardial fat pads and alterations in the thoracic cage, particular pectus excavatum. In these instances other cardiac imaging techniques (particularly echocardiography and, more recently, computer tomography and magnetic resonance imaging) will provide the requisite detail.

Several ratios and indices have been devised using parameters of the chest X-ray and body build which purport to indicate various degrees of heart enlargement. Probably the best known method, at least to clinicians, is the cardiothoracic (CT) ratio, which is the ratio of the transverse diameter of the heart shadow (i.e. the sum of the greatest extension of the right border to the right of the medium line and the greatest extension of the left border to the left) to the maximum internal diameter of the thorax above the diaphragm.

Table 15.34. CT ratio for degrees of heart enlargement.

CT ratio (%)	Heart enlargement
Under 50	None
50–54	Slight
54–58	Moderate
Over 58	Marked

Another method of estimating heart size from a chest X-ray, and one that was specially devised for use in life insurance medicine, is that of Ungerleider and Clark.[6] By this method the observed transverse diameter of the heart is expressed as a ratio of the transverse diameter predicted for height and weight. Predicted values are read off from a specially prepared table, a modified version of which is shown in Tables 15.36 and 15.37, using metric and imperial units respectively.

Degrees of heart enlargement originally proposed by Ungerleider and Clark by calculation from their table are shown in Table 15.35.

Table 15.35. Degrees of heart enlargement.[a]

Percentage of predicted	Heart enlargement
Under 110	None
110–115	Slight
115–125	Moderate
126 and over	Marked

[a]Source: Ungerleider and Clark.[6]

The table of Ungerleider and Clark has been in use for over 40 years, but for some time more liberal limits have been used by many insurance companies to define the upper limits of normal heart size, generally in the range 112–118 percent. In 1976 Siber and his colleagues[7] at the New England Life Insurance Company set out to analyze the distribution of the observed transverse diameter of the cardiac silhouette in relation to that predicted by the table of Ungerleider and Clark, utilizing the data from 4,962 insurance applicants who had had a chest X-ray and an ECG during the period 1954–66. The results of this study were reported in 1979. Compared with the 100 percent mean of the table of Ungerleider and Clark, the distribution of heart diameter for 2,137 men aged 20–49 issued standard insurance gave a mean of 96·5 percent, and for 959 men aged 50–74 a mean of 98·8 percent, the difference between the age groups being highly significant. In contrast, women showed no significant difference with age. A consistently higher heart diameter was also noted in the older men who were rated for cardiovascular and non-cardiovascular impairments.

Applying these findings to practical underwriting Siber and his colleagues made certain recommendations. Although a new table for mean heart diameters could be constructed, they considered this unnecessary and recommended that the original table could still be used; the percentage of observed-to-predicted heart diameter should be obtained in the usual way, then 3 percent added to adjust for the smaller mean predicted heart diameter found in the 1979 study. If the effect of age is also to be included, this can be done by using an adjustment of +4 percent for applicants under the age of 45, +3 percent for those aged 45–54 and +2 percent for those aged 55 and over.

The question of what value should be used as the upper limit of normal heart diameter was considered next. The New England Life Insurance Company team, using a standardization of +7·1 percent and 95 percent confidence limits, calculated an upper limit of 111 percent using the original table unadjusted, or 114 percent using the average adjustment of +3 percent for the ages 45–54. It is suggested, therefore, that the original values proposed by Ungerleider and Clark in Table 15.35 be superseded by those shown in Table 15.38.

Table 15.36. Predicted transverse diameters of the heart silhouette and aortic arch for various heights and weights using metric units.[a]

Body values are Weight (kg).

Height (cm)										Transverse diameter (mm)	
152	157	163	168	173	178	183	188	193	198	Heart silhouette	Aortic arch
39·5	41·0	42·0	43·0							102	47
43·0	45·0	46·5	47·5	49·0	50·5					107	49
47·5	49·0	50·5	52·0	53·5	55·5	56·5	58·5			112	52
51·5	53·5	55·5	56·5	58·5	60·5	62·0	64·0	65·5	67·0	117	54
56·0	58·0	60·0	61·5	63·5	66·0	67·5	69·5	71·0	73·0	122	56
61·0	63·0	65·0	67·0	69·0	71·0	73·0	75·5	77·0	79·5	127	58
66·0	68·0	70·5	72·5	74·5	76·5	79·0	81·0	83·5	85·5	132	61
71·0	73·5	75·5	78·0	80·5	82·5	85·5	87·5	90·0	92·0	137	63
76·0	79·0	81·0	84·0	86·0	89·0	91·5	94·0	96·5	99·0	142	65
81·5	84·5	87·0	90·0	92·5	95·5	98·0	100·5	103·5	106·0	147	67
87·0	90·5	93·0	96·0	99·0	101·5	105·5	107·5	110·5	113·5	152	70
		99·5	102·5	105·5	108·5	111·5	115·0	118·0	121·0	157	73
						119·0	122·5	125·5	129·0	162	75

[a]Source: Ungerleider and Clark.[6]

Table 15.37. Predicted transverse diameters of the heart silhouette and aortic arch for various heights and weights.[a]

Weight (lb)	Height										Transverse diameter (mm)	
	5ft 0in	5ft 2in	5ft 4in	5ft 6in	5ft 8in	5ft 10in	6ft 0in	6ft 2in	6ft 4in	6ft 6in	Heart silhouette	Aortic arch
	87	90	92	95							102	47
	95	99	102	105	108	111					107	49
	105	108	111	115	118	122	125	129			112	52
	114	118	122	125	129	133	137	141	144	148	117	54
	124	128	132	136	140	145	149	153	157	161	122	56
	134	139	143	148	152	157	161	166	170	175	127	58
	145	150	155	160	164	169	174	179	184	189	132	61
	156	162	167	172	177	182	188	193	198	203	137	63
	168	174	179	185	190	196	202	207	213	218	142	65
	180	186	192	198	204	210	216	222	228	234	147	67
	192	199	205	212	218	224	231	237	244	250	152	70
			219	226	233	239	246	253	260	267	157	73
							262	270	277	284	162	75

[a]Source: Ungerleider and Clark.[6]

Table 15.38.   Adjusted figures for degree of heart enlargement.

Percentage of predicted by Ungerleider and Clark		Heart enlargement
Unadjusted %	Adjusted %	
Under 111	Under 114	None
111–116	114–118	Slight
116–125	118–125	Moderate
126 and over	126 and over	Marked

The results of a follow-up to the 1979 study were presented to the Annual Meeting of the Association of Life Insurance Medical Directors of America in Cambridge, Massachusetts in October 1981 by Singer.[8] The object of the study was to investigate the mortality in 4,143 insured applicants with ECGs and chest X-rays in relation to cardiovascular and other risk factors, including relative heart diameter. The essential findings were that in cardiovascular-rated cases there was a trend for mortality ratios to increase with increases in relative heart diameter for age groups 20–49 and 50–74, starting with relative heart diameters as low as 90–96 percent of average. By contrast, in standard cases and cases rated for non-cardiovascular reasons there was no significant effect of relative heart diameter on mortality ratios even for diameters 105 percent and above (there were relatively few cases with diameters exceeding 115 percent).

Although a heart diameter of 111 percent unadjusted or 114 percent adjusted is within the normal range for cases with no ratable cardiovascular impairment, the upward trend of mortality ratios with increasing heart diameters for cases with a ratable cardiovascular impairment implies a need to be more conservative about the possible use of debits for borderline increases in heart diameter. Singer has suggested minimal debits for such cases where heart diameters are within the range of 105–111 percent unadjusted or 108–114 percent adjusted.

Cardiac volume as estimated from a chest X-ray has been a popular method of measuring increases in heart size on the continent of Europe. Upper limits of normal for heart volume have been defined as 500–540 ml/m^2 of body surface in males and 450–490 ml/m^2 in females.[9]

Rating

When heart enlargement exists the primary cause will nearly always be apparent from the history or clinical signs (e.g. valve lesions, hypertension etc), and interdependence of the two impairments will invariably mean that the combined mortality for both will be rather more than that indicated by the simple addition of the mortality for each. When the combined rating for heart enlargement (*see* p. 339) and a particular primary cause is not stated in the text, it may be calculated approximately by the method of compounding the mortality of two interdependent impairments (*see* Chapter 5).

Specimen ratings for various degrees of heart enlargement at different ages:

	Rating		
Age at entry	Slight	Moderate	Marked
Under 30	+75	+150	Refer to CMO or MD
30–49	+50	+100	+300
50–59	+25	+75	+200
60 and over	+10 to +25	+50	+100

Aortic Dilatation

The width of the aortic shadow on a PA chest radiograph can be measured in the same way as the heart, and the observed width compared with the predicted width for various builds using the Sheridan Index, which is incorporated in Tables 15.36 and 15.37. Up to 15 percent greater than predicted is considered within normal limits, 15–20 percent greater is slight dilatation and over 20 percent is moderate-to-marked dilatation.

The cause of alterations in aortic arch is obviously the prime consideration in the overall rating; if it is suspected as being due to aneurysm, connective tissue diseases (including Marfan's) or other serious anomalies, the applicant should be declined or postponed until further medical assessment is carried out. If there is marked tortuosity or calcification present, consider as atherosclerotic disease.

It must be emphasized that in the assessment of both cardiac and aortic size if more precise information is available from other imaging techniques (including echocardiography, angiocardiography, nuclear scans, CT or MRI), the data from these techniques will clearly modify the above basic ratings.

CARDIAC IMAGING TECHNIQUES

Echocardiography (Ultrasound)

This diagnostic test uses high-frequency sound waves to map the structure and function of the heart and great vessels. It provides accurate non-invasive measurements of individual chamber size, wall thickness and ventricular function and is currently the most useful technique for the investigation of heart disease because it is non-invasive, accurate and relatively inexpensive. It is fair comment that it has revolutionalized the practice of pediatric cardiology in the past decade.

A transducer with a piezoelectric crystal converts electrical impulses into high-frequency sound impulses which are directed across the heart. Reversing the process the transducer, which transmitted the impulses, receives the reflected returning waves (echoes) converting them into electrical impulses which are displayed on an oscilloscope and recorded graphically.

The present technique uses three interrelated modalities:
M-mode: this was the original ultrasound technique using a narrow beam providing an 'ice pick' view of the heart and giving the measurement indices of LV diameter, wall thickness etc (*see* Table 15.39).

Two-dimensional: a unit scans the heart in an arc-like motion, producing cross-sectional (tomographic) slices of cardiac structures.

Doppler: this tracks the velocity of blood through the heart and great vessels using the Doppler shift principle. When sound encounters moving red blood cells the frequency of its reflected signal is altered. Gradients across stenotic valves, magnitude of valvular regurgitation and degrees of cardiac shunting in septal defects are quantifiable using combinations of pulsed and continuous methods. The two-dimensional and doppler flow techniques may be combined together with different colours proportional to blood flow direction, relative velocity and turbulence, permitting easier detection of regurgitation and shunts.[10]

Not all patients have suitable thoracic anatomy for echocardiography, and inadequate visualization may occur in obstructive pulmonary disease and obesity. Transesophageal echocardiography uses the transducer mounted on the tip of a gastroscope, placing the source of the sound closer to the atria, cardiac valves and aorta; it may produce superior information in patients with prosthetic valves and in the assessment of mitral regurgitation, endocarditis, intracardiac thrombus and aortic pathology.

Table 15.39. Normal values of M-mode echocardiographic measurements (adults).

Measurement	Normal value
Left ventricular dimension	
End diastole	4·6 ± 0·9 cm
End-systole	3·1 ± 0·7 cm
Left ventricular posterior wall thickness[a]	1·0 ± 0·2 cm
Septal thickness[a]	0·9 ± 0·3 cm
Left atrial dimension	3·0 ± 1·1 cm
Aortic root dimension	2·9 ± 0·9 cm
Shortening fraction	32 ± 7%

[a]End diastole.
Mean values = 95 percent confidence limits.

Radionuclide Imaging of the Heart; Multiple Gated Acquisition Scanning (MUGA); Gated Nuclear Angiography; Gated Blood Pool Scanning

These studies are used to detect and quantitate abnormalities of left ventricular size, EF and wall motion, both at rest and on exercise. A radioisotope, usually technetium-99M, is attached to red blood cells and injected into a vein; using either a first-pass technique or an equilibrated or (ECG) gated method, counts are recorded from several hundred cardiac cycles. The radioactive tracing outlines the heart chambers and great vessels. The normal response to exercise is a 5 percent increase in EF without development of wall motion abnormalities. Results may be abnormal in the presence of ischemia, cardiomyopathy, valvular or congenital heart disease, whereas assessment of left-to-right shunts uses a modification of the first-pass technique.

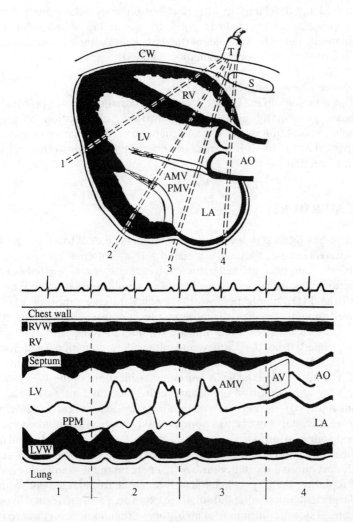

Fig. 15.1. Schematic diagrams of an M-mode echocardiographic scan through a normal heart. A long-axis section of the heart is depicted in the upper diagram. The echocardiographic movement patterns that arise from the corresponding anatomic structures are illustrated in the bottom diagram. CW = chest wall; T = echocardiographic transducer; S = sternum; RV = right ventricle; LV = left ventricle; AO = aortic root; AMV = anterior mitral leaflet; PMV = posterior mitral leaflet; LA = left atrium; RVW = right ventricular wall; AV = aortic valve; PPM = posterior papillary muscle; LVW = left ventricular wall. [Source: PC Come, Echocardiography in diagnosis and management of cardiovascular disease, *Compr Ther* 1980 6 (5): 58. Courtesty of The Laux Company, Inc., Ayer, MA.]

Magnetic Resonance Imaging (MRI)

This non-invasive technique uses no ionizing radiation but the principles of magnetic resonance. The images are formed by placing the subject within a strong magnetic field and detecting the altered radiofrequency pulse signals transmitted by hydrogen nuclei of tissues in response to stimulating radiofrequency pulses. Precise anatomic detail is available, particularly with thoracic aortic diseases; with the addition of Cine, functional evaluation is added.

Fast Computed Tomography (Cine-CT)

Completing a tomogram in 50 msec reduces the blurring effects of cardiac motion and appears particularly useful in demonstrating distribution of ventricular hypertrophy, in addition to the size and shape of cardiac chambers, great vessels and pericardial effusions. It is particularly effective in demonstrating calcification and aortic dissection.

HEART MURMURS

The life insurer's interest in heart murmurs lies in the extent to which, irrespective of the underlying cause, they are associated with a shortened life span in a group having the same murmur characteristics. It has already been pointed out that the precise nature of a cardiac or valvular lesion responsible for a murmur is not always known to the MD, simply because the medical referee reporting may not be experienced enough to make a diagnosis on purely clinical grounds. Nevertheless, when the characteristics of a murmur are considered along with other pieces of evidence gleaned from the history and physical examination (and sometimes ancillary tests), a better understanding of its significance for mortality can be obtained. For instance, in the heart murmur classifications of the *1951 Impairment Study*[11] a very large group of applicants insured as standard risks (who had an inconstant apical systolic murmur with no clinical evidence of cardiac enlargement, no history of rheumatic fever and a normal blood pressure) was studied over a long period and found to produce a mortality ratio of 107 percent. A similar group having the same clinical characteristics, except that the systolic murmur was heard constantly, produced a mortality ratio of 124 percent in the standard section. The effect of replacing the physical characteristic 'no heart enlargement' with 'slight heart enlargement' in a smaller but still large exposure group of insured lives having constant apical systolic murmur (but no history of rheumatic fever) was to increase the mortality ratio to 296 percent.

The results from the *Medical Impairment Study 1983*[1] and a survey of four individual companies' studies were summarized in *Medical Risks*[2] (*see* Table 15.40) confirming the innocent character of a non-transmitted apical systolic murmur, albeit with a slight increase in relative mortality, with ratios of 112 percent in the 1983 study and 137 percent in the *Medical Risks* study, whereas pulmonary systolic (functional) murmurs were very close to the expected, at 98 percent. It was important to note that there was a high proportion of younger people aged under 40 in all of these murmur categories. In the oldest age group, age 60–69, the male mortality ratio was 140 percent; so, in the group age 50–69 there was a mixture of cases with an increased risk factor of undetermined origin. The extra mortality by cause of death was concentrated in the cardiovascular and 'all other' causes. When the murmur is judged to be organic — that is, apical systolic murmur transmitted (mitral insufficiency) and basal systolic murmur transmitted (aortic stenosis) — the

Table 15.40. Mortality summary for various heart murmurs.[a]

Heart murmur (defect)[b]	Source	Under entry age 40 (%)	Exposure policy years E	Death claims Observed d	Death claims Expected[d] d'	Mortality ratio[d] 100(d/d') (%)	Excess deaths[d] per 1,000 per year 1000(d–d')/E
Apical systolic not transmitted (functional)	1976	67	75 399	311	227·4	137	1·1
	1983 IS	68	502 995	1 561	1 416·0	110	0·3
Apical systolic transmitted (mitral insufficiency)	1976	65	60 077	457	200·9	227	4·3
	1983 IS	66	136 891	880	499·0	176	2·6
Mitral insufficiency with rheumatic fever history	1983 IS	79	26 157	124	68·0	182	2·1
Apical diastolic (mitral stenosis)	1976	73	7 846	48	22·3	216	3·3
Basal systolic not transmitted	1976	50	6 041	49	27·7	177	3·5
Basal systolic (aortic stenosis)	1976	60	10 339	144	38·5	374	10·2
	1983 IS	62	22 992	195	76·7	254	5·1
Basal diastolic (aortic insufficiency)	1976	66	6 016	54	19·1	283	5·8
Pulmonic systolic (functional)	1976	–	29 016	86	87·4	98	–0·1
Other (atypical) heart murmurs	1976	64	42 794	297	147·4	202	3·5

[a]Source of table: *Medical Risks*.[2]
[b]Based on description of murmur on examination or other medical report.
1976: survey of four available individual company studies.
1983 IS: *Medical Impairment Study 1983*,[1] Abstracts 664–6.
[d]Expected deaths calculated on contemporaneous insurance standard select mortality rates.

mortality ratios were clearly significant, extending from 227 percent to 374 percent respectively in the 1976 study, and from 176 to 254 percent respectively in the 1983 study (*see* Table 15.40).

Although these broadly based classifications of systolic murmurs are useful to the life underwriter, generally he would prefer to know the definitive diagnosis of the lesion producing the heart murmur; thereby the prognosis can be judged more certainly enabling the broad classifications of murmurs to be narrowed considerably. It is particularly important to have a definitive diagnosis when the sum assured is large. In such an event it is usual to obtain an expert cardiologic opinion backed up by ancillary diagnostic procedures, such as electrocardiogram, chest X-ray and echocardiography.

Since the earlier editions of this book there have been rapid advances in surgical treatment of heart disease of all kinds. With improved techniques, patient care and quality of implant materials, operative mortality, once high, continues to decline. Long-term prognosis is being measured with more accuracy, clinical reports are detailing longitudinal studies of more than 20 years with heart valve replacement, and insured life statistics in these major substandard categories are now becoming available.

When unoperated cases of valve or other heart lesions are accepted for substandard insurance today, underwriters should realize that almost four-fifths of them will be subjected eventually to surgical treatment. They should also bear in mind that the average operative mortality could still be in the region of 10–80 per 1,000 despite improved techniques. If this death rate causes a shudder, the underwriter can console himself with the thought that the majority of the surgical survivors in the portfolio will enjoy a considerably extended expectation of life as a result, which should more than counter the excess operative deaths and improve the overall mortality of the group as a whole.

Defining Systolic Murmurs

As far back as 1942 Paul White recommended that 'functional' and 'organic' as applied to cardiac murmurs be dropped because of confusion over their precise meaning. 'Organic', with all its ominous implications, has come to be associated with structural deformity of a valve or with a congenital malformation, yet either of these might be quite insignificant compared with a more serious associated disease of the heart itself or of the conducting tissues. Likewise, 'functional' is generally used with an innocent connotation to describe systolic murmurs occurring in a heart where there is no structural abnormality of the chambers or valves, but it disregards the fact that the disorder of function causing the murmur may itself have a serious significance in shortening life (e.g. systemic or pulmonary hypertension, high cardiac output states due to thyrotoxicosis, severe anemia or arteriovenous fistula).

More recently, 'functional' has again been attacked as being confusing and imprecise, the suggestion being that murmurs caused by minor congenital malformations, though not functional by definition, should be termed 'innocent' when they have no hemodynamic significance and therefore no effect on shortening life. Generally speaking, the suggested terminology is realistic and might be welcomed by life underwriters so long as they are aware of the exceptions to the rule regarding effect on longevity. For instance, although the midsystolic murmur caused by turbulence of blood ejected through a congenital bicuspid aortic valve with taut commissures may have no hemodynamic significance while a subject is still young, it may well have by the time he reaches his fourth or fifth decade if aortic stenosis has developed due to progressive calcification of the valve. Also a congenitally abnormal valve is much more likely to be the locus of bacterial endocarditis, and the resulting damage could convert a minor structural defect into one responsible for major hemodynamic disturbance. Therefore, although the term innocent systolic murmur is a useful one, a life insurer has to look at it rather critically when its use implies the presence of a minor congenital abnormality of a heart valve, especially the aortic, for he is concerned not with the immediate prognosis but with the effect that a future structural change in the valve might have on long-term prognosis.

Functional Systolic Murmur

Most functional murmurs originate in the right (less commonly the left) ventricular outflow tract. Ejection vibrations can be recorded by suitable instruments in most normal hearts, and any slight increase in their intensity makes them audible with the stethoscope. These are truly functional systolic flow murmurs, for they are caused merely by forcible ejection of blood through normal aortic or pulmonic valves.

There are nearly always associated features on examination that provide clues to the functional nature of the murmur: the subject will usually be nervous, though this may be well concealed until actual physical examination when his apprehension becomes obvious; his past medical history will often reveal episodes of anxiety or anxiety equivalents; the HR will be somewhat faster than average; and the impulse at the apex, if palpable, will betray a forcible heart beat. Typically, the pulse pressure will be greater than average due to a cardiac hyperreaction pattern of the blood pressure (i.e. relatively raised systolic and relatively low diastolic pressures).

At rest the murmur is usually soft and short, occurring in early or midsystole and ending well before the second sound. It is best heard at the mitral and tricuspid areas, and almost equally well along the left sternal edge and at the aortic and pulmonic bases. The murmur sometimes has a grunting or musical quality and is usually transmitted above the right clavicle to the great vessels at the root of the neck, where it is heard as a short, sharp bruit. Exercise increases the dynamic blood flow and also the intensity, but not the character, of the murmur.

Unfortunately minimal aortic valve disease and some types of congenital bicuspid valves produce the same soft ejection murmur, and differentiation from a functional left ventricular flow murmur may be very difficult, if not impossible. Nevertheless, there are sometimes one or two useful clues which can be helpful for deciding the issue. The systolic murmur produced by minor structural changes of the aortic valve tends to be a little louder and more obvious at the aortic base than a purely functional murmur. Also, the probability of an ejection systolic murmur being organic will be somewhat greater if it occurs in a quietly acting heart with no suggestion clinically of increased stroke/volume output, especially if its intensity is louder than grade 1–2 out of 6, whilst it may often be accompanied by an early ejection click.[12]

Final differentiation of a functional benign murmur may require echocardio-graphy when no specific anatomic abnormality is visible and flow is normal on Doppler studies. A note of caution, however, is necessary: Doppler methods are extremely sensitive in detecting even trivial regurgitation, although as yet they are not accurate in quantitation. Mitral regurgitation has been detected in 5–50 percent of apparently normal subjects depending on the technique used for detection. In Popp's[10] laboratory approximately 10 percent of the subjects thought to be normal had mitral regurgitation, 40 percent had pulmonic re-gurgitation and over 75 percent had tricuspid regurgitation. Aortic regurgitation is only rarely detected in apparently normal subjects. The signal of this 'physio-logic' regurgitation in normal patients has characteristics that distinguish it from pathological regurgitation. In general, if there is no anatomical abnormality of the leaflets, subvalve apparatus or ventricle, such low-grade regurgitation should be considered to be within normal limits.

Rating

Theoretically there should be no extra risk associated with a functional or inno-cent murmur and therefore no necessity for rating, but in practice this does not always follow. Much depends on the clinical experience of the medical examiner who reports the murmur or on how well the evidence deducing its functional nature is presented in the medical report. The MD or CMO does not have the advantage of hearing the murmur; he only knows what he reads about it and has to make up his own mind after considering all the clinical data available includ-ing, perhaps, a chest X-ray and ECG.

If there are no inconsistencies and the underlying disturbance of function responsible for the murmur is not itself ratable, standard acceptance could be recommended with confidence. If, on the other hand, the characteristics of the murmur are not described (or are incompletely described) or if inconsistencies with the diagnosis of a functional murmur appear elsewhere in the medical evidence (e.g. a history of rheumatic fever, an abnormal ECG or heart enlarge-ment on X-ray), then a rating for the murmur will be justified according to the nature of the associated abnormality or according to the most appropriate schedule of ratings for systolic murmurs.

Conversely, some (often loud) ejection systolic murmurs that are not strictly functional by definition have no adverse effect on the circulation but merely draw attention to the structural abnormality causing them, which may or may not be ratable; aneursymal dilatation of an atheromatous ascending aorta would be ratable, whereas a non-stenotic, but sclerotic, aortic valve in old age would not.

Generally speaking, MDs much prefer to evaluate heart murmurs of doubtful significance on the basis of a full description of the clinical characteristics (in-cluding variation with posture, respiration etc) rather than on the unqualified diagnosis of functional or innocent. Experience has shown that these terms are not by themselves sufficiently critical for life insurance purposes.

MITRAL VALVE DISEASE

Mitral Stenosis

There has been a definite decline in the incidence of rheumatic heart disease over the past four to five decades due to a decrease in the prevalence, and possibly a diminution in the virulence, of rheumatic fever. Despite this, rheumatic heart disease remains a not unimportant cause of morbidity and mortality.

Pure or predominant mitral stenosis is the commonest chronic valvular abnormality following rheumatic fever or chorea, to which it is nearly always due, and it occurs in about 40 percent of all patients with rheumatic heart disease. The sex incidence relates to the degree of mitral regurgitation accompanying the stenosis. Female-to-male ratios are shown in Table 15.41.

Table 15.41. Female-to-male (F/M) ratios for valvular abnormalities.

Valvular abnormality	F/M ratios
Pure mitral stenosis	4:1
Equal degree of mitral stenosis and regurgitation	1:1
Predominant mitral incompetence	2:3

The earlier in childhood that the first attack of rheumatic fever occurs the higher the percentage who will later develop clinical heart disease; when the first attack occurs over the age of 20 the incidence of heart disease is small. Rheumatic chorea tends to give rise to pure mitral stenosis, whereas multiple attacks of rheumatic fever tend to give rise to a badly deformed mitral valve that is both stenotic and incompetent.

Although the peak incidence of first symptoms of mitral stenosis is in the second to fourth decades, about 23 percent do not become manifest until after the age of 50, and some of these not until old age when an acute rheumatic etiology is not always apparent.

Natural History and Prognosis

Before the days of surgical treatment, the natural history of mitral stenosis followed a fairly predictable course ending in death for the majority of patients between the ages of 40 and 50. The commonest period for the attack of acute rheumatism or chorea is between the ages of eight and 12 years. If the child survives, the typical course of events is a long latent period of up to 20 years, during which there may be no symptoms with ordinary effort and no abnormal physical signs unless elicited specifically by provocative exercise (functional Class I[a]). As the mitral orifice further narrows (less than $3 \cdot 0$ cm^2), the first symptoms appear at around the age of 30 (functional Class II[a]), after which there is an increase in the grade of severity every two to three years until the stage of total incapacity is

Table 15.42. Functional classification.[a]

Protocol (Bruce) Treadmill		Stage	Functional Class	Occurrence symptoms	Exercise tolerance (METs)[b]	Functional impairment
Speed (mph)	Incline %					
3·4	14	III	I	With unusual activity	7–8 or more	Minimal or none
2·5	12	II	II	With prolonged or slightly more than usual activity	5–6	Mild (can do light and general industrial work
1·7	10	I	III	With usual activity of daily living	3–4	Moderate (may be able to do desk job)
		0	IV	At rest	1–2	Severe (incapacitated)

[a]Modified from Hackett and Cassem.[14]

[b]1 MET = the energy requirement of the body at rest expressed as a unit of oxygen consumption = 3·5 ml O_2/kg/min.

reached after seven or eight years (functional Class IV[a]) (mitral orifice area less than 1·0 cm^2). Some observers, such as Oleson,[13] quote the interval between onset of symptoms and total incapacity at 15 years, with an average age at death of 47 years.

[a]The New York Heart Association's classification of functional capacity:
Class I — no limitation of physical activity, no symptoms with ordinary physical activity.
Class II — slight limitation of physical activity, symptoms occur with ordinary physical activity.
Class III — marked limitation of physical activity and comfortable at rest, symptoms occur with less than ordinary physical activity.
Class IV — symptoms with any physical activity and may occur at rest, symptoms increased in severity with any physical activity.
Notes
This classification was originally proposed for congestive heart failure. There have been subsequent modifications, including that of the Canadian Cardiovascular Society (CCS) which determines functional capacity in relation to angina (*see* pp. 263–4). The classes are similar. Using the New York Heart Association's classification it is important to note the patient's ordinary baseline or ordinary regular physical activity, as there are obvious differences between a fit young athlete and an elderly sedentary patient. With the advent of objective assessment of functional capacity by exercise testing, particularly in association with graded treadmill tests for ischemia, the relationships of these functional classes to standard measures of exercise tolerance (METs) and of various protocol stages to increasing speed and gradient of the treadmill provide useful shorthand classifications (*see* Table 15.42).

Gilchrist and Murray-Lyon[15] calculated the survival rates of three groups of patients with mitral stenosis: (1) men, (2) women who had borne children, and (3) women who had not. They found no great difference between these groups. In each there was a steep fall in the number surviving, so that out of 100 alive at the age of 20, less than 25 were still living at the age of 50, compared with the expected 92 for average healthy subjects. The series included all grades of mitral stenosis, from slight to severe. No doubt a better mortality experience could have been obtained by selecting for study only the most favorable cases; in other words, those who would be acceptable risks for life insurance. In Oleson's series[13] there was a survival rate of 38 percent in a group of mitral stenotics having a functional capacity of approximately Class III treated medically over a ten-year period, compared with an expected survival rate of 94 percent for a comparable sample of the general population. These earlier studies were conducted before the advent of surgical treatment of mitral valve disease, so there are only a few recent follow-up studies of medically treated patients. One of these is the Seattle Heart Watch study of 1978[16] in which 72 out of 249 patients were followed medically. There were only 19 percent with pure mitral stenosis. The improvement in overall mortality of patients with mitral stenosis reflects the advances in interventional techniques (surgery and balloon valvuloplasty), particularly in those with advanced symptoms. Nonetheless, intervention remains palliative rather than curative. In the Western world there is a tendency for a milder delayed course, particularly in older patients (contrasting with the sometimes severe progressive course in the young seen in certain parts of India, China, South East Asia and the South Pacific); although mitral stenosis remains one of the more serious forms of heart disease, the improved outlook for early unoperated milder cases must be reflected in the rating for those applicants who qualify for selection in substandard risk categories for life insurance.

Selection of Risks
The important factors to be considered in the selection of applicants having mitral stenosis are as follows:

1) The lapse of time since the last attack of rheumatic fever (though this is often not known). Since endocardial fibrous tissue continues to contract for some time after the acute rheumatic process has ceased, there must be a sufficient interval of time for the full effect of the damage to become apparent and the condition stabilized. Five years at least should be allowed, and for those who would be considered in the best category an interval of ten years is preferable.

2) The lesions should be slight and predominantly stenotic with little or no mitral regurgitation. Best risks are those in functional Class I, although those in functional Class II with moderate stenosis are also acceptable but in a higher substandard category. Those whose functional capacity is worse than Class III should be declined (or postponed until after intervention). Declinature should also apply to those who have a history of congestive heart failure or serious symptoms of pulmonary hypertension, including recurrent hemoptysis or attacks of pulmonary edema.

3) The heart rhythm should be regular and sinus in type. Atrial fibrillation present on examination or a history of recent paroxysmal atrial fibrillation should be a reason for declinature, irrespective of functional class.

4) There should be no significant defect of other heart valves.

5) There should be no generalized enlargement of the heart (see echocardiogram for assessment of individual chamber size).

Rating

1) Mitral stenosis, slight, with no mitral regurgitation; functional Class I; no rheumatic fever within ten years. Soft intensity short duration mid-diastolic murmur with no cardiac enlargement, chest X-ray and ECG normal. Echodoppler showing normal chamber dimensions, mild mitral diastolic gradient and mitral valve orifice area $3 \cdot 9 - 3 \cdot 0$ cm^2.

Age	Rating
Under 30	+150
30–49	+100
50–59	+75
60 and over	+50

2) Mitral stenosis, mild, slight exercise intolerance, mid-diastolic murmur of medium duration, chest X-ray, and ECG showing early left atrial enlargement but overall heart size normal. Echodoppler showing moderate mitral valve gradient and mitral valve orifice area $2 \cdot 9 - 2 \cdot 0$ cm^2 — increase above ratings by 50 points.

3) Mitral stenosis of moderate severity, moderate exercise intolerance (functional Class II), murmur of moderate duration, chest X-ray and ECG showing moderate left atrial enlargement and echodoppler showing increased diastolic gradient with calculated valve orifice area $1 \cdot 9 - 1 \cdot 2$ cm^2 — increase ratings by 50–100 points.

4) Several mitral stenosis — decline (postpone until six months to one year after surgery).

5) Atrial fibrillation present on examination would, as indicated above, usually be grounds for declining, but when an evaluation of the mortality risk is required for purposes other than life insurance the ratings quoted above should be increased by one-half.

6) Rheumatic fever:
Within two years — decline
Within ten years — add +100 to +25 to above ratings according to age group and time since last attack.

The prognosis following cardiac surgery in general and the surgical treatment of mitral valve disease in particular is discussed later in the chapter.

Mitral Incompetence with Regurgitation

The etiology of mitral incompetence is rheumatic in about one-third of patients. When considering other disease causes it is useful to note the pathologic basis for such regurgitation. Mitral incompetence may be due to a primary alteration of the mitral valve leaflets or commissures, pathologic or functional defects of the subvalvar apparatus (i.e. papillary muscles and chordae tendineae) and alterations of left ventricular and left atrial function. Any of these three pathologic states acting singly or in combination may cause varying degrees of regurgitation. This can be seen in the rheumatic process when acutely it is usually due to a combination of leaflet prolapse and annular dilatation. Later, there is progressive deformity of the valve with shortening of the leaflets, fusion of the commissures, with or without calcification, matting and scarring of the subvalvar apparatus and dilatation of the left ventricle leading to progressive severity of regurgitation. Among the disorders producing mitral regurgitation by alteration of the mitral leaflets or commissures there is the large group of mitral valve prolapse (MVP). In its primary form MVP may be due to myxomatous degeneration or associated with connective tissue disorders, including Marfan's and Ehlers-Danlos syndromes. MVP can be secondary to infective endocarditis with cusp destruction and, less commonly, to calcification of the mitral annulus, particularly in the elderly, and to congenital abnormalities, such as a cleft leaflet in atrioventricular canal defects. In the category of abnormal subvalvar apparatus, ruptured chordae tendineae may account for 20 percent of cases of mitral regurgitation. Rupture may be idiopathic, due to endocarditis or myxomatous degeneration or, less commonly, to thoracic trauma. Partial or complete rupture of papillary muscle may occur in the context of acute MI or, occasionally, chest trauma; papillary muscle dysfunction may result from CAD or other conditions causing localized necrosis or fibrosis, such as myocarditis and infiltrative diseases. When left ventricular and left atrial function is altered, changes in the position and direction of tension on the papillary muscles may produce mitral regurgitation seen either in generalized left ventricular enlargement (as in dilated cardiomyopathies), or in regional wall abnormalities (such as in MI). Abnormal positioning and tension on the papillary muscles may also occur in hypertrophic cardiomyopathy.

Pure mitral regurgitation affects males more than females in the ratio of 3:2. When the etiology is rheumatic the valve, as noted above, is generally more disorganized than in pure mitral stenosis. Eventually the whole valve apparatus becomes so rigid that there is a combination of stenosis and incompetence. Mitral regurgitation is progressive; there is no latent period for the appearance of physical signs, the systolic murmur and the hemodynamic effects of incompetence being present right from the date of rheumatic fever. Although the symptom-free period is rather longer than in mitral stenosis, there is a more rapid progress to complete incapacity once function has become impaired.

The incidence of atrial fibrillation increases with age and severity of regurgitation and is more common than in pure mitral stenosis, yet systemic or pulmonary embolism is less frequent. The average age at death of unoperated cases of mitral incompetence due to rheumatic fever is about 50 years.

The Murmur

The classic ausculatory signs of pure mitral incompetence are (1) a first heart sound soft or normal but never loud at the apex; (2) a murmur that is pansystolic, occupying the whole of systole and obscuring the second sound, loud and high pitched, and conducted from the mitral area to the left axilla and intrascapular region; and (3) a short mid-diastolic murmur often following a third heart sound, but no opening snap. The intensity of the systolic murmur does not correlate well with the severity of regurgitant flow.

Unfortunately, and confusing for those concerned with underwriting (and clinical medicine!), the murmur of mitral incompetence is not invariably the classic murmur described above. Sometimes it occurs in late systole preceded by a midsystolic click when the mechanism is that of mitral valve prolapse. If the posterior leaflet is flail, the regurgitant jet impinges on the left atrial wall close to the aortic root, and the systolic murmur is thus conducted to the aortic area and into the neck simulating the murmur of aortic stenosis. Conversely, a flail anterior leaflet directs the stream posteriorly. The underwriter's task is not made any easier by the differing causes of mitral incompetence that need to be considered, nor by apical systolic murmurs, which are not always typical (e.g. a history of rheumatic fever and an apical systolic murmur that would by all other criteria pass for an insignificant, functional murmur). On the face of it, it seems unfair to assign the latter to a substandard category, yet statistics clearly indicate that it should be.

Certainly it may be possible to deduce some of the non-rheumatic causes of mitral incompetence from other evidence on examination, obvious examples being a history of angina or MI, hypertrophic cardiomyopathy or marked left ventricular hypertrophy and skeletal or ocular manifestations of Marfan's syndrome. In others, however, it may not be so easy, and it is in such cases that one should have recourse to further evidence, particularly echocardiography, which is invaluable in narrowing the differential diagnosis and defining the severity of the lesion.

Selection of Risks

If all apical systolic murmurs were due to mitral incompetence, just as all apical presystolic and mid-diastolic murmurs are due to mitral stenosis, then an underwriter's life would become almost tolerable. Unfortunately that is far from the truth; even a history of rheumatic fever or chorea does not make it certain that an apical systolic murmur is due to mitral incompetence, although the chances of it being so are increased and are further increased if the murmur is the classic pansystolic or holosystolic type.

To obtain a completely homogeneous group containing only people with un-doubted mitral incompetence would entail examination of each applicant by an expert, and would often require special tests such as an echocardiogram. Conse-quently for rating purposes the most practical method of evaluating a risk is to apply the criteria of murmur characteristics, a history or otherwise of etiological significance and heart size for each applicant; in other words, the criteria used in previous studies to assess mortality of insured lives with systolic murmurs.

By this rather non-specific method of selection different classifications will invariably include apical systolic murmurs due to a wide variety of etiologies. Even groups with a history of rheumatic fever will contain a certain number of people whose murmurs are not due to mitral incompetence, as is often presup-posed, but to other lesions, some of a benign nature, either congenital or acquired. A few may be purely functional. This lack of homogeneity is one of the reasons why past studies have shown relatively lighter mortality for groups that by the criteria applied, are assumed to contain only cases of rheumatic mitral incompetence, compared with groups having an apical presystolic and mid-diastolic murmur (i.e. mitral stenosis). This difference in mortality between presumed pure mitral incompetence and pure mitral stenosis is consequently reflected in the ratings for these impairments in most underwriting manuals; it is undoubtedly justified by the method of selection used. However, the experience of clinical cardiologists indicates that there is no substantial difference between the prognosis of pure rheumatic mitral incompetence and that of pure mitral stenosis.

Perhaps another explanation for the apparently lower mortality associated with mitral incompetence is that the systolic murmur of mitral incompetence tends to be constantly present from the date of rheumatic fever. Cases can enter a mortality study having been detected early in the course of the disease when there may still be many years before symptoms begin to appear. In contrast a typical murmur of mitral stenosis cannot normally be heard at rest until several years have elapsed since the attack of rheumatic fever, when the valve becomes sufficiently stenosed, unless it is specially elicited by the usual maneuver of positioning after exercise. Mitral stenotics are therefore generally first recog-nized at a later stage in the development of the disease and would enter a study having only a short number of years to run before the development of symptoms. Therefore the selection and rating of apical systolic murmurs accord-ing to the characteristics and associated history are both practical and appropri-ate to the great majority of applicants for life insurance. However, cases of pure mitral incompetence proven beyond doubt to be such (usually by echocardio-graphy), where the degree of regurgitation is more than slight and a history of rheumatic fever is authentic, should be taken out of the non-specific category and rated similarly to pure mitral stenosis.

Rating

1) Apical systolic murmur; history of rheumatic fever or chorea ten years ago or longer; murmur described as constant, pansystolic or loud (grade 3 out of 6 or louder), or clinically designated as mitral incompetence; no cardiac enlargement, chest X-ray and ECG normal, echocardiogram; normal dimensions, echodoppler; minimal or slight regurgitation and normal exercise tolerance, Class I.

Age	Rating
Under 40	+150
40–49	+100
50–59	+75
60 and over	+50 to +25

2) Apical systolic murmur; no history of rheumatic fever or other history or signs of etiologic significance; primary mitral valve prolapse; criteria otherwise as in (1) above.

Age	Rating
Under 40	+100
40–49	+75
50–59	+50
60 and over	+25

3) Apical systolic murmur, constant, soft (grade 1–2 out of 6); not transmitted; no cardiac enlargement; murmur characteristics equivocal of organic or functional etiology.
With history of rheumatic fever ten years ago or longer:

Age	Rating
Under 40	+75
40–49	+50
50–59	+25
60 and over	Standard

No history of rheumatic fever or other history of signs of etiologic significance, or midsystolic click of mitral valve prolapse without systolic murmur — usually standard to +50.

4) As in (3) but apical systolic murmur constant or inconstant and characteristics consistent with a functional or innocent etiology; no history of rheumatic fever — standard.

5) Pure mitral regurgitation; definitive diagnosis confirmed by special techniques (such as echocardiography), degree of regurgitation mild, normal exercise tolerance or only very slight impairment, chest X-ray normal, ECG minimal

voltage increase, echo dimensions showing left ventricular LVEDD less than 55 mm, Doppler echo mild regurgitation.

History of rheumatic fever ten years ago or longer:

Age	Rating
Under 40	+200
40–49	+150
50–59	+100
60 and over	+75 to +50

No history of rheumatic fever or other history of signs of etiologic significance (e.g. ischemic disease, Marfan's syndrome, primary mitral valve prolapse):

Age	Rating
Under 40	+150
40–49	+100
50–59	+75
60 and over	+50

6) Moderate regurgitation defined as murmur grade 4 out of 6, slightly impaired exercise tolerance up to Class II, slight to moderate cardiac enlargement with cardiothoracic ratio on chest X-ray up to 55 percent; ECG increased voltages and left atrial enlargement; echo LVEDD 55–60 mm; Doppler echo moderate regurgitation.

Age	Rating
Under 40	+300
40–49	+200 to +250
50–59	+150
60 and over	+100

7) Atrial fibrillation: in many instances the presence of atrial fibrillation would warrant declinature, but where an evaluation has to be made the extra risk could be assessed as about half as much again as the ratings indicated above.

8) Rheumatic fever:
Within two years of application — decline.
Within ten years — add +25 to +100 to above ratings according to age group and time elapsed since last attack.

Mitral Valve Prolapse (MVP): Barlow's syndrome

This syndrome, which has received a lot of clinical attention in the last 20 years, continues to be a subject generating debate and controversy in almost all its aspects, including its very name (it is otherwise known as floppy valve syndrome, billowing mitral leaflet syndrome and systolic click-murmur syndrome). There is usually redundancy of mitral valve tissue, the posterior leaflet more commonly involved than the anterior, allowing aneurysmal prolapse of the leaflet into the left atrium during ventricular systole. The basic etiology is possibly due to a mismatch between the mitral valvular apparatus (including valve chordae and papillary muscle) and the systolic size of the left ventricular cavity. MVP may be primary, in that there is no apparent underlying cardiac or systemic disease to account for the prolapse, or it may be secondary to any one of a number of conditions. The association of MVP with thoracic skeletal abnormalities has suggested that a basic connective tissue disorder may affect both mitral valve and thoracic skeletal structures; interestingly, a high incidence of mitral valve prolapse among patients with anorexia nervosa has also been documented. Connective tissue disorders, such as Marfan's and Ehler-Danlos syndromes are associated with MVP and with Downs syndrome in adult patients. MVP may occur in association with some forms of congenital heart disease, particularly atrial septal defect (up to 20 percent), as a sequel of acute rheumatic fever, ischemic heart disease and cardiomyopathies.

In general, primary MVP is asymptomatic and is usually found after the age of 20 during routine physical examination or on examination for some unrelated condition. The incidence in otherwise normal individuals is 5–10 percent and there is a marked increase in frequency of MVP in first-degree relatives, so much that it raises the question of a genetically determined collagen tissue disorder. It used to be thought that many non-specific neurasthenic type symptoms were associated with MVP, including atypical chest pain, premature beats, excessive fatigue and panic attacks, but careful studies of first-degree relatives have shown a similar incidence in groups with and without MVP.

Complications include (1) progressive increase in the degree of mitral regurgitation, (2) infective endocarditis, (3) transient ischemic attacks due to fibrin emboli from the base of the prolapsing valve leaflet, (4) spontaneous rupture of chordae tendineae, (5) various serious dysrhythmias and, rarely, (6) sudden death.

The physical findings of MVP are a high-frequency midsystolic click (occasionally multiple) followed by a late systolic murmur. However, the midsystolic click can occur without the murmur, or vice versa. A pansystolic murmur that crescendos in late systole is very suggestive of MVP. The most important confirmatory diagnostic technique is echocardiography, which can demonstrate unequivocally the prolapse of one or both mitral valve leaflets and the degree of prolapse. The combined use of two-dimensional echocardiography along with Doppler estimates of the degree of mitral regurgitation, can minimize the inappropriately excessive diagnosis of MVP sometimes suggested by single-view (M-mode) echocardiography.

Prognosis
Several long-term retrospective studies of patients with midsystolic clicks and/or late systolic murmurs have been undertaken, and such studies indicate that the

incidence of mortality due directly to MVP is low. Moreover, since these were patients who presumably were referred to medical centers because of symptoms or obvious complications it is likely that mortality among asymptomatic life insurance applicants with MVP and minimal regurgitation would be lower still. These individuals can be treated in a special rating category as indicated (*see* pp. 354–5), although others with significant regurgitation should be rated accordingly. In the long-term prospective study by Duran et al[17] there was an overall death rate of 15 total deaths in 1,830 patient-years of follow-up, similar to that described by Nishamura et al in which there was an eight-year probability of survival of 88 percent, which was not significantly different from that of an age-matched control population. The most important finding from their studies was that patients with redundant, thickened leaflets on echocardiography formed a subgroup with a high incidence of complications of 10 percent, compared with less than 1 percent in those with thin leaflets. The most frequent life-threatening complication seen in patients with MVP is severe mitral regurgitation, and this was reviewed by Wilkin and Hickey from New South Wales, Australia.[18] They calculated the risk for mitral valve surgery in patients with MVP and found there was a minimum cumulative risk below the age of 50 which rose sharply over the age of 50, particularly in men. The risk for women is less than half that for men, which is consistent with the hemodynamic stresses and trauma associated with the male sex and which is important in the etiology of complications that eventually lead to valve repair or replacement.

AORTIC VALVE DISEASE

Aortic valve disease varies widely in etiology, presentation and prognosis. Thus one finds (1) known aortic stenosis of late middle age due to calcific disease affecting valves that are often congenitally abnormal, usually bicuspid, (2) aortic stenosis with moderate or important regurgitation the etiology of which is predominantly rheumatic, and (3) congenital aortic valves usually from cuspal fusion in a bicuspid or tricuspid valve in juveniles. Less often the site of stenosis may be subvalvular or, rarely, supravalvular. Incompetence of the aortic valve with regurgitation results from either intrinsic abnormalities of the aortic valve apparatus itself or disorders of the aortic root. The cusps may be damaged as a result of infective endocarditis, usually on a pre-existing abnormal valve, of rheumatic infection or of traumatic rupture. A high ventricular septal defect can also be associated with a prolapsing valve cusp. Aortic regurgitation arising from aortic root dilatation is commonly idiopathic, particularly in the elderly, although it can be caused by disease processes of the aorta, including cystic medionecrosis with or without Marfan's syndrome, syphilitic aortitis and connective tissue disorders (rheumatoid arthritis, ankylosing spondylitis, Reiter's syndrome), and occasionally by severe hypertension. Aortic regurgitation occurs in about 30 percent of cases of dissection of the ascending aorta, often with associated hypertension.

Lone Aortic Stenosis

Aortic stenosis with no or unimportant regurgitation is predominantly a disease of males. A history of rheumatic fever is unusual, and at autopsy or operation for valve replacement the cusps are almost invariably found to be heavily calcified and immobile with calcification extending into the aortic ring. If the valve is not completely disorganized and the cusps can be identified, most are seen to be congenitally abnormal, either bicuspid or having some other anomalous structure. The resultant altered mobility of these valve cusps presumably causes turbulent flow, with chronic trauma leading to progressive fibrosis and calcification.

Calcific aortic stenosis develops very slowly and can exist for many years without causing disability; this occurs only when the valve becomes narrowed to one-third of its normal aperture ($3 \cdot 0$ cm^2 orifice area). Critical obstruction ensues with increasing hemodynamic effects and symptoms appearing in the form of exertional breathlessness, syncope and angina. The left ventricle shows progressive hypertrophy which may be appreciated clinically as a thrusting apical impulse or on electrocardiography or echocardiography, although the chest X-ray will show little or no overall cardiac enlargement since the hypertrophy is predominantly concentric. The rate of progression of stenosis varies considerably, as shown by serial cardiac catheterization or echodoppler studies, with the majority of patients now presenting with symptoms in older age groups (i.e. with senile aortic stenosis).

The Murmur

The murmur of aortic stenosis is described as ejection or crescendo-decrescendo (diamond shaped) in type and is conducted into the great vessels of the neck. When the blood flow is rapid, there may be a palpable thrill, best appreciated when the patient is leaning forward and in expiration, but when the flow is greatly reduced for any reason the murmur becomes softer and the thrill absent. The murmur is classically described as rough or harsh, but the loudness of the murmur correlates poorly with the degree of severity of aortic stenosis (as occurs in left ventricular failure or in circumstances that alter the conduction of sound, such as pulmonary emphysema and obesity). In severe stenosis the murmur peaks later in systole and extends to the second heart sound; systole itself may be markedly prolonged, producing delayed closure of the aortic valve and paradoxic splitting of the second heart sound and narrowing in inspiration. However, if the valve is markedly immobile the aortic component of the second sound is likely to be inaudible. A fourth heart sound from forceful left atrial contraction is usually present.

Aortic systolic murmurs are often well transmitted to the apex, where they may be as loud or louder than at the aortic area, in which case cessation of the murmur appreciably before the second sound distinguishes it from a mitral regurgitant murmur. During the early stages of development of aortic valve disease, while there is still minimal stenosis, the murmur is soft and may be very difficult to distinguish from a functional ejection murmur. Either murmur may become moderately loud with increased stroke output from emotion, apprehension during medical examination or after exercise, but a functional murmur will tend to peak earlier in systole, whereas an abnormal aortic valve may be inferred from the presence of an accompanying aortic systolic ejection click. It is at this stage of the disease that many applicants with aortic stenosis are seen for life insurance. They will be symptomless, have hearts reputedly of normal size and will have an aortic systolic murmur as the sole sign of a diseased valve. This is the most favorable type of case as far as insurability is concerned, especially at ages under 35 years, for the natural progression of calcific aortic stenosis is slow and the incidence of mortality late, the average age of death in non-surgically treated cases being about 63 years.

In contrast, by the time the classic signs of aortic stenosis have appeared, the valve will be significantly obstructed and symptoms, if not already present, will not be long in appearing. It is doubtful that more than a handful of applicants in this category are insurable. Frank et al[19] studied the natural history of 15 patients who had hemodynamically significant aortic obstruction and in whom the progression of events was uninterrupted by operation. Their age range was 32–59 years at commencement of the study, and the age at onset of symptoms averaged 47 years. They were followed up for 11·7 years or until death. All had abnormal ECGs and all except three had symptoms ranging from functional Class I to III, including some with angina and syncopal attacks. The prognosis was poor, two-thirds being dead at the end of the follow-up period. Mortality, corrected for the number of patients followed, was 36 percent at three years and 52 percent at five years; of those who were followed up for ten years 90 percent had died. The onset of symptoms dramatically alters the course of natural history, with approximately 15 percent of patients dying within five years after the development of angina, 50 percent dying within two years of the development of syncope and 50 percent dying within one to two years after the development of heart failure.

Selection of Risks

The most difficult task facing the life underwriter is to distinguish those aortic systolic murmurs that are purely functional due to a high output state from very similar murmurs due to a minimal aortic valve obstruction or to some congenital anomaly of the valve without obstruction. The distinction has been discussed earlier. In either case there will usually be no symptoms, no cardiac enlargement and no ECG abnormalities, and the MD may decide to classify those atypical murmurs in a lower rating category than aortic systolic murmurs that have some of the more obvious characteristics of aortic stenosis. Many, indeed, can be included in a standard classification if the hemodynamics are consistent with a left ventricular ejection flow murmur, there being no other evidence to suggest aortic valve disease.

When a murmur is described as being typical of aortic stenosis, either because of its loudness or prolonged ejection time or because of a palpable thrill present at the aortic base or over the carotid artery, insurability will depend on the degree of obstruction in the valve. Bearing in mind that this has to be judged on the clinical signs and symptoms elicited during an insurance medical examination, the estimate will be approximate at best. Nevertheless the presence or absence of symptoms can be a valuable guide. Completely symptom-free applicants will have a functional capacity of Class I and will generally be acceptable as substandard risks. The *Medical Impairment Study 1983* showed an overall mortality ratio of 254 percent when the murmur was described as an aortic basal systolic murmur (*see* Table 15.40) and an excess death rate at duration beyond ten years of 15 extra deaths per 1,000. A few applicants having a functional capacity of Class II might be considered borderline but the majority will be declined, as will those with a definite history of angina or syncope.

Another good indication of the degree of aortic valve stenosis is hypertrophy of the left ventricle. Unfortunately the position of the apical impulse on clinical examination is often misleading since concentric left ventricular hypertrophy may be considerable before producing any overall cardiac enlargement, although the character of the impulse is likely to be forceful and thrusting. Likewise, a significant increase in the transverse diameter of the heart on a chext X-ray is a late effect, although the cardiac silhouette is usually abnormal with rounding of the left lower cardiac border. The electrocardiogram is accurate in assessing the severity of stenosis in about three-quarters of patients and for estimating progression by comparing serial tracings, but the absence of electro-cardiographic signs of left ventricular hypertrophy does not exclude severe obstruction. In a study of 49 patients with lone aortic stenosis, Hancock and Fleming[20] showed that in the nine patients judged to have mild aortic stenosis (valve area less than 0.7 cm^2/m^2 body surface area) none had negative T-waves in leads V5 or V6, although most were abnormally low (in the region of 0 to $+2$ mm); in the remainder who were judged to have moderate and severe stenosis the T-waves in V5 and V6 became progressively more negative the greater the mean systolic pressure gradient across the aortic valve. If, therefore, on medical examination any doubt exists about the degree of aortic stenosis, an ECG should be carried out as an additional test. Those shown to have left ventricular hypertrophy, particularly with a negative T-wave in either V5 or V6, should be considered severely impaired or decline risks, depending on the depth of the T-wave inversion.

Echocardiography has become the major form of assessment in patients with aortic stenosis. A non-valvular site of left ventricular outflow obstruction (including hypertrophic cardiomyopathy) will be clearly differentiated, and by determining the velocity flow across the aortic valve with Doppler one can obtain a direct measurement of valve gradient and so calculate the valve area. This follows the natural course of the disease and allows more precise timing of the management of intervention. The degree of calcification, the restriction of movement of the valve cusps, the amount of left ventricular hypertrophy directly measured as wall thickness, along with indices of left ventricular function and the recognition of other cardiac lesions, complete the evaluation.

Rating

The following schedules of ratings are representative of the practice of many life insurance companies both in North America and in Europe. Care should be exercised in assigning an applicant to the 'no cardiac enlargement or hypertrophy' category on clinical signs alone unless they are quite definite. Chest X-ray and ECG are especially desirable, particularly if the clinical signs suggest aortic stenosis of more than modest severity. If there is any doubt, postponement may be necessary until careful evaluation by echocardiography or Doppler has been carried out. Doppler-derived measurements of aortic valve area and pressure gradients correlate well with those of cardiac catheterization and may be more accurate in low output states and coexisting valvular regurgitation.

1) Minimal or slight aortic stenosis, murmur grade 1–2 out of 6, normal exercise tolerance, no cardiac enlargement, chest X-ray and ECG normal. Echo: normal dimensions, Doppler gradient less than 20 mm/Hg.

Age	Rating
Under 40	+150/100
40–49	+75
50–59	+50
60 and over	+25/standard

2) Mild stenosis, murmur grade 2–3 out of 6, normal exercise tolerance, no cardiac enlargement, chest X-ray left ventricular prominence, ECG normal to slight QRS voltage increases in chest leads. Echo: LV thickness less than 1·5 mm; Doppler echo gradient 20–40 mm Hg.

Age	Rating
Under 40	+200 to +150
40–49	+125
50–59	+75
60 and over	+50

3) Moderate aortic stenosis, murmur grade 3–4 out of 6 intensity, normal effort tolerance (perhaps slightly impaired) to slight heart enlargement with cardiothoracic ratio less than 54 percent, ECG mild LVH with normal upright T-waves. Echo: LV thickness 1·5–1·7 mm, Doppler echo gradient 40–60 mm Hg, aortic valve area greater than 0·7 cm^2.

Age	Rating
Under 40	+300 to +200
40–49	+175
50–59	+125
60 and over	+100

4) Severe aortic stenosis, murmur grade 4/6, fourth heart sound, moderate cardiac enlargement, ECG moderate to severe LVH with ST and T-wave changes. Echo: LV thickness more than 1·7 cm, Doppler echo gradient greater than 60 mm Hg with aortic valve area 0·6 cm^2 or less. May still be symptomless, but decline with any cardiac symptoms.

Rheumatic Aortic Stenosis

In contrast with calcific aortic stenosis, the valve cusps in rheumatic aortic stenosis are thickened, contracted and fused at the commissures, showing calcification only later in life. The stenosis so produced is commonly accompanied by an important degree of aortic regurgitation and by clinically detectable mitral valve disease.

The hemodynamic effects of combined aortic stenosis and incompetence will depend on the degree of regurgitation that exists. If substantial, left ventricular hypertrophy will become more apparent clinically than in pure aortic stenosis, and the onset of left ventricular failure will occur earlier. On the other hand, lesser degrees of rheumatic aortic stenosis and incompetence may progress very slowly, the onset of symptoms being delayed for many years. When rheumatic disease of the mitral and/or tricuspid valve coexists with aortic stenosis and incompetence, the long-term prognosis deteriorates significantly. Such multivalvular disease generally would not be an acceptable insurance risk.

Congenital Aortic Stenosis

The main causes of aortic stenosis in infants are congenital fusion of the valve cusps (which are usually bicuspid), subvalvular stenosis of a fixed or discrete nature and, rarely, aortic supravalvular stenosis. When valvular stenosis is severe, intervention by balloon valvuloplasty or open commissurotomy (rarely valve replacement) may be necessary. Localized subaortic stenosis (as distinguished from diffuse muscular subaortic stenosis, now more commonly known as hypertrophic cardiomyopathy) may occur in isolation or in association with other structural heart defects, such as a fibrous shelf or a long fibromuscular narrowing. In the infant this needs further differentiation from other causes of left ventricular outflow tract obstruction, (e.g. malaligned ventricular septal defects). Fixed subaortic stenosis progresses in severity and may present as an acquired condition; only rarely will there be a fixed localized membrane situated 0·5–2 cm below the level of the aortic valve, excision of which possibly allowing for a near-total cure. The anatomic spectrum and nature of progression of fixed aortic stenosis and its recurrence following surgical treatment are reviewed by Choy[22] and Chan.[23]

Many children with a lesser degree of congenital aortic stenosis are not recognized until school age when a typical murmur is discovered by chance on routine examination. Most of these children survive to adult life without requiring surgery, and if they apply for life insurance they should be evaluated by the same criteria as suggested for lone aortic stenosis, with the proviso that the usual clinical symptoms, signs and ECG findings are less reliable for the assessment of severity than in older patients, more reliance needing to be placed on echodoppler studies. As their valves are usually abnormal and mostly of a bicuspid nature, prognosis is essentially that of congenital bicuspid valves in general (see below).

Bicuspid Aortic Valve

A bicuspid aortic valve is the commonest congenital malformation of the heart and occurs in about two in every 100 live births, at least 80 percent being males. It also occurs in over 50 percent of people with coarctation of the aorta. Some of the dangerous complications that this malformed aortic valve can give rise to have been mentioned already, including progressive calcification and obstruction with consequent stenosis or regurgitation. In addition, infective endocarditis and its complications (including cusp damage and aortic root abscesses) give rise to aortic regurgitation.

Until the advent of echocardiography it was possible to recognize the presence, or probable presence, of a bicuspid valve only when it became symptomatic (i.e. when it produced an aortic systolic murmur indicating turbulent flow from varying degrees of aortic stenosis) or when there was a history of infective endocarditis followed by an aortic diastolic murmur, or occasionally when an experienced observer correctly interpreted the significance of an aortic systolic ejection click just following the first heart sound. An ejection sound indicates mobility of the aortic cusps and, when present in a patient with coarctation, usually implies a bicuspid aortic valve, although aortic root dilatation due to hypertension or aneurysm of the ascending aorta are other causes.

The increasing use of echocardiography in screening 'at risk' subjects who have a family history of aortic stenosis or those found to have an equivocal aortic systolic murmur on examination presents life underwriters with an increasing amount of information about such applicants who have been screened in this way. What action should then be taken regarding these symptomless bicuspid aortic valves? The natural history of bicuspid aortic valves indicates that about 25 percent are significantly calcified by the age of 40, rising to 50 percent in the 50–60 age group. The mean age at death due to lone aortic stenosis is in the early 60s, with a wide age spread ranging from the third and fourth decades, when death is due mainly to congenital aortic stenosis, to the late 70s, after which aortic stenosis due to a bicuspid aortic valve becomes increasingly rare.[24] It is evident, therefore, that by no means all people with congenital bicuspid aortic valves die prematurely; in fact, a good number actually exceed their expectation.

Aortic incompetence is a well known complication of infective endocarditis involving a bicuspid valve. The attack incidence of infection is somewhat less than 1 percent, out of which about 10–20 percent will develop regurgitation sufficiently severe to shorten life expectancy. Although there has been a sharp decline in the mortality from endocarditis in recent years,[12] due to improved antimicrobial therapy and a more aggressive surgical approach to patients with resulting heart failure, the mortality and morbidity of patients with this complication remains significant.[25]

The factors that determine whether calcification of the bicuspid valve will occur early in middle life or be delayed until old age have still not been clearly identified. Systemic arterial hypertension appears important, since if the cusps cannot retract completely during systole, altered mobility causes chronic trauma with progressive fibrosis and earlier calcification. Likewise, factors known to predispose to premature arteriosclerosis are likely to hasten calcific degeneration, as seen in familial homozygous hypercholesterolemia.

Rating

There is no clear consensus on whether a bicuspid aortic valve should be rated or not. Many insurers are accepting these valves at standard rates, although a small extra rating of up to +75, equivalent to five to six years off the life span, may be a more realistic estimate.

1) Bicuspid aortic valve found by chance following echocardiography or as a

systolic murmur diagnosed clinically no louder than grade 1 out of 6 and following an ejection click; no factors predisposing to arteriosclerosis.

Age	Rating
Under 40	+50
40 and over	Standard

2) With ratable blood pressure or two or other factors predisposing to arteriosclerosis.

Age	Additional rating[a]
Under 40	+50
40 and over	+25

[a]Add to rating for predisposing factor(s).

3) Murmur louder than grade 2 out of 6. Doppler gradient greater than 10 mm Hg, more obvious signs of aortic valve disease (e.g. aortic diastolic murmur) — rate as aortic stenosis or aortic regurgitation.

Aortic Valve Incompetence: Aortic Regurgitation

The late prognosis of aortic incompetence depends not only on the degree of regurgitation with resulting left ventricular hypertrophy and dilatation but also on whether the defect lies in the valve itself or in the valve ring. In general, aortic incompetence due to dilatation of the aortic ring has a worse prognosis because of the etiological factors involved, such as Marfan's syndrome and syphilitic aortitis, whereas minimal aortic incompetence of rheumatic etiology is a relatively benign lesion[26] compatible with a near-normal expectation of life if subacute infective endocarditis and further attacks of active rheumatism can be avoided.

Moderate or marked aortic incompetence, however, has an adverse hemodynamic effect on the left ventricle, which progressively hypertrophies and dilates to compensate for the increased workload that it has to bear. Even when the heart is considerably enlarged, symptoms may be few and exercise tolerance may remain surprisingly good up to the onset of left ventricular impairment/failure, which usually marks a rapid and progressive path towards complete functional disability. A diastolic murmur may occur at the onset of rheumatic fever, and after approximately ten years regurgitation usually becomes hemodynamically significant but well tolerated for periods averaging 10–30 years. Significant symptoms of left ventricular failure then appear, followed by further deterioration over three to ten years. The average duration of rheumatic aortic incompetence from time of onset to death varies from 20 to 30 years.

Selection of Risks

When reporting on an applicant with aortic incompetence the following points are important to the life underwriter in his evaluation of the risk:

1) *Etiology*. When there is no history of rheumatic fever is there any historical indication of other etiology?

2) *Other valve lesions*. When the etiology is rheumatic, coexistent mitral stenosis or incompetence is not uncommon, but care should be taken not to misinterpret a rumbling mid-diastolic Austin-Flint murmur at the apex as mitral stenosis. The former may be distinguished from mitral stenosis by the absence of a presystolic murmur and the fact that the first heart sound is soft rather than accentuated. Also, an aortic ejection systolic murmur audible at the apex should not be confused with rheumatic mitral incompetence.

3) *Left ventricular hypertrophy*. The presence or absence of left ventricular hypertrophy considerably affects the insurability of an applicant with aortic incompetence, and an estimation of overall heart size should be made as accurately as possible by the usual clinical methods. As always, confirmation is desirable by chest X-ray and ECG.

4) *Degree of regurgitation*. This is judged by the dynamics of the peripheral circulation. Forceful large volume arterial systolic pulsation may be noted as well as various signs, including visible capillary pulsation, a 'collapsing' pulse (Corrigan's pulse) and a biphasic femoral bruit heard during mild compression of the artery with a stethoscope (Duroziez's sign) indicating moderate to severe aortic incompetence. For underwriting purposes the best index of degree of aortic reflux is the pulse pressure. [Pulse pressure = diastolic blood pressure taken at fourth phase (muffling or change of sound) subtracted from the systolic blood pressure]. Some life insurance companies use a pulse pressure of 70 mm Hg as the dividing line between moderate and severe regurgitation; others use a pulse pressure of one-half the systolic blood pressure as the critical level. The latter method has the advantage of eliminating false high pulse pressures due to associated hypertension, although the pulse pressure may not reflect the severity of aortic regurgitation in young patients with compliant vessels.

5) *Investigative findings*. An electrocardiographic pattern of left ventricular 'strain' with ST-T repolarization changes usually implies severe chronic aortic regurgitation, recognized as a risk factor for poorer outcome. In mild aortic regurgitation the ECG may be completely normal, but as the severity of regurgitation increases, there is concomitant increase in cardiac enlargement, usually accurately reflected in the chest X-ray. Doppler echocardiography is more sensitive than auscultation in diagnosing the presence of aortic regurgitation, and pulmonary regurgitation can be differentiated with this technique, as can the murmurs of mitral stenosis and aortic regurgitation. The echocardiogram shows structural abnormalities of the aortic valve and changes in the aortic root, including, vegetations of infective endocarditis or dissection of the ascending aorta. It is becoming increasingly useful in evaluating ventricular function with measurements of wall thickness, left ventricular diameter in diastole and systole, and calculated EF or percentage fractional shortening, which may help in the difficult problem of optimal timing for aortic valve replacement before irreversible left ventricular dysfunction prevents a good long-term postoperative result. Earlier

studies have suggested that this stage might be reached when echocardiographic measurement of systolic left ventricular dimensions exceeds 55 mm with fractional shortening less than 25 percent, an EF less than 0·45 or failure of the EF to increase on exercise. However, the onset of symptoms usually represents a reasonably good guide to the timing of operative intervention.

Rating

Aortic incompetence, pure or predominant or of important degree when combined with aortic stenosis: no rheumatic fever within ten years.

1) Minimal or trivial regurgitation; sole lesion; symptomless; no cardiac enlargement; pulse pressure less than 50 percent of systolic blood pressure or pulse pressure less than 70 mm Hg; normal ECG. Echo: LVEDD less than 45 mm. Doppler echo: minimal regurgitation.

Age	Rating
Under 40	+100
40–49	+75
50–59	+50
60 and over	+25 to standard

2) Mild regurgitation; normal exercise tolerance, pulse pressure less than 50 percent of systolic blood pressure or less than 70 mm Hg; borderline cardiac enlargement; cardiothoracic ratio on chest X-ray less than 52 percent. ECG normal. Echo: LVEDD less than 55 mm. Doppler echo: mild regurgitation.

Age	Rating
Under 40	+150
40–49	+100
50–59	+75
60 and over	+50

3) Moderate regurgitation. Symptomless (functional capacity Class I); pulse pressure ± 70 mm Hg; slight cardiac enlargement with cardiothoracic ratio less than 55 percent. ECG increased voltages but normal T-waves. Echo: LVEDD up to 55 mm. Doppler Echo: moderate regurgitation.

Age	Rating
Under 40	+200
40–49	+150
50–59	+100
60 and over	+75

4) Severe regurgitation. Symptomless (functional capacity Class I); pulse pressure greater than 70 mm Hg; mild to moderate cardiac enlargement with cariothoracic ratio less than 58 percent; ECG increased voltages; Echo LVEDD 55–60 mm; Doppler echo: moderate to marked regurgitation.

Age	Rating
Under 40	+300 up
40–49	+250
50–59	+150
60 and over	+100

T-wave in V5 and V6 inverted 1 mm or deeper — decline.

5) Aortic incompetence due to Marfan's syndrome — usually decline.
Syphilitic aortitis — add +50 to the above ratings provided that syphilis has been adequately treated and is considered cured.

6) Significant lesions affecting other valves (excluding aortic stenosis) — individual consideration.

7) Active rheumatic infection within two to ten years of application — add +100 to +25 to the above ratings according to year of infection and age group.

8) With operation — as for aortic valve surgery (see pp. 384–5).

Tricuspid valve disease

Isolated tricuspid valve disease is uncommon but may occur as a congenital abnormality in Ebstein's anomaly (see pp. 403–4), in valve prolapse or occasionally following trauma, or with clefts in the valve with associated atrioventricular canal defects. When tricuspid valve disease results from the rheumatic process, left-sided valvular involvement, usually mitral, is present, and the clinical course and outcome will be largely dependent on the severity of the left heart lesions.

CARDIAC SURGERY

Before considering the prognosis and risk evaluation of the individual heart and valve lesions following surgical correction, it is necessary to make some general observations on the factors that have a bearing on the prognosis of the postsurgical heart.

Since the first successful correction of patent ductus arteriosus in 1938 and of coarctation of the aorta in 1945, surgical treatment of heart and great vessel disorders has progressed rapidly, and now even complex abnormalities can be tackled with complete success. Today there are few people with significant disability due to acquired or congenital heart disease who cannot be offered surgical treatment with the prospect of considerable relief of symptoms and, in many cases, complete cure with reversion to a normal expectation of life. It is not surprising, therefore, that the number of applicants for life insurance with postsurgical hearts is increasing each year, and opinions on their eligibility have had to be revised drastically from those held only a few years ago.

Non-surgical interventional techniques have increased dramatically in the last few years; physicians and radiologists gained experience from coronary percutaneous transluminal angioplasty following the first clinical application by Gruntzig in 1977, which followed the first balloon atrial septostomy for transposition of the great vessels by Rashkind in 1966. Hubner[27] has reviewed cardiac interventional procedures carried out in the UK in 1989; during that year there was a very marked increase in the number of balloon dilatations of valves in adults (see Table 15.43). Table 15.43 reflects the still early learning curve in the UK, as shown by the small numbers involved and the death rate of 3·6 percent for mitral valve dilatation in 112 cases; 22 coarctations of the aorta were dilated with no deaths. The UK operation rate for coronary percutaneous angioplasty was 126 per million population in 1989, markedly less than for most other countries in Europe; the corresponding rate for the US was 1,028 per million. Pediatric interventional procedures are detailed on

Table 15.43. Balloon dilatation of valves in adults in the UK in 1989.

Type	Units	Number	Deaths	Complications
Pulmonary	11	14	0	0
Aortic	18	83	5 (6%)	1
Mitral	16	112	4 (3·6%)	8
Coarctation of aorta	5	22	0	1
Miscellaneous	4	4	0	0

Table 15.44. Pediatric interventional procedures in the UK in 1989.

Procedure	Units	Number	Death	Complications
Pulmonary valve dilatation	17	212	1	3
Aortic valve dilatation	12	78	1	0
Coarctation of aorta	11	105	0	1
Closure of ductus arteriosus	10	115	0	2
Mustard conduit dilatation	8	15	0	0
Pulmonary artery or branch dilatation	8	22	0	0
Fallot's tetralogy dilatation	3	30	1	0
Shunt dilatation	3	2	0	0
Blade septostomy	5	8	0	0
Embolization	4	11	0	0
Miscellaneous	3	12	0	0

Table 15.44. Witness the number and range of procedures carried out at low mortality and morbidity. For the insurer the outcome of these interventional procedures can be assessed in a similar manner to those following cardiac surgery.

Prognosis

For those who survive operations the immediate prognosis is very favorable and is becoming even more so. There are many reports of ten- to 15-year follow-ups, with occasionally 20–25-year-old follow-up periods after initial valve replacement in the early 1960s, but long-term outcome still remains difficult to assess, particularly with the introduction of newer prosthetic valves and grafts. The expectation of life for patients treated with the more recently produced valves is likely to be better than for those who have had earlier types of prosthesis inserted, and the same can be said about inadequate surgical corrections in the past compared with the improved techniques of the present. In general, the more recent the cardiac surgery the better the prognosis is likely to be.

The life insurer, however, needs more definite guidelines to assist the selection of risks in this most difficult area of underwriting. A useful classification of what ought to be the late prognosis of various surgically treated heart lesions from a technical point of view was given by Schumaker.[28] A condensed and rearranged version of this classification has been produced below and includes the more common postsurgical heart and vascular disorders encountered in underwriting. Schumaker defined five categories according to the probable expectation of life. These range from the excellent, where there is no reason to believe that the normal life span should not be attained, to the comparatively poor, with expectation of life unknown but obviously compromised.

Category A
Excellent prognosis for normal expectation; mainly single abnormalities where complete repair is possible leaving no recognizable cardiovascular defects.

Patent ductus arteriosus
Ventricular septal defect
Atrial septal defect (secundum) } Complete repair, normal pressures
Partial anomalous venous return
Isolated infundibular stenosis
Recurrent non-specific (acute benign) pericarditis treated by subtotal peri-
    cardectomy

Category B
Very good prospects of achieving normal expectation. Simple defects repaired with some remaining abnormality of a minor nature.
Pulmonary valve stenosis
Aortopulmonary window
Isolated pulmonary arteriovenous fistula treated by lobectomy
Traumatic aneurysm of thoracic aorta

Category C
Prospects for longevity good; defects incompletely corrected but compatible with

normal activity and good health. Complex lesions; complete repair with no known residual functional impairment. Abnormalities in a high pressure circuit repaired with synthetic materials believed to maintain their strength indefinitely.

Atrial septal defect
Ventricular septal defect } With small residual defect, normal pressures
Ruptured aneurysm of the sinus of Valsalva
Coarctation of aorta
Tetralogy of Fallot
Constrictive pericarditis treated by subtotal pericardectomy
Coronary artery fistula, physiologic repair

Category D
Variable prognosis; some may have reasonably good prospects of longevity, others have disastrous complications.

Mitral stenosis
Congenital aortic stenosis } Treated by valvotomy
Congenital subaortic diaphragmatic stenosis
Mitral stenosis and/or mitral incompetence } Treated by valve replacement
Aortic stenosis or aortic incompetence
Pulmonary arteriovenous fistulas in more than one lobe
Total anomalous pulmonary venous return
Ischemic heart disease treated by aortocoronary bypass

Category E
Comparatively poor prognosis; disorders treated palliatively. Complex lesions whose long-term follow-up is not known. Disorders which, though treated effectively from the point of view of alleviating symptoms, are basically progressive or are associated with progressive cardiovascular disease.

Tricuspid atresia
Truncus arteriosus
Transposition of the great vessels
Atrial septal defect
Ventricular septal defect
Patent ductus arteriosus } With marked residual pulmonary hypertension
Aortopulmonary window
Dissecting aneurysm of thoracic aorta
Arteriosclerotic aneurysm of thoracic aorta
Cardiac transplantation

Other Prognostic Factors

It is obvious from what has been said that the late prognosis of postoperative hearts depends on more than just repairing structural defects. The whole conduct of the surgical procedure has a bearing not just on the perioperative results but on the late results as well. Therefore the diligence of preoperative preparation, anesthesia, whole body perfusion and myocardial protection, and the individual skill of the surgical operative and postoperative care in minimizing complications will all contribute to the overall results. Previously such results were only available from the more academic units in the published literature, but the process of medical audit (extending to all fields of medical/surgical intervention) will make such results more widely available in the future.

Pulmonary vascular disease (whether it arises from high pressure shunts, passively from pulmonary venous hypertension secondary to a raised left atrial pressure as in mitral disease or from primary lung disease and its subsequent secondary effects on right-sided heart structures) will be considered separately, as will the functional status of the left ventricle and the degree to which changes of dilatation and hypertrophy may regress after successful functional repair of acquired or congenital defects.

Heart Valve Replacement

The first prosthetic heart valves became generally available in 1962. Since then, continuing changes have been made in the design of these prostheses, usually with improvement in quality, although not all have stood the test of time. Also, improved intraoperative techniques, particularly with myocardial preservation and gentle handling of tissues and postoperative management, have resulted in a striking decrease in both early and late mortality. Nevertheless there is still no ideal valve substitute available, and the combined goals of freedom from thrombogenicity, long-term wear and hemodynamic restriction have not yet been obtained in a single valve. However, in the past decade it is the non-valve prostheses-related factors (patient factors) that have assumed an increasing importance in determining late survival following valve replacement.

Types of Valve

Prosthetic valves may be classified according to the origin of their material components (e.g. mechanical or tissue valves) and their mode of functioning (e.g. central flow valves, lateral flow valves or semi-central flow valves). The commonly used mechanical valve includes the cage ball valve variety (Starr-Edwards), the original model first implanted in 1960 and which has proven durability. It has lateral flow with some hemodynamic restriction and, like all mechanical valves, requires continuous anticoagulation. The current incidence of thromboembolism averages 1–2 percent, being higher in the initial five years and declining thereafter.

Tilting-disk valves, particularly of the bileaflet variety, which have central flow characteristics, are increasing in popularity. An example is the St Jude valve, first implanted in 1977, which has proven durability for more than ten years, has hemodynamics equal to or better than the single disk valves and a lower thromboembolism rate suggesting that less intense anticoagulation can be considered, particularly in the aortic site. Other tilting-disk type valves with a semi-central flow characteristic include the Omni-science valve, the Medtronic Hall valve and the Bjork-Shiley valve. Certain valves of the Bjork-Shiley type, namely the convexo-concave, have shown an increased incidence of strut fracture, with catastrophic valve failure estimated to be 0·295 percent per annum in valves implanted between 1976 and 1986.

The overall risk is greater in patients with a large mitral prosthesis and in younger patients. Treasure[29] discusses the management of such patients and argues against widescale elective replacement of all such valves, citing the risk of death with reoperation on the mitral valve of 16 percent of 206 cases operated on in UK units in 1989, and aortic valve re-replacement risk increasing from 4 percent for the primary operation to nearly 9 percent. Although these high figures are for clinically indicated reoperations (including patients with catastrophic states), such as endocarditis and sudden valve failure, more recent figures from Holland indicate that high-risk categories could benefit from elective reoperation.

Tissue valves were promoted to avoid the thrombogenic tendency of mechanical valves; they are of a semi-lunar design mimicking the aortic valve and are therefore of a central flow type. There is some limitation of hemodynamics, particularly with the smaller valves; examples include the heterograft (porcine) aortic valve (e.g. Hancock and Carpentier-Edwards) and the homograft aortic valve. Although tissue valves do not require anticoagulation, they are more prone to infection and later deterioration necessitating reoperation; in one series ten years postoperatively, 71 percent of patients were free of valve degeneration, but by 15 years only 31 percent were free of structural failure. The present practice of heart valve surgery in the UK was summarized by Taylor[30] in 1991 utilizing experience from the UK Cardiac Surgical Register. Approximately 5 thousand artificial valves are implanted each year in the UK, and this figure has remained remarkably stable since 1977; single valves make up 90 percent of implants, double valves 10 percent and triple valves less than 0·2 percent. Aortic valve replacement accounts for more than 60 percent of procedures, mitral valve replacement 40 percent and tricuspid less than 1 percent. The reduction in rheumatic etiology has been balanced by an increase in degenerative valve disease, with an increasing proportion at the aortic site.

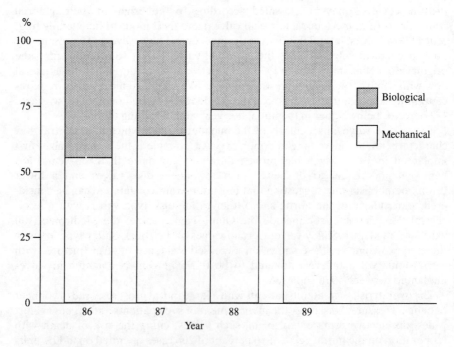

Fig. 15.2. Percentage use of biological and mechanical heart valve prostheses in the UK (1986–89) (data from United Kingdom Heart Valve Registry).

There is a trend towards using mechanical valves and away from using bioprosthetic tissue valves (*see* Fig. 15.2), homograft valves now accounting for less than 1 percent of total implants. Figure 15.3 shows the types of mechanical heart valve prostheses in use and the increasing percentage of bileaflet valves. These trends are similar to those seen in the USA. The proportion of operations for heart valve replacement is increasing in older age groups, reaching 37 percent in people over 65 years of age in 1989, with 60 percent of replacements being for the aortic valve. This trend is likely to continue, as is the trend towards conservative valve surgery, particularly mitral repair, as surgeons gain more experience.

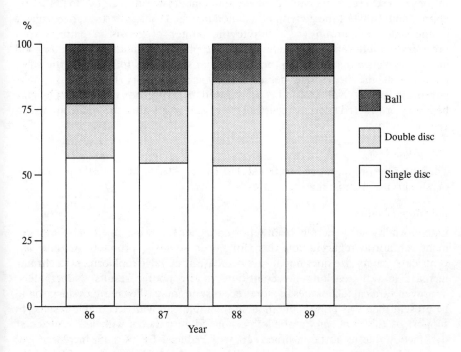

Fig. 15.3. Percentage use of main types of mechanical heart valve prostheses in the UK (1986–89) (data from United Kingdom Heart Valve Registry).

There have been few prospective randomized clinical trials comparing mechanical and tissue valves. Bloomfield et al[31] reported a 12-year comparison of Bjork-Shiley valves with porcine bioprostheses following an analysis of 541 patients who underwent valve replacement from 1975 to 1979. There was an overall 8·2 percent early hospital death rate and an improved actuarial survival after 12 years with the Bjork-Shiley mechanical prostheses compared with tissue valves, although this was not statistically significant. The group with the Bjork-Shiley valve had an overall 12-year patient survival of 51·5 percent versus 44·4 percent with the tissue valve, the Bjork-Shiley valve carrying an attendant increased risk of bleeding associated with the need for anticoagulant prophylaxis. Their conclusions were echoed by those of Collins,[32] writing in the same journal, who recommended that patients should generally receive a mechanical valve, particularly in the mitral area, although porcine valves may be considered for elderly patients whose life expectancy may not exceed that of the prosthesis used.

Factors Affecting Prognosis

Left Ventricular Dysfunction

Secondary changes in the left ventricle as a result of long-standing aortic valve disease are one of the major determinants of early and late mortality after aortic valve replacement. However, when aortic valve replacement is performed prior to the onset of severe, irreversible cardiac enlargement late survival (five to ten years) approximates that of the general population matched for age and sex, particularly in the older age groups.[33,34] Despite the poorer prognosis in patients with preoperative left ventricular failure, hypertrophy or dysfunction, there is good indirect evidence that if during the first four to six months following aortic valve replacement the heart size decreases, myocardial injury may reverse, thus improving late survival. Monrad et al[35] showed that regression of hypertrophy may be a very protracted process occurring over many years after the reduction in left ventricular load.

Functional Class

The better the preoperative functional class (*see* p. 349) the higher is the percentage of late survival in most reported series.

Functional Lesion

Late mortality has generally been reported higher following aortic valve replacement for aortic regurgitation than for aortic stenosis, probably because left ventricular cavity size does not always decrease after valve replacement; a chronic increase in wall tension may contribute to the poorer results. Nonetheless, improved surgical techniques in more recent series may allow more dysfunction to be present than was reasonably thought tolerable, yet with acceptable results. In support of this concept Carabello[36] examined 14 patients with left ventricular dysfunction due to aortic insufficiency, with reduced EF of 0·45, increased end systolic dimension 57 mm and reduced average shortening fraction of 0·23 with average end systolic volume index 111 mm/m^2; 12 of these 14 patients had marked symptomatic improvement and an increase of EF into the normal range when examined nearly two years after surgery. Similar results were reported by Taniguchi,[37] where survival was 92 percent at 6·5 years postoperatively when the end systolic volume index was less than 200 mm/m^2 but only 51 percent when the end systolic volume index exceeded 200 mm/m^2. However, Copeland et al[38] found that the difference between survival of patients with aortic regurgitation and those with aortic stenosis was primarily due to early postoperative deaths alone. After the first 30 postoperative days, survival curves for these patient groups were approximately parallel; therefore long-term survival rates were nearly identical. Kinsley[33] concurs with these findings; 93 percent of his patients with aortic stenosis and 91 percent with aortic regurgitation were alive at five years.

Associated CAD

The deleterious effects of associated CAD on survival have been well established, and it is now the practice to perform coronary artery bypass grafting when necessary in addition to aortic valve replacement. However, the late results of aortic valve replacement and coronary artery bypass grafting are inferior to those of aortic valve replacement alone. Malm and Bale[39] reported on a study of 632 patients who received porcine valve replacements at the Columbia Presbyterian Hospital between September 1974 and December 1979 followed through to August 1980. The series was divided into two groups: those who had aortic or mitral valve replacement or both, and those who had valve replacement along with some additional procedure (usually coronary artery bypass grafting). Of the 485 patients who had simple valve replacement without any associated procedure, 49 (10 percent) died during the period of the study; of 140 patients who had valve replacement together with associated procedures 19 (13·6 percent) died.

Using the data of Malm and Bale,[39] Robinson[40] made an estimate of the mortality ratios to be expected for the group who had simple replacement of the aortic and/or mitral valves without additional procedures. This was approximate because the age distribution of death was not given, but 77 percent of the replacements were carried out between the ages of 50 and 77, with a peak at ages 60–64. Assuming the patients were all aged 60 at the time of operation, with 101 deaths per 1,000 over the five-year period the cumulative mortality ratio would approximate 225 percent; if they were all aged 50 it would approximate 400 percent.

There was a high proportion of deaths in the first 12 months after operation, and since it is usual life insurance practice to postpone acceptance of intracardiac surgery cases until after the first post-operative year, a more realistic assessment of the risk can be made. After one year there were 54 deaths per 1,000 over the following five years. Assuming the patients were all aged 60 at the time of operation, the cumulative mortality ratio would approximate 125 percent; if they were all aged 50 it would be approximately 250 percent. Intermediate values of mortality ratios can be similarly calculated.

Czer et al[41] reported the results of aortic valve surgery in 474 patients; in the group of 185 patients with no associated coronary disease the operative mortality waas 2·2 percent but increased significantly to 8·2 percent in the group with coronary disease who did not undergo bypass surgery, and to 7·1 percent in the group with coronary disease who did undergo surgery. After ten years of follow-up, patients without coronary disease had a much higher survival (77 percent ± 4 percent) than patients with coronary disease who had bypass surgery (41 percent ± 6 percent) or patients who had coronary disease and did not have bypass (26 percent ± 11 percent). Although the trend favored higher survival for those patients who had coronary disease and bypass surgery, the difference was not statistically significant. A similar trend was commented on by a UK group, Schofield et al,[42] indicating from their more recent series operative mortality of 3 percent for isolated aortic valve disease, 8 percent for the group who underwent coronary artery bypass grafting in addition, and 13 percent for those who had coronary disease but did not undergo grafting. After three years, survival in the isolated aortic valve group was 83 percent, 76 percent for the group who had the additional procedure of coronary artery bypass grafting and 62 percent in those with coronary disease but without grafting.

Operative Mortality

Results of surgery for valve replacement have continued to improve since it began in the early 1960s, in part due to better myocardial protection from the late 1970s onwards. Composite figures from many different institutions tend to give higher mortality figures than those of individual institutions, and include figures for emergency operations, reoperations, patients in a poor functional class, those with poor left ventricular function and with concomitant CAD. Monro et al[43] reported overall mortality of 4·7 percent for valve replacement procedures (3 percent for single valve elective procedures, 3 percent for isolated valve procedures, 4 percent for double valve procedures) against a 1·3 percent early mortality for coronary artery bypass grafting. Scully,[44] reviewing the prognosis of valve replacement in 1986, reported the overall risk of aortic valve surgery as 2–4 percent, of isolated mitral valve replacement as 4–8 percent and of aortic and mitral valve replacement as 8–12 percent, with concomitant coronary artery grafting increasing the risk to 8–10 percent. Butchart,[45] reviewing surgery for heart valve disease in 1990, indicated that most units now achieve a hospital mortality of less than 1 percent for elective isolated aortic valve replacement and less than 4 percent for elective isolated mitral valve replacement, providing the etiology for mitral valve disease is not ischemic. These later figures are a considerable improvement on those summarized in *Medical Risks*,[2] where the most recent series is that from 1977 to 1982 when operative mortality for mitral valve replacement was 8·8 percent and aortic valve 5·4 percent. It should be noted that there are now clear guidelines for the reporting of morbidity and mortality after cardiac valvular operations.[46] They are designed to facilitate comparisons between the experiences of different surgeons who treat different cohorts of patients at different times with different techniques and materials. Hospital mortality is defined as death from any cause during or after operation within 30 days, with morbidity including structural deterioration and non-structural dysfunction, thromboembolism, anticoagulant related hemorrhage and prosthetic valve endocarditis.

Late Mortality

Late mortality results for individual aortic and mitral valve surgery will be discussed in relation to their ratings (*see* pp. 383, 384–5). The series from Starr's group in Oregon[47] gives a ten-year survival for isolated aortic and mitral valve replacement of 56 percent with 45 percent for double valve replacement, and at 15 years near identical aortic and mitral valve survivals of 44 percent and 43 percent. Allowing for a 10 percent early mortality, this still gives an average annual mortality of approximately 3 percent per year. A large series reported from Sweden by Lindblom et al[48] of 2,805 patients who underwent aortic and/or mitral valve replacement between 1969 and 1983 had an overall ten-year survival rate of 63 percent against the expected rate of 87 percent, confirming the better survival for aortic as opposed to mitral valve replacement and better long-term results for those with stenosis rather than regurgitation. They also reported a 57 percent survival for double valve replacement; elderly patients with aortic stenosis achieved a near normalized survival pattern.

Results from the Wessex Cardiac Unit in Southampton, England, discussed by Monro,[49] showed a 72 percent ten-year survival for all valve replacement procedures for 1,650 patients operated on between 1972 and 1982. There was an early one-year overall mortality of 10 percent which might equate to an annual death rate of 2 percent per year, but this included patients who had coronary artery bypass grafting, emergency valve operations, multiple valve replacements, valve repair and ascending aortic replacement.

There is little published evidence from insurance companies on their claims experience in relation to valve replacement surgery. Croxson and Tyler in their presentation to the 1989 COINTRA Symposium[50] detailed the preliminary results from the Mercantile and General Reinsurance Company from the period July 1983 to July 1988 (see Tables 15.45 and 15.46). During this period 3,062 cases for which valve-related disorder was the main or sole impairment were considered; this included 1,023 who had valve replacement surgery. Reflecting in part the high premiums for such substandard business, only 654 policies were subsequently issued with valvular disease as the primary diagnosis; this included 230 valve replacements and 23 open valve repair operations. Of the 654 policies for operated and non-operated valve disease, there were 35 claims giving an observed-to-expected mortality ratio of 84 percent in the first year and 103 percent in the second year.

There were eight aortic open valve repairs and 15 open mitral valve repairs with no death claims. Analyses were by policies issued rather than lives and are summarized in Tables 15.45 and 15.46. For aortic valve replacement there were 130 policies with 11 claims, three claims being policies from the one patient; for mitral valve replacement there were 100 policies issued with three claims. Review of the four claims in the aortic valve replacement category revealed that three had additional factors that with hindsight could have persuaded the underwriter to make a worse prognosis: one had mild aortic regurgitation postoperatively with impaired exercise tolerance requiring diuretics; a second had an ascending aortic graft replacement and a mitral valve patch for infective endocarditis; the third required antihypertensive treatment at the time of policy issue with a statement of moderate cardiac enlargement, the ECG being suggestive of an old inferior wall infarct. Five of the 12 death claims had MI and CAD given as the main cause of death, and in only three of the cases was death directly attributed to valve failure.

Rating
Suggested ratings for mitral and aortic valve surgery can be found elsewhere (see pp. 383, 384–5).

Mitral Valve Disease

Pure Mitral Stenosis
Pure mitral stenosis with no or trivial regurgitation usually implies a valve that is supple and undistorted (suspected clinically and confirmed by Doppler echocardiography) and therefore amenable to commissurotomy either by closed valvotomy or open repair (utilizing heart/lung bypass) or by transcatheter balloon valvuloplasty. Valvotomy affords excellent relief of symptoms at a low (operative) mortality. An optimum functional result and excellent long-term prognosis can be expected

Table 15.45. Aortic valve replacement, preliminary results, Mercantile and General Reinsurance Company, July 1983 to July 1988.[a]

	Uncomplicated		Complicated	
	Number of cases	Number of claims	Number of cases	Number of claims
Aortic valve prosthesis (118 cases)				
Operation within 5 yr	27	1	34	4
Operation within 5–10 yr	13	3	29	3
Thereafter	4	–	11	–
Total	44	4	74	7
Aortic bioprosthetic valve (tissue) (12 cases)				
Operation within 5 yr	3	–	2	–
Operation within 5–10 yr	1	–	3	–
Thereafter	–	–	3	–
Total	4	–	8	–

[a] Source: Croxson and Tyler.[50]

Table 15.46. Mitral valve replacement, preliminary results, Mercantile and General Reinsurance Company, July 1983 to July 1988. [a]

	Uncomplicated		Complicated	
	Number of cases	Number of claims	Number of cases	Numbers of claims
Mitral valve prosthesis (mechanical) (89 cases)				
Operation within 5 yr	10	—	31	3
Operation within 5–10 yr	12	—	24	—
Thereafter	4	—	8	—
Total	26	—	63	3
Mitral bioprosthetic tissue valves (11 cases)				
Operation within 5 yr	1	—	5	—
Operation within 5–10 yr	2	—	3	—
Thereafter	—	—	—	—
Total	3	—	8	—

[a]Source: Croxson and Tyler.[50]

under the following conditions: when the heart is small; when there is no calcification of the valve; when there is no significant subvalvar fusion; when valvotomy is complete, leaving no or trivial incompetence; when the cardiac rhythm is regular; and when there is no other valve lesion. For best cases operative mortality is now less than 1 percent; over a ten-year period a survival rate of 90 percent can be expected, compared with a survival rate of 95 percent from the general population of similar age and sex composition.[51]

Turi et al[52] described a prospective randomized trial comparing commissurotomy by balloon valvuloplasty with surgical closed valvotomy in 40 patients with severe rheumatic mitral stenosis; there were no deaths, strokes or MIs and one case of severe mitral regurgitation occurred in each group. At eight-month follow-up, improvement had occurred in both groups with mitral valve area $1\cdot6$ cm^2 in the balloon group and $1\cdot8$ cm^2 in the surgical group, and the authors concluded that valvulotomy by balloon valvuloplasty and surgically closed valvotomy resulted in comparable hemodynamic improvement sustained through eight months of follow up, the likelihood being that there would be equivalent long-term results. An interesting side issue was that cost analysis revealed that balloon valvuloplasty may substantially exceed the cost of closed surgical valvotomy in developing countries, whereas it may represent significant savings in industrialized nations. Providing the institution performing the balloon valvuloplasty had a low prevalence of untoward events this would be the initial procedure of choice for patients with important mitral stenosis with mobile leaflets and minimal chordal thickening.[53] In a combined experience reported from the National Heart, Lung and Blood Institute Balloon Valvuloplasty Registry some 24 co-operating centers with 738 patients reported a 30-day follow-up in which 3 percent had died, 4 percent had required mitral valve surgery and 83 percent had their overall condition improved.

Factors influencing late prognosis after closed mitral valvotomy are likely to be similar to those after balloon valvotomy and are discussed below.

Atrial Fibrillation

When this persists after valvotomy it is associated with a moderate reduction in percentage survival compared with a similar group with regular rhythm. When all other criteria, including optimum survival, were present in a group who were fibrillating, the ten-year survival rate in the study reported by Ellis and Harken[54] became 78 percent compared with 90 percent in the group who were not.

The *1979 Atrial Fibrillation Mortality Study (see* Table 15.32) confirms the heavy mortality in mitral stenosis accompanied by atrial fibrillation. Mortality is likely to be no less heavy when atrial fibrillation persists after valvotomy. Similarly, mortality in those with a history of temporary or intermittent atrial fibrillation immediately prior to mitral valvotomy, but remaining in sinus rhythm thereafter, is still likely to be significantly higher than in those who have never fibrillated.

Embolisation

There is no evidence to suggest that valvotomy will decrease the threat of thromboembolism if it occurred preoperatively, although it is reasonable to believe the tendency will be reduced. Fatal pulmonary and peripheral embolism is a continuing risk in established fibrillation, particularly in the presence of a large left atrium; anticoagulation is mandatory. Even after a good valvotomy with sinus rhythm, there is a low but not insignificant incidence of late embolisation, presumably due to the ultimate development of atrial fibrillation as the age of the group increases.

Calcification

Calcification of the mitral valve at the time of operation and the subsequent development of moderate-to-severe regurgitation are both major adverse factors indicating a poorer long-term prognosis after closed mitral valvotomy.

Restenosis

This condition still remains a problem even after a good interventional result; the incidence is highest when valvotomy has been inadequate, often because the valve is calcified and there is subvalvar chordal fusion. The number of patients requiring a second intervention increases sharply with the passage of time, being about 5 percent after five years, rising to 20 percent after nine years. Moreover, although some of these patients could have a second balloon or closed valvotomy, most will require direct open heart surgery with an increase in frequency of valve replacement as second option, thus being exposed to the further hazard of substantial operative mortality associated with this technique.

Preoperative Functional Capacity

There is an optimum point during the stages of increasing functional incapacity when mitral valvotomy should be performed: when there is increasing risk and significant disability due to high left atrial pressure, but before irreversible damage to the lungs, right ventricular myocardium and liver has occurred. With increasing experience from balloon valvotomy there may be a tendency to earlier intervention in less symptomatic patients. However, if surgery has been delayed until there is severe pulmonary hypertension, generalized cardiac enlargement, massive dilation of the left atrium and tricuspid incompetence, both the immmediate and late prognosis will be markedly worsened.

Age

Advanced age by itself is not a contraindication to the surgical treatment of mitral stenosis, but taken as a whole there is a higher incidence of poor end-results in the elderly because the number of complicating factors that militate against success occur with increasing frequency as age advances: valve calcification, atrial fibrillation, ischemic heart disease and chronic obstructive airways disease. Nevertheless a small proportion of elderly subjects who have no or minimal complicating features are suitable for closed valvotomy or balloon valvuloplasty and achieve a good functional result. With careful selection many of these would be insurable within substandard premium limits.

Mitral Stenosis with Mitral Regurgitation

When moderate or severe mitral regurgitation exists with stenosis, the prognosis without operation is worse than for either alone. The mitral valve is usually severely distorted and often calcified, and the only treatment with any hope of success is replacement of the diseased valve by open heart surgery. Operative mortality with this form of treatment is much higher (about 4–5 percent) than with valvotomy alone for pure mitral stenosis but should improve as more patients are treated before reaching the stage of chronic heart failure.

If the preoperative state of the patient is good, replacement of the mitral valve can produce an excellent functional result, but there remains a constant threat to life in the postoperative years from thromboembolism and infection, hazards which, nevertheless, are showing signs of reducing in frequency with the newer types of prostheses. Continuous anticoagulant treatment, however, is still required.

Rheumatic Mitral Incompetence
Surgical treatment of pure mitral incompetence also requires an open heart technique. Since the valve is not usually as distorted or calcified as it is in mixed stenosis and incompetence, plastic repair is sometimes possible, although repair rather than replacement is more often feasible in patients with degenerative valve disease than in those with a rheumatic etiology.

Non-Rheumatic Mitral Incompetence
This group includes mitral incompetence due to chordal rupture, papillary muscle dysfunction, primary prolapse of the mitral valve leaflets, congenital defects of the valve cushions, dilatation of the mitral ring and malpositions, as may be seen in hypertrophic cardiomyopathy. Open heart surgery is required, except in the case of slight regurgitation due to primary mitral valve prolapse — which has a reasonably good long-term prognosis without surgery. Long-term prognosis depends largely on the etiology of the original condition causing incompetence. For example, MI that has resulted in dysfunction of the papillary muscles and abnormal wall movement has a substantial mortality risk of its own, and cardiovascular involvement in Marfan's syndrome is likely to be more widespread than just the mitral valve. There is increasing enthusiasm among surgeons for valve repair rather than replacement, tempered, however, by the learning experience when only a few of the patients they see have pathology suitable for repair rather than replacement. Cooper et al[55] reported their results in 62 patients undergoing mitral valve repair by one surgeon between 1979 and 1989 using the techniques described by Carpentier. During the study period a total of 454 mitral valve operations were performed, of which 62 were repairs, 42 percent rheumatic, 42 percent degenerative, 10 percent postendocarditis and 6 percent ischemic. Five patients died within 30 days of operation (operative mortality 8 percent) and there were six late deaths; five patients, all with rheumatic mitral valve disease, required reoperation. Actuarial survival, including operative deaths, was 79 percent at five years and 62 percent at nine years. Review of seven other series gave operative mortality varying from 5·4 percent to 1·4 percent. Long-term actuarial survival varied from 73 percent at 15 years and 98 percent at eight years to 76 percent at five years. Singer[56] reviewed the University of Alabama results of mitral valve repair in which there was a 3·5 percent hospital mortality for isolated mitral valve repair and a five-year mortality ratio of 235 percent (late mortality), with a mean annual mortality rate of 14 excess deaths per 1,000. In Lindblom's Swedish series[48] long-term relative survival rates for mitral valve replacement for regurgitation had a ten-year survival of only 53 percent, compared with 65 percent for those operated on for mitral stenosis; most series show a similar better prognosis for mitral stenosis. In the Mayo Clinic,

patients undergoing valve replacement between 1963 and 1971 for symptomatic, isolated regurgitation had a ten-year postoperative survival of 50 percent and a 15-year of 40 percent, most of the survivors improving symptomatically by at least one functional class. Following valve replacement for mitral regurgitation, most patients show a decrease in EF of 10–20 percent after successful valve replacement, in part due to the removal of the low resistance pathway through the incompetent mitral valve into the low pressure left atrium.

Rating (Surgical Treatment)
1) Mitral stenosis. Valvotomy (balloon, closed or open):
Within one year — postpone.
Thereafter — rate as non-operated mitral stenosis according to degree of residual lesion.
2) Mitral incompetence. Valvuloplasty (valve repair):
Within one year — postpone.
Thereafter — rate as non-operated mitral regurgitation according to degree of residual lesion.
With no postoperative insufficiency — rate as moderate mitral regurgitation and credit 50 points.
With postpoperative regurgitation — rate for degree of mitral insufficiency and add 50 to 100 points.
Prosthetic valve replacement (mechanical or tissue):
  Within one year — postpone.
  Thereafter:

Age	Rating
Under 40	+200 and 7 per mil
40–49	+175 and 7 per mil
50–59	+150 and 7 per mil
60 and over	+125 and 7 per mil

Aortic Valve Disease
Except for congenital aortic valve stenosis in infancy and childhood, when intevention is either by balloon or open valvotomy, the surgical treatment of all forms of aortic valve disease, from pure stenosis to pure incompetence, is by replacement with an artificial valve; increasingly the choice is a mechanical prosthesis. The long-term results of aortic valve decalcification and balloon valvuloplasty, particularly in elderly sub-groups who are severely symptomatic and unfit for heart/lung bypass, are not sufficiently good or detailed to consider for underwriting purposes except in occasional individual cases. As the long-term durability of tissue valves is increasingly questioned, with freedom from structural valve degeneration of 71 percent at ten years but only 31 percent at 15 years (with an acceleration of deterioration after about six or seven years), there is less enthusiasm from both surgeons and patients for reoperation, even though

electively this may incur a mortality rate only slightly above that of initial replacement.

Generally speaking, relief from symptoms is good after successful aortic valve replacement, although pre-existing CAD may result in occasional functional limitation. Left ventricular hypertrophy regresses, not always completely, and late survival figures are usually better for aortic stenosis than for aortic regurgitation.

Cumming[57] reviewed the factors important in underwriting the cardiac risk after aortic valve replacement and arrived at a composite ten-year mortality six months after successful valve replacement of 24 percent, which gave mortality ratios at age 40 of 600 percent and at age 50 of 240 percent and at age 60 of 90 percent. He further delineated the underwriting requirements for optimal cases (*see below*). If all these requirements were met, a minimal rating of +50 for those aged 60 and over could be envisaged.

Selection of Risks

The following guidelines are suggested:

1) A period of one year should have elapsed after operation in which an artificial (mechanical), bioprosthetic or homograft valve was used.
2) Subject to the initial period of deferment, the more recent the valve replacement the better the risk. The longer a valve has remained in place, even if trouble free, the shorter the time remaining before possible replacement may be required, particularly in bioprosthetic and homograft valves.
3) No complications of a potentially lethal nature should have occurred since valve replacement (e.g. thromboembolism, partial dehiscence of the valve seating giving rise to aortic regurgitation, infective endocarditis, angina, left ventricular failure or persistent ventricular dysrhythmias).
4) Left ventricular hypertrophy should be no more than slight. For underwriting purposes the following measurements may be regarded as the upper limit of acceptability:
a) T-waves in the left chest leads of the electrocardiogram (V5 and V6) should not be inverted deeper than 1 mm.
b) Cardiothoracic ratio should not exceed 54 percent.
5) EFs should be greater than 45 percent.
6) There should be no arterial hypertension, although treated hypertension under good control may be permitted.
7) There should be no other valve lesion of hemodynamic significance.

Rating

Aortic valve replacement rating has to take into account valve-related and patient-related risks. Ratings for patient-related risks should be added to basic ratings.

1) Valvotomy for congenital aortic stenosis — rate as non-operated aortic stenosis or regurgitation, depending on nature and severity of residual lesion.
2) Surgical repair of subvalvular or supravalvular stenosis — refer to MD.
3) Replacement with mechanical prosthesis or tissue valve, no postoperative complications, no more than slight heart enlargement or limitation of effort tolerance.

Within 1 yr of operation — postpone.
More than 1 yr since operation:

Age	Rating
Under 40	+150 and 7 per mil
40–49	+125 and 7 per mil
50–59	+100 and 7 per mil
60 and over	+50 and 7 per mil

The above ratings are for 'average' cases; with no valve-related risks and normal function, more favorable terms would be possible.

4) Additional factors:
Arrthymias — add rating.
Poor left ventricular function — decline.
Prior lesion predominantly stenosis — credit 50 to 25 points.
Coronary artery bypass grafting — add rating.
History of postoperative complications (embolism, hemorrhage, endocarditis) — individual consideration.
Heart enlargement (moderate) — add rating.
Heart enlargement (severe) — decline.
Limitation of effort tolerance, more than slight — individual consideration; decline if severe.
Multiple or second valve replacement operation — individual consideration.
Aortic root plus valve replacement, (e.g. Marfan's syndrome) — refer to MD, usually decline.

It should be noted that many of the non-rheumatic conditions causing aortic regurgitation would themselves be associated with excess mortality, and a rating, if any, for cause should be additional to that for the postsurgical risk. Certain primary conditions may, of course, be unacceptable for life insurance, with particular caution being necessary with Marfan's syndrome, hypertrophic cardiomyopathy and ischemic heart disease.

Optimal Cases

For a case of aortic valve replacement to be considered optimal for underwriting, it has to meet all the requirements below:

1) No mitral lesion.
2) Normal coronary arteries.
3) ECG returns to normal.
4) Heart size and X-ray return to normal.
5) LV function normal (echo, MUGA).
6) No arrhythmia.
7) Good anticoagulation, stable no complications.
8) Valve size less than 25, mechanical valve.
9) Good treadmill performance.

Cardiac Transplantation

Cardiac transplantation is being offered increasingly to patients with end-stage congestive cardiac failure, not only to improve symptoms but to prolong life. One-year survival rates in excess of 80 percent and five-year survival rates in excess of 60 percent have been reported from the registry of the International Society for Heart Transplantation. With the increasing use of triple antirejection therapy, there is the prospect of further improvement on long-term results, the limiting factor being the development of coronary occlusive disease. The main indications for cardiac transplantation are end-stage dilated cardiomyopathy and severe CAD. The current high late mortality precludes routine insurance underwriting except perhaps for experimental short-term five- or, at most, ten-year policies. An analysis of the major hazards, from the Papworth group, following heart transplantation is detailed by Sharples et al.[58]

CONGENITAL DISORDERS OF THE HEART AND GREAT VESSELS

Heart disease due to congenital anomalies is worldwide; the estimated incidence is 0·8 percent of all births. The most gross defects are incompatible with more than a few weeks of life, and by twelve months only one-half of all those born with congenital anomalies will have survived. In the remainder, the incidence of mortality has been changing gradually in the last few decades, so that more deaths are now being reported at later ages than hitherto. This is undoubtedly due to the impact of surgical treatment, which has enabled many patients to revert to a normal, or near-normal, expectation of life while extending a much curtailed expectation in others.

Congenital defects of other structures tend to occur more frequently in those with heart defects than in those without; when they do, they provide a useful diagnostic clue when a doubtful cardiac murmur is being considered. Congenital heart defects may also occur as additional abnormalities in certain defined syndromes, such as Marfan's, Ehlers–Danlos, Ellis–van Creveld, Turner's and Down's. Although the overall sex distribution of congenital heart disease is about equal, there are individual variations according to type: patent ductus arteriosus and atrial septal defect are more common in females, whereas aortic valve stenosis, coarctation of the aorta, tetralogy of Fallot and transposition of the great vessels are more common in males.

General speaking, congenital heart disease presents to the life underwriter in one of several ways: (1) as a symptomless murmur previously unsuspected by the applicant; (2) as a murmur previously investigated and judged to be due to a defect too insignificant to warrant surgical correction; or (3) as a history of various congenital defects treated surgically, with either full correction or only palliative or partial correction. Life underwriters will, in fact, meet very few cases of congenital heart disease that have gone undetected in the past and that actually require surgical treatment. A notable exception is coarctation of the aorta which is not uncommonly recognized for the first time after a chance finding of arterial hypertension at a medical examination for life insurance. Most other cases, asymptomatic or otherwise, will have been fully evaluated by a cardiologist, and the nature of the lesion would normally become known to the underwriter through the attending physician. Categories (1) and (2) above might include such defects as mild pulmonic valve stenosis and small ventricular septal defect of the Roger type, both of which are benign, but they might also include cases of mild congenital aortic valve stenosis and bicuspid valve, both of which are much more important in terms of longevity.

As for surgical treatment where complete correction of single defects has been accomplished without the use of artificial materials, where the systemic and pulmonary blood pressures are normal and where there is no chamber hypertrophy, the prognosis for a normal expectation of life is excellent. Prognosis may also be equally good in some instances where more than one defect has been completely corrected. Mortality must, however, be considered above average in groups where artificial materials, such as Teflon, have been used, since the long-term effect of foreign material on cardiac muscle function is still not known, nor is it certain that artificial patches or tubes can retain their strength indefinitely or at least for the lifetime of a patient (which, in the case of congenital heart disease, may be as long as 40–50 years). Mortality will also be above average in those who, despite adequate correction of defects, are left with residual chamber hypertrophy, especially of the ventricles. These and several other factors need to be taken into consideration when evaluating the insurance risk of some of the postsurgical congenital heart conditions to be dealt with in the following pages.

Congenital heart disease can be broadly grouped into cyanotic and acyanotic types. Heart disease in the cyanotic group not treated surgically would rarely be considered insurable; this group includes Fallot's tetralogy (which is itself responsible for two-thirds of all cases of cyanotic heart disease of congenital type), pulmonary stenosis with patent foramen ovale and various combinations of lesions with dextro-position of the aora. In the acyanotic group there are several examples with a left-to-right shunt: atrial septal defect (ASD), ventricular septal defect (VSD), persistent ductus arteriosus (PDA), aortopulmonary window (AW), aortic sinus fistula (ASF), coronary arteriovenous fistula (CAF) and anomalous coronary origin. The first three are common; the remainder are rare.

Atrial Septal Defect (ASD)

An ASD is a common congenital heart defect which can sometimes be found still unoperated in adult life. The usual type is the ostium secundum defect which is generally uncomplicated and located in the midseptal region. The less common ostium primum defect lies lower in the interatrial septum and is a complicated lesion with a poor prognosis because the defect extends into one or both of the atrioventricular valves, deforming the leaflets and causing incompetence. In extreme cases there may even be a common atrioventricular canal and a defect of the superior part of the interventricular septum. The foramen ovale, which normally closes at birth, remains patent in 20 percent of cases; but in some of these, shunting of blood is prevented by the valve action of a flap of septum at the foramen, whereas in the remainder the shunt is trivial. A patent foramen ovale is rarely a source of trouble unless the pressure in the right atrium exceeds that in the left for any reason (e.g. pulmonary hypertension, or associated congenital pulmonic stenosis, or during the acute stage of pulmonary embolism).

Prognosis

In uncomplicated ostium secundum ASD the prognosis depends essentially on the size of the defect: the larger the defect the worse the prognosis. When small, the left-to-right shunt is trivial and causes no or minimal hemodynamic disturbance. When the defect is large, the mean pressure in each atrium becomes the same, and the large volume of blood shunted from left to right causes diastolic overfilling of the right ventricle and a torrential blood flow through the pulmonary arteries. In moderate-sized defects significant pulmonary vascular resistance does not usually occur until middle life, despite the increased pulmonary blood flow. Children and young adults are usually asymptomatic, but beyond the age of 40 symptoms begin to appear and are often aggravated by the development of supraventricular tachycardias or atrial fibrillation. After the age of 50 symptoms become progressively worse owing to severe pulmonary hypertension, which leads eventually to reversal of the shunt between right and left atria and, finally, cardiac failure.

Selection of Risks

It would be unusual in these days of modern heart surgery for a life underwriter to see applications from people with unoperated moderate or large ASD, but in such an event each case would have to be considered on its merits.

Complicated ostium primum defects and the larger secundum defects with gross enlargement of the right atrium and ventricle are rarely insurable, but applicants with moderate shunts who are symptomless and show right ventricular hypertrophy of slight or moderate degree could be considered for limited plans of insurance. The natural history of moderate-sized ASD indicates that survival is usual to age 50 at least and, in many cases, to age 60.

Rating

Any rating for moderately large ASDs, particularly in young applicants, must take into account the operative mortality of heart surgery should this be undertaken at a future date, and a rating equivalent to three or four extra deaths per thousand per annum for plans maturing at age 60 should cover the risk adequately.

Small, isolated ASDs of secundum type with trivial shunts are much more likely to be seen among applicants for life insurance: most will have been advised against surgical treatment since this would not add appreciably to their already near-normal expectation of life. Applicants in this category can be considered favorably; indeed many can be issued with standard insurance provided cardiac screening is satisfactory.

In less thoroughly screened applicants it would be usual to rate +150 at ages 20–30 ranging down to standard at age 60 and over.

ASD after Surgical Closure

Selection of Risks

From the underwriting point of view there are two generalizations to be made:

1) The longer the duration between closure of an ASD and application the better the risk.
2) The younger the age at closure of an ASD the better the risk.

Looking at (1), in the immediate years following operation insufficient time will have elapsed to allow proper appraisal of the way the right ventricular myocardium and pulmonary pressures are going to adjust to the altered hemodynamics. Therefore a basic extra mortality rating on a reducing scale has to be applied, particularly when the underwriting information is only that gained from the usual medical examination. On the other hand, when the operation and postoperative follow-up data are available to the MD from the attending surgeon or the attending physician a much more accurate evaluation of the long-term risk can be made; if entirely favorable, credits can be set against any basic rating that applies.

Looking at (2), the best results are obtained when an ASD is closed before pulmonary hypertension becomes established and before right ventricular hypertrophy reaches a stage where permanent damage to the muscle will remain, even after closure of the defect. The optimum time for operation is therefore in childhood, usually after the age of five years. Applicants who have had a single defect closed in childhood and who present in adult life with normal physical signs on examination would be standard risks, even though precise operative data may no longer be available.

Excellent results may still be obtainable after operation during teenage years, but with every year that closure is delayed after the age of 20 the more frequently will problems arise due to irreversibility of pulmonary hypertension. Closure of a moderate or large ASD at about age 40 may be technically possible but is more likely to be palliative than curative.

Finally, an evaluation of the postsurgical risk would also include the current clinical findings and, where possible, an ECG and chest radiograph. The presence of significant murmurs or right ventricular hypertrophy would be rated according to the characteristics of the murmur and to the degree of hypertrophy — whether slight, moderate or severe. Such ratings would be added to the basic rating, if any, without a combination factor being applied.

Rating

The following schedule of ratings, according to age at operation, for ASD after surgical closure reflects the practice of many life insurance companies. Basic ratings are given in the table; the credits and debits listed below it are applied to the basic ratings as appropriate.

	Age at operation		
Time since operation	Under 20	21–30	31–40
Within 1 yr	Postpone	Postpone	Postpone
2nd yr	+150	+150	+150
3rd yr	+75	+100	+100
4th yr	+50	+75	+100
Thereafter	+25 to 0[a]	+50	+75

[a]If closure performed below age ten.

1) Operation after age 40 — +200 up.

2) Report from operating surgeon and/or attending physician confirming secundum defect as the sole congenital abnormality and pulmonary pressures normal at operation or reverting to normal on follow-up — reduce basic ratings by one-half.

3) Current normal ECG and chest radiograph — reduce basic ratings, or resultant ratings, by one-half.

4) Heart enlargement (right ventricular hypertrophy) on examination — add rating according to degree of hypertrophy direct to basic (*see* pp. 333–7).

5) Heart murmur on examination — add rating, if any, according to murmur characteristics (*see* p. 354).

6) Dysrhythmia present on examination — add appropriate rating.

Ventricular Septal Defect (VSD)

Although a VSD is a common isolated congenital anomaly, it occurs almost as frequently as a component of multiple congenital heart defects. This section, however, will be concerned with the isolated variety only.

Small VSDs of the Roger type are relatively benign and cause no symptoms. In this type of defect there is a large pressure gradient between left and right ventricles, and the loudness of the pansystolic murmur (maximal in the third and fourth interspaces to the left of the sternum) is disproportionate to its hemodynamic significance. The ECG and chest radiograph are normal; the only complication of importance is subacute bacterial endocarditis, which occurs more frequently in small ventricular defects than large. Because of the low risk to life, surgical closure of the defect is not usually warranted.

Prognosis

In contrast to small VSDs, large and moderately large defects pose a serious threat to longevity if they persist into adult life without surgical closure. There will almost always be signs of left ventricular hypertrophy clinically, and this can be confirmed by electrocardiography and ultrasound, which may also reveal evidence of biventricular hypertrophy. Marked right ventricular hypertrophy would suggest the presence of established pulmonary hypertension, which would almost always be accompanied by symptoms of effort dyspnea.

With moderately large VSDs the clinical picture would be: cardiac enlargement; a forceful left ventricular impulse; a pansystolic murmur transmitted all over the precordium and maximal in the third and fourth interspaces to the left of the sternum; a systolic thrill palpable at the lower left sternal edge; and the usual signs of increased flow across the pulmonary valve. Without operation, death from congestive cardiac failure can be expected some time in the fifth decade.

Not all VSDs recognized at birth persist. A good proportion of quite large defects may close spontaneously in early infancy or become relatively smaller as the heart grows naturally until adulthood.

Rating

Applicants with large VSDs and significant functional disability should be declined. Those with moderate-sized defects should be rated according to the degree of heart enlargement on examination (*see* pp. 333–7), and this rating should be compounded with a basic rating of +75, which would usually mean in effect a final rating of something over +200 for applicants with slight heart enlargement to about +300 for moderate enlargement at ages under 30. When symptoms of greater severity than Class I are present, further substantial additions to the rating will be required.

When the clinical criteria for a small uncomplicated defect are fulfilled, applicants can be accepted for life insurance at a percentage mortality rating varying from +75 at young age groups to +25 at ages 60 and over, but if a Roger defect is confirmed by catheter or other studies the risk can be accepted as standard.

VSD after Surgical Closure

People in whom an isolated VSD has been closed by direct suture or with autologous tissue and who have normal pulmonary pressures can be considered to have a normal life expectancy.

Where closure has been effected using a synthetic patch results have been equally good to date. The material becomes endothelialized and incorporated into the cardiac tissue, thus minimizing the danger of thromboembolism, and modern prosthetic materials used in cardiac surgery are thought to maintain their strength indefinitely. Some physicians, however, have voiced reservations about what effect a foreign material embedded in the interventricular septum might ultimately have on ventricular function, say, in 30 or 40 years' time. No one yet knows the answer to this question, yet it is important to the life insurer, since VSDs may have been closed with synthetic patches at young ages when normal life expectancy is in the region of 55–65 years. It seems reasonable, therefore, that some account should be taken of this probable late incidence risk factor in the rating.

Selection of Risks

The criteria for selection of postsurgical VSD risks are much the same as those applicable to ASD after surgical treatment.

Rating

The rating schedule for ASDs could be used, substituting 'VSD' for 'ASD' or 'secundum defect' as appropriate. The following provisos would also apply:

1) Synthetic patch used to close a ventricular defect — add +25 to the final rating after taking into account all the debits and credits.
2) RBBB produced during repair of a VSD — disregard and credit the ECG if it is otherwise normal.

Heart enlargement would include left or biventricular hypertrophy.

Patent Ductus Arteriosus (PDA)

A patent ductus usually occurs as an isolated abnormality but is sometimes associated with coarctation of the aorta. The left-to-right shunt from aorta to pulmonary artery causes a very large blood flow in the pulmonary circuit, and the left atrium and ventricle hypertrophy in order to deal with the increased return of blood from the pulmonary veins. When the defect is large there is a wide systemic pulse pressure and bounding peripheral pulses; as age increases so does the risk of established pulmonary vascular disease and secondary hypertrophy of the right ventricle. Subacute bacterial endocarditis is also a hazard in PDA whether the shunt is large or small. In untreated cases the expectation of life is inevitably reduced, most patients dying in the fifth decade or shortly thereafter.

Rating

Unoperated cases of PDA with major hemodynamic complications should be declined; indeed it would be unusual these days for life underwriters to encounter such cases. In rare instances where the shunt is minor and not causing a hemodynamic problem the rating would be similar to that for a small secundum ASD, ranging from standard to +75.

PDA after Surgical Ligation

When persistence of the ductus arteriosus is the sole abnormality surgical ligation in infancy is virtually curative and has a very low operative mortality. Delay in closure of a ductus beyond childhood, unless the shunt is trivial, increases the risk of postoperative residual left ventricular hypertrophy and, in the least favorable cases, pulmonary vascular disease with associated pulmonary hypertension and right ventricular hypertrophy.

Selection of Risks

Except perhaps when operation was carried out in infancy or early childhood, a report should be obtained from the attending surgeon and the physician supervising follow-up checks. Also, when there is any doubt about the integrity of the heart a current chest radiograph and ECG should be obtained in addition to the usual medical examination.

In some instances persistent dilatation of the pulmonary artery may be revealed by ultrasound or chest radiography, but this is not necessarily an adverse finding. It is the opinion of Edwards[59] that although the prime factor causing dilatation of the pulmonary artery is virtually always increased pulmonary vascular resistance, it can, if not too far advanced, resolve after closure of the ductus. Therefore if the sound of pulmonic valve closure is normal and the ECG does not show right ventricular hypertrophy, persistent dilatation of the pulmonary artery can be accepted as a residual only and of no particular importance.

Rating

Virtually all PDAs are now ligated in infancy with resulting cure, and there is no question of such individuals being standard risks both in childhood and later in adult life. Those who have been operated on in adolescence or later and who show persisting pulmonary hypertension should be rated according to the degree of abnormality; these ratings might range from +100 to +250.

Other Congenital Arteriovenous Shunt Diseases

These conditions are also characterized by a shunt of blood from the arterial to venous systems. They are rare but deserve mention since they are now more likely to be diagnosed during life, thanks to modern investigational techniques, and most are amenable either to radical or palliative surgery. On the whole, it is only those who have had successful surgical treatment whose applications for life insurance are seen in underwriting departments, and therefore a brief description of the basic defects and hemodynamic consequences will be given, together with a note on the likely postsurgical prognosis.

Aortopulmonary Window

This defect consists of a communication, usually large, between the aorta and pulmonary artery just distal to the semilunar valves. The hemodynamic effects of the shunt are similar to those caused by left-to-right shunts in general, and when it is large the vastly increased blood flow in the pulmonary circuit leads to pulmonary vascular disease, pulmonary hypertension and biventricular hypertrophy. Unoperated cases of aortopulmonary window should be declined for life insurance except when the shunt has been shown to be trivial and surgical closure thought unnecessary, in which case the same criteria would apply to risk evaluation as for PDA (*see above*).

Surgical closure of an aortopulmonary defect would normally be carried out in childhood or early adult life if the left-to-right shunt is large or moderately large, and this would usually entail the use of a patch of synthetic material. Applicants who have undergone successful closure of a defect would be rated using the same criteria applicable to surgically corrected VSD but with no additional rating for the synthetic patch.

Aortic Sinus Fistula

An aortic sinus fistula is caused by rupture of an aneurysm of the sinus of Valsalva, usually the right coronary sinus, through which arterial blood tracks back into the right ventricle or right atrium. The great majority of aneurysms of the sinus of Valsalva are solitary and congenital in etiology, but a few have been reported due to diffuse aortic disease such as syphilitic aortitis or Marfan's syndrome.

An aortic sinus aneurysm may be completely symptomless and its presence unsuspected until it ruptures, usually during the third or fourth decade of life, or it may, like other aneurysms, reveal its presence by pressure on neighboring structures. When it arises from the non-coronary sinus or the posterior part of the right coronary sinus, it may cause atrioventricular block due to pressure on the conducting tissues. It may also cause aortic valve incompetence due to displacement of the associated valve cusp.

When an aneurysm ruptures, the onset of symptoms may be sudden, with the development of a continuous murmur where none existed previously, but the more usual mode of onset is insidious. Characteristically there is a collapsing pulse and a murmur, which may be continuous in type or pansystolic and diminuendo diastolic, maximal down the left sternal border. Cardiomegaly due to biventricular hypertrophy gradually develops, and the ultimate prognosis associated with an untreated fistula is extremely poor. There is no doubt, therefore, that people with an unrepaired aortic sinus fistula would be speculative risks and generally uninsurable.

Surgical closure of an aortic sinus fistula and amputation of the aneurysmal sac under cardiopulmonary bypass is the treatment of choice, but is not always successful in restoring a completely normal circulation. Wright[60] reviewed several of the larger series of cases reported in the literature since 1960, in which a total of 53 patients were treated surgically with six deaths, 16 patients being left with either a small residual fistulous shunt or aortic valve incompetence.

Occasionally other congenital defects are present in addition to an aortic sinus fistula, and these are normally repaired at the same time as the fistula. For example, an aneurysm with an immediately subjacent high ventricular septal defect and aortic regurgitation usually requires replacement of the aortic valve with a prosthesis in order to close the defect at the aortic root. Likewise, a prosthetic valve may be required if a cusp is badly distorted as a result of repair of the fistula, or if it is found to be extensively fibrosed or calcified and bicuspid.

It is clear, therefore, that applications for life insurance from those with a history of repair of an aortic sinus fistula must be carefully selected, and only those in whom the defect has been completely closed should be considered. Applicants who have been left with a slight aortic leak after operation may, however, be insured with an additional rating appropriate to the degree of aortic regurgitation present (*see* pp. 366–7).

Anomalous Origin of Left Coronary Artery

In this rare defect the left coronary artery originates from the pulmonary artery, and in those who survive infancy and childhood wide anastomotic channels develop between the right and left coronary arteries, allowing a reverse flow from the right to left coronary artery, thence into the pulmonary artery. Thus a left-to-right shunt is produced through the coronary circulation. The anomaly can be treated by simple ligation of the left coronary artery at its origin, so closing the shunt, or the left coronary artery may be anastomosed to a systemic artery or to the aorta by means of a venous or arterial autograft.

The postsurgical risk will depend largely on the state of the myocardium, whether or not there has been earlier damage due to infarction or more generalized fibrosis. Where the resting ECG is normal, an exercise ECG will be a useful screening adjunct to determine the perfusion adequacy of the coronary circulation. Applicants who have had the shunt closed and who show no residual myocardial abnormalities could be accepted for life insurance at standard rates.

Coronary Arteriovenous Fistula

This is a rare anomaly in which there is communication between the right coronary artery and the right atrium or ventricle. Since the shunt is usually small, there is insignificant hemodynamic effect and the arterial blood supply to the myocardium is usually adequate.

Surgical obliteration of the fistula can generally be carried out without recourse to artificial patches. Where the defect is an isolated one, expectation of life would be considered average for age, if the physical signs in the heart remain normal after operation.

Obstructive Congenital Defects

Isolated Pulmonic Stenosis

Congenital stenosis of the pulmonic valve is the commonest form of obstruction to the outflow from the right ventricle. Less commonly the level of obstruction is subvalvar or infundibular, but prognosis depends almost entirely on the degree rather than the level of obstruction. For clinical and underwriting purposes stenosis can be graded conveniently as mild, moderate or severe. Measurement of the pressure gradient across the obstruction in the right ventricular outflow tract enables the most accurate grading of severity to be made: a pressure gradient of less than 50 mm Hg would be consistent with mild pulmonic stenosis, 50–100 mm Hg with moderate stenosis and over 100 mm Hg with severe stenosis.

Mild Pulmonic Stenosis

This is a benign lesion causing no adverse hemodynamic effects. It gives rise to no symptoms, and the only abnormal physical sign is a midsystolic murmur at the pulmonic base which may sometimes be misleadingly harsh, but the chest radiograph reveals no cardiac enlargement or right ventricular hypertrophy and the ECG is likewise normal. Moreover, there is no tendency for a mild pulmonic stenosis to increase in severity as age advances. The only complication worthy of remark is subacute infective endocarditis. There is no significant hazard to life due to isolated pulmonic stenosis, and applicants with such a lesion can be accepted as standard risks for life insurance. The reason rating manuals of most insurance companies list an extra premium for mild pulmonic stenosis is because the life underwriter is rarely in receipt of the full investigational details of the case, having to rely on the clinical data recorded on examination at the time of application, with sometimes a chest X-ray and ECG. For this reason, it is often uncertain that a pulmonic stenosis is the sole lesion or that the obstruction is indeed mild, so a rating is justified on the grounds that in a large group of similar applicants, though most will be properly classified as mild, some will be impaired. If, however, an applicant has had full catheter or echodoppler studies and angiocardiography carried out in the past and the data are available to the underwriter confirming the obstruction as mild and the pulmonic stenosis as the sole lesion, acceptance as a standard risk will be justified.

Moderate and Severe Pulmonic Stenosis

These conditions have a much more serious prognosis than the mild type. Clinical signs of right ventricular hypertrophy may be evident and symptoms will be present. The ECG will confirm the presence of right ventricular hypertrophy in moderate pulmonic stenosis and right ventricular strain pattern in severe stenosis; the X-ray may not show significant cardiac enlargement if the stenosis is only moderate, though it would when the obstruction is severe. Unlike mild pulmonic stenosis, the severity of the obstruction tends to increase with time, possibly due to progressive hypertrophy of cardiac muscle surrounding the right ventricular outflow tract, causing infundibular narrowing. In both moderate and severe pulmonic stenosis that have not been treated surgically failure of the right ventricle and death from congestive heart failure can be expected in late middle life.

Pulmonic Stenosis after Surgical Treatment

Surgical intervention is unnecessary for mild pulmonic stenosis but is indicated for moderate degrees of valvar and subvalvar obstruction. Valvotomy and, when necessary, widening of an infundibular stenosis can afford good symptomatic relief following reduction or obliteration of a pressure gradient, but the patient is always left with an abnormal valve. Varying degrees of pulmonary regurgitation can result from operation, and the risk of subacute infective endocarditis still remains.

Rating

1) Mild pulmonic stenosis; clinical diagnosis only.

Age	Rating
Under 20	+150
20–29	+100
30–49	+50
50–59	+25
60 and over	+0

a) Current normal ECG and chest X-ray — reduce above ratings by one-half.
b) Full data regarding previous echodoppler or catheter studies confirming the stenosis as mild and the absence of any other cardiac lesion; all ages — standard.
2) Moderate pulmonic stenosis:

Age	Rating
Under 20	+400
20–60	+300 to +75 reducing by successive age groups

3) Severe pulmonic stenosis — decline.
4) Pulmonic stenosis after surgical treatment.
Within one year of operation — postpone.
Thereafter — rate as for mild pulmonic stenosis (*see above*), making appropriate additions according to the degree of residual cardiac enlargement or right ventricular hypertrophy, if any, persisting.

Congenital Aortic Stenosis

There are two main types of congenital aortic stenosis: (1) valvar and (2) discrete subvalvar.
1) In the valvar type, the aortic valve is bicuspid, but if there is no commissural fusion and the cusps are supple, there will be no symptoms or obvious signs during infancy or childhood, these being delayed until the third or fourth decade of life

when the valve becomes calcified and rigid, leading to calcific aortic stenosis. The problem of congenital bicuspid aortic valves and calcific aortic stenosis has already been discussed under aortic stenosis (*see* pp. 357–61).

If, however, commissural fusion between the valve cusps is present at birth, typical signs and symptoms of aortic stenosis will be apparent; if obstruction to left ventricular outflow is unrelieved it will lead to death, usually during the second decade. Surgical treatment undertaken in childhood is therefore necessary to save life. This consists of commissurotomy, which, though it relieves obstruction, is only a palliative measure: the valve is bicuspid and will eventually become restenosed in adult life when it calcifies, necessitating valve replacement with a prosthesis or xenograft.

Applicants with a history of surgical treatment of congenital valvar aortic stenosis in childhood will usually be unacceptable insurance risks.

2) The rarer form — discrete subvalvar congenital aortic stenosis — is caused by a membranous diaphragm attached to a fibrous ridge encircling the left ventricular outflow tract just below the base of the aortic valve. The severity of symptoms due to aortic stenosis depends on the size of the opening in the diaphragm; when it is critically small, surgical intervention is indicated. Occasionally it is possible to excise the diaphragm and fibrous ridge completely, and if the aortic valve itself is normal, the chance of complete cure is excellent.

Selection of Risks

The acceptability of applicants who have had radical correction of discrete subvalvar aortic stenosis in childhood will depend on full details of the operation being available to the life underwriter. If the aortic valve itself is confirmed to be tricuspid and there is no evidence of residual aortic stenosis or left ventricular hypertrophy on examination, the insurance risk could be considered standard.

Coarctation of the Aorta

Coarctation of the aorta is a relatively common congenital abnormality and is found about four times more often in males than females. In its adult isolated form stenosis occurs at the junction of the arch and descending aorta distal to the origin of the left subclavian artery at, or just below, the opening of the ductus arteriosus. In the postductal type of coarctation the ductus arteriosus is usually closed. The degree of narrowing of the aorta can vary from that which is barely perceptible, even at autopsy, to complete stenosis. An important accompanying anomaly is a bicuspid aortic valve, which is present in about half the cases of coarctation of the aorta.

Prognosis

In unoperated coarctation it is the level of arterial blood pressure proximal to the lesion that determines the clinical course. The severity of hypertension depends partly on the degree of stenosis and partly on the efficiency of the collateral circulation. When coarctation is moderately severe and the collateral circulation is inadequate, a humoral mechanism arising in the poorly perfused kidneys is brought into play, which further increases an already severe hypertension. But even a tight coarctation may be associated with only a modest elevation of blood pressure if the collateral circulation is efficient; Abbott[61] recorded the case of a man who lived to the age of 92 with complete coarctation of the aorta. This, of course, is exceptional; moderate to severe hypertension is the rule, with death occurring by the fourth or fifth decade from left ventricular failure, rupture of the aorta or subarachnoid hemorrhage from rupture of a congenital aneurysm of the circle of Willis.

Selection of Risks

Applicants for life insurance with uncorrected coarctation of the aorta would almost universally be declined, except in rare instances where the blood pressure is normal or only minimally elevated and the ECG normal. Best cases would be those who have been investigated and in whom the surgeon has elected not to operate because of an insignificant pressure gradient (20 mm Hg or less) across the coarctation, and in whom no other significant defect exists.

Rating

Rating would vary from +200 to +75, depending on age and on the amount of technical data available to the MD.

Coarctation of the Aorta after Surgical Treatment

Ideally treatment is resection of the coarcted segment of aorta with end-to-end anastomosis and is best carried out before adolescence. Occasionally the narrowed segment of aorta is too long to allow the free ends to be brought together for direct suture, in which case it is necessary to use a graft or tube of artificial material to fill the gap. When a tube graft has been used any complications likely to arise from it will usually appear within the first six months. If after this period nothing untoward has occurred, Edwards[59] considers that such patients should not be at any greater risk than those who have had an end-to-end anastomosis.

Selection of Risks

Applications for life insurance should be deferred for a minimum of one year following operation, but from the applicant's point of view he is likely to obtain much better terms if this period can be extended to, say, three years, for by then his heart and vascular system should have become optimally adapted to the new conditions.

   Evaluation of the postsurgical risk should take into account the following:
1) The state of the left ventricle as judged by electrocardiography, and the size of the heart as measured on a chest X-ray. When preoperative hypertension has been severe and long-standing, persistent residual left ventricular hypertrophy is almost inevitable; this should be rated according to its degree.
2) Repair of a coarcted aorta is not always successful in restoring the blood pressure to normal levels, possibly due to persistence of the humoral mechanism in the kidneys. Residual blood pressure elevation on examination should be rated in the usual way.
3) Very close attention should be paid to the state of the aortic valve, in view of the high incidence of bicuspid deformity in coarctation of the aorta. If there is any suspicion that a bicuspid valve is present and the auscultatory signs suggest that it is already beginning to stiffen and calcify, the appropriate rating should be applied as indicated in the earlier section on bicuspid aortic valve or aortic stenosis (*see* pp. 362–4). Modern echocardiography is the best way of confirming whether an

aortic valve is bicuspid, and Doppler echocardiography can measure the degree of aortic regurgitation, if any, or the gradient between left ventricle and aorta if there is early calcific aortic stenosis. Any aortic incompetence or stenosis revealed by these investigations should be rated in addition.

4) No additional rating need be applied for the use of an artificial tube graft.

It will be evident, therefore, that when most or many of the adverse features mentioned above are present the mortality risk will be extremely high, despite the successful resection or dilatation of a coarctation, and even when postoperative residuals are few and slight, a modest extra mortality rating will still be required in many instances. On the other hand, if a coarctation has been repaired at the ideal age of late childhood, the majority of individuals will most likely be standard risks when they apply for life insurance in adult life.

COMPLEX CONGENITAL DEFECTS

Tetralogy of Fallot

The tetralogy of Fallot is the commonest form of congenital heart disease causing cyanosis after the age of one year. Of the four components making up the tetralogy, obstruction to right ventricular outflow is the one that determines the degree of cyanosis and severity of symptoms; the greater the obstruction to right ventricular outflow the larger the shunt of venous blood from the hypertrophied right ventricle through the high ventricular septal defect into the overriding aorta. In the acyanotic type of Fallot's tetralogy (pink Fallot) the obstruction to right ventricular outflow is slight and the shunting of venous blood from right ventricle to aorta is not appreciable.

The cyanotic type of tetralogy of Fallot would be uninsurable even if adult life were reached without mishap, but insurability of the acyanotic form, which is much less liable to serious complications arising from cyanosis (such as polycythemia, coagulation defects and cerebral infarction), can be considered on its merits. The rating would be about +200 for the most favorable cases.

Tetralogy of Fallot after Surgical Treatment

Palliative surgery, such as the Blalock procedure, may be necessary during infancy as a life-saving measure, postponing total correction of the defects until later childhood or adolescence when the child's general condition is much more suited to radical surgery. If complete corrective repair of all the defects can then be accomplished, leaving normal postoperative pressures, Shumaker[28] considers the prospect of achieving a normal life expectancy to be very good.

Closure of the VSD and communication with the overriding aorta pose no special problems, but complete elimination of obstruction to the right ventricular outflow tract may be more difficult to achieve. Infundibular stenosis is the sole cause of right ventricular outflow obstruction in about half the cases of tetralogy of Fallot, and the funnel can be enlarged leaving a normal pulmonic valve. However, in a further quarter of cases valvar stenosis coexists with infundibular stenosis, requiring a surgical attack at both sites. In the case of valvar stenosis, obstruction may be relieved only at the expense of an incompetent valve, or the valve may sometimes be replaced by a xenograft. Nevertheless, complete anatomical correction and restoration of normal function is now possible in a larger proportion of cases of the tetralogy of Fallot.

Selection of Risks

Best results can be expected when total correction has been carried out in childhood or early adolescence, whether or not this follows an earlier palliative operation. If applications for life insurance are made at late teenage or in the early 20s, they can be considered very favorably. Each application should, of course, be considered on its merits and, as in most postsurgical heart situations, a report from the attending surgeon on the operation and postoperative data will be essential for the proper evaluation of the risk by the MD. If optimum terms are to be expected, the following criteria should be fulfilled: (1) the pressure gradient across the obstruction to right ventricular outflow should have been abolished or reduced to about 20 mm Hg or less; (2) there should be no incompetence of the pulmonic valve; (3) the ECG at application should show no or only minimal right ventricular hypertrophy; (4) the chest radiograph should show normal lung vascularization; and (5) the cardiac shadow should show no selective chamber enlargement.

In the case of multiple defects, such as occur in the tetralogy of Fallot, it is desirable for a period of two years to elapse between operation and application for insurance. Thereafter best cases could be accepted at a minimal extra premium with a possibility of standard acceptance after a five-year interval, whereas others would be rated according to whatever anatomical or functional defects are still present.

Complete Transposition of the Great Vessels

Complete transposition of the great vessels is a gross congenital anomaly in which the aorta arises from the right ventricle and the pulmonary artery arises from the left ventricle, resulting in two parallel circulations which can sustain life only when there is communication between them; usually this is an ASD, PDA or VSD, or some combination of these. Cyanosis of varying severity is always present, and even those with the best bidirectional shunts rarely survive to adult life.

A hazardous surgical procedure involving a rearrangement of the systemic and pulmonary venous return to the heart, together with correction of intracardiac defects, offers the only hope of restoring the systemic and pulmonary circulations to normal. A successful correction abolishes cyanosis and enhances the probability of survival to much later ages. But even when complete correction of defects has been accomplished, there remains a possible limiting factor to longevity, namely, the ability of the right ventricle, which is the 'systemic ventricle', to sustain its unusual functional task into old age without failing.

It would be rare indeed (but probably less rare in the future) for an underwriter to see a proposal for life insurance from a person who has undergone complete surgical correction of transposition of the great vessels. Such an applicant need not be rejected out of hand but could be considered on his merits, if not for whole of life insurance then for endowment or other more restricted plans. The best postsurgical cases might be evaluated as risks not measurably greater than those having uncomplicated corrected transposition of the great vessels (*see below*).

Corrected Transposition of the Great Vessels

People with uncomplicated corrected transposition of the great vessels have functionally normal systemic and pulmonary circulations and, being symptomless, the defect may go undetected for many years. Eventually attention may be drawn to the defect by, perhaps, an unusual ECG tracing taken in the course of a routine pre-employment or life insurance medical examination, or by an unusual appearance of the cardiac silhouette on chest radiography, or by the onset of Stokes–Adams attacks due to complete atrioventricular block that had previously been symptomless and unrecognized as a pathological dysrhythmia.

The essential defects in corrected transposition of the great vessels are: (1) anteroposterior reversal of the aorta and pulmonary trunks and (2) reversal of the two ventricles. The systemic venous blood is carried as usual by the venae cavae draining into a normal right atrium. It then passes through a bicuspid atrioventricular valve (the mitral valve) into a ventricle that is morphologically the same as the left ventricle. This venous 'left ventricle' discharges into the pulmonary trunk, the blood being carried to the lungs, oxygenated and returned by the pulmonary veins to a normal left atrium. From there it passes through a tricuspid atrioventricular valve to a ventricle that is morphologically similar to a right ventricle. Finally the arterial 'right ventricle' discharges into the aorta and thence to the systemic arterial system.

Where no other defect exists a person with corrected transposition will appear to be a perfectly normal, healthy individual with full functional capability. There will be no abnormal physical signs in the heart on ordinary clinical examination, and if examined for life insurance he would undoubtedly be accepted as a standard risk. Only if an ECG were included as an additional test would suspicion arise that an anomaly existed.

Selection of Risks

Applicants known to have corrected transposition of the great vessels but with no other intracardiac or conduction defects would not quite fall within standard acceptance limits because of the possibility that the systemic ventricle (anatomical right ventricle) might fail prematurely due to the unusual hemodynamic load it is called upon to carry. Perloff[62] cited a case of death at 45 in a woman whose chamber pressures were known to have been normal, the cause of death being failure of the systemic (right) ventricle. On the other hand, survival past the age of 70 is also on record.

Rating

A rating of +100 in young age groups would seem to be called for in applicants who have uncomplicated corrected transposition of the great vessels, reducing to +50 at ages over 40. Coexisting elevation of the blood pressure would be an adverse factor putting additional strain on an already compromised systemic ventricle. Elevated blood pressure should be debited at least one and a half times the usual tabular rating if it is mild or moderate, and the risk declined outright if it is substantial.

Applicants in whom corrected transposition is complicated by other congenital cardiac defects, such as atrioventricular block, should also be declined, but special consideration could be given to cases of atrioventricular block where artificial cardiac pacing has been instituted.

Transposition of the Pulmonary Veins

Total Anomalous Pulmonary Venous Return

In the case of total anomalous pulmonary venous return, applications for life insurance would be considered only from those who have undergone complete surgical correction of the defect. This entails redirection of the pulmonary venous trunk from the right to the left atrium, together with closure of the associated ASD, a procedure that produces an eminently satisfactory result provided there is no residual pulmonary hypertension. If total anomalous pulmonary venous return is the only defect present (and this is so in two-thirds of cases) and operation is carried out in early childhood, the majority of patients will be restored to normal health and have a near-normal life expectancy.

Selection of Risks and Rating

The factors are the same as for partial transposition of the pulmonary veins (*see below*).

Partial Transposition of the Pulmonary Veins

The circulatory abnormality of partial transposition of the pulmonary veins is somewhat similar to that of the total anomalous defect but less severe in that only one or two branches of the pulmonary veins, usually from the upper lobes or from the right upper and middle lobes, drain into the right atrium, and there may or may not be an interatrial communication. The hemodynamic effects are very similar to those of ASD.

If, after complete surgical correction of the defects, the pressures in the lesser circuit remain normal, the prognosis for longevity is excellent.

Selection of Risks

Unoperated cases of total anomalous pulmonary venous return and partial transposition of the pulmonary veins would normally be declined except, perhaps, where partial transposition involved only one branch of the pulmonary vein and the hemodynamic effect was no worse than that produced by a small or moderate-sized ASD. In such circumstances partial transposition could be rated similarly to ASD without operation (*see* pp. 389–90).

In the case of postsurgical correction of total anomalous pulmonary venous return and partial transposition of the pulmonary veins, the usual principles regarding selection of postsurgical risks would generally apply. The rating would depend on the normality or otherwise of the physical signs at time of application, on the additional information afforded by a current ECG and chest radiograph and on the availability or otherwise of technical data on the operation itself and subsequent follow-up checks.

The more information the MD has at his disposal the more often will best cases of surgically corrected total anomalous pulmonary vascular return and partial transposition of the pulmonary veins be offered standard acceptances for life insurance.

Rating

The surgically corrected transposition syndromes of the pulmonary veins should be rated similarly to ASD after operation (*see* pp. 389–90).

Other Congenital Heart Defects

Many other forms of congenital heart disease exist, most being rare and involving complex defects. Such diseases need only be mentioned briefly and can be dismissed as far as ordinary life insurance is concerned, at least in the unoperated state. For most of these defects surgery, if undertaken at all, is usually only palliative. The first example to be mentioned is, however, an exception.

Cor Triatriatum

If recognized early enough, cor triatriatum can be completely corrected, leaving no functional residual defect. It is possible, therefore, that an operated patient will present in later life as an applicant for life insurance. The defect is an abnormal diaphragm which divides the left atrium into two chambers: the posterosuperior, draining the pulmonary veins; and the anteroinferior, communicating with the mitral valve. The diaphragm usually has one or more openings; the size of these determines the degree of obstruction to pulmonary venous return. If the fibro-muscular diaphragm is excised before pulmonary vascular disease develops, complete cure can be expected.

Cor Triloculare Biatrium

In this defect there is a right and left atrium but only a single ventricle. The degree of mixing of the venous and arterial streams determines the severity of cyanosis and the length of survival, which can be up to the third or fourth decade. There is little useful that can be done surgically for patients with this defect.

Ebstein's Anomaly

Ebstein's anomaly of the tricuspid valve, in which the septal and posterior leaflets are elongated and displaced towards the apex of the heart, causes tricuspid regurgitation of variable severity. It accounts for about 0·5 percent of congenital heart disease. Cyanosis occurs because of right-to-left shunting at atrial level via a patent foramen ovale or ASD, and arrhythmias occur because of the frequent presence of an accessory atrioventricular conduction pathway. This may be manifest on the surface ECG as a short PR interval with a delta wave indicating ventricular pre-excitation (WPW syndrome). Management is usually conservative. However, drug therapy may be required for arrhythmias or heart failure; occasionally surgical closure of the foramen ovale, repair or replacement of the tricuspid valve and/or division of an accessory conducting pathway may be necessary. In some instances where function of the right ventricle is inadequate a palliative operation may be performed aimed at increasing pulmonary blood flow by diverting the systemic venous return away from the right atrium to the lungs through an anastomosis between the superior vena cava and right pulmonary artery.

Rating should be as for an ASD operated or unoperated as the case may be, with any further rating necessary due to a history of arrythmia or for replacement of the tricuspid by a prosthetic valve.

Persistent Truncus Arteriosus

This is a rare and serious anomaly which is usually fatal in childhood. Corrective surgery has so far met with little success, and the operation of banding the pulmonary artery in order to diminish blood flow through the lungs is only palliative.

Tricuspid Atresia

Operative treatment has so far met with little success in this congenital defect.

Lutembacher's Syndrome

This is an example of combined congenital and acquired heart disease. The syndrome consists of an atrial septal defect and mitral stenosis, the latter usually of rheumatic origin. The prognosis following surgical treatment will depend on the manner of correction of the mitral stenosis, whether by closed valvotomy, by valvoplasty or by prosthetic valve replacement (see p. 383).

Eisenmenger's Syndrome

The complex, as described by Eisenmenger, can be defined as pulmonary hypertension with reversed interventricular shunt, although the shunt can also be situated at other levels, such as an ASD or PDA. The pulmonary hypertension seems to be determined primarily by high pulmonary resistance at birth and not wholly by a direct shunt acting over a long period. The physiological situation is less serious than may at first appear. The naturally high systemic resistance tends to prevent too great a right-to-left shunt and so ensures a fair pulmonary blood flow. At the same time, the high pulmonary resistance is prevented from overburdening the right ventricle by the defect acting as a safety valve in the pulmonary circulation.

The main symptom of this syndrome is life-long dyspnea, with those having an ASD most incapacitated (average Class III). Those with PDA fare best (average Class II), and those with a VSA are midway between the two extremes. Other symptoms are angina and syncopal attacks, usually provoked by effort.

Prognosis

The shunt is usually bidirectional, although in a few cases there may be no shunt either way or the shunt may be wholly reversed. Any murmurs produced can therefore be very variable and sometimes inaudible.

Of 35 fatal cases of Eisenmenger's complex reported in the literature up to 1951,[63] eight died in infancy, four died between the ages of three and ten, and five, seven, seven, one and three died in each subsequent decade, the oldest being aged 60. Figures for shunts at the ASD and PDA levels should be similar.

Those suffering from Eisenmenger's syndrome who have survived to adult life are therefore capable of leading a fairly reasonable existence for many years, as long as they exercise within their capabilities. Most favorable cases might be expected to survive to the fifth or sixth decade. Operative treatment is definitely contraindicated except for those with a PDA and ASD when the shunt is still predominantly left to right.

Rating

Applicants with Eisenmenger's syndrome would usually be declined for life insurance, but it might be possible to offer terms to selected cases if plans are designed to mature not later than age 55, with a rating of 4 or 5 per mil throughout.

Congenital Dextrocardia

Dextrocardia without transposition, in which the heart is rotated and lies in the right side of the chest, is almost invariably associated with a serious congenital anomaly. Dextrocardia with transposition, whereby the left chambers lie on the right side and form the right border and apex, and the right chambers lie on the left side, is almost always accompanied by complete situs inversus of the abdominal viscera; when this is so, the heart is usually perfectly normal apart from being a mirror image of the normal anatomical configuration. As far as the heart and circulation are concerned, dextrocardia with situs inversus in no way affects longevity, but it should be noted that there is a higher incidence of bronchiectasis, presumably congenital, in this condition than in the general population.

PERICARDITIS

The causes of pericarditis are many and include bacterial and viral infections, connective tissue diseases of the auto-immune type, metabolic disorders, trauma, neoplasia and postradiation. Pericarditis occurring as part of systemic disease syndromes will be discussed later where appropriate, but there are three types that require special mention because of the confusion they sometimes cause in underwriting, due to the similarity of their symptoms to those of more serious conditions.

Acute Benign Pericarditis

Acute benign (or idiopathic) pericarditis is important, not because it is particularly dangerous to life but because the symptoms during the acute attack may easily be confused with those of MI, which has a vastly different prognosis. This error is liable to occur at various levels of the underwriting process, particularly if the applicant is unaware of the precise nature of his 'heart' complaint, and the medical examiner misinterprets his symptoms at the time of application. The mere mention in a life insurance history of severe substernal pain that has required admission to hospital and where an ECG was found to be abnormal is enough to make most MDs or CMOs extremely suspicious of ischemic heart disease.

The error is likely to be compounded if the attending physician is unable to confirm the true diagnosis because of, for example, inadequate or missing records. Finally, it is not unknown for a misdiagnosis of CAD to be made in hospital, especially if the attack of pericarditis was mild or if admission to hospital had been delayed until the acute phase had passed and evolution of the typical ECG changes had already proceeded to the final negative T-wave pattern. Moreover, the T-wave changes can occasionally persist for months or years, adding to the diagnostic confusion long after the event.

On the other hand, a history of acute benign pericarditis disclosed in the application or to the medical examiner should always be corroborated by a report from the hospital that made the initial diagnosis. This is to ascertain that it was based on sound evidence and was not merely a convenient label for 'other chest pain' where clinical and investigational findings were negative.

Differentiating Features

The clinical features of acute benign pericarditis are too well known to warrant comprehensive comment here, but it is as well to point out one or two of the features that differentiate it from MI. Although no single clinical feature can exclude MI, it is possible to do so by a combination of several clues.

The pain of pericarditis is very often influenced by movement of the chest, by posture (particularly by lying supine) and by swallowing, features that are not typical of ischemic pain. There is absence of pain in the arms of pericarditis, although it is commonly felt across both shoulders. In pericarditis the ECG abnormalities do not tend to be localized, as in MI, but are widely distributed in all leads. Problems can occur in the interpretation of the ECG where there is a so-called normal junctional elevation of the ST segment which is almost impossible to differentiate in the acute phase from that of pericarditis. A previous ECG or the lack of evolution of the pattern will confirm the true nature of the cardiographic findings. The widespread use of thrombolytic therapy often results in dramatic limitation of evolving ECG changes in acute MI, and a subsequent exercise stress ECG and/or thallium stress ECG may well help to differentiate pericarditis from MI. Pericardial friction in the absence of elevated cardiac enzymes plus a substantially raised sedimentation rate are typical of pericarditis but not of MI.

Evidence is accumulating that acute benign pericarditis is due to a tissue sensitivity phenomenon which may be provoked by a variety of noxious agents, including Coxsackie and other viral infections, some antibiotics and other drugs. Many who suffer from acute benign pericarditis are known to suffer from other forms of allergy, such as hay fever, eczema and asthma, and since the pericarditis usually responds promptly to the administration of oral corticosteroid drugs this would seem to be further evidence of the immunopathologic basis of the disease.

Prognosis

Cardiac tamponade is the chief danger to life; a few reported deaths in acute benign pericarditis have been due to this. Tamponade due to hemopericardium has also been responsible for some deaths, and this has usually been precipitated by anticoagulants given because of a mistaken diagnosis of MI.

A characteristic of the condition is a tendency to relapse; pericardectomy has occasionally been carried out to obviate recurrences, but this is rarely necessary. Judicious use of corticosteroid drugs usually forestalls serious relapses.

Rating

Acute benign pericarditis may still be described as a benign condition despite the few reported deaths; it would not usually warrant a rating when there is a history of only one attack, provided there is good documentation confirming the diagnosis. When there is a history of recurrent attacks a rating of +75 in the first year of full recovery from the last attack, +50 to +25 in the second year and standard thereafter ought to cover the risk adequately.

Postcardiac injury syndrome

The postcardiac injury syndrome is similar in many respects to acute benign pericarditis and may arise a week or two following injury to heart muscle, such as occurs with cardiotomy in heart surgery, stab wounds or contusion of the myocardium by crush or blow injuries to the thoracic cage. It may also follow MI due to coronary occlusion (Dressler's syndrome). In these syndromes pericardial effusions are more commonly demonstrated on echocardiography, and there may be accompanying pleural reactions.

Postcardiac injury pericarditis seems to be an antigen-antibody reaction originating from damaged heart muscle, and skeletal or heart muscle antibodies can usually be demonstrated in the serum.

Selection of Risks

For the selection of risks, the significance of pericarditis due to these heart injury syndromes is again the differentiation from MI, which may have complicated cardiac trauma, or from a second infarct when it arises after an original coronary occlusion. Great vigilance is necessary on the part of all underwriting personnel to prevent such mistakes occurring, but this is only possible if the fullest information about the event can be obtained from the attending physician, hospital or clinic. If confirmed, postcardiac injury pericarditis would be rated in the same way as acute benign pericarditis, but also taking into account the nature of the original etiology, particularly if it was MI.

Chronic Constrictive Pericarditis

Constrictive pericarditis would normally present as a problem in underwriting only after the operation of pericardectomy. The reason for the markedly thickened pericardium is usually obscure; in past years many cases were due to tuberculosis, and this may still be so in tropical Africa and India. Constriction is known to follow connective tissue disorders, neoplastic diseases, trauma and irradiation; uncommonly it results from acute benign pericarditis and virtually never after the acute pericarditis of rheumatic fever. Usually there is no intrinsic disease of the heart and the classic signs are due purely to mechanical constriction of the heart and great vessels; they consist of increased jugular venous pressure, hepatomegaly, soft heart sounds, Kussmaul's sign, ascites, peripheral edema, a pericardial knock, pulsus paradoxus and, less commonly, atrial fibrillation. These signs are less frequently present when there is an effusive constrictive type of pericarditis. The longer the heart has been encased by the thickened cortex of pericardium the more atrophied the underlying myocardium becomes and the more often atrial fibrillation develops.

Prognosis

If the heart and great vessels can be freed by adequate decortication, there is often a striking immediate improvement, which continues progressively over a period of several months as the semi-atrophied myocardium regenerates. Experience at the Mayo Clinic was reviewed by McCaughan,[64] who assessed the later outcome of 231 patients who underwent pericardectomy for constrictive pericarditis between 1936 and 1982. The risk of early postoperative death was strongly influenced by the severity of the patients' preoperative disability, such that the risk was 1 percent for patients in Class I or II and 46 percent for patients who were in Class IV. Current operative mortality should be substantially less than the 6 percent quoted during the 1960s, and late follow-up has shown significant continued clinical improvement in the vast majority (greater than 90 percent) of patients. It has become evident that long-standing pericardial restriction may be associated with irreversible atrophic changes in the myocardium, and the functional status of the heart would have to be carefully evaluated postoperatively with echocardiography should there be doubts about full recovery.

Rating

If the heart is basically sound and in sinus rhythm, the late prognosis should be excellent. This being so, the risk could be covered by a temporary extra premium, say 3 per mil for two or three years from the second year following pericardectomy. Some insurance companies rate by a permanent extra premium equivalent to 100 percent extra mortality in the second year, reducing to zero in stages in the subsequent three years.

ACUTE MYOCARDITIS

Myocarditis is said to be present when the heart is involved in an inflammatory process, usually the result of an infectious agent with auto-immune mechanisms implicated, as in rheumatic fever. Non-infectious myocarditis may be due to chemical agents, drugs, radiation and as part of general system disease, as in the connective tissue diseases. In general, acute myocarditis is caused by viruses, and those commonly found are the viruses of influenza and Coxsackie B strain. Acute myocarditis may also occur during the course of generalized viral diseases, such as mumps, glandular fever, measles and poliomyelitis, and is frequently associated with acute benign pericarditis, especially when it is caused by one of the Coxsackie B viruses or Echoviruses. Other infectious forms of acute myocarditis result from bacterial infection (diphtheria, typhoid, tuberculosis), spirochetal (relapsing fever, Lyme disease), rickettsial (typhus, Rocky Mountain spotted fever), fungal and protozoal (Chagas' disease). HIV is associated with myocarditis in up to 50 percent of patients dying of AIDS, and although viral, protozoal, bacterial, fungal and opportunistic pathogens have been identified in some histologic sections, the cause of the myocarditis remains idiopathic.

Acute viral myocarditis is usually a self-limiting condition and patients recover without residuals. The ECG may show transient ST-T-wave abnormalities during the acute phase, a variety of cardiac arrhythmias may occur and, occasionally, congestive heart failure may be precipitated. A transient apical systolic murmur may be heard, and a friction rub if there is an associated pericarditis.

Selection of Risks

As far as life insurance is concerned the problem is mainly confirming the true nature of the acute illness. This is sometimes difficult if specific viral antibody titers were not performed at the time. Confusion may also arise if the ECG is later reviewed outside the context of the symptomatology of the acute attack. Mistakes are less likely to occur if the acute myocarditis has complicated one of the generalized viral infections, since these are more readily identifiable.

Rating

When acute myocarditis has accompanied acute benign pericarditis the rating would be as for the latter condition. Otherwise the risk would be standard after full ECG and clinical recovery. Persisting ECG changes would be looked on with some reserve in view of evidence that some cases of dilated cardiomyopathy may have had their origin in acute viral myocarditis. If in doubt, echocardiographic functional status may have to be obtained.

CARDIOMYOPATHY

There has been general agreement to follow the definition and broad classification of the WHO/ISFC[65] task force which met in 1980 and which redefined cardiomyopathies as heart muscle diseases of unknown cause. They were classified into restrictive, hypertrophic and dilated cardiomyopathies. The group previously known as secondary cardiomyopathies is now called specific heart muscle disease and includes disorders of heart muscle of either known cause or association with disorders of other systems; it therefore includes infective, metabolic (endocrine, familial storage diseases, deficiencies, amyloid), general system diseases (connective tissue disorders, infiltrations and granulomas), heredofamilial disorders (muscular dystrophies, neuromuscular disorders) sensitivities and toxic reactions. This group also includes alcoholic and peripartum heart disease.

Clinically the two important types of cardiomyopathy are hypertrophic and dilated (formerly known as congestive). It may seem rather pointless to discuss cardiomyopathies in a textbook devoted to selection of life insurance risks, since the prognosis of symptomatic cardiomyopathy is uncertain and mortality ratios generally so high in relation to select life mortality that life insurance for this type of heart disease can be little more than speculation. Nonetheless there are studies suggesting that the incidence of these disorders may not be as uncommon as originally suspected and that survival may be better in certain subsets. Examples of previously undiagnosed, symptomless cardiomyopathy continue to turn up regularly in underwriting departments, the applicants having no relevant past history but with abnormal ECGs showing gross left ventricular hypertrophy. Most of these cases are examples of hypertrophic cardiomyopathy, and it is this symptomless group that requires closer examination in relation to insurability. Prognostic aspects of the cardiomyopathies, with particular reference to insurability, were reviewed at the 15th International Conference of COINTRA in 1985.[66]

Hypertrophic Cardiomyopathy

Hypertrophic cardiomyopathy is characterized by disproportionate hypertrophy of the left ventricle (occasionally also the right ventricle), which typically involves the septum more than the free wall but which occasionally is concentric. The left ventricular volume is normal or reduced; systolic gradients are common. There is diastolic compliance dysfunction, but systolic contraction is normal or increased. Inheritance is usually by an autosomal dominant gene with incomplete penetrance. Characteristic morphologic changes, usually most severe in the septum, have been described comprising myocardial cell disarray.

There is a wide variation in the clinical presentation and outcome in hypertrophic cardiomyopathy, indicating that this is likely to be a heterogeneous disorder with differing genetic mutations responsible. The wide variety of clinical presentations has given rise in the past to different names for this condition (for example, muscular subaortic stenosis or idiopathic hypertrophic subaortic stenosis where the accent has been on large systolic gradients within the left ventricle) and a smaller subgroup of purely apical hypertrophy, often associated with giant negative T-waves, or to a group of genetically affected family members whose only abnormality may be a minor alteration of the ECG without echocardiographic evidence of hypertrophy.

An increasing majority of cases of hypertrophic cardiomyopathy are likely to have a genetic basis. Except for unexpected sudden deaths in infancy and childhood, and systematic screening of first degree relatives, most cases of hypertrophic cardiomyopathy present with symptoms in the second or third decade. Deaths are frequently sudden, often in a previously asymptomatic person, with an incidence higher in younger than older age groups, but sudden death can also occur late in the course of the disease as a result of congestive cardiac failure.

Symptomatology
The main presenting symptoms of hypertrophic cardiomyopathy are exertional breathlessness, anginal pain, syncope, presyncope and palpitations. The classic physical findings in patients with hypertrophic cardiomyopathy apply to those with left ventricular outflow gradients: jerky arterial pulses, a thrusting apical impulse often with a palpable fourth heart sound, giving a double impulse, and an ejection systolic murmur maximum towards the lower left sternal edge. Lembo et al[12] have re-emphasized the value of bedside maneuvers enabling the careful physician to distinguish the murmur of hypertrophic cardiomyopathy from all other murmurs by its increased intensity during the Valsalva maneuver and during squatting to standing, and by its decreased intensity with standing to squatting. When such signs and symptoms appear in patients over the age of 50, care should be taken not to

confuse them with the manifestations of cardiovascular diseases that are more common at this time of life, such as atrial fibrillation (which may occur in 10 percent of older people), coronary and hypertensive heart disease, mitral incompetence and calcific aortic stenosis. Now that echodoppler studies can define the functional abnormality and morphologic varieties of the disease, invasive studies are less often necessary. A typical case will show marked hypertrophy of the ventricular septum with the ratio of septum to posterior wall being greater than 1·5:1, a small ventricular cavity and systolic anterior motion of the mitral valve. It is with the advent of the detailed echocardiographic analysis that varying patterns of ventricular hypertrophy have been described. So far, however, these different patterns have not been particularly helpful in prognosis.

Epidemiology
The condition is more common than previously thought. Bagger et al carried out a retrospective study of hypertrophic cardiomyopathy in western Denmark, producing an incidence of 3·6 per 10 million of the population per year, whereas population-based information from the Rochester–Olmsted epidemiology project suggests an incidence rate for hypertrophic cardiomyopathy of 2·5 per 100,000 person years, with an age- and sex-adjusted prevalence rate of 18·8 per 100,000 population.

Prognosis and Natural History
The natural history is highly variable, up to 75 percent of patients presenting with hypertrophic cardiomyopathy remaining stable over several years' follow-up and 25 percent dying or showing deterioration. Deterioration is not well correlated with the outflow gradient, but the onset of atrial fibrillation often heralds clinical worsening, and about 10 percent of patients will go on to experience congestive heart failure. This may be accompanied by a decrease in the size of the left ventricular outflow gradient. In 1981 McKenna et al[67] reported a retrospective experience of 254 patients followed up for 23 years (with a mean of six years). This showed that 48 patients had died, 32 of them suddenly. The deaths in other patients were mainly the result of congestive heart failure. No definite features predictive of sudden death were detected at that time, but subsequently Goodwin[68] highlighted the clinical criteria of young age, strong family history and progressive symptoms all indicating a worse prognosis. Figure 15.4 illustrates the cumulative survival curves for medically treated patients from McKenna's series.[67] The adverse prognostic features in this study were the combination of (1) young age (14 years or younger), (2) syncope at diagnosis, (3) severe dyspnea at last follow-up, and (4) a family history of hypertrophic cardiomyopathy and sudden death. Patients who had been diagnosed in childhood were usually asymptomatic, had an unfavorable family history and a 5·9 percent annual mortality. In those aged 15–45 at diagnosis there was a 2·5 percent annual mortality rate, syncope being the only prognostic feature. Among those diagnosed between the age of 45 and 60, breathlessness and exertional chest pain were more common in the patients who died, and the annual mortality rate was 2·6 percent. Poor prognosis was better predicted by the history at the time of diagnosis and by changes in symptoms during follow-up than by any ECG or hemodynamic measurement.

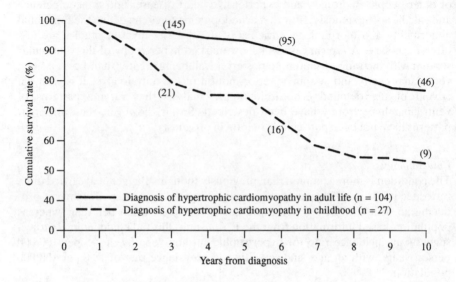

Fig. 15.4. **Cumulative survival curve from the year of diagnosis for 211 medically treated patients. The probability of death equals the total number of deaths for the year divided by the adjusted number at risk, minus the number of deaths due to other causes. [Source: Mckenna et al.[67]]**

It has been suggested that the likely cause of sudden death in hypertrophic cardiomyopathy is by ventricular arrhythmias, and Holter ECG monitoring has identified a subgroup with a high incidence of such arrhythmias, often unrecognized by the patient. Unsustained ventricular tachycardia on ambulatory monitoring is both sensitive and specific; in particular it has a very high (97 percent) negative predictive accuracy. Ventricular tachycardia has a low positive predictive accuracy for sudden death (23 percent), indicating that not all patients with non-sustained ventricular tachycardia are at risk; further risk stratification in this group is necessary. There is some evidence that treatment with amiodorone suppresses ventricular tachycardia and improves prognosis.

Figure 15.5 illustrates the natural history of hypertrophic cardiomyopathy as is seen typically in tertiary referral centers, where there is an estimated total mortality of 56 percent in 15 years or a pooled average mortality rate of 3–3·5 percent per year. However, data from tertiary centers may introduce a bias because such patients may have more symptoms and be at higher risk for events. Experience of outpatient populations in district hospitals suggests that incidence of symptoms, clinical deterioration and death rates may be lower. Shapiro[69] reviewed a five-year experience of hypertrophic cardiomyopathy at a district general hospital; 39 cases were diagnosed representing 8 percent of patients investigated for angina and 0·7 percent of the total outpatients, with an age range of 15 to 76. The 'typical' form with asymmetrical hypertrophy and a gradient was found in only one-third of patients. Serious ventricular arrhythmias were probably more common than in the

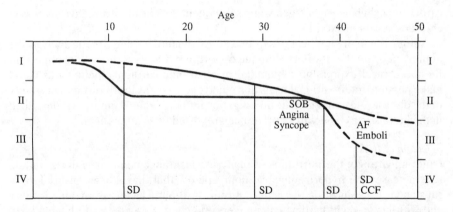

Fig. 15.5. A suggested natural history of hypertrophic cardiomyopathy. The vertical axis represents the New York Heart Association functional class (*see* p. 349). The developmental myocardial abnormality is probably present from birth and a murmur usually precedes symptoms. The average age at onset of symptoms was 28 years. The average duration of symptoms before death was nine years. Many patients, however, deteriorated only slowly, although some developed atrial fibrillation with a striking increase in symptoms. Sudden death may occur at any age.

SOB, dyspnea; SD, sudden death, CCF, congestive cardiac failure; AF, atrial fibrillation.

general population, and no deaths occurred during a relatively short follow-up period (mean 3·1 years). Ten of these patients were asymptomatic, 12 had a family history of hypertrophic cardiomyopathy and two had a family history of sudden death. The authors concluded that hypertrophic cardiomyopathy occupied a 'not insignificant proportion' of cardiac workload and that unselected cases presenting to a district general hospital represented a relatively mild form of the disease wthout the more serious prognosis suggested by the more specialized units.

Some surgical series tend to support improved survival, but this probably reflects the patient-selection process as there have been no randomized medical-surgical trials. In 1987 the National Institute of Health reported 240 patients operated on between 1960 and 1980. There was an 8 percent operative mortality and a late mortality of only 1·5 percent per year. Results from the Mayo Clinic indicate a general consensus that operation does not alter the natural history of the disease or reduce mortality. The Mayo Clinic studies produced an annual mortality of 2·2–3·5 percent, contrasting with a medical annual mortality of 3 percent.

Genetic aspects
Rosenweig et al[71] described the preclinical diagnosis of familial hypertrophic cardiomyopathy by genetic analysis of blood lymphocytes, identifying a novel missense mutation in a patient with familial hypertrophic cardiomyopathy. There was perfect agreement in the evaluation of 15 of the patients' relatives, with the clinical diagnosis of eight affected and seven not affected. Further analysis of 14 children of these family members revealed one child with echocardiographic features diagnostic of familial hypertrophic cardiomyopathy, although genetic analysis showed that six other children also had inherited missense mutation and might later manifest the disease. Mutation in the beta

cardiac myosin heavy chain gene, and subsequent defects in cardiac myosin, was in chromosome 14 in exon 13.

Among the many implications of preclinical diagnosis using genetic analysis the authors indicate that it offers a unique opportunity to assess the factors important for the clinical expression of familial hypertrophic cardiomyopathy; this could make possible interventional trials that could decrease the morbidity and mortality of the disease. A similar genetic investigation into the original family first described in the literature by Teare in 1958 has been reported by Watkins et al.[72]

Selection of Risks

Quite unwittingly the portfolios of many life insurance companies must contain several cases of hypertrophic cardiomyopathy that have been insured in a substandard classification of systolic murmur, without a history of rheumatic fever and with no or slight cardiac enlargement, no chest X-ray or ECG having been carried out at the time of application. Generally speaking, applicants in whom a diagnosis of hypertrophic cardiomyopathy has been confirmed have not normally been considered insurable in the past. Certainly the quoted death rate of 2–3 percent per year could not be said to inspire the confidence of a life underwriter. But too pessimistic a view is probably unjustified. It should be remembered that the cases in the studies quoted above were those referred to tertiary centers, and many had symptoms when they first entered the studies. Therefore it is conceivable that by excluding those with symptoms and those in whom there is a clinical pointer to a high risk of sudden death a group may be found with an estimated mortality that would allow acceptance for life insurance within the usual range of substandard premium pricing. Apart from being symptom free, individuals in the most favorable mortality group should have had onset of recognition of disease after the age of 30, with no family history of hypertrophic cardiomyopathy with sudden death. They should be normotensive and in sinus rhythm, and cardiologic evaluation should be available, including stress testing and Holter monitoring.

Rating

As a guide to risk evaluation of hypertrophic cardiomyopathy a rating schedule, based on the practice of one UK reinsurer, is shown below.

Always symptomless, no family history of premature or sudden or cardiac death, no rhythm disturbances, minor ECG changes only:

Age	Rating
Under 30	Refer to MD or CMO
30–39	+350 to +250
40–49	+250 to +200
50–59	+150 to +100
60 and over	+75 to +50

With more marked ECG changes (deeper T-wave inversion) or occasional ectopic beats — add +50 up depending on age and number and severity of unfavorable features.

History of more serious tachyarrhythmias or with continuing symptoms (e.g. dyspnea, angina) or positive family history — decline.

Until large mortality studies of hypertrophic cardiomyopathy have been carried out, ratings must necessarily be empirical.

Other Types of Cardiomyopathy

Only the main features of the other types of cardiomyopathy need be mentioned briefly, since the severity of their condition and poor long-term prognosis almost always indicate declinature.

Idiopathic Dilated Cardiomyopathy (Congestive Cardiomyopathy)

This condition is recognized by dilatation of the left or right ventricle or both. Dilatation often becomes severe and is invariably accompanied by hypertrophy. Systolic ventricular function is impaired, and congestive heart failure may or may not supervene. Presentation with disturbances of ventricular or atrial rhythm is common; death may occur at any age. Incidence studies in Sweden revealed 5·3 cases per 100,000 population, and postmortem studies 7·5 cases per 100,000. Population-based studies in Olmsted county, Minnesota, confirmed these data, with an incidence of 6 per 100,000. It is likely that the clinic incidence of idiopathic dilated cardiomyopathy is significantly underestimated, and in non-industrialized countries non-hypertensive heart disease patients may have an incidence of 10–20 percent.

By definition the cause is unknown, although viral and auto-immune hypotheses have received attention. The extremely poor prognosis is generally agreed, with two-fifths to one-half of patients dying within the first two years of diagnosis, usually from progressive congestive heart failure. In many the abruptness of the terminal event indicates an arrhythmic mechanism, although treatment with antiarrhythmic agents has not been shown to improve prognosis. In a long-term follow-up of symptomatic patients with dilated cardiomyopathy from the Mayo Clinic, 77 percent of patients had an accelerated course to death within the first two years and 23 percent had a normal survival, the majority of these showing clinical improvement and decreased or normal heart size. Many patients with dilated cardiomyopathy are candidates for heart transplantation (see p. 386). In a smaller group of patients with documented improvement, experimental underwriting could be considered after a two-year postponement period.

Alcoholic Cardiomyopathy

Those especially predisposed may develop dilated cardiomyopathy after excessive consumption of alcohol over a long period. The disease is characterized by frequent ventricular ectopic beats or atrial fibrillation and by the occurrence of intermittent episodes of congestive heart failure related to alcoholic bouts or for no apparent reason.

Just as the fatty liver of the alcoholic can be reversed by complete abstinence, so too can alcoholic cardiomyopathy, at least in its early stages. It is unlikely, however, for people with a history of alcoholic cardiomyopathy to be insurable unless they have observed total abstinence for several years with evidence that the heart has returned completely to normal.

Peripartum Cardiomyopathy

It is possible that some cases of fully regressed peripartum cardiomyopathy may apply for life insurance in later years. The most favorable examples are those arising in the first three months after childbirth, in which case the great majority will regress completely. If the cardiomyopathy arises later than three months after childbirth and persists after the sixth month, the chance of regression is very small, and mortality high. A history of perinatal cardiomyopathy could be considered insurable after complete recovery provided there had been no symptoms for at least two years and the heart was normal on investigational procedures.

Restrictive Cardiomyopathy

This may exist with or without obliteration of the ventricular cavities; it includes endomyocardial fibrosis and Löffler's cardiomyopathy and could be described as eosinophilic myocardial disease. There is restriction to filling of the heart by scarring affecting one or both ventricles and, although involvement of the atrioventricular valves is common, the outflow tracts are spared. There may be difficulty in differentiating this condition from constrictive pericarditis. Restrictive cardiomyopathy is uncommon, the long-term prognosis uncertain; it would not normally be considered an insurable entity.

PULMONARY HEART DISEASE

Acute Cor Pulmonale

Acute cor pulmonale is caused by acute massive obstruction of the pulmonary circulation due, in the majority of cases, to a large pulmonary embolus originating from systemic phlebothrombosis, usually in the veins of the legs or pelvis.

Rating

The occurrence of pulmonary infarction is one of the main reasons for the slightly increased mortality risk associated with a history of phlebitis or deep vein thrombosis, but after full recovery from an infarction the risk would only be that of further emboli. A permanent rating of +50 may be required if significant residuals remain, in the form of a swollen and tense limb complicating deep venous thrombosis, or varicose ulceration complicating varicose veins.

Recurrent pulmonary embolism will usually require a higher rating, bearing in mind that even minor episodes of repeated thromboembolism, particularly in older age groups, are commonly the starting point of inexorably progressive cardiopulmonary disease. Much will depend on the state of pulmonary function at the time of application as judged by special tests, the degree of exercise tolerance and the clinical signs in the lungs and heart. When normal, rating could be up to +75 depending on the state of the veins of the lower limbs and duration since last attack, but when abnormal the case should be classified as chronic cor pulmonale and rated accordingly (see below).

It should be noted that the clinical diagnosis of both pulmonary embolism and deep venous thrombosis is unreliable; even with the advent of non-invasive techniques, such as Doppler flow studies, impedance plethismography and radionuclide techniques (including ventilation-perfusion scans), angiography is still frequently needed to confirm the diagnosis. The chance of recurrence of acute pulmonary embolism is low, particularly in subjects in whom a definite acute and temporary predisposing factor, such as recent surgery or trauma, can be identified. When there is no such predisposing factor careful assessment is needed to define the situation to ensure that there is no evidence of some systemic illness, such as malignancy or a rare clotting disorder (e.g. antithrombin III deficiency). When no acute predisposing factor can be identified or there are repeated events, long-term anticoagulation beyond an initial three months is usually required.

Chronic Cor Pulmonale

Chronic cor pulmonale is primarily the result of long-standing hypertension in the pulmonary circulation. It is the end result of many chronic lung diseases, such as pulmonary emphysema, chronic bronchitis and pulmonary fibrosis from whatever cause. It is the common end result of various chest deformities, such as severe kyphoscoliosis or funnel deformity of the chest of a degree sufficient to cause mediastinal displacement and compression. It can also result from repeated small pulmonary emboli and from pulmonary vascular disease complicating congenital heart disease where significant left-to-right shunts exist or have existed prior to operation. Chronic pulmonary heart disease manifests itself predominantly over the age of 50, and the incidence rises steeply after the age of 60.

This type of heart disease has tended to increase in recent years owing to the fact that the lives of so many sufferers from chronic bronchitis and emphysema are being prolonged by the use of modern antibiotics, so that the ultimate cause of death is now more often right-sided heart failure than lung infection.

In the UK chronic bronchitis with emphysema used to account for not less than nine-tenths of all cases of chronic cor pulmonale, but the relative frequency of the condition as a cause of heart failure has been gradually decreasing over the past 20 years with the widespread introduction of clean air programs and a decrease in cigarette smoking among the population. Nevertheless, pulmonary heart disease due to chronic bronchitis and emphysema still exists as a public health problem.

Primary pulmonary hypertension is a rare condition. The female-to-male ratio is about 2·5:1 and the average age at onset is 35. The clinical course is of inexorable progression to death, with approximate three-year survival of only 50 percent. There are rare instances involving reversal or regression of pulmonary hypertension, and occasional survival durations beyond ten years have been reported. Such cases are candidates for heart-lung transplantation, and both heart-lung transplants and single lung transplants are being used in suitable candidates with end-stage chronic cor pulmonale. Medium-term results from heart-lung transplantation and single lung transplantation are not yet sufficiently well documented to provide even experimental short-term ratings; cases should be declined for the present.

Selection of Risks

Chronic cor pulmonale should not often cause undue difficulty in underwriting, for even in mild types some degree of cardiopulmonary impairment will usually be obvious; more advanced cases will produce a typical clinical picture that will leave no doubt about decision to be taken. Any history of congestive cardiac failure, even slight, occurring during the course of an exacerbation of acute infection is sufficient reason for declining a risk for life insurance.

As a rule, the underwriting of chronic cor pulmonale is rather similar to that for chronic bronchitis and emphysema (*see* Chapter 17).

CARDIOVASCULAR SYPHILIS

Heart disease due to acquired syphilis is now rare because of efficient methods of treatment of the primary infection and good public health control and propaganda. Congenital syphilis does not give rise to cardiovascular disease. Onset of symptoms of cardiovascular syphilis is approximately during the fourth decade, but asymptomatic lesions may sometimes be recognized earlier during the course of routine life insurance examinations. The most common interval between primary infection and the appearance of cardiovascular symptoms is about 20 years, although there are wide variations.

The three main lesions of cardiovascular syphilis are: (1) aortic incompetence, which is by far the most common; (2) aneurysm of the aorta; and (3) inflammatory involvement of the origins of the coronary arteries giving rise to symptoms of myocardial ischemia.

Aortic Incompetence

When an aortic diastolic murmur is discovered and there is some doubt as to its etiology, syphilis must always be excluded, because an untreated case progresses steadily, and once symptoms become apparent the prognosis is poor. On the other hand, when there is a history of syphilis known to have been treated adequately in the past, the prognosis will be much better, and an applicant so treated might be considered insurable in a substandard category when the degree of incompetence is no more than slight and when there is no radiological evidence of aortic aneurysm. Mortality is generally somewhat higher than with aortic insufficiency of rheumatic or congenital origin.

Syphilitic Aortic Aneurysm

Syphilitic aortic aneurysms are dangerous but fortunately are now very rare. Despite thorough antisyphilitic treatment these aneurysms are liable to progress, and applicants with an aortic aneurysm, however small, are best declined. On the other hand, modern reparative vascular surgery has greatly improved prognosis of aortic aneurysm, and postsurgical risks could be accepted substandard at a rating of +100 to +50, depending on the extent of the prosthetic repair, plus a temporary extra of 5 per mil for five years in the first year of acceptance.

Myocardial Ischemia

Anginal pain due to syphilitic narrowing of the ostia of the coronary arteries is very rare, but the possibility must be kept in mind. The diagnosis would be supported by other stigmata of syphilis found during clinical examination, but confirmation would depend on the result of serological tests and angiography, although the demonstration of ostial narrowing is often difficult even with special views.

When there is a history of anginal pain considered to be due to syphilis and that has completely remitted after adequate antisyphilitic treatment, the risk may be accepted six months after freedom from all symptoms, provided there is no aortic aneurysm, aortic regurgitation or significant coronary artery disease as demonstrated by angiography. Rating is as for aortitis without aneurysm (*see* p. 912).

Precordial pain is often a feature of the late stages of syphilitic aortitis with free aortic regurgitation, being due to relative ischemia in a grossly hypertrophied left ventricle. Such a case would, of course, be quite uninsurable.

PERIPHERAL VASCULAR DISEASES (PVD)

Arteriosclerosis is an inexact term which has come to embrace several kinds of arterial disorders. When the different types have to be defined, more exact terminology is necessary. Four terms are used:

1) *Monckeberg's or medial sclerosis.* This is characterized by pipe-stem arteries due to degeneration of the medial coat of the medium arteries, focal calcification being common. It is a feature of diabetes, long-term corticosteroid administration and old age, and affects both sexes equally. In the lower limbs it may be associated with atherosclerosis leading to occlusive disease, and there is an increased association with senile calcification of the aortic valve.
2) *Diffuse arteriolar sclerosis.* This arises from hypertrophy of the muscular coat of the small arteries, commonly affecting the precapillary arterioles of the kidneys and other viscera. It is typically associated with persistent systemic hypertension.
3) *Atheroma or atherosclerosis.* This lesion occurs first as a thickening of the intimal coat, especially of the aorta and its main branches and of the coronary and cerebral arteries. It is followed later by lipid deposition, fibrosis and calcification.
4) *Elastosis.* This is due to weakening of the elastic fibers of the vessel wall and is characteristically exemplified by the corkscrew temporal arteries of people past middle age.

Of all these conditions the one mainly responsible for high mortality in cardiovascular disorders is atherosclerosis, since it is generalized, affecting particularly the coronary and cerebral arteries. Some atheroma is usually present in most people past middle age but unfortunately there is no easy way of measuring its extent, and its presence may only become apparent when it causes symptoms. Indirect evidence of a predisposition to develop generalized arterial atheroma can be obtained by studying the lipoprotein profile (*see* pp. 315–19). Those with familial type III hyperlipoproteinemia (dyslipoproteinemia or broad beta band disease) are said to be particularly likely to develop peripheral arterial atheroma and may be recognized clinically by the finding of palmar or tuberous xanthomas.

Intermittent Claudication

Intermittent claudication is the usual clinical manifestation of an obstructed arterial supply to the lower limbs and is always of serious import. The pain, which is due to muscle ischemia, is typically provoked by walking and occurs characteristically in the calf, anterior tibial compartment or the foot, depending on the site of arterial obstruction. In the great majority of cases intermittent claudication is due to atherothrombotic occlusion of one of the larger arterial trunks supplying the limb. Other less common causes are classical thromboangiitis obliterans, arterial thrombosis secondary to trauma, peripheral arterial embolism, arteritis (systemic lupus erythematosis and Takayasu's disease), fibrosis (idopathic diffuse and postradiation), developmental anomalies (including coarctation and popliteal entrapment) and adventitial cystic disease. The relative frequency of these conditions as a cause of intermittent claudication is shown in Table 15.47.

Table 15.47. Analysis by cause of 162 cases of peripheral ischemia of the lower limb.[a]

Etiology	Number of cases
Thrombosis secondary to trauma	4
Thromboangiitis obliterans	6
Atherothrombotic obliterans	149
Peripheral arterial embolism	3

[a]Source: Mavor et al.[73]

It is worthwhile attempting to differentiate the various causes of claudication, since the prognosis of each differs sufficiently to be of importance in underwriting.

The late prognosis of claudication due to peripheral embolism depends on the primary cause as well as the site of occlusion. For example, the overall risk associated with a peripheral embolus emanating from a rheumatic or cardiomyopathic heart in atrial fibrillation would be very much greater than a similar embolism arising from a mural thrombus complicating a myocardial infarction or from an atherothrombotic lesion in a more proximal large main artery.

Claudication due to thrombosis in a traumatized artery of a lower limb would probably have the best prognosis of all, especially if the occluded portion has been successfully treated surgically. Needless to say, it should be established that trauma was not merely an incidental occurrence in a vessel already severely affected by atherothrombotic disease.

Thromboangiitis Obliterans
As described by Buerger, thromboangiitis obliterans is a disease of young people, seldom starting after the age of 35; the extremes of age in Mavor's series[73] were 13 and 35. It is a disease of the small arteries and veins of the lower extremities, beginning characteristically in the digital or plantar arteries of the foot and ascending to involve arteries at a more proximal level with each succeeding attack.

The condition inevitably becomes bilateral. The typical initial symptom is claudication pain in the arch of the foot or perhaps gangrene affecting a toe. With succeeding attacks, exercise pain may spread up the anterior compartment of the lower leg and occasionally to the lower calf region. It is doubtful that the large arterial trunks of the legs are ever involved in classic thromboangiitis obliterans, although expert opinion differs on this point.

The disease is more common in Asia that in Western countries and is likely to become even more common as more Asians become regular cigarette smokers.

Prognosis

According to Eastcott,[74] the smoking of tobacco, particularly cigarette smoking, was the initiating cause of thromboangiitis obliterans; if stopped, the result would be complete recovery, provided that gangrene was not already present. There does appear to be a genetic predisposition with an increased incidence of HLA-B5 and A9 antigens. Certainly the progress of the disease is usually cut short when smoking is stopped. If smoking continues, the disease progresses relentlessly, with repeated attacks of arteritis and phlebitis, often with Raynaud's phenomenon; these lead to gangrene requiring amputation, at first local and peripheral, but then at successive proximal levels until the whole lower limb or limbs may be lost.

Nevertheless, despite recurring peripheral arteritis, there is usually no evidence of degenerative disease of the arteries, and it is uncommon to find significant arterial atheroma elsewhere (although sporadic reports of cerebral, visceral and coronary vessel involvement have been noted). It is the important feature of the lack of generalized arterial disease that makes the prognosis for life in thromboangiitis obliterans better than that in atherothrombotic occlusive disease. The risk is virtually only that associated with gangrene and its complications (infection and amputation).

Rating

1) Last attack of arteritis within one year:
Still smoking or quit less than one year ago — +150.
Quit smoking more than one year ago — +75 to +50.
2) 2nd year or longer since last attack:
Quit smoking more than one year ago — standard.
Still smoking — +100.

Atherothrombotic Disease

Dormandy et al[75] summarized the natural history of intermittent claudication noting the incidence studies from Framingham and Basle which showed the risk of claudication increasing rapidly from 0·2 percent in men aged 45 to 0·5 percent in men aged 55–65; in the same population the incidence of stroke and ischemic heart disease were about one-half and fourfold that of claudication respectively. The Basle study showed a higher incidence partly because of the more careful assessment of patients, including the use of non-invasive physiologic measurements. About one-third of patients with hemodynamically significant arterial disease did not have symptoms of claudication; this is consistent with autopsy studies in CAD, in which 30 percent of subjects with occlusions experienced no symptoms before death. Studies show a 1–1·5 percent prevalence rate in men aged under 50, rising rapidly with age to more than 5 percent in the older age groups. About 75 percent of patients improve or stabilize, usually within one to two years of onset; 25 percent deteriorate. Nevertheless the underlying atheromatous disease most certainly progresses both locally and generally unless there has been 'aggressive' attention to underlying risk factors, of which cigarette smoking has the highest ranking. For example, the amputation rate is 1·7 percent in epidemiologic studies but higher in heavy smokers and in those who continue to smoke.

Eastcott[74] compiled figures from several large-scale studies of atherothrombotic occlusive disease of the lower limbs, mainly of the femoropopliteal type, observed at the Mayo Clinic, Manchester Royal Infirmary, St Bartholomews Hospital and the Oslo city hospitals. From these it transpired that the prognosis for life was actually worse than that for the affected limb. Patients died from MI or cerebrovascular disease within five years of onset of symptoms (20–25 percent), whereas the amputation rate was about 10 percent. In cases of diabetes included in this survey, the limb prognosis was much worse, the amputation rate being 25 percent in five years. Dormandy,[75] writing 26 years after Eastcott, quotes similar figures for overall mortality. After five, ten and 15 years of follow-up the total mortality rates from all causes were approximately 30 percent, 50 percent and 70 percent respectively.

In the Whitehall Study, Davey Smith et al[76] confirmed the doubling of mortality and significant reduction of life expectancy in subjects with peripheral arterial disease, mostly due to cardiovascular deaths. They assessed 18,388 subjects aged 40–64 using a questionnaire; over a 17-year follow-up period 38 percent and 40 percent of the probable and possible cases died, and there were increased cardiovascular and all-cause mortality rates after adjusting for coronary risk factors (cardiac ischemia at baseline, systolic blood pressure, plasma cholesterol concentration, smoking behavior, employment grade and degree of glucose intolerance) (see Table 15.48).

Selection of Risks

Medical Treatment

Like angina pectoris, the pain of intermittent claudication is caused by ischemia of muscle, but there the similarity ends; whereas the heart is a vital organ the leg is not. Therefore it follows that mortality associated with stabilized intermittent claudication will, age for age, always be lower than mortality associated with stabilized angina pectoris. Nevertheless, both are due to arterial atheroma, which is a generalized disease, and the predominant cause of death in those who suffer from intermittent claudication is MI, the less frequent causes arising directly from lower limb ischemia itself: namely, gangrene, infection and amputation.

The state of the coronary circulation must therefore be as great a concern to the life underwriter as the state of the circulation in the lower limbs when considering applications from people with a history of intermittent claudication.

From the underwriting point of view, the risk is best when there is a history of intermittent claudication that, after onset, improves with the passage of time and finally disappears, presumably because of the presence of good collateral channels. The longer the duration since last symptoms the smaller the risk becomes. Almost as favorable is the group with potential claudication where ischemic pain is only felt

Table 15.48. Relative mortality rates and 95 percent confidence intervals for men with probable or possible intermittent claudication versus no intermittent claudication.[a]

| Cause of death | Adjustments | Intermittent claudication | | | |
| | | Possible | | Probable | |
		RR	95% CI	RR	95% CI
Coronary heart disease	Age only	2·54	1·7, 3·6	3·08	2·2, 4·3
	Full[b]	2·12	1·4, 3·0	2·90	2·0, 4·1
Cerebrovascular disease	Age only	3·00	1·3, 6·8	2·79	1·1, 6·8
	Full[b]	2·44	1·1, 5·6	2·53	0·9, 7·3
Cardiovascular disease	Age only	2·46	1·8, 3·3	2·92	2·2, 3·9
	Full[b]	2·05	1·5, 2·8	2·69	2·0, 3·7
Non-cardiovascular disease	Age only	1·83	1·3, 2·7	0·80	0·4, 1·4
	Full[b]	1·70	1·2, 2·5	0·71	0·4, 1·3
Lung cancer	Age only	2·07	1·0, 4·2	0·58	0·1, 2·3
	Full[b]	1·73	0·8, 3·7	0·46	0·1, 1·8
All cancers	Age only	1·66	1·0, 2·7	0·87	0·4, 1·7
	Full[b]	1·58	1·0, 2·6	0·73	0·3, 1·5
All causes	Age only	2·15	1·7, 2·7	1·91	1·5, 2·5
	Full[b]	1·86	1·5, 2·4	1·72	1·3, 2·3

[a]Source: Davey Smith et al.[76]
[b]Fully adjusted relative rates are adjusted for age, systolic blood pressure, cholesterol, smoking habits, employment grade and degree of glucose intolerance.
RR = relative rates.

after exceptional exertion and remains stable with no tendency to deteriorate. A history of intermittent claudication that is provoked by the minimum of exertion or that shows evidence of worsening cannot be considered insurable, or at best it should be postponed until the limb is revascularized.

Surgical Treatment

The surgical options available for lower limb ischemia are as follows.

1) *Aortoiliac reconstruction.* Prognosis is best when the atherothrombotic lesion is localized, as is generally the case when the disease is above the inguinal ligament in the aortoiliac vessels. The subject is usually younger and the distal arteries patent allowing a good run-off after end-arterectomy or bypass procedures. If the occlusion or stenosis is localized to a short length of vessel, percutaneous angioplasty is effective and can be repeated if there is restenosis. Arterial grafts in this region have high patency rates (95 percent at five years) with a low incidence of reoperation. Therefore revascularization for aortoiliac disease produces very satisfactory results provided the status of the coronary arterial circulation has been shown to be sound.

2) *Femoropopliteal reconstruction.* Percutaneous techniques are not as effective in revascularization of the femoropopliteal segment as they are in the aortoiliac segment. Although balloon dilatation has a role in the management of localized stenosis of the superficial femoral artery, an isolated lesion of this type rarely produces critical ischemia. However, most patients with disease in this region undergo femoropopliteal bypass. Patency rates at three years range from 80 percent for autologous vein bypass to the proximal popliteal artery to 55 percent for prosthetic bypass to the distal popliteal artery. These figures can be maintained over many years if there is a good surveillance program to detect stenosis in a graft and take appropriate action to deal with the problem.

3) *Femorocrural reconstruction.* When occlusive vascular disease extends beyond the popliteal artery into the three crural vessels (the peroneal artery and the anterior and posterior tibial arteries) percutaneous techniques are of no value in primary revascularization. The options then are to insert a femorocrural bypass graft or, rarely, to carry out a primary amputation if the disease is considered to be unreconstructable. Unfortunately conventional preoperative arteriography often fails to show the distal vessels and may give the false impression that revascularization is technically impossible, with the result that the patient is denied surgery to save the limb. Sayers et al[77] urge that further specialized vascular techniques, including Doppler ultrasonography and pulse-generated run-off, be used to identify possible patent calf vessels which; if they were confirmed, femorodistal bypass could be performed using an *in situ* saphenous vein when possible, thus avoiding major amputation.

4) *Amputation.* Amputation must be regarded as a last-resort treatment for an ischemic limb, but it is often inevitable because of associated disease (e.g. diabetes, atherothrombotic stenoses too extensive to permit revascularization) or failed vascular surgery. Among the general public, amputation is still regarded as a fate not much better than the announcement of a terminal illness, and probably with some reason, for mortality and morbidity are both high. As already mentioned, overall hospital mortality 30 days after operation is about 10 percent; considerable

later morbidity can also be expected, with less than one-third of patients walking independently outside the home and over one-third being confined to a wheelchair or bed.

Mortality

Previously survival of patients who presented with critical leg ischemia suggested a five-year mortality of anything between 40 percent and 100 percent regardless of management. More recently, however, Cheshire and Wolfe[78] have reported improved survival rates; up to 80 percent of patients may be expected to survive three years, and operative mortality after reconstruction compares very favorably with that after amputation (about 1 percent and 10 percent respectively). Femorocrural reconstruction in particular can therefore be undertaken safely in patients with critical leg ischemia, most of whom will survive many years after operation. It should not be forgotten, however, that although a patient can be made symptom free by good surgery, the basic arterial disease remains, as does the excess mortality.

Rating

Medical Treatment

Life insurance companies' methods of rating intermittent claudication differ. Most agree that a reasonable interval of time should elapse between the onset of symptoms and issue; this varies from six months to one year. A basic rating is indicated by some companies, from which credits may be deducted if a normal ECG is obtained at examination or if risk factors, such as cigarette smoking, have been eliminated. Other companies indicate a lower rating but make a normal current ECG obligatory and debit other unfavorable factors such as continued cigarette smoking. An example of the first method of rating is presented below.

Within six months of onset — postpone.
Thereafter, symptoms continuing, mild, stabilized — +150.

Symptom-free period	Rating
1 yr	+125
2 yr	+100
3 yr	+75
4 yr and over	+50

With normal resting ECG at application — credit 25 points.
With maximal or submaximal effort ECG (when practicable) negative for ischemia — credit 50 points (provided that the indicated rating is not reduced by more than one-half).
No cigarette smoking since diagnosis, or none within one year of application — credit 25 points.

Surgical Treatment

The best prognosis can be expected when surgical reconstruction has been confined to the aortoiliac vessels alone, indicating localized disease.

1) Aortoiliac arteries: endarterectomy with or without prosthetic patch; aortoiliac bypass; claudication pain abolished.
Within six months of operation — postpone.

Time since operation	Rating
6–24 mth	+100
3rd yr	+75
Thereafter	+50

2) Femoropopliteal bypass graft — postpone one year and, if symptom free, rate as for aortoiliac reconstruction.
Claudication still present:
Mild — rate as medical treatment of intermittent claudication (*see* p. 425).
Severe — decline.
3) Femorocrural bypass graft — postpone one year and, if symptom free, add 25 points to the ratings for aortoiliac surgery (*see above*).
Claudication still present:
Mild — add 25 points to ratings for medical treatment (*see* p. 425).
Severe — decline.
Ratable blood pressure with PVD — add to rating.
Ischemic heart disease combined with PVD — when this situation arises it is the cardiac impairment that is the major risk to life and should receive the full appropriate rating. The rating for PVD alone already discounts the risk of death from ischemic heart disease, and so, when the two impairments are combined, only one-half to one-third the rating for PVD need be added to that for ischemic heart disease.

Arteriosclerotic Aneurysm of the Abdominal Aorta

Untreated, the prognosis of aneurysms of the abdominal aorta is poor, and rupture can be predicted within a few years of diagnosis. In contrast, modern surgical treatment of these aneurysms by excision and repair with prosthetic materials produces technically excellent results, so that after full recovery from operation the prognosis becomes merely that of the pre-existing generalized atherosclerosis.

Selection of Risks
The life risk could be rated similarly to aortoiliac atherothrombotic stenosis treated by endarterectomy or reconstruction (*see above*).

Varicose veins

There would seem to be no extra risk associated with uncomplicated varicose veins judging by the experience of the *1951 Impairment Study*,[11] in which no significant excess mortality was revealed by age or duration in the classification of varicose veins in the standard and substandard sections, and no cause of death showed a mortality ratio significantly above that expected. It is clear, therefore, that no special attention need be paid to uncomplicated varicose veins in underwriting, and it is probably of little consequence whether a support is worn or not.

The favorable experience regarding varicose veins in the *1951 Impairment Study*[11] presumably reflects careful selection of risks. However, when complications, such as varicose ulceration or extensive eczema, are present on examination or where the nutrition of the skin over the lower part of the legs is so poor that varicose ulceration is inevitable, a modest extra premium would be chargeable.

Thrombophlebitis: Phlebitis: Deep Vein Thrombosis

Observations on some of the mechanisms initiating thrombophlebitis have already been made in Chapter 9. The mortality experience in the section of the *1951 Impairment Study*[11] dealing with phlebitis was appreciably above normal. Those included in the study had a history of one attack of phlebitis at any time prior to application for insurance, and in the standard section of the study mortality ratios ranged from 125 percent to 145 percent; when calculated by age and duration, mortality ratios were appreciably and consistently above 100 percent. Deaths from diseases of the heart and circulation were above the expected, as were deaths from diseases of the digestive tract.

Some care must, therefore, be exercised in selection when there is a history of phlebitis or deep vein thrombosis; it is the practice of most life insurance companies to rate +75 to +50 within one year of an attack, and +25 to standard in the second year. A history of recurrent attacks of phlebitis or deep vein thrombosis increases the risk; a rating half as much again as for a single attack would be applied.

The benefit of anticoagulation probably cancels out the risk of its complications, and therefore no adjustment to the rating for thrombophlebitis is necessary when anticoagulants are being administered.

Raynaud's Disease: Raynaud's Phenomenon

Raynaud's Disease
This is essentially bilateral, with symmetrical pallor and numbness of the extremities (induced by cold or excitement), usually of the upper limbs and occurring in various degrees of severity. The condition occurs predominantly in young females, and in its simplest form there is an hereditary tendency to 'cold fingers'. On exposure to low temperature the fingers become blanched due to spasm of the digital arteries and arterioles; they may remain so for a few minutes or a few hours. In long-standing cases of Raynaud's disease nutritional changes may occur at the finger tips, occasionally with small superficial areas of gangrene, but never more than this.

Raynaud's disease is due to an idiopathic sensitivity of the digital arteries to cold and, by definition, is a benign condition. Since there are no significant complications, applicants for life insurance with a history of Raynaud's disease would be considered standard risks.

Raynaud's Phenomenon

This is defined as when the signs and symptoms described above occur secondary to other diseases or conditions. Since some of these have a poor prognosis it is essential that the underwriter knows which primary disease is present for proper evaluation of the risk.

Raynaud's phenomenon should always be suspected if digital ischemia first arises in a person over the age of 30. Generally the primary disease is quite apparent, but sometimes it is not, particularly in the case of scleroderma which may first present in a young female mimicking typical Raynaud's disease. It is often extremely difficult to differentiate between the two, but scleroderma should always be suspected if the episodes of pallor of the fingers are prolonged and severe and have caused more extensive gangrene of the finger tips than one would expect to find in Raynaud's disease.

The following diseases may give rise to Raynaud's phenomenon: collagen diseases, especially scleroderma (systemic sclerosis) in which Raynaud's phenomenon is one of the elements of the CREST phenomenon (*see* p. 816); thromboangiitis obliterans; atherothrombotic arterial disease; non-cardioselective beta-blocking drugs; cervical rib; sickle cell disease; cold hemagglutinins; and vibratory tool disease.

The prognoses of the more important causes of Raynaud's phenomenon are reviewed in the appropriate sections of this book.

REFERENCES

1 *Medical Impairment Study 1983*. Vol 1. Boston: Society of Actuaries and Association of Life Insurance Medical Directors of America, 1986.
2 Lew EA, Gajewski J (editors). *Medical Risks: trends in mortality by age and time elapsed*, Vols 1 & 2. New York, Westport, London: Praeger, 1990.
3 Rodstein M, Wooloch L, Gubner RS. A mortality study of the significance of extrasystoles in an insured population. *Trans Assoc Life Insur Med Dirs Am* 1970; 54: 91.
4 Kennedy HL, Witlock JA, Spragg MK et al. Long term follow-up of asymptomatic healthy subjects with frequent and complex ventricular ectopics. *N Engl J Med* 1985; 312: 193–4.
5 *1979 Atrial Fibrillation Mortality Study*. New York: Association of Life Insurance Medical Directors of America/Society of Actuaries.
6 Ungerleider HE, Clark CP. *Trans Assoc Life Insur Med Dir Am* 1938; 25: 84.
7 Siber FJ, Brown AE, Singer RB, Pittkin FI. A cardiovascular survey of chest X-ray and nearly five thousand life insurance applicants: normal standards and distribution curves for relative heart diameter. *Trans Assoc Life Insur Med Dir Am* 1979; 53: 159.
8 Singer RB, Siber FS et al. Mortality in 4100 insured applicants with ECG and chest X-ray. *Trans Assoc Life Insur Med Dir Am* 1981; 65: 180.
9 Amundsen P. The diagnostic value of conventional radiologic examination of the heart in adults. *Acta Radiol* 1959 (Suppl) (Stoch); 181.
10 Popp RL. Medical progress. Echocardiography. *N Engl J Med* 1990; 323: 101–9, 165–72.
11 *1951 Impairment Study*. New York: Society of Actuaries, 1954.
12 Lembo NJ, Dell'Italia IJ, Crawford MH, O'Rourke RA. Bedside diagnosis of systolic murmurs. *N Engl J Med* 1988; 318: 1572–8.
13 Olesen KH. *Mitral Stenosis: a follow up of 351 patients*. Copenhagen: Munksgaard, 1955.
14 Hackett TP, Cassem NH. Psychologic aspects of rehabilitation following myocardial infarction. In: Wenger NK, Hellerstein HK (editors). *Rehabilitation of the Coronary Patient*. New York: John Wiley & Sons, 1978.
15 Gilchrist AR, Murray-Lyon RM. *Edinburgh Med J* 1933; 40: 587.

16 Hammermeister KE, Fisher L, Kennedy JW, Samuels S, Dodge HT. Prediction of late survival in patients with mitral valve disease from clinical, hemodynamic, and quantitative angiographic variables. *Circulation* 1978; 57: 341–9.

17 Duren ER, Becker AE, Dunning AJ. Long term follow up of idiopathic mitral valve prolapse in 300 patients. *J Am Coll Cardiol* 1988; 11: 42–7.

18 Wilken DL, Hickey AJ. Lifetime risk for patients with mitral valve prolapse on developing severe valve regurgitation requiring surgery. *Circulation* 1988; 78: 10–14.

19 Frank S, Johnson A, Ross J. Natural history of valvular aortic stenosis. *Br Heart J* 1973; 35: 41.

20 Hancock EW, Fleming PR. Aortic stenosis quarterly. *Q J Med* 1960; 29: 209.

21 Kelly TA, Rothbart RM, Cooper CM, Kaiser DL, Smucker ML, Gibson RS. Comparison of outcome of asymptomatic to symptomatic patients older than 20 years of age with valvular aortic stenosis. *Am J Cardiol* 1988; 61: 123–30.

22 Choi JY, Sullivan ID. Fixed subaortic stenosis; anatomical spectrum and nature of progression. *Br Heart J* 1991; 65: 280, 286.

23 Chan KY, Redington AN, Rigby ML, Gibson DG. Cardiac function after surgery for subaortic stenosis: non invasive assessment of left ventricular performance. *Br Heart J* 1991; 66: 161–5.

24 Pomerance A. *Mod Geriat* 1972; 140.

25 Bayless R, Clarke C, Oakley CM, Summerville W, Whitfield AGW, Young SEJ. Incidence, mortality and prevention of infective endocarditis. *J R Coll Phys (Lond)* 1986; 20: 15–20.

26 Campbell JM. Life assurance for applicants with heart disease, *Trans Assur Med Soc* 1958; 29.

27 Hubner PJB. Cardiac interventional procedures in the United Kingdom in 1989. *Br Heart J* 1991; 66: 469–71.

28 Schumaker HB. The post surgical heart is a risk for insurance. *Trans Assoc Life Insur Med Dir Am* 1971; 55: 192.

29 Treasure T. Management of patients with Bjork-Shiley prosthetic valves. *Br Heart J* 1991; 66: 333–4.

30 Taylor KM. Heart valve surgery in the United Kingdom: present practice and future trends. *Br Heart J* 1991; 66: 335–6.

31 Bloomfield P, Wheatley DJ, Prescott RJ, Miller HC. Twelve year comparison of Bjork-Shiley mechanical heart valve with porcine bioprosthesis. *New Engl J Med* 1991; 324: 573–9.

32 Collins JJ. The evolution of heart valves. *N Engl J Med* 1991; 324: 624–6.

33 Kinsley RH. Valve replacement. *Life Insur Med* 1980; 6: 185.

34 Livesey S, Caine N, Speigelhalter DJ, English TAH, Wallwork J. Cardiac surgery for patients aged 65 years and older: a long term survival analysis. *Br Heart J* 1988; 60: 480–4.

35 Monrad ES, Hess OM, Murakami T, Nonogih H, Corin WJ, Krayenbuehl HP. Time course of regression of left ventricular hypertrophy after aortic valve replacement. *Circulation* 1988; 77: 1345–55.

36 Carabello BA, Ursher BW, Hendrix GH, Assey ME, Crawford FA, Leiman RB. Predicters of outcome for aortic valve replacement in patients with aortic regurgitation and left ventricular dysfunction: a change in the measuring stick. *J Am Coll Cardiol* 1987; 10: 991–7.

37 Taniguchi K, Nakano S, Hirose H, Matsuda H, Shirakura R, Saki K, Kawamoto T, Sakai S, Kawashima Y. Pre-operative left ventricular function: minimal requirement of the successful late results of valve replacement for aortic regurgitation. *J Am Coll Cardiol* 1987; 10: 510–18.

38 Copeland GJ, Griepp RB, Stinson EB, Shumway NE. Long term follow up after isolated aortic valve replacement. *J Thorac Cardiovas Surg* 1977; 74: 875.

39 Malm JR, Bale GS. *Trans Assoc Life Insur Med Dir Am* 1980; 64: 430.

40 Robinson JC. *J Insur Med* 1981; 12: 11.

41 Czer SC, Grey RG, Stewart ME, De Robertis M, Choux A, Matloff JM. Reduction in sudden late death by concomitant revascularization with aortic valve replacement. *J Thorac Cardiovasc Surg* 1988; 95: 390–401.

42 Jones M, Schofield PM, Brooks NH, Dark JF, Moussalli H, Deiraniya AK, Lawson

RAM, Rahman AN. Aortic valve replacement with combined myocardial revascularization. *Br Heart J* 1989; 62: 915.

43 Monro JL, Ross JK, Manners JM, Edwards JC, Lewis B, Hyde I, Ogelvy BC, Keaton BR, Conway N, Johnson AM. Cardiac surgery in Wessex. *Br Med J* 1983; 286: 361–5.

44 Scully HE. Prognosis in valve replacement. *Assoc Life Insur Med Dir Am* 1986; 70: 129–34.

45 Butchart EG. Surgery for heart valve disease. *Hospital Update* 1990; 16: 963–74.

46 Edmunds LH, Clark RE, Cohn LH, Miller DC, Weisel RD. Guidelines for reporting morbidity and mortality after cardiac valvular operations. *J Thorac Cardiovasc Surg* 1988; 96: 351–3.

47 Teply J. Grunkemeier G, Sutherland HD, Lambert L, Johnson D, Starr A. The ultimate prognosis after valve replacement; an assessment at 20 years. *Ann Thorac Surg* 1981; 32: 111–19.

48 Lindblom D, Lindblom U, Qvist JJ, Lundstrom H. Long term relative survival rates after heart valve replacement. *J Am Coll Cardiol* 1990; 15: 566–73.

49 Monro JL. Wessex Cardiac Unit 10 year survival valve replacement procedures. Personal communication.

50 Croxson RS, Tyler AW. Underwriting aspects of heart valve replacement. *16th International Conference of COINTRA* 1989; 241–54.

51 Ellis LB, Harken DE. *Ann Life Insur Med* 1977; 3: 149.

52 Turi ZG, Reyes VB, Raju BS, Raju AR, Kumar DM, Rajagopalp et al. Percutaneous balloon v surgical closed valvuloplasty for mitral stenosis. *Circulation* 1991; 83: 1179–85.

53 Kirklin JW. Percutaneous balloon v surgical closed commissurotomy for mitral stenosis. *Circulation* 1991; 83: 1450–1.

54 Ellis LB, Harken DE. Closed valvuloplasty for mitral stenosis. A 12 year follow-up study of 1571 patients. *N Engl J Med* 1964; 270: 643.

55 Cooper GJ, Wright EM, Smith GH. Mitral valve repair: a valuable procedure with good long term results even when performed infrequently. *Br Heart J* 1991; 66: 156–60.

56 Singer RB. Valve repair for mitral insufficiency without stenosis. *J Insur Med* 1988; 20: 21–3.

57 Cumming GR. Underwriting the cardiac risk after aortic valve replacement. *Assoc Life Insur Med Dir Am* 1987; 71: 151–61.

58 Sharples LD, Cane N, Mullens P, Scott JP, Solis E, English TAH, Large SR, Schofield PM, Walwork J. Risk factor analysis for the major hazards following heart transplantation — rejection, infection and coronary occlusive disease. *Transplantation* 1991; 52: 244–52.

59 Edwards JE. Second conference on congenital cardiac defects and rheumatic heart disease. *Trans Assoc Life Insur Med Dir Am* 1965; 49: 281, 285.

60 Wright JS. Ruptured aneurysm of the sinus of Valsalva. *QJ Med* 1970; 39: 493.

61 Abbott ME. Coarctation of the aorta of the adult type II. A statistical study and historical retrospect of 200 recorded cases with autopsy of stenosis or obliteration of the ascending arch in subjects above the age of two years. *Am Heart J* 1928; 3: 574.

62 Perloff JK. The changing population of congenital heart disease. *Trans Assoc Life Insur Med Dir Am* 1974; 58: 140.

63 Wood P. *Diseases of the Heart and Circulation*. London: Eyre Spottiswood, 1956.

64 McCaughan BC, Schaff HV, Piehler JM, Danielson GK, Orzulak TA, Puga FG, Bluth JR, Connolly DC, McGoon DC. Early and late results of pericardectomy for constrictive pericarditis. *J Thorac Cardiovasc Surg* 1985; 89: 340–50.

65 Report of the WHO ISFC task force on the definition and classification of cardiomyopathies. *Br Heart J* 1980; 44: 672–3.

66 Croxson RS. Prognosis of cardiomyopathies. *15th International Conference of COINTRA* 1985.

67 McKenna W, Deanfield J, Faruquia, England D, Oakley C, Goodwin J. Prognosis in hypertrophic cardiomyopathy: role of age and clinical electrocardiographic and haemodynamic features. *Am J Cardiol* 1981; 46: 1532–8.

68 Goodwin JF. The frontiers of cardiomyopathy. *Br Heart J* 1982; 48: 1–18.

69 Shapiro LM, Zezulka Alexander. Hypertrophic cardiomyopathy: a common disease with

a good prognosis. 5 year experience of a district general hospital. *Br Heart J* 1983; 50: 530–3.

70 Maron BJ, Epstein SE, Morrow AG. Symptomatic status and prognosis of patients after operation for hypertrophic obstructive cardiomyopathy; efficacy of ventricular septal myotomy and myectomy. *Euro Heart J* 1983–4; Suppl F: 175–85.

71 Rosenzweig A, Watkins H, Swang DS, Miri M, McKenna W, Traill T, Sideman JG, Sideman CE. Preclinical diagnosis of familial hypertrophic cardiomyopathy by genetic analysis of blood lymphocytes. *N Engl J Med* 1991; 325: 1753–60.

72 Watkins H, Seidman CE, MacRae C, Sideman JG, McKenna W. Progress in familial hypertrophic cardiomyopathy: molecular genetic analysis in the original family studied by Teare. *Br Heart J* 1992; 67: 34–8.

73 Mavor GE. Thromboangiitis obliterans, clinical and arteriographic findings, with discussion on clinical diagnosis. *QJ Med* 1955; 24: 229.

74 Eastcoff HHG. Prognosis in peripheral vascular disease. *Trans Assur Med Soc* 1965; 77.

75 Dormundy JA. Natural history of intermittent claudication. *Hospital Update* 1991; 17: 314–20.

76 Davey Smith G, Shipley MJ, Rose G. Intermittent claudication, heart disease risk factors and mortality: the Whitehall Study. *Circulation* 1990; 82: 1925–31.

77 Sayers RD, Thompson MM, London NJM, Bell PRF. Critical ischemia of the lower limb: femorodistal bypass in preference to amputation. *Br Med J* 1992; 304: 898.

78 Cheshire NJW, Wolfe JHN. Critical leg ischemia: amputation or reconstruction. *Br Med J* 1992; 304: 312–14.

CHAPTER 16

ELECTROCARDIOGRAPHY

LEONARDO CHAIT

This chapter assumes that the reader is proficient in electrocardiogram (ECG) interpretation. Its aim is to spotlight items of special interest to the insurance industry; it includes a lengthy section on exercise electrocardiography.

Life insurance medical underwriters, veterinarians and pediatricians share a common problem: the frequent unavailability of a reliable medical history. Underwriters are in an even worse predicament because the applicant may be interested in hiding or not disclosing adverse information. This is called antiselection.

Because of the need to make prompt decisions on the basis of limited and sometimes unreliable information, medical underwriters must often violate the most important rule of clinical electrocardiography: the ECG should always be interpreted in the context of the clinical picture.

Medical underwriters are often confronted with an abnormal ECG plus a 'normal' history and physical examination. At a minimum the ECG should be interpreted within the context of sex, age and risk factors for arteriosclerotic heart disease.

Patterson and Horowitz[1] have emphasized the importance of probability of disease based on heredity, age, sex, blood pressure, smoking status and lipid values.

Arriving at a causal diagnosis is sometimes impossible and often unwarranted. It increases costs and delays the processing of the application. Some physicians develop a zeal for diagnostic certainty that is not always justified in clinical medicine and even less justified in insurance medicine.[2] The medical underwriter's aim is not individual case diagnosis but appraisal of risk as it would apply to a statistically similar group of applicants.

When there is a definite diagnosis, the ECG becomes one more element of the total clinical picture; in those instances the reader should consult the relevant chapter. This chapter specifically addresses instances in which the ECG is the main or only unexplained abnormality and there are studies that provide a useful basis for underwriting. Mortality reported in clinical series often runs at higher levels than is usually found in insured lives; this is probably due to the fact that most clinical studies have been done in symptomatic patients who are sick enough to be referred to subspecialty services.

Many insurance applicants are males over the age of 50 whose most common lethal impairments are cardiovascular. The insurance industry has extensive experience in using the ECG as a screening-rating tool in this group. Although in clinical medicine the ECG has been partially dethroned by nuclear tests and echocardiography, it is unrivaled in insurance medicine because there is a long experience of ECG use, it is inexpensive, non-invasive, easily available, simple, reproducible, provides a wealth of information and allows serial studies showing the progression or regression of hypertrophy or ischemia.

It has been said that a diagnostic ECG is valuable but a normal one gives no assurance of normality. This caveat applies, however, to most medical tests. The newer tests are more accurate but less available and not cost effective for the insurance industry.

The need to include other subjects in the medical curriculum has shrunk the amount of time devoted to learning how to interpret ECGs; many doctors feel that interpretation can be done efficiently by computer. Computer reading of ECGs has improved remarkably. Some programs can read ECGs more accurately than the average cardiologist.[3] Approximately 10 percent of the more than 100 million ECGs taken each year in the USA are computer-processed;[4] the number continues to increase.

The computer is at its worst in diagnosing arrhythmias, right ventricular hypertrophy and old inferior myocardial infarction. It has difficulty in recognizing P-waves when they occur 'out of place' instead of just before QRS complexes. Another major weakness is the comparison of serial ECGs. Equivocal ECGs should be compared with the applicant's prior ECGs if available. What appeared to be an equivocal change could indicate a serious problem if it signaled a significant difference from a previous tracing.

Most current computer programs are oversensitive and the flagged abnormalities are frequently over-read by the cardiologist as 'normal variants' or 'not clinically significant.' A computer diagnosis of 'normal' is usually dependable without need for physician over-read. In the USA approximately 90 percent of the ECGs interpreted by a life insurance medical director (MD) are normal. It is likely that in the future this part of his work will be taken over by computers. An interesting by-product is the remote ECG interpretative workstation, which allows the physician to read ECGs from his home or office. High-resolution screens have images as sharp as high-quality tracings.

ECGs transmitted by fax. Inscription is made with overlapping bar lines which vitiate any attempt to measure critical time intervals, especially Q-wave duration. ST–T morphology is not disrupted. Tracings may be acceptable as long as they do not show borderline Q-waves. Fax transmission saves much time. Medical underwriters have to weigh the convenience of fax transmission against the frequent need to see the original tracing.

The ECG remains a valuable screening tool and medical underwriters should have a thorough grounding in electrocardiography. The most difficult areas are the recognition of unusual variants of normal, borderline cases and technical errors that may lead to erroneous diagnoses. Computer interpretation is weak in the same areas, but is consistent.

The choice of criteria to interpret any test as normal or abnormal moves specificity and sensitivity in opposite directions. Stringent criteria increase specificity at the expense of sensitivity. This trade-off is called a receiver-operator characteristic (ROC) curve.[5] No important new diagnostic ECG criteria have emerged recently. Specificity is high in populations with a low probability of disease, and diagnostic accuracy increases in parallel with the degree of abnormality of the electrocardiographic findings. According to Surawicz,[6] the standard ECG has reached the limits of possible accuracy for diagnosing chamber enlargement. The same probably applies to most other ECG diagnoses.

The concept that the prognosis in most patients with ECG abnormalities, including arrhythmias, is related to the presence or absence of underlying cardiac disease evolved gradually. The ECG will often find an abnormality without yielding an etiological diagnosis. The findings are frequently called non-specific, but they are not necessarily benign. Follow-up of individuals carrying these 'disease markers' has been long enough to allow underwriting based only on the ECG. Under these circumstances underwriting is often more conservative than when the medical underwriter has more complete information.

The rating for non-diagnostic ECG abnormalities depends on whether they are present in a 'normal' or 'abnormal' heart. The likelihood of identifying a cardiac disease as potential cause of an electrocardiographic abnormality depends on the thoroughness with which the applicants are evaluated and on what conditions are accepted as potential causes. Unless the MD or the underwriter communicates with the attending physician, the thoroughness of the work-up is outside their knowledge. Rating is based on statistical likelihood of disease.

Talking with the attending physicians and obtaining a copy of their records, including specialized tests and serial ECGs, is sometimes warranted, especially in the USA where many individuals are being thoroughly studied by their attending physicians. This additional information sometimes allows a more accurate and competitive rating, with placement of business which would otherwise have been lost. Agents certainly appreciate this effort.

Most of the ECGs done for insurance purposes are performed by paramedic organizations; quality control is often inadequate, although this has improved in the past few years. A faulty tracing raises unfounded suspicion of heart disease; besides causing untold inconvenience and anxiety, it may compromise the chances of being accepted for life insurance at a standard premium. Medical underwriters have to recognize these faulty tracings and, depending on the likelihood of disease, decide whether to have them repeated by a reputable operator or waive the repetition. Redoing ECGs creates a serious problem for the insurance agent and should be avoided whenever possible. Common errors and how to deal with some of them are discussed in this chapter.

ELECTROCARDIOGRAPHIC TECHNIQUE

Physicians or paramedics who have been asked to obtain an ECG for insurance purposes should bear in mind that the tracing they produce may, in all likelihood, be reviewed by reinsurance companies in Zurich, New York, London or Toronto, among other centers of insurance. The ECG may need to be compared with others recorded from the applicant in the past. This is one of the reasons why proper technique and a uniform presentation are so essential in life insurance medicine.

The date, applicant's name, age and signature, and any medication being taken should appear at the beginning of the tracing; each lead should be clearly marked.

The standardization signal is an essential part of the tracing; voltages cannot be measured in its absence. The signal should be imprinted at the beginning of the tracing as a minimum requirement, but preferably in circuit once during the recording of each lead, between the T-wave and succeeding P-wave.

The first step in reading an ECG is checking for errors. Except in dextrocardia,

P-waves should be upright in Lead I and inverted in aVR. It is not unusual for P III to be biphasic (+ −) but it should never be (− +). Einthoven's law should be fulfilled (lead II = lead I + lead III), as well as its corollary (aVr + aVL + aVF = 0).

Common Faults

1) Somatic tremor due to failure to have the applicant comfortably relaxed. This interferes with the measurement of Q-wave duration but may be disregarded in younger individuals, when no suspicious Q-waves are seen and there is no reason to suspect the presence of arteriosclerotic heart disease. Somatic tremor may also be a clue to the presence of Parkinson's disease.

2) AC interference due to poor insulation or improper grounding of the electrocardiograph. This is a fairly common problem when the tracings are obtained at the applicant's office or residence. It does not change the general configuration of the tracing but vitiates measurements of Q-wave duration.

3) Wandering baseline. Down-sloping baselines magnify ST depression or mask ST elevation. Up-sloping baselines magnify ST elevation or mask ST depression.

4) Misplacement of precordial electrodes, usually one interspace too high. This may cause poor R-wave progression and lead to an erroneous suspicion of anterior myocardial infarction. Biphasic or inverted P-waves in V2 and V3 may alert one to this technical error but they are not always present. Tracings should be repeated with careful attention to precordial electrode placement.

5) Mislabeling leads during mounting. This can be recognized by applying Einthoven's law to the peripheral leads. Lead V6 often resembles lead I. Each precordial lead is transitional in form between the lead preceding it and the lead following it. Mounting errors can usually be rearranged correctly by the person who reads the ECG. Use of a three-channel recorder eliminates cutting and mounting time and avoids mounting errors.

6) ECGs obtained in a sitting position. These show changes in the frontal plane axis and morphology of the peripheral leads (as compared with other tracings that may have been submitted by the attending physician). It creates difficulties in the evaluation of inferior Q-waves.

7) Imperfect skin preparation or dirty electrodes. These cause low-voltage and bizarre movements of the stylus due to high resistance between skin and electrode.

Failure to insert standardization signal. This impairs the use of voltage criteria of suspect LVH and the estimate of over- or under-damping from the rectangular shape of the signal. This does not usually warrant repetition of the tracing.

8) Over- or under-damping of the writing stylus. Over-damping is more serious: it abolishes fine details, and may cause slurring of the QRS complex and depression of the ST segments. It is easily misdiagnosed as pathological and often warrants repetition of the tracing, especially in applicants over the age of 50.

9) Smearing electrode paste across the skin areas prepared for application of chest electrodes. This leads to short-circuiting between some V positions (notably between V3, V4, V5 and V6). The complexes look almost identical, representing a mean value of the short-circuited positions.

10) Interchanging electrode cables.

a) Switching the cables of both arms creates a mirror image of lead I and interchanges leads II and III. The ECG may look like a lateral myocardial infarction but P I is inverted. Only two conditions may cause an inverted P I: dextrocardia and arm cable switching.

b) Switching the cables for the left arm and the left leg inverts the ECG in lead III and interchanges leads I and II. The tracing does not appear abnormal, with the exception that a diphasic P III becomes (− +) instead of (+ −).

c) Switching the cables for the right arm and the left leg inverts all leads and, furthermore, interchanges leads I and III. The unusual ECG, with inverted P-waves in leads II and III, may be confused with a junctional rhythm.

d) Clockwise displacement of all cables inverts leads I and II and places them after lead III; the normal ECG resembles an inferior myocardial infarction.

e) Counterclockwise displacement of all cables inverts leads II and III, places them before lead I and looks like a lateral myocardial infarction. Inverted P-waves in leads I and sometimes II are telltale signs.

COMPARISON OF SERIAL ELECTROCARDIOGRAMS

Whenever available, serial ECGs should be carefully compared. This yields invaluable information on unstable ischemia, silent myocardial infarctions, and progression and regression of hypertrophy.

AGE AND THE ELECTROCARDIOGRAM

Frontal Plane Leads

At birth there is right axis deviation of up to 120°. At six to eight months the axis reaches the normal adult range of +30° to +90°. Any degree of left axis deviation present before the age of 16 should be viewed as abnormal.

Precordial Leads

The right ventricular preponderance present at birth causes large R-waves in the right precordial leads. They gradually decrease in size and reach the adult pattern by the age of six.

The T-waves in leads V1 to V3 or V4 are usually upright during the first three weeks of life; they then become sharply inverted. In adolescence they usually revert to positive, but in some cases the T inversion may persist in what has been called a juvenile pattern.

Ferrer[7] has recently reviewed the literature and confirmed that aging *per se* does not cause any further changes in the ECG.

INDICATIONS FOR OBTAINING AN ELECTROCARDIOGRAM

Large Sums Assured; Antiselection

Although the mortality experience associated with very large sums assured is lighter than for overall business, insurers still have to be on their guard against antiselection when substantial sums of money are at risk. If an applicant deliberately suppresses a history of, for example, angioplasty, cardiac pain, heart murmur, or knowledge of some ECG abnormality, an ECG may detect some abnormality, protecting the insurer against such antiselection. This will be even more effective if a stress ECG is included.

Age

The incidence of heart disease rises with increasing age. For this reason, it is prudent to include an ECG in the medical requirements as an additional aid to selection for applicants over the age of 50, especially when the sum assured is substantial.

Arterial Hypertension

Mortality associated with different levels of blood pressure becomes proportionately higher with increasing degrees of left ventricular hypertrophy in the ECG.

Cardiac Murmurs

Although the ECG is not often helpful in the diagnosis of doubtful cardiac murmurs, a negative tracing has a favorable prognostic implication and can influence the final underwriting decision.

When a known valve lesion or congenital defect is present, an ECG can be of immense value in determining the proper risk category for rating by demonstrating the presence and degree of selective chamber hypertrophy appropriate to the particular lesion.

Medical History

A current ECG should form part of the underwriting evidence when there is a history of myocardial infarction or angina. The Lincoln National follow-up study by Cochran and Buck[8] showed conclusively that mortality in the group of insured lives having a definite history of coronary artery disease but with normal ECGs at application was consistently lower than in the group who had no current ECGs.

Applicants who have a previous history of undiagnosed chest pain which, from its characteristics, is suspicious of myocardial ischemia should have an ECG at the time of examination. In this type of case an exercise ECG would be of even greater value and, if negative for ischemia, would enable considerable credit points to be set against any rating for 'other chest pain'.

A history of peripheral vascular disease is an indication for including an ECG in the medical evidence required at the time of application for life insurance.

Dysrhythmias

Irregularities of rhythm reported on examination or a history of paroxysmal arrhythmia would require a current ECG for proper assessment of the risk.

ELECTROCARDIOGRAPHIC EVALUATION OF ARTERIOSCLEROTIC HEART DISEASE — SOME DILEMMAS

'Old Myocardial Infarction Cannot Be Ruled Out'

This statement, often seen in physician's reports and computer printouts gives a false impression to the lay underwriter. Not even a completely normal ECG can rule out an old myocardial infarction. It is not unusual for Q-waves to shrink to normal dimensions, R-waves to regrow and ST–T to return to normal. Many medical tests behave in this fashion; most medical diagnoses are 'rule in', based on statistical probability, rather than 'rule out', and most of the time we deal with different degrees of uncertainty.

'Possible Old Myocardial Infarction'. Differentiation of Normal from Abnormal Q-Waves

There is a borderline area in which normal and abnormal Q-waves overlap. Development of new Q-waves or their presence in leads where they should not be seen is usually abnormal.

The initial forces of ventricular activation are oriented right and anteriorly. This gives rise to the normal septal Q-wave seen in leads I, aVL, V5 and V6.[9] These initial forces may be directed upwards or downwards. When they point up, a Q-wave is generated in leads III, aVF and sometimes in II. These normal Q-waves may be identical to those caused by a small inferior myocardial infarction.

Normal Q-waves in the limb leads are generally small (less than 3 mm deep), narrow (less than 0·03 s) and unnotched. The exceptions are leads III and aVR. In lead III a Q or QS may be recorded in normal subjects.

In the precordial leads a QS deflection may occasionally be seen in lead V1 in normal adults. It is uncommon in lead V2 and rare in V3.

In ventricular hypertrophy, including hypertrophic cardiomyopathy, Q-waves may become unusually deep without any widening, notching or slurring.

Lack of electrical activation of a large and properly located myocardial area generates abnormal Q-waves, which for many years were attributed to necrosis of myocardial tissue. This was confirmed by the absence of thallium uptake and by decreased or absent wall motion. The realization that these abnormalities sometimes revert after revascularization led to the concepts of stunned myocardium and hibernating myocardium.[10] These areas of transiently stunned or chronically hibernating myocardium are at high risk and, although not necrotic, should not change our current underwriting practices.

Retrospective Diagnosis of Myocardial Infarction

Antiselection is complicated by the fact that silent or undiagnosed myocardial infarctions are very common. When the acute ST–T changes are no longer present, the only marker that may be left is a Q-wave and its characteristics may overlap with those of the normal Q-waves.

In the Framingham Study[11] more than 25 percent of myocardial infarctions documented by clear-cut ECG changes did not prompt a visit to the attending physician or went unrecognized. Almost half of the unrecognized infarctions were totally silent. Others caused atypical symptoms that escaped diagnosis. The prognosis of unrecognized myocardial infarctions was as serious as that of recognized infarctions. These findings have been confirmed recently by Yano and MacLean.[12] The true incidence of unrecognized myocardial infarctions may be much higher than 25 percent because many infarctions do not leave ECG sequelae detectable at routine periodic examinations.

Cox and Lond[13] showed that in the absence of recurrence in 5·6 percent of well documented Q-wave infarctions the ECG had returned to normal within four years. The figure increased to 54·5 percent for non-Q-wave infarctions. In some cases this could be due to revascularization and consequent recovery of hibernating myocardium.

Inferior Myocardial Infarction

One of the most nagging problems that confronts the medical underwriter is the presence of a 0·03–0·04 s Q-wave in aVF. Mazzoleni and coauthors[14] studied this problem in patients diagnosed on the basis of clinical picture, angiography and wall motion abnormalities. Using the traditional criteria for ECG diagnosis of inferior myocardial infarction (Q-wave duration in leads II and/or aVF up to 0·04 s and Q/R ratio less than 0·25), the authors found that specificity was 100 percent but sensitivity was only 42 percent. They pointed out that the choice of criteria depends on whether the goal is to achieve better specificity or sensitivity. If specificity is more important, the traditional criteria are best. If sensitivity is more important, a Q-wave of 0·03 s is better; specificity falls only to 96 percent and sensitivity rises to 52 percent.

QS complexes in aVF had a very poor diagnostic value, probably related to the direct-writing ECG recorders failing to record small brief R waves preceding a 'pseudo QS'.

Anterior Myocardial Infarction

Warner and colleagues[15] tested five ECG criteria for diagnosis of anterior infarction in patients with diagnosis proven by coronary angiography and ventriculography. All criteria had over 93 percent specificity but sensitivity varied between 36 percent and 78 percent. De Pace and coworkers[16] have demonstrated that poor R-wave progression is an insensitive marker for anterior infarction.

It is obvious that our screening ECGs miss a large number of myocardial infarctions. Many of these applicants go unrated and increase the mortality and basic rating of the standard group.

Rating for Borderline Q-Wave Abnormalities

Borderline Q-wave abnormalities interpreted as possible old myocardial infarction create an underwriting dilemma. Probability of disease becomes paramount. Guilt by association, unacceptable in our legal system, is very useful in medical diagnosis. If the ECG shows P-, ST- or T-wave abnormalities, the likelihood of disease increases significantly. Risk factors, including age and sex, should be taken into consideration. The final interpretation (as well as the underwriting decision) should be based on a careful analysis of all factors. Most insurance companies do not rate applicants who have a 0·03 s Q in a VF, normal ST–T and no acknowledged adverse history.

Q-Wave versus Non-Q-Wave Myocardial Infarction ('Transmural' versus 'Subendocardial')

Pipberger and Lopez[17] concluded in 1980 that the attempt to distinguish transmural from subendocardial infarcts on the basis of the presence or absence of Q-waves was not justified by any clinical, pathologic or experimental data.

Although Q-wave myocardial infarctions are not transmural and non-Q-wave infarctions are not subendocardial, they constitute two different groups with somewhat different prognosis. Pathological and angiographic studies have shown that 85–90 percent of the subjects with evolving Q-wave myo- cardial infarctions had total thrombotic occlusion of a coronary artery.[18,19] Many non-Q-wave infarctions are partially aborted infarctions which have large areas of jeopardized but viable myocardium at high risk for infarction extension.

Roberts[20] has stressed that before the advent of thrombolysis one-month mortality was approximately 20 percent for Q-wave myocardial infarction, versus 8 percent for non-Q wave myocardial infarction. At two years, however, the rates were similar, due to a high incidence of reinfarction during the first year after non-Q-wave infarction. Boden et al[21] pointed out that non-Q-wave myocardial infarction patients without ST–T changes have a much better prognosis.

Applicants who have experienced a non-Q-wave myocardial infarction may be subdivided into two groups. The group with post-infarction angina, acute ST–T changes during the hospitalization, and an abnormal exercise test before discharge has a very high incidence of early extension of the infarction. The best prognosis pertains to patients with enzyme-confirmed myocardial infarction, lack of definite ECG changes and normal exercise test before discharge. This low-risk group may encompass 20 percent of all non-Q-wave myocardial infarction patients.

Rating for Non-Q-Wave Myocardial Infarctions

No other adverse information; no post-infarction angina; normal exercise test (before hospital discharge or current); prognosis is good and most of these applicants will not have undergone cardiac catheterization.

Time since infarction	Rating
Up to 1 mth	Postpone
Thereafter	+50 to +75

Time since infarction	Rating
Up to 1 yr	Postpone
Thereafter	Rate as other infarctions (*see* Chapter 15)

Old, Strictly Posterior Myocardial Infarction

Prominent initial anterior forces manifested by an R/S ratio of up to 1 in V1 may be seen in old strictly posterior myocardial infarction. Mazzoleni et al[14] have determined that this is neither a sensitive nor a specific marker for this infarction. Strictly posterior infarctions are rare, they usually extend into lateral and inferior areas and, besides V1, cause changes in the inferior and/or lateral leads. Normal variants, incomplete right bundle branch block, right ventricular hypertrophy, pulmonary embolism and chest deformity are more likely diagnoses, especially if the history and risk factors are not suggestive of arteriosclerotic heart disease. During the acute period ST is depressed and T is upright in V1, but these changes are of short duration and seldom present at the time of application.

Rating
Possible old, strictly posterior myocardial infarction.
No adverse findings from attending physician statement and/or review of previous ECGs — standard (disregard as probable normal variant).
Adverse findings adding to a significant likelihood of arteriosclerotic heart disease — rate as infarction (*see* Chapter 15).

Electrocardiographic Estimation of Infarct Size

Multiple studies have shown unmistakably increased mortality from clinical infarcts carrying a history of a previous infarct. This also applies to infarctions only diagnosed by ECG.[22]

Bounous et al[23] have developed a score system for estimating infarct size and its reflection in the severity of wall motion abnormalities and level of left ventricular ejection fraction. It is based on measurements of Q- and R-wave durations, and R/Q and R/S amplitude ratios in the standard 12-lead ECG. It appears to be valuable but, even in its simplified form, is somewhat cumbersome for routine use.

Prognostic Implications of Anterior versus Inferior Myocardial Infarction

Most authors have reported a higher mortality for anterior infarctions, and some have attributed it to a larger size.[24–29] Other authors disagree.[30,22]

Non-specific ST–T Abnormalities

The T-wave is the most labile component of the ECG; the transition from a normal to an abnormal wave may be so gradual that any division is somewhat arbitrary. Moreover, the configuration of ST and T can be affected by a great variety of physiological and pathological states, as well as certain medications. There is no rule for distinguishing benign, inconsequential T-wave changes from those caused by disease. However, it is possible to go one step beyond the diagnosis of 'non-specific changes'. ST–T abnormalities should be classified into primary and secondary. Changes in the sequence of activation trigger changes in the sequence of repolarization. In a ventricular extrasystole, ST–T is opposite to the main QRS deflection. The same occurs in bundle branch block and in marked ventricular hypertrophy. These 'secondary ST–T abnormalities' are caused by changes in the QRS complex.

ST–T abnormalities that are not opposite to the main QRS deflection have been called 'primary ST–T abnormalities'. These are non-specific and due to changes in myocardial metabolism. Causes include ischemia, pericarditis, myocarditis, electrolyte imbalances, myxedema, drug effects, neurological changes, hyperventilation, postprandial changes and changes in position. The ST–T morphology sometimes allows an educated guess at the cause (digitalis sagging of ST, hyperkalemic tenting of the T-waves, large U-waves of hypokalemia etc). Classifying ST–T abnormalities into primary, secondary and mixed is more helpful than lumping all of them together under 'non-specific'.

The Prudential Insurance Company of America has been able to supply much useful information about the mortality and morbidity associated with T-wave changes in the ECG. ECG records from all Prudential employees have been kept since 1933, and follow-up studies have been conducted from time to time by Kiessling and coworkers.[31] The authors demonstrated that mortality was related to the degree of T-wave abnormality; unfortunately the conception of what constitutes adequate T-wave voltage is a subjective standard.

T-wave changes were classified into major and minor. Although this separation is arbitrary and not in clinical use, it has prognostic value and fulfills underwriting needs. The authors included biphasic T-waves in the major abnormality group. It is perhaps preferable to consider them minor abnormalities in most cases. The major-minor classification should not be applied to secondary T-wave abnormalities. The inverted T-wave present in lead I in a complete left bundle branch block is part of this entity's ECG pattern and should not be additionally rated as a major T-wave abnormality.

Definition of Primary Minor and Major T-Wave Changes

There is a relationship between the normal voltage of R and T; therefore criteria for the individual leads vary with the QRS configuration.
1) With a normal but tall R-wave in leads I, II, V2 to V6, aVL in a 'horizontal heart' and aVF in a 'vertical heart':
Minor T-wave changes — low, flat, notched or biphasic T-waves.
Major T-wave changes — inverted T-waves.
2) With a normal but moderate-to-small R-wave in leads I, II, V2 to V6, aVL in a 'horizontal heart' and aVF in a 'vertical heart'.

Minor T-wave changes — low, flat, notched, biphasic or slightly inverted T-waves.
Major T-wave changes — deeply inverted.

Kiessling's paper[31] delves into finer details of this classification.

Arteriosclerotic heart disease is the most common cause of ST depression in middle-aged men in the USA. In an Oriental population, where hypertension is more prevalent than arteriosclerosis, it becomes the most common cause of ST depression.

Primary ST–T-wave abnormalities are sometimes the clue for a work-up leading to a diagnosis of silent ischemia.

Primary Minor T-Wave Abnormalities

Minor T-wave abnormalities in apparently normal individuals allow for some latitude in interpretation. The underwriter should look closely at the P-waves and also search for risk factors for arteriosclerotic heart disease. It is likely that the risk will be greater when minor changes occur in multiple leads, or in a group of leads reflecting a particular area of the myocardium. A broad guideline for the interpretation of borderline changes in aVL and aVF is that the frontal plane T-wave axis should not be more than 30° to the left or 60° to the right of the QRS axis. Comparison with previous ECGs may be helpful, as the risk diminishes if it is known that the abnormality has been unchanged for many years.

In his evaluation of applicants for life insurance, the medical underwriter must come to a prompt decision based on the information at his disposal. Apart, perhaps, from an exercise ECG, he cannot embark on other more sophisticated investigations. The question arises, therefore, of how to evaluate individuals who show T-wave changes but who, as far as can be determined, have no abnormal history or gross abnormality.

Obviously in any large group there will be many whose T-wave changes are not related to cardiac disease, and there will be some whose T-wave changes will be evidence of ischemic heart disease or other cardiac pathology.

Rating

Since this heterogeneous group produces increased mortality and it is impossible to identify the heart disease cases from the resting ECG alone, there is no alternative but to charge a small extra premium (+50) to most members of the group. If the exercise tracing is negative for ischemia, the rating for minor T-wave changes in the resting ECG can usually be reduced to zero.

Primary Major T-Wave Abnormalities

Major changes in T-waves as an isolated finding without a pertinent history of clinical abnormality are exceedingly rare. In the Prudential studies of company employees the mortality ratio varied between 302 percent and 158 percent, depending on the length of follow-up. The medical histories of Prudential employees are more likely to be dependable than those obtained from life insurance applicants; accordingly, the experience is probably lighter than one would expect to find among applicants for life insurance.

Rating

The medical underwriter should look at major T-wave changes with considerable suspicion. Close attention should be paid to the P-waves and to the presence of risk factors for arteriosclerotic heart disease; the medical history should be thoroughly checked, and the physical examination should be supplemented by all other available aids.

Major T-wave changes, cause known — rate for cause.

Major T-wave changes, cause unknown, no other adverse information:

Depth of T-wave inversions	Rating
Up to 3 mm	+ 100 to +150
Over 3 mm	+ 150 to +200

Unstable ST–T-Wave Pattern

Lyle[36] demonstrated that individuals whose ECGs originally showed minor T-wave changes but later reverted to normal had higher mortality ratios than those whose minor T-wave abnormalities remained unaltered throughout the study. This emphasizes the fact that a changing pattern in the ECG is more likely to indicate active myocardial pathology than if the pattern is stable over a long period. Therefore T-wave abnormalities that disappear cannot be ignored, for their disappearance does not prove that the abnormalities were of no significance.

Ventricular Arrhythmias: Ventricular Ectopic Beats (VEBs) (Premature Ventricular Complexes (PVCs), Ventricular Extrasystoles (VEs)), Ventricular Tachycardia

The standard ECG is a poor screening method for assessing the prevalence of VEs. Attempts at quantifying the number of ventricular premature beats per minute present on mounted tracings are biased by the tendency to select for mounting the portions of strips that display premature beats.

VEs are found in about 1 percent of routine ECGs obtained on clinically normal individuals. Their prevalence increases to between 50 percent and 73 percent when assessed by continuous monitoring on 24-hour ambulatory ECGs. Frequent, complex and R-on-T ventricular premature beats are present, although at a low frequency in ambulatory-monitored normal subjects.

Few impairments have undergone wider swings in the interpretation of their significance than ventricular ectopy. The belief that the intermittent pulse has a universally poor prognosis and may lead to sudden death was stated by Galen and persisted for over 17 centuries.

It is still being debated whether chronic VEs are a direct manifestation of underlying electrical instability and a primary factor in the genesis of sustained ventricular tachycardia and fibrillation or an epiphenomenon in the electrically unstable heart.

From Morgagni[33] to Osler,[34] there were authors who disagreed with this teaching.

Lyle[35,36] followed 11 thousand employees of the Prudential Insurance Company for 27 years. Those with simple extrasystoles had a mortality risk ratio of 1·2; those with bigeminal, consecutive and multiform patterns had a mortality risk ratio of 1·3.

The Tecumseh prospective study, published in 1969, and studies of myocardial infarction patients while in the coronary care units and after discharge demonstrated that those with ventricular arrhythmias were at a higher risk of sudden death. The hypothesis that an increased number of ventricular premature beats may constitute a risk factor for sudden death (by causing ventricular fibrillation) was extrapolated to the general population.[37-39]

Hierarchical classifications of arrhythmias were proposed by Lown[40] and Myerburg. These classifications emphasize the frequency and complexity of the PVCs and assume that there is a gamut of increasing severity, which starts with infrequent PVCs and continues with frequent PVCs, polymorphic PVCs, couplets, triplets, R-on-T phenomenon, non-sustained ventricular tachycardia, sustained ventricular tachycardia and ventricular fibrillation. The implication is that preventing the PVCs will prevent the more complex forms and decrease the risk of sudden death.

Surawicz reviewed the evidence in 1989 and concluded that the common denominator in most fatal electrical accidents seems to be ischemia; he stressed that too much attention may have been paid to the ventricular arrhythmias. Meanwhile, longitudinal studies published in the 1970s showed that extrasystoles have a much better prognosis when unaccompanied by other cardiac abnormalities.[41-43]

Rodstein and coworkers[41] (Equitable Life Assurance Society of the United States) studied individuals considered to be standard risks except for the presence of extrasystoles. The mortality ratios for the entire group, as well as for subgroups displaying simple or complex, supraventricular or ventricular extrasystoles, ranged between 94 percent and 124 percent, well within the standard insurance premium classification. When VEBs were present in subjects with hypertension or other cardiac abnormalities the mortality ratio increased to 223 percent.

Crow and colleagues[44] analyzed the available evidence, including their own 12 thousand cases, and criticized Rabkin[39] for his failure to explore the role of other potentially important variables, such as hypertension, cigarette smoking and sample size. Crow opined that ventricular ectopy, in and of itself, does not justify an adverse prognosis.

In a six-and-a-half-year follow-up, Kennedy and coworkers[45-49] showed that asymptomatic frequent and complex ventricular ectopy (including ventricular tachycardia present in 26 percent) in a group of 72 asymptomatic subjects without evidence of cardiac disease or a family history of cardiomyopathy and/or sudden death showed no increased risk of death compared with that of the healthy US population.

Ruskin,[50] in an editorial discussing Kennedy's studies, emphasized that the natural history of patients with frequent or complex ventricular ectopy occurring in association with mild abnormalities of cardiac function (such as mitral valve prolapse or early cardiomyopathy) or in the setting of a family history of cardiac disease or sudden death is unknown.

Contribution of Ambulatory Electrocardiography

This technique was originally used for the documentation and diagnosis of arrhythmias suspected of causing various symptoms during the course of everyday life. In the USA it is frequently called Holter monitoring after its developer,

Norman Holter.[51] Scanning was initially very demanding but contemporary technology is almost entirely automated. However, tracings still need careful over-reading by an individual well versed in arrhythmia interpretation. Holter monitoring is frequently used to detect ventricular arrhythmias and evaluate patients' response to treatment. It may be of help in assessing the prognosis of patients with hypertrophic cardiomyopathy, a group with a high incidence of sudden death due to arrhythmias.

Ambulatory Electrocardiography in the Post-Myocardial Infarction Patient

Ambulatory electrocardiography has a proven value for risk stratification of the post-acute-myocardial infarction patient, as demonstrated by various investigators.[39,52–55]

More than 50 percent of patients Holter-monitored for the twenty-four hours preceding hospital discharge have less than one premature ventricular beat per hour. The two-year mortality rate of this group is about 5 percent. Of post-infarction patients monitored in the same way, 15–25 percent display 10 or more PVCs per hour; their two-year mortality rate is less than 20 percent. The presence of more than three PVCs per hour or one couplet in 24 hours markedly increases the risk of death over a several-year follow-up period. Survival decreases even further with increasing complexity of the arrhythmias.

Sinus Rate Variability

Heart rate (HR) variability (the standard deviation of all R–R intervals in sinus rhythm) may be automatically measured from ambulatory ECG recordings.

In a large trial the Multicenter Postinfarction Research Group[56] demonstrated that heart rate variability had a greater univariate correlation to mortality than the presence of left ventricular ejection fraction of less than 30 percent, rales, or complex ventricular premature beats. This may represent decreased vagal tone and enhanced sympathetic tone during ischemia, which could facilitate the development of ventricular fibrillation. These findings, if confirmed, would provide a very valuable underwriting parameter.

Intracardiac electrophysiologic testing has been tried for prognosis and as a guideline for therapy in patients with ventricular arrhythmias.

In patients with coronary artery disease and ventricular arrhythmias, Gomes and coworkers,[57] showed that when programed ventricular stimulation induced sustained ventricular tachycardia the one-year mortality rate, even on anti-arrhythmic therapy, exceeded 30 percent. It was only 2 percent when ventricular tachycardia could not be induced. As there are no randomized trials to confirm the validity of this approach, the use of electrophysiologic studies to evaluate ventricular ectopic activity occurring late after myocardial infarction remains controversial.[58] The electrophysiologic study of patients who develop ventricular tachycardia or cardiac arrest within the first 48 hours of a myocardial infarction has little or no prognostic value.[59]

Signal-averaged electrocardiography is receiving increasing attention as a method that may help define subsets of patients at high risk for sustained ventricular tachycardia.[60]

Sustained Ventricular Tachycardia

This is a dangerous arrhythmia which should always elicit a careful evaluation. Prognosis varies according to the context in which it appears. Ventricular tachycardia occurring within the first 24 hours of an acute myocardial infarction and sometimes leading into ventricular fibrillation is a complication of this acute phase and does not aggravate the prognosis of the infarction.[61,62] Alternatively, if ventricular tachycardia arises in what appears to be a stable situation, recurrence is likely and the prognostic outlook becomes less favorable, especially if this occurs in the context of coronary artery disease with a low ejection fraction.

When sustained ventricular tachycardia originates in the right ventricle the prognosis may be more favorable than when it emanates from the left ventricle.

Ventricular Arrhythmias Occurring During Exercise

Faris et al[63] studied the prevalence and reproducibility of increased ventricular ectopy on exercise in clinically normal policemen aged 25 to 54 and repeated the testing two to nine years later. The authors concluded that the presence of VEs during exercise in clinically normal individuals appears, in itself, to be of little or no diagnostic or prognostic importance. There is poor reproducibility on repeat testing and the risk of coronary events or sudden death is not increased.

Fleg and Lakata[64] analyzed findings from the Baltimore Longitudinal Study on Aging. As this is a community study, the participants, healthy asymptomatic volunteers, somewhat resemble insurance applicants. Out of one thousand people, 10 had exercise-induced ventricular tachycardia with runs lasting up to 6 beats; nine of them were aged 65 years or older. The tachycardia occurred near peak exercise and some people had multiple runs. These 10 individuals had normal thallium scans and their coronary risk factors did not differ from those of other members of the study. In two years of follow-up no subject died suddenly, had syncope or developed any symptom or sign of heart disease or worsening of the arrhythmia. Sustained ventricular tachycardia has been defined as lasting more than 30 seconds at a heart rate ± 110/min.

Risk Classification

The lowest risk category consists of applicants in whom structural heart disease is not identifiable by thorough cardiovascular evaluation, including echocardiography and stress testing. These individuals have simple or complex VEBs and even short runs of 'non-sustained' ventricular tachycardia (considered benign in this set-up). Sustained ventricular tachycardia is extremely infrequent in the absence of documented heart disease. Long-term follow-up of such patients has demonstrated that the incidence of cardiac death or sudden death has been no greater than that in the general population.

The highest risk category encompasses individuals who have advanced structural heart disease; many have a history of sustained, symptomatic, ventricular tachycardia or ventricular fibrillation. Their ventricular arrhythmias have been called malignant.

The intermediate-risk group is probably the largest. They have mild-to-moderate abnormalities of cardiac structure and/or function, such as early cardiomyopathy, slight ischemia, or a family history of cardiac disease or sudden death. Their ventricular arrhythmias are considered potentially malignant. These applicants' risk of sudden death covers a wide range.

Rating

Suggested ratings for ventricular arrhythmias occurring at rest:

Low-risk, benign — standard.

Intermediate-risk — add +50 to +200 to the rating for cause.

High-risk, malignant — decline.

Note: The intermediate-risk group encompasses many conditions with varying degrees of severity. Furthermore, a long-term follow-up is not available. Its underwriting requires sound and conservative clinical judgment.

EXERCISE TESTS

Exercise tests are an important risk selection tool in the USA. They provide important information and are often available at no additional cost as part of the attending physician's statement (APS).

ECG exercise test is a term covering all graded stress tests with ECG tracings taken during or after exercise. In the USA the most common is the treadmill exercise test performed according to the Bruce protocol. The bicycle exercise test appears to be more prevalent in Europe.

The Master's Two-Step Test is considered obsolete by the insurance industry. Besides its low sensitivity, many doctors are reluctant to exercise a patient without ECG monitoring. Most American insurance companies accept it only when a treadmill test cannot be obtained and if an HR over 114/min has been achieved. It is usually performed as a double Master's test.

Exercise tests are useful and cost-effective in the evaluation of large-amount applicants who also have:

1) Moderate likelihood of arteriosclerotic heart disease, based on a combination of resting ECG abnormalities, symptoms, risk factors and age. The additional information enhances risk classification and sometimes allows a more competitive rating.

2) Known arteriosclerotic heart disease. Exercise tests are indicated to evaluate its severity and/or progression and achieve a more accurate underwriting.

It is difficult to justify doing ECG exercise tests in young, apparently healthy individuals only on the basis of insurance amount. Most abnormal tests in young individuals, especially in females, are false-positive and only create delays and ill will. MDs should be especially careful when ordering treadmill tests in elderly individuals who have poor balance and may fall and sustain injury.

Exercise tests occasionally yield useful information on other impairments (i.e. completion of Stage 2 of the Bruce protocol suggests that a respiratory impairment is probably minor). Intermittent claudication of the lower extremities may become apparent during an exercise test.

Under Bayes' theorem, good clinical judgment has become quantitative. It allows a calculation of the pre-test probability of disease based on symptoms and risk factors, and of how it changes according to the test results.[65] It is possible to develop these concepts into an underwriting point system, but they are cumbersome and time consuming for an underwriter to use. This approach may have a future as part of the software of an automated expert underwriting system.

Exercise Testing Protocols

These may be symptom-limited (maximal) or arbitrarily-limited (submaximal).

1) Symptom-limited (maximal) tests are limited by symptoms or predetermined signs. Exercise is continued until the patient develops angina, inappropriate dyspnea, inappropriate fatigue, pallor and abnormal cerebral function, drop in BP or HR, marked ST–T abnormalities, electrical alternans or dangerous cardiac arrhythmias (unless the test is performed for arrhythmia assessment). Maximal tests are more sensitive than the submaximal and allow a more accurate assessment of functional capacity.

2) Submaximal tests are terminated at an arbitrarily chosen target HR or if the applicant develops indications for test termination before achieving the target level. Under these circumstances a test planned as submaximal may really be maximal. A frequent target is 85 percent of the maximum predicted HR for the patient's age. The maximal predicted HR is roughly 220 minus the age. Athletes have slower HRs both at rest and during exercise. There are tables that give the maximal predicted target HRs for age, sex and physical condition. Some applicants, on beta-blocking medications, are unable to reach 85 percent of their maximal predicted HR. Others become fatigued and stop the test prematurely.

American Insurers' Requirements

The following criteria are often used by American insurers for accepting an exercise ECG as normal (negative test).

1) Treadmill or bicycle ergometer:
a) Achievement of at least 75 percent of maximal predicted HR.
b) Achievement of double product (DP) (Systolic BP × HR) ≥ 20,000.
c) Otherwise negative test by clinical and ECG criteria.

2) Double Master's (unacceptable for many US companies):
a) Faithful implementation of the Master's protocol. The heart rate in the tracing recorded immediately after exercise must be over 114/min.
b) Otherwise negative test by clinical and ECG criteria.

Occasionally it becomes necessary to compare tests performed under different

Table 16.1. Comparison of Exercise Protocols.

METs		Treadmill Tests				Step test Naughton 30 steps/m Step Ht.cm	Bic Ergom For 70kg Wt kg–m/min
		Bruce mph/% elevation	Kattus	Balke mph/% elevation	DeBusk		
5–6	Stage	I 1·7mph 10%	I 2 mph 10%	III 3 mph 5–7·5%	IV 2 mph 10·5–14%	III–IV 12–16 cm	III–IV 450–600
7	Stage	II 2·5mph 12%	II 3 mph 10%	V 3 mph 10%	VI 2 mph 17·5%	V 20 cm	V 750
9–10	Stage	III 3·4mph 14%	IV 4 mph 14%	VII 3 mph 15%	VIII–IX 3 mph 15%	VII 28 cm	VI–VII 900–1050
13	Stage	IV 4·2mph 16%	V 4 mph 18%	X 3 mph 22·5%	> IX —	> X >40 cm	X 1500

protocols. Table 16.1 compares common exercise protocols on the basis of the METs (*see* Chapter 15) required at different levels of exercise.

Orthopedic, arthritic or peripheral vascular impairments may limit the applicant's ability to perform on a bicycle or treadmill. It is sometimes possible to substitute a non-standardized test exercising the upper extremities.

Intravenous infusion of dipyridamole or adenosine unmask ischemia through a 'coronary steal' mechanism. Dobutamine infusions increase cardiac work and oxygen demand. These new tests are not yet widely available. A 24-hour ambulatory ECG performed with FM equipment and reliable recording of the ST segment may also show abnormal changes but it is less sensitive than the exercise test.

Risk of Exercise Testing

Stuart and Ellestad[66] surveyed 518,448 tests performed in 1,375 centers and found a mortality rate of 0·5 deaths per 10,000 (0·005 percent) and a combined morbidity/mortality rate of 8·86 per 10,000. Exercise testing is eminently safe, especially if personnel are aware of the contraindications and when to terminate testing. Personnel should be trained for handling any emergency that might arise.

The following are a few technical points of importance to the MD:
1) Exercise electrodes are placed on the torso to avoid motion and muscle contraction artifacts. This changes the voltage and morphology of leads I, II, III, aVR, aVL and aVF. Therefore they should not be used for diagnosing hypertrophy or infarction.
2) Proper technique requires obtaining a standard ECG before the exercise ECG. Unfortunately some physicians skip this step, and thereby risk missing interval changes that may have occurred in the standard ECG. Tracings are often labeled 'recumbent, control' without specifying that the leads are not standard. This is confusing when an unwary interpreter tries to compare them with standard tracings.
3) The sensitivity of the ECG exercise test drops significantly if the monitored lead does not display a prominent R-wave.
4) Labile repolarization can lead to false-positive diagnoses. It may be detected by looking for ST–T changes induced by hyperventilation and/or by change in position.
5) Artifacts may be reduced by bandpass filtering and/or computer averaging. If the tracing is being averaged by computer, all aberrant beats (mainly PVCs) should be deleted from the averaging system; their inclusion distorts the tracing. This is a reason for the medical underwriter to review copies of the actual tracings rather than the computer-averaged complexes only.

Computerized Exercise ECG Systems

These have become widespread in the USA. Some systems can measure the ST segment slope and/or its integral. This is a triangular area bounded by the ST segment, a horizontal line drawn through the isoelectric point and a vertical line at 0·08 s after the J-point. It should not measure less than 7·5 microvolt-sec. The ST segment integral takes into account both ST displacement and slope.[67–69]

Computer measurements do not replace interpretation by an experienced ECG reader. The measurements should be reviewed carefully to make sure they are consistent with visual inspection of the actual tracings. It is not yet clear which method of measurement yields the best sensitivity and specificity for our purposes.

Detection of Myocardial Ischemia by Exercise Electrocardiography

Myocardial ischemia may cause repolarization changes at rest, during exercise and after exercise. ST segment changes occurring with exercise attracted early attention, but sensitivity and specificity are significantly enhanced by also looking at test duration, development of chest pain, fatigue, dyspnea, arrhythmias, rales, murmurs, rate and blood pressure changes. Goldschlager et al[70] determined the probability of a greater than 50 percent narrowing of one or more coronary arteries according to the degree of ST segment changes on the exercise electrocardiogram.

Most cardiologists consider abnormal an ST segment depression or elevation of 1 mm (0·1 millivolt) measured 0·08s after the J-point. The PR segment is the baseline reference voltage.

If the J-point is not depressed and the T-wave is negative, the ST-segment has to go down in order to merge with the T-wave; this should not be interpreted as a downsloping ST-segment. The true downsloping pattern of ST depression starts from a depressed J-point. The down-sloping ST depression pattern is associated with a higher incidence of subsequent coronary events than either the horizontal or the up-sloping pattern.

ST elevations often signal more severe ischemia than ST depressions; sagging ST depressions are equivocal.

A positive test during Stage I of Bruce protocol (low double product), is very likely to represent left main or triple vessel disease. The same applies to ST depression persisting for more than 8 min after exercise.[71]

Double Product (DP), Rate-Pressure Product

The metabolic workload imposed on the myocardium can be estimated by the 'double product' (DP): the product of the maximal heart rate and the maximal systolic blood pressure. They are usually attained simultaneously and at the peak of exercise. A DP of less than 20,000 constitutes a very low work load; it will elicit abnormal changes only in the presence of very severe disease. At this load, only abnormal tests are useful; other tests are unacceptable. DPs over 30,000 carry very high work loads. Slight ST abnormalities found under these circumstances may be due to either ischemia or a false-positive test. Most tests will fall between these two extremes.

Some companies allow up to 100 credits for a DP of more than 30,000. The credit

Table 16.2. Suggested electrocardiographic criteria for abnormal Master's test.

Level of abnormality	mm
Equivocal	0·4
Slightly abnormal	0·5–0·9
Moderately abnormal	1·0–1·9
Moderate to markedly abnormal	2·0–2·5
Markedly abnormal	>2·6

is applicable only to cancel debits due to resting ECG abnormalities suspicious of ischemia.

Relating the degree of ST change to the corresponding HR or to the double product helps to establish degrees of abnormality.

Clinical criteria for exercise test abnormality:

1) Chest, neck or arm pain suspicious of angina.
2) Severe dyspnea or fatigue, disproportionate to the amount of exercise.
3) S3 gallop or a new mitral insufficiency murmur (papillary muscle dysfunction).
4) Abnormal systolic blood pressure response to progressive exercise. Beware of inaccurate BP measurements on a moving patient in a noisy environment.

   Flat response (less than 10 mmg Hg rise for two stages) is markedly abnormal if the measurement is reliable.

   Sustained decrease of more than 10 mm Hg is markedly abnormal if the measurement is reliable.

5) Inability to complete more than 3 min of the Bruce Protocol because of any of the above is markedly abnormal (unless psychogenic or due to other disabilities).

Electrocardiographic criteria for graded exercise test abnormality:

1) 1 mm or more of horizontal ST depression in excess of the control ECG.
2) Up-sloping ST depression which 80 min after the J-point is 1 mm below the isoelectric line.
3) Down-sloping ST depression.
4) Development of ST elevation.

ST changes developing in leads that display 'infarction waves' are not reliable for diagnosing significant ischemia.

Table 16.3. Estimation of degree of ST abnormality; analysis based on heart rate (HR) at maximal ST depression.

ST depression (mm)	HR at maximal ST depression		
	<110/min	110–140/min	>140/min
<0·6	Equivocal	Normal	Normal
0·6–1·0	Equivocal	Normal	Normal
1·1–1·5	Slightly abnormal	Slightly abnormal	Equivocal
1·6–2·9	Moderately to markedly abnormal	Moderately abnormal	Moderately abnormal
⩾3·0	Markedly abnormal	Markedly abnormal	Markedly abnormal

Other findings suggestive of high-risk coronary artery disease on exercise electrocardiographic stress tests are exercise angina occurring at less than 4 METs, failure to achieve more than 4 METs, abnormal or inadequate blood pressure response, ST depression persisting for 8 or more minutes into recovery and ST depression accompanied by exercise-induced complex ventricular arrhythmias.

False Negative Exercise Tests

Puzzling reports of patients with negative exercise tests who, shortly after being reassured by their physicians, developed an acute myocardial infarction have recently found a satisfactory explanation. Non-flow limiting coronary plaques, undetectable by our current non-invasive methods, may crack and precipitate a thrombotic occlusion leading to infarction. Thrombotic occlusions occur more frequently on higher-grade stenosis, but mild plaques are more numerous.[72]

False-Positive Exercise Tests

Ventricular hypertrophy, causing relative ischemia, may cause abnormal ST changes in the presence of normal coronary arteries. Mitral valve prolapse, left bundle branch block, Wolff-Parkinson-White (WPW) syndrome and primary ST–T abnormalities due to medications and/or electrolyte imbalances may also cause false-positive tests. Sometimes the cause is unknown.

Exercise ST changes are valid in right bundle branch block and in the evaluation of primary ST–T abnormalities not due to medications or hypokalemia. The baseline used to measure the additional ST changes should be the ST level in the control tracing. This issue has recently been reviewed by Kligfield et al.[73]

Digitalis, quinidine, other antiarrhythmic agents, hypokalemia and a few psychiatric medications may interfere with the interpretation of ST changes elicited by exercise. According to Nasrallah and collaborators,[74] interpretation of exertional ST depression in digitalized patients may be facilitated by using 1·5 mm depression as a criterion and by relating such changes to the HR.

Rating

Suggested rating for ECG-exercise test when there is no documented diagnosis of ASHD and no chest pain:
1) Normal to HR up to 150/min or DP up to 30,000 — give up to 100 credits against resting ECG abnormalities.
2) Abnormal: try to obtain a copy of the attending physician's records, which may clarify the diagnosis and allow to rate for cause. Otherwise:

Degree of abnormality	Rating	
	Men aged ≤39 Women aged ≤49	Men aged ≥40 Women aged ≥50
Equivocal	0[a]	Usually 0[a]
Slightly abnormal	0[a]	0[a] to +50
Moderately abnormal	+50[b] to same as current angina	+75[b] to same as current angina
Markedly abnormal	Most should be declined unless further work-up establishes that they constitute an insurable risk	

[a]These favorable ratings assume that the test is most likely a false-positive. To make this assumption there should be no history of suspicious chest pains and the risk factors should be favorable.
[b]These ratings assume a moderate likelihood of disease. They may be decreased or waived if the applicant completes a normal radionuclear or echocardiographic study to a satisfactory level of exercise.

Other ECG changes occurring during or minutes after exercise.
1) Subsidence of ST abnormality within 1 min (rapid recovery) — credit 50.
2) Less than 20,000 — inadequate test, valuable only if abnormal.
30,000–32,000 — credit 50 against ECG abnormalities suspicious of ischemia.
Greater than 32,000 — credit up to 100 against ECG abnormalities suspicious of ischemia.
3) Labile repolarization (ST–T changes caused by pre-exercise standing or hyperventilation): consider the likelihood of a false-positive test.
4) CLBBB developing transiently during exercise (rate dependent CLBBB): With favorable PS: +50.
No current AP — use one-half of basic CLBBB rating, see p. 464.
5) CRBBB developing transiently during exercise — 0.
6) ST elevation (frequently indicates severe coronary disease or ventricular aneurysm) — rate as severe angina or decline.
7) T-wave changes without ST depression or elevation — 0.
8) Failure of HR to rise greater than 20 percent over control (test stopped without explanation):
Well-conditioned athlete or on beta-blocker medication (test may be inadequate) — no additional rating.
Others — may indicate severe disease (chronotropic insufficiency).

Arrhythmias and Conduction Disturbances During Exercise Testing

Prognosis depends on the underlying disease rather than on the arrhythmia. Arrhythmias in normal hearts are essentially benign. In insurance medicine this applies only to reliable applicants who have had thorough cardiological evaluations. When the attending physician's work-up has not been thorough and when there is more risk of antiselection, insurance companies are more conservative.

Rating

Suggested ratings for arrhythmias developed during ECG exercise test; no documented diagnosis of heart disease and no chest pain.
1) PVCs:

	Rating		
	Unifocal		Multifocal or couplets
	<10/min	>10/min	
During exercise			
Noted at rate >145/min	0	0	Individual consideration
Noted at rate <145/min	0	0	Add 0·5 mm to ST
Disappear at higher rate	0	0	Individual consideration
Persist at rate <145/min	0	Add 0·5 mm to ST	Add 1 mm to ST
After exercise			
Appear or reappear	0	Add 0·5 mm to ST	Add 0·5 mm to ST

2) PACs — usually ignore.
3) Atrial fibrillation:
Short duration, noted at rate >150/min — usually ignore.
Otherwise — add 0·5 mm to ST.

Abnormal ECG Exercise Test and Normal Nuclear or Echo cardiographic Exercise Test

Nuclear tests are more sensitive and more specific than the ECG exercise test and usually over-rule it. The medical underwriter should verify that the nuclear test was technically correct and carried to at least the same level of exercise as the abnormal ECG exercise test. It is also important to consider the tests in the context of likelihood of disease. Nuclear tests may have false-negative results. If there is high likelihood of disease, a nuclear test should not be allowed to over-rule the abnormal results of an ECG test.

Atrial and Ventricular Hypertrophy

Left Atrial Abnormalities

Echocardiographic and hemodynamic studies have shown that the P-waves show similar changes in left atrial hypertension, dilatation, hypertrophy and interatrial conduction defects.[75]

Some computer programs read as abnormal any biphasic P in V1. This leads to over-diagnosis of left atrial abnormality. When several signs of left atrial abnormality coexist, however, the diagnosis carries a higher weight and should influence the interpretation of borderline clinical or ECG findings. Left atrial abnormalities significantly increase the likelihood of disease.

The earliest electrocardiographic change in arterial hypertension is left atrial abnormality. It appears much earlier than left ventricular hypertrophy and may help the MD in differentiating labile hypertension from early hypertensive heart disease.

Rating

Left atrial abnormalities are seldom, if at all, rated *per se*. If clear-cut, they should prompt further investigation, mainly a request for an APS. When left atrial abnormalities accompany borderline Q-waves or ST–T abnormalities they should tip the balance towards rating, rather than giving the applicant the benefit of the doubt.

Left Ventricular Hypertrophy

Echocardiographic studies have confirmed the shortcomings of the electrocardiogram: the echocardiograph can make an early diagnosis of left ventricular hypertrophy or differentiate between concentric ventricular hypertrophy and dilatation, and/or a combination of both.

Autopsy, angiography and, more recently, echocardiography have established that the ECG achieves only a 50–65 percent sensitivity in the diagnosis of moderate or severe left ventricular hypertrophy. Despite this poor performance, it is still the best method for detecting hypertrophy in the context of insurance medicine. Except in rare unusual cases of balanced biventricular hypertrophy with cancellation of opposite ventricular forces, the ECG is far more sensitive than the chest X-ray or the physical examination. It also allays concern aroused by slightly increased CT ratios in normal anatomically horizontal hearts.

The ability of the ECG to diagnose left ventricular hypertrophy declines in the presence of biventricular hypertrophy, myocardial infarction and treatment with digitalis or antiarrhythmic drugs.

ECG findings suggestive of ventricular dilatation or hypertrophy are of considerable importance in insurance medicine because they signal advanced disease and increased risk over and above that associated with the primary cause.

Voltage criteria

Apart from P-wave changes, the earliest electrocardiographic evidence of left ventricular hypertrophy is an increase in voltage of the QRS complexes in leads reflecting left ventricular muscle mass. Unfortunately voltage criteria yield too high an incidence of false-positive diagnosis when applied to a population with low prevalence of heart disease.[6]

Among the constitutional variables, age has the greatest effect on the amplitude of the QRS complex, especially in the precordial leads. The QRS voltage is higher in adults under the age of 40 than in those over 40. The amplitude of the maximum spatial QRS vector decreases at an average rate of 6·5 percent with the advance of each decade of adult life.[76]

It is suggested that excessive voltage as a sole abnormality in the ECG should be disregarded, unless there is corroborative evidence of left ventricular hypertrophy in the form of left atrial abnormalities, a chest radiograph suggestive of left ventricular enlargement or an abnormal clinical examination of the heart.

Degrees of Left Ventricular Hypertrophy

A greater diagnostic accuracy occurs when a left ventricular strain pattern appears. This name has fallen into disfavor because it is not appropriate to describe an electrical event. The presence of secondary ST–T abnormalities with ST and T oriented in a direction opposite to the larger QRS deflections signals advanced disease and a significantly shorter life expectancy unless the cause is reversed.

Romhilt and Estes[77] improved diagnostic accuracy by combining multiple criteria and giving them weighted scores. They used QRS amplitude, ST–T changes, P-wave abnormalities, left axis deviation, QRS width and delayed intrinsicoid deflection as parameters.

Rating

Slight left ventricular hypertrophy: positive voltage criteria plus disproportionately low T-wave voltages in the left chest leads — +50 to +75.

Moderate left ventricular hypertrophy: positive voltage criteria plus ST depression and/or T-wave inversion up to 3 mm in depth in the left chest leads — +100 to +150.

Marked left ventricular hypertrophy: positive voltage criteria plus ST depression and/or T-wave inversion deeper than 3 mm in the left chest leads — usually decline.

Athlete's Heart and Hypertrophic Cardiomyopathy

The most common ECG abnormalities in hypertrophic cardiomyopathy are increased QRS voltage, repolarization changes, deep thin Q-waves and arrhythmias. Contrary to theoretical prediction, studies correlating the depth of the Q-waves with the thickness of the interventricular septum, as measured by echocardiography, have shown no correlation.[78]

Since athletes can have hypertrophy and repolarization abnormalities, it is sometimes difficult to separate the physiologic from the pathologic. The ECG should be viewed in context with the medical history and physical examination. If this raises any suspicion of hypertrophic cardiomyopathy, either a rating 'as is' or an echocardiogram would be advisable. Even the echocardiogram does not always differentiate the athlete's heart of a weight lifter from that of a patient with hypertrophic cardiomyopathy. Ratios relating left ventricular mass to left ventricular volume are helpful.[79]

Pelliccia et al[80] evaluated 947 highly trained athletes, most of them involved in soccer, rowing, cycling and track events. Only 16 showed left ventricular wall thicknesses of 13 mm or more. Of the 16, 15 were rowers or canoeists, and one was a cyclist. Each of these 16 athletes had an end-diastolic-left-ventricular-cavity dimension of less than 55 mm, and only seven had ECG abnormalities. 'Jogging' should not be an acceptable explanation for ECG abnormalities.

Right Atrial Abnormality; Right Ventricular Hypertrophy

These are only rarely seen in applicants for life insurance. In the context of life insurance medicine, right atrial abnormality is mainly seen at an advanced stage of obstructive lung disease, although it may transiently develop during an acute episode of asthma or hypoxemia. This is different from clinical medicine where it may also be a manifestation of congenital heart disease, pulmonary hypertension or tricuspid valvular disease.

According to Calatayud et al[81] correlation with lung function was consistently better for the P axis than for P amplitude, and the rightward axis shift was the most discriminating P-wave change in evaluating the severity of chronic obstructive lung disease.

Right ventricular enlargement may also be seen in an occasional applicant with chronic obstructive lung disease. The ECG may sometimes show poor R-wave progression in the precordial leads and inverted T-waves.[82]

Patients who develop severe pulmonary hypertension may show a typical right ventricular hypertrophy pattern with tall R-waves in the right precordial leads. Shift of QRS axis to the right, increased P amplitude and QRS changes suggestive of right ventricular hypertrophy are seldom present until the FEV_1 is less than 45 percent of predicted normal value.

Rating

Although the ECG is a poor indicator of slight or even moderate right ventricular hypertrophy, neither is a chest radiogram, and reliable evidence from clinical signs depends largely on the skill, experience and interest of the examining physician. Spirometry in lung disease and an echocardiogram in other conditions are of greater help.

ECG abnormalities, when present in chronic obstructive lung disease, indicate an advanced stage and usually lead to further investigation and a decision to decline. It is not uncommon for these patients to display secondary polycythemia, which may be an additional clue in the absence of a reliable history.

Congenital Heart Disease

Most adult applicants with ratable congenital heart disease have had surgery and/or tell-tale scars or murmurs. An APS will allow rating for cause.

Atrial septal defect may be well tolerated and undiagnosed until well into adult life. The right ventricular enlargement that occurs in atrial septal defect usually manifests as complete or incomplete right bundle branch block; these patterns may warrant further investigation when present in young adults.

CONDUCTION DEFECTS

Sinoatrial Block (S–A Block) and Sinus Pauses

S–A Block is relatively uncommon. Brodski et al[83] studied 50 male medical students using 24-hour Holter recordings. They found severe bradycardia (less than 40 beats/min) during sleep in 24 percent, with sinus pauses exceeding 1·5 s in 68 percent. It is evident that vagal tone may suppress nodal function in healthy asymptomatic individuals. On the other hand, most instances of S–A block, especially in older individuals, are due to structural disease or drug toxicity.

Rating

Young individuals without evidence of heart disease — standard.
Age 50 and over — usually rate as sick sinus syndrome.

Atrioventricular Block (A–V Block)

It is important to keep in mind that the same individual may present different degrees of block depending on the HR. A 2-to-1 block accompanying an atrial flutter of 300/min is a physiologic phenomenon. The same block accompanying a supraventricular tachycardia of 200/min denotes a slight impairment in A–V conduction; in the presence of a sinus rate of 70/min it represents a severe degree of A–V block.

Atrioventricular block occurs when the sinus impulse is conducted with delay, or is not conducted at all, to the ventricle at a time when the AV junction is not physiologically refractory. It has three different degrees of severity.

First-Degree A–V Block

This is manifested by prolongation of the PR interval to more than 0·20 s in the adult.

The PR or PQ interval is a measure of the conduction time from the sinoatrial node through the atrial muscle, atrioventricular node, bundle of His and Purkinje fibers, at which point the QRS commences. PR intervals of more than 0·20 s duration are, in most circumstances, a normal variant due to vagotonia, especially in young and/or athletic individuals. Other causes are non-specific fibrosis affecting the bundle of His, myocarditis, medication, ischemic heart disease and congenital anomalies.

When the prolonged PR interval is attributable to a known cardiac impairment there is no difficulty in classifying the risk and rating for cause. Very often, however, a prolonged PR interval is the sole abnormality present. No large, long-term mortality studies of insured lives with first-degree A–V block have been made, and any estimation of the risk must be deduced from studies derived mainly from other populations. An extensive survey was undertaken by Johnson and coworkers[84] to ascertain the incidence and cause of A–V block among 67,375 healthy, asymptomatic men of the US Air Force. First-degree A–V block was found in 350, an incidence rate of 5·2 per thousand. Only five were found to have evidence of organic heart disease. The PR interval could be brought back to normal in most of these individuals by using various means of altering the vagal tone. The authors concluded that most of the examples of A–V block in their series were normal physiological variations.

Blackburn and collaborators[85] studied a different population and found that those with first-degree A–V block on routine ECG recording had a risk ratio of 1·8 for coronary artery disease when compared with controls appropriately matched for age, obesity, systolic blood pressure, serum cholesterol, smoking and physical activity.

In normal hearts atropine, standing, exercise and isoproterenol shorten the prolonged PR interval. This does not occur with artificial atrial pacing. In diseased hearts an increase in rate is frequently associated with lengthening of the PR interval. Increased vagal tone, however, may both slow the heart rate and prolong the PR interval.

Rating

Cause known — rate for cause.
Cause unknown; PR interval (in seconds):
1) To 0·29 — 0.
2) 0·30–0·39:

	Rating		
Duration since onset of first degree block	Heart rate per min		
	<66	66–90	>90
0–2 yr	0	+50[a]	+100[a]
Over 2 yr or duration unknown; no progression	0	0	+50[a]

[a]Shortens with exercise to normal or near normal — standard.

3) 0·40 and over — increase the above ratings by 25–50 debits depending on PR length.

Second-Degree A–V Block

In second-degree A–V block some sinus impulses are not conducted to the ventricle at a time when physiological interference is not involved.

Second-Degree A–V Block (Mobitz Type I): Wenckebach Phenomenon

In this type of block there is a progressive beat-by-beat prolongation of the PR interval until one impulse completely fails to be conducted to the ventricles.

Mobitz Type I A–V block can occur in normal individuals, especially in healthy children[86] and in well-trained athletes (increased vagal tone). It sometimes complicates posteroinferior myocardial infarction or digitalis intoxication, but often the cause is unknown. It is uncommon to find Mobitz Type I A–V block in insurance ECGs. The prevalence varies from 0·0004 percent in airmen to 2 percent in trained athletes.

In young individuals and adults Mobitz Type I A–V block with a normal QRS complex is usually benign, and does not progress to more advanced forms of A–V conduction disturbance. In older people Type I A–V block, with or without bundle branch block, has been associated with a clinical picture similar to Type II A–V block.

Rating
1) Cause known — rate for cause.
2) Cause unknown; no apparent heart disease:
   ECG otherwise normal — 0.
   Otherwise abnormal ECG — add +50 to abnormal ECG rating.

Second-Degree A–V Block (Mobitz Type II)

In Type II second-degree A–V block the PR interval remains constant prior to the blocked P-wave. Type II A–V block in an applicant with a normal QRS complex is likely to be a Type I A–V nodal block that exhibits very small increments, easily missed, in the PR interval. When Type II A–V block occurs in association with a bundle branch block it is localized to the His-Purkinje system.

Rating
1) Transient, caused by medication toxicity — rate for cause.
2) Others, no symptoms — rate as third-degree A–V block (*see below*).
3) With history of symptoms (angina, dizziness, syncope):
   No pacemaker — usually decline.
   With well functioning pacemaker — use basic pacemaker rate (*see below*).

Third-Degree Heart Block: Complete Heart Block

Rating
1) Congenital (known to have been present since childhood or adolescence); serial ECGs all show complete heart block; otherwise negative work-up by cardiologist, no symptoms (syncope, palpitations, dizziness, Stokes-Adams attacks); no pacemaker needed — credit 50 from basic pacemaker rating (*see below*).
2) Acquired — rate for cause plus basic pacemaker rating (*see below*).

Basic Pacemaker Rating
1) Pacemaker inserted for 0–5 years; no current complications:

Age	Rating
Up to 14	Decline
14–30	+125
30–49	+75
50–59	+50
60 and over	+25

2) Pacemaker inserted for more than 5 years; no current complications — 0.

3) Pacemaker with current complications — usually postpone.

4) Pacemaker cases associated with other disorders.
   Cardiomyopathy, valve disorders — usually decline.
   Coronary artery disease — usually very high rating or decline (*see* Chapter 16).
   Sick sinus syndrome or hypertension:
   0–1 yr — postpone.
   Thereafter — rate for cause plus basic pacemaker rate (*see above*).

5) Temporary pacemaker (e.g. placed at time of inferior wall infarction, currently removed) — rate for cause.

6) Abandoned pacemaker (no longer needed but wires not removed) — 0.

Intraventricular Conduction Disturbances

Complete Left Bundle Branch Block (CLBBB)

There is absolutely no way to determine if bundle branch block is 'complete' or not; the 0·12 second definition is entirely arbitrary.[88]

The terms complete and incomplete bundle branch block will be used to describe patterns of conduction delay. They do not always indicate an organic pathologic lesion, especially when intermittent.

When either right bundle branch block (RBBB) or LBBB appears during an episode of ischemic heart disease, its significance is obvious. If, however, it is discovered by chance in the routine ECG of an asymptomatic individual, its prognostic significance is far from clear.

Singer[89] made an important contribution in a prospective and retrospective study of 966 life insurance applicants to the New England Mutual Life Insurance Company. He also followed up the non-issued cases and determined that excess mortality in all types of bundle branch block and in wide QRS cases correlated well with the associated major cardiovascular disorder, being largest in coronary heart disease and moderate in arterial hypertension, borderline blood pressure elevation and other ratable cardiovascular impairments. Where there was no associated ratable cardiovascular impairment, excess mortality was minimal for applicants with complete right or left bundle branch block (CRBBB or CLBBB), and the mortality ratio for applicants with intraventricular or incomplete right bundle branch block (IRBBB) was actually below the 1955–60 standard intercompany level. Another important finding emerging from the study and that has practical underwriting significance was the striking decrease in mortality ratios with advancing age. In this respect, bundle branch blocks follow the age-related pattern of mortality found with other cardiovascular impairments.

Left Bundle Branch Block

The concept that the prognosis in patients with LBBB is related to the presence or absence of underlying disease evolved gradually.

In the USA the most common underlying disease in patients with CLBBB is coronary artery disease, occurring in approximately 25 percent of asymptomatic young men with acquired CLBBB as shown on routine electrocardiographic examination.[90] The incidence is even higher in the elderly. A frequent error is attributing bundle branch block in asymptomatic subjects to arteriosclerotic heart disease just because the subjects are old. Conduction abnormalities may be caused by other disorders, such as Lenegre's disease, Lev's disease, fibrosis of the summit of the muscular septum and calcification of the aortic valve.

The presence of primary T-wave changes was found to be of less value as an indicator of underlying disease in patients with LBBB than in patients with RBBB. Exercise ST changes have shown poor specificity for CAD, even when the 2 mm criterion is used. Unfortunately exercise thallium scintigraphy, nuclear ventriculography and echocardiography also have limited value in diagnosing arteriosclerotic heart disease in patients with LBBB.[91-93]

About 80 percent of all patients encountered with chronic complete or incomplete left bundle branch block have left ventricular hypertrophy. Researchers have not agreed on whether voltage and axis criteria are useful in separating patients with LBBB and hypertrophy from those that show no hypertrophy. The echocardiogram is the crucial tool in diagnosis of hypertrophy and/or cavity dilatation.

Patients with LBBB and left axis deviation greater than $-30°$ in the frontal plane frequently show more widespread lesions involving the conduction system.[94]

It is rare for LBBB with left axis deviation to progress to the point of requiring insertion of a cardiac pacemaker.

Persons with chronic LBBB have decreased survival. It is not clear, however, that the conduction system abnormalities are the cause. In most cases the adverse effect on survival results from associated heart disease. Progression to complete heart block is infrequent.

Flowers reviewed several large series with long-term follow-up published in the medical literature. She concluded that LBBB in the absence of clinical evidence of heart disease is rare and has a mortality risk ratio of about 1·3. Newly acquired LBBB has a mortality risk ratio of 10. The longer studies suggest an increase in the mortality risk ratio for subjects developing LBBB, especially for those over the age of 44. The presence of a normal ECG before the onset of CLBBB is a favorable factor.

In the Framingham study, 55 out of 5,209 individuals developed LBBB during an 18-year follow-up period. Coincident with, or subsequent to, the onset of LBBB, 48 percent developed clinical coronary disease or congestive heart failure for the first time. It is of interest that throughout the entire period of observation only 11 percent remained free of clinically apparent cardiovascular abnormalities and that within 10 years of the onset of LBBB 50 percent had died of cardiovascular diseases. A comparison with age- and sex-matched control subjects free of LBBB confirmed that in the general adult population newly acquired LBBB is commonly a hallmark of advanced hypertensive or ischemic heart disease, or both. However, the mean age of onset of the LBBB was 62 years, and the prognostic data acquired from such a population may not be applicable to clinically normal individuals developing the conduction defect at an earlier age.

Benign Left Bundle Branch Block

LBBB unassociated with coronary heart disease or left ventricular hypertrophy has a good prognosis. Many of these patients have degenerative disease of the cardiac conduction system detectable by electrophysiologic studies; some have other abnormalities of the septum, including scars from old focal myocarditis.

Rating

1) Cause known — rate for cause with associated BBB (*see* Chapter 15).
2) Cause unknown. This creates an underwriting dilemma because LBBB masks electrocardiographic evidence of infarction and of LVH and invalidates most of the information obtainable from exercise tests.

With current negative work-up by cardiologist, including a satisfactory resting and exercise echocardiogram or a resting echocardiogram and a nuclear exercise test — standard.

No cardiology work-up — basic CLBBB rating (*see below*).

| | Basic CLBBB Rating Age at discovery | |
Duration	50 and under	51 and over
0–6 mth	Postpone until 6 mth from initial detection	
6 mth–3 yr	+150	+100
3–5 yr	+125	+75
Thereafter	+75	+50 to 0

Complete Right Bundle Branch Block (CRBBB)

CRBBB is arbitrarily defined by the presence of slow terminal QRS forces directed to the right, anteriorly and either superiorly or inferiorly, with a QRS duration of at least 0·12 s. The initial 0·08 s of the QRS complex experiences little or no modification as compared with the morphology before the onset of the block. Therefore it does not mask the presence of abnormal Q-waves or QRS evidence of left ventricular hypertrophy. The QRS axis should be measured on the first 0·08 s of the QRS complex; this is important in order to be able to diagnose bifascicular blocks.

Fleg et al[95] followed a cohort from the Baltimore Longitudinal Study on Aging for over eight years. This group is a true population study, in which the individuals resembled insurance applicants. They had no evidence of heart disease at the beginning of the observation. The subsequent mortality and morbidity were no higher in the RBBB group than in the controls who had no RBBB. The RBBB block and the control group were fairly well matched.

Barrett et al concluded that CRBBB may be present in about 0·3 percent of clinically normal individuals, a prevalence about three times greater than that of CLBBB. The abnormality is rarely complicated by syncope or documented A–V block, and there is little or no increased risk of death from coronary artery disease over an average follow-up period of nine years. Barrett et al also state that this probably applies mainly to young individuals who are clinically normal.

Rating

1) Cause unknown.

No ratable cerebrovascular, cardiovascular, peripheral vascular or blood pressure impairment; well-documented and detailed case history — standard.

With any of the above mentioned ratable impairments:

If the rating for the underlying impairment is less than +50 — rate +50.

If the rating for the underlying impairment is +50 or more — rate for this with a minimum of +100.

2) With incomplete clinical evidence, duration up to 0·14 s, or clearly abnormal P-waves but no other ratable features:

Age	Rating
Under 50	+100
50–59	+75
60 or over	+50

Incomplete Bundle Branch Block

The pattern indicates a delay in activation of a ventricle, resulting from delayed conduction within the ipsilateral bundle branch. The involved ventricle may be partially activated by the impulse from the contralateral bundle.

Incomplete Left Bundle Branch Block (ILBBB)

The existence of ILBBB as an electrocardiographic entity has long been debated. The generally accepted criteria are frequently seen in patients with left ventricular hypertrophy. As a result, the question has been raised as to whether this conduction defect coexists with, or whether the changes are secondary to, left ventricular hypertrophy.

Rating   Rate ILBBB as moderate LVH.

Incomplete Right Bundle Branch Block (IRBBB)

The diagnosis of IRBBB may be made when QRS duration is between 0·10 s and 0·12 s and the terminal QRS forces point to the right and anteriorly. Some authors make the diagnosis even when the QRS duration is less than 0·10 s. The pattern of IRBBB may occur in right ventricular hypertrophy. It may also be observed as a normal variant and in some skeletal abnormalities, such as pectus excavatum or straight back syndrome.

Hiss and Lamb[96] reported a prevalence of 2·4 percent in a large series of normal young subjects.

Rating   Cause known (IRBBB pattern as a manifestation of RVH) — rate for cause (*see* Chapter 15).
With ratable cardiovascular or blood pressure impairment — rate for impairment only (*see* Chapters 14 and 15).
Sole abnormality — standard.

Fascicular Blocks; Hemiblocks
The left branch of the His bundle splits into three relatively distinct fascicles: a narrower anterior fascicle, a broader, earlier branching posterior fascicle and many branches forming a third or septal segment. Rosenbaum accumulated clear-cut evidence and coined the term hemiblock in 1968.

Left Anterior Hemiblock (LAHB) Versus Left Axis Deviation (LAD)
The development of criteria to separate LAHB from simple left axis deviation has been a problem because in many cases LAD is an incomplete LAHB and gradually evolves into it. Fortunately for the medical underwriter, neither is usually rated.

Left Axis Deviation (LAD)
The term LAD should be reserved for a QRS frontal plane axis lying between $-30°$ and $-45°$. Epidemiological studies by Blackburn et al[85,97] have shown that LAD in a general population may be a benign concomitant of aging.

Ostrander[98] analyzed data from the Tecumseh Communities Health Study and concluded that the prognosis does not appear to depend so much on the electrocardiographic abnormality as on conditions associated with it.

When present as an isolated abnormality, LAD constitutes a benign finding and can be disregarded in a way similar to IRBBB.

Rating   Suggested rating for LAD — standard.

Left Anterior Hemiblock (LAHB)
Rosenbaum's original definition of LAHB[99] required a frontal plane QRS axis of $-45°$ to $-80°$, QRS duration equal or more than 0·11 s, and a small septal Q-wave equal to or less than 0·02 s in leads I and aVL. It should be appreciated, however, that there is no discrete point at which left axis deviation magically becomes left anterior fascicular block. It is likely that most leftward shifts of the QRS axis represent some point in the spectrum of acquired intraventricular conduction delay. The $-45°$ cut-off point may eliminate some false-positive patterns not directly due to involvement of the branches of the left anterior fascicle.

Schaaf[100] reviewed the ECG files of Prudential employees and found 273 with a QRS axis of $-45°$. The number of lives involved was too small to permit definite assertions, but in this group LAHB did not adversely affect mortality until ages 60 and above, and then only to a moderate degree. About one-third of the unimpaired cases were observed to develop LAHB gradually over several to many years, sometimes even slipping back below $-45°$ left axis before finally establishing a permanent LAHB; this suggests that the underlying cause, be it 'normal' or pathological, was not abrupt or rapidly progressive, as might be anticipated with coronary heart disease or an inflammatory process.

Barrett et al reviewed the literature until 1981 and concluded that the risk of coronary events or death is probably not increased by the mere presence of LAHB in clinically normal individuals.

The underwriting importance of LAHB is that it may complicate the electro-cardiographic diagnosis of old myocardial infarction. It can cause both false-positive and false-negative diagnoses of anteroseptal infarction. It may also mask inferior infarction.

The diagnosis of left and right ventricular hypertrophy becomes even less precise in the presence of LAHB.

Rating   LAHB occurring in an otherwise normal heart — standard.
LAHB associated with other cardiac impairments — rate for cause.

Left Posterior Hemiblock (LPHB)

Of the three divisions of the left bundle branch, the posteroinferior is the less liable to interruption because it is shorter, wider and is supplied by more than one artery. Lesions that cause LPHB are larger than those that cause LAHB. LPHB is found only rarely, and its diagnostic criteria are clinico-electrocardiographic. They require a right axis deviation of +105° or greater, Q-waves in leads II, III, aVF and initial R waves in leads I and aVL in the absence of right ventricular hypertrophy. As this is an unusual electrocardiographic finding, there are no series large enough for adequate prognostic evaluation. The general consensus is that it represents more widespread disease than left anterior fascicular block.

Barrett et al found 20 cases in clinically normal individuals followed for seven to ten years. There were no deaths and no cases of documented A–V block, but there was one case of syncope after one year.

Rating   Suggest further underwriting work-up to verify cardiac status and rule out RVH. At a minimum this should include an APS. Rate almost as CLBBB (*see* p. 462).

Bifascicular Block

Bifascicular block is usually manifested as a combination of RBBB and LAHB. The left axis deviation should be measured on the first 0·08 s of the QRS complex (*see* p. 464).

There is no general consensus on the prognosis of bifascicular block.[99] Surawicz[101] reviewed conflicting data and opinions and placed them in perspective. Barrett et al, in a review of the literature up to 1981, concluded that 'the data suggest that although mortality and coronary events are not increased by the presence of RBBB and LPH on the ECG, the risk of developing advanced A–V block is about 6 percent over six years'. They pointed out that in all probability there are at least two broad categories of patients with chronic bifascicular block. One group, composed of younger and clinically normal individuals, seems to have a benign primary conduction abnormality without clinically manifest cardiac disease. Another group, composed of older patients and with a frequent association of hypertension and/or arteriosclerosis, had an average risk of developing advanced A–V block of 19 percent over five years. The prognosis seems to be related to the underlying or associated cardiovascular disease rather than to the observed conduction disturbance.

Pine et al[102] did a 12-year study comparing a group of patients with CRBBB and LAHB with a matched group without this conduction disturbance. After omitting patients with moderate and severe congestive heart failure present at entrance in the bifascicular block group, they found a mortality of 147 percent. This small extra mortality could, in part, be due to patients with mild heart failure; the authors seem to have disregarded this possibility.

Only rarely does bifascicular block progress to the point of requiring insertion of a cardiac pacemaker.

Rating

Rate as CLBBB (*see* p. 462).

REFERENCES

1 Patterson RE, Horowitz SF. Importance of epidemiology and biostatistics in deciding clinical strategies for using diagnostic tests: a simplified approach using examples from coronary artery disease. *J Am Coll Cardiol* 1989; 13: 1653–65.
2 Kassirer JP. Our stubborn quest for diagnostic certainty. A cause for excessive testing. *N Eng J Med* 1989; 320: 1489–91.
3 Sheffield LT. Computer-aided electrocardiography. In: Geiser EA, Skorton DJ (editors). Seminar on computer applications for the cardiologist VII. *J Am Coll Cardiol* 1987; 10: 448–55.
4 Sridharan MR, Flowers NC. Computerized electrocardiographic analysis. *Modern Concepts of Cardiovascular Disease* 1984; 53: 37–41.
5 Lusted LB. *Introduction to Medical Decision-Making*. Springfield, IL: Charles C Thomas, 1968; 1–46.
6 Surawicz B. Electrocardiographic diagnosis of chamber enlargement. *J Am Coll Cardiol* 1986; 8: 711–24.
7 Ferrer MI. Age and the electrocardiogram. *J Insur Med* 1989; 21: 196–8.
8 Cochran HA Jr, Buck NF. Coronary artery disease and other chest pain. A fourth report. *Trans Assoc Life Insur Med Dir Am* 1970; 54: 63–90.
9 Sodi Pallares D, Rodriguez MI, Chait LO, Zuckerman R. The activation of the interventricular septum. *Am Heart J* 1951; 41: 569–608.
10 Tillisch J, Brunken R, Marshall R, Schwaiger M, Mandelkern M, Phelps M, Schelbert H. Reversibility of cardiac wall-motion abnormalities predicted by positron tomography. *N Engl J Med* 1986; 314: 884–8.
11 Kannel WB, Abbott RD. Incidence and prognosis of unrecognized myocardial infarction. An update on the Framingham study. *N Engl J Med* 1984; 311: 1144–7.
12 Yano K, MacLean CJ. The incidence and prognosis of unrecognized myocardial infarction in the Honolulu, Hawaii, Heart Program. *Arch Intern Med* 1989; 149: 1528–32.
13 Cox CJ, Lond MB. Return to normal of the electrocardiogram after myocardial infarction. *Lancet*. 1967; 1: 1194–7.
14 Mazzoleni A, Hagan AD, Glover MV, Vieweg WVR. On the relationship between Q waves in leads II and aVF and inferior-posterior wall motion abnormalities. *J Electrocardiol* 1983; 16: 367–77.
15 Warner RA, Roger M, Hill NE, Mookherjee S, Smulyan H. Electrocardiographic criteria for the diagnosis of anterior myocardial infarction: importance of the duration of precordial R waves. *Am J Cardiol* 1983; 52: 690–2.
16 DePace NL, Colby J, Hakki A–H, Manno B, Horowitz LN, Iskandrian AS. Poor R wave progression in the precordial leads: clinical implications for the diagnosis of myocardial infarction. *J Am Coll Cardiol* 1983; 2: 1073–9.

17 Pipberger HV, Lopez EA. 'Silent' subendocardial infarcts: fact or fiction? *Am Heart J* 1980; 100: 597–9.
18 Davies MJ, Woolf N, Robertson WB. Pathology of acute myocardial infarction with particular reference to occlusive coronary thrombi. *Br Heart J* 1976; 38: 659–64.
19 DeWood MA, Spores J, Nooke R et al. Prevalence of total coronary occlusion during the early hours of transmural myocardial infarction. *N Engl J Med* 1980; 303: 897–902.
20 Roberts R. Symposium sponsored by Baylor College of Medicine, Houston, 1989 Hilton Head, South Carolina.
21 Boden WE et al. Enzymatic non-Q-wave infarction without diagnostic ST–T wave changes on admission associated with favorable long-term outcome (abstr). *Circulation* 1988; 78: II–579.
22 Wasserman AG, Bren GV, Ross AM, Richardson DW, Hutchinson RG, Rios JC. Prognostic implications of diagnostic Q waves after myocardial infarction. *Circulation* 1982; 65: 1451–4.
23 Bounous EP, Califf RM, Harrell FE, Hinohara T, Mark DB, Ideker RE, Selvester RH, Wagner GS. Prognostic value of the simplified Selvester QRS Score in patients with coronary artery disease. *J Am Coll Cardiol* 1988; 11: 35–41.
24 The Coronary Drug Project Research Group. The prognostic implications of the electrocardiogram after myocardial infarction. *Ann Intern Med* 1972; 77: 677–89.
25 Kannel WB, Sorlie P, McNamara PM. Prognosis after initial myocardial infarction: The Framingham Study. *Am J Cardiol* 1979; 44: 53–9.
26 Kennedy HL, Goldberg RJ, Szklo M, Tonascio JA. The prognosis of anterior myocardial infarction revisited: a community-wide study. *Clin Cardiol* 1979; 2: 455–60.
27 Geltman EM, Ehsani AA, Campbell MK, Schectman K, Roberts R, Sobel BE. The influence of location and extent of myocardial infarction on long-term ventricular dysrhythmia and mortality. *Circulation* 1979; 60: 805–14.
28 Faxon DP, Myers WO, McCabe CH, Davis KB, Schaff HV, Wilson JW, Ryan TJ. The influence of surgery on the natural history of angiographically documented left ventricular aneurysm: The Coronary Artery Study. *Circulation* 1986; 74: 110–18.
29 Hands ME, Lloyd BL, Robinson JS, de Klerk N, Thompson PL. Prognostic significance of electrocardiographic site of infarction after correlation for enzymatic size of infarction. *Circulation* 1986; 73: 885–91.
30 Weinberg SL. Natural history six years after acute myocardial infarction. Is there a low risk group? *Chest* 1976; 69: 23–8.
31 Kiessling CE, Schaaf RS, Lyle AM. Mortality studies of isolated electrocardiographic T-wave change. *Trans Assoc Life Ins Med Dir Am* 1955; 39: 5–24.
32 Lyle AM. Selection of applicants for insurance with isolated T-wave abnormalities in the electrocardiogram. *Trans Soc Actuaries* 1965; 17:357–66.
33 Morgagni GB. *The Seats and Causes of Diseases*. London: Millar Cadell Johnson & Payne, 1769; Vol 1: 732.
34 Osler W. *The Principles and Practice of Medicine*. New York: D Appleton & Co, 1918.
35 Lyle AM. Study of premature beats by electrocardiogram. *Trans Soc Actuaries* 1953; 14: 493.
36 Lyle AM. Coronary disease as an underwriting problem. *Trans Soc Actuaries* 1963; 15: 324–50.
37 Ruberman W, Weinblatt E, Goldberg JD, Frank CW, Shapiro S. Ventricular premature beats and mortality after myocardial infarction. *N Engl J Med* 1977; 297: 750–7.
38 Bigger JT Jr, Fleiss JL, Kleiger R, Miller JP, Rolnitzky LM. The relationships among ventricular arrhythmias, left ventricular dysfunction, and mortality in the two years after myocardial infarction. *Circulation* 1984; 69: 250–8.
39 Rabkin SW, Mathewson FAL, Tate RB. Relationship of ventricular ectopy in men without apparent heart disease to occurrence of ischemic heart disease and sudden death. *Am Heart J* 1981; 101: 135–42.
40 Lown B, Wolf M. Approaches to sudden death from coronary heart disease. *Circulation* 1971; 44: 130–42.
41 Rodstein M, Wolloch L, Gubner RS. Mortality study of the significance of extrasystoles in an insured population. *Circulation* 1971; 44: 617–25.
42 Fisher FD, Tyroler HA. Relationship between ventricular premature contractions on

routine electrocardiography and subsequent sudden death from coronary heart disease. *Circulation* 1973; 47: 712–19.

43 Elkon KB, Swerdlow TA, Myburgh DP. Persistent ventricular ectopic beats: a long-term study. *S Afr Med J* 1977; 52: 564–6.

44 Crow R, Prineas R, Blackburn H. The prognostic significance of ventricular ectopic beats among the apparently healthy. *Am Heart J* 1981; 101: 244–8.

45 Kennedy HL, Pescarmona JE, Bouchard RJ, Goldberg RJ. Coronary artery status of apparently healthy subjects with frequent and complex ventricular ectopy. *Ann Intern Med* 1980; 92 (Pt 1): 179–85.

46 Horan MJ, Kennedy HL. Characteristics and prognosis of apparently healthy patients with frequent and complex ventricular ectopy: evidence for a relatively benign new syndrome with occult myocardial and/or coronary disease. *Am Heart J* 1981; 102: 809–10.

47 Kennedy HL, Pescarmona JE, Bouchard RJ, Goldberg RJ, Caralis DG. Objective evidence of occult myocardial dysfunction in patients with frequent ventricular ectopy without clinically apparent heart disease. *Am Heart J* 1982; 104: 57–65.

48 Horan MJ, Kennedy HL. Ventricular ectopy. History, epidemiology and clinical implications. *JAMA* 1984; 251: 380–6.

49 Kennedy HL, Whitlock JA, Sprague MK, Kennedy LJ, Buckingham TA, Goldberg RJ. Long-term follow-up of aymptomatic healthy subjects with frequent and complex ventricular ectopy. *N Engl J Med* 1985; 312: 193–7.

50 Ruskin JN. Ventricular extrasystoles in healthy subjects. *N Engl J Med* 1985; 312: 238–9.

51 Holter NJ. Historical background and development of ambulatory monitoring: the nature of research. In: Jacobson N, Yarnall S (editors). *Ambulatory ECG Monitoring*. Seattle: MCSA, Inc, 1976; 1–10.

52 Pasternak RC, Brunwald E. Sobel BE. Acute myocardial infarction. In: Zipes DP. Management of cardiac arrhythmias: pharmacological, electrical and surgical techniques. In: Brunwald E (editor). *Heart Disease: a textbook of cardiovascular medicine*, 3rd ed. Philadelphia: WB Saunders, 1988; 1222–313.

53 The Multicenter Postinfarction Research Group. Risk stratification and survival after myocardial infarction: *N Engl J Med* 1983; 309: 331–6.

54 Kostis JB, Byington R, Freidman LM, Goldstein S, Furberg C for the BHAT Study Group. Prognostic significance of ventricular ectopic activity in survivors of acute myocardial infarction. *J Am Coll Cardiol 1987*; 10: 231–42.

55 Scheidt S (editorial). Ventricular premature complexes as villains: still an important part of the problem. *J Am Coll Cardiol* 1987; 10: 243–5.

56 Kleiger RE, Miller JP, Bigger JT Jr, Moss AJ for the Multicenter Postinfarction Research Group. Decreased heart rate variability and its association with increased mortality after acute myocardial infarction. *Am J Cardiol* 1987; 59: 256–62.

57 Gomes JAC, Hariman RI, Kang PS, El-Sherif N, Chowdhry I, Lyons J. Programmed electrical stimulation in patients with high-grade ventricular ectopy: electrical findings and prognosis for survival. *Circulation* 1984; 70: 43–51.

58 Gunnar RM, Bourdillon PDV, Dixon DW, et al. Guidelines for the early management of patients with acute myocardial infarction: a report of the American College of Cardiology/American Heart Association Task Force on Assessment of Diagnostic and Therapeutic Cardiovascular Procedures (Subcommittee to Develop Guidelines for the Early Management of Patients With Acute Myocardial Infarction). *J Am Coll Cardiol* 1990; 16 249–92.

59 Zipes DP, Akhtar M, Denes P et al. Guidelines for clinical intracardiac electrophysiologic studies: a report of the American College of Cardiology/American Heart Association Task Force on Assessment of Diagnostic and Therapeutic Cardiovascular Procedures (Subcommittee to Assess Clinical Intracardiac Electrophysiologic Studies). *J Am Coll Cardiol* 1989; 14: 1827–42.

60 Gomes JA, Winters SL, Stewart D, Horowitz S, Milner M, Barreca P. A noninvasive index to predict sustained ventricular tachycardia and sudden death in the first year after myocardial infarction: based on signal-averaged electrocardiogram, radionucleide ejection fraction and Holter monitoring. *J Am Coll Cardiol* 1987; 10: 349–57.

61 Cobb LA, Hallstrom AP, Weaver WD, Copass MK, Haynes RE. Clinical predictors and characteristics of the sudden cardiac death syndrome. In: *Proceedings of the USA/ USSR First Joint Symposium on Sudden Death*. Bethesda, Maryland: Department of Health, Education, and Welfare, 1978; 99–116.

62 Myerburg RJ, Kessler KM, Zaman L, Conde CA, Castellanos A. Survivors of prehospital cardiac arrest. *JAMA* 1982; 247: 1485–90.

63 Faris JV, McHenry PL, Jordan JW, Morris SN. Prevalence and reproducibility of exercise-induced ventricular arrhythmias during maximal exercise testing in normal man. *Am J Cardiol* 1976; 37: 617–22.

64 Fleg JL, Lakata EG. Prevalence and prognosis of exercise-induced nonsustained ventricular tachycardia in apparently healthy volunteers. *Am J Cardiol* 1984; 54: 762–4.

65 Rifkin RD, Hood WB Jr. Bayesian analysis of electrocardiographic exercise stress testing. *N Engl J Med* 1977; 207: 681–6.

66 Stuart RJ Jr, Ellestad MH. National survey of exercise stress testing facilities. *Chest* 1980; 77, 94.

67 Sheffield LT, Holt JH, Lester FM, Conroy DV, Reeves TJ. On-line analysis of the exercise electrocardiogram. *Circulation* 1969; 40: 935–44.

68 Ellestad MH, Savitz S, Bergdall D, Teske J. The false positive stress test. Multivariate analysis of 215 subjects with hemodynamic, angiographic and clinical data. *Am J Cardiol* 1977; 40: 681.

69 Hollenberg M, Budge WR, Wisneski JA, Gertz EW. Treadmill score quantifies electrocardiographic response to exercise and improves test accuracy and reproducibility. *Circulation* 1980; 61: 276–85.

70 Goldschlager et al. *Ann Int Med* 1976; 85: 277.

71 Lavine P, Kimbiris D, Segal BL, Linhart JW. Left main coronary artery disease: clinical, arteriographic and hemodynamic appraisal. *Am J Cardiol* 1972; 30.

72 Epstein SE, Quyymi AA and Bonow RO. Sudden cardiac death without warning. Possible mechanisms and implications for screening asymptomatic populations. *N Engl J Med* 1989; 321: 320–4.

73 Kligfield P, Meisen O, Okin PM. *Circulation* 1989; 79: 245.

74 Nasrallah AT, Garcia E, Benrey J, Jall RJ. Treadmill exercise testing in the presence of digitalis therapy or non-specific ST–T changes: correlation with coronary angiography. *Cath Cardiovasc Diagn* 1975; 1: 375.

75 Josephson ME, Kastor JA, Morganroth J. Electrocardiographic left atrial enlargement: electrophysiologic, echocardiographic and hemodynamic correlates. *Am J Cardiol* 1977; 39 967–71.

76 Chou T. Variations in the normal electrocardiogram. *Practical Cardiol* 1983; 9: 6; 37–51.

77 Romhilt D, Estes EH Jr. A point-score system for the ECG diagnosis of left ventricular hypertrophy. *Am Heart J* 1968; 75: 752–8.

78 Moro C, Tascón J, Muela A. Correlation between electrical and echocardiographic data in hypertrophic myocardiopathy. *Int J Cardiol* 1983; 3: 381–2.

79 Menapace FJ, Hammer WJ, Ritzer TF et al. Left ventricular size in competitive weight lifters: an echocardiographic study. *Med Sci Sports Exerc* 1982; 14: 72–5.

80 Pelliccia A, Maron BJ, Spataro A, Proschan MA and Spirito P. The upper limit of physiologic cardiac hypertrophy in highly trained elite athletes. *N Engl J Med* 1991; 324: 295–301.

81 Calatayud JB, Abad JM, Khoi NB, Stanbro WW, Silver HM. P wave changes in chronic obstructive lung disease. *Am Heart J* 1970; 79: 444–53.

82 Selvester RH, Rubin HB. New criteria for the electrocardiographic diagnosis of emphysema and cor pulmonale. *Am Heart J* 1965; 69: 437–47.

83 Brodski M, Wu D, Denes P, Kanakis C, Rosen KM. Arrhythmias documented by 24-hour continuous electrocardiographic monitoring in 50 male medical students without apparent heart disease. *Am J Cardiol* 1977; 39: 390–5.

84 Johnson RL, Averill KH, Lamb LE. Electrocardiographic findings in 67,375 asymptomatic subjects. Atrioventricular block. *Am J Cardiol* 1960; 6: 153.

85 Blackburn H, Taylor HL, Keys A. The electrocardiogram in prediction of 5 year-coronary heart disease incidence among men aged 40 through 59. *Circulation* 1970; 41–2 (suppl I): I–154.

86 Southall DP, Johnston F, Shinebourne EA, Johnston PGB. 24 hour electrocardiograph study of heart rate and rhythm patterns in population of healthy children. *Br Heart J* 1981; 45: 281–91.

87 Shaw DB, Kekwick CA, Veale D, Gowers J, Whistance T. Survival in second degree atrioventricular block. *Br Heart J* 1985; 53: 587–93.

88 Willems JL, Robles de Medina E, Bernard R, Coumel P, Fisch C et al. Criteria for intraventricular conduction disturbances and pre-excitation. World Health Organization/International Society and Federation for Cardiology Task Force Ad Hoc. *J Am Coll Cardiol* 1985; 5: 1261–75.

89 Singer RB. Mortality in 966 life insurance applicants with bundle branch block or wide QRS. *Trans Assoc Life Insur Med Dir Am* 1969; 52: 94–114.

90 Froelicher VF, Thompson AJ, Wolthuis R, Fuchs R, Balusek R, Longo MRJr, Triebwasser JH, Lancaster MC. Angiographic findings in asymptomatic aircrewmen with electrocardiographic abnormalities. *Am J Cardiol* 1977; 39: 32–8.

91 Hirzel HO, Senn M, Nuesch K, Buettner C, Pfeiffer A, Hess OM, Krayenbuehl HP. Thallium-201 scintigraphy in complete left bundle branch block. *Am J Cardiol* 1984; 53: 764–9.

92 Braat SH, Brugada P, Bar FW, Gorgels APM, Wellens HJJ. Thallium-201 exercise scintigraphy and left bundle branch block. *Am J Cardiol* 1985; 55: 224–6.

93 Rowe DW, Oquendo I, DePuey EG, de Castro CM, Garcia E, Burdine JA, Hall RJ. The noninvasive diagnosis of coronary artery disease in patients with left bundle branch block. *Texas Heart Inst J* 1982; 9: 397–406.

94 Rosenbaum MB. Types of left bundle branch block and their clinical significance. *J Electrocardiol* 1969; 2: 197–206.

95 Fleg JL, Das DN, Lakatta EG. Right bundle branch block: long term prognosis in apparently healthy men. *J Am Coll Cardiol* 1983; 1: 887–92.

96 Hiss RG, Lamb LE. Electrocardiographic findings in 122,043 individuals. *Circulation* 1962; 25: 947–61.

97 Blackburn H, Vasquez CL, Keys A. The aging electrocardiogram. A common aging process or latent coronary artery disease? *Am J Cardiol* 1967; 20: 618–27.

98 Ostrander LD. Left axis deviation: prevalence, associated conditions and prognosis. An epidemiologic study. *Ann Intern Med* 1971; 75: 23–8.

99 Rosenbaum MB, Elizari MV, Lazzari JO et al. The differential electrocardiographic manifestations of hemiblocks, bilateral bundle branch block and trifascicular blocks. In: Schlant RC, Hurst JW (editors). *Advances in Electrocardiography*. New York: Grune & Stratton, 1972; 145–82.

100 Schaaf RS. Left anterior hemiblock; the Prudential experience. *Trans Assoc Life Insur Med Dir Am* 1974; 58: 197–216.

101 Surawicz B (editorial). Prognosis of patients with chronic bifascicular block. *Circulation* 1979; 60: 40–2.

102 Pine MB, Oren M, Ciafone R, Rosner B, Hirota Y, Rabinowitz B, Abelman WH. *J Am Coll Cardiol* 1983; 1: 1207.

CHAPTER 17

RESPIRATORY DISORDERS

R D C BRACKENRIDGE
R J MILLS

Apart from an increase in pneumonia-attributable deaths in young people in association with the human immunodeficiency virus (HIV), mortality from acute respiratory infections, which occur mostly at the extremes of life, continues to decline. On the other hand, chronic lung diseases, particularly those caus- ing airway obstruction, remain a major health problem, with deaths increasing una- bated year by year in the US,[1] although there was a 5 percent reduction in these deaths (ICD 490–496) in England and Wales between 1985 and 1989.[2] Death rates from malignant neoplasms of the trachea, bronchus and lung continue to increase for women, although rates for men now show a small decline.

There is a strong familial tendency to diseases of the respiratory system gener- ally which, when adverse environmental factors are present in addition, greatly increases the chances of a person developing respiratory disease.

PULMONARY FUNCTION TESTS (PFTs)

As there is no single test that can adequately describe the performance of the system, the evaluation of respiratory function requires a set of standardized procedures. It is convenient to base the tests that are used on a simple three compartment model (see Fig. 17.1). The three compartments in the model are ventilation, diffusion and perfusion. Although each compartment is considered in isolation relative to the tests that may be employed, physiologically they are interdependent in terms of the function of the respiratory system, and interac- tion between the compartments does occur.

Ventilation

The ventilatory compartment concentrates on the bellows action of the lungs, and relates to the size of the air-containing spaces (static lung volumes and capacities) and the ability to move air rapidly in and out of the lungs (dynamic lung volumes and forced ventilatory flow rates).

Static Lung Volumes
The subdivisions of the lung volume are shown in Figure 17.2. The commonly measured volumes are listed below.

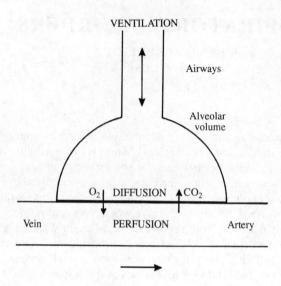

Fig. 17.1 Simple three compartment model of the respiratory system.

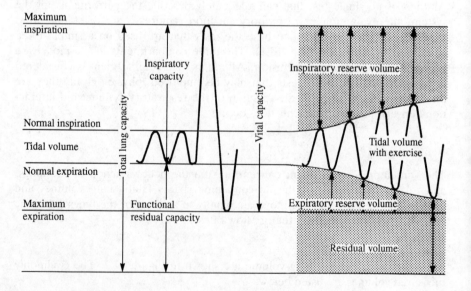

Fig. 17.2 Subdivisions of lung volume.

Vital Capacity (VC)

This is the volume of air that can be completely exhaled following a full inspiration. The rate at which the maneuver is performed is not relevant to the measurement.

Residual Volume (RV)

RV is the volume of air remaining in the lungs after a maximal expiration.

Total Lung Capacity (TLC)

This is the volume of air in the lungs following a maximal inspiration and is equal to the sum of the VC and RV.

Functional Residual Capacity (FRC)

FRC is the volume of air in the lungs at the end of a normal expiration, being equivalent to the sum of the Expiratory Reserve Volume (ERV) and the RV.

Tidal Volume (TV)

TV is the volume of a single natural breath, the size of which will vary depending upon factors such as the level of activity and emotional state.

Dynamic Lung Volumes

These volumes are assessed during forced breathing when maximal effort is applied throughout the respiratory maneuver. Expiratory indices are obtained that relate to the caliber of the intrapulmonary airways. The procedure is seldom used to measure inspiratory indices except where there is suspected airflow obstruction in the extrathoracic airways.

The indices are derived from measurements of airflow rates continuously measured during a vital capacity maneuver performed with maximum effort. The measured flow rates may be related to the time or to the volume expired from the commencement of the expiration (volume-time curve or flow-volume curve).

The indices in general use are explained below.

Forced Vital Capacity (FVC)

A vital capacity maneuver is performed with maximum effort sustained for the complete expiration. Essentially the same as the slow VC in healthy people, the FVC may give a lesser value in the presence of airways obstruction.

Forced Expired Volume in 1 second (FEV$_1$)

This is the volume of air expired in the first second of the FVC. The FEV$_1$ is often reported as a percentage of the forced vital capacity (FEV$_1$/FVC%). This is extensively used as an index of airflow limitation rather than the FEV$_1$ volume, which can have a low value in restrictive lung disease without the presence of obstruction.

Peak Expiratory Flowrate (PEFR)

This is the maximum flow produced during a forced expiration that commences at a full inspiration, and is indicated by the peak on the flow-volume curve. The PEFR is particularly reduced in diffuse airways obstruction and is a useful measurement in the assessment of the variable obstruction seen in asthma.

Maximum Mid-Expiratory Flowrate (MMEF)

This is a measure of the maximum expiratory flowrate achieved at a lung volume corresponding to 50 percent of the VC remaining in the lungs. The MMEF is potentially useful for the detection of early abnormalities as it is more sensitive to increased obstruction in smaller airways. This is in contrast to the FEV_1 and PEFR which are more affected by changes in the caliber of the large and medium sized airways.

Measurement and Assessment

Volume changes of the lungs are measured at the mouth by spirometry. The classic bell spirometer with a water seal is a cumbersome instrument: it is adequate for measuring slowly occurring displacements but has a limited response to fast changes in volume. Modern spirometers have a bell with a dry rolling seal which improves the dynamic response of the system as well as promoting a portable instrument.

Alternatively the prime measurement can be the flowrate at the mouth as produced by a pneumotachograph (which presents little impedance to the respiratory system). The flow signal is instantaneously converted to volume by an inbuilt micro-computer which will also calculate the results that can be derived from the measured data. Spirometry is, to some degree, effort dependent and relies on the full co-operation of the subject; and to assess the quality of the effort, the spirogram can usually be displayed on a monitoring screen or output to a printer.

The body plethysmograph is a complex instrument which allows the measurement of lung volumes and will directly assess airways resistance. In the presence of obstructive airways disease it will provide a truer, more rapid measure of the residual volume than the conventional spirometric method which requires a prolonged period of rebreathing of a helium-air mixture. The body plethysmograph is also able to detect small changes in airway caliber; for this measurement a forced expiratory maneuver is not required.

Bronchial hypersensitivity in extrinsic asthma may be usefully assessed by a histamine provocation test. The subject is challenged with serial concentrations of histamine in aerosol form ranging from 0·03 mg/ml to 16 mg/ml, each one being applied for a fixed time. Starting with the weakest of the standardized solutions, a measure of FEV_1 is made following each application. The concentration of histamine is increased until a value is reached that produces a fall in FEV_1 of 20 percent from the control value. This is used as an index of bronchial reactivity, and the lower the concentration at which this occurs, the greater the degree of hypersensitivity. A normal response would produce no significant fall in FEV_1, even with the highest concentration of histamine that is used.

Diffusion

Diffusion is concerned with the ability of gases to transfer across the gaseous-liquid interface of the alveolar membrane, and is a recommended measurement in the investigation of interstitial lung disease. The disposal of carbon dioxide is not considered in this context, as the elimination of this gas is influenced mainly by the level of the alveolar ventilation and not by the diffusion characteristics of the lung.

Thus it is the oxygen exchanging property of the lung parenchyma that is relevant in the measurement of diffusion. A technique requiring the breathing of a test gas containing a low concentration of carbon monoxide is usually employed. Any abnormality in this measurement reflects an impairment in oxygen transfer, which is not solely related to an impairment of diffusion: many factors apart from diffusion affect gas transfer in the lung, and so the term 'transfer factor' is preferred to 'diffusing capacity'. The measurement relates the rate of transfer of gas to its partial pressure gradient across the alveolar-capillary membrane (ml/min/mm/Hg).

Perfusion

Adequate perfusion of the pulmonary vasculature is necessary for efficient gas exchange as reflected by the level of the arterial blood gases. Measurement of the arterial oxygen tension (PaO_2) is applicable to the detection of arterial hypoxemia, and is more appropriate than arterial oxygen saturation (SaO_2) in the higher range of PaO_2 where there is little detectable change in the oxygen saturation. The arterial carbon dioxide tension ($PaCO_2$) gives a satisfactory way of assessing the adequacy of alveolar ventilation.

Recent technical developments have produced a non-invasive technique for the measurement of arterial blood gas tensions from micro-electrodes placed on the forearm. The transcutaneous gas tensions so measured reflect the arterial tensions, and have a use in exercise testing and in the investigation of the sleep apnea syndrome. Ventilation and perfusion are inexorably linked in the maintenance of adequate blood gas levels. Regional variations occur in both ventilation and perfusion; if, however, they are appropriately matched in all regions, optimum gas exchange is maintained.

Ventilation-perfusion imbalance implies variations in the level of ventilation of a region relative to its perfusion. Imaging techniques requiring radioisotopes are now available, for which a gamma camera is used to give a picture of the distribution of radioactivity in the lungs. First the patient breathes radiolabeled Xenon from which a picture of the distribution of ventilation is obtained. After clearance of this material a second picture is taken following the intravenous injection of radiolabeled macro-aggregated albumin, which displays the distribution of pulmonary perfusion. This technique has more or less replaced right heart catheterization and pulmonary arteriography in the investigation of pulmonary embolism.

Interpretation of PFTs

It is customary to compare the results of lung function tests with reference values in order to assess the degree of abnormality, if any, in the data. Biochemical measurements tend to have a fixed normal range of values applicable to the whole population, as is the case with blood gas data. Values obtained from most respiratory tests, however, are influenced by one or several of the following parameters: stature, age, sex and body mass. Reference values used should be deduced from prediction formulae or tables that involve the relevant parameters.

Little consideration has been given to ethnic variations in pulmonary function, although it has been demonstrated that variations do exist. It has been reported that subjects of African origin tend to have lung volumes at least 10 percent lower than Caucasians.[3]

Modern respiratory testing equipment is usually provided with a data processing facility that will compare the calculated values with reference values appropriate to the patient. These are derived from prediction formulae obtained from published data and are usually based on samples of a white population. Comparison of the measured value with the mean predicted normal gives an index of percentage predicted. From this an interpretation of the results, in terms of the degree of abnormality, can be made; in some instances this will be arrived at by computation within the testing equipment.

Standardization of lung function testing is a subject that has been dealt with in several reports; those from the European Community[4] and the Intermountain Thoracic Society[5] are the most recent. Both sources survey the current literature of reference values and provide tables as well as prediction formulae for lung volumes, flowrates and gas transfer.

HEMOPTYSIS

A history of coughing up blood must still be taken seriously by the life insurer despite the decreasing importance of active tuberculosis as a cause. Such a history would be a warning signal to the life underwriter to obtain further information from the medical attendant. When hemoptysis refers merely to blood flecking or staining of the sputum the cause will often turn out to be something quite innocuous, such as bleeding gums or a hemorrhagic postnasal drip from an infected nasopharynx.

It is rarely necessary to obtain a current chest X-ray for applicants with a history of hemoptysis unless the event is recent or abnormal signs are reported in the lungs on examination. Despite a current negative chest X-ray, it may still be necessary to postpone a decision for six months if the applicant is middle-aged or older, is a cigarette smoker and has had a very recent hemoptysis, because carcinoma of the bronchus does not always produce unequivocal radiological signs of abnormality in its early stages.

Other causes of hemoptysis, apart from active tuberculosis (which still should not be dismissed lightly), are bronchiectasis, pneumonia, lung abcess, acute pharyngo-tracheo-bronchitis and chronic fibroid lung disease with secondary invasion of cavities by fungus, usually *Aspergillus*. All of these primary conditions would generally be recognized from the history, by sputum examination or by radiology. A bronchial angioma or bronchial telangiectasis may give rise to repeated hemoptyses and cause some difficulty in diagnosis, as may one of the bleeding disorders if it has not been previously diagnosed on other grounds. Injuries, particularly penetrating wounds of the lung, are obvious causes of blood spitting. Finally, there are two common cardiovascular causes of hemoptysis: (1) pulmonary embolism and infarction, which would be recognized from the typical history, and (2) mitral stenosis, which would be recognized from the physical signs on examination.

PULMONARY INFARCTION

This has been discussed in detail elsewhere (*see* p. 416).

PNEUMONIA (PNEUMONITIS)

Pneumonia can be caused by a host of different agents — bacterial and viral — and is often referred to according to the infecting organism (e.g. pneumococcal, *Haemophilus legionella*, mycoplasmal, Friedlander's or viral pneumonia). Viral pneumonias account for about 75 percent of all acute pulmonary infections, but the causal virus is rarely identified except when specific antibodies are sought in hospitalized patients or during severe epidemics of, for example, influenza A. During the last dozen or so years acute pneumonia due to the multiflagellate protozoon *Pneumocystis carinii* has complicated the acquired immune deficiency syndrome (AIDS); infection is usually preceded by several months of ill health, tends to be recurrent and is commonly terminal.

A single, uncomplicated attack of pneumonia or pneumonitis that has completely resolved would, other things being equal, be disregarded in underwriting, but recurrent attacks would arouse suspicion of the existence of some predisposing factor, such as bronchiectasis, chronic bronchitis or AIDS, which would then determine the rating. With no such cause and a full clinical and radiological recovery the risk would usually be standard.

PLEURISY

Fibrinous (Dry) Pleurisy

Primary pleurisy causing acute pleurodynia is usually viral and is commonly due to one of the group B coxsackie viruses. It is sometimes epidemic as in Bornholm disease. Pleurisy of this type is self-limiting and recovery is complete. Fibrinous pleurisy frequently accompanies lung infections, especially pneumonia, in which case the prognosis is that of pneumonia itself. Involvement of the serous membranes, including the pleura, is a feature of the collagen group of diseases, such as systemic lupus erythematosus, progressive systemic sclerosis, rheumatoid arthritis and polyarteritis nodosa. Therefore when there is a history of an unduly prolonged illness in which pleurisy was a feature, the underwriter should be alert to the possibility that he is dealing with one of those diseases and classify the risk accordingly.

Pleurisy with Effusion

This is often a natural sequel to dry pleurisy and the causes are similar. When the effusion is large the possibility of tuberculosis should be kept in mind, particularly in young people; the possibility of malignant disease should be kept in mind in older people. A pleural effusion may sometimes occur after a peripheral pulmonary infarct. In each case a diagnosis will generally be established. In those conditions where eventual full recovery is possible, the information will usually be available to the life underwriter if the person concerned applies for life insurance within a few years of the attack. Rating would be according to the prognosis of the causative disease. When a history of pleurisy with effusion is remote and full recovery is disclosed, the condition can usually be assumed to have been tuberculous.

EMPYEMA

Some applicants are still seen, particularly in older age groups, who have had a pneumonic empyema treated by rib resection and drainage in the days before antibiotics were available. Despite the presence of some pleural thickening and mediastinal traction, applications need not be adversely underwritten provided there is no significant restrictive defect and the lungs are otherwise sound. Similar remarks would apply to pleural thickening following a tuberculous empyema, a common complication of artificial pneumothorax in the pre-chemotherapeutic era.

Owing to the liberal use of broad-spectrum antibiotics for respiratory infections, a frank empyema is relatively rare today, having been supplanted by the sterile pleural effusion. Although this prolongs the illness, ultimate resolution of the effusion can be assured by repeated needle aspiration and continued use of antibiotics. A history of acute pneumonitis complicated by a pleural effusion would still be underwritten as standard after full recovery.

CHRONIC OBSTRUCTIVE PULMONARY DISEASE (COPD)

Although an association between chronic bronchitis and emphysema is by no means inevitable, the current facts suggest that most patients suffering from chronic airway obstruction have both bronchitis and emphysema, and that pure bronchitis or pure emphysema are relatively rare — probably less than 5 percent each. However, certification practices in different countries have given the causes of chronic airway obstruction a spurious emphasis.

COPD, also known as chronic obstructive lung disease (COLD), is a classification introduced by the National Center for Health Statistics because of the increasing use of the term by physicians in death certificates in preference to the more specific diagnoses of chronic bronchitis or emphysema. The ninth revision of the International Classification of Diseases (ICD) lists 490–496 as 'chronic obstructive pulmonary disease and allied conditions', which include chronic bronchitis, emphysema, asthma and several less common lung diseases causing airflow limitation. In practice, the bulk of the classification ICD 490–496 is made up of cases of chronic bronchitis, emphysema, and more usually both combined. Asthma (ICD 493), which is reversible obstructive pulmonary disease, is usually separated from the main classification for descriptive and epidemiologic purposes and will be discussed later (see pp. 487–90).

Trends

In Britain and the USA mortality rates from COPD have been increasing steadily from 1960 to the present, and in the US COPD and allied conditions consistently rank fifth among the leading causes of mortality. The US figures from 1979 to 1987 (*see* Table 17.1) illustrate how COPD mortality rates have been increasing for both sexes, but more dramatically for women than men. This difference appears to be a reflection of the changes in smoking habits between the sexes over the years. Although the prevalence of smoking in the USA has been declining steadily since 1965, the decline among women has been slower. Among men aged 20 or over cigarette smoking declined from 50 percent in 1965 to 32 percent in 1987; among women the prevalence rate dropped from 32 percent to 27 percent respectively.[6] A similar pattern of reduction has been reported in Britain.

Table 17.1. Trends in mortality from chronic obstructive pulmonary disease (COPD), USA 1979 to 1987.

Year	Age-adjusted rate[a,b]			Crude rate[a]			Number of deaths
	Total	Male	Female	Total	Male	Female	
1987	18·7	26·9	13·2	32·2	39·7	25·1	78380
1986	18·8	27·6	12·8	31·8	40·1	23·8	76559
1985	18·7	27·9	12·5	31·3	40·1	22·9	74662
1984	17·7	27·0	11·4	29·2	38·3	20·7	69100
1983	17·4	27·0	10·9	28·3	37·9	19·2	66246
1982	16·2	25·5	9·8	25·8	35·2	16·9	59869
1981	16·3	26·2	9·5	25·7	35·7	16·2	58832
1980	15·9	26·1	8·9	24·7	35·1	15·0	56050
1979	14·9	24·7	7·9	22·7	33·0	12·9	49933

[a]per 100,000.
[b]Adjusted on the basis of age distribution of the US total population, 1940.
Source: Various reports from the National Center for Health Statistics.

Cigarette Smoking and COPD

It has been estimated that more than 80 percent of COPD mortality is attributable to cigarette smoking,[7,8] and despite the fact that the prevalence of smoking continues to fall, COPD deaths continue to rise. This is because COPD is a slowly progressive disease and a reduction in the ventilatory reserve of the lungs sufficient to cause death takes many years. Thus mortality from COPD has a late-age incidence; death rates only begin to increase over the age of 45, and dramatically so after the age of 65.

In identifying the risk of developing chronic irreversible airway obstruction it is necessary to take into account the two main factors in the equation: (1) a genetic predisposition to respiratory disease and (2) the smoking of tobacco, particularly cigarettes. So the formula can be written simply:

hereditary factor + cigarette smoking = chronic bronchitis and emphysema

The genetic mechanisms at play are so far not well understood, but may include some unidentified fault in the immunologic chain, a mildly impaired ability to inactivate proteolytic enzymes, as in heterozygotic alpha$_1$ antitrypsin deficiency (*see* pp. 483–4), or some other genetic characteristic so far undiscovered.

In a life insurance medical examination it is not possible to delve in detail into remote family history, but for practical purposes it is reasonable to assume that an applicant has a hereditary predisposition if there is a history of lung disease of any sort in the immediate family (i.e. one or both parents and/or one or more siblings). Unfortunately, unless specially elicited by the medical examiner, the information about family history is sometimes ambiguous or misleading: for example, a death from cor pulmonale may be reported simply as heart failure, or a death from cancer of the bronchus may be listed merely as cancer. Nevertheless, despite the apparent absence of a positive family history, an applicant can still be assumed to have a genetic predisposition to respiratory disease if there is a history of pneumonia, recurrent bronchitis or chestiness in childhood before smoking age. The genetic factor, whatever it is, presumably acts by rendering the respiratory mucosa more vulnerable to infection and chronic irritants.

However, it is the inhalation of tobacco smoke that is the more important in initiating the pathologic process of mucus hypersecretion and in causing relentless progression to the stage of irreversible airway obstruction in the form of chronic bronchitis and emphysema. Atmospheric pollution, which is now being increasingly suppressed in the industrialized world, probably plays only a secondary role as a bronchial irritant by aggravating established chronic bronchitis.

It is a common experience both in clinical and life insurance medicine to find cigarette smokers, often heavy smokers, who appear to be immune to the irritant effects of smoking and who never develop symptoms of mucus hypersecretion. Furthermore, of those smokers who *are* subject to habitual throat clearing or expectoration, only a minority progress to respiratory disability, although they are very likely to be victims of other target organ diseases such as myocardial infarction. The reason for this apparent inconsistency lies in the fact that these individuals are not genetically predisposed to lung affections; their family histories will reveal no respiratory disorders among parents or siblings. Knowledge of the family history and smoking habits is very important where the underwriting of reversible or irreversible airway obstruction is concerned.

Cessation of Smoking and COPD Mortality

The following paragraphs have been extracted from the authors' overview of respiratory diseases in *Medical Risks*.[9]

There is little evidence that present day therapeutics can alter the course of COPD. The only hope of reducing the mortality from these diseases is by prevention: in other words, by encouraging people not to start smoking or to stop smoking if they have already started. There is abundant evidence that cessation of cigarette smoking reduces the mortality from COPD, although it may take several years to produce significant results.

The Surgeon General's 1984 Report[7] cites two main studies, the British Doctors and the US Veterans, which substantiate the value of quitting smoking. In both, the mortality ratios for COPD reduced as the number of years of cessation increased over ten, but there was still a residual risk compared with non-smokers at 20 years and longer. In the British Doctors study, there was no change in mortality in the first five years of cessation and an increase in the second five years. This was thought to be related to the presence of many physicians in this group who stopped smoking for health reasons. A similar pattern of increased mortality in the first nine years of quitting smoking was seen in the US Veterans study, but the reason for this was not clear since the ex-smokers entered in the study were supposed to have quit smoking for reasons other than ill health.

The relationship between cessation of smoking and incidence of chronic bronchitis and emphysema was studied by Fletcher et al[10] using one of the chief prognostic variables, the FEV_1, as an index. The FEV_1 is an accurate and reproducible measurement of airway caliber; in non-smokers it declines continuously and smoothly over a lifetime, the rate of loss accelerating in old age. The loss, however, never reaches the point of causing disability. In susceptible individuals cigarette smoking causes a more rapid decrement in the slope of the FEV_1 curve, producing symptoms of disability when the level of FEV_1 reaches around one liter. If the individual quits smoking, the rate of decline of his FEV_1 reverts to normal from that point on the curve at which he stopped smoking. But if he has smoked for many years and does not quit until he is 55 or 60 years of age, the natural decrement of FEV_1 after cessation of smoking may mean that he reaches the critical level of disabling symptoms of COPD when he is 65 or 70. In other words, the shorter the duration of cigarette smoking and the earlier in life one stops the less likely it is that disabling symptoms of COPD will appear.

Emphysema

As mentioned earlier, emphysema occurs most often in combination with chronic bronchitis, when it is simply part of a general obstructive airway syndrome. However, in a small proportion of cases it occurs in pure form, in which case it is termed primary or essential emphysema. Emphysema is defined in pathologic terms as an increase in the size of the air spaces distal to the terminal bronchioles with destruction of their walls. The two important types of emphysema are (1) centriacinar, involving the respiratory bronchioles and alveolar ducts in the center of the acinus, and (2) panacinar, involving the whole acinus. Centriacinar emphysema is most commonly found in the upper part of the upper and lower lobes, whereas panacinar emphysema is predominantly basal. In severe cases both types of emphysema may be found in the same lung, and both may be associated with cigarette smoking. However, centriacinar emphysema is the classic form found in cigarette smokers as they grow older.

The cause of primary emphysema has been linked to the genetic absence or deficiency of the antienzyme alpha$_1$ antitrypsin which, in conjunction with tobacco smoking, is responsible for the widespread atrophy of alveolar tissue. Briefly, there are several Pi phenotypes of alpha$_1$ antitrypsin, designated M, D, Z, O and so on. The great majority of the population is of the homozygous MM phenotype, having normal levels of alpha$_1$ antitrypsin; a much smaller proportion is of the heterozygous MS and MZ phenotypes, having normal or near-normal levels of alpha$_1$

antitrypsin. The rare homozygous ZZ and the heterozygous SZ phenotypes have low or absent levels of alpha$_1$ antitrypsin, and consequently severe deficiency of serum elastase inhibitory function. Elastase, which can hydrolyze the peptide bonds of native elastin, is released either from pulmonary alveolar macrophages or from polymorphonuclear leucocytes, both of which are present in increased numbers in the lungs of smokers. This elastase is continuously inhibited in health by normal levels of alpha$_1$ antitrypsin, but when the balance between elastase activity and its inhibition is altered in cigarette smokers parts of the lung are autodigested, with the production of emphysema.

In primary emphysema the airways are generally quite free of mucus or fibrosis right to the terminal bronchioli: nevertheless airway obstruction does occur because the small bronchi collapse prematurely during expiration owing to loss of elastic support of surrounding normal alveolar tissue. This can be demonstrated in pulmonary function tests by a severely reduced maximum expiratory flow. The flow-volume curve has a brief peak, possibly caused by airways collapse, following which flow falls slowly. Expiratory wheezing or pursed lip breathing would be expected. The emphysematous subject assumes a more inspiratory respiratory position to increase the elastic tension in the lungs; this provides extra support to the airways so that more ventilation can occur. Such persistent hyperinflation may contribute to stretched and narrowed alveolar capillaries, progressive trophic changes, loss of elastic tissue and dissolution of alveolar walls. The thoracic cage assumes the inspiratory position and the diaphragm becomes low and flat. The vital capacity is diminished and tidal volume decreases, whereas residual volume increases. There is not only a reduction in the area of alveolar membrane available for gas exchange, as indicated by an abnormal transfer factor, but also perfusion of non-ventilated areas and ventilation of non-perfused parts of the lung (i.e. ventilation/perfusion abnormalities).

On examination of the chest the percussion note is hyper-resonant and the area of cardiac and liver dullness is diminished or abolished, but the outstanding clinical sign on auscultation is the 'silent lung'. Pulmonary function studies show a decrease in vital capacity, FEV$_1$, closing volume and maximum voluntary ventilation, and an increase in residual volume. In early cases the PaO$_2$ may be normal at rest and after exercise, but in the late stage there is hypoxia owing to continued perfusion of non-ventilated parts of the lung, which leads to a reduction in the capillary bed, pulmonary arterial hypertension and finally increased cardiac output and right ventricular failure.

Other forms of emphysema, none of which gives rise to airway obstruction, are:

1) *Periacinar or paraseptal emphysema*: at the surface of the lung or near fissures blebs can develop which may rupture and cause a pneumothorax or, if they occur in groups, may over-expand to produce bullae.

2) *Scar emphysema*: enlarged air spaces occur irregularly within the acini around fibrotic or calcified lung scars.

3) *Compensatory emphysema*: this occurs, for example, following lobectomy or pneumonectomy.

4) *Over-inflated lungs*: this is due to uncomplicated asthma.

Insured Life Mortality Studies

The following long-term mortality studies give some guidance to the life underwriter for evaluating the risk associated with COPD. The largest of these studies is the Medical Impairment Study 1983 (MIS 1983)[11] covering the years 1962 to 1977. In the section on COPD, mortality was analyzed separately for chronic bronchitis and emphysema. Unfortunately data on an important risk factor, smoking, was unavailable for separate analysis, which may account for the fact that mortality was consistently underestimated by the underwriters in the standard, slightly and moderately impaired sections of the study for both chronic bronchitis and emphysema.

In the standard section of chronic bronchitis, males had a mortality ratio of 137 percent (standard mortality = 100 percent based on modified 1965–70 Basic Tables); those rated slightly substandard (up to 175 percent) had a mortality ratio of 239 percent, and those rated moderately substandard (180–250 percent) had a mortality ratio of 281 percent. The overall mortality ratio for substandard male issues was 240 percent. The overall mortality ratio for substandard females (235 percent) was similar to that for males.

In the emphysema section, standard males had a mortality ratio of 128 percent; those rated slightly substandard (up to 175 percent) had a mortality ratio of 309 percent, and those rated moderately substandard (180–250 percent) had a mortality ratio of 341 percent. The overall mortality ratio for substandard male issues was 323 percent, the second highest relative mortality in the 1983 MIS after myocardial infarction. In a much smaller exposure, overall female substandard experience gave a mortality ratio of 252 percent based on standard mortality.

These results suggest that there had been a too liberal approach to the underwriting of COPD; this could possibly have been corrected had the smoking status of applicants been known, or if well conducted pulmonary function tests, such as the timed vital capacity, had been obtained in doubtful cases in addition to the clinical appraisal.

In a smaller intracompany study of COPD by the Swiss Reinsurance Company[12] the mortality associated with chronic bronchitis and emphysema was also analyzed separately. For chronic bronchitis there were 48 policy deaths, giving an overall mortality ratio of 210 percent compared with standard risks issued by the Swiss Reinsurance Company over the same period of observation (1958–82). Mortality associated with emphysema alone was 235 percent, a little higher than for chronic bronchitis alone (210 percent), and higher still when emphysema was combined with chronic bronchitis (345 percent). This adverse effect of emphysema combined with chronic bronchitis was also seen in the study by the Prudential Assurance Company of London.[13] Among insureds aged 39–49 at entry there were 35 deaths, giving a mortality ratio of 323 percent and an excess death rate of 13·5 per thousand, and 45 deaths at ages 50 and older giving a mortality ratio of 196 percent and an excess death rate of 20·3 per thousand.

Rating

Chronic Bronchitis and Emphysema Combined: COPD
To avoid errors in classifying COPD for rating purposes, the following popular misconceptions should be mentioned:

1) There is poor correlation between a radiological diagnosis of emphysema and true destructive panacinar emphysema. The radiological appearance of emphysema is caused mainly by air trapping, as in asthma or when bronchospasm complicates chronic bronchitis. Therefore a chest X-ray report of emphysema should not be used as a criterion of impairment in evaluating COPD unless supported by other evidence.[14,15]

2) A clinical impression of barrel-shaped chest has been shown to be unrelated to functional signs of emphysema.[16]

3) A subnormal chest expansion should not be used as diagnostic evidence of emphysema unless adequately supported by other clinical data; a poor chest expansion is more commonly due to reasons other than lung disease (see p. 60).

Early Stage

Recurrent mucoid or mucopurulent expectoration or throat clearing; normal lung signs or catarrhal rhonchi dispersed by coughing; lungs otherwise normal. Expected range of pulmonary function test values: FEV_1 less than 65 percent predicted; FEV_1/FVC less than 70 percent.

1) Currently smoking — +25.
2) With known hereditary predisposition:
    Currently smoking or within past 12 months — +25 to +50.
    Smoking ceased for more than 12 months — standard.

Intermediate Stage

As in early stage (see above) with, in addition, persisting signs of airway obstruction on auscultation. History of dyspnea on moderate exertion but not at rest or on ordinary activity (e.g. no shortness of breath on dressing or undressing). Expected range of pulmonary function test values: FEV_1 50–65 percent predicted.

1) No known hereditary predisposition; smoking currently or within past 12 months — +50 to +75.
2) With known hereditary predisposition; smoking currently of within past 12 months — +100 to +150.

Smoking ceased for longer than 12 months — credit 25 points.

Late Stage

Manifest dyspnea with ordinary day-to-day effort or at rest, and obvious signs of irreversible airway obstruction on auscultation; able to carry out sedentary work but history of frequent absences because of respiratory disability; intermittent exacerbations of acute respiratory infection requiring institutional or domiciliary care. Expected range of pulmonary function test levels: FEV_1 40–49 percent predicted (moderate disability); FEV_1 35–39 percent predicted (severe disability).

Rating will vary according to whether disability is judged to be moderate or severe:
    Moderate — +150 to +200.
    Severe — +200 up.
If currently smoking — + 50 points to rating.

Primary (Essential) Emphysema

From the point of view of functional impairment and prognosis, mild primary emphysema corresponds roughly to the intermediate stage of combined chronic bronchitis and emphysema (*see* p. 486). Likewise, moderately advanced and severe primary emphysema correspond to the late stage of combined chronic bronchitis and emphysema. Therefore the debits shown in the rating schedule for combined chronic bronchitis and emphysema under the headings of intermediate and late stages may be used to underwrite primary emphysema of equivalent functional or clinical severity.

Applicants with COPD who have a history of, or currently show, two or more of the following should be declined:

1) FEV_1 less than 35 percent predicted.
2) Heart rate over 100 beats per minute.
3) Persistent reduction of PaO_2 to less than 7·98 kPa (60 mmHg), with $PaCO_2$ more than 6·65 kPa (50 mmHg).
4) ECG or echocardiographic evidence of more than slight right ventricular hypertrophy.
5) Pulmonary hypertension.
6) An episode of edematous heart failure.
7) Use of oxygen at home.

ASTHMA

Asthma is an ill-defined syndrome manifested clinically by reversible airway obstruction, the severity of obstruction and the degree of reversibility being unequivocal and clinically recognizable. It is usual to divide the clinical syndromes of reversible airway obstruction into (1) extrinsic asthma, which is mediated by a type I allergic reaction, but sometimes by type III and occasionally by both, (2) intrinsic, non-atopic or infective asthma in which no allergen can be identified, and (3) exercise-induced asthma. As a group, asthmatics exhibit the phenomenon of increased bronchial reactivity in which there is excessive responsiveness of the tracheobronchial tree to a multiplicity of stimuli. There is widespread narrowing of the airways due to bronchoconstriction that may be a direct effect of an allergen or irritant on the tissues, or a reflex response mediated by the vagi, or both. Thus, in addition to the more easily recognized allergic reactions in atopic patients, asthma may be triggered by bronchial infections, exercise, dust, smoke or even emotional stress. Bronchial reactivity may also occur in chronic bronchitis and emphysema causing wheezing and complicating the clinical picture. In some cases it is allergic in origin with eosinophilia in the sputum and blood, and a history of atopy; in others it is not.

Some cases of severe asthma, particularly those whose treatment has been mismanaged, continue to have airway obstruction between acute attacks and are in danger of developing COPD. The latter complication is also likely to affect asthmatics who continue to smoke cigarettes. On the other hand, true panacinar emphysema, as opposed to simple hyperinflation, is rare in asthmatics who have never smoked and whose asthma has been kept well controlled.

Mortality in Asthma

Bronchial asthma can occur at any age, although its onset is predominantly in childhood when it is typically extrinsic in type. Approximately 70 percent of asthmatics will have developed the disease before they reach the age of 40. Compared with chronic irreversible obstructive lung disease, the number of deaths from asthma is relatively low. Moreover, deaths from asthma tend to be spread fairly evenly over the age range of 10 to 50, thereafter showing a moderate increase, whereas deaths from chronic irreversible lung disease are concentrated at the older ages, increasing dramatically from the age of 55 onwards.

A few epidemics of asthma deaths have occurred in recent years; mortality increased substantially during the 1960s in Australia, New Zealand and the United Kingdom, although there was no appreciable increase in the USA, Canada and countries in mainland Europe.[17] The most notable increases occurred in New Zealand where in 1966 the mortality rate rose to 2·8 per 100 thousand and again in 1979 when it rose to 4·1 compared with 0·8 in the UK. Although the excessive use of pressured aerosols, especially those containing isoproterenol (isoprenaline), may have been a contributory factor in the rise in asthma deaths in the 1960s and 1970s, it is now thought that the excessive use of these aerosols simply reflects over-reliance on home therapy, leading to late self-referral and inadequate use of corticosteroids. This appears to be the most likely explanation of the two epidemics in New Zealand.[18]

Several years on, and despite a better understanding of the pathophysiology of asthma and the introduction of more sophisticated drugs, the problem of asthma control remains undecided. It has become apparent in the past ten or so years that there is a gradual increase in the morbidity and mortality from asthma in the USA and several Western countries. From 1980 to 1987 total deaths from asthma in the USA increased from 2,891 to 4,360, representing a 31 percent increase in the death rate from 1·3 per 100 thousand to 1·7 per 100 thousand.[19]

Increases in asthma death rates have also been reported from Canada, the United Kingdom and countries in northern mainland Europe. The increases in the UK are even greater than those reported in the USA, with a 50 percent increase in recorded mortality from asthma among the 5–34 age group between 1974 and 1984.[20] However, mortality from asthma in England and Wales has since shown a slight reduction. In 1985 the death rate for the 5–34 age group was 0·87 per 100 thousand and the corrresponding rate for 1989 was 0·79.[21,22] One of the possible reasons for this welcome improvement in mortality may be a shift in the approach to management of asthma, not only by British but also by European and antipodean physicians, which has not been whole-heartedly embraced by their counterparts in the United States, namely that the genesis of the acute asthmatic attack is inflammatory rather than purely bronchospastic, and that it should be treated accordingly. Therefore first-line therapy for acute asthma in the UK is now inhaled corticosteroids, using very high doses if necessary, reserving beta-agonist bronchodilators as reserve medication on an as-needed basis.[19]

Insured Life Mortality

In a relatively large exposure the mortality of insured asthmatics was analyzed in the *Medical Impairment Study 1983* (MIS 1983)[11] and gives valuable information to underwriters in classifying these risks. In contrast to COPD exposure of asthmatics was concentrated at ages under 40, with a slightly higher proportion of females than males. Most of the substandard risks were classified as slightly substandard.

Among males classified as standard risks the mortality ratio was 108 percent (standard = 100 percent), confirming the general opinion among clinicians that mild asthma, at least for young males, is a benign condition. However, females accepted as standard risks fared less well, with a mortality ratio of 160 percent.

Males who were rated slightly substandard (up to 175 percent) and moderately substandard (180–250 percent) had mortality ratios well over these expected levels (186 percent and 298 percent respectively), the comparable mortality ratios for females being even worse (242 percent and 386 percent respectively). Because the mortality ratio for standard females was unexpectedly high at 160 percent, a more detailed review of the experience was made. This showed that mortality ratios were elevated only at ages 40 and over, suggesting that milder cases of asthma, which are of little significance at younger ages, must be carefully underwritten at ages 40 and over, especially for females. A similar pattern was found for standard males but to a much lesser degree.

People with a history of asthma who were issued insurance between 1958 and 1982 formed the basis of a mortality study by the Swiss Reinsurance Company.[12] The subjects, males and females combined, were divided into two groups: (1) chronic, severe and (2) occasional, seasonal. The chronic, severe asthmatics had a mortality ratio of 255 percent based on standard mortality, whereas the occasional, seasonal group returned a mortality ratio of 105 percent. As in the *Medical Impairment Study 1983* (MIS 1983),[11] the underwriters badly underestimated the mortality of the substandard or severe group of asthmatics, but managed to classify the mild, occasional group nearly correctly.

Both the above studies reinforce the opinion that truly mild asthma is a relatively benign disease but that anything more severe requires careful underwriting evaluation.

Selection of Risks

Asthma may be classified as mild, moderate or severe depending on its clinical behavior over a period of time, say two years, prior to application.

In life insurance practice severe asthmatics will be greatly outnumbered by those in the mild and moderate categories, and usually the underwriter will have no great difficulty in identifying them. For example, there may be a history of unstable asthma with recurring acute attacks, some requiring systemic corticosteroids for relief, or even hospitalization for life-threatening status asthmaticus. Asthmatics infected with *Aspergillus fumigatus* generally suffer from severe asthma because of the development of additional hypersensitivity to the fungus, and many will require continuous systemic steroids in order to keep well. Also in the severe category are those chronic asthmatics who have developed airway obstruction between acute episodes either through neglect or mismanaged treatment.

There has been a slow change in the attitude of underwriters to the handling of asthmatic applicants on continuous corticosteroid therapy. At one time these individuals were automatically classified as severe, and a further addition was made to the premium to cover the corticosteroid risk. Certainly there is a risk from long-term systemic corticosteroids, but the mortality risk for severe asthmatics if corticosteroids are witheld is much higher. The lesson of the epidemic of asthma deaths in New Zealand in the 1960s and 1970s makes this point quite clear (*see* p. 488).

As mentioned earlier, the classification of severity of asthma for insurance should be based mainly on the clinical status as maintained over a period of time irrespective of treatment. Thus a severe asthmatic treated successfully on continuous oral corticosteroids may in time become well-controlled and revert to a moderate category or better, and be rated accordingly so long as the rating does not fall below that required to cover the steroid risk. In fact, the number of asthmatics being treated with continuous systemic corticosteroids is now decreasing. Most can be changed successfully to modern aerosol steroids with metered doses, together with inhaled bronchodilators when necessary, thus avoiding the adverse effects of systemic therapy.

Mild asthma would include occasional, infrequent wheezing easily controlled by aerosol bronchodilators, or mild, exertional asthma or nocturnal wheezing where daily treatment is used. Pulmonary function tests would be normal. Asthma that occurs only during the pollen season would not attract a rating for life insurance.

The moderate category would usually include asthmatics who require regular daily treatment to keep free of wheezing but who, perhaps once or twice a year, have a more severe attack of bronchospasm requiring systemic corticosteroids on a domiciliary or even an in-patient basis to stabilize the condition. Between attacks pulmonary function tests would generally be normal or only slightly impaired.

Rating

The following basic ratings for asthma are suggested:

Severity	Rating
Mild	0 to +75
Moderate	+75 to +150
Severe	+150 to +200

1) Cigarette smoker, current or within 12 months, depending on number per day — + 25 to +50.
2) Asthma complicated by chronic bronchitis — rate as asthma or COPD according to severity, whichever is the higher.

BRONCHIECTASIS

Bronchiectasis may be familial, arising from fetal malformation of the alveoli (e.g.

Kartagener's syndrome), which is also associated with dextrocardia and sinusitis, and the immotile cilia syndrome; or it may be acquired as the result of lung fibrosis, extrinsic or intrinsic bronchial obstruction, atelectasis or the late stage of chronic bronchitis.

The outlook for bronchiectatic patients has greatly improved since the introduction of antibiotics. When treatment is combined with the intelligent use of physiotherapy, localized and even more widespread bronchiectasis can be satisfactorily controlled by medical measures alone; surgical treatment is not often indicated today. Confluent lung abscess, secondary cerebral abscess and amyloid disease, which were the classical complications of bronchiectasis in pre-antibiotic days, are now rare.

Risk Factors

COPD in the form of chronic bronchitis and emphysema is a common accompaniment of bronchiectasis, and its presence or absence is a major factor determining overall prognosis. In fact, surgical treatment of bronchiectasis would be contraindicated in the presence of irreversible COPD. If the lungs are otherwise healthy, the risk to life associated with bronchiectasis can be considered proportional to the extent of the disease, being low and insignificant when it is localized to one segment of one lobe. The risk is much increased when it is more widely distributed involving several segments of more than one lobe.

Selection of Risks

The following factors should be taken into account when evaluating the risk associated with bronchiectasis:

1) The extent of the disease and whether it is localized or widespread. If the result of a bronchogram is available, the extent may be conveniently expressed as the number of segments of a lobe or lobes affected.
2) The integrity, or otherwise, of remaining lung tissue.
3) The frequency and severity of secondary infections, often referred to as attacks of pneumonia, with or without pleurisy.
4) Smoking habit.

Rating

Medical treatment

Minimal

Acute respiratory infection, pneumonia or pleurisy; bronchiectasis localized to not more than two segments of a lobe or to the right middle lobe or lingular lobe.

| Duration | Age | | |
since last attack	Under 30	30–49	50 and over
Within 2 yr	+50	+35	+25
Over 2 yr	0	0	0

Moderate

Affecting one or two segments in two major lobes.

Duration	Age		
since last attack	Under 30	30–49	50 and over
Within 2 yr	+100	+75	+50
3–4 yr	+ 75	+50	+25
Thereafter	0	0	0

Severe

Widespread bronchiectasis.

Duration	Age		
since last attack	Under 30	30–49	50 and over
Within 2 yr	+150	+100	+75
3–4 yr	+100	+ 75	+50
Thereafter	+ 75	+ 50	+25

1) With associated chronic bronchitis and emphysema — add debit according to stage (*see* p. 486).
2) Current smoker, or within 12 months — +25.
3) With other associated lung diseases — add appropriate debits.

Surgical Treatment

Although surgical resection for bronchiectasis is now undertaken only in special circumstances, people who have been treated in this way in previous years are still seen from time to time as applicants for life insurance. As in the case of medical treatment, the integrity of the remaining lung tissue is important for the best prognosis, in which case rating will depend simply on the amount of lung tissue resected. The body compensates well for the loss of a limited volume of lung tissue, especially at young ages, and overall function is virtually unaffected by the resection of, for example, one upper lobe or two of the three major segments of a lower lobe.

1) Right or left upper lobectomy or segmental resection of right or left lower lobe, or equivalent; all ages — standard.
2) Right or left lower lobectomy or equivalent.

	Age	
Duration since surgery	Under 30	30 and over
Within 5 yr	3 per mil for 2 yr	5 per mil for 2 yr
Over 5 yr	Standard	Standard

3) Resection of two major lobes or equivalent; all ages and at all durations — +75.

4) Pneumonectomy; all ages and at all durations — +100 to +75.

With associated chronic bronchitis and emphysema (COPD) — add the appropriate debit according to stage and smoking history (*see* p. 486).

Immotile Cilia Syndrome

This is a genetically determined disorder and includes Kartagener's syndrome (*see* pp. 490–1). It is characterized by immotility of the cilia in the respiratory tract epithelium, sperm and other cells. These changes lead to continuing and long-standing recurrent bronchitis, sinusitis and otitis. The condition may be suspected if there is a family history of bronchiectasis or dextrocardia, and confirmed by bronchial or nasal biopsy. In the male the spermatozoa are immotile, causing infertility.

In the course of time bronchiectatic areas develop, producing COPD that tends to remain at a stable level of impairment changing relatively little over the years. The prognosis can be equated to that of modern COPD, and rating for life insurance should be as for moderate or severe bronchietasis (*see* pp. 491–2) with an addition of 50 percentage points. A milder form of the disease exists in which the respiratory cilia are dyskinetic rather than immotile.

CYSTIC FIBROSIS (CF)

Although CF causes profound systemic disturbance as a result of nutritional deficiency, it is the changes in the lungs that are the most disabling. The disease is manifested in an autosomal recessive manner, its effects generally appearing in infancy, although some cases may not be recognized as CF until much later in life. The defect is carried by one in every 20 people, and one in four children born to a couple who are carriers will have CF. Bowel problems cause meconium ileus and intestinal obstruction in 10 percent of all CF babies, and pancreatic ducts become plugged with viscid secretions leading to malabsorption of fat and the clinical picture of steatorrhea and malnutrition. The most serious problem, however, is recurrent bronchial infection causing pulmonary damage and severe obstructive airway disease.

Prognosis

Since CF was first recognized as an entity in the late 1930s, mean survival of those affected has gradually increased, but despite the best available treatment most patients die before they are 40.[23] The improved survival is thought to be partly because of earlier recognition and treatment of the disease and partly because mildly affected cases of CF discovered in screening programs have been included in follow-up studies. This information is collected by the Cystic Fibrosis Foundation from 120 affiliated CF centers around the USA. The Foundation maintains current year follow-up data for the preceding decade, and the most recent ten-year follow-up (1976–85), involving about 14 thousand patients, has been analyzed by Butz.[24]

By 1985 more than half of the patients reached 25 years of age, a considerable improvement in average survival during the previous ten years (*see* Fig. 17.3). Mortality in CF is higher among females (*see* Table 17.2), the outlook for males being somewhat better at every age (*see* Table 17.3). The annual mortality rate plotted against age demonstrates a nearly linear relationship showing an approximate annual increase in mortality rate of 0·2 percent or a 2 percent increase with each passing decade.

Although the proportionate improvement in mortality from CF in recent years has been dramatic, it does not represent a major breakthrough in the care of these patients. The figures in Tables 17.2 and 17.3 make it obvious that mortality in CF still far exceeds insurable levels, and unfortunately the position will remain so until there is a significant advance in medical science to deal with this tragic affliction.

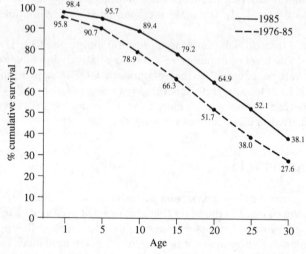

Fig. 17.3 Cumulative survival of cystic fibrosis patients.

Table 17.2. Cystic fibrosis in females, ten-year follow-up 1976–1985.

Ages	e	d	d'	Mortality ratio %	Annual average mortality rate	Estimated ten-year survival rate	EDR
1–4	1145·5	10	0·55	1800	0·0087	0·916	8·3
5–9	1355·8	23	0·32	7200	0·0170	0·842	16·7
10–14	1039·8	31	0·24	12900	0·0298	0·739	29·6
15–19	828·1	40	0·38	10500	0·0483	0·610	47·9
20–24	582·1	26	0·32	8100	0·0447	0·633	44·1
25–29	304·0	22	0·18	12200	0·0724	0·472	71·8
30+	233·9	14	—	—	—	—	—

e = exposure in person-years.
d = actual deaths.
d' = expected deaths estimated from US population mortality rates.
EDR = excess death rate per thousand.

Table 17.3. Cystic fibrosis in males, ten-year follow-up 1976–1985.

Ages	e	d	d'	Mortality ratio %	Annual average mortality rate	Estimated ten-year survival rate	EDR
1–4	1186·2	7	0·73	950	0·0059	0·943	5·3
5–9	1452·6	15	0·46	3250	0·0103	0·902	10·0
10–14	1194·4	23	0·42	5500	0·0193	0·823	18·9
15–19	1017.1	32	1·26	2550	0·0315	0·726	30·2
20–24	703·5	32	1·22	2600	0·0445	0·628	37·3
25–29	446·1	27	0·76	3550	0·0605	0·536	58·8
30+	372·7	25	—	—	—	—	—

e = exposure in person-years.
d = actual deaths.
d' = expected deaths estimated from US population mortality rates.
EDR = excess death rate per thousand.

LUNG ABSCESS

A lung abscess is usually secondary to bronchial obstruction, and the commonest cause after middle life is carcinoma of the bronchus. Aspiration of vomit into the lungs during a drunken stupor and inhalation of a foreign body or septic material during emergency anesthesia outside the ordered routine of the operating theater are also very common causes of bronchial obstruction and subsequent lung abscess. Causes other than bronchial obstruction are pneumonia due to *Staphylococcus aureus*, infected pulmonary emboli and direct extension of a liver abscess through the diaphragm.

Since a lung abscess causes considerable systemic upset, it will normally require urgent treatment followed by a period of observation until it is considered inactive. Investigations to determine the cause of the abscess will also have been carried out in most cases. Any applicant with a history of lung abscess will, therefore, have relevant information regarding the event filed by the attending physician, and this should be obtained by the insurance company, especially if the history is recent.

Selection of Risks

A history of lung abscess should be evaluated from the point of view of the chest history as a whole, including smoking habits, as well as from the nature of the abscess itself: whether it drained freely and responded promptly to antibiotics, or whether it was complicated, for example, by a pyopneumothorax or bronchopleural fistula requiring prolonged treatment. Careful enquiry should be made about current and past alcohol habits if the history suggests that an abscess followed aspiration of vomit.

Rating

1) History of lung abscess or abscesses:
Uncomplicated, with full recovery and no symptoms — standard.

Complicated by pyopneumothorax or bronchopleural fistula but full recovery without residuals.

Within one year — 5 per mil for two years.

Thereafter — standard.

2) With residual abscess cavity or cavities — rate as bronchiectasis according to distribution and history of infective episodes (*see* pp. 491–2).

3) With surgical resection of affected segments or lobes — rate as surgical treatment of bronchiectasis (*see* pp. 492–3).

Add to above any rating for primary cause of lung abscess if applicable.

PNEUMOTHORAX

By definition a pneumothorax is a collection of free air between the visceral and parietal pleura causing the space to become real instead of potential.

Artificial Pneumothorax

A pneumothorax may be artificially induced as a diagnostic procedure. It was also used in the treatment of respiratory tuberculosis in pre-chemotherapeutic days to collapse and splint the diseased lung.

Traumatic Pneumothorax

Any perforating wound of the chest, including tearing of the parietal pleura by the free end of a fractured rib, may allow air to enter the pleural space. Standard acceptance for life insurance would be the rule after full recovery.

Secondary Pneumothorax

This is caused by clearly defined disease of the underlying lung, such as bullous emphysema, tuberculosis, lung abscess, cysts, asthma, bronchial carcinoma, sarcoidosis and other fibrosing lung diseases. The primary disease, if not already known, would generally become apparent after re-expansion of the affected lung. Applicants with a history of secondary pneumothorax would be rated according to the nature of the causative lung disease.

Benign Idiopathic Spontaneous Pneumothorax

This is the commonest form of pneumothorax. It occurs in previously fit young adult males between the ages of 20 and 35 without any obvious clinical or radiological abnormality of the underlying lung. Air simply escapes into the pleural space through a small, usually congenital, subpleural bleb. The four types are described below.

Simple Pneumothorax
A simple pneumothorax absorbs spontaneously if left alone, but it may take several

weeks for the lung to re-expand completely. More rapid expansion — in five or six days — may be achieved by means of a Heimlich flutter valve inserted into the pleural space through the second intercostal space anteriorly.

Tension Pneumothorax
In tension pneumothorax, which is a medical emergency, a positive pressure builds up in the pleural space, leading to mediastinal shift, shock and hypotension. The increased pleural pressure must be relieved promptly by underwater seal drainage.

Recurrent Pneumothorax
After several episodes of spontaneous pneumothorax pleurodesis or parietal pleurectomy may be carried out to prevent further recurrences.

Chronic Pneumothorax
Surgical resection of a fistulous communication between lung and pleural space is usually required for cure of chronic pneumothorax.

Rating

The possibility of a pneumothorax occurring in the other lung while one side is still collapsed exists, but is a rare complication in practice. A history of one or more attacks of benign idiopathic spontaneous pneumothorax treated conservatively or by pleurodesis would generally be considered a risk within the limits of standard premium pricing.

WIDESPREAD PULMONARY FIBROSIS

A great variety of entirely distinct processes may initiate widespread fibrosis in the lungs. In some cases the acute process is short-lived. In others activity continues alongside the fibrosing response over prolonged periods. In either event the resulting fibrosis progressively impairs lung function and often leads to premature death.

The causes of widespread pulmonary fibrosis may be grouped broadly into four main categories:

1) Granulomas: sarcoidosis, extrinsic fibrosing alveolitis (farmer's lung, bird-fancier's lung), berylliosis.
2) Pneumoconioses: silicosis, asbestosis, coal miner's lung.
3) Alveolar exudates: chronic left ventricular failure, certain drugs (e.g. busulphan, hexamethonium).
4) Unknown causes: cryptogenic fibrosing alveolitis.

The conditions liable to give rise to widespread pulmonary fibrosis that present most commonly as underwriting problems in life insurance are discussed below.

Sarcoidosis

In 1869 Jonathan Hutchinson in London and Carl William Boeck in Oslo described the first two cases of sarcoid of the skin, but it was not until many years later that sarcoidosis was recognized as a disorder involving most tissues in the body. Nevertheless the subject is discussed here because the majority of cases of sarcoidosis present with an intrathoracic lesion, either hilar lymphadenopathy or pulmonary infiltration, or both. Moreover mortality in sarcoidosis is almost wholly due to widespread lung fibrosis, with some deaths due to renal failure from hypercalcemia and hypercalciuria. CNS and cardiac involvement account for the few remaining deaths.

Presentation and Prognostic Stages

Evidence is accumulating that the various forms of sarcoidosis can be explained on an immunopathological basis,[25] depending on the immune response which develops when the body is challenged by the antigen responsible for sarcoidosis. For example, sarcoidosis ushered in by vigorous lymphoproliferation is accompanied by high concentrations of immunoglobulins and has a distinct tendency to spontaneous remission. In contrast, when pulmonary granuloma formation is predominant and insidious in onset there is no increase in immunoglobulins, but cell-mediated immunity is normal or increased. Intrathoracic sarcoidosis may present as follows:

1) Bilateral hilar lymphadenopathy without lung infiltration, which is ushered in by an acute febrile illness with erythema nodosum and sometimes iritis, has the best prognosis of all the syndromes of sarcoidosis; one can expect complete, spontaneous resolution of the lesions within six months to two years from onset. Once resolution is complete, relapse does not occur and life expectancy is unaffected. Until resolution is complete there is a slight possibility of lung infiltration appearing, but this in turn is likely to regress without fibrosis. Infiltration that persists unchanged or partially regressed for longer than two years from onset is unlikely to worsen.

2) Acute-onset sarcoidosis with hilar lymphadenopathy together with mottling of the lungs has a slightly less favorable prognosis than purely hilar lymphadenopathy. In a small group of patients in this category followed up for a five- to ten-year period, Scadding[26] found a higher proportion with radiological residua, and of those with persisting infiltration 8 percent had symptoms, mainly of breathlessness, and were considered slightly impaired lives. However, the larger proportion whose pulmonary lesions regressed completely were considered to be no longer at risk.

3) Widespread pulmonary infiltration may occur without previous evidence of hilar lymphadenopathy. Generally there is no history of acute onset, and in many instances the lesions are symptomless. Such cases are often found by chance on routine chest radiography. Those who have symptoms will usually be treated with long-term oral corticosteroids, mostly with benefit. However, it is only those whose pulmonary infiltration resolves and does not relapse after steroids have been withdrawn for a period of six months or more who can be considered to have a prognosis as good as patients whose infiltration has resolved spontaneously.

Once relapse occurs repeated relapses are more likely, and this is an indication for long-term, low-dose maintenance therapy. In a group of 152 patients with incapacitating pulmonary sarcoidosis who were given corticosteroids, John et al[27] found that clinical response was almost uniformly good but often not complete or sustained. Although 21 percent remained asymptomatic after the initial course of treatment (10–12 months), 78 percent had relapses when treatment was withdrawn; 10 percent died during the short period of observation.

4) Patients presenting with established pulmonary fibrosis have the worst prognosis of all, and despite corticosteroid treatment mortality is excessive in the group.

Other Factors Determining Prognosis

Cutaneous sarcoidosis

In the absence of intrathoracic disease, this is benign, but when there is associated lung infiltration large, fixed skin lesions usually mean that established lung fibrosis will ultimately ensue.

Hypercalcemia

This is an uncommon manifestation of sarcoidosis but is dangerous if untreated, leading to nephrocalcinosis and progressive renal failure. If recognized early enough, the increased serum calcium concentration can be effectively reduced to within normal range and maintained there by corticosteroid drugs until the tendency to hypercalcemia subsides spontaneously. The risk associated with hypercalcemia would be additional to that of an intrathoracic sarcoid lesion, should it exist.

Hepatic Sarcoidosis

Liver biopsy, which is one of the tests carried out to confirm a diagnosis of intrathoracic sarcoidosis, is positive in 75–80 percent of cases, showing sarcoid granulomas even though there is no clinical evidence of hepatic involvement. Nevertheless only a relatively small proportion of people having a positive liver biopsy progress to liver damage and biliary cirrhosis. If there is any doubt about the existence of significant granulomatous hepatic disease, such as unexplained fever or an enlarged liver, liver function tests should be carried out before acceptance for life insurance is considered.

Pulmonary Function

Chest radiography is an unreliable and often misleading method of evaluating the degree of impairment of pulmonary function: occasionally asymptomatic subjects have chest X-rays that appear to show widespread fibrosis; also, subjects with symptoms may show no significant abnormality on the X-ray. Pulmonary function tests are a better guide to prognosis in the stage of pulmonary infiltration and fibrosis. Typically, lung volumes are reduced, indicating a restrictive ventilatory defect. There is usually a serious impairment of the transfer factor and there may be cyanosis. Tests of airway obstruction are not particularly impaired unless there is coexisting chronic bronchitis and emphysema. Severely affected cases will usually have evidence of cor pulmonale in the ECG.

Selection of Risks

Applications for life insurance should be postponed six months from the onset of symptoms or diagnosis. This serves to exclude the lymphoreticular malignancies from the differential diagnosis of hilar and paratracheal lymphadenopathy, and allows time for a definitive diagnosis to be made. A current chest X-ray film should be obtained if possible, in addition to an attending physician's statement or clinic report. The information contained in the latter can be invaluable to the life underwriter, enabling him to check the clinical and radiological progress of the disease, as well as the important biochemical values, such as serum calcium and liver function tests. In the case of chronic pulmonary infiltration or fibrosis, the result of any pulmonary function tests that may have been carried out would also provide helpful additional information when forming an opinion of the risk.

Rating
Within six months of onset or diagnosis — postpone.
Thereafter:
1) History of hilar lymphadenopathy; no pulmonary infiltration; acute onset with erythema nodosum, iritis or arthralgia.
Chest X-ray normal — standard.
Hilar lymphadenopathy still present:
   Within one year — 2 per mil for two years.
   After two years — standard.
2) As in (1) but with a history of pulmonary infiltration.
Chest X-ray normal — standard.
Pulmonary infiltration still present, but not increased; symptomless:
   Within two years — 3 per mil for two years.
   3–5 years — +75.
   After five years — standard.
3) History of pulmonary infiltration with or without hilar lymphadenopathy, insidious onset or discovered by chance.
a) Resolution of pulmonary infiltration.
   Spontaneous — standard.
   Corticosteroid-induced, no relapse:
      Within six months of steroid withdrawal — +75.
      Thereafter — standard.
b) With relapse and continuous or intermittent corticosteroid medication:
Slight pulmonary infiltration or fibrosis on X-ray; no symptoms and no or minimal impairment of pulmonary function tests — +100.
Moderate pulmonary infiltration or fibrosis on X-ray; effort-induced dyspnea; slight to moderate impairment of pulmonary function tests (diffusing capacity, oxygen unsaturation with exercise) — +150 to +200.
Widespread pulmonary infiltration or fibrosis on X-ray: dyspnea at rest or on minimal effort; marked impairment of pulmonary function tests (oxygen unsaturation at rest); ECG evidence of cor pulmonale — +300 to decline.
4) Hypercalcemia:
Untreated — decline.
Well controlled by corticosteroid therapy — +50.
Constant proteinuria or other evidence of renal calcinosis — add ratings for proteinuria, history of renal calculi, or extent of renal calcification (see Chapter 18).

5) Hepatic sarcoidosis (positive liver biopsy):
Normal liver function tests; no hepatomegaly; no treatment — standard.
History of abnormal liver function tests or hepatomegaly; controlled with corticosteroids; no progression — +100.
Progressive impairment of liver function tests or frank cirrhosis — decline.
6) Sarcoidosis of the CNS — usually decline.
7) Cutaneous sarcoid; no intrathoracic lesion; quiescent — standard.
With intrathoracic lesion — rate according to stage (*see above*).
8) Cardiac sarcoid presents most commonly as ventricular arrhythmia, heart block or with heart failure, although in sarcoidosis generally cardiac involvement is not often recognized clinically.
Symptomatic cardiac sarcoid; disease still active — decline.
Conduction defect only; disease inactive — rate for defect (*see* Chapter 15).

Note Where dosage of corticosteroid drugs is regularly or frequently greater than 15 mg prednisolone, or its equivalent, per day add 50 points to above ratings.

Extrinsic Allergic Alveolitis: Farmer's Lung Disease (FLD)

The term extrinsic allergic alveolitis refers generically to reactions, partly inflammatory, partly granulomatous, in the peripheral gas-exchanging parts of the lungs associated with antigen-antibody reactions to inhaled organic dusts. The number of organic antigens known to induce an allergic alveolitis is steadily increasing.

Since repeated or intensive exposure to antigens is needed to cause disease in non-atopic subjects, allergic alveolitis is mostly related to occupation or hobbies. Thus FLD, which is the prototype of this form of lung disease, is caused by inhalation of thermophilic actinomycetes in the dust of hay that has overheated in going moldy. Fungal spores are known to cause allergic alveolitis in other occupations, such as maple bark stripping, malting, mushroom farming and the sugar cane industry. Animal proteins known to induce an allergic alveolitis include avian protein (bird-fancier's lung), and bovine and porcine protein in pituitary snuff (pituitary snuff-taker's lung).

Mode of Presentation and Prognosis

The frequency and intensity of exposure seem to be the principal determinants of the mode of presentation of allergic alveolitis. In the case of farm workers, exposure to the antigen is intermittent, of short duration and in relatively heavy concentrations. Therefore FLD is characterized by acute attacks of disabling dyspnea, tightness in the chest and cough directly related to exposure to moldy hay during the winter months. The number of recurrences of acute attacks appears to be important in long-term prognosis; Braun et al[28] studied 92 patients who had FLD for an average period of 14·8 years in order to determine the long-term effects of the disease and the factors influencing the outcome. The main findings were that patients with a history of five or more symptomatic recurrences had significantly smaller values for vital capacity, total lung capacity and CO diffusing capacity than those patients with less than five recurrences. The authors concluded that the number of symptomatic recurrences may be the most important factor in determining the danger of progressive disease.

At the other extreme, non-atopic subjects who are exposed to low concentrations of antigen over a long period of time, as in the case of bird fanciers, may experience no recognizable acute attacks. Instead, pulmonary fibrosis develops insidiously, and by the time significant symptoms appear widespread fibrosis of the lungs is already far advanced with pulmonary function tests showing marked ventilatory and circulatory impairment. At this stage, no form of treatment can alter the relentless downhill course to chronic hypoxia, pulmonary hypertension and congestive heart failure.

Applicants for life insurance who suffer from extrinsic allergic alveolitis will therefore present in several ways:

1) There may be a definite history of acute respiratory symptoms related to occupation confirmed to be, for example, farmer's lung or maltworker's lung, by specific precipitin tests. Although there may have been radiological evidence of micronodular mottling in the past, the lungs may be clinically and radiologically clear on examination if there has been no exposure to the antigen for several months. Nevertheless while the individual remains in the same occupation he will continue to be periodically at risk in spite of precautions, and a rating of +50 to +100 would be appropriate depending on the number of symptomatic recurrences reported. On the other hand, should the person cease to be exposed because of a change of occupation, standard rates could apply.

2) There may be a long history of recurrent attacks of allergic alveolitis with evidence of respiratory impairment on examination, and dense, diffuse mottling or established widespread fibrosis of the lungs on X-ray. Rating would be similar to that for the pulmonary fibrosis of sarcoidosis of equivalent extent (see pp. 500–1), and an additional +50 should be applied if exposure to the antigen continues.

3) Widespread pulmonary fibrosis may be discovered either by chance or when a chest X-ray has been carried out because of abnormal signs in the lungs reported on examination. As before, the risk may be evaluated according to the extent of pulmonary fibrosis or the degree of impairment of PFTs, also taking into account whether or not exposure to the offending antigen is continuing.

Cryptogenic Fibrosing Alveolitis: Chronic Interstitial Pneumonia

Cryptogenic, intrinsic, fibrosing alveolitis, known also as chronic interstitial pneumonia, is an uncommon disease with a poor long-term prognosis which is being diagnosed less often as more extrinsic antigens are discovered. By definition, cryptogenic fibrosing alveolitis excludes interstitial lung fibrosis caused by extrapulmonary multisystem diseases such as rheumatoid arthritis, progressive systemic sclerosis or systemic lupus erythematosus, or by an other identifiable causes, such as radiotherapy or drug sensitivity. Yet there remains a hard core of true intrinsic cases which are thought to be perpetuated by an auto-immune mechanism.

The disease affects both sexes, usually at ages over 40 but occasionally younger, and the clinical picture itself can often suggest the diagnosis: progressive exertional dyspnea without bronchospasm, gross clubbing of the fingers, dry cough and coarse basal crepitations on auscultation. The end result is progressive impairment of ventilation and perfusion, hypoxia and pulmonary hypertension. The course of the disease is variable but relentless, some patients advancing rapidly to death within a year or two, whereas others who are more responsive to treatment progress at a slower rate and survive for 12 to 15 years or longer. The reason for this variation may lie in the two different pathologic abnormalities found in chronic interstitial pneumonia.

The most common pattern of disease is known as 'usual' interstitial pneumonia (UIP) and is characterized by an increase in cellular thickening of the alveolar wall, which contains excess fibrous tissue; a less common form is known as 'desquamative' interstitial pneumonia (DIP), in which there is an accumulation of mononuclear cells in the distal air spaces. Of the two types, the histologic appearance indicating DIP carries a more favorable prognosis than one showing UIP. Carrington et al[29] carried out a prospective longitudinal study of patients with confirmed interstitial pneumonia who were initially classified histologically into desquamative (n = 40, age range 17–67 years) and usual (n = 53, age range 15–72 years) types, and followed for 1–22 years. Mortality in DIP was 27·5 percent and mean survival 12·2 years, compared with 66·0 percent and 5·6 years respectively in UIP. Without treatment 21·9 percent with DIP, but none with UIP, improved. With corticosteroid therapy 61·5 percent with DIP and only 11·5 percent with UIP improved, whereas 27·0 percent and 69·2 percent respectively, worsened.

Selection of Risks
From what has been said above it is obvious that idiopathic pulmonary fibrosis of either histologic type is a serious condition, often presenting sporadically in chronic and misleadingly benign form. Since relapse frequently occurs after corticosteroids are withdrawn, only those who have remained in continuous remission for six to 12 months after cessation of therapy can be given individual consideration for insurance, the risk diminishing as the duration of remission lengthens. Such applicants would usually have the desquamative type of the disease, and depending on the level of pulmonary function might be ratable +300 in the second year reducing to +100 by the fifth year after cessation of immunosuppressive drugs. Applicants currently receiving corticosteroids or other immunosuppressives are best declined.

Beryllium Granulomatosis (Berylliosis)

Chronic berylliosis is essentially an occupational disease occurring in people engaged in the processing of the metal or its salts. Chronic granulomatous nodules develop in the lungs, often several years after exposure. There is thickening of the alveolar walls causing symptoms of respiratory insufficiency arising from impaired gaseous diffusion. Beryllium granulomatosis closely resembles pulmonary sarcoidosis in its pathology and ultimate effect on lung function. If corticosteroid therapy is instituted early enough, it can cause a remission with apparent resolution of lung lesions and a return to normal pulmonary function. In other cases the lesions fail to regress completely and permanent pulmonary fibrosis ensues.

Chronic beryllium granulomatosis may be evaluated for life insurance in the same way as the pulmonary infiltration or fibrosis of sarcoidosis (see pp. 500–1).

Chronic Pulmonary Histoplasmosis

Chronic pulmonary histoplasmosis is a relatively uncommon infectious disease caused by inhalation of dust containing the spores of *Histoplasma capsulatum*. There is a high incidence of sensitivity to histoplasma in animals and man in central USA, suggesting widespread subclinical infection; chest X-ray surveys in these areas have revealed many residents having asymptomatic lesions, sometimes calcified.

The early, acute lesions of histoplasmosis are relatively benign and some 80 percent heal permanently. In the remaining 20 percent the lesions break down, forming persistent infected cavities. From this local infection there is bronchogenic dispersion of antigen to areas of the lung distant from the cavity, leading to progressive pulmonary fibrosis; sometimes there is a more disseminated hematogenous spread of the fungus to distant organs such as the liver, spleen, adrenals, and lymphatic system.

Prognosis

As might be expected, those with persistent lung cavitation have the worst prognosis, and this was borne out in a combined follow-up study over a period of 20 years (1955 to 1975) by Goodwin et al[30] of 228 patients with chronic pulmonary histoplasmosis. Thirty-one people died of histoplasmosis itself, and of these, 61 percent had persistent lung cavitation. It is noteworthy that in one of the populations included in the study all but two of the 118 patients were established smokers, giving credence to the view that it is rare for histoplasmosis to affect healthy lungs.

The number of patients in the combined study (228) was too small to derive meaningful age-related mortality. However, an overall mortality ratio of 451 percent (mean age of 51 years at entry) was calculated in *Medical Risks*[9] using as a basis of comparison the 1970–74 mortality experience of men covered by group life insurance (in other words, men actively at work).

Selection of Risks

Applicants with only a few asymptomatic, non-cavitating and preferably calcified lesions of pulmonary histoplasmosis would constitute the best risk group for insurance and could be accepted at standard rates. Those with more widespread, non-cavitating lesions should be evaluated according to the extent of fibrosis as judged by pulmonary function tests. Those with persisting cavitation should be declined.

Pulmonary Histiocytosis X

The various forms of histiocytosis X (HX) are described elsewhere (*see* pp. 926–7). When the lungs alone are involved the condition is called eosinophilic granuloma of the lung or primary pulmonary HX and is comparable with solitary eosinophilic granuloma of bone. Lung shadowing is often found by chance in asymptomatic subjects if they have a chest X-ray carried out for some other purpose. Generally the extent of initial shadowing correlates well with the subsequent course of the illness, and in the most favorable cases the lung shadows disappear altogether. Such cases comprised nearly one-half of a series of 78 young adults with pulmonary HX studied retrospectively by Basset et al[31] over a ten-year period. The remaining cases deteriorated with the radiographic appearances of honeycomb fibrosis and bullous changes, and one-half of these patients died.

Selection of Risks

Carefully selected applicants with a history of pulmonary HX that has cleared spontaneously or who have limited lung shadowing that has remained stable for two to three years may be considered standard or slightly substandard insurance risks. Those with more extensive lung shadowing, or with a bullous or honeycomb appearance, should be postponed or declined, especially if systemic HX coexists.

Pneumoconiosis

Pneumoconiosis is the accumulation of dust in the lungs and the tissue reactions to its presence. Dust in this context means an aerosol composed of solid inanimate particles. The tissue reactions fall into the two categories below.

1) *Benign (non-collagenous) pneumoconiosis*: tissue reaction resulting from the inhalation of biologically inert matter, such as iron, tin oxide, barium sulphate and carbon, is minimal and normal alveolar architecture is preserved.

2) *Collagenous pneumoconiosis*: this results in permanent scarring in the lungs and is caused either by fibrogenic dust, such as silica or asbestos, or by an altered tissue response to a non-fibrogenic dust. Complicated coal worker's pneumoconiosis or progressive massive fibrosis is an example of such altered response.

Stages of Pneumoconiosis

In evaluating the risk associated with pneumoconiosis, three cardinal features must be considered together: (1) occupation, (2) the clinical history, (3) chest radiography (to which should be added pulmonary function tests). If this is not done, mistakes could be made: for example, the chest X-ray of siderosis showing small discrete rounded shadows disseminated throughout the lungs might be interpreted as silicotic nodulation and an unfavorable prognosis given if radiology were the sole criterion of diagnosis. If first it had been ascertained that the man in question was completely symptom-free and that he had been engaged in steel welding for 25 years, this misdiagnosis would not have been made. Siderosis is a benign pneumoconiosis caused by inhalation of fumes containing iron particles and has no adverse effect on longevity.

Similarly, one coal worker may have no, or minimal, radiological signs and yet suffer from exertional dyspnea, whereas another may have quite widespread, discrete nodulation and no cough or dyspnea. When symptoms are present in simple coal worker's pneumoconiosis the cause is very often something other than pneumoconiosis, such as cigarette smoking with mucus hypersecretion or the later stages of chronic obstructive bronchitis. Such complications must also be taken into account in assessing the risk associated with pneumoconiosis.

Complicated Pneumoconiosis

Progressive Massive Fibrosis

In some coal miners simple nodular fibrosis progresses to the extent that large fibrotic masses develop, eventually occupying as much as one-third of the area of each lung field on a chest radiograph. Terminal bronchioles become distorted, scar emphysema develops and dyspnea of hypercapneic type inevitably becomes more severe. Lung volumes show a restrictive pattern, and arterial hypoxia and cor pulmonale occur as late complications.

Removal from dust exposure at the stage of progressive massive fibrosis seems to make no difference to the relentless course of the disease. There is evidence that progressive massive fibrosis is due to a secondary tissue response of immunopathological type, since many of those so affected have been shown to have circulating antibodies, e.g. antinuclear, anticollagen and antiglobulins (rheumatoid factor), whereas those antibodies do not occur in exposed but unaffected individuals.[14]

Silicosis

Silicosis is a fibrogenic pneumoconiosis caused by inhaling crystalline-free silica dust. It is characterized first by nodular pulmonary fibrosis and, in its later stages, by coalescence of fibrotic areas and impairment of pulmonary function similar to the progressive massive fibrosis of coal worker's pneumoconiosis. The occupations in which silicosis is liable to occur are the mining of copper, silver, gold and hard coal, sandstone and granite quarrying and cutting, sandblasting and the manufacture of silica abrasives.

From the life insurance point of view, permanent removal from an occupational hazard is the ideal and would attract credit points in any system of rating. Often it is not possible, nor indeed desirable, on socioeconomic grounds to remove a person from the only trade or skill he knows. Much more damage may be done to health psychologically than if a person is allowed to continue working under stricter supervision for anti-dust precautions.

Rating

The figures quoted apply to all forms of pneumoconiosis except asbestosis.

1) No symptoms:
Non-collagenous pneumoconiosis (siderosis etc) — standard.
Collagenous pneumoconiosis (coal workers and all occupations in which silicosis is a hazard):

a) Uncomplicated.
Linear opacities — +0 to +25.
Small opacities: punctuate, micronodular or nodular — +50 to +75.

b) Complicated.
Large opacities — +100 to +200.

2) With symptoms.
Cough and/or dyspnea with moderate exertion — add +50.
Cough and/or dyspnea at rest or with minimal exertion — add +100.

Smoking continued — add +25.

Asbestosis

Asbestosis being a fibrogenic dust disease is also one of the pneumoconioses, but since it has unique pathogenic properties it is dealt with separately. Asbestos is an almost indispensable material in modern mechanized society. It has long been an essential ingredient of thermal, acoustic and electrical insulation products. Asbestos-containing pipes, chimneys, roofing, boards and panels have been used extensively in the building and shipbuilding industries. There is no good substitute for it in friction materials, such as brake and clutch linings, and in gaskets.

Exposure to asbestos fiber dust may occur at any stage from the mine or mill, during transportation, and during processing, application or removal of the modified product. In general, the risks are increased by handling as the fibers are broken down to a respirable size. The diseases caused by asbestos dust that are of importance in life underwriting are (1) pulmonary fibrosis, (2) carcinoma of the lung, and (3) mesothelioma.

Pulmonary Fibrosis

Asbestos fibers measuring 10–100μm in length are the most dangerous in producing the fibrotic reaction. The continued presence of this fibrogenic material in the lungs may stimulate non-specific antibodies, particularly antinuclear and rheumatoid antibodies, which accelerate the fibrotic reaction. As the disease progresses, irregular shadowing in the lower zones becomes coarser and more extensive, resulting in death from respiratory failure or cor pulmonale.

Carcinoma of the Lung

This a much commoner cause of death than pulmonary heart failure in people occupationally exposed to any type of asbestos dust. Cigarette smoking seems to be an essential cofactor; it is unusual to find carcinoma of the lung in asbestos workers who do not smoke.

Of 370 asbestos workers studied by Selikoff et al,[32] 283 had a history of regular cigarette smoking and 24 died of lung cancer within the 52-month period of the study. It was estimated that among men who smoked, only three would have died of lung cancer within the same length of time if not exposed to asbestos dust. The authors were careful to point out, however, that their findings do not prove that such exposure has no influence on lung cancer among non-smokers.

Mesothelioma of Pleura and Peritoneum

This is an invariably fatal tumor, death usually occurring within one year of diagnosis. There is a long latent period from exposure to asbestos dust — mainly the hydrous silicate of sodium and iron (crocidolite or blue asbestos) — to the onset of mesothelioma. The risk associated with exposure to amosite (brown asbestos) and chrysotile (white asbestos) is considerably lower and the latent period before appearance of the tumor longer — more than 25 years. The risk of developing mesothelioma is related to the degree of exposure of asbestos: for each tenfold increase in fiber concentration in the lung the risk increases 29·4 times for blue asbestos, 15·7 times for white and 2·3 times for brown.[33]

Australians have the highest incidence of mesothelioma in the world. Annual notifications almost tripled in the last decade, to 314 in 1990, and known deaths since 1980 number 1,455, mostly among men. According to the Australian National Institute of Occupational Health and Safety[33] a further 6000 cases of mesothelioma can be predicted over the next 20 years. The latency period of 25– 50 years between initial exposure and onset of mesothelioma means that the incidence in Australia will continue to rise until about 2010 and then fall as the tight controls on exposure implemented in the 1970s take effect.

Selection of Risks
Crocidolite is no longer used in any asbestos products manufactured in the industrialized world, but there is still the residual risk of exposure for people engaged in removing old insulating materials (which often contain large amounts of crocidolite), especially when power tools are used in the process. Mortality from asbestos and asbestos-related diseases will therefore continue at a significant level for some years to come. Also, the hazard of carcinoma of the lung will still remain a problem among workers exposed to asbestos dust who continue to smoke cigarettes, however good the current anti-dust precautions. Cigarette smoking is thus an important factor in risk selection for life insurance, but equally important is the ability of the underwriter to identify those occupations where asbestos dust is a hazard.

Rating
1) History of, or current occupational exposure to, asbestos dust; negative chest X-ray; no symptoms.

Years of exposure	Ratings Non-smoker	Cigarette smoker
Under 10	0 to +25	+75
10 or more	+50	+100

2) With radiological evidence of asbestosis.

Radiological features	Ratings Non-smoker	Cigarette smoker
Linear shadows	+75	+150
'Ground glass' shadowing in lower zones	+100	+150
Dense nodular shadowing	+150 to +300	+175 to +350

3) Calcified pleural plaques — no additional debit.

Alveolar Exudates

Widespread pulmonary fibrosis developing from alveolar exudates would be evaluated first according to the nature of the primary disease causing the exudate, or the nature of the primary disease for which an offending drug responsible for the exudate was given. Generally the primary disease in question would indicate a decline risk (e.g. chronic left ventricular failure, severe mitral stenosis, chronic nephritis or leukemia being treated with busulphan). Where, however, terms can be quoted for the primary disease, the extent of any residual pulmonary fibrosis should be assessed separately according to its extent (as judged by radiology, pulmonary function tests and symptoms) and the rating added to that of the primary disease. Fibrosis may be caused by certain drugs and therapeutic agents, such as nitrofurantoin (for urinary tract infections), sulphasalazine (ulcerative colitis), hexamethonium bromide (hypertension — no longer used) and oxygen (pre-maturity).

Pulmonary Alveolar Proteinosis

This is a rare disease of unknown etiology usually occurring in previously healthy people. Males are affected more than females, and it occurs mostly between the ages of 20 and 50. The alveoli, which are otherwise normal, are plugged with amorphous granules containing lipoproteins and plasma proteins causing reduction in vital capacity, residual volume, functional residual capacity, total lung capacity and transfer factor. The disease may be diffuse or localized and may progress, remain stable or clear spontaneously.

Depending on the degree of lung involvement, symptoms may vary from none to severe respiratory insufficiency, although extrapulmonary symptoms are rare. Fine inspiratory crepitations may be heard over affected areas, and the chest X-ray appearance is of infiltration spreading outwards from the hila. There is no hilar lymphadenopathy and the pleura are not involved.

Bronchopulmonary lavage has now been shown to be the most effective treatment, and many patients will remain symptom-free after one such treatment; others, however, may require further lavage.

Prognosis
Death is unusual in pulmonary alveolar proteinosis unless symptoms are severe and have not been treated by bronchopulmonary lavage. Patients with minor symptoms would usually be treated conservatively in the hope that spontaneous cure will ensue.

Rating
1) Treated by bronchopulmonary lavage.
Within three years of lavage — +100, reducing by 25 points each year.
After three years symptom-free — standard.

2) Treated medically.
Condition stable, but still minor symptoms — +75.

PULMONARY EOSINOPHILIA

Except for helminthic and aspergillosis infections, the cause of eosinophilic pneumonia is unknown. There is a hypersensitivity reaction in which the characteristic pathology is of alveoli filled with large mononuclear cells and eosinophils, with edema and infiltration of the interstitial spaces. The bronchioles may be plugged with mucus.

Eosinophilic pneumonias of unknown etiology are relatively benign and may be divided into the three categories below.

1) *Loeffler's syndrome*: in this syndrome there are rapidly developing and disappearing pulmonary infiltrates in various lobes at varying times accompanied by low-grade fever but few respiratory symptoms. The condition generally clears spontaneously within four weeks.

2) *Prolonged pulmonary eosinophilia*: this is similar to Loeffler's syndrome but lasts longer than four weeks. Fever and systemic symptoms may be more pronounced, but spontaneous recovery eventually ensues.

3) *Pulmonary eosinophilia accompanied by asthma*: in this case the usual treatment of asthma is indicated. Severe symptoms respond dramatically to oral corticosteroid drugs.

Rating

Standard rates would be usual after pulmonary eosinophilia has resolved and the chest X-ray has become normal. Cases complicated by asthma, especially if recurrent, should be rated as asthma according to severity.

Allergic Eosinophilic Granulomatosis of the Lungs

This is a variant of polyarteritis nodosa, and the risk should be handled accordingly (*see* p. 818).

OBSTRUCTIVE SLEEP APNEA (OSA)

In OSA the pharyngo-glottal area of the upper airway becomes blocked on inspiration, requiring a marked effort on the part of the individual to overcome the obstruction and so allow respiration to resume.

Those subject to OSA appear physically normal except for a high incidence of obesity; closer inspection may reveal a bulky tongue and a small pharyngeal lumen. There may be a history of diurnal hypersomnolence and a past tendency to noisy snoring (often reported by the spouse). In these individuals negative pressure in the pharynx during inspiration causes the posterior pharyngeal wall to collapse onto the back of the tongue causing obstruction and apnea. This negative pressure can be accentuated by partial obstruction higher up the airway, such as a deviated nasal septum, large adenoids, swollen turbinates or a broken nose.

Repeated apneas are life-endangering, causing hypoxemia and hypercapnia with cyanosis and polycythemia; if untreated, the subject either dies suddenly during a prolonged apnea or more slowly develops pulmonary hypertension, cor pulmonale and respiratory failure. Webster[34] describes the apnea index (AI) as a measure of severity of OSA, being the number of apneas lasting longer than 10 seconds per hour of sleep. These periods can be measured by a tape recorder or by the spouse. An AI of less than 10 has a better prognosis for survival than an AI of greater than 10, and there is a further reduction in survival with both indices at ages over 50 years.

Treatment

Conservative treatment, essentially weight reduction and corrective nasal surgery, suffices for most cases of mild OSA. Tracheostomy is a definitive cure and would be necessary for severe cases as a life-saving measure while other treatments are being considered. Continuous positive airway pressure (CPAP) delivered by sealed nasal canulae has been a very efficient and successful method of overcoming OSA, but uvulopalatopharyngoplasty (UPP), an operation to remove redundant pharyngeal tissue, has so far not been shown to improve survival significantly compared with tracheostomy and CPAP.[34]

Rating

Webster recommends that the life insurance risk be evaluated in terms of the AI, age and treatment modality employed. Rating philosophy varies with different insurance companies, but the following schedule is suggested:

	Rating	
Treatment	Under age 50	Over age 50
Conservative treatment		
AI<20	+50 to standard	+100
AI>20	+100	+200 up
Tracheostomy	Standard	+50 to standard
CPAP	Standard	Standard
UPP	+50	+100

Note Ratings for additional impairments (e.g. overweight, diabetes, COPD) should be added to the above.

PULMONARY TUBERCULOSIS

Tuberculosis is a curable disease, and mortality rates in technologically advanced countries now run at less than 1 per 100 thousand of the population. This would appear to be a very satisfactory state of affairs. However, there is still a residuum of active disease in certain groups, causing transmission of new infection in urban centers and among the young; this may perpetuate the tuberculosis problem, small though it is, well into the next century.[35]

There are several reasons for this. First, as the threat of tuberculosis has receded, the vast public health infrastructure for controlling the infection, which had been in place up to the 1970s, has gradually run down, and with it the diagnostic awareness and skills of management of the disease. Secondly, notification rates of tuberculosis, which had been steadily reducing both in the USA and UK since the 1960s, have leveled off because of the introduction of new infection by the large number of immigrants from developing countries where there is still a very high incidence of tuberculosis. Thirdly, a steady pool of infection exists among certain groups of the community because of poor co-operation, leading to inadequate treatment and a higher than average relapse rate (e.g. some psychiatric patients, psychopaths, alcoholics, drug abusers, the homeless, and the elderly and infirm). So long as these uncontrolled sources of infection exist there is always the likelihood of transmission of tuberculosis to contacts, especially the very young.

The risk of contracting tuberculosis is relatively high among immunocompromised individuals, such as those on long-term corticosteroid therapy, and specifically among those suffering from AIDS where drug resistance is a particular problem and where management generally is difficult because of coexistence of other opportunist infections, such as *P. carinii* and legionella pneumonia.

Factors Influencing Mortality

Adequacy of Chemotherapy
This remains by far the most important factor influencing the relapse rate and mortality in tuberculosis. Adequate treatment must now be redefined in the light of the success of modern regimes of antituberculous drugs. Rifampicin plus INAH for nine months supplemented initially by ethambutol is more acceptable than the 18–24 months of previous standard chemotherapy, is highly effective in producing sputum conversion and has resulted in no relapses over a nine-month follow-up period.[36] Such treatment is much more acceptable to patients than the old regime, which included PAS, and is much more likely to be followed without default for the shorter period.

Extent of the disease
Whether the initial tuberculous infiltration is minimal or extensive is now of little importance in prognosis. If the mycobacterium is sensitive to the drugs, an exudative lesion, however extensive, can melt away with treatment, ultimately leaving no trace of its presence.

Relapse
A person who has completed a course of chemotherapy adequate for the nature of the lesion can be considered virtually free from risk of relapse thereafter. If relapse does occur, it can usually be traced to default by the patient in taking the drugs or to

the unrecognized development of drug resistance during treatment. Relapse almost always occurs within five years of the start of the treatment.

Residual Pulmonary Fibrosis: Open-healed Cavities: Tuberculous Bronchiectasis

These lesions are virtually always relics of treatment undertaken in the era prior to adequate chemotherapy. Although the disease may have been considered healed and inactive for many years, there is always the possibility of reactivation of infection, especially if any of the risk factors mentioned earlier are present. Also, open cavities or tuberculous bronchiectasis may be secondarily invaded by fungi, such as *Aspergillus*, producing mycetomas.

Rating

Rating for a history of active tuberculosis must now be judged against a background of mortality which is negligible, particularly in groups under 60 years of age. Even in applicants who have relapsed because of default in initial treatment, or because of drug resistance or the risk factors mentioned previously, mortality would be considered standard if they have completed, without complications, a subsequent course of antituberculous chemotherapy judged to be adequate by modern standards. If there is any risk after adequate treatment, it would be the presence of open-healed cavities or significant fibrotic disease, with or without bronchiectasis.

Follow-up observation of infectious tuberculosis after primary treatment with adequate chemotherapy has been completed is now considered unnecessary.

1) Initial treatment with chemotherapy.
Within three months of commencement or until return to full-time employment (whichever is the longer) — postpone.
Thereafter, while chemotherapy continues — +2 per mil for two years.
After completion of designated course of chemotherapy, X-ray normal or minimal scarring — standard.

2) Second or subsequent course of chemotherapy following relapse from whatever cause.
Treatment with antituberculous drugs continuing — postpone.
Designated treatment completed without complications — standard.

3) Where doubts exist about the adequacy or control of treatment.
Within two years of cessation of treatment — +2 per mil for two years.

4) Residuals of tuberculosis: no active infection.
Open-healed cavity(-ies) or bronchiectasis — rate as bronchiectasis according to distribution and extent (*see* pp. 491–2).

5) Surgical treatment of tuberculosis.
Segmental resection of a lobe, lobectomy and pneumonectomy — rate as for surgical treatment of bronchiectsis (*see* pp. 492–3).
Thoracoplasty:
    Single stage (up to six ribs) — standard.

Two or more stages — +25 to +100 (according to volume of lung involved).

NON-RESPIRATORY TUBERCULOSIS

Non-respiratory tuberculosis is dealt with in those chapters covering the affected organs or tissues. Generally speaking, the risk would be evaluated first as tuberculosis-the-infection and rated similarly to respiratory tuberculosis above. Secondly the risk would be rated according to the nature and extent of any organ damage persisting after cure of the infection.

REFERENCES

1 *Statistical Bulletin*. New York: Metropolitan Life Insurance Company. Deaths from chronic obstructive pulmonary disease in the United States, 1987. Jul–Sept 1990: 20–6.
2 Mortality Statistics. Review of the Registrar General on deaths by cause, sex and age in England and Wales, 1985 (Series DH2 No 12) and 1989 (Series DH2 No 16). Office of Population Censuses and Surveys, London: HMSO.
3 Rossiter CE, Weill H. Ethnic differences in lung function: evidence for proportional differences. *Int J Epid* 1974; 3: 55–61.
4 Quanger PhH (editor). Standardized lung function testing. *Bull Physiopathol Resp* 1983; 19: Suppl. 5.
5 Morris AH (editor). Clinical pulmonary function testing. Utah: *Intermountain Thoracic Society*, 1983.
6 Centers for Disease Control *Reducing the health consequences of smoking: 25 years of progress — a report of the Surgeon General, 1989*. Rockville, Maryland: US Department of Health and Human Services, Public Health Service, 1989; DHSS Pub No (CDC) 89–8411.
7 US Department of Health and Human Services. *The health consequences of smoking: a report of the Surgeon General*. Public Health Service, Office on Smoking and Health, 1984.
8 Centers for Disease Control. Chronic disease reports. Chronic obstructive pulmonary disease mortality — United States, 1986 and State-specific smoking attributable chronic obstructive pulmonary disease mortality — United States, 1986. *MMWR* 1989. 38(32): 549–552, 552–561.
9 Lew EA, Gajewski J (editors). *Medical Risks: trends in mortality by age and time elapsed*. New York, Westport CT, London: Praeger, 1990.
10 Fletcher CM, Peto R, Tinker C, Speizer FE. *The Natural History of Chronic Bronchitis and Emphysema: an eight-year study of early chronic obstructive lung disease in working men in London*. Oxford, England: Oxford University Press, 1976.
11 *Medical Impairment Study 1983*. Vol 1. Boston: Society of Actuaries and Association of Life Insurance Medical Directors of America, 1986.
12 Fessel M. Mortality of policyholders suffering from obstructive pulmonary disease. 36th Meeting of Swiss Life Assurance Physicians, Zurich, 1984.
13 Clarke RD. Mortality of impaired lives. *J Inst Actuar* 1979: 106: 15.
14 Hudson LD. Clinical spirometry in chronic airway obstruction. *Trans Assoc Life Insur Med Dirs Am* 1972; 56: 139.
15 Thurlbeck WM, Simon G. Radiographic appearance of the chest in emphysema. *Am J Radiol* 1978; 130: 429–40.
16 Fletcher CM. The clinical prognosis of pulmonary emphysema — an experimental study. *Proc Roy Soc Med* 1952; 45: 577.
17 Speizer FE, Doll R, Heath P. Observations on recent increase in mortality from asthma. *Br Med J* 1968; 1: 335–9.
18 The nebuliser epidemic (editorial). *Lancet* 1984; 2: 789–90.

19 Buist AS, Vollmer WM. Reflections on the rise in asthma morbidity and mortality (editorial). *JAMA* 1990; 264: 1719–20.
20 Burney P. Asthma deaths in England and Wales 1931–85: evidence for a true increase in asthma mortality. *J Epidemiol Community Health* 1988; 42: 316–20.
21 Mortality Statistics 1985, England and Wales (Series DH2 No 12). Office of Population Censuses and Surveys, London: HMSO.
22 Mortality Statitistics 1989, England and Wales (Series DH2 No 16). Office of Population Censuses and Surveys, London: HMSO.
23 Hudson ME. Diseases of the respiratory system: bronchiectasis and cystic fibrosis. *Br Med J* 1978; 1: 971.
24 Butz RH. Cystic Fibrosis Mortality. *J Insur Med* 1988; 20: 14–15.
25 Iwai K, Hosada Y (editors). *Proceedings of the 6th International Conf on Sarcoidosis*. Tokyo: University Press, 1974.
26 Scadding J G. *Trans Assur Med Soc* 1966: 1.
27 John CJ, Zachary JB, Ball WC Jr. A ten-year study of corticosteroid treatment of pulmonary sarcoidosis. *Johns Hopkins Med J* 1974; 234: 271.
28 Braun SR, doPico GA, Tsiatis A, Horvath E, Dickie HA, Rankin J. Farmer's lung disease: long-term clinical and physiologic outcome. *Am Rev Respir Dis* 1979; 119: 185–91.
29 Carrington CB, Gaensler EA, Coutu RE, Fitzgerald MX, Gupta RG. Natural history and treated course of usual and desquamative interstitial pneumonia. *N Engl J Med* 1978; 298: 801–9.
30 Goodwin RA Jr, Owens FT, Snell JD *et al.* Chronic pulmonary histoplasmosis. *Medicine* 1976; 55: 413–52.
31 Basset F, Corrin B, Spencer H et al. Pulmonary histiocytosis X. *Am Rev Respir Dis* 1978; 118: 811–20.
32 Selikoff IJ, Churg J, Hammond EC. Asbestos exposure, smoking and neoplasia. *JAMA* 1968; 204: 106.
33 Pockley, P. White asbestos and mesothelioma. *Br Med J* 1991; 302: 675.
34 Webster RL. Obstructive sleep apnea: recent mortality studies and their implications. *J Insur Med* 1989; 21: 86–8.
35 Kearns TJ, Russo PT. The control and eradication of tuberculosis: a summary report from Massachusetts Department of Public Health. *N Engl J Med* 1980; 303: 812–14.
36 British Thoracic and Tuberculosis Association. Short-course chemotherapy in pulmonary tuberculosis. *Lancet* 1975; 1: 119.

CHAPTER 18

DISEASES OF THE KIDNEYS AND URINARY TRACT

HOWARD L MINUK

The kidneys are important organs and are intimately related functionally to the cardiovascular system. Diseases of the kidneys and their outflow tracts are therefore of special importance in life underwriting. In addition to primary renal diseases the kidneys may be secondarily involved in systemic disease processes; they may be congenitally deformed, or they may become diseased by lesions affecting their respective outflow tracts.

URINALYSIS

There have been changes in the type of urinalysis performed on many North American applicants within the past five years. Historically, the urine dipstick was the main method used for the detection of protein and hemoglobin (RBCs), and a microscopic urinalysis was not performed. Within the last few years most North American insurance applicants applying for amounts greater than $100,000 also have a microscopic urinalysis performed for the detection of red blood cells, white blood cells, hyaline or granular casts. Automated immunoassays are routinely employed for the detection of proteinuria. These techniques allow for the detection of protein concentrations as low as 2 mg/dl. A cut-off value of 12 mg/dl is usually employed: urines containing protein concentrations below 12 mg/dl are reported negative, whilst levels greater than 12 mg/dl are quantitated.

A specific gravity is performed with all quantitively positive protein determinations, since random urine protein concentrations are markedly influenced by the urine concentration: protein excreted into a more concentrated urine results in a higher protein measurement than the same amount of protein excreted into a dilute urine. Urines are routinely quantitated for the level of nicotine or its metabolite, cotinine, as a method of circumventing non-disclosure of cigarette smoking in insurance applicants seeking the discounted non-smoking insurance policies. Urine is also screened to detect the presence of diuretics and oral hypoglycemic agents, and many North American insurance companies are routinely screening for drugs of abuse such as cocaine. For lower amounts of insurance many North American insurance companies are using the urine HIV test to screen for AIDS.

In the UK and Europe the traditional dipstick for the detection of proteinuria and hematuria has remained, and most urines are neither subjected to microscopic urinalysis nor screened for drugs of abuse or nicotine.

A more rigorous urinalysis performed for North American insurance applicants should enhance the risk classification process, but there are no studies as yet pointing to an improved mortality experience using these protocols as compared with the traditional dipstick technology.

PROTEINURIA

When an underwriter is faced with the finding of an elevated protein determination on a single random urine specimen it is customary to repeat that urinalysis two more times. For insurance purposes, proteinuria occurring in two-thirds or more of urine specimens is considered constant or persistent; less frequent proteinuria is considered to be transient or intermittent.

Constant proteinuria is generally an indicator for the presence of renal disease and excess mortality. The *Medical Impairment Study 1983* determined that male insurance applicants who had proteinuria greater than 30 mg/dl on two or more specimens had an overall mortality ratio of 194 percent. Those issued standard insurance contracts still had a mortality ratio of 170 percent.[1] Several of the companies contributed data for constant proteinuria according to the amount of protein: for males 'small amount proteinuria' revealed a mortality ratio of 232 percent, 'moderate proteinuria' 270 percent and 'large proteinuria' 336 percent. Diseases of the heart and circulatory system were the most important causes for excess mortality. Since most of the above insurance applicants never had their proteinuria investigated, undetected glomerulonephritis, tubular interstitial nephropathy and renal vascular diseases (such as nephrosclerosis) probably contributed some of this excess mortality.

The gold standard for the detection of pathologic proteinuria is a 24-hour urine collection for the measurement of protein. The upper limit of normal is generally considered to be 150 mg;[2] amounts below this level are considered physiologic, higher amounts pathologic.

The healthy kidney contains about 1 million nephrons. Each nephron consists of a single glomerulus of capillaries with an attached renal tubule. The glomerular capillaries consist of three layers: an inner layer of endothelial cells, a mid basement membrane and an outer epithelial layer of cells called podocytes. This capillary basement membrane unit has permeability characteristics such that red blood cells, white blood cells and larger molecular weight proteins (including albumin) are relatively impervious. Due to its large size, only 500 mg of albumin are filtered in a 24-hour period; most of the filtered albumin is resorbed by healthy tubules, so that in a 24-hour period the upper limit of normal for albumin is only 30 mg.[3] Trace amounts of larger molecular weight proteins, such as immunoglobulins, enzymes and peptide hormones, are found in a normal 24-hour urine. The ability to detect such trace amounts of immunoglobulins in the urine is the basis for measurement of HIV-specific antibodies in the urine. Smaller molecular weight proteins, such as beta-2 microglobulin and lysozyme, are freely filtered through the glomerular capillary basement unit, but only small amounts are detected in the urine since these small proteins are almost completely resorbed by healthy tubules. In fact, 60 percent of all proteins found in a 24-hour urine are derived from filtered plasma proteins, albumin being the most common. The remaining 40 percent of protein found in the urine is derived from renal and urogenital tissues, the most common being Tamm-Horsfall mucoprotein.[4]

With glomerular disease the glomerular permeability to larger molecular weight proteins increases. The proteinuria, which often exceeds 2,500 mg in 24 hours (250 mg/dl assuming a one liter 24-hour urine volume), is composed mainly of albumin. With tubular interstitial disease the 24-hour proteinuria, which rarely exceeds 1,500 mg (150 mg/dl assuming a 1 liter 24 hour urine volume), is composed mainly of smaller molecular weight filterable proteins (dependent on resorption by healthy tubules). The 24-hour albumin is never more than 500 mg (50 mg/dl).

The finding of proteinuria on a routine single specimen for insurance purposes is not uncommon. When two subsequent urinalyses are repeated without any attention to posture or activity, and are negative, the insurance applicant is felt to have transient or intermittent proteinuria. In some applicants, particularly females, this may be on the basis of vaginal contamination of the urine. In others this benign transient proteinuria may occur as a consequence of a highly concentrated urine, exercise, febrile illnesses, stress or exposures to cold. This type of transient proteinuria may be termed functional, and a long-term prognosis is considered to be favorable. Normal renal biopsies are found in the majority of such individuals.[5]

The finding of constant proteinuria is more likely to indicate renal disease. When subjected to a complete evaluation some individuals with constant proteinuria are found to have glomerular, tubular interstitial, or vascular renal disease. However, others have a benign urinalysis and a completely negative evaluation. Such individuals are considered to have constant isolated proteinuria, but if they should undergo renal biopsies, abnormalities will be present that are likely to contribute to excess mortality. Biopsy findings are generally heterogeneous with minor abnormalities noted in the glomeruli and/or interstitial regions.[5] For underwriting purposes it is generally felt that the higher the average proteinuria reading in individuals with presumed isolated constant proteinuria, the worse the mortality.

Orthostatic Proteinuria

Orthostatic proteinuria refers to the entity characterized by the presence of proteinuria when the individual is upright (during the day) but absence of proteinuria in the supine position. Such orthostatic proteinuria is defined as fixed and reproducible when it is consistently present in the upright position but consistently absent in the supine position. The total daily excretion of protein is generally low, below 1·5 g in 24 hours. The significance of fixed orthostatic proteinuria remains somewhat controversial.[5] Biopsy studies of some of these individuals have demonstrated alterations in renal glomeruli and tubules in about 50 percent.[6] Nonetheless, 20-year follow-up studies thus far have been favorable, without any excess mortality. One 50-year follow-up of six people also revealed no excess mortality.[7] A follow-up of 127 individuals revealed proteinuria persisting less than five years in 52 percent, five to ten years in 25 percent and greater than ten years in 23 percent.[7] Several studies have demonstrated an increased frequency of renal anomalies in people with fixed reproducible orthostatic proteinuria. It appears at present that the mortality is favorable in this group of individuals, but a sophisticated evaluation is necessary to separate this condition from the increase in proteinuria seen with orthostasis in people with chronic, serious renal disease.

In one particular study of 27 individuals with renal disease and proteinuria, standing increased the random urine protein concentration by as much as tenfold.[8] In one individual with chronic renal disease, standing for 90 minutes increased the urine protein concentration from 24 mg/dl to 247 mg/dl. The mean increase in proteinuria in these individuals with orthostasis was from 36 mg/dl to 121 mg/dl. An important distinguishing feature between this group of individuals having excess mortality and the more favorable fixed reproducible orthostatic proteinuria is that in the former most of the individuals had an abnormal renal sediment examination and all individuals had the presence of supine proteinuria, albeit in small amounts in some.

Transient orthostatic proteinuria is an entity characterized by the intermittent occurrence of orthostatic proteinuria. This is the most common type of orthostatic proteinuria, occurring in 70–75 percent of all individuals with orthostatic proteinuria. Long-term studies of this group of individuals are rare, but it is generally considered that this entity is favorable, and this is supported by the fact that most kidney biopsies are completely normal. It is considered that some of these individuals may, in fact, have the transient functional proteinuria noted previously due to exercise, fever, stress, or exposure to cold.[5]

Urine Sediment

A urine sediment evaluation is an important component of any microscopic urinalysis. The nephron segments produce a peculiar protein of unknown biologic function, known as the Tamm-Horsfall protein, which gels at high urine concentrations or when exposed to albumin, red blood cells, tubular cells or debris. As the protein gels, it traps whatever is in its vicinity. The casts are named for their contents, such as a red blood cell cast, a leucocyte cast, an epithial cell cast, a granular cast or a fatty cast. Empty casts are called hyaline casts. Red blood cell casts define nephronal hematuria and are essentially pathognomonic for proliferative glomerulonephritis. Leucocyte casts occur with proliferative glomerulonephritis or other imflammatory conditions, such as pyelonephritis or tubular interstitial nephritis. Epithelial casts are composed entirely of tubular epithial cells and may occur with acute tubular injury, glomerulonephritis or the nephrotic syndrome. Leucocyte or epithelial cell debris may cause granular casts, and this may occur with glomerular or tubular interstitial disease. Fatty casts (which are really hyaline casts containing fat droplets) and epithelial casts occur with massive proteinuria. Hyaline casts occur in normal people after exercise or with dehydration; they may also be seen with glomerular proteinuria. Waxy casts are casts that have remained stagnant in the tubules long enough to become completely homogenized. They are usually indicators of advanced renal failure. Pyuria in the urine sediment usually indicates infection somewhere in the urogenital tract. Hematuria is discussed below.

Quantitative and Qualitative Measurement of Proteinuria

Quantitative measurement of protein refers to the utilization of sensitive radioimmunoassays for the measurement of protein concentration in the urine. These techniques are automated and highly sensitive. Most insurance applicants have a protein concentration of 2–9 mg/dl. This would be reported as negative (many insurance laboratories report any protein concentration of less than 12 mg/dl as negative).

Qualitative measurement of urine protein refers to the use of dipstick methodology to determine proteinuria. The technique is cheap, easy to perform but clearly lacks the sensitivity of a quantitative immunoassay. The sensitivity of the technique is reputed to be 80–90 percent, which means that false negative occur 10–20 percent of the time. The lowest level of detection, a trace, corresponds to 15–25 mg/dl, 1+ represents around 25–35 mg/dl, 2+ represents 35–100 mg/dl, and 3+ and 4+ usually indicate 300 and 1,000 mg/dl.[2,4] These differing levels of proteinuria are detected by a color change from yellow to deepening shades of green with increasing proteinuria.

False negative values for protein occur when the urine is dilute, since pathological amounts of protein may be diluted below the level detectable by this method (about 15 mg/dl). False negative results may also be seen with dipsticks because of their relative insensitivity to proteins other than albumin.[2] Additionally, dipsticks may be falsely negative in tubular proteinuria where non-albumin proteins predominate. False positives occur with highly concentrated urines, gross hematuria and in urinary tract infections with urea-splitting organisms. One study found that in random urine samples from patients where 24-hour urine protein was definitely abnormal (150 mg to 1000 mg), 19 percent of the dipstick results were false negative and 30 percent were trace positive of questionable significance.[9] Therefore it appears that the dipstick methodology significantly underestimates the presence of pathologic proteinuria.

A major problem with quantitative measurements of random urine specimens is that repeat values may differ widely. This is not surprising since urine protein concentration may be markedly influenced by posture, exercise, febrile illnesses and, most importantly, by urine concentration.[8] Additional studies have also demonstrated that the protein excretion by a kidney differs according to the time of day, being lowest during the sleeping hours and highest in the late afternoon.[10]

Protein-to-Creatinine Ratio

This ratio represents the protein concentration in a single random urine divided by the creatinine concentration in the random urine. It has been widely used in clinical medicine since a 1983 report indicated that this measurement actually approximates the amount of protein that would be present in an individual's urine had it been collected for a period of 24 hours.[11] Other studies have validated this approach, and in clinical medicine the cumbersome time-honored 24-hour urine protein is often being replaced by a random urine protein-to-creatinine ratio. In insurance medicine one North American laboratory has been providing this ratio since 1990.

If an individual, for example, had a random urine protein concentration of 100 mg/dl and urine creatinine concentration of 150 mg/dl, the urine protein-to-creatinine ratio would be 0·67 g of protein for every 1 g of creatinine. Since about 1 g of creatinine is found in a 24-hour urine, the 0·67 g of protein equates to the amount of protein that would be found in the urine had it been collected for a period of 24 hours. Detailed analysis of this test has appeared in the more recent clinical literature between 1970 and 1989, and in insurance literature in 1991.[9-16]

Numerous studies suggest that the upper limit of normal for a protein-to-creatinine ratio is 0·2. This refers to 0·2 g of protein, or 200 mg of protein in a 24-hour urine. For underwriting purposes, glomerular proteinurias are suggested when the protein-to-creatinine ratio is greater than 1·5, whereas tubular interstitial, glomerular, orthostatic or isolated proteinurias have ratios between 0·2 and 1·5.

Rating for Proteinuria

Intermittent Proteinuria
Proteinuria present in one out of three specimens — +0.

Constant Proteinuria
Proteinuria present in two or more specimens.[a] The mean rating applies.

mg/dl	Rating
1–25	+0
26–50	+25
51–75	+50
76–100	+100
101–150	+150
Greater than 150	Decline

[a]Credit for a specific gravity greater than 1·030 for each level of proteinuria; debit 25 for specific gravity less than 1·005 for each level of proteinuria.

If protein-to-creatinine ratios are given and proteinuria is constant, it would be preferable to use the mean protein-to-creatinine ratio to determine the rating for proteinuria. The following ratings apply:[a]

Mean protein-to-creatinine ratio	Rating
Less than 0·20	+0
0·21–0·50	+25
0·51–0·75	+50
0·76–1·00	+75
1·01–1·50	+100
1·51–2·00	+150
Greater than 2·01	Decline

[a]If the mean protein concentration is less than or equal to 15 mg/dl the rating is +0 regardless of the calculated protein-to-creatine ratio.

Proteinuria Complicated by Other Findings
Elevated blood pressure — the sum of the ratings for proteinuria and hypertension should be increased by 1/4.

Abnormalities of Urinary Sediment
1) Hyaline casts — +0.
2) Granular casts:

Casts per slide	Rating
Less than 10	+0
Greater than 10	+50

3) Red blood cell casts — rate as glomerulonephritis.
4) Pyuria:

Cells per high power field (HPF)	Rating
Less than 20	+0
21–40	+25
Greater than 40	+50

Orthostatic Proteinuria
1) Investigated, normal renal function:
   Transient or intermittent — +0.
   Fixed reproducible:
      24-hour protein less than 1·5 g (protein-to-creatinine ratio less than 1·5) — +0.
      Greater than 1·5 g — +100
   With abnormal renal function — decline.
2) Not investigated, normal renal function — use ratings for constant proteinuria.
3) Abnormal renal function — decline.

HEMATURIA

Asymptomatic Hematuria

The presence of blood in the urine is always cause for alarm as it may be a harbinger for serious genital urinary diseases such as a tumor or glomerulonephritis. Hematuria is called gross or macroscopic when it can be detected by the human eye. When it cannot be detected by the human eye it is considered to be microscopic.

It is not uncommon in the insurance setting for hematuria to be detected during the medical or paramedical examination by a routine dipstick. This chemical test is highly sensitive for the presence of hemoglobin in the urine. False positives may occur in rare situations where myoglobin is found in the urine. The color change is relatively easy to assess: different color shades corresponding to trace, 1+, 2+, 3+, and 4+, are indicators of increasing amounts of hematuria. When freshly voided urines are centrifuged and the sediment microscopically analysed for red blood cell quantification, an approximate relationship between the chemical dipstick and microscopic findings can be ascertained (*see* Table 18.1).

Table 18.1. Approximate relationship between chemical dipstick and microscopic findings.

Dipstick	Microscopic (RBC per HPF)
Trace	0–2
1+	3–5
2+	6–10
3+	11–20
4+	>20

However, two important factors influence this relationship. Firstly, when the urine is dilute it would not be unexpected to find fewer red blood cells (RBC) per high power field (HPF) for each respective degree of dipstick positivity. The reverse is true for highly concentrated urines: higher numbers of RBC are found for each dipstick reading. The second factor influencing this relationship is the length of time between voidance of urine and microscopic urinalysis. Once more than 48 hours have elapsed, progressive RBC distintegration occurs. It is not unusual for life insurance applicants to have a delay of some four days or longer between voidance of urine and the microscopic analysis. This delay leads to an underestimation of hematuria by the microscopic method. As many as 15–20 RBC per HPF may disintegrate and hence not be detected microscopically when 'outdated' urines are analyzed. The dipstick is actually preferable in these settings since hemolyzed red blood cells not detectable microscopically will yield positive dipstick reactions.

It is important to emphasize that sources of urine contamination with blood should always be considered. In young women menstruation should always be suspected. Therefore it is customary to repeat the urinalysis, preferably on two more occasions, to determine whether the hematuria is intermittent or constant. Most cases of gross hematuria usually will have been investigated previously, and the source and cause for the bleeding will have been found. It should be noted that red cells can enter the urinary system anywhere from the glomerulus to the urethral meatus, and therefore the cause for hematuria may reflect abnormalities in the kidneys, ureters, bladder, prostate in the male, and in the urethra. Red blood cells arising from the glomerulus must penetrate the glomerular basement membrane. The tight squeeze through this capillary unit may result in distortion of the shape of the red blood cells in the urine. The finding of such dysmorphic red blood cells is an indicator of glomerular origin for hematuria. Hematuria may be caused by disorders such as infections, kidney or bladder tumors, urinary tract stones or glomerulonephritis, or genetically acquired disorders such as polycystic kidney disease, Alport's syndrome or benign familial hematuria (BFH). Although most insurance companies do not finance the investigation of individuals with asymptomatic microscopic hematuria, it is customary to obtain an attending physician's statement (APS) or medical attendant's report (MAR) to determine at least the duration of the problem and to ascertain exactly what investigations have been done. Certainly a diagnosis of a urinary tract tumor or proliferative glomerulonephritis would be highly unlikely if there was a long-standing history of stable microscopic hematuria in a healthy individual without a family history of hematuria, other urinary sediment abnormalities (such as red blood cell casts) and without complicating proteinuria or hypertension, and with normal renal function.

It is not uncommon for an applicant who has been declined or postponed for life insurance because of asymptomatic hematuria to return following a negative investigation. This investigation may have included a cystosopy to exclude urethral, prostate or bladder inflammation or tumors, and an ultrasound to exclude changes in renal morphology, which may result from renal tumors, polycystic kidney disease, chronic glomerulonephritis or chronic tubular interstitial renal disease.

In BFH[17,18] one or more individuals in a family have persisting hematuria. Light microscopic findings are rare, but electron microscopy reveals extensive diffuse thinning of the glomerular basement membranes. The clinical course of such individuals has been generally considered benign without progression to chronic renal failure; however, a recent report revealed three individuals with this entity developing progressive renal insufficiency. This disorder needs to be differentiated from Alport's syndrome,[19] which is manifested initially by recurrent microscopic hematuria, usually progressing to terminal renal failure in the second or third decade of life. This is usually accompanied by an associated disorder of sensorineural deafness, but the latter finding may not be present in one of the genetic variants. Renal biopsy reveals fairly characteristic electron microscopic findings consisting of a fragmented, split glomerular basement membrane.

Rating

Even when the cause of the hematuria is not known, it may be possible, at the discretion of the medical director (MD), to offer terms for life insurance on the basis of several urine dipsticks and/or the mean count of the red cells in several specimens of urine; this would be combined with his clinical impression that a tumor in the genitourinary system is unlikely. The following ratings may be applied with either dipstick or microscopic hematuria.

1) Microscopy (RBC/HPF) and/or dipstick result, no proteinuria:

Microscopy	Dipstick	Rating
1 to 5	Trace, 1+	+0
6 to 20	2+	+25 to +50
21 to 50	3+	+50 to +75
Over 50	4+	Refer to MD

When discrepant results occur due to the presence of a dipstick and/or a microscopic, use the rating for microscopic when the urinalysis is analyzed within 48 hours of voiding; for older urines the ratings for the dipstick apply.
2) Hematuria with proteinuria — refer to MD (*see* glomerulonephritis).
3) History of hematuria.
Negative investigation:
Current specimen negative — consider +0.
Current specimen positive — credit 25 to the above ratings.
Positive investigation — rate for cause.
4) Benign familial hematuria (BFH).
With normal renal function and proteinuria:

mg/dl	Rating
Less than 25	+50
25–75	+100
Greater than 75	Decline

5) Alport's syndrome — decline.

RENAL FUNCTION

Renal function refers to the ability of the kidney to eliminate waste products. Nitrogenous waste products are filtered through the glomerulus and are eliminated in the urine. In the clinical setting, a 24-hour urine is often collected to measure the creatinine clearance as an estimate for the glomerular filtration rate. The normal glomerular filtration rate of young men and women averages 125 and 115 ml per minute respectively. At ages over 65 there is a gradual but natural loss of nephrons, so that the glomerular filtration rate becomes only about 70 percent of that of younger adults. When significant glomerular disease and/or tubular interstitial disease occurs, filtration is reduced and waste products, such as creatinine and blood urea nitrogen (BUN), increase in the blood. Such rises are bad prognostic indicators for individuals with renal disease. However, significant renal function abnormalities may be present before any rises in creatinine or BUN occur, since the creatinine clearance or the glomerular filtration rate must be reduced to about 50 percent of normal before rises in serum creatinine or BUN[3] are seen. Therefore it is apparent that the earliest rises in creatinine and BUN will underestimate the existing impairment of renal function. However, slight rises in creatinine need not be due to renal disease. Creatinine may increase after the ingestion of cooked meat (creatinine is formed from creatin during cooking and is absorbed) or from medications such as aspirin, cimetidine, trimethoprim and sulphamethoxazole (Septra, Septrin, Bactrim) which lead to an impairment of tubular secretion of creatinine. Additionally, heavily muscled men may produce more creatinine than normal individuals and typically have creatinine levels at the higher end of normal or slightly above the accepted normal range. BUN is less specific than creatinine as an indicator for renal disease. BUN elevations with normal renal function may occur in individuals consuming high protein diets, with gastrointestinal (GI) bleeding, or secondary to diuretic medication. Conversely, low BUN levels in the presence of deteriorated renal function may occur with low protein diets; low BUN levels may also occur with impaired liver function, since urea is synthesized in the liver.

Rating

In general, individuals with renal insufficiency secondary to any type of disease are not considered for life insurance. However, individuals who have had an acute bout of renal insufficiency with complete recovery could be considered at the discretion of the MD.

GLOMERULONEPHRITIS

Glomerulonephritis refers to disease processes resulting in glomerular injury and inflammation. When the damage occurs to the glomerulus largely as a result of a disease confined to the kidney, the term primary glomerulopathy is used. Immunological mechanisms appear to be pathogenically responsible for glomerular injury in these disorders. Experimental injection of antiglomerular basement membrane antibodies into animals reproduces the clinical syndrome.[5] Advances in light and electron microscopy, combined with newer immunofluorescent techniques, have resulted in a better understanding of the histopathological processes resulting in glomerular injury.

The glomerulus is able to respond to injury only in a finite number of ways, which lend themselves to clinical entities such as acute glomerulonephritis, the nephrotic syndrome, rapidly progressive glomerulonephritis or asymptomatic urinary abnormalities. As far as a bout of acute glomerulonephritis is concerned, when recovery is complete the underwriting handling of this problem would be straightforward. At the other end of the spectrum are applicants with the rapidly progressive glomerulonephritis and renal insufficiency, who would be declined. However, problems arise when applicants present with an active urine sediment consisting of red blood cells, red blood cell casts, and proteinuria with or without a prior history of glomerulonephritis. Such individuals might be labeled as having asymptomatic urinary abnormalities following a bout of acute glomerulonephritis, or they may be given a diagnosis of chronic glomerulonephritis. It is in these situations that renal histopathology can be used as a predictor for subsequent morbidity and mortality.

Pathologic Clinical Correlation

Glomerulonephritis may be classified histopathologically as either non-proliferative or proliferative. The three types of non-proliferative glomerulonephritis are minimal change glomerulopathy, focal and segmental glomerular sclerosis, and membranous glomerulopathy. There are five types of proliferative glomerulopathy: focal IgA-IgG proliferative (Berger's), mesangioproliferative, membranoproliferative glomerulonephritis, acute glomerulonephritis and crescentic glomerulonephritis. Each of these types may be produced by a systemic disease (*see* Table 18.2).

Table 18.2. Systemic illness associated with glomerular diseases.[3]

Morphology	Systemic diseases
Minimal change glomerulopathy	Hodgkin's and non-Hodgkin's lymphomas Interstitial nephritis due to non-steroidal anti-inflammatory agents (e.g. fenoprofen)
Mesangioproliferative glomerulonephritis	Henoch-Schönlein purpura Systemic lupus erythematosus Resolving post-infectious glomerulonephritis Diabetes mellitus
Focal and segmental glomerular sclerosis/hyalinosis	Heroin abuse Healed focal proliferative lesions due to systemic lupus erythematosus, systemic vasculitis, bacterial endocarditis Hemodynamic factors related to nephron loss: vesicoureteric reflux, aging, unilateral renal agenesis, sickle cell disease Schistosomiasis (mansoni)
Membranous glomerulopathy	Infections: syphilis, malaria, hepatitis B Autoimmune diseases: systemic lupus erythematosus, rheumatoid arthritis Cancer Drugs (e.g. gold, penicillamine, captopril)
Membranoproliferative glomerulonephritis Type I	Related to infections (e.g. bacterial endocarditis, 'shunt nephritis', visceral infections, schistosomiasis, malaria, hepatitis B) Chronic lymphocytic leukemia, lymphoma Systemic lupus erythematosus Cryoglobulinemia Congenital complement deficiency
Type II	Partial lipodystrophy
Acute glomerulonephritis	Viral and bacterial infection Systemic lupus erythematosus, systemic vasculitis Henoch-Schönlein purpura

Morphology	Systemic diseases
Crescentic glomerulonephritis	
Type I	Goodpasture's syndrome
Type II	Related to infections (e.g. poststreptococcal glomerulonephritis, bacterial endocarditis, bacterial sepsis or visceral infection, hepatitis B)
	Systemic lupus erythematosus
	Henoch-Schönlein purpura
	Systemic vasculitis

Minimal Change Glomerulopathy

Minimal change glomerulopathy is distinguished by the relative absence of abnormal findings on light microscopy. Because the proximal tubules may contain lipid droplets the lesion was originally called lipoid nephrosis. By electron microscopy, minimal change glomerulopathy is characterized by fusion of the glomerular epithelial cell foot processes. Immunofluorescence is unremarkable. Clinically, individuals present with edema and nephrotic-range proteinuria. Hypoalbuminemia and hyperlipidemia characterize the laboratory picture. Of individuals presenting with the nephrotic syndrome, minimal change glomerulopathy will be found in 90 percent of children under the age of six and in 20 percent of adults. Microscopic hematuria occurs in a minority, whilst gross hematuria is rare.

Prognostically, 90 percent of children and a somewhat smaller percentage of adults will respond within one month to high doses of prednisone. Failure to respond should raise suspicion of another disease entity, especially focal and segmental glomerular sclerosis. Of those who respond initially, 60 percent will have relapses, which can be treated either with repeat doses of prednisone or with the immunosuppressant cyclophosphamide.[20] Death from complications is now rare, although the International Study of Kidney Disease in Children (ISKDC) has demonstrated that excess mortality from complications still exists. Of the ten children who died in the ISKDC followed for seven to 15 years, six died from infection and one died from a dural sinus thrombosis.[21] In Cameron's own study of 183 unselected children with the nephrotic syndrome and biopsy-proven minimal lesion disease, there were 11 deaths during the subsequent 15- to 22-year follow-up.[22] Seven of those deaths were related to the nephrotic syndrome or its treatment, including infections, septicemia and hypovolemia. The only death in the past eight years in this group was a boy who suffered brain infarction from a sagittal sinus thrombosis during relapse.

Focal and Segmental Glomerular Sclerosis

Of adults and children with nephrotic syndrome, 10–20 percent will reveal microscopic changes consistent with focal and segmental glomerular sclerosis (or FSGS). This entity may represent the end stage of the way a glomerulus is able to respond to a number of insults (see Fig. 18.1). Many nephrologists believe that focal and segmental glomerular sclerosis in children is a distinct clinical pathologic entity, especially when found in biopsies early in the course of a patient's disease. Light microscopy reveals the presence of sclerotic changes in portions of some, but not all, of the glomeruli; hence the term segmental and focal. Advanced lesions may become sclerotic and eventually involve the entire glomerulus. By immunofluorescent microscopy, IgM and a complement component are commonly found in the affected area.

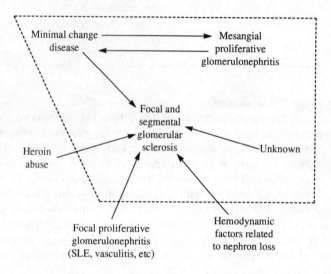

Fig. 18.1. Causes of focal and segmental gomerular sclerosis/hyalinosis.[3]

Nephrotic individuals with focal and segmental glomerular sclerosis cannot be distinguished from patients with other underlying histopathology on clinical grounds, although the diagnosis may be suspected on the basis of failure to respond to steroids, presence of hypertension, renal insufficiency and gross hematuria. Additionally, the glomerulus in this entity is freely permeable both to albumin and larger molecular weight proteins such as gammaglobulins, whereas the proteinuria of minimal lesion disease tends to be more selective; that is, proportionately more albumin is found in the urine than gammaglobulin. Approximately 50 percent of individuals will be in renal failure within ten years of the diagnosis. However, 20 percent of individuals show steroid responsiveness, which carries a more favorable prognosis. One study suggests that only 10 percent of such responders are in renal failure after six years of follow-up, compared with 53 percent of non-responders. The presentation with non-nephrotic-range proteinuria is also associated with a markedly better prognosis (*see* Fig. 18.2).

Membranous Glomerulopathy

This is the most common morphologic lesion causing the nephrotic syndrome in adults, with incidence ranging from 17 to 42 percent of all adult cases of nephrotic syndrome. This entity is defined by its microscopic findings. By light microscopy,

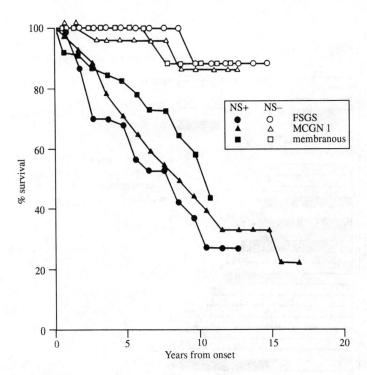

Fig. 18.2. Survival in patients with and without a nephrotic syndrome at onset.

glomeruli tend to be uniformly involved and lesions are generally confined to the basement membrane. The glomeruli may appear normal in the earlier stages; later in the disease the glomerular basement membrane becomes thickened, and immunofluorescent microscopy always reveals granular deposition of IgG and complement along the capillary walls. In some cases due to secondary diseases, deposits of known antigens, such as DNA, thyroglobulin, tumor-associated antigens or hepatitis B, may be found.

The majority of individuals are more than 35 years of age and the onset is insidious without a prior infection. Over 80 percent present with massive proteinuria and the overt nephrotic syndrome; the other 20 percent have asymptomatic proteinuria and microscopic hematuria.[3] Depression of serum complement, circulating immune complexes or anti-DNA should suggest a diagnosis of secondary lupus. Of older patients with membranous nephropathy, 6–11 percent will have cancer, usually of the gastrointestinal tract.

Prognostically, 10–30 percent of adults with nephrotic syndrome from membranous glomerulopathy experience a complete and lasting remission of proteinuria and maintain a stable level of renal function. A life table analysis from Guy's Hospital[22] (*see* Fig. 18.2) shows a ten-year survival of 40 percent in individuals presenting with nephrotic syndrome; survival in the minority presenting with lower-level proteinuria is about 88 percent in ten years. The longer-term follow-up of individuals with membranous nephropathy suggests that this disease is very indolent and that terminal renal failure may eventually occur after more than 20 years. The clinical

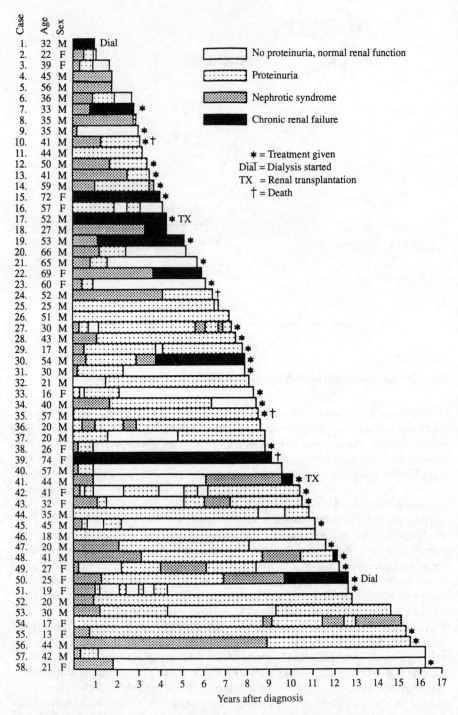

Fig. 18.3. Clinical course of the patients who were followed up for one year or more after the first renal biopsy.[23]

course of 58 individuals is revealed in Figure 18.3. This data does emphasize the fact that when the urinalysis has been normal for five years remissions are sustained.

The long-term prognosis of patients on a very short course of steroids remains to be determined. Many experts, however, do advocate a trial of steroid treatment for adults with recently diagnosed idiopathic membranous glomerulonephropathy, nephrotic syndrome and normal serum creatinine concentration. When renal function deteriorates, the use of immunosuppressants, such as cyclophosphamide, may stabilize the disease; however, the natural history remains unaltered.

Acute Glomerulonephritis

Acute glomerulonephritis is a clinical syndrome and is characterized by the sudden onset of hematuria, proteinuria, declining renal function, edema, hypertension and, occasionally, pulmonary edema.[24] The prototype of this disease is acute poststreptococcal glomerulonephritis. Although the classic presentation of acute nephritis is common, insurance applicants may present with mild disease and exhibit only asymptomatic urinary abnormalities. Of those with symptomatic acute nephritis, 50 percent will excrete less than 500 mg of protein per day; 25 percent will produce greater amounts, between 500 and 3,000 mg, over a 24-hour period.

Pathogenically acute poststreptoccocal glomerulonephritis is probably an example of antigen-antibody immune complex disease with deposition in the renal glomeruli and subsequent inflammation.

The long-term prognosis of individuals with poststreptococcal glomer-ulonephritis remains controversial. A study from Trinidad, mainly of children, reveals that only 3·6 percent of 534 patients followed for 12 to 17 years had asymptomatic urinary abnormalities and that none of them had an elevated serum creatinine.[25] This contrasts with the results of a New York study which followed 168 patients for up to 15 years with the finding that 50 percent had evidence of chronic renal impairment as evidenced by proteinuria and hypertension.[26] Six patients were uremic and one-third had mild elevations of serum creatinine. The Trinidad experience actually mirrored large pediatric study groups with post-streptococcal glomerulonephritis in Minnesota and Texas. This has led to the generalization that the long-term prognosis in children is good, but poorer in adults. It was also felt that the poor long-term prognosis in the New York study may well have reflected more severe acute disease in these patients, all of whom were hospitalized. Those individuals destined to develop chronic renal dysfunction generally tend to have a more severe acute illness followed by a second phase usually marked by persistent urinary abnormalities, hypertension and, finally, diminished renal function. Focal and segmental glomerular sclerosis are late histopathologic findings preceding renal insufficiency. The importance of these studies for underwriting purposes lies in the fact that individuals with asymptomatic non-nephrotic-range proteinuria may have a progressive disease whose natural history is only revealed after 15–20 years.

Berger's Disease

Worldwide, Berger's disease is the most common form of primary glomerular disease. In Japan, Australia and France Berger's disease accounts for 20–50 percent of all primary glomerular diseases. Individuals may present with gross or microscopic hematuria immediately following an upper respiratory tract infection.[27] Myalgias and fatigue are common. Frank nephrotic syndrome and acute glomerulonephritis are rare clinical presentations in most studies.

Pathologically, most patients with Berger's disease have mild mesangial hypercellularity associated with IgA or IgG deposition. Similar histopathologic findings are noted in Henoch-Schönlein purpura and in the glomerulonephritis associated with liver disease. The disorder was first described by Berger and Hinglais in 1968. Since that time many reports of large series of patients have emerged; it is now clear that although this disease was initially considered to be quite benign and innocent, significant numbers may actually progress to end-stage renal failure.[27,28]

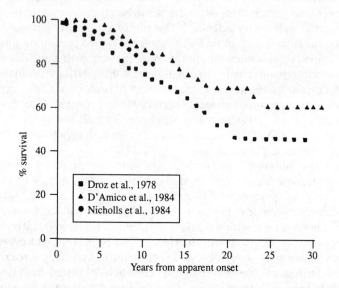

Fig. 18.4. Life table analysis of the survival of renal function in patients with IgA-associated nephropathy. Data from these series are shown: Droz et al 1978, D'Amico et al 1984 and Nicholls et al 1984. It can be seen that, in general, the evolution of IgA-associated disease into renal failure in adults is slower than for other forms of idiopathic glomerulonephritis.[22]

Most papers on IgA-associated disease in adults suggest that Berger's disease is usually an indolent disease, with the entry into renal failure taking up to 20 or 30 years. Several large series of patients suffering from IgA nephropathy have been reported, and the long-term outcome is indicated in Figure 18.4. Additionally, the largest collected Japanese series of Katajima et al involving 1,394 adult-onset patients followed up for a mean of 39 months indicates that 8 percent (or 112) had gone into chronic renal failure or died, while a further 18 percent had progressive disease with reduction in renal function.[29] There are few data on the proportion of individuals going into a complete remission and one study did suggest that it was under 10 percent. At present, it is clear that at least 25 percent of patients, and possibly up to 50 percent, will eventually end up in renal failure, but what proportion of the remaining group will develop renal failure subsequently is not known.[27,30]

Poor prognostic features in individuals with Berger's disease, who often present with asymptomatic microscopic or macroscopic hematuria and proteinuria, include an onset of proteinuria that is greater than 2 g in 24 hours, hypertension and onset in an older age group. At the histological level, crescents, glomerular sclerosis and interstitial damage are bad features.

Mesangioproliferative Glomerulonephritis

This remains an ill defined entity where mesangioproliferative change occurs without IgG or IgA deposition. It may not be possible clinically to differentiate this group from Berger's glomerulonephritis, and the indications are, once again, that this is a chronic indolent disease with significant percentages progressing to renal failure.

Crescentic Glomerulonephritis

This clinical syndrome is also called rapidly progressive gomerulonephritis, extracapillary proliferative glomerulonephritis or subacute gomerulonephritis. There are at least two types of this disease. In Type I disease, making up one-third of all patients with rapidly progressive glomerulonephritis, there is linear deposition of antiglomerular basement membrane antibodies on the glomeruli.[3] In Type II disease the antiglomerular basement membrane antibodies are not present; immune complex mediated diseases may be present. Of individuals with crescentic glomerulonephritis, 60 percent have primary renal disease; the remainder have systemic disorders such as Goodpasture's syndrome (Type I crescentic glomerulonephritis and pulmonary hemorrhage), collagen vascular disease or post-infective glomerulonephritis. Primary renal crescentic glomerulonephritis begins insidiously with signs and symptoms of uremia and fluid retention. Myalgias, fever and abdominal pain are common, but the features of nephrotic syndrome are uncommon. These symptoms may not differ significantly from crescentic glomerulonephritis attributable to secondary causes.

Five-year survival rates for Types I and II are 50–60 percent.[31] Various combinations of therapy, including prednisone, cyclophosphamide and plasma exchange, have been tried and may successfully halt disease progression. In the long term, survivors may function normally with mild chronic renal insufficiency; this, however, may progress at a later time. Complete remissions are rare.

Membranoproliferative Glomerulonephritis

This disorder is also known as mesangiocapillary glomerulonephritis (MCGN) or lobular glomerulonephritis. About 10 percent of individuals with the nephrotic syndrome will have lesions that characterize membranoproliferative glomerulonephritis on biopsy. In this disorder proliferative change occurs in the mesangial region as well as in the glomerular capillary walls. Histopathologically, it has been separated into several subclasses on the basis of electron microscopic findings.

In Type I disease, or classic membranoproliferative glomerulonephritis, enlargement of the mesangial matrix occurs to such a degree that prominent lobules are formed. Electron-dense deposits are found in the subendothelial region. In Type II disease, also known as dense deposit disease, the glomerular basement membrane is markedly thickened and contains dense deposits. Light microscopic changes are similar in both types.

Of individuals with both types of glomerulonephritis, 50 percent present with heavy proteinuria and nephrotic syndrome, 30 percent with asymptomatic proteinuria and 20 percent with acute glomerulonephritis. Diminished renal function, hypertension and progression to nephrotic syndrome are poor prognostic features. The disorder most commonly occurs in individuals between the ages of five and 30. The ten-year actuarial survival of renal function varies between 40 and 70 percent (see Fig. 18.5). Survival is worse when presentation is with the nephrotic syndrome (see Fig. 18.2).

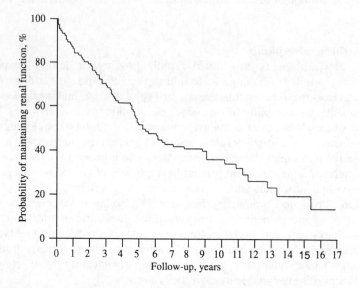

Fig. 18.5 Probability of maintaining renal function (survival curve) in 220 patients with Type I membranoproliferative glomerulonephritis.[32]

In the longer term, one study of 220 patients[33] revealed that preservation of normal renal function for 17 years occurred in only 10 percent (see Fig. 18.5).

Treatment is a matter of debate; some studies have claimed success using combinations of steroids, antiplatelet agents and indomethacin. The best treated survival figures shown in Figure 18.6 are from the Cincinatti experience using alternate day prednisone.[34] Cumulative renal survival is 60 percent at 20 years.

Chronic Glomerulonephritis

This entity represents the end stage of many of the histopathologic glomerular diseases discussed. The kidneys are found on ultrasound to be small; biopsy, not unexpectedly, reveals glomerular and interstitial fibrosis, and tubular atrophy. Determination of the type of disease that it originally began with may be difficult because these are end-stage changes. Serum creatinine concentration is significantly elevated.

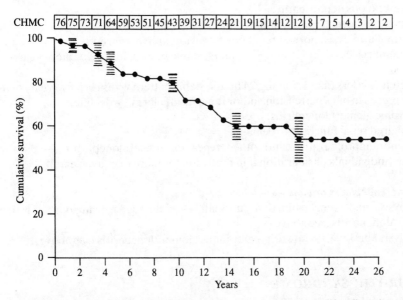

Fig. 18.6. Actuarial renal survival in patients with membranoproliferative glomerulone-phritis, plotted against years after disease onset in 76 children in the Cincinnati experience from 1957 to 1989. Confidence intervals (95 percent) are indicated by bars. *CHMC*, Children's Hospital Medical Center (Cincinatti).[34]

Ratings for Glomerulonephritis

Confirmed by renal biopsy
1) Minimal change nephropathy:

Time since end of treatment or last abnormal urinalysis	Rating
Within 1 yr	+100
2nd and 3rd yr	+50
Thereafter	Standard

Urinalysis abnormal or continuing treatment — +150
2) Mesangioproliferative glomerulonephritis, Berger's disease (focal proliferative glomerulonephritis).
In remission, normal urinalysis, normal renal function — +150.
Abnormal urinalysis, normal renal function, hematuria, nephrotic range pro-teinuria — decline.
Hematuria, low-level proteinuria (less than 1,500 mg/24 hours):
    Without hypertension — +300.
    With hypertension and/or impaired renal function — decline.

3) Membranous nephropathy.

In remission, normal urinalysis and renal function — +150.

Abnormal urinalysis, normal renal function without hypertension:

Proteinuria less than 1,500 mg/24 hours, stable pattern for five or more years — +300.

Proteinuria less than 1,500 mg/24 hours, stable pattern within last five years or in the presence of hypertension and/or renal insufficiency — decline.

4) Chronic glomerulonephritis:

Impaired renal function — decline.

5) Membranoproliferative and other types of glomerulonephritis — usually decline (individual consideration if in remission for more than five years).

Without renal biopsy or biopsy unknown

Urinalysis and renal function normal — rate as mesangioproliferative glomerulonephritis (*see* above).

Urinalysis abnormal — rate as membranous glomerulonephritis (*see* above).

NEPHROTIC SYNDROME

This is a syndrome characterized by glomerular proteinuria above 3·5 g in 24 hours, depression of the serum albumin level, edema and hypercholesterolemia. The major factors determining the prognosis of the nephrotic syndrome are the types of histopathology present, and the presence or absence of treatable systemic processes. The likelihood of a particular pathologic process is related to the age at onset (*see* Table 18.3). It should be noted that diabetes is under-represented in this study as many centers do not routinely biopsy nephrotic diabetics.

Diabetic nephropathy and renal failure were responsible for 18 percent of all the end-stage renal failures in Canada between 1981 and 1986.[35] The mortalities from the histopathologic appearances of any of the primary types of glomerulonephritis have been outlined in the previous sections. The nephrotic syndrome secondary to metabolic and systemic disorders (such as amyloid, lupus and diabetes) does not have a good prognosis and should be declined for life insurance.

NEPHROSCLEROSIS

Essential hypertension is by far the major cause of atherosclerotic vascular changes in the kidney known as nephrosclerosis. Arteriosclerotic changes are most marked in the afferent arterioles and interlobular arteries. Thickening of the arterial wall contributes to glomerular fibrosis with subsequent renal insufficiency.

There is often a history of poorly controlled hypertension for about ten years. The presentation of nephrosclerosis may be by the chance finding of an elevated creatinine level in the hypertensive patient or by the finding of proteinuria on a routine urinalysis. The urinalysis generally shows only modest proteinuria in the absence of malignant hypertension. Twenty-four hour urine protein excretion is generally less than 2 g, but several reports have indicated that higher amounts of proteinuria up to 6·5 g in 24 hours may occur with severe hypertensive

Table 18.3. The underlying histopathological appearances in 506 adult-onset nephrotic patients in Guy's Hospital, 1964–1984.

Age at onset	Minimal change	FSGS	Membrane	MCGN	Other proliferative	Diabetes	Amyloid	Lupus	Other	Total
15–19	18 (28%)	12 (19%)	3 (5%)	10 (20%)	13 (16%)	0	0	8 (12%)	0	64
20–29	22 (24%)	17 (18%)	4 (4%)	18 (20%)	12 (13%)	0	0	18 (21%)	1[a]	92
30–39	16 (20%)	9 (11%)	21 (27%)	4 (5%)	12 (15%)	1 (1%)	2 (3%)	13 (17%)	1[b]	79
40–49	22 (27%)	3 (4%)	20 (24%)	6 (7%)	13 (16%)	2 (2%)	3 (4%)	12 (14%)	2[b,c]	83
50–59	15 (16%)	15 (16%)	22 (24%)	7 (7%)	13 (14%)	2 (2%)	14 (15%)	3 (3%)	3[b,c]	94
60–69	13 (19%)	3 (5%)	22 (33%)	4 (6%)	14 (21%)	2 (3%)	8 (12%)	1 (1%)	0	67
70–79	5 (21%)	0	7 (29%)	1 (4%)	5 (21%)	1 (4%)	3 (13%)	0	1[c]	23
80	2		1							3
	113 (22%)	60 (11·8%)	100 (19·7%)	50 (9·8%)	82 (16·0%)	8 (1·7%)	30 (5·9%)	55 (10·8%)	8 (1·5%)	506

[a] Alport's syndrome.
[b] Schönlein–Henloch purpura.
[c] Microscopic polyarteritis.

nephrosclerosis.[36] As a guideline, the proteinuria with hypertensive nephrosclerosis tends to be clearly related to the degree of hypertension control. The individual with neprosclerosis often has evidence of hypertensive changes in the retinal vessels and of left ventricular hypertrophy.[37,38]

The morbidity and mortality from hypertensive nephrosclerosis remain high. In North America hypertensive nephrosclerosis accounts for 20–25 percent of all end-stage renal diseases; in Europe it is closer to 10 percent. In the USA there is as yet no evidence of reduction in the incidence of end-stage renal disease attributable to nephrosclerosis, despite the fact that effective anti-hypertensive agents have led to a decline in morbidity and mortality from stroke and myocardial infarction. This has led to speculation that some of the anti-hypertensive agents used may well lower systemic hypertension without affecting intraglomerular hypertension, which seems to persist. Several studies have demonstrated the effectiveness of the angiotensin-converting enzyme inhibitors in the reduction of the proteinuria in hypertensive nephrosclerosis, and there is renewed enthusiasm that these agents may be able to halt progression of renal failure where other agents have failed.

Selection of Risks

The risk associated with hypertension combined with proteinuria should be evaluated in the usual way: find the numerical rating for each and add 1/4 of their sum because of the interdependence of impairments. When hypertension is severe and proteinuria constant, the total mortality rating would generally indicate a decline. Even when nephrosclerosis is deemed to be mild by low levels or intermittent proteinuria, other complications from hypertension, such as the development of cerebral vascular disease or left ventricular hypertrophy, might be the determinants of an adverse outcome in the application for life insurance. The finding of an elevated creatinine level in the long-standing hypertensive individual, even though hypertension has come under control, would still be adequate grounds for declining, since nephrosclerosis may be a progressive disease regardless of the control of the blood pressure.[39] Similarly, persisting electrocardiographic abnormalities attributable to irreversible hypertensive cardiovascular disease or asymptomatic coronary artery disease may be major matters for concern in the underwriting process.

Senile Nephrosclerosis

The pathological lesion of senile nephrosclerosis is almost identical to that of hypertensive nephrosclerosis, but is seemingly unrelated to the level of arterial hypertension. The onset of senile nephrosclerosis is insidious, and it may be difficult to distinguish from chronic obstructive nephropathy unless there is a clear-cut history suggesting the latter. The insurability of elderly applicants showing albuminuria due to senile nephrosclerosis may be determined by a simple test of renal function, such as the serum creatinine or BUN, which, to be acceptable, should be normal for age or show no more than a slight impairment.

Malignant Nephrosclerosis

Medial necrosis of the renal arterioles is the typical lesion of malignant or accelerated hypertension. It is of relatively rapid onset, and death from progressive uremia is the usual outcome unless treatment is instituted early. Only individuals with the mildest cases of malignant nephrosclerosis that have responded to treatment and who have survived without permanent renal damage could be considered insurable, and then only after a prolonged deferment period.

TUBULAR INTERSTITIAL NEPHRITIS (TIN)

This is a group of disorders primarily affecting the renal interstitium and tubules. They are quite separate from the disorders affecting primarily the glomeruli and from the vascular disorders such as nephrosclerosis.

Acute Tubulointerstitial Nephropathy (ATIN)

Acute injury to the tubules and interstitium of the kidney generally occurs through allergic immunologic or idiosyncratic mechanisms, or following infections.[3] In immunologic mediated ATIN, drug-induced hypersensitivity reactions include fever, rash and arthralgias, occurring 10–20 days after drug exposure. Laboratory findings include deterioration in renal function with an increase in creatinine associated with eosinophilia. Mild tubular-range proteinuria is the rule with 24-hour proteins less than 2 g and random urine protein concentrations less than 100 mg/dl. Hematuria and pyuria are commonly seen, but red blood cell casts are absent.

Penicillin derivatives (especially methacillin) and many other classes of antibiotics have been implicated. Non-steroidal anti-inflammatory medications, diuretics, cimetidine, allopurinol and phenobarbital may also produce this picture.[40]

Pathogenically, direct humeral, immunologic and cellular mechanisms appear to precipitate this acute tubular injury.[40] Although dialysis may be necessary in 20 percent of individuals during the acute phase, cessation of the offending drug generally results in normalization of renal function and sediment. However, disorders that may cause ATIN, such as lupus and Sjøgren's syndrome, may irreversibly damage tubules resulting in chronic tubular interstitial nephritis.

Selection of Risks

A history of ATIN due to drugs with complete normalization of the urine sediment, and resolution of proteinuria and renal function would not necessitate a rating. When abnormalities of renal function persist six months after the event, a diagnosis of chronic renal insufficiency would be made, and the risk for progressive renal deterioration would be too prohibitive to insure. The problem of persisting abnormal renal sediment with proteinuria and hematuria (with normal renal function) should warrant a complete investigation to exclude a systemic collagen-vascular disease or a primary glomerulonephritis. With a favorable investigation, including normal renal function one year after the bout of ATIN, a rating of +100 to +150 would apply.

Acute Infectious Tubulointerstitial Nephritis (Acute Pyelonephritis)

Although bacteria may invade the kidney through the systemic circulation, by far the most common route of infection is the lower urinary tract. Urinary tract infection in the younger ages is predominantly a female disease, and it has been estimated that 10–20 percent of all women have at least one urinary tract infection in their lives.[41] Increase in the risk of urinary tract infection occurs when there is any anatomic abnormality in the urinary tract.

Urine in the bladder is generally sterile, and colonization in the bladder is minimized through the act of urination, by the resistance of the bladder surface to some types of bacteria, and also by the chemical composition of the urine itself. However, the urethra may be contaminated by GI flora; this may allow bacteria to enter the bladder where colonization may occur despite the defense mechanisms outlined above. At times this is completely asymptomatic, but at other times symptoms of suprapubic pain, dysuria and frequency may occur; the disorder is then known as cystitis. Even without antibiotic therapy symptoms generally subside within 48 to 72 hours and bacteruria disappears in 75–80 percent of individuals.

However, in 30–50 percent of lower urinary tract infections the kidneys may be seeded. Such ascending infection is favored if there is a coexistent anatomic obstruction, such as prostatic hypertrophy in the male, or if there is vesicoureteric reflux that is either spontaneous or induced by the infection itself. The clinical picture may be variable, from virtually no upper tract symptoms to severe flank pain, fevers and chills in a symptom complex called acute pyelonephritis. In general, a two- to six-week course of antibiotics is given for these upper tract infections; if recurrences of symptoms occur, low dose prophylactic antibiotics may be given for six or more months.

When urinary tract infections occur in men or small children an investigation is warranted because there may be an associated anatomical abnormality impairing drainage of urine from the kidney. These problems should be identified to allow either surgical correction or chronic antibiotic prophylaxis. This is important because deterioration of renal function almost never occurs with a urinary tract infection unless there is a significant problem impairing drainage of urine. The entity previously known as chronic pyelonephritis, thought to occur from unapparent upper urinary tract infections, is now thought not to exist. Instead renal failure stemming from recurring upper urinary tract infections seems to occur only if there is superimposition of a urinary tract abnormality which predisposes the kidneys to intra-renal reflux of urine. Therefore it is important to eliminate stasis induced by kidney stones and prostatic hypertrophy, and surgically to correct vesicoureteric reflux.

Selection of Risks

A single bout of acute bacterial interstitial nephritis adequately treated without recurrence would not be associated with any excess mortality. If recurring bouts of acute pyelonephritis have been reported in the APS or MAR, it would be important for the underwriter to determine whether the upper urinary tracts have been appropriately evaluated for the presence of anatomic anomalies. This might include evaluation with ultrasounds, IVPs and cystoscopies. If the urinary tract itself proved to be anatomically normal, a standard rating should be considered. However, if specialized testing were not performed, it would be appropriate to rate such individuals at +50 if the last attack had occurred within two years of underwriting. However, if evidence of anatomic abnormalities existed in a setting of urinary tract infections, the issue of insurance would depend on the frequency of clinical symptoms, stability of renal function, the presence of systemic symptoms, hypertension and the appropriateness of the medical follow-up.

Chronic Tubular Interstitial Nephritis (CTIN)

These entities[42] were previously lumped under the term chronic pyelonephritis; this terminology is no longer appropriate since a purely infective etiology is not thought to be causally pathogenic. Many cases of what was previously considered to be chronic pyelonephritis are actually due to chronic reflux nephropathy. Studies in animals and humans have demonstrated that intra-renal urine reflux reproduces the chronic atrophic changes of chronic pyelonephritis.

The principal difference between ATIN and CTIN is the fact that the immunological mechanisms operative in drug-induced ATIN are not present in CTIN. Rather, actual physical chemical injury occurs to the tubules. Subsequent tubule damage is a slow but progressive process. It is important to recognize when chronic CTIN is present, since chronic renal damage can be arrested if the appropriate interventions are introduced. Therapeutic interventions are considered to be highly important, since as many as 30–40 percent of end-stage renal diseases in the USA are attributable to CTIN. Table 18.4 outlines the possible causative factors for this entity. Pathologically, the kidney in CTIN may be normal or small, but acute inflammatory cells are absent and the cellular infiltrate consists mainly of mononuclear cells. There is fibrosis and, as the disease progresses, glomerular obliteration and sclerosis may occur, eventually resulting in renal failure.

Table 18.4. Chronic Tubulointerstitial nephropathies.[a]

Drugs and toxins
    Analgesics
    Cis-Platinum
    Methyl CCNU
    Streptozotocin
    ? Lithium
    Balkan nephropathy (toxin presumed but not proven)
    Cyclosporine A
Heavy metals
    Lead
    Cadmium
    Mercury
    Copper (Wilson's disease)
Metabolic disturbances
    Hypercalcemia/hypercalciuria
    Hyperuricemia/hyperuricosuria
    Hyperoxaluria
    Cystinosis

Sickle cell disease
Paroxysmal nocturnal hemoglobinuria
? Hypokalemia
Urinary tract obstruction
Immunologic disorders
    Usually associated with glomerulonephritis
        Systemic lupus erythematosus
        Anti-GBM disease
        Essential mixed cryoglobulinemia
        Membranoproliferative glomerulonephritis
    Not usually associated with glomerulonephritis
        Sjøgren's syndrome
        Transplant rejection
        Chronic active hepatitis
        Primary biliary cirrhosis
        Thyroiditis
Neoplastic disorders
    Multiple myeloma
    Light-chain nephropathy
    Leukemia and lymphoma
Hereditary and cystic diseases
    Alport's syndrome (predominantly glomerular disease)
    Polycystic disease
    Medullary cystic disease
    Medullary sponge kidney
    Familial interstitial nephritis
Miscellaneous disorders
    Sarcoidosis
    Retroperitoneal fibrosis
Idiopathic

[a]Source: Clinical nephrology.[3] Adapted in part from Cogan MG. Classifications and patterns of renal dysfunction. In Cotran RS, Brenner BM and Stein JH (eds). *Tubulointerstitial Nephropathies*. Churchill Livingstone, Inc, New York 1983.

The presentation of the disease may very well depend on the disorder causing it. For example, the metabolic disorders of hypercalciuria and hyperuricuria may present with a kidney stone, whereas a genetic disease such as familial polycystic kidney disease may present with hypertension and hematuria. The presentation, however, may be totally asymptomatic and recognizable only by the chance finding of low-level proteinuria (less than 100 mg/dl in a random urine) in an individual who, for example, has been using many analgesics or non-steroidal anti-inflammatory medications over the years. Small molecular weight proteins, such as lysozyme and beta-2 microglobulin, may be found in the urine, since the unhealthy tubules are not able to resorb them. If the proximal tubules have been damaged more than the distal tubules, there will be defective resorption of glucose, uric acid and aminoacids, and these will be found in the urine in increased quantities. An inability to concentrate the urine may occur, especially if the interstitium and the medulla of the kidney have been involved. This may lead to nephrogenic diabetes insipidus.

Of all the causes of CITN, excessive analgesic abuse is certainly a very important one.[43] It has been estimated that excessive consumption of these analgesics may be responsible for 10–20 percent of all chronic renal disease in the USA. The analgesic mixtures in European countries have commonly contained antipyrine, phenazine and caffeine; in North American countries aspirin, caffeine, and codeine combined with phenazine or acetaminophen have been implicated.[42] Studies seem to indicate that in analgesic combinations containing aspirin, phenazine and caffeine the aspirin appears to be a major nephrotoxin, whereas phenazine synergizes with it. The renal medulla and the renal papillae are extremely sensitive to the high concentration of these nephrotoxic analgesics. Capillaries and venules in the renal papillae show thickening, and when significant flow obstruction occurs in this microangiopathic process ischemic necrosis occurs. The tubules become atrophic, interstitial fibrosis ensues and progressive bilateral scarring occurs, leading to renal insufficiency. Concomitant urinary tract obstruction due to necrotic papillae or a renal calculus may hasten the process.

Selection of Risks

A number of factors contribute to the overall prognosis when underwriting applicants with chronic tubular interstitial nephropathy. At one extreme is the individual whose disease process is so far advanced that creatinine concentration is elevated, and he is in either early or late chronic renal insufficiency. These individuals would, of course, not be insurable. The cause of the disease would also have a direct bearing on the overall prognosis, since disease progression can be predicted on the basis of the presence or absence of reversible features. For example, the elimination of analgesics in the individual at an early stage of disease revealing only minimal proteinuria and hematuria would be associated predictably with a good prognosis. A rating of +75 would be appropriate if supervening urinary tract infections or hypertension were not present. However, CTIN attributable to chronic nephrolithiasis whose metabolic abnormality was never corrected might predictably lead to further damage and the development of renal insufficiency in the future. Such individuals would need a high substandard rating to a decline.

The presence of unilateral scars in a particular kidney (atrophic pyelonephritis) may result from a combination of infection and impaired drainage, and should have a good prognosis for overall kidney function if the contralateral kidney is free from disease. Excess mortality, however, could occur from the development of hypertension or from sepsis related to obstructions in the affected kidney.

When CTIN is judged to be early and minimal in extent, and both kidneys are functioning normally, especially if the diagnosis has been made on purely radiological grounds (e.g. scarring of the cortex), a rating of standard to +50 is appropriate. For clinically established CTIN the rating should be increased to +150, and if the blood pressure is raised, whether under treatment or not, the appropriate rating should be added to the basic rating for CTIN. Finally, any obstructive lesion persisting in the urinary tract should be rated additionally and according to its nature; this could vary from +50 to +100, depending on the practice of the individual insurance company. This scheme of rating ensures that the best cases of CTIN are offered the most favorable terms, whereras those with complications indicating a more serious prognosis are declined or rated extremely heavily.

PROSTATITIS: EPIDIDYMITIS

Neither acute nor chronic prostatitis is usually a risk as far as life insurance is concerned. Acute bacterial prostatis is often associated with fevers, chills, dysuria, and a very tender prostate on physical exam. Vigorous prostate massage of an inflamed gland may result in bacteriemia and be a cause of significant morbidity. Response to the appropriate antibiotic is generally the rule, although morbidity may arise when treatment has been inadequate resulting in abscess formation, epididymo-orchitis, seminal vesiculitis and residual chronic bacterial prostatitis.

Chronic bacterial prostatitis may follow an acute episode of bacterial prostatitis, or be a consequence of a non-specific urethritis; a viral or chlamydial cause seems likely in many cases. Most individuals with non-bacterial prostatitis are sexually active men and, since many cases follow a non-specific urethritis, it is felt that the causative agent is sexually transmitted. Individuals with chronic prostatitis may have variable symptoms: some are totally asymptomatic, whereas others have diverse symptoms, including dysuria, aching and discomfort in the perineal region. Long-term antibiotic treatment is generally employed with the aim of suppressing symptoms and sterilizing the urine. However, chronic symptoms causing morbidity rather than mortality may persist despite antibiotic treatment.

Testicular ultrasound is an ideal modality for differentiating the testicular pain associated with epididymitis from either torsion of the testicle or testicular tumor. Transabdominal and preferably transrectal ultrasonography of the prostate gland may sometimes reveal prostatic calculi, which may be a nidus for infection or other complications, such as a prostatic abscess.

Selection of Risks

As far as the life risk is concerned, no adverse underwriting action need be taken as long as investigations have shown no important obstructive complications affecting the kidneys or urinary tract that would cause wider dissemination of pathogenic organisms from the prostate or epididymis.

CYSTIC DISEASES OF THE KIDNEYS

The increased use of ultrasound and CT scanning imaging modalities has resulted in an increased detection of renal cysts.[44] The overwhelming majority of these cysts are found by chance when such a study is performed to evaluate an individual with urinary tract symptoms or other abdominal pelvic symptomatology. Of the several types of cystic disease affecting the kidneys, only those that become apparent after early infancy will be considered here.

Simple Cysts

These are the most common of all of the types of cystic disorders of the kidney, and have been estimated to occur in at least 50 percent of all people over the age of 50. This is the most common cystic lesion that the underwriter will encounter. The cysts range in size from 1 cm to 15 cm and are often multiple and bilateral. There are definite ultrasonographic characteristics of a simple cyst, and if these are all met the underwriter can be assured that the cystic lesions are in fact benign.[44] Doubts about an applicant's insurability only arise when such criteria are not met and the possibility of a solid component to the tumor representing a hypernephroma is entertained. Additionally, a cystic mass with multiple septations (walls) is sometimes detected on ultrasound. Although this can merely be a confluence of benign simple cysts, differentiation from a multi-locular cystic nephroma or a cystic renal cell carcinoma is necessary before insurance can be issued.

Multilocular Cystic Nephroma

This is a rare non-hereditary cystic neoplasm[45] occurring in the very young or in the middle ages. If symptomatic, presentation may be with pain or hematuria, but most are incidental findings during an evaluation for other problems. Ultrasound reveals a multilocular cystic mass. Pathologically, the thick capsule separates the lesions from the adjacent renal tissue, and contains numerous capillaries and blood vessels. This lesion is usually benign but clearly has malignant potential, substantiated by the rare occurrence of distant metastases.

Selection of Risks
Individuals with benign lesions treated appropriately either by a complete or heminephrectomy may be issued insurance at standard rates. Otherwise the tumor should be treated as other renal cell carcinomas (*see* Chapter 20).

Medullary Sponge Kidney[3,45]

Medullary sponge kidney or tubular ectasia is a non-inherited developmental defect in the medullary portion of the kidney, and this is characterized by dilatation of the distal collecting tubules. Most individuals would be asymptomatic, but the tubular ectasia predisposes to stasis, infection and stone formation, resulting in polyps; a urinalysis may include hematuria and pyuria. Pathologically, the kidney has cysts ranging in size from 1 mm to 6 mm. Calculi may be seen within these cysts. Uncomplicated cases are associated with normal kidney function tests and urinalysis, and the disorder is generally non-progressive with normal life expectancy.

Rating

A rating is rarely required for asymptomatic medullary sponge kidney even when minimal calcification is present. A rating in the range of +50 to +75 will only be necessary when the cysts are large and calcification is heavy, or when recurring bouts of renal colic occur with secondary complications such as pyelonephritis or hydronephrosis.

Medullary Cystic Disease

Medullary cystic disease[45] is an autosomal dominant disorder characterized pathologically by cysts predominantly within the renal medulla bilaterally. Renal failure generally occurs in the third or fourth decade, although there are case reports of individuals living well into the seventh decade. Renal transplant may improve function, and the transplanted kidney does not undergo cystic changes.

Rating

Life insurance applicants with this disorder, even though they may be healthier at the younger ages, are not insurable.

Familial Polycystic Disease of the Kidneys

Familial polycystic kidney disease is an autosomal dominant cystic disease of the kidneys characterized by multiple renal cysts that increase in size and number with age. It is one of the most common genetic diseases and occurs in between 1 and 400 and 1 in 1,000 people.[46] It presently accounts for about 12 percent of individuals with end-stage renal disease in the USA. Cysts also occur in the liver, pancreas, spleen, ovaries and testes. The disorder is associated with an increased incidence of cardiovascular abnormalities. In one particular study 18 percent of all patients hospitalized with polycystic kidney disease and 27 percent of all autopsy patients with this ailment had one or more cardiovascular abnormalities.[47] Acquired myxomatous degeneration of the mitral and/or aortic valve may occur. Degenerative changes may occur in the aortic root resulting in dilatation and aortic insufficiency. Congenital lesions may include bicuspid aortic valve, mild aortic stenosis and coarctation of the aorta. Saccular aneurysms of the circle of Willis have been described in as many as 15 percent of cases. These may contribute to excess morbidity and mortality.

Pathologically, the kidneys contain innumerable cysts throughout the cortex and medulla, ranging in size from barely visible to several centimetres in diameter. The result is a distortion of the renal parenchyma with eventual destruction of the nephrons and tubules, leading to progressive renal insufficiency. Assuming the facilities for dialysis and renal transplantation are available, the current suggested life expectancy is well into the sixth decade of life. Adverse prognostic features include uncontrolled hypertension, frequent bouts of pyelonephritis, presence of significant aortic valvular disease or the presence of cerebral aneurysms.

Assuming ideal blood pressure control and the availability of transplantation and dialysis, Levey et al have calculated survival data for various age groups of individuals with polycystic kidney disease[48] (*see* Table 18.5).

Table 18.5. Life expectancy in patients with polycystic kidney disease.[48]

Age (years)	Mean survival (years)	Probability of survival	
		Five-years	To age 80–84
20–24	40	0·99	0·042
25–29	35	0·99	0·042
30–34	30	0·98	0·043
35–39	26	0·96	0·043
40–44	22	0·93	0·045
45–49	18	0·90	0·046
50–54	15	0·85	0·054
55–59	12	0·79	0·064
60–64	9	0·71	0·081
65–69	7	0·62	0·115
70–74	6	0·52	0·187
75–79	4	0·36	0·362

Selection of Risks

Once elevated creatinine concentrations are present, early renal insufficiency is evident and individuals are not insurable. However, with normal renal function and controlled hypertension the most favorable individuals with polycystic kidney disease would have extra mortality in the range of 200 percent to 300 percent. The presence of other associated congenital cardiac anomalies would require a further debit.

A problem arises when an individual who has one parent with polycystic kidney disease applies for life insurance. This individual has a 50 percent chance of developing the disease. At present it is considered that individuals who are free from cysts after the age of 35 are unlikely to carry the gene for polycystic kidney disease and can be issued insurance at standard rates. Individuals with a negative ultrasound scan at the age of 25 could be offered a temporary flat extra of, for example, about 5 per mil; this would cease at the age of 35, assuming that the ultrasound remained normal. Issuing an insurance contract to individuals below the age of 25 is somewhat speculative, but it may be possible to issue contracts based on the observed mortality data in Table 18.5.

It is an interesting fact that the gene for familial polycystic kidney disease is located on chromosome 16,[46] and current data suggest that there may be two different genes causing this disorder. In the future the development of molecular probes for the defective gene will determine whether an individual at risk has inherited the disorder. Identification of affected individuals could take place much earlier than present technology allows.

OBSTRUCTIVE UROPATHY

Hydronephrosis

Hydronephrosis is defined as dilatation of the pelvis of the kidney and usually of the renal calyces; the calyces may also show various degrees of clubbing. In some cases the ureters share in the dilatation. Hydronephrosis is caused essentially by obstruction to the free passage of urine anywhere in the renal tract, from the infundibula of the kidney to the urethral meatus. It is especially likely to occur if the obstruction is partial or gradual in onset and continues for a long period of time. It may be unilateral (particularly if the obstruction is above the bladder) or bilateral (if the obstruction is below the bladder). Prolonged severe hydronephrosis will ultimately result in pressure atrophy of the renal parenchyma, affecting first the collecting tubules, later the proximal tubules and finally the glomeruli; this will result in CTIN with gradual deterioration of renal function if the disorder is bilateral, and in a non-functioning kidney if the disorder is unilateral.

Presentation

Hydronephrosis usually presents to the life underwriter in APSs or MARs. It may be mentioned merely as a complication of a primary symptomatic disorder, usually obstructive, that has been corrected surgically; or a large hydronephrosis itself may have given rise to symptoms and so drawn attention to its presence, previously unsuspected. This latter manner of presentation is typical of chronic hydronephrosis due to a congenital malformation such as a ureteric-pelvic stricture. Again, appropriate surgical measures would usually have been taken to relieve the obstruction.

Very occasionally symptomless hydronephrosis may be discovered because of an abnormality found on medical examination for life insurance, such as a palpable swelling in the flank or persistent proteinuria, leading to subsequent investigations revealing a hydronephrosis. Care should be taken to exclude the presence of earlier CTIN (*see* p. 543), which is sometimes an unfortunate complication of hydronephrosis, especially when there is a history of recurrent urinary tract infections prior to surgical relief of the obstruction. Even without prior urinary tract infections, intra-renal reflux of urine may result in significant tubular interstitial damage, atrophy and scar formation; these results are pathologically identical to the process, previously termed chronic pyelonephritis, thought to result from bacterial infection.

The persistence of arterial hypertension after free drainage of the urinary tract has been achieved should be viewed with some concern especially if renal function has been permanently impaired, as in the case of unilateral hydronephrosis. The risk would be substantially greater than that indicated by the level of blood pressure alone, and the blood pressure debit should be increased by one-half. Where there is residual impairment of renal function affecting both kidneys, as in the case of bilateral hydronephrosis, the coexistence of hypertension would generally indicate a decline risk or, at best, a rating calculated by compounding the mortality rating for each impairment.

Evaluation of the Hydronephrosis Risk

It can be said straightaway that evaluation of the risk when there is a history of hydronephrosis can be a most complex matter; in order to piece together the essential facts the underwriter is frequently dependent on the attending physician or surgeon for technical information. It is probably best to tackle the problem of risk evaluation by considering first the nature of the primary obstructing lesion. The causes of obstruction are many; some have a serious individual prognosis (malignancy), whereas others are relatively benign (kidney stones for example) and can be completely removed. It is imperative to relieve the obstruction because of the risk of progressive renal function deterioration and sepsis. The transurethral approach may be employed by the urologist to insert a stent into the ureter, passing the obstructing lesion if it cannot be removed and allowing the distal end to remain in the bladder. If such an approach is not feasible, a percutaneous nephrostomy may be inserted under ultrasound guidance by the radiologist. This may end up being the definitive procedure, for example, if a malignancy is obstructing a ureter. It may also be the initial procedure designed to decrease morbidity from, for example, a surgical procedure to extract kidney stones.

Some of the principal causes of urinary tract obstruction are listed below.

1) Congenital causes: these include obstruction at the ureteropelvic junction due to compression by an aberrant renal artery or fibrous bands, or to a developmental stricture at this point; kinking of a ureter caused by a malpositioned kidney or kidneys (e.g. a horseshoe kidney); vesicoureteric reflux due to absence of the normal protective valve action at the lower end of the ureters where they enter the bladder; congenital valves at the bladder outlet; urethral or meatal structures and phimosis.

2) Acquired causes: these are even more numerous and include obstruction from a urinary stone lodged in the kidney, renal pelvis, ureter or bladder; tumors of the renal pelvis, ureter or bladder; schistosomal strictures of the ureter; extrinsic compression of the ureter by whatever cause; neuropathic (cord) bladder which predisposes in due course to acquired vesicoureteric reflux; bladder neck obstruction from benign or carcinomatous enlargement of the prostate, or acquired strictures.

Having identified the nature of the obstructing lesion the following questions then arise:

1) Is obstruction to free urinary flow still present, or has it been completely eliminated surgically or otherwise?

2) Is the condition responsible for the obstruction itself ratable?

The consequences of urinary tract obstruction — namely hydronephrosis and the state of the kidney or kidneys — should be examined next:

1) Was (or is) the hydronephrosis unilateral or bilateral?

2) Was (or is) the degree of hydronephrosis slight, moderate or severe?

3) Is there any evidence of residual damage to the renal parenchyma causing diminished function or even complete loss of function?

Owing to the extremely varied clinical presentation it is not possible to give precise guidance on the handling of hydronephrosis; each case has to be evaluated individually. There are, however, some general principles which can be stated. When an obstructing lesion causing bilateral hydronephrosis has been completely relieved and is unlikely to recur, and no permanent damage has been done to the renal parenchyma, the prognosis for a normal expectation of life should be excellent. A good prognosis would still be expected even though a degree of calyceal hydronephrosis remains as a residual structural abnormality, renal function being normal, for there would be no reason to anticipate an increased incidence of infection so long as there is free drainage of urine and competent ureterovesical valves; other things being equal, there is no question that the underwriting risk would be standard. Where residual hydronephrosis is more severe and renal function has failed to recover completely after removal of the obstruction, the risk would be considered substandard depending on the degree of functional impairment. Progressive deterioration, however, need not be anticipated.

In the case of unilateral hydronephrosis the underwriting principles are a little different. So long as the unaffected kidney is completely normal in all respects, diminished renal function in the hydronephrotic kidney would not necessarily debar an applicant from standard insurance acceptance, provided the obstructing lesion had been eliminated. Even if little or no useful renal function remained in the hydronephrotic kidney after adequate drainage, ultimate insurability as a standard risk would still be possible, especially if the sound kidney was shown to be hypertrophied, indicating that it had been compensating for the deficient function of its fellow kidney for several years. Standard acceptance would be even more certain after the non-functioning hydronephrotic kidney had been removed surgically.

Congenital Defects of the Urogenital Tract

Congenital defects occur in the urogenital tract more often than in any other system, and some have been mentioned already in connection with the causation of hydronephrosis and cystic disease. The essential point as far as the life risk is concerned is whether a particular developmental abnormality does or does not produce obstruction to the free passage of urine. If it does, then complications resulting from urinary stasis are almost inevitable, including infection, renal stone formation and, ultimately, hydronephrosis and chronic tubular interstitial nephropathy.

Some congenital deformities not causing obstruction will rarely give rise to complications and will not usually require surgical correction. Since, in such circumstances, the kidneys would not be particularly liable to suffer damage and functional impairment, expectation of life should be unaffected. Deformities falling into the above category are duplex kidneys, whether unilateral or bilateral, double renal pelvis and double ureter. These are frequently found by chance in the investigation of some unrelated condition and, if there is no evidence of hydronephrosis and urinalysis is normal, the risk would be standard. If, however, hydronephrosis has been demonstrated by excretion urography or by ultrasound, an obstructing lesion must be assumed, whether this has been investigated or not, and the risk must therefore be considered substandard. Likewise, if a congenital anomaly found by chance has been further investigated and an obstructive lesion demonstrated (e.g. vesicoureteric reflux in the case of a duplex kidney or double ureter), the chances of future damage to renal tissue would be greatly increased, and a small rating to cover this eventuality would be appropriate.

One particular congenital anomaly that can be considered completely benign as far as length of life is concerned is unilateral renal agenesis. This is usually diagnosed by chance when one kidney is found to be hypertrophic, and there is no renal shadow and no excretion of dye on the opposite side. Confirmation that the kidney is in fact congenitally absent and not simply an atrophic pyelonephritic kidney can often be obtained on cystoscopy by demonstrating the absence of a trigone and ureteral orifice on that side.

Congenital abnormalities of the urogenital tract are so many and varied that quite often an individual evaluation of the risk is required, but whatever the type of lesion it should always be borne in mind that the overriding consideration is whether or not there is associated obstruction to urinary flow. Gross deformities would not normally be seen as an underwriting problem until after some surgical reconstruction. Bladder ectopy, for example, may require urinary diversion.

Urinary Diversions

There are a number of urinary diversions that underwriters will encounter. All are designed to maintain free flow of urine, minimize the likelihood of upper tract infections, and thereby reduce the chances for progressive renal insufficiency. In an ileo- or sigmoid conduit an isolated loop of ileum or sigmoid colon is anastomosed to the proximal bowel segment. The distal end is brought to the abdominal skin surface where a stoma is fashioned and a urinary appliance is used to collect the urine. In these instances the bowel functions only as a conduit to carry urine to the skin surface. The ureters themselves may be diverted directly to the skin, and this is known as a cutaneous ureterostomy. Both procedures may be extremely successful at maintaining normal renal function, as long as anastomotic obstruction does not occur in the former and stomal stenosis does not lead to hydronephrosis and upper tract infections in the latter. Stomal stenosis frequently occurs with ureterostomies, necessitating conversion to a bowel conduit.

In another urinary diversion procedure, known as a ureterosigmoidostomy, the ureters are joined to the sigmoid colon with bowel continuity remaining. Although feces and urine intermix, technical advances in the ureteric-sigmoid anastomosis have resulted in good results comparable to ileo- and sigmoid conduits. The major advantage of this procedure is that there is bowel and urinary continuity without external stomas. Creating a proximal colostomy to the ureterosigmoidostomy will eliminate intermixing of urine and feces and reduce the risk for urinary infections, but the thought of maintaining a colostomy is esthetically unpleasant to many given the alternative of urinary diversion techniques.

Ideally, continuity of the intact urinary system is desirable, as long as the risk from recurring upper tract infection (pyelonephritis) is minimized and free flow of urine without reflux or hydronephrosis is achieved. Re-implantation of the ureter into the bladder may achieve this result when reflux is related to sphincteric incompetence and adequate bladder function exists. Should the bladder become chronically contracted, leading to frequency, urgency, suprapubic pain and frequent urinary tract infections, the bladder may be reconstructed using isolated pieces of ileum. These new ileo-bladders, medically called ileocystoplasties, may be complicated by failure to empty, and intermittent catheterization may be necessary to prevent infection attributable to urine stasis. If adequate emptying occurs, long-term results are excellent.

Rating

1) Ileo- or sigmoid conduit with normal renal function and urinalysis, normal imaged kidneys:

Ileo- or sigmoid conduit	Basic rating
With 0–2 UTI/yr	+75
With 3–5 UTI/yr	+150
Greater than 5	Decline

With mild unilateral hydronephrosis or pyelonephritis (cortical scarring) — no additional rating.
Mild bilateral hydronephrosis or pyelonephritis, normal renal function — add +100.
Otherwise — individual consideration.
2) Ureterosigmoidostomy:
With proximal colostomy — credit 75 to ileo-conduit rating.
Without proximal colostomy — rate as ileo- or sigmoid conduit.
3) Cutaneous ureterostomy — add 25 to ileo-conduit rating.
4) Ileal bladder, no reflux — credit 75 to ileo-conduit rating.
  With mild unilateral reflux — add +0.
  With moderate unilateral reflux or mild bilateral reflux, normal renal function — add +50.
  Otherwise — decline.

Vesicoureteric Reflux

Vesicoureteric reflux has been mentioned in the preceding paragraphs as an important cause of hydrostatic damage to the kidney. The defect may be congenital but can also be acquired as a result of recurrent cystitis in a paralysed bladder or following long-continued bladder neck obstruction. Vesicoureteric reflux is a major cause of chronic tubulointerstitial nephropathy.[42] In one study, over 90 percent of children and 50 percent of adults with phyelonephritic scars had vesicoureteric reflux on voiding cystourethrogram. In 89 percent of adults with scars, cystoscopic exam revealed abnormal ureteral orifices suggesting ureteral reflux.[42] The damage that occurs in the kidneys depends on the degree of incompetence of the vesicoureteral valves, the magnitude of pressure that develops, and the length of time that the reflux persists before correction. Reflux nephropathy not only induces the pathologic changes of chronic tubulointerstitial nephropathy noted previously: glomerular changes that are also commonly encountered are ischemic in nature, consisting of sclerosis and obsolescence. When examined by immunofluorescent microscopy affected glomeruli may also contain IgM and complement components, suggesting an immunologic mechanism.

Vesicoureteric reflux may be corrected either by implantation of the ureters elsewhere in the bladder wall or, in the case of the neuropathic bladder, by primary diversion to an ileal bladder or to the skin surface (*see* p. 553). Following successful elimination of the reflux, the life risk will depend upon the degree, if any, of permanent residual damage to the kidney.

In adults vesicoureteric reflux existing as the sole impairment of the urogenital tract with a negative history would not usually call for surgical correction. Instead the patient would be instructed in the technique of timed voidance of urine, so that the reservoir in the ureter is drained at each micturition. Nevertheless a hazard to renal function certainly exists in females, especially those who are particularly susceptible to asymptomatic bacteriuria, but once the abnormality is known to the individual the chances of serious complications arising due to neglect would be markedly reduced.

Lone vesicoureteric reflux with a negative history and normal examination findings would not usually warrant a rating, but if there is a history of recurrent urinary tract infections a rating of +75 to +100 would be appropriate.

Maldescended Testicle: Cryptorchidism

Failure of the testicle to descend into the scrotal sac is known as cryptorchidism. By the age of one year 47 percent of all males have at least one cryptorchid testis. The location may be intra-abdominal in 10 percent, in the inguinal canal in 20 percent, high in the scrotum in 40 percent or obstructed due to a physical barrier in 30 percent.[49] Two complications of cryptorchidism are important: spermatogenesis cannot occur at the temperature of the abdominal cavity and there is a tenfold to fortyfold greater risk of developing testicular cancer.[49] Of interest is the fact that both the cryptorchid testicle and the contralateral normally descended testicle are at this increased cancer risk, suggesting that some underlying testicular defect contributing to maldescent and malignancy exists. Although it has not been established that bringing the testicle down surgically into the scrotum decreases the risk of cancer, it certainly increases the likelihood of earlier detection of a testicular cancer.

Under normal underwriting circumstances an undescended testicle, even if not surgically corrected, would not be ratable.

Hydrocele

A hydrocele known to have been present for a long time, sometimes many years, without obvious cause, is often termed idiopathic, although some may have a congenital origin. These chronic hydroceles are benign and would not be considered important as underwriting risks despite the fact that they may be large and tense, and that the testicle cannot be properly felt.

A hydrocele reported to be of recent onset requires much more careful consideration by the life underwriter since it could be symptomatic of a malignant disease of the testicle, especially if its development has been insidious and associated with non-tender enlargement of the testicle. In such circumstances testicular ultrasound is necessary to exclude a complicating malignancy.

Other cystic swellings that commonly occur in the scrotum, and that have to be differentiated from a hydrocele, are spermatoceles and varicoceles; these refer respectively to small cystic accumulations of semen in the spermatic cord and blood in the testicular vein. They are invariably benign as far as the life risk is concerned. Likewise, direct and indirect inguinal hernias with sacs extending into the scrotum would not usually be considered ratable unless they were incarcerated and not reducible.

URINARY CALCULI: RENAL AND URETERIC COLIC

Approximately 2–3 percent of people in the USA and western Europe run the risk of having an attack of renal colic during their lifetime. The risk of recurrence after initial episode is 20–50 percent over the subsequent ten years.[50] Of those who develop recurring stones an endocrine, metabolic or infective cause will be found in a majority. Disorders such as primary hyperparathyroidism, renal tubular acidosis, hyperoxaluria, hyperuricosuria, cystinuria and infections, particularly with the proteus species of bacteria, can be found. In the past many stones could only be removed by open surgery, but alternative approaches are now being employed with increasing frequency. A technique known as extracorporeal shock-wave lithotripsy was introduced in Germany and has now gained worldwide acceptance in the industrialized world. In this technique an anesthetized patient is submerged in a water bath, and hydraulic shock waves are generated by an electric discharge in the bottom of the tank. The shock waves are carefully aimed and the stone is bombarded. For average size stones the procedure might last for about an hour, and longer for larger stones. Treatment has been successful in 90 percent of individuals, with a decrease in morbidity that is not yet possible with more invasive surgical procedures. Of interest is the fact that 99 percent of urologists questioned about treatment for kidney stones would prefer this technique if they themselves had a renal stone that required removal.[50]

Mortality and Urinary Stone Disease

The long-term mortality associated with a history of urinary stones showed surprisingly low ratios in the *1951 Impairment Study*[51] and the *Medical Impairment Study 1983*[1], both figures being remarkably similar. In the 1983 study, 139 policies issued from 1952 to 1976 at standard or substandard premiums were followed through to 1977. Of all the policies issued for kidney stones, 92 percent were issued at standard and 8 percent at substandard; 92 percent were issued to men and only 8 percent to women. The overall mortality ratio for the entire group was 97 percent in men and 85 percent in women. For those applicants rated at standard, the mortality ratio for men was 95 percent. There were too few substandards in either the male or female categories to reach statistical significance. The highest mortality ratio, 128 percent, was in male applicants who were rated at over 250 percent. In the 1951 study, standard and substandard combined, mortality ratios for men and women were 105 percent and 130 percent respectively. The favorable substandard experience probably reflects good underwriting selection; in cases of renal colic the outcome of excretion urography is usually available to the underwriter, thus eliminating applicants with serious structural kidney damage.

Bladder Stone

Although primary bladder stone is still a major problem in the Middle East, the Far East and India, it is now quite rare in temperate climates. In Eire, Smith and O'Flynn reviewed 652 examples of bladder stone treated at the Meath Hospital, Dublin between 1952 and 1972.[52] The great majority of these stones were thought to be primary: only 3 percent of patients gave a history of ureteric colic, indicating that these stones had descended to the bladder from the kidney. Five patients were below the age of ten and 80 percent aged 50 and over. Males made up 92 percent of the cases, and among them two-thirds had bladder outlet obstruction (benign prostatic hypertrophy, carcinoma and stricture). Only 15 of the total number of patients had no other disease apart from vesical calculi.

A history of bladder stone should be underwritten as for renal stone (*see below*), bearing in mind that a rating will frequently also be required for the predisposing cause.

Selection of Risks

The following ancillary aids can provide the life underwriter with valuable information for classifying the risk in urinary stone disease:

1) Excretion urography or ultrasonography will demonstrate (1) whether or not renal calculi or calcification are still present after the original stone has passed, been treated by lithotripsy or been surgically removed, (2) whether or not there are any structural abnormalities of the kidneys or urinary tract, or (3) whether or not there is vesicoureteric reflux if a voiding cystometrogram has been performed.

2) Microurinalysis showing unexplained pyuria or hematuria may indicate the presence of either further renal calculi or inflammation surrounding the area of a prior calculus.

3) The blood chemistry profile will help to indicate whether some metabolic disorder of urinary stone formation is operative and, combined with the microurinalysis, checks the integrity of renal function.

Rating

The following guidelines apply when urinary stone disease is idiopathic. Primary metabolic diseases that produce urinary calculi require individual evaluation and should be rated in addition to the renal manifestations. Likewise, obstructive lesions of the urogenital tract other than stone should be rated additionally.

History of stone or urinary tract colic:
1) Medical treatment: stone(s) passed naturally (including lithotripsy).
Up to four attacks — standard.
More than four attacks:
  Within one year — +50.
  Thereafter — 0 to +30.
2) Without residuals — standard.
3) Stones present on examination:

Description	Rating	
	Unilateral	Bilateral
Specks of calcification	Standard	Standard
Up to 3 mm in diameter	+0	+25
Over 3 mm in diameter	+25	+50
Staghorn calculus	5 per mil for 1 yr	Postpone
No signs or symptoms } for 3 yr or longer }	Reduce ratings by one-half	Reduce ratings by one-half

BENIGN HYPERTROPHY OF THE PROSTATE (BHP)

Benign prostatic hyperplasia (BPH) is an extremely common disorder in men over the age of 50.[49] It is characterized by the presence of discrete nodules in the paraurethral region of the prostate. When sufficiently large, these nodules compress and narrow the urethral orifice causing partial and sometimes complete obstruction to urine flow. Autopsy studies reveal nodular hyperplasia to be present in 20 percent of men at the age of 40, a figure that increases to 70 percent by the age of 60, and 90 percent by the eighth decade of life. However, not more than 5–10 percent of men with this condition require surgical relief for urinary obstruction, and in the remainder there is very little clinical significance. Individuals with symptomatic obstruction generally have frequency, nocturia, difficulty starting and stopping the stream of urine, diminished force of the urinary stream and dysuria. The urine may become retained in the bladder with subsequent distension and hypertrophy of the bladder, and hydronephrosis, cystitis and pyelonephritis occur as a consequence of obstruction and infection.

Traditional treatment has been surgical, either through a transurethral prostatic resection or a suprapubic prostatectomy. There is, however, significant morbidity and some mortality during prostatic surgery in older patients; this has lead to trials of pharmacologic agents designed either to shrink prostatic volume or decrease the tone of the prostatic smooth muscle.[53] Further controlled trials are necessary to define the efficacy of these treatment regimes.

Selection of Risks

Preoperative
Many insurance companies now include prostatic examination as part of the medical examination particularly in North America. This practice has not yet become as widespread in European insurance companies. The finding of benign hypertrophy on an evaluation is to be expected in the older age group. Symptoms such as dysuria, dribbling and poor urinary stream are suggestive of outflow obstruction. A concomitant finding of pyuria and hematuria on a urinalysis suggest that there is a concomitant urinary tract infection or complicating prostatitis. An elevated blood creatinine suggests post-renal failure.

If symptoms are significant, the risk should be postponed until the applicant is evaluated. At present such evaluations should include ultrasonography where the size of the prostate can be measured, and post-void residual bladder volumes to determine the magnitude of the obstruction. If a suspicious nodule has been palpated on an insurance rectal examination, a transrectal ultrasound will be necessary in the diagnostic work-up to exclude a malignancy.

The use of screening tests, such as prostate-specific antigen (PSA), is gaining more widespread acceptance in the insurance market, particularly in North America.[54] When PSA readings are extremely high (over 10 ng/ml), the specificity of such a finding for the presence of a prostrate carcinoma is as high as 95 percent in some series. This antigen may be detected by sophisticated radio-immunoassays but is secreted both by hypertrophic and malignant prostate glands. Figure 18.7 outlines the frequency of abnormalities of prostate specific antigen in individuals with benign prostatic hypertrophy versus malignancy.[54]

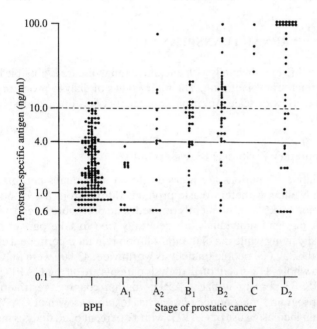

Fig. 18.7. Preoperative values for PSA in patients with BPH, clinically localized prostatic cancer or metastatic prostatic cancer. Solid line denotes the upper limit of the level of PSA in normal men; dashed line denotes the upper limit in patients with BPH.[54]

Using these findings as a basis, it would be most prudent to decline individuals with PSA levels greater than 10 ng/dl. Applicants with PSA levels of 6–10 ng should be evaluated, if this has not already been done. Applicants with PSA levels of 4–6 ng should at least have a rectal examination before insurance is issued.

Postoperative
In the uncomplicated case the prognosis following a prostatectomy is generally excellent and the risk could be considered standard after recovery has taken place, providing the urinalysis is normal and symptoms have been relieved. When,

however, there has been a history of prolonged surgical or medical preparation prior to prostatectomy, indicating that there were major complications of obstruction, the postoperative prognosis would depend largely on the degree of residual damage to the kidneys, ureter and bladder. Recovery will be slower than for the uncomplicated case of BHP and therefore applicants for life insurance should be postponed six months following operation. Thereafter the risk could be evaluated according to the state of renal function, as judged by the serum creatinine and microscopic urinalysis.

Persisting pyuria or a history of recurring urinary tract infections after prostatectomy may indicate complicating bladder diverticula, vesicoureteric reflux or chronic reflux nephropathy. These complications could be excluded by imaging modalities such as cystometrograms and ultrasonography. Depending on the findings, the risk could range from standard all the way up to decline.

DIALYSIS AND RENAL TRANSPLANTATION

Prolongation of life in individuals with end-stage renal disease is possible by means of dialysis or renal transplantation. The major types of dialysis programs that are available on a worldwide scale are chronic ambulatory peritoneal dialysis (CAPD) and hemodialysis.

Chronic Ambulatory Peritoneal Dialysis (CAPD)

In CAPD, dialysate solutions are infused into an individual's peritoneal cavity through an indwelling catheter. Waste products diffuse from the blood into the dialysate solution which is subsequently drained. The procedure is repeated four to five times per day and individuals are generally free to take part in the usual activities of daily living while the dialysate solution is in their peritoneal cavity.

By 1988 of the 330,000 people on dialysis worldwide, 43,000 were on CAPD.[56] In Europe as a whole, 11 percent of all dialysis patients are on the CAPD program, but in the UK 33 percent utilize CAPD. In that country, restriction of the hemodialysis program for economic reasons has fostered growth of CAPD. In the USA there is an increasing use of CAPD, with 17 percent of all dialysis individuals now using this method.[56]

Hemodialysis

In hemodialysis, waste products are removed from the individual's body by diffusion across a semi-permeable membrane, the major component in a hemodialysis unit. One major obstacle to the long-term use of this technique was the necessity of maintaining vascular access. In 1960 Quinton, Dillard and Scribner developed an arterial-venous shunt[55] connecting the radial artery to the cephalic vein through the respective insertion of silastic cannulas into the artery and vein and connecting them together by a Teflon tubing. Long-term morbidity was high due to clotting, bleeding and infection, but alternative and successful techniques are now employed for chronic vascular access. Currently, acute access to the vascular system is initiated by the percutaneous insertion of a double lumen catheter either into the internal jugular or femoral vein. Chronic vascular access is generally obtained through the use of an arteriovenous fistula which was first introduced in 1966. It generally takes eight weeks for the fistula to mature and thereafter dialysis may be performed without the morbidity of the Scribner shunt.

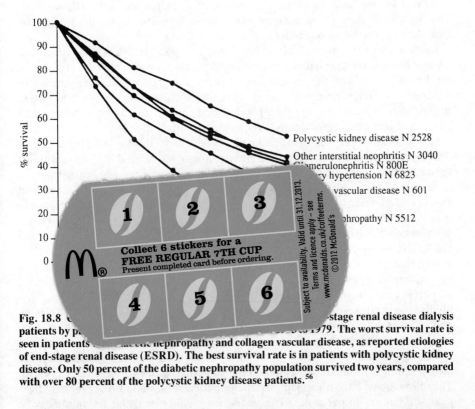

Fig. 18.8 ... stage renal disease dialysis patients by p... 979. The worst survival rate is seen in patients ... nephropathy and collagen vascular disease, as reported etiologies of end-stage renal disease (ESRD). The best survival rate is in patients with polycystic kidney disease. Only 50 percent of the diabetic nephropathy population survived two years, compared with over 80 percent of the polycystic kidney disease patients.[56]

The mortality from optimally performed peritoneal dialysis is very similar to the mortality from hemodialysis.[56] Figure 18.8 graphically indicates the mortality in over 26,000 Americans dialysed from 1973 to 1979.[56] It is noteworthy that dialysed diabetic patients do very poorly. An analysis of the recent US experience in the treatment of end-stage renal disease by dialysis and transplantation was reported in 1983.[57] This report included almost all individuals on dialysis in the USA, totalling over 65,000. The annual mortality rate for individuals treated either by hemodialysis or peritoneal dialysis was 19 percent per year for the first four years after initiating treatment. The annual mortality ratio was calculated to be 1,100 percent for males and 1,900 percent for females.[58] Over 50 percent of all deaths from dialysis may be related to cardiac disease and/or infection. The foregoing data reveal that dialysed individuals would not usually be insurable.

Renal Transplantation

The first renal transplant was performed between identical twins in 1950 in Boston. Later, transplantation between unrelated donors became possible with the use of immunosuppressant drugs. Most of the individuals with end-stage renal failure who meet the criteria for insurability will have had a renal transplant. Several factors can influence survival: young age groups have a better survival than older ones; applicants with a living related donor kidney have a better survival than those with a cadaver kidney, and the closer the compatibility match the better the survival. The higher the dose of maintenance immunosuppressive drugs, the higher the mortality, especially among older applicants.

Recurrence of the original disease in a transplanted kidney is always a hazard and is more likely if the original diagnosis was glomerulonephritis. Disease recurrence can be suspected with the appearance of proteinuria, or the new occurrence of hypertension. Recurrences are more likely within five years of grafting. Most studies also indicate that the transplanted diabetic has the worst survival of all patients having other renal diseases requiring transplantation.

An American study following 849 patients with renal disease for a period of 12 years clearly demonstrates superior survival for living related donor transplants versus cadaver transplants, both of which have superior mortality to dialysis treated patients.[59] More recent data suggest that the poor survival figures in cadaver related transplantation, as compared with living related donor transplantation, may be partially explained by a high frequency of HLA-DR typing mismatches.[60] Using sophisticated DNA technology, cadaver transplanted HLA-DR antigen matches have a success rate nearly as good as HLA matched sibling transplants. Data from the Collaborative Transplant Study showed a one-year success rate of 93 percent for 842 HLA identical sibling grafts compared with a 90 percent success rate for DNA HLA-DR correctly matched cadaver transplants.[61] It is not known whether the results of DNA HLA-DR matched sibling and cadaver transplants will yield similar survival figures five to ten years post-transplant, but the early results are certainly encouraging.

The Canadian renal failure register is a population-based disease register incorporating an annual follow-up feature for people with end-stage renal disease. The follow-up of 2,436 transplanted patients between 1981 and 1986 revealed a five-year survival of 86 percent.[35] The yearly probability of dying for non-diabetic individuals who received a transplant was constant at about 2 percent per year for each of the five years, whereas diabetics had an adjusted risk of death 3·7 times the mean non-diabetic risk. In males 50 percent of the overall deaths were attributable to cardiovascular disease and 22 percent were related to infection, undoubtedly a consequence of immunosuppressive medication. The calculated mortality ratio for diabetic males was 1,100 per cent, and for non-diabetic males was 300 percent. For female diabetics the mortality ratio was 2,000 percent, and for non-diabetics was 700 percent. The mortality experience in the first year post-transplant is generally high.

In the US transplant experience,[58] a 95 percent one-year and a 91 percent three-year survival were noted in living related donor transplants, whilst cadaver transplants were associated with 86 percent one-year and 77 percent three-year survivals.[59] This translated to mortality ratios of 1,700 percent for cadaver transplants and 1,150 percent for living related donor transplants. When high first-year mortality is eliminated, as would occur in a postponement period for life insurance, the mortality ratios for second and third years for all ages combined were 1,100 percent for cadaver transplants and 800 percent for related donor transplants.

A special situation arises when a monozygotic twin with end-stage renal failure receives an HLA identical kidney not requiring immunosuppressive therapy. In this ideal situation survival should be optimal, but recurrence of autoimmune disorders, such as glomerulonephritis, will occur with equal frequency as in a non-identical kidney match.

In the long term, immunologic matching between the donor and the recipient is important for successful renal transplantation, since rejection is a major problem. Acute rejection occurs in about 80 percent of cadaver transplants and about 50 percent of living related transplants, and may respond fully to immunosuppressive therapy. In the longer term, chronic rejection may lead to a transplant failure, and such individuals present with hypertension, proteinuria and renal insufficiency. This rejection may sometimes be reversed with increasing doses of immunosuppressive medications. This type of clinical picture must be differentiated from late graft failure resulting from recurrence of the original disease.

As has been shown above, it is indeed possible that with more sophisticated immunological matching, improvement in survival will be seen, not only with cadaver renal transplants but also with living related transplants. In addition, newer immunosuppressive regimens, including analogues of cyclosporin-like agents and application of various monoclonal antibodies, are likely to improve renal survival and decrease mortality.

Selection of Risks

For life insurance purposes only those applicants who are being followed and closely monitored at a transplant clinic can be considered. The presence of uncontrolled hypertension is a poor prognostic feature and applicants with this should be declined. Since cardiovascular diseases are the major causes of mortality, individuals with ischemic cardiac or cerebral vascular disease would not be considered insurable. The transplanted diabetic has a poor prognosis and should also be declined. Additionally, individuals with other organ diseases, such as chronic obstructive pulmonary disease or chronic hepatitis, would not be considered candidates for insurance. The occurrence of frequent episodes of rejection requiring high doses of immunosuppressive agents is rather worrisome and would most likely dictate a decline. Similarly, the occurrence of frequent infections or the occurrence of secondary tumors as a result of immunosuppressive agents has prognostically unfavorable features.

Cadaver and Living Related Transplants
The following rating scheme may be used for favorable kidney transplant recipients following a one-year postponement period:

Age (yr)	Cadaver transplant[a]	Living related transplant
Less than 20	Decline	Decline
21–40	+700	+500
41–50	+600	+400
Over 50	+400	+200

[a]Cadaver kidneys transplanted after 1989 using the DNA HLA-DR technique of matching can be rated as living related transplants.

An alternative method of rating renal transplants used by some companies is as follows:
1) Within one year of transplant — postpone.
Ages 16–60 — +100 and 10 per mil.

Transplant from monozygotic twin
Within one year of transplant — postpone.
Original disease causing end-stage failure:
    Glomerulonephritis — 5 per mil for four years.
    Other than glomerulonephritis — standard.

Hemodialysis, CAPD
Within three years — postpone.
Thereafter, best cases — individual consideration.

REFERENCES

1 *Medical Impairment Study 1983*. Vol 1, Boston: Society of Actuaries and Association of Life Insurance Medical Directors of America, 1986.
2 Abuelo JG. Proteinuria: diagnostic principles and procedures. *Ann Intern Med* 1983; 98: 186–91.
3 Brenner BM, Coe FL, Rector MD. *Clinical nephrology*. WB Saunders Co. Philadelphia, 1987.
4 Travis LB, Brouhard BH, Kalia A. *An Approach to the Child with Hematuria and Proteinuria*. Appleton-Century-Crofts. Norwalk CT, 1985.
5 Robinson RR. Isolated proteinuria in asymptomatic patients. *Kidney Int* 1980; 18: 395–406.
6 Robinson RR, Glover SN, Phillipi PJ et al. Fixed and reproducible orthostatic proteinuria: light microscopic studies of the kidney. *Am J Pathol* 1961; 39: 291–306.
7 Rytand DA, Spreiter S. Prognosis in postural proteinuria. *N Engl J Med* 1981; 305: 618–21.
8 King SE. Postural adjustments and protein excretion by the kidney in renal diseases. *Ann Intern Med* 1957; 46: 360–77.
9 Shaw A, Risdon P, Lewis-Jackson J. Protein creatinine index and albustix in assessment of proteinuria. *Br Med J* 1983; 287: 929–32.
10 Koopman MG, Krediet RT, Koomen GCM et al. Circadian rhythm of proteinuria: consequences of the use of urinary protein: creatinine ratios. *Nephrol Dial Transplant* 1989; 4: 9–14.
11 Ginsberg JM, Chang BS, Matarsee RA et al. Use of single voided urine samples to estimate quantitative proteinuria. *N Engl J Med* 1983; 309: 1543–46.
12 Schwab SJ, Christensen RL, Dougherty K el al. Quantitation of proteinuria by the use of protein to creatinine ratios in single urine samples. *Arch Intern Med* 1987; 147: 983–4.
13 Kristal B, Shasha SM, Labin L et al. Estimation of quantitative proteinuria by using the protein to creatinine ratio in random urine samples. *Am J Med Nephrol* 1988; 8: 198–203.
14 Minuk H. Understanding glomerular disease. *On the Risk* 1985; 3: 9–13.
15 Minuk H, Weir R. Understanding proteinuria and the protein/creatinine ratios. *On the Risk* 1991; 8: 18–27.
16 Barratt TM, McLaine PN, Soothill JF. Albumin excretion as a measure of glomerular dysfunction in children. *Arch Dis Child* 1970; 45: 496–501.
17 Yoshikawa N. Benign familial hematuria. *Arch Pathol Lab Med* 1988; 112: 794–7.
18 Bailey RR. Familial hematuria due to thin basement membrane nephropathy. *NZ Med J* 1990; 103: 312–13.

19 Sessa A, Meroni M, Battin G (eds). Hereditary nephritis. Contrib Nephrol. Basel: Karger, 1990; 80: 95–100.
20 Shrier RW, Gottschalk CW (eds). *Diseases of the Kidney*, 1988; Little, Brown and Co, Boston/Toronto.
21 International study of kidney disease in children. Minimal change nephrotic syndrome in children. *Pediatrics* 1984; 173: 497.
22 Cameron JS. The long term outcome of glomerular diseases. In: Schrier RW, Gottschalk CW (eds). *Diseases of the Kidney*, 1988; 2127–89.
23 Honkanen E. Survival in idiopathic membranous glomerulonephritis. *Clin Nephrol* 1986; 25: 122–8.
24 Madaio MP, Harrington JT. The diagnosis of acute glomerulonephritis. *N Engl J Med* 1983; 1299–1302.
25 Potter EV, Lipschultz SA, Abidh S et al. Twelve to seventeen year follow-up of patients with poststreptococcal acute glomerulonephritis in Trinidad. *N Engl J Med* 1982; 307: 725–9.
26 Baldwin DS. Post streptococcal glomerulonephritis: a progressive disease. *Am J Med* 1977; 62: 1–11.
27 Schena F. A retrospective analysis of the natural history of primary IgA nephropathy worldwide. *Am J Med* 1990; 89: 209–15.
28 Alamartine E, Sabatier J, Guerin C et al. Prognostic factors in mesangial IgA glomerulonephritis. An extensive study with univariate and multivariate analysis. *Am J Kid Dis* 1991; 18: 12–19.
29 Katajima T, Murakami M, Sakai D. Clinical pathological features in Japanese patients with IgA nephropathy 1983; *Jpn J Med* 22: 219.
30 Beukhof J, Karchaun O, Schaafsma W et al. Toward individual prognosis of IgA nephropathy. *Kidney Int* 1986; 29: 549–56.
31 Heilman RL, Offord MS, Holley KE. Analysis of risk factors for patient and renal survival in crescentic glomerulonephritis. *Am J Kid Dis* 1987; 9: 98–107.
32 Cameron JS, Turner DR, Heaton J et al. Idiopathic mesangiocapillary glomerulonephritis. *Am J Med* 1983; 74: 175–92.
33 Schmitt H, Bohle A, Reineke T et al. Long term prognosis of membranoproliferative glomerulonephritis type 1. *Nephron* 1990; 55: 242–50.
34 McEnery PT. Membranoproliferative glomerulonephritis. The Cincinatti experience — cumulative renal survival from 1957 to 1989. *J Pediatr* 1990; 116:109–14.
35 Silina, J. Fortier L, Mao Y et al. Mortality rates among patients with end-stage renal disease in Canada 1981–1986. *CMAJ* 1989; 141: 667–82.
36 Luke R. Nephrosclerosis. In: Schrier RW, Gottschalk CW (eds) *Diseases of the Kidney*, 1988; 1573–95.
37 Toto, R, Mitchell HG, Lee H et al. Reversible renal insufficiency due to angiotensin converting enzyme inhibitors in hypertensive nephrosclerosis *Am Intern Med* 1991; 115: 513–19.
38 Keane WF, Anderson S, Aurell M et al. Angiotensin converting enzyme inhibitors and progressive renal insufficiency. *Am Intern Med* 1989; 111: 503–16.
39 Rostand S, Brown G, Kirk K et al. Renal insufficiency in treated essential hypertension. *N Engl J Med* 1989; 320: 684–8.
40 Grun J, Klienknecht D, Droz D. Acute interstitial nephritis. In: Schrier RW, Gottschalk CW (eds). *Diseases of the Kidney*, 1988; 1461–87.
41 Lipsky B. Urinary tract infections in men. *Am Intern Med* 1989; 110: 138–50.
42 Eknoyan G. Chronic tubulointerstitial nephropathies. In: Schrier RW, Gottschalk CW (eds). *Diseases of the Kidney*, 1988; 2197–221.
43 Dubach UC, Rosner B, Pfister E. Epidemiologic study of abuse of analgesics containing phenacetin. *N Engl J Med* 1983; 308: 357–62.
44 Bosniak M. The current radiological approach to renal cysts. *Radiology* 1986;158: 1–10.
45 Madewell J. Hartman D, Lichtenstein J. Radiologic-pathologic correlations in cystic disease of the kidney. *Radiol Clin N Amer* 1979; 17: 261–79.
46 Kimberling WJ, Fain PR, Kenyon JB et al. Linkage heteregeneity of autosomal dominant polycystic kidney disease. *N Engl J Med* 1988; 319: 913–18.

47 Leier CV, Baker PB, Kilman JW et al. Cardiovascular abnormalities associated with adult polycystic kidney diseases. *Ann Intern Med* 1984; 100: 683–8.
48 Levey AS, Pauker SG, Kassirer JP. Occult intracranial aneurisms in polycystic kidney disease. *N Engl J Med* 1983; 308: 986–94.
49 Cottram RS, Kumur V, Robbins SL. *Robbins Pathologic Basis of Disease*, 4th edition. WB Saunders Co, 1989.
50 Maffly RH. Nephrolithiasis. In: *Scientific American Medicine*. Rubenstein, Federman (eds). 1986; 8: 1–10.
51 *1951 Impairment Study*. New York: Society of Actuaries, 1954.
52 Smith JM, O'Flynn JD. Vesical stone: the clinical features of 652 cases. *J Irish Med Assoc* 1975; 68: 85.
53 Jardin A, Bensadoun H, Delauche-Caxallier MC et al. Alfuzosin for treatment of benign prostatic hypertrophy. *Lancet* 1991; 337: 1457–61.
54 Gittes R. Carcinoma of the prostate. *N Engl J Med* 1991; 324: 236–45.
55 Tolkoff-Rubin N. Dialysis and transplantation. In: *Scientific American Medicine*. Rubenstein, Federman (eds), 1991; 11: 1–25.
56 Greca GL, Feriam M, Dell'Aquila R et al. Updating on continuous ambulatory peritoneal dialysis. Contrib Nephrol. Basel: Karger, 1990; 84: 1–9.
57 Rosansky SJ, Eggers PW. Trends in the US end-stage renal disease population 1973–1983. *Am J Kid Dis* 1987; 9: 91–7.
58 Kakaver H. Grauman JS, McMullan MR et al. The recent US experience in the treatment of end-stage renal disease by dialysis and transplantation. *N Engl J Med* 1983; 308: 1558–63.
59 Lew EA, Gajewski J (eds). *Medical Risks: trends in mortality by age and time elapsed*. New York, Westport CT, London: Praeger, 1990; 10: 14–70.
60 Vollmer WM, Wahl P, Blagg CR. Survival with dialysis and transplantation in patients with end-stage renal disease. *N Engl J Med* 1983; 304: 1553–8.
61 Opelz G, Mytilineos J, Scherer S et al. For the collaborative transplant study. Survival of DNA HLA-DR typed and matched cadaver kidney transplants. *Lancet* 1991; 338: 461.

CHAPTER 19

DISEASES OF THE LIVER AND ALIMENTARY TRACT

MAX L HEFTI

R D C BRACKENRIDGE

PART I: LIVER AND BILIARY SYSTEM

MAX L HEFTI

The alimentary tract, perhaps more than any other system, reflects the feeling of well-being, or otherwise, of an individual. Indigestion, dyspepsia, abdominal pain, vomiting and diarrhea can arise as the result of almost any functional or organic disease of the digestive tract including the liver, biliary system and pancreas; even ischemic heart disease may give rise to symptoms akin to indigestion. When indigestion is reported in a medical history the examiner should attempt to interpret its meaning; otherwise its significance to the life underwriter could be far from clear.

HEPATOMEGALY

A liver palpable on physical examination does not automatically mean liver enlargement (hepatomegaly). This, however, is likely to be present if the lower edge of the liver descends more than 3 cm (1½ finger-breadths) below the right costal margin in the mid clavicular line with deep inspiration in subjects of average build. In hyposthenic subjects a normal-sized liver may be palpated up to 8 cm (4 finger-breadths) below the costal margin. In pyknic subjects, on the other hand, even an enlarged liver may escape palpation. Reporting the location of the edge of the liver in terms of the costal margin without describing the consistency (soft, firm, hard) of the liver and the nature of its surface (smooth, nodular) is bad medical practice. Indeed, a liver that feels hard and nodular is likely to be pathological even if its lower edge can only just be palpated beneath the costal margin. And a liver of borderline size is more likely to be truly enlarged if it feels firm rather than soft.

The relative mortality associated with hepatomegaly as an isolated finding varies between 200 percent (European policyholders) and 370 percent (Japanese declined lives).[1,2]

With an unsuspicious history and otherwise normal physical examination it is sometimes appropriate to accept applicants with a soft liver palpable 3-4 cm (1½–2 finger-breadths) below the right costal margin. If the liver is larger, especially if described as firm, hard or nodular, liver function tests are mandatory before a reasonable risk assessment can be made.

ABNORMAL LIVER FUNCTION TESTS

The laboratory tests most commonly used to evaluate and monitor liver integrity and function consist of the measurement, in the serum, of liver cell-derived enzymes and products of liver metabolism. Unfortunately they all lack sensitivity and, especially, specificity.

Elevated enzyme activity in the serum may primarily reflect liver cell necrosis or cholestasis (biliary retention). The major indicators of liver cell necrosis are alanine aminotransferase (ALT, formerly called SGPT) and aspartate aminotransferase (AST, formerly called SGOT). Lactate dehydrogenase (LDH) also belongs to this group. Alkaline phosphatase (AP) is the major indicator of cholestasis. Other cholestasis enzymes include 5'-nucleotidase and gamma-glutamyl transferase or transpeptidase (GGT or GGTP). Elevation of the latter may have a double meaning: cholestasis or alcohol-induced leakage of liver cells. The methods used to measure enzyme activity in the serum vary, and the results of measurement are expressed in different units. A simple way to compare results is to express them as a multiple of the particular laboratory's upper limit of normal.[3]

Serum bilirubin concentrations are an indicator of the excretory function of the liver. Serum levels in excess of 17 μmol/l (1·0 mg/dl) are referred to as hyperbilirubinemia. Other 'true' liver function tests include measurement of serum albumin concentration and of the prothrombin-time. However, hypoalbuminemia and prolonged prothrombin-time, both pointing to impaired synthetic liver function, are signs of advanced liver disease.

Common Underwriting Scenarios

Abnormal liver tests may be the sole problem of two common underwriting scenarios: (1) a history of acute hepatitis with full clinical recovery where liver tests have not yet returned to normal, and (2) the chance finding, on routine screening, of abnormal liver tests in an applicant without history or clinical evidence of liver disease.

Scenario 1
If abnormalities involving multiple tests, say several liver enzymes and serum bilirubin, persist despite apparent recovery from acute hepatitis, applications for life insurance should be postponed for a period of six months. If the tests are then still abnormal, there would be a strong suspicion of chronic hepatitis. If, on the other hand, the sole abnormality is persisting mild elevation of the aminotransferases with a record of steadily falling values on serial testing, most would consider the risk to be standard. It must be stressed, however, that the finding of abnormal liver tests more than twelve months after the alleged clinical recovery from acute hepatitis indicates either chronic hepatitis or a disorder unrelated to the reported acute disease. Applications should be handled as indicated under scenario 2 (*see below*).

Scenario 2
If the abnormalities involve multiple tests, applications should be postponed for a period of six months. Liver function tests should then be repeated and tests for serologic markers of HBV and HCV infection performed. If the liver tests are still abnormal, there would be a strong suspicion of chronic liver disease, particularly of chronic viral hepatitis if HBsAg and/or anti-HCV were positive.

If a single test is mildly abnormal there is a high probability of abnormality secondary to chance alone.[4] Most underwriters would disregard it.

JAUNDICE

The range of normal serum bilirubin values is 5·1–17 μmol/l (0·3–1·0 mg/dl), the conjugated form accounting for no more than 6·8 μmol/l (0·4 mg/dl). Hyperbilirubinemia up to 26 μmol/l (1·5 mg/dl) goes clinically unnoticed. With bilirubin values in excess of 34 μmol/l (2·0 mg/dl) jaundice becomes patent. The major causes of jaundice include liver disease, biliary obstruction, excessive hemolysis and inborn or drug-induced impairments of the bilirubin metabolism. The long-term prognosis of persistent or recurrent jaundice cannot be evaluated without knowing the etiology.

Benign Forms of Recurrent Jaundice

Gilbert's Syndrome

Gilbert's syndrome or familial unconjugated non-hemolytic hyperbilirubinemia (or Meulengracht's juvenile icterus, as it is described in German literature) is a benign hereditary condition which affects about 5 percent of adolescents. It is due to reduced bilirubin absorption by the liver cells combined with a mild deficiency of the bilirubin-conjugating enzyme, glucuronyl transferase.

Affected people may give a history of attacks of jaundice occurring intermittently over many years, often since childhood. The attacks may be triggered by physical stress, infection, prolonged fasting and oral contraceptives. They tend to disappear with increasing age. Misinterpretation as relapsing or even chronic hepatitis is not uncommon. Apart from unconjugated hyperbilirubinemia, which usually runs at 26–68 μmol/l (1·5–4 mg/dl), the biochemical liver tests are completely normal. There is typically no bilirubinuria and no signs of increased hemolysis.

Dubin-Johnson's Syndrome

Dubin-Johnson's syndrome (or idiopathic chronic familial jaundice) is an uncommon benign hereditary condition due to impaired excretion of the conjugated bilirubin into the biliary canaliculi by the liver cells.

Intermittent attacks of jaundice occur throughout life, favored by physical stress, infection, alcohol consumption and oral contraception. Affected people are more jaundiced than ill. Serum values of conjugated bilirubin may reach 257 μmol/l (15 mg/dl) or more during attacks. The biochemical liver tests are normal. The diagnosis is made from the pathognomonic result of the bromsulphthalein test (normal bromsulphthalein retention by the liver 45 minutes after injection, regurgitation into the circulating blood 90 minutes after injection) and by demonstrating the typical black pigmentation of the liver on laparoscopy or liver biopsy.

Rotor's Syndrome

Rotor's syndrome is identical to Dubin-Johnson's syndrome, the only difference being that the black pigmentation of the liver is missing.

Benign Intrahepatic Familial Recurrent Cholestasis

Benign intrahepatic familial recurrent cholestasis (or Summerskill-Tygsturp's syndrome) is a relatively rare benign condition of unknown etiology. A familial incidence can be traced in many instances.

The first attack, characterized by jaundice and cholestasis which may last for several weeks, usually occurs before the age of 20. It subsides spontaneously only to occur later in life. During attacks the serum values of the aminotransferases and AP are significantly elevated (two to six times and three to four times the upper normal limit respectively). Hyperbilirubinemia is of the conjugated type. Liver biopsy shows only cholestasis, and no obstruction of the biliary tree is found on retrograde cholangiography. During remissions liver function tests and biopsy are completely normal.

Prognosis and Selection of Risks

Long-term prognosis of Gilbert's syndrome, Dubin-Johnson's syndrome, Rotor's syndrome and benign intrahepatic familial recurrent cholestasis is good. Applicants in whom the diagnosis of one of these benign forms of recurrent jaundice has been established can be insured as standard risks.

HEPATITIS

Hepatitis is a diffuse inflammatory reaction of the liver with cellular infiltration and degeneration or necrosis of liver cells in response to infection, toxic substances or drugs. The extent of inflammatory infiltration and loss of liver parenchyma varies greatly with etiology, severity and duration of the disease. In many cases hepatitis is an acute self-limiting process. It can, however, be a chronic disease from the start or progress to chronicity later.

Acute Hepatitis

Application from individuals with a history of acute hepatitis should be considered depending upon the answers to the following questions:
1) Was it acute self-limiting hepatitis (e.g. hepatitis A)?
2) Was it an acute exacerbation of chronic disease (e.g. alcoholic hepatitis)?
3) Was it the acute start of potentially chronic disease (e.g. hepatitis B)?
4) Is recovery complete (e.g. following toxic fulminant hepatitis)?

Often the time elapsed since acute illness or the applicant's assertion of full recovery is all that is needed to make an underwriting decision. In other cases more information, such as a statement from the attending physician or liver function tests and serology, may be necessary.

If chronic disease can be excluded and liver function is restored, most cases could be accepted at standard rates six months after onset of acute hepatitis and three months since recovery.

Fulminant Hepatitis

Fulminant hepatitis is a clinical variety of hepatitis characterized by precipitous collapse of liver function due to massive liver cell necrosis. It may occur in viral hepatitis (particularly in hepatitis B with delta coinfection, and in hepatitis E in pregnant women), toxic hepatitis and drug-induced hepatitis.

Mortality ranges between 50 and 80 percent.[5] Emergency liver transplantation is the only therapeutic chance for many patients. The final outcome of those who survive fulminant hepatitis with medical care alone depends on recovery of liver function and the underlying liver disease. It could mean normal life expectancy.

Chronic Hepatitis

Chronic hepatitis is diffuse necroinflammation of the liver persisting for more than six months. With such an arbitrary cut-off point, overlapping of acute and chronic hepatitis is likely to occur. The major causes of chronic hepatitis include HBV infection (with or without delta coinfection or superinfection), HCV infection, alcohol and other toxic substances, a number of drugs and auto-immune mechanisms.

Chronic hepatitis is conventionally subdivided into two major forms, based on clinical, serum biochemical, serologic and histologic findings: chronic persistent hepatitis (CPH) and chronic active hepatitis (CAH). The line of separation may be blurred, and fluctuation between the two forms occurs due to changing disease activity or immune response (e.g. in hepatitis B), or due to treatment.

Chronic Persistent Hepatitis (CPH)

This is low grade inflammation of the liver which may persist for decades. It is by no means a necessary or automatic precursor of CAH. Its usual causes are hepatitis B and hepatitis C. Histologically, CPH is characterized by spotty necrosis and restriction of the inflammatory infiltrate to the portal tracts. Clinically, the disease is generally silent. There is often hepatomegaly but never cutaneous lesions and ascites. Serum bilirubin does not exceed 26 μmol/l (1·5 mg/dl). The amino-transferases may be moderately elevated.

When confirmed, CPH is generally assumed to be non-progressive. However, progression to CAH or cirrhosis has been observed in some cases, especially in HBeAg-positive patients with HBV-induced disease. The overall five-year survival rate is 95 percent.[6,7]

Well-selected and well-documented cases could be accepted for life insurance with a rating of +50 to +100 depending on age. Credit could be considered if serology confirms the absence of HBeAg.

Chronic Active Hepatitis (CAH)

This is progressive necroinflammation of the liver, also called chronic aggressive hepatitis, which may be associated with cirrhosis in the very early stages. The major causes of CAH are viral hepatitis B and C, auto-immune disease and drugs (such as oxyphenacetin, methyldopa, isoniazid and nitrofurantoin).

Histologically, the disease is characterized by conspicuous extension of the portal infiltration into the periportal area with piecemeal necrosis. Severe bridging necrosis and multilobular necrosis associated with collapse and fibrosis pave the way to cirrhosis. Clinically, CAH may be silent or associated with chronic illness, or fluctuate between acute exacerbations and prolonged periods of remission. Depending on severity of the disease, there may be jaundice, spider nevi, hepatosplenomegaly, ascites and signs of encephalopathy. Although liver function tests do not correlate well with the clinical, serological and histologic state, marked elevation of serum bilirubin, aminotransferases, gamma-globulin and pathological liver function tests tend to be associated with more severe disease.

Viral CAH

About 40 percent of HBV-induced and 50 percent of HCV-induced CAH progress to cirrhosis. Progression is most rapid in HBeAg-positive hepatitis B (four-and-a-half years on average) and in hepatitis C in general, especially if associated with alcohol-induced liver disease (four years on average).[8] On the other hand, CAH may remain stable for many years or even resolve clinically and histologically. This may occur spontaneously or as a result of interferon therapy in both hepatitis B and C. Relapse after the cessation of treatment is, however, common.[9]

The estimated five-year survival rate for patients with viral CAH without evidence of cirrhosis is 86 percent on average.[6] Clinically stable cases in which liver function tests indicate little disease activity and serial liver biopsies show a stable pattern with only little necrosis and fibrosis may be accepted for life insurance at substandard rates. For applicants over the age of 45 the rating should be +200 to +300 depending on age.

Drug-Induced CAH

Withdrawal of the offending agent usually halts progression of the disease, and long-term prognosis depends mainly on the damage to the liver already done as judged on biochemical and histologic evidence. For selected cases with normal liver function tests and stable minimal histologic changes a rating of +100 to +150, depending on age, might be adequate.

Auto-immune CAH

This is hepatitis presumed to be initiated by auto-immune disease. It was originally called lupoid hepatitis, since the LE cell test is positive in some 15 percent of patients. Auto-immune hepatitis is a multisystem disease which may be accompanied by arthralgia, hemolytic anemia, inflammatory bowel disease, nephritis and thyroiditis. Antimitochondrial, antinuclear and anti-smooth-muscle antibodies are found in 70 percent of patients, and HCV antibodies in many.

The disease affects practically only women, usually aged 15 to 25 or older than 45. It is particularly frequent in Australia. Although the disease usually responds well to immunosuppression, cirrhosis cannot be prevented in the long term. The five-year survival rate in treated patients is 85 percent, compared with 40 percent in the untreated.[10]

Carefully selected cases showing no evidence of cirrhosis or multisystem involvement might be considered for life insurance. If successfully treated for at least two years, a rating of +200 to +300, depending on age, might be correct. This might be reduced by half if drugs have been finally withdrawn for at least one year without relapse, or even more if liver biopsy reveals healing with no, or only minimal, fibrosis.

Viral Hepatitis

If viral hepatitis is being referred to, it usually means a systemic infection that predominantly affects the liver. This definition restricts the scope of viral hepatitis to infections with the so-called hepatitis viruses; it excludes infections with other viruses (such as the herpes simplex viruses, varicella-zoster virus, Epstein Barr virus, cytomegalovirus and a number of tropical hemorrhagic fever viruses) in which inflammation of the liver is not the predominant feature.

Five so-called hepatitis viruses have been so far identified: A, B, D (delta agent) and the two non-A, non-B viruses, C and E. All may cause acute hepatitis (symptomatic or asymptomatic) and fulminant hepatitis, but only HBV, HDV and HCV infection carry the risk of chronic hepatitis, cirrhosis and hepatocellular carcinoma.

Enterically Transmitted Viral Hepatitis

Hepatitis A

Hepatitis A, formerly called infectious hepatitis, is caused by the hepatitis A virus (HAV), an RNA virus belonging to the group of picornaviruses. It is transmitted by the fecal-oral route and may occur sporadically or in large outbreaks that can be traced to contaminated water or food. Travel in developing countries has become a common source of infection for adults from areas with advanced sanitation.

Primary infection in childhood tends to cause subclinical disease, whereas infection in adulthood produces clinical disease in 50–80 percent of the infected. Fulminant hepatitis is rare and mainly occurs in people over the age of 40.[11] Hepatitis A never develops into chronic liver disease or a viral carrier state, although a prolonged course of disease, including relapsing hepatitis and persistent cholestasis over a period of up to 12 months, has been reported.[12]

The diagnosis of hepatitis A is made by demonstrating specific viral antibodies (anti-HAV) of the IgM class in the serum during acute infection or of the IgG class later in life.

Long-term prognosis is good, and applicants with a history of hepatitis A can be accepted at standard rates three months after recovery.

Hepatitis E

The etiological agent of enterically transmitted hepatitis non-A, non-B has been recently shown to be an RNA virus belonging to the caliciviruses, and has been named hepatitis E virus. The disease spreads through the fecal-oral route, and it usually occurs in large outbreaks after contamination of water supplies. It has been identified in India, South East Asia, Africa and Central America, and in travelers to these areas.

Hepatitis E is more common in adults than in children and the incidence is especially high in pregnant women. The incidence of fulminant hepatitis varies from about 5 percent to 15 percent depending on the epidemic. Pregnant women have a mortality of up to 39 percent.[13] Hepatitis E never progresses to chronic liver disease and there is no chronic virus carrier state.

The diagnosis of hepatitis E by demonstrating the presence of the HEV genome in the stools by means of reverse transcription-polymerase chain reaction is still reserved for research work. In clinical medicine the diagnosis relies on epidemiologic features and exclusion of HAV, HBV, HDV and HCV infection.[14]

The vast majority of patients (including most survivors from fulminant hepatitis) make a complete recovery within three months. They can be insured for life at standard rates three months after recovery.

Hepatitis B

Hepatitis B, formerly called serum hepatitis, is caused by a DNA virus from the hepadnavirus family, the hepatitis B virus (HBV). The complete virus (Dane particle) consists of a core and an envelope or coat. The core encloses the viral genome (HBV DNA) and the HBV-specific DNA-polymerase, and contains at least two antigenic structures, the hepatitis B core antigen (HBcAg) and the closely related HBeAg. The hepatitis B surface antigen (HBsAg) is the major coat antigen.[11]

The prevalence of HBV infection varies greatly. It is highest in Africa, South East Asia, eastern and southern Europe and India (6–11 percent of the total population) and is lowest in the Americas, Australia and northern and western Europe (0·1–1·5 percent).[15] Transmission is primarily parenteral and through sexual exposure. Since screening of blood donors and effective sterilization of needles and surgical tools have become nearly universal, blood transfusions, blood products and surgical and dental procedures are no longer common sources of infection. In low prevalence areas the classic high-risk groups (health care workers, gay men) have been replaced by new ones (heterosexuals with multiple partners, intravenous drug users) over the last 10 years.[16] Infection usually occurs in adolescence or adulthood. In high prevalence areas perinatal infection from mother to child is a major route of transmission (vertical transmission). Depending on the country 10–25 percent of children below the age of five are already infected.

HBV is not considered to be directly hepatotoxic. Hepatitis results from the immune response against infected liver cells. In adults with an intact immune system infected liver cells tend to be destroyed and the virus eliminated within a few weeks. Primary infection is asymptomatic in as many as 60 percent and fewer than 5 percent develop chronic infection. In infants and small children with an immature immune system (as well as in the immunocompromised) the destruction of infected liver cells and the clearance of the virus is delayed. The acute stage is asymptomatic in 90 percent, and chronic infection occurs in 90 percent of infants and 20 percent of pre-school-aged children. The major forms of chronic infection are CPH, CAH and chronic HBsAg carrier state. All may progress to cirrhosis and hepatocellular carcinoma. Fulminant hepatitis occurs in fewer than 1 percent of cases, usually in HCV or HDV superinfection or coinfection.

Recovery in self-limited cases is generally complete. Anti-HBc temporarily associated with anti-HBs is the lifelong marker of recovered hepatitis B.[16] Applications from individuals with a history of acute hepatitis B of at least six months can be accepted standard provided there is no evidence of ongoing liver disease and viral replication.

Chronic HBsAg carriers

Patients who have HBsAg persisting in the serum for more than six months are usually referred to as chronic HBsAg carriers. This is, however, a very confusing term, since such patients vary enormously in their clinical, serum biochemical, serologic and histologic features and, last but not least, in their long-term prognosis. To overcome this confusion a classification into carriers with chronic liver disease and asymptomatic or 'healthy' carriers has been proposed. The distinction is often made based on the presence of clinical manifestations and/or elevation of serum aminotransferases. This approach is not always reliable, and new definitions, which are based not only on clinical and serum biochemical findings but also on histologic evidence of liver disease and on the state of viral replication, should be used.

The prevalence of chronic HBsAg carriers varies a great deal in different geographical areas, depending on the most frequent route of transmission and the usual age at infection. It ranges from less than 1 percent in western Europe and the USA to 10–15 percent in South East Asia and China.[17]

HBsAg Carriers with Chronic Liver Disease A virus carrier with chronic HBV-related liver disease will typically have elevated serum aminotransferases plus one of HBeAg, HBV DNA or DNA polymerase in the serum. Liver biopsy will reveal some degree of chronic hepatitis and/or cirrhosis. Depending on the severity of hepatitis, there could be jaundice, spider nevi, hepatomegaly and ascites. The markers of active viral replication, HBcAg and 'free' HBV DNA in the liver cells, would be detectable using special technology.[18]

Healthy Chronic HBsAg Carriers This is a person who has no clinical manifestations of liver disease, normal serum aminotransferases and no detectable HBeAg, HBV DNA and DNA polymerase in the serum. Anti-HBe would usually be detectable. Liver biopsy, if carried out, should be normal or only minimally abnormal, the most common abnormality being ground-glass hepatocytes (liver cells packed with HBsAg). No markers of viral replication (i.e. HBcAg and 'free' HBV DNA) should be present in liver cells, but small amounts of viral DNA integrated into the host's DNA could be detected using advanced technology.

The classification of the chronic HBsAg carrier state is neither clear cut nor definitive, since many distinctive features are quantitative rather than qualitative; the state of HBV replication and the disease activity can change over time, and about 1 percent of chronic carriers annually lose their HBsAg.

Prognosis and Risk Evaluation Data from Taiwan clearly show that death from cirrhosis is 24 times more frequent in chronic HBsAg carriers than in non-carriers, and the incidence of hepatocellular carcinoma (HCC) 94 times greater in carriers than in non-carriers.[1-19] Prospective studies from Japan and the UK researching risk and incidence in carriers compared with the general population show estimates consistent with the Taiwan data.[20,21] Although carriers with evidence of chronic liver disease and healthy carriers were not studied separately, it can be assumed that a high proportion are likely to have been healthy carriers, since the examinees were either active civil servants, eligible blood donors or active railway employees.

About 50 percent of chronic carriers will eventually die of cirrhosis or HCC.[22] Even in the absence of progression to cirrhosis 'all persons who remain HBsAg carriers will', according to R P Beasley, 'develop hepatocellular carcinoma if they live long enough and are not killed by other causes first.'[19] The major risk factors, besides cirrhosis and already existing silent carcinoma, include seropositivity for IgM anti-HBc, HBeAg and HBV DNA, infection during birth or at pre-school age, male sex, age over 45 and black African or Asian background.

It might be assumed that the mortality of healthy chronic HBsAg carriers is significantly higher in a country like China, where most are infected early in life, than in western Europe, where infection usually occurs in adult life. This assumption, however, is not entirely correct. In China the extra risk due to the age at infection is to some extent reduced by the fact that it is shared by up to 15 percent of the adult population and is therefore, at least partially, included in the standard mortality. In western Europe, on the other hand, the extra risk, though lower for the individual carrier infected in adult life, is not offset by a high prevalence in the general population. Therefore it seems reasonable to consider that the final extra mortality (which, among others, depends on the two inversely related factors, usual age at infection and prevalence of infection) is about the same worldwide. A rating of +50 to +125 is suggested, depending on factors representing a better chance or a greater risk in the market concerned.

Hepatitis D

Hepatitis D, also called delta hepatitis, is caused by the hepatitis D virus (HDV) or delta agent always found associated with hepatitis B virus. The HDV is coated in hepatitis B virus surface antigen (HBsAg) and depends on pre-existing or concomitant HBV infection for propagation.

In endemic areas, such as northern Africa, the Middle East and southern Europe, the disease is predominantly transmitted by close personal contact. In non-endemic areas, such as North America and northern Europe, it is mainly transmitted through the parenteral route. Coinfection and superinfection with HDV may cause fulminant hepatitis or exacerbation of pre-existing chronic hepatitis B.

The diagnosis of hepatitis D coinfection or superinfection in patients with chronic hepatitis B is made by demonstrating anti-delta antibodies (anti-HDV) of the IgM class during acute infection and of both IgM and IgG in chronic infection.

Applicants for life insurance with a history or with evidence of hepatitis D should be underwritten based on the concomitant hepatitis B.

Hepatitis Non-A, Non-B

It has been recognized for a long time that hepatitis viruses A and B do not account for all forms of epidemic, transfusion-associated and sporadic viral hepatitis. These forms caused by as yet unidentified viruses have been globally named hepatitis non-A, non-B – although it was clear from the beginning that there were at least two distinct viruses or groups of viruses: one transmitted by the fecal-oral route, another transmitted parenterally.

The major virus causing transfusion-associated hepatitis non-A, non-B was identified in 1988 (hepatitis virus C); the virus responsible for water-borne epidemics was successfully cultivated in 1989 (hepatitis virus E). There are good reasons to believe that there is still at least one unidentified parenterally transmitted 'non-B, non-C virus'.

Enteric hepatitis non-A, non-B, is discussed in the section on hepatitis E (*see* pp. 573–4), and the parenteral form is dealt with in the section on hepatitis C (*see below*).

Hepatitis C

Most cases of parenterally transmitted hepatitis non-A, non-B and many sporadic cases of the disease are presently recognized as hepatitis C. The hepatitis C virus (HCV) can be indirectly traced by demonstrating an antibody directed against an antigen derived from the viral genome (referred to as anti-HCV), or sequences of the viral RNA (HCV RNA) in the serum. The HCV is an RNA virus and a distant parent of the togavirus or flavivirus family.[11,23] It has not yet been demonstrated, and there is no test as yet to detect circulating HCV antigens. Anti-HCV is a late marker of infection, appearing in the serum two to nine months (15 weeks on average) after infection and disappearing over the years in 30 percent of cases, regardless of whether cured or with chronic liver disease. Sequences of HCV RNA appear in the serum as early as one to two weeks after primary infection. They disappear in cured cases when HCV is definitely eliminated from the body, but persist in cases with ongoing viremia.[24,25] The HCV RNA test, which is not yet universally available, is currently the only marker that can discriminate between overcome infection and ongoing disease.

Transmission of hepatitis C is predominantly by the parenteral route. As far as the sexual route is concerned, it is interesting to note that transmission by homosexual contact seems to be less efficient than by multi-partner heterosexual contact. Perinatal transmission, if it occurs at all, is not an important mode of infection. About 40 percent of patients with acute hepatitis C have no identifiable source of infection. The anti-HCV seroprevalence in healthy adults (usually volunteer blood donors) is estimated at about 1 percent in western Europe, the USA, Taiwan and Japan. Higher proportions were reported in high-risk groups, including health workers (1·75 percent in New York), female prostitutes (3·5 percent in Taiwan), hemophiliacs (74·4 percent in Japan) and intravenous drug users (48 to 89 percent in the USA).[26–29]

Hepatitis C occurs as the direct result of the cytotoxic effects of HCV. The acute disease is often asymptomatic and only about 25 percent of patients become ill with jaundice. A self-limiting course is observed in about 50 percent of people affected, and fulminant hepatitis develops in under 5 percent. Recovery from self-limiting acute hepatitis C is usually complete. HCV RNA disappears from the serum. Anti-HCV may become detectable only after the cure of the disease and remain positive for up to 30 years.[24,25,27]

In about 50 percent of patients with acute disease there is a slow sequential progression to chronic hepatitis, cirrhosis and, eventually HCC. In the USA more than 40 percent of patients with transfusion-associated chronic hepatitis who underwent liver biopsy within five years after onset had histologic evidence of CAH, and 10–20 percent had evidence of cirrhosis. In contrast, the proportion of community-acquired CAH with cirrhosis and HCC was less than 20 and 3 percent respectively.[8] It has been suggested recently that early interferon therapy might prevent the progression to chronicity.[30]

According to recent surveys from Korea and Japan, hepatitis C might account for up to 80 percent of all CAH and for 65 percent of cirrhosis and HCC. It could be responsible for the sharp increase in HCC in HBsAg negative patients in Japan: from 5·6 per 100 thousand in 1968–78 to 12 per 100 thousand in 1984–85. The risk of HCC is 3·5 times greater in hepatitis C than in hepatitis B.[29,31]

Chronic HVC Carriers

HCV RNA has been detected in the serum of individuals with a history of proven hepatitis C for up to 14 years after primary infection. Anti-HCV did not remain detectable in all.[23,24] Bearing in mind that the presence of HCV RNA in the serum indicates actual replication of the C virus, whereas the persistence of HBsAg in the serum only means that the coat of the B virus is still being produced, with or without ongoing viral replication, chronic HCV RNA carriers cannot be considered the analogue of chronic HBsAg carriers. For underwriting purposes applicants with HCV RNA persistent in their serum for more than six months should be treated like those with chronic HCV-related liver disease, regardless of their anti-HCV status.

HEPATIC CIRRHOSIS

Cirrhosis of the liver is progressive, with irreversible hardening and shrinking of the liver resulting in liver failure and portal hypertension. From a morphologic point of view, two major forms of cirrhosis can be distinguished: micronodular cirrhosis (also called regular or portal or Laennec's cirrhosis) and macronodular cirrhosis (also called irregular or postnecrotic cirrhosis).

The major causes of cirrhosis are chronic alcohol consumption (alcoholic cirrhosis), chronic hepatitis B and C (posthepatitic cirrhosis), hemochromatosis, prolonged biliary obstruction (biliary cirrhosis), inherited metabolic disorders and a large number of drugs. The cause remains obscure in nearly 10 percent of cases (cryptogenic cirrhosis).

Cirrhosis is histologically characterized by pseudolobular regeneration of necrotic liver cells and invasive fibrosis disrupting the normal architecture of the liver and distorting its vascular bed. Clinically, cirrhotic patients may be nearly asymptomatic except for induration of the liver. The liver may be enlarged in early stages, or no longer palpable under the costal margin in advanced cases. Alternatively cirrhotics may be ill with jaundice, spider nevi, ascites, encephalopathy and signs of portal hypertension. Depending on the activity of the disease, serum enzymes may vary from normal to markedly elevated; depending on the loss of liver cell mass, liver function tests may vary from nearly normal to highly pathological.

The three major complications of cirrhosis are hepatic encephalopathy, upper gastrointestinal bleeding and HCC. In posthepatitic cirrhosis acute exacerbations of the underlying hepatitis, due to reactivation of the causative virus or superinfection with another virus, may precipitate the natural course of the disease.

Prognosis and Risk Evaluation

The combined annual death rate from encephalopathy, esophagogastric variceal bleeding and HCC is 6–8 percent on average.[32] In the first five years liver failure and variceal bleeding are the main causes of death; later liver failure is less common, with variceal bleeding and hepatoma as the principal causes of death. The five-year survival rate of cirrhosis is 55 percent on average;[6] it tends to be lower in anti-HCV-positive patients and higher in alcohol-induced cirrhosis, partly due to the fact that the risk of HCC in posthepatitic cirrhosis is more than twice as high as in alcoholic cirrhosis.[27,33]

The majority of applicants with established hepatic cirrhosis will not qualify for life insurance cover. Carefully selected cases may, however, be accepted. Such cases would typically be individuals with alcoholic cirrhosis who have ceased alcohol consumption entirely for many years. Cirrhosis should be of the micronodular type, inactive and stable for several years, without a history or evidence of decompensation (jaundice, coagulation disorders, ascites, hepatic encephalopathy) or portal hypertension (hypersplenism, upper gastrointestinal bleeding). Best cases would have only mildly elevated serum aminotransferases, normal serum alpha-fetoprotein values and no detectable esophagogastric varices or liver tumors. Cases of this type over the age of 40 could be insured at a rating in the range of +200 to +300.

Biliary Cirrhosis

Biliary cirrhosis is a form of liver cirrhosis which is secondary to prolonged partial or total obstruction of the common bile duct or its major branches, or which results from injury to the biliary tree.

Secondary Biliary Cirrhosis
In adults secondary biliary cirrhosis most commonly occurs with post-operative strictures of the common bile duct, gallstones (cholangiolithiasis), chronic pancreatitis and idiopathic sclerosing cholangitis. In children the most common causes are congenital biliary atresia and cystic fibrosis of the pancreas.

Like any other form of cirrhosis, biliary cirrhosis eventually ends in death from liver failure or complications of portal hypertension if biliary obstruction is not relieved in time. Relief of obstruction by surgical or endoscopic means may result in a significant improvement, even in patients with established cirrhosis.

Primary Biliary Cirrhosis
This is the possible end-product of chronic non-suppurative destructive cholangitis, an auto-immune disease affecting and slowly destroying medium and small intrahepatic bile ducts. It may progress to cirrhosis or come to a stop before full scale cirrhosis has developed. The disease typically affects women between the ages of 35 and 60 and is frequently associated with other auto-immune diseases.

Elevated serum GGT and markedly accelerated erythrocyte sedimentation rate, to be followed by elevated alkaline phosphatase (two to five times the upper limit of normal), are the first signs of chronic non-suppurative destructive cholangitis. Most patients are asymptomatic at this stage and the disease is detected on routine laboratory screening. The diagnosis is confirmed by the finding of high titers of antimitochondrial antibodies in the serum (1:80 or higher) and the typical lesions of the intrahepatic bile ducts on liver biopsy.

In 30–60 percent of patients symptoms appear within four years from diagnosis.[34] In the majority the first symptom is pruritus and it often remains isolated for many years. Early jaundice or hepatomegaly are prognostically ominous signs. The clinical features of fully developed primary biliary cirrhosis include darkening of the exposed area of skin, xanthelasma and xanthomas, and osteoporosis and osteomalacia. Serum cholesterol is elevated.

Immunosuppressive therapy is being used in an attempt to halt the auto-immune process leading to the destruction of the intrahepatic bile ducts, but there is no cure for established primary biliary cirrhosis short of liver transplantation.

Risk Evaluation
Survival is strongly related to symptom appearance. The ten-year survival rate of symptomatic patients is 48 percent, compared with 78 percent in the asymptomatic without associated auto-immune disease.[35,36] Applicants with established biliary cirrhosis are uninsurable. Selected asymptomatic cases may, however, be insured. The selection should be based on the following: stable condition for at least one year, serum bilirubin not exceeding 1·5 mg/dl (26 μmol/l), prothrombin time normal and no evidence of portal hypertension. For applicants aged 35–55 a rating of +200 to +250 would be appropriate.

PORTAL HYPERTENSION

Portal hypertension indicates an increased resistance to blood flow from all organs drained by the portal vein: stomach, small and large intestine and spleen. The block to blood flow may be situated proximally to the hepatic blood bed (presinusoidal block) or distally to the sinusoids (postsinusoidal block).

The main causes of presinusoidal block are schistosomiasis and thrombosis of the portal vein. Combined sinusoidal and postsinusoidal block is present in cirrhosis, and postsinusoidal block may result from occlusion of the hepatic veins (e.g. in the Budd-Chiari syndrome) or pericardial and myocardial disease obstructing the venous outflow from the liver.

Chronically increased pressure in the portal system causes congestive spenomegaly, esophagogastric varices and congestive gastropathy.

Congestive Splenomegaly

Congestive splenomegaly, formerly called Banti's syndrome, is enlargement of the spleen due to obstruction of the venous outflow with increased pooling of blood cells resulting in hemolytic anemia, leucopenia and thrombocytopenia (hypersplenism).

Esophagogastric Varices

Esophagogastric varices result from dilatation of collateral veins by the venous blood in its attempt to reach the inferior vena cava by bypassing the obstacle in the portal system. Esophageal and gastric varices may rupture and lead to repeated gross bleeding.

About one-third of cirrhotic patients with portal hypertension can be expected to die from hemorrhage. There are several therapeutic options, including variceal sclerotherapy, reduction of the gastroesophageal blood flow by drugs and portacaval shunt surgery. There is no evidence yet that any of these improves the long-term outcome.

Congestive Gastropathy (Portal Hypertensive Gastropathy)

This is diffuse dilatation of the mucosal capillaries and submucosal veins of the stomach due to obstruction of the venous outflow. Diffuse gastric lesions are the cause of up to 50 percent of episodes of gastrointestinal bleeding in cirrhotic patients with portal hypertension.[37]

Portal Vein Thrombosis

Thrombotic occlusion of the portal vein with secondary extra-hepatic portal hypertension occurs most often in infancy and is usually a complication of umbilical sepsis, which spreads to the portal system via the umbilical vein. Portal vein thrombosis arising initially in adulthood is less commonly of infective etiology but due to causes such as tumors, polycythemia, myeloproliferative disorders and liver cirrhosis. In many instances no obvious cause can be found.

Prognosis and Risk Evaluation

The prognosis of portal hypertension of extra-hepatic origin is better than the prognosis following liver cirrhosis, since liver function is usually better preserved. There is, however, a substantial extra mortality.

Insurance cover at substandard rates may be granted in cases without history of gastrointestinal bleeding, with normal liver function tests and where the cause of portal vein thrombosis is not itself associated with significant extra mortality. The rating would be +150 to +250, depending on age.

Portacaval Shunt Surgery

The purpose of portacaval shunting is portal decompression to prevent or arrest bleeding from esophagogastric varices or gastric mucosa in congestive gastropathy. Depending on the site of the portal block and local anatomy, blood from the high-pressure portal system can be shunted into the low pressure venacaval system by portacaval, splenorenal or mesenterico-caval anastomosis, at the price of possible worsening of liver function and portasystemic encephalopathy.

Several controlled studies suggest that, although mortality from esophagogastric hemorrhage is substantially reduced, increased mortality from other causes, especially liver failure and encephalopathy, more than redress the balance. It appears, therefore, that the risk associated with portal hypertension will be the same whether a surgical shunt has been carried out or not.

ALCOHOL-INDUCED LIVER DISEASE

The liver is a preferred target organ of the toxic effects of ethyl alcohol (ethanol, C_2H_5OH). Amount and duration of alcohol consumption are the most important determinants of alcohol-induced liver injury. Although there is no threshold below which alcohol cannot induce liver disease, practically no cirrhotic was found to drink less than 80 g of ethanol per day in a classic French study in the 1950s.[38] This amount is equivalent to about 25 dl of whisky, 50 dl of port or sake, nearly 1 liter of wine and more than 1 liter of beer. These findings have been confirmed by the Japanese Group for the Study of Alcoholic Liver Disease.[39] According to this body a daily consumption of 80 g of ethanol for five years is necessary to cause alcoholic liver disease in general, and 140 g per day for ten years to cause alcoholic cirrhosis. These values apply to males of average body mass. Corresponding values for females are about one-third lower. However, factors other than gender and amount and duration of alcohol consumption must have a role in the pathogenesis of alcohol-induced liver disease, since only 10–20 percent of heavy and steadfast drinkers develop cirrhosis, and since cirrhosis of the liver and chronic pancreatitis seem to occur in different subsets of alcoholics.[40]

Identifying individuals at increased risk of alcohol-induced liver disease and proving the alcoholic origin of evident liver disease is difficult, due to the fact that people suffering from alcohol dependence are poor witnesses of their own drinking habits. Experience shows that the actual alcohol consumption of an individual suspected of drinking more than the accepted norm usually amounts to anything up to twice the quantity admitted. The following anamnestic data and findings point to excessive alcohol consumption: a history of driving incidents or fighting injuries, mild fluctuating arterial hypertension, unexplained arrhythmia and signs of peripheral neuropathy, more pronounced elevation of AST than ALT, elevation of serum transferases, elevation of GGT of more than 2·5 times the upper normal limit, hypertriglyceridemia and hyperuricemia, and macrocytosis.[3,41]

The incidence and prevalence of alcohol-induced liver disease vary widely between different geographical and ethnic groups, and over time as alcohol consumption per head of population changes. The extra mortality associated with alcohol-induced liver disease is mainly due to liver cirrhosis, violent death and cardiovascular disease. Alcohol, often combined with cigarette smoking, is indeed a frequent contributing factor to arterial hypertension.[42]

Fatty Liver (Hepatic Steatosis)

This is diffuse infiltration of liver cells by neutral fats, mainly triglycerides. The proportion of cells affected indicates the severity of steatosis. There is no or only minimal inflammation and portal and periportal fibrosis in uncomplicated cases. The most common causes of fatty liver are alcohol consumption, marked obesity and poorly controlled diabetes. Fatty liver occurs in most heavy drinkers. It usually builds up progressively over a period of years, but it may occur within a month or even weeks of particularly heavy drinking. The condition is completely reversible if its cause is eliminated. It is not an inevitable precursor of cirrhosis. In fact, cirrhosis develops in only 10–15 percent of cases, very often when there is superimposed alcoholic hepatitis.

Slowly developing fatty liver is usually asymptomatic. The only clinical sign is a uniformly enlarged, firm and smooth liver. Liver enzymes and serum bilirubin are usually normal or borderline, except for occasional GGT elevation pointing to the alcoholic genesis of the condition. The diagnosis may be confirmed based on increased echogenicity and decreased ultrasound penetration, or by finding large fat droplets within one-third or more of liver cells.[43]

It may be assumed that extra mortality in alcohol-induced fatty liver is similar to that observed in hepatomegaly of unknown etiology (i.e. about 50–100 percent).[1]

Alcoholic Hepatitis

This is inflammation of the liver with necrosis of groups of liver cells and fibrosis induced by heavy alcohol drinking. It may occur in a fatty liver as well as an apparently intact liver.

Although alcoholic hepatitis is a chronic process from the beginning, it may manifest itself with episodes of acute exacerbation with fever, right upper abdominal pain and leucocytosis. The finding, on biopsy, of so-called Mallory bodies (alcoholic hyaline) within the cytoplasm of hepatocytes is typical, though not pathognomonic, of alcoholic hepatitis. The condition is reversible in early stages provided alcoholic drinks are strictly avoided. However, it is usually the starting point of cirrhosis, and 30 percent of severe alcoholic hepatitis progresses to cirrhosis within three years.[39]

In the absence of any meaningful statistical data it is safe to estimate the risk of an individual with alcoholic hepatitis who is still drinking or has only stopped drinking for a few months as nearly as high as in fully developed cirrhosis. Most applicants will therefore be uninsurable. Best cases (i.e. reformed drinkers for several years without evidence of cirrhosis) might be underwritten as for alcohol-induced fatty liver (*see above*).

Alcoholic Cirrhosis

Cirrhosis occurring in the alcoholic is usually of the regular micronodular type (Laennec's cirrhosis). It is often associated with steatosis and may be complicated by alcoholic hepatitis. If alcohol is withdrawn, the active progressive disease may be transformed into a stable latent scar stage with few, if any, clinical and biochemical manifestations.

For long-term prognosis and rating see the section on cirrhosis (*see* pp. 578–80).

POLYCYSTIC DISEASE OF THE LIVER

Polycystic disease of the liver is a congenital condition characterized by the formation of multiple non-bile-containing cysts in the liver due to defective development of the bile ducts within the portal tracts. The lobular architecture is not disturbed and the liver cells are normal.

Hepatomegaly first becomes evident in about the fourth or fifth decade of life and may range from slight to filling the whole abdomen, depending on the number of cysts. The cholestatic enzymes may be moderately elevated but liver function always remains normal. It is estimated that more than 50 percent of patients with polycystic disease of the liver also have polycystic disease of the kidneys. Other organs, such as the spleen, pancreas and lung, may also be affected.

Polycystic disease affecting only the liver is compatible with normal longevity. Involvement of the kidneys, however, is associated with a high extra mortality. The exclusion of associated polycystic disease of the kidneys is therefore the key step in the risk assessment of applicants with polycystic disease of the liver. Any suspicion of renal involvement on examination, such as proteinuria or arterial hypertension, should lead to further investigations, including abdominal ultrasonography. When renal involvement can be confidently excluded applicants can be insured at standard rates, but if the liver is grossly enlarged and causing significant pressure symptoms an extra mortality rate of +50 would be appropriate.

HEPATOCELLULAR CARCINOMA (HCC)

HCC is a primary malignant tumor of the liver cells or hepatocytes (primary hepatoma). It is the most common cancer in sub-Saharan Africa and the second most common in South East Asia and China. In western Europe and the USA it accounts only for about 2 percent of all malignancies.

HCC most commonly develops in a cirrhotic liver. The etiology of the underlying cirrhosis varies in various geographic areas: 85–95 percent chronic HBV infection in South East Asia and China, compared with 10–25 percent in western Europe and the USA; 75 percent chronic HCV infection in Japan; and 15 percent alcohol-induced liver disease in Europe and the USA. However, HCC can arise in a liver without detectable cirrhosis (e.g. in chronic HBsAg carriers). This is a strong argument in favor of the thesis that HBV is a direct oncogenic factor.[8,17,33,44] In alcoholic cirrhosis HCC usually develops late in life, often many years after cirrhosis has been recognized. In posthepatitic cirrhosis the tumor tends to develop at younger ages, often before cirrhosis is first detected. Typical ages at diagnosis are 35–45 in Africa, 45–55 in China and Japan, and over 55 in western Europe and the United States.[45]

Diagnosis at an early stage, when resection is still possible, is based on alpha-fetoprotein in the serum and abdominal ultrasonography. Elevated alpha-fetoprotein values (upper limit of normal 25 ng/ml) are found in 85 percent of HCCs. A single value of 400 ng/ml or more is considered pathological, as are repeated values of 30 ng or more with a rising trend.[17,46]

The three-year survival rate, even of early diagnosed and resected cases, does not exceed 60 percent.[47] Declining is the usual underwriting decision (*see* p. 632).

GALLSTONES

The prevalence of gallstones in a nation or community seems to rise in proportion to its level of affluence. In South East Asia, for example, the prevalence at autopsy is less than 3 percent in contrast to the USA where autopsy series have shown gallstones in 8 percent of men and more than 20 percent of women over the age of 40. Between the ages of 40 and 50 the annual incidence is about 3 percent.[48]

Gallstones consist of normal and abnormal bile constituents. Three types may be distinguished: cholesterol stones, pigment stones and mixed stones. In industrialized countries more than 80 percent are cholesterol stones. Super-saturation of bile with cholesterol, destabilization of bile and stasis of bile in the gallbladder are the major pathogenetic factors.

Today more and more symptomless gallstones are being discovered during the course of routine abdominal ultrasonography. On the whole, the natural history of silent gallstones is benign. The cumulative risk for the development of symptoms or complications requiring surgery is relatively low: 10 percent at five years and less than 20 percent at 15 years. Patients then remaining asymptomatic are unlikely to develop symptoms later on.[49]

There is general agreement that cholecystectomy is the definitive treatment for symptomatic gallbladder stones and that silent gallstones do not require surgery or medical treatment. There is no agreement, however, on the need for cholecystectomy in every symptomatic patient. Non-surgical approaches, like dissolution with bile acids (usually ursodeoxycholic acid) and disintegration by shock waves generated outside the body (extracorporeal shock wave lithotrypsy) or a combination of both, are highly successful in carefully selected patients with cholesterol stones. Unfortunately all forms of treatment in which the gallbladder remains *in situ* share the major drawback of stone recurrence: 50 percent at five years.[50]

Prognosis

Analysis of the experience with 19,646 life policies issued in the USA from 1952 to 1976 at standard or substandard premium rates to people with cholelithiasis and cholecystitis not treated surgically indicates an overall mortality ratio of 101 percent for men and 86 percent for women. However, in the two years following issue of insurance the mortality ratio was higher.[51]

Rating

Gallstones with or without cholecystitis, not treated surgically.
1) Silent gallstones:

Time since diagnosis	Rating
Up to 12 mth	2·5 per mil for 1 yr
Thereafter	Standard

2) Symptomatic gallstones.
Biliary colic without acute cholecystitis and jaundice:

Time since last attack	Rating
Up to 12 mth	5 per mil for 1 yr
2nd yr	2·5 per mil for 2 yr
3rd yr	2·5 per mil for 1 yr
Thereafter	Standard

With attacks of acute cholecystitis or evidence of chronic cholecystitis:

Time since last attack	Rating
Up to 12 mth	5 per mil for 2 yr
2nd yr	5 per mil for 1 yr
3rd yr	2·5 per mil for 2 yr
4th yr	2·5 per mil for 1 yr
Thereafter	Standard

GALLBLADDER SLUDGE

Biliary sludge is a mixture of granules of calcium bilirubinate and cholesterol crystals within bile that contains a high concentration of mucus which collects in the dependent part of the gallbladder. Biliary sludge is essentially an ultrasonographic diagnosis.

Follow-up studies of patients with gallbladder sludge indicate that in the majority the characteristic echo patterns disappear or have a fluctuating course of disappearance and reappearance. This suggests that the precipitation of cholesterol crystals is not an irreversible process. In one study about 15 percent of patients developed gallstones, more than half asymptomatic, and 6 percent had complications without gallstone formation ('acalculous' cholecystitis, acute pancreatitis).[52]

From the underwriting point of view the finding of asymptomatic gallbladder sludge may be disregarded, whereas gallbladder sludge associated with biliary colic should be rated like symptomatic gallstones.

CHOLECYSTITIS AND CHOLANGITIS

Cholecystitis (inflammation of the gallbladder) and cholangitis (inflammation of the biliary tree) usually occur as the result of obstruction of the cystic duct or the extrahepatic bile ducts respectively, with secondary bacterial infection.

Cholecystitis

More than 90 percent of cases of acute cholecystitis result from obstruction of the gallbladder outlet by gallstones. Acute cholecystitis is a serious condition and cholecystectomy remains its mainstay therapy. Of patients who undergo remission without surgery 25 percent will experience at least one recurrence within one year, and more than 50 percent within five years. Acute attacks are associated with frequent complications, including gallbladder empyema, hydrops, gangrene and perforation, with a surgical mortality of up to 30 percent.

The prognosis and rating are as for gallstones (*see* p. 585).

Cholangitis

Cholangitis is usually due to bacterial infection of the entire biliary tree secondary to obstruction of the extrahepatic bile ducts by stones (choledocholithiasis), tumor or stricture. If the bile flow is not rapidly restored, cholangitis may become chronic and progress to secondary biliary cirrhosis.

Primary Sclerosing Cholangitis
Primary sclerosing cholangitis is a chronic fibrosing inflammation of both the intrahepatic and the extrahepatic bile ducts progressing towards obliteration of the intrahepatic bile ducts and secondary biliary cirrhosis.

The etiology is still unknown, but the importance of the immune system in its pathogenesis is strongly suspected. Primary sclerosing cholangitis occurs principally in young men: At the time of diagnosis 70 percent are less than 45 years of age. The disease is most often associated with chronic inflammatory bowel disease[53] or with fibrosclerosing syndromes, including retroperitoneal fibrosis, Riedel's struma and pseudotumors of the orbit.

The onset of the disease is insidious and an average of two years precedes the diagnosis. Liver tests reveal a cholestasis profile with predominantly increased AP, GGT and bilirubin. Endoscopic retrograde cholangiography demonstrates multifocal strictures involving the intraheptic and extrahepatic ducts.

Two treatment possibilities are currently being evaluated, methotrexate and bile salts, in an attempt to decrease liver cell damage secondary to biliary stasis. However, liver transplantation seems to provide the best hope for cure of the disease. The long-term prognosis is poor, and relentless progression is the rule. In a recent survey of 454 patients, 45 of whom were asymptomatic at the initial evaluation, the average duration of survival after symptoms developed was six years.[54] In terms of life underwriting, this unfortunately usually means decline.

Chronic Non-Suppurative Destructive Cholangitis
Chronic non-suppurative destructive cholangitis is an auto-immune disease affecting and slowly destroying medium and small intraheptic ducts; it may progress to primary biliary cirrhosis.

Prognosis and risk evaluation are as for primary biliary cirrhosis (*see* pp. 579–80).

CHOLECYSTECTOMY

There are two approaches to the removal of the gallbladder: (1) conventional open cholecystectomy via an abdominal incision (laparotomy) and (2) laparoscopic cholecystectomy using instruments introduced into the abdominal cavity through canulas and monitored using an endoscope (laparoscope, peritoneoscope, celioscope).

The overall post-operative mortality of open cholecystectomy is 0·5–3·0 percent for acute cholecystitis and interventions on the common bile duct,[55] the higher values being observed in patients over the age of 60. The average hospitalization time is seven to ten days. The use of laparoscopic cholecystectomy was first reported in 1989. Since then, more than 3 thousand cases have been reported, with an overall post-operative mortality of less than 1 per mil and an average hospitalization time of two to two-and-a-half days.[56,57]

Is the gallbladder really physiologically irrelevant as Carl Langerbuch, who first successfully removed a gallbladder for cholelithiasis in 1882, believed? The fact is that no significant metabolic or functional impairment as a direct sequel of cholecystectomy has yet been convincingly demonstrated. However, as many as 30 percent of patients complain of various symptoms following removal of the gallbladder, collectively referred to as postcholecystectomy syndrome.[58] In less than half of these patients organic causes can be demonstrated. These include residual gallstones that escaped surgery, recurrent gallstones secondary to traumatic papillary stenosis, a long cystic duct stump or traumatic stricture of the choledochus and pre-existing disorders of the esophagus, stomach, duodenum and pancreas.

Prognosis

Overall, the long-term prognosis following cholecystectomy for benign disease is good. Analysis of the experiences with 90,168 life policies issued in the USA from 1952 to 1976 at standard or substandard premium rates to people with a history of cholecystectomy within the last five years indicates an overall mortality ratio of 105 percent for men and 93 percent for women. The mortality ratio for substandard cases was slightly higher, with 121 percent in men and 128 percent in women.[59]

Rating

1) Cholecystectomy for benign disease, full recovery:

Time since surgery	Rating
Less than 6 mth	Postpone
7–12 mth	2·5 per mil for 2 yr
2nd yr	2·5 per mil for 1 yr
Thereafter	Standard

2) Cholecystectomy for benign, postcholecystectomy syndrome.
Residual or recurrent gallstones, papillary stenosis, choledochus stricture:

Time since surgery	Rating
Less than 12 mth	Postpone
2nd yr	5 per mil for 2 yr
3rd yr	5 per mil for 1 yr
Thereafter	Standard

Disorders of the esophagus, stomach, duodenum and pancreas — rate according to underlying disorders.

PANCREATITIS

Pancreatitis or inflammatory disease of the pancreas may be classified into acute pancreatitis and chronic pancreatitis, based on clinical, biological and morphologic criteria. The incidence of acute pancreatitis in reported series ranges from 2 to 24 per 100,000 in different countries. The wide variation may be partly a result of different approaches to case selection rather than true regional differences.

Gallstones and alcohol together account for about 80 percent of cases. However, the part played by each causative factor in different parts of the world is variable. In the UK alcohol-related disease accounts for 15–25 percent of cases, in the USA for more than 40 percent and in Sweden for more than 65 percent.[60] About 5–10 percent of pancreatitis cases are caused by diverse factors, including hypertriglyceridemia, hypercalcemia, viral infection, various drugs and major surgery. The remaining cases are still labeled idiopathic pancreatitis.[61]

Acute Pancreatitis

The main clinical features of acute pancreatitis are abdominal pain, elevated serum amylase levels and, in severe cases, hypovolemic shock resulting from exudation and vasodilatation. Frequent local complications include pancreatic abscess and pseudocysts. The pathologic spectrum varies from mild edematous pancreatitis to severe necrotizing pancreatitis.

Treatment of acute pancreatitis consists of supportive measures and elimination of the causative factors in order to prevent relapses and chronicity.

Prognosis
Overall mortality associated with the first acute attack is about 15 percent[60] but tends to diminish with subsequent attacks.

Rating

1) Biliary pancreatitis
Biliary obstruction corrected (e.g. cholecystectomy or papillotomy):

Time since last attack	Rating
Up to 12 mth	5 per mil for 1 yr
2nd yr	2·5 per mil for 1 yr
Thereafter	Standard

Biliary obstruction still present:

Time since last attack	Rating
Up to 12 mth	5 per mil for 3 yr
2nd yr	5 per mil for 2 yr
3rd yr	5 per mil for 1 yr
Thereafter	Standard

2) Alcohol-induced pancreatitis.
Up to two attacks:

Time since last attack	Rating
Up to 12 mth	5 per mil for 3 yr
2nd yr	5 per mil for 2 yr
3rd yr	5 per mil for 1 yr
Thereafter	Standard

Three or more attacks — rate for chronic pancreatitis (*see below*).
   3) Acute pancreatitis of other etiology — rate for causative disorder.
   4) Acute idiopathic pancreatitis — rate as biliary pancreatitis, obstruction still present (*see above*).

Chronic Pancreatitis

Advanced chronic pancreatitis is characterized by the triad of steatorrhea due to exocrine deficiency, impaired glucose tolerance due to endocrine deficiency and intraductal calcification. The natural history of chronic pancreatitis is characterized in early stages by recurrent episodes of acute inflammation superimposed on previous pancreatic injury (relapsing chronic pancreatitis) and progressive pancreatic dysfunction (with or without calcification in late stages).

   Early diagnosis is hardly possible due to the natural history of the disease. In the early stages recurrent episodes of acute inflammation dominate the clinical picture, and there is no way of definitely distinguishing recurrent acute pancreatitis from chronic relapsing pancreatitis. Decreasing severity of successive attacks is an argument in favour of chronicity. Definite diagnosis, however, depends on the appearance of progressive pancreatic dysfunction with or without calcifications, and this occurs at an average of five-and-a-half years after onset of pancreatitis.[62] In late stages pain may disappear, and there are cases of proven chronic pancreatitis that never experienced any pain. In other words, the key to classification of pancreatitis into acute and chronic disease is its long-term clinical course. Even histology may not always differentiate residuals from acute damage from chronic lesions. In case of doubt, a history of more than one acute attack should be interpreted as early chronic pancreatitis.

Elimination of the cause (e.g. biliary surgery or abstinence from alcohol) may stop the progression of the disease. Exocrine and endocrine pancreatic deficiency may be controlled by substitution therapy. Surgery may be the only means of controlling pain.

Prognosis
In two recent studies from France and Japan an extra mortality of about 200 percent was observed, as compared with the age– and sex-matched general population.[63,64] If these patients had been compared with standard lives, the extra mortality rate may be assumed to be around 350 percent. Whether or not alcohol-induced chronic pancreatitis has a higher mortality than non-alcohol-induced pancreatitis is still controversial.

Rating
The rating should be +150 to +200, depending on severity of exocrine and endocrine pancreatic deficiency, and likelihood of surgery.

REFERENCES

1 Fessel M, Scholl L, Hefti ML. Die isolierte Hepatomegalie und ihre Folgen auf die Lebenserwartung. *Lebensversicherungsmedizin* 1984; 36: 136–9.
2 Lew EA, Gajewski J (editors). *Medical Risks: trends in mortality by age and time elapsed.* New York: Praeger 1990; 9: 70–1.
3 Reichling JJ, Kaplan MM. Clinical use of serum enzymes in liver disease. *Dig Dis Sci* 1988; 33: 1601–14.
4 Desbien NA, Turney SL, Gani KS. Multichannel 18-test panels: are 60% of panels abnormal by chance? *J Lab Clin Med* 1990; 115: 292–7.
5 Fagan EA, Williams R. Fulminant viral hepatitis. *Br Med J* 1990; 46: 462–80.
6 Weissberg JI, Andres LL, Smith CI et al. Survival in chronic hepatitis B: an analysis of 379 patients. *Ann Int Med* 1984; 101: 613–16.
7 Andershvile J, Dietrichson O, Skinhoj P et al. Chronic persistent hepatitis: serological classification and meaning of the hepatitis Be system. *Hepatology* 1982; 2: 243–6.
8 US Department of Health and Human Services. Public Health Service inter-agency guidelines for screening donors of blood, plasma, organs, tissues and semen for evidence of hepatitis B and hepatitis C. *MMWR* 1991; 40 (RR–4): 1–17.
9 Davis GL, Balart LA, Schiff ER et al. Treatment of chronic hepatitis C with recombinant interferon alpha: a multicenter randomized controlled trial. *N Engl J Med* 1989; 321: 1501–6.
10 Kirk AP, Jain S, Pocock S et al. Late results of the Royal Free Hospital prospective controlled trial of prednisolone therapy in hepatitis B surface antigen negative chronic active hepatitis. *Gut* 1980; 21: 78–83.
11 Valenzuela P. Hepatitis A, B, C, D and E viruses: structure of their genomes and general properties. *Gastroenterol Jpn* 1990; 25 (Suppl 2): S62–S71.
12 Lesnicar G. A prospective study of viral hepatitis A and the question of chronicity. *Hepato-gastroenterol* 1988; 35: 69–73.
13 Gupta H, Joshi YK, Tandon BN. Enteric non-A, non-B hepatitis in India. *J Gastroenterol and Hepatol* 1990; 5: 288–95.
14 Ray R, Aggarwal R, Salunke PN et al. Hepatitis E virus genome in stools of hepatitis patients during large epidemic in North India. *Lancet* 1991; 388: 783–4.
15 Sobeslavsky O. Prevalence of markers of hepatitis B virus infection in various countries: a WHO collaborative study. *Bulletin WHO* 1980; 58: 621–8.

16 Alter MJ, Hadler SC, Margolis HS et al. The changing epidemiology of hepatitis B in the United States. *JAMA* 1990; 263: 1218–22.

17 Di Bisceglie AM, Rustigi VK, Hoofnagle JH et al. Hepatocellular carcinoma. *Ann Int Med* 1988; 108: 390–401.

18 Hoofnagle JH, Shafritz DA, Popper H. Chronic type B hepatitis and the 'healthy' HBsAg carrier state. *Hepatology* 1987; 7: 758–63.

19 Beasley RP. Hepatitis B virus: the major etiology of hepatocellular carcinoma. *Cancer* 1988; 61: 1942–56.

20 Hall AJ, Winter PD, Wright R. Mortality of hepatitis B positive blood donors in England and Wales. *Lancet* 1985; i: 91–3.

21 Samkuma K, Takahara T, Okuda K et al. Diagnosis of hepatitis B virus surface antigen carriers in relation to routine liver function tests: a prospective study. *Gastroenterol* 1982; 83: 114–17.

22 Popper H, Shafritz DA, Hoofnagle JH. Relation of the hepatitis B virus carrier state to hepatocellular carcinoma. *Hepatology* 1987; 7: 764–72.

23 Hepatitis C virus upstanding (editorial). *Lancet* 1990; 335: 1431–2.

24 Farci P, Alter HJ, Wong D et al. A long-term study of hepatitis C virus replication in non-A, non-B hepatitis. *N Engl J Med* 1991; 325: 98–103.

25 Aramaki T, Wakayama Y, Akaike M et al. Long-term status of antibody to hepatitis C virus and the relation to the outcome of hepatitis: a restrospective study using stored sera from patients with Sashima epidemic hepatitis. *Gastroenterol Jpn* 1991; 26 (Suppl 3): 209–11.

26 Klein RS, Freeman K, Taylor PE et al. Occupational risk for hepatitis C virus infection among New York City dentists. *Lancet* 1991; 338: 1539–42.

27 Hepatitis C (parenterally transmitted non-A, non-B hepatitis). *WHO Wkly Epidem Rec* 1991; 34: 251–4.

28 Sakamoto M, Hirohashi S, Tsuda H et al. Increasing incidence of hepatocellular carcinoma possibly associated with non-A, non-B hepatitis in Japan, disclosed by hepatitis B virus DNA analysis of surgically treated cases. *Cancer Research* 1988; 48: 7294–7.

29 Chen DS, Kuo GC, Sung JL et al. Hepatitis C virus infection in an area hyperendemic for hepatitis B and chronic liver disease: the Taiwan experience. *J Infect Dis* 1990; 162: 817–22.

30 Omata M, Yokosuka O, Takario S et al. Resolution of acute hepatitis C after therapy with natural beta interferon. *Lancet* 1991; 338: 914–15.

31 Nishioka K. Hepatitis C virus infection in Japan. *Gastroenterol Jpn* 1991; 26 (Suppl 3): 152–5.

32 Liaw YF, Lin DY, Chen TJ et al. Natural course after the development of cirrhosis in patients with chronic type B hepatitis: a prospective study. *Liver* 1989; 9: 235–41.

33 Hadengue A, N'dis N, Benhamou JP. Relative risk of hepatocellular carcinoma in HBsAg positive versus alcoholic cirrhosis. A cross-sectional study. *Liver* 1990; 10: 147–51.

34 Nyberg A, Loof L. Primary biliary cirrhosis: clinical features and outcome, with special reference to asymptomatic disease. *Scand J Gastroenterol* 1989; 24: 57–64.

35 Roll J, Boyer JL, Barry D et al. The prognostic importance of clinical and histologic features in asymptomatic and symptomatic primary biliary cirrhosis. *N Eng J Med* 1982; 308: 1–7.

36 Beswick DR, Klatskin GD, Boyer JL. Asymptomatic primary biliary cirrhosis: A progress report on long-term follow-up and natural history. *Gastroenterol* 1985, 89: 267–71.

37 Portal hypertensive gastropathy (editorial). *Lancet* 1991; 338: 1045–6.

38 Péquignot G. Die Rolle des Alkohols bei der Aetiologie von Leberzirrhosen in Frankreich: Ergebnisse und Bedeutung einer systematischen Umfrage. *Münch Med Wschr* 1961; 31: 1464–8.

39 Takada A, Galambos JT. Diagnosis of alcoholic liver disease: an international conference. *Gastroenterol Jpn* 1990; 25 (Suppl 1): 3–53.

40 Angelini G, Merigo F, Degani G et al. Association of chronic alcoholic liver and pancreatic disease: a prospective study. *Am J Gastroenterol* 1985; 80: 998–1003.

41 Braun RE. A probabilistic approach to underwriting suspected alcohol abuse. *J Insur Med* 1989; 21: 255–62.

42 Alexander JF, Lischner MW, Galambos JT. Natural history of alcoholic hepatitis: the longterm prognosis. *Am J Gastroenterol* 1971; 56: 515–25.

43 Ekberg D. Aspelin P. Ultrasonography in asymptomatic patients with abnormal biochemical liver tests. *Scand J Gastroenterol* 1986; 21: 573–6.

44 Nishioka K, Watanabe J, Furuta S et al. A high prevalence of antibody to the hepatitis C virus in patients with hepatocellular carcinoma in Japan. *Cancer* 1991; 67: 429–33.

45 Hasan F, Jeffers LJ, de Medina M et al. Hepatitis C-associated hepatocellular carcinoma. *Hepatology* 1990; 12: 589–91.

46 Nakamura RM, Molden DP. Hepatoma screening in hepatitis B carriers. *JAMA* 1984; 252: 2067–8.

47 Pearce N, Milne A, Moyes C. Hepatitis B virus: the importance of age at infection. *NZ Med J* 1988; 101: 788–90.

48 Paumgartner G, Sauerbruch T. Gallstones: pathogenesis, *Lancet* 1991; 338: 1117–21.

49 Gracie WA. Ransohoff DF. The natural history of silent gallstones. The innocent gallstone is not a myth. *N Engl J Med* 1982; 307: 798–802.

50 Sauerbruch T, Paumgartner G. Gallbladder stones: management. *Lancet* 1991; 338: 1121–4.

51 Herzog U, Bertschmann W. Postoperative Letalität in der Chirurgie der Cholelithiasis: eine retrospektive Analyse aus den Jahren 1972 bis 1980. *Schweiz Rundsch Med Prax* 1990; 79: 287–90.

52 Thistle JL, Cleary PA, Lachin JM et al. Steering Committee National Cooperative Gallstone Study Group. The natural history of cholelithiasis. *Ann Int Med* 1984; 101: 171–5.

53 Rabinovitz M, Gavaler JS, Schade RR et al. Does primary sclerosing cholangitis occurring in assocation with inflammatory bowel disease differ from that occurring in the absence of inflammatory bowel disease? *Hepatology* 1990; 11: 7–11.

54 Porayko MK, Wiesner RH, LaRusso NF et al. Patients with asymptomatic primary sclerosing cholangitis frequently have progressive disease. *Gastroenterol* 1990; 98: 1594–1602.

55 Cucchiaro G, Watters CR, Rossitch JC et al. Deaths from gallstones. Incidence and associated clinical factors. *Ann Surg* 1989; 209: 149–51.

56 Cuschieri A, Dubois F, Mouriel J et al. The European experience with laparoscopic cholecystectomy. *Am J Surg* 1991; 161: 385–7.

57 The Southern Surgeons Club. A prospective analysis of 1,518 laparoscopic cholecystectomies. *N Engl J Med* 1991; 324: 1073–8.

58 Tondelli P, Gyr K, Stalder GA et al. Postoperative Syndrome nach Cholecystekomie. In: Siewert JR, Blum AL (editors). *Postoperative Syndrome* Berlin: Springer, 1980; 315–35.

59 Lew EA, Gajewski J (editors). *Medical Risks: trends in mortality by age and time elapsed.* New York: Praeger, 1990; 9: 75–6.

60 Thomson SR, Hendry WS, McFarlane GA et al. Epidemiology and outcome of acute pancreatitis. *Br J Surg* 1987; 74: 398–401.

61 Reber HA. Acute pancreatitis: another piece of the puzzle? *N Engl J Med* 1991; 325: 423–5.

62 Ammann R, Buehler H, Bruehlmann W et al. Acute (nonprogressive) alcoholic pancreatitis: prospective longitudinal study of 144 patients with recurrent alocholic pancreatitis. *Pancreas* 1986; 1: 195–203.

63 Levy P, Milan C, Pignon JP et al. Mortality factors associated with chronic pancreatitis. Unidimensional and multidimensional analysis of a medical-surgical series of 240 patients. *Gastroenterol* 1989; 96: 1165–75.

64 Miyake H, Harada H, Ochi K et al. Prognosis and prognostic factors in chronic pancreatitis. *Dig Dis Sci* 1989; 34: 449–55.

PART II: ESOPHAGUS, STOMACH AND DUODENUM

R D C BRACKENRIDGE

NON-ULCER DYSPEPSIA: NERVOUS DYSPEPSIA

A high familial incidence of alimentary disorders in people who suffer from peptic ulceration is also found in those subject to non-ulcer dyspepsia, suggesting that the two conditions have a common factor and are not completely separate entities. Where the dividing line lies is sometimes difficult to determine but becomes important in risk appraisal because it can mark the division between average and higher-than-average mortality in the respective groups.

Symptoms can be notoriously misleading when attempting to distinguish clinically between peptic ulcer and non-ulcer dyspepsia. Frequently one has to fall back on contrast radiography and/or fiberoptic endoscopy to provide the criteria for classification; even so, accuracy cannot be guaranteed. A barium meal will fail to detect 5–10 percent of gastric ulcers and an even higher proportion of duodenal ulcers, although fiberoptic endoscopy has a much better record of ulcer detection.

Non-ulcer dyspepsia can usually be assumed when there is a chronic history of atypical intermittent dyspepsia, when the duration of exacerbations is short and morbidity is not a feature, or when one or more barium gastrointestinal X-ray series is reported as showing no evidence of ulcer. Sometimes symptoms are so mild that they never warrant X-ray examination or even the advice of a physician. A more subtle point of distinction is the heart rate; in functional or stress dyspepsia it is usually in the higher than average range, whereas in peptic ulcer it is typically slow and vagotonic.

Mortality

It is the experience of most life insurance companies that non-ulcer dyspepsia as an isolated impairment has a low mortality risk. This is borne out statistically in the Prudential mortality study of assured lives reported by Preston and Clarke in 1965.[1] In the classification 'dyspepsia, chronic, ulcer not suspected' there was a mortality ratio of only 102 percent ± 16 percent in 11,573 lives exposed to risk between 1947 and 1963. It is a safe rule, therefore, that an applicant with a history of atypical dyspepsia that is judged to be non-ulcer in character can be considered a standard insurance risk, other things being equal.

On the other hand, the rather faint dividing line separating standard from substandard risks may sometimes become more distinct when the clinical history is strongly suggestive of peptic ulcer despite negative investigations. A small but definite excess mortality in a similar clinical group was found in the Prudential study.[1] The classification 'dyspepsia, suggestive of ulcer, but not proved' showed a mortality ratio of 142 percent ± 18 percent among 14,560 lives exposed to risk. However, times have changed since 1965. Symptoms of acid hypersecretion where investigations have shown pathology short of actual ulceration (e.g. duodenal spasticity, irritability, deformity or duodenitis) can now be easily controlled by modern inhibitors of acid secretion, allowing healing of the pre-ulcer state. It would now be unusual to rate such a history once symptoms have been controlled by medical treatment. Such a policy is confirmed by the results of the *Medical Impairment Study 1983* (MIS 1983),[2] in which a history of indigestion (without known ulcer) produced mortality ratios of 89 percent for males and 97 percent for females. Substandard males had an overall mortality ratio of 118 percent, but most were rated only slightly substandard. It is noteworthy that half of the extra deaths among substandard males were due to malignancy, these predominantly being in policy years 11 and over.

ESOPHAGEAL DISORDERS

Globus Hystericus

Globus hystericus is a disturbing sensation of a persistent lump in the throat occurring predominantly in women of a nervous disposition. The globus does not interfere with swallowing and is caused by muscular spasm in the upper esophageal sphincter. The condition is benign and can usually be relieved by explanation and reassurance.

Diverticula of the Esophagus

Diverticula of the esophagus occur in three situations: (1) at a natural weakness of the pharyngeal wall, (2) in midesophagus, and (3) epiphrenic, which is often associated with achalasia (*see below*). Pharyngeal pouches can become large and filled with food consumed several days previously, causing halitosis and dysphagia. They require surgical excision for cure, after which the life insurance risk would be standard. Small, or even moderate-sized, midesophageal and epiphrenic diverticula are often asymptomatic and do not usually carry a risk.

Mallory-Weiss Syndrome

This syndrome is laceration at the esophagogastric junction during violent retching and vomiting, causing arterial bleeding, hematemesis and melena. First described in alcoholics, it is by no means confined to this group. Bleeding usually ceases spontaneously, but the lacerated vessel may require ligation in a few cases. The life insurance risk would be standard after recovery, although the underwriter should first exclude alcohol abuse as a cause.

Achalasia of the Esophagus

In this rare condition, previously known as cardiospasm, there are four cardinal changes: (1) a failure of the cardia to relax; (2) the disappearance of normal esophageal peristalsis and its replacement by segmental and tertiary contractions; (3) dilatation and hypertrophy of the esophagus above the cardia; (4) an increased sensitivity of the esophagus to cholinergic drugs. It is believed that these changes are due to degeneration or absence of the ganglion cells in Meissner's and Auerbach's plexuses. The cause of these neurological faults is unknown.

Achalasia results in a functional obstruction at the cardia which can be overcome only when a sufficient column of food and fluid builds up in the esophagus to force a small quantity through the tight sphincter. Characteristically there is a long history of gradually increasing dysphagia, starting in early adult life. Eventually the esophagus becomes enormously dilated and full of stagnating food and mucus which may regurgitate during sleep, causing an aspiration pneumonitis or lung abscess. If the condition remains untreated, weight may be lost due to starvation.

Mild cases of achalasia may be helped by eating a semi-solid diet and taking calcium channel antagonists, such as nifedipine. It is also possible for the patient to reduce temporarily the tension of the sphincter by the daily passage of bougies, a method not without danger. The treatment of choice at the moment is the use of balloon dilatation of the lower esophageal sphincter in order physically to stretch and rupture the muscle fibers. This method has a high chance of success in experienced hands, and has the advantage over Heller's operation (surgical division of the circular muscle layer of the sphincter) in that it is non-invasive and is followed less frequently by reflux esophagitis, ulcer and stricture.

Selection of Risks
Dysphagia can be a symptom of several conditions with a prognosis much worse than achalasia of the esophagus (e.g. carcinoma of the esophagus or gastric fundus, malignant mediastinal tumors, dermatomyositis or an aneurysm of the aorta). Therefore applicants with a recent history of dysphagia that has not been fully investigated should be postponed.

Rating
1) Mild, medical treatment only — standard.
2) Regular or occasional use of bougies — +50 to +75.
3) With operation or balloon dilatation to destroy sphincter:
No further use of bougies — standard.
Dilatation with bougies still required — +50 to +75.

Hiatus Hernia

The common type is the sliding hiatus hernia, which allows reflux of digestive juices into the esophagus when the body assumes certain postures, such as stooping, sitting hunched forward or lying in bed decubitus. Symptoms are not inevitable even when a hiatus hernia is large. If esophagitis develops as the result of reflux, the usual complaints are heartburn, flatulence, difficulty in swallowing and acid/bile regurgitation into the mouth. Repeated small bleeds from a congested mucosa or a frank peptic ulcer in the lower esophagus can cause significant anemia.

The burning retrosternal pain of peptic esophagitis may be mistaken for the pain of myocardial ischemia (*see* pp. 272–3), especially if it radiates up to the neck, but careful history taking can usually avoid such an error. Another common trap that some physicians fall into (incidentally dragging not a few life underwriters with them) is to assume too readily that once a hiatus hernia has been demonstrated no further cause of pain need be sought. In order to avoid a misdiagnosis other causes of dyspepsia and retrosternal pain such as chronic gall bladder disease, chronic pancreatitis, myocardial ischemia and even gastric and duodenal ulcer, should always be carefully eliminated before unwittingly ascribing symptoms to hiatus hernia.

Some 10–20 percent of hiatus hernias are of the paraesophageal type, where the gastroesophageal junction remains in its normal position below the diaphragm and part of the cardia herniates into the chest. There is no reflux, and symptoms arise from pressure by the hernia on structures within the thoracic cavity. Occasionally the intrathoracic portion of the stomach becomes obstructed.

Rating

Medical Treatment

Applicants with a history of uncomplicated hiatus hernia that has responded to medical treatment would generally be considered standard life insurance risks. When a hiatus hernia has been complicated by an esophageal ulcer or significant hemorrhage from peptic esophagitis, the risk can be considered similar to that of a duodenal ulcer of equivalent severity and duration, and rated accordingly (*see* pp. 601–2).

In contradistinction to the burning pain of peptic esophagitis, retrosternal pain that is gnawing in character, as if a ball were lodged deep inside the chest, can be produced by inappropriate contractions of the esophagus. The pain may sometimes be relieved, even if only temporarily, by swallowing a large bolus of food or air, thus distinguishing it from cardiac pain. Investigations, however, often fail to reveal a hiatus hernia. If the typical relieving factor cannot be elicited from the history, the innocence of the pain may be open to question, even though a resting ECG is normal, in which case investigations should be taken a stage further with a graded exercise ECG and, if necessary, an exercise thallium scan.

Surgical Treatment

Only a minority of cases of hiatus hernia require surgical treatment; when this is called for, a highly selective vagotomy is usually carried out in addition to repair of the hernia. The post-operative risk would normally be considered standard, except when the presence of a chronic esophageal ulcer raises doubts about the future development of a stricture. In these circumstances a rating of 2 per mil for two years should be charged in the first post-operative year only.

PEPTIC ULCER

By definition, a peptic ulcer is one that occurs in the mucous membrane anywhere in the alimentary tract bathed by the acid/pepsin digestive juices and that penetrates the muscularis mucosa. The peptic ulcers that will be considered are gastric, duodenal, pyloric, esophageal and (following anastomotic surgery) stomal ulcers. Acute erosions are not strictly peptic ulcers since they do not penetrate the muscularis mucosa. These erosions can be found in the stomach, duodenum or other parts of the gastrointestinal tract, especially after severe injuries, burns, acute sepsis or during medication with corticosteroid drugs or salicylates. Acute ulcers are not prone to recur or become chronic, although they are frequently referred to as peptic ulcers.

Patterns of Mortality

Unquestionably there has been a gradual decline in the mortality of peptic ulcer since the beginning of the century. This is not altogether accounted for by better medical and surgical handling of the disease, at least during the first 50 years. Changes have also taken place in the character of peptic ulcer disease. Since the mid-19th century gastric ulcer, then a disease of young women, has been replaced by duodenal ulcer as the commonest variety, and both are increasingly becoming diseases of the elderly.

The incidence of ulcer morbidity and mortality in relation to socioeconomic status has also changed. Fifty years ago mortality from duodenal ulcer was distinctly higher in Social Class 1 than in any other, but a complete reversal has taken place: morbidity and mortality from gastric and duodenal ulcer have now become higher in the impoverished and socially underprivileged.

Mortality from peptic ulcer increases with age, since major complications and surgery are badly tolerated at this time of life. For males in the USA with duodenal ulcers the death rate in 1978 rose from a low of 0·9 per 100,000 at ages 35–44 to 37·6 per 100,000 at ages 75 and over.[3]

In the case of duodenal ulcer the majority of young people affected will gradually lose their symptoms once they have reached the age of 40, and will remain in permanent remission thereafter. The mortality risk in people under the age of 40 with a history of duodenal ulcer is therefore a gradually decreasing one. Even for the minority whose ulcers continue to relapse and remit past the age of 40 the histamine H_2-receptor antagonists (cimetidine, ranitidine, famotidine, nizatidine) can heal 85–90 percent of duodenal ulcers. Maintenance treatment prevents recurrence in the majority and prolongs the period before recurrence in others. Nevertheless for some, hemorrhage and perforation will become ever-increasing hazards to life. Treatment by elective surgery, which has a mortality of its own, will often be required when medical measures fail to control symptoms adequately or when complications demand it.

In age groups up to 40 the mortality risk associated with peptic ulcers treated medically is now so low that a rating is rarely necessary for uncomplicated cases whose symptoms are well controlled by therapy. In more refractory cases with a recent history, a small temporary extra premium would be appropriate. In these age groups the generally favorable experience of most insurance companies endorses this practice. At ages over 40 the same principles would apply, except that, if an ulcer is chronic and the history long-standing and recurrent a permanent addition to the premium, based on percentage extra mortality, is more appropriate. This is due to excess deaths arising later from causes apparently unconnected with peptic ulceration.

Deaths by Cause
As might be expected, the predominant cause of death in those with a history of peptic ulcer is from complications arising directly from the ulcer itself, but excess mortality also occurs from other causes, notably cancer, suicide and, to a lesser extent, cardiovascular diseases. This pattern of excess deaths is a consistent finding not only in mortality studies of insured lives,[1,4] but also in studies of hospital patients with peptic ulcer treated medically or surgically.[5,6]

The pattern of mortality by cause associated with a history of peptic ulcer is an excellent educational model for life underwriters. It illustrates why, in evaluating a risk, one should allow for mortality arising not only from the impairment in question, but also from other causes, perhaps not obviously connected with the impairment but nevertheless associated with it in some way. In the case of peptic ulcer, the consistent excess of deaths from accident and suicide is not altogether surprising when one considers that peptic ulcer disease is now thought to be an anxiety or depression equivalent by many clinicians. For less obvious reasons late mortality from cancer and cardiovascular disease in excess of that expected is regularly found in those with a history of chronic, relapsing peptic ulcer, even though they have been treated surgically.

Surgical Treatment

The general decline in the incidence of peptic ulceration, together with the more recent dramatic effects of the histamine H_2-receptor antagonists, have reduced the frequency with which patients are referred to surgery for treatment of chronic duodenal ulceration. Nevertheless there are still clear indications for surgery. The main indications for elective surgical treatment of peptic ulcer are as follows:

1) Frequent relapse of ulcer symptoms that occur in spite of apparently adequate medical measures and that so interfere with a person's employment record that they endanger his livelihood.
2) Scarring and fibrosis of a healed ulcer resulting in pyloric stenosis, hour-glass stomach or cup-and-spill stomach.
3) Chronic anemia, mostly in men over the age of 40, as a result of repeated small losses of blood from an ulcer, or more than one large hemorrhage warranting blood transfusion.

Types of Operation

Today there are all sorts of elective operations designed for duodenal and gastric ulcers. Subtotal gastrectomy is still performed, but some form of vagotomy with pyloroplasty, antrectomy or gastroenterostomy is more common. Proximal vagotomy, or highly selective vagotomy (HSV), without drainage is a currently popular technique which has produced encouraging results since it was introduced.

The approximate operation mortality and ulcer recurrence rates for the main types of elective surgery are as follows:

Subtotal gastrectomy: operation mortality is 2 percent and recurrence rates are 3 percent for duodenal ulcers and 1 percent for gastric ulcers. There is a high incidence of dumping symptoms and nutritional sequelae following subtotal gastrectomy. These include deficiencies of iron, vitamins and calcium and, exceptionally, a protein deficiency of severe degree. Osteomalacia has been reported.

Vagotomy and pyloroplasty: operation mortality is 0·8 percent, but the recurrence rate is moderately high, at 5–8 percent. Postvagotomy diarrhea is the most notable complication of vagotomy and pyloroplasty but it is only disabling in about 1 percent of patients.

Vagotomy and antrectomy: operation mortality is 1·1 percent, but the recurrence rate of ulcer is very low, at 0·5 percent.

Proximal (highly selective) vagotomy without drainage: operational mortality is low — about 0·3 percent[7] — but the overall incidence of recurrent ulcer after this form of vagotomy, reported from many centers throughout the world, is between 15 percent and 20 percent.[8] Although highly selective vagotomy is a promising development in the treatment of peptic ulcer, it is still too early to be certain of the long-term prognosis. Ischemic necrosis of the lesser curvature is a problem that has still to be overcome, and gastric stasis caused by fibrotic contraction of a healing duodenal or gastric ulcer lying adjacent to the pyloric canal may require a further operation to provide adequate drainage.

Emergency surgery is required for an acute or chronic ulcer that perforates into the peritoneal cavity. The usual procedure is to oversew the perforation and proceed later to elective surgery if symptoms persist or recur, which they do in 50 percent of cases when the ulcer is chronic but rarely if the ulcer is acute. Emergency surgery for gastroduodenal hemorrhage is only required if massive bleeding continues or recurs despite intensive transfusion therapy for 24 hours. Laparotomy will usually determine the source of bleeding and the type of operation required to deal with it. A gastrocolic fistula complicating a stomal ulcer requires urgent, if not emergency, surgery for its closure, followed later by elective operation for more radical treatment of the original ulcer.

Mortality Following Surgical Treatment

Previous studies of insured lives have always shown a higher mortality following operation for gastric or duodenal ulcer than for ulcers treated medically. The *1951 Impairment Study*[4] included a sizeable experience of insured lives with a history of gastric or duodenal ulcer surgically treated, but because the operations being performed during the period covered by the study were mainly simple gastroenterostomy and subtotal gastrectomy without vagotomy, the results cannot be applied to the evaluation of risks treated by present-day surgical techniques. Nevertheless it is interesting to recall that mortality following surgically treated ulcers prior to 1951 ran at about twice average for the first ten years before falling to a lower level of 35 percent extra mortality thereafter. In the *Medical Impairment Study 1983*[2] data on substandard males surgically treated for duodenal ulcer showed mortality ratios of 146 percent (226 policy deaths) for gastrectomy or vagotomy, and 153 percent (101 policy deaths) for other forms of surgery. In a more limited experience, cases of gastric ulcer treated by surgery showed a higher mortality than those treated surgically for duodenal ulcer; for those undergoing gastrectomy or vagotomy the mortality ratio for substandard males was 179 percent (40 policy deaths); the mortality ratio was 191 percent (24 deaths) for other forms of surgery.

Exposure for substandard females operated on for gastric and duodenal ulcer was much less than for males, but mortality was higher, especially in cases of duodenal ulcer treated by surgery other than vagotomy or gastrectomy (mortality ratio 344 percent with 15 policy deaths).

The consistently higher mortality following surgical, as opposed to medical, treatment in most studies probably reflects the greater number of severe types of peptic ulcer in the surgical groups, as well as the sometimes serious complications which often followed earlier surgical techniques. Undoubtedly, however, recent experience of surgically treated peptic ulcer shows an improvement in both short- and long-term mortality, due partly to more modern investigational and surgical techniques, and partly to the improvements that have taken place over the years in general patient care in blood transfusion and correction of serum chemistry abnormalities before and after operation.

Selection of Risks

The attitudes of life insurance companies towards the underwriting of histories of peptic ulcer differ considerably. Most, however, take the view that for most medically treated ulcers the mortality risk is low and relatively early, decreasing with lapse of time. For chronic ulcers rating would generally take the form of a decreasing temporary extra premium dating from the last relapse, with or without an additional permanent extra, depending on age, the number and severity of relapses and the total duration of history. The usual practice is to charge histories of gastric ulcer on a slightly higher scale of rating than the equivalent history of duodenal ulcer, except when the lesion has been confirmed to be an acute erosion, in which case insurance at standard rates could be considered. Standard acceptance is now the rule for uncomplicated duodenal ulcers where relapses have been infrequent and symptoms respond promptly to modern inhibitors of acid secretion.

Rating

Duodenal and gastric ulcer: medical treatment.
1) Acute erosion, with or without bleeding; no symptoms before or since; subsequent X-ray or endoscopy negative for peptic ulcer; after recovery — standard.
2) Short history; ulcer confirmed by X-ray or endoscopy; complete recovery — standard.
3) Long history; infrequent relapses; ulcer confirmed at any time since onset; prompt response to treatment — standard.
4) Long history; more frequent relapses, or chronic ulcer, or one or more episodes of bleeding:

Time since last symptom	Rating
Within 2 yr	+75 to +50
Thereafter	Standard

Duodenal and gastric ulcer: surgical treatment.

1) Perforation, simple closure:
Acute ulcer following severe stress, injuries, burns etc; no prior or subsequent symptoms of dyspepsia; after return to full-time work — standard.
With history of prior or subsequent dyspepsia or chronic ulcer — rate as medical treatment (see above).
2) Subtotal gastrectomy:
Within one year — 3 per mil for five years.
Thereafter — 3 per mil for $(4-t)$ years, where t is the number of complete years since operation.
3) Gastroenterostomy; antrectomy; pyloroplasty (all usually with vagotomy) — 2 per mil for $(3-t)$ years.
4) Proximal (highly selective) vagotomy without drainage — 2 per mil for $(2-t)$ years.
5) Recurrence of ulcer or development of stomal ulcer after operation — rate as medical treatment (see above).
Subsequent corrective operation — rate as if primary operation.
6) Total gastrectomy — rate as for subtotal gastrectomy, taking care to ascertain that the reason for this operation was not a lesion other than a benign ulcer (e.g. Zollinger–Ellison syndrome, see below, or carcinoma).

Note Diminishing symptoms of ulcer during the first nine months following elective operation may be disregarded unless severe.

ZOLLINGER–ELLISON SYNDROME

In this condition a tumor of the alpha-cells of the islets of the pancreas secretes large amounts of the hormone gastrin, which provokes a copious secretion of highly acid juice and leads to the formation of particularly active, and frequently multiple, peptic ulcers. In over 50 percent of cases the tumor is of low-grade malignancy and eventually spreads to the liver and lymph nodes, or even to more distant sites. The secondary growths are usually capable of secreting gastrin.

The Zollinger–Ellison syndrome is often first suspected when a peptic ulcer is unusually severe or rapidly progressive, particularly if it recurs frequently, perforates more than once or bleeds profusely. When the syndrome is confirmed or suspected on good grounds, applications for life insurance should be postponed pending surgical treatment. If the pancreatic tumor is found to be malignant at operation, the risk would naturally be declined. If the tumor is benign and confined to the pancreas (and this cannot be guaranteed at the time), it would be removed, along with surrounding pancreatic tissue, and a total gastrectomy carried out.

Even in the most favorable cases it would be necessary to postpone acceptance for life insurance for at least one year following radical operation for the Zollinger–Ellison syndrome. If subsequently there is good evidence that no ectopic gastrin-secreting tumors exist, applications may be considered at a rating equivalent to that for total gastrectomy for benign peptic ulcer in the first post-operative year (see above).

GASTRITIS

The term gastritis covers a wide variety of pathologies from acute inflammatory to chronic degenerative changes in the gastric mucosa. Since the diagnosis of gastritis can be based on several factors, such as clinical symptoms, endoscopic appearances or histologic findings, the classification tends to be imprecise. However, the life underwriter is probably less concerned with the semantics of classification than the causes of gastritis and their effect, if any, on mortality. For example, acute erosive or hemorrhagic gastritis can be due to medications such as aspirin, non-steroidal anti-inflammatory drugs or corticosteroids, or to alcohol excess. On the other hand, chronic atrophic gastritis may give rise to no symptoms at all and may only be found by chance during investigations of anemia that uncover achlorhydria, megaloblastosis and parietal cell antibodies. Giant hypertrophic gastritis (Ménétriere's disease), characterized by large, convoluted rugae of the gastric mucosa, can cause various dyspeptic symptoms; it can also cause hypoalbuminemia and edema due to loss of protein from exudates into the lumen of the stomach. Medical treatment can usually control symptoms, but occasionally gastrectomy is required. This condition should be rated similarly to chronic relapsing peptic ulcer (*see above*).

REFERENCES

1 Preston TW, Clarke RD. *J Inst Actuar* 1965; 92: 27.
2 *Medical Impairment Study 1983*. Boston: Society of Actuaries and Association of Life Insurance Medical Directors of America, 1986.
3 *Statistical Bulletin*. New York: Metropolitan Life Insurance Company, April 1982: 7.
4 *1951 Impairment Study*. New York: Society of Actuaries, 1954.
5 Swynnerton BF, Tanner NC. Chronic gastric ulcer. A comparison between gastroscopically controlled series treated medically and a series treated by surgery. *Br Med J* 1953; 2: 841.
6 Harvey JS, Langman MJS. The late results of medical and surgical treatment for bleeding duodenal ulcer. *Quart J Med* 1970; 39: 539.
7 Johnston D. Operative mortality and postoperative morbidity of highly selective vagotomy. *Br Med J* 1975; 4: 545.
8 When vagotomy fails (editorial). *Br Med J* 1982; 284: 1815.

PART III: INTESTINES

MAX L HEFTI

CELIAC DISEASE (GLUTEN-SENSITIVE ENTEROPATHY)

Celiac sprue is a chronic disease in which there is characteristic, though not specific, atrophy of the villi of the mucosa of the jejunum induced by the ingestion of gluten, resulting in impaired nutrient absorption by involved bowel. Mucosal lesions, as well as absorption, typically improve on withdrawal of gluten, hence the new name, gluten-induced enteropathy, for what had previously been termed celiac disease in children and non-tropical sprue in adults. Although it is clear that gluten (or rather its toxic fractions: gliadins in wheat; prolamins in barley, rye and oat) somehow damages the intestinal mucosa, the role played by enzyme deficiency, genetic factors and immune mechanisms remains obscure.

Celiac disease occurs largely in Caucasians, although the disease has been documented in Asians from India and Pakistan. Prevalence rates in Europe range from 1 in 300 in Ireland to 1 in 1,000 or 2,000 in other regions.[1] Since a substantial number of patients have no or only mild symptoms the true prevalence is likely to be higher. Reports from Great Britain, Italy and Sweden indicate significant fluctuation in incidence, which was on the increase in the 1970s and 1980s.[2] No data from the USA are available.

The classic clinical features include steatorrhea, weight loss and malabsorption induced conditions, such as iron-deficiency anemia, folate deficiency and osteopenic bone disease. Untreated disease or interruption of treatment in childhood and adolescence may affect growth as evaluated by final height. The symptoms vary tremendously from patient to patient and appear to depend largely on the length of small bowel affected.

Celiac disease may present at any time in life. It may start in infancy and later remit completely or reappear. Alternatively it may arise unexpectedly in adult life following some stressful situation, such as pregnancy or major surgery, probably in previously undiagnosed latent disease. There is a well established association of celiac disease with dermatitis herpetiformis, Type 1 diabetes mellitus and selective IgA deficiency.

The diagnosis is based on clinical, laboratory and radiologic evidence and jejunal biopsy, and is confirmed by the response to gluten withdrawal.

Patients with celiac disease (whether symptomatic or latent) are exposed to the double risk of the sequelae of malabsorption and the increased incidence of malignant conditions, especially lymphoma (predominantly malignant histiocytosis of the small bowel). Clinical symptoms, histologic changes and intestinal absorption respond rapidly and well to gluten-free diet. Refractory cases are rare. However, as shown in a study from the Children's Hospital in Zurich, 87 percent of patients relapse within two years following interruption of gluten-free diet, and another 12 percent relapse later.[3] Any residuals from malabsorption are amenable to oral or parenteral replacement therapy. A recent study from Birmingham (UK) suggests that the incidence of malignancies is reduced among patients who adhere to a lifelong strict gluten-free diet.[4]

Prognosis and Risk Evaluation

The overall mortality rate of patients with celiac disease is somewhat increased. The quotient of actual and expected mortality in a cohort of 653 patients was 1·86 in a recent survey from Scotland.[5] The increased mortality was greatest within the first year of diagnosis and steadily declined over time, with the excess mortality being concentrated at ages 45–54 in men and 55–64 in women. The mortality in adults diagnosed during childhood as having celiac disease was practically standard.

Best-risk applicants are those with a history of celiac disease diagnosed in childhood that has responded well to withdrawal of gluten, and who have adhered to a strict gluten-free diet since, without significant relapse. The longer the duration of uninterrupted treatment the greater the chances that the patient will comply with his diet throughout his life. Best-risk applicants can be accepted for life insurance at nearly standard rates. Applicants with disease discovered in adulthood should be rated substandard, especially within the first years following diagnosis and if there is evidence of subclinical malabsorption, most notably anemia. Ratings of +50 to +100, depending on time elapsed since successful treatment, seem adequate. Those straying from the diet or refractory to diet with or without evidence of malabsorption should be rated +100 to +150, and more after the age of 50 if malignant conditions have not been excluded.

TROPICAL SPRUE

Tropical sprue is a disease with a symptomatology similar to that of celiac disease (gluten-sensitive enteropathy) confined to specific endemic regions located mainly between the Tropic of Cancer and the Tropic of Capricorn. It may occur in natives of, visitors to, and expatriates from, these regions. In expatriates the initial manifestations of the disease may appear in temperate countries up to years after emigration.

The cause of tropical sprue remains obscure. However, epidemiology suggests that exposure to an infectious or other environmental agent is crucial. Persistent contamination of the proximal small bowel with coliform bacteria has been demonstrated in many, though not all, patients.[6,7]

The natural history of tropical sprue is variable. Some patients improve spontaneously within six months. In others chronic illness develops and, if untreated, persists for years, causing long-standing malabsorption as evidenced by cachexia, megaloblastic anemia and osteopenic disease. The diagnosis of tropical sprue is clinical, since there is no single pathognomonic symptom, sign or laboratory test, including intestinal mucosal biopsy. The clinical diagnosis is corroborated by the exclusion of other causes of chronic wasting diarrhea (AIDS and enteric parasitic infections, including giardiasis, coccidiosis and strongyloidiasis) and by the response to adequate treatment.

The currently accepted therapy consists of an appropriate antibiotic, such as tetracycline, combined with folate for about a month in travelers and expatriates, and for six months in more chronically ill residents in the tropics. Even then, the recurrence rate in residents is high for the first few years after completion of therapy.[8]

Prognosis and Risk Evaluation

Applicants having made a full recovery after proper treatment may be insured at standard rates if residing in a temperate climate. If residing in tropical environments, a rating of +25 to +75 would be indicated, depending on the presence or absence of sequelae of malabsorption.

IRRITABLE BOWEL SYNDROME

The irritable bowel syndrome is a benign disease of young and middle-aged adults affecting twice as many women as men. Patients may present either with abdominal pain and constipation ('spastic colon') or intermittent painless diarrhea ('nervous diarrhea'), or with alternating constipation and diarrhea. The term 'mucous colitis' is deprecated since there is no inflammatory component in irritable bowel syndrome. There is a strong relation of the basic alterations of intestinal motility with environment and emotional stress. Nocturnal diarrhea, bloody diarrhea, blood intimately mixed with the stools and wasting are not signs of the irritable bowel syndrome and, if present, must arouse suspicion of a more serious condition.

Irritable bowel syndrome is neither a precursor of inflammatory bowel disease nor a risk factor for intestinal cancer. Irritable bowel syndrome and diverticulosis of the colon may occur in the same patient. The current view is that it is a coincidental rather than causative relationship.

The diagnosis of irritable bowel syndrome is based on the clinical symptomatology and the exclusion of organic gastrointestinal disease and malabsorption. There is no measurable excess mortality. The only concern in life underwriting is misdiagnosis of severe organic disease for irritable bowel syndrome. If the diagnosis is based on a convincing medical report or if more severe conditions can be reasonably excluded due to a long unsuspected course of the disease, life cover can usually be granted on standard terms.

DIVERTICULAR DISEASE OF THE COLON

Diverticular disease of the colon is a common disease of the second half of life in Western populations. It consists of the development of multiple diverticula (more exactly, pseudodiverticula) in the large bowel. It is called diverticulosis if not accompanied by inflammation.

Colonic diverticula are sac-like protrusions of the intestinal mucosa through the muscular coat of the colon. Thickening of the muscularis in most patients with diverticulosis suggests that diverticula are caused by increased intraluminal pressure secondary to colonic contractions related to reduced fecal bulk with a fiber-deficient diet.

Two classic surveys have provided information on the occurrence of diverticulosis in the asymptomatic general population in England, and on the areas of the large bowel involved in patients with diverticular disease in the USA, respectively. Diverticulosis was discovered by a barium follow-through examination in 18·5 percent of people in the age group 41–59, in 29·2 percent in the age group 60–79, and in 42·1 percent in those over the age of 80.[9] The sigmoid was involved in 95 percent of patients with diverticulosis; in 47 percent alone and in 48 percent together with the colon.[10] A recent paper from Singapore reported the prevalence of diverticular disease in 20 percent of Asian patients referred to hospital for barium enema. Interestingly, there was right-sided diverticulosis sparing the sigmoid in 70 percent of cases.[11]

Uncomplicated diverticulosis is generally symptomless and usually remains undetected throughout life. Symptomatic diverticular disease without clinical or pathologic evidence of complications is usually due to the coincidence of diverticulosis and the irritable bowel syndrome, both common in the same population groups.[12] Complications are frequent, particularly in patients with extensive disease, and they tend to increase with increasing age. The longitudinal observation of 294 patients with diverticulosis over a period of 20–30 years showed that 24·8 percent had at least one attack of acute diverticulitis, most commonly presenting as 'left-sided appendicitis'. Nearly 40 percent had secondary complications of diverticulitis: perforation into the peritoneal cavity or an adjacent organ, such as the bladder and vagina, or pericolonic abscess with formation of an inflammatory tumor causing intestinal obstruction. Eight percent had massive hemorrhage caused by erosion of a vessel by a fecolith within the diverticular sac, independently of diverticulitis.[13] Unlike diverticulitis that generally develops in the vicinity of the colosigmoidal junction, bleeding most commonly occurs in the ascending colon.

For acute diverticulitis without signs of perforation and intestinal obstruction, treatment is medical. Repeated attacks of diverticulitis in the same area are an indication for elective resection of the segment involved. Cases with suspected perforation or obstruction require emergency surgery. This may consist of a simple diverting colostomy, followed later by resection of the diseased bowel and reanastomosis. Depending on circumstances these three steps may be carried out in one operation. Cases with perforation and fecal peritonitis still have a high fatality rate.

Prognosis

The experience of 9,888 life insurance policies issued to people with diverticulosis in the USA from 1952 to 1976 showed a slightly elevated relative mortality of 104 percent overall; it was somewhat higher in men under the age of 40 and significantly lower in women. The most important cause of excess mortality was malignancy.[14] This is not surprising since the diagnosis of cancer may be extremely difficult with gross changes of the large bowel by diverticular disease.

The reported mortality ratio might be too optimistic, since only 11 percent of the policies issued were at ages 50–59 (the ages at which diverticulosis becomes common) and about 2 percent at ages 60–69. In addition, no classification based on history of acute diverticulitis was carried out.

Rating

1) Diverticulosis; asymptomatic, no history of diverticulitis or hemorrhage — +0 to +50, depending on extent of bowel involvement, number of polyps and reliability of cancer exclusion.
2) Diverticulitis, medical treatment:

Number of attacks and time since last attack	Rating
Single attack:	+0 to +50[a]
Within 1 yr	Plus 5 per mil for 1 yr
Thereafter	No flat extra premium
More than 1 attack:	+0 to +50[a]
Within 1 yr	Plus 5 per mil for 3 yr
2nd yr	Plus 5 per mil for 2 yr
3rd yr	Plus 5 per mil for 1 yr
Thereafter	No flat extra premium

[a]Depending on extent of bowel involvement, number of polyps and reliability of cancer exclusion.

3) Diverticulitis, surgical treatment:

Type of surgery and time since surgery	Rating
Emergency treatment only (drainage, temporary colostomy)	Postpone
Radical treatment (sigmoidectomy, partial colectomy) with or without colostomy:	
Within 6 mth	Postpone
6–12 mth	5 per mil for 1 yr
Thereafter	Standard
More than one operation or closure of fistulas etc:	
Within 1 yr	Postpone
2nd yr	10 per mil for 2 yr
3rd yr	5 per mil for 1 yr
Thereafter	Standard

INFLAMMATORY BOWEL DISEASE

The term inflammatory bowel disease, in common medical parlance, does not refer to all categories of inflammatory diseases of the intestine but only to its chronic idiopathic forms. These encompass two major forms, ulcerative colitis and Crohn's disease, and several more gentle and subtle forms, including collagenous colitis and lymphocystic colitis. The origin and pathogenesis of inflammatory bowel disease remain an enigma. A role for infectious agents and alterations of the immune system is suspected. The contribution of genetic factors has been strongly supported by a recent survey which found that first-degree relatives of patients with ulcerative colitis or Crohn's disease in Copenhagen County had a tenfold increased risk of having the same disease, compared with the general population.[15] Increasing evidence suggests that ulcerative colitis and Crohn's disease are indeed distinct entities. In some patients, however, it may not be possible to distinguish with confidence between ulcerative colitis and Crohn's disease affecting the colon.

Ulcerative Colitis

This is an inflammatory process confined to the mucosa and superficial submucosa of the large bowel, usually affecting the rectum and extending proximally in a continuous fashion. Depending on the length of proximal extension, ulcerative colitis may be classified as distal (left-sided colitis) and total (pancolitis). Ulcerative disease confined to the anorectal segment (ulcerative or hemorrhagic proctitis) seems to be different from extensive ulcerative colitis, based on differences in temporal trends and other epidemiological characteristics.[16] The prevalence of ulcerative colitis varies widely around the world and its incidence has remained relatively stable over the years, except for the Far East where it is on the increase.[17]

The main pathologic features of active ulcerative colitis are superficial changes of the mucosa of the affected bowel. Depending on the intensity of the inflammatory process these range from diffuse granularity and friability to extensive confluent ulceration, often with pseudopolyps. On a microscopic level, microabscesses of the crypts are typical.

The cardinal symptom of active colitis is bloody diarrhea. Periods of active disease characteristically alternate with periods of remission. The frequency, duration and severity of the recurrent flares of activity are highly variable. Almost all patients have at least one relapse during a ten-year period. Some have a practically uninterrupted active course.[18]

Crohn's Disease

This is an inflammatory process involving the full thickness of the wall of the segments of the affected alimentary tract (transmural disease). Although involvement of the terminal ileum, colon or both is most common, any site of the gastrointestinal tract can be affected. Disease restricted to the small bowel is often referred to as regional enteritis. Crohn's colitis is typically segmental and the rectum is frequently spared. The prevalence of Crohn's disease varies widely but, unlike ulcerative colitis, its incidence is on a steady increase (or was, at least until recently).

From a pathological point of view Crohn's disease is characterized by thick inflammatory masses with deep linear or fissure-like ulcers, and a propensity for fibrotic scarring and fistula formation. Biopsies of the affected segments reveal non-caseating granulomas in approximately 50 percent of patients. The clinical picture is dominated by abdominal pain and diarrhea, often associated with symptoms of intestinal obstruction and systemic signs, including fever and loss of weight. Crohn's disease follows a chronic recurring course and nearly all patients have at least one relapse within ten years of their initial attack.[19]

Collagenous Colitis; Lymphocytic Colitis

These are mild forms of colitis in which the inflammatory process is discrete and often only in the microscopic range. In both collagenous colitis and lymphocytic colitis infiltration of the intestinal epithelium is predominantly by lymphocytes. In addition, collagenous colitis is characterized by strictly subepithelial deposition of collagen, which gives the condition its name.[20]

Clinically these forms of colitis present as chronic watery diarrhea, as compared with the bloody diarrhea of ulcerative colitis.

Complications

Both ulcerative colitis and Crohn's disease are associated with a wide variety of secondary effects of the inflammatory process in the gastrointestinal tract, as well as with intestinal and extraintestinal complications. The complications include toxic megacolon, arthritis affecting the spine, sacroiliac joints and isolated large joints, uveitis, erythema nodosum and pyoderma gangrenosum. In addition, ulcerative colitis may be associated with primary sclerosing cholangitis (see p. 587). Crohn's disease, on the other hand, is often complicated by fistulas connecting different segments of the gastrointestinal tract or with other organs, such as the bladder and the vagina, or with the skin, particularly of the perineum (perianal disease).

Inflammatory Bowel Disease and Cancer

Some classic dogmas about the risk of cancer in inflammatory bowel disease need revision. First, cancer now seems equally common in ulcerative colitis and Crohn's disease.[21] Second, in ulcerative colitis the cancer risk is identical for all ages at onset of colitis and for patients with left-sided colitis and pancolitis. There is, however, no increased risk in hemorrhagic proctitis.[22] Third, cancer is a complication of long-standing disease in both ulcerative colitis (mean interval from onset of colitis to diagnosis of cancer 14 years) as well as in Crohn's disease (mean interval 22 years).[22,23]

The quotient of observed and expected number of cancers in inflammatory bowel diseases ranges between 2·0 and 5·6, according to recent studies of large numbers of cases over several decades.[23,24]

Management

Medical therapy is the first option in the management of both ulcerative colitis and Crohn's disease, although it can at best control active disease and reduce the frequency and severity of relapses in quiescent disease.

Sulfasalazine remains the standard drug for the control of active ulcerative colitis as well as for preventing relapses in quiescent disease. Corticosteroids are best for the treatment of severe bouts of colitis but they are of no use in the prevention of recurrences. Corticosteroids, sometimes in combination with sulfasalazine, are the most effective drugs for the control of active Crohn's disease. Azathioprine and other immunosuppressive agents have emerged over the past several years as an efficient means of controlling active disease and preventing relapses in quiescent disease.[25]

Surgical therapy may be required in the management of refractory cases and complications of inflammatory bowel disease. In addition, cancer prophylaxis in long-standing ulcerative colitis used to be a major indication for colectomy. Since about 1980, patients with duration of disease of more than eight to ten years are instead included in effective biopsy surveillance programmes for muscosal dysplasia and carcinoma.[26,27]

In ulcerative colitis the resection of colon and rectum (proctocolectomy) is curative for the patient. In a representative study, about 10 percent of patients, mostly with total colitis, had a colectomy during the first year after diagnosis, 4 percent during the second year and 1 percent annually during subsequent years. The overall 25-year cumulative colectomy rate was 45 percent and that of patients with total colitis 65 percent.[26] Fecal diversion may be achieved by ileostomy or ileoanal anastomosis, both conventional or combined with the construction of an ileal reservoir (pouch). These reservoirs may, however, cause mechanical problems or develop inflammation that resembles ulcerative colitis ('pouchitis'). As many as 15 percent of pouch carriers require reoperation.[19]

In Crohn's disease resection of the involved bowel is unlikely to be curative. In addition, recurrence of Crohn's disease immediately proximal to the anastomosis is common. Hence surgery is reserved for the management of complications, and resection limited to areas affected by gross disease. An yet unpublished survey from Denmark indicates that approximately 30 percent of patients required surgery within the first year of diagnosis. The remainder had surgery at a rate of 5 percent per year.[19] In a large British series 94 percent had surgery at least once during the observation period.[24]

Prognosis

Long-term prognosis in both ulcerative colitis and Crohn's disease has significantly improved within the last decades and has become nearly similar in the two diseases. Cancer of the digestive tract is now the most common disease-related cause of death in both.

For ulcerative colitis a mortality ratio of 170 percent for men and 200 percent for women (standard: lives insured at standard premium rates) was found, based on the analysis of 10,179 life insurance policies issued to people with ulcerative colitis in the USA from 1952 to 1976.[14] A survey of 1,274 patients who were diagnosed as having ulcerative colitis in Stockholm County during the period 1955–79 showed a fall in the mortality ratio (standard: general population) from 280 percent during the period 1955–69 to 170 percent during the period 1970–79. In patients with total colitis at onset mortality was greater than for other patients during the first year of the disease, and increased with duration of the disease after the initial ten years.[28] A recent publication from Japan reports comparable observations.[17]

The excess mortality in Crohn's disease has also decreased but still exists, as shown in two recent studies, one involving 671 patients seen in Leiden, The Netherlands, between 1934 and 1984, the other involving 769 patients seen in Birmingham, England, between 1944 and 1984.[24,29] The mortality ratio observed (standard: general population) has decreased from 260 percent during the period 1964–73 to 190 percent during the period 1974–83. It was significantly higher in women than in men, in patients whose disease had started before the age of 20, and during the first year after diagnosis.

There are no sufficient mortality data available on collagenous colitis and lymphocytic colitis. The very few clinicopathological studies published so far suggest that the natural history of these diseases is benign and that no significant excess mortality is to be expected.[30]

Rating

Ulcerative Colitis
1) Medically treated.

Time since diagnosis	Rating
Less than 1 yr	+100 to +250[a] and 5 per mil for 2 yr
2nd yr	+75 to +200[a] and 2·5 per mil for 1 yr
Thereafter	+50 to +150[a]

[a]Depending on the extent and severity of disease, frequency of relapses and quality of cancer surveillance.

Additional rating of +50 for corticosteroid therapy (continuous or repeated).

2) Surgically treated:

Time since surgery	Rating
Less than 6 mth	Postpone
Thereafter:	
For proctocolectomy and conventional ileostomy	2·5 per mil for 3 yr
For proctocolectomy and ileoanal anastomosis with ileal pouch	5 per mil for 3 yr
For simple colectomy with ileorectal anastomosis	+25 to +75 throughout[a] and 5 per mil in 1st yr

[a]Depending on severity and frequency of relapses in the rectum and quality of cancer surveillance.

Crohn's Disease

Time since diagnosis	Rating
Less than 1 yr	+100 to +250[a] and 5 per mil for 3 yr
2nd yr	+75 to +200[a] and 2·5 per mil for 2 yr
Thereafter	+50 to +150[a]

[a]Depending on age at onset (worse for onset before age 20), severity of disease, frequency of relapses and evidence of complications.

Additional rating of +50 for corticosteroid therapy (continuous or repeated).

With surgery — no additional rating, but refer to MD if complex.

Collagenous Colitis and Lymphocytic Colitis
Suggested rating — +25.

ISCHEMIC COLON DISEASE (ISCHEMIC COLITIS)

Ischemic colon disease is a condition resulting from deficient arterial blood supply to part of the large intestine. The segments most frequently involved are the splenic flexure, the descending colon and the sigmoid. The rectum is usually spared because of excellent collateral circulation. However, if it is involved, the prognosis is usually bad.[31]

The most common cause of colonic ischemia is non-occlusive arterial disease (i.e. no definite occlusion of a major vessel) due to atherosclerosis. Ischemic colon disease is therefore mainly a disease of the elderly.

The extension and severity of damage to the affected segment of large intestine depends on the degree and duration of ischemia and its rate of development. Edema of, and hemorrhage into, the mucosa and submucosa, and necrosis of the mucosa are regular pathologic features of ischemic colon disease. In mild cases necrosis is only superficial. In severe cases it affects the full thickness of the mucosa.

Acute fulminant ischemic colitis is a dramatic medical emergency with abdominal pain, massive rectal bleeding and hypotension. Surgical resection may be required in some patients to remove gangrenous bowel. Others may respond to medical management. Subacute ischemic colitis is the most common variant of ischemic colon disease. Most cases resolve within a few weeks and do not recur. Secondary stricture of the affected segment may lead to intestinal obstruction and require surgery.

The long-term prognosis of ischemic disease of the colon after full resolution (with or without segmental resection) is that of the underlying arterial disease, usually generalized atherosclerosis, less commonly arteriopathy associated with one of the connective tissue diseases; applicants should be rated for the underlying cause.

HIRSCHSPRUNG'S DISEASE (CONGENITAL OR AGANGLIONIC MEGACOLON)

Hirschsprung's disease is congenital lack of peristalsis in the distal large intestine combined with achalasia of the internal anal sphincter, causing obstinate constipation. The inability of circular muscle fibers to relax results from the absence or scarcity of the parasympathetic ganglion cells (aganglionosis) in the mesenteric and submucosal plexuses (Auerbach's and Meissner's, respectively) due to deficient embryonic development. Aganglionosis most commonly affects a segment of the rectosigmoid 5–20 cm long. If it is limited to a very short segment of the rectum the condition is called short-segment Hirschsprung's disease. If it involves the whole colon and possibly part of the distal small intestine, the condition is termed total aganglionosis coli. Hirschsprung's disease usually presents shortly after birth. It is more frequent in boys than girls and it may be familial. Association with trisomy 21 has frequently been noted.

The characteristic findings on sigmoidoscopy and barium enema are narrowing of a distal segment of gut with secondary distension of the colon proximal to the functional stenosis. Distension may be grotesque (megacolon) and the distended bowel packed with solid feces.

With a long agangliomic segment, fecal retention is complete and such infants die if not operated on early. With shorter aganglionosis where constipation can be corrected by medical means, resection of the aganglionic segment and division of the internal anal sphincter may be delayed until the age of three to ten years. Mild cases may be managed medically lifelong. However, complications, such as life threatening enterocolitis and severe fecal impaction, may occur at any time, typically after a spell of accidental constipation. Surgery may then be required, not infrequently as an emergency.[32]

There is no excess mortality in adults with a history of Hirschsprung's disease corrected by adequate surgery. However, in patients with persistent aganglionosis, though successfully compensated by medical means, there is a significant risk of severe complications and recourse to surgery.

It seems safe to accept applications for life insurance from adults with a history of surgically cured disease at standard rates, and to charge applicants with persisting disease a flat extra premium of 5 to 7·5 per mil for 3 years.

COLORECTAL POLYPS AND GASTROINTESTINAL POLYPOSES

A polyp is a tumor that projects from the mucosa into the lumen of the gut and which may be peduculated or sessile. The terms polyp (the individual tumor-like lesion) and polyposis (the occurrence of multiple polyps) are clinical terms. The benign or malignant nature of polyps in general and the potential for malignancy of benign polyps (the factors determining long-term prognosis) can only be established with accuracy after histological examination of the entire polyp, including its stalk.

Benign polyps may be classified into two groups: those with a potential for malignancy and those lacking this potential. Only the neoplastic epithelial polyps (i.e. the adenomatous polyps) have a tendency to become malignant. The non-neoplastic epithelial polyps and the mesenchymal polypoid tumors have no potential for malignancy. The non-neoplastic epithelial polyps include hyperplastic polyps, inflammatory polyps, hamartomatous polyps (adenomatous change and, hence, tendency to become malignant may occur in the Peutz–Jeghers syndrome; see pp. 619–20) and lymphoid pseudopolyps (an increased incidence of lymphatic malignancy has been observed in diffuse lymphoid pseudopolyposis; see p. 620). The mesenchymal polyps include fibroma, myoma, lipoma and hemangioma.

Polyps of the colon and rectum may occur as solitary lesions (numbering up to perhaps a score) or in their hundreds or thousands and extending to more proximal parts of the gut (polyposes). Whether it is a solitary polyp or polyposis, the overriding consideration for the life insurer is that adenomatous polyps have a tendency to become malignant whereas non-adenomatous polyps have not.

Solitary Colorectal Polyps

Adenomatous polyps, hyperplastic polyps, inflammatory polyps, hamartomatous polyps and lymphoid pseudopolyps may all occur as solitary lesions. In about 20 percent of cases the potentially malignant adenomatous polyps are associated with truly benign hyperplastic polyps.[33] Unfortunately these are endoscopically indistinguishable. In a large retrospective cohort study the overall risk of developing cancer was 5·1 times greater in patients with (histologically undefined) colorectal polyps than in the general population. The risk was reduced to 2·3 by polypectomy.[34]

Adenomatous Polyps

Adenomatous polyps are epithelial in origin and include tubular adenomas, villous adenomas (papillomas) and tubulovillous adenomas.

A very recent survey of asymptomatic elderly men in the USA showed a prevalence of solitary adenomatous polyps of 41 percent. The mean polyp size was 6·5 mm, and the size was less than, or equal to, 10 mm in 92 percent. Histologically 19 percent were villous or tubulovillous in nature. High-grade dysplasia was found in 32 percent and invasive adenocarcinoma in 4 percent.[35] The size of the polyps, the extent of the villous component of the polyps and increasing age of the patient have been recognized as independent risk factors for high-grade dysplasia and invasive cancer. Multiplicity and location of polyps and the gender of the patient have no direct impact on the risk.[36] The risk of malignant change was increased by a factor of 3·3 in medium-sized polyps (10–20 mm) and of 7·7 in large-sized polyps (more than 20 mm), compared with small polyps (less than 10 mm); by a factor of 2·7 to 8·1 for polyps with increasing extent of the villous component, compared with tubular adenomas; and by a factor of 1·8 in people over the age of 60.

Hyperplastic Polyps

Hyperplastic polyps were found in 34 percent of asymptomatic elderly men in the USA and 2 per 1,000 in the resident population of eastern France.[33,35] They were located in the rectum in nearly 60 percent of cases and 91 percent were smaller than 55 mm. Malignant change was never observed.

Risk Selection

The histologic nature of a polyp is the overriding single factor that determines long-term prognosis. Only neoplastic epithelial polyps (i.e. adenomatous polyps) have a potential for malignant change. Carcinoma *in situ* and carcinoma occurring at the tip of a pedunculated tubular adenoma and not invading the stalk have an excellent prognosis if removed surgically or by endoscopic loop resection. All other forms or locations of carcinomatous change must be regarded as invasive carcinoma of the colon or rectum for underwriting purposes. On the other hand, hyperplastic polyps, inflammatory polyps, solitary hamartomatous polyps and solitary lymphoid polyps can usually be disregarded.

When underwriting polyps of unknown histology the following factors should be taken into account:

1) Number of polyps: the risk of cancer rises in proportion to the number of polyps found on endoscopy.
2) Shape of polyps: the risk of cancer is greater in sessile polyps than in pedunculated polyps, and much greater in villous polyps than in smooth polyps.
3) Size of polyps: the risk of cancer rises fast in proportion to the size of polyps. Cancer incidence is under 1 percent in polyps that measure less than 10 mm, rising to nearly 50 percent in polyps over 20 mm.
4) Age of the patient: the risk of polyps progressing to malignancy increases significantly after the age of 60.

Rating

1) Adenomatous polyps:

Treatment	Rating
Removed, no malignancy on histology	Standard
Removed, carcinoma *in situ* or non-invasive carcinoma:	
Within 1 yr	7·5 per mil for 3 yr
2nd yr	5 per mil for 2 yr
3rd yr	2·5 per mil for 1 yr
Thereafter	Standard
Not removed	Postpone

2) Polyps of unknown histology:

Characteristics of polyps and treatment	Rating
Removed, no recurrence on endoscopic follow-up for:	
1 yr	7·5 per mil for 3 yr
2 yr	5 per mil for 2 yr
3 yr	2·5 per mil for 1 yr
More than 3 yr	Standard
Up to 3 polyps 3 mm or less in diameter, not removed, no increase in size on endoscopic follow-up for:	
1 yr	Postpone
More than 1 yr	+50
Up to 10 polyps or polyps up to 10 mm in diameter, not removed, no increase in size on endoscopic follow-up for:	
2 yr	Postpone
More than 2 yr	+50 to +100[a]
More than 10 polyps or villous polyps or polyps greater than 10 mm in diameter, not removed	Postpone[b]

[a]Depending on number, shape and size of polyps.
[b]When histology known, rate accordingly.

Familial Adenomatous Polyposis (FAP)

FAP is an inherited disease characterized by the early development of hundreds, or even thousands, of adenomatous polyps in the gut, particularly in the colon and rectum, and by congenital hypertrophy of the retinal pigment epithelium.[37,38] Two major variants have been described, depending on the association with extraintestinal manifestations: Gardner's syndrome and Turcot syndrome. Their distinction has, however, become blurred because of marked overlapping between them.[39] FAP has an autosomal dominant mode of inheritance, which means that offspring, both male and female, of patients with FAP have a 50 percent risk of developing polyposis. The condition can also occur without a preceding family history because of a spontaneous mutation. The genetic defect responsible for the disease has been localized within a small region of chromosome 5.[40,41]

Polyps in FAP rarely appear before puberty but can usually be detected in affected individuals by the age of 25, and in 90 percent of patients they are present by the age of 40.[42] The mean age of symptomatic presentation (usually cancer) in untreated patients is in the fourth decade (age 36 in the polyposis registry of St Mark's Hospital, London); colorectal carcinoma will develop in almost all patients at risk before the age of 40. In addition, there is an increased risk of upper gastrointestinal cancer and, in young women, of cancer of the thyroid gland.[43,44] The diagnosis of FAP is based on family history and endoscopic and histologic evidence of multiple adenomatous polyps of the colon and rectum. Among offspring of patients with FAP, carriers of the gene can be identified by fundoscopic evidence of hypertrophy of retinal pigment epithelium and by genetic markers before the polyps develop.[37,38,45] Screening of all members of families at risk by fiberoptic colonoscopy or contrast radiography should start at about ages 12–14 and continue every two or three years. As age increases over 25 the chances of developing the disease decrease, until by age 35 the risk becomes negligible.

The only foolproof prevention of colorectal cancer is surgical removal of the entire colon and rectum (panproctocolectomy). In a series of patients who underwent less radical surgery (subtotal colectomy with ileorectal anastomosis) 7·5 percent developed cancer in the retained portion of the rectum.[46] A policy of subtotal colectomy with ileorectal anastomosis with conscientious lifelong endoscopic follow-up thereafter is nevertheless advocated by many. Unfortunately colectomy, whether total or partial, does not prevent carcinoma of the upper gastrointestinal tract or other locations.

Gardner's Syndrome
This is a variant of FAP in which desmoid tumors (benign tumors of subcutaneous tissues, muscle and joints), osteomas (particularly of the mandible and skull) and other neoplasms occur together with multiple adenomas of the colon and rectum. Polyps usually develop later than in classic FAP, practically never before the age of 20.[47] Gardner's syndrome should be rated as FAP and any associated extraintestinal tumor.

Turcot Syndrome
This is a rare variant of FAP in which multiple adenomas of the colon and rectum are associated with neural tumors, particularly with gliomas and medulloblastomas. The brain tumor typically occurs prior to, or early in, the development of colorectal polyps.[48] Applicants should usually be declined.

Ratings
1) Familial Adenomatous Polyposis (FAP):

Type of treatment	Rating
No surgery	Decline
Partial colectomy with ileorectal anatomosis:	
Within 6 mth	Postpone
Thereafter	+100 to +150[a]
Panproctocolectomy:	
Within 12 mth	Postpone
Thereafter	+50[b]

[a]Depending on the number of polyps in the retained portion of the rectum; add rating for carcinoma *in situ* or invasive carcinoma discovered on colectomy or subsequent endoscopic follow-up.
[b]Add rating for carcinoma *in situ* or invasive carcinoma discovered on colectomy.

2) Family history of familial adenomatous polyposis (FAP):

Age at, and findings on, screening	Rating
Age 30 and under:	
No polyps on endoscopy	5 per mil for 5 yr
No polyps on endoscopy and no evidence of hypertrophy of the retinal pigment epithelium	3 per mil for 5 yr
Ages 31–40:	
No polyps on endoscopy	3 per mil for 3 yr
No polyps on endoscopy and no evidence of hypertrophy of the retinal pigment epithelium	2 per mil for 2 yr
Ages over 40	Standard
All ages; no genetic markers of FAP	Standard

Non-Adenomatous Polyposis

Non-adenomatous polyposis is a heterogeneous group of diseases that have one thing in common: the involvement of the gut by multiple polyps of non-adenomatous nature. Some of these diseases are inherited, others are not. Some are associated with typical extraintestinal manifestations, others are not. They are basically not precancerous, although an increased incidence of malignancy has been observed in the Peutz–Jeghers syndrome and in diffuse lymphoid pseudopolyposis.

Juvenile Polyposis

This is involvement of the rectum, colon and, rarely, the small intestine by inflammatory polyps which may be solitary or (more often) multiple. They occur in childhood and usually disappear during puberty. They may occasionally be found in adults and are macroscopically not distinguishable from adenomatous polyps. Juvenile polyps may cause bleeding, intestinal obstruction or prolaps. They are considered to be benign with no potential for malignancy.[49]

Applicants with a history or evidence of solitary inflammatory polyps or juvenile polyposis can be accepted standard for life insurance.

Peutz–Jeghers Syndrome

This is familial polyposis in which harmatomatous polyps occur in any part of the gastrointestinal tract, although most frequently in the jejunum. Polyposis is associated with melanin spots in mucocutaneous tissues, especially the mouth and lips. Inheritance is autosomal dominant. Since the polyps in the Peutz–Jeghers syndrome are harmatomatous in nature, the condition should not be precancerous. However, gastrointestinal malignancy has been observed in an increasing number of patients in whom polyps had undergone adenomatous change. In fact, two of the 12 affected members of one of the original Peutz–Jeghers families reported by

Jeghers developed gastrointestinal cancer.[50] In all cases published so far, the adenomatous change occurred in the stomach or duodenum. In addition, ovarian neoplasms have been reported in women affected by Peutz–Jeghers syndrome.

Keeping in mind the increased incidence of cancer in patients with gastric and duodenal polyps, and in women in general, applicants for life insurance with Peutz-Jeghers syndrome should be carefully selected and rated +50 to +100, depending on sex and the part of the gastrointestinal tract involved.

Cronkhite–Canada Syndrome

This is generalized polyposis of the gastrointestinal tract associated with diffuse pigmentation of the skin, alopecia and dystrophy of the nails. The polyps are non-adenomatous in nature and the condition is apparently not genetically determined. Cronkhite–Canada syndrome usually becomes manifest after the age of 40 and presents with uncontrollable diarrhea and steatorrhea. Malabsorption and enteric loss of plasma proteins and electrolytes frequently lead to death within a short period of time. The condition, though not precancerous, is uninsurable.

Diffuse Lymphoid Pseudopolyposis

This is a condition in which the mucosa of rectum and colon is packed with conglomerates of hyperplastic lymph follicles macroscopically suggesting polyposis. The abdominal lymph nodes may be enlarged; the peripheral lymph nodes and the spleen are not. Diffuse lymphoid pseudopolyposis is a slowly progressing disease of the elderly presenting with diarrhea. Since an increased incidence of malignant lymphoma and Hodgkin's disease has been reported, diffuse lymphoid pseudopolyposis is considered to be a premalignant condition.[51] Pseudopolyps and diarrhea disappear with treatment with alkylating drugs, such as chlorambucil.

For carefully selected elderly lives whose disease has been adequately treated, standard rates for life insurance would apply. For less than satisfactory control an appropriate years-to-age rating is suggested.

REFERENCES

1 Trier JS. Celiac sprue. *N Eng J Med* 1991; 325: 1709–19.
2 Ascher H, Krantz I, Krishansson B. Increasing incidence of coeliac disease in Sweden. *Arch Dis Child* 1991; 66: 608–11.
3 Shmerling DH, Franckx J. Childhood celiac disease: a long-term analysis of relapse in 91 patients. *J Pediatr Gastroenterol Nutr* 1986; 5: 565–9.
4 Holmes GKT, Prior P, Lane MR et al. Malignancy in coeliac disease — effect of a gluten-free diet. *Gut* 1989; 30: 333–8.
5 Logan RFA, Rifkind EA, Turner ID et al. Mortality in celiac disease. *Gastroenterology* 1989; 17: 265–71.
6 Glynn J. Tropical sprue — its aetiology and pathogenesis. *J Roy Soc Med* 1986; 79: 599–606.
7 Beaugerie L, Baetz A. Discussion diagnostique: diarrhée chronique chez un Haitien. *Ann Gastroentérol Hépatol* (Paris) 1986; 22: 41–6.
8 Case records of the Massachusetts General Hospital. Case 15–1990. A 78-year-old woman from the Dominican Republic with chronic diarrhea. *N Engl J Med* 1990; 322: 1067–75.
9 Manousos DN, Truelove SC, Lumsden K. Diverticular disease of the colon. *Br Med J* 1967; 3: 62–5.
10 Horner JL. Natural history of diverticulosis of the colon. *Am J Dig Dis* 1958; 3: 343–450.

11 Chia JG, Wilde CC, Ngoi SS et al. Trends of diverticular disease of the large bowel in a newly developed country. *Dis Colon Rectum* 1991; 34: 498–501.
12 Olle JJ, Larsen L, Andersen JR. Irritable bowel syndrome and symptomatic diverticular disease — different diseases? *Am J Gastroenterol* 1986; 81: 529–31.
13 Boles J, Jordan JM. The clinical significance of diverticulosis. *Gastroenterology* 1958; 35: 579–82.
14 *Medical Impairment Study 1983*. Boston: Society of Actuaries and Association of Life Insurance Medical Directors of America, 1986.
15 Orholm M, Munkholm, Langholz E et al. Familial occurrence of inflammatory bowel disease. *N Engl J Med* 1991; 324: 84–8.
16 Ekbom A, Helmick C, Zack M et al. Ulcerative proctitis in Central Sweden 1965–1983: a population-based epidemiological study. *Dig Dis Sci* 1991; 36: 97–102.
17 Hiwasashi N, Yamazaki H, Kimura M et al. Clinical course and long-term prognosis of Japanese patients with ulcerative colitis. *Gastroenterol Jpn* 1991; 26: 312–18.
18 Hendriksen C, Kreiner S, Bruder V. Long term prognosis in ulcerative colitis. *Gut* 1985; 26: 158–63.
19 Podolsky D. Inflammatory bowel disease. *N Engl J Med* 1991; 325: 928–36, 1008–16.
20 Yardley JH, Lazenby AJ, Giardiello FM et al. Collagenous, 'microscopic', lymphocytic and other gentler and more subtle forms of colitis. *Hum Pathol* 1990; 21: 1089–91.
21 Softley A, Clamp SE, Watkinson G et al. The natural history of inflammatory bowel disease: has there been a change in the last 20 years? *Scand J Gastroenterol* 1988; 23 (Suppl 144): 20–3.
22 Kvist N, Jacobsen O, Kvist HK et al. Malignancy in ulcerative colitis. *Scand J Gastroenterol* 1989; 24: 497–506.
23 Ekbom A, Helmick C, Zack M et al. Increased risk of large-bowel cancer in Crohn's disease with colonic involvement. *Lancet* 1990; 336:357–9.
24 Andrews HA, Lewis P, Allan RN. Mortality in Crohn's disease — a clinical analysis. *Quart J Med* 1989: 71: 399–405.
25 Marchow H, Ewe K, Brandes JW et al. European cooperative Crohn's disease study (ECCDS): results of drug treatment. *Gastroenterology* 1984; 86: 249–66.
26 Leijinmerck LE, Persson PG, Hellers G. Factors affecting colectomy rate in ulcerative colitis: an epidemiologic study. *Gut* 1990; 31: 329–33.
27 Nugent FW, Haggitt RC, Grilpin PA. Cancer surveillance in ulcerative colitis. *Gastroenterology* 1991; 100: 1241–8.
28 Broström O, Monsén U, Nordenwall B et al. Prognosis and mortality of ulcerative colitis in Stockholm Country 1955–1979. *Scand J Gastroenterol* 1987; 22: 907–13.
29 Weterman IT, Biemond I, Pena AS. Mortality and causes of death in Crohn's disease: review of 50 years' experience in Leiden University Hospital. *Gut* 1990; 31: 1387–90.
30 Sloth H, Bisgard C, Grove A. Collagenous colitis: a clinicopathological follow-up study. *Eur J Gastroenterol Hepatol* 1989; 1: 73–6.
31 Boot H, Rauwerda JA, Hoitsman HFW et al. Ischaemic colitis with rectal involvement: clinical features, endoscopic assessment and management. *Eur J Gastroenterol Hepatol* 1989; 1: 69–72.
32 Powell RW. Hirschsprung's disease in adolescents. Misadventures in diagnosis and management. *Am Surg* 1989; 55: 212–18.
33 Chatrenet, Milan C, Arneux P et al. Les polypes hyperplasiques colo-rectaux dans la population du Départment de la Côte-d'Or, entre 1976 et 1985. *Bull Cancer* (Paris) 1991; 78: 229–35.
34 Murakami R, Tsukuma H, Kanamori S et al. Natural history of colorectal polyps and the effects of polypectomy on occurrence of subsequent cancer. *Int J Cancer* 1990; 46: 159–64.
35 Di Sario JA, Foutch PG, Mai HD et al. Prevalence and malignant potential of colorectal polyps in asymptomatic, average-risk men. *Am J Gastroenterol* 1991; 86: 941–5.
36 O'Brien MJ, Winawer SJ, Zauber AG et al. The National Polyp Study. Patient and polyp characteristics associated with high-grade dysplasia in colorectal adenoma. *Gastroenterology* 1990; 98: 371–9.
37 Romania A, Zakov ZN, McGannon E et al. Congenital hypertrophy of the retinal pigment epithelium in familial adenomatous polyposis. *Ophthalmology* 1989; 96: 879–84.

38 Chapman PD, Church W, Burn J et al. Congenital hypertrophy of retinal pigment epithelium: a sign of familial adenomatous polyposis. *Br Med J* 1989; 298: 353–4.
39 Haggitt RC, Reed BJ. Hereditary gastrointestinal polyposis syndromes. *Am J Surg Pathol* 1986; 10: 871–87.
40 Kinzler KW, Hilbert MC, Su LK et al. Identification of FAP locus genes from chromosomes 5q21. *Science* 1991; 253: 661–5.
41 Nishisho S, Nakamura Y, Miyoshi Y et al. Mutations of chromosome 5q21 genes in FAP and colorectal cancer patients. *Science* 1991; 253: 665–9.
42 Vasen HF, Griffioen G, Offerhaus GJ et al. The value of screening and central registration of families with familial adenomatous polyposis. A study of 82 families in The Netherlands. *Dis Colon Rectum* 1990; 33: 227–30.
43 Jagelman DG, DeCosse JJ, Bussey HJ. Upper gastrointestinal cancer in familial adenomatous polyposis. *Lancet* 1988; 1: 1149–51.
44 Plail RO, Bussey HJ, Glazer G et al. Adenomatous polyposis: an association with carcinoma of the thyroid. *Br J Surg* 1987; 74: 377–80.
45 Nakamura Y, Lathrop M, Leppert M et al. Localization of the genetic defect in familial adenomatous polyposis. *Am J Hum Genet* 1988; 43: 638–44.
46 Sarre RG, Jagelman DG, Beck GJ et al. Colectomy with ileorectal anastomosis for familial adenomatous polyposis: the risk of rectal cancer. *Surgery* 1987; 101: 26–8.
47 Herrera-Ornelas L, Elsiah S, Petrelli N et al. Causes of death in patients with familial polyposis coli. *Semin Surg Oncol* 1987; 3: 109–17.
48 Kropilak M, Jagelman DG, Fazio VW et al. Brain tumours in familial polyposis. *Dis Colon Rectum* 1989; 32: 778–82.
49 Mestre JR. The changing pattern of juvenile polyps. *Am J Gastroenterol* 1986; 81: 312–14.
50 Foley TR, McGarrity, Abt AB. Peutz–Jeghers syndrome: a clinicopathologic survey of the 'Harrisburg family' with a 49-year follow-up. *Gastroenterology* 1988; 95: 1535–40.
51 Weill JP, Monath C, Farcot JM et al. Pseudopolypose lymphoide diffuse rectocolique. *Arch franç Mal Appar dig* 1972; 61: 485.

CHAPTER 20

ONCOLOGY

ROBERT D RUBENS

THE NATURE AND BEHAVIOR OF TUMORS

Tumors arise when the mechanisms of cell regulation are disturbed so that uncontrolled proliferation occurs, a process termed neoplasia. In recent years there has been a remarkable increase in our understanding of the genetic processes involved in neoplasia. Genes have been identified that encode for cell growth factors and receptor proteins for these factors. Over-expression of these genes is often associated with the development of tumors. Conversely, genes for the production of proteins necessary to control growth may be absent or functionally abnormal in some tumors.

Tumors are described as either benign or malignant. With benign tumors the abnormal cell proliferation is relatively orderly and the neoplastic cells bear a close resemblance to the normal cells from which they originate. The tumor is well circumscribed and the cells do not spread into adjacent tissues. The majority of benign tumors are harmless and can be cured by surgical excision. However, they can occasionally cause serious complications and be life-threatening when sited in a critical position, for example within the cranium.

In malignant tumors (cancers) the constituent cells have acquired the property to infiltrate surrounding tissues. The cancerous cells can gain access to the circulation and spread elsewhere in the body, a process known as metastasis. In the presence of metastases, cure cannot be achieved only by surgical removal of the primary tumor. Even without metastases, local growth and invasion may sometimes be so extensive as to render the tumor inoperable.

The histological (microscopic) features of malignant tumors give information of the probable behavior of cancer. When there is a resemblance to the normal tissue of origin, the tumor is designated well differentiated. These cancers are often slowly growing and late to disseminate. When the histological appearances differ markedly from normal tissue, usually with a high frequency of mitoses, the tumor is said to be poorly differentiated or anaplastic and is likely to behave in an aggressive fashion.

The majority of cancers arise in epithelial tissues (the skin, respiratory tract and alimentary system, and their appendages) and are termed carcinomas. The prefix 'squamous cell' or 'adeno-' indicates the type of epithelium from which the tumor arises. Cancers arising in other sites are given other specific names (e.g. sarcomas arise in connective tissues, lymphomas in lymphatic tissues).

Before carcinomas invade surrounding tissues, they proliferate at the site of origin. If diagnosed at this stage, before invasion has occurred, they are termed *in-situ* and are readily curable. Although the majority of malignant tumors are potentially life threatening, one type, basal cell carcinoma of the skin (rodent ulcer), does not metastasize and can be cured by either surgery or radiotherapy;

only if they remain untreated and become very extensive do they present a threat to life.

DIAGNOSIS AND STAGING

Biopsy is essential for the histological diagnosis of cancer. Once established, a series of staging investigations are undertaken to identify the extent and distribution of the cancer. This has implications both for determining prognosis and planning treatment. Staging includes physical examination and a series of laboratory, imaging and radiological investigations. A useful general staging system is given below.

Stage 0: in situ disease without invasion.

Stage I: the tumor is invasive, but confined to its tissue or organ of origin; it has not invaded surrounding structures, has not spread to regional lymph nodes and there is no evidence of distant spread; it is amenable to complete surgical removal.

Stage II: the primary tumor has the characteristics of Stage I, but it has also spread to the regional lymph nodes; although still removable by surgery, additional treatment by radiotherapy and/or chemotherapy may be given.

Stage III: there has been invasion of surrounding organs or structures; the disease is inoperable and usually treated by radiotherapy.

Stage IV: distant metastases have occurred; treatment is usually palliative and may involve hormones, cytotoxic drugs or only symptomatic and supportive care (which may include surgery or radiotherapy for the relief of symptoms).

For certain cancers (e.g. lymphomas, melanoma, colorectal cancer) special staging systems are used; these are described in the relevant sections.

TREATMENT AND PROGNOSIS

Stage I and II tumors are normally resectable by radical surgery; the intention of treatment is to eradicate the disease entirely. Stage III tumors are often inoperable, but because they are localized, cure may sometimes be achieved by radical radiotherapy. For disseminated tumors, systemic treatment (endocrine treatment or chemotherapy) is needed, but cure is not a realistic prospect for most common cancers and the purpose of treatment is palliative. Nevertheless, certain disseminated tumors can be cured by chemotherapy; these include chorio-carcinoma, testicular cancer and some lymphomas.

Why should localized cancer (Stages I and II) treated by apparently successful radical surgery subsequently relapse with distant metastases? The reason is illustrated in Figure 20.1. It is assumed that a malignant tumor arises from a single mutant cell which has escaped from cell regulation mechanisms. This proliferates exponentially, so that after 30 tumor doublings approximately 10^9 (one billion) tumor cells will have been produced. This is still a relatively small volume of cells, approximately 1 cm^3. It still takes some more doublings before there is a sufficient tumor mass for the cancer to become symptomatic. Yet, after only a few further doublings (40 from the original cell) a kilogram of tumor will be present, which is likely to be overwhelmingly lethal. Hence, when cancer is recognized clinically for the first time, it is in a relatively late stage of tumor evolution and the process of metastasis may have already occurred. These microscopic secondary deposits continue to grow after intended curative surgery and are responsible for the failure of radical treatment.

Understanding these principles has led to the use of systemic anti-cancer treatment to complement surgery in the initial treatment of cancer at high risk of recurrence. This is termed adjuvant systemic treatment. It has achieved significant success in reducing mortality from cancer, particularly carcinoma of the breast, and has been responsible for a marked improvement in the outlook for children with cancer.

The most important determinants of outcome for patients with cancer are the tumor type, staging, histological differentiation and treatment received. Considerable variations in mortality are also seen according to race, social

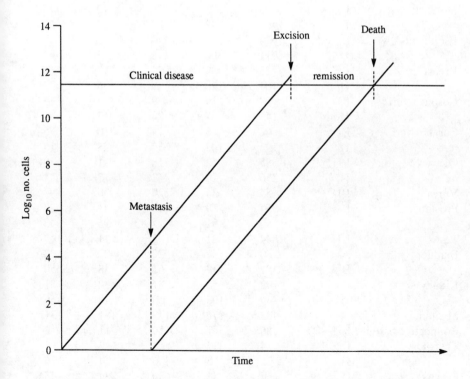

Fig. 20.1. A model to explain the frequent incurability of cancer by local treatment.

class, life style, occupation and environment. Information on mortality comes from various cancer registers; a particularly useful source is from the program for Cancer Surveillance Epidemiology and End Results Reporting (SEER) in the USA, which has been reviewed by Lew and Gajewski.[1] Table 20.1 shows the variability in mortality according to different tumor types. This information is essential for a scientific and logical approach to underwriting for life insurance.

Table 20.1. Mortality for various cancers expressed as extra deaths per thousand with time elapsed from diagnosis.[a]

Site	Stage	Extra deaths per mil for time intervals Diagnosis (years)				
		0–2	2–5	5–10	10–15	15–20
Lung	I	307	104	55	55	48
	II	575	228	69	36	12
Colon	A/B	70	49	19	11	8
	C	184	124	37	3	5
Rectum	A/B	78	61	24	11	9
	C	203	177	62	16	9
Stomach	I	203	105	29	12	15
	II	467	242	83	27	22
Esophagus	I	614	304	113	—	—
	II	711	306	112	12	—
Breast	I	23	39	24	17	16
	II	104	120	69	36	33
Corpus Uteri	I	28	19	9	7	15
	II	145	57	24	13	—
Cervix Uteri	I	62	35	14	10	5
	II	192	102	32	28	18
Ovary	I	85	52	18	11	19
	II	236	120	42	13	4
Vulva	I/II	54	34	20	30	—
Prostate	I	54	59	46	41	29
	II	86	91	77	95	43
Testis	I/II	44	21	3	11	7
Bladder	A	80	37	22	27	22
	B	381	119	61	38	50
Kidney	I	102	55	31	32	31
	II	249	106	60	46	66
Myeloma	—	422	276	178	181	131
Connective tissue	I/II	86	47	14	11	2
Thyroid	I	4	2	3	2	5
	II	25	5	6	4	6
Larynx	I	67	38	30	34	43
	II	283	143	60	36	—

Site	Stage	Extra deaths per mil for time intervals Diagnosis (years)				
		0–2	2–5	5–10	10–15	15–20
Pharynx	I	232	141	64	61	23
	II	368	175	87	53	66
Floor of mouth	I	106	71	63	65	24
	II	287	121	96	95	122
Mouth (other)	I/II	124	96	47	27	3
Lip	I/II	17	21	15	14	29
Salivary gland	I/II	26	24	19	11	3
Tongue	I	154	103	58	45	65
	II	396	196	103	42	96

[a] Source: *Medical Risks.*[1]

UNDERWRITING

The well established approach to underwriting cancer risks is illustrated in Figure 20.2. In the early years after diagnosis and primary treatment, extra mortality is too high for terms to be offered. This is followed by a period of lower extra mortality when terms can be offered at an increased premium. It is assumed that in time the mortality of previous cancer sufferers approximates to that of the normal population, provided recurrence has not occurred; therefore applicants can be accepted at ordinary rates. However, long-term studies demonstrate a considerable late residual extra mortality for many tumors (*see* Table 20.1). There are probably several reasons for this, in addition to late mortality from the cancer itself. These include late harmful effects of the treatment necessary to achieve long-term survival in the first place and, perhaps, an applicant's inherent genetic susceptibility to develop further malignancy. Nevertheless, in underwriting, applicants known to have relapsed will normally be excluded from policies, so this important cause of late residual mortality will be of relatively little importance. In other words, we select the more favorable subsets of patients for life insurance, namely those who are alive and free from recurrence (*see* Fig. 20.3). This more favorable survival of insured lives is taken into consideration in rating schedules.

For practical purposes, the model described in Figure 20.2 serves well for most cancers. However, there are some for which there is no possibility of eradication by treatments currently available, but which follow a relatively indolent course over many years (e.g. low-grade non-Hodgkin's lymphoma and chronic lymphocytic leukemia). For these, a permanent extra mortality rating can be applied and the duration of policies limited.

For most cancers a temporary extra premium will suffice after a period of postponement. The tumors can be placed in an appropriate rating category

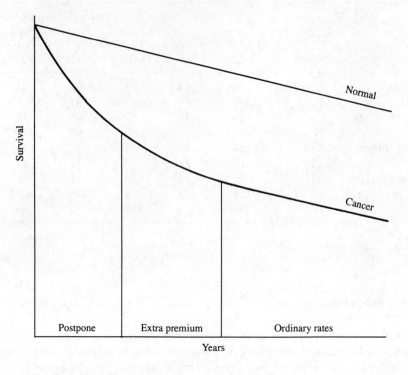

Fig. 20.2. Model for rating cancer risks.

Table 20.2. Specimen rating schedule for localized cancer.

Years from primary treatment	Ratings[a]						
	Class A	Class B	Class C	Class D	Class E	Class F	Class G
0–6 mth	Postpone	Postpone	Postpone	Postpone	Postpone	6 for 4 yr	5 for 3 yr
6–12 mth	Postpone	Postpone	Postpone	Postpone	8 for 5 yr	6 for 4 yr	5 for 2 yr
2nd yr	Postpone	Postpone	Postpone	12 for 5 yr	8 for 4 yr	6 for 3 yr	3 for 2 yr
3rd yr	Postpone	Postpone	12 for 5 yr	12 for 4 yr	8 for 3 yr	6 for 2 yr	Standard
4th yr	Postpone	17 for 5 yr	12 for 4 yr	12 for 3 yr	6 for 2 yr	2 for 2 yr	
5th yr	17 for 7 yr	12 for 5 yr	12 for 3 yr	8 for 2 yr	2 for 2 yr	Standard	
6th yr	17 for 6 yr	12 for 4 yr	8 for 3 yr	4 for 2 yr	Standard		
7th yr	12 for 6 yr	12 for 3 yr	8 for 2 yr	Standard			
8th yr	8 for 6 yr	8 for 3 yr	4 for 2 yr				
9th yr	8 for 4 yr	8 for 2 yr	Standard				
10th yr	8 for 2 yr	4 for 2 yr					
11th yr	4 for 2 yr	Standard					
Thereafter	Standard						

[a]Extra units of currency per mil insured.

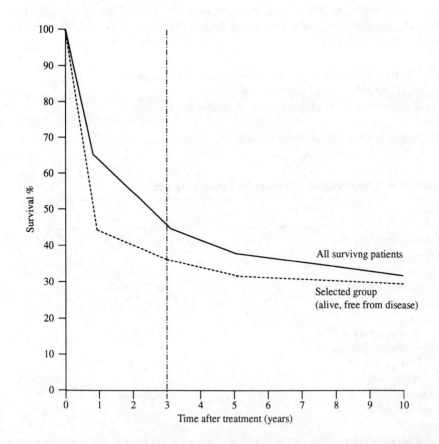

Fig. 20.3. Survival of patients with time after treatment of localized cancer: all surviving patients and the subgroup alive and free from disease (the group selected for life insurance after the appropriate postponement period).

according to the risk involved. Insurance companies differ in the details of their individual approaches; an example is shown in Table 20.2. It is based on considering the extra mortality in successive time periods after diagnosis for different ages and converting this into extra deaths per thousand in order to give the monetary per mil extra premium. This method gives a more intelligible picture of excess mortality than using table ratings because the risk is early, falling sharply with time elapsed since treatment. Table 20.3 shows how the rating schedule is applied to the various tumors. For some tumors, different ratings are specified for different stages. Unfortunately, full information is not always available from medical attendants' and medical examiners' reports; when this is so, caution dictates the use of a rating for a high staging.

Ratings have not been given for most Stage III and IV cancers as mortality is so high that terms can rarely be considered. However, for the few applicants who have been treated for these stages and are free of disease five or more years later, individual terms may be cautiously considered. Similar consideration can be applied to applicants who have been treated for a localized recurrence. For example, the following modifications to Stage I (localized) cancer ratings may be used:

Stage II (nodal involvement): one rating class higher than for Stage I.
Stages III and IV: +100[a] plus Class A rating.
Local recurrence +50[a] plus the usual rating for the tumor.

[a]Rating usually discontinued after ten disease-free years.

Table 20.3. Classification of tumors for rating purposes.

Tumor	Class
Adenolymphoma (parotid)	Standard
Adrenal cortex	
adenoma	Standard
carcinoma	B
Adrenal medulla	
ganglioneuroma	D
neuroblastoma	B
pheochromocytoma	
benign	*see* p. 718
malignant	B
Angioma	Standard
Angiosarcoma	B
Anus	
adenocarcinoma	B
squamous cell carcinoma	C
Appendix	
carcinoid	Standard
carcinoma	B
Arrhenoblastoma	B
Astrocytoma	
Grade 1	D
Grade 2	C
Grade 3	B
Grade 4	A
Basal cell carcinoma	Standard
Bone	
chondroma	Standard
chondrosarcoma	B
ecchondroma	Standard
enchondroma	Standard
eosinophilic granuloma	Standard (*see* p. 926)
Ewing's sarcoma	B
exostosis	Standard

Tumor	Class
osteoblastoma	F
osteoclastoma	D
osteosarcoma	B
Bowen's disease	Standard
Breast	
carcinoma	
intraduct only, non-invasive	
simple mastectomy	G
excision only	F
infiltrating	
Stage I	B
Stage II	A
cystosarcoma phyllodes	F
fibroadenoma	Standard
fibrosarcoma	B
intraduct papilloma	Standard
mammary duct ectasia	Standard
sclerosing adenosis	Standard
Brenner tumor of ovary	Standard
Bronchus	*see* 'Lung'
Carcinoid	
appendix	Standard
bronchus	D
colon	B
small intestine	B
stomach	B
Cervix uteri	
carcinoma	
in situ	Standard
invasive	
Stage Ia	F
Stage Ib	C
Stage II	B
Cholangiocarcinoma	A
Cholesteatoma (intracranial)	E
Chordoma	C
Choriocarcinoma (including hydatidiform mole)	
hydatidiform mole	
HCG levels normal	
< 6 months	Postpone
≥ 6 months	Standard
choriocarcinoma	
occult in mole	
HCG levels normal	
< 6 months	Postpone

Tumor	Class
≥ 6 months	G
invasive	B
Colon	
carcinoma	
Dukes' Stage A	C
Dukes' Stage B	B
Dukes' Stage C	A
Corpus uteri	
carcinoma	C
Craniopharyngioma	E
Cylindroma	
bronchial	D
salivary glands	B
skin	Standard
Dermatofibroma	Standard
Dermatofibrosarcoma	B
Dermatofibrosarcoma protuberans	F
Desmoid	Standard
Dysgerminoma	B
Ependymoma	B
Esophagus	
carcinoma	A
leiomyoma	Standard
Eye	
melanoma	B
retinoblastoma	B
Fibroid	Standard
Fibroma	Standard
Fibromyoma	Standard
Fibrosarcoma	B
Gall-bladder	
carcinoma	A
Glioma	B
Grawitz's tumor	B
Hamartoma	Standard
Hemangioblastoma	D
Hemangiopericytoma	
benign	Standard
malignant	B
Hepatoma	A
Histiocytoma	
benign	Standard
malignant fibrous	B
Hodgkin's disease	
lymphocyte predominant	

Tumor	Class
Stage I	F
Stage II	E
Stage III	C
Stage IV	B
nodular sclerosing, mixed cellularity	
lymphocyte depleted	
Stage I	E
Stage II	D
Stage III	B
Stage IV	A
Hypernephoma	B
Kaposi's sarcoma	A
associated with AIDS	Decline
Kidney	
carcinoma	B
Wilm's tumor	B
Larynx	
carcinoma	
in situ	F
invasive	B
chondroma	Standard
fibroma	Standard
papilloma	Standard
polyp	Standard
Leiomyoma	Standard
Lieomyosarcoma	B
Leukemia	*see* p. 685
Lip	
carcinoma	D
Lipoma	Standard
Liposarcoma	B
Liver	
cholangiocarcinoma	A
hepatocellular carcinoma (hepatoma)	A
Lung	
adenoma	D
carcinoid	D
carcinoma	
adenocystic	B
alveolar cell	A
large cell anaplastic	A
oat cell	A
small cell	A
squamous cell	A
Lymphoma, non-Hodgkin's	

Tumor	Class
low-grade	
Stage I	C
Stage II	B
Stage III	A
Stage IV	A
high-grade	
Stage I	B
Stage II	A
Stage III	A
Stage IV	A
Medulloblastoma	B
Melanoma (malignant, Stage I)	
cutaneous	
tumor thickness	
0–0·75 mm	Standard
0·76–1·0 mm	G
1·01–1·25 mm	F
1·26–1·5 mm	D
> 1·5 mm	A/B
Clark level	
I(*in situ*)	Standard
II	G to standard
III	E
IV	B
V	A
ocular	B
Meningioma	F
Mesothelioma	A
Mouth (floor of)	
carcinoma	A
Myeloma	Decline
Myxoma	Standard
Myxosarcoma	B
Nasopharynx	
carcinoma	A
Nephroblastoma	B
Neurofibroma	Standard
Neurilemmoma	Standard
Neuroma	
acoustic	Standard
elsewhere	Standard
Oligodendroblastoma	B
Oligodendroglioma	C
Osteosarcoma	B
Ovary	

see also pp. 643–4

Tumor	Class
adenoma	Standard
arrhenoblastoma	B
Brenner tumor	Standard
carcinoma	B
cystadenoma	Standard
dermoid cyst	Standard
dysgerminoma	B
fibroma	Standard
granulosa cell carcinoma	B
Krukenberg tumor	A
pseudomucinous cystadenocarcinoma	B
serous cystadenocarcinoma	B
teratoma	
benign	Standard
malignant	B
Pancreas	
carcinoma	A
cystadenoma	Standard
islet cell adenoma	Standard
islet cell carcinoma	A
Parathyroid	
adenoma	Standard
carcinoma	B
Parotid gland	
adenocarcinoma	B
adenoid cystic carcinoma	B
adenolymphoma	Standard
mixed tumor (pleomorphic adenoma)	Standard
Penis	
carcinoma	C
Pharynx	
carcinoma	A
Pinealoma	C
Plasmacytoma	A
Prostate	
carcinoma	
in situ	Standard
invasive	
confined to prostate	B
extracapsular	A
Rectum	rate as 'Colon'
Rhabdomyosarcoma	A
Rodent ulcer	Standard
Stomach	
adenomyoma	Standard

see also pp. 645–6 (for prostate carcinoma invasive)

Tumor	Class
carcinoid	B
carcinoma	A
Synovial sarcoma	A
Testis (seminoma, teratoma)	
Stage I	E
Stage II	D
Stage III	C
Stage IV	B
Thymoma	
benign	Standard
malignant	B
Thyroid	
adenoma	Standard
carcinoma	
alveolar	B
anaplastic	B
follicular	D
Hurthle cell	B
medullary	B
papillary	E
Tongue	
carcinoma	A
Tonsil	
lymphoepithelioma	A
carcinoma	A
Urinary bladder	
benign papilloma	
single	G
multiple	F
in situ carcinoma	
single	F
multiple	E
invasive carcinoma	
Stage A	
single	E
multiple	D
Stage B1	
single	C
multiple	B
Stage B2	B
Vulva	
adenocarcinoma	B
squamous cell carcinoma	C
Wilms' tumor	B

see also p.641

SPECIFIC TUMORS

Lung Cancer

Carcinoma of the lung is the commonest cancer in the UK and accounts for about 17 percent of all new cases of cancer. At least 90 percent of cases are caused by tobacco smoking, a habit probably accounting for one-third of all cancer deaths. Most lung cancers are not amenable to radical treatment, but when surgical resection is possible, about a quarter of patients survive five years in the best series, compared with about 5 percent following radical radio-therapy.[2] There have been no important developments in treatment that have had a major impact on survival. Small cell carcinoma of the lung is highly sensitive to chemotherapy, but its use only extends median survival prospects by some months. Only about 5 percent of all patients with lung cancer are alive five years after diagnosis.

Despite the high prevalence of lung cancer, these appalling mortality statistics ensure that very few sufferers become eligible for life assurance. For the small proportion who have radical resections of the tumor and are disease-free four years later, terms can be considered, but at severe ratings (*see* Table 20.3) when the high late residual mortality is noted (*see* Table 20.1).

Colorectal Cancer

Cancers of the colon and rectum are common and, as causes of death from cancer, are surpassed only by lung cancer in men and breast cancer in women. Curative treatment is by resection of the involved bowel together with the mesentery containing its draining lymph nodes. After surgery, colorectal cancer is staged using Dukes' classification (*see* Table 20.4).

Table 20.4. Dukes' classification for colorectal cancer.

Dukes' Stage	Extent of disease
A	Tumor confined to mucosa and sub-mucosa.
B	Invasion has occurred through the muscularis without nodal metastases.
C	Involvement of mesenteric lymph nodes.

Survival figures at five years for Dukes' A, B and C are about 90 percent, 70 percent and 35 percent respectively.[3] Recent clinical trial results indicate that cure rates for Dukes' C colorectal cancer may be improved by the use of post-operative adjuvant chemotherapy.[4]

Three non-malignant conditions predispose to the development of colorectal cancer: villous adenomas, familial adenomatous polyposis and ulcerative colitis. (*see* Chapter 19). Provided villous adenomas are completely resected, the risk of cancer is eliminated. Familial adenomatous polyposis, on the other hand, almost invariably leads to the development of colorectal cancer and, for this condition, prophylactic colectomy is necessary. Total colectomy with ileorectal anastomosis is the preferred treatment, provided the rectum is free from polyps; lifelong proctoscopic examination thereafter at six-monthly intervals is needed to remove any polyps that develop and to observe for the early development of cancer.[5,6]

For underwriting, a temporary extra of 7 to 10 per mil for three to four years is warranted following the removal of villous adenomata, if histological confirmation confirms the lesion to be benign or shows carcinoma *in situ*; if invasive cancer is present, the rating is as for carcinoma of the colon (*see* Table 20.3). For familial adenomatous polyposis, terms can only be offered if colectomy has been carried out. Following colectomy with ileorectal anastomosis it is reasonable to impose a permanent rating of +50 to cover the risk of cancer developing in the rectal stump; this is not necessary after pan-proctocolectomy. The approach to underwriting ulcerative colitis is discussed elsewhere (*see* pp. 610–12).

Breast Cancer

Breast cancer is the most common malignancy affecting women in developed countries. In the UK it accounts for 20 percent of all female cancers, and the lifetime risk of a woman developing this tumor is 1 in 12. With the implementation of breast cancer screening, the incidence must be expected to increase, but with a higher proportion of cases being curable there should be an ultimate lowering of mortality from this cause. Breast cancer is conveniently staged using the general system outlined (*see* p. 624). This staging is useful both for planning treatment and estimating prognosis.

Conventional treatment for Stages I and II has been by total mastectomy, often with axillary clearance. However, in recent years techniques enabling radical treatment with breast preservation have been developed. As far as survival is concerned, all the evidence points to these conservation procedures being equivalent to mastectomy. Stage III disease cannot normally be treated by radical surgery and the mainstay of treatment is radiotherapy. In disseminated disease (Stage IV), treatment is palliative. Survival according to stage is shown in Figure 20.4; the minority of patients presenting with Stages III and IV disease are not eligible for life insurance. In recent years the use of adjuvant systemic treatment has been used extensively as post-operative treatment, particularly in Stage II disease. A meta-analysis of clinical trials has shown convincingly that this approach significantly reduces mortality.[7] The most marked effects are seen with adjuvant chemotherapy in pre-menopausal patients, and tamoxifen in post-menopausal patients, which lead to a reduction in the annual odds of death of about 25 percent, equivalent to an absolute reduction in the death rate of 10 percent at ten years.

The most powerful predictor of prognosis in breast cancer is whether or not axillary nodes are involved by metastatic disease (compare Stages I and II in Figure 20.4). Nevertheless it is possible to refine prediction further by noting the size of the primary tumor, histological appearances and indices of the rapidity of tumor cell proliferation. Unfortunately such detailed information is only occasionally available to underwriters; but when it is, risk evaluation is enhanced considerably. For example, in Stage I breast cancer, consideration of tumor size and histological or proliferation characteristics can define, on the one hand a group

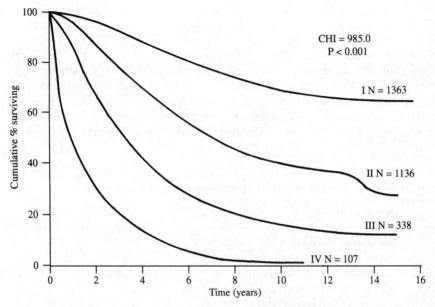

Fig 20.4. Survival of patients with breast cancer from diagnosis according to stage of disease at presentation. [Source: author's database at Guy's Hospital, London.]

of patients with a survival expectancy no different from normal women and, on the other, a group with an outlook similar to node-positive disease.[8] It has also been noted that the timing of surgery in relation to the menstrual cycle can have a major impact on survival in pre-menopausal patients.[9]

One of the factors associated with an increased risk of developing breast cancer is a strong family history. This is particularly marked for women with mothers who developed the disease pre-menopausally and had bilateral disease; the risk for these women is increased about fourfold. The use of this information for underwriting is questionable, but an applicant with such a family history is unlikely to be eligible for critical illness cover.

In situ cancer of the breast will become more common with screening programs. An entity known as lobular carcinoma *in situ* is often an incidental finding and is associated with a relatively low risk of invasive cancer. This type of *in situ* disease can probably be disregarded for life insurance, but would exclude critical illness policies. Ductal carcinoma *in situ*, on the other hand, is associated with a significant incidence of subsequent invasive cancer unless adequately treated. Paradoxically in these days of breast preservation procedures for invasive cancer, mastectomy has been the standard treatment for ductal carcinoma *in situ*. Clinical trials are now taking place to see if breast preservation is safe using radiotherapy or tamoxifen to treat this condition. A guide to underwriting ductal carcinomas *in situ* is given in Table 20.3.

Gynecological Cancer

Carcinoma of the uterine cervix is particularly prevalent in developing countries, notably in China and Latin America where it is the commonest female cancer.[10] Risk is increased by early commencement of sexual activity and number of partners; there is some evidence implicating herpes and papilloma viruses in its etiology. It is possible to screen for carcinoma of the cervix by cytological examination, the appearances being categorized as cervical intra-epithelial neoplasia (CIN). CIN I indicates mild dysplasia, CIN II moderate dysplasia, and CIN III describes either severe dysplasia or *in situ* carcinoma. CIN III can be treated adequately either by cone biopsy, cryotherapy or laser ablation performed at colposcopy. Table 20.5 shows how invasive carcinoma of the uterine cervix is staged.

Table 20.5. Classification for invasive carcinoma of the uterine cervix.

Stage	Extent of disease
I A	Microinvasive (up to 3 mm invasion)
I B	Occult invasive (up to 5 mm invasion)
II A	Extension beyond cervix but not infiltrating the parametrium
II B	With parametrial invasion
III A	Involvement of lower third of vagina
III B	Extension to pelvic wall and/or ureteric obstruction
IV A	Involvement of bladder and/or rectum or extension beyond pelvis
IV B	Metastases to distant sites.

The earlier stages of invasive cancer (I and IIA) can be treated by either radiotherapy or surgery (Wertheim hysterectomy); survival at five years can be over 80 percent, and a guide to underwriting is given in Table 20.3. Higher stages of the disease may be amenable to radiotherapy, but such patients are unlikely to become eligible for life insurance.

Carcinoma of the corpus uteri (endometrial cancer) usually presents at an early stage following the complaint of post-menopausal bleeding. The cure rate following hysterectomy is high, with a five-year survival of about 80 percent. By contrast, carcinoma of the ovary presents relatively late in most patients. Even when disease is confined to the ovaries (Stage I), five-year survival is only about 60 percent. The comparative differences between these gynecological cancers are reflected in the late residual mortality (*see* Table 20.1) and taken into account in underwriting (*see* Table 20.3).

Testicular Tumors

Testicular cancer is the commonest cancer in young men aged 20–40. Of testicular tumors, 95 percent are germ cell tumors, either teratomas or seminomas. The only established risk factor is cryptorchidism, but only 10 percent of patients have such a history. Table 20.6 shows how testicular cancer is staged.

Table 20.6. Staging for testicular cancer.

Stage[a]	Extent of disease
I	Confined to testis.
II	Involvement of abdominal lymph nodes.
III	Involvement of lymph nodes above diaphragm.
IV	Spread to other tissues.

[a]The equivalent North American classification is: Stage I = Stage A; Stage II = Stage B; Stages III and IV = Stage C.

There have been remarkable advances in the treatment of testicular cancer which may involve, depending on stage, surgery, radiotherapy and/or chemotherapy. Modern chemotherapy can even eradicate Stage IV disease. Management is greatly facilitated by monitoring the serum markers human chorionic gonadotropin (HCG) and alfa-fetoprotein (AFP).[11] This is the only cancer, apart from the rare choriocarcinoma, where there is a routine role for tumor markers in management. Overall, more than 90 percent of patients with testicular cancer are alive five years after treatment, effectively cured of the disease.

Because of the unique mortality characteristics of testicular malignancies in terms of their response to treatment and their long-term management, some insurance companies have used an alternative rating schedule to that shown in Table 20.3. This is set out below.

Treatment completed; with or without chemotherapy or radiotherapy; markers negative.

Stage	Rating
I	5 per mil for 3 yr
II	7 per mil for 4 yr
III	
Within 1 yr	Postpone
2nd yr	10 per mil for 3 yr
IV	
Within 2 yr	Postpone
3rd yr	10 per mil for 4 yr

For recurrences identified by rising marker values — rate from time of re-treatment.

Where combined chemotherapy has been used in excess of the planned initial regime (e.g. to treat recurrences), +50 throughout may be added to the above ratings to cover the risk of late secondary malignancies.

Bladder Cancer

Most, at least 90 percent, of urothelial bladder tumors are of the transitional cell variety. They are usually papillary and often multicentric. Papillary tumors seem to have relatively less tendency to invade the muscularis and have a better prognosis than non-papillary lesions, which have a propensity to deeper invasion. The distinction between benign papillomas and malignant urothelial tumors is not always clear-cut. Even benign transitional cell papillomas have a recurrence rate of up to 50 percent, warranting six-monthly cystoscopic observation. Bladder tumors are categorized according to Marshall's staging system (*see* Table 20.7).

Table 20.7. Marshall's staging system for bladder tumors.

Stage	Extent of disease
0	Confined to mucosa.
A	Infiltration of submucosa.
B_1	Infiltration of superficial muscle.
B_2	Infiltration of deep muscle.
C	Infiltration of perivesical fat.
D_1	Infiltration of adjacent organs or lymph nodes.
D_2	Extension beyond pelvis.

Carcinoma *in situ* presents a specific problem in patients with transitional cell carcinoma. It is non-invasive, but has a high potential for subsequent invasion. It is multifocal and diffuse, reflecting the potential for the entire urothelial surface to react to carcinogens. Limited carcinoma *in situ* can be treated by either fulguration or intravesical chemotherapy, but unresponsive or more extensive lesions necessitate cystectomy.[12] These considerations are relevant to risk evaluation (*see* Table 20.3).

Lymphoma

Primary tumors of the lymphatic system are classified as Hodgkin's disease or non-Hodgkin's lymphomas. Hodgkin's disease is characterized by the presence of multinucleate giant cells (Reed Sternberg cells) which are not present in the non-Hodgkin's lymphomas. In Hodgkin's disease the tumor arises in a group of nodes and spreads in a contiguous fashion to other nodal areas. Non-Hodgkin's lymphomas have a less orderly mode of spread and often have a multifocal origin. Accurate staging of lymphomas is essential for adequate treatment planning and requires certain imaging tests, which may include MRI, computerized tomography (CT scanning), lymphography, isotope scanning or ultrasonography. For Hodgkin's disease, laparotomies have been done in some centers for accurate staging by sampling intra-abdominal lymph nodes and undertaking splenectomy for histological examination. With improved imaging techniques and treatment, staging laparotomy is being performed less often. The staging system for lymphomas is as follows:

Stage I: disease confined to one group of lymph nodes (I) or a single extra lymphatic site (IE).
Stage II: disease confined to lymph nodes either above or below the diaphragm, but not both (II), with or without local involvement of extralymphatic tissue (IIE).
Stage III: disease confined to lymph nodes on both sides of the diaphragm (III) with or without involvement of the spleen (IIIS) or a localized extralymphatic site (IIIE).
Stage IV: disseminated involvement of one or more extralymphatic organs or tissues (e.g. liver, bone marrow, bone, pleura, lung, skin).

To the above staging, the suffix 'A' is added if there is absence of weight loss, fever and sweating; the suffix 'B' is added in the presence of weight loss, fever or sweating.

Hodgkin's Disease
The incidence of Hodgkin's disease rises during chilhood to a peak at about the age of 20, after which it falls, to rise again steadily after the age of 50. Four histological types of Hodgkin's disease are described, which are, in order of worsening prognosis for a given stage, lymphocyte predominant, nodular sclerosis, mixed cellularity and lymphocyte depleted; nodular sclerosis accounts for one-half of cases, with mixed cellularity being the next most frequent. For Stages IA and IIA, high cure rates are achieved with radiotherapy. This involves irradiating the total nodal areas either above or below the diaphragm, known as mantle or inverted Y fields respectively. When 'B' symptoms are present or for Stage III disease, although nodal irradiation can be undertaken, the results are less good and are improved by incorporating chemotherapy into the primary treatment plan. Chemotherapy, which can also be curative for Stage IV disease, utilizes cytotoxic drugs in combination. The usual regimens contain either an alkylating agent, mustine or chlorambucil, a vinca alkaloid (vincristine or vinblastine), procarbazine and prednisolone (e.g. MOPP, MVPP or ChlVPP) or doxorubicin (adriamycin), bleomycin, vinblastine and dacarbazine (ABVD). These treatments, particularly when combined with radiotherapy, are associated with a low (but significant) risk of long-term morbidity, particularly the development of acute lymphoblastic leukemia. Nevertheless the risk of dying from Hodgkin's disease is far greater than the hazard of another subsequent malignancy.[13]

Non-Hodgkin's Lymphomas
The non-Hodgkin's lymphomas steadily increase in incidence with age. Although occasionally localized, they are usually disseminated lymphomas. Classification is complex and a variety of systems have been unified into a working formulation, which categorizes non-Hodgkin's lymphoma into low, intermediate and high grades.[14] The low-grade lymphomas are relatively

indolent and include the previously designated nodular and well differentiated lymphocytic lymphomas. The intermediate and high grades are progressively more aggressive and include those previously classified as diffuse poorly differentiated lymphomas, lymphosarcoma, reticulum-cell sarcoma and Burkett's lymphoma. Short-term survival after diagnosis is much worse for the high-grade lymphomas, but, paradoxically, these are more amenable to cure by chemotherapy and the long-term survival for those cured of high-grade lymphoma exceeds that for low-grade tumors. In other words, the approach to the chemotherapy of high-grade lymphoma is curative, but palliative in intent for low- grade. Only for the uncommon Stage I non-Hodgkin's lymphomas can radiotherapy be curative. Because of the relatively indolent course of the low-grade non-Hodgkin's lymphomas and their predominant occurrence in older people, an alternative underwriting approach to that outlined in Table 20.3 is to impose a permanent extra mortality rating of +200 after they have been in remission for at least two years.[15]

Melanoma

Malignant melanoma is the only potentially lethal skin cancer. Exposure to sun is the main etiological factor and the incidence of, and mortality from, this tumor has increased in recent years. There is wide international variation and the disease is almost ten times as common in Australia as it is in Europe. Malignant melanoma needs to be distinguished from benign melanocytic naevi, which only very rarely give rise to malignant lesions. Lentigo maligna (Hutchinson's melanotic freckle) is a more definite precursor of malignancy. Clinically, malignant melanomas are described as either superficial spreading or nodular, the latter penetrating more deeply and carrying a worse prognosis. The prognosis of melanoma is defined with some precision following excision, by either noting the thickness of the lesion or using Clark's classification of the level of invasion (see Table 20.8).

Table 20.8. Clark's classification for melanoma.

Level	Extent of disease
I	Confined to epidermis.
II	Papillary dermis invaded.
III	Extension to papillary-reticular junction.
IV	Reticular dermis invaded.
V	Subcutaneous tissue invaded.

Tumor thickness is the single most important prognostic factor and a mathematical model has been described which shows a simple non-linear relationship between thickness and ten-year mortality.[16] Either thickness or Clark level can be used in underwriting (see Table 20.3).

Although most malignant melanomas arise in the skin, they also account for 70 percent of primary cancers arising in the eye. The standard treatment for these tumors has been enucleation of the eye, but the metastasis rate is only about 10 percent and a growing body of evidence suggests that observation and laser treatment are safe options.[17]

Tumors of the Nervous System

There are a variety of brain tumors, the majority being gliomas which arise from the connective tissue of the central nervous system. The commonest glioma is the astrocytoma, others being ependymomas, oligodendrogliomas and medulloblastomas. Astrocytomas are graded according to the aggressiveness of the histological appearances, survival being progressively lower from Grade I to Grade IV. Other important intracranial tumors include those arising from the pituitary (adenomas and craniopharyngiomas) and meningiomas. If possible, surgical removal of brain tumors is desirable, both for histological diagnosis and, sometimes, definitive treatment. Radiotherapy is frequently employed, either as an adjunct to surgery or as definitive treatment. The results of treatment are highly variable and are related to the grade of the tumor; for all grades, incomplete removal is associated with a worse prognosis. The high morbidity and mortality from gliomas make relatively few sufferers eligible for life assurance. The outlook for pituitary tumors and meningiomas, which are more amenable to surgical excision, is much better. Primary tumors of the spinal cord are rare; they cause considerable neurological morbidity but have relatively less adverse implications for survival than brain tumors.

Childhood Cancer

Cancer in childhood is rare, but is now the second most common cause of death at ages 1–14 years in developed countries after accidents and violence. The commonest childhood cancer is acute lymphoblastic leukemia, accounting for a third of malignancies in this age group. Brain tumors account for almost a quarter of all childhood cancers and, with the leukemias, are the cause of over half of childhood cancers. The embryonal cancers in children are virtually never seen in adults; they include Wilms' tumor (nephroblastoma), neuroblastoma, retinoblastoma, hepatoblastoma and rhabdomyosarcoma.

The outlook for children with cancer has improved markedly since the introduction of effective chemotherapy.[18] Probably at least half of childhood cancers are now cured, and 80 percent of three-year survivors are alive ten years later.[19] The importance of these results for life assurance medicine is that underwriters must now expect to see more survivors of childhood cancer as applicants for life insurance. It is still too early to know what the ultimate long-term survival of these patients will be and whether or not the treatment they have had confers an adverse legacy. Nevertheless, in the absence of recurrence or residual disability it is now reasonable to combine caution with optimism and accept these applicants on standard terms after ten years.

Prostatic Cancer

The incidence of cancer of the prostate rises steadily from middle-age onwards. It is often found to coexist with benign prostatic hyperplasia, although the latter is not a risk factor for development of malignancy. Tumors are usually adenocarcinomas, poorly differentiated lesions (Gleason[20] score 6 or over — higher grade) having a worse prognosis than those that are well differentiated (Gleason score less than 6 — low grade). Metastasis occurs particularly to the regional lymph nodes and skeleton. Staging of localized lesions relates to the extent of the tumor within the prostate gland and whether or not there has been extension outside its capsule. In this respect, the underwriter should realize that accurate staging and differentiation of the tumor depends on adequate investigational procedures having been carried out, such as ultrasound or other imaging techniques and prostatic biopsy. When such information is available it allows a more precise evaluation of the risk to be made, and a rating schedule embracing these criteria is shown below.

Recent interest in biological markers for prostatic cancer has focussed on prostate-specific antigen (PSA).[21] It is elevated in most patients with prostatic cancer and is more sensitive than prostatic acid phosphatase, although specificities are similar. The antigen titer increases with advancing clinical stage and is proportional to the estimated volume of the tumor. These findings raise the question of whether or not measurement of PSA might be used as a screening test for prostatic cancer with potential application for life insurance. However, this seems premature and inappropriate at the present time for two reasons. First, the test lacks adequate specificity, PSA frequently being elevated in men with benign prostatic hypertrophy. Secondly, although elevated PSA levels correlate with the presence and extent of prostatic cancer, there are no data on the effect of detection by screening on outcome nor on how the prognosis of screen-detected prostatic cancer differs from that presenting clinically. These considerations are particularly relevant to an elderly population, many of whom have subclinical malignant change in the prostate of uncertain significance.

Rating
Adenocarcinoma of prostate.

Stage	Extent of disease	Low grade	Higher grade
A_1	On-*in situ* non-palpable focus.	0	0
A_2	More than one or diffuse non-palpable foci.	F	E
B_1	One palpable nodule less than 1·5 cm in size, confined to the prostate gland (intracapsular).	E	D
B_2	More extensive intracapsular tumor.	D	C
C_1	Minimal extracapsular tumor invasion (e.g. to sulcus or one seminal vesicle).	C	A
C_2	More extensive local extracapsular tumor invasion (e.g. to bladder).	+50 & A	+50 & A
D	Very extensive local invasion or metastatic to lymph nodes or another organ system (e.g. bone).	+100 & A	+100 & A

Note The staging criteria and ratings apply to both surgically treated and irradiated tumors. Most tumors treated by radioactive implants will be in Stages A_2, B or C_1. External irradiation may be used to treat Stage B or C_1 tumors or as a palliative for metastatic disease.

Thyroid Cancer

Thyroid cancer has an extremely variable behavior. Although it is the most common endocrine cancer, it accounts for less than 1 percent of all deaths from cancer. It affects all age groups, but has a more aggressive course in older patients. Thyroid cancer usually follows an indolent clinical course and many patients, particularly the young, have minimal morbidity and a normal life expectancy; only 9 percent of patients with thyroid cancer die from this cause.[22] Post mortem studies reveal a high incidence of occult thyroid cancer and indicate that well under 1 percent of thyroid cancers ever become clinically evident.

Histological categorization provides the basis for underwriting thyroid cancer risks (*see* Table 20.3). The most common type is papillary cancer, which accounts for 80 percent of all thyroid malignant tumors. Many are associated with a normal life expectancy, although some high-risk follicular variants carry an 80 percent ten-year mortality. Size is an important prognostic factor; cancers less than 1 cm in diameter have little adverse affect on survival. Anaplastic thyroid cancer is the most lethal type, with a median survival of four months and a five-year life expectancy of less than 4 percent. Medullary thyroid cancer arises from calcitonin-producing cells and is often inherited as part of the syndrome of multiple endocrine neoplasia (*see* p. 726). It is a relatively aggressive form of thyroid cancer. When thyroid cancer metastasizes, it commonly affects the skeleton. Metastatic sites from well differentiated follicular cancers take up radioactive iodine administered therapeutically. This can control the disease for several years, but the approach is not applicable to the treatment of either anaplastic or medullary tumors.

REFERENCES

1 Lew EA, Gajewski J (editors). *Medical Risks: trends in mortality by age and time elapsed.* New York: Praeger, 1990.
2 Minna JD, Pass H, Glatstein E, Ihde DC. Cancer of the lung. In: De Vita VT, Hellman S, Rosenberg SA (editors). *Cancer: principles and practice of oncology.* Philadelphia: JB Lippincott Co, 1989.
3 Cohen AM, Shank B, Friedman MA. Colorectal cancer. In: De Vita VT, Hellman S, Rosenberg SA (editors). *Cancer: principles and practice of oncology.* Philadelphia: JB Lippincott Co, 1989.
4 Moertel CG, Fleming TR, Macdonald JS, Haller DG, Laurie JJA, Goodman PJ et al. Levamisole and fluorouracil for adjuvant therapy of resected colon carcinoma. *N Engl J Med* 1990; 322: 352–8.
5 Bussey HJR, Eyers AA, Ritchie SM, Thomson JPS. The rectum in adenomatous polyposis: the St Mark's policy. *Brit J Surg* 1985; 72 (suppl): S29–S31.
6 Sarre RG, Gagelman DG, Beck GJ, McGannon E, Fazio VW, Weakley FL et al. Colectomy with ileorectal anastomosis for familial adenomatous polyposis: the risk of rectal cancer. *Surgery* 1987; 101: 20–6.
7 Early Breast Cancer Trialists Collaborative Group. Effects of adjuvant tamoxifen and of cytotoxic therapy on mortality in early breast cancer: an overview of 61 randomized trials among 28,896 women. *N Engl J Med* 1988; 319: 1681–92.
8 O'Reilly SM, Camplejohn RS, Barnes DM, Millis RR, Rubens RD, Richards MA. Node negative breast cancer: prognostic subgroups defined by tumor size and flow cytometry. *J Clin Oncol* 1990; 8: 2040–6.
9 Badwe RA, Gregory WM, Chaudary MA, Richards MA, Bentley AE, Rubens RD et al. Timing of surgery during menstrual cycle and survival of premenopausal women with operable breast cancer. *Lancet* 1991; 337: 1261–4.

10 Parkin DM et al. Estimates of the worldwide frequency of 16 cancers in 1980. *Internat J Cancer* 1988; 14: 184–97.

11 Lange PH, McIntire KR, Waldmann TA, Hakala TR, Fraley EE. Serum alphafetoprotein and human chorionic gonadotropin in the diagnosis and management of non-seminomatous germ cell testicular cancer. *N Engl J Med* 1976; 295: 1237–40.

12 Richie JP, Shipley WU, Yagoda A. Cancer of the bladder. In: De Vita VT, Hellman S, Rosenberg SA (editors). *Cancer: principles and practice of oncology.* Philadelphia: JB Lippincott Co, 1989.

13 Bookman MA, Longo DL, Young RC. Late complications of curative treatment in Hodgkin's disease. *JAMA* 1988; 260: 280–3.

14 Rosenberg SA, Berard CW, Brown BW et al. The non-Hodgkin's lymphoma pathologic classification project: National Cancer Institute sponsored study of classification on non-Hodgkin's lymphomas: summary and description of working formulation for clinical usage. *Cancer* 1982; 49: 2112–35.

15 Illango RK. Non-Hodgkin's lymphomas: a medical underwriting perspective. *J Insur Med* 1990; 22: 145–8.

16 Balch CM, Houghton A, Peters L. Cutaneous melanoma. In: De Vita VT, Hellman S, Rosenberg SA (editors). *Cancer: principles and practice of oncology.* Philadelphia: JB Lippincott Co, 1989.

17 Albert DM, Earle JD, Sahel JA. Intra-ocular melanomas. In: De Vita VT, Hellman S, Rosenberg SA (editors). *Cancer: principles and practice of oncology.* Philadelphia: JB Lippincott Co, 1989.

18 Stiller CA, Bunch KJ. Trends in survival for childhood cancer in Britain diagnosed 1971–1985. *Br J Cancer* 1990; 62: 806–15.

19 Hawkins MM. Long-term survival and cure after childhood cancer. *Arch Dis Childhood* 1989; 64: 798–807.

20 Gleason DF. The Veterans Administration Cooperative Urological Research Group: histologic grading and clinical staging of prostatic carcinoma. In: Tannebaum M (editor). *Urologic Pathology: the prostate.* Philadelphia: Lea & Febiger, 1977. 171.

21 Stamey TA, Yang N, Hay AR, McNeal JE, Freiha FS, Redwine E. Prostate-specific antigen as a serum marker for adenocarcinoma of the prostate. *New Engl J Med* 1987; 317: 909–16.

22 Robbins J. Merino MJ, Boice JD, Ron E, Ain KB, Alexander HR et al. Thyroid cancer: a lethal endocrine neoplasm. *Ann Int Med* 1991; 115: 133–47.

CHAPTER 21

BLOOD DISORDERS

MAURICE BRAZEAU

In the context of insurance medicine, hematological disorders occupy a relatively limited place. In a sense, this is unfortunate, given that accessibility and ease of sampling of blood and bone marrow make blood diseases among the best studied of all impairments.

The hematology system comprises the formed and fluid elements of blood, the bone marrow and, in addition, those organs or systems having to do with production, transport, processing or destruction of the components of blood.

This chapter covers selected hematological impairments that may be encountered in medical life underwriting.

HEMATOLOGY LABORATORY VALUES

It is helpful to have available lists of selected normal laboratory values in common usage in hematology tabulated in both traditional and SI units, along with a conversion factor and an indication of testing specimen used. Such values are site and procedure specific; reported results are always to be assessed in conjunction with the procedure used and with normal ranges for the reporting laboratory.

Given the variability of testing procedures, reporting units and normal ranges, there is merit in having available more than one such list, extracted from different sources. They may be obtained from laboratories servicing the insurance industry, other private laboratories, university or hospital centers, or medical publications.[1-3]

ANEMIAS

Anemia, defined as a reduction in the oxygen carrying capacity of blood, is, in practice, recorded by the finding of a reduced red cell count, reduced hematocrit or reduced hemoglobin level. The clinical suspicion of anemia is often imprecise and should always be confirmed by laboratory measurement. A cause for anemia is undoubtedly present in all cases, although even a diligent search may at times fail to disclose one.

Anemia may be an isolated finding or it may occur in the context of a background illness; it may or may not be accompanied by variation in other hematological cell lines. In clinical practice, anemia may be classified in different ways, the commonest being morphological or by mechanism. Although classifying by mechanism (under-production, blood loss, destruction) is perhaps logical, it should be remembered that in a number of cases multiple mechanisms are operative. In addition, assigning to a specific pathophysiologic mechanism is often only possible in retrospect.

Whether anemia is symptomatic or not depends on the cause, the degree, the speed at which anemia develops and on the background health of the individual, in particular the cardiorespiratory status.

Anemia by any definition is extremely common. The incidence and prevalence vary by country and by race (among other factors) but the numbers are striking in both fully industrialized nations and in those less well developed.

An influence of hemoglobin or hematocrit level on well-being, growth and development, work capacity, infection risk and mortality has been demonstrated.

When an underlying disease is the cause of anemia, the risk is included in that of the causative illness. Otherwise, the following generalizations are offered.

1) Mortality is less at hemoglobin levels around the mean and increases at both extremes of the distribution curve. This relationship appears to hold true whether one is assessing the hemoglobin at a single initial visit (here the influence on mortality is relatively modest) or whether the anemia is constant.

2) Surgery performed on moderately or severely anemic patients presents a mortality risk.

3) In any group of random anemia patients there will be some with established causes.

4) Those with undiagnosed anemias may evolve over time to reveal a specific disease entity or cause.[4-6]

Rating

1) Cause of anemia known — rate for cause.
2) Cause or details unknown.
Corrected — +0 to +25.
Not corrected:
   Hemoglobin ≥ 12 g/dl (hematocrit ≥ 36 percent) — +0.
   Hemoglobin 11–11·9 g/dl (hematocrit 33–35·9 percent) — +25.
   Hemoglobin 10–10·9 g/dl (hematocrit 30–32·9 percent) — +50.
   Hemoglobin 8–9·9 g/dl (hematocrit 24–29·9 percent) — +100.
   Hemoglobin < 8 g/dl (hematocrit < 24 percent) — decline.

Aplastic Anemia

Aplastic anemia is a rare hematological disorder featuring peripheral pancytopenia and bone marrow hypoplasia without dysplastic features and unassociated with a specific disease state such as subleukemic leukemia or myelofibrosis. It is customary not to include those cases caused by the intentional use of cytotoxic drugs or radiotherapy, and to consider separately paroxysmal nocturnal hemoglobinuria (PNH).

Most large series reveal a modest prominence of men, and the condition is most common in the Orient. Two age peaks have been noted: under 20 and over 40. In North America the incidence in children under 15 is about 2 to 4 per million, and in the general population 3 to 6 per million.[7,9]

Marrow aplasia may be constitutional or may result from a variety of acquired etiologies.[10] Fanconi's anemia is the most common constitutional aplasia. Acquired aplasia may reflect the influence of viruses (hepatitis, Ebstein-Barr virus etc), drugs (chloramphenicol, gold, phenylbutazone etc) or environmental toxins (benzene, accidental irradiation etc), although fully 70 percent are idiopathic. Like incidence rates, presumed causes tend to vary by country. In most cases the mechanism of aplasia is unclear, with stem cell, bone marrow microenvironment and immunological factors being postulated.

Aplastic anemia may be transient (uncommon) or persistent (usual) and the severity may be mild, moderate or marked. Patients at highest risk are those with chronic severe aplasia, defined most often as two of (1) neutrophils below 0.5×10^9/liter, (2) platelets less than 20×10^9/liter, and (3) corrected reticulocytes under 1 percent and either (a) marrow cellularity of less than 25 percent of normal or (b) cellularity less than 50 percent of normal with under 30 percent residual hematopoietic cells (Aplastic Anemia Study Group criteria).

The risk in aplastic anemia is roughly proportional to the counts and to disease duration. Consequently, causes of death in several series revolve around infection, hemorrhage, severe anemia, transfusional hemosiderosis and complications of treatment.

Those with transient aplasia recover spontaneously. Mild persistent aplasia primarily requires supportive and prophylactic care. Active intervention is called for in those with moderate or severe disease.

Before the advent of specific treatment options, supportive measures alone were associated in severe aplastics with a mortality rate of 50–60 percent at six months, 90 percent by one year. The prognosis improved with availability of platelet support and potent antibiotic cover.[8]

Bone marrow transplantation (BMT) has proven to be the definitive treatment of choice for the younger patient who has a histocompatible donor (at present only one-quarter of the group).[11] In the best centers, ten-year survival is around 80 percent, results being best when recipients are untransfused. The importance of age is evident in the five-year survival rate: in one series it was 79 percent for those under the age of 20, 40 percent for those aged 20–35 and 25 percent for those over 35. BMT recipients, of course, face the added hazards of transplantation, including graft versus host disease (GVHD). Aside from the 10 percent or so who suffer significant GVHD, long-term BMT survivors tend to return to a normal life and do not suffer relapse of aplasia. Rare reports of acute leukemia in long-term survivors are recorded.[12]

More than 50 percent of severe aplastic anemia patients are over the age of 40. For them and for younger patients unsuitable for BMT, the best available option is in the form of immunosuppression. With antithymocyte (ATG) or antilymphocyte (ALG) globulin a collective hematological response occurs in about 55 percent, with survival of 42–75 percent of these at 12–55 months. For those surviving two years, actuarial mortality was 22 percent at eight years.[13] This modality appears more effective in moderate rather than severe aplasia, and in aplasia due to certain specific causes (e.g. gold-induced aplasia). Response may be incomplete, some 10 percent relapse and over 40–50 percent may be at risk (at eight years) for acute leukemia, myelodysplasia or PNH.

Preliminary results suggest superiority of cyclosporin over ATG and ALG, as well as a lesser relapse risk. A variety of new agents are also under study.

Corticosteroids and anabolic steroids alone probably do not prolong survival of the group, despite benefit in isolated cases. They continue to be used as adjuncts and in the case of corticosteroids for control of side effects of other therapies.

Rating

Description	Rating
Transient, complete recovery	
1st yr	Postpone
2nd & 3rd yr	+50
Thereafter	+0
Persistent	
Mild	
1st yr	Postpone
Thereafter	+50
Moderate or severe	
Untreated	Decline
Support only	Decline
BMT	
1st & 2nd yr	Postpone
Recovery complete	
3rd yr	+200
4th yr	+100
5th yr	+50
Thereafter	+0
Recovery incomplete, stable	Add +50
GVHD	
Mild	Add +50
More than mild	Decline
Immunosuppression	
1st & 2nd yr	Decline
Thereafter	
Recovery	
Complete	+300
Incomplete	+400 to decline

Fanconi Anemia (FA)

FA, the commonest form of constitutional (inherited) marrow failure, is a disorder transmitted in autosomal recessive fashion and characterized by progressive marrow aplasia, congenital malformations, lymphocytic chromosomal instabilities and a predisposition to development of acute leukemia. The incidence of heterozygotes is probably about 1 in 300, and parental consanguinity is not uncommon.

The congenital malformations are not universally present and may be absent in some cases; others may include various combinations of the following: skin pigmentation, microcephaly, modest retardation, short stature, skeletal anomalies, hypogonadism and cardiac or renal defects.

In addition to the hematological and clinical findings, lymphocytic chromosomal instabilities are a prominent feature of FA. Characterized primarily by breaks, gaps, rings or translocations accentuated by cytotoxics in particular alkylating agents, the unstable genetic regions may be in part responsible for the leukemia risk and for adverse effects of some BMT pre-conditioning regimes.

The clinical course is quite variable, both within families and between different families. Marrow aplasia may onset any time from birth to the mid-twenties but most commonly surfaces between the ages of five and ten. Non-hematological congenital anomalies may occur in virtually any combination, pigmentary and skeletal findings being among the most common.

The diagnosis of FA rests on the clinical picture, family history, marrow aplasia and chromosomal breaks accentuated by cytotoxics, in particular alkylating agents. Hemoglobin F levels are often elevated. The diagnosis may be difficult in those with pure aplasia, those with partial cytopenias only or those with a negative family history.

Rarely, spontaneous recovery of aplasia may be seen, usually coinciding with onset of puberty. Otherwise, untreated FA is invariably fatal, secondary to progressive marrow aplasia, acute leukemia or, less commonly, other cancers. Median survival in this setting is less than five years after onset.

It is not unusual to observe a response to the use of anabolic steroids, but the virilizing effects and hepatotoxicity, along with increased risk of leukemia in FA, limit long-term use.

Early attempts at BMT were associated with long-term survival in 38 percent, a considerable improvement but disappointing in comparison with results in idiopathic aplastic anemia patients of similar age.[14] It was later discovered that pre-conditioning regimes incorporating alkylating agents were partly to blame for the dismal results.

It is now common practice to avoid use of alkylating agent conditioning, to verify the effects of cytotoxics on lymphocyte chromosome preparations and to ascertain that potential donors are not FA heterozygotes. With these precautions, actuarial survival of FA patients after BMT is about 80 percent, with GVHD observed in about one-quarter.

Rating

Description	Rating
Spontaneous recovery	
1–5 yr	+100
Thereafter	+0
Active	
Untreated	Decline
Androgens, recovery	
1st & 2nd yr	Postpone
Thereafter	+200
BMT	
1st & 2nd yr	Postpone
Thereafter	Rate as for aplastic anemia (*see above*)

Paroxysmal Nocturnal Hemoglobinuria (PNH)

PNH is a rare acquired disorder of uncertain cause in which young cholinesterase-deficient red blood cells are unusually sensitive to the lytic effect of serum complement.[15] The resultant intravascular hemolysis classically occurred intermittently and during sleep, hence the descriptive name. The estimated prevalence is at least 1 case per 500 thousand people.

PNH typically causes a chronic hemolytic state varying in different individuals from mild to severe, and bearing at least a rough relationship to the percentage of defective red cells. The stable background hemolysis is then often punctuated by episodic hemolytic crises at times precipitated by infection, vaccination, surgery, exercise, menstruation or other stressful situations. A relationship to sleep is now only evident in about one-quarter of those affected.

Patients with PNH are often young adults, although people any age may be affected. Some series mention a slight male predominance. Clinical features include abdominal or back pains, severe headaches, hepatosplenomegaly (in some) and dark urine.

Laboratory studies reveal hemolysis with or without anemia, often leukopenia and thrombocytopenia and a variably cellular marrow that is not infrequently hypoplastic. Serum iron is often low (urinary loss), as is the leukocyte alkaline phosphatase. Diagnosis rests on the clinical picture, elimination of other causes, the laboratory findings mentioned and confirmation of PNH by a screening test (sucrose lysis) or the more definitive Ham acid hemolysis test.

Of particular concern is a series of potential significant complications, running the gamut from extreme hemolysis to arteriovenous thrombosis, aplastic crises, renal dysfunction, acute leukemia, complications related to transfusion support and the effects of low counts (i.e. infection or hemorrhage). Others have a lessening of PNH manifestations over time; in some, all features disappear entirely.

It should be mentioned that PNH red blood cells may appear in other conditions, including aplastic anemia, FA and myelofibrosis.

Management options, individualized and reserved for those with significant disease manifestations, include transfusion with washed red blood cells, iron replacement, folic acid support and management of complications as they arise. Although not uniformly beneficial, selected patients have responded to corticosteroids, androgens or splenectomy. A variety of less conventional therapies, including heparin and tranexamic acid, have also produced erratic results overall.

Histocompatible BMT provides the only potential for cure in those with life-threatening cytopenias or complications.

Rating

Description	Rating
Recovered	
1st yr	Postpone
Thereafter	+50 to +100

Description	Rating
Persistent	
Mild	+100 to +200
Moderate, stable, followed	+200 to +400
Severe	
Supportive care only	Decline
BMT	Rate as for aplastic anemia (*see above*)
Response to medical treatment	Credit +50

Iron Deficiency Anemia

Without doubt, iron deficiency is the most common cause of anemia worldwide. Despite internal schemes for reutilization of released iron, free passage between the various iron compartments, expected external loss limited to 1 mg daily or less, as well as ready availability of iron in nature, iron depletion is universal and resultant anemia frequent.

Absorption from food requires that iron be in ferrous form, and takes place most effectively within the proximal duodenum; in times of depletion the iron absorptive area may extend throughout most of the small bowel. Multiple factors influence the absorption of iron, not the least of which are factors within gastric secretions, mucosal saturation mechanisms and the effect of certain foodstuffs, such as milk and vitamin C.

Various stages of iron lack have been described. These range from reduced stores to depleted stores, followed by frank anemia and finally hypochromic microcytic indices.

Potential causes of iron deficiency include limited intake (poverty, unsupplemented bottle feeding, over-indulgence in foods with little nutritional value), poor absorption (surgery, malabsorption states), blood loss (menstruation, gastrointestinal (GI) or urinary loss, frequent phlebotomy) and increased demands (pregnancy, lactation, growth spurts), or various combinations of these causes.

Clinical features may include fatigue, headaches, pallor, stomatitis, cheilosis, nail spooning, esophageal discomfort or webs, and, rarely, trace splenomegaly.

The diagnosis of iron deficiency anemia is based on the appropriate setting, clinical picture, finding of hypochromic microcytic indices, low MCHC, and recording of reduced serum iron with raised transferin levels (iron binding capacity). Only if the basic study is atypical should recourse to measurement of serum ferritin (low) and bone marrow iron stores (depleted) be required. In addition, unless a probable cause is readily evident (e.g. poor dietary intake, heavy menstruation), a search for the condition at fault should be instituted.

Management of iron deficiency revolves round iron replacement and, when possible, correction of the cause. Oral iron is always preferred for reasons of convenience, cost and safety. Only rarely should IV infusions be required, and IM injections should preferably not be used. The duration of replacement will depend on the response and on the ability to correct the cause. When the cause is chronic, recurrent or permanent and cannot be eliminated, long-term replacement will be required.

Rating

Description	Rating
Underlying cause identified	Rate for cause
Cause not known	
Anemia corrected	
Under age 60	+0
Age 60 or over	+50
Anemia not corrected	Rate as anemia (*see* p. 650)

Megaloblastic Anemia

Megaloblastosis is a term used to describe a distinctive cellular appearance, the characteristic feature of which is nucleocytoplasmic asynchrony (out-of-step maturation of nucleus and cytoplasm). With rare exceptions, megaloblastosis is a reflection of deficiency of vitamin B12 or folic acid, lack of either impairing DNA synthesis. At the cellular level, B12-deficient megaloblastic change may well be mediated by functional deficiency of folic acid.

Although the hallmark of megaloblastosis is hematological, it should be noted that (1) deficiency of vitamin B12 or folic acid may impair neurological integrity in the absence of hematological findings,[16] and (2) other tissues with rapid cell turnover (GI mucosa, uterine cervix etc) may show megaloblastic change.

The peripheral blood findings of megaloblastosis include oval macrocytosis, Howell–Jolly bodies, neutrophil nuclear hypersegmentation and occasional nucleated red blood cells. In florid cases leukopenia and thrombocytopenia are not unexpected. The bone marrow reveals megaloblastic erythroid precursors and giant neutrophil forms. As a consequence of ineffective erythropoiesis, serum LDH and bilirubin are often elevated.

The clinical setting may help establish whether one is dealing with B12 or folic acid deficiency, and why.

Vitamin B12 Deficiency

Since neither vitamin B12 nor folic acid is produced by humans in amounts sufficient to satisfy needs, both must be absorbed from food.

Following oral intake, vitamin B12 combines with intrinsic factor (IF) produced by gastric parietal cells. The complex later attaches to ileal receptor sites; the B12 is absorbed and then transported by a series of carrier proteins, known as transcobalamins, to the liver for storage, and ultimately to functional sites throughout the body.

Given the sequence described, it is understandable that vitamin B12 deficiency may result from inadequate dietary intake (extreme malnutrition, vegans), increased requirements, unavailability of IF (molecular non-function, immunological interference, disease or surgery of the stomach), intestinal competition for B12 by parasites, malabsorption states, lack of availability of ileal receptor sites (congenital absence, ileal disease or resection) or transcobalamin deficiency. Examples of each have been recorded.

Because daily requirements are small, a B12 deficiency state may take up to five years to become manifest, depending on the adequacy of pre-existing stores.

Pernicious Anemia (PA)

Addisonian PA is a B12 deficiency state caused by absence or non-function of gastric IF, such that the IF–B12 complex is then not available for ileal binding and B12 absorption. In most cases the process is auto-immune and accompanies atrophic gastritis.

In its classic form, PA is a disease of the elderly in which onset is insidious and symptoms non-specific. Affected individuals may be pale, jaundiced and lethargic. Glossitis and stomatitis are common and other auto-immune disorders occur with greater frequency than expected (e.g. diabetes mellitus, hypothyroidism). With time, neurological features (peripheral neuropathy, subacute combined degeneration of the spinal cord, psychiatric) may become manifest; the risk of gastric carcinoma is also increased over time.[17]

Accompanying the blood, marrow and biochemical findings of megaloblastic anemia in general, serum B12 levels are found to be low and the Schilling test records minimal urinary excretion (and therefore absorption) of B12 after an oral dose with normal excretion following an IF–B12 combined dose. In centers with a special interest, parietal cell or intrinsic factor antibody can be demonstrated. Finally, gastric achlorhydria is an expected feature. When other investigations are atypical or equivocal, levels of methylmalonic acid or homocysteine have been found to be useful indicators of cellular B12 deficiency.

Treatment consists of intramuscular B12 injections given frequently until recovery, then monthly for life. In some cases iron stores are also low and have to be replaced. Conversely, folic acid is to be avoided for fear of worsening neurological dysfunction. Early deaths have occurred from hypokalemia as rapidly regenerating megakaryocytes responding to B12 use up large amounts of potassium; replacement has been recommended.

Barring complications or accompanying conditions, hematological recovery is expected to be complete. When mild, neurological sequelae may also fully recover, whereas recovery will be partial at best in advanced cases.

Rating
Treated, recovered, ongoing replacement — +0.
Treatment interrupted, severe neurological impairment, or incomplete hematological recovery — +100 to +200.

B12 Deficiencies other than PA

The deficiency of vitamin B12 anticipated after distal small bowel resection or after removal of more than half the stomach is readily corrected by prophylactic intramuscular B12 administration beginning one to two years after the operation or as dictated by hematological findings.

The B12 deficiency associated with small bowel disease or malabsorption states is addressed by anticipation, treatment of the background disorder and appropriate B12 replacement. The risk in this setting is primarily that of the background disease.

B12 lack related to a single correctable cause, such as parasitic competition, requires elimination of the competitor and temporary B12 replacement.

Congenital defects of ileal receptor sites or deficiency of transport proteins call for lifelong B12 replacement.

In all of the above situations, the challenge is the diagnosis of the underlying cause of B12 deficiency. The duration of B12 replacement (from a few weeks to lifelong) will depend on the cause, its potential for control and the hematological response to B12. In all cases B12 is best provided by the intramuscular route, although in selected settings oral replacement in massive dose could theoretically correct the deficiency.

Rating
Appropriate B12 replacement — rate cause.
B12 replacement unsatisfactory or unknown — add +50.

Folic Acid Deficiency

Folate deficiency is capable of producing a hematological picture identical to that of vitamin B12 deficiency, although blood and marrow findings are generally somewhat more subtle.

Daily requirements of folic acid vary by age, and in women by pregnancy or lactation status. Folic acid is ubiquitous in nature and in food (green leafy vegetables and liver are two prime sources) but may be destroyed by boiling. Daily requirements of this and other nutrients are listed in a number of standard reference sources. Absorption is in the upper small bowel; complex enzyme systems are involved in absorption, metabolism and cellular incorporation. Because serum levels are so labile, red blood cell levels are a better measure of true status.

Given that folate stores in humans are modest, a deficiency state may develop within weeks. Possible causes include poor intake, interference at different stages by drugs (antiepileptics, contraceptives, certain chemotherapeutic agents), malabsorption states (including sprue, Crohn's disease), increased requirements (pregnancy, lactation, hemolytic disorders) and insufficient replacement during specialized medical procedures (such as dialysis or parenteral nutrition).

Regardless of the cause and in addition to the hematological consequences, folic acid deficiency may induce glossitis, stomatitis and GI symptoms. There is also suspicion that folate lack may interfere with neurological integrity in the developing fetus or post-natally. However, a picture of subacute combined degeneration of the spinal cord analogous to that of B12 deficiency does not develop.

The diagnosis rests on the clinical picture, the appropriate setting, the blood and marrow findings of megaloblastic anemia in florid cases and on accurate documentation of true reduction in serum or red cell folate levels.

Principles of therapy revolve round eliminating correctable causes, controlling (to the utmost) underlying disease states, improving diet (where appropriate) and replacing folate (orally when at all possible). Dosages and duration of therapy will depend on the cause of folate depletion. As always, an accurate diagnosis is essential; providing folate to B12-deficient individuals may prove disastrous neurologically.

Rating
Because folic acid deficiency is readily diagnosed, is often anticipated in given clinical settings and because replacement therapy is consistently effective in correcting the deficiency, folate depletion *per se* need not be rated and a debit need not be added to a pre-existing background illness.

Sideroblastic Anemias (SA)

Like a number of other hematological disorders, sideroblastic anemia is not a single entity. Sideroblastic anemias may be congenital or acquired, and the latter idiopathic or secondary.

Sideroblasts are developing red blood cells which, on iron staining of marrow preparations, reveal characteristic iron deposits within the cytoplasm. The deposits in SA differ from the occasional deposit seen in normals in that they represent defective iron utilization or incorporation in the heme synthetic process such that mitochondriae, the site of heme-iron linkage, become iron engorged. As mitochondriae are located primarily around the nucleus, the deposits appear in ring form surrounding the nucleus. These characteristic ring sideroblasts are the hallmark of sideroblastic anemias.

Congenital SA exists in a sex-linked and an autosomal form. Both are rare. The severity of anemia is variable, splenomegaly may be present, iron levels are raised, a dual red cell population is common (reflecting normal and sideroblastic precursors) and ringed sideroblasts are demonstrable, as is ineffective erythropoiesis. When transfusions are required, iron overload is accentuated. Some 50 percent of the sex-linked variants are fully or partially responsive to pyridoxine in large doses; the autosomal variants are refractory. The clinical course tends to parallel the severity of anemia and ranges from death in infancy to diagnosis only in adulthood.

When acquired SA develops in response to drugs (isoniazid, chloramphenicol, chemotherapy), alcohol, lead or a host of disease states including malignancy, it is said to be secondary. Clinical and basic laboratory details are not importantly different from those listed above. The pathogenesis in each setting varies, is often complex and sometimes unknown or poorly understood. The approach will vary by case. Drug-related or toxic causes tend to correct on discontinuance of the offending agent (with or without temporary pyridoxine or folate supplementation). Those accompanying disease states or malignancy may or may not respond to pyridoxine and correction of the background illness.

Idiopathic (primary) acquired SA may again be divided into two groups:[18] pure sideroblastic anemia (PSA), which is confined to defective red cell formation, and refractory anemia with ringed sideroblasts (RARS), which is characterized by additional defective granulopoiesis and platelet formation as well as a greatly enhanced risk of leukemic transformation (five-year cumulative risk 48 percent compared with 1·9 percent for pure SA in one series).

Most affected individuals in these two classes are middle-aged or older. Iron stores vary from depleted in those who bleed, to severely overloaded, particularly in those requiring transfusion. About 20 percent will respond, at least temporarily, to pyridoxine orally or to pyridoxine phosphate parenterally. In those with clear iron excess, phlebotomy or iron chelation (if practicable) may prove beneficial.

Although some have prolonged survival, all individuals are at risk from anemia and iron overload. Infection and hemorrhage are frequent causes of death in RARS but less so in PSA. Overall survival at five years was estimated at 69 percent for PSA and 19 percent for RARS.

Rating

Description	Rating
Congenital	
Pyridoxine responsive or discovered in adulthood	+50 to +100
Pyridoxine unresponsive or severe	Decline
Acquired	
Secondary	+0 to +50 and rate for cause
Idiopathic PSA pyridoxine responsive	+200 to +300
pyridoxine unresponsive	Decline
RARS	Decline

Auto-immune Hemolytic Anemia (AIHA)

When an immunological reaction is initiated against autologous (self) red blood cell surface antigens, the condition is termed AIHA, even when hemolysis is absent or is fully compensated; the hallmark is the positive Coombs test. The process is analogous to that of autoimmune thrombocytopenic purpura in the case of platelets. In general, three types are recognized, each of which may be idiopathic or secondary.

Warm Antibody AIHA

This type of AIHA, characterized by autoantibody maximally active at body temperature, is not uncommon; it affects women slightly more often than men, and is most often seen above the age of 30. Roughly half the cases are idiopathic; the rest accompany lymphoreticular neoplasms (lymphocytic leukemia, lymphomas), auto-immune disorders, infections, use of medications (in particular alpha methyldopa) or a miscellaneous group of entities. Antibody reactivity is usually directed against the Rh system.

As antibodies are formed and coat the red cell surface, the potential for hemolysis is present. If it occurs, it is primarily reticuloendothelial, including splenic. Hemolysis may range from non-existent to fulminant, even with seemingly identical antibody loads, and red cell breakdown is not uncommonly episodic.

With decompensated hemolysis, pallor, jaundice, fevers and splenomegaly may result and share the clinical spotlight with the underlying disease if present. Thrombophlebitis may also occur. There will be the usual blood, biochemical and marrow evidence of hemolysis, and platelets and white blood cell counts may be low. Most importantly, the anti-RBC antibodies may be found on the cell surface (direct Coombs), in the serum (indirect Coombs) or in the red cell eluate in most patients with warm AIHA.

Management is dictated by the severity of hemolysis and by the underlying process if present. For hemolytic anemia, all the following may play a part: general support, slow, truly compatible transfusion when needed, corticosteroids (60 percent satisfactory response anticipated), splenectomy for more serious steroid unresponsive cases and immunosuppressants for potentially fatal cases.

Unless a single correctable cause can be eliminated (drugs, infection), the typical course is one of waxing and waning with outcome dictated by the underlying process, ongoing hemolysis, and complications of disease or therapy. Some 50–75 percent will succumb to hemolysis or background disease over time and even the pure AIHA warm antibody type has a mortality of 10–40 percent.

Rating
1) Correctable cause:
Active — postpone.
Corrected, hematological recovery — +0.
2) Idiopathic or persistent cause:
Mild, controlled — +100.
Moderate — +200 to +400.
Severe despite active intervention — Decline.

Cryopathic Hemolytic Syndromes: Maximal Autoantibody Activity 32°C or Less

Cold Agglutinin Disease (CAD)

CAD is red cell agglutination and hemolysis on cold exposure due to complement-fixing IgM (usually) antibody reactivity against the I–i group of red cell surface antigens. Again, idiopathic and secondary (lymphoreticular malignancies, infections) forms are known to exist.

More common in older women, typical features include pallor, acrocyanosis, Raynaud's phenomenon, diffuse skin mottling and, in severe cases, gangrene of exposed protruding surfaces. Mild splenomegaly is not unusual. Anemia is usually mild, signs of modest hemolysis being found, and intense red cell agglutination is visible on smear. Cold agglutinins are the laboratory hallmark of the disease.

The mainstay of therapy is avoidance of cold exposure and treatment of background disease if present. Corticosteroids and splenectomy are often disappointing. Immunosuppressants have proved beneficial in some, and washed red cell transfusions are sometimes required.

Post-infectious forms of CAD tend to resolve spontaneously. Idiopathic forms are usually lifelong, often reasonably well tolerated, but overall life span is shortened.

Rating
Rate as for PCH (*see below*).

Paroxysmal Cold Hemoglobinuria (PCH)

PCH is a rare hemolytic auto-immune disorder often characterized by fulminant episodic hemolysis following cold exposure and by the presence of a peculiar dual phase IgG antibody. This Donath-Landsteiner or D–L antibody, directed most often against red cell surface antigen P, fixes to the cell surface along with early complement sequences on cold exposure; on rewarming, complement fixing continues and lysis occurs.

PCH may occur in idiopathic form or follow disease, usually infectious (viral, syphilis). Typically, manifestations are variable. Back and abdominal pains, nausea, fever, dark urine and Raynaud's phenomena are usual in florid crises.

Infection-related cases tend to recover spontaneously on disappearance of the infection. Idiopathic cases should avoid cold exposure and may benefit from steroids, splenectomy or immunosuppression, but these measures are usually disappointing. Despite the dramatic appearance of crises, the overall prognosis is good with lengthy survival not uncommon.

Rating
1) Accompanying infection — postpone.
2) On recovery — +0.
3) Idiopathic:
Mild — +100.
Severe — +200.

Hereditary Spherocytosis (HS)

HS is a congenital, clinically heterogeneous disorder characterized most often by the presence of spherocytic red blood cells and, in some, by varying degrees of hemolysis, anemia, jaundice and splenomegaly. Described in virtually all races, the condition is most common in people of Northern European ancestry. In the US the incidence is roughly 1 in 5000 or 220 per million.[19]

The root of the problem is believed to lie in a deficiency or dysfunction of certain red cell membrane proteins, particularly spectrin or the spectrin binding protein ankyrin. The resultant cell acquires an increased permeability, has an altered volume/surface ratio and is osmotically and mechanically fragile, leading to its destruction within the splenic microcirculation. It should be mentioned that spherocytes are not unique to HS: they have been reported in a number of hemolytic states of different pathophysiologies.

There are several different types of HS with different degrees of severity.[20] Some 75 percent are autosomal dominant and exhibit a mild or moderate hemolytic state. The remaining 25 percent have an autosomal recessive character. Heterozygotes have only the trait, are discovered often coincidentally during family studies and are characterized by membrane protein defects without hemolysis and often without spherocytosis. Homozygotes suffer a severe hemolytic state, often present in infancy, and are at greater risk of disability and death. All hemolysers are candidates for gallstone formation and, in the severest forms, skeletal development may suffer.

The clinical picture is highly variable, ranging from an insignificant or fully compensated hemolytic state without clinical findings to a severe uncompensated hemolysis with severe anemia. Moderate to severely affected patients tend to have detectable splenomegaly, may be intermittently jaundiced and (as in numerous other hemolytic conditions) their clinical course may be punctuated by episodes of hyperhemolytic or aplastic crises, often following infection (parvovirus B19 being a prime culprit).

Although most clinically evident forms are detected in childhood or adolescence, some 25 percent are diagnosed after age 20; a few patients come to light only beyond the age of 60 or 70. At the other extreme are newborns with severe neonatal jaundice calling for exchange transfusions.

The diagnosis of HS may be straightforward or involved and rests on a combination of the clinical picture, family history, presence of spherocytes, absence of other conditions capable of leading to formation of spherocytosis, and demonstration of augmented red cell osmotic fragility with or without prior incubation. Evidence of response to hemolysis should be looked for in the form of reticulocytosis, raised LDH and elevated bilirubin. In select circumstances and where facilities exist, membrane protein studies provide confirmatory evidence.

Splenectomy corrects the red cell destruction in all but the severest cases without altering the basic biochemical defect and without eliminating spherocytes from the circulation. Splenectomy is called for in all HS patients with more than borderline hemolysis to correct the hemolytic state, prevent hemolytic or aplastic crises and restore well-being. It should be postponed if possible in the very young, given the risk of post-splenectomy sepsis, but it may be indicated even in infancy when hemolysis is fulminant. Splenectomized children should receive antibiotics thereafter until beyond adolescence; there is a case to be made for the use of pneumococcal vaccine as well.

For those who cannot be splenectomized, transfusions (with their attendant risk) and folic acid supplementation may be required to correct symptomatic anemia. For HS discovered beyond the age of 50 in those without a significant history, monitoring and folate support may be a valid approach, with splenectomy reserved for complications. Some debate exists as to whether fully compensated HS patients with only borderline hemolysis should be routinely splenectomized.

Splenectomy is curative in the commonest forms of HS, and subsequent life span is normal. In the severest forms splenectomy is also beneficial, but response may be incomplete. In rare individuals post-splenectomy transfusion support cannot be abandoned.

Rating
1) Splenectomy:
Hemolysis corrected — +0.
Incompletely corrected — +50 to +100.
Before age 16 — add +25 to 0.
2) Not splenectomized:
Trait — +0.
Mild — +25.
Moderate — +50 to +100.
Severe — +200.

Hereditary Elliptocytosis (HE): Hereditary Ovalocytosis (HO)

HE is a clinically, morphologically and biochemically heterogeneous disorder, numerous variants having been described. With one notable exception, transmission is autosomal dominant. The prevalence of all forms of HE is approximately 250–500 per million. HO is given as a synonym because of common usage, although red blood cells in HE are elliptical rather than oval.

The characteristic feature of HE is the finding of numerous elliptocytic red blood cells, a change that appears to onset after marrow release. A membrane defect has been identified in most;[21] among the more common are abnormalities of spectrin and protein 4.1. In different cases elliptocytes may number anything from about 15 percent to 100 percent of total circulating red cells.

The majority of HE patients are heterozygous and either do not hemolyse or are fully compensated. Less than 10 percent hemolyse and only a fraction of these become anemic, symptomatic or require treatment. There appears to be little correlation between the genetic variant, the membrane protein defect, the red cell morphology and the clinical effect.

Diagnosis rests on the finding of substantial numbers of elliptocytes (probably less than 1 percent in normals) in the peripheral blood, in absence of another cause for ovalocytosis. In some variants and in the homozygous form, red blood cell morphology may be bizarre. In those who hemolyse there will be evidence of a hemolytic state; when severe, splenomegaly and jaundice are sometimes recorded. The spleen is the major site of red cell destruction in HE. Documentation of the membrane defect may be of enormous importance for other reasons, but has little relevance in the individual case in clinical practice unless features are greatly atypical.

HE without hemolysis requires no treatment and is not in itself a mortality risk. Those who hemolyse are cured by splenectomy, which is indicated for all patients who decompensate or are symptomatic.

Rating

Description	Rating
No hemolysis or fully compensated	+0
Hemolysis, uncompensated	
Splenectomy	+0
Splenectomy planned	Postpone
Splenectomy not possible or not done	
Mild	+25 to +100
Moderate or severe	Decline

Glucose 6 Phosphate Dehydrogenase (G6PD) Deficiency

G6PD deficiency is a common hereditary abnormality[22] in which the red blood cell hexose monophosphate shunt enzyme G6PD is reduced in amount or functionally defective. The clinical potential is that of a hemolytic state occurring particularly in response to certain oxidant drugs (e.g. certain antimalarials, sulfonamides, analgesics), infections (bacterial, viral etc) certain foods (fava beans), stressful conditions (such as diabetic ketoacidosis) or during the neonatal period. One variant, with continuous rather than sporadic manifestations, takes the form of a congenital non-spherocytic hemolytic anemia.

The condition is very common. Numerous molecular variants have been described, all manifesting reduced enzyme levels, altered enzyme function or defective substrate affinity. The two principal variants are the Mediterranean, which has very low enzyme activity and affects 30 percent of individuals in some countries, and the African, affecting some 10 percent of black American males and having 5–15 percent or so of enzyme activity.[23] Among Caucasians of different races and from different countries, forms of G6PD deficiency may affect anything from 1 in 1,000 to 1 in 2 individuals. Several variants are also described in the Orient.

Genetic transmission is sex-linked in most cases. Carrier females have varying amounts of G6PD and may range from fully normal to fully affected.

Under the conditions described and through complex biochemical interactions, hemoglobin is denatured and red blood cell survival is reduced. The resultant hemolysis is the only clinical effect and may vary in severity from fully compensated to life-threatening.

In drug-induced cases the clinical onset is usually abrupt, begins one to three days after ingestion and progresses rapidly. Those with the African variant usually have self-limiting disease, given that young cells have higher G6PD levels than older cells. This is not often the case with the Mediterranean variant. In addition to splenic red blood cell destruction, severe cases may develop significant intravascular hemolysis with back pain and dark urine. Infection-related cases are usually milder, favism cases severe.

Those individuals with continuous non-spherocytic hemolytic variants may also have different degrees of severity (*see* PKD, pp. 666–7) and are prone to cholelithiasis in the long term.

Diagnosis revolves around documentation of hemolysis with or without anemia under the conditions described, demonstration of Heinz bodies (denatured hemo-globin fragments) in red cells and finding of reduced G6PD levels by screening tests or by direct analysis. Identification of specific variants is a more involved procedure.

Management consists principally of avoiding agents capable of inducing hemolysis, promptly treating accompanying conditions and providing blood support for those with symptomatic decompensated hemolysis. For those with severe continuous hemolysis, transfusion support (as needed) and splenectomy (in select cases) may be required. Infants with neonatal jaundice on the basis of G6PD deficiency may require exchange transfusion.

The risk with G6PD deficiency is proportional to the degree and continuity of hemolysis, as well as the frequency of attacks and, to some extent, the enzyme variant.

Rating
1) Acute intermittent hemolysis:
Within 1 yr — +150 to +200.
2nd yr — +75 to +100.
3rd yr — +50 to +0.

When particularly serious episode — add +50.
When self-limited — credit −50.
2) Chronic hemolysis:
Mild — +100.
Severe or transfusion-dependent — decline.

Pyruvate Kinase (PK) Deficiency

PK is an enzyme within the anaerobic glycolytic metabolic pathway of red blood cells. Deficiency of PK may result in a congenital non-spherocytic hemolytic state. PK deficiency was one of the first described and is the second most common (after G6PD deficiency) inherited enzyme deficiency in human red blood cells.[24]

In most cases transmission is autosomal recessive, clinical manifestations being restricted to those who are homozygous or doubly heterozygous. Singly heterozygous carriers tend to have half the normal enzyme levels and are generally asymptomatic. Parental consanguinity is recorded but is not common. Rare cases of autosomal dominant inheritance are reported.

Numerous molecular variants have been described in PK deficiency, resulting in either reduced enzyme levels or limited functional capacity. (The International Committee for Standardization in Haematology established criteria for diagnostic analysis in 1979.)

PK deficiency may affect either sex; it is said to be more common in those of Northern European ancestry but has been described in several races and from several geographic locations.

Clinical manifestations include the effects of anemia, jaundice and hepatosplenomegaly in about 50 percent of cases. Cholelithiasis at young ages is not uncommon.

Clinical onset in symptomatic cases is usually between infancy and early adulthood, rarely at older ages. Clinical and genetic heterogeneity is striking; PK levels correlate poorly with hemoglobin levels or with the degree of hemolysis, which may range from fully compensated to a chronic severe transfusion-dependent state. Anemia may also fluctuate in a given case with hemolysis increasing in response to infection or stress. Aplastic crises have also been reported.

In early childhood cases with initially severe hemolysis, one-third remitted, one-third improved and only one-third had sustained severe hemolysis.[25]

The diagnosis of PK deficiency rests on the finding of non-spherocytic hemolysis, reduction in red cell PK levels and elimination of other causes of hemolysis. Bone marrow erythroid hyperplasia reflects the response to red cell destruction, and in roughly half the cases one finds reduced osmotic fragility and augmented RBC autohemolysis (effect of glucose, ATP). Serum ferritin is usually increased, unrelated to severity of hemolysis, transfusion requirements or splenectomy status.

Treatment usually consists of transfusions when the degree of anemia warrants, splenectomy for those with unpalatable transfusion requirements and folate replacement as indicated for significant hemolysis of any cause.

An acquired form of PK deficiency has been described, usually accompanying hematological malignancies or myelodysplastic syndromes. PK levels in such cases are usually in the range of heterozygotes, but may be more severely depressed and lead to severe anemia. The background disease is believed to be the cause and the PK deficiency may add to the risk.

In general the risk in PK deficiency is proportional to the degree of hemolysis and to complications of treatment. The implications of iron overload also need to be considered. The risk is especially high when hemolysis is active and anemia severe.

Rating

Description	Rating
Congenital	
Compensated	+0
Mild chronic anemia, infrequent	
transfusion requirements	+50
Severe hemolysis with or without	
splenectomy	
children	Postpone
adults	+100 to +200
Frequent transfusion requirements	
or iron overload	Decline
Acquired	Rate as for underlying disease (add +50 if significant hemolysis)

HEMOGLOBIN DISORDERS

The normal human hemoglobin molecule is composed of two pairs of unlike globin chains and a heme component. Beyond the neonatal period, three types of hemoglobin are normally present, each named according to its constituent globin chain composition. Hemoglobin A (HbA), containing alpha and beta chains, makes up over 95 percent of the total beyond six months of age. The remainder is a mix of hemoglobin A2 (HbA2), containing alpha and delta chains, and fetal hemoglobin (HbF), which contains alpha and gamma globin chains. Additional hemoglobins present during intrauterine life have disappeared or remain present in only trace amounts after birth.

When globin chains are produced in normal amounts but contain a variant structural component, the result is a hemoglobinopathy that may (e.g. sickle hemoglobin or HbS) or may not affect hemoglobin function or characteristics. The thalassemia syndromes are characterized by reduced or absent production of one or another of otherwise normal globin chains.

By and large, inherited hemoglobin disorders follow the laws of mendelian genetics. In the case of the thalassemias, inheritance patterns may be somewhat involved. In beta-thalassemia, beta chain production may be either limited (β^+)

or absent (β^0); with alpha-thalassemia there are two separate sets of genes which control alpha chain production, and the various combinations influence clinical disease patterns.

Sickle Cell Disease

Sickle cell disease represents an outstanding example of the potentially catastrophic effect of a single mutant gene product. The substitution of valine for glutamic acid at the 6 position on the beta chain of human hemoglobin produces a variant referred to as sickle hemoglobin or HbS. The homozygous state, sickle cell anemia (or SSA) (HbSS), results from the inheritance of an HbS gene from each parent.

When HbS is inherited from one parent and another hemoglobin variant from the other parent, the result is a doubly heterozygous sickle hemoglobinopathy (e.g. HbSC) or sickle thalassemia syndrome (e.g. HbSβ). The term sickle cell disease includes these variants as well as SSA (HbSS).

Sickle Cell Anemia (SSA)

SSA is the chronic hemolytic state resulting from the homozygous autosomal recessive inheritance of HbS (*see above*). Worldwide, this serious disease is probably currently responsible for some 100 thousand deaths yearly.

Confined almost exclusively to non-Caucasians and in particular to blacks, the deleterious consequences of the presence of HbS relate to its ability to sickle. A number of factors contribute to the sickling process, the principal being the state of oxygenation. Under the influence of significant hypoxia, HbS forms a semi-solid gel alignment causing the entire red cell to assume a crescent shape. These distorted rigid cells both obstruct small vessels and, being fragile, die a premature death.

Clinically, SSA patients manifest anemia and are prone to a series of clinical events which include increased risk and severity of sepsis, periodic crises (painful, hand-foot, sequestration, hemolytic or aplastic), permanent vascular occlusion (e.g. cerebrovascular) and, in the long term, to organ dysfunction (particularly renal, cardiac and pulmonary). Less life-threatening but nevertheless bothersome manifestations include stunted growth, chronic leg ulcers, cholelithiasis and aseptic bone necrosis. Splenomegaly at young ages soon gives way by auto-infarction to a small shrunken spleen.

The diagnosis of SSA is based on the clinical picture, an appropriate racial background (in most cases), documentation of a hemolytic state (with the expected blood, marrow and biochemical consequences) as well as in vitro evidence of red cell sickling and, finally, hemoglobin electrophoresis demonstration of abnormally migrating HbS consistent with HbSS.

Managing the SSA patient calls for education, anticipation, provision of good general health care and appropriate milestone vaccination/immunization. Antibiotic prophylaxis at younger ages, prompt treatment of established infections and aggressive management of crises are all mandatory. Painful crises require hydration and analgesia; hemolytic and aplastic crises require transfusion support; sequestration crises may or may not call for splenectomy. Transfusion with or without exchange has shown benefit in select situations (e.g. CVA, pregnancy).

A number of prophylactic measures aimed at reducing the sickling tendency or raising the level of HbF (which appears protective) have proved disappointing, toxic or inconsistent. No such consistently safe and effective measure is currently available.

Finally, support for deteriorating renal, cardiac or pulmonary function and management of chronic complications (e.g. leg ulcers) are indicated.

Individual patients with particularly stormy disease have undergone BMT. This option is not available to the majority.

The outlook for SSA patients has improved since the mid 1960s.[26] Major credit for this improvement belongs to general health care, supportive measures during crises, preventive care (vaccination, prophylactic penicillin), education programs and specific strategies in given situations (e.g. transfusion programs during pregnancy). Despite this, no cure exists for SSA.

Although individual survival into the fifth or sixth decade is not uncommon, overall mortality remains high. A recent major study[27] in the US of people under the age of 20 with sickle cell disease revealed 0·5 deaths per 100 person years (or 2·6 percent), most of these in individuals with HbSS. Deaths were highest between the ages of one and three years, followed by adolescence, the major cause at ages one to three being infections (*S. pneumonia*, hemophilus, salmonella). Above the age of ten, cerebrovascular, traumatic and other SS-related events led the list. Overall, mortality was equal for boys and girls. Low average HbF and low average Hb concentrations were associated with increased risk of death, with high white cell count a factor at certain ages. Of sickle cell disease patients, 89 percent lived to the age of 20 (85 percent of SS), up from 50 percent in the mid 1960s.[28]

A separate study has revealed a 60 percent survival to the age of 50 for SS patients, although age at entry could have skewed the findings.

A major beneficial influence in early childhood has been demonstrated by the prophylactic use of penicillin. Trials are currently taking place to determine if benefit may extend to older childhood ages. In older adults, organ dysfunction represents a principal cause of death.

Rating

Age	Rating
Under 15	Decline
15–20	+300
21–50	+200
Over 50	+100

Sickle Cell Trait (HbAS)

When a sickle hemoglobin gene is inherited from one parent and a normal hemoglobin gene from the other, the result is HbAS or sickle cell trait.

Some 8 percent of black North Americans are singly heterozygous for HbS (i.e. have sickle cell trait). The incidence is much the same or higher in black populations elsewhere. Such individuals are not anemic and, as a general rule, are considered healthy. The most consistent findings are hyposthenuria, hematuria in 4 percent of those affected at some stage of their life and a raised incidence of urinary tract infection during pregnancy. Only infrequently does the hematuria become significant enough to require treatment (bicarbonate, diuretics, fibrinolysis inhibitors, transfusion).

Prolonged hypoxia (unpressurized or incompletely pressurized aircraft, casual general anesthesia) may induce sickling in trait patients; deaths have been recorded in this setting. It is customary to recommend good oxygenation in potentially hypoxic environments and to avoid such settings when the condition is known.

A recent report has reactivated the debate over strenuous physical exertion by sickle cell trait patients. It is known that black athletes in North American football leagues have the same incidence of HbAS as other black Americans yet do not suffer crises during strenuous practice or game conditions. The same was believed to apply to military exertion (e.g. basic training) but Kark et al[29] recently reported that the risk of sudden death in this setting was 28 times higher in black military recruits with sickle cell trait than in black recruits without the trait, and 40 times higher than all other recruits. The risk increased with age. The death rate in this highly select group (1 in 3,200) is impressive but not representative of the risk in sickle cell trait patients with non-comparable daily activities.

Rating

Overall — +0.

Note Individual caution will be necessary for those sickle cell trait patients whose occupation or avocation places them in contact with hypoxic situations and for military inductees about to undergo basic training. Postponing such applicants may be a valid decision.

Other Hemoglobin Disorders

Other than HbS and the thalassemias, the more common hemoglobin variants encountered worldwide are C, D, E and various combinations of the five together. In general, the diagnosis rests on the clinical picture, racial origin, smear appearance, presence of sickling, family history and hemoglobin electrophoretic study. Because screening electrophoresis may not distinguish all cases, various techniques in different media and at different pH may be required. More in-depth study is rarely called for in routine practice.

Hemoglobin SC Disease

HbSC disease is a doubly heterozygous hemoglobinopathy with HbS inherited from one parent and HbC (another beta 6 variant) from the other. Again more common in blacks, clinical involvement may range from minimal to severe, but is generally less significant than with SSA. Of those with symptoms, one-half present in childhood, the rest in adolescence or adult life. More or less common manifestations include combinations of the following: hemolytic anemia (usually mild), splenomegaly, hematuria, aseptic necrosis of the femoral head, retinal changes, higher than expected risk of complications during pregnancy and occasional sickling crises.

Life expectancy is slightly reduced in comparison with the general population.

Rating

Rate at one-half SSA ratings (*see* p. 669).

Hemoglobin CC Disease

Homozygous C hemoglobinopathy features mild to moderate hemolysis and splenomegaly. Abdominal and joint pains are common and cholelithiasis may occur. Mild anemia is common and target cells are prominent. Infrequently, hemolytic or aplastic crises may punctuate the otherwise stable background picture. In general, the prognosis is excellent and there is probably no significant shortening of life span.

Rating

Age	Rating
Up to 40	+50
Over 40	+0

Hemoglobin SD

A number of D variants have been described and SD disease has been reported in several races, including whites. Usually milder than sickle cell anemia, sickling may occur and splenomegaly is reported in up to one-third.

Rating

Rate at one-half SSA ratings (*see* p. 669).

Hemoglobin E

This is a beta chain variant (position 26) not uncommon in South East Asia (but not in the Chinese). Heterozygotes (HbAE) are asymptomatic; homozygotes (HbEE) may have a mild to moderate hemolytic anemia. The combination with beta-thalassemia (HbEβ) is usually associated with severe clinical involvement.

Rating

Heterozygotes — +0.
Homozygotes — +75 to +50.
HbEβ — +300.

Sickle Beta-Thalassemia

This is a not uncommon combination in the US, West Indies and western Africa. The severity is dependent on the type of beta-thalassemia gene. Those with β^0 tend to be severe, not unlike SSA, and special studies may be required to diagnose. Those with β^+ are more similar to sickle cell trait than SSA. Unlike sickle trait, there is more HbS than A; again, special studies may be needed to firm the diagnosis.

Rating

Sickle β^0 — one-half to full SSA rating (see p. 669).
Sickle β^+ — +0.

Thalassemias

The thalassemia syndromes are a heterogeneous group of disorders characterized by reduced synthesis of one or another of the globin chains of hemoglobin, leading to ineffective erythropoiesis and red cell destruction. Collectively one of the commonest inherited disorders of mankind, the thalassemias have traditionally been named after the globin chain whose synthesis is affected, hence the two main categories of alpha- and beta-thalassemia.

Beta-Thalassemia

Linked to a defect in the gene site on the short arm of chromosome 11, beta chain production in beta-thalassemia may be reduced or entirely absent. For practical purposes three clinically relevant types are recognized: minor, intermedia and major.

Beta-thalassemia is extremely common in areas bordering the Mediterranean, particularly Italy, Greece and certain Arabic states, and in the Far East. In addition, sporadic cases are not uncommonly found in virtually every racial group and in every country.

Beta-thalassemia minor causes little or no anemia and is either symptomless or minimally so. Clinical findings are absent, or limited to mild pallor and trace splenomegaly, whereas the hemoglobin is invariably in excess of 100 g/l. Characteristic laboratory findings include hypochromic microcytic red blood cells with normal MCHC, smear findings of target and tear-drop cells and hemoglobin electrophoresis showing raised HbA2 or, less commonly, HbF.

Survival is affected little or not at all, although pregnant women with beta-thalassemia minor tend to become more anemic than expected. A number of unrecognized patients are inappropriately treated with iron preparations because of their red cell indices; they risk becoming iron overloaded as a result.

Beta-thalassemia major is a severe hemolytic state present from early childhood and characterized classically by growth retardation, skeletal changes due to expansion of the marrow cavity, hepatosplenomegaly and transfusion dependency. Both the disease and the inevitable transfusion-related siderosis combine to lead to organ dysfunction, cardiomyopathy being a particularly worrisome development. Death in adolescence or early adult life is not unusual. With hypertransfusion programs (to reduce endogenous defective RBC production) and iron chelation, survival to the age of 30 is becoming more common, although compliance with parenteral iron chelators is an issue, particularly in adolescence. An even better outlook may follow selective transfusion of young red cells and oral iron chelation therapy; one such oral agent is currently on trial. In select cases BMT is potentially curative.[30] Various experimental drugs have been tried with minimal success; genetic engineering is likely to become an issue in the future.

In a 1982 report, the mortality of a series of Greek patients with thalassemia major and intermedia was similar to that of the general population at up to six years of age; it then increased gradually, with only 24 percent alive at the age of 28. In Italy patients managed with hypertransfusion and iron chelation since the mid-1970s were reported in 1989.[31] Survival estimates at the age of 15 after the first decade of life were 81 percent for subjects born 1960–4, 84 percent for those born 1965–9 and 97 percent for those born 1970–4. At the age of 20, survival from age 10 in the first two cohorts was 59 percent and 70 percent; at the age of 25, survival from age 10 was 41 percent in the first cohort. Overall survival from birth for those born 1970–4 was 97 percent at the age of 10, and 94 percent at the age of 15. The most common causes of death were heart disease, infection, liver disease and malignancy.

At present there is debate between proponents of hypertransfusion and iron chelation on the one hand, and BMT on the other, for patients with beta-thalassemia major. Although BMT is potentially curative, there is a 15 percent mortality, a distressingly high percentage given that the procedure should be done early and that life expectancy by five-year cohorts is improving rapidly with medical management. On the other hand, compliance with hypertransfusion and iron chelation is a problem in that 95 percent survival at the age of 15 and greater than 50 percent survival past the age of 30 may be possible only in select centers with aggressive follow-up.

Beta-thalassemia intermedia is a useful clinical designation for those individuals having manifestations intermediate between the above two extremes. Survival beyond middle-age is expected with or without intermittent transfusions, as dictated by symptomatic anemia. Delta-beta-thalassemia homozygotes may also be classified in this category.

The terms beta-thalassemia minima or trait are sometimes encountered. These correspond to the least affected thalassemia minor patients; their outlook, as expected, is compatible with a normal life span. In this category would be included those with heterozygous delta-beta-thalassemia.

Rating
Minor, minima or trait — +0.
Intermedia — +100 to +200.
Major — decline.
BMT, successful — rate as for aplastic anemia (*see* p. 652).

Alpha-Thalassemia

This condition is most common in South East Asia, some parts of Africa and the Caribbean. The genetic defect lies on chromosome 16.

As stated, two sets of alpha globin genes are believed to exist with clinical events in alpha-thalassemia corresponding to the number of gene defects present. Given that alpha chains are common to all three adult hemoglobins, hemoglobin electrophoresis is only useful in some cases of alpha-thalassemia where tetramers of opposing globin chains form. Otherwise, the diagnosis, which is not usually difficult, revolves around the clinical picture, family study, smear appearance, red cell inclusions and alpha-beta globin synthesis ratios.

Silent carriers (including individuals with heterozygous Hb Constant Spring) may have deletion of a single alpha gene and show no clinical or laboratory abnormality. Most often, they are discovered in the course of family studies. Survival is unaffected.

Minor or trait patients (including homozygous Hb Constant Spring) may have a two-gene deletion and, in general, exhibit hypochromia and microcytosis but little or no anemia. Again, survival would be anticipated to be normal.

HbH disease demonstrates variable clinical severity, corresponding roughly to the picture associated with beta-thalassemia intermedia or major. The findings include hemolysis, anemia, splenomegaly, bony changes, smear abnormalities and HbH (beta chain tetramers) inclusions in red cells.

Finally, deletion of all four alpha genes is the probable background for Hb Bart's (gamma tetramers) hydrops fetalis. All alpha chain synthesis is absent and the condition is incompatible with sustained survival. Severe neonatal pallor, hydrops and death within the first few hours of extrauterine life are expected.

Rating

Silent carriers — +0.
Trait or minor — +0.
HbH disease — +100 to decline.
Hb Bart's — not insurance applicants.

MARCH HEMOGLOBINURIA

The forceful striking of a part of the body against a hard surface results in intravascular mechanical erythrocyte damage and destruction. The condition is most common in strenuous walkers or joggers (hence the term) but the same process has been recorded in karate practitioners, Conga drum players, head bashers and others.

The hemolytic event tends to accompany the stress, produces hemoglobinemia and hemoglobinuria and, at times, a modest reticulocyte response. Clinical features are usually non-existent (mild jaundice rarely) and anemia is borderline at worst. Full recovery is usually prompt on cessation of exertion.

Accurate diagnosis and elimination of other types of hemolysis constitute the principal challenge. When diagnosis is secure, reassurance and advice on the particular causative activity are the only necessities. Mortality implication is nil.

Rating

March hemoglobinuria — +0.

HEREDITARY COAGULATION DISORDERS

Hemophilias

The term hemophilia has been used inconsistently over the years. From antiquity it identified a congenital bleeding disorder of unknown cause primarily affecting boys. With the discovery of soluble clotting factors and an understanding of the coagulation cascades, the term was restricted to a congenital deficiency of factors VIII and IX. In recent years the label has been loosely applied by both lay and medical personnel to a variety of inherited (and sometimes acquired) bleeding disorders. This and the source of the diagnosis should be considered when reviewing medical underwriting information.

The majority of congenital hemostatic disorders involve soluble plasma protein factors (as opposed to cellular or vascular factors) and most of these revolve round deficiency or dysfunction of clotting factors VIII and IX: classical hemophilia A (factor VIII deficiency), Christmas disease or hemophilia B (factor IX deficiency) and von Willebrand's disease.

Hemophilia A and Christmas disease are similar disorders in terms of inheritance, clinical patterns and management approach. The main distinctions are the factor affected, incidence and replacement product. There is reason to believe that a high mutation rate for hemophilia A serves to maintain current prevalence rates.

Classical hemophilia A results from the sex-linked inheritance of reduced level or dysfunctional factor VIII clotting factor. The same clinical picture may result from acquired inhibition of normally inherited factor VIII. Three levels of severity are recognized, defined partly by the clinical picture and partly by the level of factor VIII clotting activity: severe hemophilia (less than 1 percent), moderate hemophilia (1–5 percent) and mild hemophilia (more than 5 percent).

The clinical risk is primarily bleeding, in particular muscle hemorrhage, hemarthrosis and internal bleeding. The most feared eventuality is intracranial hemorrhage. Bleeding may be spontaneous or induced, and varies with the severity of clotting factor deficiency and, to some extent, with age, reflecting activity-related trauma of childhood and adolescence as well as longer survival of milder forms. In particularly mild cases bleeding may only follow invasive procedures or some other reason for blood loss.

The diagnosis is based on the clinical picture, family history, prolonged partial thromboplastin time (reflecting intrinsic pathway integrity) and level of factor VIII clotting activity. When indicated, the presence of inhibitors may need to be documented.

Aside from the general measures of supportive care, avoidance of circumstances likely to induce bleeding and avoidance of medications capable of interfering with hemostatic integrity (e.g. aspirin), management calls for factor replacement in the form of cryoprecipitate or factor VIII concentrates, in severe cases prophylactically or on demand, or at earliest sign of bleeding in lesser forms. Amounts and duration of replacement are dictated by the situation at hand.

Hemophilia A patients with greater than 5–10 percent of activity may derive benefit from use of DDAVP (desmopressin), which stimulates endogenous factor production and enhances platelet function and has proven useful in select circumstances. For dental work, the use of fibrinolysis inhibitors has also proven valuable.

To the consequences of hemorrhage both short- and long-term (e.g. crippling deformities, pseudotumors) should be added the risks associated with treatment, particularly blood-product-related disease transmission (hepatitis, HIV etc).

With modern regimes, chronic complications are on the decrease, and genetically engineered factors or ultra-purified concentrates give promise of avoiding the risks associated with natural blood products.

The various management strategies called for in patients with inhibitors are beyond the scope of this brief review.

Christmas disease or factor IX deficiency is associated with a clinical picture not unlike that of classical hemophilia A. Genetic inheritance and risks are also similar. Factor assays serve to distinguish the two.

Replacement strategy in Christmas disease calls for the use of plasma or concentrates of factors II, VII, IX and X. Again, amounts used and duration of treatment are dictated by the situation at hand. A monoclonal antibody purified IX preparation containing negligible amounts of other vitamin K dependent factors in early trial has achieved control of bleeding episodes equivalent to experience with II, VII, IX and X concentrates.[32]

Life expectancy in hemophilia was very low prior to the introduction of clotting factor preparations. Severe hemophiliacs rarely lived beyond early adulthood; survival in mild hemophilia was about two-thirds of normal life span. A UK study covering the period 1969–74 revealed the average age at death was 43 years for hemophilia A, 34 years for hemophilia B. Between 1961 and 1980 the median life expectancy for severe hemophiliacs improved to 57 years.[33]

Survival data in a large cohort of AIDS-free Dutch hemophiliacs (both A and B) covering the period 1973–86 reveal that, as a group, observed over expected mortality was 2·1 (2·9 for severe and 1·6 for mild hemophilia). Mean age at death was 49 years, with mean life expectancy 66 years compared with 74 for the Dutch male general population.[34] As expected, patients with inhibitors fared worse, having a 5·3 times higher risk of dying than those without an inhibitor. Severe hemophiliacs without inhibitors who received prophylaxis fared better than those who did not.

Causes of death in this cohort included bleeding, neoplasms, stroke, renal failure, myocardial infarction, suicide and unknown events. (Other series have also shown an excess of liver disease.) Cancer deaths were higher and MI deaths lower than expected.

Rating
1) HIV positive — decline.
2) At risk for HIV — test.
3) HIV negative or not at risk:
Mild — +25 to +50.
Moderate — +75 to +100.
Severe — +100 to +200.
4) With inhibitors — add +100.
5) Age above 50 — reduce ratings by −25 to −50.

Von Willebrand Disease (VWD)

In its simplest form, VWD is a hereditary bleeding disorder with elements of disturbed hemostasis related to dysfunction of both soluble clotting factor VIII and platelets.

Like so many other hematological disorders, in-depth study has led to the recognition that VWD is a heterogeneous disorder from the genetic, clinical, laboratory and pathophysiologic points of view.

Von Willebrand factor (VWF) is a large multimeric (several subunits) glycoprotein produced by vascular endothelial cells and megakaryocytes. One portion serves to transport factor VIII procoagulant activity, another serves as an intermediate in platelet aggregation and is responsible for ristocetin aggregation, one of the crucial *in vitro* diagnostic tests for VWD. The factor also expresses its antigenic determinants.[35]

VWD is due to a quantitative, qualitative or selective subunit abnormality of VWF. The genetic defect lies on the short arm of chromosome 12.

Numerous subtypes of VWD have been identified. No systematic classification is agreeable to all, but currently three main types are recognized (*see* Table 21.1); the first two are segregated by analysis of VWF structure, the third by clinical features. Multiple variants are described in each main category.

Table 21.1. Types of VWD.

Type	Description
1	All multimers of VWF are present but decreased.
2	Large multimers of VWF are selectively reduced.
3	A severe form presenting in early life.

From a practical point of view, the severity of bleeding determines the clinical import. Types 1 and 2 above are probably transmitted in autosomal dominant fashion and Type 3 autosomal recessive. The usual clinical picture is a spontaneous or induced blood loss, usually mucocutaneous. Expistaxis, heavy periods, easy bruising and lengthy bleeding after cuts or invasive procedures are all common. Type 3 presents early in life with severe hemorrhages, the clinical picture being not unlike that of classical hemophilia. As seen, clinical manifestations in VWD may range from trivial to life threatening.

An acquired form of VWD has been described. With manifestations similar to the hereditary mild or moderate variants, it has been identified in association with lymphoreticular, myeloproliferative and auto-immune disorders.

The diagnosis of VWD rests on the clinical picture and laboratory assessment. The latter reflects the dual hemostatic nature of the underlying defect. Included are combinations of prolonged bleeding time, reduced factor VIII clotting activity (reflecting reduced transport), reduced VIII antigenic material and decreased or absent platelet aggregation with ristocetin.[36] Whilst these tests form the basis for the diagnosis of VWD, combinations of laboratory findings will vary by type and subgroups. Various other uncommon findings, including thrombocytopenia, may be recorded in some variants. Multimeric structure determination is, of course, more involved.

The treatment of VWD in the event of bleeding or in preparation for invasive procedures has to be individualized. The mildest form with modest clinical events may benefit from use of DDAVP; in some of the more serious variants its use may be contraindicated. For the majority of cases infusions of plasma or cryoprecipitate (the latter providing more 'activity' per volume and therefore preferred, particularly where large volume use is anticipated) are the treatments of choice. In addition to replacing VWF, endogenous VIII synthesis is stimulated. The usual factor VIII concentrates address only one aspect of the problem and are of limited benefit, but recently new pasteurized VIII concentrates (Humate P) have provided hemostasis in severely hemorrhaging patients who had proven unresponsive to DDAVP and cryoprecipitate.[37] Its mechanism of action is conjectural.

Again, the amounts, routes of administration and duration of treatments are beyond the scope of this chapter.

Rating
Mild — +25.
Moderate — +75 to +50.
Severe — +150.

MYELOPROLIFERATIVE SYNDROMES

This term groups together a series of disorders having in common autonomous clonal overproduction of one or more marrow derived non-lymphoid cell lines (i.e. red blood cells, platelets, granulocytes and fibroblasts).

Of the several conditions included under this heading, the most commonly encountered are polycythemia rubra vera (PRV), essential thrombocythemia, myelofibrosis and chronic myelogenous leukemia. These alone are discussed in this chapter.

It is customary to present these entities separately, as a firm diagnosis is usually possible. It is worth remembering that in a small percentage the distinction between them is somewhat arbitrary and overlap syndromes are not rare. Furthermore, evolution during the course of illness from one form to another is recorded; in particular, myelofibrosis and leukemic transformation are not uncommon terminal events.

Polycythemia Rubra Vera (PRV)

PRV is a condition characterized by an absolute increase in directly measured red cell mass. In this it differs from spurious polycythemia in which red blood cells appear increased because of a reduction in plasma volume. Like PRV, secondary polycythemias represent a form of true polycythemia, but as a response to stimuli promoting red blood cell production rather than autonomous growth.

The textbook PRV patient may be of either sex, is past middle age and demonstrates ruddy complexion, splenomegaly, raised hemoglobin and hematocrit, neutrophilia, thrombocytosis and is at risk for thrombohemorrhagic complications. To provide uniformity, particularly in less than classical cases, various study groups, including the PRV Study Group, have established diagnostic criteria. In addition, red cell precursors are known to grow autonomously in appropriate tissue culture and to be unusually sensitive to erythropoietin.

The untreated polycythemia vera patient is at risk of vascular events due to sludging of thick blood or thromboembolic complications related to hyperviscosity and platelet hyperaggregability. Paradoxically, hemorrhage may also occur, a reflection, in part, of dysfunctional platelets.

Therapy is best accomplished by venesection until the hematocrit returns at least to the normal range. Initially, phlebotomy may be required every few days then as needed to maintain the hematocrit in the desired range (ideally induce a borderline iron depletion). Myelosuppression with ^{32}P, an alkylating agent, hydroxyurea or some other similar drug may be called for in those who require frequent maintenance venesection, those with massive thrombocytosis, painful spleno-megaly or those with thrombohemorrhagic events. It is unlikely that these modalities prolong survival much beyond that obtained with simple phlebotomy. Those with hyperactive platelets or prior thrombotic events may benefit from aspirin.

The average survival in untreated established PRV is about six to 18 months. Patients treated by casual phlebotomy alone have a median survival between eight and 15 years and 1 percent of these will develop acute non-lymphoblastic leukemia. A more closely supervised phlebotomy program will be associated with survival only slightly reduced from normal. The risk of leukemia with any myelosuppres-sion varies from a low of 2 percent in European series to about 25 percent in American series (about 11 percent PRV Study Group, onsetting later with ^{32}P than with alkylating agents). When multiple agents are used the leukemia risk may be as high as 32 percent.[38] In one series acute leukemia developed at a mean of about ten years after diagnosis and four years following myelosuppression. In these settings leukemia remission is difficult to achieve and survival is short.

Rating
1) Phlebotomy:
1st yr — postpone.
Thereafter — +50 to +100.
Major thrombohemorrhagic event while under treatment — add +50.
Poor control or default in treatment — +200 up.
2) Myelosuppression:
1st yr — postpone.
Thereafter — +300.

Idiopathic Myelofibrosis (Agnogenic Myeloid Metaplasia)

Myelofibrosis is characterized by a primary excessive accumulation of fibrous connective tissue in the bone marrow. Idiopathic myelofibrosis is distinguished from marrow fibrosis accompanying other myeloproliferative disorders and from all other entities leading to bone marrow fibrosis, such as hairy cell leukemia, metastatic malignancies, chronic infections and auto-immune disorders.

Typically, idiopathic myelofibrosis presents in older individuals with non-specific symptoms, marked splenomegaly and characteristic peripheral blood findings: leukoerythroblastosis (nucleated red blood cells and immature neutrophils), platelet anisocytosis and red blood cell tear-dropping. The marrow aspirate is usually dry, whereas a biopsy discloses intense fibrosis. Initial blood counts are highly variable and a number of non-specific biochemical and auto-immune findings may be recorded.

The outlook in myelofibrosis is poor. Supportive care is the mainstay of therapy. Various treatments (including cytotoxics, splenic irradiation, corticosteroids, androgens, multiple bone marrow punctures etc.) have had only modest, inconsistent or poorly reproducible influence on survival. Splenectomy is sometimes indicated to control pain, cytopenias or massive size but does not improve longevity and is performed at the risk of acceleration of hepatomegaly and disease progression.

The following represent complications encountered at some stage of the disease in one large series: infections (63 percent), cardiovascular events (50 percent), thromboembolic phenomena (40 percent), hemorrhage (33 percent) and symptomatic anemia.[39]

From the myelofibrosis group in general is segregated the entity of acute myelofibrosis, characterized by pancytopenia, absence of splenomegaly, severe bone marrow fibrosis, variable numbers of blast cells and a rapid evolution. Survival is measured in months.

Chronic idiopathic myelofibrosis is compatible with survival lasting several years in select patients; overall, survival of five to ten years after diagnosis is usual.

Rating
Acute myelofibrosis — decline.
Chronic myelofibrosis — decline.

Thrombocytosis and Thrombocythemia

Up to 10 percent of patients admitted to general hospitals may be shown to have an increase in platelet count during their hospital stay. When an absolute increase in platelet count occurs as a marrow response to an external stimulus or when platelet removal is inhibited, the condition represents reactive or secondary thrombocytosis. Such a finding is very common, occurs in a vast number of settings and is in general innocuous, the risk being that of the background cause.

When platelet numbers are excessive because of isolated autonomous clonal over-production, the individual is said to have primary or essential thrombocythemia. Autonomous platelet over-production may occur in the other myeloproliferative diseases (MPDs) as well. Although a distinction can usually be made, overlap syndromes are not uncommon. In particular, PRV and thrombocythemia may be at opposite ends of a common spectrum.

Essential thrombocythemia (ET)[40] usually presents beyond middle age (average age at presentation is 50–60), may affect either sex (female–male ratio is about 1·7 : 1) and is associated with a risk of thrombohemorrhagic complications. Typical hematological findings are pronounced thrombocytosis, variation in platelet size (including giant forms), dysfunctional platelet activity and marked increase in dyspoietic megakaryocytes in the bone marrow. The PRV Study Group has established specific diagnostic criteria for ET.[41]

Thrombocythemia usually comes to light in one of four ways: (1) by chance (hematological findings or documentation of splenomegaly), (2) frank thrombohemorrhagic event, (3) transient, usually neurological dysfunction believed to be due to platelet plugging (e.g. TIA), and (4) vasomotor manifestations (e.g. burning, acrocyanosis).

Younger patients with ET were once thought to have a more benign course than those over 40.[42] Indeed, some authorities had suggested withholding treatment in otherwise well young ET patients regardless of platelet count. Recent evidence does not support this contention, a number of young ET patients having suffered catastrophic complications. At all ages correlation between hematological parameters and clinical events is not ideal.

Reduction in platelet mass with melphalan or hydroxyurea is indicated when platelets in ET approach one million per mm^3 or when complications have occurred. The potential of both alkylating agents and hydroxyurea to be associated with long-term leukemia development should be kept in mind. Recently alpha-interferon has been shown to have an effect in lowering platelets in ET, but its exact place in the treatment scheme is not yet established. In crisis situations plateletpheresis may reduce platelets rapidly, and in those with hyperactive platelets aspirin cover is beneficial.

The major causes of death in several series were thrombohemorrhagic and late development of acute leukemia. In one study,[43] the probability of survival to 100 months was 80 percent; in another the probability of survival to ten years was 64 percent, to 15 years 51 percent. Considering the age at diagnosis, life expectancy was close to normal.

Rating
Essential thrombocythemia.
Controlled asymptomatic — +50.
Average control or prior thrombohemorrhagic event — +100.
Poor control or symptomatic — decline.
Untreated — postpone.

HEMOLYTIC UREMIC SYNDROME (HUS)

There is reason to believe that the frequency of HUS is, at least in North America, increasing. Clinical manifestations are believed to reflect intravascular platelet aggregation with resultant occlusion of arterioles and capillaries. It differs from the related thrombotic thrombocytopenic purpura (TTP) principally by age, predominant target organ involvement, management priorities and long-term outlook.

Characterized principally by microangiopathic hemolysis, thrombocytopenia and renal impairment, HUS is a leading cause of acute renal failure in childhood. Affecting boys and girls equally, the mean age of childhood cases is 3·8 years and cases predominate in summer. A number of cases are idiopathic; others are temporally related to infections, drug use or, in adult females, to pregnancy. A particularly close link is believed to exist with verocytotoxic strains (0157:H7) of E. coli.[44]

Presenting symptoms include vomiting, diarrhea (often bloody) abdominal cramps, fever, lethargy and, less commonly, seizures. Some have no distinct prodrome.[45] Management strategies revolve round supportive care, treatment of infection, elimination of cause, use of heparin and renal support (including dialysis if necessary). Additional measures in individual cases have included those affecting hemostasis or fibrinolysis, IV immunoglobulin, plasma exchange etc. The mean hospital stay in one series was 15 days; mean dialysis time in those requiring it, was 12 days. Twenty-three percent had a stormy course and the case fatality rate was 3·4 percent, with renal, neurological, GI and treatment-related complications representing prime causes of mortality. Predictors of more serious disease included short duration, admission leukocytosis, bloody diarrhea and possibly early CNS manifestations. Those who died tended to deteriorate from onset (i.e. it was unlikely that a patient would recover after relapse).

Rating

1) Active disease — decline.
2) Full recovery:
Within 6 mth — postpone.
Thereafter — +0.
3) Dialysis dependent — decline.

THROMBOTIC THROMBOCYTOPENIC PURPURA (TTP)

TTP is a serious but relatively rare disorder, the main features of which are fever, microangiopathic hemolytic anemia, thrombocytopenia, renal impairment and fleeting, changing neurological dysfunctions. In contrast to HUS, to which it bears a resemblance, adults are usually affected, renal impairment is less impressive than neurological and the outlook is worse. The incidence is estimated at one case per million, peak presentation is in the third or fourth decade and 60 percent of cases occur in women.[46]

A number of cases of TTP are idiopathic; others demonstrably follow infections (again, E. coli 0157:H7), medications, toxins, pregnancy or other triggers. The pathogenesis is presumed to involve endothelial cell damage resulting in small vessel occlusion by platelet-fibrin thrombi. Possible mediators include von Willebrand factor multimers, a calcium-dependent protease known as calpain, or absence of an inhibitor of platelet aggregation.[47]

TTP patients often present acutely with fulminant evidence of part or all of the pentad outlined above. Other organ systems may be involved, the gut and myocardium being prime targets. Diagnosis is usually straightforward, based on the clinical presentation, laboratory findings and sometimes hyaline thrombi in biopsy material.

Modern therapies have reduced early and late mortality from over 90 percent to about 20 percent but the incidence of relapse remains high,[48] complications are frequent and a chronic smoldering course is not uncommon. Pregnancy-related cases have been known to recur in subsequent pregnancies.

The list of available therapies is vast, indicating that no single treatment is universally effective. This list includes antiplatelet agents, corticosteroids, vincristine, plasma infusions, splenectomy, plasma exchange, IV immunoglobulins, prostacyclin and immunosuppressives. Each is aimed at correcting one or other aspect of postulated etiology or pathogenesis. Some of these therapies are primarily of historical interest, others are unproved, others still (platelet infusions) are potentially hazardous.[49] The best results are currently achieved with a combination of plasma exchange and vincristine, with other modalities often added as well.[50] Response to a given therapy is often impressive in one patient, unhelpful in another. For this reason and because of the urgency of treatment in fulminant cases, most patients receive more than one mode of therapy.

Rating

Description	Rating
Idiopathic	
Acute	
Single episode	
Active	Decline
Recovered	
Within 1 yr	Postpone
1–3 yr	+200
3–5 yr	+100
Thereafter	+0
Relapse	
Active	Decline
Recovered	Add +50 to single episode ratings
Chronic smoldering	
Mild	+200
Severe	Decline
Secondary	
Fixed cause, no longer present or	
unlikely to recur	+50 to +0
Possible recurrence	+100

AUTO-IMMUNE THROMBOCYTOPENIC PURPURA (ATP): IDIOPATHIC THROMBOCYTOPENIC PURPURA (ITP)

Immune platelet destruction is the likely common pathophysiological mechanism of many thrombocytopenic states. A disorder in which immune thrombocytopenia is induced by auto (self) antibodies and is the primary and only defect is referred to as idiopathic auto-immune thrombocytopenic purpura. Before the discovery that platelet destruction in this condition is mediated by platelet autoantibodies, ATP was known as idiopathic thrombocytopenic purpura (ITP); this term is still frequently used.

In ATP, IgG antibodies interact with platelet-specific membrane glycoproteins, sometimes attracting complement as well. The whole is then destroyed in the reticuloendothelial system, particularly that of the spleen and liver. The same mechanism may be operative in the platelet destruction of several disease states, particularly auto-immune and infectious disorders. When ATP is accompanied by auto-immune hemolysis, the term Evan's syndrome is used.

ATP (ITP) may be seen in acute or chronic form.[51] Acute ATP usually presents fairly suddenly, has a peak occurrence in childhood and another in young to mid-adulthood, where women are affected more often than men by a ratio of 2:1 or 3:1. Although peak incidences are useful study concepts, ATP may be seen at any age. Indeed, a third peak in the elderly has been postulated. Clinical events are generally limited to petechiae, bruising and bleeding (most often mucocutaneous). The main concern is catastrophic bleeding, usually GI or neurological. Blood loss may lead to anemia. Other than mild splenomegaly, there are no clinical findings, and muscle hemorrhage or hemarthrosis is not a feature. Indeed, additional clinical findings should prompt a review of the diagnosis. By arbitrary definition, cases persisting over six months are termed chronic.

The diagnosis of idiopathic ATP revolves round the clinical picture, documentation of true thrombocytopenia, increased size of circulating platelets (outpouring of young forms from the bone marrow) and prominent marrow megakaryocytes. In cases of doubt and where available, documentation of shortened platelet life span and of raised antiplatelet IgG levels may prove useful.

The clinical course of ATP is variable. In children acute ATP is often sudden, post-viral and self-limited. With or without the use of corticosteroids, full recovery is the rule, with intravenous immunoglobulin or splenectomy reserved for the occasional non-responder. There is no firm evidence that steroids hasten recovery. In adults with acute disease,[52] treatment with corticosteroids is called for when the platelet count is less than about 30,000 per mm^3 or when there is bleeding. A full or satisfactory response is expected in three-quarters of patients. In the event of steroid failure or frequent relapse, splenectomy is curative in some 80 percent of cases.

The line between acute and chronic ATP is sometimes blurred. In ATP of long duration, corticosteroids are certainly less often beneficial. Incomplete responders to splenectomy may or may not require additional treatment. A platelet count in excess of 30–35,000 per mm^3 will usually be well tolerated unless accidents, dental extractions, surgery or childbirth occur, at which times special preparation and precautions will be necessary. When the platelet count is less than 30,000 per mm^3 or bleeding recurs, additional therapy is generally required, presents a therapeutic challenge and may take one of several forms as dictated by the circumstances; the options include repeat corticosteroids, removal of accessory spleens if found, vincristine, IV immunoglobulin, danazol, vincristine-treated platelets, plasma exchange and immunosuppressive agents.[53]

The outlook is good for the majority of acute childhood cases and for adults responding satisfactorily to corticosteroids or splenectomy. Of splenectomy failures who respond incompletely to additional measures (about 50 percent), some 10–20 percent will have a particularly stormy course, and mortality risk is high (bleeding, development of auto-immune disorders or malignancies). The mortality of chronic ITP as a whole is about 5 percent.[51]

Pregnant women with ATP represent a special concern and it should not be forgotten that ATP is a well documented potential complication of HIV infection.

Recent published reports have suggested a rather benign course in mother and child for thrombocytopenia in pregnancy unless there is a pre-existing diagnosis of ATP or circulating antiplatelet antibodies are present.

Rating

Description	Rating
Acute	
Single episode, full recovery	
(spontaneous, steroid or splenectomy induced)	
Under 6 mth	Postpone
6–12 mth	+50
Thereafter	+0
More than one episode or incomplete recovery	Rate as chronic
Chronic (regardless of treatment)	
Stable platelet count >100,000	+0
Stable platelet count 50–100,000	+50
Stable platelet count 30–50,000	+75
Platelet count <30,000	
Stable, on minimal treatment	+100 to +200
Active, aggressive treatment	Decline
Other	
Pregnancy	Postpone
HIV related	Decline
Current corticosteroids, immunosuppressants, vincristine	Add + 50

LEUKEMIAS

As a group these malignant disorders of blood cells constitute one of the prime causes of mortality directly related to a hematological process. Space limitations allow no more than a cursory review of the main types. The individual leukemias are named according to the cell involved and to the rapidity of evolution in the absence of intervention. Deaths related to leukemia tend to reflect disease infiltration of tissue, effects of cytopenias (i.e. infection or hemorrhage) from the disease and its treatment, or other complications, such as organ failure.[54]

Chronic Lymphocytic Leukemia (CLL)

CLL is a clonal overproduction of immunoincompetent lymphocytes, most often of B-cell lineage, affecting primarily older individuals. The overall median survival of all CLL patients from time of diagnosis and regardless of therapy is between five and ten years; some 10 percent die within one year of diagnosis.

Several staging systems have been devised to identify factors of relevance to longevity and survival. Based on various combinations of these factors (age, sex, performance status, tumor bulk, height of lymphocyte count, marrow cellularity, cytopenias and certain biochemical parameters) low-, intermediate- and high-risk groups have been identified. More normal counts, lesser lymphocytes in blood and marrow, and minimal evidence of disease are all indicative of a better risk.

Best-risk groups, about 25–50 percent of the total, have an annual death rate of 2–9 percent (9–23 percent for intermediate and 31–42 percent for high risk) over ten years and a five-year survival of 75 percent (59 percent for intermediate risk and 14 percent for high risk).

A number of aggressive and sometimes novel therapies in intermediate- and high-risk groups have had limited impact on survival or are incompletely evaluated. One study[55] recently subdivided best-risk patients further and established that those with smoldering disease (a somewhat arbitrary definition) had survival rates close to those of the general population but were difficult to segregate absolutely in advance.

Rating

1) Best risk:

Age	Rating
Under 50	+200
50–59	+150
60 and over	+100

2) Intermediate and high risk — decline.

Acute Lymphoblastic Leukemia (ALL)

The most important form of cancer and an important cause of death in North American children, the principles of ALL management include remission induction, treatment of potential sanctuary sites, consolidation regimes and chemotherapy maintenance. A study begun at St Jude's in 1967 followed this plan and produced the best early evidence of potential cure of ALL in children. Of 35 children treated, 31 entered a complete remission and 18 were alive and well in 1986. Refinements have allowed complete remission rates to surpass 90 percent, and five-year survival now exceeds 60 percent. Patients off treatment for four years in sustained first remission are considered potentially cured.

Treatment complications, in the form of tumors, have surfaced as a mortality consideration in ALL survivors. This complication affects about 8 percent of survivors at 10–20 years after treatment, the risk being some 10–20 times greater than the risk of first neoplasm in an age-matched general population.

ALL in adults has not the same promising outlook and is more analogous to ANLL (*see below*).

Rating

Description	Rating
ALL in childhood, treated	
Within 5 yr	Decline
Thereafter	
No relapse, clinically and	
hematologically well	5 per mil for 5 yr and + 100
Relapse	Decline
After further yr	Individual consideration
ALL in adult	Rate as for ANLL (*see below*)

Chronic Myelogenous Leukemia (CML)

CML is a clonal disorder affecting non-lymphoid hematological elements. Untreated or palliated by standard measures (busulfan, hydroxyurea), even markers of 'good' prognosis, such as Ph1 chromosome, identify individuals with median survival of only about 3·5 years. Eventual evolution to acute leukemia with or without an accelerated phase awaits CML patients; over three-quarters will be non-lymphoblastic, some 20 percent lymphoblastic. Overall treatment responses at this stage are disappointing or brief.

Autologous BMT provides temporary palliation only. Allogeneic or syngeneic BMT in chronic stable phase normalizes hematological parameters and eliminates Ph1 markers in over 80 percent. The five-year survival is 50–60 percent. Results in accelerated or blastic phase are strikingly worse, only 20 percent surviving to five years. BMT is a more important option in CML than CLL, given the broader age range of those affected.

Rating
1) Without BMT — decline.
2) With BMT:
Within 5 yr — decline.
Over 5 yr, stable and well — 7·5 per mil for 5 yr and + 50.

Acute Non-Lymphoblastic Leukemia (ANLL)

ANLL is an encompassing term for all acute leukemias of non-lymphoid lineage. Current FAB (French, American, British) classification identifies seven subgroups. In practice, similar management schemes apply except that the monocytic has a greater likelihood of CNS involvement and the promyelocytic variant an associated coagulopathy.

Regardless of type and treatment regime, long-term survival correlates best with length of healthy disease-free post-induction interval. Current best chemotherapy regimes induce complete remission in 50–90 percent but most relapse within 18–24 months. Some 10 percent, however, remain leukemia-free for years. For suitable candidates, BMT in first remission produces long-term survival and probable cure in 50 percent, an option currently available to a minority only.

Rating
1) Within 5 yr — decline.
2) Thereafter; disease-free and well regardless of treatment — 5 per mil for 5 yr and + 50.
See BMT if applicable.

Promyelocytic Leukemia (PC)
PC is one variant of ANLL and is separated from the rest because of recent evidence of cell differentiation and disease control using oral all-trans retinoic acid.[56] Hospital stay is limited and periods of control in excess of one year are regularly achieved. Although the condition should still be regarded in the same

light as ANLL for the time being, there is hope that PC may prove to be a controllable or potentially curable condition. Developments in this area will be followed with interest.

LEUKOCYTOSIS

In men a white blood cell count in excess of 9,000 appears to be an independent predictor of all-cause mortality compared with those with lower values (mortality rates increased 1·8 to 2·5 times in each of three age groups).[57] The excess risk associated with an increasing WBC was evident even within the normal range. It could be considered reasonable to apply a small debit to men with a consistently greater than borderline leukocyte increase in the absence of a firm diagnosis. Those with a demonstrable background process should be rated for cause.

BONE MARROW TRANSPLANTATION (BMT)

Human BMT has achieved the status of accepted (preferred in some cases) option in the management of selected hematological impairments. As a means of repopulating the depleted marrow compartment with viable healthy cells, BMT is currently indicated primarily in states of marrow under-production (aplasia), marrow replacement (leukemias) and selected life-threatening genetic disorders (e.g. SSA, thalassemia major, immune deficiency states, hereditary enzymopathies). Autologous (self) marrow rescue following intense chemoradiotherapy for malignant disease other than leukemia is a separate issue.

While disease states for which BMT is performed retain the underwriting implications appropriate and proportional to their post-transplant evolution, the transplant procedure itself may impact morbidity and mortality and hence call for an added independent rating. (The consideration of BMT patients is prompted by the information that some diseases for which the procedure is performed are curable following successful transplantation.)

Very briefly, the steps involved in allogenic or syngeneic marrow transplantation include (1) presence of a disease state for which BMT is a viable option, (2) identification of a suitable, as compatible as possible, related or random donor, (3) elimination of host marrow with chemotherapy and/or radiotherapy, (4) intravenous infusion of donor marrow in sufficient quantity, (5) supportive and prophylactic measures, including use of blood product support, antibiotic cover and use of anti-rejection drugs, (6) constant watch for, and prompt aggressive treatment of, complications, including rejection, infection with a variety of potential pathogens, interstitial pneumonitis and graft versus host disease (GVHD) both acute and chronic, and (7) long-term follow-up.

The procedure is being constantly modified and improved by fine tuning of preparatory regimes, modification of prophylactic and treatment anti-infectious regimes, refinement of immunosuppression and addition of options (such as marrow purging of T-cells and suppression of interleukin 2 and tumor necrosis factor in an attempt to reduce GVHD severity). It should be mentioned that alternatives to the use of marrow are being explored, including the harvesting and infusion of stem cells from compatible circulating or cord blood.

The complications[58] of most concern include lack of engraftment (rare), marrow rejection (uncommon), treatment (e.g. immunosuppression) complications, complications related to low counts (i.e. infection and hemorrhage), GVHD, recurrence of primary disease and risk of secondary diseases (e.g. leukemia). Chronic GVHD, recurrence of the primary disorder and long-term malignancy risk constitute the most worrisome delayed complications. The risk of each depends to some extent on the basic disease, the preparatory regime, the compatibility of the donor and the adequacy of immunosuppression (among other factors).

Chronic GVHD with skin, gut, joint and other manifestations is a particular concern, and its implications may range from inconvenience to a life threat.

Peculiarities of haploidentical or autologous BMT are beyond the scope of this brief overview. In principle, GVHD should be minimal or non-existent and complications of immunosuppression not a factor.

It may well be that as medical treatment modalities are perfected, BMT may disappear as a therapeutic option. Alternatively the adverse concerns associated with the procedure may be overcome, rendering the process uniformly simple, effective, safe and complication free. Until either of these scenarios prevails, the following approach to BMT seems appropriate.

Although it is sometimes difficult to separate the impact on mortality of the basic disease from that of treatment complications, acute and chronic GVHD clearly have an impact on overall survival post-BMT in several published studies.

Rating

See primary disease; otherwise as below.
1) Within 5 yr for leukemia, 2 yr for aplasia or congenital disorders — decline.
2) Over 5 yr or 2 yr as above:
No recurrence of primary disease, counts normal, minimal or no GVHD, no other complications — +100.
No recurrence of basic disease, counts normal, moderate GVHD — +300.
Severe GVHD — decline.
Complications other than GVHD — individual consideration.
Note Add rating for underlying disease if appropriate.

MONOCLONAL GAMMOPATHY OF UNDETERMINED SIGNIFICANCE (MGUS)

Monoclonal proteins are those single immunoglobulin components believed to be produced by an individual clone of plasma cells; they are detected most commonly as a dense band on protein electrophoresis, as a sharp peak on a densitometer tracing or as a distinct prominent arc on immunoelectrophoresis.

A number of monoclonal proteins reflect the presence of a plasma cell dyscrasia syndrome (myeloma, macroglobulinemia, heavy chain disease, amyloidosis of primary immunoglobulin origin); others accompany a variety of other disorders (e.g. chronic infections, non-lymphoreticular neoplasms, auto-immune diseases). The latter may be loosely termed secondary monoclonal gammopathies.

These two categories aside, there remains a group of otherwise well individuals who are documented to have a monoclonal gammopathy without detectable cause or associated disease process.[59] The term benign monoclonal gammopathy was originally applied to this group, but because a certain percentage evolve over time, the term MGUS is preferred. The incidence of MGUS is uncertain but probably affects 1 percent of adults in general, about 3 percent of individuals over the age of 70 and 4–5 percent over the age of 80. Sixty percent are IgG, 14 percent IgA, 18 percent IgM and the rest IgD, light chain or multiclonal.

In contrast to the situation with multiple myeloma, MGUS patients typically have a low level of immunoglobulin which remains stable over time, a low percentage of bone marrow plasma cells which appear for the most part morphologically normal, no bony lesions, a limited amount of urinary light chain (Bence Jones protein) and absence of complications.

In a number of series a certain percentage of MGUS patients who appear typical at onset have evolved to myeloma; a few others have developed a separate process which may or may not be related to the gammopathy. In one particular series, which combined true MGUS and secondary gammopathies, 25 percent improved or remained stable, 50 percent died without developing plasma cell dyscrasias (cardiac, CVA, malignancies, infections, miscellaneous or unknown), while roughly 22 percent progressed to plasma cell disease (PCD). The remaining few had increase in protein but remained well. Median interval to development of non PCD illness was eight years; rate of progression to PCD was 17 percent at ten years, 33 percent at 20 years. As such, long-term follow-up is called for. For the rest, the outlook is favorable.

Rating

Description	Rating
1st yr	Postpone
Thereafter	
Stable	
First 5 yr	+50 to +100
Thereafter	+25 to +50
Changing protein levels, bony lesions, other	
complications suggestive of plasma cell dyscrasia	Decline
Development of a separate disease,	
not plasma cell dyscrasia	Rate separately

MULTIPLE MYELOMA

Multiple myeloma is a malignant neoplasm of committed plasma cells producing detectable monoclonal proteins and capable of causing bony changes, cytopenias, hypercalcemia and especially renal impairment. Melphalan and corticosteroids remain the mainstay of treatment. Five-year survival, all stages, all races, is barely 26 percent and has improved little in the past decade, despite advances in supportive care and trials with a number of new therapeutic approaches. Particularly disappointing, and in contrast with some of the leukemias, is the lack of a sustained remission in most of those achieving some measure of control.[60]

Based on general experience and on survival data, multiple myeloma remains an uninsurable condition.

HAIRY CELL LEUKEMIA (HCL): LEUKEMIC RETICULOENDOTHELIOSUS (LRE)

HCL is a descriptive term for a condition believed to be a neoplasm of B lymphocytes, the hallmark of which is a morphologically distinctive cell; effective long-term control appears possible at present.[61]

The hairy cell is a medium-sized mononuclear cell with hair-like cytoplasmic projections and an eccentric, often indented nucleus. The nucleus stains with acid phosphatase that is tartrate resistant (TRAP positive). The bone marrow may reveal only patchy hairy cell infiltration, is usually heavily fibrotic and may be somewhat hypocellular. Typical hairy cells are seen infrequently in other hematological conditions and the hairy cells in HCL patients are not always fully typical.

The HCL patient presents most often with non-specific symptoms, modest splenomegaly, the presence of hairy cells in blood, bone marrow and tissues, and various degrees of cytopenia. A few have an associated arteritis.

A few HCL patients will have an indolent course. In others with pancytopenia and splenomegaly, splenectomy may provide long-term control. For others or for splenectomized patients with continued disease manifestations, alpha-interferon or deoxycoformycin have proven beneficial. The latter appears to provide a greater chance of complete remission but has more adverse effects, and the long-term advantage of one over the other has not yet been demonstrated.[62] Whilst interferon, in particular, may produce only partial remission, judicious use of all options in sequence should contribute to making most cases of hairy cell leukemia a chronic, controllable, non-debilitating condition.

Rating

1) Indolent — +50 to +100.
2) Active:
Splenectomy, controlled — +100 to +200.
Interferon or deoxycoformycin — +100 to +200.
3) Progressive — decline.

NEUTROPENIA

Neutropenia refers to a decrease in peripheral blood polymorphonuclear leukocyte (neutrophil) count, a measure that gives a reasonably accurate picture of the entire neutrophil pool in most circumstances. Neutrophils being essential to combat a variety of foreign agents, the principal risk associated with neutropenia is a susceptibility to infection. Although granulocytopenia is technically a more general term (it encompasses other granulocytic white blood cells in addition to neutrophils), it is often used synonymously with neutropenia. Agranulocytosis, an extreme degree of granulocytopenia, usually refers to near absence of neutrophils.

The lower limit of neutrophils in healthy North Americans and Europeans is roughly 1,500 per mm^3. Counts vary somewhat by race, being noticeably lower in blacks in particular.

In fighting infection, adequate numbers and function of neutrophils are both required. When neutrophils function normally, the predisposition to sepsis related to decreasing neutrophils is roughly proportional to the count. Between 500 and 1000 per mm^3 the risk is moderate; below 500 per mm^3 the risk is extreme.

There are numerous potential mechanisms and causes of neutropenia. Counts may be low because of decreased production, increased destruction (mechanical, immune, ineffective cellular integrity), excess utilization, vascular margination, reduced marrow release to the circulation or loss from the body. Specific causes acting through one or more of these mechanisms may include congenital or acquired variants; the latter may be idiopathic or secondary (drugs, toxins, radiation, infections, sequestration etc). With defined causes, such as drugs, the neutropenia may be predictable (e.g. dose related) or idiosyncratic (i.e. unpredictable).

It is not possible to summarize the specifics of all neutropenic states, of which there are dozens of variants.

The management of neutropenia depends on the cause, severity, correctability and degree of risk: in acquired cases management involves elimination of potential causes, avoidance of sources of sepsis, antibiotic cover (after culture for established infection) and, in some cases, compatible leukocyte infusions; persistent cases warrant addition of measures to raise neutrophil counts in the form of corticosteroids, androgens, lithium or a variety of other measures and, in select cases, splenectomy to eliminate a prime site of presumed destruction.

For underwriting purposes, the main concern relates to ongoing risk of sepsis in persistent neutropenia or to the possibility of associated diseases then or later.

Rating

Description	Rating
Single episode	
Known cause, full recovery	+0
Incomplete recovery	Rate as persistent
Persistent	
Known cause	Rate for cause
Idiopathic or familial	
1,000–1,500/mm^3	+0
500–1,000/mm^3	+100
<500/mm^3	+200
Blacks	One-half above ratings
History of sepsis	
No serious episode for 3 yr	Credit −50
Frequent	Add +50
On steroids, immunosuppressants	Add +50

CHRONIC GRANULOMATOUS DISEASE (CGD)

When phagocytes meet suitably prepared bacteria or other stimuli, they activate a special internal pathway which produces antimicrobial activity. This burst of metabolic activity, available for call-up on demand, is mediated by a complex enzyme system dormant in resting leukocytes and known as respiratory burst oxidase.

CGD is an inherited disorder characterized by a phagocyte molecular defect making it impossible to mount an effective respiratory burst. As a result, affected individuals suffer recurrent infections. These infections, usually bacterial, sometimes fungal, tend to be frequent, severe, protracted and difficult to treat.

Clinical events usually onset in infancy or childhood, although mild cases may occasionally not be diagnosed until adulthood. Transmission is sex-linked in 60 percent (i.e. affecting primarily boys) and autosomal recessive in most of the remainder where sex incidence is equal.

Infections are often deep-seated, may occur in almost any site and are most often due to catalase-producing organisms. Additional clinical manifestations may include hepatosplenomegaly, delayed growth, granuloma formation with obstructive features and, in the long term, fibrosis or tissue destruction in various organs. Interestingly, patients tend to have no problem with streptococci or pneumococci, perhaps because these organisms provide CGD phagocytes with materials necessary for the bacterium's own destruction.

Documentation of the neutrophil defect is demonstrated by inability to express a respiratory burst (most commonly with the nitroblue tetrazoleum or NBT test) or deficient microbial killing potential.

Treatment calls for prevention and treatment of infection as dictated by circumstance (antibiotics, drainage, granulocyte infusions). Prophylactic antibiotic cover has proved valuable and, recently, regular gamma-interferon has been shown to reduce the relative risk of severe infection and reduce length of hospitalization. A variety of other unusual medications has been tried with limited success. BMT has cured individual patients, but well known BMT complications make this a last resort for a disease whose outlook is improving.[63]

Rating

Description	Rating
Mild form (discovery in adulthood)	+50
Common form	
Mild to moderate	+100 to +200
Severe	
General support	Decline
BMT	Rate as for BMT (see p. 652)
Gamma-interferon	+100

SPLENOMEGALY

The normal spleen performs the functions of filtration, phagocytosis and immune modulation. To be palpable in an average-sized normally developed adult, the spleen must be increased in volume some two-and-a-half times.

College-aged students may have transiently palpable spleens; a normal spleen may be palpated at times in postpartum women, very thin individuals or in those with low lying diaphragms (e.g. emphysema). These few exceptions apart, it is generally accepted that consistently palpable splenomegaly is abnormal and that the larger the spleen the likelier that pathology is present.

A cause can usually be assigned after investigation in most cases of splenomegaly, and it is difficult to find a published study relating mortality to undiagnosed splenomegaly *per se*. Several published series, however, do report splenectomy findings after in-depth non-surgical investigation failed to reveal an explanation for the enlarged spleens. [64,65] (In several studies roughly 10 percent of splenomegaly cases referred for splenectomy were for diagnostic purposes,[66] a percentage that is falling given availability of new diagnostic techniques.)[67] The vast majority of such spleens were found to be abnormal, the commonest pathology being infiltrative (in particular, hematological malignancies), congestion, inflammation, cysts, accentuation of normal physiological functions or a variety of miscellaneous causes.[68]

Of the 25 percent or so who remain undiagnosed after splenectomy (usually younger patients with smaller spleens), some 25 percent will develop a hematological malignancy within three years. Continued observation is therefore recommended after splenectomy performed for splenomegaly when pathology findings are non-diagnostic.

Those cases of splenomegaly for which a diagnosis can be established should be rated for cause. When an enlarged spleen is discovered during an insurance evaluation, postponing the application and referring to the attending physician is a reasonable course of action. Those cases being simply followed or those remaining undiagnosed after splenectomy may be rated as follows, subject to absence of symptoms, signs or laboratory anomalies. Cases remaining well for extended periods could then be looked on favorably.

Rating

Splenomegaly.
1) No other finding clinical or laboratory:
Mild ($\leq$2 cm) — +50.
Moderate (2–5 cm) — +100.
Large (>5 cm) — decline.
2) Symptoms, signs or low counts — decline.
3) Remaining well over 5 yr — +50 to +0.

SPLENECTOMY

That splenectomized children are at risk post-operatively for overwhelming sepsis with encapsulated organisms has been known for some time. The risk appears greater before adolescence and in those splenectomized for hematological disorders, and has been minimized by the use of prophylactic antibiotic cover (and possibly by the use of pneumococcal vaccine) as well as by prompt recognition and management of septic episodes.

It has more recently become evident that a mortality risk also exists for adults splenectomized for reasons of trauma (i.e. when no hematological or other condition is known to affect the spleen). The excess mortality risk in this case is from pneumonia, ischemic heart disease and (not significantly) cirrhosis.[69]

Rating

At present a number of insurers would accept otherwise well, splenectomized individuals at standard rates, but available evidence suggests a debit of +25 would not be unreasonable. Those splenectomized for rated hematological causes would likely be covered by the rating for the underlying disease.

HEREDITARY HEMORRHAGIC TELANGIECTASIA (HHT)

HHT is a vascular anomaly involving primarily the skin and mucous membranes; in most cases it is transmitted as an autosomal dominant trait. The US incidence is approximately 1 in 50–100,000, although pockets of much higher incidence there and elsewhere are not unknown.

The vascular lesion involves venule or capillary endothelial cell discontinuity and weakening of perivascular support. This becomes visible clinically as angiomas, telangiectasias or nodular vasculomas which are typically non-pulsatile and blanch on pressure. Lesions are seen most commonly on facial skin, fingertips, buccal and nasal mucosa, as well as internally, predominantly in the GI tract. Urinary tract involvement is uncommon. Arteriovenous fistulae in lungs or liver may present a particularly challenging form of HHT.

In general, tests of hemostasis are normal. One patient subset has a picture not incompatible with von Willebrand's disease.

Age of onset is quite variable, depending in part on manifestations and on the clinical acumen of examiners. A childhood presentation is not uncommon and clinical severity generally increases with age. Epistaxis, the most common feature (96 percent) in one large fixed-time series, was evident by the age of 20 in 58 percent, by the age of 45 in 90 percent.[70] Cutaneous telangiectasias were found in 74 percent, the presentation often being abrupt and the course progressive. In this series 25 percent suffered a visceral bleed, almost all from angiodysplasia in the GI tract.

The most serious sequelae, and those accounting for the greatest morbidity and mortality, are those of (1) intractable bleeding, (2) effects of A–V shunts,

(3) cirrhosis, and (4) intracranial vascular abnormalities resulting in epilepsy, cerebrovascular events or abscesses.

No specific treatment is available to modify the course of the lesions. Management may be simple or difficult depending on the clinical event and on accessibility of offending lesions. Those with a single A–V shunt amenable to surgical correction tend to do well. The approach to the more common HHT presentation involves avoidance of trauma, supportive care, nasal packs for epistaxis, cautery of bleeding lesions, iron replacement if indicated and blood transfusion for symptomatic anemia or profuse bleeding. Estrogens, once commonly used, are of unproven benefit and may be associated with distressing side effects. There may be a place for fibrinolysis inhibitors.

In general, the risk revolves round the complications mentioned above along with the frequency and severity of bleeding and accessibility of bleeding sites.

Rating

1) Single A V shunt surgically corrected:
Within 12 mth — postpone.
Thereafter, no further events — +0.
2) More typical presentation:
Infrequent accessible bleeds — +50.
Frequent severe bleeds poorly accessible or requiring more than one transfusion — +200.
3) Epilepsy — rate as for epilepsy (*see* pp. 739–40).

HEMOCHROMATOSIS

In contrast to other conditions of iron excess, hemochromatosis is an autosomal recessive primary iron-overload state in which iron deposition occurs preferentially in parenchymal cells of solid tissues. Resultant damage to affected organ systems accounts for the principal clinical manifestations of hepatic cirrhosis, diabetes mellitus, cardiomyopathy, hypogonadism, arthritis and skin bronzing. The genetic defect responsible for this relatively common disorder is believed to lie on the short arm of chromosome 6 in close proximity to the site of the HLA–A complex.[71] At the time of writing, the gene product remains unknown.

Intestinal dietary iron absorption in excess of need is believed to be operative in hemochromatosis. Additional physiological impairments are postulated to account, in particular, for preferential iron deposition within parenchymal rather than reticuloendothelial cells.

Iron stores in normal individuals total approximately 3–4 g and are present in various sites in functional and/or storage forms. All is available for mobilization and use. In hemochromatosis, increased absorption in the range of 1–3 mg per year has been recorded with a total pool of 15–50 g accumulated over four to five decades, corresponding to onset of clinical manifestations.

Caucasians of European ancestry are most often affected. Approximately 10 percent of whites carry one gene for hemochromatosis (heterozygotes) with 1 in

300–1,000 being homozygous. Men are affected more often than women, by a ratio of about 10:1; this is partly due to iron loss by women through menstruation.

Depending on the case and presentation, diagnosis of hemochromatosis rests on a combination of the clinical picture, increased transferrin saturation, elevated serum ferritin levels and biopsy proof of parenchymal iron deposition without reticuloendothelial overload. Recent published reports suggest that non-invasive procedures, such as liver CT and MRI scans, may play a role in diagnosis. HLA typing is valuable in the course of family studies.

Management of hemochromatosis consists of removing iron excess by phlebotomy. Initially phlebotomy may be performed every week and then a few times yearly, the object being to reduce iron stores to virtually nil. Aiming to obtain a borderline iron deficient state is a reasonable goal.

The prognosis of untreated hemochromatosis is poor. Prior to 1935, death occurred within one to five years of presentation. Ready availability of insulin brought survival to some four to five years. Early attempts at phlebotomy carried survival to between five and 15 years. Results from phlebotomy have continued to improve, even within the past decade, probably related to discovery and treatment of less severely affected cases.

A recent large series of cases, aggressively treated and carefully followed, has outlined current survival data and causes of death in hemochromatosis:[72]
1) Overall life expectancy remains shortened. Causes of death include liver neoplasm, cirrhosis, diabetes and cardiac dysfunction.
2) Non-cirrhotics and non-diabetics have survival curves virtually identical to age- and sex-matched controls.
3) The above holds true even though certain non-fatal complications, such as arthritis, may persist or even progress in spite of phlebotomy.
4) Removal of excess iron may halt progression of hepatic fibrosis in those with evident liver injury, but the risk of hepatoma remains.

Rating

Non-cirrhotic, non-diabetic, treated and followed — +0.
Early liver fibrosis or mild diabetic — +100.
Established cirrhosis, stable with treatment — rate as cirrhosis (see p. 579).
Diabetes — rate for severity (see Chapter 13).
Cardiomyopathy — decline.
Clinical information only — +100 up.
Heterozygotes — +0.

PORPHYRIAS

The hemoglobin molecule consists of two pairs of globin chains and the iron-containing heme component. In contrast to the hemoglobinopathies and thalassemia syndromes, which reflect globin chain disturbances, the porphyrias[73] are a group of disorders having in common an over-production of porphyrins and related compounds which are essential components of heme synthesis.

Heme synthesis is a complex multistage intracellular process regulated by a series of enzymes catalyzing the different steps in the biosynthetic pathway, a process which begins and ends within the mitochondrion and whose intermediate steps take place within the cytosol. A partial enzyme blockage at any step in the pathway results in an over-production of precursors and is associated with clinical disease. The disease entity reflecting a specific enzyme blockage tends, itself, to be more or less specific.

As heme production takes place primarily in developing erythroblasts and in the liver, the prophyrias are generally referred to as erythropoietic, hepatic or both.

With the exception of congenital erythropoietic porphyria, the porphyrias share an autosomal dominant inheritance pattern. In addition, clinical manifestations may exhibit periods of quiescence and exacerbations and, in some, inducibility. Finally, although the basic defect is enzymatic, assays of several of the enzymes are complex and laborious, to the extent that precursor over-production is relied on more commonly for laboratory assessment.

Erythropoietic Porphyrias

Erythropoietic Protoporphyria: Erythrohepatic Porphyria (EP)
EP is an autosomal dominant condition causing over-production of protoporphyrin by both erythroblasts and liver cells, occurring in roughly 4 per 100,000 of the population. Onsetting in childhood and more common in males, symptoms of photosensitivity range from itching and edema to blistering and ulceration, and eventually to scarring and altered pigmentation. Hepatic dysfunction is common but hepatomegaly, cirrhosis and liver failure rare. Mild anemia and cholelithiasis may occur. The clinical picture, family history and raised red cell protoporphyrins without other cause form the basis for diagnosis. Decreased sun exposure, beta-carotenes and oral iron are considered beneficial. Measures useful in other porphyrias, such as hematin and cholestyramine, are under study. Note that sunscreens are not protective.

Rating
Skin only, mild — +0.
Skin severe or hepatic component — +50.
Severe liver involvement — +200 to decline.
Cholelithiasis — rate separately (*see* p. 585).

Congenital Erythropoietic Porphyria (CEP)
CEP is a very rare autosomal recessive state marked by rebound over-production of uroporphyrinogen 1 and coproporphyrinogen 1. Manifestations, evident in infancy or early childhood, include staining of bones and teeth, extreme photosensitivity with vesiculation, scarring, alopecia, eye damage, significant hemolysis with dark urine and splenomegaly. Extensive mutilation is common and survival to middle age is rare. Available management includes transfusion for anemia (reduces intrinsic red cell production but has attendant risk of iron overload), splenectomy in select cases, reduced sun exposure and, recently, use of cholestyramine or charcoal (both probably reduce prophyrin reabsorption from the intestine). Use of hematin and beta-carotene are being assessed.

Rating

All cases, currently — decline.

Hepatic Porphyrias

Acute Intermittent Porphyria (AIP)

A not uncommon autosomal dominant disorder, AIP is caused by reduced amounts or dysfunction of porphobilinogen (PBG) deaminase. More common in women (about 75 percent) and onsetting clinically most often in adolescence or early adult life, the process shares with other hepatic porphyrias the common manifestations of pain, neuropsychiatric events and precipitation of crises by drugs, the perimenstrual state, malnutrition or other illnesses (particularly infections). The US prevalence is about 5–10 per 100,000.

Clinical events are varied and tend to fluctuate, but typical features include pain (most often abdominal), a multitude of neuropsychiatric and mood alterations, dark urine, hyper- or hypotension, and GI symptoms. Of precipitating factors, a number of drugs have been implicated, including alcohol, anesthetics, barbiturates, hypoglycemics, antiepileptics and sulfonamides. A family history is common and clinical manifestations range from modest to life threatening, the latter most often from widespread paralysis and respiratory failure. Photosensitivity is not a feature.

Diagnosis rests on the clinical picture, family history, dark urine and elevated urine levels of aminolevulinic acid (ALA), PBG, uroporphyrin and coproporphyrin (universal during attacks, less often found in between). Management includes symptomatic pain relief, glucose infusions, close monitoring for neurological crises, avoidance of non-essential surgery and, in severe cases, infusions of hematein (which probably serve to induce enzymes).

In an older study, mortality was 25 percent at five years, deaths being most often from general or respiratory paralysis. When continuous respiratory support is required, short-term survival is likely to be less than 50 percent.

The current outlook is probably not as bad as previously outlined, given newer diagnostic techniques, earlier diagnosis of less severe cases, newer treatment modalities and aggressive respiratory support.

Rating

Age	Rating
Under 20	Decline
20–39	+200
40–59	+100
60 and over	+50

Variegate Porphyria (VP)

VP is relatively common in white South Africans and is due to a decrease in the targeted enzyme resulting in over-production of protoporphyrinogen, coproporphyrinogen and uroporphyrinogen in urine, stools or red cells. During acute attacks ALA and PBG are also increased. Clinical features often include photosensitivity, mechanical skin fragility, hypertrichosis, neuropathy and pains. The variable clinical picture may make it hard to distinguish VP from other porphyrias, including AIP and HC. The distinction rests on the biochemical parameters, particularly elevated stool protoporphyrin. Precipitating factors, treatment regimes and outlook are not remarkably different from AIP.

Rating

Rate as for AIP (*see above*).

Hereditary Coproporphyria (HC)

In this, the least common of the hepatic porphyrias, the inheritance pattern is autosomal dominant and the enzyme block leads to over-production of coproporphyrin and its precursors. Clinical features, prophylaxis, exacerbating stimuli and treatment are not unlike those of AIP or VP. ALA and PBG may also be raised during episodes.

During acute attacks, urinary PBG and stool coproporphyrins will be found. As coproporphyrin is not entirely specific for HC, the demonstration of reduced lymphocyte levels of coproporphyrinogen oxidase would be diagnostic.

Rating

Rate as for AIP (*see above*).

Porphyria Cutanea Tarda (PCT)

PCT is the most common of the hepatic porphyrias. A number of cases are familial and autosomal dominant, others are sporadic. Males are affected more commonly (about 75 percent) and clinical onset is slightly later than with AIP. Uroporphyrin levels are elevated. Because of different induction at the biochemical level, precipitating agents are not necessarily the same as in AIP and acute neurological events are not a feature.

Series of PCT patients include a sizeable number of alcoholics. Clinical features include photosensitivity, liver disease, iron overload and, in some, hepatoma. Alcohol, estrogens and chemicals are common inducers, and associated diseases are not uncommon in particular infections and auto-immune disorders.

Rare homozygote cases demonstrate hemolysis, splenomegaly and dental discoloration.

The urine shows raised uroporphyrin, whereas the chemical features of AIP, VP and HC are not found. Along with clinical details, these features support the diagnosis. Again, enzyme estimation is more specific but not always available.

Treatment consists of avoiding precipitating causes, phlebotomy to remove excess iron (monitored against uroporphyrin excretion) and, in those unfit for phlebotomy, desferroxamine. Chloroquine has been beneficial in some by mobilizing tissue porphyrins.

Rating

Homozygous familial cases — decline.
Alcohol excess by history — decline.
Non-alcohol abusers, but hepatic dysfunction — +200.
Iron depleted, liver function normal or near normal — +100.

ADDITIONAL DISORDERS

Space limitations restrict the number of hematological impairments that may be legitimately covered at length. In closing, the following list is presented. Without in-depth review, it is felt that sufficient is known of the natural history of these disorders to allow segregation of those that may be accepted unrated (list A) or declined outright (list C) and those that are likely to be acceptable rated insurance risks subject to full details and individual consideration by medical staff (list B). Inclusion on the list is limited to those disorders of a primarily or exclusively hematological nature and not to those processes usually accompanying other impairments, such as disseminated intravascular coagulation (DIC).

List A
Infectious mononucleosis, uncomplicated, recovered.
Eosinophilia-myalgia syndrome, recovered.
Malaria, treated successfully, recovered.
Purpura simplex.
Senile purpura.
Amyloidosis of aging.
Auto erythrocyte sensitization.
Auto DNA sensitization.
Gaucher's disease Type I.
Deficiency of clotting factor XII (Hageman trait).
(Primary) syndrome of sea blue histiocytes.
Histiocytosis X (eosinophilic granuloma syndromes) onsetting after age five years
    (*see* p. 926).

List B
Pure red cell aplasia.
Methemoglobinemia.
Sulfhemoglobinemia.
Spurious polycythemia.
Some types of amyloidosis other than primary and age-related.
Deficiency of blood clotting factors V, VII, X, XI, XIII.
Most unstable hemoglobins.
Hypercoagulable states related to inherited deficiencies of antithrombin III,
    protein C and protein S.
Most congenital platelet dysfunctions, including Bernard Soulier syndrome,
    thrombasthenias and storage pool disorders.
Hodgkin's disease.
Some non-Hodgkin lymphomas.
List C
Amyloidosis of immunoglobulin origin (primary).
Gaucher's disease Types II and III.
Niemann Pick disease.
Tay-Sachs disease.

Erythroleukemia.
Waldenstrom's macroglobulinemia.
Gamma heavy chain disease.
Alpha heavy chain disease.
Preleukemias.
Systemic mastocytosis.

It is possible for impairments to migrate from one list to another, subject to a change in disease evolution. It is equally possible for a disease, after study, to be included on more than one list, depending on severity of manifestations. Finally, individuals with declinable disorders in principle may become acceptable risks subsequent to definitive curative therapy (e.g. BMT, enzyme replacement or (in the future) gene manipulation).

REFERENCES

1 Scully RE (editor). Case records of the Massachusetts General Hospital. *N Engl J Med* 1986; 314: 39–49.
2 Dunagan WC, Ridner ML (editors). Table of laboratory values. *Manual of Medical Therapeutics*, 1989; 26th edition: 505–11.
3 Williams WJ, Beutler E, Erslev AJ, Rundles RW (editors). SI unit conversion table. In: *Hematology* (2nd edition), 1977; 1663.
4 Fleming. FF. Iron deficiency in the tropics. In: Disorders of iron metabolism. *Clins in Hematology* 1982; 11 (2): 365–88.
5 Elwood PC. The clinical evaluation of circulating hemoglobin level. In: Anemia and hypoxia. *Clins in Hematology* 1974; 3 (3): 705–18.
6 Carson GL, Spence RK, Poses RM, Bonavita G. Severity of anaemia and operative mortality and morbidity. *Lancet* 1988; 1: 727–9.
7 Webb DKH. Aplastic anaemia: continued cause for concern. *Br Med J* 1990; 1105–6.
8 Hamajima N, Sasaki R, Aoki K, Shibata A. A notable change in mortality of aplastic anemia observed during the 1970s in Japan. *Blood* 1988; 72 (3): 995–9.
9 Hine LK, Gerstman BB, Wise BP, Tsang Y. Mortality resulting from blood dyscrasias in the United States, 1984. *Am J Med* 1990; 88: 151–3.
10 Pineo GF. Acquired severe aplastic anemia. *Annals of Royal College of Physicians and Surgeons of Canada* 1989; 22 (2): 105–8.
11 Bone marrow transplantation for aplastic anemia. In: Lew EA, Gajewski J (editors). *Medical Risks: trends in mortality by age and time elapsed*. New York: Praeger, 1990. Abstract 1413: 14–36, 14–37.
12 Witherspoon RP. Long-term results of bone marrow transplantation for leukemia or aplastic anemia. *Proc ALIMDA* 1988; 144–54.
13 De Planque MM, Bacigalupo A, Howe JM et al. Long-term follow-up of severe aplastic anaemia patients treated with antithymocyte globulin. *Br J Haem* 1989; 73: 121–6.
14 Gluckman E. Bone marrow transplantation for Fanconi's anemia. In: *Baillière's Clinical Hematology* 1989; 2: 153–62.
15 Rotoli B, Luzzatto L. Paroxysmal nocturnal hemoglobinuria. In: *Baillière's Clinical Hematology* 1989 (1); 2: 113–35.
16 Lindenbaum J, Healton EB, Savage DG et al. Neuropsychiatric disorders caused by cobalamin deficiency in the absence of anemia or macrocytosis. *N Engl J Med* 1988; 318: 1720–8.
17 Brinton LA, Gridley G, Hrubec Z et al. Cancer risk following pernicious anaemia. *Br J Cancer* 1989; 59: 810–13.
18 Gattermann N, Aul C, Schneider W. Two types of acquired idiopathic sideroblastic anaemia. *Br J Haem* 1989; 74: 45–52.
19 Agre P. Hereditary spherocytosis: grand rounds at the Johns Hopkins Hospital. *JAMA* 1989; 262: 2887–90.

20 Eber SW, Armbrust R, Schroter W. Variable clinical severity of hereditary spherocytosis: relation to erythrocytic spectrin concentration, osmotic fragility and autohemolysis. *J Pediatrics* 1990; 117: 409–16.

21 Palek J. Hereditary elliptocytosis and related disorders: the red blood cell membrane. *Clins in Hematology* 1985 (Feb): 45–87.

22 Beutler E. Glucose 6-phosphate dehydrogenase deficiency. In: Williams WJ, Beutler E, Erslev AJ, Rundles RW (editors). *Hematology* (2nd edition), 1977; 466–79.

23 Yoshida A, Beutler E. G6PD variants: another update. *Ann Human Genetics* 1983; 47: 25–38.

24 Zanella A, Colombo MB, Miniero R et al. Erythrocyte pyruvate kinase deficiency: 11 new cases. *Br J Haem* 1988; 69: 399.

25 Boivin P, Ottenwaelter T. Anémie hémolitique héréditaire par déficit de pyruvate-kinase: pronostic des formes néo natales. *La Nouvelle Presse Medicale* 1982; 11: 917–19.

26 Smith JA. The natural history of sickle cell disease. In: Sickle cell disease. *Annals of the New York Academy of Science* 1989; 565: 104–8.

27 Leiken SL, Gallagher D, Kinney TR et al. Mortality in children and adolescence with sickle cell disease. *Pediatrics* 1989; 84: 500–8.

28 Murthy VK, Haywood LJ. Survival analysis by sex, age group and hemotype in sickle cell disease. *J Chron Dis* 1981; 34: 313–19.

29 Kark JA, Posey DM, Schumacher HR, Ruehle CJ. Sickle cell trait as a risk factor for sudden death in physical training. *N Engl J Med* 1987; 317: 781–7.

30 Lucarelli G, Galimberti M, Polchi P et al. Bone marrow transplantation in patients with thalassemia. *N Engl J Med* 1990; 322: 417–21.

31 Zurlo MG, DeStefano P, Borgna-Pignatti C. Survival and causes of death in thalassaemia major. *Lancet* 1989; 2: 27–30.

32 Kim HC, McMillan CW, White GC. Clinical experience of a new monoclonal antibody purified factor IX: half-life, recovery and safety in patients with hemophilia B. *Seminars in Hematology* 1990; 27 (2): 30–5.

33 Hemophilia. In: Lew EA, Gajewski J (editors). *Medical Risks: trends in mortality by age and time elapsed.* New York: Praeger, 1990. Vol 2, Abstract 1412: 14–34, 14–35.

34 Rosendaal FR, Varekamp I, Smit C et al. Mortality and causes of death in Dutch haemophiliacs, 1973–1986. *Br J Haem* 1989; 71: 71–6.

35 Ruggeri ZM, Zimmerman TS. Von Willebrand factor and Von Willebrand disease. *Blood* 1987; 70: 895–904.

36 Miller JL. Von Willebrand disease: platelets in health and disease. *Hematology Onc Clin N Am* 1990 (Feb): 107–28.

37 Rose E, Forster A, Aledort LM. Correction of prolonged bleeding time in Von Willebrand disease with humate P. *Transfusion* 1990; 30: 381.

38 Nand S, Messmore H, Gross Fisher S et al. Leukemic transformation in polycythemia vera: analysis of risk factors. *Am J Hematology* 1990; 34: 32–6.

39 Hasselbalch H. Idiopathic myelofibrosis: a clinical study of 80 patients. *Am J Hematology* 1990; 34: 291–300.

40 Tobelem G. Essential thrombocythemia. *Baillière's Clinical Hematology.* Platelet Disorders, 1989 (July): 719–28.

41 Belluci S, Janvier M, Tobelem G et al. Essential thrombocythemia: clinical evolutionary and biological data. *Cancer* 1986; 58: 2440–7.

42 Millard EM, Hunter CS, Anderson M et al. Clinical manifestations of essential thrombocythemia in young adults. *Am J Hematology* 1990; 33: 27–31.

43 Hehlmann R, Jahn M, Baumann B, Kopcke W. Essential thrombocythemia: clinical characteristics and course of 61 patients. *Cancer* 1988; 61: 2487–96.

44 Kaplan BS, Proesmans W. The hemolytic uremic syndrome of childhood and its variants. *Seminars in Hematology* 1987; 24 (3): 148–60.

45 Martin DL, MacDonald KL, White KE et al. The epidemiology and clinical aspects of the hemolytic uremic syndrome in Minnesota. *N Engl J Med* 1990; 323: 1161–7.

46 Bell WR, Braine HG, Ness PM, Kickler TS. Improved survival in thrombotic thrombocytopenic purpura — hemolytic uremic syndrome: clinical experience in 108 patients. *N Engl J Med* 1991; 325 (6): 398–403.

47 Kwaan HC. Clinicopathologic features of thrombotic thrombocytopenic purpura.

Seminars in Hematology 1987; 24: 71–81.
48 Rose M, Eldor A. High incidence of relapses in thrombotic thrombocytopenic purpura: clinical study of 38 patients. *Am J Med* 1987; 83: 437.
49 Rock GA, Shumak KH, Buskard NA et al. Comparison of plasma exchange with plasma infusion in the treatment of thrombotic thrombocytopenic purpura. *N Engl J Med* 1991; 325 (6): 393–7.
50 Welborn JL, Emrick P, Acevedo M. Rapid improvement of thrombotic thrombocytopenic purpura with vincristine and plasmapheresis. *Am J Hematology* 1990; 35: 18–21.
51 Stefanini M. Idiopathic thrombocytopenic purpura (ITP): an analysis of 1122 cases. *Nouvelle Revue Fr d'Hématologie* 1990; 32: 129–35.
52 Berchtold P, McMillan R. Therapy of chronic idiopathic thrombocytopenic purpura in adults. *Blood* 1989; 74 (7): 2309–17.
53 Pizzuto J, Ambriz R. Therapeutic experience on 934 adults with idiopathic thrombocytopenic purpura: multicentric trial of the cooperative Latin American Group on hemostasis and thrombosis. *Blood* 1984; 64 (6): 1179–83.
54 Brazeau M. Outlook in leukemias. *Proc CLIMOA* 1988. 43rd Annual Meeting: 24–32.
55 French Cooperative Group on chronic lymphocytic leukaemia: natural history of stage A chronic lymphocytic leukaemia in untreated patients. *Br J Haem* 1990; 76: 45–57.
56 Wiernik PH. Acute promyelocytic leukemia: another pseudoleukemia? *Blood* 1990; 76 (9): 1675–7.
57 Delabry LO, Campion EW, Glynn RJ, Vokonos PS. White blood cell count as a predictor of mortality: results over 18 years from the normative aging study. *J Clin Epidem* 1990; 43 (2): 153–7.
58 Deeg HJ. Delayed complications and long term effects after bone marrow transplantation. *Hematology Onc Clin N Am* 1990; 4(3): 641–55.
59 Kyle RA, Lust JA. Monoclonal gammopathies of undetermined significance. *Seminars in Hematology* 1989; 26 (3): 176–200.
60 Cancer Statistics Review 1973–1987. National Cancer Institute, Division of Cancer Prevention and Control Surveillance Program. US Dept of Health and Human Services, 1989: IV–9, V–33.
61 Catovsky D, Golde DW, Golomb HM. The third international workshop on hairy cell leukemia. *Br J Haem* 1990; 74: 378–9.
62 Horning S. Toward defining an optimal therapy for hairy cell leukemia. *J Nat Cancer Inst* 1989; 81 (15): 1120–1.
63 Babior BM, Woodman RC. Chronic granulomatous disease. *Seminars in Hematology* 1990; 27 (3): 247–59.
64 Bowdler AJ. Splenomegaly and hypersplenism. In: The spleen. *Clins in Hematology* 1983 (June): 467–88.
65 Hermann RE, DeHaven KE, Hawk WA. Splenectomy for the diagnosis of splenomegaly. *Annals of Surgery* 1968; 896–901.
66 Goonewardene A, Bourke JB, Ferguson R, Toghill PJ. Splenectomy for undiagnosed splenomegaly. *Br J Surg* 1979; 66: 62–5.
67 Mitchell A, Morris PJ. Surgery of the spleen. In: The spleen. *Clins in Hematology* 1983 (June): 565–90.
68 Letoquart JP, Casa C, Grosbois B et al. La splenectomie a visée diagnostique. A propos de trente huit cas. *Annales de Chirurgie* 1990; 44: 342–7.
69 Robinette CD, Fraumeni JF Jr. Splenectomy and subsequent mortality in veterans of the 1939–1945 war. *Lancet* 1977; 127–9.
70 Plauchu H, deChadarévian JP, Bideau A, Robert JM. Age related clinical profile of hereditary hemorrhagic telangiectasia in an epidemiologically recruited population. *Am J Med Genetics* 1989; 32: 291–7.
71 Smith LH Jr. Overview of hemochromatosis. *Western J Med* 1990; 153: 296–308.
72 Strohmeyer G, Niederau C, Stremmel W. Survival and causes of death in hemochromatosis: observations in 163 patients. In: Hemochromatosis. Proceedings of the First International Conference. *Ann New York Acad Sci* 1988; 526: 245–57.
73 Rubenstein E, Federman DD (editors). The porphyrias. *Sci Am Med* 1988; Section 9: V-1 to V-12.

CHAPTER 22

ENDOCRINE DISORDERS

RICHARD J MACKLER

Endocrine glands are organized collections of specialized cells that synthesize and release into the blood stream chemical products affecting other glands, tissues, and organs. The effects are extremely varied, and include growth, energy production, sexual development and function, and electrolyte secretion. One of the commonest endocrine disorders, diabetes mellitus, has such far-reaching effects on morbidity and mortality that it requires a chapter to itself (see Chapter 14). Disorders of the endocrine glands usually produce their clinical effects by overproduction or underproduction of the hormones.

HYPOTHALAMUS AND PITUITARY GLAND

The hypothalamus is made up of interconnected clusters of groups of cells located at the base of the brain. Below the hypothalamus, and connected to it by a stalk, is the pituitary gland or hypophysis, which is divided into an anterior lobe (adenohypophysis) and a posterior lobe (neurohypophysis). The hypothalamus communicates with the anterior lobe by capillaries that carry hypothalamic releasing hormones; the releasing hormones stimulate the discharge of hormones synthesized in the anterior pituitary. The hypothalamus communicates with the posterior lobe by a nerve transport system that carries hormones produced in specific hypothalamic nuclei to the pituitary for secretion directly into the blood under appropriate stimulus. The pituitary gland lies in a depression of the sphenoid bone, the sella turcica, and is covered by a layer of tissue called the diaphragma sellae, through which the pituitary stalk passes. Tumors of the pituitary gland large enough to extend above the diaphragma sellae are said to have suprasellar extension.

Formerly the cells of the anterior pituitary were divided into three types according to their histological staining characteristics, and the accumulations of cells comprising tumors of the pituitary were named accordingly. For example, tumors secreting excessive growth hormone were called eosinophilic tumors, tumors secreting excessive ACTH were called basophilic tumors, and non-secretory tumors were called (and often are still) chromophobe adenomas. Currently, the hormones of the pituitary are readily detectable in the blood, and not only can the quantities be measured precisely, but the hormone levels can be suppressed and stimulated by injecting various substances into the patient. When the tumor is removed, new immunocytological staining techniques can localize the granules of hormone in the cells, and these granules can be seen by electron microscopic examination. Therefore the pituitary cells and the pituitary tumors are currently classified according to their functional capacity: we speak of growth-hormone secreting cells and tumors (or acromegaly), and ACTH-secreting cells and tumors (or Cushing's disease).

The cells of the anterior lobe of the pituitary gland secrete several different polypeptide hormones of clinical significance. Those referred to in this chapter are TSH or thyroid stimulating hormone (also called thyrotropin), ACTH or adrenocorticotropic hormone, FSH or follicle stimulating hormone, LH or luteinizing hormone, GH or growth hormone, and PRL or prolactin. Other important hormones have been identified, but their role in disease processes is not clear, and many other hormones await identification. The polypeptide hormones secreted by the pituitary act on the endocrine end-organs (thyroid, adrenal, ovary, testis, and other tissues diffusely), but the pituitary in turn is subject to the release of small peptides secreted by the hypothalamus. These chemical messengers are transported from small groups of cells in the hypothalamus to the pituitary, acting to stimulate or inhibit the release of TSH, ACTH, FSH, LH, GH and PRL. The hypothalamic hormones that have been characterized include thyrotropin releasing hormone (TRH), which provokes the release of TSH and PRL, corticotropin releasing hormone (CRH), which stimulates release of ACTH, gonadotropin releasing hormone (GnRH or LHRH), which stimulates release of both LH and FSH, growth hormone releasing hormone (GRH), which stimulates release of GH, and somatostatin (also called growth hormone release inhibiting hormone), which acts to inhibit the release of GH and several other hormones. Most of these hypothalamic hormones are available for dynamic testing of the pituitary gland, and one, GnRH, is currently used for the treatment of gonadal failure caused by hypothalamic deficiency.

The posterior pituitary secretes two peptide hormones, which are synthesized in the hypothalamus and transported directly by nerve axons. The first is the antidiuretic hormone or ADH, which enhances reabsorption of water from the renal glomerular filtrate, decreasing urine flow in states of dehydration. A second hormone, oxytocin, acts chiefly to promote contraction of the pregnant uterus and to eject milk during lactation.

HYPOTHALAMIC-PITUITARY-ENDOCRINE GLAND FEEDBACK

Many complex interactions govern the secretion of the endocrine hormones into the bloodstream, but in general terms it is correct to say that the hypothalamic hormones stimulate the pituitary hormones, which in turn stimulate the endocrine end-organs to release their own hormones, which finally act in part to suppress the hypothalamus and the pituitary. This concept of feedback mechanism is basic to the investigation of endocrine disorders. In cases where an endocrine gland fails to produce hormones, the pituitary stimulatory hormone will increase. For example, as the ovary ceases to function in menopause, the estrogen levels decline, and consequently the levels of LH and FSH rise. When estrogens are administered in menopause, they are not used to correct a disease state, but to control the symptoms of flushing and mental distress, to prevent osteoporosis, and to restore atrophic vaginal tissue. (The goal of therapy is not to restore the LH and FSH to normal, but to improve symptoms.) When the thyroid gland fails to function, the TSH rises as the levels of thyroxine and triiodothyronine decline. In this case the TSH becomes a useful diagnostic test, for after the administration of thyroxine in adequate dose the TSH falls to normal.

In some cases the endocrine end-organ becomes overactive and autonomous, independent of the hypothalamus and pituitary. In these situations the pituitary hormones are suppressed, and such suppression is a useful diagnostic test. For example, in cases of autonomous tumors of the adrenal gland, the cortisol level is increased and the ACTH is suppressed; in cases of hyperthyroidism, the TSH levels may be suppressed while thyroxine and triiodothyronine are elevated.

The many levels of endocrine function mean that failure of a gland to produce the expected hormone can be caused by the 'primary' failure of the gland due to intrinsic disease, by the 'secondary' failure of the gland because of pituitary disease, or by 'tertiary' failure of the gland because of hypothalamic dysfunction. For example, primary hypothyroidism is caused by intrinsic thyroid disease; secondary hypothyroidism is caused by an impaired release of TSH by the pituitary; and tertiary hypothyroidism is caused by an impaired release of TRH by the hypothalamus. In all three cases the serum levels of thyroxine are low, but in the first the TSH is elevated, in the second the TSH is not elevated but responds to stimulation when TRH is injected, and in the third the TSH does not respond to TRH. In all three cases administration of the principal thyroid hormone, thyroxine, corrects the deficiency.

ANTERIOR PITUITARY

Adult Hypopituitarism

Complete or partial destruction of the anterior pituitary gland leads to deficiency of all or some of its hormones. The most important deficiencies are those caused by failure to secrete TSH and ACTH, because the secretions of the thyroid and the adrenal are necessary to support life. Thyroid deficiency is very easy to treat: the thyroid hormone (usually thyroxine) is administered only once daily, and because the half-life of the compound in the body is longer than a week, the omission of a dose or two is of no clinical significance whatever. Adrenal replacement is a more difficult matter. Usually the adrenal hormones are administered in a pattern that mimics the secretion of the gland, with the major dose taken in the morning and a smaller dose in the late afternoon. If the hormone is not taken on a regular basis, the patient experiences all the symptoms and all the dangers of Addison's disease (*see* pp. 717–18). The normal adrenal gland is able to increase its secretion tenfold in periods of stress. The patient dependent on adrenal hormones for life must learn to increase the replacement medication when warranted by major stress (e.g. trauma, infection, surgical procedures, severe emotional disturbance) to avoid the life-threatening complication of adrenal crisis. Therefore patients with ACTH deficiency have to develop the same expertise and judgment in adjusting the daily corticosteroid dosage as patients with Addison's disease.

Deficiency in the other pituitary hormones (GH, FSH and LH) has lesser clinical consequences than TSH and ACTH deficiency. Without FSH and LH the female is infertile, and the male not only infertile but sexually impotent. The administration of estrogens and androgens is not difficult and has little effect on mortality. GH is of little importance clinically once adult height is attained.

Therefore the risk to life in hypopituitarism is dependent on (1) the nature of the causative lesion, and (2) the proper replacement of thyroid and adrenal hormones. The cause of anterior pituitary deficiency might be a tumor of the pituitary, of the pituitary stalk (craniopharyngioma), or of the hypothalamus, and the tumor might be primary or metastatic from another site. The cause might be sarcoidosis, histiocytosis X, hemochromatosis, infection (e.g. syphilis), or trauma. A well known cause of hypopituitarism is necrosis of the anterior pituitary following postpartum blood loss with hypotension, called Sheehan's syndrome. Other causes are iatrogenic, such as hypophysectomy performed to arrest diabetic retinopathy and metastatic breast carcinoma.

Prognosis and Rating

The postoperative mortality risk associated with pituitary and related tumors has already been discussed (*see* p. 645); any additional risk depends on the resultant deficiency of ACTH. The risk is theoretically a constant one regardless of age, but is rather higher in the first few years of treatment as the patient gains experience in adjusting the dose of corticosteroids. Where there is no mortality rating for the primary lesion of the pituitary (e.g. postpartum necrosis), the ratings for panhypopituitarism requiring corticosteroid replacement would be:

Time since start of treatment	Rating
Within 1 yr	Postpone
2nd yr	3 per mil for 3 yr
3rd yr	2 per mil for 2 yr
4th yr	2 per mil for 1 yr
Thereafter	Standard

Note 1 If the primary lesion responsible for panhypopituitarism is ratable (e.g. a pituitary adenoma or craniopharyngioma), the additional debit for corticosteroid replacement need only be applied during the first three years of treatment.

Note 2 In partial hypopituitarism where corticosteroid replacement is unnecessary the need to replace other hormones, such as T4 or the sex steroids, is not normally considered a significant hazard to life. In such circumstances no additional rating would be required.

Most cases of hypopituitarism are now adequately characterized before an application for life insurance is made. This is due to the availability of (1) dynamic testing using the hypothalamic hormones to assess pituitary reserve, and (2) the new imaging techniques. However, the life underwriter may have to face cases where the investigation was incomplete by current standards and where no precise diagnosis has been made. There is a risk that a slowly progressive tumor might have escaped diagnosis on initial imaging studies. In these circumstances it would be prudent to defer applications for a period of two years from the time of diagnosis to see whether a tumor manifests itself. Where modern scanning techniques have been used with negative findings, the deferment period may be shortened if a repeat scan is negative.

Following the deferment period, and provided the applicant has fully recovered and remained stable on hormone replacement therapy, the ratings outlined above would be appropriate. If, however, there is any suggestion of poor control of corticosteroid dosage a table rating of +50 to +75 should continue after the 4th year.

Childhood Hypopituitarism

In childhood, deficiency of GH will lead to growth retardation, and the deficiency can be remedied by injection of synthetic GH. GH deficiency may occur in isolation, or in association with a deficiency of the other pituitary hormones. When the cause is a tumor, the applicant must be refused until there has been a radical cure. Cases of isolated GH deficiency would be standard. Cases with combined hormone deficiencies without known cause may be rated analogously with adults.

Growth Hormone Hypersecretion: Acromegaly

When the body is exposed to excess GH before the skeleton has matured, there is a marked increase in height (gigantism); but when there is a prolonged excessive circulation of growth hormone after the epiphyses have fused, there is a characteristic overgrowth of skeletal parts and soft tissues (acromegaly). Initially the changes are insidious, but with time there is not only enlargement of the hands and feet, but coarsening of the features, with prominent supraorbital ridges, thickened lips, enlarged tongue and prognathism. Although the physical appearance may become static, the disease is rarely 'burned out', and the oversecretion of GH continues until treatment is initiated. Because the disease is often discovered late, many patients have headaches and visual field defects from tumor enlargement, and often some degree of hypopituitarism from tumor compression of the anterior pituitary.

Untreated acromegaly does not have the short-term fatality associated with other untreated endocrine hypersecreting states, such as Cushing's disease and thyrotoxicosis, but it carries an increased mortality from a strong association with hypertension, heart disease and diabetes mellitus; respiratory disease is also more common than normal.

The vast majority of cases of acromegaly are caused by GH-secreting tumors of the pituitary. There are rare cases where ectopic tumors, usually malignant, secrete GH, and cases where the tropic hormone of the hypothalamus, GHRH, is secreted by a tumor.

Treatment and Prognosis

The goal of treatment is to reduce GH levels to normal, reversing some of the soft tissue changes as well as diabetes mellitus and hypertension. The majority of cases are currently treated by transsphenoidal surgery. In cases of very large tumors, the considerably more dangerous transfrontal approach may be needed. Other therapeutic approaches include heavy-particle radiation (available in few centers), external pituitary irradiation using a linear accelerator or supravoltage, and intrasellar implantation of radioactive yttrium or gold. Radiation is slower than surgery and more likely to lead to hypopituitarism. Bromocriptine in large doses decreases the GH levels in acromegalic patients, but is usually used when surgery has not been wholly successful.

Rating

Untreated acromegaly, no large suprasellar extension of tumor, no hypopituitarism, no hypertension, heart disease or diabetes — +200.
Medical treatment alone, continuing — +150.
Successful surgery or radiotherapy, with or without adjunct medical therapy, with growth hormone oversecretion corrected and tumor removed or arrested:

Time since start of treatment	Rating
Within 1 yr	+150 and 3 per mil for 2 yr
2nd yr	+150
3rd yr	+100
4th yr	+75
Thereafter	+50

Hyperprolactinemia: Prolactinoma

Prolactin is secreted by cells of the anterior pituitary. Its secretion is regulated by the hypothalamus, which tonically inhibits its release by the small peptide, dopamine. The medications used to reduce PRL are therefore dopamine agonists, and the most commonly used is bromocriptine. Because PRL is under tonic inhibition, tumors which press on the hypothalamus or the pituitary stalk may interfere with the secretion or passage of dopamine and therefore cause hyperprolactinemia, even though these tumors in themselves do not secrete PRL. Primary hypothyroidism may cause not only elevation of TSH but elevation of PRL as well. Hyperprolactinemia is also found in pregnancy, situations of physical and emotional stress, and in patients receiving a variety of common drugs, including cimetidine, antihypertensives (alphamethyldopa), tricyclic antidepressants, and antipsychotic medications (chlorpromazine, haloperidol).

The commonest cause of hyperprolactinemia is a tumor of the anterior pituitary called a prolactinoma. The clinical manifestations of prolactinoma in the female include galactorrhea and amenorrhea with anovulation. In males galactorrhea is less common, but sexual impotence is frequent. Most tumors are under 10 mm and are called microadenomas. Larger tumors, greater than 10 mm in diameter, are called macroadenomas; when they are large enough to produce a mass effect they may lead to visual field defects or headaches, or may interrupt the secretion of other anterior pituitary hormones. The actual PRL level is not a reliable indicator of the size of the tumor: small tumors may produce very high PRL levels, and large tumors may be poor secretors of PRL. The discovery of the tumor in males is usually late, when the tumor is a macroadenoma. CAT scanning is an indispensable tool of investigation, and establishes the size of the tumor.

Prognosis

There is no risk to life from the purely hormonal effects of hyperprolactinemia. The risk is mainly that associated with large extrasellar macroadenomas, which require a transfrontal surgical approach for their removal. However, the long-acting dopamine agonists (bromocriptine and analogues) are so effective in this disorder that they not only reduce the blood levels of PRL but even cause reduction in size of the prolactinoma, so long as the medication is continued. The therapies of choice are (1) transsphenoidal removal of the tumor and (2) bromocriptine therapy; in a few cases recourse is made to (3) external radiation. Because PRL measurement is part of the investigation of female infertility, many women with prolactinomas are placed on bromocriptine to induce ovulation; the medication is stopped after conception has occurred. Pregnant women with microadenomas suffer little morbidity; those with macroadenomas may experience enlargement of the tumors with visual field defects, requiring reinstitution of bromocriptine or even surgical intervention.

Rating

Medical treatment, ceased or continuing:
    Hyperprolactinemia, no cause found — standard.
    Microadenoma — standard.
    Macroadenoma, no suprasellar extension — +50.
    Macroadenoma, suprasellar extension — +100.
Surgical treatment, with or without subsequent medical treatment.
    Transsphenoidal, after recovery — standard.
    Transfrontal, within 1 yr — 3 per mil for 2 yr.
    Transfrontal, after 1 yr — standard.
Pregnancy, no medical treatment:
    Microadenoma — standard.
    Macroadenoma — 3 per mil for 1 yr.
    Following radiotherapy — standard.
Permanent replacement with cortiocosteroids — 2 per mil for 3 yr; thereafter standard.

POSTERIOR PITUITARY

Vasopressin Deficiency: Diabetes Insipidus

Diabetes insipidus is a disease characterized by an inability to secrete adequate amounts of antidiuretic hormone (ADH, also called vasopressin), which is necessary for urinary concentration. Patients excrete large, dilute amounts of urine, at least three liters daily and as many as twelve, causing intense thirst. The causes of diabetes insipidus include all the causes of anterior pituitary deficiency, including tumors, and surgical or radiation treatment of anterior pituitary tumors, as well as trauma, infection and infiltrative processes. There are also inherited forms of ADH deficiency.

Rating

Just as in anterior pituitary disease the rating in posterior pituitary disease is for the primary cause. Control of the hormonal deficiency is provided by an analogue of vasopressin, desmopressin or arginine vasopressin, which may be administered intranasally. Mild cases may take agents that are less expensive than desmopressin, such as the oral hypoglycemic chlorpropamide, which sensitizes the renal tubular cells to endogenous ADH. Therefore when diabetes insipidus is controlled or stable, and there is no rating for the primary cause, the risk is standard.

ADRENAL GLAND

The adrenal glands are divided anatomically and functionally into an outer layer (the cortex) and a central area (the medulla). The cortex produces three types of hormones: glucocorticoids, mineralcorticoids and sex hormones. The most important of the glucocorticoids is cortisol (also called hydrocortisone), which is controlled by the pituitary release of ACTH. Cortisol is a hormone essential for life, and is secreted in large amounts during periods of stress. The mineralocorticoids, of which the most important is aldosterone, act to prevent salt losses by the body. The adrenal sex hormones are androgens which play a role in the development of the secondary sexual characteristics of women. The medulla produces catecholamines, chiefly epinephrine (adrenalin) and norepinephrine (noradrenalin), which have widespread effects on cardiac rate and vascular tone.

Cushing's Syndrome; Adrenocortical Hyperfunction

Cushing's syndrome includes a number of clinical symptoms and signs caused by an exposure of the body to prolonged and excessive levels of cortisol or analogues of cortisol, either from overproduction by the adrenal glands or by administration for medical reasons. The clinical features include excess fat centrally distributed, especially in the cheeks (moon facies), chest (truncal obesity), upper dorsal region of the spine (buffalo hump), and above the clavicles (supraclavicular fat pads). Other clinical features include thin, atrophic and easily bruised skin, acne, facial plethora, weakness of the proximal muscles, osteoporosis with fractures, hypertension, abnormal glucose tolerance, and abnormalities in mood ranging from emotional lability to frank psychosis. Gastrointestinal ulceration may occur.

Untreated, Cushing's syndrome is not insurable. The risk associated with the successfully treated syndrome will depend on the nature of the underlying disorder that caused overproduction of the glucocorticoids by the adrenal gland.

The simplest cause of Cushing's syndrome is a benign tumor or adenoma of one adrenal gland, leading to overproduction of glucocorticoids, suppressing the ACTH production of the pituitary, and consequently causing atrophy of the contralateral adrenal gland. After the tumor is successfully removed, there is a cure, although the patient will require the administration of cortisol (or an analogue) to sustain life until the suppressed pituitary again secretes ACTH and the suppressed adrenal tissue responds with endogenous cortisol. A small temporary extra premium would cover the risk for the first year or two following surgery, after which the rating would be standard. If the pathological finding reveals that the tumor removed was an adenocarcinoma, the rating would be the same as that for a malignancy in this site.

Cushing's syndrome may be caused by neoplasms which produce ACTH, leading to hypertrophy of the adrenal glands; ACTH produced outside the pituitary gland is called ectopic ACTH. The diseases associated with ectopic ACTH include malignancies (e.g. bronchial oat-cell carcinoma and islet cell tumors of the pancreas), and some benign tumors (e.g. thymoma, bronchial carcinoid tumor, and pheochromocytoma). The prognosis in each case depends on the prognosis of the underlying tumor after treatment.

The majority (80 percent) of cases of Cushing's syndrome are caused by Cushing's disease, which specifically means pituitary-dependent adrenal hyperplasia. In these cases both adrenal glands are hypertrophied in response to overproduction of ACTH by the pituitary gland. The tumors responsible for the disorder may be exceedingly small, sometimes 2 mm across, and therefore often cannot be visualized by CT scan of the pituitary.

Treatment and Prognosis

There have been important changes in the treatment of Cushing's disease over the past two decades. When there was no radiological evidence of pituitary tumor, the treatment used to be removal of both adrenal glands. The treatment was effective, but entailed two disadvantages. First, the adrenalectomized patient was wholly dependent on corticosteroid replacement for life, experiencing the same problems as the patient with Addison's disease (see pp. 717–18). Secondly, in over 30 percent of the cases the initially undetectable pituitary tumor would grow, sometimes producing compression of the optic chiasma or deficiency in other pituitary hormones, and causing hyperpigmentation of the body through the massive overproduction of ACTH (Nelson's syndrome). The tumor that became evident after bilateral adrenalectomy was often aggressive in nature and difficult to resect.

The treatment of choice, where available, is transsphenoidal removal of the microtumor; in cases where the tiny tumor is not identified by the surgeon, core resection of the pituitary may be undertaken. Sometimes petrosal sinus sampling may help to locate the microtumor for the neurosurgeon. If the disease remits promptly after pituitary miscrosurgery, there is usually a permanent cure, and recurrence occurs in less than 3 percent of patients. In some cases where the initial microsurgery is unsuccessful, total hypophysectomy can be undertaken. The patient then will be cured of Cushing's disease, but will have the same morbidity as patients with panhypopituitarism.

Other modalities of therapy are the same as in acromegaly: external radiation using supravoltage or linear accelerators, heavy-particle irradiation, and implantation of radioactive yttrium or gold. These other modalities will damage other parts of the pituitary and lead eventually to hypopituitarism.

Rating

Applicants who have Cushing's syndrome at the time of application should be declined or deferred. Those who have been treated and who still have the disease or who have relapsed should also be declined or deferred.

Bilateral adrenalectomy, pituitary microsurgery, hypophysectomy, implant or external irradiation with remission:

Time since last treatment	Rating
Within 1 yr	Postpone
2nd yr	+150
3rd yr	+100
4th yr	+50
Thereafter	Standard

Adrenocortical Steroid Therapy

Hormone replacement therapy with glucocorticoid drugs for the treatment of primary hypoadrenalism or hypoadrenalism secondary to pituitary disease has already been discussed. Since these hormones are administered only in physiological amounts, no complications arising from the drugs themselves would be expected. The debits are given only to patients who are still inexperienced in the handling of the drugs and are therefore at risk of experiencing acute adrenal insufficiency.

In the majority of patients, cortisol (hydrocortisone) and its synthetic analogues are administered not for adrenal insufficiency but for the control or palliation of other diseases, where the dose requirement is far in excess of the physiological requirement. Complications are frequent, and these appear to depend on the corticosteroid dosage and the duration of therapy.

It is useful to have as a reference the various compounds administered to replace normal adrenal function (*see* Table 22.1).

Table 22.1. Average daily dose of various compounds for adrenal insufficiency.

Compound	Average daily dose (mg)	
	morning	afternoon
cortisone acetate	25	12·5
cortisol	20	10
prednisone	5	2·5
methylprednisolone	4	2
dexamethasone	0·75	0·375

Doses of corticosteroids in excess of double the usual morning dose lead to the symptoms described as Cushing's syndrome. In addition to these serious metabolic disturbances, withdrawal of the corticosteroid drugs can precipitate adrenal insufficiency similar to Addison's disease, because of the feedback suppression of pituitary ACTH with consequent atrophy of the adrenal glands. Withdrawal of the corticosteroids may also lead to relapse of the disease for which the drugs were instituted. (In a few cases the physician may administer ACTH rather than exogenous corticosteroids; this is to ensure that the adrenal glands do not become atrophic, though the symptoms of Cushing's disease still may occur.) In many disease states, the complications of the corticosteroids may be decreased by administering the medication only in the morning (to avoid suppressing the normal nocturnal surge of ACTH) and, when possible, on alternate days.

Common disease states for which corticosteroids are administered are asthma, sarcoidosis, inflammatory bowel disease, glomerulonephritis, organ transplantation, collagen-vascular disease, various forms of dermatitis, and leukemia.

The insurability of people receiving long-term corticosteroid therapy depends largely on the nature of the disease being treated. Diseases that have responded to the corticosteroids, with resolution of the inflammatory lesions, and that have become stable enough for an insurance offer, require an extra premium to cover the risks of long-term corticosteroid treatment. Topical administration of these compounds has less risk, because the therapy is rarely excessive and usually interrupted. Therefore aerosols, ointments and enemas are unlikely to suppress the adrenal glands or produce the symptoms of Cushing's syndrome.

Rating

The debits below should be added to those for the disease being treated. Oral corticosteroids, continuous treatment:
1) Dosage not exceeding 15 mg prednisone (or equivalent) per day:

Duration of treatment	Rating
Less than 4 yr	+50[a]
More than 4 yr	+75[b]

[a]Combined rating should not be less than 2 per mil.
[b]Combined rating should not be less than 3 per mil.

2) Dosage frequently more than 15 mg prednisone (or equivalent) per day — add +25 to above ratings.
3) History of significant complications: myopathy, osteoporosis with fractures, hypertension, diabetes, severe depression, gastrointestinal bleeding — minimum +100.

Congenital Adrenal Hyperplasia (CAH)

There are many enzymatic steps in the adrenal cortex leading to the production of cortisol and aldosterone. Defects in the enzymes may lead to a deficiency of cortisol, reducing the normal feedback to the pituitary, which responds to such deficiency by increasing the secretion of ACTH. The increased ACTH causes hypertrophy and hyperplasia of the adrenal cortex, sometimes restoring the cortisol level to normal, but at the cost of overproducing intermediary metabolites, which produce disease states in the body. The commonest enzymatic deficiency is called 21-hydroxylase defect. The overproduction of ACTH in this disease leads to an accumulation of androgens in the body, which in the female fetus causes masculinization of the genitalia (in the severest cases leading to wrong gender identification at birth). If untreated, the disease causes premature pubic and axillary hair, increased muscular development, and premature fusion of the epiphyses with short stature. Some female patients are diagnosed after childhood because of hirsutism and infertility; this disease is called late-onset 21-hydroxylase deficiency. Some patients, particularly in the vulnerable period of childhood, are subject to dehydration under stress. Patients with this tendency to fluid and electrolyte loss are called 'salt-losing'.

Since the primary abnormality in CAH is deficiency of cortisol and/or aldosterone, the rationale of treatment is to provide physiological quantities of glucocorticoids and mineralcorticoids, which will correct the deficient state, suppress the pituitary ACTH, and therefore prevent the overproduction of adrenal androgens.

Prognosis

If the disease is recognized early and treated properly, most patients with CAH should be able to lead normal lives. Some patients will require surgical correction of abnormal external genitalia. The main risk to life is the possible occurrence of an adrenal crisis during stressful illness, particularly in those patients with the salt-losing variety of 21-hydroxylase deficiency.

Rating

Stable endocrine status with treatment; no history of salt-losing episodes or adrenal insufficiency — standard.

History of salt-losing episodes or severe adrenocortical deficiency, currently stable:

Age	Rating
Under 10	Decline
10–19	+100
20 and over	Standard

Primary Hyperaldosteronism: Conn's Syndrome

Mineralcorticoid hypersecretion (chiefly aldosterone) by the adrenal cortex leads to sodium retention with resultant hypertension, and to potassium loss with resultant muscular weakness and cardiac irritability. When the cause is a unilateral benign adenoma, excision of one adrenal corrects the symptoms and the laboratory abnormalities. When the cause is bilateral hyperplasia of both adrenals, surgery is no longer recommended, and patients are treated with drugs that antagonize aldosterone, such as spironolactone or amiloride.

Rating

Disease due to unilateral adenoma successfully removed:

Time since removal	Rating
Within 1 yr	3 per mil for 2 yr
2nd yr	2 per mil for 1 yr
Thereafter	Standard

Disease present, electrolyte abnormalities corrected by aldosterone antagonists, normal blood pressure — +100.

Addison's Disease: Adrenocortical Hypofunction

Life cannot be sustained without the hormones produced by the adrenal cortex: the glucocorticoids (chiefly cortisol) and the mineralocorticoids (chiefly aldosterone). Addison's disease is the eponym for adrenocortical insufficiency. Formerly, the main cause of the disease was tuberculosis; currently most cases are idiopathic, caused by a presumed autoimmune process (similar to the process that leads to diabetes through islet cell destruction in the pancreas). Idiopathic Addison's disease is frequently accompanied by other autoimmune processes, such as pernicious anemia or hypothyroidism. Other causes of adrenocortical failure include metastatic tumor, intra-adrenal hemorrhage, hemochromatosis, and surgical excision of the adrenal glands. Incautious withdrawal of glucocorticoid therapy that has been administered long enough to suppress adrenal function may also lead to adrenal failure.

The clinical manifestations are usually slow and insidious, including weakness, weight loss, anorexia, postural hypotension, dehydration, hypoglycemia and increased pigmentation in the skin, mucous membranes and pressure areas (from the elevated ACTH levels in the absence of feedback suppression). There is a marked inability to withstand stress: when the patient is subject to major stress, such as infection, trauma or surgery, a life-threatening adrenal crisis takes place. This leads to shock and then death, unless adrenal hormones and fluids are promptly and aggressively administered.

Prognosis
With the availability of glucocorticoid and mineralcorticoid therapy, adrenal insufficiency is readily treated. Patients must learn how to increase their replacement medication to cover acute illness or stresses when they arise, and be instructed to go to their doctor or hospital for parenteral medication when they cannot tolerate pill replacement. Therefore deaths during Addisonian crisis in patients known to have adrenocortical insufficiency are rare, though not unknown.

Selection of Risks
Following diagnosis and institution of replacement therapy, there should be an initial period of deferment to allow full recovery and enable the applicant to gain experience in the self-administration of the medications. The main mortality is from acute adrenal crisis, which is expected to be highest in the first years following diagnosis and treatment.

Rating

Time since diagnosis and treatment	Rating
Within 1 yr	Postpone
2nd yr	2 per mil for 2 yr
Thereafter	Standard

Pheochromocytoma: Adrenal Medullary Hyperfunction

Pheochromocytoma is a tumor, usually of the adrenal medulla (90 percent of cases), which secretes excessive amounts of catecholamines (epinephrine and norepinephrine), hormones that have a rapid and profound effect on the cardiovascular system. Most tumors are benign, but 10 percent are malignant, and about 10 percent are bilateral (i.e. located in both adrenals). Since the tumors arise from cells of the sympathetic nervous system, they may originate wherever these cells are found outside the adrenal medulla, including the ganglia of the sympathetic chain, the ganglia of the aorta, even the urinary bladder. Uncontrolled, the disease leads to hypertension, either paroxysmal or persistent, which may be very severe, causing death from cerebral hemorrhage or cardiac arrhythmia. Symptoms include hypertension, palpitations, headache, pallor, sweating, and impaired glucose tolerance. The diagnosis is made by finding excessive levels of the catecholamines in the blood and in urinary collections; the urine is measured not only for epinephrine and norepinephrine but also for their metabolites, the metanephrines and vanillylmandelic acid (VMA). In addition to hormonal measurements, a variety of imaging procedures are used to localize the tumors before surgery. Malignancy is determined less by cell type than by extension into other tissues. Before surgery, specific medications – alpha-blockers (phenoxybenzamine, phentolamine) and beta-blockers (propranolol) – must be administered to block the effect of the catecholamines, in order to avoid death from intraoperative hypertension when the tumor is handled by the surgeons. When tumor resection has not been complete, these agents may be used postoperatively.

Rating

Applications for life insurance are postponed for one year after surgery to allow for physiological readjustment and return of blood pressure to normal. If after one year the symptoms have disappeared and the blood pressure is normal the rating would be standard.

Benign disease, no residual hypertension:

1)

Time since treatment	Rating
Within 1 yr	Postpone
Thereafter	Standard

2) Slight to moderate blood pressure impairment on examination — rate for blood pressure.

3) Persistent need for alpha-blockers, persistent hypertension — decline.
4) Operative evidence of malignancy — *see* Chapter 20.

THYROID GLAND

Non-toxic Goiter

Goiter is a term meaning enlargement of the thyroid gland. A toxic gland is one which causes overproduction of the thyroid hormones: thyroxine (called T4 because of the presence of four iodide atoms on the molecule) and triiodothyronine (called T3 because of the presence of three iodide atoms on the molecule). A non-toxic goiter is an enlarged gland that does not produce biochemical and clinical evidence of hypersecretion of the thyroid hormones. The 'simple' goiter is a diffusely enlarged gland; later it may become nodular.

Endemic goiter refers to thyroid enlargement found in a large proportion of a population under study, usually as a consequence of iodine deficiency in the diet. Such areas include the mountainous regions of the Andes and Himalayas, the Alps, New Guinea, and also areas of Central Africa and Indonesia. The deficiency in iodine, which is required for the production of T4 and T3 by the gland, leads to a decreased secretion of these two hormones. In some populations there is a consumption of foodstuffs (called goitrogens) that impair functioning of the thyroid gland. The pituitary gland responds to the deficiency by an increase in TSH, which leads to hypertrophy of the gland.

Sporadic goiter occurs in only a small fraction of the population. The causes are varied: rarely iodide deficiency, more commonly abnormalities, acquired or inherited, in the many biochemical steps which take place in the thyroid gland. These steps start with the concentration of iodide by the gland and culminate in the release of T4 or T3 into the bloodstream. Goiters are common in pregnancy, when placental hormones contribute to the enlargement of the gland. Most sporadic goiters are smooth and uniform, but if the gland hypertrophies it may become nodular; it is then referred to as a non-toxic nodular goiter.

Treatment
Endemic goiter is treated by adding iodine to the diet. Most cases of sporadic goiter are treated with thyroxine (T4), an inexpensive medication even when administered for life. It suppresses the production of TSH by the pituitary and therefore reduces the most important stimulus for thyroid growth. Surgery is an important form of therapy (though surgeons think otherwise) only when (1) there is suspicion of malignancy or (2) the gland is massive, causing compression of the trachea, impairment of the venous return, or stretching of the laryngeal nerves that innervate the vocal cords. After surgery, thyroxine is administered to prevent hypertrophy of the remnant of the thyroid and the development of hypothyroidism.

Selection of Risks
Euthyroid patients with non-toxic goiters not causing pressure symptoms can be considered standard insurance risks. Where there is a history of pressure symptoms, applications should be postponed until the goiter is removed surgically,

because of the many vital organs in the surgical field. After successful surgery, standard rates apply. In most cases, surgical subjects are prescribed thyroxine for life.

Solitary Thyroid Nodule

The clinical handling of a euthyroid patient whose thyroid gland contains a solitary nodule is still controversial, the point at issue being whether or not the nodule is likely to harbor carcinoma. The factors associated with increased risk of carcinoma in these lesions include sex (females are at greater risk, since nodules are commoner in women), age (children and older adults are at greater risk) and size (nodules larger than 2 cm are especially suspect). The risk of cancer is particularly elevated in subjects who have had a history of radiation to the neck (formerly prescribed for thymus enlargement and acne). Prior to surgical excision the most useful tests to detect carcinoma in the solitary nodule are thyroid scan and fine needle aspiration. Nodules that preferentially concentrate radioactive iodine compared with the rest of the gland are called 'warm' or 'hot', and are unlikely to be cancerous. Nodules which are 'cold' on scan, showing no uptake of the radioactive tracer, are suspicious for malignancy. In such cold nodules the technique of fine needle aspiration is useful, for aspirates that show normal cells are less likely to harbor cancer. (However, it is difficult to distinguish follicular adenoma from follicular carcinoma by aspiration). Most centers treat unoperated nodules with thyroxine to suppress the TSH, which may be a stimulus to nodule growth. If the nodule decreases in size (or at least stays stable) malignancy is less likely than if the nodule increases in size.

Rating

If no investigations have been carried out to determine the function of the nodule, a rating of +100 would represent a minimum; but patients under the age of 20 and over the age of 50 should be postponed pending investigation. Applicants whose nodules are functioning (warm or hot) may be accepted at standard rates. Applicants whose nodules are non-functioning (cold) and have not been subject to fine needle aspiration and a trial of thyroxine should be declined until surgical excision has taken place. Nodules found to be benign at surgery do not require a rating. Malignancies should be rated according to histology (*see* p. 636).

Autoimmune Thyroid Disease and Hashimoto's Disease

Many thyroid disorders are caused by autoimmune processes that alter the function, the histological appearance, and even the external contour of the gland. The commonest disorder is Hashimoto's thyroiditis, which is usually characterized by an enlarged gland, often multinodular, that histologically shows infiltration with lymphocytes and lymphoid follicles. The serum of patients with Hashimoto's disease usually has thyroid antibodies (usually microsomal antibodies), and the activity of the gland is often depressed. Such patients are treated for hypothyroidism. (In a few cases the gland may become hyperactive (Hashitoxicosis), and is then treated as Graves' disease.)

Hypothyroidism

There are many causes of hypothyroidism; the main categories have already been outlined (*see* pp. 720–1). Rare cases are caused by hypothalamic disease, some cases by pituitary disease; the large majority are caused by primary thyroid disorders. The disorders may be congenital (thyroid screening shortly after birth is widespread in North America and Europe) or acquired. Most cases are caused by a variant of Hashimoto's disease, in which the gland is sometimes atrophic; other cases are caused by the therapy used to treat hyperthyroidism (radioactive iodine and surgery). Initial symptoms of hypothyroidism are mild, with fatigue, weight gain, constipation, cold intolerance, dry skin and some hair loss. In later stages severe hypothyroidism or 'myxedema' (a non-pitting edema) develops, which may be accompanied by facial puffiness, deepened voice, effusions in body cavities, and, in the severe cases, mental obtundation and even coma.

Rating

Most cases of hypothyroidism are simply treated with thyroxine and have a standard rating. Cases diagnosed when the disease was advanced but which have become normal on replacement therapy are similarly standard. The rare applicants who have had neglected myxedema with residual heart disease after therapy should be strictly rated for the cardiac impairment. Where the adequacy of the medical follow-up is in doubt, the standard thyroid tests may be requested (TSH and T4).

Thyrotoxicosis or Hyperthyroidism

Overproduction of the thyroid hormones (T4 and T3) is caused by three diseases of the thyroid gland: (1) Graves' (or Basedow's) disease, also called toxic diffuse goiter, (2) toxic multinodular goiter, and (3) toxic uninodular goiter. Most cases of hyperthyroidism occur in females. Graves' disease affects a younger age group, and toxic multinodular goiter tends to be a disease in older people.

Symptoms common to all causes of hyperthyroidism are due to the oversecretion of T4 and T3: anxiety, irritability, insomnia, heat intolerance, sweating, palpitations, weight loss and increased bowel movements. Physical findings include tachycardia, increased pulse pressure, warm moist skin, tremulousness of the outstretched hands, hyperactive reflexes, and proximal muscle weakness.

Toxic multinodular goiter usually develops in a multinodular gland containing functioning thyroid nodules that have become autonomous (i.e. independent of pituitary TSH stimulation). Because the disease occurs in older patients whose myocardial tissue is sensitive to thyroid hormones, cardiac complications, such as atrial fibrillation, congestive heart failure, and angina, may occur before the other symptoms listed above. When there is a single hyperfunctioning nodule in an otherwise normal gland, the disease is called toxic uninodular goiter or Plummer's disease.

Unlike toxic multinodular goiter, Graves' disease is an autoimmune disorder associated with antibodies to the thyroid gland (microsomal and thyroglobulin) and immunoglobulins that interact with the TSH receptors of the thyroid. In addition to these abnormal laboratory findings there may be physical findings, which most characteristically relate to the eyes: exophthalmos and diplopia from swelling of the external ocular muscles, lid retraction, and conjunctival inflammation. Sometimes the ocular abnormalities appear before hyperthyroidism occurs. Graves's disease may also be accompanied by a thick non-pitting edema usually of the shin, called pretibial myxedema (a term confusing to the student because 'myxedema' is generally used to describe severe hypothyroidism).

Complications
In younger patients tachycardia and hypermetabolism revert to normal after successful treatment, and atrial fibrillation, if it has been present, is temporary. Among older patients hyperthyroidism can seriously aggravate pre-existing heart disease, and the residual cardiac status may require rating.

Treatment
There are marked regional preferences in the treatment of hyperthyroidism. Whatever the treatment chosen, patients must be monitored periodically: over the years hypothyroidism commonly develops, earlier in those given radioactive iodine, somewhat later in those treated with surgery; it even develops in a large percentage of those who have entered remission with antithyroid drugs. Initial treatment is usually an antithyroid drug (carbimazole, methimazole, propyl-thiouracil) to relieve symptoms and attain normal levels of T4 and T3. These drugs carry the small but definite risk of causing a reversible agranulocytosis. Often beta-blockers are given to slow the pulse and provide more rapid symptomatic improvement. About one third of patients given the drugs will go into remission, particularly those with small glands and low titers of thyroid-receptor antibodies. Definitive therapy is either subtotal thyroidectomy (with attendant risks to the parathyroid glands, and the nerves supplying the vocal cords) or the administration of radioactive iodine. Whatever the form of therapy, the patient must be followed for the detection of hypothyroidism.

Rating
History of hyperthyroidism, without recurrence, euthyroid on examination.

1) Medical treatment with antithyroid drugs:

Time since start of treatment	Rating
Within 6 mth	+75
More than 6 mth	+50

Time since end of treatment	Rating
Within 3 mth	+50
Thereafter	Standard

2) Surgical treatment with adequate follow-up — standard.
3) Radioactive iodine with adequate follow-up — standard.

PARATHYROIDS

There are usually four parathyroid glands, two embedded in the superior poles of the thyroid and two in the inferior poles. There is considerable individual variation in size and even in number. The glands release a hormone, parathormone (PTH), which acts to raise the serum calcium by increasing bone reabsorption, decreasing urinary excretion of calcium, and increasing calcium absorption from the gastrointestinal tract.

Hyperparathyroidism

Hyperparathyroidism is the term applied to the disorders associated with an increase in PTH. In primary hyperparathyroidism often (80% of cases) a single enlarged hyperactive parathyroid gland (usually a benign adenoma) causes excessive secretion of PTH, leading to hypercalcemia. The hormone may cause bone disease (usually osteomalacia and rarely osteitis fibrosa cystica), peptic ulcer disease, kidney stones and, in advanced cases, nephrocalcinosis. The medical student learns the triad of 'bones, groans and stones'. With the availability of automated blood testing, most cases of hyperparathyroidism are diagnosed quite early, when the patient has asymptomatic hypercalcemia without the attendant complications. When there is a single adenoma, the other parathyroid glands may be suppressed by the high serum calcium. In other cases there are multiple adenomas or even hyperplasia of all the parathyroid glands.

There are other causes of hyperparathyroidism. Secondary hyperparathyroidism is caused by hypocalcemia, with resultant overproduction of PTH; the hypocalcemia may be caused by vitamin D deficiency, vitamin D resistance, or renal disease. When the hypocalcemia is treated, the overproduction of PTH ceases. Tertiary hyperparathyroidism takes place when the parathyroid glands in long-standing secondary hyperparathyroidism no longer respond to serum calcium and develop autonomous hypersecretion of PTH. Among the commonest causes of secondary and tertiary hyperparathyroidism is chronic renal failure; patients on hemodialysis sometimes require parathyroid surgery.

Treatment

Treatment of primary hyperparathyroidism is surgical. When there is a single hyperfunctioning adenoma it is excised, but only after the surgeon has ascertained that the other glands appear small. When there is hyperplasia of all the parathyroid glands, three of them are excised and part of the fourth left in place. The insurance risk after surgical cure depends on the residual renal damage, if present. A short waiting period is wise after surgery to eliminate the risk of persistent hyperparathyroidism due to incomplete excision of the hyperfunctioning tissue, and also to allow time for the atrophic glands ro resume functioning. Many cases of low-grade hypercalcemia are detected by routine blood tests without noticeable symptomatology. These cases are often not referred to surgery, but followed by periodic calcium determinations.

Rating

Unoperated stable hypercalcemia, calcium less than 2.75 mmol/l (11 mg/100 ml) — +50.

Primary hyperparathyroidism, surgical cure, within 3 mth — postpone.

Primary hyperparathyroidism, surgical cure, after 3 mth — standard.

Hypoparathyroidism

The term hypoparathyroidism is applied to those disorders with hypocalcemia due to defective secretion or defective action of PTH. The hypocalcemia may cause (1) neuromuscular irritability with carpopedal spasm, particularly spasm of the hand following occlusion of the brachial artery by the blood pressure cuff (a common clinical test), (2) paresthesias, and (3) generalized seizures. The commonest cause of hypoparathyroidism is damage to the glands during surgery to the neck (including thyroid surgery). Less common is idiopathic atrophy of the parathyroids, sometimes as an isolated deficiency and sometimes associated with other autoimmune disorders, including adrenal insufficiency. The treatment of PTH deficiency is administration of vitamin D in one of the many forms available, sometimes with supplemental calcium. Vitamin D administered in excess can cause prolonged hypercalcemia and hypercalciuria. For that reason a new short-acting (and expensive) metabolite of vitamin D is used when the patient can afford it (1,25-dihydroxycalciferol).

In some cases of hypocalcemia the parathyroid glands secrete PTH but the tissues are insensitive; this disorder, pseudohypoparathyroidism, is associated with skeletal abnormalities and mental retardation.

Rating

Continuous treatment and good control — +50 to standard.

Poor control with convulsions or tetany — +150 to +100.

GONADAL DYSGENESIS

Unequal division of the chromosomes of the germinal cells in the testis or ovary, or during the early divisions following fertilization, can lead to an abnormal complement of sex chromosomes. The male normally has XY chromosomes in each cell, and the female normally has XX. Two common developmental abnormalities are Klinefelter's syndrome in the male and Turner's syndrome in the female.

Klinefelter's Syndrome

Klinefelter's syndrome is the most common disorder causing male hypogonadism. Patients with this syndrome have an XXY chromosomal pattern, though other varieties have more than one extra X chromosome. Many patients are detected among men who seek treatment for infertility. There is a wide variation in the physical appearance of the affected males: all have small testes, some have gynecomastia, some are eunuchoid in appearance. Treatment is androgen replacement when indicated. The defective spermatogenesis cannot be treated. The insurance rating is standard.

Turner's Syndrome

The female with Turner's syndrome has an XO chromosome pattern (i.e. she lacks the second X chromosome). The consequences of this abnormality are short stature, small streak-like ovaries, and amenorrhea. The disease is associated with a number of congenital abnormalities, some of which are cosmetic (webbed neck, lymphedema, shield-shaped chest, retruded mandible); others may be serious health impairments (congenital renal anomalies, coarctation of the aorta, aortic stenosis, intestinal telangiectasia causing bleeding). Osteoporosis may be treated by estrogen therapy. The insurance risk depends on the presence of the congenital abnormalities considered to be health impairments; if these are absent the risk is standard.

Sex Change

Various surgical procedures on the genital organs may be necessary in some intersex states in order to change or emphasize sexual identity. These disorders range from true hermaphroditism to testicular feminization, a form of male pseudohermaphroditism. In cases of testicular feminization the phenotype is female, with normal female external genitalia and developed breasts, but the vaginal pouch is blind and the uterus is absent. In these cases the chromosome pattern is XY, and the tissues are completely insensitive to androgens. Rudimentary testes lying in the labial folds or inguinal canals are usually removed to prevent malignant change. In these individuals the life risk would be standard after recovery from surgery.

Most sex change operations are performed for transsexuals. Male transsexuals are phenotypically and genetically normal males who feel that they are psychologically female, and who choose to undergo the extensive surgical and medical treatment in order to be able to perform a female social role. The changes include penectomy, creation of an artificial vagina, occasional laryngeal surgery, breast augmentation and extensive electrolysis. Underwriting in these cases is extremely difficult: in some series of cases patients have died from metastatic breast carcinoma because of excessive estrogen administration; in some cities transsexuals have a significant presence in the population of prostitutes and are at risk of HIV infection. Male transsexuals are best considered individually. The operation is now performed more selectively than in the past.

Female transsexuals who seek operations to acquire a male phenotype are subjected to mastectomy, hysterectomy, oophorectomy, and receive androgenic hormone to promote beard growth and a deeper voice. The rating in such cases depends on the success of the psychological adaptation to the male role. Where the patient is psychiatrically stable, a temporary extra premium should be appropriate.

HYPOGLYCEMIA

When blood glucose level falls, there is usually a stimulus to the sympathetic nervous system in the normal human being, causing characteristic adrenergic symptoms: sweating, pallor, trembling, anxiety, palpitations, hunger, weakness. When the level of glucose is low enough to deprive the cerebral cortex of sufficient substrate for normal function, the symptoms that occur are called neuroglycopenic: these include lack of concentration, stupor, diplopia, irrational behavior, seizures, coma and even death. The commonest cause of hypoglycemia is the use of insulin or oral hypoglycemic agents prescribed for the treatment of diabetes mellitus. Other causes of hypoglycemia include insulin-secreting islet tumors of the pancreas (insulinomas), inadequate glucose production from the liver caused by a variety of hepatic diseases, absence of the adrenocortical hormones (Addison's disease, hypopituitarism), and a variety of malignancies. The insurance rating in all these cases depends on the underlying disorder. If an islet cell tumor is resected and found to be benign, with resolution of the symptoms the rating would be standard.

Reactive hypoglycemia occurs when a person experiences the adrenergic symptoms several hours after food ingestion; the symptoms are usually controlled by diet therapy. The disorder is an overdiagnosed one, and carries a standard rating.

MULTIPLE ENDOCRINE NEOPLASIA (MEA)

The insurance underwriter should be aware that tumors of the endocrine glands causing hyperfunctioning frequently occur in families, and are frequently associated with other quite distinct endocrine tumors. The tumors do not appear at the same age in any given family tree, nor do the associated tumors appear simultaneously. Three general syndromes have been described:
1) MEA Type 1: hyperparathyroidism (benign), pituitary tumors (benign), pancreatic tumors (often malignant).
2) MEA Type 2: hyperparathyroidism (benign), pheochromocytoma, medullary carcinoma of the thyroid.
3) MEA Type 2b or 3: neuromas of the conjunctiva, labial and buccal mucosa and GI tract, pheochromocytoma, medullary carcinoma of the thyroid.

The rating of these cases depends on the successful excision of the benign tumors and the attentive medical follow-up to detect malignancies before they occur. In particular, patients who carry the Type 2 or Type 3 disease can be considered for insurance only when they are subject to at least yearly testing for calcitonin levels, to be certain that microscopic medullary carcinoma of the thyroid is absent.

CHAPTER 23

DISEASES OF THE NERVOUS SYSTEM AND ASSOCIATED DISORDERS

F CLIFFORD ROSE
R D C BRACKENRIDGE

Affections of the nervous system may be divided into several categories, each having its own significance for life underwriting: (1) diseases or disorders that are curable or self-limiting, have no tendency to progress or recur and that may or may not leave residual neurological defects (e.g. infections, trauma) (2) functional disorders of the nervous system (e.g. idiopathic epilepsy, migraine), (3) secondary lesions of nervous tissue caused by diseases of other systems, of which the prognosis is mainly that of the primary system disease (e.g. hypertension, atherothrombotic vascular disease), and (4) progressive diseases in which premature death is usual, some being genetically determined, some having an immunopathological basis and others having an as yet unknown etiology. The dividing line between the categories may not be as distinct as the classification implies, for several diseases occupy an intermediate position.

INFECTIONS

The simple infections with pyogenic bacteria causing meningitis or cerebral abscess are readily curable by antibiotics, with or without surgical drainage. A history of such conditions may be disregarded in life underwriting provided there are no residuals, such as hydrocephalus, epilepsy or psychiatric disturbance. Uncomplicated cases of tuberculous meningitis could also be considered for standard insurance after an adequate course of antituberculous chemotherapy has been completed. In the case of a brain abscess that has required surgical drainage, a period of postponement, say one year, would be advisable before accepting the risk as standard.

Poliomyelitis

Poliomyelitis is a self-limiting disease in which the maximum damage to nervous tissue occurs during the early stages of infection. Thereafter paralysis may be permanent, or motor function may recover partially or completely, but there is never any subsequent extension of the disease. The incidence and severity of poliomyelitis has now been reduced to negligible proportions in countries that have pursued aggressive vaccination programs; in some underdeveloped countries epidemics are still rife, especially among the underprivileged.

Like other viral diseases, poliomyelitis may occur in epidemic or sporadic form. Those who succumb, particularly to sporadic infection, will generally be constitutionally susceptible because of their hereditary or environmental background. On examination many individuals with a history of paralytic poliomyelitis will be found to hyper-react by tachycardia and elevation of the systolic blood pressure, and not a few will suffer from frank hypertension. This association between poliomyelitis and hypertension has been recognized in both clinical[1] and life insurance[2] surveys.

In the selection of risks for life insurance a history of paralytic poliomyelitis may be disregarded even if recovery has been incomplete. A risk would be present only if paralysis was so severe and extensive that locomotor function was markedly impaired, or when there was evidence of weakness of the respiratory muscles. The presence of hypertension or other impairments would, of course, be taken into account in the final evaluation.

Herpes Zoster (Shingles)

By itself, a history of shingles could be ignored in underwriting provided there were no significant residuals. However, a very recent history of herpes zoster must be viewed more critically, since in some instances the infection may be a harbinger of a more serious underlying disease. In those so predisposed, and especially in the elderly, shingles may be the starting point of intractable neuralgia leading in turn to prolonged invalidism, surgical interventions, reactive depression and even drug addiction.

Viral Meningitis, Encephalitis and Encephalomyelitis

In acute viral meningitis or aseptic meningitis, inflammation is confined to the meninges, whereas in encephalitis it involves the brain itself. In encephalomyelitis the spinal cord is also affected. The inflammatory lesions are self-limiting and due either to direct invasion by a virus or to hypersensitivity in response to viral infection. Mortality during the acute stage of encephalitis is sometimes high but varies from epidemic to epidemic and with the type of infecting virus. Aseptic meningitis virtually always recovers without residuals, but focal neurological deficits of varying severity may persist after recovery from the acute stage of encephalitis or encephalomyelitis.

Applicants may be accepted as standard risks after complete recovery from the acute phase of the infection. The presence of residual focal lesions of a minor character not causing interference with vital functions would not preclude standard acceptance, but permanent major impairments, such as epilepsy, hydrocephalus, mental disorder or paraplegia, would call for appropriate underwriting.

Neurosyphilis

The three main manifestations of neurosyphilis (tabes dorsalis, general paralysis and meningovascular syphilis) have declined markedly in the past 50 years but are not yet so rare that they can be forgotten. Mixed or atypical forms of neurosyphilis are said to be appearing more frequently in recent years. It is advisable, therefore, to have anyone who presents with unusual neurological signs screened for syphilis.

Of untreated syphilitics, 10 percent will eventually develop neurosyphilis but, because of the efficacy of penicillin in eradicating the infecting spirochete and thus preventing the development of other tertiary lesions, mortality due to neurosyphilis itself is now very low. Premature deaths are more likely to be caused by late complications of the established disease, such as renal failure as a result of obstructive uropathy in tabes dorsalis. Dementia and its consequences in general paralysis are also likely to result in early death.

Prognosis

Meningovascular syphilis has a good prognosis after treatment, and the risk to life will depend largely on any residual neurological damage that had developed prior to treatment; for example, a dense hemiplegia following a cerebrovascular accident (CVA). Antisyphilitic treatment appears to have no effect in halting the very slow progression of tabes dorsalis, and its effect on general paralysis is variable. About one-third of patients show a marked recovery of function and one-third show a lesser degree of recovery; the rest remain static or deteriorate. It is evident, therefore, that many sufferers from neurosyphilis in its early stages who have been adequately treated and followed up will be acceptable risks in a substandard category. The evaluation of syphilis as a life insurance risk is discussed in Chapter 31, where suggested ratings for the various stages of the disease are given (*see* p. 912).

PERIPHERAL NEUROPATHY: POLYNEURITIS

Disease of the peripheral nerves produces muscular weakness and atrophy of the muscles supplied by the affected nerves, and sensory loss along their distribution. Typically there is absence of tendon reflexes and of cutaneous and proprioceptive sensation. When symmetrical, sensory loss is usually of the 'glove and stocking' type. Subjective sensations of tingling and other paresthesiae are common.

The causes of peripheral neuropathy and polyneuritis are many and varied, and will not be listed in detail here. They range from mechanical causes producing pressure on nerves to toxic agents (such as heavy metals and organic compounds), metabolic disturbances (such as diabetes mellitus and nutritional deficiencies, including alcoholism), some malignant neoplasms and infectious diseases.

If the cause of a neuropathy is known, the prognosis will usually be that of the causative disease or agent. When the cause is unknown and the neuropathy is of recent onset and persisting, the possibility of a serious underlying pathology, such as carcinoma of the bronchus, should be considered and applications for insurance postponed in order to eliminate the early risk. Fortunately most cases of mild peripheral neuritis recover if the causative agent can be identified and removed, although recovery may not always be complete. Nevertheless, residual nerve damage that does not produce interference with vital functions need not be considered an additional risk.

Acute Infectious Polyneuritis (Guillain-Barré Syndrome)

This is a specific form of neuropathy of immune etiology characterized by symmetrical, ascending motor weakness, distal sensory impairment and a cerebrospinal fluid which contains excess protein but relatively few white cells. Mortality during the acute phase is less than 10 percent due to involvement of the bulbar and respiratory muscles, but in those who survive the prognosis for full recovery is excellent. Applicants for life insurance with a history of acute infectious polyneuritis can be considered standard risks soon after return to work.

TUMORS

The underwriting handling of tumors of the brain and spinal cord following appropriate treatment is discussed in Chapter 20. The ratings in Table 20.2 are designed to cover the risk associated with the type of tumor, its recurrence and the risk of post-surgical or post-radiation complications, such as infection or epilepsy. Temporary ratings are shown where endocrine deficiency involves replacement therapy with corticosteroids. The significance of residual neurological deficits following treatment of brain and spinal cord tumors is discussed below.

Residual Neurological Deficits

Damage to nervous tissue may occur because of compression by a tumor within the cranium or spinal canal before its removal or during subsequent surgical or radiation treatment. A certain amount of recovery of nervous function can take place within the first six to 12 months of treatment, but thereafter any deficit is likely to be permanent. Since the lesions are, in a sense, traumatic, no progression need be anticipated. Minor deficits that have little or no effect on vital functions can usually be disregarded in underwriting. These would include lesions of cranial nerves or their nuclei and of anterior or posterior spinal roots, excepting the cauda equina. Residual hemiplegia or hemianesthesia arising from intracerebral damage may also be disregarded provided it does not interfere significantly with locomotion.

Major neurological deficits are those that can shorten life by affecting vital functions, and a rating in addition to the tumor rating will usually be required when they are present. The most important of these is a neuropathic (cord) bladder which commonly complicates tumors of the spinal cord or cauda equina and some tumors of the brain. Depending on the site of the lesions, the bladder becomes either atonic or exhibits urinary retention with over-flow, or spastic producing automatic reflex emptying, often against urethral resistance. In either case, urinary stasis predisposes to infection of the bladder, vesicoureteric reflux and calculus formation in the kidneys or bladder. Permanent urinary diversion may be required in cases of complete neuropathic bladder in order to protect renal function. The following ratings are suggested for neuropathic bladder where renal function is normal (*see also* pp. 553-4):

Extent	Rating	
	Aged under 45	Aged 45 and over
Complete	+100	+75
Incomplete	+75	+25

Other major neurological deficits associated with brain tumors are psychiatric, such as depersonalization, organic psychosis and dementia. These would normally warrant declination for life insurance. Intellectual impairment of lesser degree would probably warrant an additional rating of 30–50 points.

Serious interference with locomotor function may follow the surgical treatment of cerebellar tumors or tumors involving the cerebellar connections; an additional rating of up to 50 points would be appropriate according to the degree of residual disability. Complete or partial paraplegia (including neuropathic bladder) may result from, or follow the treatment of, some spinal tumors. The additional rating would be similar to that for traumatic paraplegia (*see* p. 734).

SPINAL CORD INJURIES: PARAPLEGIA; TETRAPLEGIA

The prognosis for the paraplegic today is vastly different from what it was 40 years ago. This is due to the new approach to the management and treatment of paraplegia prompted by the great increase in the number of cases during World War II. Special units were set up to deal specifically with cases of traumatic paraplegia in service personnel and have since developed into national centers in every country where research and comprehensive programs of dynamic rehabilitation on modern lines, including all medical and social aspects of paraplegia, are carried out. Today the majority of paraplegics, especially those due to injury, receive specialized treatment and rehabilitation in one of these units.

Prognosis

A long-term study of mortality associated with injuries of the spinal cord was reported by Guttmann[3] in 1959 and served as a guide for the insurance of paraplegics during the 1960s. The study comprised 482 consecutive cases of spinal paralysis who were admitted to the National Spinal Injuries Centre at Stoke Mandeville, England, from 1944 to 1958. Most of the patients were between 20 and 30 years of age at the time of injury, and injuries involved lesions at different levels of the cord producing complete or incomplete paralysis. Mortality (92 deaths) in the group at the end of the observation period was compared with the mortality (14·44 deaths) among a contemporaneous group of first-class insured lives over the same period, giving a mortality ratio of 637 percent. From this it was calculated, by employing the usual process of medical selection, that a group of paraplegics in the age range 20–30 years might reasonably be insured at rating equivalent to 400–500 percent of standard mortality (i.e. +300 to +400), and in the age range 31–50 at rating equivalent to 300–400 percent of standard mortality (i.e. +200 to +300).

Despite improved medical, surgical and rehabilitation techniques for the management of injuries of the spinal cord, mortality still remains high. In 1977 Geisler et al[4] reported on 1,501 traumatic spinal cord injuries (including tetraplegia) treated between 1945 and 1973. The 428 deaths (28·5 percent) are analyzed by cause in Table 23.1.

Table 23.1. Cause of mortality in follow-up of 1,501 traumatic spinal cord injuries.

Cause of death	Number of deaths	%
Renal insufficiency	132	30·8
Heart/circulatory diseases	87	20·4
Diseases of respiratory organs	52	12·2
Neoplasms	42	9·8
Strokes	29	6·8
Decubitus ulcer	19	4·4
Suicides	18	4·2
Gastrointestinal diseases	18	4·2
Others	31	7·2
Total	428	100·0

The authors noted that although there had been a steady improvement in mortality over the years up to 1966, there had been no demonstrable improvement from 1967 to 1973. This observation they ascribed to the increased number of tetraplegics entering the study in the later years.

Devivo and Fine[5] calculated life expectancy of 1,517 men at different ages who had suffered spinal cord injuries of various types. From these values an actuarial colleague determined the mortality ratios (see Table 23.2) for each type of injury using as a basis the A1967–70 life tables and after applying a discount of 30 percent for selection. The results are independent of age at discharge from hospital and are approximate (in view of the lack of data for the period of study).

Table 23.2. Mortality ratios for spinal cord injuries.

Extent of paralysis	Mortality ratio (%)
Complete tetraplegia	850
Incomplete tetraplegia[a]	225
Complete paraplegia	475
Incomplete paraplegia	150

[a]Presumably incomplete paralysis of all four limbs.

Tetraplegia

Injuries to the cervical spine have become more frequent in recent years with a consequent increase in the incidence of tetraplegia.

A report by Hardy[6] on the long-term survival of 331 tetraplegics admitted to the Sheffield Spinal Injuries Centre, England, from 1948 to 1972 confirms the very poor prognosis associated with complete lesions. Mortality in complete tetraplegia was found to be excessively high in the first year, and especially in the first three months following injury. Thereafter there was a lower but steady mortality throughout the remaining period of observation. For those under the age of 45, observed survival at 20 years was 7 percent, compared with an expected survival of 94 percent in a comparable sample of the general population of England and Wales. For those over the age of 45, observed survival at ten years was 3 percent, as against an expected 82 percent.

A smaller study by Carter[7] reviewed 67 complete tetraplegics with motor levels at C4 and above admitted to the Texas Institute for Rehabilitation and Research between 1959 and 1977. Of the 67 patients, 18 (27 percent) died, half of the deaths being after discharge from hospital. Adjusted for loss to follow-up (five patients), the mortality became 34 percent, the major cause of death being cardiorespiratory. These figures reflect the enormous advance in the standard of treatment of high cervical lesions in recent years. Nevertheless, even if the very high early mortality is eliminated by a period of postponement, complete tetraplegia would still be considered a risk too speculative for life insurance.

The prognosis of incomplete tetraplegia is known to be better than for the complete lesion; this was confirmed in the Sheffield study.[6] Observed and expected survival curves for both age groups followed a closer and parallel course for the first 12–14 years before beginning to diverge a little due to increased patient mortality. For those under the age of 45 with incomplete tetraplegia, observed survival after 20 years was 80 percent, compared with an expected survival of 94 percent in the general population. For those over the age of 45, the corresponding observed and expected survival rates after 20 years were 32 percent and 52 percent, respectively.

Non-Traumatic Paraplegia

The prognosis of paraplegia secondary to disease will generally be worse than that of purely traumatic paraplegia, merely because many of the causative diseases are themselves associated with increased mortality (e.g. multiple sclerosis, occlusive vascular disease of the spinal arteries, malignant lymphomas arising in the spinal canal and intramedullary spinal tumors). On the other hand, paraplegia due to diseases or conditions of a non-recurring or non-progressive nature is likely to have a prognosis similar to that of traumatic paraplegia and holds a similar risk for life insurance. Primary conditions of this type would include osteomyelitis of the spine with intrathecal abscess, spinal tuberculosis, benign intradural tumors following removal, prolapse of a thoracic intervertebral disc and iatrogenic damage by radio-opaque contrast medium.

Selection of Risks

The following factors should be taken into account in evaluating the risk of applicants with a history of spinal injury:

1) Incomplete lesions of the cord have a better long-term prognosis than complete lesions.

2) The mortality of paraplegics with dorsal or lumbar spine injuries is clearly higher than that of standard insurance risks, but significantly less than the mortality of complete tetraplegics with high cervical spine injuries.

3) Mortality associated with incomplete tetraplegia due to a lower cervical spine injury does not differ greatly from that associated with dorsolumbar paraplegia.

4) Best-risk cases are those who have received specialized treatment and rehabilitation at a special unit. They should be able to lead an active life in a wheelchair and be employed in work compatible with their disability.

5) In order to allow adequate physical and mental adaptation to the changed circumstances a suitable interval should have elapsed between the injury and issue of insurance. Generally, insurance should not be issued until a paraplegic has completed at least six months of independent existence outside the spinal unit.

6) The leading cause of death in complete paraplegia is renal failure, although the incidence has been markedly reduced in recent years by better patient management. Avoidance of internal catheterization and the use of external sphincterotomy tends to prevent the development of vesicoureteric reflux and upper tract damage. A history of occasional attacks of urinary tract infection is to be expected in paraplegics and, of course, is allowed for in the risk evaluation, but the presence of established renal disease, such as chronic pyelonephritis, would be sufficient reason for declination. Likewise, trophic changes in the anesthetic areas would not be unexpected, but should there be chronic intractable ulceration over pressure areas or elsewhere the risk should be postponed or declined.

Rating

1) Traumatic complete paraplegia; applicant fully rehabilitated and gainfully employed; regular urological surveillance; normal renal function; no significant skin problems:

Time since injury	Rating	
	Aged under 45	Aged 45 and over
Within 4 yr	+300	+150
Thereafter	+200	+100

2) Mild paraplegia; no, or minimal, residuals; normal bladder function; walks without aids — standard.

3) Incomplete paraplegia; when the applicant is able to walk unaided or with the use of callipers, stick, crutches, etc and has only occasional recourse to a wheelchair — one-half the rating for complete paraplegia (see p. 731) or that for neuropathic bladder, depending on the degree of paraplegia.

4) Complete tetraplegia — decline.

5) Incomplete tetraplegia — rate as complete paraplegia (see above).

6) Other factors.
Impaired renal function:
 Slight — add 75–100 to basic ratings.
 Moderate or marked — decline.
When renal function tests are not available the findings on urinalysis may be used to assess the state of the renal tract. A more equitable judgment can be made if three urine specimens are examined on separate days and the results averaged.
 Albuminuria — add one-half the ratings for albuminuria (*see* p. 522).
 Pyuria — add one-half the ratings for pyuria (*see* p. 523).
If there is established chronic pyelonephritis, if one kidney is non-functioning or if there are renal calculi present on examination, the risk would usually be declined.

No additional rating would normally be required for a history of surgical operations to improve bladder drainage, but a urinary diversion (e.g. an ileal conduit) may require a separate rating (*see* pp. 553–4).

An intravenous urogram reported as normal within the past year may be credited up to 50 points.
7) Non-traumatic paraplegia: causal disease is non-progressive or has been cured, or where the cause has been removed — rate as for traumatic paraplegia (*see above*) plus the rating for the primary cause, if any.

EPILEPSY

In 1881 Gowers made two meaningful observations: (1) epilepsy is a symptom of brain dysfunction of multiple causation and is not a disease *sui generis*; (2) any brain stressed sufficiently can respond with a seizure, and therefore a single convulsion does not constitute epilepsy. Today epilepsy is regarded as a syndrome of multiple etiology characterized clinically by repeated paroxysmal disturbances of motor, sensory or psychic function, and physiologically by repeated paroxysmal discharges of cerebral neurones.

Despite the wide range of new antiepileptic drugs available for treatment, mortality associated with epilepsy as a whole still remains above normal, although it varies slightly according to the type and frequency of fits and reduces with increasing duration since the last attack. Among epileptics the causes of death that are above the average expected are chiefly accident and suicide.

Classification

There are many local and systemic conditions that cause convulsions and loss of consciousness; some are obvious clinically and others can be identified only after painstaking investigations. However, in the majority of epileptics no cause can be found (idiopathic epilepsy). In selecting risks for life insurance it is important to know if a cause has been identified, since the prognosis of some primary diseases (e.g. brain tumor, cerebral infarction) may be much worse than that of the epilepsy they trigger. Figure 23.1 illustrates the etiology of epilepsy at various ages of onset. The overall high incidence of epilepsy of unknown origin will be noted, as well as the higher yield of known causes at the extremes of age.

The simple clinical classification of epilepsy shown in Table 23.3 is a convenient way of referring to the different types under discussion, but no useful purpose is served by making too many subdivisions of epilepsy for risk evaluation, since the character of certain seizures often changes over the years. Thus the absence attacks or akinetic seizures of centrencephalic epilepsy in childhood (petit mal) often give way to, or alternate with, grand mal attacks as adolescence is passed, though still originating in the centrencephalon. Focal epilepsy that progresses to generalized seizures can be modified by anticonvulsants so that the manifestations of the attack remain focal without a convulsion occurring. Temporal lobe epilepsy in adults without generalized convulsions is frequently misreported as petit mal, which very rarely arises for the first time after 15 years of age. For these reasons it is more practical to underwrite a history of epilepsy according to the frequency of attacks, irrespective of type.

Table 23.3. Classification of epilepsy.

Focal seizures (with or without subsequent generalized convulsions)
    Motor or sensory   Temporal lobe

Centrencephalic seizures (with or without subsequent generalized convulsions)
    a) Absence attacks
    b) Myoclonus
    c) Atonic spells

Generalized seizures without focal or centrencephalic signs

Special Forms of Epilepsy

Sleep Epilepsy

The prognosis of epilepsy that occurs exclusively during sleep is relatively benign, although a proportion of such patients will eventually develop additional waking attacks. In the study by Henriksen et al[10] a mortality ratio of 149 percent was found in the group of 256 patients with epilepsy occurring only during sleep, but among 1,015 patients who had both sleep and waking epilepsy the mortality ratio was 302 percent.

Television Epilepsy

An increasing number of people are being seen who have fits only when watching television. At least half have normal EEGs except when exposed to intermittent photic stimulation; and if the stimulation is applied with one eye closed, only insignificant abnormalities, or none at all, appear in the EEG. For these persons an effective prophylactic against a fit being induced by too close proximity to the television screen or by other flickering light is to cover one eye completely with the palm of the hand. If the basic EEG shows no abnormality and there is no history of fits other than those associated with flickering light, no significant extra mortality need be anticipated.

Traumatic Epilepsy

This may follow head injuries of all kinds, the fits usually being focal in type (*see* pp. 752–4).

The Single Fit

It has already been mentioned that a single fit or seizure does not constitute epilepsy. However, a very practical difficulty faces the life underwriter when there is a history of a single fit, or perhaps a group of two or three fits within a short period, followed by an asymptomatic period, sometimes without treatment. After what period since the first fit is it safe to issue life insurance?

In the days before sophisticated methods of neurological investigation, it used to be customary to postpone such applications for two years because even though initial investigations were negative, a few cases of early tumor would be missed, only to become evident one, two or three years later.

As more accurate methods of investigation became available, the postponement period was reduced to one year. Today, for cases screened by computerized tomography or magnetic resonance imaging (MRI), a six-month period would seem to be sufficient. The only reason for deferring applicants is to eliminate the early risk due to primary or secondary neoplasia. Also, where the EEG shows an unequivocal synchronous 3Hz spike and wave pattern of classical centrencephalic epilepsy there would be no reason to postpone for longer than six months from the initial attack.

Mortality Studies

Several studies of the mortality of epileptics have been carried out both on insured lives and on patients. In the *1951 Impairment Study*[8] a mortality ratio of 318 percent was found in the classification of lives with a history of grand mal epilepsy, standard and substandard sections combined. The Prudential Assurance Company in the UK (Preston and Clarke, 1965[9]) and Henriksen et al[10] in Denmark studied the mortality of epileptics among insured lives and patients. Their findings are summarized in Table 23.4. In the study of Henriksen et al the 2,763 epileptics had no impairment other than epilepsy, which would make them substandard risks for life insurance. They were selected from a total of 3,671 epileptics seen at four neurology clinics in Denmark. Expected deaths were calculated from the first-class life experience of Danish life insurance companies for the corresponding ages and durations.

Table 23.4. Results of several studies of the mortality of epileptics.

Study	Type of epilepsy	Years covered	Exposed to risk	Expected deaths	Actual deaths	Mortality ratio (%)
Preston and Clarke[9]	Grand mal	1947–63	5155	8·156	25	292
Henriksen et al[10]	All types	1950–64	2763	44·2	123	278
	Temporal lobe (with fits)	1950–64	587	14·7	41	279

A surprising consistency is apparent in the levels of mortality of epileptics reported from the USA, UK and Denmark.

More up-to-date data on the mortality of epilepsy are available from the *Medical Impairment Study 1983*[11] (*see* Table 23.5).

Table 23.5. Mortality associated with epilepsy.[a]

		Standard (%)	Substandard rating			Total (%)
			Under 175 (%)	175–250 (%)	Over 250 (%)	
	Sex					
Grand mal	M	(101)	141	224	360	229
	F	—	—	232	408	248
Petit mal	M	(147)	(112)	(193)	—	168
	F	—	—	—	—	—

Key: ( ) = 10–34 policy deaths
— = <10 policy deaths
[a]Data from *Medical Impairment Study 1983*.[11]
Note Mortality ratios are based on modified 1965–70 life tables and are shown under standard and substandard categories, the latter being divided into slight, moderate and heavy according to the original rating.

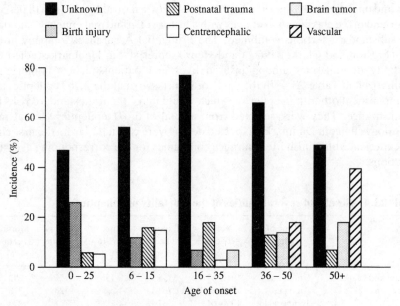

Fig. 23.1. Etiology of epilepsy in terms of its onset at various ages.

Surgical Treatment

Where focal epilepsy cannot be adequately controlled by medical means alone, excision of the triggering focus may be attempted. This is often successful in abolishing attacks completely, but where it is not, fits are usually reduced sufficiently to be amenable to control by anticonvulsant drugs.

Rating

1) Grand mal or generalized seizures; focal epilepsy (temporal lobe, motor or sensory) with or without generalized seizures; petit mal, non-convulsive or modified epilepsy.
Within one year of diagnosis — usually postpone.
   Selected cases may be insurable after six months.
a) Medical treatment.
Up to two attacks per year:

Time since last attack	Rating
Within 1 yr	+75 to +100
2nd yr	+50 to +75
3rd–5th yr	+25 to +50
Thereafter	Standard

More than two but less than seven attacks[a] per year:

Time since last attack	Rating
Within 1 yr	+100 to +150
2nd yr	+75 to +100
3rd–5th yr	+25 to +50
Thereafter	Standard

More than six attacks[a] per year — +200 to +300.
History of status epilepticus:
   Within one year — postpone.
   Thereafter — rate as number of attacks per year.
b) Surgical treatment (removal of epileptic focus).
No further fits:

Time since surgery	Rating
Within 6 mth	Postpone
7th–12th mth	3 per mil for 2 yr
Thereafter	Standard

With continuing fits — rate as medical treatment.
2) Sleep epilepsy.

Time since last attack	Rating
Within 2 yr	+50
Thereafter	Standard

With waking epilepsy in addition — rate as epilepsy (*see above*).
3) Photic (television) epilepsy — standard.
4) Single seizure, negative investigations (including CT scan or MRI):

Time since seizure	Rating
Within 6 mth	Postpone
Thereafter	Standard

[a]If attacks are wholly or predominantly minor (no generalized seizure), use lower rating of range.

NARCOLEPSY AND CATAPLEXY

Narcolepsy is a disorder characterized by daytime episodes of irresistible sleep. It is commonly accompanied by cataplexy (a sudden loss of muscle tone frequently induced by emotion), sleep paralysis (episodes of inability to perform voluntary movements on falling asleep or waking) and hypnagogic hallucinations (dreaming and hallucinatory episodes, sometimes of a terrifying nature, which occur on falling asleep). The diagnosis depends mainly on the history, although the EEG may show a characteristic disturbance. Whereas in normal persons an interval of an hour or so elapses between falling asleep and the first appearance of rapid eye movement (REM) sleep on the EEG tracing, sleep in a patient with the narcoleptic syndrome may begin abruptly with a period of REM. Some patients with narcolepsy alone, however, do not show this feature and therefore there is a distinction between those with REM-type narcolepsy (narcolepsy with cataplexy) and non-REM narcolepsy (simple hypersomnia). Narcolepsy is usually amenable to treatment with dextroamphetamine, but the other features of the narcoleptic syndrome (cataplexy, sleep paralysis and hypnagogic hallucinations) require the addition of tricyclic antidepressant drugs.

Rating

Where investigations have revealed no organic brain disease, applicants with a history of narcolepsy and cataplexy can be accepted as standard.

SYNCOPE

When the previous medical history refers to an episode of 'black-out' or fainting, it is possible that the cause has been syncope rather than epilepsy. Syncope may be defined as loss of consciousness due to an acute decrease of cerebral blood flow. If a person stands upright, the effective filling pressure of the heart falls, but in normal subjects the moderate decrease in stroke output in the erect position is fully compensated by baroceptor construction. Syncope will only result when decrease in stroke output is considerable, and this is often found in soldiers who faint on the parade ground after standing to attention for long periods, especially in very warm weather. In these circumstances there tends to be diminished vascular tone and gross pooling of blood in the veins of the lower part of the body, leading to a decrease in cardiac filling pressure, low stroke output and cerebral anemia.

Cough syncope is a condition which sometimes occurs in powerfully built, middle-aged men with chronic bronchitis who have episodes of prolonged, violent coughing that lead to increased intrathoracic pressure to 200–400 mm Hg, causing an acute decrease in venous filling pressure of the heart. A similar syncope can be artifically induced by Valsalva's maneuver, particularly in subjects with poor vasomotor tone. This is also the mechanism which sometimes causes fainting when straining at stool. Rising quickly to the erect position out of a warm bed may cause an acute drop in venous filling pressure of the heart and produce syncope; the same sort of thing occurs in people under treatment with ganglion-blocking drugs or who have had an extensive dorsolumbar sympathectomy. In each of these situations there is excessive pooling of blood in the lower parts of the body in the erect position, and in the case of the last two conditions it is due to blocking of the normal constrictor baroceptor responses.

Syncope may, of course, be a symptom of disease; an obvious example would be cerebral anoxia which occurs in a Stokes-Adams attack. Also, syncope may result when the decrease in cardiac output that sometimes follows acute myocardial infarction or massive pulmonary embolism is so gross that the normal physiological baroceptor constrictor mechanism is insufficient to counteract it.

An important, though rare, form of syncope occurs during or shortly after exercise in those suffering from primary pulmonary hypertension or other conditions affecting the right side of the heart. Acute right ventricular failure causes a steady rise in venous filling pressure with a fall in cardiac output, thereby overcoming the normal compensatory peripheral constrictor reflexes. Finally, some cases of syncope are hysterical in origin and arise from hyper-ventilation.

VERTIGO

Vertigo is defined as the disordered orientation of the body in space, and may be experienced in movement of the external world (rotatory or oscillatory) as a sensation of movement of the body itself (either in rotation or a feeling of falling) or as a sensation of unsteadiness (particularly of the lower limbs). Vertigo may result from disordered function at several different levels of the central nervous system, and is one of the presenting symptoms of vertebrobasilar ischemia (see p. 747).

Giddiness is commonly a symptom of an anxiety reaction. In many instances there will also be an associated elevation of blood pressure; this, however, is not usually a causal factor. Functional vertigo is not in itself a ratable impairment, although any associated hypertension would call for a debit.

A history of Ménière's syndrome is not infrequently reported in the examination for life insurance, but the term tends to be used rather loosely to describe giddiness or tinnitus not of the classical type. The diagnosis of Ménière's syndrome should be made only when there are the characteristic symptoms of recurrent severe giddiness, usually with vomiting and prostration, and associated with tinnitus and increasing deafness. The condition runs a long course with a tendency for tinnitus to disappear as deafness increases. It is predominantly a disorder of middle age; according to Brain[12] one-third of all patients are first affected after the age of 60. As in giddiness of psychogenic origin there is no excess mortality associated with Ménière's syndrome. In the 1951 Impairment Study[8] vertigo and syncope were considered together, and mortality ratios for the combined experience in the standard sections were below 100 percent of expected in all age groups under 50, and slightly above at issue ages 50 and over.

MIGRAINE

The clinical picture of typical migraine is so well known that it need not be repeated here. Environmental stresses tending to produce anxiety and fatigue may precipitate attacks of migraine in susceptible people.

The first published mortality experience of insured lives with a history of migraine appeared in the 1951 Impairment Study.[8] For lives insured at standard premium rates mortality was found to be within 80 percent of expected, whereas for those insured as substandard it ranged from 105 percent to 140 percent of expected. In the 1983 Medical Impairment Study[11] migraine, as such, was not studied; the symptom headache was substituted instead. For those accepted as standard risks the mortality ratio was 91 percent, and for those rated mildly substandard the mortality ratio was 119 percent. There were too few deaths in the higher substandard categories to make analysis significant. Both experiences may be taken as a guide to underwriting, and it would be usual practice to disregard a history of migraine provided there were no other ratable impairments.

Some varieties of migraine require particular mention, since they may simulate organic disease. One of these, ophthalmoplegic migraine, is typified by paralysis occurring in one or more oculomotor nerves, usually of brief duration. When, however, ocular palsies with diplopia have lasted more than an hour or two the diagnosis of migraine must be in doubt, and many people diagnosed as having ophthalmoplegic migraine have, in fact, had transient ischemic attacks or a congenital aneurysm. Also, when an attack of aphasia, paresthesia or weakness of a limb or limbs occurs without headache, a diagnosis or migraine must be supported by a history of previous attacks of a similar or almost similar nature that have a periodicity typical of migraine; otherwise a diagnosis of transient cerebral ischemia or even stroke should be considered.

VASCULAR DISEASES OF THE NERVOUS SYSTEM

Mortality from cerebrovascular disease continues to decline, although it is still the third leading cause of death. In 1974 it was responsible for approximately 11 percent of all deaths; by 1979 the figure had dropped to 8·8 percent. For standard ordinary policyholders of the Metropolitan Life Insurance Company, cerebrovascular disease accounted for 6·7 percent of all deaths in 1979, a reduction of 17 percent over the years 1974–78.[13]

A decline in mortality from cerebrovascular disease has been reported throughout the West, and it is probable that more effective drug therapy in the control of hypertension has contributed to the decline.

Stroke

The clinical end-product of cerebrovascular disease is a transient ischemic attack (TIA), a completed stroke or strokes, or various combinations of these. But to define the prognosis of cerebrovascular disease with any accuracy is almost impossible, since the term is generic and covers a number of conditions differing in etiology, pathology and site of lesion. Theoretically it should be possible to subdivide the various causes of TIA and completed stroke and evaluate the prognosis of each separately, but in practice this is not feasible because the clinician's ability to determine with certainty the cause of a stroke in the individual patient is possible only with the help of modern imaging techniques.

In evaluating the prognosis of cerebrovascular disease it is generally agreed that certain causes of stroke should be excluded. Among these are intracranial hemorrhage due to primary causes (such as congenital aneurysms or angiomas), embolism originating from heart disease, cerebral disturbance due to cardiac dysrrhythmia or hypotension, and generalized diseases characterized by arteritis. Most of these causes can be relatively easily identified in the course of routine investigation, and the prognosis of each can be evaluated separately. The etiology of cerebrovascular disease, as it is generally understood, would then include all other causes, such as arterial hypertension and intracerebral hemorrhage, atherothrombotic disease producing stenosis of extracranial arteries and embolic foci, and primary intracerebral thrombosis. But for the purpose of long-term study, the best classification of cerebrovascular disease is not by cause but by the clinical end result; in this form it is also meaningful to the life underwriter.

Prognosis; Mortality Studies

The study by Marquardsen[14] of 769 patients carefully observed in the acute phase of a stroke and then followed up for ten to 23 years is an important contribution to prognosis. The study was carried out in the small Danish town of Frederiksberg, where the hospital department of neurology received for admission almost all cases of stroke, however mild, from a wide catchment area. The study comprised 303 men (mean age 67·3 years) and 466 women (mean age 69·9 years). Marquardsen analyzed three phases after the stroke: the immediate prognosis, the functional recovery of the immediate survivors and the long-term mortality. During the first phase, which was taken as three weeks, the mortality was 50·5 percent for men and 44·8 percent for women. There were 407 immediate survivors, and of these about one-half became fully independent. A further 20 percent were able to walk unaided. The remaining patients were more severely disabled and 12 percent were completely incapacitated.

Apart from neurological evidence of severe cerebral damage, other poor prognostic factors were lack of improvement in motor function, persistent confusion and apathy, incontinence and extracerebral complications. Right-sided cerebral lesions had a less favorable prognosis than left-sided lesions, owing to the accompanying defects in visuomotor, temporal and spatial concepts. Indeed certain defects of higher nervous function are probably present in those who fail to regain independence despite the absence of obvious adverse factors.

Using life tables to assess long-term survival in those alive at the end of the first three weeks, Marquardsen found that mortality in the first year in men was 19 percent — five times that expected. After three years 46 percent of the patients had died, compared with an expected mortality of 12 percent. The median survival time was 3·5 years for the patients with strokes as against more than ten years in the corresponding general population. The average annual probability of dying remained remarkably constant and, in comparing results with other series, survival curves after the first year tended to become parallel, indicating that long-term survival is determined by the steady progression of the underlying generalized disease. Atherosclerotic lesions tend to develop in parallel in different arterial systems, coronary lesions usually preceding cerebral by a decade.

Further strokes occurred in 37 percent of the immediate survivors in Marquardsen's series. The factors associated with an increased liability to recurrence included more than one previous stroke, a history of heart failure, a primary stroke with slight or no residual disability, atrial fibrillation, ECG abnormalities and arterial hypertension.

An important contribution to the statistics of survival after stroke has been made by Haberman,[15] who analyzed in detail 110 papers from the medical literature dealing with the natural history of cerebrovascular disease. The object of the survey was to measure mortality associated with various types of stroke and to compare this with a standard experience suitable for application to life underwriting. In order to express his results, Haberman used the 'ratio of average death rates' (RAD); this ratio expressed as a percentage is approximately the same as the more familiar mortality ratio (actual to expected deaths percent).

Cerebrovascular disease primarily affects individuals over the age of 50; the average ages at onset for various types of stroke in Haberman's series are given in Table 23.6.

Table 23.6. Average age at onset for various types of stroke.

Type of stroke	Average age at onset
a) Cerebral infarction	70
b) Cerebral embolism	70
c) Intracerebral hemorrhage	67
d) Subarachnoid hemorrhage	51
e) Transient ischemic attacks	62

Death rates in the first few hours and weeks after a stroke are very high, and therefore the results of the study shown in Table 23.7 exclude the first year mortality. This follows usual underwriting practice.

Table 23.7. Effect of age at onset on RAD values[a] (at one year or more) for pathological types of cerebrovascular disease: first attack and no history of heart failure.[15]

Age at onset	Cerebral infarction	Cerebral embolism	Cerebral hemorrhage	Subarachnoid hemorrhage	Transient ischemic attacks
40	955	1100	365	225	280
50	585	880	280	175	215
60	360	540	205	125	150
70	220	335	130	100	100
80	140	205	100	100	100

[a]100 = standard.
Note The RAD values decrease as age at onset of a stroke increases. This is not altogether surprising, since the measurement of relative mortality in substandard lives at older ages is greatly influenced by the high level of 'expected' mortality prevailing at these ages.

The phenomenon of reducing mortality ratios with time elapsed, which is common to most medical impairments, does not seem to apply to cerebrovascular accidents. Haberman found no appreciable fall in the RAD index with time elapsed in most of the clinical studies he analyzed, and a similar finding was reported from Japan[16] among 1,532 men who were declined insurance because of a CVA: mortality ratios remained virtually unchanged by time elapsed even after the fifth year. This tends to support Marquardsen's observation that there is a constant annual mortality after the first year following a completed stroke and should be taken into account in the underwriting of these risks.

Also of interest is the relatively favorable mortality associated with intracerebral hemorrhage after one year compared with that for thrombotic and embolic strokes. Again the reason for this is understandable; intracerebral hemorrhage is much more closely associated with arterial hypertension, usually substantial, than other types of stroke and is often the sole pathology. Mortality is, of course, excessive in the early period following a hemorrhage. Baum and Robins,[17] in a national survey of stroke in the USA involving 1,846 subjects hospitalized for an initial stroke, found the in-hospital mortality among those with intraparenchymal hemorrhage to be 67·9 percent compared with 25·8 percent among patients with a thrombotic stroke. However, those who survive a hypertensive stroke are invariably treated with antihypertensive drugs and, if the blood pressure can be well controlled, the chances of a further hemorrhage are considerably reduced.

Risk factors, such as uncontrolled hypertension, heart failure and a previous history of stroke, had the effect of increasing the above RAD values substantially for all types of stroke.

Selection of Risks

A stroke is a serious illness and applicants with such a history must be carefully selected. Those with established systemic disease, particularly of the heart, should be excluded, as should those with substantial hypertension. If hypertension is being treated medically, it must be shown to have been under good control for an adequate period of time.

Neurological deficit following a completed stroke would be the rule, but would not necessarily call for additional rating unless there was also deterioration of higher cerebral functions leading to intellectual impairment, inability to communicate or loss of independent existence.

Rating

Known primary causes of stroke should be rated according to cause (e.g. mitral valve disease, atrial fibrillation, mitral or aortic valve replacement, meningiovascular syphilis etc). Stroke due to the contraceptive pill can be accepted standard after recovery provided the offending medication has been completely withdrawn. Transient focal neurological deficits (or even cerebral infarction) following an attack of migraine (*see* p. 747) would not attract a rating, but the diagnosis should be supported by a pre-existing history of typical migraine, and other causes of stroke should have been rigorously excluded.

Add rating for blood pressure with or without treatment. Applicants with substantial hypertension should usually be declined.

1) Single attack: cerebral infarction, thrombosis or embolism.

Time since attack	Ages		
	Under 50	50–59	60 and over
Within 1 yr	Postpone	Postpone	Postpone
2–5 yr	+400	+250	+150
6–10 yr	+300	+200	+125
Over 10 yr	+200	+150	+100

No neurological deficit on examination — credit 50 points.
More than one attack — usually decline.

2) Single attack: intracerebral hemorrhage, hypertensive stroke.

Time since attack	Ages		
	Under 50	50–59	60 and over
Within 1 yr	Postpone	Postpone	Postpone
2–3 yr	+150	+100	+75
4–5 yr	+125	+75	+50
Thereafter	+100	+50	+25

Minor blood pressure impairment — add rating (*see* Chapter 14).
More severe blood pressure impairment — decline.
More than one attack — usually decline.

Transient Ischemic Attacks (TIAs)

A TIA is an episode of brief neurological deficit secondary to temporary interruption of the arterial blood supply to a part of the brain. The resulting symptomatology will depend on the territory of supply affected. The attack usually lasts from a few minutes to several hours but, by definition, must be shorter than 24 hours. If neurological signs or symptoms persist longer than one day, even if minor, the episode is termed a stroke.

Transient cerebral ischemia may occur in territories supplied by either carotid or vertebrobasilar arteries. In 50 percent of cases attacks are caused by multiple microemboli originating from an ulcer in an atheromatous plaque situated in one or other of the cervical extracranial arteries. More rarely TIAs are caused by reduction of perfusion through extracranial arteries grossly narrowed by atheroma, and attacks are often precipitated by conditions causing hypotension. When there is significant atherostenosis a localized bruit in the neck will often be heard with the stethoscope.

Vertebrobasilar ischemia may also be related to movements of the neck suggesting compression of the artery by cervical osteophytes or, if the radial pulse is absent, to the subclavian steal syndrome when the arm is exercised.

Symptoms
The symptoms of transient ischemia arising in the territory of the carotid artery include amaurosis fugax, which is sudden monocular visual loss on the same side as the affected artery; the attack is usually brief, lasting about five minutes. Sometimes bright yellow cholesterol crystals or whitish fibrin platelet plugs may be seen traversing the retinal arterioles, a sign giving incontrovertible proof that the cause of the TIA is microemboli. Other symptoms include transient weakness or heaviness of an arm or leg on the contralateral side, sometimes accompanied by facial weakness. Sensory symptoms include tingling, pins and needles and numbness in the contralateral limbs and side of face. Transient ischemia in the dominant hemisphere may also cause dysphasia, usually expressive, but sometimes receptive.

Transient ischemia in the vertebrobasilar territory causes symptoms related to the structures in the brain stem, cerebellum and occipital lobe. The commonest symptom is vertigo which occurs in nearly half the attacks; this is often accompanied by marked unsteadiness while standing or walking. Rarely there is a hemianopic episode, but transient diplopia is quite common. Other symptoms reflect the involvement of the long sensory pathways and the pyramidal tracts on their passage through the brain stem, giving rise to transient hemipareses or hemisensory symptoms with facial involvement on the opposite side to the affected limbs. Circumoral sensory symptoms with involvement of both sides of the tongue may also occur.

Prognosis

The importance of a history of TIAs in the carotid territory is that a completed stroke may occur in about 30 percent of cases within the next three years. In the case of TIAs occurring in the territory of the vertebrobasilar artery the prognosis is rather better, despite the fact that attacks may be more numerous.

Treatment

Radical surgery is sometimes possible when TIAs have been caused by atheroma in one or other carotid artery. If the lesion is localized, as demonstrated by four-vessel angiography, thromboendarterectomy can prevent the occurrence of a disabling stroke in the next two or three years. Thromboendarterectomy now carries a mortality rate of less than 1 percent, and neurological damage may be expected in less than 3 percent of patients as a direct result of surgery itself, although some lesions cause only transient manifestations. Follow-up studies show that 10 percent of operated cases will die of a stroke within the next ten years.

Patients deemed unsuitable for surgery because of multiple stenoses are treated with antiplatelet agents which diminish the risk of stroke by one-third.

Selection of Risks

Mortality associated with TIAs is less than that following cerebral infarction and much less if vertebrobasilar ischemia is due only to external compression of the artery in the cervical spine. Care should be taken not to diagnose vertebrobasilar ischemia too readily on the single symptom of vertigo unless there is a good supporting evidence of vascular disease, or the pattern of onset is typical.

The prognosis following thromboendarterectomy of a localized atheromatous lesion is now proven to be favorable.

Rating

TIAs (including amaurosis fugax).

Time since last attack	Ages		
	Under 50	50–59	60 and over
Within 6 mth	Postpone	Postpone	Postpone
6–12 mth	+125	+75	+50
2–3 yr	+100	+50	+50
4–5 yr	+75	+50	+25
Thereafter	+25	Standard	Standard

1) Surgical treatment (thromboendarterectomy, bypass procedures):
Within six months — postpone.
Thereafter — no additional rating.
2) Carotid bruits, asymptomatic — standard.

3) Angiographic or imaging evidence of extensive or ulcerating lesions — rate as TIAs.

Minor Ischemic Stroke

This category is sometimes used for single attacks of minor stroke that do not fulfill the criteria for a TIA in that the neurological deficit persists for longer than 24 hours but resolves completely within the next few weeks. These attacks are usually embolic producing a limited infarction that may or may not be identified by imaging techniques. A modified rating could be justified for these minor strokes, and the schedule for intracerebral hemorrhage (single attack) is appropriate (*see* (2), p. 746). In cases where the neurological signs persist for longer than three months, though eventually disappearing, rating should be as for cerebral infarction (embolism) with any credit due for no neurological deficit on examination (*see* (1), p. 746).

Subarachnoid Hemorrhage

Spontaneous rupture of a congenital aneurysm of the circle of Willis is responsible for most examples of hemorrhage into the subarachnoid space. Less often it is bleeding from an angioma or extension of a hypertensive intracerebral hemorrhage into the ventricular system.

Congenital Aneurysms

The presence of a congenital intracranial aneurysm would be suspected only if it bleeds or enlarges sufficiently to cause pressure on surrounding structures. Therefore, unless it has been found by chance during the investigation of some unrelated condition, a congenital aneurysm will only become an impairment from the life underwriter's point of view after it has given rise to symptoms.

Mortality

The incidence of, and mortality from, subarachnoid hemorrhage increases with age, at least up to 60, and although bleeding from a congenital aneurysm may occur in the absence of hypertension it is likely that a rise of blood pressure in later life may be responsible, if not for the formation of the aneurysm, at least for its rupture.

The mortality rate of all subarachnoid hemorrhages is still almost one in three, and since second episodes of bleeding in those surviving an initial attack are common, surgical treatment is carried out whenever possible in order to forestall a further hemorrhage. McKissock et al[18] made a follow-up study of 94 patients with posterior communicating aneurysms, 48 of whom had been treated conservatively and 46 by surgery. Of the group treated conservatively, 42 who had been in good clinical condition had a mortality rate of 36 percent, and five of the six critically ill patients died. The bulk of deaths occurred in the first year following the initial bleed, mostly in the second and third weeks.

Surgical treatment

Four-vessel angiography is usually carried out on the third or fourth day after a subarachnoid hemorrhage. If the source of the bleeding is shown to be an aneurysm, surgery may be undertaken depending on its situation. For posterior communicating aneurysms a direct attack, by clipping the neck of the aneurysm, is the operation of choice. This offers over a 90 percent chance of completely eliminating the aneurysm. For technical reasons a direct attack on the aneurysm may not be possible, in which case the internal carotid artery on the same side is ligated. The latter operation has the disadvantage of eliminating from the cerebrovascular supply a major vessel and may prove critical if vascular insufficiency elsewhere develops subsequently or if another aneurysm develops. Also, at least half the aneurysms so treated fill with contrast medium at a subsequent angiography.

Selection of Risks

Subarachnoid hemorrhage is still frequently unrecognized as such, especially if the aneurysm has only leaked. Symptoms of unique headache, often recurrent and intense, and associated with nausea or actual vomiting, may precede a frank hemorrhage by several days or even months. Therefore when there is a recent history of severe headaches which are uncharacteristic for the applicant and which have not been investigated by angiography, the medical director would be justified in advising postponement of the applicant for several months.

Rating

Subarachnoid hemorrhage due to rupture of a congenital aneurysm, or other symptoms without hemorrhage; no, or minor, residual neurological deficit.
1) Medical (conservative) treatment.
Single attack:

	Rating	
Time since attack	Aged up to 40	Aged over 40
Within 1 yr	Postpone	Postpone
2nd yr	+250	+150
3rd yr	+200	+125
4th yr	+150	+100
5th yr	+125	+75
Thereafter	+100 to +50	+50

More than one attack — usually decline.
Ratable blood pressure — add to basic rating.

2) Surgical treatment.
Radical (direct obliteration of aneurysm):

Time since surgery	Rating
Within 6 mth	Postpone
6–24 mth	+5 per mil for 2 yr
Thereafter	Standard

Palliative (ligation of internal carotid artery) — rate as medical treatment.
Where four-vessel angiography fails to demonstrate an aneurysm or angioma —
rate as surgical treatment, radical.

Cerebral Arteriovenous Malformation (AVM): Cerebral Angioma

Cerebral AVMs may give rise at any time to hemorrhage, epilepsy or progressive
deterioration of cerebral function. The fatality rate from recurrent hemorrhage is
approximately 1 percent per year,[19] which nevertheless is less than that from
ruptured congenital aneurysms treated conservatively.[20]

Small AVMs, though they bleed profusely in the first attack, tend to have the
best outcome if they are situated superficially in a silent area in a neurologically
intact young patient. Hemorrhage from medium-sized AVMs is often slight but
repeated. Large, deeply seated lesions in patients with neurological damage have
the highest mortality and morbidity whatever type of management is followed.
Sometimes a cerebral AVM can be detected with a stethoscope; if the lesion is an
arteriocavernous fistula, it can be heard by the patient himself.

Cerebral AVMs are much less amenable to surgical treatment than congenital
aneurysms, mainly because of the inaccessibility of some, and because morbidity
and mortality associated with the surgical removal of others would be worse than
that associated with conservative treatment. For AVMs that cannot be removed,
radiotherapy, with or without clipping of feeding vessels, or artificial embolization
may be attempted with some degree of success.

Iansek et al[19] have published probability estimates for the outcome of AVMs
calculated from various published data. These, which are shown in Table 23.8,
compare the results of conservative and surgical management.

Table 23.8. Probability estimates for AVM.

Feature	Mean (%)	Mean (%)
Natural history (untreated over 20 years)		
Hemorrhage		
Annual rate	1	0·6–1·6
20-yr cumulative total	18	11·3–28
Sequelae of hemorrhage		
Immediate death	14	8–19
Morbidity	20	17–24
Surgical management		
AVM that has not bled		
Mortality	10	Unavailable
Morbidity	27	Unavailable
AVM that has bled		
Mortality	8	4–11
Morbidity	23	19–26

Rating

1) Without operation: no significant neurological deficit.
No history of bleeding:
  Small, superficial — +50.
  Large or deeply situated — +150 to +100.
With a history of bleeding — rate as ruptured congenital aneurysm, medical (conservative) treatment (*see* p. 750).
2) With operation or radiotherapy.
Complete obliteration of AVM — rate as congenital aneurysm, surgical, radical treatment (*see* p. 750).
Incomplete obliteration of AVM:
  Within six months — postpone.
  Thereafter — rate as congenital aneurysm, medical (conservative) treatment (*see* p. 750).
3) Associated epilepsy should be rated in addition as focal epilepsy (*see* pp. 738–40).

HEAD INJURIES

The commonest type of head injury results from direct or indirect violence, a blow or fall on the head, or a shock wave transmitted through the spine by jumping from a height and landing on the heels. The brain may be concussed, contused, lacerated and, if there is intracranial hemorrhage, compressed.

Although serious brain damage can occur without the skull being fractured, it is generally the case that closed head injuries are less serious and have a better late prognosis than injuries that have resulted in a compound, depressed fracture of the skull and a torn dura, or a fracture involving the nasal air sinuses or the middle ear.

A second prognostic sign of value is the duration of post-traumatic amnesia (for events prior to the period of unconsciousness); for increasing durations over 24 hours, the late prognosis for morbidity and mortality becomes worse, whereas periods of less than 24 hours indicate a mild injury with a favorable outcome.

The third prognostic factor is the occurrence of an epileptic fit in the first week after injury (early epilepsy). This considerably enhances the risk of late epilepsy which, in spite of an apparently good recovery, may develop several months or even years after the initial injury. Late epilepsy makes a significant contribution to the overall mortality following head injury, and its incidence requires closer scrutiny.

Jennett[21] calculated the initial risk (at the end of the first week) of late epilepsy in patients with compound, depressed fractures of the skull with a dural tear and varying combinations of risk factors, including post-traumatic amnesia longer than 24 hours and early epilepsy. When only one risk factor was known the initial risk of late epilepsy for each is as shown in Table 23.9. When all three risk factors were present together the incidence of late epilepsy rose to 70 percent. In almost half the patients in whom late epilepsy eventually developed, the first fit was delayed for a year or longer.

Table 23.9. Risk of late epilepsy associated with risk factors.

Risk factor	Risk of late epilepsy (%)
Post-traumatic amnesia of more than 24 hr	39
Dural tear	30
Early epilepsy	28

Mortality

In the *1951 Impairment Study*[8] the combined mortality experience of insured lives with a history of fractured skull was higher than that due to simple cerebral concussion, but was about the same when skull fractures requiring operation were excluded. Although the numbers in the operated group were small, the mortality ratio in those accepted as substandard risks approached 300 percent; and for all groups of fractured skull combined, the mortality ratio in the standard section was 127 percent, and 193 percent in the substandard section.

The *Medical Impairment Study 1983*[11] analyzed mortality following fractured skull (with or without operation) among male and female insureds. Males accounted for 92 percent of entrants, and 89 percent were under the age of 40 at time of issue. Relative mortality under the age of 40 was a modest 137 percent, but this tended to rise as age increased, reaching almost 200 percent in the 60–69 age group. Female exposure was too small to provide accurate results.

Selection of Risks

Particular attention should be paid to a history of psychiatric sequelae, since mortality from suicide in the *1951 Impairment Study*[8] was appreciably above the average expected, with deaths largely concentrated at ages under 40 at issue. The higher mortality in the substandard section of fracture of the skull with operation seemed to be accounted for mainly by diseases of the nervous system itself, such as epilepsy, meningitis and cerebrovascular disorders.

Rating

The duration of consecutive (or post-traumatic) amnesia after head injury has been mentioned as a valuable prognostic factor, but in practice it is difficult for the life underwriter to obtain accurate information about this from the applicant or the attending physician. Instead the duration of unconsciousness following injury has been found to be a reasonably reliable substitute, and one about which information is easier to obtain.

The rating schedules that follow illustrate the general practice of handling a history of head injuries. Unless stated otherwise, epilepsy occurring during the first week following head injury may be disregarded.

A history of epilepsy occurring more than one week after head injury should be rated as focal epilepsy (*see* pp. 738–40), with no further period of postponement, and added to the rating for head injury (*see below*).

1) Head injury, with or without skull fracture; no bone depression; no operation; full recovery; no residuals.
a) Unconscious less than six hours:
    No early epilepsy — standard.
    With early epilepsy — rate as (b) (*see below*).
b) Unconscious six to 48 hours:

Time since injury	Rating
Within 6 mth	Postpone
6–12 mth	2 per mil for 1 yr

c) Unconscious longer than 48 hours:

Time since injury	Rating
Within 6 mth	Postpone
6–12 mth	3 per mil for 3 yr
2nd yr	3 per mil for 2 yr
3rd yr	3 per mil for 1 yr

2) Head injury; with skull fracture and bone depression; surgical correction, closure of bony defect by prosthetic plate, or intracranial hemorrhage, epidural or subdural; full recovery with no, or minimal, residuals:

Time since injury	Rating
Within 1 yr	Postpone
2nd yr	5 per mil for 3 yr
3rd yr	5 per mil for 2 yr
4th yr	5 per mil for 1 yr

3) At ages 60 and over — increase the above temporary ratings by 2 per mil.

PROGRESSIVE DISEASES OF THE NERVOUS SYSTEM

Multiple Sclerosis: Disseminated Sclerosis

Multiple sclerosis has a very definite geographical distribution, being commonest in latitudes above 30°N and below 35°S. It is particularly prevalent in Western Europe and North America. It is commoner in the northern states of the USA than in the southern ones. An exception is Japan where the incidence of multiple sclerosis is uniformly low.

Multiple sclerosis is a chronic disease characterized clinically by a group of neurological symptom complexes which can remit, wholly or partially, and recur over a period of many years. The clinical picture is determined by the position of foci of demyelination, which have a predilection for certain parts of the nervous system. Microscopically, the striking feature of one of these lesions is the disappearance of medullary sheaths from the nerve fibrils due to loss of myelin. Despite this, the axis cylinders persist and are capable of transmitting impulses for a long time until they, too, are ultimately destroyed. In an old lesion reactive over-growth of neuroglia gives it the appearance of a plaque.

Etiology

Although the etiology of multiple sclerosis is not yet known, there is strong circumstantial evidence implicating infection; this may act by altering the antigenicity of the cell membrane of oligodendrocytes (which produce myelin in the central nervous system,) so that the body's immune mechanism attacks these cells, not recognizing them as 'self', causing a breakdown of myelin sheaths. This auto-immune reaction of the host is constitutionally determined, and the hereditary component can often be recognized by a higher incidence of multiple sclerosis among relatives of affected people. On the environmental side there is ample documentation of stressful situations preceding the onset of a relapse of multiple sclerosis, such as disturbing life events, severe injuries and infections, pregnancy and, especially, the puerperium. Therefore stress is capable of lowering auto-immune reactions in susceptible people.

Evaluating Early Symptoms

In its initial manifestations the diagnosis of multiple sclerosis can be difficult. Typically the onset is marked by sensory symptoms, signs often being transitory or absent. In the monosymptomatic form, for example, there may be a history of unilateral numbness and tingling in the fingers and hand, or of the whole arm, or vision may be lost in one eye. In the polysymptomatic form motor and sensory symptoms appear together, the commonest being loss of power in a lower limb causing dragging of the leg and unsteadiness of gait, paresthesiae and weakness of ocular muscles. These symptoms generally last for a few weeks before gradually disappearing. Such a history poses great problems for the life underwriter: should it be considered multiple sclerosis or might it be something quite benign? An agreed international classification of multiple sclerosis divides it into possible, probable and definite. Although raised levels of IgG in the cerebrospinal fluid, delayed visual or auditory evoked responses and the presence of a low-density lesion in a computerized tomography (CT) scan provide useful clues in the evaluation of a patient suspected of having multiple sclerosis, the definitive diagnosis is by magnetic resonance imaging (MRI). The certainty of the diagnosis is increased by the clinical picture.

Unlike the clinician, the life underwriter does not have the opportunity of waiting for the passage of time and of repeated examinations to make the diagnosis of multiple sclerosis certain. Instead he has to evaluate the risk from the evidence presented to him at any given moment in the course of the disease. In the case of a history of early symptoms where the clinical diagnosis of multiple sclerosis is indefinite, any rating would be based on a system of probabilities depending on the nature of the symptoms and their onset, and whether or not they have remitted and relapsed. Where there is laboratory support (especially MRI), the task is much easier.

Prognosis

The prognosis of confirmed multiple sclerosis is notoriously unpredictable. In a few instances one or two episodes of demyelination in the nervous system have been followed by lifelong remission, whereas in a few others death has been known to occur rapidly within several months of onset. The majority of cases, however, fall between the two extremes.

Müller[22] studied 810 cases of multiple sclerosis in Sweden. He found the average relapse rate over a period of ten years to be one every two years, the number of relapses being greatest in the first year of the disease and decreasing in frequency over the next five years. It was on the assumption that most damage to the nervous system occurs during the first five years, any subsequent progression being due to the effects of slow neuroglial scarring, that Alexander[23] based a prognosis of multiple sclerosis. This is that the fewer the physical signs present five years after onset the better the chances of a mild and prolonged course, and the more physical signs present the more severe the course of the disease and the shorter the expectation of life. A benign form of multiple sclerosis has always been emphasized by McAlpine and Compston[24] who studied 241 cases observed for 10–30 years and found that 34 percent were unrestricted in that they were capable of employment. A further study in 1964[25] showed that of the 78 capable of employment, 62 still remained unrestricted, and McAlpine suggested that 20 percent of people might be expected to remain unrestricted some 20 years after the onset of multiple sclerosis.

Retrospective surveys are subject to many fallacies, but prospective studies of multiple sclerosis are rarely practicable since the duration of the disease may exceed 25 years. However, a study by the United States Veterans Administration[26] comes nearer to a prospective study of multiple sclerosis than most. The series comprised 762 men of the US armed forces who were diagnosed as having multiple sclerosis during the period 1942–51 and who were followed up to 1962. Of these cases, 527 were classified as definite or probable multiple sclerosis; in one-half of them the onset attack had preceded the attack that led to diagnosis in the army. Of these men, 76 percent were alive 20 years and 69 percent 25 years after the onset of their disease. This represents a mortality rate approximately three times that of the general population of the USA adjusted for age and sex.

As far as it is possible to be dogmatic in a disease such as multiple sclerosis, several facts generally pertain. Early relapses are particularly common in patients developing the disease after the age of 25; later relapses tend to be of longer duration and tend to leave residual neurological deficit in their wake. Extremely long latent periods between the first and second attacks are quite common, and this is particularly true of patients presenting with acute optic (retrobulbar) neuritis (*see* pp. 758–9). For this reason, early optic neuritis is generally reputed to be a sign of favorable prognosis.

A chronic progressive stage occurs in many patients after frequent early relapses, and also in the 10–20 percent of cases in which a slowly progressive course is observed from the onset. A decline in neurological function may be extremely insidious and quite compatible with many years of useful and fairly active existence. The slowly progressive course is more common in patients in whom the first symptom occurs after the age of 40. In general, it may be stated that an onset (acute or subacute) affecting the posterior columns, brain stem or optic pathways followed by a low relapse rate with relatively slight effect on pyramidal and cerebellar pathways characterizes the benign form. In contrast, frequent relapses with persisting paraplegia, ataxia or urinary bladder paresis usually point to a progressive course.

Medical Examination

When there is a history of confirmed or possible multiple sclerosis the examining physician should extend his review of the central nervous system beyond the usual routine points requested in the proforma. It is always of great assistance to the medical director in his evaluation of a risk to know what actual signs, if any, of multiple sclerosis are present (e.g. nystagmus, intention tremor, inco-ordination or spasticity of limbs, absent abdominal reflexes or extensor plantar responses), because the currently reported physical signs can often be compared with those found in previous examinations, allowing an opinion to be formed of the progress, or otherwise, of the disease.

Rating

1) Tentative or possible diagnosis of multiple sclerosis; usually monosymptomatic (excluding optic neuritis); no neurological signs on examination:

Time since diagnosis	Rating	
	Single episode	Two episodes*
Within 1 yr	+75	+125
2nd yr	+50 to 0	+75
3rd yr	Standard	+50 to +25
Thereafter		Standard

*More than two attacks — rate as multiple sclerosis.

2) Definitive clinical diagnosis; usually polysymptomatic, with or without relapse. No abnormal neurological signs on examination:

Time since onset	Rating	
	Aged under 40	Aged 40 and over
Within 1 yr	+300	+200
2nd–3rd yr	+200	+150
4th yr	+150	+75
5th yr	+100	+50
8th–10th yr	+50	+25
Thereafter	Standard	Standard

Minimal signs on examination, no functional disability — add 50 and 25 points respectively, for under 40 and 40 and over (*see above*).

Moderate neurological abnormalities on examination; moderate impairment of function (but independent of wheelchair):

Time since onset	Rating	
	Aged under 40	Aged 40 and over
Less than 10 yr	+400 up	+250 up
More than 10 yr	Decline	Decline

Major neurological abnormalities (paraplegia, cord bladder, ataxia); use of wheelchair — decline.

Optic (Retrobulbar) Neuritis

When all other causes have been eliminated, acute, isolated optic neuritis of one eye is due to multiple sclerosis. The presenting symptom is unilateral blurring of vision due to a central scotoma, which generally enlarges over a few days, persists for several weeks and then gradually improves. Pain on movement of the eyeball is an additional symptom in the majority of cases.

Of those who develop an initial attack of optic neuritis, at least 10 percent will already have evidence of demyelination elsewhere, and some 30–50 percent of the remainder will ultimately develop further demyelination of the nervous system if they are followed up for many years. Since an isolated episode of acute optic neuritis may precede other manifestations of multiple sclerosis by several years, the underwriting risk will be much less than for confirmed multiple sclerosis, being highest in the first year following the attack, decreasing rapidly thereafter.

Gradual loss of vision is an infrequent occurrence after optic neuritis, but in the form of multiple sclerosis known as neuromyelitis optica, bilateral blindness characteristically precedes or accompanies signs of an acute or subacute myelitis. Occasionally, however, the picture is less dramatic. One or more attacks of optic neuritis affecting each eye in turn and eventually causing blindness may, months or years later, be accompanied or followed by paraplegia and other evidence of multiple sclerosis.

Rating

Optic neuritis; CNS otherwise normal:

Time since attack	Rating	
	Single attack	One recurrence*
Within 1 yr	+75	+100
2nd yr	+50	+75
Thereafter	Standard	+50 to 0

*More than two attacks — rate as multiple sclerosis.

Motor Neurone Disease (MND)

MND is a progressive, degenerative disease of the nervous system, worldwide in distribution, with an excess of male deaths in the ratio 1·5:1. Age-specific death rates rise from almost nil near the age of 50 to a maximum at the age of 70. The term MND embraces three clinical syndromes — progressive muscular atrophy, amyotropohic lateral sclerosis and progressive bulbar palsy — which often occur together in mixed form with one or other syndrome predominating. The onset is insidious and early signs may easily be missed on routine examination. If, however, the medical examiner makes it his practice always to inspect the hands, the typical wasting of the muscles of the thenar or hypothenar eminences or the interosseous spaces, particularly the first, may often provide a clue to the diagnosis. The characteristic fine fasciculation in the wasting muscles is a confirmatory sign of progressive muscular atrophy; weakness, increased deep reflexes and spasticity, particularly in a lower limb, indicate involvement of the pyramidal tracts.

The average duration of MND from onset to death is about four years,[27,28] but one-tenth of patients are known to survive ten years or longer, particularly those with progressive muscular atrophy. Expectation of life is shorter if the bulbar muscles are involved, but longer in progressive muscular atrophy.

There is no treatment that has the slightest effect in halting the relentless progression of MND, and with such a natural history it is obvious that applicants in whom the disease has been confirmed are uninsurable. A possible exception exists in the case of elderly applicants with recently diagnosed non-bulbar disease, whose average expectation of life closely matches the expected duration of the disease.

Peroneal Muscular Atrophy: Charcot-Marie-Tooth's Disease

Peroneal muscular atrophy is a hereditary disease of the nervous system, one type of which behaves as a medelian dominant, affecting and being transmitted by both sexes. It differs from progressive muscular atrophy not least because onset is very much earlier, most cases being recognized in late childhood. It is characterized by symmetrical muscular wasting and weakness affecting typically the small muscles of the foot and the peroneal muscles leading to the deformities of talipes equino varus and pes cavus. Many years later wasting may also appear in the hands, but wasting in the upper limbs does not extend higher than the elbows, nor in the legs higher than the junction of the middle and lower third of the thighs, producing a very typical appearance. Although peroneal muscular atrophy has been included for convenience in the section on progressive disorders of the nervous system, the essential feature of the disease is that it does not appear to shorten life.

In partial forms of the disease functional disability is minimal, but when muscular atrophy is complete it can be considerable, especially in the elderly. Nevertheless it is now the usual practice of most life insurance companies to accept applicants with peroneal muscular atrophy as standard risks.

Parkinsonism

Parkinsonism is a syndrome characterized by tremor, rigidity and hypokinesia. The condition may result from several causes, yet none has been found for the commonest form, widely known as paralysis agitans or Parkinson's disease. This large group may be referred to as idiopathic parkinsonism, although a few rare cases are genetically determined.

Etiology

Fifty years ago parkinsonism of known etiology was usually a sequel of encephalitis lethargica, but today postencephalitic parkinsonism is a condition of dwindling importance. If encephalitis lethargica still occurs, it does so only on a very small scale, and those people now suffering from postencephalitic parkinsonism are long-term survivors of the original epidemic. The implication is that this type of parkinsonism will soon disappear altogether and that the preponderance of idiopathic cases will become progressively greater.

Today parkinsonism of known etiology is, in most instances, drug induced, the phenothiazine derivatives being the most commonly implicated. It is noteworthy that an increased family incidence of parkinsonism is also to be found among people who develop drug-induced parkinsonism. Other known (but rare) causes are carbon monoxide and manganese poisoning and repeated head injury. Arteriosclerotic parkinsonism is now thought by most neurologists to be the idiopathic type occurring fortuitously in people suffering from cerebral arteriosclerosis.

Some or all of the features of parkinsonism may be present in hepatolenticular degeneration (Wilson's disease) and in the rigid akinetic form of Huntington's chorea, both of which will be discussed later in this chapter. Other rare neurological conditions that may show parkinsonism are the Shy-Drager syndrome, Creutzfeldt-Jakob disease and progressive supranuclear palsy.

Course and Prognosis

Parkinsonism is a common disorder, but its prevalence is difficult to determine; it tends to be under-diagnosed because of the insidious nature of its onset and because some of its manifestations are often wrongly considered to be normal features of aging. Mortality statistics are also misleading: the cause of death is usually something other than parkinsonism, and therefore parkinsonism does not always appear on death certificates.

Although parkinsonism induced by drugs is usually, but not invariably, reversible, the idiopathic type is progressive. In a comprehensive study of the subject of Hoehn and Yahr,[29] the average survival of patients with idiopathic parkinsonism was found to be nine years from the onset of symptoms, although there was a wide variation. In postencephalitic parkinsonism the mean duration of survival was nearly three times as long, partly reflecting the earlier age of onset. This confirms the generally held impression that the disease process of most postencephalitic patients seems to reach a plateau beyond which only very slow progression occurs. Parkinsonism with tremor as the initial symptom was found to progress more slowly than if it presented in other ways. The commonest causes of death in all age groups were arteriosclerotic heart disease, bronchopneumonia, malignant neoplasms, vascular lesions of the central nervous system and infections of the urinary tract.

Levodopa is by far the most effective treatment yet discovered for parkinsonism. Four patients out of five improve with a mean 40–50 percent reduction in disability, and many maintain some benefit for at least five years of levodopa treatment; it is now known that the life expectancy of those who respond best is increased by several years. Nevertheless treatment with levodopa presents many problems: 10–25 percent of patients on long-term therapy develop psychiatric symptoms, the common problems being agitation, irritability and insomnia. Occasionally anxiety, fear and apprehension acquire paranoid features and progress to hypomania; some patients become depressed and may attempt suicide. These manifestations of drug toxicity are reversible when levodopa is stopped. Nevertheless evidence is accumulating that there is an increased prevalence of dementia in parkinsonism which cannot always be attributed to treatment or concomitant cerebrovascular disease.

Shaw et al[30] studied 178 parkinsonian patients followed up for six years. All were treated with levodopa, with some 70 percent initially showing a marked to moderate response to the drug and a mean 50 percent reduction in disability. After two years 35 percent of the patients had stopped levodopa either because of inadequate response or because of side effects of treatment, and by the end of six years 50 percent had ceased treatment. Using UK population statistics as a basis, the mortality ratio for all patients over the six years of study was calculated to be 145 percent. For those unable to tolerate levodopa for longer than two years it was 238 percent, and for those able to sustain medication for the whole period it was 100 percent of expected. Therefore there is adequate evidence of increased survival in parkinsonian patients who can continue with levodopa treatment; moreover they enjoy an improved quality of life.

Rating

Idiopathic and postencephalitic parkinsonism cannot be distinguished with certainty but can be considered together for the purpose of risk evaluation. Applicants may be grouped according to their clinical state on examination:

1) Those with early symptoms of localized tremor, without rigidity and not usually requiring specific treatment.

2) Those having a history of more widespread tremor, with or without slight to moderate rigidity; currently on treatment with levodopa for two years or more, with or without anticholinergic drugs; good toleration and response to treatment; minimal disability.

3) Those showing the typical parkinsonism triad of tremor, rigidity and hypo-kinesia, unable to tolerate levodopa or other dopamine agonists, but not dependent on others and showing no intellectual deterioration.

Clinical state	Rating		
	Under 50	50–59	60–65[a]
1	+75	+50	+25
2	+100	+75	+50
3	+200	+150	+100

[a]For ages over 65 rating is best calculated as an addition of years to age.

Significant deterioration in intellectual capacity, dementia or chronic depression — decline.

Drug-induced parkinsonism would not usually require a separate debit; it would be sufficient to rate the primary condition for which the drugs were being prescribed.

Essential Tremor

Essential tremor is a chronic, benign, monosymptomatic disorder of unknown etiology which progresses very slowly over several decades. The peak incidence is in early adult life, and there is often a positive family history. The tremor varies widely in amplitude and frequency, at first being noticeable only on movement but later also appearing at rest. It affects the head much more often than does parkinsonian tremor, but nearly always spares the legs. There are no other abnormal neurological signs, such as rigidity or hypokinesia, and significant incapacity does not develop. A similar tremor appearing in old age is referred to as senile tremor. If there is a positive family history, the condition is usually called familial tremor. No extra risk need be anticipated in applicants with essential tremor.

Wilson's Disease: Hepatolenticular Degeneration

Thirty years ago there would have been little point in mentioning Wilson's disease in the context of life insurance since it was invariably fatal within five to ten years of onset of symptoms. However, the prognosis has changed so dramatically since the introduction in 1956 of penicillamine, the first effective form of treatment for the disease, that applications for life insurance are now being made by people with

Wilson's disease who are under treatment, well controlled and asymptomatic. It is therefore necessary to take a closer look at the disease with a view to identifying those who are likely to have the best long-term prognosis and who might be suitable candidates for life insurance.

Hepatolenticular degeneration, or Wilson's disease, is a rare hereditary disease of copper metabolism which behaves as an autosomal recessive and is usually transmitted to offspring by parents who are each heterozygous to the abnormal gene. Starting soon after birth, dietary copper absorbed from the intestine is stored in excess in the liver and later released to be deposited in the brain, kidneys, corneae and other organs.

Symptomatology

The symptomatology of Wilson's disease is due entirely to the toxicity of excess copper in the organs where it accumulates. Thus disease of the liver starts as steatosis and proceeds through the stage of chronic active hepatitis to postnecrotic cirrhosis with all the usual complications.

In the brain the basal ganglia are mainly affected, and clinically there may be tremor and chorea or choreoathetoid movements, but the most characteristic sign is a mixture of parkinsonism and cerebellar ataxia. Kayser-Fleischer rings are invariably present in the corneae when the brain is affected, but may be absent when the mode of onset is hepatic disease. In the kidneys anomalies of reabsorption occur in the proximal renal tubules, producing aminoaciduria, uricosuria, glycosuria or phosphaturia. Renal involvement usually indicates a poor prognosis despite treatment with penicillamine.

Diagnostic tests

Wilson's disease is confirmed by a combination of abnormal biochemical tests (see Table 23.10).

Table 23.10. Biochemical values in Wilson's disease and normal subjects.

Assay	Normal	Wilson's disease
Serum, copper (mg/dl)	81–147	10–80
Ceruloplasmin (mg/dl)	25–43	0–20
Urine copper (μg/24-hr)	5–25	100–4000
Liver copper (μg/g dry weight)	18–45	250–2000

It is important to remember that biochemical abnormalities may also be present in some heterozygotes. This can lead initially to an incorrect diagnosis of Wilson's disease, although the true nature of the condition will usually become apparent after further investigation and observation. The serum copper may be slightly low, in the range 60–80μg/dl, the ceruloplasmin decreased to 5–20 mg/dl, and the liver copper increased by up to 200 μg/g dried weight. Copper excretion in the urine is not, however, significantly increased. Despite their biochemical anomalies, these heterozygotes will always be symptomless, will not require specific chelating therapy and can be accepted as standard risks.

Course and Prognosis

Clinical symptoms, apart from hemolytic anemia, are rare during the first five years of life. Thereafter the course of the disease is extremely variable. A peak incidence of symptoms occurs in the second decade. Hepatic symptoms are more frequent in people with an early onset, whereas those whose symptoms first occur later usually present with neurological disease.

Strickland et al[31] analyzed the relationship of treatment to prognosis in 142 patients from the UK and Taiwan with Wilson's disease; there were 55 Chinese from Taiwan and 87 subjects from the UK. Of the total, 122 had the initial onset of symptoms, or had the diagnosis established, between the ages of five and 25 years. Eighty-eight patients (71 symptomatic and 17 asymptomatic) who were treated with penicillamine given for periods of up to 16 years were followed either to death or to the end of the study in 1972. Of the symptomatic patients, 35 were treated with penicillamine; 31 of these remained alive and 18 became asymptomatic. All but one of the symptomatic patients not receiving penicillamine therapy died, and the remaining one had severe disease. All but one of the treated asymptomatic patients were alive and remained asymptomatic. The four symptomatic patients who did not respond to penicillamine died between four and 12 months after commencing treatment; three had renal tubular acidosis and in the other renal involvement was not excluded. Other workers have also reported excellent therapeutic response to penicillamine in cases of Wilson's disease, both symptomatic and asymptomatic.

Clearly the prognosis is best when treatment has commenced before symptoms have appeared and before significant tissue damage has been caused. This is often the case when an individual has been screened as a result of a sibling already developing overt Wilson's disease. Patients who are symptomatic when they commence penicillamine therapy generally respond well, and some may eventually become asymptomatic; but even in those who do not, liver function usually improves, tremor and rigidity become less and mental changes disappear. Unfortunately a small proportion of patients develop toxic reactions to penicillamine; the most serious of which are the nephrotic syndrome and a lupus-like disease. They have to be treated with other chelating agents, such as triethylene tetramine dihydrochloride (Trien) or BAL. However, serious complications are rare in patients with Wilson's disease, and lesser toxic reactions can usually be controlled by corticosteroid cover.

Selection of Risks

It may take from six to 12 months from the commencement of therapy before the excess copper has been removed from the body and the stage of maintenance therapy and negative copper balance is reached. Therefore it is suggested that applicants with Wilson's disease should be postponed for at least two years from commencement of treatment. The case data should be well documented, with information on serial liver function tests and liver biopsies available to the underwriters.

The risk will be highest in the early years of treatment, gradually reducing with time elapsed and the absence of complications. Since the disease is rare and treatment regimes with penicillamine and other drugs have only been in use for a relatively short time, statistics of mortality are not yet adequate to make accurate predictions about long-term survival. But clinical impressions are so far extremely favorable, and it is suggested that best-risk cases of Wilson's disease could reasonably be insured at a premium equivalent to 250 percent extra mortality in the third year of treatment, reducing to 150 percent by the sixth year, and 100 percent thereafter. Additions to the basic ratings would be required for applicants showing residual symptoms but maintaining a stable pattern. Those with significant renal tubular abnormalities should be declined.

Huntington's Disease

Huntington's disease (or chorea) is a degenerative disorder of the central nervous system characterized pathologically by atrophy of the ganglion cells in the forebrain and corpus striatum. It is inherited according to the laws of autosomal dominance with almost complete penetrance, although occasional sporadic cases occur. The usual clinical picture is of choreoathetoid movements and dementia starting in middle life mainly between the ages of 30 and 45, although onset at as late as 71 has been reported.[32] A juvenile form, with onset before the age of 20, has also been described. The onset of Huntington's disease is insidious and the progress generally slow; although some people may survive up to 30 years from the onset of symptoms, the average duration of life is only about 10–15 years, death being due to intercurrent infection or other diseases and, in not a few instances, suicide.

Data on mean age of onset, duration and age at death in Huntington's disease can be derived from a composite of studies reported between 1934 and 1970 (*see* Table 23.11). However, Newcombe[32] considers that age at death reported in older studies, such as those mentioned, tended to be biased because they excluded heterozygotes who had not manifested the disease by the termination of the studies. By including all definite or possible unaffected heterozygotes in his own study, Newcombe[32] observed a mean ± SD age at onset of 41·60 ± 12·29 years, both sexes combined, a considerably older age than had previously been reported.

Table 23.11. Huntington's disease: age at onset, mean duration and age at death, studies reported 1934–70.

Age at onset		Mean duration	Age at death	
Males	Females	(yr)	Males	Females
38·4	38·4	13·5	53·0	53·5

Selection of Risks

Obviously, people who have already developed symptoms of Huntington's disease would be uninsurable. The difficult problem in underwriting arises in the case of a young person who, at the time of application, is asymptomatic but who has a family history of the disease. There is a prior genetic risk of 50 percent, 25 percent or 12·5 percent, according to whether the last forbear known to be heterozygous (i.e. manifested the disease) was the parent, grandparent or great-grandparent. Age is also crucially important: it has been calculated that between 21–34 percent of all eventual sufferers from Huntington's disease will have shown symptoms by the age of 30. Therefore the probability of manifesting the disease decreases as the individual gets older, particularly after the age of 45.

In addition to the applicant's age, an evaluation of the risk would also take into account all other known factors of the case, such as the ages of onset of symptoms and at death of all affected relatives going back, if possible, as far as great-grandparents. For example, if the last forbear known to be heterozygous was a grandparent, the chances of a grandson or grand-daughter ever becoming affected would be virtually nil, provided the parent at risk was still asymptomatic by the time he or she had reached the age of 60.

Predictive Tests

It is now possible to predict whether an asymptomatic offspring of a Huntington's chorea family is carrying the affected gene.[33,34] Genetic testing can be employed for both presymptomatic and prenatal exclusion of Huntington's disease when the individuals specifically request it, but pre-test counseling becomes so all-important when dealing with such a serious disease that, as a result, many presymptomatic people eventually withdraw from the test program.

Knowledge of an accurate predictive test would be invaluable to a life underwriter in the evaluation of an at-risk applicant, allowing standard rates when the test is negative, or a correspondingly lower extra premium if it shows a substantially reduced risk of developing Huntington's disease in the order of 5 percent or less[34] depending on age.

Rating

The following schedule may be used as a basis for rating asymptomatic applicants with a family history of Huntington's disease in one or other parent or a sibling (genetic risk 50 percent) when no predictive tests have been performed. In theory, ratings could be suitably modified if the last forbear known to be heterozygous was (1) a grandparent (genetic risk 25 percent) or (2) a great-grandparent (genetic risk 12·5 percent); in practice, however, family histories in a life insurance setting tend to be incomplete and unsubstantiated so that the underwriter usually has no option but to consider the genetic risk 50 percent and rate accordingly.

Age	Rating
Under 21	Decline
21–35	7 per mil for 10 yr
36–45	5 per mil for 10 yr
46–55	5 per mil until age 55
56 and over	Standard

Predictive Genetic Tests
1) Negative for heterozygosity — standard.
2) Risk of heterozygosity 5 percent or less:
Under age 40 — 3 per mil for 3 yr.
Age 40 and over — standard.
3) Risk of heterozygosity greater than 5 percent up to 50 percent — rate as schedule above.
4) Otherwise — decline.

Congenital Diplegia: Cerebral Palsy

The diseases grouped under the heading of congenital diplegia are characterized by bilateral and symmetrical involvement of the motor cortex, the cerebellum or extrapyramidal system, either alone or in combination. Spastic weakness is the most common manifestation, the legs being involved more than the arms. The degree of severity may range from a very mild form to the most severe in which there is marked spasticity of all extremities together with dysarthria and dysphagia from involvement of bulbar muscles. Cerebellar ataxia or choreoathetosis may dominate the clinical picture or accompany the spasticity. Mental retardation of all degrees may be present, but often this is only apparent because of slowness in development due to the motor disabilities; with proper management normal intelligence is frequently attained.

The disabilities are present from birth and do not progress; in fact, some children improve with training. Many congenital diplegics who survive to adult life are insurable, but standard acceptance should be limited to those who show no significant mental defect and whose motor disability is only moderate. Those having a more severe motor impairment, but who are still able to work and live independently, would be ratable in the range +50 to +100. Epilepsy should be rated as an additional impairment, but those having significant involvement of the bulbar muscles should be declined.

Occasionally the question of insuring large groups of 'spastics' may arise in connection with a group pension scheme, since several types of employment exist where they can work conveniently together. Provided they are employed full-time, insurance within the group arrangement may be undertaken with an appropriate premium loading.

Friedreich's Ataxia

Friedreich's ataxia is a progressive hereditary disorder characterized by degeneration of the posterior columns, lateral columns and spinocerebellar tracts, which gives rise to the typical ataxia; other congenital abnormalities, such as spina bifida, pes cavus and scoliosis, are also commonly present. Symptoms usually appear before adolescence, but in a few instances may be delayed until early adulthood. The span of life varies with the age at onset of symptoms, being longer the later the age at onset. In a study of 82 fatal cases of proven Friedreich's ataxis, Hewer[35] found that 39 patients who developed ataxia between the ages of one and ten had a mean duration of life of 20·7 years (range one to 41 years) and 32 who developed ataxia between the ages of 11 and 20 years had a mean duration of life of 29·4 years (range eight to 48 years). The average age at death for the whole series was 36·6 years. The commonest causes of death in Friedreich's ataxia are heart failure and diabetes mellitus or its complications.

The heart is abnormal in a large proportion of cases of confirmed Friedreich's ataxia, the characteristic lesion being hypertrophic obstructive cardiomyopathy.[36] Harding and Hewer[37] reviewed 115 patients with carefully defined Friedreich's ataxia and found normal ECGs in 25 percent, major ECG abnormalities in 66 percent and minor abnormalities in the remaining 9 percent. Of the patients with major ECG abnormalities, 95 percent had widespread T-wave inversions and were diagnosed as having definite cardiomyopathy. The commonest symptoms were exertional dyspnea and palpitations, affecting 60 percent of the 115 patients, mostly with abnormal ECGs; four had typical angina of effort due to hypertrophic cardiomyopathy. Heart failure seems to be a late feature of Friedreich's ataxia and is often preterminal, the mean period to death after the onset of failure being 2·2 years.

For expectation of life, Harding and Hewer[37] thought there can be little doubt that ECG abnormalities do have a prognostic significance, since the proportion of patients with abnormal ECGs fell with increasing duration of the disease, implying that those with Friedreich's ataxia live longer if they do not have heart disease. The mean duration of neurological disease in their series was 22·0 ± 12·8 (range two to 61) years.

It is evident, therefore, that most cases of Friedreich's ataxia will be uninsurable, but special consideration may sometimes be possible for applicants in adult life whose neurological disabilities are slight, and whose ECGs are normal or show only insignificant abnormalities.

Familial Cerebellar Ataxia: Familial Spastic Paraplegia

The genetic trait of Friedreich's ataxia can also assume diverse clinical patterns, among which are progressive forms of familial cerebellar ataxia and familial spastic paraplegia. These also lead to severe disability and ultimate crippling, necessitating confinement to a wheelchair or bed; as a general rule, all would be unacceptable insurance risks.

Syringomyelia; Syringobulbia

Syringomyelia is a progressive disorder of the nervous system in which central cavitation occurs, particularly in the cervical part of the spinal cord. The syrinx may extend downwards in the spinal cord or upwards to the medulla; in the latter situation the disease is called syringobulbia.

Typically, dissociated anesthesia occurs in the upper limbs and in a cape or half-cape distribution over one or both shoulders. Usually the condition also causes atrophy of upper limb muscles and absent tendon reflexes, but pyramidal tract involvement of the lower limbs is generally a later sign. When syringobulbia is present, there is also dysphagia due to involvement of the muscles of swallowing. The symptoms of syringomyelia usually become apparent in early adult life, tend to progress up to a certain point over the course of several years and then remain unchanged for long periods.

A congenital lesion with cavitation or with abnormal glial tissue in the center of the cord is the most widely held explanation of syringomyelia. An increasing number of cases, however, are being explained by a Chiari malformation at the foramen magnum causing dilatation of the central canal of the spinal cord which may form diverticula and, in turn, dissect downwards along the centre of the cord. If syringomyelia due to a Chiari malformation is diagnosed early enough, surgical decompression at the foramen magnum may result in the complete resolution of the symptoms and signs of the disease.

Because of their tendency to cystic formation, intramedullary tumors of the cord in the cervicodorsal region (gliomas, hemangioblastomas or ependymomas) may give rise to signs and symptoms almost identical with those of syringomyelia. The distinction from syringomyelia can be made by modern non-invasive techniques which show a well-filled cystic syrinx contrasting with the more typical collapsed intramedullary cyst of syringomyelia. Also, the protein content of the cerebrospinal fluid is raised in the case of tumors, whereas it is normal in syringomyelia. The presence of congenital skeletal abnormalities, such as cervical ribs, spina bifida occulta and scoliosis, may be useful clues supporting the diagnosis of syringomyelia in doubtful cases.

Selection of Risks

Applicants with syringobulbia or with signs of a cervicodorsal syrinx for which a tumor etiology has not been excluded should be declined. Similarly applicants with evidence of advanced syringomyelia producing Charcot joints, spasticity of the lower limbs and loss of sphincter control would be uninsurable. Even best-risk cases of non-progressive syringomyelia showing minimal evidence of dissociated anesthesia and lower motor neurone signs in the upper limbs without involvement of the pyramidal tracts would be eligible only for limited plans of insurance, ceasing by the age of 60 or 65, at a rating of about +200.

Where there is a history of operation to correct a Chiari or other malformation, that has resulted in the disappearance of signs of syringomyelia, standard acceptance may be considered one year after operation, or with a suitable rating if there are significant residual neurological abnormalities.

Spina Bifida Occulta

Spina bifida occulta is a minor malformation of one or two spinous processes and laminae in which there is a gap in the vertebral arches. The cord and membranes are normally positioned.

The condition is often symptomless and is frequently noted fortuitously in routine radiograms of the spine. In other cases symptoms arise in adolescence or later due to traction on the anterior part of the cord by a fibrous band connecting the dura mater with the deep surface of the skin. There may be a localized motor paresis resulting in bilateral deformity of the feet, especially claw foot. In some cases paralytic dilatation of the bladder occurs, or there may be nocturnal enuresis. Symptomless spina bifida occulta can be disregarded in underwriting, but if it is complicated by a cord bladder an appropriate rating would be required (*see* p. 731).

Subacute Combined Degeneration of the Cord

This has been considered elsewhere (*see* pp. 656–8).

Hydrocephalus

Cerebrospinal fluid is normally secreted by the choroid plexuses, passes through the ventricular system to the cisterna magna and over the surface of the brain, and is absorbed into the large venous sinuses. Hydrocephalus is an increased volume of cerebrospinal fluid with increased pressure due to a disturbance of the formation, circulation or absorption of the fluid. In some cases one, two or all of these factors operate. Here, the concern is the insurability of applicants with surgically treated obstructive hydrocephalus. Obstruction to the cerebrospinal fluid may occur at three points: (1) in the aqueduct of Sylvius, (2) at the foramina in the roof of the fourth ventricle, and (3) around the midbrain where it is gripped by the tentorium.

Postmeningitic adhesions, which occlude the foramina of the fourth ventricle, are responsible for the majority of cases of hydrocephalus. A frequent cause is the Arnold-Chiari malformation at the foramen magnum, which prevents cerebrospinal fluid from passing round the brain stem to reach the cerebral subarachnoid space. This malformation is commonly associated with spina bifida and myelomeningocele. Stenosis of the aqueduct of Sylvius is occasionally caused by the pressure of a tumor, but more often by a congenital malformation or scar tissue in the lumen. Table 23.12 shows the causes of hydrocephalus and their relative occurrence in a series of 297 operated cases reviewed by Sloan Robertson et al.[38]

Table 23.12. Causes of hydrocephalus in 297 patients.[38]

Cause	Number of patients	%
Postmeningitic	64	21·5
Tumors	62	20·9
Myelomeningocele/Arnold-Chiari	55	18·5
Aqueduct stenosis	27	9·1
Various	89	30·0
Total	297	100·0

Shunts

Although the introduction of various shunting and bypassing operations has transformed the management of hydrocephalus, morbidity and mortality often depend more on the cause of hydrocephalus than on the particular drainage technique employed. The following shunt procedures are used.

Ventriculoatrial: a silicone tube placed in the lateral ventricle is brought out through a burr hole in the skull and led down the neck buried in the subcutaneous tissue to enter the jugular vein and thence to the right atrium. A Spitz-Holter valve is fitted to the tube to prevent backflow. This technique is widely adopted as the standard treatment of hydrocephalus.

Torkildsen tube: this drains cerebrospinal fluid from a lateral ventricle to the basal arachnoid cistern.

Ventriculoperitoneal tube: a tube draining the lateral ventricle is led by the subcutaneous route to the abdomen where it ends by draining into the preitoneum above the liver. No intervening valve is necessary.

The main complications of shunts are blockage (especially of a valve), infection and, in atrial shunts, thromboembolic phenomena. Revision of a shunt is necessary when it becomes blocked; this is relatively easy to accomplish when a ventriculoperitoneal shunt blocks at its distal end, but extremely difficult in ventriculoatrial shunts once venous thrombosis has occurred. Because of this, ventriculoatrial shunts are often revised prophylactically at regular intervals whether blockage has occurred or not. All the patients in the series reviewed by Sloan Robertson et al[38] had ventriculoperitoneal shunts and were adequately followed up. Although 44 percent required revision, one-third of these remained well and without complications for three years from the original operation.

Selection of Risks
If hydrocephalus is secondary to an intracranial tumor (e.g. a pinealoma), the risk should be evaluated according to the nature of the tumor and whether or not it has been radically treated. If a tumor has not been treated radically, any bypass operation becomes a palliative measure; as such the risk would be uninsurable. If, as occasionally happens, hydrocephalus is due to an unsuspected tumor, which has escaped detection during initial investigations, the early risk can be considerably lessened by having an adequate postponement period following insertion of a bypass. However, the problem of undetected tumors has diminished with modern imaging techniques.

Apart from the risk associated with the primary lesion, there remains the risk following insertion of a shunt, and this is considerable. The overall infection rate associated with shunts of any kind is high, and the higher the rate in studied groups the greater the reported mortality. The revision rate of shunts is also a good prognostic index. In those who die the revision rate is always appreciably higher than in long-term survivors.

It is evident, therefore, that only a very few carefully selected applicants with a history of hydrocephalus treated by a shunt procedure would be suitable candidates for life insurance. Before applications can be considered, it is suggested that a postponement period of one year is necessary following the establishment of a shunt, during which time there should be no episodes of significant infection (meningitis, septicemia), thromboembolic phenomena or blockage of the shunt.

Rating
Establishment of a shunt or revision of a shunt because of a blockage; no subsequent history of major infection:

Time since shunt/revision	Rating
Within 1 yr	Postpone
2nd yr	+100 and 10 per mil for 3 yr
3rd yr	+100 and 10 per mil for 2 yr
4th yr	+100 and 5 per mil for 2 yr
Thereafter	+100

2) Meningitis or other serious infection since shunt established — decline.
3) More than one revision for blockage — decline.
4) Planned revisions, no blockage — disregard.
5) Where the etiology of the hydrocephalus is tumor — rate, according to its type, after treatment (*see* pp. 630–6) and add to rating for hydrocephalus.
6) Operation to correct an Arnold-Chiari malformation; no artificial shunt:

Time since operation	Rating
Within 1 yr	Postpone
Thereafter	Standard

Benign Intracranial Hypertension

This is a form of hydrocephalus, due to impaired absorption of cerebrospinal fluid from the arachnoid villi, of obscure etiology, but not due to known serious causes, such as intracranial tumor or impediment to the venous drainage from the head by raised intrathoracic pressure in the case of pulmonary neoplasm or severe emphysema. Impaired absorption may be due to obliteration of some arachnoid villi by previous meningitis or to thrombosis of the superior longitudinal and lateral sinuses as a result of middle ear infection.

There are the usual signs of increased intracranial pressure, including papilledema, which can be relieved by repeated lumbar punctures until the condition resolves, usually after a few months. There are no serious complications of benign intracranial hypertension; the risk may be covered by a small temporary extra premium while treatment continues, but would become standard after the cerebrospinal fluid pressure had stabilized at normal levels for a period of six months.

NEUROMUSCULAR DISEASES

Muscular Dystrophy

Muscular dystrophy is not common, but it is one of the most important of the neuromuscular diseases. It is always inherited and is the result of a primary degenerative process involving the muscle cells.

Naturally some types of muscular dystrophy in which the prognosis for life is universally poor cannot be considered for life insurance. Other types compatible with moderately long survival may be suitable for specially designed plans of insurance, whereas a few with an excellent prognosis for normal survival can be considered for ordinary life insurance without undue risk to the insurer. To aid recognition of the different varieties of muscular dystrophy a short description of each will be given; they are classified according to genetic criteria as recommended by Walton.[39] It should be pointed out, however, that the accurate diagnosis of muscle diseases is a problem requiring considerable expertise, knowledge and full investigative facilities, and without an accurate diagnosis there can be no accurate prognosis. Therefore before an applicant suffering from one of the neuromuscular diseases is issued insurance the underwriter should make certain that the diagnosis has been authenticated by a competent neurologist.

Electromyography and muscle biopsy are useful in confirming a diagnosis of muscular dystrophy but are otherwise non-specific. Serum enzyme estimations have proved to be more sensitive. Serum aldolase and creatine phosphokinase (CPK) are markedly elevated in the early stages of Duchenne muscular dystrophy and while the patient is still ambulant, but values return to normal in the late stages of the disease. CPK may be elevated in asymptomatic carriers. In facioscapulohumeral muscular dystrophy the enzymes remain normal, except for the serum CPK which is slightly elevated.

Duchenne Type

Duchenne muscular dystrophy is the commonest and most severe type of muscular dystrophy. It is transmitted in a sex-linked recessive manner by a symptomless female carrier so that half her sons may be dystrophic and half her daughters may be carriers. The usual form of the disease begins in about the third year of life with slowness and clumsiness in walking and running, frequent falling, and difficulty in climbing stairs and rising from the floor. There is a steady deterioration until, by the time the boy is about ten years old, he is unable to walk and is confined to a wheelchair. Eventually he becomes bedridden and dies, usually before the end of the second decade. Life underwriters are unlikely to see examples of Duchenne muscular dystrophy in the course of their work.

Becker Type

The Becker type of muscular dystrophy is also transmitted as a sex-linked recessive but is much more benign than the Duchenne type, which it resembles closely in its clinical manifestations (except that the first symptoms arise at a substantially later age and progress at a much slower pace). Muscular weakness usually develops in the late teens or early 20s, sometimes preceded by a phase of diffuse muscle hypertrophy, but most of these patients can walk until they are 40 or 45 years of age when they become confined to a wheelchair. Many live for a further 15 years. It is often possible to offer plans of insurance for up to 25 years at an appropriate extra premium to selected applicants with Becker muscular dystrophy whose onset of symptoms occurred at about the age of 20 or later. The genes for both Duchenne and Becker dystrophies have now been located on the same chromosome.

Limb Girdle Muscular Dystrophy

This form of muscular dystrophy is inherited as an autosomal recessive and therefore affects either sex. The onset is usually in the second decade, but in a few instances symptoms do not develop until middle age. Typically, weakness begins asymmetrically in the shoulder or pelvic girdle muscles. If in the shoulder, the weakness may remain confined to the muscles of this region for ten to 15 years, or even longer, before the pelvic girdle muscles become involved. If the dystrophic process begins in the muscles of the pelvic girdle, mainly the quadriceps and hamstrings, weakness generally proceeds more rapidly and involves the shoulder girdle within ten years. Most of these patients have to take to a wheelchair during the fourth or fifth decade.

People in whom shoulder girdle symptoms arise in the late teens or the early 20s might be expected to live for about 30 years from onset. Appropriate plans of insurance may, therefore, be offered to selected risks in this category provided that progress is known to be slow and that the muscles of the hip girdle are still unaffected.

Fascioscapulohumeral Muscular Dystrophy

Of all the non-myotonic dystrophies, this form has the best prognosis for life; those affected may reach near to their normal expectation, though increasingly disabled. The disease is transmitted in an autosomal dominant manner, affecting first the facial muscles and those round the shoulder girdle. Weakness of these muscles advances very slowly and eventually affects the muscles of the pelvic girdle, producing exaggerated lumbar lordosis, a typical waddling gait and progressive difficulty in walking. Frequently those suffering from facio-scapulohumeral muscular dystrophy have abortive forms of the disease in which weakness remains confined to the face and shoulder girdle. In some, weakness of the facial muscles is minimal, dystrophic changes being confined to only one or two groups of muscles around the shoulders. Neither of these forms is prone to develop weakness of the pelvic girdle muscles and both are compatible with survival to normal age.

Many people suffering from fascioscapulohumeral dystrophy could be issued ordinary life insurance (whole of life). For those with the abortive form, the risk would be minimal and most could be considered at standard rates of premium, whereas those with the slowly progressive form would be moderately substandard and ratable in the 75–150 percent extra mortality class.

Ocular Myopathy

This is a rare but distinctive form of muscular dystrophy in which there is progressive bilateral ptosis and external ophthalmoplegia. Weakness spreads to the muscles of the neck, trunk and upper limbs, and dysphagia occurs in about half the cases. No consistent pattern of inheritance has yet emerged. Ocular myopathy runs an extremely benign course and most patients survive to their normal expectation.

Congenital Muscular Dystrophy

Little need be said about this rare variety of dystrophy which starts in infancy and is characterized by marked weakness of muscles at birth, often with gross contractures. Affected children are unable to stand or even sit unaided, and most inevitably die of a respiratory infection within the first 12 years of life.

Benign Congenital Myopathies

Many relatively benign and non-progressive congenital myopathies have been described in recent years which, in the past, have been wrongly regarded as forms of muscular dystrophy. Among these benign myopathies is central core disease, in which the great majority of muscle fibers contain a nonfunctioning central core. Another type is nemaline myopathy, in which many muscle fibers contain rod-like bodies of unknown constitution. Other types have been described in which there are abnormal mitochondria. All of these rare conditions are relatively mild, non-progressive and of good prognosis.

Mytonic Muscular Dystrophy

Myotonia Congenita: Thomsen's Disease

Myotonia congenita is a rare disease of muscles which is inherited as an autosomal dominant and is characterized by the inability of muscles to relax quickly after voluntary contraction. The condition often appears initially in childhood and has a tendency to improve in later years. Myotonia can be abolished or greatly relieved by certain drugs, notably sodium hydantoinate. Life expectancy is completely normal for those suffering from myotonia congenita, and applicants can be accepted as standard risks for life insurance.

Dystrophia Myotonica: Myotonia Dystrophica

Dystrophia myotonica is a hereditary disorder having an autosomal dominant transmission. The fully developed syndrome is characterized by muscular atrophy (affecting particularly the sternomastoids, facial and shoulder girdle muscles), myotonia and several dystrophic disturbances (such as cataract, frontal balding and gonadal atrophy). The disease causes progressive incapacity over several years due to muscular wasting; death eventually occurs in about late middle life from intercurrent infection or an associated cardiomyopathy.

Dystrophia myotonica may manifest itself in some generations only as cataract, before eventually appearing in its fully developed form. Therefore a family history of cataract occurring in young or middle-aged parents should suggest the diagnosis of dystrophia myotonica in an offspring who shows signs of muscular hypotonia.

Generally speaking, dystrophia myotonica has a poor prognosis and those suffering from it should be declined for life insurance.

MUSCULAR ATROPHY

Werdnig-Hoffmann Disease (Infantile Spinal Muscular Atrophy)

This disease is characterized by muscular atrophy due to progressive degeneration of the cells of the anterior horn and medulla. Clinical signs of hypotonia and flaccid paralysis are usually apparent by the age of three months. Later, dysphagia appears and death generally occurs before the age of two years. However, spontaneous arrest may sometimes occur, leaving the child with chronic muscular weakness that is non-progressive. It is aborted cases such as these which sometimes present for life insurance in adolescence or adult life, many of them being acceptable risks. Depending on the degree of residual disability, rating might range from +75 to +150 or a minimum extra premium if applicable.

Kugelberg-Welander (K-W) Syndrome

The K-W syndrome, or pseudomyopathic spinal muscular atrophy, is a benign variant of Werdnig-Hoffman's disease (*see above*). It can affect either sex. Since it is characterized by weakness affecting the proximal muscles of the upper or lower limbs producing an exaggerated lumbar lordosis and waddling gait, it is frequently misdiagnosed as a muscular dystrophy of the Duchenne, Becker or limb girdle type, depending on age at onset and sex. The diagnosis, however, can be confidently made by muscle biopsy. The disease often becomes permanently arrested. If it begins in adolescence or later, a normal or near normal expectation of life can be expected by many individuals. Depending on the degree of disability, the insurance risk would range from standard to 75 percent extra mortality.

MYOPATHY

Polymyositis

Polymyositis gives rise to limb girdle and proximal limb weakness which may develop acutely or insidiously at almost any age. The neck and bulbar muscles, and sometimes the distal limb muscles, are affected. Occasionally when the onset is acute the muscles may be painful and tender, but this is not a constant feature. If in young subjects the onset is insidious, there may be great difficulty in distinguishing polymyositis from limb girdle muscular dystrophy. In about half the cases there are associated cutaneous manifestations, this combination being designated dermatomyositis (*see also* p. 819).

Prognosis
The majority of patients improve, sometimes dramatically, with oral corticosteroids (which are usually continued for up to one year); the erythrocyte sedimentation rate (ESR) falls and the CPK subsides to normal values. A few patients recover completely, but usually a little non-disabling weakness of the shoulder muscles remains. The few deaths that occur are due to respiratory or cardiovascular-renal complications. Muscle biopsy may not be positive in otherwise typical cases of polymyositis, a possible explanation being that the muscle may be affected in a patchy manner causing sampling difficulties in the taking of biopsies.

Selection of Risks
A proximal myopathy identical with polymyositis may occur in association with malignant neoplasms most commonly of the bronchus, gastrointestinal tract, breast or ovary, and may even antedate the detection of the underlying tumor,

occasionally by as much as three years. Moreover, neoplastic myopathy will respond initially to corticosteroids. Extreme care must therefore be taken in selecting life insurance applicants with a history of polymyositis.

Since the risk will tend to be highest in the early stages of the disease, it would be wise to postpone applications for one year from the onset of symptoms. Thereafter a rating of +150, reducing to +100, (including the corticosteroid debit) would be appropriate during the period of active treatment. Standard rates could be offered six months after corticosteroid therapy has ceased. An attending physician's statement would be advisable in the first two years of acceptance to confirm that screening tests for occult malignancy had been carried out. Failing that, a current chest X-ray should be considered in order to exclude carcinoma of the bronchus.

Other Myopathies

Other forms of myopathy occur, some hereditary and some secondary to other diseases or metabolic disorders. The myopathy of thyrotoxicosis, hypopituitarism, Addison's disease and Cushing's disease resolves with effective treatment of these conditions and has a similar prognosis to the disease in which it occurs.

Familial Periodic Paralysis
In the group of conditions called familial periodic paralysis there are attacks of widespread muscle weakness. One variety is due to hypokalemia, whereas in another the serum potassium rises during an attack. In a third variety the serum potassium remains normal but recovery follows the administration of sodium. The cause of paralysis in these cases appears to be the movement of potassium across the muscle fiber, and once each type is identified the appropriate therapy cuts short an attack. All varieties of periodic paralysis, though somewhat alarming in their effects, carry an excellent prognosis, and the great majority of sufferers live to normal age.

McArdle's Disease
This is the most important of the myopathies associated with glycogen storage disease of voluntary muscles. It is characterized by muscle pain and cramp occurring during exercise in people who are otherwise physically well. The condition is due to a deficiency of the enzyme myophosphorylase, which is concerned with the breakdown of glycogen in contracting muscle.

Although McArdle's disease is rare, it is being diagnosed with increasing frequency; and despite the fact that there is no specific treatment, symptoms can be averted if those affected learn to exercise within the limits of their disability. The prognosis is excellent and expectation of life is normal.

There are several other rare forms of glycogen storage diseases of muscle but most cause death in early life.

MYASTHENIA GRAVIS

Myasthenia gravis is an auto-immune disorder of neuromuscular function causing increased fatigability in striated muscle. The antigenic target is the acetylcholine receptor, an integral protein of the postsynaptic membrane at the neuromuscular junction. Acetylcholine receptor antibody is a heterogeneous IgG antibody detectable in the serum of over 90 percent of patients with generalized symptoms and in 75 percent of those with restricted ocular disease. The presence of the antibody leads to the loss of functional acetylcholine receptors with a consequent disorder of neuromuscular transmission. The antibody is specific for myasthenia gravis. Muscle weakness is characteristically worse after effort and is improved by rest, the muscles commonly affected being the extraocular, bulbar, neck, limb girdle, distal limb and trunk, in that order.

Myasthenia gravis occurs at all ages but there is a bimodal onset, the primary peak being around the age of 20 and the secondary in the fifth decade. Females predominate at younger ages, but after the age of 45 there is a preponderance of males.

Natural History

There is a tendency for myasthenia gravis to remit early after onset, but complete remissions are not prolonged and are rarely repeated. An exception is the ocular form, in which a complete remission may occur within two years of its onset. Moreover, patients with the purely ocular form do not commonly develop generalized myasthenia if symptoms remain confined to the extraocular muscles for more than one year. In generalized myasthenia gravis, mortality is highest in the first year of the disease with a further peak in the fifth to seventh years; thereafter mortality falls. In those who survive more than ten years from onset death from myasthenia gravis is rare.

Treatment

Broadly, there are two approaches to the treatment of myasthenia gravis: the symptomatic and the immunological.

The symptomatic approach depends principally on antiacetylcholinesterase preparations, such as neostigmine and pyridostigmine, which aim to compensate for the reduced number of acetylcholine receptors by potentiating the effect of acetylcholine. Although this form of therapy has contributed greatly to the management of the disease over the past 40 years, it does not correct the primary abnormality and is of greatest value in mild cases.

Immunological treatment, by contrast, aims to eliminate acetylcholine receptor antibody and thus correct the immunological abnormality. The earliest form of immunological treatment, though not at first recognized as such, was thymectomy.

Thymectomy

The histology of the thymus gland is always abnormal in myasthenia gravis, and there is good reason to believe that thymus-related immunological abnormalities are involved in decreasing the number, and possibly the sensitivity, of acetylcholine receptors at the motor endplates of muscle. It has long been recognized that the earlier thymectomy is performed in myasthenia gravis the better the prognosis, although the hazards of operation prior to 1960 were so great that few patients who were well controlled on medical treatment were submitted to it. But with a sound theoretical rationale for removing the thymus in myasthenia gravis, and with advances in anesthesia and assisted respiration producing a currently low morbidity and mortality, the practical benefits of thymectomy early in the disease are now beyond doubt.

In a study at Mount Sinai Hospital of 353 patients who underwent thymectomy for myasthenia gravis, Genkins et al[40] produced evidence that the duration of the disease and the presence of germinal centers within the thymus influenced the response to surgery. The shortest interval between thymectomy and complete remission occurred in patients with abundant germinal centers and a short history of myasthenia (60 percent showed immediate post-operative improvement), whereas no immediate improvement was seen in patients with few germinal centers and a long history. Although thymectomy may sometimes fail to produce a remission, it will generally arrest the progress of the disease so that fewer patients will develop the more severe forms of myasthenia.

In patients with thymoma, a thymectomy does not usually improve muscle weakness and, since many thymomas are malignant, the prognosis is correspondingly worse. The presence of a thymoma is therefore an absolute indication for thymectomy.

Corticosteroid Therapy

Alternative immunological treatment in the form of prednisolone may be used in those patients for whom thymectomy has been ineffective or is not indicated. Striking benefit can be achieved with prednisolone, the disease improving or remitting in over 80 percent of cases; ocular myasthenia responds particularly well to small maintenance doses. Unfortunately immune regulation by corticosteroid drugs lacks specificity and can cause unwanted side effects. Other forms of immunosuppressive therapy that have been tried, either alone or in combination with prednisolone, are azathioprine and plasma exchange transfusion. The efficacy of the latter has now been fully proven.

Selection of Risks

A postponement period of one year from the onset of symptoms of myasthenia gravis is necessary to avoid the heavy early mortality of the fully developed disease. It also serves to distinguish those applicants with the benign ocular form of the disease if the myasthenia has remained confined to the extraocular muscles.

Where thymectomy has been carried out a report of the histology should always be obtained from either the attending physician or surgeon. The prognosis of myasthenia gravis following thymectomy can usually be judged by the number of years after onset of symptoms at which it was performed and by the severity of post-operative, compared with preoperative, symptoms. Myasthenic or cholinergic crises are serious complications indicating poor control. A history of such crises within one year would warrant postponement of an application for life insurance.

Rating

1) Medical treatment.
Myasthenia confined to extraocular muscles (ocular type):

Time since onset	Rating
Within 1 yr	Postpone
2nd yr	+75
3rd yr	0 to +50

True myasthenia gravis; well stabilized on treatment:

Time since onset	Rating
Within 1 yr	Postpone
2nd–7th yr	+100 and 5* per mil for 6 yr reducing in annual stages
8th–10th yr	+75
Thereafter	+50

*3 per mil at ages 30 and under.

If oral corticosteroids are being used — add appropriate rating.
Myasthenic or cholinergic crisis or other major complication, within one year — postpone for one year from date of attack.
2) Surgical treatment (thymectomy).
Malignant histology — rate as malignant tumor (*see* Chapter 20).
Benign histology.
Within six months — postpone.
Thereafter — rating depends on the clinical response:

Unchanged: drug requirement similar to preoperative dosage — rate as medical treatment (*see above*) according to year since onset of symptoms.

Improved: regular drug requirement, but much reduced compared with preoperative dosage — rate as medical treatment (*see above*) according to year since onset of symptoms but omitting temporary extra premiums.

Markedly improved: complete remission; no drugs required or only on rare occasions; remission of less than 1 year — +75; remission of longer than one year — 0 to +50.

REFERENCES

1 Hypertension from poliomyelitis (editorial). *Lancet* 1959; 2: 120.
2 Raestrup O. Effects of poliomyelitis on the heart and circulation. *Trans 13th Int Congress Life Ass Med.* Karlsruhe: Verlag Versicherungswirtschaft, 1976; 221.
3 Guttmann L. The place of our spinal paraplegic fellowman in society (Second Dame Georgiana Buller Memorial Lecture, 1959). *Rehabilitation* 1959; 30: 15.
4 Geisler WO, Jousse AT, Wynne-Jones M. Survival in traumatic transverse myelitis. *Paraplegia* 1977; 14: 262.

5 Devivo MJ, Fine PR. The prevalence of spinal cord injuries. A re-estimation based on life tables. *Spinal Injuries Digest* 1980; 1.

6 Hardy AG. Suvival periods in traumatic paraplegia. *Paraplegia* 1976; 14: 41.

7 Carter RE. Experiences with high tetraplegics. *Paraplegia* 1979; 17: 140.

8 *1951 Impairment Study*. New York: Society of Actuaries, 1954.

9 Preston TW, Clarke RD. Investigation into the mortality of substandard lives. *J Inst Actuar* 1965; 92: 27.

10 Henriksen B, Juul-Jensen P, Lund M. The mortality of epileptics. *Proc 10th Int Congress Life Ass Med*. London: Pitman Medical and Scientific, 1970; 139.

11 *Medical Impairment Study 1983*. Vol 1. Boston: Society of Actuaries and Association of Life Insurance Medical Directors of America, 1986.

12 Brain WR. *Diseases of the Nervous System*, 6th ed. Oxford: Oxford University Press, 1962.

13 *Statistical Bulletin*. New York: Metropolitan Life Insurance Company, 1980; April–June: 15.

14 Marquardsen J. The natural history of acute cerebrovascular disease: a retrospective study of 769 patients. *Acta Neurol Scand* 1969; 45: Suppl 38: 11.

15 Haberman S. Scientific underwriting: stroke as a model. *J Inst Actuar* 1983; 110 Part III: 445–55.

16 Mortality investigation of declined lives in Japan. Tokyo: The Life Insurance Association of Japan, 1979.

17 Baum HM, Robins MR. National survey of stroke. Ch 5: Survival and prevalance. *Stroke* 1981; 12 (Suppl 1): 1.59–1.68.

18 McKissock W, Richardson A, Walsh L. Posterior communicating aneurysms. *Lancet* 1960; 1: 1203.

19 Iansek R, Elstein S, Balla JI. Application of decision analysis to management of cerebral arteriovenous malformations. *Lancet* 1983; 1: 1132.

20 Cerebral angiomas (editorial). *Lancet* 1968; 1: 1296.

21 Jennett WB, Teather D, Bennie S. Epilepsy after head injury. Residual risk after varying fit-free intervals. *Lancet* 1973; 22: 652.

22 Müller R. Studies on disseminated sclerosis with special reference to symptomatology, course and prognosis. *Acta Med Scand* 1949; 133: Suppl 222.

23 Alexander L. New concept of critical steps in course of chronic debilitating neurologic disease in evaluation of therapeutic response; longitudinal study of multiple sclerosis by quantitative evaluation of neurologic involvement and disability. *Arch Neurol Psychiat* 1951; 66: 253.

24 McAlpine D, Compston N. Some aspects of natural history of disseminated sclerosis, incidence, course and prognosis; factors affecting onset and course. *Q J Med* 1952; 21: 135.

25 McAlpine D. The benign form of multiple sclerosis: results of a long-term study. *Br Med J* 1964; 2: 1029.

26 Kurtzke JF. *Acta Neurol* 1970; 22: 215.

27 Bobowick AR, Brody JA. Epidemiology of motor-neuron diseases. *N Engl J Med* 1973; 288: 1047.

28 Kurtzke JF. Motor neuron(e) disease. *Br Med J* 1982; 1: 141.

29 Hoehn MH, Yahr MD. Parkinsonism: onset, progression and mortality. *Neurology* 1967; 17: 427.

30 Shaw KM, Lees AJ, Stern GM. The impact of treatment with levodopa in Parkinson's disease. *Q J Med* 1980; 40: 283.

31 Strickland GT, Frommer D, Leu M-L, Pollard R, Sherlock S, Cummings JN. Wilson's disease in the United Kingdom and Taiwan. I General characteristics of 142 cases and prognosis; II A genetic analysis of 88 cases. *Q J Med* 1973; 42: 619.

32 Newcombe RG. A life table for onset of Huntington's chorea. *Ann Hum Genet* 1981; 45: 375–85.

33 Gusella JF, Wexter NS, Conneally PM et al. A polymorphic DNA marker genetically linked to Huntington's disease. *Nature* 1983; 306: 234.

34 Brock DJH, Curtis A, Barron L, Dinwoodie D, Crosbie A, Mennie M et al. Predictive testing for Huntington's disease with linked DNA markers. *Lancet* 1989; 2: 463–6.

35 Hewer RL. Study of fatal cases of Friedreich's ataxia. *Br Med J* 1968; 3: 649–52.
36 Cote M, Bureau M, Leger C. Evolution of cardiopulmonary involvement in Friedreich's ataxia. *Can J Neurol Sci* 1979; 6: 1.
37 Harding EA, Hewer RL. The heart disease of Friedreich's ataxia; a clinical and electrocardiographic study of 115 patients. *Q J Med* 1983; 52: 489–502.
38 Sloan Robertson J, Maraqa MI, Jennett WB. Ventriculoperitoneal shunting for hydrocephalus. *Br Med J* 1973; 2: 289.
39 Walton JN. The prognosis of some neuromuscular diseases. *Trans Assur Med Soc* 1970; 13.
40 Genkins G, Papatestas AE, Horowitz C et al. Studies in myasthenia gravis: early thymectomy. *Am J Med* 1975; 58: 517.

CHAPTER 24

PSYCHIATRIC DISORDERS

MAURICE LIPSEDGE

The mentally ill are known to have a higher mortality than the general population.[1-3] The purpose of this chapter is to demonstrate the specific risks of excess mortality associated with specific diagnoses (the diagnostic system used is based on DSM III R). In the past, severely disturbed psychiatric patients would at times remain agitated and malnourished for long periods, leading to debilitation, predisposition to infection and cardiovascular problems, all resulting in an increased risk of premature death. There has been a progressive decline in excess mortality associated with psychiatric illness over the past 30 years, since the introduction of effective psychotropic drugs.[4] This fall in deaths can be partly attributed to deinstitutionalization: in the era of protracted hospitalization the excess of natural deaths in psychiatric patients was mainly due to infections.[3,5]

The high death rates previously recorded for psychiatric patients relative to the general population,[2,3,6,7,8] which were mainly seen in patients receiving substandard care for intercurrent medical illnesses and prolonged periods of extreme psychiatric symptoms, are now less marked with the reduction in duration of hospitalization and improvements in the provision of general medical care. In particular a decrease in natural deaths has been noted. However, there is still a high death rate relative to the general population, and excessive deaths are now attributable mainly to suicides and accidents, which tend to occur within a short interval after discharge. Fifteen percent of depressives will commit suicide, and psychiatric patients generally still have an increased expectation of early death[3] relative to age and sex-matched controls in the general population. This is despite the advent of ECT and effective psychotropic drugs which allow more rapid control of extreme symptoms.[1,3]

Since the introduction of effective psychotropic drugs there has been a 30 percent reduction in mortality among patients hospitalized for less than a year and a 50 percent reduction among longer-stay patients.[4] However, psychiatric illness is not invariably associated with excess mortality, as indicated by the low mortality in somatization disorder (*see* p. 795).

A general problem with mortality studies in psychiatry is that the number of patients is too small and the follow-up too short to yield a precise estimate of mortality ratios. One relatively large-scale study was that carried out during a follow-up, over nine and a half years, of 1,436 first admissions to a psychiatric hospital in Toronto.[3] During the follow-up period there were 153 deaths, constituting 143 percent of the expected figure, and 43 of these deaths were due to unnatural causes (i.e. suicides and accidents). There was no evidence of an excess mortality due to natural causes. The risk of premature death was greater among female patients and among patients below the age of 65. The diagnostic groups that contributed most to the excess mortality in these psychiatric patients were the affective disorders and addictions.

Despite deinstitutionalization and effective treatment, several recent studies have shown an excess number of natural deaths in psychiatric patients. This might be because patients with serious but undetected physical disorders are selectively referred to psychiatric clinics.[8]

There is still a marked excess in unnatural deaths. In a follow-up of 500 psychiatric outpatients over a six- to twelve-year period, death from unnatural causes occurred at three and a half times the expected rate, a significant elevation.[8] The rates of suicide were nearly 15 times that expected, and homicide nearly five times that expected. Accidents, including overdoses not ruled as suicides by the coroner, were seen at more than twice the rate expected. Excessive rates of unnatural deaths, especially suicide, have been observed in virtually every study of mortality in psychiatric patients.[3]

Former psychiatric inpatients were similarly shown to be at great risk for unnatural deaths in a prospective comparison of standardized mortality ratios for suicide in various diagnostic and demographic groups.[9] Of a cohort of 5,412 patients admitted to the University of Iowa psychiatric hospital between 1972 and 1981, 331 died during the follow-up period, significantly more than expected. Comparison with standardized mortality ratios suggests a relatively greater risk for women and younger people. Women were twice as likely, and men one and a half times as likely, to die during follow-up than age and sex-matched controls. The risk was associated with all psychiatric diagnoses. Suicide and accidental death were more frequent than expected and were responsible for two-thirds of the excess deaths. Suicides were clustered in the first two years after discharge.

The results of this study are similar to previous prospective studies[10] which demonstrated similar age, sex and diagnostic distribution among the suicide victims, with the commonest diagnoses, in descending order, being depression, schizophrenia, alcoholism, personality disorder and neurosis. Other studies[11] have also demonstrated that deaths among psychiatric patients tend to cluster around the first one to two years of follow-up, especially deaths from suicide. Thus in a 35-year follow-up of schizophrenics and patients with affective disorder, the risk was confined to the first decade after discharge.[2] The relative frequency of schizophrenia in association with suicide among psychiatric patients[9] compared with suicides in the general population is due to the fact that schizophrenia is relatively rare outside psychiatric hospitals and therefore makes a relatively small contribution to suicide figures in the general population.

Despite the overall reduction in mortality in psychiatric inpatients there is still a relatively high death rate during the first year because psychiatric patients in general have disproportionately more concomitant physical illnesses, which are often missed on physical examination prior to referral for psychiatric care.[4] Taking death due to natural causes as an outcome variable, both schizophrenia and affective disorders manifest significantly higher mortality during the first decade following admission than in the general population of comparable age and sex.[12] In a 30- to 40-year follow-up study of 685 patients with schizophrenia, affective disorders and surgical controls,[13] the patients with schizophrenia, the manic depressives and depressives had a shortened survival compared with the general population. In addition to suicide and accidents, the causes of excess deaths were infective and circulatory system diseases, and there was a suggestion of a paucity of deaths due to cancer in the major psychoses. This study confirms other reports[3] that psychiatric patients in general have consistently high mortality rates relative to the general population. That this applies to both outpatients and inpatients was demonstrated by the ascertainment of mortality status for 494 randomly selected psychiatric outpatients during a mean follow-up period of seven years.[5] With 43 deaths at follow-up there was an observed mortality nearly twice that expected. Nevertheless this excess was regarded by researchers as relatively modest, and the discrepancy in comparison with earlier results could be due to the availability of effective physical treatments and the reduction in protracted hospitalization. A surprising result was the lack of excess mortality associated with primary affective disorder. Excess mortality tends to be associated with secondary affective disorder in alcoholics, addicts, patients with antisocial personalities and patients with organic brain syndromes.

The causes of death were studied in a cohort of 200 schizophrenics, 100 manic and 225 depressive patients who were followed up in a prospective study.[13] In all three diagnostic groups, deaths due to unnatural causes were significantly in excess. Cardiovascular disease contributed to excess mortality in female mania, and deaths from infective diseases were excessive in both sexes with schizophrenia. Despite the alleged lower cancer death-risk among mental patients,[14] in this study[13] deficiencies were not found in neoplasm death in either schizophrenia or affective disorders when absolute mortality rates were used, but the deficiencies were noted when proportional mortality analysis was carried out. The results based on actual rates of disease, as in the absolute method, are clearly more valuable than those based on numerators of the rates, as in the proportional mortality method. Hence it must be concluded from this data that there is no decrease in neoplasm deaths among schizophrenic and manic depressive patients.

SCHIZOPHRENIA AND MORTALITY

The traditional textbook view that repeated episodes of schizophrenia lead invariably to residual symptoms and lasting social deficits and deterioration has been challenged by the recent demonstration and considerable deteriogeneity in the long-term outcome with deteriorated states as the exception. In a review of five studies comprising over 1,300 subjects with schizophrenia studied for longer than 20 years, between one-half and two-thirds achieved recovery or significant improvement.[15] Nevertheless the suicide rate in schizophrenia is extremely high, especially in the early years.

A poor outcome for schizophrenia two years after first admission to hospital is associated with male sex, poor response to medication within the first five weeks of the first admission and negative schizophrenic symptoms.[16]

A few basic facts have been established concerning mortality of schizophrenia. It is known from a number of studies, that patients with schizophrenia have a higher mortality than the general population.[2,6,8,13,17] The excess mortality from all causes has been found consistently to be around twice that of the general population, but mortality from suicide has been by far the dominating cause of this excess, being up to ten or more times greater than that of the general population. A series of follow-up studies has demonstrated that 10 percent of schizophrenics die by suicide, the risk being particularly high during the early years of the illness.[11,18,19]   So, a diagnosis of schizophrenia predicts a reduced life expectancy relative to that of the general population matched for age and sex. There is extensive literature demonstrating both this relatively high mortality of patients with schizophrenia and the greatly increased suicide rate, especially among young patients.[2,3,8,9,13,17,20] Thus in the Iowa 500 study a 40-year follow-up of 200 schizophrenics admitted from 1934 to 1944 using sex- and age-standardized mortality ratios showed a significantly increased risk of death, especially among females, compared with the general population.[2] The risk covered both unnatural deaths and those due to infections such as tuberculosis, pneumonia and gastroenteritis. These patients were more likely to have been in hospital for long periods prior to modern psychiatric medical treatment, hence the higher death rate.

Whilst other studies also show relatively high mortality from natural causes in patients with schizophrenia,[3,8,17,20] one study found that only unnatural deaths were excessive and early deaths occurred most often within two years of discharge, especially among younger patients.[9] Until about 40 years ago high mortality rates were reported among institutionalized schizophrenics. Nowadays young people with a diagnosis of schizophrenia still tend to have a reduced life span, since they are disproportionately the victims of suicide or accidents. In fact, suicide is the leading cause of premature death among schizophrenic patients.[20]

Psychiatric case registers linked with a register of cause of death constitute a useful sampling frame for psychiatric mortality studies, as they provide a large patient sample and reasonably long follow-up periods. This strategy was used in the Oxford Case Register Investigation of physical disease in schizophrenia, which found that mortality among 600 schizophrenics was about twice the population norm.[17] There was a significant excess for both unnatural death (trauma and poisoning, especially in the young) and natural death due to ischemic heart disease, which was the commonest cause of death overall in both sexes, as in the general population.

In the ten-year mortality study performed on 1,190 patients with schizophrenia discharged from Stockholm County Hospital in 1971, there was an approximately twofold increase in overall mortality compared with the general population, as found in previous studies.[20] The excess mortality pertained to all causes of death but was particularly high for suicides, which were ten times higher in male schizophrenics and 18 times higher in female schizophrenics than in the general population. Many of the suicides occurred immediately or soon after discharge and some actually occurred during inpatient care. As in the Oxford study,[17] there was a high excess mortality due to ischemic heart disease. Two other investigations differ in this respect. In neither of these two studies was there any significant excess in natural death.[8,21]

A second Scandinavian study consisted of a 29-year follow-up of over 6 thousand patients with a clinical diagnosis of schizophrenia.[22] The study confirms the finding of other surveys that schizophrenic patients have an overall increased mortality rate compared with the general population. Surprisingly, the suicide mortality did not differ significantly from that of the general Danish population, but this may be explained by the fact that the subjects were predominantly old long-stay patients who had survived the initial phases of the disorder and had therefore survived the period during which suicide risk is highest.

Rating

Single attack; acute schizophrenic episode; short duration; full recovery and return to work; otherwise favorable features:

Time since recovery	Rating
Within 1 yr	Postpone
2nd yr	5 per mil for 3 yr reducing to
5th yr	Standard

More than one attack; hospitalization; maintenance treatment; able to work; some less favorable features:

Time since recovery	Rating	
	Under 30	30 and over
Within 1 yr	Postpone	Postpone
2nd–3rd yr	+300	+200
4th–5th yr	+150	+100
6th–10th yr	+75	+50
Thereafter	+50 to 0	+50 to 0

DEPRESSION AND MORTALITY

According to traditional medical teaching, patients with affective disorders generally recover from acute episodes and return to their premorbid level of functioning. Even though some patients will have recurrent episodes, it is assumed that there will be no residual symptoms between these recurrences, unlike schizophrenia which generally runs a deteriorating course.

Energetic medical or physical treatment seems to have reduced the risk of suicide in primary affective disorder. A 40-year follow-up of psychiatric inpatients found that most suicides among patients with primary affective disorders occurred prior to 1955.[23] However, this may have occurred simply because the risk of suicide is greatest early in the course of such illness. It has been claimed that when energetic treatment is offered to patients with primary affective disorders there is a change in the epidemiology of suicide with less representation of patients with pure affective disorder.[7] In a recent study not a single patient having the diagnosis of primary affective disorder died of an unnatural cause.[7] However, unnatural death occurred in patients with depression secondary to alcoholism, antisocial personality and drug addiction at nearly eight times the expected rate. A second study has also found that suicide tends to occur among patients with secondary, but not primary, depressive disorders.[24]

However, a number of more recent studies[25,26] have demonstrated that a substantial number of patients with severe depression will continue to have significant symptoms for at least two years.

In one follow-up study of 97 patients, over one-fifth (20 out of 97) still had severe symptoms after two years, and the majority suffered from severe depressive symptoms throughout the two years of this prospective follow-up.[25] A review of the literature concluded that although most patients do indeed recover from episodes of major depression, a substantial proportion, at least 25 percent, begin a chronic course.[27]

The poor prognosis for a substantial proportion of depressives has been confirmed by the study of the long-term outcome of 89 consecutive admissions to the Maudsley Hospital with primary depressive illness.[26] Mortality among these patients was almost twice that expected, with a sevenfold increase for women who were aged under 40 when originally admitted. Less than one-fifth of the survivors had remained well during the 18-year follow-up period and one-third had suffered unnatural death or severe chronic distress. Ten percent died of unnatural causes. Although patients at the psychotic end of the depressive spectrum had the poorest outcomes in terms of relapses and re-admissions, there was no significant difference in mortality between the patients diagnosed as suffering from neurotic depression and those diagnosed as psychotic depressives.

This twofold increase in mortality is in accord with the findings of the Iowa 500 series[2] which showed a similar increase in a retrospective 40-year follow-up. A sevenfold excess in women under 40 adds further support to the recent evidence that the greatest excess in mortality in depressive illness is among young women.[21]

The natural history of patients admitted to the Maudsley Hospital with depression, indicating that the long-term outcome for between one-fifth and one-half of such patients is extremely poor,[26] gives no support to the view,[7] derived from an outpatient study, that modern treatments have virtually eliminated the risk of unnatural death in primary depressives.

Another study of 500 psychiatric outpatients followed up under blind conditions for 6–12 years found that no patient with an index diagnosis of primary affective disorder died of unnatural cause.[8] Alcoholism, addiction and antisocial personality seemed to be, however, highly predictive of unnatural death. The overall picture is more consistent with the gloomy conclusions of a review of 17 follow-up studies of patients with affective disorders, which demonstrated that approximately 15 percent ended their lives by suicide; this is 30 times the risk in the general population.[28] The risk of suicide is highest relatively early in the course of the disorder. On a short-term follow-up of just a few years, the proportion of suicides was close to 35–60 percent of total deaths.

Depressive illness in old age is often characterized by frequent and prolonged relapses. In a follow-up study of 92 elderly depressed inpatients, after an interval of three years only 26 percent had made a sustained recovery and 12 percent had been continuously ill throughout the three-year follow-up period.[29] In a one-year prospective study of 124 elderly depressed patients, by the end of the follow-up year just over one-third of the patients had made a good recovery despite the use of antidepressant medication, ECT and social support via day hospital and outpatient facilities.[30] Poor outcome was associated with severity of illness, those with depressive delusions doing particularly badly. Physical health problems and major adverse life events were also associated with a poor outcome. A group of elderly depressed inpatients who had enlarged lateral ventricles on CT scan had a higher mortality rate than depressed elderly subjects with normal CT scans.[31]

Rating

Depression (including anxiety, reactive, endogenous and psychotic depression).

1) Simple reactive depression (e.g. grief reaction); duration less than three months; no specialist referral; isolated episodes — usually standard.

2) Anxiety/depression; reactive; more than one attack:

Time since last attack	Rating
Within 1 yr	3 per mil for 3 yr
2nd yr	3 per mil for 2 yr
Thereafter	Standard

3) Deeper depression; reactive/endogenous; specialist referral — 3 per mil throughout.
No attacks for five years — standard.

4) Manic depression, including severe endogenous depression; good response to treatment:

Time since last acute episode	Rating
Within 1 yr	Postpone
2nd yr	5 per mil for 4 yr
3rd yr	5 per mil for 3 yr
4th yr	5 per mil for 2 yr
5th yr	3 per mil for 2 yr
Thereafter	Standard

SUICIDE

There has been considerable progress in identifying groups at high risk of suicide. In an extensive review of the literature it has been demonstrated that, when compared with psychiatric patients who do not commit suicide, those who do eventually kill themselves are more often widowed or unmarried, unemployed, living alone, have a history of admission to a mental hospital and are depressed at the time of suicide.[32] However, knowledge of risk factors, whether diagnostic, familial or social, is of limited value for predicting individual suicides, owing to the low sensitivity and specificity of identification procedures, compounded by the low base rate of suicide.[6,10]

Both manic depressives and schizophrenics are at increased risk of suicide.[19] Although there is no evidence that suicide in first degree relatives increases the suicide risk in schizophrenics, there does seem to be a familial association of suicide and affective disorder.[33] A striking relationship between affective disorder and a positive family history of suicide was demonstrated in a study of 365 patients with affective disorder, in which 25 had lost parents or siblings by suicide or probable suicide.[34] This association with suicide and manic depressive disorder might reflect a genetic component, as suggested by twin and adoption studies of suicide.

Although suicide may range from 10 percent to 15 percent in various mental disorders, the great majority of mentally disturbed individuals do not commit suicide.[11] It is very difficult to predict which patients will commit suicide because suicide is a relatively rare event, and any risk factor significantly associated with suicide also characterizes many patients who will not commit suicide.[10,30,32]

In a prospective study that attempted to identify people who subsequently committed or attempted suicide in a sample of 4,800 psychiatric inpatients, it was found that too many false positive cases were identified, using a variety of measures including those previously reported as predictive of suicide. Therefore the low base rates and the great number of false positives render accurate identification impossible.[10]

Although certain demographic data help to single out those groups who are at greater than average risk (e.g. the single, widowed and divorced), they are too general to be of practical use, since they identify large numbers of individuals who are never at risk, suicide being an infrequent event. The low base rate of suicide in even the highest risk groups limits the discriminatory power of predictive factors.

Suicide rarely occurs in the absence of psychiatric illness;[35] even then, only a minority of psychiatric patients will commit suicide. Risk factors vary with the population under consideration: for example, whether outpatients with depression or inpatients with schizophrenia are under consideration.[36] The majority of suicides are associated with a relatively small number of conditions. On the basis of a number of follow-up studies it has been estimated that the following percentage of affected individuals will die by suicide: depression (both endogenous and reactive), 15 percent; alcoholism 15 percent (especially late in the course of the addiction, and especially with the onset of cirrhosis); schizophrenia, 10 percent; psychopathic personality disorder, 5 percent; and opiate addiction, at least 10 percent.[11] Therefore the great majority of mentally disturbed individuals do not commit suicide.

Of all suicides, half have an affective disorder, a quarter suffer from alcoholism and a fifth suffer from schizophrenia.[35] Suicide is particularly likely to occur in alcoholics following the recent loss of a close personal relative.[37] Another association in successful suicide is chronic physical illness (in epilepsy there is a fivefold increase in the risk of suicide). The death of a parent during childhood and the recent death of a spouse or parent also increases the risk of suicide, as does a family history of suicide, previous history of attempted suicide and unemployment.

The demographic and diagnostic features of suicide tend to vary according to whether the general population or a population of psychiatric patients is studied.[7] Three systematic retrospective studies of a total of 342 consecutive coroner-identified suicides from the general population in St Louis,[38] Seattle[39] and England[35] found similar results. They showed that almost all of the deceased had a recognizable psychiatric illness at the time of death: 48 percent had a primary affective disorder, 22 percent were alcoholics and 6 percent had schizophrenia. Males exceeded females by a ratio of 2:1 and most of those who committed suicide were middle-aged. In contrast, the proportion of schizophrenic suicides within a psychiatric population as opposed to the general community would be much higher, and inpatient suicides tend to occur at a younger age than those in the general population.[40]

Many studies have shown that a history of psychiatric illness is one of the most powerful predictors of suicide.[11,41] A longitudinal study of a cohort of over 50 thousand Swedish men conscripted for military service in 1969–70 demonstrated that the risk for suicide was much higher for those who had been admitted to a psychiatric hospital at some point during the 13-year follow-up period than among those who had been diagnosed as suffering from a psychiatric disorder at their original screening assessment prior to starting military service.[42] There was a relative risk of suicide of 3·1 among those diagnosed as psychiatrically ill at conscription and of 16·7 among those who received psychiatric inpatient care during the follow-up period. However, although a history of psychiatric inpatient care is known to be a predictor of suicide,[10,43,44] only 44 percent of the 247 Swedish conscripts who committed suicide had ever undergone treatment as psychiatric inpatients, confirming the low specificity of psychiatric hospital admission as a predictor of suicide.[36]

Deaths by suicide in the psychiatric population tend to occur at a younger age, and involve males and females in almost equal proportions.[3] The risk of suicide among the psychiatrically ill in general is about 15 times that for the general population.[28] A comparison of psychiatric patient suicides and general population suicides found 48 suicides among 12,500 adult psychiatric patients, giving a ratio of suicide by psychiatric patients to suicides within the general population of about 5:1.[7] Suicides were twice as common among men than women and were younger than suicides in the general population.

The rates were especially high for schizophrenia and bipolar affective disorder. Suicides occurred seven times more frequently in bipolar patients than in unipolar patients. This might be because bipolar affective disorder is less responsive to treatment than unipolar affective disorder. Other diagnoses associated with an increased risk of suicide are personality disorder and secondary alcoholism, and Murphy and Robins[37] found that a significantly large proportion of suicides with affective disorder and alcoholism were living alone.

The social and psychiatric risk factors for suicide were determined in a matched control study of 90 psychiatric patient suicides in Toronto.[32] The suicide group contained significantly more patients with chronic schizophrenia or recurrent affective disorder than the control group. Nearly a half of the Toronto suicide group had made a previous suicide attempt and 65 percent were diagnosed as depressed at the time of their last psychiatric contact prior to the suicide. Socio-demographic variables that characterized the suicides were young age, being single and social isolation. The majority were unemployed and living alone. Over a half of the outpatient suicides had seen a psychiatrist in the previous week and of those who had been admitted, 40 percent committed suicide within a month of discharge. Other research has similarly demonstrated that the social risk factors for suicide among psychiatric patients include being single or widowed,[45] being unemployed,[46] and living alone.[35]

In the Toronto study, the use of prospectively collected data enhanced both completeness and accuracy by avoiding reliance on the retrospective analysis of secondary sources, and by permitting the collection of data on attitudes and behavior that would not otherwise be available.[32]

The mortality among nearly 2 thousand suicide attemptors followed up over a period of eight years[44] turned out to be extremely high: in fact, over three times higher than expected. Suicide was the main reason for this, but death from other causes was also important. Suicide occurred in 2·8 percent, making the rate of suicidal deaths nearly 27 times the expected rate. The highest risk of suicide was in the first six months following the attempt. Factors identified at the time of the

Table 24.1. Suicide and deliberate self-harm: a summary of various variables.

Demographic, diagnostic and other variables	Completed suicide	Deliberate self-harm (para-suicide)[a]
Sex	Male:female, 2:1.	Female:male, 2:1.
Age	Mainly over 35.	Mainly under 35.
Marital Status	Mainly single, widowed or divorced.	Divorced men and women, teen-age wives, young single men and women.
Presence of serious psychiatric morbidity	Present in 90 percent — mainly depression and alcoholism. (Mainly depression, especially re-current depression, but not necessarily of psychotic intensity. Life-time risk of suicide in depression 15 percent.)	One third to one half have personality disorder; alcoholism also common.
Degree of planning	Planned in advance, car-ried out in private, inter-ruption avoided, rapidly effective.	Impulsive, makes provision for rescue, uses slowly effective or ineffective means.
Overdose	25 percent.	Over 90 percent.
Purpose of the act	To end life (up to one-third have a history of previous attempts).	Survival and impact on other people (about one-quarter will repeat the act).

[a]Ten percent of parasuicides progress to completed suicide.

attempt, which were associated with suicide risk, included being male, advanced age (only for females), the presence of psychiatric disorder (especially schizophrenia), the long-term use of hypnotics, poor physical health and repeated attempts.

Surprisingly, there were more than double the expected number of deaths from natural causes, mainly among females. Markedly high death rates were found for endocrine, circulatory and respiratory disease and accidents. This eventual relatively high mortality rate from natural causes among suicide attemptors confirms a previous study.[47]

In summary, there is no pathognomonic symptom or feature associated with suicide. Prediction on the basis of demographic variables is unsatisfactory because of low base rates (i.e. the frequency of each of the statistically related characteristics is high, whereas the number of suicides among those possessing these characteristics is very low).

Because suicide is statistically a rare event there is a high risk of false positives. In other words, because any risk factor significantly associated with suicide also characterizes many patients who do not commit suicide, none of the predictor characteristics are unique to the group that commit suicide (i.e. they are shared by large numbers of people who do not commit suicide). That suicide is indeed a rare event was shown by Pokorny, who ascertained a rate of 67 out of 4,800 subjects over a five-year period.[40]

Rating

Attempted suicide (parasuicide): self-poisoning; overdose of medication; impulsive; or other methods of self-harm but half-hearted; no significant background mental disorder.

Time since attempt	Rating
Within 1 yr	Postpone
2nd yr	3–5[a] per mil for 4 yr
3rd yr	3–5[a] per mil for 3 yr
4th yr	3–5[a] per mil for 2 yr
Thereafter	Standard

[a]Use higher of the two ratings for more than one attempt, or for other more determined methods of self-harm.

For rating of attempted suicide in affective and schizophrenic disorders see p. 787.

SUICIDE AND AFFECTIVE DISORDER

A review of the course and outcome of affective disorders indicated a very high suicide rate, with suicide accounting for approximately 15 percent of all deaths in patients with bipolar and unipolar disease. The ultimate risk of suicide for patients with primary affective disorder is approximately 30 times that of the general population.[28]

A 40-year follow-up study comprising 100 manic depressives and 225 depressive patients, using sex- and age-standardized mortality rates, showed a significantly increased mortality risk for patients with affective disorder in the first decade following admission.[2] It has been suggested that this excess mortality might be due to the combination of suicide and the presence of a high degree of physical ill health influencing the decision for hospital admission, since there was an excess of cardiovascular deaths among the manics.[48]

It has been claimed that the risk of suicide in affective disorder can be dramatically reduced. If the Iowa 500 study is combined with other large-scale methodologically rigorous studies, there seems to be a substantially lower risk of suicide nowadays than in the decade 1935 to 1944.[5,21,23] However, although it has been found that aggressive treatment of primary affective disorder has reduced the mortality risk and the risk of suicide,[8] there is still evidence of excess mortality in the affective disorders.[26] Two controlled studies of depressed patients who eventually committed suicide compared with surviving depressives showed that the following characteristics were more common among the suicides: male sex, an older age group, single status, living alone and having a history of previous suicidal behavior (seven times more frequent).[49,50] Pessimism and hopelessness were valuable predictive symptoms; other symptoms that distinguished the suicides were insomnia, impaired memory and self-neglect. Almost half the suicides showed retardation. Depressed patients with delusions may be at greater risk than similar patients without delusions.

SCHIZOPHRENIA AND SUICIDE

There is general agreement that when suicide occurs in schizophrenia it often happens in the early phase of the illness.[11,18] Therefore research based on older, more chronic samples is likely to underestimate the actual number of suicides. The most consistent findings relate to gender and to the period of greatest risk. Thus 75–90 percent of suicides in this diagnostic group are committed by men, and suicide is most common during the first ten years of the illness.[51] It has been found that there is a 10 percent incidence of suicide within the first ten years of the illness and a 15 percent lifetime incidence.[52]

On the basis of a comparison of 30 chronic schizophrenics who killed themselves with 30 surviving chronic schizophrenics, the risk factors for suicide included being young, male, unemployed with a chronic relapsing illness, with a past history of depression and recurrent depressive episodes, and recent discharge from hospital.[18] Another study found that schizophrenic suicides tended to occur during the relatively non-psychotic phase of the illness.[53] The depression or despair preceding suicide would be expected to be most intense in the early phases of the illness as patients begin to recognize the potential chronic nature of their disorder. A strong association between suicide and negative expectations about the future has been postulated. In the Toronto series the three variables that predicted suicide were fears of mental disintegration, suicide threats and hopelessness.[18] Other factors that might increase the risk of suicide in schizophrenia include akathisia[54] and the abrupt withdrawal of medication.[55]

Although young age is one of the most important characteristics of suicide in schizophrenia, studies of older patients have revealed that suicide might occur throughout the lifespan and at all stages of the illness.[56]

Studies of suicide in schizophrenia have shown strikingly similar mortalities among hospitalized and non-hospitalized patients.[8,20] In an analysis of prospectively gathered data on 80 young adults who committed suicide during an ongoing longitudinal study of long-term treatment of schizophrenia in the community,[55] the subjects who eventually committed suicide had reported significantly more distress and dissatisfaction at the time that they entered the study. The suicide group obtained high scores on a measure of hopelessness but also admitted to feelings of loneliness and dissatisfaction with social relationships. Various schizophrenic symptoms, such as feelings of disintegration and persecution, are associated wtih suicide in schizophrenia, but because of the high base rate of these symptoms they are not helpful in identifying patients at risk. Hopelessness is a more powerful predictor of suicide. Other predictors include loss of family support, poor social and sexual functioning, negative attitudes towards treatment and better premorbid functioning. A number of studies have shown that the suicide risk for psychiatric patients is inversely proportionate to the time spent under psychiatric treatment;[57] of the 107 Icelandic patients with a first presentation of schizophrenia followed up for 20 years, the suicide rate was approximately 20 times the national suicide rate and most of the suicides were committed during the first year.[58] The best discriminators between suicidal and non-suicidal schizophrenic patients included depression (not surprisingly), aggressiveness, substance abuse, physical illness and progressive impairment in social functioning together with lack of family support.

SOMATIZATION DISORDER AND MORTALITY

A 42-year follow-up of 76 women with somatization disorder provided no evidence of excess mortality, whereas a matched group of patients with primary unipolar depression did show an excess mortality compared with local population figures.[59] Suicide and other unnatural deaths accounted for the excess mortality in the group with primary depression.

In somatization disorder the tendency to have multiple surgical procedures and the association with antisocial behaviour tend to suggest excess mortality from both natural and unnatural causes. However, these factors may be offset by the positive effects of frequent visits to physicians, with the resulting early diagnosis of conditions such as cancer and hypertension. This also demonstrates that psychiatric illness is not invariably associated with excess mortality, supporting the view that there is a low risk of suicide in hysteria.[60] A follow-up study of 500 outpatients over a six- to 12-year period demonstrated that despite a frequent history of suicide attempts, hysteria was not associated with an excess of unnatural mortality.

Rating

In general, applicants with a history of somatization or psychosomatic disorders can be accepted as standard risks provided that the physical impairment or impairments manifested do not in themselves attract a rating, or that there is no additional ratable mental disorder present.

THE NEUROSES AND MORTALITY

Neurosis used to be regarded as benign and a very rare cause of death. Anxiety states in particular were regarded, until relatively recently,[35] as carrying a minimal risk of suicide. However, in 1973 a report of a 12-year follow-up study of neurotic patients treated in hospital showed an increased mortality.[61] It has since been shown that a variety of neurotic conditions carry an increased risk of suicide.[62] After a period of nearly 11 years 1,482 patients with neurosis were followed up. These were all relatively severely disturbed patients who had been inpatients. Of the sample, 91 percent were traced and 139 patients were found to have died. There was a highly significant increase in mortality for both sexes for all causes of death. The risk was especially high during the year after discharge. Many patients had a diagnosis of depressive neurosis, but the suicide risk was high even when this diagnostic group was excluded. Although suicide and accidents contributed disproportionately, particularly in the early part of the follow-up, there was still a markedly increased mortality from the combined categories of nervous, respiratory and cardiovascular disease, which was more evenly distributed in time.

Further evidence for an excess mortality of neurotic patients as a group is provided by a 35-year follow-up study in Iowa of 113 former patients with panic disorder, in which both men and women were found to have an excessive number of deaths due to unnatural causes compared with the expected values predicted by age and sex-specific local population data.[63] Suicide accounted for 20 percent of the deaths, a higher rate than in a control group of unipolar depressives. Men with panic disorder, but not women, also had an excess number of deaths due to disease of the circulatory system.

The risk of suicide was high in patients with panic disorder but not in those with obsessive compulsive disorder.[64] Patients with a history of high blood pressure at the index evaluation were excluded, so panic attacks were not an early manifestation of hypertension in these patients.

It is known that patients with anxiety neurosis not infrequently develop depression and/or alcoholism, both of which are notoriously associated with completed suicide. In those cases the diagnosis at the time of death will probably be as alcoholism or depression, thus leading to under-reporting of anxiety states as a diagnosis that might be associated with suicide.

Of 112 patients with anxiety neurosis, 44 percent reported episodes of depression during a six-year follow-up, compared with only 7 percent in a group of surgical controls.[65] These secondary depressions tended to occur mainly in women, were reactive in nature, generally lasted three months or less and developed in those patients with a more severe and chronic anxiety neurosis. It has been reported that as many as 50 percent of patients with anxiety neurosis give a history of secondary depression.[66] The association and outcome of panic and depression were surveyed in a longitudinal study carried out in Zurich which incorporated a seven-year follow-up period. Patients with a combination of panic and depression had a high rate of suicide attempts, confirming that patients with both panic and depression have a more severe outcome than patients with only one of these disorders.[67] In another study,[9] patients of either sex with neurosis were at risk of unnatural death, while women were at risk of natural death as well.

There has been at least one other report of death by suicide and other unnatural causes in a follow-up study of patients with panic disorder.[68] However, none of the anxiety neurotics in another study died of circulatory disease, and the two who died of unnatural causes suffered from alcoholism as well.[8]

Mortality among insured lives with a history of psychoneurosis was examined in the *Medical Impairment Study 1983* (MIS 1983)[89] and confirmed only a slightly elevated death rate among those applicants accepted as standard risks compared with somewhat higher mortality for those accepted in substandard categories.

The data base for psychoneurosis was large, representing over 5 percent of the total substandard exposure for the whole study. Using the modified 1965–70 Basic tables as the basis for comparison, there were 353 male deaths in the standard category, giving a mortality ratio (MR) of 111 percent, virtually all of the extra deaths being due to suicide. The corresponding figures for females were 59 deaths giving an MR of 112 percent. The total number of deaths in the substandard categories was 393 for males (MR of 166 percent) and 151 for females (MR of 156 percent).

The *Medical Impairment Study 1983* demonstrated a high incidence of psychoneurosis among the insured population, especially among women. By careful selection it should be possible for the life underwriter to identify the milder cases of psychoneurosis that could be offered insurance at standard rates of premium, assigning the more severe and chronic cases to the slightly, moderately or highly substandard categories of risk.

Rating

Psychoneurosis, including anxiety and phobic reactions, obsessive compulsive states, conversion hysteria, anxiety/depression.

1) Mild.
Single (e.g. grief reaction) or infrequent episodes, no hospitalization — usually standard.

2) Moderate.
More frequent episodes, outpatient specialist advice, no hospitalization:

Time since last episode	Rating
Within 1 yr	3 per mil for 2 yr
2nd yr	2 per mil for 2 yr
Thereafter	Standard

3) Severe.

Chronic, recurrent anxiety with episodes of deeper depression, hospitalization —
2–3 per mil throughout.

No symptoms for five years — consider standard.

ORGANIC MENTAL DISORDERS AND MORTALITY

Organic mental disorder predisposes to early death, mainly from natural causes.[40]
Of 548 patients with organic mental disorders admitted to the University of Iowa
psychiatric hospital during a ten-year period, 87 died.[69] The conditions considered
in this survey were senile and presenile organic psychoses, alcohol- and drug-
related psychosis and transient organic psychosis. Mortality was significantly in
excess of that of a control population. Patients of all ages were at risk of premature
death, especially those under the age of 40, and risk was greatest during the first two
years of follow-up. Death from natural causes tended to be due to cancer and heart
disease in women, and influenza or pneumonia in young men. During the first two
years of follow-up, men were also at risk of death from accident or suicide.

This survey confirms the view that organic mental disorders are associated with
particularly high death rates, mainly from medical disease rather than accident or
suicide.[3] Other workers have also found a significant excess in natural mortality
among patients with organic brain syndromes.[8,69]

ADDICTION AND MORTALITY

In the series of 500 outpatients followed up for between six and 12 years, initial
psychiatric diagnoses highly predictive of unnatural death included drug addiction,
alcoholism and antisocial personality disorder.[8] Affective disorder secondary to
these conditions was also predictive of excess unnatural mortality.

In a seven-year follow-up of 128 heroin addicts, 15 (12 percent) had died.
Abstinence from opiates had been achieved by at least 40 subjects and 33 had
abstained for at least two years;[70] abstinence did not seem to have been replaced by
dependence on other drugs, including alcohol. However, 48 percent were still using
opiates. The mean age at death was 28·9. The death rate was 16·7 per thousand
heroin addicts yearly, which was appreciably lower than the rate (27 per thousand)
for male British heroin addicts in the 1960s.[71] All the patients in this study had been
physically dependent and were receiving daily prescriptions for heroin at the outset
of the study. The risk of suicide among drug addicts is known to be very high, and
James[71] suggested that the risk of suicide among male heroin addicts is 20 times that
of the general population. A similar study was carried out by Stimpson in London
in the1970s.[70]

A Swedish study[72] reports on mortality within a cohort of 115 street heroin
addicts who were studied over a period of five to eight years. Mortality was 63 times
that expected compared with official statistics for a group of this age and sex
distribution. Study of mortality among a control group of heroin addicts given
maintenance methadone treatment showed that the methadone program drastically

reduced the death rate. However, even those in the methadone treatment program had a mortality eight times that expected compared with a non-drug-using population matched for age and sex. The reasons for this moderately elevated death rate include the contraction of potentially life threatening diseases before entry into the program. Thus methadone treatment programs seem to protect against drug-abuse-related morbidity and death among heroin addicts.

The HIV seropositive rate in drug abusers in this Swedish series was 52 percent. Seropositive rates of 38–65 percent among drug abusers have been reported in three other studies.[73–75]

Rating

Rating for drug abuse is covered elsewhere (*see* Chapter 30).

ALCOHOLISM AND MORTALITY

A review of ten long-term follow-up studies of alcohol abuse, which covered periods ranging from seven to 35 years, found a wide range of deaths in the samples which varied from 5 percent to 62 percent.[76] One of the most methodologically sound follow-up studies reviewed the progress of 100 severe alcoholic men and women for a period of eight years after they had been admitted to hospital for detoxification.[76] At the end of the follow-up period 25 percent had achieved stable abstinence for at least three years; whereas 29 percent had died. Only 26 percent were experiencing continuing serious problems with alcohol. The death rate in that series was roughly three times that expected of non-alcoholic men and women of comparable age. Five of the deaths were due to myocardial infarction, eight were associated with homicide and accidents, four died from cirrhosis and four from cancer of the pharynx, lung or stomach. One of the remaining deaths was from suicide. A predictor of good outcome was premorbid social stability.

A 15-year longitudinal study of 96 alcoholic men with an average age of 47 years also demonstrated a high mortality rate.[77] The alcoholics in this Swedish study were classified as abusers (daily drinkers with repeated intoxications and amnesic spells), addicts (alcohol-dependent with craving, withdrawal symptoms and relief drinking) or chronics (alcohol-dependents with medical sequelae such as cirrhosis, pancreatitis or convulsions). These alcoholics received only limited treatment and, when reviewed 15 years later, the combined death rate was almost 25 percent: one-fifth of the abusers, one-quarter of the addicts and as many as half of the chronics had died. The causes of death in this series were similar to those observed in other follow-up studies of alcoholics: the most frequent causes were cardiovascular disease, unnatural death (including three suicides), gastrointestinal disease and infections. The predictors for a poor prognosis included severity of the involvement with alcohol, increased age, chronic unemployment and social isolation.

Over a 17-year follow-up of 1,832 white Americans originally aged 40–45 with a daily alcohol intake of six drinks there was a marked increase in age-adjusted risk of death from cancer, cardiovascular disease, coronary artery disease and other causes of death. Although some of the increased mortality in this group could be explained by cigarette smoking or baseline elevation of blood pressure, there continued to be a statistically significant excess mortality which could not be explained by the higher risk of these variables in the six-drinks-per-day group.[78]

Some studies indicate that the lifetime risk of suicide in alcoholism is 11–15 percent.[79] However, it has been demonstrated that at least some of these studies overestimate the risk by a factor of at least 3.[80] Nevertheless, despite the relatively small lifetime risk of suicide, there is a mortality risk from suicide of 3·4 among previously hospitalized alcoholics in English-speaking countries, so that the likelihood of suicide in conservatively diagnosed alcoholism is still between 60 and 120 times that of the general population, with alcoholism contributing about a quarter of all suicides.[80]

Suicide among alcoholics tends to occur relatively late after the development of the disorder, in contrast to the affective disorders.[38] Factors that distinguish alcoholic suicides from surviving alcoholics[81] include poor physical health, poor work record in the previous four years, a previous history of suicidal behavior and the development of secondary depression. The recent loss of a close relationship through separation or death is also common among alcoholic suicides.[37]

Once alcoholic cirrhosis has developed, the five-year survival rate is only 36 percent, according to a 20-year prospective study of cirrhosis.[82] Only complete abstention from alcohol affected survival. If abstinence could be achieved in patients with compensated alcoholic cirrhosis, five-year survival more than doubled.

Alcoholism and other drug abuse have been linked to high death rates, young men and middle-aged women being at greatest risk of death, mostly from unnatural causes. Women alcoholics tended to die later than men, probably because of the later onset of drinking. In a detailed study of 935 alcoholics hospitalized between 1954 and 1957, both natural and unnatural deaths were significantly greater than expected. Suicide and accidents were leading causes of death, followed by cancer, circulatory and respiratory disorders.[83] Unnatural death and alcohol-related physical disorders, such as cirrhosis and pancreatitis, accounted for most deaths among young alcoholics in the US Navy.[84]

Alcoholism and drug addiction (as well as antisocial personality) were highly associated with unnatural death in a six- to 12-year blind follow-up study of 500 outpatients.[8] Affective disorder that was antedated by alcoholism addiction or antisocial behavior was also predictive of a very high rate of mortality due to unnatural causes.[8]

Rating

Rating for alcoholism is covered elsewhere (*see* Chapter 30).

ANOREXIA NERVOSA

Outcome and Prognosis

In a follow-up study of 100 women with anorexia nervosa who were reviewed between four and eight years after their first presentation, 20 had a poor outcome and there had been two deaths. The poor outcome was associated with longer duration of the illness, older age of onset on presentation, lower weight during illness and at original presentation, and the co-existence of symptoms such as bulimia, vomiting and anxiety when eating with others. Unfavorable prognostic features were poor childhood, poor social adjustment and poor parental relationships.[85] There had been only one death in the Bristol series of 78 patients (half of whom were outpatients) followed up for a mean period of nearly six years,[86] but in the Maudsley series of 41 anorexic inpatients, 5 percent had died after a mean follow-up of between four and ten years.[87]

Rating

A history of mild anorexia nervosa of short duration with full recovery under the age of 20 can usually be disregarded in underwriting. For durations over 12 months, especially if recovery is delayed until over the age of 20, a temporary extra premium of 2 per mil for three years in the first year of recovery and decreasing annually would be indicated. Where full recovery has not yet been achieved — e.g. continuing amenorrhea and body weight less than 103 lb (47 kg) — a rating of +200 to +100 (or a minimum extra premium if indicated) depending on duration of symptoms and severity should be considered. Applicants who have attempted suicide or whose body weight is below 84 lb (38 kg) (irrespective of height) should be declined.

PERSONALITY DISORDER

People with severe personality disorder are at risk of premature death, especially from suicide and accidents.[1] Up to 10 percent of suicides suffer from sociopathic disorders,[88] and those individuals who are most at risk are those who show marked lability of mood, aggressiveness, impulsivity, alienation from peers and alcohol or drug abuse.

Rating

Applicants diagnosed as having the more benign forms of personality disorder (e.g. neurotic or obsessive personalities) can usually be insured as standard risks unless complicated by ratable depression. On the other hand, those with the more severe aggressive or psychopathic personalities would require a rating of +100 up.

REFERENCES

1 Black DW, Warrack G, Winokur G. Excess mortality among psychiatric patients. The Iowa record linkage study. *JAMA* 1985; 253: 58–61.
2 Tsuang MT, Woolson RF. Mortality in patients with schizophrenia, mania, depression and surgical conditions. A comparison with general population mortality. *Br J Psychiat* 1977; 130: 162–6.
3 Eastwood RM, Stiasny SHM, Meier R, Woogh CM. Mental illness and mortality. *Comprehensive Psychiatry* 1982; 23: 377–85.

4 Craig TJ, Lin SP. Mortality among psychiatric inpatients. Age adjusted comparison of populations before and after psychotropic drug era. *Arch Gen Psychiat* 1981; 38: 935–8.
5 Martin RL, Cloninger R, Guze SB, Clayton PJ. Mortality in a follow up of 500 psychiatric outpatients. Cause specific mortality. *Arch Gen Psychiat* 1985; 42: 58–66.
6 Tsuang MT, Woolson RF. Excess mortality in schizophrenia and affective disorders. Do suicides and accidental deaths solely account for this excess? *Arch Gen Psychiat* 1978; 35: 1181–5.
7 Morrison JR. Suicide in a psychiatric practice population. *J Clin Psychiat* 1982; 43: 348–52.
8 Martin RL, Cloninger R, Guze SB, Clayton PJ. Mortality in a follow up of 500 psychiatric outpatients. Total mortality. *Arch Gen Psychiat* 1985; 42: 47–54.
9 Black DW, Warrack G, Winokur G. The Iowa record linkage study. Suicides and accidental deaths among psychiatric patients. *Arch Gen Psychiat* 1985; 42: 71–5.
10 Pokorny AD. Prediction of suicide in psychiatric patients. Report of a prospective study. *Arch Gen Psychiat* 1983; 40: 249–57.
11 Miles CP. Conditions predisposing to suicide. *Nerv Mental Dis* 1977; 164: 231–46.
12 Tsuang MT, Woolson RF, Fleming JA. Long term outcome of major psychoses. Schizophrenia and affective disorders compared with psychiatrically symptom free surgical conditions. *Arch Gen Psychiat* 1979; 36: 1295–1301.
13 Tsuang MT, Woolson RF, Fleming JA. Premature deaths in schizophrenia and affective disorders. An analysis of survival curves and variables affecting the shortened survival. *Arch Gen Psychiat* 1980; 37: 979–83.
14 Modrzewska K, Book JA. Schizophrenics and malignant neoplasms in a north Swedish population. *Lancet* 1979; I: 275–6.
15 Harding CM, Zubin J, Strauss JS. Chronicity in schizophrenia: fact, partial fact or artifact? *Hosp and Commun Psychiat* 1987; 38: 477–86.
16 McCreadie RG, Wiles D, Grant S et al. The Scottish first episode of schizophrenia study. Two year follow up. *Acta Psychiat Scand* 1989; 80: 597–602.
17 Herrman HE, Baldwin JA, Christie D. A record linkage study of mortality and general hospital discharge in patients diagnosed as schizophrenic. *Psycholog Med* 1983; 13: 581–93.
18 Roy A. Suicide in chronic schizophrenia. *Br J Psychiat* 1982; 141: 171–7.
19 Winokur G, Tsuang M. The Iowa 500: Suicide in mania, depression and schizophrenia. *Am J Psychiat* 1975; 132: 6: 650–1.
20 Allebeck P, Wistedt B. Mortality in schizophrenia. A ten year follow up based on the Stockholm County inpatient register. *Arch Gen Psychiat* 1986; 43: 650–3.
21 Black DW, Warrack G, Winokur G. The Iowa record linkage study. Excess mortality among patients with 'functional' disorders. *Arch Gen Psychiat* 1985; 42: 82–8.
22 Mortensen PB, Juel K. Mortality and causes of death in schizophrenic patients in Denmark. *Acta Psychiat Scand* 1990; 81: 372–7.
23 Tsuang MT. Suicide in schizophrenics, manics, depressives and surgical controls. A comparison with general population suicide mortality. *Arch Gen Psychiat* 1978; 35: 153–5.
24 Akiskal H, Bitar AH, Puzantoin VR, Rosenthal TL, Walter P. The nosological status of neurotic depression: a prospective 3–4 year follow up examination in light of the primary-secondary and unipolar dichotomies. *Arch Gen Psychiat* 1978; 35: 756–66.
25 Keller MB, Klerman GL, Lavori PW, Coryell W, Endicott J, Taylor J. Long term outcome of episodes of major depression. Clinical and public health significance. *JAMA* 1984; 252: 788–92.
26 Lee AS, Murray RM. The long-term outcome of Maudsley depressives. *Br J Psychiat* 1988; 153: 741–51.
27 Bebbington PE. The course and prognosis of affective psychoses. In: Wing JK, Wing L (eds). *Handbook of Psychiatry* 1982. Vol 3. Cambridge: Cambridge University Press.
28 Guze SB, Robins E. Suicide and primary affective disorders. *Psychiat* 1970; 117: 437–8.
29 Post F. The management and nature of depressive illnesses in late life: a follow through study. *Br J Psychiat* 1972; 121: 393–404.
30 Murphy E. The prognosis of depression in old age. *Br J Psychiat* 1983; 142: 111–19.
31 Jacoby RJ, Leoy R, Bod JM. Computed tomography and the outcome of the affective

disorder: a follow up study of elderly patients. *Br J Psychiat* 1981; 139: 288–92.

32 Roy A. Risk factors for suicide in psychiatric patients. *Arch Gen Psychiat* 1982; 39: 1089–95.

33 Tsuang MT. Risk of suicide in the relatives of schizophrenics, manic depressives and controls. *J Clin Psychiat* 1983; 43: 396–400.

34 Pitts FN, Winokur G. Affective disorder III: Diagnostic correlates and incidence of suicide. *J Nerv Mental Dis* 1964; 139: 176–81.

35 Barraclough B, Bunen J, Nelson B, Sainsbury P. A hundred cases of suicide: clinical aspects. *Br J Psychiat* 1974; 125: 355–73.

36 Murphy GE, Problems in studying suicide. *Psychiatric Developments* 1983; 4: 339–50.

37 Murphy GE, Robins E. Social factors in suicide. *JAMA* 1967; 199: 303–8.

38 Robins E, Gassner S, Kayes J, Wilkinson RH and Murphy GE. The communication of suicidal intent: a study of 134 consecutive cases of successful (completed) suicide. *Am J Psychiat* 1959; 115: 724–33.

39 Dorpat TL, Ripley HS. A study of suicide in the Seattle area. *Comprehensive Psychiatry* 1960; I: 349–59.

40 Pokorny AD. Suicide rates in various psychiatric disorders. *J Nerv Mental Dis* 1964; 139: 499–506.

41 Hawton K. Assessment of suicide risk. *Br J Psychiat* 1987; 150: 145–53.

42 Allebeck P, Allgulander C. Psychiatric diagnoses as predictors of suicide. A comparison of diagnoses at conscripton and in psychiatric care in a cohort of 50,465 young men. *Br J Psychiat* 1990; 157: 339–44.

43 Murphy GE. On suicide prediction and prevention. *Arch Gen Psychiat* 1983; 40: 343–4.

44 Hawton K, Fagg J. Suicide and other causes of death, following attempted suicide. *Br J Psychiat* 1988; 152: 359–66.

45 Flood R, Seager C. A retrospective examination of psychiatric case records of patients who subsequently committed suicide. *Br J Psychiat* 1968; 114: 443–50.

46 Myers D, Neal C. Suicide in psychiatric patients. *Br J Psychiat* 1978; 133: 38–44.

47 Pederson AM, Teft MA, Babigian HM. Risk of mortality of suicide attempters compared with psychiatric and general populations. *Suicide* 1975; 5: 145–57.

48 Tsuang MT, Woolson RF and Fleming JA. Causes of death in schizophrenia and manic depression. *Br J Psychiat* 1980; 136: 239–42.

49 Barraclough BM, Pallis DJ. Depression followed by suicide: a comparison of depressed suicides with living depressives. *Psycholog Med* 1975; 5: 55–61.

50 Roy A. Suicide in depressives. *Comprehensive Psychiatry* 1983; 24: 487–91.

51 Johns CA, Stanley M, Stanley B. Suicide in Schizophrenia. *Ann NY Acad Sci* 1986; 487: 294–300.

52 Nyman AK, Jonsson H. Patterns of self destructive behaviour in schizophrenia. *Acta Psychiat Scand* 1986; 73: 252–62.

53 Drake RE, Gates C, Cotton PG. Suicide among schizophrenics: a comparison of attempters and completed suicides. *Br J Psychiat* 1986; 149: 784–7.

54 Drake RE, Ehrlich J. Suicide attempts associated with akathisia. *Am J Psychiat* 1985; 142: 499–501.

55 Cohen S, Leonard C, Farberow N, Schneidman ES. Tranquillizers and suicide in the schizophrenic patient. *Arch Gen Psychiat* 1964; 11: 312–21.

56 Yarden P. Observations on suicide in chronic schizophrenics. *Comprehensive Psychiatry* 1974; 15: 325–33.

57 Copas J. Fryer M. Density estimation and suicide risks in psychiatric treatment. *J R Statist Soc* [A] 1980; 143: 167–76.

58 Helgason L. Twenty years' follow up of first psychiatric presentation for schizophrenia: what could have been prevented? *Acta Psychiat Scand* 1991; 81: 231–5.

59 Coryell W. Diagnosis specific mortality. Primary unipolar depression and Briquet's syndrome (somatization disorder). *Arch Gen Psychiat* 1981; 38: 939–42.

60 Woodruff RA, Clayton PJ, Guze SB. Hysteria: studies of diagnosis, outcome and prevalence. *JAMA* 1971; 215:425–8.

61 Sims A. Mortality and neurosis. *Lancet* 1973; 2: 1072–5.

62 Sims A, Prior P. The pattern of mortality in severe neuroses. *Br J Psychiat* 1978; 133: 299–305.

63 Coryell W, Noyes R, Clancy J. Excess mortality in panic disorder. A comparison with primary unipolar depression. *Arch Gen Psychiat* 1982; 39: 701–3.
64 Coryell WH. Obsessive-compulsive disorder and primary unipolar depression. *J Nerv Mental Dis* 1981; 169: 220–4.
65 Clancy J, Noyes R, Hoenk PR, Slymen DJ. Secondary depression in anxiety neurosis. *J Nerv Mental Dis* 1978; 166: 846–51.
66 Woodruff RA, Guze SB, Clayton PJ. Anxiety neurosis among psychiatric out patients. *Comprehensive Psychiatry* 1972; 13: 165–70.
67 Vollrath M, Angst J. Outcome of panic and depression in a seven year follow up: results of the Zurich study. *Acta Psychiat Scand* 1989; 80: 591–6.
68 Noyes R, Clancy J, Hoenk PR, Seymen D. The prognosis of anxiety neurosis. *Arch Gen Psychiat* 1980; 37: 173–80.
69 Black DW, Warrack G, Winokur G. The Iowa record linkage study. Excess mortality among patients with organic mental disorders. *Arch Gen Psychiat* 1985; 42: 78–81.
70 Stimson GV, Oppenheimer E, Thorley A. Seven year follow up of heroin addicts: drug use and outcome. *Br Med J* 1978; 1: 1190–2.
71 James IP. Suicide and mortality among heroin addicts in Britain. *Br J Addiction* 1967; 62: 391–8.
72 Gronbladh L, Ohlund LS, Gunne LM. Mortality in heroin addiction: impact of methadone treatment. *Acta Psychiat Scand* 1990; 82: 223–7.
73 Brettle RP, Bisset K, Burns S et al. Human immunodeficiency virus and drug misuse: the Edinburgh experience. *Br Med J* 1987; 295: 421–4.
74 Robertson JR, Bucknall ADV, Wiggins P. Regional variations in HIV antibody sero-positivity in British intravenous drug users. *Lancet* 1986; 1: 1435–6.
75 Pentherer SF, Edmond E, Simmonds P, Dickson JD, Bath GE. HTLV–III antibody in Edinburgh drug addicts. *Lancet* 1985; 2: 1129–30.
76 Vaillant GE, Clark W, Cyrus C, Milofsky ES, Kopp J, Wulsin VW, Mogielnicki NP. Prospective study of alcoholism treatment. Eight year follow up. *Am J Med* 1983; 75: 455–63.
77 Ojesjo L. Long term outcome in alcohol abuse and alcoholism among males in the Lundby general population, Sweden. *Br J Addiction* 1981; 76: 391–400.
78 Dyer AR, Stamler J et al. Alcohol consumption and 17 year mortality in the Chicago Western Electric Company study. *Preventative Med* 1980; 9: 78–90.
79 Murphy G, Armstrong J, Hiermele S. Suicide and alcoholism. *Arch Gen Psychiat* 1979; 21: 753–60.
80 Murphy GE, Wetzel RD. The lifetime risk of suicide in alcoholism. *Arch Gen Psychiat* 1990; 47: 383–93.
81 Motto JA. Suicide risk factors in alcohol abuse. *Suicide and Life Threatening Behaviour* 1980; 10: 230–8.
82 Saunders JB, Walters JRF, Davies P, Paton A. A 20 year prospective study of cirrhosis. *Br Med J* 1981; 282: 263–6.
83 Nicholls P, Edwards G, Kyle E. Alcoholics admitted to four hospitals in England. II general and cause–specific mortality. *Quart J Stud Alcohol* 1974; 35z: 841–55.
84 Schuckit MA, Gunderson EKE. Death among young alcoholics in the US naval service. *Quart J Stud Alcohol* 1974; 35: 856–62.
85 Hsu LKG, Crisp AH, Harding B. Outcome of anorexia nervosa. *Lancet* 1979; 8107: 61–5.
86 Morgan HG, Purgold J, Welbourne J. Management and outcome in anorexia nervosa. *Br J Psychiat* 1983; 143: 282–7.
87 Morgan HG, Russell GFM. Value of family background and clinical features as predictors of long term outcome in anorexia nervosa. *Psycholog Med* 1975; 5: 355–71.
88 Ovenstone IMK, Kreikman N. Two syndromes of suicide. *Br Jr Psychiat* 1974; 124: 336–45.
89 *Medical Impairment Study 1983*. Vol 1. Boston: Society of Actuaries and Association of Life Insurance Medical Directors of America, 1986.

CHAPTER 25

THE RHEUMATIC GROUP OF DISORDERS

NEIL CARDOE

The rheumatic group of disorders represents over 200 different clinical entities. These diseases affect the musculoskeletal system, a system made up not only of joints, but also of the tissues acting on, supporting or surrounding the joints. The three main components are (1) the synovium, which lines the joint and is responsible for its nutrition and for the secretion of joint fluid (which lubricates the joint and separates the joint surfaces), (2) the cartilage, which acts as a cushion between the joint surfaces, and (3) the tissues that act on the joint, that is the muscles, tendons, their sheaths, and the stabilizing mechanism of the joint, the ligaments and capsule. Any one of these tissues may be involved in the disease process, and, because there is considerable overlap in the tissues involved, classification is difficult.

The exact cause of most of the rheumatic diseases is not known but the histopathology in many of them indicates an autoimmune process with genetic, viral, environmental, social, physical and even geographical factors influencing the outcome. Genetic profiling may identify those people susceptible to some of these conditions, such as rheumatoid arthritis and systemic lupus, but the trigger mechanism for each disease, whether it is viral, infective or due to other factors, has still to be identified.

Clinically the signs and symptoms of many of the rheumatic diseases are similar: pain on movement, often swelling of the affected joint and loss of function with subsequent disability. Many of the conditions have systemic involvement affecting the major organs.

Few of the rheumatic diseases have an early mortality, but they do have a high morbidity due to the disability they cause; not being a killing disease, statistics are scarce.

CLASSIFICATION

1) Rheumatoid arthritis, including juvenile chronic arthritis.
2) Seronegative arthritis, including ankylosing spondylitis, psoriatic arthritis, reactive arthritis, enteropathic arthritis, Behçet's disease and Sjøgren's disease.
3) Osteoarthritis.
4) Crystal depositon disease.
5) Systemic lupus erythematosus.
6) Systemic sclerosis and mixed connective tissue disease.
7) Polyarteritis and related arteritic syndromes.

8) Polymyositis and dermatomyositis.
9) Polymyalgia rheumatica and other myalgic syndromes.
10) Other arthritides.
11) Soft tissue rheumatism.
12) Nerve entrapment syndromes.
13) Intervertebral disc lesions.
14) Hypermobility syndromes.

RHEUMATOID ARTHRITIS

Despite intensive research in the past few years, the cause of rheumatoid arthritis is still not known, although recent advances in immunology and molecular biology are contributing to the understanding of the pathogenic mechanism of the disease. Rheumatoid arthritis can be rapidly progressive, but more often has a fluctuating course with remissions and relapses. It can cause severe disability due to joint destruction and can remit after one attack, never to reappear, leaving no disability. It is a systemic disorder affecting mainly the peripheral joints and is usually symmetrical in distribution; it often shows extra-articular manifestations. No age group is exempt, but it is more common in the third and fourth decades. It is more common in females, but conflicting evidence exists suggesting that the use of the contraceptive pill or hormone replacement therapy may protect against the disease.

The onset can be acute or insidious, the patient presenting with a symmetrical, peripheral, polyarthropathy, but it can remain monarticular throughout its course. As a rule it is associated with morning stiffness lasting more than an hour, an elevated erythrocyte sedimentation rate or plasma viscosity, and the rheumatoid factor will be present in the serum of at least 85 percent of cases. There is often a low grade fever, anorexia, weight loss, lassitude and fatigability. Twenty percent of cases will show skin nodules; serious cases may show evidence of vasculitis, pleural effusion, pulmonary fibrosis, and even obstructive bronchiolitis. Of those with skin nodules, 55 percent show evidence of cardiovascular involvement. Ocular, neuropathic and renal abnormalities are not unusual in the severe progressive disease.

The clinical course of the disease is variable, but the factors that suggest a poor prognosis are:
1) failure to respond to the first line drugs (i.e. nonsteroidal anti-inflammatory drugs).
2) the presence of erosive changes on X-ray of the small joints early in the disease.
3) poor functional capacity early in the disease.
4) the presence of extra-articular manifestations, particularly anemia, nodules, eye changes and vasculitis.
5) persistently elevated ESR or plasma viscosity.
6) a high IgM rheumatoid factor titer or the presence of anti-nuclear factor.
7) tissue type HLA DR3 or DR4, which may indicate a risk of side effects developing when the second line drugs are used.

Mortality

Mortality in rheumatoid arthritis is probably underestimated as it is not always recorded on the death certificate, but most studies do indicate a reduction in life expectancy with rheumatoid arthritis, the increased mortality being associated with lung disorders, long duration of the disease, severe disabling arthritis, bacterial infections, renal disease and evidence of systemic involvement. Sometimes the treatment is more toxic than the disease: there is an increased mortality associated with the use of the second line drugs such as gold, penicillamine, methotrexate and the immunosuppressive or cytotoxic drugs.

If there is great loss of function within one year of the onset of the disease, the prognosis is poor; the five-year survival in those severely disabled is less than 55 percent, similar to the prognosis in three-vessel coronary artery disease. Poor function seems to indicate a high mortality. The five-year survival of those patients with extra-articular manifestations is less than 60 percent and it is particularly bad for those with pulmonary fibrosis, pericarditis, eye involvement or vasculitis.

Rating

Mild Disease
Cases with minimal disease activity, negative rheumatoid factor, a sedimentation rate of less than 30, few joints involved, no extra-articular manifestations and control feasible with non-steroidal anti-inflammatory drugs — 0 to +50.

Moderate Disease
Cases showing chronic active disease that continues in episodic fashion with the presence of nodules, a hemoglobin of less than 11 g per dl, and an ESR of up to 55 — +50 to +100.

Severe Disease
In these cases the disease is acute, with the presence of nodules, an ESR above 55, rheumatoid factor positive, the presence of systemic manifestations, marked disability and the use of second line drugs (particularly corticosteroids) — +100 to +250.

Additional Debits
If there is also a history of peptic ulceration, an extra +50 should be added because of the risk of perforation or hemorrhage from the ulcer due the effects of therapy. If a peptic ulcer is present and active, the decision should be postponed until the ulcer has been treated. The use of steroids in the treatment of rheumatoid arthritis warrants an extra +50 because of the risks associated with long-term therapy. There are special surgical risks associated with rheumatoid disease, especially those cases treated with steroids; the infection rate is increased and, as several joints may have to be replaced, there will be an increased rate of joint failure. The drug treatment of rheumatoid arthritis may be straightforward, but in severe cases toxic drugs, known as disease-modifying agents, have to be used. Gold can cause severe skin reaction and damage to the kidneys and bone marrow; penicillamine can cause

loss of taste, bone marrow suppression, anemia and proteinuria. Sulphasalazine has similar side effects to penicillamine and may also affect the liver and reduce male fertility. The anti-malarial drugs, such as hydroxychloroquine may induce photosensitivity and, with high doses, retinopathy. When methotrexate, cytotoxic or immunosuppressive drugs are used regular monitoring of the blood and the urine is essential.

Juvenile Chronic Arthritis

This is a group of diseases which begin before the 16th birthday. G F Still first described the major disease of the group in 1897, and it is still referred to in some areas as Still's disease. In many aspects this condition is similar to adult rheumatoid arthritis, but it can be divided into three distinct types, each with a different prognosis.

Systemic
The onset is associated with fever, skin rashes, lymphadenopathy, splenomegaly, pleurisy, pericarditis and progressive polyarthritis. This type accounts for 25 percent of the cases seen.

Polyarticular
This type is associated with multiple joint involvement and a negative rheumatoid factor. It has a course very similar to adult rheumatoid arthritis but with a better prognosis. This is the commonest type and accounts for 40 percent of cases.

Pauciarticular
This type is characterized by the involvement of only one or two joints (up to a maximum of four); up to 50 percent show eye involvement in the form of iridocyclitis, which, if not treated early, can lead to blindness. This type accounts for 35 percent of the cases seen.

Prognosis
Patients with the best prognosis are monarticular where the child presents to the doctor with a limp: these cases usually remit within five years. Bad prognostic signs in juvenile chronic arthritis are
1) Onset before fifth birthday.
2) Disease remaining active after five years.
3) Cardiac involvement.
4) Thrombocytosis or a raised IgA level.
5) Severe functional limitation when first seen by the rheumatologist.
   In 15 percent of cases of juvenile chronic arthritis the pattern resembles that of adult rheumatoid disease and has to be treated as such; in another 15 percent of cases the progress of the disease resembles ankylosing spondylitis and has to be treated accordingly.

Rating
For the younger age groups needing treatment with steroids or other second line drugs — +100 to +150.

When the disease has been inactive for five years — 0 to +50.

In the case of children with eye involvement, care must be taken when offering permanent health insurance as untreated disease can lead to blindness.

Jaccoud's Arthritis

This condition is a rare sequel to rheumatic fever when the attack has been unusually severe or recurrent. The joints of the hands develop deformities similar to rheumatoid disease, but the course is benign and not progressive, and so may be accepted at standard rates.

SERONEGATIVE SPONDYLO-ARTHRITIS

The disorders in this group have in common a negative test for rheumatoid factor, a high propensity for the tissue type HLA B27, a tendency to axial-skeletal joint involvement and a strong association with ankylosing spondylitis.

Ankylosing Spondylitis

Ankylosing spondylitis is a chronic inflammatory disease of the spine beginning in the sacro-iliac joints and spreading up the spine to involve the costovertebral joints and 30 percent of the large proximal joints, in particular the hip and shoulder joints. This may lead to hip joint replacement at an early age, and to progressive restriction of spinal movement.

The HLA B27 tissue type is present in 94 percent of cases. It is predominantly a male condition, starting before the age of 30, and is associated with an elevated ESR; 20 percent of cases have eye changes in the form of an iritis, and about 4 percent have a non-specific aortitis leading to aortic valve incompetence. In addition, 5 percent have heart conduction defects, usually in the form of a bundle branch block. It has been estimated that about 6 percent will develop amyloid disease resulting in renal dysfunction. Ankylosing spondylitis has a variable course but the majority remit by the mid-30s and remain quiescent; these cases do not present an insurance risk and most remain in full employment.

At risk are those with proteinuria (possibly indicating amyloid disease), aortic incompetence and any previously treated with deep X-ray therapy. The latter risk factor is due to the increased risk of leukemia and skin cancers arising at the site of irradiation. Patients showing long-term disease activity, progressive disease and a persistently elevated ESR will need continuous treatment and/or surgical intervention in the form of hip joint replacement or spinal deformity correction.

Rating

Active disease requires rating of +75 to +100. Inactive disease not needing therapy for at least one year and with no significant spinal deformity can be taken at standard rates. Patients with marked spinal deformity, ankylosis of the hips or shoulders, or those with aortic incompetence or conduction defects will require an additional rating of +50 to +150. Those with a history of more than one course of radiotherapy need an extra +50. Any showing proteinuria of more than 2 g in twenty-four hours should be declined; those with a protein excretion of less than 2 g in twenty-four hours warrant an additional debit of +100.

Psoriatic Arthropathy

Psoriasis is a common skin disorder; 7–10 percent of patients develop an associated arthritis, presenting as a condition not dissimilar to rheumatoid arthritis with the same consequential deformity and disability, which in some cases is severe. The clinical features are predominantly those of distal interphalangeal joint involvement in the hands and feet, usually asymmetrical, often associated with dactylitis. Severe deforming arthritis with widespread ankylosis or mutilans can occur, but the majority are rheumatoid-like and show a benign course; about 5 percent have spinal involvement indistinguishable from ankylosing spondylitis. Nodules are not a feature of this condition, which is always seronegative; and the prognosis is if anything better than that of rheumatoid arthritis. However, those showing extensive progressive disease may require toxic drugs, such as methotrexate, to halt progress. These cases are at risk.

Rating
Rating is 0 to +150, depending on activity of the disease and the therapy used.

Reactive Arthropathy

This type of arthritis is seen when an inflammatory synovitis develops in association with infection at a site distant to the joints.

Reiter's Disease

This disease is characterized by the triad of seronegative polyarthritis, conjunctivitis and nonspecific urethritis. Two types are described. The first is genital in origin and occurs after sexual encounters; it is sometimes referred to as sexually acquired reactive arthritis (SARA). The second type occurs after an intestinal infection such as bacillary dysentery, salmonella or yersinia infections; 60–80 percent of those affected are HLA B27 positive. Of patients attending a clinic for sexually transmitted disease because of non specific urethritis, 2 percent go on to develop Reiter's syndrome. The majority of cases are self-limiting, but 30 percent have relapses with evidence of continued disease activity. Approximately 11–15 percent of these latter cases are severe enough to cause long term unemployment and about 15 percent progress to a state indistinguishable from ankylosing spondylitis.

Rating
A single attack with no signs of recurrence can be accepted at standard rates. Those with relapses need a rating of +50 to +100, depending on the degree of activity present.

Other reactive arthropathies, such as those associated with viral infections, can be accepted at standard rates unless the underlying condition warrants a rating in its own right.

AIDS (HIV Infection)

This infection can present with an acute peripheral seronegative arthritis (*see* Chapter 28).

Enteropathic Arthropathy

Arthritis can be associated with primary bowel disease, the two main disorders being Crohn's disease and ulcerative colitis. It has also been described in Whittle's disease and following intestinal by-pass operations for obesity. Approximately 12 percent of patients with ulcerative colitis have either arthropathy or spondylitis. In Crohn's disease approximately 20 percent have an associated arthritis and 1 percent have spondylitis. Joint involvement is more common with extensive disease and the knee is the most commonly affected joint.

Rating
Rating is as for the underlying disease; the joint complications can be ignored unless very severe.

Behçet's Syndrome

This condition is characterized by oral and genital ulceration; as iritis may feature in the symptoms it may be mistakenly diagnosed as Reiter's syndrome. Behçet's is a chronic episodic disease and 60 percent of cases have arthritis of the large joints. If there is evidence of neurological involvement the prognosis is poor.

Rating
Unless the disease has been in remission for at least five years a heavy rating of +150 to +200 is indicated. Where there is evidence of neurological involvement the case should be declined.

Sjøgren's Syndrome

This syndrome represents a group of diseases characterized by inflammation of the exocrine glands, the salivary and lacrymal glands being principally involved, giving rise to dryness of the eyes and mouth. It can be classified as primary, where the disease exists on its own, or secondary, where it is associated with other autoimmune disorders (e.g. rheumatoid arthritis, systemic lupus erythematosus). The majority of patients have a high ESR, anemia and hypergammaglobulinemia, and 80 percent have antibodies to Ro (SS-A); 25 percent have renal tubular defects, and, since it is possible that this syndrome is related to the EB virus, an increased risk of malignancy is said to be present.

Rating
In primary Sjøgren's disease standard rates are indicated. When the disease is secondary to an autoimmune disorder the rating is for that disorder with an extra +25 to cover the increased risk of malignant disease.

OSTEOARTHRITIS (OA)

Osteoarthritis is the commonest rheumatic condition; between one and two of every three of the population over the age of 35 will show some aspect of OA in at least one joint. This condition is also referred to as osteoarthrosis or degenerative arthritis. This arthritis, at times disabling, affects the synovial joints, especially after the fifth decade; research indicates that it is not just a degenerative disorder.

OA is characterized by the loss of articular cartilage from the bone surface and the formation of osteophytes at the joint margins. It is mainly a non-inflammatory condition and asymptomatic in the early stages, but at times there are inflammatory episodes due to the appearance in the joint of microcrystals, which cause the joint to become hot and swollen. The condition is diagnosed by X-ray and, in the acute phase, by radioactive isotope scan.

The most commonly affected joints are the first metacarpal, distal inter-phalangeal and proximal interphalangeal joints of the hands, the hips, knees and the first metatarsal joint of the foot. OA is not always symptomatic: up to 50 percent of subjects with X-ray changes have no symptoms. It is treated both by non-steroidal anti-inflammatory drugs and surgery. Total joint replacement is probably the treatment of choice when large joints are affected; anti-inflammatory drugs are used when the symptoms are mild, although these drugs do not alter the course of the disease.

Rating

Not being a life threatening disease, the risk factors are those associated with treatment (i.e. the unwanted side effects of the drugs used and the complications of joint replacement). Unless either of these factors is present, standard rates can be offered.

Postoperative mortality for elective hip replacement is strongly age related and is highest in the early months following operation. Mortality is lower for women than for men (*see* Table 25.1). Except perhaps for applicants under the age of 60, insurance should be postponed for at least six months following surgery; for those under the age of 60 awaiting hip replacement an appropriate single extra premium should be charged according to age and sex.

For applicants awaiting hip replacement who otherwise have no, or only minor ratable impairments, the following schedule of single extra premiums is suggested:

Age	Rating
45	No extra rating
45–54	3 per mil (male)
	2 per mil (female)
55–59	5 per mil (male)
	2 per mil (female)
60 and over	Postpone

Table 25.1. Number of deaths, postoperative mortality per 1,000 and relative mortality ratio in the first 90 days at various ages for men and women who had elective hip replacement.[a]

Age (years)	Patients	Deaths	Postoperative mortality (per 1,000)	Relative mortality ratio
		Men		
<45	166	0	0	0
45–54	296	1	3·4	2·9
55–64	937	8	8·5	2·8
65–74	1361	16	11·8	1·8
75–84	537	19	35·4	3·0
≥85	18	2	111·1	>10
Total	3315	46	15·7[b]	2·38
		Women		
<45	148	0	0	0
45–54	396	1	2·5	0·9
55–64	1166	3	2·6	1·4
65–74	2171	16	7·4	2·3
75–84	1233	24	19·5	3·0
≥85	79	3	58·0	8·5
Total	5193	47	8·4[b]	2·54

[a]Based on figures from ten hospitals in the Oxford Health Authority, England.[1]
[b]Age standardized rates.

CRYSTAL DEPOSITION DISEASE

Gout, calcium pyrophosphate dihydrate (CPPD) deposition disease and hydroxy-apatite-associated diseases are the three main conditions in this group. The diagnosis is made in the case of gout by measuring the uric acid levels in the serum; in the case of CPPD it is made by joint aspiration and examination of the fresh fluid under polarized light for the crystals. Diagnosis is made by electron microscopy looking for apatite crystals in conditions associated with these crystals. Joints and synovial tissues are susceptible to mineral deposition; when this occurs in a joint it may be referred to as chondrocalcinosis, a condition affected by age, metabolic disturbances and connective tissue damage. The crystals in the joint may be harmless but they can also trigger off an acute inflammatory reaction, which, if recurrent, may lead to joint damage.

Gout

Gout is a disorder of purine metabolism characterized by hyperuricemia and the deposition of monosodium urate crystals in joints, causing an acute arthritis. There is no evidence that a raised uric acid level in itself is a risk factor; it only becomes so when associated with clinical gout. The main symptoms are the sudden onset of an acute arthritis, bursitis or tenosynovitis. The affected part becomes red, hot and extremely painful. Without treatment the attack will subside in about ten days, but repeated attacks will lead to joint damage and periarticular urate deposits known as tophi. If untreated, urate will be deposited in the kidneys, leading to the formation of stones, and in about ten percent of patients this leads to hypertension and renal failure. Gout is now a treatable condition and, with the advent of allopurinol, such complications can be avoided. However, the treatment must be lifelong, so evidence of good compliance and regular blood testing is essential if standard rates are to be offered. Poor risk factors are, therefore, lack of long-term treatment, the presence of renal stones or hypertension, obesity, impaired renal function or lack of regular supervision.

Rating
1) Asymptomatic hyperuricemia — standard.
2) History of clinical gout:
     Well controlled and supervised — standard.
     No prophylaxis:
          Infrequent attacks — standard.
          Frequent attacks — +50.
     Complicated gout (proteinuria, hypertension,
          renal calculi) — rate additionally for complication.
3) Secondary gout — rate for cause.

Calcium Pyrophosphate Dihydrate Deposition Disease

When crystals of calcium pyrophosphate are deposited in a joint they can cause a reaction in the joint similar to that of gout; this has led to the condition also being known as pseudogout. It commonly occurs in the elderly and is therefore an age related condition. The serum uric acid levels are normal, and the condition is diagnosed by aspirating fluid from the joint and identifying the crystals in the fresh fluid under polarized light. It can be a slowly progressive condition but subjects are usually able to lead normal lives.

Rating
Standard rates apply.

Hydroxyapatite Deposition Disease

When crystals of hydroxyapatite are deposited either in the soft tissues around the joint or in the joint, a reaction occurs. The crystals are identified by electron microscopy. Deposition around the shoulder joint may result in a calcific periarthritis causing considerable pain and disability. The condition is difficult to treat and surgical intervention may be the only way to prevent continued pain and progressive disability.

Rating

This is not a life threatening condition and standard rates may be offered, except in the case of PHI, where a rating according to disability is indicated.

SYSTEMIC LUPUS ERYTHEMATOSUS (SLE)

SLE is a non-specific inflammatory condition affecting the connective tissues, and is a condition in which the body becomes allergic to its own tissues. The resulting autoantibodies produce an inflammatory reaction in multiple systems. The disease is characterized by polyarthropathy, fever, fatigue, a paranasal skin rash, an abnormal skin response to light, hair loss, pleurisy, pericarditis, psychosis, neuropathy and kidney disease. Being a mainly musculoskeletal disorder it mimics rheumatoid arthritis. The diagnosis is made by finding abnormal blood tests: leucopenia, thrombocytopenia, an elevated ESR, an elevated C-reactive protein, and the presence of antinuclear antibodies (ANA) and anti DNA antibodies.

The prognosis of SLE has imrpoved considerably in recent years with the use of steroids, and survival figures are improving year by year. In 1964 the five- and ten-year survival figures were 70 percent and 54 percent respectively; now the figures are 95 percent and 90 percent. Those with mild disease have at least a 98 percent chance of surviving for five years. The prognosis depends on the extent of renal involvement and, to a lesser extent, central nervous system disease. The worst prognosis is in those cases that on renal biopsy show a diffuse proliferative nephritis; the best show neither renal disease nor impaired renal function. The majority of those developing renal changes do so within the first five years of the disease.

Rating

Those cases with evidence of active renal or cerebral disease should be declined. It would be unwise to insure those patients requiring more than 15 mg of prednisolone or equivalent steroid therapy daily. However, applicants with the mild or localized form of the disease who have been stable for at least a year (perhaps suppressed on a small dose of steroids or an antimalarial drug such as hydroxychloroquine) can be accepted. The suggested ratings are as follows:

1) Mild localized forms of SLE, well controlled with steroids not exceeding 15 mg prednisolone per day or equivalent, or an antimalarial such as hydroxychloroquine not exceeding 600 mg daily, and with no evidence of nephropathy or cerebral involvement:

Time since diagnosis	Rating
Within 1st yr	Postpone
2nd yr	+300 upwards
3rd to 4th yr	+300 to +200
5th yr	+150
Thereafter	+100 to +50

Standard rates may be offered five years after treatment has ceased.

2) Any case with nephropathy, cerebral lupus or multisystem disease should be declined.

PROGRESSIVE SYSTEMIC SCLEROSIS (PSS)

PSS is a chronic connective tissue disease characterized by increased collagen deposition in the dermis and other organs, resulting in fibrosis of those tissues. When the skin alone is involved the term scleroderma is used. The skin usually becomes affected first, followed by the intestinal tract. Fibrosis of the lower two-thirds of the esophagus causes dysphagia; the lungs may show interstitial fibrosis, and the joints may show changes that resemble rheumatoid arthritis. Fifty percent of patients have renal involvement, and the myocardium is occasionally affected. When the condition is focal it may be called morphea; this is a benign condition and very rarely spreads to other organs. Once PSS is established it tends to persue a chronic, relentless course to death. Remissions are rare, and less than 20 percent of patients are alive ten years after the onset of visceral symptoms. No therapy is known to alter the course of this disease. The principal cause of death is acute renal failure and malignant hypertension.

In the case of scleroderma, 50 percent of patients may be alive at ten years after diagnosis. The worst prognosis is in those cases where (1) the onset is after the age of 40, (2) there is evidence of either renal, pulmonary, or cardiac disease, and (3) the skin of the trunk becomes involved.

Rating

Those individuals having only the localized form of the disease can be offered standard rates. In a few rare cases where scleroderma appears to have gone into remission for at least five years, a rating of +150 to +300 could be considered. Most cases should be declined.

Crest Syndrome

This condition is another localized form of systemic sclerosis, where calcinosis, Raynaud's phenomenon, esophageal dysfunction, sclerodactyly and telangiectasia exist as a separate syndrome. Because the esophagus is the only visceral organ involved the prognosis is better in this condition than in PSS.

Rating
Patients over the age of 65 can be accepted at standard rates, otherwise a rating ranging from +50 to +150 is indicated.

Eosinophilic Fasciitis

Eosinophilic fasciitis was first described by Schulman in 1974. It is a scleroderma-like syndrome characterized by a widespread fascial sclerosis especially affecting the limbs, and is associated with eosinophilia and hypergammaglobulinemia. It is a chronic condition with a tendency to spontaneous remission; oral steroids may help to induce remission.

Rating
Unless on long term steroids, which warrants a rating of +50, standard rates can be offered.

Mixed Connective Tissue Disease

This disease shows the features of several conditions and so is also known as the 'overlap syndrome'. The conditions are SLE, polymyositis, scleroderma and rheumatoid arthritis. The prognosis is variable, with a few cases going into remission, but the majority drift into the realm of one or other of the above diseases. The diagnosis is made by finding a raised ESR, positive ANF, negative anti DNA and a positive ENA test in the serum.

Rating
This disease should be rated according to the nearest condition it simulates when the disease has become chronic.

VASCULITIS

Vasculitis represents a group of uncommon diseases characterized by necrosis and inflammatory cell infiltration of the blood vessel wall. It may arise without cause or be a secondary feature to such connective tissue disorders as rheumatoid arthritis and SLE. The vasculitides can be classified according to the size of the blood vessels affected.
Small and medium arteries: Classical polyarteritis nodosa and its variants, arteritis of rheumatoid arthritis, SLE, Sjøgren's syndrome etc, and when associated with granulomatosis, as seen in Wegener's granulomatosis and the Churg-Strauss syndrome.
Large arteries: Giant cell arteritis, including temporal arteritis, Takayasu's arteritis, aortitis associated with ankylosing spondylitis, etc.
Small vessel vasculitis: Henoch-Schönlein purpura, essential mixed cryoglobulin-emia etc.
The size of the vessels involved and the presence or absence of renal involvement are the two most important factors affecting prognosis. Despite recent therapeutic advances, up to 40 percent of patients with polyarteritis, 20–30 percent of patients with rheumatoid vasculitis and 10–20 percent with Wegener's granulomatosis die within one year of diagnosis. Those with small vessel vasculitis and predominantly large artery disease have the best prognosis. Less than 10 percent of patients with Henoch-Schönlein purpura develop significant renal involvement; giant cell arteritis and Takayasu's arteritis are rarely fatal, but can be associated with significant morbidity. Cytotoxic drugs and steroids are often used in the treatment of these conditions.

Polyarteritis Nodosa (PN)

The underlying lesion in PN is inflammation of the vessel wall producing an arteritis and vasculitis. The clinical features are those of malaise, anorexia, intermittent fever, weight loss, myalgia and arthralgia; as it is a multisystem disease, symptoms relating to any of the major systems may arise, peripheral neuropathy being common. The diagnosis may be confirmed by renal biopsy. The outcome is not easy to predict as there is such a wide variation in the disease; about 80 percent will survive five years, but involvement of the vital organs is, as a rule, a bad prognostic sign. If the disease is not treated it will be fatal within one to two years. Fortunately there is usually a good response to steroid therapy, although the presence of renal failure or hypertension carries a bad prognosis.

Rating

While PN is active a decision should be postponed. Once there is evidence of remission lasting at least one year, rating can be considered (dependent on evidence of normal renal function) starting with +300 and reducing according to the duration of the remission, so that after three years +150 could be offered reducing to a minimum of +50 provided no suppressive therapy has been given for at least three years. If there is evidence of impaired renal function the case should be declined.

Temporal Arteritis

This is a disease of late middle age mainly affecting the extra-cranial arteries of the head. It may start with a general constitutional upset or may occur as a complication of polymyalgia rheumatica. The most feared complication is blindness due to ischemic optic neuritis. The ESR is elevated and the diagnosis is confirmed by temporal artery biopsy. There is, as a rule, a dramatic response to oral steroid therapy.

Rating

The rating is +50 to +75 if the applicant is on long-term steroid therapy and the dose is below 10 mg prednisolone daily. Standard rates may be offered six months after therapy has been withdrawn if there is no sign of clinical activity.

Takayasu's Disease

This condition is also known as the aortic arch syndrome or pulseless disease and is characterized by occlusion of major vessels, especially those arising from the aortic arch; it has a chronic course with remissions and relapses. The arterial complications may prove fatal, but treatment with steroids and anticoagulants (and occasionally surgical intervention) may arrest the progress of the disease.

Rating

Decline all cases.

Henoch-Schönlein Purpura

This condition often follows a streptococcal infection and is characterized by the presence of both arthritis and purpura. The arthritis rapidly resolves, usually within a week, and unless there is renal involvement total resolution is expected within six weeks.

Rating

Standard rates may be offered two months after remission.

DERMATOMYOSITIS AND POLYMYOSITIS

These are uncommon inflammatory conditions of muscle characterized by weakness of the proximal muscles. Both diseases are associated with increased muscle enzymes, especially creatine phosphokinase. The electromyographic pattern is abnormal, usually showing a mixed picture of both myopathy and denervation. The diagnosis is confirmed by muscle biopsy, which will show muscle fibre necrosis and inflammation. In dermatomyositis the muscle changes are associated with a distinctive rash of the face and eyelids.

Both conditions may be associated with malignant tumours except when they occur in children. Although the reported incidence of malignancy varies from 6 to 50 percent, it is thought that malignancy occurs in 15 percent of cases of dermatomyositis and 10 percent of cases of polymyositis. The five-year survival rate in both diseases is about 80 percent and the majority become asymptomatic three to four years after starting steroid therapy. The highest mortality occurs in the first year, especially in those cases where there is either cardiovascular or pulmonary involvement.

Rating

Postpone all cases for at least one year after diagnosis to allow time for any associated malignancy to manifest itself; the rating will then depend on the duration of remission or the dose of steroids needed to control the disease. Once steroids have been discontinued for at least one year and there is no evidence of active disease then standard rates may be quoted.

POLYMYALGIA RHEUMATICA AND OTHER MYALGIC SYNDROMES

Polymyalgia rheumatica, fibromyalgia, eosinophilia-myalgia syndrome and relapsing polychondritis are the main diseases that have painful muscles in common.

Polymyalgia Rheumatica

This is a connective tissue disorder of older age groups, seldom diagnosed before the age of 60. It is characterized by severe pains in the muscles of the shoulder and pelvic girdles, often associated with malaise, weight loss, fever and morning stiffness. The condition is associated with temporal arteritis in one-third of cases and always has an elevated ESR. The response to oral steroid therapy is dramatic, and this response may be used as a diagnostic test.

Rating
If the disease is still active, as judged by an elevated ESR, then acceptance should be postponed until the disease is in remission and the maintenance dose of steroids is down to 5 mg of prednisolone or less daily. The risk is then only that of the steroids, so a small rating (such as +25 to +50, according to period of stabilization) is justified.

Fibromyalgia

Fibromyalgia is a pain syndrome of uncertain origin that is becoming more widely recognized. There is conflicting evidence about whether or not this syndrome is associated with psychiatric illness, it having previously been referred to as fibrositis or psychogenic rheumatism. It is characterized by widespread muscle pains associated with areas of muscular tenderness. All investigations are negative.

Rating
Standard rates can be offered unless there is an obvious underlying ratable psychiatic disorder.

Eosinophilia-Myalgia Syndrome

This condition is associated with the use of preparations containing L-tryptophan. Over 1,400 cases have been identified in the USA, and 19 deaths have been reported. Patients complain of intense and disabling fatigue and myalgia, and it may also be associated with arthralgia, fever, cough and dyspnea, rashes, limb edema and eosinophilia. In some cases the condition resolves after stopping the preparation, but improvement is often slow and the disease may even progress after stopping the drug. A few patients develop a progressive and potentially fatal ascending polyneuropathy. The use of high-dose steroid therapy has been recommended but its efficacy has yet to be proved.

Rating
Postpone until at least six months after withdrawal of the offending preparation. Then, if there is no sign of neuropathic disease, standard rates may be offered. If evidence of polyneuropathy is present, the applicant should be declined.

Relapsing Polychondritis

Relapsing polychrondritis is an episodic, progressive and inflammatory disease of cartilage. The sites of the cartilage affected are commonly the aural, nasal and ocular structures. It has a 20–30 percent mortality rate with a five-year survival of about 75 percent. The poor prognostic signs are saddle nose deformity, the presence of laryngo-tracheal strictures, systemic vasculitis, microhematuria and anemia, especially if these signs present in patients below the age of 50. Fifty percent of deaths are related to the respiratory tract.

Rating
Only those cases that have shown no progress for at least five years can be considered, and then a heavy rating, such as +200 to +300 is indicated.

OTHER ARTHRITIDES

Arthritis and arthralgia are commonly associated with systemic disease, the commonest perhaps being that associated with rubella. However, similar joint symptoms can occur with disorders such as acne, amyloid disease, neoplasia, erythema nodosum, familial Mediterranean fever, sickle cell anemia, hyperlipidemia, ochronosis, endocrine disorders and many others. In all these cases the rating is that of the primary disease and not that of the arthritis, which usually disappears when the primary disease has been treated. Special mention must be made of Lyme disease because with this condition 48 percent show articular involvement and 24 percent develop a chronic and at times disabling arthritis.

Palindromic Rheumatism

This condition is characterized by recurrent, acute, self-limiting attacks of arthritis. It affects people aged about 30, and women more than men. The severe joint pain can resemble gout and the skin over the joint can become red. The attacks can occur at regular or irregular intervals several times a year, and between each attack the joint remains normal. The attacks can last from a few hours to a few days and all tests for rheumatoid arthritis are negative. The prognosis is excellent.

Rating
All cases may be accepted at standard rates.

Soft Tissue Rheumatism

The soft tissues around a joint, other than the muscles already dealt with, can become inflamed, causing pain and disability. Some of these disorders are work related, some are due to leisure activities, and some occur spontaneously without apparent cause. The majority of disorders in this group are self-limiting and have no mortality and little morbidity, except those cases that are work related. Occupational overuse syndromes, such as repetitive strain injury and tenosynovitis, are the second commonest disorders for which compensation claims are made; unfortunately psychological factors are of importance and may cloud the issue. These conditions, apart from those mentioned, include medial and lateral epicondylitis (otherwise known as golfer's and tennis elbow), DeQuervain's stenosing tenosynovitis and other types of tenosynovitis, some referred to as trigger fingers, capsulitis of the shoulder (causing frozen shoulder), bursitis and tendinitis. Apart from the fact that chronicity of these conditions may lead to depression there are no long-term effects and most respond to local steroid injections.

Rating
All applicants may be accepted at standard rates.

Nerve Entrapment Syndromes

These conditions, also known as compression neuropathies, are caused by pressure on various peripheral nerves. The common features are pain and paresthesia, especially at night; the commonest lesions involve (1) the median nerve at the wrist, known as the carpal tunnel syndrome, (2) the posterior tibial nerve at the ankle, known as the tarsal tunnel syndrome, and (3) the lateral cutaneous nerve of the thigh, also called meralgia parasthetica. All these syndromes are relieved by either hydrocortisone injection or surgical decompression.

Rating
Standard rates may be offered in all cases.

Intervertebral Disc Lesions

The symptoms associated with intervertebal disc lesions can be acute or chronic: when acute they are often referred to as acute proplapse of the disc; when chronic as disc degeneration or spondylosis. Discs can prolapse in any region of the spine (cervical, thoracic or lumbar), but they most frequently occur in the lumbar region, where the disc protrusion causes symptoms relative to the sciatic or femoral nerves. On the other hand, chronic disc degeneration or spondylosis is commonest in the cervical region, being a frequent cause of neck, shoulder and arm pain. Intervertebral disc lesions do not cause death, but chronic disability is common, especially in manual workers, excluding many from permanent health insurance. Chronic spinal problems can cause continuous pain and induce a reactive depression or a chronic anxiety state due to time lost from work (*see also* p. 148).

Rating
Standard rates for life insurance apply unless there is a recurrent history of depression or anxiety, which in themselves may warrant a small loading.

Hypermobility Syndromes

Double jointedness, joint laxity and increased joint flexibility are benign inherited connective tissue disorders. They are characterized by weakness and fragility of collagen-bearing tissues (such as ligaments, tendons, muscles, bones, cartilage and skin). Because of the increased laxity, increased movement of the affected joints is obtained. Acute soft tissue lesions are common in occupations where the increased range of movement is used to advantage, such as dancers, musicians and acrobats.

Certain syndromes (such as Marfan's, Ehlers Danlos, osteogenesis imperfecta, Turner's and Down's) have joint laxity as part of the disease; hypermobility itself is not a cause of death, although it can lead to disability later in life.

Rating

Standard rates apply unless the underlying syndrome warrants an extra premium because of major system disease.

DISORDERS NOT MENTIONED

As there are over 200 arthritic and arthralgic disorders it is inevitable that many have been omitted from this chapter. It may be assumed that those conditions not specifically mentioned may be accepted as standard risks.

REFERENCE

1 Seagroatt V, Tan HS, Goldacre M, Bulstrode C, Nugent I, Gill L. Elective total hip replacement: incidence, emergency readmission rate, and postoperative mortality. Br Med J 1991; 303: 1431–35.

CHAPTER 26

DISORDERS OF THE SKELETON

R D C BRACKENRIDGE

Although some bone lesions have a purely local pathology, disorders of the skeleton as of the skin frequently reflect a more widespread pathological process. In some deformities, such as those caused by infantile rickets, the systemic disorder is a thing of the past, the only remaining evidence being skeletal changes. On the other hand, a primary bone disease may give rise to systemic effects; for example, extensive Paget's disease of bone can cause a profound haemodynamic disturbance leading to high-output congestive cardiac failure. Excluding malignant tumors, skeletal disorders that are not part of a primary systemic disease would usually have little effect by themselves on longevity unless there was anatomical interference with vital structures, such as pressure effects on nervous tissue or on the heart or lungs.

Malignant bone tumors should be underwritten according to the general principles set out in Chapter 20. Other growths peculiar to cartilage and bone, mainly of a benign nature, are discussed later in this chapter.

INFECTIONS OF BONE

Osteomyelitis

Infection, either pyogenic, tuberculous or syphilitic, affecting bones and joints is of less importance in underwriting today than it was forty years ago. Before the advent of penicillin, osteomyelitis was a disease dangerous to life both in the acute stage from septicemia and in the chronic stage from amyloid disease. However, antibiotics have revolutionized the treatment of acute osteomyelitis, and mortality has now been reduced to negligible levels. A history of acute osteomyelitis, treated either medically alone or in combination with surgery, can be disregarded so long as the condition has responded to treatment and there is no evidence of chronicity with the presence of open sinuses on examination. The outlook has not improved similarly in chronic osteomyelitis in which the infection is usually mixed, and the organisms deep-seated in sclerotic bone and scar tissue where antibiotics cannot penetrate. Chronic osteomyelitis may complicate local bone trauma such as a compound fracture, gunshot wound or an amputation. A continuing discharge indicates sequestra and persisting infection which may require surgical drainage with removal of dead bone. Those who suffer from chronic osteomyelitis with open discharging sinuses face a definite risk of developing amyloid disease.

In the 1983 *Medical Impairment Study*[1] standard and substandard experience was combined and covered the years 1962 to 1977, but only the experience on male lives was large enough to warrant analysis.

The overall mortality ratio for males with a history of osteomyelitis was 178 percent, being lower at issue ages under 40 and higher at ages 40 and over. In the first five years following issue of insurance relative mortality was only 75 percent based on 8 eight deaths, but was close to 200 percent thereafter.

Rating

The rating for chronic osteomyelitis with recurrent relapses and a history of surgical drainage or curettage might be: for a single bone +75 within one year reducing to standard in the third year; or where three or more bones are affected +100 within the first two years, +75 in the third and fourth years and +50 to standard in the fifth year or later. Where there is an open, discharging sinus or sinuses on examination, rating should be as for chronic osteomyelitis within one year.

Bone and Joint Tuberculosis

This type of tuberculosis is now rare, but when it occurs it has an excellent prognosis similar to that of tuberculosis of other organs, so long as chemotherapy has been adequate by present-day standards. The underwriting handling of a history of bone or joint tuberculosis would be similar to that described for respiratory tuberculosis (*see* p.513).

Syphilitic Periostitis: Gumma of Bone

A history of syphilitic periostitis or gumma of bone would be rated as tertiary syphilis (*see* p. 912). If typical sabre tibiae or other skeletal abnormalities suspicious of syphilis are present on examination, but no definite history of specific treatment can be obtained, applications for life insurance should be postponed until quantitative serological tests for syphilis have been carried out.

NUTRITIONAL AND METABOLIC BONE DISORDERS

Rickets: Osteomalacia

Bone is a highly specialized form of connective tissue having mechanical rigidity which is due to orderly deposition of calcium salts on an uncalcified matrix, the osteoid. If calcium salts for some reason are not deposited on newly formed osteoid tissue, the result is an excess of uncalcified matrix and loss of structural rigidity. This is the characteristic feature of the disease due to vitamin D deficiency which is known as rickets in children and osteomalacia in adults.

Vitamin D is necessary for the mineralization of osteoid. Cholecalciferol (Vitamin D_3), the naturally occurring compound in man, is formed in the skin from 7-dehydrocholesterol by ultraviolet irradiation. In the absence of sufficient endogenous synthesis of cholecalciferol, particularly in northern latitudes with limited ultraviolet exposure, the dietary intake of vitamin D becomes important. Under these circumstances the consequent rickets or osteomalacia is usually termed nutritional.

Infantile rickets was common in the UK until 1945 when the addition of cholecalciferol to dried milk for infant feeding virtually eliminated the disease. However, vitamin D deficiency reappeared in 1962 when rickets and osteomalacia were reported in Glasgow in Indian and Pakistani immigrants. The deficiency has since been found in almost every center of immigrant population. Asians have a striking propensity for developing vitamin D deficiency. In contrast with indigenous white children who develop rickets below the age of three, active rickets in Asian children occurs not only in infancy but throughout school life, with a peak incidence at puberty; children of all socioeconomic groups are affected. The reasons for the prevalence of Asian rickets are not clear but genetic differences in intermediary vitamin D metabolism may be partly responsible. There is much less of a problem of rickets and osteomalacia in North America, where vitamin D fortification of food is carried out on a much wider scale.

Selection of Risks

Apart from the manifestations of active rickets or osteomalacia which include hypocalcaemic tetany, thoracic, back and limb pains, pseudofractures and general ill health, there are the late effects on the skeleton such as genu valgum and other limb deformities which often require osteotomies. In male applicants for life insurance even marked deformities of the skeleton can be disregarded so long as respiratory function is unimpaired. The only other circumstance in which rachitic deformities might be a risk to life would be in females of child-bearing age when there is sufficient deformity of the pelvis to prevent natural childbirth. The risk would be greatest in primiparous women but much less at subsequent childbirth after the necessity for cesarean section had been established. Hence it would probably be wise to postpone applications for insurance from such women while pregnant and to reconsider after the puerperium.

Applicants with a history of symptoms which have been shown to be due to active osteomalacia should be postponed until they have been treated and are subsequently being maintained on an adequate regular supplement of vitamin D.

Osteoporosis

There is a universal loss of bone tissue with advancing age which becomes increasingly common in women after the menopause and in men over the age of 50. This is the state known as senile osteoporosis and is the commonest bone disease in old age. A net loss of bone may be the result of an increase in the rate of bone destruction, a decrease in the rate of bone formation, or both, but the primary disturbance which causes loss of bone with age is not known. Certainly, ultraviolet deprivation and inadequate dietary vitamin D intake in many elderly people aggravates the steady deterioration in bone status which is generally accepted as an aging process.

Osteoporosis may come to the attention of the life underwriter in various ways: it may be reported by a radiologist from the appearance of the bones following routine chest X-ray of an applicant who is otherwise symptomless. It may be suspected if fractures have occurred as the result of unusually slight violence, to be confirmed later after a more extensive skeletal survey and metabolic studies have been carried out.

Obviously osteoporosis would be a significant underwriting problem for long-term care (LTC) insurance and permanent health insurance (PHI), but it would also be of concern to the life underwriter if osteoporosis was discovered to be more advanced than expected for age, in which case a secondary cause should be suspected. Thyrotoxicosis, hyperparathyroidism, Cushing's syndrome, intestinal malabsorption states (celiac disease, tropical sprue), corticosteroid admin- istration and osteomalacia are some of the conditions causing excessive loss of bone. The underwriting handling of osteoporosis due to any of these would depend on the nature of the primary disease and whether or not it is being ade- quately treated.

Osteoporotic fractures commonly occur at the wrist, hip and vertebrae. Wrist fractures, which increase in frequency after the age of 50, heal readily without surgical intervention, but fractures of the hip are much more troublesome; they require major surgery which is not well tolerated by the very elderly, and most patients require prolonged convalescence, some never regaining full mobility. Some 20 percent die as a result of complications.[2] Between the ages of 65 and 85 muscle strength in the lower limbs decreases by about 35 percent[3] and this is an additional problem, causing a feeling of instability with resulting falls and the risk of a hip fracture.

Perhaps the most serious complication of osteoporosis is collapse fractures of vertebrae. Deformity caused by these fractures cannot be repaired and results in progressive reduction in the quality of life over many years. Dorsal kyphosis causes progressive loss of height, and many patients suffer chronic back pain, stiffness and increasing inactivity.

Since osteoporosis is part of the natural aging process premium rates for life insurance already reflect the risk of the various complications that can occur in the elderly. Standard rates would therefore apply to applicants with uncomplicated osteoporosis and also to those who had recovered fully from a fractured hip. Vertebral fractures should be rated according to the number of fractures, the degree of deformity and the severity of ongoing symptoms, and might range from standard rates for a single fracture with minimal deformity, to +50 to +100 at ages 65 and under for several fractures and moderate deformity. An equivalent years-to-age rating would apply to applicants over the age of 65. Those with multiple vertebral fractures or with severe kyphosis should be declined insurance.

Osteitis Fibrosa Cystica

Osteitis fibrosa cystica is a rare bone disease complicating hyperparathyroidism and usually occurs only if the latter is severe, or is of long duration as in chronic renal hemodialysis (see pp. 723, 560). Increased osteoclastic resorption causes a rarefying osteitis with the formation of cysts and fibrosis in the marrow of affected bones, and the disease can be readily distinguished on radiography.

The life risk would only be acceptable after correction of the primary or secondary hyperparathyroidism.

Clubbing of the Fingers: Hypertrophic Osteoarthropathy

Clubbing of the fingers is a valuable clinical sign which may indicate the presence of systemic disease not always detectable clinically. It may be present in certain diseases of the chest or lung such as bronchial carcinoma, chronic lung or pleural suppuration and pulmonary vascular anomalies, in celiac disease, hepatic cirrhosis, congenital cyanotic heart disease and subacute infective endocarditis.

The finger-tip deformity is due to increased vascularity, hyperplasia of the fibrous tissue and edema, and various theories have been advanced to account for the changes. Hypertrophic osteoarthropathy, which occasionally accompanies clubbing of the fingers, is usually regarded as an extension of the same process to the joints and periosteum at the ends of the long bones.

The hereditary form of finger clubbing is a benign condition which can be disregarded. It is easily recognized as such by simply asking the applicant about it: he will generally be able to inform the doctor that his fingers have always been clubbed and that they have frequently excited medical interest in the past. On the other hand, if finger clubbing is of recent onset and no cause is immediately apparent, further investigations would be obligatory before the risk could be properly evaluated.

PAGET'S DISEASE OF BONE (OSTEITIS DEFORMANS)

Osteitis deformans is a primary disorder of bone of unknown cause in which there is a mixture of excessive bone resorption with increased synthesis of abnormally textured new bone. Certain bones (skull, pelvis, femur, tibia, vertebrae and clavicle) are commonly affected. It is said to affect up to 3 percent of people over 40 years of age, and the pattern of evolution is very varied. A slow and relentless progression over several decades represents one part of the spectrum of the disease. Rarely it extends rapidly over a period of a few months. In some persons the disease seems to become quiescent and the radiological abnormalities persist unchanged for many years.

Paget's disease of bone is usually found by chance either when biochemical screening reveals an elevated serum alkaline phosphatase or when X-rays of any part of the body happen to show the characteristic radiological changes. Only a small number of people in whom the diagnosis is made have any symptoms, and an even smaller number develop serious complications such as pathological fractures, cranial nerve, brain stem or spinal cord compression, sarcomatous change, or high-output cardiac failure. Bone pain may be the only symptom, but it is sometimes persistent and distressing.

The treatment of Paget's disease has received renewed attention since the introduction of calcitonin and the diphosphonates, both of which have been shown to produce biochemical remission of the disease. These treatments are especially valuable in abolishing bone pain.

Rating

	Rating	
Feature	Below 60	60 and over
Asymptomatic, localized; found by chance	Standard	Standard
Moderately extensive or symptomatic (pain); no complications	Standard	Standard
Widespread, or with minor complications	+75	+25
With major complications (e.g., congestive heart failure, spinal cord compression)	Decline	Decline

FIBROUS DYSPLASIA (ALBRIGHT'S SYNDROME)

Fibrous dysplasia is a rare disease of bone whose etiology is unknown; the condition does not appear to have a hereditary basis. The X-ray appearance is that of a radiolucent area in the bone having a well defined smooth border, with thinning of the adjacent cortex. Occasionally the cyst-like area appears multilocular. The disease appears in three forms: (1) monostotic, (2) polyostotic, and (3) Albright's syndrome.

1) In the monostotic form of fibrous dysplasia the lesions are confined to single bones, the craniofacial bones and ribs being most often involved. There may be no symptoms, but the condition is commonly detected between 20 and 30 years of age because of pathological fractures.

2) In polyostotic fibrous dysplasia the bone lesions are more widespread, sometimes involving half the skeleton, with signs of deformity and fractures appearing in childhood. Generally speaking, the earlier the onset of clinical signs the more severe and deforming the disease. Complications occur mainly in the polyostotic form and, apart from skeletal deformities, include epilepsy and cranial nerve palsies when the skull and facial bones are involved, a high cardiac output state similar to that in Paget's disease and, very rarely, sarcomatous change in a lesion, particularly if it has been subjected previously to X-radiation.

3) Albright's syndrome is more common in females. It is characterized by macules or sheets of light brown pigmentation of the skin, usually confined to one side of the midline and often overlying the bone or bones affected by fibrous dysplasia. In addition, sexual precocity may be found in some females.

Rating

Applicants with the localized, monostotic form of fibrous dysplasia can usually be accepted as standard. Those with polyostotic fibrous dysplasia should be postponed until after puberty; thereafter rating would range from +200 to +100, depending on the extent of the lesions, but with a minimum of +2 per mil. Albright's syndrome should be rated according to whether the fibrous dysplasia is monostotic or polyostotic.

DWARFISM

A dwarf may be arbitrarily defined as an adult who is less than 56 in (142 mm) in height. Since the etiological factors concerned in some forms of dwarfism have an adverse effect on longevity, life underwriters should be alerted to make special enquiries about the circumstance if applications are received from adults whose stature is below the defined limit of normal. The probable risk associated with different types of dwarfism is indicated below.

Primordial Dwarfism

A dwarf may be a normal short-statured person or a primordial dwarf due to inherent factors. Persons in this category have no evidence of endocrine abnormality, are proportionately built and have normal secondary sex characters. They would be insurable as standard risks.

Dwarfism due to Hereditary or Chromosomal Abnormalities

Hereditary and chromosomal abnormalities may give rise to dwarfism by influencing the tissues of the body as a whole including the skeleton or, as in achondroplasia (see below), the skeleton alone.

Achondroplasia
This is a hereditary disorder in which bones preformed in cartilage are short due to defective endochondral ossification, whereas bones formed in membrane are normal. The appearance of the achondroplastic dwarf is so well known that description is unnecessary. There is a high still-birth rate and many die soon after birth, but expectation of life becomes normal for those who survive to adulthood. A small risk exists for female achondroplastics up to the end of the child-bearing period; because of the abnormal pelvic outlet natural childbirth is impossible, and cesarean section is necessary with each pregnancy.

Down's Syndrome (Mongolism)
The degree of mental retardation (IQ about 50) found in Down's syndrome would generally disqualify these persons from life insurance, despite the fact that many who reach adult life without a significant congenital heart defect survive to old age. However, carefully selected risks over the age of 20 who are guaranteed a protected environment may be insured at a rating in the range +100 to +200.

Hurler's Syndrome (Gargoylism)
Because of the combination of important defects (mental retardation, blindness, deafness, kyphotic deformity leading to cor pulmonale) which occur in Hurler's syndrome only very few survive to adult life, and even for them life expectancy is severely curtailed.

Turner's Syndrome
This is primarily a chromosomal defect with secondary endocrine disorders and is considered elsewhere (see p. 725).

Osteogenesis Imperfecta

This is a hereditary disease in which the basic pathology is a generalized disorder of connective tissue affecting bone, teeth, sclerae, ligaments, tendons and skin. The clinical manifestations are blue sclerae, slender brittle bones which predispose to multiple fractures, progressive deafness due to otosclerosis (usually starting in the third decade) and laxity of joints. Of the main types of osteogenesis imperfecta, only one is compatible with life into adulthood. After puberty the bones become stronger although fractures still occur; growth is stunted, the long bones are bowed, and frequently there is severe kyphoscoliosis. Even in the most benign form of osteogenesis imperfecta life expectancy is modestly curtailed.

Applications for life insurance should be declined under the age of 18. Best-risk cases with minimal functional deformity of the skeleton and no aminoaciduria might be accepted at a rating of +50 to +100. Those with marked chest deformity require an additional rating (*see* p. 839).

Cardiovascular or Chronic Renal Disease

Dwarfism resulting from major congenital cardiovascular abnormalities or chronic renal disease is unlikely to be met in a life insurance context.

Nutritional Disturbances

Dwarfism can result from nutritional disturbances due to (1) inadequate food, vitamin or mineral intake as seen in various deficiency diseases, (2) defective absorption of food, and (3) defective utilization of food after absorption because of metabolic or endocrine disorders. The latter group includes hypopituitarism and hypothyroidism, both important causes of dwarfism which can be prevented by appropriate hormone replacement starting early enough in life.

Hypothyroid Dwarfs

Cretinism is the term used to describe infants suffering from deficiency of thyroid hormone at birth. Juvenile hypothyroidism is a similar condition developing in infants or children who were normal at birth. In either case physical and mental retardation is inevitable if untreated, and dwarfism is the rule by adult life. Even if thyroid replacement therapy is started early in infancy mental retardation of some degree may remain, although physical development usually proceeds normally. Of the two types juvenile hypothyroidism responds better to treatment.

Adults who are dwarfed because of hypothyroidism in infancy will almost certainly be mentally retarded to a degree which will make them, at best, insurable only as highly substandard risks, despite the fact that they may be receiving hormone replacement therapy currently.

Pituitary Dwarfism

There are three types of pituitary dwarfs, each with a different etiology and prognosis, but having in common a deficiency of human growth hormone (hGH).

Idiopathic hypopituitarism All the hormones of the anterior pituitary including hGH are deficient in this type of pituitary dwarfism, which is more common in males. Puberty does not appear because gonadotropic hormones are lacking. The adult dwarf has normal body proportions but often has an appearance older than his true age. Osseous development is retarded, the external genitals are infantile and the secondary sex characters are only partially developed. Impotence and sterility are usual.

From the life-underwriting point of view, idiopathic pituitary dwarfs may be handled similarly to persons with adult panhypopituitarism (*see* pp. 708–9).

Familial pituitary dwarfism This is due to selective deficiency of hGH, the other hormones of the anterior pituitary being unaffected. The adult dwarf is normally proportioned and has normal secondary sex characters and reproductive capacity. Familial pituitary dwarfs have a normal expectation of life and can be insured at standard rates of premium.

Lorrain-Levi syndrome The name is given to dwarfism secondary to pituitary damage after birth, usually from a craniopharyngioma. Since the tumour grows very slowly, the individual may survive to early adult life without the true nature of the cause of his dwarfism being suspected. In most cases, however, signs of a space-occupying lesion would become evident before insurance age was reached (e.g. diabetes insipidus or visual field defects due to pressure on the hypothalamus and optic chiasma, respectively).

Lorrain-Levi dwarfs would only be acceptable risks for life insurance after their craniopharyngiomas had been removed surgically. Thereafter the risk would be evaluated according to the time elapsed since operation (*see* p.632) and the need for adrenocortical hormone replacement in the first few years of therapy (*see* p. 708).

As more hGH becomes available for the treatment of pituitary dwarfism fewer examples of gross dwarfism are likely to be seen in the future, but the principles underlying the selection of risks of this nature will remain the same whether they are dwarfed or not.

BENIGN TUMORS OF BONE

The following tumors of bone deserve brief mention since they may feature from time to time in medical histories, or may present as an exercise in differential diagnosis if discovered on examination. They are all benign and produce their effects by (1) pressure on other structures, (2) pain and tenderness, or (3) pathological fractures.

Osteochondroma (Cancellous Osteoma)

Osteochondroma is the most common benign tumor of bone. It generally arises from the metaphysis of a long bone, especially just above or below the knee. It is due to ossification of a displaced portion of epiphysial cartilage onto the surface of the bone, and ossification continues during the whole period of skeletal growth. The tumor may only become apparent in early adult life when it may be symptomless or cause pressure on a related nerve or interference with the movement of a joint.

Single tumors remain benign, but multiple chondromata are said to have a greater than 10 percent chance of developing secondary malignant chondro-sarcoma. Persons in the latter category applying for critical illness plans would, therefore, have to be declined insurance.

Benign chondromas usually occur within the marrow cavity and appear as lytic lesions on X-ray. Chondroblastoma and chondromyxofibromas are rarer benign tumors appearing near the end of long bones.

Exostosis

Exostosis is the term applied to any bony mass projecting from the skeleton and includes the osteomas described above. An exostosis can also be secondary to chronic trauma, such as a rider's spur at the adductor insertion on the femur. A subungual exostosis arises from the terminal phalanx of a toe, generally the great toe, and causes pressure under the nail. It may have to be removed because of pain.

Ivory Osteoma

An ivory osteoma nearly always arises from the skull, especially the outer table, and grows slowly forming a smooth, rounded painless lump. It may predispose to sinusitis if it grows inwards towards the frontal sinus, or it may displace the eye-ball if it should arise in the orbit, or produce deafness when it is in relation to the ear.

Osteoid Osteoma

This benign lesion occurs most commonly in the long bones and is characterized on X-ray by a small radiolucent zone surrounded by a large sclerotic zone. Pain is a feature and is relieved by surgical removal of the small radiolucent zone.

Benign Osteoblastoma

This tumor grows at the end of long bones or in the spine and is the large version of the osteoid osteoma. The tumor causes much pain and surgical excision is the treatment of choice.

Giant Cell Tumor

Giant cell tumor of bone occurs most commonly in young adults and is situated in the epiphysis of long bones. It produces a lytic appearance on X-ray and may erode the surrounding normal bone. Excision by curettage followed by bone grafting is the treatment of choice for small lesions, but for large lesions more radicle surgery is required. Benign giant cell tumors have a great tendency to recur, and sarcomatous change is said to occur eventually in less than 10 percent of cases.

Unicameral Bone Cyst

Unicameral bone cyst is not a true neoplasm. It occurs in the long bones of children causing pathological fractures. In some cases a cyst will heal spontaneously after a fracture; in others curettage and bone grafting may be necessary.

Aneurysmal Bone Cyst

This cyst occurs in adolescence and early adult life usually in the metaphyseal region of long bones or in the spine. The cyst grows slowly and presents as a swelling or as pain. Complete surgical removal is the treatment of choice, or radiotherapy if the lesion is inaccessible as in the spine.

OSTEOCHONDRODYSPLASIA

There are several types of osteochondrodysplasia all producing skeletal deformities which, although striking, may nevertheless have very little effect on longevity. The basic defect is perversion of the normal process of endochondral ossification in certain bones which is neither symmetrical nor universal. The main types recognized are considered below.

Achondroplasia

Achondroplasia is the commonest example of this group and has already been discussed under dwarfism (*see* p. 831).

Hereditary Multiple Ossifying Endochondromata (Multiple Cartilagenous Exostoses)

The condition is characterized by multiple palpable bony tumors usually near the knee, shoulder, hip, ankle and wrist joints. Various other deformities of bones may be found such as a disproportionately short ulna or fibula in relation to the radius or tibia respectively. The main danger is pressure by one of the tumors on nerve tissue such as the spinal cord or its roots, or on vascular structures.

Multiple Chondromata

This is a rare condition in which cartilagenous swellings, usually of the fingers and toes, start in early life and gradually increase in size. Great deformity of the feet and hands eventually occurs.

Unilateral Chondrodysplasia (Ollier's Disease)

The feature of this syndrome is the completely unilateral nature of the defect, which is usually first noticed in early infancy when one limb is found to be shorter than its fellow due to a different rate of growth. The deformity becomes progressively greater as the child grows older.

Multiple Epiphyseal Dysplasia

This condition often presents with dysplasia of the hip with the probable risk of future osteoarthrosis of the joint.

Selection of Risks

Insurance of persons so affected is best deferred until adult life when bone growth has ceased and deformities have reached their maximum. Selection would then depend on the degree of functional disability as regards locomotion and on the ability of the applicant to participate in ordinary day-to-day activities.

In the more severe types, secondary arthrosis of related joints is a complication which may have the effect of immobilizing an already crippled individual. Each risk would, however, be treated on its merits.

JUVENILE EPIPHYSITIS (OSTEOCHONDRITIS)

Juvenile epiphysitis includes a variety of lesions, the more common of which are Perthes's disease of the femoral head, Osgood–Schlatter's disease of the tibial tuberosity and Scheuermann's disease of the vertebrae. The condition is generally believed to result from avascular necrosis of the epiphyses, occurring mainly in boys and at characteristic age periods varying with the particular epiphysis. The bony nucleus of the epiphysis undergoes a characteristic change which looks like fragmentation on radiography. During the active phase it may be deformed by weight-bearing or by the pull of muscles inserted into it, but after some weeks or months the structure of the bone returns to normal, although some deformity may persist. Only the severity of the skeletal deformities and their potential consequences have any significance in underwriting.

Perthes's Disease

This disease starts typically between the ages of three and 11 years. The prognosis for a good functional hip joint is related to the extent to which the epiphysis undergoes ischemic change, but with good management it has been found that four-fifths of patients are fully active and free from pain 30 years after the onset of Perthes's disease, despite the fact that many have demonstrable deformity of the femoral head on radiography.[4]

Rating

It would be usual practice to accept as standard applicants with a history of Perthes's disease, even though there is moderate functional impairment of the hip joint. For those having grosser deformity and incapacity, the risk would be evaluated similarly to osteoarthrosis of the hip joint (see p. 812).

Scheuermann's Disease

Scheuermann's disease is epiphysitis affecting the ossification centres of one or more vertebral bodies, the usual age of onset being between 12 and 30 years. The acute stage is short and self-limiting, but the important feature is the secondary deformity of the spine which may result. This takes the form of a rounded kyphosis with a radiographic appearance of slight wedging of the affected vertebrae.

Rating

Mild or moderate deformities of the chest may be disregarded in underwriting, but impairment of cardiopulmonary function is likely to be a late complication when deformity is severe, and would constitute an extra risk (see p. 840).

Osgood–Schlatter's Disease

This disease of the tibial tuberosity is a condition allied to other forms of osteochondritis or epiphysitis. It occurs mainly in adolescent males between the ages of 13 and 17, and like other forms of epiphysitis is self-limiting. Any resulting deformity can be disregarded as far as life underwriting is concerned.

CONGENITAL AND FAMILIAL ABNORMALITIES OF SKELETON

Congenital abnormalities of the skeleton may vary from the very gross defects such as absence of whole limbs, or part of a limb, to minor abnormalities such as fusion of two adjoining ribs, absence of a rib, or cervical ribs.

Marfan Syndrome

In the Marfan syndrome, which is inherited or occasionally sporadic, the main skeletal characteristics are long, thin fingers (arachnodactyly) with a metacarpal index[a] greater than 8·4, arm span which exceeds the height by more than 3·2 in (8 cm), and a distance from pubic symphysis to heels which exceeds that from crown to symphysis by more than 2 in (5 cm). Other abnormalities commonly present are pectus excavatum (funnel depression of the sternum), pigeon chest, high-arched palate and talipes equinovarus. Apart from chest deformity caused by a very deep pectus excavatum (see p. 840), the skeletal abnormalities do not themselves constitute a ratable impairment, but serve to draw attention to the possible presence of the more serious cardiovascular manifestations of the Marfan syndrome, namely dilatation of the aortic and mitral valve rings, and medionecrosis affecting the ascending and descending aorta (see p. 364). Atrial septal defect, coarctation of the aorta and patent ductus arteriosus may be present and are probably associated congenital defects rather than etiologically part of the syndrome. The third part of the Marfan syndrome is characterized by ectopia

[a]Metacarpal index = average length of the second to fifth metacarpals divided by their average width measured from a radiograph.

lentis, severe myopia, cataract, nystagmus, squint and a liability to detachment of the retina.

Osteopetrosis (Albers Schönberg Disease)

This is the common autosomal dominant or benign form of osteosclerosis. It is characterized by increased bone density, particularly in the skull and spine. The nasal sinuses may become obliterated and the cranial foramina may become overgrown causing facial palsy and deafness from nerve compression. The condition may be quite asymptomatic and is often found by chance when X-rays are performed for some unrelated purpose. A mild anemia is an infrequent complication.

Applicants suffering from the autosomal dominant form of osteopetrosis can be considered standard life risks.

Osteopetrosis of the autosomal recessive or malignant type is, on the other hand, a lethal disorder. It presents in infancy with over-growth of bone and marrow dysfunction. There is increasing anemia and thrombocytopenia with compensatory hepatosplenomegaly, and death usually occurs in early childhood. It is quite distinct from the autosomal dominant form and need not be considered further in the context of insurance.

Hyperostosis Frontalis Interna

This abnormality is often found by chance on radiography of the skull for some other purpose. It is a smooth enostosis of the inner table of the frontal bones not usually exceeding 1 cm at its greatest thickness. Hyperostosis frontalis interna is found almost exclusively in women, some of whom suffer from a variety of neuro-psychiatric complaints, although others appear perfectly healthy. There is no good evidence that the bony enostosis has any pathological significance.

Pigeon Chest

Pigeon chest, often unilateral, is another frequently observed congenital deformity not to be confused with the deformity due to infantile rickets. It does not usually interfere with respiration and may be disregarded.

Cervical Rib

Cervical rib and postfixed plexus is a congenital abnormality which would not normally be a ratable impairment despite the fact that there may have been symptoms arising from it. The condition can be easily remedied surgically if it should cause troublesome symptoms.

Spina Bifida: Spina Bifida Occulta

These conditions are of importance only insofar as they may give rise to neurological deficits (*see* p. 769).

Congenital Dislocation of the Hips

This condition is recognizable from birth, and if promptly treated much distressing disability can be prevented in later life. If, however, the defect has been neglected there can result a permanent disabling limp or gait. Unless an individual is severely incapacitated congenital dislocation of the hips would require no particular weighting in life underwriting.

CHEST DEFORMITIES

Scoliosis: Kyphoscoliosis

The commonest cause of spinal curvature is idiopathic scoliosis, which has also been called genetic scoliosis because of its high familial incidence. Congenital scoliosis due to vertebral anomalies and scoliosis secondary to neurological disease, of which neurofibromatosis is the commonest, are the next most frequent and important causes.

Moderate degrees of scoliosis are not inconsistent with normal longevity, but severe scoliosis, which is usually accompanied by some degree of kyphosis, produces gross deformity of the thoracic cage leading ultimately to impaired cardiopulmonary function. The degree of curvature of a spine is usually expressed as an angle with reference to the vertical. Thus slight scoliosis would measure 20° or less, moderate scoliosis from 21° to 50°, and severe scoliosis greater than 50°. With thoracic scoliosis over 75° the lung is severely compressed between the spine and chest wall, causing diminished ventilation and an imbalance between ventilation and perfusion which ultimately leads to pulmonary hypertension and right heart failure. Mortality in this severe group has been estimated in clinical studies[5,6] to be twice that expected for similar age groups in the population.

Orthopedic correction of scoliosis when undertaken early enough and before the curvature reaches 50° is generally successful in returning most children to a near- normal state.

Mortality experienced by insured lives with spinal curvature was analyzed in the *1951 Impairment Study*.[7] In the standard section, which presumably included persons with only mild or moderate deformities, the morality ratio was within 120 percent, but in the substandard section, which would have included the more severe deformities, it was significantly higher being in the range 200–230 percent of standard. Deaths from tuberculosis, pneumonia and influenza were significantly more than expected, but it should be remembered that antibiotics were not freely available during the period covered by the study.

Another mortality study of insured lives with chest deformities was reported by Singer and Levinson.[8] These were applicants having abnormal curvature of the spine, including kyphosis and scoliosis, insured as substandard risks by the New York Life Insurance Company between 1954 and 1970 followed to policy anniversaries in 1971. The results by age showed that the highest mortality ratio, 290 percent, was experienced by males under the age of 40; in the age group 40–49 it was 157 percent, and at the ages of 50 and over 210 percent. By duration, all ages combined, the mortality ratio for the first five years was 285 percent, and for durations five to 17 years 182 percent. The major cause of death was diseases of the heart and circulation, the mortality ratio being 370 percent.

Lew and Gajewski, in *Medical Risks*,[9] describe the mortality experience associated with spinal curvature reported in the 1983 *Medical Impairment Study*.[1] There were 8,319 policies issued from 1952 through 1976 at standard (85%) or substandard (15%) premium rates, and follow-up covered the experience between 1962 and 1977. The age distribution of applicants with spinal curvature was strongly skewed towards younger ages.

Mortality among all men with spinal curvature was favourable with a mortality ratio of 99 percent suggesting that most men in this classification had only a mild degree of deformity. Men with spinal curvature to whom policies were issued at substandard premium rates produced a mortality ratio of 163 percent based on 41 deaths, with much higher relative mortality at issue ages under 40 (285 percent based on 21 deaths).

The experience among all women with spinal curvature produced a mortality ratio of 188 percent based on 42 deaths in a much smaller volume of data than that for men. Those women issued insurance as substandard risks registered a mortality ratio of nearly 400 percent based on 22 deaths, whereas those to whom insurance was issued at standard rates recorded virtually normal mortality.

The excess mortality for both men and women was due mainly to heart and circulatory diseases and to 'all other diseases'.

Rating
Scoliosis or kyphoscoliosis, with or without operation.
1) Slight to moderate deformity, no cardiorespiratory complications; all ages – standard.
2) Severe deformity; no cardiorespiratory complications:

Age	Rating
Below 40	+150
40 and over	+50 to +100

3) With complications (effort dyspnea, pulmonary hypertension): +200 up to decline.

Pectus Excavatum

A debit would be required only if the sternal depression is so deep as to embarrass the heart by compression, by displacement, or by kinking of the major arteries or veins. For such applicants the rating listed under scoliosis with severe deformity (*see above*) would be appropriate, but no weight need be given to pectus excavatum of lesser degree. With any degree of funnel depression of the sternum the possibility of congenital defects elsewhere, particularly of the heart and great vessels, should be kept in mind (*see* p. 170).

REFERENCES

1 *Medical Impairment Study 1983*, Vol 1. Boston: Society of Actuaries and Association of Life Insurance Medical Directors of America, 1986.
2 Harrison JE. Osteoporosis – new ideas for an old problem. *Trans Assoc Life Ins Med Dir Am* 1986; 70: 53–71.
3 Duursma SA. Osteoporosis. *Trans Assoc Life Ins Med Dir Am* 1989; 73: 115–120.
4 Ratcliffe AHC. *J Bone Joint Surg* 1967; 49B: 102.
5 Nachemson A. A long term follow-up study of non-treated scoliosis. *Acta Orthop Scand* 1968; 39: 456.
6 Nilsonne U, Lundgren K-D. Long term prognosis in idiopathic scoliosis. *Acta Orthop Scand* 1968; 39: 456.
7 *1951 Impairment Study*. New York: Society of Actuaries, 1954.
8 Singer RB, Levinson L. *Medical Risks: patterns of mortality and survival*. Lexington: DC Heath, 1976.
9 Lew EA, Gajewski J. *Medical Risks: trends in mortality by age and time elapsed*. Vol 2. New York, Westport Conn., London: Praeger, 1990.

CHAPTER 27

PREGNANCY AND FEMALE GENITAL DISORDERS

POLLY M GALBRAITH

Over the last 50 years medical and socioeconomic advances have resulted in dramatically increased life expectancy, particularly in women. In developed countries women now have lower mortality rates than men at all ages. Females aged 0–75 can now expect approximately three to seven years additional lifespan compared with males. Women are much less likely to die of violent causes, such as accidents, suicide and homicide, in every age group. They presently have far fewer deaths due to HIV disease, although this is increasing. Women appear also to have better mortality experience from chronic obstructive lung disease and cardiovascular causes, including hypertension. Cirrhosis of the liver continues to be a leading cause of death for men, but not for women. However, more women than men die from diabetes and cerebrovascular diseases, particularly in older age groups. Cancer deaths continue at approximately the same rate in both sexes. Pregnancy related mortality has declined to the point that it is now rare for a woman to die in the process of normal childbirth. Since 1930 there has been a thirtyfold decrease in the maternal death rate. Cardiovascular disease and malignancies continue to account for the majority of deaths in women.[1,2]

PREGNANCY

In general, pregnancy in developed countries presents no significant mortality hazards unless complications occur or other medical impairments are present. In developed countries there are now approximately 5–8·4 direct maternal deaths per 100,000 live births in all ethnic groups, compared with 9·6 in 1978 and 7·2 in 1980. Maternal deaths in minorities are continuing to trend at 18–22 per 100,000. The deaths from sepsis, hemorrhage and abortion have been replaced by mortalities from pregnancy-induced hypertension (20 percent), embolism (20 percent), ectopic pregnancy (10 percent) and anesthesia (4 percent).[3]

Pulmonary embolism and pregnancy-induced hypertension account for the majority of maternal deaths. A strong association is evident with maternal age greater than 35 years, obesity, restricted activity, operative intervention and high parity. Elevated blood pressure may act as the link between these factors. Factors driving an increased mortality rate are poor nutrition, low educational attainment, low socioeconomic class, increased age, high parity and short intervals between births.[4]

The critical factors affecting maternal mortality are the availability of contraception, prenatal care, blood replacement, medical facilities for anesthesia and operative intervention. Underlying health problems and obstetric disorders play a more important role in the insured populations of the USA and Europe. Generally insurance companies assume as standard risk any pregnancy documented to be without complicating factors. However, the following risks must be considered if present:

Maternal Age

Pregnancy is safest when maternal age is 20–30 years. Conception under the age of 16 and over the age of 35 is associated with particularly increased risk of morbidity and mortality. In the older age groups there is approximately a two to six times increased chance of dying from pregnancy related causes. For those over the age of 45 the risk is approximately nine times greater than for women aged 20–25.

Reproductive history

Overall, second pregnancies have the lowest mortality rate. Parity of five or more creates a moderate increase in risk, and parity of eight or more creates a significant increase in risk. Previous hypertensive disease history has approximately a 25 percent recurrence rate. Additional factors that place patients at lesser degree of risk include previous operative delivery (such as cesarean section, mid-forceps or breech extraction), borderline pelvic measurements, previous prolonged labor or dystocia, severe emotional problems or pregnancy less than three months after last delivery.

Pre-existing Conditions With Pregnancy

Underlying medical impairments may seriously complicate pregnancy. Certain chronic diseases exert a deleterious effect during pregnancy and are themselves exacerbated, thus increasing mortality. Chronic hypertension, renal disease, pulmonary disorders, maternal cancers, gastrointestinal and liver disease and seizure disorders should be carefully evaluated in both the pre-pregnant state as well as during the pregnancy. Some insurance companies may elect to postpone these applicants, depending on the severity of the condition, until well after recovery. On the other hand some conditions may be so mild and under such excellent control that a standard rating is justified.

Diabetes mellitus, especially insulin dependent, is associated with a tenfold increase in mortality as a result of complications such as ketoacidosis, underlying hypertension, renal disease and pre-eclampsia. Pre-existing non-insulin-dependent diabetes does not appear to carry as much risk; however, some cases do require insulin control during pregnancy. Evaluation of the medical course during pregnancy appears to be important in these cases. If an applicant appears compliant and well-controlled on diet, rating appropriate for diabetes only may be given (*see* p. 226). Presently almost all pregnant women are screened for gestational diabetes. Thus, very mild cases of gestational diabetes (glucose intolerance) are being diagnosed and followed very closely, and are doing extremely well. If, however, insulin is required to control the condition, these cases would warrant more caution. Studies do indicate that approximately 40 percent of women with glucose intolerance during pregnancy will develop overt diabetes in

10–20 years, particularly if associated with obesity. If repeat testing postpartum shows glucose intolerance, a diabetic rating will certainly be appropriate. Companies do vary in their handling of a history of gestational diabetes in the face of a current normal glucose tolerance test.

Maternal heart disease now complicates 1 percent of pregnancies as a result of improved survival rates among those with congenital heart disease. Of these women 15 percent have pregnancy-induced hypertension as well as spontaneous abortion and poor fetal outcomes. The New York Heart Association classification is quite useful in determining the risk (*see* p. 349). Pregnant Class I and II patients have a 10 percent risk of heart failure but only a 0·3 percent mortality. Class III patients have a 30–80 percent risk of heart failure. Class III and IV patients have a 4–7 percent mortality rate associated with pregnancy. Those with mild valvular stenosis and moderate valvular regurgitation with normal pulse pressure and normal chamber size have a slightly increased mortality. Those diagnosed with moderate valvular stenosis, significant valvular regurgitation and prosthetic heart valves with normal function have a moderately increased risk. Those diagnosed with severe valvular stenosis or regurgitation, atrial fibrillation and compensated heart failure have a considerably increased mortality risk. Those with congestive heart failure, pulmonary hypertension, Eisenmenger's syndrome or the Marfan syndrome with aortic valve insufficiency have an unacceptable mortality risk and would rightfully be cautioned to avoid pregnancy or undergo therapeutic abortion. Most companies would postpone or decline all but the best of these cases during pregnancy.

Coagulopathies or venous disorders should be viewed with concern, especially in light of a history of deep vein thromboses, transient ischemic attack, stroke, pulmonary embolism or thrombophlebitis. The risk of thrombosis during pregnancy is increased threefold during the postpartum period and threefold to sixteenfold after cesarean section. Severe varicosities can also increase the risk of thromboembolic phenomenon. As the pregnant hormonal state predisposes to hypercoagulability, these applicants would normally be postponed until fully recovered. Smoking during pregnancy (especially when in excess of two packs per day or combined with other factors, such as hypertension, morbid obesity or heart disease) further complicates a high-risk pregnancy.

Pregnancy-induced hypertension is a significant complication solely as a result of the pregnant state and dissipates within a few weeks after delivery. The incidence of pre-eclampsia and eclampsia (toxemia) is estimated at about 7 percent of all obstetric cases. Pre-eclampsia is characterized by elevated blood pressure, proteinuria and edema. With eclampsia convulsions and/or coma also develop; and acute renal failure accompanying this state can go on to varying degrees of chronic renal failure, although this is rare. The etiology is unknown but is associated with vascular diseases, multiple pregnancies, primigravida, oligohydramnios, molar pregnancy, dietary deficiency and a familial tendency. Mortality rates in developed countries have been reduced by half but, even so, 5–10 percent of eclampsia patients die. A history of eclampsia or severe toxemia is associated with increased hypertension in later years, as well as a very high risk of recurrence of toxemia in a subsequent pregnancy.

In the USA, the cesarean section rate has risen to 25 percent of all deliveries. The disadvantages of a rising cesarean section rate may be partially offset by more being done electively or expectantly, preferably with epidural anesthesia. The increased mortality is due in part to complications such as embolism, hemorrhage and infection, and in part to anesthesia. Following emergency cesarean sections the fatality rate is 0·36 per 1,000, approximately four times the risk of vaginal delivery. After elective cesarean section the death rate is 0·09 per 1,000, somewhat higher than for vaginal deliveries.

Extrauterine Pregnancy

An extrauterine or ectopic pregnancy is one in which a fertilized ovum implants outside the uterine cavity (i.e. tubal, ovarian, intestinal, peritoneal and cornual sites). The incidence is 1 per 100 pregnancies, and its occurrence is more frequent in infertility patients, patients with previous pelvic inflammatory disease, IUD users and those with a history of previous ectopic pregnancies. Extrauterine pregnancy is also clearly age related, with women aged 35–44 having ectopic rates three times higher than those for women aged less than 25. The risk of death is ten times higher than for vaginal delivery.[5]

Hemorrhage is the major cause of maternal death. Intestinal obstruction and fistulas may develop after hemoperitoneum and peritonitis. New technologies, such as trans-vaginal ultrasound and sensitive serum human chorionic gonadotropin assays, have made early detection possible, avoiding many of these life-threatening complications. Maternal mortality in ectopic pregnancy is 1–2 percent. Tubal pregnancy will recur in 10 percent of cases treated.

Consideration of an applicant's age, gynecologic history, treatment and presence of residual problems is important in underwriting this condition. In general, documentation of full recovery would indicate a standard risk.

Abortion (Miscarriage)

Spontaneous abortion is the natural termination of pregnancy before 20 weeks' gestation, or before the fetus is viable. This occurs very frequently (15–50 percent of all abortions and miscarriages) and generally carries no increased mortality risk. Hemorrhage, sepsis and intravascular coagulation are some lethal complications, but death is exceedingly rare. Prognosis is excellent with prompt treatment, and once fully recovered the risk is standard.

Elective legal abortions are associated with approximately 1 per 100,000 deaths, which is much lower than the risk from childbirth. First trimester abortions are associated with much less risk than later trimesters. Even with serious underlying medical conditions, the risk associated with abortion appears to be less than that associated with childbirth. Once fully recovered from any type of abortion or miscarriage, the life risk would be considered negligible.

FEMALE GENITAL DISORDERS

Uterine Myoma (Fibroids, Fibromyoma, Leiomyoma, Myofibroma or Fibroma)

This is the most common uterine tumor, but the vast majority are asymptomatic and benign. They appear to be hormone-sensitive and thus only clinically significant during the menstrual years. Myomas are usually multiple, discrete uterine masses.

Symptoms occur in approximately 25–50 percent of myomatous patients. Abnormal endometrial bleeding occurs in about 30 percent, most likely due to distortion of blood vessels and/or ulceration of overlying endometrium. Menorrhagia (prolonged, heavy menses) usually occurs as only one variant in the entire spectrum of abnormal menstrual bleeding patterns that may be seen. It frequently produces an iron deficiency anemia. Pain is uncommon, but when present indicates tumor degeneration after circulatory occlusion, infection, torsion, or contractions to expel a myoma from the uterine cavity. More commonly pelvic discomfort, heaviness or backache may be described. Large myomas can cause intestinal obstruction, urinary obstruction, pelvic venous congestion and lower leg edema.

Because presentation is often a pelvic mass, diagnosis should be confirmed by pelvic and abdominal examination and ultrasound. CT scan and MRI may occasionally be used. Hysterography and/or hysteroscopy may be required to identify submucosal myomas. Laparoscopy or laparotomy may be needed to establish definitively the exact origin of the mass, as well as to rule out malignant transformation. Between the ages of 40 and 60, 1 percent of women with presumed uterine myomas producing symptoms necessitating hysterectomy had malignant leiomyosarcoma diagnosed postoperatively.[6]

Common indications for treatment are menorrhagia, rapid increase in size, pain or pressure, infertility and adjacent organ compromise. Hysteroscopic laser or rectoscope is being used for submucous types. Medical therapy with hormones, danazol and GnRh analogues have had some success. Hysterectomy is curative. Mortality associated with hysterectomy is 0·1–0·3 percent. Myomectomy may be corrective but 15 percent recur and 10–60 percent require further surgery. If hysterectomy, myomectomy or confirmatory biopsy has been performed with full recovery and no evidence of malignancy, then the risk could be considered standard.[7]

If an unoperated fibroid is small and there are no significant symptoms, and there has been competent evaluation and diagnosis, the risk would be standard. On the other hand, if the tumor is large and there are significant symptoms, and the diagnosis is questionable, the applicant should be postponed until the condition has been fully evaluated, particularly if her age is over 40.

Ovarian Cysts and Tumors

Of all the female disorders, new growths arising in the reproductive system are probably the most notable and are responsible for almost half of the deaths from malignancy. Attention should be paid to any pelvic mass or suspicious clinical history. As age increases, the probability also increases that gynecological procedures, such as hysterectomy and salpingo-oophorectomy, have been performed because of cancer. If the history is recent, it may be advisable to obtain pathology reports.

Benign ovarian cysts are one of the most common surgical conditions in young women. Symptoms include pelvic pain, infertility and menstrual dysfunction.

Functional cysts (follicular and corpus luteum) are common and benign. If persistence longer than 60 days is noted, the diagnosis is not a functional cyst and further investigation is warranted. Neoplastic cysts may be benign or malignant. Benign tumors once removed are not a cause for concern. All ovarian cysts are problematic until removed or biopsied and pathologically diagnosed. Over the age of 50, 50 percent of ovarian cysts are malignant.[8]

Polycystic ovarian disease (Stein-Leventhal syndrome) is characterized by bilaterally enlarged, polycystic ovaries, secondary oligomenorrhea and infertility. Many affected are also hirsute and obese; because of this, adrenocortical hyperplasia or tumor should be ruled out. Ultrasound, laparoscopy and hormone tests are the accepted diagnostic techniques. Well differentiated endometrial cancer does occur occasionally, but with proper evaluation to exclude malignancy the life risk should be standard after appropriate treatment.

Endometriosis

Endometriosis is defined as the presence of endometrial tissue outside the uterine cavity. Typically it is manifested by pelvic pain, dysmenorrhea, adnexal mass and/or infertility. Diagnosis is properly made by laparoscopy or laparotomy. Prevalence in the reproductive age group is estimated at 0–50 percent depending on the study. The disease may develop as the result of mechanical factors, such as retrograde menstrual flow, and requires estrogen stimulation. The severity of the disease has been staged mild, moderate, severe and extensive. Bowel adhesions, peritonitis, ureteral and intestinal obstruction can be unusual complications. Hysterectomy with bilateral oophorectomy is considered definitive treatment and, when the patient has fully recovered, constitutes a standard risk. Endometriosis is rarely fatal and all but the most complicated or severe cases would be standard risks.

Endometrial Hyperplasia

The endometrial hyperplasias comprise a whole spectrum of altered states of the endometrium, ranging from physiologically normal to endometrial carcinoma. The terminology for these disorders is not standardized at present. Generally accepted categories that denote increasing risk for developing cancer if untreated are endometrial polyps, cryptic hyperplasia, adenomatous hyperplasia and atypical adenomatous hyperplasia. The cause of endometrial hyperplasia is unopposed estrogen stimulation. The irregular and/or heavy vaginal bleeding can be properly classified with an endometrial biopsy or cervical dilation and fractional curettage (D & C), and serum estradiol determination to rule out endogenous estrogen sources, such as granulosa-theca-cell tumors, ovarian cortical stromal thecosis, or other gonadal stromal or metastatic neoplasms to the ovary. A pathology report indicating adenomatous hyperplasia in a perimenopausal or postmenopausal patient demands attention, as 8 percent develop adenocarcinoma within ten years of onset.[9]

Atypical hyperplasia or endometrial adenocarcinoma has been found in 25 percent of those with postmenopausal bleeding. Associated risk conditions were obesity, nulliparity and age over 60. The prevalence of endometrial neoplasia, even in asymptomatic women over the age of 45, is 4 per 1,000.

The menopausal woman who presents with abnormal vaginal bleeding should be postponed until a D & C and hormone evaluation are performed, whether she is on estrogen replacement therapy or not. Once carcinoma has been ruled out, most of these women can be treated successfully with hormones, D & C and/or hysterectomy; they would then be considered standard risks.

Endometrial polyps are a frequent cause of irregular vaginal bleeding. In premenopausal women these polyps have little or no malignant potential. In the postmenopausal woman, however, 10–15 percent are associated with malignancy. Of particular interest are those polyps that exhibit active hyperplasia after the menopause. These seem to represent a focal form of hyperplasia that may be related to malignant transformation. Once evaluated and treated, these can be considered standard risks.

Dysmenorrhea

Dysmenorrhea refers to the cramping pelvic pain that occurs before and during menstruation. Sixty percent of women suffer from either primary dysmenorrhea (i.e. no evidence of organic defect) or secondary dysmenorrhea related to organic pelvic disease. Primary dysmenorrhea is effectively treated in the majority of cases and is of little underwriting significance. Secondary dysmenorrhea should be appropriately investigated to confirm or eliminate the finding of pelvic pathology. Endometriosis and adenomyosis are the most common causes of secondary dysmenorrhea. Other causes include salpingitis, cervical stenosis, uterine fibroids, polpys and possibly uterine malposition. It is important to document cause and rule out malignancy. Once effective treatment is completed, this condition is usually a standard risk.

Premenstrual Syndrome (PMS)

PMS is a cyclical syndrome complex consisting of mood, behavioral and physical changes that occur during the luteal phase of most menstrual cycles; the severity of symptoms varies with each woman. If only those with symptoms severe enough to affect personal relationships and occupation are considered, the incidence is 10–20 percent of reproductive women. If the diagnosis is appropriately confirmed, physical aspects are of little underwriting significance. Most commonly reported symptoms are psychologic, such as anxiety, depression and emotional lability. Serious psychoneurotic conditions can be masquerading under the PMS diagnosis or significantly exacerbated in the presence of PMS. People requiring psychiatric consultation, hospitalization or psychopharmacologic medications would warrant a rating commensurate with the severity and duration of the condition (see Chapter 24).

Pelvic Inflammatory Disease

Acute salpingitis is manifested by the acute onset of pelvic and lower abdominal pain, fever and tenderness. Both gonococcal and non-gonococcal infections are causative. Complications range from peritonitis, abscess formation with adnexal destruction, intestinal adhesions and obstruction, to septic shock and death. Early diagnosis and treatment with intravenous antibiotics are directly related to a favorable outcome. These applicants must be postponed until fully recovered.

Chronic or recurrent pelvic infection implies episodes of acute reinfection, chronic pelvic pain, and the presence of pelvic tissue changes, and peritoneal adhesions. Hydrosalpinx or a tubo-ovarian abscess may be present. The chances of ectopic gestation are much increased with ensuing episodes. Clinical records should be evaluated in the underwriting process, and ratings may range from standard (after definitive surgical procedures, such as hysterectomy and salpingectomy) to postpone (during active infection).

REFERENCES

1 Centers for Disease Control. *MMWR* 1988; 30: 637.
2 National Center for Health Statistics. Births, marriages, divorces and deaths for Feb 1988. *Monthly Vital Stat Report* 1988; 37: 3.
3 Rochat ET, Koonan AL. Maternal mortality in the United States: report from maternal collaberative. *Am J Obst Gyn* 1988; 72: 91.
4 Rosenberg MJ. Reproductive mortality in the United States: recent trends and methodologic considerations. *Am J Pub Health* 1987; 77: 833.
5 Marchbanks PA. Risk factors for ectopic pregnancy: a population based study. *JAMA* 1988; 259: 1823.
6 Leibsohn S, d'Ablaing G. Leiomyosarcoma in a series of hysterectomies performed for presumed uterine leiomyomas. *Am J Obst Gyn* 1990; 4: 968–76.
7 Hutchins F. Uterine fibroids: current concepts in management. *Female Patient* 1990; 15: 29–41.
8 Parazzini F. Risk factors for endometrioid, mucinous and serous benign ovarian cysts. *Int J Epidem* 1989; 48: 108–12.
9 Schlaerth JB. Endometrial hyperplasia: management of common problems. *Am J Obst Gyn* 1988: 427–30.

CHAPTER 28

HIV AND AIDS

ROBERT K GLEESON

The spread of the human immunodeficiency virus (HIV) has presented the late 20th century with a morbid opportunity to study a major world-wide epidemic. Although we have a reasonable understanding of methods of transmission, the genetics of the virus and the cause of the infection, considerable advances or breakthrough still seem remote prospects, especially while significant scientific controversy is aroused over the role of the HIV itself. Although progress is being made on therapeutic regimes, no truly effective treatment, let alone a cure or a vaccine, can yet be anticipated.

If little else, this chapter provides a historical guide to life insurance understanding and underwriting of the epidemic. The insurance industry was among the first institutions to understand clearly the serious nature of the epidemic. When other officials stated that *only* 5–15 percent of the people infected with the AIDS virus would die from AIDS within five years, the industry anticipated that this was an understatement and that the death rate per year was likely to continue well into the future. Insurers focused on the entire course of the disease, as opposed to focusing on the final clinical stage, AIDS. They also realized the predictive value of HIV antibody testing and knew that highly accurate antibody tests could be performed in a confidential manner.

EPIDEMIOLOGY

In 1981 several previously healthy young males died from Kaposi's sarcoma or pneumocystis carinii pneumonia. These cases were later identified as having an underlying immune deficiency. In the early 1980s other cases began to appear in otherwise healthy hemophiliacs or blood transfusion recipients. It soon became apparent that all these cases represented a new infectious disease descriptively called the acquired immune deficiency syndrome or AIDS. The Centers for Disease Control (CDC) described the cases clinically so that an accurate epidemiologic picture could be developed.[1]

In 1983 both Dr Montagnier of France and Dr Gallo of the USA described a retrovirus as the causative agent responsible for AIDS. The virus carried several different names, but most commonly it was called the HTLV-III or human T-cell lymphotropic virus, type III because of its predilection for T cells. In 1986 the International Committee on Taxonomy of Viruses officially named this the human immunodeficiency virus or HIV. A further classification of the original AIDS virus as HIV-1 became necessary in late 1985 when an AIDS-similar disease was identified in patients in Western Africa; this second retrovirus, also capable of causing AIDS, became known as HIV-2. HIV-1 and HIV-2 appear to have identical modes of transmission, considerable genetic homology, and both are capable of causing the disease AIDS.

The identification of HIV-1 enabled researchers to develop a test for antibodies to HIV-1 infections. In March 1985 the American Food and Drug Administration first licensed tests for the identification of antibody to HIV-1. These highly accurate antibody tests have promoted further study of the epidemiology and clinical course of HIV infection. A test for antibody to HIV-2 became commercially available in late 1990.

Antibody testing has confirmed that both HIV-1 and HIV-2 diseases are spread primarily by sexual contact, but blood-to-blood contact, including shared needles during intravenous (IV) drug use, blood product transfusions in the absence of routine antibody testing and transplacental transmission, are also possible means of transmission.

In the industrialized world HIV disease was first identified in the homosexual and bisexual male community. This led to the assumption that AIDS was somehow a 'gay disease'. In 1981 homosexual males made up virtually all of the AIDS cases; by 1985 homosexual and bisexual males accounted for 75 percent of all AIDS cases but by 1990 the figure was down to 62 percent, according to the CDC. This percentage will continue to decrease both as safe sex and monogamy increase among the informed homosexual population and the number of heterosexual cases increases.

The second wave of AIDS patients in industrialized societies is the IV drug user (IVDU). HIV disease is spread efficiently by shared needles used during illicit IV drug use. As of mid-1990 IVDUs already account for more AIDS cases than other risk groups in some European countries. In the USA almost a third of all AIDS cases and over half of all females with diagnosed AIDS in 1989 had used IV drugs.

Seroprevalence studies of HIV infection rates among IVDUs indicate that infection usually spreads rapidly once it enters the drug abusing community. In the USA the seroprevalence rates among IVDUs vary from nearly 50 percent, particularly in the large cities in the east coast, to only 1 percent in midwest cities such as Minneapolis. In Quebec, Canada, there were no reported HIV positives in the IVDU population prior to 1988, but since then IVDUs have accounted for 8·8 percent of all seropositives. And again, seroprevalence rates recently emerged from Thailand indicating the number of HIV-infected IVDUs had risen from virtually zero in 1987 to 500,000 in 1990.

Furthermore, IV drug use represents an efficient mode of transmission into the heterosexual community. IVDUs have a high prevalence of other sexually transmitted diseases (STDs), which increase the ease of HIV transmission, and frequently resort to prostitution to pay for drugs. The combination of IV drug abuse, prostitution and poverty is potentially disastrous, greatly promoting the heterosexual spread of HIV disease.

In Africa, the Caribbean, South America and Asia the disease is more likely to affect males and females in equal numbers. Heterosexual HIV disease is increasingly likely to become the pattern observed throughout the industrialized world. There is no reason for the industrialized world to believe that AIDS is not a heterosexual disease.

As of September 1990 the World Health Organization (WHO) had reported 283,010 AIDS cases but estimated that the actual number of cases approached 700 thousand. Only 21 of 157 countries belonging to the WHO have reported no AIDS cases. In 1988 the WHO estimated that there are between 8 and 10 million infected individuals world-wide. However, in August 1990 the WHO indicated that within the next two years they are going to increase significantly their estimate of HIV cases because the rate of spread within just the past two years in some countries has far exceeded their initial projections.[2]

AIDS is now a world-wide epidemic which will only increase in severity for the foreseeable future. At this time, the zenith of the epidemic cannot be determined because of the long time lag between infection and clinical illness, the continued spread of the virus and the lack of an effective vaccine. The relatively larger case numbers reported in the industrialized world primarily reflect better identification and reporting methods. However, major increases in AIDS cases are likely to occur in nations without adequate education-prevention systems, and adequate testing and case identification methods.

HIV-2 disease appears to be more limited than HIV-1 disease: as at 1990 only 600 cases of HIV-2 AIDS have been reported in 36 countries. The majority of these cases are in western Africa where some studies have indicated that up to 1 percent of the population is infected with HIV-2. However, only 26 cases have been reported in North America. The transmission of HIV-1 and HIV-2 are identical, but the course of the disease caused by HIV-2 may be more prolonged than HIV-1. The future spread of this epidemic remains even less clear than the more common HIV-1. However, in November 1990 the CDC completed a study of the blood banking system and determined that during the two-year study no cases of HIV-2 had been identified. Therefore the CDC indicated that blood banks did not need to test for HIV-2 antibody.[3]

CLINICAL MANIFESTATIONS

HIV disease is a chronic infection of the immune system, just as Hepatitis B is an infection of the hepatic system. Infection, which is detected by the presence of antibody to HIV, is characterized by a long latent period before the clinical expression of disease. Some authorities believe that HIV is quiescent until reactivation occurs; others believe that the virus is continually active and progressively destroys CD4 lymphocytes. HIV is a retrovirus, so named because it uses the enzyme reverse transcriptase to synthesize DNA from its own RNA, a reversal of the normal process. The HIV genetic material is actually inserted into the infected host cell which then becomes a 'slave' to produce HIV at the direction of the new genetic material.

HIV infection attacks the immune system because the HIV envelope marker gp-120 interacts with a cell receptor found primarily on cells of the CD4 lymphocyte. As the infection continues, HIV destroys its host cells. CD4 markers can also be found on macrophages, certain brain cells and gastro-intestinal cells; these are also infected with HIV.

HIV infection proceeds along a rather predictable and prolonged course of which AIDS itself is only the last manifestation. The focus of attention should be on the entire course of HIV infection; the use of the terms AIDS and ARC should be limited to defining late clinical states. In the average patient, the period from HIV infection to the onset of clinical AIDS is 11 years.[4] At this time, there is no logical reason to assume that the annual mortality rate of 5000 percent total mortality will not continue.

An approximation of HIV disease's progression with time for the average patient illustrates that subclinical infection is the most common phase. A minority of patients develop a transient mononucleosis-type illness at the time of seroconversion, which usually occurs four to 12 weeks after infection. The symptoms at this time may include fever, a roseola-like rash, myalgias and lymphadenopathy, or transient neurological syndromes, including Guillain-Barré or other acute neuritis. Antibodies to HIV can be detected at, or shortly after, this episode. For the next perhaps six years the average patient feels clinically well; the only evidence of infection is the presence of antibody to HIV and possibly subclinical and subtle deterioration of the immune system as HIV infects more CD4 cells. Finally HIV infection weakens the immune system so much that constitutional symptoms become manifest. These include persistent generalized lymphadenopathy, fever for more than one month, involuntary weight loss of more than 10 percent, unusual dermatologic conditions and oral thrush. This phase of the infection is clinically called AIDS related complex (or ARC), a useful but unscientific determination. As the immune system deteriorates even further, opportunistic infections occur and the diagnostic criteria for CDC-defined AIDS is finally met, on average, some nine years after the initial infection with HIV.

During the entire time after HIV infection the only constant method of confirming the diagnosis of infection is the HIV antibody test. This is a major reason for the widespread use of the HIV antibody test by insurers.

The clinical conditions associated with the symptomatic phase of HIV infection known as ARC are varied. Among the most common symptoms is persistent generalized lymphadenopathy. The enlarged nodes are typically seen in the posterior cervical, axillary and inguinal regions. A biopsy of the enlarged node reveals only benign hyperplastic changes.

ARC is a variously defined condition referring to the clinical state of mild immune dysfunction that exists before the onset of CDC-defined AIDS. Most commonly the definition includes at least two signs or symptoms from a list that includes chronic fevers, night sweats, diarrhea, unintentional weight loss, multi-dermatomal herpes zoster, oral thrush and hairy leukoplakia.

The development of laboratory markers to measure the progression of disease will lead to a more refined and rational understanding of the course of the infection; in turn this will lead to improved treatment programs based on the status of the host's immune system. Today's laboratory markers of potential value include CD4 cell counts, the ratio of CD4 to CD8 cells, serum levels of HIV p24 antigen, serum and urine neopterin levels, anemia and sedimentation rates.

There are currently two major classification systems of HIV disease. The CDC classification system (see Table 28.1) keys off its initial definition of clinical AIDS and remains clinically based; it is not designed for prognostic use. The Walter Reed classification system (see Table 28.2) was the first major classification system to recognize the importance of serological markers, in this case CD4 cell counts, and anergy in the various stages of HIV infection. The WHO has proposed an HIV staging system based on four clinical marker divisions, with subclassification based on laboratory lymphocyte and CD4 cell counts where available. At the time of writing, the WHO system has not yet been published.

Table 28.1. CDC classification system of HIV disease.

Group I   Acute infection occurring at the time of infection
Group II   Asymptomatic infection
Group III Persistent generalized lymphadenopathy
Group IV Other disease
        a) Constitutional disease
        b) Neurologic disease
        c) Secondary infectious disease
           1) Specified opportunistic infectious diseases listed in the CDC surveillance definition.
           2) Other specified conditions
        d) Secondary cancers
        e) Other conditions

Table 28.2. Walter Reed classification system for HIV.

Stage	HIV antibody	Enlarged lymph nodes	CD4 count	Anergy	Oral thrush	Opportunistic infections
WRO	−	−	>400	none	−	−
WR1	+	−	>400	none	−	−
WR2	+	+	>400	none	−	−
WR3	+	+	<400	none	−	−
WR4	+	+	<400	partial	−	−
WR5	+	+	<400	complete/partial	+	−
WR6	+	+	<400	complete	+	+

TREATMENT

Treatment programs have been found to be beneficial and are increasingly tailored to the stage of HIV infection. Most regimens are based on the use of zidovudine (AZT, azidothymidine) and aerosolized pentamidine. The initial use of medical therapy was directed at the patient with frank AIDS. However, studies have now shown that prophylatic treatment is beneficial if instituted when the individual's CD4 cell counts are below 200. This treatment seems to delay the onset of opportunistic infections by perhaps several months. Further treatments will undoubtedly improve on these early successes. Currently, treatment programs do not increase survival enough to make life insurance available. However, it is hoped that treatment will continue to improve so that insurance on a rated basis may be feasible. These treatment programs are, however, likely in the short-term to increase health and disability costs. A vaccine would be a most welcome development. In theory, both a post-infection vaccine similar to the rabies vaccine and a preventive vaccine similar to polio vaccines are possible. Unfortunately there are significant difficulties in developing these products because of the intricate nature of retroviral cell biology.

TESTING

Testing for HIV infection continues to be a sensitive issue and is qualitatively different from other tests insurers might perform. The knowledge that an applicant has HIV disease has significant implications for that individual. Regardless of what we would like to believe about the goodness of mankind and the willingness of humans openly to accept HIV-infected individuals as equal members of society, this goal is unfortunately seldom realized. Now that treatment programs are available and testing accuracy is beyond question, antibody testing has become more widely accepted. In addition, society benefits when knowledge of test results prevents further spread of the infection.

HIV antibody testing should be performed with pre-test notification and confidential post-test notification and referral. Pre-test notification should include a clear statement that HIV antibody testing is going to be performed, the significance of a positive test and the eventual distribution of the results. When an applicant has further questions about the implications of an HIV antibody test, referral to an AIDS service organization is appropriate. If the test results are positive, the applicant should be notified confidentially. The current US practice is to send a registered letter to the applicant indicating that his application has been declined because of an abnormal laboratory result, then asking for permission to mail the results to a physician. After signed authorization is returned, the results are forwarded to the personal physician, who provides notification and counseling. Some states allow positive results to be sent directly to the proposed insured. In these instances the notification letter should include a referral to a local AIDS support organization and literature regarding the significance of a positive test from a neutral organization, such as the American Red Cross.

Results of HIV tests should not be released without the specific authorization of the individual. These tests should also be safeguarded in the Home Office against unprotected distribution. Most companies have written guidelines for the security of positive HIV results and keep the results separate from other applications.

Most serum tests for HIV disease detect the antibody to HIV. Patients infected with HIV will develop antibodies within 12 weeks, although rare cases of prolonged seronegative periods have been reported.

The most common testing protocols begin with an enzyme-linked immunosorbent assay, or ELISA or EIA screening test. If the ELISA is doubly reactive, a confirmatory test, such as the Western Blot or RIPA, should be done. This is particularly true when testing low risk populations such as insurance applicants. A 1989 study among 630,190 units from 290,110 blood donors in Minnesota indicated the specificity rate for the testing series of ELISA, ELISA Western Blot was 99·9994.

The ELISA methodology begins with HIV antigen preparation, either from viral lysate or genetic recombinant material, which is coated onto a microliter plate. During the test the patient's serum reacts with the antigen. The plate is washed with anti-human antibody followed by a colorometric conjugate. This produces a change in color of the wells containing antibody to HIV. These plates can be read mechanically and values compared to cut-off absorbence thresholds. Values above control are considered reactive. There are several approved ELISA tests commercially available which approach 100 percent sensitivity and specificity. Nonetheless, false positive tests do occur, particularly in low-risk populations with ELISAs prepared from viral lysate. These false positives are primarily caused by underlying auto-immune disease, prior pregnancies or transfusions, polygammopathy or liver disease. False positives are much less common in genetically prepared recombinant assays.

The Western Blot detects immune response to specific viral proteins via immuno-electrophoresis. Purified viral proteins or antigens are spread throughout a polyacrylamide gel according to molecular weight. The proteins are transferred to a nitrocellulose strip. During testing this strip is bathed in the patient's serum and incubated with anti-human globulin. An enzyme then reacts with the substrate to produce a detectable band wherever an antigen-antibody complex forms between the plated proteins and the patient's serum.

The Western Blot bands specific for HIV are found at discrete molecular weights indicating specific viral gene products. The envelope glycoproteins (env) are gp41, gp160 and gp120; the core proteins (gag) are p17, p24 and p55; and the polymerase proteins (pol) are p31, p51 and p66.

Most HIV antibody-positive sera will react with all of the proteins mentioned above. Several criteria have been established for the minimum banding pattern required for a positive test; the other banding patterns are assumed to be indeterminate results. US criteria for a positive Western Blot are listed in Table 28.3.

Table 28.3. US criteria for a positive Western Blot test.

Organization/source	Criteria
CDC	Any two of p24, gp41 and gp120/160
Association of State of Territorial Public Health Laboratory Directors	Any two of p24, gp41 and gp120/160
FDA-licensed DuPont test	p24 and p31 and either gp41 or gp120/160
American Red Cross	One band from each group: gag and pol and env
Consortium for Retrovirus Serology Standardization	Two bands: p24 or p31 plus either gp41 or gp120/160

If an individual has some bands on the Western Blot but does not fulfil the criteria listed above for a positive test, they have an indeterminate test. Approximately 15 percent of the US adult population has some bands on a Western Blot. When the Western Blot was first approved by the Federal Drugs Administration (FDA) in 1987, the significance of an indeterminate test was not clear. The FDA-approved package insert indicated that indeterminate tests should be repeated in three to six months. Further testing has indicated that in a low-risk population represented by the insurance applicant most indeterminate tests are truly negative. An indeterminate is usually negative on further testing in the low-prevalence insured population. This is particularly true for non-specific bands such as p17.

Most major American laboratories follow the protocol developed by the Walter Reed Armed Forces HIV Testing Protocol. This protocol splits all blood reactive after two ELISAs into both Western Blot and the more specific genetically engineered recombinant ELISA testing.[5] This offers a verification of both negative and positive specimens which must be concordant in their results. It also clarifies indeterminate Western Blot tests. The logic of this method has been substantiated by the now five-year-long study of the US Armed Forces involving more than 10 million HIV antibody tests.

Newer testing techniques for the detection of HIV antibody are being developed. These tests include peptide assays and polymerase chain reaction. Testing techniques will probably continue to change in the future. However, confirmation of screening tests using a highly sensitive testing technique, such as the Western Blot, is likely to remain a standard procedure because of the sensitivity and implications of a positive test for antibody to HIV.

Recent advances in testing technology have prompted the development of non-serological tests for HIV antibody in both urine and saliva. As of 1990 the urine antibody test has been introduced by some insurance laboratories but is not well documented in the clinical literature. The saliva test has not yet been released but is under intensive study. In the near future these non-serological tests are likely to be employed by insurers.

ACTUARIAL STUDIES

Since the first clinical recognition of the disease AIDS, cases have been described in virtually all countries of the world. The majority of the reported cases are in the industrialized world, reflecting the higher level of health care and greater public recognition of the epidemic. Future projections have been made based on the known number of cases, approximations of the rate of new infections and the half-life from infection to death based on specialized studies. Unfortunately national seroprevalence studies are not available to provide the key information on the extent of the infection in the population. However, the epidemic seems far greater than initially projected by the WHO.

Recent international studies have indicated that the epidemic is spreading much more rapidly than previously anticipated. For example, WHO studies in sub-Saharan Africa have found that the number of people infected with HIV-1 has doubled in just three years and may now number over 5 million. In many African cities up to 20 percent of sexually active adults are infected, and the infection is moving from the cities to the countryside. In Thailand only a handful of HIV-1 cases were identified in 1987; by 1990 there were an estimated 500 thousand infected people, primarily IVDUs and prostitutes.

In July 1990 the WHO released a report indicating that AIDS is 'accelerating dramatically in some parts of the world.' This report increased the WHO estimates of the current HIV-1 infected population by 2 million from its 1989 report, up to

8–10 million. The report attributed most of this increase to heterosexual cases and indicated that future reports might contain significantly higher projections. The report also indicated that 3 million women and children were likely to die from AIDS during the 1990s. In conjunction with World AIDS Day the WHO released an interview of Dr Micheal Merson, director of the Global Program on AIDS at WHO, who said that on the basis of current infection trends there may be a cumulative total of 25–30 million men, women and children infected with HIV by the year 2000.[6]

The 32 European countries reporting to the WHO have documented a 61·9 percent increase in AIDS cases in the 23 months since the previous report of March 1989. The European countries have now reported a total of 35,376 AIDS cases.

The CDC maintains ongoing tallies of AIDS cases and deaths, and makes projections of the future extent of the epidemic. Their data based on projections made in July 1988 is indicated in Table 28.4 for both historical and projected cases, compared with the actual cases observed.[7]

Table 28.4. CDC data for the US population.

Year	AIDS cases		AIDS deaths	
	Annual	Cumulative	Annual	Cumulative
Historical				
1982		1371		317
1983	2856	4227	975	1292
1984	5832	10059	2373	3665
1985	10957	21016	4496	8161
1986	18115	39131	8140	16301
1987	27976	67107	11608	27909
Projected				
1988	35291	102398	22601	56446
1989	45137	147535	31195	87641
1990	55129	202664	40707	129348
1991	64737	267401	50414	178767
1992	73440	340841	59876	238634

The American Society of Actuaries (SOA) has devoted considerable resources to the study of the HIV infection. Its report recognizes three major limitations to any attempt to project the course of the HIV epidemic: (1) good prevalence studies are not available to indicate the extent of the disease outside known high-risk groups, (2) the continuing development and effect of treatment on the course of the disease is not known, and (3) a vaccine may be developed, which would significantly alter the course of the epidemic. The study also recognizes the complicating factors caused by the long latency period between infection and clinical AIDS; it also recognizes the fact that the spread of infection is related to specific, controllable (at least in theory) behaviors.

The SOA has made projections based on the available data using a methodology slightly different from that of the CDC, but both organizations have produced similar results for short-term projections. The SOA data are based on probable low and high scenarios showing the broad ranges possible in the future. For example, the 1987 estimates of HIV-infected US individuals varies from 700 thousand to 1·7 million. These figures for the general US population do not necessarily reflect an insurer's risk because of fundamental differences between the general population and an insured population. Additionally, any underwriting action, including antibody testing, taken by an insurer will limit future claims. The results of the SOA study predicting the future number of AIDS cases are shown in Figure 28.1.

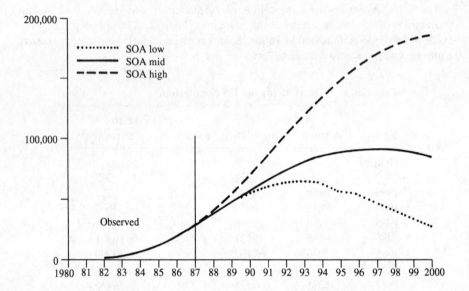

Fig. 28.1. New AIDS cases per year.

The SOA has also projected the range of possible HIV claims on the insurance industry. The projections are based on the number of recognized HIV claims reported in 1987, which has the obvious limitation of being based only on reported AIDS claims. Nonetheless the US industry-wide claims are projected at between $50 billion and $125 billion by the end of the 1990s. By the end of 1989 the life and health industry had paid a cumulative total of $2·38 billion since 1986 in AIDS-related claims; $1 billion was paid in 1989 alone.

The SOA recommends that companies take adequate steps to avoid financial difficulties as the epidemic matures. First, companies should underwrite this disease as they underwrite other identifiable diseases: the basic underwriting tool is confidential HIV antibody testing. Other approaches include increased reserves to cover projected claims. As the epidemic matures, future projections for both the size and identity of the infected population groups will obviously be improved as more data are collected. However, the SOA projections for the early years have proved to be remarkably accurate.

UNDERWRITING

HIV infection carries a very significant increase in mortality expectation because the average survival after infection is only 11 years. The mortality rate can be calculated at nearly 5000 percent extra mortality for a 35-year-old male, the average age at death of an insured AIDS patient. Approximately 5 percent of the HIV-infected population dies per year, or 50 deaths per thousand. This is in sharp contrast to the expected death rate of only 1 per thousand at age 35 in most insured populations.

Underwriting HIV disease can be understood by analyzing the spectrum from risk behavior to the stages of infection to frank AIDS. The underwriting of risk behaviors is interpreted differently in different countries. In the USA the National Association of Insurance Commissioners (NAIC) has issued guidelines for the underwriting of HIV disease risk behaviors which conclude that a gay or bisexual life style is not by itself sufficient reason to order an HIV antibody test or take adverse action on the application. The NAIC believed that risky behavior, regardless of sexual preference, was the concern. This has led to relatively low HIV antibody testing limits across the board, with lower testing limit distinctions being made for entire high-risk states; thus, for example, an insurer in New Jersey is allowed to test at a lower limit than Iowa.

NAIC guidelines are given as follows:
1) General considerations:
   a) No inquiry in an application for health or life insurance coverage, or in an investigation conducted by an insurer or an insurance support organization on its behalf in connection with an application for such coverage, shall be directed toward determining the applicant's sexual orientation.
   b) Sexual orientation may not be used in the underwriting process or in the determination of insurability.
   c) Insurance support organizations shall be directed by insurers not to investigate, directly or indirectly, the sexual orientation of an applicant or beneficiary.
2) Medical life style applications, questions and underwriting standards:
   a) No question shall be used that is designed to establish the sexual orientation of the applicant.
   b) Questions relating to the applicant having, or having been diagnosed as having, AIDS or ARC are permissible if they are factual and designed to establish the existence of the condition. For example, insurers should not ask, 'Do you believe you may have . . .?' but rather, 'Do you know or have reason to know . . .?'
   c) Questions relating to medical and other factual matters intending to reveal the possible existence of a medical condition are permissible if they are not used as proxy to establish the sexual orientation of the applicant, and the applicant has been given the opportunity to provide an explanation for any affirmative answers given in the application. For example: 'Have you had chronic cough, significant weight loss, chronic fatigue, diarrhea, enlarged glands . . .?' This type of question should be related to a finite period of time preceding the completion of the application and should be specific. All of the

questions above should provide the applicant the opportunity to give a detailed explanation.

d) Questions relating to the applicant's having, or having been diagnosed as having, or having been advised to seek treatment for a STD are permissible.

e) The marital status, living arrangements, occupation, gender, medical history, the beneficiary and the zip code (or other territorial classification) of an applicant may not be used to establish, or aid in establishing, the applicant's sexual orientation.

f) For purposes of rating an applicant for health and life insurance, an insurer may impose territorial rates, but only if the rates are based on sound actuarial principles or are related to actual or reasonably anticipated experience.

g) No adverse underwriting decision shall be made because medical records or a report from an insurance support organization shows that the applicant has demonstrated AIDS-related concerns by seeking counseling from health care professionals. This subsection does not apply to an applicant seeking treatment and/or diagnosis.

h) Whenever an applicant is requested to take an AIDS-related test in connection with an application for insurance the use of such a test must be revealed to the applicant and his written consent obtained. No adverse underwriting decision shall be made on the basis of such a positive AIDS-related test unless an established test protocol has been followed.

In a majority of American states legislators and regulators have ruled on how and when HIV antibody tests can be performed. The majority of these regulations indicate that written informed consent should be given before the test is performed, sexual orientation should not be used in underwriting and that the test should follow an accepted protocol with confirmation of reactive specimens.

The British have taken a somewhat different approach. The Association of British Insurers has recommended that AIDS strategy include increased reserves, increased/variable premiums, removal of high-risk options and more stringent underwriting, including proposal form questions, life style questions, HIV blood tests and exclusion clauses for permanent health insurance and certain term assurances. The proposal form questions include the wording 'Have you ever been counseled or medically advised in connection with AIDS (HIV) or any sexually transmitted disease or had an AIDS (HIV) blood test?' These proposal questions can lead to life style questions, which ask about membership of the high- risk groups: homosexual or bisexual men, IVDUs, hemophiliacs or sexual partners of any of the preceding groups. HIV antibody testing limits across the board are frequently set according to marital status or sex, with females having a higher testing threshold than males, and married males having a higher limit than single men.[8]

The SOA has indicated that prudent companies will HIV-antibody test at least some portion of new business placed on their books. The portion tested and the testing threshold limits will vary according to the company's goals, its mix of business and the amount of HIV disease present in its own state, territory or country. HIV antibody testing both detects applicants with HIV infection and serves as a deterrent to prevent those infected from antiselecting against the company. The true value of HIV antibody testing cannot be determined because the preventative value of testing cannot be determined, except in comparison with the excess claims of companies that chose not to test.

Testing for HIV antibody should be done as a routine age and amount requirement or when sufficient medical information exists on the file to warrant a test (the so-called 'for cause' testing). This is consistent with all other test requirements for other impairments.

The simplest testing rules are based on age and amount limits. These indicate that all applicants over a specified age applying for more than a preset amount of insurance should be tested. This rule applies to all applicants regardless of sex, race or sexual orientation. The other reason for testing is 'for cause'. This implies that the applicant applied for an amount of insurance below the age and amount testing limits, and that the application contains sufficient valid information to indicate that antiselection is probable or that the applicant has a high likelihood of HIV infection. For example, since HIV disease is transmitted by sexual contact, applicants with a history of syphilis or other STDs might logically be tested.

Symptoms during the early stages of symptomatic HIV infection can be confused with those of other diseases or they may be unrelated to any medical condition; this can make it difficult to know when to test for HIV antibody. For example, the applicant's non-medical form could indicate night sweats, a recent visit to a physician due to a mouth infection or considerable weight loss. The first two could be symptoms of Hodgkin's disease and aphthous ulcers respectively; the last could simply be due to a weight loss program. Alternatively, all three could be signs of symptomatic HIV infection. In general it is appropriate to order an HIV antibody test of all applicants fulfilling certain preset medical requirements. However, many conditions associated with HIV infection may also be associated with other serious impairments. For example, if an applicant has bilateral axillary adenopathy, it will make little sense to order an HIV antibody test: even if the test is negative, the underlying cause of the enlarged nodes will still not have been clarified.

If an applicant has unequivocal medical evidence of HIV infection, an HIV antibody test may not be required to support the declinature. It is important to remember that a physician may not wish to divulge the diagnosis of AIDS preferring to give adequate hints instead. For example, the physician may indicate that his patient has lymphopenia and anergy, and is being treated with aerosolized pentamidine. The straightforward declinature 'for confidential reasons' may better protect the applicant's confidentiality in his dealings with an agent than the requirement of a further blood test.

CONCLUSION

HIV disease is a new infectious epidemic which has spread widely throughout the world. Unfortunately treatment has proven very difficult, and current therapies have been only marginally beneficial. A vaccine seems to be even further off than good therapy.

At this time we can only hope for improved treatments, support prevention and education strategies, and provide compassion and support to those infected with HIV. It is hoped by all that treatment will soon increase the life expectancy of HIV-infected individuals and that a more optimistic chapter can be written for the next edition of this publication.

REFERENCES

1 Centers for Disease Control. Pneumocystis pneumonia — Los Angeles. *MMWR* 1981; 30: 250–2.
2 World Health Organization data 1990; updated and published monthly.
3 *MMWR* 1991.
4 Lemp GF et al. Projections of AIDS morbidity and mortality in San Francisco. *JAMA* 1990; 263: 1497–1501.
5 Burke D. The diagnosis of human immunodeficiency virus infection by immunoassay using molecularly cloned and expressed virus envelope polypeptide. *Ann Immunol* 1987; 106: 671–6.
6 Centers for Disease Control. *AIDS Weekly*. December 10, 1990; 5.
7 Society of Actuaries' final report to the ACLI-HIAA CEO task force on AIDS by the ACLI-HIAA ad hoc group on AIDS data. March 1989.
8 Reynolds MA. AIDS: the British insurance response. *J Insur Med* 1990; 22 (1): 44–5.

CHAPTER 29

TROPICAL AND TRAVEL-ACQUIRED DISEASES

DAVID LAWEE

R D C BRACKENRIDGE

The problem of life insurance in tropical or subtropical climates can be studied from two aspects: firstly as it applies to inhabitants of temperate zones visiting, travelling or residing in the tropics; secondly as it applies to indigenous populations. The former, in addition to being subject to the diseases peculiar to their race, are exposed to hazards of climatic conditions and tropical diseases, which may vary in severity from area to area.

A hot, humid climate is very trying, but there is no evidence that prolonged residence in the tropics affects longevity or morbidity in those who adjust themselves to the climatic conditions and observe reasonable hygienic precautions. Persons, however, who are unable to adjust psychologically to a tropical environment are unlikely to remain well for long.

There are also other hazards of tropical residence. Living conditions may lead to the abuse of alcohol or to anxiety and depression. The homicide rate tends to be high in countries with an indigenous population that places a relatively low value on human life, and there is an increased hazard to life in areas of unstable government when political unrest leads to violence.

Twenty million residents from the industrialized countries visit developing countries annually and the number is increasing. There is also an increase in the number of visitors, immigrants and refugees from developing countries to developed countries.[1]

Travelers' diarrhea is the most common health problem associated with travel abroad. Toxinogenic *Escherichia coli* is the etiological agent in more than 80 percent of cases. However, the disease is self-limiting and has no implications for the life insurer. The remaining 20 percent of post-travel diarrhea is caused by a variety of etiological agents. Furthermore, diarrhea can be a presenting symptom of several diseases known to have significant morbidity and mortality: for example, severe and life-threatening *Plasmodium falciparum* infection.[2]

Life style morbidity (sexually transmitted diseases or STDs) and mortality (road accidents) assume a greater significance. The age-specific mortality rates for cardiovascular diseases of US travelers are similar to those at home. In contrast, death due to injury is two to three times greater in travelers aged 15–44. Both short- and long-term travelers practice casual, unprotected sex. In sub-Saharan Africa seropositivity for the human immunodeficiency virus (HIV) among Belgians is reported to be 1·1 percent. Among Danish volunteers the rate is 6·8 percent. These rates are significantly higher than those for the general European population.[3,4]

From available population statistics there is evidence that overall mortality is higher in subtropical than temperate zones, and higher still in the tropics, but the general trend is always towards improvement due to rising standards of living, better hygiene and bold public health measures, such as schemes for the eradication of malaria and helminth infections. Advances in medical science are also available to indigenous tropical populations, but the still high doctor–population ratio makes it more difficult for these advances to be used to the best advantage. Tuberculosis, for example, is still a problem among the population of some tropical countries because, owing to the terrain and the numbers involved, supervision of treatment by chemotherapy is difficult and segregation of 'open' cases sometimes impossible. The cost of modern drugs is also a drawback when vast numbers of people in an economically poor area need to be treated.

Cities and large urban areas in the tropics have a much better record of public health than remote jungle areas, and this fact should be kept in mind when evaluating the underwriting risk of applicants from temperate zones resident in the tropics. Indeed, it is now unusual for life insurance companies to charge extra premiums for such residence or travel unless a particular hazard exists in the country concerned.

As for business conducted by local life insurance companies among populations indigenous to the tropics or subtropics, the tendency has been for the bulk of insured lives to be drawn from the higher social classes, such as the professions, businessmen, merchants, teachers and civil servants, a group not truly representative of the population as a whole. As standards of living in these territories rise, more of the population moves into the higher socioeconomic classes and becomes potentially insurable. There is, therefore, an ever-changing composition in the portfolios of insurance companies doing business wholly in the developing countries.

A major disadvantage in these countries is the inadequacy of population statistics relating to births and deaths; since insured life mortality is usually also lacking, the underwriting of impaired lives poses great problems. Often judgment has to be based largely on empirical assumptions from knowledge of local conditions, standards of living, occupation, housing conditions and adequacy, or otherwise, of medical facilities. However, as time passes, statistics will accumulate and the mortality experience of the various insurance companies will become a more faithful guide to future operations of both standard and substandard business.

Although the operations of nationally based life insurance companies in developing countries are of great importance to life insurance as a whole, the subject matter of this chapter has probably more relevance to the insurance of applicants from developed countries resident in tropical or subtropical zones, and to the reinsurance of standard or substandard applicants indigenous to tropical or subtropical countries by insurance companies in North America or Europe.

PROTOZOAL DISEASES

Malaria

Malaria is still the most important disease of the tropics despite a global program of eradication launched in 1957 sponsored by the World Health Organization

(WHO). Much has been achieved. It is estimated that about 73 percent of the 1,945 million people living in originally malarious areas of the world were free of endemic disease by the end of 1974. However, some 525 million are still exposed in greater or lesser degree to the infection in Central and South America, in Asia, in the south west Pacific, and particularly in tropical Africa where only in its northern and southern zones has there been any significant improvement.

A major cause of concern is the resurgence of malaria in several tropical countries where eradication had advanced promisingly in the ten years since 1964. This applies particularly to Afghanistan, Burma, India, Nepal, Sri Lanka, Thailand and Pakistan. A similar situation is arising in the Philippines, Indonesia and Vietnam.[5]

Part of the problem of the rising wave of malaria today lies in the emergence of drug-resistant strains of *P. falciparum, P. vivax* and *P. malariae*; the vectors, too, are becoming increasingly resistant to insecticides. Resurgence of malaria in Central America and India has been attributed to intensified agriculture in these countries and the associated increase in the use of pesticides.[6] Artificially created malaria arising from inadequate water management in irrigation schemes or dam sites is also on the increase.

Nevertheless, training programs to strengthen the scientific manpower of institutions in developing countries are going ahead, and intensive research is being conducted to find alternative drugs and, hopefully, an effective vaccine. In 1982 the WHO launched its Seventh General Programme of Work for the period 1984–9.[7] It shows the year 1989 as a target for all countries with an established health-care system to reduce their annual malaria morbidity to less than 1 percent of the population, and to mount a strong attack on malaria mortality in children and pregnant women.

Imported Malaria

Malaria imported to regions where it is not endemic may appear in immigrants and travelers who have been exposed in endemic areas. Many cases are recrudescences or relapses. Primary attacks are usually seen in travelers who, because of the speed of modern air transport, may enter a non-endemic area during the incubation period of an infection; thus malaria has become an important possibility in the differential diagnosis of febrile illness.

The number of imported cases of malaria to Europe continues to rise: 7,300 cases reported in 1987 compared with 6,900 in 1986 and 6,400 in 1985. It is likely that these figures are underestimates because of acknowledged under-reporting, and variation in reporting and surveillance systems.[8] Between 1978 and 1988 an average of 1,843 cases of malaria were reported annually in the UK, with a significant and steady rise towards falciparum. In the UK the mortality rate for *P. falciparum* infection is estimated to be 1 percent even with all the advanced diagnostic and therapeutic facilities now available.[9]

Since 1984 the Centers for Disease Control (CDC) have documented a doubling in the number of US travelers acquiring *P. falciparum* infections. Of the 7 million who travel to malaria-endemic areas, only 10 percent travel to malarious areas in Africa. However, 80 percent of the *P. falciparum* infections in US travelers were acquired in Africa.[10] Similar trends have been observed in Canada,[11,12] France[13] and the Netherlands.[14]

Indigenous Malaria

Indigenous malaria occurs in some hundred countries. The global incidence of clinical malaria is estimated at 103 million cases annually, and the prevalence of infection is in the order of 264 million parasite carriers. Excluding the WHO African region, where reporting is fragmentary and irregular, there is an upward trend in the number of cases reported in the Americas and some Asian countries. Almost 83 percent of the total number of cases reported annually to the WHO are found in Afghanistan, Brazil, China, India, Mexico, Philippines, Sri Lanka, Thailand and Vietnam.

Malaria-specific mortality rates are unknown; these are mostly reported from non-endemic areas. Antimalarial services in endemic areas seem to concentrate on measuring infection, except as it relates to children and pregnant women. In Gambia up to 25 percent of childhood mortality (1–4 years) may be attributable to malaria.[15]

Airport Malaria

When favorable climatic conditions exist, infected imported mosquitoes can survive locally and cause limited outbreaks of malaria. A mini-epidemic involving five cases in 1988 in Geneva emphasizes the need for systematic spraying with insecticides of aircraft coming from malaria-endemic areas, and for physicians to be alert to the possibilities of such occurrences.[16]

The Infection

Human malaria is caused by infection with sporozoa of the genus *Plasmodium*, transmitted in nature by the bite of female *Anopheles* mosquitoes. Four species are involved: *P. vivax*, which is called vivax malaria, *P. ovale*, called ovale (tertian) malaria, *P. malariae*, called quartan malaria, and *P. falciparum*, previously called malignant tertian malaria but now known internationally as falciparum malaria.

Clinical Patterns

The clinical manifestations of malaria are caused by the invasion of the red blood cells and the progress of the asexual erythrocytic E parasites. In non-immune people *P. falciparum* differs from other species in that it causes an acute, rapidly progressive disease in which serious and diverse complications may occur; it is often fatal if unchecked. Recrudescences occur in incompletely treated infections. The other species of parasite give rise to serious and unpleasant, but more benign, illnesses in which complications are unusual. Fatality is rare and the diseases are self-limiting, but relapse is common.

Rating

When a special rate of premium is being charged, either to white residents in the tropics or to applicants native to the area, a history of mild uncomplicated attacks of malaria may be disregarded. This is because the residential extra premiums would already cover the risk. However, where tabular premium rates applicable to North American or European lives are being charged the following ratings would usually apply:

1) No complications:

| Time since attack | Rating | |
	Single attack	Recurrent attacks
Within 6 mth	+25	+50
6–12 mth	+15	+30
Thereafter	Standard	Standard

2) Spleen palpable on examination — add 50 points to above ratings.

Applicants with a history of *P. falciparum* malaria during the 12 months prior to repatriation should be charged an additional single extra premium of 3 per mil within one year of their return to a temperate climate.

Tropical Splenomegaly (TS)

TS deserves mention if only to differentiate the condition from other tropical diseases in which splenomegaly is a feature (e.g. malaria, schistosomiasis and leishmaniasis). The precise cause of TS is unknown and may differ in different populations. There does, however, seem to be a causal relationship with chronic malarial infestation; TS is found only where malaria is endemic, and its incidence is known to have decreased in those parts of India where mass malarial chemo-prophylaxis has been practiced. One hypothesis in the etiology of TS is that some people, perhaps for genetic reasons, react to malaria in an atypical manner. They form autoantibodies in response to immune complexes containing malarial antigen. These autoantibodies are in turn responsible for the very high levels of serum IgM and the proliferation of macrophages in the spleen and liver which cause the clinical syndrome.

TS has been defined as a disorder characterized by massive splenomegaly, hepatic sinusoidal infiltration, high malaria antibody titres and very high levels of serum IgM; malarial parasties are rarely found in the blood. TS leads to wasting and ill-health, and there is considerable morbidity and mortality in the untreated disease. However, long-term treatment with antimalarials has produced promising results, causing the spleen to reduce in size or disappear entirely below the left costal margin, and the level of serum IgM to reduce in parallel with the reduction in the size of the spleen.

Rating

Applications for life insurance from people with a history of TS are likely to be few in view of the socioeconomic level of the indigenous population usually affected. Those who do apply should be postponed for at least one year from commencement of treatment (preferably continuing), and the spleen should be no more than moderately enlarged. A rating of +150 would be required in the early years, reducing to +50 with duration of treatment; standard rating would apply if the applicant now resides in a temperate climate.

African Human Trypanosomiasis

There are two forms of African human trypanosomiasis, one resulting from infection by the trypanosome species *T. gambiense* and the other by *T. rhodesiense*. The vector is the tsetse fly, genus *Glossina*, *G. palpalis* being responsible for the transmission of *T. gambiense* and *G. morsitans* for the transmission of *T. rhodesiense*. Animals are known to act as reservoir hosts of *T. rhodesiense*, although there is as yet only scanty evidence of any animal reservoir of *T. gambiense*.

T. gambiense occurs throughout west and west central Africa: from Angola in the south through Zaire northwards to Cameroon and the south-east corner of Chad, and thence westwards through Nigeria to southern Senegal and Gambia. The main endemic area for *T. rhodesiense* runs from the Uganda/Tanzanian border in the north as far south as the Zambesi Valley in Zimbabwe and the Okavango Delta in Botswana. Data from the WHO suggest that the level of transmission in the old endemic countries is increasing and that the disease is spreading to neighboring regions.[17]

Clinical Features
Both forms of trypanosomiasis produce first a chancre at the site of the original tsetse bite followed by lymphadenopathy in the lymph drainage of the affected area, and later generalized enlargement of lymph nodes. There is irregular fever, and after a variable length of time there is invasion of the central nervous system (CNS) by trypanosomes producing a progressive leptomeningitis and, finally, irreversible damage to brain tissue. The most favored index of CNS involvement is the level of cerebrospinal fluid (CSF) protein, which most workers regard as abnormal if it rises higher than 25 mg/dl (0·25 g/l). Mattern[18] has shown that an appreciable increase of IgM in the CSF not only occurs early in the disease, even before increase of CSF cells and total protein, but also is virtually pathognomonic of trypanosomiasis. In the experience of Mattern, levels of 100 μg/ml are always reached in meningoencephalitic trypanosomiasis and in no other disease.

The course of *T. gambiense* infections is chronic, and the period from infection to death in untreated cases may vary from about one year to several years; in the later stages involvement of the CNS leads typically to marked lethargy and sleeping, hence the common name sleeping sickness. The course of *T. rhodesiense* infections is more acute, death in untreated cases usually occurring within a period of from three months to one year and commonly within five to nine months.

Prognosis
If trypanosomiasis is diagnosed and treated the prognosis depends entirely on the type of the disease and how far it has progressed. Whereas early *T. rhodesiense* infection is virtually 100 percent curable with suramin, the best cure rates of the early Gambian form are usually upwards of 95 percent. Soon after the onset of CNS involvement the chances of cure are still around 90 percent, but steadily decrease as the CNS lesions advance causing increasing damage to the brain. Melarsoprol has the ability to penetrate the CNS and is an important agent in preventing later relapses.

The degree of brain damage also determines the final outcome, even if a cure is achieved. The onset of damage and degeneration is relatively late, but once such degeneration has occurred it is irreversible and, even if completely cured, the individual will be left with permanent mental defects which may vary from very slight to severe.

Rating
History of infection with *T. gambiense* or *T. rhodesiense*; single attack adequately treated.

1) No CNS involvement:

Time since treatment completed	Rating	
	Early infection	Late infection
Within 6 mth	Postpone	Postpone
6–12 mth	+100	+150
2nd yr	+50	+100
3rd yr	0 to +25	+50
Thereafter	Standard	Standard

With relapse — rate as late infection above.

2) CNS involvement, no or slight mental defect:

Time since treatment completed	Rating
Within 1 yr	Postpone
2–4 yr	+200 to +50
Thereafter	+25 to 0

3) More than slight mental defect — decline.

South American Trypanosomiasis (Chagas' Disease)

In 1907 Carlos Chagas first found the causative organism, *T. cruzi*, in its anthropod vector triatomid bugs. Transmission is effected by contamination of the host's skin by the bug's feces.

Chagas' disease occurs in every country in South America and cases have been reported from Central America, Trinidad, Curaçao and Aruba. It is a particularly serious public health problem in Brazil, Argentina, Chile and Venezuela. Poor housing conditions in these countries predispose to easy breeding of the vector bugs in cracks in the mud walls and in thatched roofs.

Clinical Features

Acute Phase

The acute phase of Chagas' disease is rarely recognized even in endemic areas, particularly in young children. Older children and adults may experience only a mild febrile illness with regional lymphadenopathy corresponding to the site of entry of infection. Thereafter generalized dissemination of the infection results in fever, muscular pains, malaise and some degree of generalized lymphadenopathy and hepatosplenomegaly. The complement fixation test becomes positive after about 30 days. After the acute phase has subsided an asymptomatic period of ten to 20 years ensues.

Chronic Phase

The chronic phase is seen most often during the second to fifth decades and is characterized chiefly by cardiomyopathy which usually presents with signs of congestive heart failure. There is marked cardiomegaly, and dilatation of the atria and ventricles produces the murmurs of functional mitral and tricuspid incompetence. Arrhythmias are present in as many as two-thirds of cases, and conduction defects, such as atrioventricular block, bundle branch blocks, hemiblocks and bifascicular blocks (see pp. 459–68), are also exceedingly common. Intractable heart failure and sudden death due to cardiac arrest or ventricular fibrillation are frequent end results of Chagasic cardiomyopathy.

The other main complication of the chronic phase is dilatation of the gut, mainly the esophagus and colon, due to destruction of related autonomic ganglia by the parasite. These dilatations, known as the mega syndromes, cause much disability, although they are not a major cause of mortality.

Underwriting Considerations

The treatment of established South American trypanosomiasis is still unsatisfactory, although nifurtimox is effective in the treatment of the acute stage of the disease. The prognosis for chronic infection is therefore poor, and any applicant known to be harboring the infection would be regarded as a speculative risk for life insurance. However, the importance of Chagas' disease to the life underwriter is not the insurability of proven cases but in the elimination of the disease as a possible cause of cardiac arrhythmias, conduction defects and systolic murmurs in applicants from areas where the infection is known to be endemic. Even in areas where *T. cruzi* infections are common, other forms of cardiovascular disease are more frequently responsible for heart failure. It is essential, therefore, that before insurance is issued to applicants from endemic zones who are found to have a cardiac arrhythmia or block pattern in the ECG, additional, more sensitive tests, such as the complement fixation, should be carried out.

Leishmaniases

This is a group of clinically differing diseases caused by infection with protozoa of the genus *Leishmania*. *L. donovani* causes visceral disease, *L. tropica* cutaneous leishmaniasis (oriental sore), and *L. braziliensis* and various subspecies cause South American cutaneous, mucocutaneous and diffuse cutaneous leishmaniasis.

The vectors are female sandflies of the genera *Phlebotomus*, and the parasistes are injected into the skin when they bite, generally at dusk or during the night. The various cutaneous and mucocutaneous forms of leishmaniasis are less important than those of the visceral form in terms of longevity and will be mentioned later (*see* p. 874).

Visceral Leishmaniasis (Kala-azar)

Visceral leishmaniasis is probably the most important member of the group of leishmaniases from the insurance point of view. The incubation period tends to be long — three to six months or more — and visitors or businessmen who spend short tours of duty in an endemic area may become infected and return home unaware that they are suffering from kala-azar. Vague ill health may be attributed initially to debility following residence in a humid, tropical climate.

Endemic areas are scattered throughout the world in tropical and subtropical zones, the main ones being Bangladesh, the Ganges and Brahmaputra basins and Madras in the Indian subcontinent, northern Kenya, northern Nigeria, Guinea, Cameroon, Zaire and the Sudan in Africa, and the Mediterranean basin and islands.

Course

Except in the Sudanese type the onset of the disease is generally insidious, the main complaints being listlessness, tiredness and gradual loss of weight. Fever may appear at irregular intervals, but there are few pathognomonic signs until the classical picture emerges several months later. The most striking sign at this time is a markedly enlarged spleen without a corresponding increase in the size of the liver, together with extreme wasting, remittent fever, which may show the typical double diurnal peak, and tachycardia.

Selection of Risks

It is possible that a person who has visited an area endemic for visceral leishmaniasis and become infected may apply for life insurance before significant symptoms have appeared. However, the spleen generally becomes palpable about two months after the initial infection with *L. donovani*, and may be the only objective sign of the disease. The finding of splenomegaly in an applicant with a suggestive travel history should lead to automatic postponement of his application pending further investigations.

In the early stages of the disease the diagnosis may be elusive. Leukopenia, thrombocytopenia and a great increase in gammaglobulin would raise suspicions of leishmaniasis, but the diagnosis would be clinched by demonstrating Leishman–Donovan bodies in suitably stained tissue, such as mononuclear cells in the peripheral blood, lymph nodes or bone marrow, or from tissue obtained by percutaneous liver or splenic biopsies. Proven cases of visceral leishmaniasis can be cured by sodium stibogluconate, although several courses may be required to eradicate the infection. Tests of cure would be carried out for several months thereafter. Infection with *L. donovani* produces considerable immunity to further infection with the homologous organism and also to *L. tropica* which causes oriental sore.

Rating

Applicants with a history of visceral leishmaniasis should be postponed for six months following completion of treatment; a single extra premium of 3 per mil in the sixth to 12th month following cure, and standard rates thereafter, would be an appropriate handling of the risk, provided the spleen has become impalpable, gammaglobulins have returned to normal and anemia and thrombocytopenia have been corrected. On the other hand, visceral leishmaniasis in an immunocompromised individual is considered to be an opportunistic infection, and such an applicant should be declined insurance.[19]

Cutaneous Leishmaniasis (Oriental Sore)

In 1989 Mansour et al[20] reported 113 cases of cutaneous leishmaniasis among soldiers of the Multinational Force and Observers (MFO) who were drawn from various countries and stationed in East Sinai. A case of cutaneous leishmaniasis has also been reported in a 21-year-old woman after a sojourn in Central America.[21] More recently the US Department of Defense reported 22 cases of leishmaniasis among the more than 500,000 soldiers who returned from the Gulf war zone.[22] All of these cases were caused by *L. tropica*; 15 were cutaneous and, unexpectedly, seven were viscerotropic. In each of these seven cases *L. tropica* was recovered from the bone marrow. The natural history of this viscerotropic form is unknown. The serum indirect immunofluorescent antibody test used in this investigation is not yet commercially available. As with visceral leishmaniasis, sodium stibogluconate is the treatment of choice, and applicants can be accepted as standard risks after eradication of the infection.

Amebiasis

Amebiasis is a state of infection with *Entameba histolytica* which may or may not be symptomatic. Infection takes place by swallowing the cysts of *E. histolytica* which change to the trophozoite form in the gut. The active amebae then establish themselves in the large bowel where they may either live for long periods without causing symptoms or invade the mucosa destroying tissue and causing amebic dysentery. If *E. histolytica* gains access to the radicles of the portal vein it can be carried to the liver where it may set up active inflammation called hepatic amebiasis.

E. histolytica is distributed widely throughout the world but causes symptomatic amebiasis mainly in endemic areas of Africa, central and South East Asia and in South America where sanitation is poor and standards of living are low. Infection is disseminated by people with chronic and often symptomless disease, in which state the trophozoites encyst to be passed in the stools where they can survive for long periods and so contaminate food and drinking water. The cysts are resistant to gastric acid and the low concentration of chlorine commonly used in commercial water purification systems. On the other hand, people with active dysentery pass motile trophozoites which have only a short survival outside the body.

Sexual transmission, either through oral-anal-genital contact or by direct inoculation of traumatized tissue, and an outbreak related to the use of contaminated enemas illustrate alternative modes of transmission. The prevalence of *E. histolytica* in male homosexuals attending STD clinics in New York, San Francisco and Seattle has been variably estimated to be in the range of 25 to 30 percent.

Amebiasis in Temperate Zones

It has been estimated that up to 5 percent of the population of countries in temperate zones harbor the parasite, but if sanitation is good, clinical disease rarely occurs. The number of deaths in England and Wales certified as caused by amebiasis between 1962 and 1971 was 31; four deaths were reported in 1982. Stamm[23] estimates that about 200 new cases of clinical amebiasis occur annually. Many of the deaths in temperate zones are due to failure or delay in diagnosis because amebiasis, being relatively rare, is not given its proper place in the differential diagnosis of intestinal or hepatic disease.

On the other hand, dysenteric or hepatic forms of amebiasis are unlikely to go undetected for long among white residents in hot climates or the higher socioeconomic classes of the indigenous population, and efficient treatment nearly always results in cure.

It was amply demonstrated that the prognosis following treatment of all forms of amebiasis is excellent by the negligible mortality and late complications that occurred among substantial numbers of US, British and Dominion troops who contracted amebiasis while serving in the tropics during World War II.

Hepatic Amebiasis

Hepatic amebiasis is invariably secondary to bowel infection, although bowel symptoms may often be minimal or absent. The hepatic lesion is always suppurative and the organ always enlarged, and although the abscesses may be very small initially, they may later become confluent to form one or more large cavities. Diffuse non-suppurative amebic hepatitis does not exist as a pathological entity.[24] Amebic liver abscess can be a fatal disease; the mortality rate in adults is between 3 and 5 percent. Rupture into the pericardium or peritoneum is especially dangerous, although rupture into the lung carries a good prognosis except when complicated by empyema.

Despite the fact that an amebic liver abscess may attain a very large size with destruction of much liver tissue, successful treatment is not followed by any impairment of liver function, and scarring is minimal. In fact, almost all forms of invasive amebiasis are amenable to treatment; subsequent impairment of function is rare and complete cure is the rule.

Rating

Amebiasis, intestinal or hepatic; one or more attacks; tests of cure satisfactory:
1) Medical treatment — standard.
2) Surgical treatment (drainage etc.); sinuses healed:
   Within six months — 3–5 per mil, depending on age, for one year.
   Thereafter — standard.

Applicants living in an endemic area who are not subject to a residential debit may be rated as above except when there is a history of recurrent attacks of amebic infection, in which case a rating of +100 to +50 would usually be necessary in the three years following the last attack.

Giardiasis

Giardia lamblia is a flagellate protozoon which lives and multiplies in its trophozoite form in the duodenom and upper jejunum of man. As the trophozoites pass along the gut they encyst and, in the absence of diarrhea, pass out in stools. Cysts are capable of infecting others by the direct fecal-oral route or in drinking water or food, and the cycle is completed by the release of trophozoites in the new host. Giardiasis occurs as an endemic disease and in large water-borne outbreaks. Direct person-to-person spread (day care centers, sexually active males and chronically institutionalized patients) is frequent because of the small inoculum required (less than 100 cysts).

Clinical features

Clinical giardiasis most commonly presents with the passage of frequent, loose stools which may be bulky and often offensive. Anorexia, nausea and flatulence are usual accompaniments. Characteristically diarrhea persists for more than one week and may cause considerable loss of weight. Some patients show villous atrophy in the small intestine with functional malabsorption of fat and, possibly, folic acid. Lactase and other disaccharidases within the epithelial cells have been shown to be reduced in some patients.

Giardiasis should always be considered in people who have recently traveled abroad in tropical or subtropical regions; even in temperate zones infections of epidemic proportions have been reported, notably in Leningrad in 1972–4 where the drinking water was probably the source of the infection.[25]

Prognosis

Once the diagnosis is established symptoms due to *G. lamblia* are usually rapidly controlled by treatment with mepacrine or metronidazole, although more than one course may be required to eradicate the infection. There are no complications that would materially affect the underwriting risk, and applicants with a history of giardiasis can be accepted as standard after completion of specific treatment.

Toxoplasmosis

Although *Toxoplasma gondii* has been known since 1908, it is only since the middle of the century that the clinical features of toxoplasmosis in man have been recognized and the wide distribution of infection in the animal kingdom, including man, revealed.

T. gondii is a protozoon of warm-blooded vertebrates measuring only 5–7 μm long. It occurs in almost all domestic animals, but so far only cats and other felines have been shown capable of producing coccidian oocysts which develop after a gametogonic cycle in the intestinal mucosa of the ileum. The oocysts are passed in the feces contaminating soil and are extremely resistant, long-lived and highly infective. Man is probably infected by ingesting the oocysts in the cat's feces, particles of which adhere to its paws and fur and so become mixed with ordinary house dust. Undercooked beef and lamb are other sources of infection.

The disease in man

In man the parasite is found in two forms: (1) the proliferative stage (or pseudocyst); and (2) the cyst. After ingestion or inhalation the organism invades the lymphoid macrophages where it multiplies forming a pseudocyst; this bursts, disseminating parasites to distant organs, including the lungs, tonsils, brain, lymph nodes and placenta. If cysts develop they can lie dormant in the brain or muscles for years provoking no reaction and apparently producing no signs or symptoms. If, however, the acute proliferative stage of the disease occurs, extensive damage is caused to the brain, and in congenital transplacental spread calcifications take place which can be seen in radiographs of the skull.

Acquired toxoplasmosis in man is usually latent, and no symptoms are recognized except possibly transient fever, which usually goes unnoticed.

The next most common form is lymphadenopathy, usually accompanied by pyrexia, sore throat and a rash. Moderately enlarged, soft and usually painless nodes can be felt in most areas. The disease is relatively mild, although it may persist for weeks and is often confused with infectious mononucleosis or a lymphoma. Probably about 10 percent of patients suspected of having glandular fever but with a negative Monospot or Paul–Bunnell test are suffering instead from toxoplasmosis.

A more malignant type of the disease is meningoencephalitis; this is somtimes the terminal event in cancer, leukemia or Hodgkin's disease where the patient's resistance to an accompanying but latent infection with *T. gondii* has been lowered by irradiation or immunosuppressive drugs. In such circumstances the organism undergoes a change to the proliferative stage and multiplies rapidly in the brain and meninges causing extensive necrosis.

Ocular Toxoplasmosis

The typical lesion is a focal chorioretinitis with necrosis and scarring producing characteristic pale areas surrounded by dark rings of pigment. The organism probably remains viable in the retina for many years.

Congenital Toxoplasmosis

The fetus becomes infected from the mother who has acquired the infection in the first trimester of pregnancy. If the fetus survives, it is usually born with hydro- or microcephaly, chorioretinitis, cerebral calcification and mental deficiency. Generally the child dies soon after birth.

Distribution of Toxoplasmosis

The incidence of toxoplasmosis infection in various populations has been determined by serological or toxoplasmin skin test surveys. In some countries (e.g. Trinidad), the infection rate is as high as 90 percent in people over 20 years of age, whereas in the USA and Europe a rate in adults of up to 30 percent has been found, as shown by a positive Sabin–Feldman dye test.

Selection of Risks

Applicants for life insurance who show signs of the common overt form of the disease, namely lymphadenopathy with occasional hepatosplenomegaly, should be postponed until all signs and symptoms have subsided. A positive Sabin–Feldman dye test in a titer of 1 in 16 is usually taken to be indicative of active infection, although a rising titer three to four weeks later is even more diagnostic. A more sensitive test of active disease is the complement fixation test, which becomes positive later in the course of the illness and negative soon after infection subsides.

Rating

When clinical signs of overt toxoplasmosis have disappeared and serological tests have become negative, applicants for life insurance would generally be considered standard risks. Individuals who have had the latent form of toxoplasmosis will be unaware that they have been infected. In them a Sabin–Feldman dye test will be positive and remain so for many years, although it will not show a rising titer. In such circumstances applicants for life insurance would be acceptable as standard risks.

Tropical Sprue

See p. 605.

BACTERIAL INFECTIONS

Leprosy

Leprosy is a chronic disease of the peripheral nervous system, commonly involving the skin and less often the mucosa of the mouth and upper respiratory tract, the reticuloendothelial system, eyes, bones and testes. The disease is caused by *Mycobacterium leprae*, a micro-organism similar in appearance to *M. tuberculosis*. The latent period between infection and the appearance of definite clinical signs is between one and five years.

Most of the world's estimated 15 million cases of leprosy originate in the tropical and subtropical areas of Africa, Asia, the Near East and Latin America. Endemic areas exist in south-east Texas, Louisiana, Florida and Hawaii, but three-quarters of the known cases of leprosy in the USA were acquired in other countries. The transmission of leprosy under normal social conditions in the developed countries is virtually negligible, although the possibility may exist in special circumstances: for example, where there is overcrowding in living conditions and where standards of hygiene are low.

Clinical Types

There is a remarkable diversity of manifestations in people infected with *M. leprae*. The spectrum of clinical, immunological, bacteriological and histological features is almost continuous from the polar lepromatous type at one extreme and the polar tuberculoid type at the other, with some individuals in the middle showing features of both polar types (referred to as borderline).[26] The position of a patient on the leprosy spectrum is related to his capacity to mount a cell-mediated response (cell-mediated immunity, CMI) to *M. leprae*. Thus, people suffering from tuberculoid leprosy who carry very few leprosy bacilli have a high degree of CMI, reflected in infiltration of their lesions and the paracortical areas of their lymph nodes by lympocytes. In contrast, lepromatous patients who carry a massive load of bacilli have gross depression of CMI and few lymphocytes in their lesions and lymph nodes.

Lepromatous Leprosy

Although patients with lepromatous leprosy have a CMI deficiency, they are capable of producing high titers of circulating antimycobacterial antibodies. When the patients are treated using chemotherapy large numbers of mycobacteria are killed; they act as antigenic material which, together with high titers of anti-mycobacterial antibodies, forms circulating immune complexes responsible for the acute leprosy reaction of *erythema nodosum leprosum*. Deposition of immune complexes in and around blood vessels is responsible for severe systemic manifestations such as arthritis, iridocyclitis, orchitis, neuritis, lymphadenopathy and nephritis. Since patients with lepromatous leprosy have a deficient cell-mediated response they are liable to develop other diseases. They have a high incidence of pyelonephritis, glomerulonephritis and urinary tract infections, and in the USA renal amyloid disease contributed to as many as 38 percent of deaths in one series.[27] Lepromatous leprosy is progressive and the response to treatment is variable. Late relapse is often seen either because patients stop their treatment early or because of the development of dapsone resistance, which may occur two to 24 years or more after starting treatment. However, it is hoped that multidrug therapy using dapsone, rifampicin and either clofazimine or prothionamide will help to overcome the problem of drug resistance and shorten the duration of treatment.

Tuberculoid Leprosy

The only tissues involved are nerves and skin. In patients with a very high degree of immunity the infection may not proceed further and pure neural tuberculoid leprosy results; if resistance is inadequate to anchor the infection within nerves, one or two skin lesions develop. Most commonly the patient will present with dermal as well as neural symptoms. In untreated cases peripheral nerves become thickened, and there will be associated anesthesia or muscle wasting depending on the type of nerve involved; serious deformity may eventually result.

The diagnosis of tuberculoid leprosy requires a high index of suspicion when dealing with people from endemic areas. The combination of neuropathy and non-healing ulcerations, particularly of an extremity, should suggest the diagnosis. However, the definitive diagnosis requires the demonstration of bacilli in the tissues.

Some non-lepromatous lesions are self-limiting, but usually tuberculoid and intermediate forms require treatment for about five years or until all signs of activity have ceased; borderline patients are treated for five to 15 years depending on their position in the spectrum. The prognosis of tuberculoid leprosy treated efficiently at an early stage is excellent, especially with multidrug therapy.

Selection of Risks

Leprosy as an underwriting impairment is likely to be encountered more often in the future because of the rapid social emancipation of hitherto poorer populations from which the majority of cases of leprosy spring. Generally speaking, life insurance should be limited to those with the tuberculoid type of leprosy, although some borderline or intermediate types may be acceptable. In neural cases there should be no more than minimal loss of function, either motor or sensory. The longer the infection has been inactive and the milder and more localized the disease, the better the risk.

Rating

1) Lepromatous leprosy, best cases:

Time since remission	Rating
Within 2 yr	Postpone
3rd and 4th yr	+150 to +100
5th yr	+75
Thereafter	+50 to 0

2) Tuberculoid or borderline leprosy, cured, inactive or non-progressive:

Time since diagnosis or commencement of treatment	Rating	
	Mild, localized lesions	More extensive neural or disseminated cutaneous lesions
Within 2 yr	+100	+150
3rd yr	+50	+100
4th yr	Standard	+75
5th yr		+50 to 0

Household contact under medical supervision — standard.

Brucellosis

Brucellosis is the term used to describe the reaction of the human host to the various infections caused by organisms of the genus *Brucella*. These reach man almost exclusively from domestic animals. *B. melitensis* infects goats and sheep. It is found in most tropical and subtropical countries as well as in some temperate zones of Europe and the USA. *B. abortus* infects cattle. It is widespread throughout the world. It is the only form of brucellosis endemic in the British Isles. *B. suis* infects pigs or hogs. It persists in some countries of the European mainland, the USA and the Far East.

Human brucellosis is contracted by direct contact with secretions and excretions, and by ingesting milk or milk products containing viable *Brucella*. The disease is rarely transmitted from person to person. Brucellosis is most prevalent in rural areas and is an occupational disease among veterinary surgeons, farmers, meat packers and livestock producers. Holidaymakers and other travelers may contract brucellosis by drinking infected milk.

The disease is characterized by an acute febrile stage with few localizing signs. This is followed by a chronic stage with more prolonged fever and symptoms of weakness, perspiration and vague (or sometimes agonizing) pain in the back and hips.

Prognosis
Antibiotic treatment early in the acute phase of the infection is generally effective, but becomes decreasingly successful as the disease passes into the chronic stage. Nevertheless the prognosis for life in brucellosis is good, and although chronic infection may result in a state of ill health for several years, it is rarely fatal. Consequently applicants for life insurance with a history of brucellosis can generally be accepted as standard risks.

HEAT HYPERPYREXIA; HEAT EXHAUSTION

Heat hyperpyrexia is caused by a disturbance of the heat regulating mechanism, the predisposing factors being a high humidity coupled with a high temperature, long residence in the tropics, the coexistence of other bodily infirmities such as heart, kidney or lung disease, alcoholism and old age. The dark-skinned races are less susceptible than the white ones, except for white women, who are rarely affected.

The fatality rate from heat hyperpyrexia is high. Those who survive a severe attack with coma may be permanently disabled with mental changes resembling those occurring in senility. Epilepsy may also occur, with attacks persisting for some time after the coma, and there is a distinct danger of suicide in a small percentage of survivors. Although dementia may complicate the more severe cases, lesser degrees of cerebral disturbance, such as loss of memory, recurrent headaches and neurasthenic symptoms, are generally more common.

Heat exhaustion, unlike heat hyperpyrexia, has a quite different etiology, being dependent on sodium depletion. The condition is generally benign and responds well to treatment, and convalescence is usually short and complete.

Rating
1) Heat hyperpyrexia with coma.
No epilepsy and no significant mental residuals:

Time since successful treatment	Rating
Within 6 mth	Postpone
6–12 mth	+50
Thereafter	Standard

With epilepsy — rate as epilepsy (*see* pp. 739–40).

With mental disorder (no dementia) — add rating for neurosis (*see* p. 797) or psychosis (*see* p. 789) as appropriate.

With dementia:

Within one year — postpone.

Thereafter

Severe, unemployable — decline.

Mild/moderate, employed — +100.

2) Heat exhaustion, after recovery — standard.

CESTODE INFECTIONS

Hydatid Disease

Hydatid disease is caused by the larval stage of the tapeworm *Echinococcus granulosus* which normally inhabits the intestines of dogs, wolves and jackals. The intermediate hosts are usually sheep, cattle, camels and dogs. Man is also an intermediate host and develops the disease by swallowing food or water contaminated with infected canine feces, or simply from close association with an infected dog. Hydatid disease is common in sheep-breeding countries such as Australia, New Zealand, Argentina and South Africa, and is endemic in Greece, Cyprus and other eastern Mediterranean countries.

After ingestion of the eggs by man, the embryos hatch and metastasize mainly to the liver, usually its right side, where they develop into hydatid cysts. Less frequently cysts develop in the lungs, muscles, bones, kidneys and brain. The natural history of hydatid disease depends on the site of the cyst, and the initial symptoms may be due either to local pressure effects or to rupture of the cyst into the peritoneum, bronchus or a vein.

In general, hydatid disease is a serious condition which is particularly dangerous to life when cysts occur in bone, brain or the spinal canal. The prognosis is best with hydatid cysts of the liver; in this site small to moderate-sized cysts of up to 7 cm in diameter would usually be left alone if they were causing no symptoms, because in the course of time they will calcify and degenerate resulting in spontaneous cure. On the other hand, the accepted treatment of hydatid cyst of the lung is removal along with the segment or lobe in which it is situated.

Selection of Risks

Applicants suspected of having hydatid disease because of occupation, residential or travel history, and with signs on medical examination that are consistent with the disease (e.g. bulging in the right hypochrondrium, a cystic swelling in the abdomen or a spherical shadow in a chest radiograph) should be postponed pending investigations, particularly ultrasound and computed tomography. Serological tests of diagnosis are useful but tend to be fallible because of poor specificity or sensitivity, or because they produce positive reactions too long after a cyst has died or been removed surgically. However, some workers claim advantage of specificity coupled with an absence of false positive reactions for the immunoelectrophoresis test of Capron using whole hydatid cyst fluid as antigen.[28]

Rating

Applicants proved to be harboring viable hydatid cysts should be declined. On the other hand, a small or moderate-sized hydatid cyst of the liver that is known to have been present and symptomless for several years and showing well-marked calcification on X-ray can be regarded as safe and an insignificant underwriting risk. However, a similar cyst in the lung would still be a risk merely because it is a foreign body producing reactive fibrosis and distortion of surrounding bronchi. A rating similar to that for localized bronchiectasis would be appropriate, *see* pp. 491–2.

Applicants who have had a viable hydatid removed surgically or marsupialized should be postponed for six months; thereafter, if no further cysts have been discovered, they may be rated as follows:

Time since application	Rating
6th–12th mth	+100
2nd yr	+50
Thereafter	Standard

If surgery is contraindicated, treatment with oral mebendazole or albendazole for up to 11 months may produce total regression. Rate as for surgery.

Cysticercosis

Although not strictly a tropical disease, cysticercosis is found mostly in people who have been resident in hot climates, particularly India. The incidence is also high in eastern Europe and in Central and South America, but low in western Europe. Cysticercosis in humans is caused by the accidental ingestion of the larval stage of a tapeworm, usually *Taenia solium*. The adult tapeworm is found only in man, and the cysticercoid or larval stage normally in the pig. Man is infected by eating undercooked pork containing cysticerci, by ingesting food or drink contaminated by human feces containing ova, or by autoinfection by the anal–oral route if he is himself the host of the tapeworm. He may also be autoinfected during violent vomiting if the gravid segments are returned to the stomach by reverse peristalsis; the human cysticercoid stage will then develop. The larvae penetrate the intestinal wall and are carried in the bloodstream all over the body, where the cysts may be identified clinically by palpation of the reactive nodules in the subcutaneous tissues or muscles, or by radiography of skeletal muscle or the brain after they calcify.

The important feature about cysticercosis is the liability of those affected to develop cerebral symptoms, usually epilepsy, and occasionally increasing intracranial pressure, which may require decompression. As the interval between primary infection and the appearance of symptoms may vary from a few weeks to several years, there is no period during the disease that can be said to be more dangerous than another. Generally speaking, however, the prognosis improves as the symptom-free period increases, especially after three years, and in those who have had fits the frequency of attacks tends to diminish after about ten years.

Dixon and Hargreaves[29] analyzed the fate of 284 cases of cysticercosis who were followed up to 1944, 99 of whom had developed the disease sometime in the previous 52 years. The results are shown in Table 29.1.

Table 29.1. Fate of 284 cases of cysticercosis.

	Number of cases
Alive	
Worse	20
Unchanged	92
Improving	81
Symptom-free (3 years or more)	33
Never any symptoms	15
Total	241
Dead	
Fits within 3 years of death	32
Fits ceased	7
Never any symptoms	4
Total	43
Causes of death	
Cysticercosis	22
After operation	4
Other causes	17
Total	43

A follow-up study of 450 cases of cysticercosis in British military personnel was made in 1961 by Dixon and Lipscomb.[30] Of these, 98 percent contracted the disease in India, and a history of intestinal teniasis was found to be eight times higher in those cases than in other troops from the area, thus underlining the danger of autoinfection.

The chief symptom was epilepsy, which occurred in 92 percent; 8·7 percent had mental changes and 6 percent suffered from intracranial hypertension. A few (3 percent) were entirely free from symptoms. Of the 450 cases, most of whom had been infected for 12 years or longer, 42 had died, but many had remained symptom-free for many years.

Selection of Risks
Obviously there is considerable morbidity and mortality associated with cysticercosis and it is essential that applicants with a history of the disease are

carefully selected. The following features are known to be associated with increased mortality:

1) Evidence of heavy infection, judged by the number of calcified cysts revealed by radiography.
2) Continuing epilepsy despite treatment.
3) A history of increased intracranial pressure within the previous five years.
4) A short interval between presumed infection and onset of symptoms (usually implying a massive initial infection).
5) Non-resectable neural lesions. These are treated with praziquantel, and to avoid associated drug reactions (cerebral edema, seizures and anaphylactic reactions) patients with neurocysticercosis are pre-medicated with corticosteroids.

A long interval between presumed infection and application for insurance, preferably longer than ten years, would indicate a favorable prognosis; this would be further enhanced if there had been no symptoms of any kind, as might be the case if the diagnosis were made accidentally in the course of radiographic investigation of some unrelated condition. The prognosis would also tend to be more favorable if epileptic fits had become less frequent and severe, or had ceased altogether three years or more prior to application.

Rating
Calcified cysticerci found accidentally on radiography; no history of symptoms, initial infection judged to be:

Time since initial infection	Rating
Less than 10 yr	+50 to +30
10 yr or longer	Standard

Palpable subcutaneous cysts, no radiological calcification, no history of symptoms — +100 to +75.
Epileptic fits — rate as epilepsy (*see* pp. 739–40) and add 25–50 points.

TREMATODE INFECTIONS

Schistosomiasis: Bilharziasis

Schistosomiasis is probably responsible for more severe disability and more deaths than any other form of helminthiasis, and its control is a problem even more intractable than that of malaria itself. The urinary form of the disease is known to have existed in Egypt 3,000 years ago: the characteristic ova have been found in ancient mummies.

Most major endemic infectious diseases in tropical countries have shown a proportional decrease in prevalence with the increase in their economic growth. Schistosomiasis is an exception: in many other areas economic development consequent on the provision of water resources, either for irrigation or for hydroelectricity, has caused an increase in the number of water snails, the intermediate hosts of the parasites. The result has been that the disease has not only become more prevalent in much of the tropical world but its severity, which is related to the parasite density in the individual, has also increased owing to more intense transmission.

The three main forms of schistosomiasis are caused by *Schistosoma hematobium*, *S. mansoni* and *S. japonicum* respectively. Both *S. hematobium* and *S. mansoni* are widely distributed throughout the continent of Africa, giving rise to systemic disease in humans which, if untreated, can produce serious and fatal complications several years after the initial infection. Schistosomiasis is therefore a disease requiring careful consideration by life insurance companies transacting business in endemic areas.

Geographic Distribution

The geographic distribution of *S. hematobium* is along the whole of the north African coast and Israel, extending through Egypt, the Sudan, Ethiopia and down the east coast to South Africa. It also occurs in west Africa from Senegal to Nigeria.

S. mansoni coexists with *S. hematobium* in some parts of Egypt, the Sudan and east and west Africa, and extends down the Congo basin. It is also found alone in the West Indies and the northern part of South America, from Venezuela through Guyana to the Amazon valley and the north coast of Brazil.

S. japonicum is distributed in eastern Asia, in parts of Japan, in the valley of the Yangste River, and can be traced in central and southern China, parts of the Philippine Islands, Singapore and the Shan states of north-east Burma.

Life Cycle

The schistosome worm, which varies from 7 to 20 mm in length, inhabits the blood vessels of man: *S. mansoni* and *S. japonicum* in the mesenteric and intestinal veins, *S. hematobium* in the pelvic and vesical venous plexuses. The eggs, which are characteristic for each species, are laid in the blood vessels and find their way to the bowel wall and feces, and to the bladder wall and urine respectively. The discharged eggs can develop only in fresh water, where they hatch to produce free-swimming miracidia which then enter the body of the appropriate intermediate host, a freshwater snail. After a further stage of development in the snail lasting several weeks, fork-tailed larvae or cercariae escape into the water in large numbers. On contact with human skin larvae penetrate it and make their way to the venous plexuses of the portal and pelvic systems where they mature into adult worms, so completing the life cycle.

It will be evident, therefore, that schistosomiasis is a disease encouraged by insanitary habits of populations in areas where there is a low standard of public health. In South Africa town dwellers are unlikely to become infected; in the country districts the infection is generally low but increases as one travels northwards until in Zimbabwe and central Africa as much as 100 percent of the indigenous population living in villages may suffer from the disease. It is almost impossible for them to escape, since they wash in, launder in or walk through infected water almost daily.

Morbidity and Mortality

Acute symptoms of the primary invasion of schistosome cercariae may come on within minutes of their penetration, and pruritus on emerging from the water is not unusual. Later, fever malaise and allergic skin rashes may appear after an incubation period of four to seven weeks, but only if the infection was heavy. Thereafter symptoms depend on the type of schistosomiasis. With *S. hematobium* hematuria is the most constant symptom and often the only one, but secondary urinary tract infection with pyogenic organisms may supervene at any time. The later complications are due to fibrous strictures of the urinary tract, particularly of the ureters, leading to progressive hydronephrosis, pyelonephritis, secondary hypertension and ultimately uremia (*see* pp. 550–2), but these may not occur until a person has been infected for several years and usually heavily so.

When infection is with *S. mansoni* and *S. japonicum*, symptoms of vague abdominal pain and mild diarrhea may occur, associated occasionally with blood in the stool or tenesmus. Later there may be liver involvement leading eventually to cirrhosis with hepatosplenomegaly. This is particularly the case in *S. japonicum* infection and is usually fatal. Pulmonary schistosomiasis produces respiratory symptoms with the development of pulmonary hypertension and eventual right heart failure.

The longevity of the schistosomal worm in the human host is well documented and may certainly be over 20 years. During these years the patient may be substantially free of symptoms and physical signs. A reminder that latent schistosomiasis is more than a theoretical consideration is given by Wood *et al*[31] who reported the case of a US citizen who developed paraplegia and skin lesions due to *S. mansoni* some seven years after his last possible exposure to infection.

Prognosis

In general, schistosomal infection in residents of temperate zones visiting, or living temporarily in, endemic areas is usually light and is often due to accidental exposure on one or two occasions. Between 1975 and 1990 there have been seven documented outbreaks of schistosomiasis in European and US tourists visiting endemic areas of Africa.[32] In these circumstances the disease is usually mild and, provided it is efficiently treated and followed up, the risk of late complications is negligible. In fact the clinical outcome of praziquantel-treated schistosomiasis is usually excellent.

Individuals of middle and lower socioeconomic groups who are indigenous to endemic zones run the highest risk of heavy schistosomal infection, especially if they live in rural areas, and a high incidence of late complications may be anticipated among them.

Selection of Risks

Schistosomiasis is so chronic and insidious that its detection during the routine clinical examination for life insurance may be impossible. Even when there is a history of schistosomiasis treated by one of the recognized methods, there can be no guarantee that the infection has been eradicated simply because symptoms are absent. A person can only be regarded as cured when no viable ova are found over a period of six to eight months.

One or more of the following features elicited during the medical examination of an exposed applicant should call for further screening tests to exclude schistosomal infection:

1) A history of treated schistosomiasis, but no record of follow-up tests of cure.
2) A history of hematuria, particularly if terminal, or dysuria, neither of which has been investigated.
3) Persistent proteinuria.
4) A history of uninvestigated abdominal discomfort or tenesmus with the passage of blood in the stools.
5) Enlargement either of the liver alone or both the liver and spleen.

Unfortunately the expense factor tends to limit the scope of further pathological examinations when life insurance business is being conducted among an indigenous population of the tropics, except in cases where the sum insured is large. Any tests requested must be carefully chosen to give the maximum amount of information.

Screening Tests for Schistosomiasis
The following direct tests are recommended for screening applicants for life insurance:

1) A terminal specimen of urine passed first thing on rising in the morning is slowly centrifuged for a few minutes and the sediment examined for living schistosomal ova. Most positive cases can be detected by this method. If, however, ova are scanty, the chances of obtaining a positive result will be increased by examining a pooled collection of terminal urines passed during a 24-hour period.
2) Through a proctoscope small snippets of rectal mucosa are taken with a cutting curette and examined unstained under the low power lens of the microscope. This is a reliable test which has the advantage that ova of either *S. hematobium* or *S. mansoni*, or both, can be demonstrated.

Unfortunately the various indirect immunodiagnostic tests that have been developed all suffer from the same defects in that they often produce non-specific cross-reactions with other helminths, and especially with other species of schistosomes from birds and animals. Thus false positive results are common, and even a negative result by no means excludes a diagnosis of schistosomiasis. Also, the eosinophil count is unhelpful: although eosinophilia is common early in the infection, it often disappears in the later stages.

Rating
Non-residents who are now living outside an endemic area may be accepted as standard six months after treatment with praziquantel if evidence of cure is established. When there is a history of more than one attack or heavy infection, rate as for 'residents' below.

Residents in endemic areas; no current symptoms; well-treated with adequate follow-up tests of cure; single attack:

Time since successful treatment	Rating
Within 6 mth	Postpone
6–24 mth	3 per mil for 2 yr
Thereafter	Standard

NEMATODE INFECTIONS

Ankylostomiasis (Hookworm Disease)

Human ankylostomiasis is caused by two species of nematodes. *Ankylostoma duodenale* and *Necator americanus*, both species occurring in tropical and subtropical regions where there is heavy rainfall and bad sanitation. It causes a vast amount of morbidity among the poorer sections of indigenous populations, resulting in lower working efficiency and consequent economic loss. There is also significant mortality due to ankylostomiasis in less civilized communities because the disease may go unrecognized until it is too late for any treatment to be effective. In temperate countries it can occur among workers in mines and tunnels, where the atmosphere is hot and humid and standards of sanitation are poor. It is estimated that one-fifth of the population of the world suffers from ankylostomal infection of greater or lesser degree.

For the life cycle to be continued hookworm eggs must gain access to the soil, and this is possible only if it is contaminated by the feces of infected people. After incubation, larvae hatch out from the eggs and may remain viable for three to four months in warm, damp soil or fecal matter. They are infective and enter the human body by penetrating the unbroken skin, and therefore the risk of infection is greatest in people walking barefoot. The larvae are carried in the venous blood to the lungs and make their way up to the trachea and larynx into the esophagus, and thence to the stomach and small intestine where they mature. They attach themselves to the mucosa and feed on blood from the host; the resulting anemia is slight and well compensated in normally nourished people who have only a mild infection, but it may become profound and fatal in heavily infected, undernourished individuals.

Studies using ^{51}Cr-labelled red blood cells have demonstrated that the amount of blood lost in *N. americanus* infection is about 0·05 ml per day due to each worm; in *A. duodenale* infection the blood loss is somewhat greater. Thus a worm load of about one hundred ankylostomes seldom produces anemia, but worm loads of 2–3 thousand may cause a daily blood loss of 250 ml. In addition to the loss of red cells, albumin is also lost in the gut; in chronic infections this leads to hypoalbuminemia and edema.

Rating

Ankylostomiasis would not usually present a significant underwriting problem among white residents in the tropics or people native to the area who enjoy a good standard of living, and who would normally constitute the insuring class of the community. Their standard of medical care is generally good, and it is likely that the disease would be detected and treated early if there were suspicious symptoms. Ankylostomal infection can be easily and quickly eradicated from the body. Applicants suspected of having ankylostomiasis because of anemia may either be postponed or rated according to the level of their hemoglobin (*see* p. 650).

Toxocariasis

Toxocariasis is an infection in man with larvae of *Toxocara canis* or *T. cati* which hatch from swallowed toxocaral eggs in the intestine and migrate via the portal blood to the liver, lungs and other tissues of the body, where they cause a granulomatous reaction.

Infection in dogs with the adult worm is cosmopolitan: a prevalence rate of 82 percent has been reported in Calcutta, 37·5 percent in Nigeria and 10–20 percent in south-east England. There is less information about the prevalence of feline infection, but Woodruff[33] found approximately 20 percent of cats in south-east England infected with *T. cati*.

In view of the high prevalence of infection with adult worms in dogs and cats it is likely that considerable numbers of humans become infected, and evidence points to toxocariasis being responsible for much morbidity and pathology hitherto regarded as being idiopathic or of undetermined origin.[33] Confirmation of human infection is difficult because the larvae, being so small, often escape detection in biopsied tissue, and other tests are either non-specific or give false positive results by cross-reaction with other nematodes.

In proven cases of toxocariasis it is the eye which is mainly affected. A granuloma of the retina, usually unilateral, can result in complete loss of or greatly impaired vision, especially when it involves the macula. Granulomas in the liver cause a mild hepatitis and slight hepatic enlargement. Granulomas in the cerebral cortex can give rise to epilepsy.

Rating

Treatment with diethylcarbamazine is usually successful in eradicating human infection, but pre-existing damage to the retina remains. Applicants with a history of toxocariasis will almost certainly have been treated and, if there are no residual impairments, can be accepted as standard risks for life insurance. Continuing epilepsy due to residual cortical scarring should be rated as such (*see* pp. 739–40).

Filariasis

Filariasis is a group of disorders produced by infection with nematodes of the supergenus *Filaroidea*. After being inoculated by the bite of the intermediate host, a blood-sucking insect, the worm invades subcutaneous tissues and lymphatics of man producing reactions ranging from acute inflammation to chronic scarring. Each type of filarial worm produces its own distinctive clinical picture. The term filariasis is commonly used to describe the diseases produced by *Wuchereria bancrofti* or *Brugia malayi*, both of which are responsible for elephantiasis. The other chief forms of filariasis are loiasis and onchocerciasis.

Bancroftian Filariasis

W. bancrofti is the most widely distributed of the human filarial parasites and occurs in many regions throughout the tropics and subtropics. It is found between 30°N and 30°S in the western hemisphere and 41°N and 28°S in the eastern hemisphere. It is endemic in all warm, damp regions of Africa, southern Asia and the tropical Americas. Very high prevalence rates have been reported from many south Pacific islands, and during World War II thousands of US troops had to be repatriated because of filariasis.

Life Cycle

The adult worms live coiled up in the lymphatics, the male being 35 mm and the female 80–100 mm long. The gravid female releases microfilariae into the lymphatics; from there they migrate to the peripheral blood where they appear in most abundance between 21.00 and 02.00 hours to await ingestion by a mosquito.

The principal vector is *Culex fatigans*, but anopheline mosquitoes in certain parts of Africa and aëdes mosquitoes in Brazil and the Pacific islands also carry the disease. On being taken up in the blood meals of the vector mosquito the microfilariae develop into larvae, which in turn are transmitted to man when he is bitten. The adult worms, which develop from the larvae, then take about one year to reach full maturity.

Clinical Manifestations

Most indigenous populations of endemic areas have evolved a symbiosis with the parasite and a considerable percentage of inhabitants have microfilariae circulating in their blood, often in large numbers, yet with no symptoms or apparent ill-effects. In people from non-endemic areas the first symptoms (usually lymphangitis and lymphadenopathy of the inguinal, femoral, axillary or epitrochlear nodes) arise between five and 18 months after the original infection. Recurrent lymphangitis leads to puffiness and, one or two years later, to edema of the scrotum, penis or limbs. A hydrocele is a common finding if the para-aortic lymph nodes are involved. Classical elephantiasis is a relatively unusual complication and its development is probably aggravated by secondary infection.

Diagnosis

Precise, early diagnosis of *W. bancrofti* infection is difficult since microfilariae are not readily found in the blood until the second or third year of infection. However, a confident presumptive diagnosis can usually be made from the history of exposure in an endemic area, of recurrent attacks of lymphangitis associated with fever and lymphedema, and of eosinophilia.

Prognosis

Fortunately treatment with diethylcarbamazine during the early stages of bancroftian filariasis can be relied upon to cure the infection completely, and later development of elephantiasis is unlikely. In those who have limited exposure to infection the prognosis is further enhanced if they leave the endemic area permanently. Elephantiasis, once established, does not improve with the death of the worms but tends to progress, although very slowly. If the condition becomes disabling, plastic surgery on the genitals and limbs may have to be undertaken.

Rating

History of filariasis; adequate treatment; no significant residuals:
   Single attack — standard.
   More than one attack:
      Repatriated to non-endemic area — standard.
      Still domiciled in endemic area — +50.

Elephantiasis:
   Moderate — add 50 points.
   Severe — add 100 points.

Brugian Filariasis

Infection with *B. malayi* closely resembles that with *W. bancrofti* and need not
be described separately. The disease is common in Malaysia, southern India, Sri
Lanka and Indonesia, and is transmitted by mosquitoes of the genera *Culex*,
Anopheles and *Mansonioides*. The incubation period is somewhat shorter and
the axillary lymph nodes more frequently affected than in bancroftian filariasis.

Rating

The underwriting handling is similar to that for the bancroftian infection (*see
above*).

Other Filariasis Forms

Other forms of filariasis, such as loiasis due to *Loa loa* and onchocerciasis due to
Onchocerca volvulus, have an underwriting significance similar to bancroftian
filariasis (*see above*).

Loiasis

This nematode infection is found only in Africa, the most highly endemic areas
being Cameroon, Zaire, south-western Sudan and parts of Uganda. It is characterized by recurrent swellings of the subcutaneous tissue (Calabar swellings) and
the occasional appearance of the adult worm beneath the skin and, less commonly, the conjunctiva. The adult female measures 5–7 cm in length and the
male 3 cm.

Onchocerciasis

The distribution of this infection is the tropical regions of Mexico, Guatemala
and Colombia, and Africa between latitudes 15°N and 13°S. It is also found in
the south-east of the Arabian peninsula and Yemen. The most important
manifestation of the disease is blindness, which may be caused in various ways:
the host's reaction to dead microfilariae in the conjunctiva can produce keratitis
and, in the anterior chamber, chronic iridocyclitis and glaucoma; in the posterior chamber chorioretinitis and optic atrophy may occur. It is estimated that
onchocerciasis is responsible for more than a quarter of a million cases of
blindness in the world.

REFERENCES

1 Steffen R. Travel medicine: prevention based on epidemiological data. *Trans Roy Soc Trop Med Hyg* 1991; 85: 156–62.
2 Kozarsky P, Lobell HO, Steffen R. Travel medicine 1991: new frontiers (editorial). *Ann Int Med* 1991; 115 (7): 574–5.
3 Von Reyn CF, Mann JM, Chin J. International travel and HIV infection. *Bulletin of the World Health Organization, 1990*; 68: 251–9.
4 Ellis EJ. HIV infection and foreign travel [C]. *Brit Med J* 1990; 301: 984–5.
5 Bruce-Chwatt LJ. Resurgence of malaria and its control. *J Trop Med Hyg* 1974; 77: 4.
6 Chapin G, Wasserstrom R. Agricultural production and malaria resurgence in Central America and India. *Nature* 1981; 293: 181.
7 *Seventh General Programme of Work for the Period 1984–1989*. Geneva: World Health Organization, 1983.
8 Report of a meeting of European representatives responsible for malaria surveillance. First International Travel Medicine Meeting, Zurich, April 1988.
9 Bradley DJ. Current trends in malaria in Britain. *J Roy Soc Med* 1989; 82 suppl 17: 8–13.
10 Lackritz EM, Lobel HO, Haowell BJ et al. Imported *Plasmodium falciparum* malaria in American travelers to Africa: implications for prevention strategies. *JAMA* 1991; 265 (3): 383–5.
11 Yechouron A, Nguyen C, MacLean JD, Keystone J. The changing pattern of imported malaria. *Canada Weekly Diseases Report* 1988; 14: 133–6.
12 Wittes RC, Constantinidis P, MacLean JD et al. Recent Canadian deaths from malaria acquired in Africa. *Canada Weekly Diseases Report* 1989; 15: 199–204.
13 Raccurt CP, Dumestre-Toulet V, Abraham E et al. Failure of falciparum prophylaxis by mefloquine in travelers from West Africa. *Am J Trop Med Hyg* 1991; 45 (3): 319–24.
14 Wetsteyn JCFM, DeGeus A. Chloroquine-resistant falciparum malaria imported into the Netherlands. *Bulletin of the World Health Organization* 1985; 63 (1): 101–8.
15 Anonymous. World malaria situation 1988. Part I. Overview. *Weekly Epidemiological Record* 1990; 65: 189–96.
16 Anonymous. Airport malaria. A report from the Department of Medicine, Cantonal University Hospital, Geneva. *Weekly Epidemiological Record* 1990; 65: 224–5.
17 Anonymous. Trypanosomiasis: situation in the OCEAC member states. *Weekly Epidemiological Record* 1990; 50: 388–91.
18 Mattern P. Techniques et intérèt épidémiologique du diagnostic de la trypanosomiase humaine Africaine par la recherche de la beta-macroglobuline dans le sang et dans le LC-R. *Ann Inst Pasteur* 1964; 107: 415.
19 Salas A, Riera, M, Udina M et al. Visceral leishmaniasis: another HIV-associated opportunistic infection? Report of eight cases and review of the literature. *AIDS* 1991; 5 (2): 201–7.
20 Mansour NS, Youssef FG, Mohareb EW et al. Cutaneous leishmaniasis in the peace-keeping force in East Sinai. *J. Egyp Soc Parasitol* 1989; 19 (2): 725–32.
21 Anonymous. Case records of the Massachusetts General Hospital. Weekly clinicopathological exercises. *N Engl J Med* 1991; 324 (7): 476–85.
22 Leishmaniasis in military personnel returning from the Persian Gulf. *MMWR* Nov 13, 1991. Centers for Disease Control, Atlanta, GA.
23 Stamm WP. Amoebiasis in England and Wales. *Br Med J* 1975; 2: 452.
24 Lamont NMcE, Pooler NR. Hepatic amoebiasis: a study of 250 cases. *Quart J Med* 1958; 27: 389.
25 Brodsky RE, Spencer HC jr, Schultz MG. Giardiasis in American travelers to the Soviet Union. *J Infect Dis* 1974; 130: 319.
26 Ridley DS, Jopling WH. Classification of leprosy according to immunity. A five group system. *International Journal of Leprosy and other Mycobacterial Diseases* 1966; 34: 255–73.
27 Powell CS, Swan LL. Leprosy: pathologic changes observed in 50 consecutive necropsies. *Am J Pathol* 1955; 31: 1131.
28 Schantz PM. Testing for hydatid disease. *Lancet* 1976; 2: 1022.

29 Dixon HBF, Hargreaves WH. Cysticercosis (*Taenia solium*): further ten years clinical study covering 284 cases. *Quart J Med* 1944; 13: 147.
30 Dixon HBF, Lipscomb FM. *MRC Report on Cysticercosis*. London: HMSO, 1961.
31 Wood MG, Srolovitz H, Schetman D. Schistosomiasis: paraplegia and ectopic skin lesions as admission symptoms. *Arch Dermatol* 1976; 112: 690.
32 Anonymous. Acute schistosomiasis in travelers returning from Africa. *Weekly Epidemiological Record* 1990; 65: 194–5.
33 Woodruff AW. Toxocariasis. *Br Med J* 1970; 3: 663.

CHAPTER 30

DRUG ABUSE, ALCOHOL AND TOBACCO

ROGER H BUTZ
W JOHN ELDER

Substance abuse is the term currently popular to describe excessive, habitual or addictive use of psychoactive drugs. Such drugs include hallucinogens, central nervous system stimulants, central nervous system depressive, sedative substances and a few intoxicants which act by a variety of mechanisms, some even abetted by creating cerebral hypoxia. Alcohol is often classified separately, a practical approach when considering medical underwriting and one employed here, although it is a central nervous system depressant with many characteristics similar to other members of that class of substances. Narcotic substances are also members of that general group but are generally set apart as those with a more potent tendency to produce addiction in the repeated user.

The use of narcotic medications and some other designated substances is prohibited by law in many countries. Underwriting policies of some companies simply preclude the provision of insurance to users since they are engaging in inherently criminal behavior, regardless of the unique aspects of the particular substance or its usage by an applicant under consideration. This would certainly be true if there was reason to believe that the applicant was engaged in 'dealing' the drug, or in any illegal behavior to finance the purchase of personal supplies. Organized criminal elements are closely tied to illegal drug traffic, and untimely violent death appears to be a significant risk for any user outside the social mainstream. Also, it is generally accepted that the use of drugs by young people represents one aspect of a life style often associated with social maladjustment, economic instability and various psychopathology. Because of these associated risks, the underwriting must consider the entire situation.

The abuse of prescribed medications represents a unique aspect of this problem. Associated sources of mortality in that population would be expected to be of a different nature and magnitude, although reliable data are difficult to find.

Excess mortality accompanies the abuse of psychoactive substances on the basis of their pharmacologic toxicity as well as the increase in risk of intentional or unintentional injury and medical complications of metabolic, nutritional and infectious nature.[1] Among the latter are blood-borne pathogens causing epidemic outbreaks of hepatitis B and HIV disease among intravenous drug abusers who share the injection paraphernalia without practicing sterile precautions.

The abuse of drugs is ubiquitous. Although it is given much public attention in more affluent societies, it is almost universal in its geographic presence. In affluent areas it is reported to be relatively widespread among members of the highly visible entertainment industries, among people with occupational access to drugs, among military populations, and among young professional people.

Data concerning the extent, nature and natural history of the use and abuse of psychoactive drugs must be interpreted somewhat skeptically. Biases related to the selection of study populations and data sets skew the results in virtually every case. Unfortunately extrapolation from observation of limited select populations is the only basis for quantifiable information in many situations, especially when related to illegal drug use where there are strong incentives for secrecy and deception among the subjects.

In the USA the National Institute on Drug Abuse monitors several surveys which report on prevalence and trends of drug abuse. The longest-standing surveillance is by the National Household Survey on Drug Abuse conducted every two to three years since 1972.[2] This study comes closest to reflecting a representative sample of the non-institutionalized population living in households, adjusted for the known demographic variables related to population diversity. Despite considerable differences in age group, sex, racial, employment and geographic variables, overall trends suggest that hallucinogens are becoming less popular, cocaine use is increasing and that most other illegal substances show a relatively stable prevalence of use. In this study, about one-fifth of young people (ages 12–17) admit using an illegal drug one or more times during the preceding year; over one-third of young adults (ages 18–25) and about one-tenth of adults (over 26 years of age) make the same admission.

Since 1975 an annual study of drug use by high school seniors (ages 17–19) has been reported in the Monitoring the Future Study.[3] This study confirms the relative stability of utilization rates, including alcohol, with the exceptions noted in the paragraph above. Unfortunately this study omits the (high-risk) population leaving school before entering the senior class level.

A third major study is the Drug Abuse Warning Network (DAWN), reported only since 1983.[4] This study tallies reports by medical examiners and hospital emergency rooms in major metropolitan areas concerning incidents involving drug abuse. The source of the data allows no assumptions concerning prevalence, but tracks temporal trends. These figures confirm relative stability in frequency of reported use, except for burgeoning rates of cocaine.

The growing use of cocaine, its purported great propensity to lead to habitual use and several highly publicized cocaine-related deaths have made this drug the substance of most concern for life underwriters, and have caused many US insurance companies to require cocaine screening for applicants requesting large life policies. Prevalence of positive tests is reported to be less than 1 percent at insurance laboratories.[5] The efficacy of such screening is certainly not quantifiable because there are no data from which to predict the number of early deaths that were presumably avoided by detection and declination of cocaine-positive applicants. Likewise there is no information from which to predict how likely cocaine-positive insurance applicants are to be (or to become) addicted to that or another substance. Anecdotal reports of occasional or temporary use of cocaine by educated, productive people suggest that declination of every cocaine-positive applicant may not be required by valid outcome data.

CENTRAL NERVOUS SYSTEM STIMULANTS

Central nervous system stimulants subject to abuse include cocaine, methylphenidate and the amphetamines. Similarities of action include the creation of a state of excited euphoria in the user. This is manifested by disinhibition in behavior, grandiose ideation, hypervigilance, impulsiveness and hypersexuality, along with insomnia and anorexia. The altered state of consciousness may take on psychotic characteristics as exposure is prolonged, often with paranoid features and panic states. Upon cessation of use, or even after one high-dose binge (with cocaine especially), an intense depression ensues, with exhaustion, agitation and anxiety. Indeed, intense symptoms, which appear to be the reverse of the signs of intoxication, are typical of withdrawal or the 'crash' after a binge. Suicide is a risk during the acute abstinence syndrome.

Users sometimes combine narcotic depressants with stimulants to modulate the mood swings and ameliorate the depressive crash of withdrawal. When the combination is cocaine and heroin this is called 'speedballing', which has become increasingly popular. The DAWN study reports that deaths associated with this combination increased fivefold in the USA during the late 1980s.[6]

Cocaine base is sometimes smoked. This produces rapid absorption and an even more intense intoxication, and also reportedly increases the risk of addiction. The use of cocaine free base or 'crack' is also referred to as 'free-basing'.

Rating

1) Occasional use, not intravenous, no 'crack' smoking:

Time since cessation of use	Rating
Within 1 yr	+ 0 to +100
Thereafter	Standard

2) Frequent use (more than three times per week), intravenous, or use of 'crack' cocaine:

Time since cessation of use	Rating
Within 2 yr	Postpone
3rd–5th yr	+100 to +300
Thereafter	Standard

HALLUCINOGENS

Hallucinogens include a variety of manufactured substances known best by their chemical abbreviations — LSD, STP, PCP, DMT — and naturally occurring substances found in mushrooms, cacti and the cannabis (marijuana) plant. Although varying significantly in potency, all produce an intoxication accompanied by accentuated sensory perception and, as the group name suggests, may lead to the onset of hallucinations, often visual or olfactory in nature. Habituation can occur, and the substances are often part of a picture of polydrug abuse, either simultaneously or in a pattern of progressive, sequential substance abuse. The alteration of sensory experiences may interfere with reality testing, leading to a psychotic state or aggravating any pre-existing looseness of association in the schizoid or pre-psychotic individual. Panic states may be associated with the difficulty of separating reality from the drug experience. Deaths are most often violent in nature, or related to simultaneous irrational use of other substances.

Rating

1) No more than two or three exposures — standard.
2) Repeated exposures:

Time since cessation of use	Rating
Within 1 yr	Postpone
2nd–3rd yr	+50 to +150
Thereafter	Standard

CENTRAL NERVOUS SYSTEM DEPRESSANTS

The central nervous system depressants, the most commonly used and abused psychoactive drugs, include narcotic analgesics, sedative hypnotics, tranquilizers and alcohol. All of these substances are capable of acutely suppressing central nervous system function with sufficient increasing dose, progressively causing intoxication, somnolence, coma and cessation of respiration. Likewise all of these substances create addiction when prolonged exposure occurs. Addiction includes physical and psychological dependence on the substance, tolerance so that increasing doses are necessary to cause the same degree of effect, and a specific withdrawal syndrome upon abstinence.

Death can follow overdose and severe central nervous system depression, the synergistic effects of two or more dissimilar depressants used simultaneously (especially true with barbiturates and alcohol); death can also be due to catastrophic medical crisis that is undetected due to the depressed mentation and sensibilities or which is precipitated by the stress of withdrawal. Except for alcohol, serious medical problems are not otherwise common as a direct result of the central nervous system depressant. However, they can be a complication of unsterile intravenous injection of the drugs (usually opiates or synthetic analgesics) or due to the general personal and nutritional neglect common to the 'street' addict.

The recidivism rate following withdrawal from opiate addiction is reported to be very high, and monitored methadone replacement programs have been implemented in a number of countries. The goal of these programs is to transfer the addiction to methadone, a substance of limited toxicity and low cost which can then be meted out to the addict in a controlled program. The program will aim to provide for the safety and overall health of the addict with efforts to manage and perhaps eventually reduce the required intake, and all of this in a lawful environment where supply is secure without resort to criminal activity or traffic with street drug dealers. Abstinence-based treatment programs are the alternative (and probably most desirable) avenue, if achievable.

As with all substance abuse, but especially nervous system depressants, adequate underwriting requires maximum effort to get a complete history of the habit, preferably corroborated by more than one source. Any evidence of a 'cover-up' or lack of candor on the part of the applicant suggests that the illness is not under control. Denial of the problem and of the loss of control over the use of substances in the face of obvious resulting medical or social complications is a classic symptom of the addictive disease. An applicant for insurance may misrepresent the status of the substance abuse problem without malicious intent but because he truly is persuaded that he is quite in control, despite clear evidence to the contrary. The medical underwriter, then, must attempt to seek confirmation from the applicant of duration of abstinence, activity in support groups or treatment programs, or of involvement in monitored programs or surveillance.

Successful abstinence in the former addict requires a social environment that sustains functional living without the need for the numbing effect of central nervous system depressants to make life tolerable. Psychopathology that creates serious strain on an individual's ability to relate comfortably to his environment should be treated and managed as necessary. Stability of family setting, employment situation and social circle support long-term sobriety with abstinence. Regular participation in specific support groups provides uniquely valuable assistance in maintaining drug-free living. And, of course, medical problems should be treated appropriately, especially if associated with chronic pain states.

Rating

Drug-free interval	Rating
Within 3 yr	Postpone
4th–6th yr	+300 up
7th–10th yr	+100 up
Thereafter	+0 to +50

ALCOHOL

Alcoholism is the substance abuse syndrome associated with dysfunctional drinking of alcoholic beverages, either in a pattern of increasing daily intake leading to addiction and medical complications, or periodic binges of excessive drinking which most commonly lead to adverse social consequences, confrontations with constituted legal authority and/or accidental injury.

Estimates of the extent of alcoholism in North America and Europe generally place the number at 5–10 percent of the adult population who use any alcohol at all. In the USA the Behavioral Risk Factor Surveillance System, 1986, confirmed the range of heavier drinking adults to be 3·7–10·8 percent of the population in various states.[7] In addition, 7·2–29·6 percent of the surveyed adults admitted to drinking five or more drinks on a single occasion at least once during the preceding month. Also, 1·5–9·6 percent admitted driving an automobile after having 'too much to drink' at least once in the preceding month.

As with any central nervous system depressant, death can occur from acute overdose of alcohol or from excessive depression due to the synergistic effect of alcohol and another depressant. Much more common, however, are deaths due to injury, unintentional (particularly motor vehicle accidents and drowning) and intentional (suicide and homicide). For the long-term alcohol addict or heavy daily drinker, a variety of medical complications are the risk. The liver is damaged by the toxic effect of alcohol and the nutritional inadequacies accompanying alcoholism. The earliest and mildest alcoholic liver pathology is usually a fatty metamorphosis in the liver parenchyma, which is initially detectable only by biopsy; later, laboratory studies begin to manifest the metabolic injury and/or the liver size increases sufficiently to allow detection of hepatomegaly on examination. Alcoholic hepatitis may also occur, with predominant inflammatory hepatic change associated with significant elevations of liver enzyme levels on laboratory examination, and biopsy demonstrating typical inflammatory infiltrates along with deposition of alcoholic myelin. The eventual outcome of continuing alcohol abuse may be Laennec's or nutritional cirrhosis of the liver, which is seldom seen in North America or Europe except in the alcoholic population. In the USA, however, cirrhosis is the ninth leading cause of death, attesting to the prevalence of alcoholism of a severe and prolonged nature. Among people aged 25–44 and 45–64, liver cirrhosis is the sixth and fifth leading cause of death, respectively.[8]

Besides liver disease, alcoholics experience a wide variety of multisystem complications. These include pancreatitis, esophageal disease, increased incidence of peptic ulcers, certain degenerative central nervous system diseases, peripheral neuropathy, certain blood dyscrasias, nutritional and metabolic disturbances, and secondary complications of these and liver lesions, including malignancies. Efforts to estimate the mortality impact of alcohol-related conditions include the development of a structured applications software package, the Alcohol-Related Disease Impact program, by which alcohol-attributable fractions of cause-related mortality can be quantified.[9] This work suggests that in the USA alcohol can be considered the primary causative factor in 15 percent of liver and intrahepatic biliary cancers, 20 percent of gastric carcinoma, 75 percent of esophageal cancer and 40 percent or 50 percent of cancers of lip, oral cavity, pharynx and larynx for women and men, respectively. The same data show alcohol-attributable mortality fractions of 42 percent of motor vehicle accident deaths, 46 percent of homicides, 28 percent of suicides, 38 percent of drownings, 45 percent of deaths in fires, 35 percent of accidental falls and 20–25 percent of all other injuries. Among more common medical conditions, alcohol is considered accountable for 5 percent of deaths from diabetes, 5 percent of pneumonia deaths, 7 percent of cerebrovascular deaths, 8 percent of hypertension and 10 percent of disease of esophagus, stomach and duodenum.

Sudden withdrawal from alcohol abuse by the addicted individual poses yet another risk. The acute abstinence syndrome may cause tremor, hallucinations, seizures, and delirium tremens, and death may occur if careful management of the detoxification is not obtained.

Alcoholism is notably difficult to detect and accurately assess. As already mentioned, denial and concealment are commonplace for alcoholics; indeed, they may be essential if the individual wants to preserve his job, marriage and social standing. Alcoholics become quite expert at keeping the full picture hidden through long practice. Underwriting departments are unsuccessful in fully perceiving the extent of the risk, as recent industry mortality studies have demonstrated.[10] In fact, the problem is probably even worse than suspected because these data rely on death certificate diagnoses, which have been shown to under-report very significantly the incidence of alcohol-related deaths, at least in the USA.[11]

Successful programs to assist the alcoholic in achieving abstinence give a reasonably optimistic outlook for even the alcohol addict. The most successful programs rely on active participation in Alcoholics Anonymous, an international support group program for recovering alcoholics. Recidivism is still high, and continued risk of exacerbation apparently exists after many years of drug-free living.[12]

Rating

Recovering Alcoholic

Drug-free, recovering alcoholic with evidence of relative social stability and regular participation in support group meetings:

Alcohol-free interval	Rating
Within 2 yr	Postpone
3rd yr	+200 to +300
4th–5th yr	+100 to +200
6th–8th yr	+0 to +100

Current Use of Alcohol

1) Occasional drink; no criticism — +0.
2) Minor criticism; never intoxicated — +50.
3) Moderate criticism:
   a) free user; occasional intoxication; liver enzymes elevated; no physical damage — +100.
   b) as (a) plus hepatomegaly; steatosis (biopsy, ultrasound) — +150.
4) Severe criticism:
   a) heavy drinking; frequently drunk; aggressive; involvement with the law — +200 to decline.
   b) hepatic cirrhosis — decline (see pp. 578–9).
   c) cardiomyopathy — decline (see p. 415).
   d) fulfills criteria for alcoholism — decline.

Note Owing to the widely differing standards of measurement and alcohol content of beverages between countries, it is not possible to define here what constitutes a 'drink'. However, the categories of minor, moderate and severe habit criticism will normally be determined by the custom of each country and its attitude to alcohol consumption, and should easily be recognized by criteria other than the volume of alcohol consumed.

TOBACCO

Attention was drawn to the possible effect of cigarette smoking on health soon after World War II when annual national mortality statistics began to report steadily increasing numbers of deaths from malignant neoplasm of the lung and bronchus, and later from ischemic heart disease when this was coded separately from arteriosclerotic heart disease in the eighth revision of the International Classification of Diseases (ICD 8) introduced in 1968.

In order to compare the mortality between smokers and non-smokers many prospective studies were begun in the USA, UK and Canada in the 1950s. These long-duration studies, and many subsequent comparisons of mortality between smoking and non-smoking populations, conclusively show approximately twice the mortality for those who smoke cigarettes.[13-21] For every age group mortality rates rise proportionately with the number of cigarettes smoked, and excess mortality is higher the longer the duration of smoking; the shortened life expectancy of the smoker, even if he has been smoking for many years, gradually increases if he ceases smoking. On the other hand, the mortality of pipe and cigar smokers appears little different from that of non-smokers.

Cigarette Smoking and Life Insurance

Life insurance companies as a whole took very little action in the charging of lower premiums to non-smokers until about 1980–81. However, one company, the State Mutual Assurance Company of America, acting on the results of the Surgeon General's 1964 report on smoking and health[13] decided to enter the market with a new policy for non-cigarette smokers. This policy was priced at lower premium rates than for smokers and was first sold in April 1964. Apart from the usual underwriting information, the only requirement was a statement that the applicant had not smoked cigarettes for at least a year. In 1976, encouraged by the success of its non-cigarette-smoker business, the State Mutual extended the concept of non-smoker premium discount to all individual life insurance policies except those in its pension series.

In 1967 the Phoenix Mutual Life Insurance Company in the USA introduced several non-cigarette-smoker policies coupled with a build requirement. The latter condition was dropped in 1979 when the policies became purely for non-smokers. The Scottish Mutual Assurance Society in 1971 was the first office in the UK to offer policies at discounted premiums to non-smokers.

With the publication of the Surgeon General's report on smoking and health in 1979[14] and the State Mutual's mortality experience of non-cigarette-smoker life insurance policies in 1980,[20] it did not take long for other life insurance companies in North America to jump on the 'band wagon' of non-smoker policies. By the mid-1980s almost all the individual life insurance sold in North America was separated into non-smoker and smoker premiums. The practice of discounting the premium for non-smokers spread to many countries, including Australia and South Africa; in the UK nearly 90 percent of companies were discounting premiums for non-smokers in 1992.

Prevalence of Cigarette Smoking

The percentage of cigarette smokers in the adult population of the USA increased between 1955 and 1965, but from 1965 to 1987 it declined by approximately 0·5 percentage points per year. In 1988 the Centers for Disease Control (CDC) conducted a study to determine the prevalence of cigarette smoking in detail in the USA; the overall findings were that 28·1 percent of the adult population were smokers (men 30·8 percent, women 25·7 percent).[22] One of the national health objectives for the year 2000 is to reduce the prevalence of cigarette smoking among adults to 15 percent.[21] To achieve this the present decline rate must be doubled.[23]

In the UK, statistics from the General Household Survey on cigarette smoking from 1972 to 1990[18] indicate that over the 18 years since the survey began there has been a substantial overall increase in the proportion of adults, both men and women, who do not smoke cigarettes. In 1972 48 percent of men aged 16 and over were non-smokers; by 1980 this figure had increased to 58 percent, and by 1990 to 69 percent. This represents a reduction in the prevalence of cigarette smoking among men of about one-quarter during the decade 1980–90. Among women there was an increase in non-cigarette smoking from 63 percent in 1980 to 71 percent in 1990, an overall reduction in the prevalence of cigarette smoking among women during the decade of just over one-fifth.

Mortality Differentials

On the basis of numerous studies — principally in the USA, Canada and the UK — of mortality in the general population and in certain subgroups, and from special studies involving carefully controlled groups of smokers and non-smokers, the Surgeon General's reports of 1964,[13] 1979[14] and 1989[15] concluded that overall mortality for all male cigarette smokers was about 170 percent that of male non-smokers. The percentage mortality was slightly less for female smokers. Mortality rates were shown to increase with the number of cigarettes smoked; male smokers consuming 40 cigarettes a day had mortality rates equal to 200 percent of those of non-smokers.

The most recent intercompany smoker/non-smoker study of the Society of Actuaries reports the experience with individual life policies issued from 1980 to 1986 with anniversaries 1982–1987. The total mortality ratios were non-smoker 70·3 percent and smoker 152·1 percent (male 153·8 percent, female 143·4 percent), the highest was for those over the age of 50 where the mortality ratio of smokers was 2·5 times that of non-smokers. This experience has been remarkably consistent for many years. The proportion non-smoker-to-total-exposure was 83·2 percent for males and 82·7 percent for females.[21]

The principal causes of death among cigarette smokers are ischemic heart disease, cancer of the lung and bronchus, and chronic bronchitis and emphysema. These account for something like 75–80 percent of excess deaths among cigarette smokers in the UK and the USA, with a slight difference in the figures for chronic bronchitis which is less common in the USA as a cause of death. Almost all other causes of death also show an excess over the expected among cigarette smokers.

Problems Arising from Smoker/Non-smoker Policies

Insurance companies offering plans for non-smokers have had to draw up two sets of premium rates — one for non-smokers, and the other for smokers — the rates for smokers being higher to offset the loss from the composite group of the more favorable mortality non-smokers. Currently non-smoker rates for term plans are 15–25 percent less, and smoker rates 30–50 percent higher, than composite premium rates. The general and insured population experience has continued to show a sustained mortality for non-smokers approximately half that of smokers. This has lead to a permanent division of the standard premium into smoker and non-smoker rates in the USA.

In order to escape the relatively high premiums charged to smokers, some applicants misrepresent their habit in the declaration (most companies define a non-smoker as one who has not smoked cigarettes for one year or longer). The rate of misrepresentation in the USA has been found to be as high as 37 percent in some samples. In order to counter this problem, some companies estimate the nicotine (comprising nicotine and cotinine) or cotinine concentration (or more accurately the cotinine/creatinine ratio), where cotinine is the slowly excreted metabolite of nicotine, in a sample of urine passed at the time of examination. In some countries this may only be done when an application is for a large amount, but in the USA it has become routine practice to test the majority of urine specimens for nicotine or cotinine irrespective of amount. If a urine tests positive, a smoker premium is charged, unless the applicant can provide a convincing explanation of cigar or pipe smoking and the policy applied for specifically links smoker rates to the smoking of cigarettes.

Should a person who has ceased to smoke on medical advice be treated on the same basis as someone who has never smoked? Generally speaking, the rating for the impairment that lead to non-smoking (e.g. chronic bronchitis, angina, hypertension) would probably cover the risk adequately. The cessation of smoking could be regarded as a favorable change in life style.

Should a heavy smoker (i.e. 40 cigarettes or more per day be entitled to smoker rates of premium? According to the statistics, a group of heavy smokers would have a higher mortality than that allowed for in smoker rates. Therefore an addition to smoker premium rates of +25 would be justified, and +50 if the plan was based on composite aggregate rates. However, it should be recognized that it is almost impossible to obtain reliable information from applicants about the number of cigarettes smoked.

Smoking and Aggravation of Existing Impairments

There are abundant clinical data indicating the adverse effect that cigarette smoking has on several medical conditions, and their combination must be considered an aggravation of the existing impairment. Also, genetic and other factors have been shown to predispose certain individuals to the carcinogenic, thrombogenic and atherogenic effects of cigarette smoking. There is, therefore, a good case for the additional rating of applicants who smoke and who are known to have an important genetic predisposition to certain diseases, irrespective of their personal state of health at the time.

The following impairments and adverse factors combined with current cigarette smoking would make a debit for smoking obligatory (or even necessitate a declination if the applicant continues to smoke heavily): asbestosis, thromboangiitis obliterans, clinical ischemic heart disease or a history of ischemic heart disease, peripheral or cerebrovascular atherothrombotic disease, hypertension, diabetes, chronic pulmonary disease, treated cancer of the lung or bronchus, a heart rate of 96 per minute or above, and a family history of ischemic heart disease in two members below the age of 60.

Rating

Ratings for current cigarette smoking when combined with many of the above impairments or factors have already been indicated in earlier chapters. Where they have not, the following ratings, additional to those for the impairment, are suggested.

Cigarette smoking in combination with any of the above impairments or factors, depending on consumption:
Composite aggregate premium rates — +25 to +50.
Smoker premium rates — 0 to +25.

REFERENCES

1 Garson RD. In: *Medical Risks: trends in mortality by age and time elapsed.* N.Y.: Praeger, 1990; chapters 3.3 and 3.4.

2 National Institute on Drug Abuse. *National Household Survey on Drug Abuse: main findings 1988*; DHHS Pub No (ADM) 90–1682. Washington, DC: US Department of Health and Human Services, 1990.

3 National Institute on Drug Abuse. *National trends in drug use and related factors among American high school students and young adults, 1975–1986*; DHHS Pub No (ADM) 87–1535. Washington, DC: US Department of Health and Human Services, 1987.

4 National Institute on Drug Abuse. *Data from the Drug Abuse Warning Network: semiannual report, trend data through July–December 1987.* Rockville, Maryland: National Institute on Drug Abuse, 1987.

5 Sadler G. Cocaine and HIV antibody results by age and geographic area. *Insight*; 5(1): 9, 10, March 1991, Home Office Reference Laboratory, Shawnee Mission, Kansas.

6 National Institute on Drug Abuse. *Drug Abuse Warning Network, March 1988 data file.* Rockville, Maryland: National Institute on Drug Abuse.

7 Centers for Disease Control: Behavioral risk-factor surveillance in selected states — 1985. *MMWR*; 35: 441–4.

8 Williams GD et al. Trends in alcohol-related morbidity and mortality. *Public Health Reports* 1988; 103(6): 592–6.

9 Shultz JM et al. Alcohol-related mortality and years of potential life lost — United States, 1987. *MMWR* 1990; 39: 173–7.
10 *Medical Impairment Study* 1983. Vol 1, Boston: Society of Actuaries and Association of Life Insurance Medical Directors of America, 1986.
11 Pollock DA et al. Underreporting of alcohol-related mortality on death certificates of young US Army veterans, *JAMA* 1987; 258(3): 345–8.
12 Walsh DC et al. A ramdomized trial of treatment options for alcohol-abusing workers. *N Eng J Med* 1991; 325: 775–82.
13 United States Department of Health, Education and Welfare. *Smoking and health: report of the Advisory Committee to the Surgeon General of the Public Health Service*, 1964.
14 United States Department of Health, Education and Welfare. *Smoking and health: report of the Advisory Committee to the Surgeon General of the Public Health Service*, 1979.
15 Centers for Disease Control. *Reducing the health consequences of smoking: 25 years of progress — a report of the Surgeon General, 1989*. Rockville, Maryland: US Department of Health and Human Services, Public Health Service, 1989; DHHS Pub No (CDC) 89–8411.
16 Doll R, Hill AB. Mortality in relation to smoking: ten years' observations of British doctors. Part I. *Br Med J* 1964, 1: 1399.
17 Doll R, Hill AB. Mortality in relation to smoking: ten years' observations of British doctors. Concluded. *Br Med J* 1964; 1: 1460.
18 General Household Survey; cigarette smoking 1972–90. Office of Population, Censuses and Surveys. Monitor SS 91–3. Information Branch M, OPC&S.
19 Best EWR, Josie GH, Walker CB. A Canadian study of mortality in relation to smoking habits: a preliminary report. *Can J Public Hlth* 1961; 52: 99.
20 Cowell MJ, Hirst BL. Mortality differences between smokers and nonsmokers. *Trans Soc Act* 1980; 32: 185.
21 Mortality under standard individually underwritten life insurance between 1986 and 1987 anniversaries. Society of Actuaries 1991.
22 Cigarette smoking among adults — United States, 1988. *JAMA* 1991; 266: 3113–14.
23 Public Health Service. *Healthy people 2000: national health promotion and disease prevention objectives — full report, with commentary*. Washington DC:US Department of Health and Human Services, Public Health Service, 1991; DHHS Pub No (PHS) 91–50212.

CHAPTER 31

MISCELLANEOUS IMPAIRMENTS

R D C BRACKENRIDGE
I McLEAN BAIRD

SEXUALLY TRANSMITTED DISEASES (STDs)

Acquired Immune Deficiency Syndrome (AIDS)

In the latter part of the 20th century infection by the human immunodeficiency virus (HIV) has posed an even more serious threat to the life insurance industry than infection by *Treponema pallidum* did in the first half of the century. This being so, it has been necessary to devote a separate chapter to consideration of the problem of AIDS and HIV as it affects life insurance and other forms of insurance (*see* Chapter 28).

Underwriters dealing with histories of other STDs, even though these diseases may be amenable to treatment and cure, should bear in mind the possibility of concurrent HIV infection and take appropriate action to protect their companies.

Syphilis

Syphilis is caused by the spirochete *T. pallidum*; the mode of transmission is invariably sexual contact, since the treponeme is rapidly destroyed outside the body.

There were 50,233 cases of infectious syphilis reported in the USA in 1990 compared with 31,206 in 1981,[1] the largest increase since 1949. However, these bald statistics hide the difference in incidence of infection by race. Between 1985 and 1990 there was a threefold increase in the rates of infectious syphilis in black men, whereas the rates in whites and people of Asian or Pacific origin have remained low.

There has also been an almost explosive increase in reported congenital syphilis in infants younger than one year in certain inner-urban areas of the USA, and with it a corresponding local increase of infectious syphilis in females.[2] This is related to a variety of factors which combine to create a situation conducive to the spread of STDs: unemployment, poverty, poor education and inadequate health care, which lead to crime, substance abuse, prostitution and family disruption. On the other hand, deaths from syphilis in the USA have fallen from 160 in 1979 to 85 in 1988.[1]

In England and Wales, the epidemiological situation so far has been rather better than in the USA. In 1990 there were 335 cases of infectious syphilis reported by genitourinary medicine clinics (including latent syphilis in the first two years) compared with 2,512 cases in 1980.[3] Deaths from syphilis in England and Wales have also fallen, from 40 in 1985[4] to 18 in 1990.[5] The deaths from syphilis in 1985 included 14 cardiovascular, 23 neurological and 3 congenital; the 1990 deaths included 2 cardiovascular, 8 neurological and 5 congenital.

Syphilis, although far less common than other STDs, remains a potentially fatal condition if untreated or inadequately treated. Fortunately *T. pallidum* is extremely sensitive to penicillin, and the effect of treatment in the infectious stages of syphilis represents one of the great therapeutic successes of medicine. Almost all patients with primary, secondary and early latent syphilis can now be completely cured of the disease, and treatment of late latent syphilis will nearly always prevent progression to late symptomatic syphilis. Even in the late benign stage, most lesions of the skin, mucous membranes, bones and ulcerating gummas will rapidly respond to penicillin. The prognosis in late symptomatic syphilis, however, depends on the site of the lesion and the amount of damage already caused by the treponeme. Penicillin may arrest the disease, but it cannot replace damaged tissue.

One of the major problems in underwriting a history of treated syphilis is the difficulty in obtaining reliable information about the stage of the disease, the nature of the treatment given and the subsequent follow-up serology. Confidentiality of information about venereal disease is generally strict, which unfortunately may act to an individual's disadvantage if he applies for life insurance. If the full facts were known to the life underwriter, most cases of infectious and late asymptomatic syphilis, efficiently treated and followed up with the recommended tests of cure, could undoubtedly be issued with standard insurance. As it is, details of treatment and surveillance are often incomplete, and the underwriter has no option but to evaluate the risks in terms of probabilities and apply appropriate extra premiums. However, if it is possible to obtain serological tests for syphilis (STS) on application which produce non-reactive results, substantial credits can be allowed which may result in standard acceptance or a much reduced rating, depending on the stage of the disease when treatment was initiated. A negative HIV antibody test would be obligatory in most cases.

Serological Tests for Syphilis (STS)

A practical sequence of serological tests to assess the clinical activity, or otherwise, of syphilitic infection involves three stages. (1) Initial screening with the RPR (rapid plasma reagin) test. (2) If positive, the titer is checked with the VDRL (Venereal Disease Research Laboratory) test, which will give an indication of the degree of infectivity. (3) The *T. pallidum* hemagglutination assay (TPHA) test is highly specific and can be quantified (unlike the RPR test and its titer, which are non-specific). If the reagin tests are reactive, a positive TPHA test will confirm the diagnosis of syphilis. On the other hand, a reactive reagin test can be designated false positive if the TPHA test is negative. The fluorescent treponemal antibody absorption (FTA–ABS) test is also specific for syphilis, but it is expensive and tedious to perform and so is not usually used for screening. However, it is useful as a confirmatory test.

In most patients the results of reagin tests become negative one year after adequate treatment for primary syphilis and two years after treatment for secondary syphilis. The specific tests, however, may stay positive for many years. When patients are treated for latent or late syphilis, reagin tests usually show a slow decline in titer and may eventually become negative. In a few patients the titer becomes stationary and is not affected by retreatment. The TPHA and FTA–ABS tests remain positive indefinitely. For evaluating progress after treatment quantitative reagin tests are of most use; specific tests are of little value.

A problem that sometimes arises is the interpretation of positive serological tests for syphilis in people from areas where endemic treponematoses, such as *yaws* and *bejel*, are prevalent. In general, the serological rections to syphilis and non-venereal treponematoses are identical. Thus, people who have had yaws in childhood show positive specific tests and have lipoidal antigen tests that are either negative or positive in low titer — a pattern identical to that in patients with latent or late syphilis, or with a previously treated infection.

Biological False Positive Reactions (BFPRs)

The non-specific tests — like the WR (Wasserman reaction), Kahn, RPR and VDRL — may be positive in patients who have never had syphilis and in whom the specific tests, such as the TPHA, are negative. Acute BFPRs occur during the course of many infections, when the tests are positive for a short period, becoming negative after the patient has recovered. The commonest of such infections are glandular fever, infectious hepatitis, malaria and chickenpox. A false positive result also occurs in pregnancy, and in leprosy when the reaction tends to persist rather longer. BFPRs may persist for years, even for life; they are much commoner in women and develop during the course of one of the collagen diseases, such as systemic lupus erythematosus, dermatomyositis and polyarteritis nodosa. A chronic false positive reaction can be confirmed by finding a negative TPHA test.

Late Non-infectious Syphilis

This is the clinical stage of tertiary syphilis and includes cardiovascular syphilis and neurosyphilis.

Cardiovascular Syphilis

This develops in about 10 percent of untreated syphilitics after a latent period of ten to 20 years; when fully developed it has a high mortality. It may involve the aortic wall or the aortic valve, or both.

Aortitis

When aortitis is not aneurysmal it is usually asymptomatic, and can only be detected by imaging techniques or radiologically from widening of the thoracic aorta and sometimes from the diagnostic linear deposits of calcium in the ascending aorta. If adequate treatment is initiated at this stage, the vascular damage should not progress.

Syphilitic Aneurysm

When there is a definite aneurysmal swelling of the aorta producing pressure symptoms, the expectation of life is greatly curtailed, even after adequate antisyphilitic treatment. Some smaller aneurysms that have been repaired surgically may be accepted as insurable impairments after recovery and completion of antisyphilitic treatment (*see* p. 418).

Aortic Incompetence

Once cardiac failure develops, the prognosis is poor and antisyphilitic treatment has little or no effect. Untreated aortic incompetence discovered by chance with

the stethoscope, even if slight and asymptomatic should be declined; consideration may be given to rating as aortic incompetence according to degree (*see*
pp. 366–7) with an additional debit of 50 points after full antisyphilitic treatment, or if an artificial valve has been fitted (*see* pp. 384–5).

Neurosyphilis

Neurosyphilis develops in about 10 percent of untreated syphilitics, but the
incidence has declined markedly in the last 50 years.

Asymptomatic Neurosyphilis

This stage is diagnosed by an abnormal CSF. Treatment can usually forestall
frank neurosyphilis.

Meningovascular Syphilis

Symptoms are due to involvement of the meninges and cerebral blood vessels
causing meningitis, cranial nerve palsies and, in severe cases, hemiplegia if the
arteries supplying the internal capsule are involved. Meningovascular syphilis is
the form of neurosyphilis most amenable to antisyphilitic treatment. Significant
neurological deficits should be rated in addition to the debit for tertiary syphilis.

Tabes Dorsalis

Now a rare form of neurosyphilis, tabes doralis is marked by a chronic and
usually progressive degeneration of the ascending sensory neurones in the posterior columns of the spinal cord. It also affects the posterior sensory ganglia
and nerve roots. Tabes usually appears in men over the age of 35. The presenting symptoms and signs are impaired proprioception, diminished vibration
sense, Argyll–Robertson pupils, muscular hypotonia and absent tendon reflexes.
A characteristic feature is recurrent lightning pains mostly in the legs. Other
features are impotence, painless trophic ulcers over pressure points of the feet,
Charcot joints and a neurogenic bladder with overflow incontinence. Loss of
bladder function predisposes to recurrent urinary infection, and a common
cause of death in tabes is chronic pyelonephritis. Optic atrophy, which is unaffected by treatment, eventually causes blindness. Antisyphilitic treatment appears to have little effect on tabes, but progression is usually slow, the ataxia
often remaining slight and not greatly interfering with the patient's life.

Applicants who have received adequate antisyphilitic treatment at an early
stage of the disease and who have only slight locomotor disability may be
accepted for life insurance at a rating between +200 and +100. A further 50
points should be added when there is bladder dysfunction without evidence of
obstructive uropathy.

General Paralysis (GPI)

The onset of GPI is usually insidious with progressive decrease in concentration,
loss of memory, irritability, and irresponsible and slovenly behaviour. Today
most patients first present with progressive depression or epilepsy rather than
dementia (as occurred in the past). With penicillin therapy the majority sur-

vive, but the degree of functional recovery varies: about one-third improve markedly and one-third moderately, with the rest remaining static or deteriorating.

Insurance should be restricted to those cases of general paralysis diagnosed and treated in the early stage without significant mental changes. Applications should be postponed for one year from completion of treatment, following which best risk cases could be rated from +75 to +50.

Congenital Syphilis

Early Congenital Syphilis

The lesions of early congenital syphilis resemble those of the secondary acquired disease and appear before the infant is two years old. The bones, lungs and pancreas may be affected, and neurosyphilis, which occurs in about 10 percent of cases, can be life-threatening because of its resistance to treatment. Mental handicap and convulsions are common.

Late Congenital Syphilis

Interstitial keratitis is the commonest lesion of late congenital syphilis and usually develops in early teenage. Many of the typical skeletal stigmata, including a saddle-shaped nose, various dental dystrophies, periostitis of the frontal and parietal bones, and perforation of the hard palate and nasal septum, will be present. More serious are the lesions of the central nervous system, such as juvenile taboparesis, facial weakness, optic atrophy and eighth-nerve deafness, because once developed they do not respond satisfactorily to treatment. Provided the disease is recognized and treatment started in infancy, the manifestations of late congenital syphilis can be avoided.

Selection of Risks

Good documentation of the medical evidence is essential if applicants with a history of syphilis are to be offered the best terms. Different insurance companies have their own underwriting requirements, but most call for authenticated information on the thoroughness of treatment appropriate to the stage of the disease and the results of follow-up studies, including blood serology, and CSF tests when necessary. Most companies also require documented evidence of cure, which would usually mean two successive non-reactive serological tests, the last being within six months of application or, in the case of late tertiary syphilis, two consecutive serological tests showing reactive results at low titer in both specimens. This information would usually be obtained from the medical attendant or the attending venereologist.

Rating

The ratings for partial treatment (see below) should be used when there is good reason to suspect insufficient treatment or follow-up tests, or when there is incomplete information relating to the risk.

	Years since treatment	Serology negative (or no active infection)	
		Thorough treatment	Partial treatment
Acquired			
Infectious and latent asymptomatic stages	0–2	0	+100[a] to +50[a]
	3 and over	0	+50[a] to 0
Asymptomatic neurosyphilis, benign tertiary stage (gummas, skin lesions, etc.)	0–3	+100[a]	+150[a]
	4 and over	+50[a]	+100[a]
Meningovascular syphilis	0–3	+150[b]	+200[b]
	4 and over	+75 to 0[b]	+100[b]
Tabes dorsalis, general paresis	0–1	Postpone	Decline
	2 and over	*see* text	Decline
Aortitis without aneurysm	0–2	+150[a]	+200[a]
	3 and over	+75 to 0[a]	+100[a]
Other CV lesions		*see* text	Decline
Congenital (age 15 years and over)			
No evidence of system disease	0–3	+100[b]	+200[b]
	4 and over	+50[b]	+100[b]
With evidence of system disease		Rate as Acquired	Rate as Acquired

[a] Cerebrospinal fluid negative — credit 25 points.
[b] Cerebrospinal fluid negative — credit 50 points.
Where current STS indicates active infection — postpone 6–12 months.
BFPR — standard.

Gonorrhea

Gonorrhea is one of the common STDs and until recently its incidence had been steadily increasing. Notifications of gonorrhea in the USA reached a peak between 1977 and 1988; since then the incidence has been decreasing.[6] Likewise, in England and Wales the number of cases of gonorrhea reached a peak and began to fall between 1986 and 1987, followed by a steeper fall between 1987 and 1988, the decrease being greater in males than in females.[7] There is little doubt that the decrease in incidence of gonorrhea has been due to changes in sexual behavior resulting from the publicity associated with the AIDS epidemic.

The spread of gonorrhea is not easy to control. The very short incubation period makes it unusually difficult to break the chain of infection and, since some 50–60 percent of women with gonorrhea are asymptomatic, a large, hidden reservoir of infection still exists.

Complications

With effective and simple treatment available, the risk to life from gonococcal infection is negligible and arises only indirectly from complications in untreated or inadequately treated cases. Females are liable to develop gonorrheal salpingitis, which may extend to cause parametritis and pelvic peritonitis.

In the male, urethral stricture may result if treatment is neglected or inadequate; this leads to obstructive uropathy and its complications. Very occasionally syphilitic infection is contracted at the same time as gonorrhea and may be masked initially by the treatment of the gonococcal infection, only to appear much later as latent or tertiary syphilis. The proper management of gonorrhea should therefore include a STS taken before antibiotic therapy is started, followed by a further STS at least four months later.

Most life insurance companies accept as standard a history of adequately treated gonorrhea without complications, but, as with other STDs, a negative HIV antibody test would normally be a condition of acceptance if the infection was recent.

Non-specific Urethritis (NSU)

NSU is a disorder of multiple etiology, although in 30 percent of patients no micro-organisms are found. Organisms that have been incriminated in the etiology of NSU are chlamydia trachomatis, mycoplasma trichomonas vaginalis, or herpes simplex virus.

The disease is almost certainly transmitted by sexual contact, although there is often no obvious infection in the female. Symptoms arise after an incubation period of seven to 14 days and are generally milder than those of gonoccocal urethritis. The course, however, is more chronic, and relapses or reinfections occur frequently in both treated and untreated patients. The commonest complication of NSU is chronic prostatitis, which is often accompanied by urethrophobia or even frank depression. NSU is one of the classical triad of symptoms that make up Reiter's disease (non-gonococcal urethritis, seronegative arthritis and conjunctivitis), but only about 1 percent of young men with NSU eventually develop Reiter's disease.

Applications for life insurance disclosing a history of NSU should be underwritten similarly to gonorrhoea. Chronic prostatitis and Reiter's disease are discussed more fully elsewhere (*see* p. 546 and p. 810, respectively).

Other STDs

The following diseases are less important in underwriting; after cure all are acceptable for life insurance without debit. Nevertheless, their significance sometimes requires elucidation when they appear in attending physicians' statements or medical examination reports, and evidence of a negative STS and HIV antibody test is usually mandatory before insurance is issued.

Genital Warts (Condylomata Acuminata)

These warts are caused by the papilloma virus which is transmitted sexually and has an incubation period of several months. Male patients are seen twice as commonly as females at clinics in the UK, and genital warts are regarded as the third most common STDs. Warts appear on the male, and female genitals and on the perianal area, and have a tendency to spread if untreated. The smaller warts can be cured by local applications, but the larger ones may require removal by electrocautery or diathermy. Genital warts should not be confused with condylomata lata, the flat-topped anogenital papules which may appear during the secondary stage of syphilis.

Herpes Genitalis
This is caused by *Herpes simplex* virus type 2, which can be cultured from the lesions. The virus is sexually transmitted; after incubation, herpetic vesicles appear in crops on the glans, prepuce and shaft of the penis in men, and on the external genitalia and sometimes the cervix in women. The vesicles rupture to form shallow ulcers which may become secondarily infected and necrotic. Although local treatment with idoxuridine is effective, herpes genitalis tends to be recurrent over several weeks or months.

Trichomoniasis
Trichomonas vaginalis is a common cause of genital infection and is generally believed to be sexually transmitted. It causes acute vaginitis with a profuse yellow discharge or, in middle-aged women, a low-grade chronic infection with few symptoms. In men the organism causes a trichomonas urethritis which in some instances may be accompanied by a non-specific urethritis, both requiring treatment to effect a cure. As with genital warts, treatment must be followed by serological tests to exclude syphilis.

Genital Candidosis
Genital candidosis is caused by the fungus *Candida albicans* and is much more common in women, in whom it produces an intensely irritating vaginitis with a scanty white discharge. Men contract candidosis from their infected partners and develop erosive balanitis and, less commonly, urethritis. There are no serious complications of genital candidosis.

THE EYES

Examination of the eyes can yield valuable information for the diagnosis of systemic disease and sometimes, as in the case of a corneal arcus occurring under the age of 30, for the detection of preclinical disease. Among the many abnormal eye signs that may be reported, the following examples are but a few: exophthalmos, icteric sclerae, nystagmus, pupillary anomalies, hypertensive and diabetic retinopathy, choroiditis and optic atrophy. The diseases associated with these signs have already been considered in previous chapters. In addition, there are several purely local disorders of the eye which have little or no bearing on life expectancy.

Total Blindness

Total blindness is a much less common disability than partial blindness, and individual life insurance companies' experience of total blindness is generally very small. Even with the pooled experience of many companies, the numbers are relatively few, and in the *1951 Impairment Study*[8] the standard section of insured lives with total blindness was too small to make an analysis of mortality worthwhile, although a mortality ratio of 157 percent was found in the substandard section. An anomalous finding in this study was that there was not a single death due to accident. The reason for this unexpectedly low incidence is unclear.

The results of a study by the New York Life Insurance Company of insured male and female lives with total blindness have been analyzed in the Mortality Monograph.[9] The standard and substandard classifications combined, at a mean age of 35 years with 1,536 policy-years exposure, produced a mortality ratio of only 130 percent.

A more recent analysis of mortality among insured lives with total blindness was reported in the *1983 Medical Impairment Study*.[10] Those insured at standard rates were found to have better than average mortality at 82 percent. A smaller number insured in substandard categories showed an overall mortality ratio of 195 percent.

There are several factors to be taken into account in evaluating the risk associated with total blindness, the most important being the cause of blindness. Naturally mortality will be increased when blindness is due to diabetic retinopathy, recurrent retrobulbar neuritis, syphilitic optic atrophy and other causes where the primary disease itself is subject to excess mortality. On the other hand, the risk associated with total blindness is likely to be much less significant if the causal disease was temporary and no longer a hazard to life, or was localized purely to the eyes. Conditions such as meningitis, temporal arteritis, glaucoma and bilateral retinal detachment belong to the latter category. Mortality experience is likely to be most favorable in those groups where blindness was due to accidental causes.

Also of some importance is the age at onset of blindness. Longevity is more likely to be normal among those who lost their sight in adolescence or adult life than among those who have been blind since birth or early infancy.

Although blindness causes problems of adjustment to the environment which may last for up to five years, most life insurance companies consider as standard otherwise healthy blind people who have been fully rehabilitated to suitable employment and have adjusted satisfactorily to their disability. Applications on behalf of blind children should be postponed until they reach adolescence.

Blindness in One Eye

A history of blindness in one eye is relatively common, and mortality in such a group was found to be only a little above average in the *1951 Impairment Study*[8] and in the intracompany study by the New York Life Insurance Company (mortality ratio 133 percent). As in total blindness, the important factor in determining extra mortality is not the blindness itself, but its cause. Accident is by far the commonest cause of monocular blindness; when this is so, the impairment can be disregarded in underwriting. Complete unilateral amblyopia dating from childhood, often with a history of squint, is a not infrequent finding and may also be disregarded. When blindness in one eye has resulted from systemic disease such as arteritis or cerebrovascular disease, the risk would be that associated with the primary cause.

Temporary Blindness
Temporary blindness in one eye lasting a week or two is often due to *retrobulbar*

optic neuritis, which is nearly always an early sign of multiple sclerosis; its significance in risk evaluation has already been considered (*see* p. 759). *Amaurosis fugax* is a transient loss of vision in one eye lasting a variable time (from a few seconds or minutes to several hours); is most often due to microembolism of the central retinal artery with platelets or cholesterol arising from atheroma and narrowing of the internal carotid artery on the same side. Amaurosis fugax has the same significance as a transient ischemic attack, although in many instances no cause can be found after thorough evaluation of the aorta and great vessels in the neck, and of the heart. When this is the case, and especially in young age groups, the prognosis is favorable.

Diplopia

Diplopia that is an isolated symptom lasting only a few minutes is usually of little significance, whereas diplopia persisting for several days or weeks is much more likely to be due to organic disease, especially multiple sclerosis. Temporary diplopia may be due to a small rupture and leak from an intracranial aneurysm, in which case it usually develops suddenly with headache, not necessarily severe and not always accompanied by loss of consciousness. Recurrent diplopia, possibly neuritic in origin, may sometimes be a complication of diabetes, especially in the elderly.

Diplopia due to opthalmoplegic migraine can usually be identified from the history by its periodicity and the fact that it often dates from childhood or adolesence. The condition is characterized by periodic severe headaches with recurrent third-nerve palsy, and, although relatively benign, may eventually lead to permanent paralysis of the third nerve. This type of migraine was once thought to be due to intracranial aneurysm, but the majority of sufferers have normal arteriograms. Double vision may also be the first symptom of myasthenia gravis (*see* p. 778).

When diplopia is of recent onset and persistent, the possibility of intracranial tumor must be seriously considered; in these circumstances applications for life insurance should be postponed pending neurological investigation.

Retinal and Choroidal Disorders

Retinal Vasculitis

Retinal vasculitis almost always affects the retinal veins, and is characterized by white perivascular sheathing of the vessels and retinal hemorrhages, which tend to be centrally situated (central retinal vasculitis). If the vasculitis is severe, periphlebitis may cause venous occlusion and retinal neovascularization. The most common systemic diseases causing retinal vasculitis are sarcoidosis and Behçet's disease; rare cases are caused by systemic lupus erythematosus, polyarteritis nodosa and toxoplasmosis if the retinal arteries are involved rather than the veins.

Eales' disease is a retinal vasculitis of unknown etiology which usually affects the eyes alone. The condition occurs predominantly in males during the second and third decades of life, with the lesions peripherally situated and producing a syndrome of recurrent hemorrhages into the retina and vitreous. A rare complication of Eales' disease has been reported,[11] namely a neurologic lesion in the upper dorsal cord causing paraplegia.

The rating of retinal vasculitis is that of the causal systemic disease, whereas a history of Eales' disease as a localized entity generally qualifies for standard rates.

Central Serous Retinopathy

This condition of obscure etiology is localized to the eyes, usually unilaterally, and is characterized by edema of the macula. Typically there is a partial scotoma affecting central vision which usually resolves over a period of weeks or months. When the diagnosis is confirmed and vision has returned to normal, disability and life insurance can be granted at standard rates.

Chorioretinitis

Old, healed choroiditis or chorioretinitis is occasionally reported during routine examination of the optic fundus. These white and pigmented patches, denoting retinal and choroidal atrophy with the white sclera showing through, cause no noticeable visual defect if they are situated peripherally, but interfere with central vision if the macula is involved. Common causes of chorioretinitis are histoplasmosis (see p. 504), toxoplasmosis (see p. 876) and toxocariasis (see p. 890), but usually the acute phase of infection cannot be recalled. Old, inactive chorioretinitis can generally be disregarded in risk evaluation.

Iritis: Cyclitis: Iridocyclitis

Inflammation of the iris, ciliary body or, more usually, both is termed *anterior uveitis*. Generally the inflammation is non-specific, occurring as a hypersensitivity reaction to various systemic diseases (e.g. rheumatoid arthritis, Behçet's syndrome, acute sarcoidosis, primary tuberculosis and leprosy). It may also complicate local diseases of the eye such as episcleritis, keratoconjunctivitis, corneal ulcer and retinal detachment, and follow ocular trauma. In many instances the cause of iridocyclitis can never be found. The inflammation lasts a few days to several weeks and may recur; in a few cases it may become chronic and last months or years.

A history of a single attack of iritis or iridocyclitis does not warrant a rating. Recurrent or chronic attacks should be rated +50 to +25, and if long-term systemic corticosteroids are being used currently in treatment the appropriate rating should be added (see p. 715).

THE EARS

Deafness

No additional mortality need be anticipated in a selected group of individuals with complete or almost complete deafness except when it occurs as deaf mutism. The causes of deafness do not have the same serious implication for health as some of the causes of blindness, and deafness is generally not such a great handicap to an individual as blindness.

The commonest cause of deafness or partial deafness is still chronic middle ear infection, but happily the incidence is becoming much less, due to the use of antibiotics in the acute stage. Otosclerosis, nerve degeneration, Ménière's disease and a few other causes, which are not always clear, account for deafness in the remainder. When there is a recent history of unilateral deafness that is progressive and not due to obvious cause, the possibility of an acoustic neurinoma or other intracranial tumor should be eliminated before insurance is issued.

Deaf Mutism

This form of deafness is rarely seen as an impairment in life underwriting; it is a great handicap from the point of view of both educational and social development, but much has been done to help deaf mutes by special schools and training centers. The result is that many are now able to lead a reasonably normal, independent existence with regular employment. If they are otherwise healthy, people who fall into the category just described can usually be granted life insurance at standard rates. For those who fall short of the criteria for best-risk cases, a rating of +100 or a minimum extra of 2 per mil is required.

Otitis Media

Acute otitis media used to be a serious infection in the times before antibiotics were available, particularly in children. Today, however, the death rate from middle-ear infection and its complications is negligible, being only about one-fiftieth of what it was 50 years ago. Chronic otitis media with otorrhea is of two kinds, each with a different prognosis. (1) In the so-called 'dangerous' ear, a perforation is situated at the margin of the ear drum or in the attic; bone necrosis is usually present and accompanied by granulations or cholesteatoma tissue protruding through the perforation. Thrombosis of a lateral sinus or the extension of an abscess into the brain is an ever-present danger in this type of chronic otitis media. (2) If, however, a perforation of the ear-drum is central, bone necrosis will be absent and the risk of serious complications will be negligible despite otorrhea.

Rating

1) Central perforation with or without discharge — standard.
2) Marginal or attic perforation with offensive discharge, or middle-ear granulations or cholesteatoma:
One ear — +50 or 2 per mil.[a]
Both ears — +75 or 3 per mil.[a]
([a]Whichever is greater.)
After radical operation (bone curette with or without tympanoplasty) — standard.

Ménière's Disease

Care should be taken that only genuine cases of Ménière's disease (see p. 742) are classified as such before issuing life insurance. The mistaken inclusion of applicants with a history of episodic vertigo due, for example, to vertebrobasilar ischemia or temporal lobe epilepsy is likely to produce a significantly adverse mortality experience in the Ménière's group as a whole. On the other hand, mild forms of Ménière's disease without severe vertigo are often misdiagnosed as neurosis. The pathological process in Ménière's disease is benign and, despite the fact that the ultimate result will be deafness, applicants with this affliction who are otherwise healthy can usually be considered standard life risks.

SKIN DISEASES

Most primary skin diseases are benign and are not associated with excess mortality. These range from the pyodermas and the simple allergic rashes to the eczematides which occur in those whose inborn pattern of reaction to stress is dermatological. In these people the principal target organ seems to be the skin, although other target organs are occasionally involved. A few primary skin diseases have a high fatality rate and are mentioned specifically in the paragraphs that follow. Finally there are the skin lesions that occur as part of a symptom complex of systemic diseases, some of which are themselves associated with high mortality; most have been mentioned in earlier chapters and are not discussed further here.

Pemphigus

The primary conditions carrying the highest mortality of any skin disease are pemphigus vulgaris (PV) and the related diseases pemphigus foliaceus (PF), pemphigus vegetans (PVeg) and pemphigus erythematosus (PE). Pemphigus affects primarily the middle-aged, particularly between the ages of 40 and 60. The Jewish race shows a marked susceptibility.

   The commonest clinical presentation of PV is with mucous membrane lesions of the tongue and cheeks. Intact blisters are rare, but non-healing superficial ulcerations with peripheral extension are commonly seen. Initially the skin blisters are sparse but generalized blistering soon develops, and flaccid serum-filled bullae rapidly give way to painful bleeding erosions. The normal skin between lesions can often be stripped off by firm stroking with a finger. PVeg has a slightly slower tempo than PV, and PF and PE have an even more indolent clinical course.

   Pemphigus can be distinguished from the more benign bullous pemphigoid (*see* below) by the site of localization of specific IgG antibodies in the lesions. In pemphigus, immunofluorescence shows these antibodies to be located precisely to the site of acantholysis, the suprabasal cells, whereas in bullous pemphigoid they are localized on the basement membrane.

   The lesions of PE have a morphological appearance close to that of lupus erythematosus in that the scaling and erythema often occupy the butterfly area of the face with coarse scaling obscuring the underlying blisters. This type of lesion may represent a combination of pemphigus and lupus erythematosus.

Prognosis
Before corticosteroids became available PV was invariably fatal in an average time of 14 months. In contrast, PF frequently follows a relatively benign course often lasting over a decade. PVeg runs a more prolonged course than PV but early death

is the rule in the absence of treatment with corticosteroids. The lesions of PE generally spread inexorably until there is total body involvement. Death in all forms of pemphigus is due usually to secondary infection and the metabolic effects which result from large, denuded and oozing areas of the body surface.

Even with corticosteroids and immunosuppressive agents such as azathioprine, the mortality of pemphigus is still around 40 percent, and applicants for life insurance who are currently receiving suppressive therapy should be declined. For cases of pemphigus considered to be cured and not receiving suppressive therapy, a rating of +200 in the second year since cure decreasing to +0 in the fifth and subsequent years is required.

Bullous Pemphigoid

This condition is a disease of the elderly, and 80 percent of patients are over the age of 60 at onset. There is a relative absence of oral lesions, and blisters appear mostly on the central abdomen and flexor aspects of the limbs; these are often hemorrhagic and either rupture, leaving quick-healing erosions, or reabsorb spontaneously. Mortality is much lower than in pemphigus. Corticosteroids are used in treatment and, although remission is described, many patients require lifelong suppression.

Applicants in remission and not receiving suppressive treatment can be considered standard risks. Best-risk cases below the age of 65 still having suppressive treatment may be accepted at a rating of +100 to +75 including the corticosteroid extra. Applicants aged 65 and over are best evaluated as a years-to-age rating in a slight- to moderate-risk category.

Erythema Multiforme (EM)

Typical EM can occur in various forms which differ in the severity of cell damage they cause. Thus individual lesions may be macules, papules or have superimposed blisters. The mildest and commonest form of EM is the papular, which presents as dull red maculopapules up to 2 cm in diameter distributed on the hands and feet, on the extensor surfaces of the elbows and knees, or possibly more widespread.

At the other end of the spectrum of severity, blistering of the skin may be very extensive and accompanied by a high pyrexia and profound constitutional symptoms. This form of EM is known as the *Stevens-Johnson syndrome*. Characteristically the mucous membrane of the mouth is almost entirely denuded of epithelium and the eyes show a severe conjunctivitis or corneal damage. Lesions on the genitalia may give rise to retention of urine. Renal disease occurs rarely, but bronchitis or pneumonitis is a common complication. There is an appreciable mortality during the acute phase of the disease.

The etiology of all forms of EM remains obscure in most instances. A variety of stimuli have been known to trigger it off, with a latent interval of one to three weeks. These include virus and mycoplasma infections, drug sensitivities, pregnancy and radiotherapy. The drugs commonly incriminated are barbiturates, long-acting sulphonamides and phenylbutazone. This pattern of reaction suggests that EM has an immunopathological basis.

Prognosis

Systemic corticosteroids usually produce dramatic symptomatic improvement, but it is doubtful whether they have any effect in reducing mortality. However, EM in all its forms is self-limiting, and recovery can be expected to be complete in two to six weeks, with the possible exception of the more severe ocular complications. EM sometimes recurs, but little can be done to prevent recurrences apart from avoidance of offending drugs.

Rating

EM, after full recovery:
   Mild or moderate attacks — standard.
Stevens–Johnson syndrome:
   Within one year — 5 per mil for one year.
   Thereafter — standard.

Mycosis fungoides

Mycosis fungoides is a malignant, cutaneous T-cell lymphoma which always starts in the skin. Biopsy may be diagnostic, and electron microscopy may show atypical mycosis fungoides cells, which have been identified as thymus-dependent lymphocytes. Involvement of viscera is reported more often in the USA than in the UK; it is a late stage of the disease which may not occur for 20–30 years from the earliest sign of the cutaneous lesion.

Topical therapy such as the combined psoralens and long ultraviolet treatment, or whole-skin electron beam treatment, may control the cutaneous lesions for several years, and systemic chemotherapy can cause regression of visceral lesions, but the ultimate outcome for survival seems to be unchanged.

The prognosis for life depends on the stage of the disease at any particular point of time. Patients with very early premycotic-type lesions of *parapsoriasis* with equivocal biopsy findings can survive up to 30 years, whereas those with visceral involvement and a definite histological diagnosis survive for an average of five years. If there are ulcerating skin tumors and infiltration of lymphatics and nodes, average survival is only two and a half years. In a series of cases of mycosis fungoides reported by Samman,[12] 8 percent of patients had died within ten years of onset of the disease.

The most favorable terms for life insurance should be reserved for those with the early skin lesions of mycosis fungoides. Plans up to 25 years could be considered at a rating of 2 per mil for ages up to 50 and 5 per mil over age 50. Applicants with nodal or systemic involvement should be rated as lymphoma (*see* pp. 643–4, 633–4).

Xanthomatosis

This section should be read in conjunction with the section on primary and secondary hyperlipoproteinemia (*see* pp. 315–19).

Cutaneous xanthomas are the hallmark of disordered lipid metabolism and occur in primary and secondary hyperlipoproteinemia and obstructive liver disease. Xanthomas may also occur in association with reticuloendothelial disease, such as histiocytosis. The morphology and distribution of cutaneous xanthomas can often provide important clues to the nature of an underlying hyperlipoproteinemia.

Eruptive Xanthomas

These imply an abnormality in the body's handling of triglyceride. When they appear in infancy or early childhood, they are usually associated with Type I hyperlipoproteinemia, whereas those appearing in early or later adult life are usually associated with Types IV or V. The lesions consist of small reddish to yellow papules frequently with an erythematous halo. They usually appear in crops, evolve rapidly, and tend to lose their erythematous hue with age. Itching is a common symptom. Favored locations include the buttocks, the backs of the thighs and knees, the flexor surfaces of the arms, the body folds and the oral mucous membranes.

Tendon Xanthomas: Tuberous Xanthomas

Extensive tendon xanthomas and large tuberous xanthomas over the elbows, knees and friction areas are characteristic of Type II(a) hyperlipoproteinemia. Tuberous xanthomas differ from the tendinous type in that they are located in the skin and not attached to underlying structures.

Xanthelasma

Such plaques about the eyelids occurring as isolated lesions are not particularly diagnostic. They are seen commonly in Type II and Type III hyper-lipoproteinemia and in obstructive liver disease, but they occur just as frequently in apparently normal individuals.

Planar Xanthomas

These flat plaque-like lesions occurring on the palms, the volar surfaces of the fingers, and the neck and trunk are distinctive of Type III hyperlipoproteinemia. Although they also appear in obstructive liver disease, they do not occur in the other four types of hyperlipoproteinemia.

Xanthoma Diabeticorum

Diabetics who are inadequately controlled may develop secondary Type IV hyperlipoproteinemia with marked elevation of serum triglycerides and the rapid onset of erputive xanthomas (xanthoma diabeticorum). The serum triglyceride level falls rapidly and the xanthomas promptly resolve with appropriate treatment of the diabetes.

Chronic Dermatitis: Eczema

The various forms of dermatitis and eczema make up more than one-half of all the skin disorders seen in clinical practice. Except in a few instances the dermatoses are not associated with excess mortality, but they can be the cause of much time lost from work, especially in some occupations where industrial agents are responsible for skin sensitization, or where an individual is employed in food handling and comes into contact with the public in shops or restaurants. In these circumstances permanent health policies may require appropriate exclusion clauses. The main importance in risk selection is one of recognition, so that the many varieties of dermatoses may be differentiated from skin lesions occurring as part of a systemic disease or as a precursor of organic disease. Some of the chief forms of chronic dermatitis not associated with systemic disease are listed below.

Contact Dermatitis

Chemical allergens that come in contact with the skin, such as ointments, cosmetics, metals, fabrics and some plants, cause contact dermatitis. The rash resolves spontaneously when the specific cause is removed. In *photoallergic contact dermatitis*, the chemicals in, for example, soaps, perfumes and ointments, only become allergens when exposed to the ultraviolet radiation of the sun.

Seborrhoeic Dermatitis

The rash is erythematous and scaly, and occurs in people who have a naturally oily skin. The commonest site is the scalp, where diffuse scaling produces dandruff. The rash may spread to the eyebrows, lid margins (chronic blepharitis) and the external auditory meatus (otitis externa). Intertrigo in the contiguous body folds of obese people is another manifestation of seborrhoeic dermatitis.

Localized Neurodermatitis

The rash is characterized by thickened, dry, desquamating excoriated plaques associated with intense pruritus. Psychological factors play a large part in the etiology, but there is no allergic basis. Mental tension predisposes to itching of the skin, which causes scratching. This initiates the rash, which causes more itching and more scratching, and so a vicious circle is established. Neurodermatitis occurs frequently in the occipital region, in the arms and on the front of the legs. *Pruritis ani* and *pruritis vulvae* are examples of circumscribed scratch dermatitis and, when persistent, usually indicate the presence of a severe underlying stress reaction.

Drug Eruptions

A mucocutaneous reaction may develop at varying intervals during repeated administration of certain drugs, or as a result of prior use of a drug. Individuals who suffer from asthma, hay fever or other allergic disorders are particularly susceptible to drug eruptions. Sensitization to pencillin causes a particularly severe urticarial or angioedematous reaction, which is sometimes fatal.

Photosensitivity Reactions

Such reactions (other than those occurring as part of organic disease syndromes) may be induced by sulphonamides, cotrimoxazole, phenothiazines, thiazides, quinidine and dimethylchlortetracycline. Continued administration of a drug that has caused a skin reaction can result in dangerous, irreversible immunopathological damage to vital organs such as the kidneys or liver.

Psoriasis

Except when there is associated arthropathy (*see* p. 810), psoriasis does not affect general health. There are no known visceral complications, and even when lesions are widespread and confluent there is no evidence that longevity is affected.

Applicants with uncomplicated psoriasis can be considered standard insurance risks, and those with arthropathy should be rated similarly to rheumatoid arthritis according to severity (*see* p. 807).

Chronic Discoid Lupus Erythematosus

Cutaneous lupus erythematosus (LE) exists as a separate entity from systemic lupus erythematosus (SLE) and remains confined to the skin for life in the great majority of patients; only 1–3 percent are said ultimately to develop systemic disease. However, since SLE has identical cutaneous manifestations, people presenting with what seem to be typical discoid lesions must be carefully investigated to exclude system involvement. This normally includes biopsy of a skin lesion, ESR, antinuclear factor assay, LE cell preparations, differential serum protein estimation and renal function tests.

Rating
Screening tests for SLE negative, no proteinuria:
Within six months of onset — +50.
Thereafter — standard.

Dermatitis Herpetiformis

This is an uncommon disorder characterized by blister formation at the dermoepidermal junction. Males are predominantly affected and the disease may present for the first time in early, middle or late adult life. The blisters are symmetrically distributed and tend to be grouped on the elbows, knees, buttocks, upper back and at pressure points from the clothing. Unlike bullous pemphigoid, the lesions are intensely pruritic and measure from 3 to 10 mm in diameter. Although the severity of the eruption may vary from time to time, spontaneous remissions without treatment are very rare, if they occur at all. The eruption of dermatitis herpetiformis responds to dapsone, and pruritis clears within 48 hours of treatment, but when the drug is stopped the rash and irritation return. Two-thirds of patients have an associated enteropathy and the characteristic changes of celiac disease can be found in the proximal small intestine. Despite this, overt manifestations of malabsorption are mild or absent, and the bowel changes respond to a gluten-free diet. The skin eruption can also remit after a few months on a gluten-free diet.

The risk associated with dermatitis herpetiformis is not excessive, but the possibility of malignant complications arising from untreated celiac disease should be kept in mind. A rating solely for the enteropathy and the adequacy of its treatment would be appropriate (*see* pp. 603–5).

Behçet's Syndrome

Vasculitis is the basis of the lesions of this chronic relapsing disease in which the classical triad of symptoms is orogenital ulceration, uveitis and involvement of the central nervous sytem (CNS). However, a diagnosis of Behçet's disease cannot be made with certainty unless both oral and genital ulceration are present. Other

Letterer-Siwe disease

This is an acute syndrome of unknown etiology occurring in children, consisting of widespread reticuloendotheliosis affecting the viscera, lymph nodes and bones. It is distinct from the types of eosinophilic granulomas already discussed and is more akin to an aggressive malignant lymphoma. The fatality rate is high, and the condition need not be discussed further in the context of risk selection.

LYSOSOMAL STORAGE DISEASES

This is a large group of complex disorders characterized by various enzyme deficiencies which lead to the abnormal storage of substances in nervous tissue, abdominal viscera, bone and other sites, the particular substance deposited depending on the ezyme disorder involved. Each type can be identified by specific enzyme assays.

Most of the lysosomal storage diseases are autosomal recessive in transmission and occur in infantile, juvenile and adult forms. Only the adult forms that occasionally appear in a life insurance setting are discussed here.

Gaucher's Disease

The adult Type I form of Gaucher's disease is the commonest lysosomal storage disease and occurs predominantly, but not exclusively, in Ashkenazi Jews. A lipid material, glucosylceramide, is deposited within the cells of the reticuloendothelial system, showing as distinctive foam cells on marrow biopsy. Clinical manifestations include painless splenomegaly, with anemia, thrombocytopenia and leucopenia, which are secondary to hypersplenism. Bone pain can be severe, and pathological fractures can occur. There is no neurologic involvement.

Prognosis

The course of the adult disease is variable, but most patients run a mild, slowly progressive course with longevity being measured in decades rather than years. Many live to old age. Occasionally splenectomy is performed with the object of increasing the number of circulating platelets or to relieve discomfort due to the size of the organ. There is, however, a measurable mortality from infection in the years following splenectomy (*see* p. 695).

Rating

Adult Gaucher's disease Type I:

	Under age 40	Age 40 and over
Best cases; few symptoms	+100	+50
Splenectomy		
Within 5 yr	Add 50	Add 25
Thereafter	No addition	No addition
With life-threatening complications (e.g. hepatic dysfunction, pulmonary or portal hypertension etc)	Decline	Decline

Type II (Pompe) Glycogen Storage Disease

This is a lysosomal disease in which there is an accumulation of glycogen due to a deficiency of the enzyme alpha-glucosidase. Transmission is autosomal recessive and the disease occurs in infantile, juvenile and adult forms. Clinically, in adults, there is hepatomegaly and progressive weakness of skeletal muscles, but no involvement of bone or blood-forming elements. The heart muscle is not usually affected, as it is in the infantile form.

Rating

Adults only eligible; best cases; no cardiomyopathy; not confined to wheelchair — +150 to +200.

Otherwise — decline.

Von Gierke Disease

Type 1(a) glycogen disease is due to a deficiency of glucose-6-phosphatase. Symptoms of hypoglycemia and hepatomegaly appear in infancy, leading later to retardation of growth and delayed adolescence. Special feeding regimes to combat hypoglycemia and lactic acidosis are helpful in the short term, but for those patients who survive middle age, prognosis is worsened by the severe hyperlipidemia and hyperuricemia that typify the disease and that eventually lead to cardiovascular morbidity and mortality, and chronic renal failure. Type 1(b) glycogen storage disease has a slightly different enzyme deficiency but follows a clinical course similar to Type 1(a). In general, applicants having either type of von Gierke disease should be declined insurance.

RECURRENT POLYSEROSITIS: FAMILIAL MEDITERRANEAN FEVER (FMF)

Recurrent polyserositis, also known as familial Mediterranean fever (FMF), is a genetic disorder characterized by recurrent episodes of fever, peritonitis or pleuritis. Arthritis and skin lesions also occur. Onset is usually in childhood and adolescence. Those affected enjoy normal health between attacks, which last only a few days, and these tend to become less severe and frequent as age advances.

FMF occurs predominantly in people of non-Ashkenazi Jewish, Armenian and Arabic descent, but is not necessarily restricted to these groups. In Israel, where the disease has been thoroughly studied, it appears to be inherited as an autosomal recessive, and the incidence of *amyloidosis* as a late complication is very high. When amyloidosis affects the kidneys, death from renal failure is inevitable in a few years. In contrast, FMF in the USA is a relatively benign condition; amyloidosis is very rare, and the major danger is drug addiction or habituation from the treatment of recurrent attacks of fever and polyserositis.

Rating

Applications for life insurance from individuals with proven FMF who are indigenous to the eastern Mediterranean and North Africa would require careful selection. The urine should be double checked, one of the specimens being examined by a reliable clinical laboratory. If there is no proteinuria or other evidence of renal amyloidosis, a substantial rating would still be required, +200 to +300 depending on age. Those showing proteinuria should be declined.

Applicants indigenous to the USA with proven FMF and a negative urinalysis would usually be rated +50, and those with proteinuria declined.

FIBROMATOSES

This is a group of conditions of fibroblastic origin whose etiology is unknown. Their great importance, and the reason they are mentioned here, lies in the fact that they are often misdiagnosed as true malignant neoplasms.

A fibromatosis can be defined as an infiltrating fibroblastic proliferation showing none of the features of an inflammatory response and no features of unequivocal neoplasia. These lesions can occur anywhere and to any extent. They can be fatal on very rare occasions or relatively harmless, and are encountered from fetal life to old age. Tissues, such as muscle and fat, become replaced by, or infiltrated with, fibrous tissue of varying cellularity. Sometimes this is a diffuse or multifocal process and sometimes a localized nodular one. The fibroblasts are well differentiated, uniform in size and often devoid of mitotic activity. Inflammatory infiltration is not a feature. These lesions mimic a fibrosarcoma through their infiltrative capacity but do not metastasize. In many cases, however, they show a pronounced tendency to recur and lead to major problems of eradication.

Musculoaponeurotic Fibromatoses (Desmoid Tumors)

The most important of the fibromatoses is the musculoaponeurotic variety, sometimes known as desmoid tumours. It is in this group where most of the disasters occur: disasters of nomenclature and treatment. The commonest sites for the musculoaponeurotic fibromatoses in descending order of frequency are the lower limbs, chest wall and shoulder region, head and neck, abdominal wall, upper limbs, buttocks and back.

The treatment of choice of the fibromatoses may be defined as 'adequate' surgery and should be carried out preferably by a surgeon who understands the natural history of this group of conditions. If the infiltrative margins of a musculoaponeurotic fibromatosis are not excised the condition will recur. In one clinical series of 34 cases re-excision for recurrent lesions was necessary in 38 percent of cases, and in another series of 56 cases[13] at least one recurrence was notified in 41 percent. Nevertheless, major surgery, even involving complete amputation of the limb, will almost always eradicate the disease. If a desmoid tumor arises in the abdominal muscles it may infiltrate the parietal peritoneum and involve the intestines, necessitating resection of a wide area of parietal peritoneum and, possibly, excision of segments of intestine.

Selection of Risks

The major problem is correct diagnosis; once the underwriter has established that the condition is non-malignant, the risk, at least in extra-abdominal musculoaponeurotic fibromatoses, should be no more than that associated with a major surgical operation. A rating of 3 per mil in the first year following excision or re-excision should suffice. Abdominal desmoids should be rated similar to Class G tumors (*see* p. 628).

REFERENCES

1 Morbidity and Mortality Weekly Report (MMWR). Oct 4, 1991 for 1990, Vol 39, No 53. US Department of Health and Human Services. Centers for Disease Control.
2 Hunter Handsfield H. Old enemies: combating syphilis and gonorrhea in the 1990s (editorial). *JAMA* 1990; 264: 1451–2.
3 Hilton J. Infectious syphilis in England and Wales: report. HP(M)1 Division. Department of Health, London (personal communication).
4 Mortality Statistics 1985, cause. England and Wales. Series DH2 No 12. Office of Population Censuses and Surveys. HMSO.
5 Mortality Statistics 1990, cause. England and Wales. Series DH2 No 17. Office of Population Censuses and Surveys. HMSO.
6 McIntosh K. Congenital syphilis: breaking through the safety net (editorial). *N Engl J Med* 1990; 323: 1339–41.
7 Sexually transmitted diseases in England and Wales. Summary information from forms KC60 and SBH60. Department of Health, London, 1988.
8 *1951 Impairment Study*. New York: Society of Actuaries, 1954.
9 Singer RB, Levinson L (editors). *Medical Risks: patterns of mortality and survival*. Lexington: DC Heath, 1976.
10 *1983 Medical Impairment Study*. Vol 1. Boston: Society of Actuaries and Association of Life Insurance Medical Directors of America, 1986.
11 Singhal BS, Dastur DK. Eales' disease with neurological involvement. *J Neurol Sci* 1976; 27: 313–21.
12 Samman PD. Mycosis fungoides and other cutaneous reticuloses. Parkes Weber Lecture 1976. *Clin Exp Dermatol* 1976; 1: 197.
13 Mackenzie DH. The fibromatoses: a clinicopathological concept. *Br Med J* 1972; 4: 277.

APPENDIX

Système Internationale d'Unités (SI units) conversion factors.
Conventional to SI: multiply
SI to conventional: divide

Assay[a]	Conventional units	Conversion factor	SI units
Acid phosphatase	KA Units	1·77	IU/l
Alkaline phosphatase	KA Units	7·1	IU/l
Bilirubin P (total)	mg/dl	17·1	μmol/l
Blood pressure	mm/Hg	0·133	kPa
Calcium P	mg/dl	0·25	mmol/l
Calcium U	mg/24 hr	0·025	mmol/24 hr
Cholesterol S	mg/dl	0·026	mmol/l
Creatinine P	mg/dl	88·0	μmol/l
Creatinine U	g/24 hr	8·84	mmol/24 hr
Folate P	μg/dl	22·65	nmol/l
Glucose B, P, CSF	mg/dl	0·0556	mmol/l
Iron S	μg/dl	0·179	μmol/l
Iron binding capacity S	μg/dl	0·179	μmol/l
Lactate B	mg/dl	0·112	nmol/l
Lead B	μg/dl	0·048	μmol/l
Lipids S (total)	mg/dl	0·01	g/l
Magnesium S	mg/dl	0·411	mmol/l
pCO_2B	mm Hg	0·133	kPa
pO_2B	mm Hg	0·133	kPa
PBI	μg/dl	78·8	nmol/l
Phosphate S (as P)	mg/dl	0·323	mmol/l
Phospholipids S (as P)	mg/dl	0·323	mmol/l
Pyruvate B	mg/dl	115·0	μmol/l
Triglycerides S	mg/dl	0·0113	mmol/l
Urate P	mg/dl	0·06	mmol/l
Urea P	mg/dl	0·166	mmol/l
Urea nitrogen (BUN)	mg/dl	0·357	mmol/l
Urea U	g/24 hr	16·6	mmol/24 hr

[a] B, blood; P, plasma; S, serum; U, urine; CSF, cerebrospinal fluid.

ABBREVIATIONS

ACE	Angiotensin I converting enzyme
CABG	Coronary artery bypass graft
CHD	Coronary heart disease
CPK	Creatine phosphokinase
ECG	Electrocardiogram
EF	Ejection fraction
FBS	Fasting blood sugar
GXT	Graded exercise treadmill electrocardiogram
HDL	High density lipoprotein
HR	Heart rate
IMA	Internal mammary artery
LAD	Left anterior descending coronary artery
LCX	Left circumflex coronary artery
LIMA	Left internal mammary artery
LMCA	Left main coronary artery
LV	Left ventricle
LVF	Left ventricular hypertrophy
MET	Metabolic equivalent
MI	Myocardial infarction
NCA	Normal coronary artery
PET	Position emission tomography
PTCA	Percutaneous transluminal coronary angiography
RCA	Right coronary artery

INDEX